D1273863

The Author's Chair and Beyond

The Author's Chair and Beyond

Language and Literacy in a Primary Classroom

Ellen Blackburn Karelitz

HEINEMANN   Portsmouth, NH

Heinemann
A division of Reed Publishing (USA) Inc.
361 Hanover Street   Portsmouth, NH 03801–3912
Offices and agents throughout the world

Every effort has been made to contact the copyright holders for permission to reprint borrowed material where necessary. We regret any oversights that may have occurred and would be happy to rectify them in future printings of this work.

"Note Writing: A Neglected Genre" originally appeared in *Understanding Writing: Ways of Observing, Learning, and Teaching,* 2nd edition, edited by Thomas Newkirk and Nancie Atwell (Heinemann Educational Books, Portsmouth, NH, 1988).

The author and publisher would like to thank the following for permission to reprint previously published material:

p. 115   From "Common Ground: Developing Relationships Between Reading and Writing" by Ellen B. Karelitz. In *Language Arts* 61 (4). Copyright © 1984 by N.C.T.E. Reprinted by permission.

p. 129   From *Turtle Pond* by Berniece Freschet. Copyright © 1971. Published by Scribner's. Reprinted by permission of the author.

p. 198   From *Are You My Mother?* by P.D. Eastman. Copyright © 1960 by P.D. Eastman. Copyright renewed 1988 by Mary L. Eastman. Used by permission of Random House, Inc.

p. 210   From *Only the Moon and Me* by Richard J. Margolis. Copyright © 1969 by Richard J. Margolis. Reprinted by permission of HarperCollins Publishers.

Library of Congress Cataloging-in-Publication Data

Karelitz, Ellen Blackburn.
     The author's chair and beyond : language and literacy in a primary classroom / Ellen Blackburn Karelitz.
          p.   cm.
     Includes bibliographical references (p.).
     ISBN 0–435–08781–9
     1. Language arts (Primary)—New Hampshire—Case studies.
2. Classroom management—New Hampshire—Case studies. 3. Language arts (Primary)—Massachusetts—Case studies. 4. Classroom management—Massachusetts—Case studies. I. Title.
LB1529.U5K37   1993
372.6′ 044—dc 20

Book design and cover illustration by Jenny Jensen Greenleaf
Printed in the United States of America
     94 95 96 97   9 8 7 6 5 4 3 2

For my mother
Adela Beckham Blackburn
reader, writer, teacher

Contents

Preface

But there are so many good books about reading and writing—what do I have to add that's important? I asked myself this question many times as I worked on this book. Eventually, however, I answered the question and finished the book. I believe my contribution is to provide a sustained look at one classroom and one teacher's approach to education—my own education as well as the education of the children in my classroom.

Although the time frame of the book is one school year, in writing it I have drawn upon my full sixteen years of experience as a teacher. The primary data have been obtained during eight years of teaching at Great Falls School, a small neighborhood school in Somersworth, New Hampshire. This material has been supplemented by that obtained from two years of teaching in a very different setting, the Edward Devotion School, a large, metropolitan school in Brookline, Massachusetts. I try to show how a reflective teacher cycles from practice to theory to experimentation and back to theory, always observing, questioning, and testing a particular approach or activity for "goodness of fit."

Goodness of fit is important to me because I was a misfit in school. My learning style was at odds with conventional practice at the time and I was a miserable student. I drew faces on my pencils and made up stories about them when I was supposed to be listening. I hid storybooks behind my textbooks and read during lessons. I wrote pages and pages of notes to my friends instead of doing my homework. Every September I would vow to do better but by November I knew that, this year, I would once again be labeled an "underachiever." I continued my underground curriculum until I went to college. There I finally had choice in what I studied, time to ponder what I learned, and a community of readers, writers, and thinkers with whom to share ideas.

I think often of my own school experiences as I develop my curriculum and teaching methods. It is no accident that my underground curriculum as a student has become the legitimate agenda of my classroom as a teacher. I think about the time I wasted; the pain of failure; the gaps I have in my education. Looking back I see that school was a lonely time for me. Reading and writing helped me to get by and, finally, to succeed.

Reading and writing are still at the center of my life and at the center of this book. So is the notion of conversation and community. My students do not have to draw faces on their pencils for companionship. Instead, they have opportunities for real dialogue with me, with each other, with hundreds of authors through the books they read, and with the characters in the books they write.

Schools have changed a lot since I was a child, but they need to change more. I hope this book contributes to that change.

Acknowledgments

I wish to thank:

Susan Sowers, for having the confidence in me as a writer and a teacher to suggest this book.

Don Graves and Jane Hansen, who chose my classroom as a research site and who recognized and labeled "The Author's Chair" in my classroom.

Tom Newkirk, always present with suggestions, opportunities, and persistent nudging.

Don Murray, for helping me write better by telling me to lower my standards.

Dorothy Pecce, a friend and colleague, who read my drafts with a practiced and practical eye.

Toby Gordon, my editor at Heinemann, for patience and good advice.

My father, Charles Blackburn, for translating my eccentric designs for classroom furniture into reality.

All the wonderful children, parents, and teachers I've worked with and learned from in over fifteen years of teaching.

My husband, Bob, and my two children, Emily and Sam, for helping me maintain perspective and for keeping my life interesting and full of love.

Reading and Writing All Day Long

1

It's a Monday morning in late November. As I walk through the door of my first-grade classroom, sunlight breaks through the clouds and streams in the big, old windows. It brightens the yellow walls and makes the small room seem larger. After days of gloomy November weather, I welcome the sunshine.

The guinea pigs whistle their greeting more loudly than usual and I hurry to the cage, knowing that Mamma has given birth over the weekend. Yes, three furry balls scurry under the ledge as I approach. What an exciting day for my class. The children will be "parents" for the first time *and* they will finally get to have outdoor recess! Quickly I give the rest of the room my Monday-morning check. The fish are still making slow circles in the tank, the plants look a bit wilted, but the narcissus bulbs seem to have grown three inches. Finally I check the bird feeder. As I walk toward the window I hear the sound of wings fluttering and get there in time to see a pair of sparrows hurry off. I sigh. The bird feeder is one of my less successful nature projects. Birds only visit early morning before the children arrive or late afternoon after the children are gone. The other day Parks showed me an observation he'd written in *Outside Our Window,* a book my class keeps (an idea I've borrowed from Kathy Matthews [1985, 67]): "We have a bird feeder outside our window. No birds come." A lonely picture of a deserted bird feeder sticking out into empty space illustrates his words (see Figure 1–1).

I turn away from the window to look at my classroom. I remember the apprehensive looks on the faces of the children's parents when they came to visit the room before school started. Many attended Great Falls School themselves, in the fifties, when it was a parochial school. They are always surprised to find the rooms and building so transformed.

"I used to be in this same room. Yes, I sat right here, but it isn't the same now. Kids sure can have fun in this room. We didn't have much fun back when I went to school."

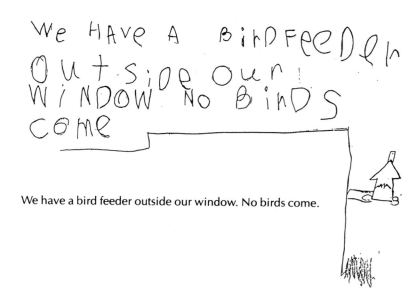

We have a bird feeder outside our window. No birds come.

FIGURE 1-1 *Parks's observation.*

In those days, Somersworth, New Hampshire, was a mill town. Many French Canadians came to work in the mills and French is still spoken in many homes. Now the largest employer in town is General Electric, in whose plant a lot of the children's parents work split shifts. The parents are interested in their children's education but do not have much time to attend meetings, come to parent/teacher conferences, or volunteer in the classroom. They are content to have me do my job and generally leave me alone to do it.

I think about the way teaching and classrooms have changed as I unscrew the lids on the paint jars and stir the colors, clipping clean paper onto each easel. Everything I do now as a teacher is different from the way I was taught as a child. The classroom is a workshop with different work areas. Since I am responsible for providing my students with information and learning experiences in art, science, social studies, and math, I set up centers around the room where they can use materials and explore concepts and skills particular to each of these subjects. During my school experience there was little opportunity for student choice. Now I build in those choices whenever possible. One way I do this is to allow my students to choose the centers they wish to work in during the first hour of the school day. When the children arrive each morning they find their name tags and hang them on the workboard next to the name of the center they've chosen. If all of the hooks are taken, they know that center is full and they must pick an alternative.

Once they have chosen a center, the children spend the first hour of the morning there. Because I expect his kind of time commitment, I must provision the centers carefully. For one thing, I make sure that each center has at least one activity that is open-ended, highly engaging, and essentially cooperative. For example, in the math area, the sorting table is an immediate draw. Four or five children can work at the table, sorting buttons, screws, or beads (also included in the collection are many small blocks and interesting natural objects: acorns, shells, pine cones).

In the art center, Playdoh™, easel painting, collage—in fact most of the activities available there—meet the above criteria. In addition there are bins of "beautiful junk": toilet paper tubes, yarn, small boxes, paper and fabric scraps, pieces of wood, old bits of jewelry, and just about anything else the parents and I can scrounge are raw material from which the children can fashion creatures, robots, vehicles, and junk sculpture.

Some centers require a bit more thought in providing open-ended activities. In the reading/language center I provide many different sets of blocks—large classroom blocks as well as smaller wooden tabletop blocks depicting houses, cars, animals, and trees. My reasoning is that these blocks encourage rich storytelling and cooperative talk.

The students typically begin the day with the large-group open-ended activities before choosing from the other commercial and teacher-made games and materials on the shelves in each center. Half these choices are group activities (such as board games) and half are individual activities (tracing wooden alphabet letters, for example). It is important to pay attention to this balance between individual and group activities. Group activities encourage dialogue and negotiation, but sharing and cooperating can be stressful. The children need to retreat into private activities too.

The more closed-ended materials challenge the children to learn and use specific skills and concepts and to demonstrate that knowledge by winning the game or completing a pattern or puzzle correctly. I believe children need these "quantitative" activities by which they can measure how much they know and compare themselves with others in finite terms. I realize this is not a popular idea in a climate that values non-competitiveness, but we all need reality checks once in a while to help us evaluate where we are in relation to our peers and to a standard of excellence against which we can set goals for improvement. The activities I provide help children do this in a gentle, constructive way.

Whichever center they choose, the students are always encouraged to read, write (stories, observations, or notes), draw, practice math, or do their worksheets. With all these options available, the students have more than enough meaningful choices to engage them for the first hour.

I add and subtract centers as needed but the mainstays are writing, reading, listening, science, math, and art. The students work in groups, at tables or on the floor. There are no desks—not even a teacher's desk. Taking a cue from a student who told me "I think more things when I write," I have tried to integrate reading and writing throughout my curriculum.

A Classroom Day

I begin to take the chairs down and wish I could be a child again myself: "I sure could have fun here." In this reflective mood, I pay particular attention to the rhythm of the day as I move through it, both a leader and a participant.

8:00 A.M.   I finish with the chairs and hurry to write a note to Parks about the sparrows I saw this morning. Next, I tape a sign to the door: "Mamma and Papa Guinea Pig are proud to announce the birth of their 3 babies this weekend." I close the door. It will be fun to see how the kids puzzle this out.

8:15 A.M.   Now that I have a few moments to myself, I enjoy a cup of coffee and listen for the first rumblings of arrival. Soon I hear, "What does this say?"

"Something about pigs—see—p-i-g pig."

"Pigs!?"

"Oh, the guinea pigs!"

"Did they have their babies?"

"Three—it says three—b-b-babies. I bet it says three babies?"

"Yeah."

"Hey Parks—does this say three babies?"

Parks, the class reading expert pushes forward and reads the sign perfectly.

"The babies! The babies!" There is much confusion and struggling to get the door open. Then twenty-three children somehow squeeze their way through the door, simultaneously it seems, and dash across the room. I scramble to position myself in front of the cage, shielding it until I restore order.

"Wait! The babies aren't used to all of you yet. Try to be quiet and I'll take one out for you to see." With some difficulty, I catch a baby. It is completely furred, eyes open, and eager to escape.

"Oh, he's so cute. Can we hold the babies?"

"Yes, after you hang up your jackets."

8:35 A.M. As the children return from the hall a few at a time, many go right to the easel at the front of the classroom to write a line of "daily news" on the chart paper clipped there. This morning much of the writing is about the guinea pigs, but usually the news is some home-related activity or concern (see Figure 1–2).

This class newspaper (another idea suggested by Kathy Matthews [1985, 64]) is read each afternoon before the children go home. Then, at the end of the week, a student teacher, parent volunteer, or school aide gathers all the sheets together and helps the children transcribe their news onto ditto masters. Copies are made and sent home on Friday for the children to share with parents and friends.

DAILY NEWS

I love my mom. I love my dad. I love my sisters. I love my cat. I love my dog. I love my brothers. Maeshan.

I drove through the clouds [fog]. Jeremy.

My stepmother has an aunt that is dead. Jamie G.

My dad got a water bed. Jamie G.

FIGURE 1–2 *Daily news.*

I dislike rushing the children into school agendas so I postpone bureaucratic details like collecting lunch money and taking attendance. In fact, most of these tasks are accomplished by the children themselves as the morning progresses. Each child has a "classroom maintenance" job. Children take attendance, order snacks, feed the animals, water the plants, clean up, and straighten up. The jobs are rotated weekly and a new list is posted on the job chart every Monday.

As some children peruse the chart for their new assignments, I listen to the conversation of others while they take turns writing their news. Often, especially on Monday mornings, children need time to make the transition from home to school. The newspaper gives them a place to hold on to home a little longer—to write about things that are happening there, and to talk about them, because, of course, the children read one another's news as it's written.

Richie pushes his way up to the easel and begins to pass out attendance cards. As I walk off, I hear him urging kids to put their cards in the pockets on our attendance chart: "Hurry up you guys, I gotta take the slip to the office." He herds stragglers to the attendance chart. When all the pockets are filled he takes the clipboard with the attendance slips on it and copies the names of any children whose pockets remain empty.

"Anybody absent today, Richie?" I ask.

"Nope. See, I writ 'Ol her.'"

"Good job," I say, glancing quickly around the classroom to double-check. Our school secretary, Gloria Chabot, is a wonderful woman who patiently decodes invented spelling.

Timmy also has a clipboard and, like a small maitre d', he's taking snack orders. Every morning our foster grandparents help the special-needs children make up snacks. The menu includes fruit (seasonal), peanuts and raisins, peanut butter crackers, peanut butter and celery, and popcorn. (The money they make goes to pay for the food.) Timmy reads the selections and their prices.

"I have thirty-five cents, Timmy, so that means I can get two peanut butter and crackers."

"No, you can't, Shawn."

"Yes, I can. Hey, Eric can't I get two peanut butter and crackers for thirty-five cents?"

Eric shrugs. "Go ask Ms. Blackburn." Soon Shawn appears at my elbow and hands me a note: "How many peanut butter crackers can you get with $.35?" I write the answer and watch as Shawn returns to Timmy, note in hand. My answer must have vindicated Shawn because I see him gloat as Timmy throws the note back at him. Having it in writing from me has made Shawn's victory more official. The snack count is done. Timmy now needs to total the amount of money he's collected—no easy task for a first grader in November. Timmy finds his friend Christopher. Together they go to the front of the classroom and start to work it out on the "minicomputer"—a kind of abacus that's part of my math program.

While Richie and Timmy have been attending to their bureaucratic duties, the other children have been checking the work board, choosing which activity center they'd like to be in.

This morning, when they finish with the snack list, Timmy and Christopher are both in the writing area, where they are free to invent stories, relate personal narratives, or write on any topic that interests them. They get their writing folders and sit down to work. Timmy writes about a birthday party he attended recently: "My friend had a G.I. Joe set. We didn't want no cake. My friend got paint, magic markers, ten helicopters. . . ." Christopher has a new loose tooth: "I got a loose tooth. When I wiggle it it hurts. . . ."

8:50 A.M. After helping the children at the writing table get started, I take a quick walk around the room. On my clipboard I make notes on my daily record sheet about what the children are working on or what they plan to work on in their centers (see Figure 1–3). Then I go back to the writing table. Jeannine is ready to read her story *I Like Simone* to

Name	Math	Writing	Reading	Science	Art
Daniel					✓ playing bakery pizza
Christina	✓ did her work papers.				
Eric		talked to Eric about war. asked what people did when they weren't fighting.	✓ Small World Blocks	Eric made connection with *How Is Far* (spaceships "sky is a playground for birds") talked about non-violent so.	
Jason		played with Eric, got a little wild crashing everything down	✓ Small World Blocks		
Joshua		✓ making a war story again? no one!			
Christopher	✓ C-rods made a tower How many times has it fallen down?		"I'm selling how many rods of each color I can use w/out it falling down." 5 times.		
Jaime				✓ G.Ps. carrying around in basket	

FIGURE 1–3 *Daily record sheet.*

the group. The children and I discuss the story and help Jeannine flesh out the details.

JEANNINE: "I like Simone. I like Simone because she got a Barbie bathtub."

EBK: And that's all you've written so far?

JEANNINE: Yeah.

EBK: What else do you like about Simone?

JEANNINE: When she invites me over to her house and stuff. 'Cause sometimes I can play some games with her.

EBK: Do you think you'll write about that?

JEANNINE: Guess what she did, she scribbled all over her doll's face.

EBK: Can she wash it off?

JEANNINE: Don't come off. It did everything, it wets . . .

EBK: Is that why you like Simone?

JEANNINE: No . . .

EBK: So what do you think you'll say? What other things make someone a good friend.

CHRISTOPHER: Because, when you play together . . . and they make friends.

MISTY: They always play together. Simone's a bad girl sometimes.

EBK: Well, everyone is sometimes.

CHRISTOPHER: I know, and you have to fight a lot of times.

EBK: Do friends fight sometimes?

MISTY: Yes, sometimes, when they get mad at each other.

EBK: Do you and Simone fight?

JEANNINE: Sometimes.

EBK: But you stay friends?

JEANNINE: Yeah.

EBK: Do you think you'll put that in your story?

JEANNINE: Yeah.

EBK: Does anyone have a question for Jeannine?

CHRISTOPHER: How are you gonna end this though?

JEANNINE: I don't know yet.

CHRISTOPHER: I know, why don't you just put, like, "We like each other" at the end. "We play a lot, we are best friends."

EBK: Do you think that's a good ending?

JEANNINE: Mmm, yeah. "We are best friends now because we don't fight any more."

9:00 A.M.   While I continue to work with the writing group, the rest of the class settles into their work in the activity centers. Everyone is busy. Mara decides to write a note to Martina. She hand delivers her note and returns to her area to wait for a response. Their exchange is shown in Figure 1–4.

Jamie wants to write to Nina but instead of hand delivering her note and interrupting Nina's writing she decides to put it in Nina's mailbox. (Each child has a "mailbox" in a row of milk cartons that have been stapled together and set on a shelf.) Jamie's note (Figure 1–5) will be more of a surprise to Nina when she discovers it there.

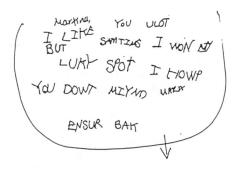

Martina,
I like you a lot, but
sometimes I want my lucky
spot [next to the bookcase].
I hope you don't mind.
Mara
Answer back.

Mara,
One day I could have the
lucky place and one day
you could have your lucky
place and we could share
the lucky place.
From Martina to Mara
Answer back.

FIGURE 1–4 *Mara's and Martina's note exchange.*

Me and you are friends.

FIGURE 1–5 *Jamie's note to Nina.*

9:15 A.M.   Ricky is having a problem with some classmates. He writes a note and brings it to me in the writing center. As the conference continues, I glance quickly at the note and write a response. Ricky and I correspond a few more times before the problem is solved. (See Figure 1–6.)

9:25 A.M.   Each child has now shared his or her writing. While they work on revisions I again cruise the classroom with my clipboard. Referring to my earlier notes, I stop in each area to find out how the children's projects and plans are turning out. I make more notes. I'll use these notes at the end of the day to refresh the children's memories about the work they did. The notes will also come in handy as the week progresses and I can see patterns of interest develop. I keep several weeks of daily record sheets on my clipboard at a time. This allows me to flip through them quickly to remind myself of what each child has done. I can refer to past efforts and interests as I'm talking with the students. This encourages them to be aware of their history as learners and helps them plan for the future.

In the art center, Amy and Christina are looking through the art postcards. "Three Candles," by Marc Chagall, has caught their attention. "She's a bride, 'cause, look . . . she's wearing a white veil," Amy says.

"She looks just like my Barbie," says Christina. I smile at the comparison.

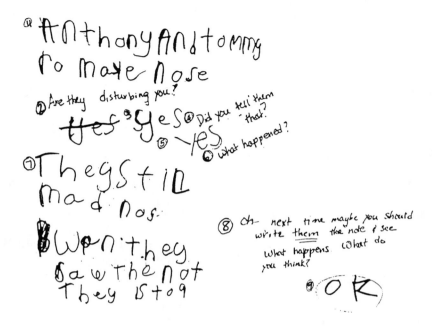

1. Anthony and Tommy are making noise.
2. Are they disturbing you?
3. Yes.
4. Did you tell them that?
5. Yes.
6. What happened?
7. They still made noise, when they saw the note, they stopped.
8. Oh–next time maybe you should write them the note and see what happens. What do you think?
9. OK.

FIGURE 1–6 *Ricky's and my correspondence.*

"Yeah, but why are they frightened? They look frightened to me."

I look at the picture over their shoulders. A bride and groom clutch at each other amidst flowers and tiny figures floating around them. "I don't know, they do look a little startled, don't they?" I answer.

"Are those fairies or angels or what?" asks Amy. "Everyone is flyin' around."

"Well, this artist often made his people float around. I always thought they were happy pictures," I tell them. "Maybe the library has a book about Marc Chagall. Why don't you go down and ask Mrs. Pod-siak to help you look." The two girls take the postcard and head for the library.

I move on to the science area, where Jay cuddles one of the baby guinea pigs. "It wasn't easy to catch him," Jay tells me. "The mother and father guinea pigs chased the babies into the corner under the shelf whenever I tried to pick one up, and then they stood in front and guarded them."

"You mean they actually protect their babies?" I ask in some amazement. I've had guinea pigs as classroom pets for eleven years and have failed to observe this simple fact of animal behavior.

"Yes, I've seen them do it a hundred times. Watch." Jay puts his pig back into the cage and sure enough the parents dash out from under the shelf and herd him back in with the rest of the family. Then with the babies tucked behind them, they face outward, ready to ward off eager little hands.

"Jay, I've never noticed that before. That's a good observation. Maybe you could write it in the guinea pig book." I pick up *Our Guinea Pig Friends,* a book I made for the children to write in, and find a blank page for Jay.

While in the science area, I notice that Erin and Becca have written some advice to me about the Halloween pumpkins we are watching decompose. On chart paper next to the pumpkins they've written, "I think it's time to throw the little pumpkin away—he is too ugly. Erin and Becca." I pause to write a response: "Erin and Becca, you're right, he is getting pretty mushy. What is making him so soft? Please write back. Ellen."

As I finish writing the note, Amy and Christina reappear with *Marc Chagall* by Ernest Raboff (1968), one of the books in the Art for Children series. "Three Candles" is in the book, and I read the interpretation for the girls. The candles are "like rockets [pointing] towards the sky. As though exploding they shower the earth with flowers and green leaves, tumbling angels. . . . The bridegroom, holding his wife in his arms looks startled and amazed." The two girls smile.

"You were right," I say, "they are a little frightened."

"Come on, Amy, let's go look at the book."

As they skip off, I turn to the math center. Sam is building a colorful cityscape with Cuisenaire™ rods. I watch for several minutes and then ask, "How much do you think those buildings are worth? I mean if you added up the value of all the rods, how much would it cost Donald Trump to buy those?"

After I explain who Donald Trump is, Sam decides to calculate the price tag. I leave him to it and walk over to the reading center, where

Lucas is making a reading worksheet. When it's finished I'll duplicate it and Lucas can pass it out to the class. Making worksheets is a challenge because the directions for completing the sheet have to be clear and the penmanship legible. The tabletop where Lucas is working is littered with crumpled paper and he's about ready to chuck the whole project.

"I can't fit all the words on the paper," Lucas complains. Lucas's writing is large and he's having difficulty fitting the directions onto the page.

"This is just a draft," I say, "do the best you can and then we can cut and paste it together." Looking relieved, Lucas sorts through the papers, salvaging some he thinks he can use. His finished worksheet is shown in Figure 1–7.

Just then Sam appears with his figures on his buildings. "Maybe you should write an ad to sell these buildings and we'll see if anyone wants to buy them," I suggest. The ad Sam wrote as a result of my suggestion is shown in Figure 1–8.

To be sure we won't forget to record accomplishments, I keep chart paper and markers in each activity center so the children can write about their projects. I also take photographs of my students' projects. After the film has been developed, the prints are put into a class scrapbook and the children write captions describing each picture. The scrap-

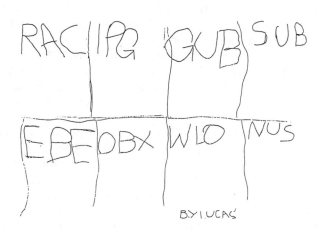

These are mixed up words. Put the letters in the right order and write the words. By Lucas.

Figure 1–7 *Lucas's worksheet.*

These two buildings are $500. The [apartment] building has an indoor swimming pool. The [jail] holds 200 people.

FIGURE 1–8 *Sam's ad.*

book is visible evidence that I value their work long after the projects have been packed up and put away. It remains as a record that parents, children, and classroom visitors can enjoy all year.

9:50 A.M.   I glance up at the clock. The morning activity period has gone on longer than usual. I return to the writing table for a final check, but the natives are restless. I hurry to blink the lights, our signal that it's time to clean up. On my way, I have to admonish Jay and Eric, who are wrestling in a corner. There is noticeable relief when I blink the lights. Most members of the class have already cleaned up and they hurry to the meeting area, eager to get this over with so they can eat their snacks.

Our morning meeting normally takes about twenty minutes to half an hour on Mondays. Today, however, it is abbreviated. I postpone reading from the daily news. I hope we'll have time for that at the end of the day. At ten o'clock I dismiss the group for snack time, and at quarter past ten the class goes out for morning recess.

These first two hours of the day have been packed with activity. The way I spend my time (see Figure 1–9) is an important factor in making the class work smoothly. It is nearly equally divided between the writing center and the other centers. Of course the children at the writing table have the benefit of more intense and focused attention, but I think the chart shows that it's possible to be an active participant within the writing group and also within the class as a whole. I am careful to stick

TIME	WRITING CENTER	OTHER CENTERS
5 mins.	Teacher helps writing group get started	Children begin work in centers
15 mins.	Writing group works on drafts	Teacher circulates to check on work in centers
25 mins.	Teacher has writing conferences	Children continue work in activity centers
15 mins.	Writing group works on revisions, reads drafts to others	Teacher circulates to activity centers
5 mins.	Teacher makes final check at writing table	Children clean up

TOTAL 65 mins.

Nonshaded areas = Teacher time spent supervising children's work

Shaded areas = Children's time spent working independently

FIGURE 1-9 *An example of my time distribution.*

to this routine because the predictability of my movement around the classroom ensures that the children know when I'll be available to them. This cuts down on the number of interruptions during writing conferences.

10:30 A.M.   When the children return from recess, they slowly settle into the meeting area for our math lesson, which today has been prepared by Parks. On Friday, he put his plan for a lesson and a sample worksheet in the dishpan labeled "Math Lessons." I discussed his idea with him, and we agreed that he could teach his lesson on Monday. Now he steps up to the chalkboard, pointer in hand, and begins to tell his math story. It is similar to one I told earlier in the year

(Comprehensive School Mathematics Program 1977, 61), but he has changed the characters and some details.

Parks draws fifteen dots on the chalkboard. "These are fifteen rabbits," he says. "Now close your eyes." Using colored chalk, Parks draws colored "strings" around the dots (see Figure 1–10). "O.K. Open your eyes. What happened?" Hands fly up.

"Oh, I remember this."

"This is easy."

"Yeah!"

Parks calls on Eric. "Are the rabbits in their nests?" asks Eric.

"No, their holes, these are holes. O.K., now which hole has the most rabbits? Jeannine." Jeannine comes to the board, takes the pointer and points to the purple string.

"Right," says Parks. "How many?"

"Five."

"Right!"

Parks continues to lead the children through the lesson, counting the dots and comparing the amounts, then grouping the dots differently. The class is enjoying this lesson because they have mastered the concept Parks is demonstrating. They challenge him to explain his points and spar with him as equals. He passes out paper and gives directions for them to diagram their own stories. The children find seats and get to work. Hands shoot up, and Parks bustles around answering questions and making admonitions about neatness. Parks and the other

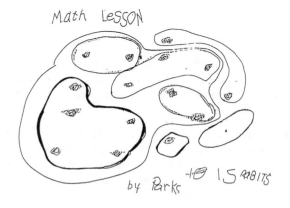

Math lesson.
15 rabbits.
By Parks.

Figure 1–10 *Park's math lesson.*

students are role-playing now, practicing skills and reinforcing concepts and making math their own.

11:45 A.M. As the children finish, Parks collects the papers and puts them in his cubby bucket. He'll correct them later. The class lines up for lunch and lunch recess. The bell rings. When the children return it will be time for reading.

During lunch, I return to my reflections of the morning. I think back to some of the things I do in the summer to prepare for my fall class. I begin in August. My first step is to read through my teaching "journal." This is a composition book in which I store quotations from books and articles I've read, ideas jotted down as they occur to me during the school year, diagrams, anecdotes, and lists. Once I read through this collection I take some time and write several paragraphs describing what I hope to accomplish.

> 8-5-85 My head has been spinning with thoughts about my classroom next year. I have so many little things I'm trying to do. Scheduling is the biggest problem. I need to work out a way this year to do everything so that it flows more naturally. I also want to extend the idea of math as being another symbol system like writing that can be worked on at any time—How can I extend the process approach to math? Math conferences? Weekly meetings to discuss math notebooks? Opportunities for children to teach math lessons? I feel like I have to push on, to keep discovering new things, but I can't keep moving ahead and not capitalizing on what I've learned. I want to have more art projects/activities going on. I felt last year that I didn't attend to art enough. I want the children to develop in their art too. Last year's group didn't work with clay or paint much. My fault??

As this excerpt shows, I think a lot about how to schedule the day and my time. I try to arrive at a schedule that has its own logical rhythm and momentum. In setting up my schedule I use the natural breaks in the day—snack, recess, lunch—and the special subjects—art, music, P.E.—to signal changes in focus or momentum. I avoid teacher-initiated interruptions of activities and I allow large chunks of time in which the class can immerse itself in a project. This may seem like common sense but it isn't. I have so many responsibilities that it's tempting at times to be a stage manager, fitting in as many scenes as possible in an attempt to cover the curriculum. Whenever I've fallen into this trap I've found stopping and starting the activities to be exhausting, because all the energy has to come from me. The children don't enjoy being "managed," either, and their resistance necessitates a kind of heavy-handedness that makes all of us uncomfortable. I believe that teaching and learning should be enjoyable if not always easy. My general schedule for any given day is shown in Figure 1-11. Of course I have to fit P.E., music, and art into this schedule on various days and I try hard to do so in spots that will disturb my main work periods as little as possible.

Between spoonfuls of yogurt, I note the morning's activities in my journal. I am pleased to see that my students' work this morning reflects at least two of my August goals: they are taking responsibility for math lessons and they are using the materials in the art area to better advantage.

12:10 P.M.   After lunch and before reading period we have a brief rest period. I circulate around the room rubbing each child's back. There are always a few embarrassed snickers at the beginning of the year, but the children enjoy this ritual and soon the snickering stops. Making the

8:30	15 mins.	Arrival, greetings, gossip
	60 mins.	Activity-center time
	20 mins.	Whole-class meeting
	25 mins.	Snack and recess
	75 mins.	Math
	35 mins.	Lunch
	85 mins.	Reading
	45 mins.	Science, art, social studies, or special projects
	20 mins.	Cleanup and end-of-the-day activities
3:00		Dismissal

FIGURE 1-11 *My general daily schedule.*

back rub a daily habit ensures that I have some loving contact with every child—a short moment to compliment and reassure.

12:20 P.M.   I finish the back rub and go to the library area. One at a time I call each table over until the entire class is assembled for our reading period. I begin the period by reading a book. Today I read *The Last Free Bird*, by H. Harris Stone (1968). The story, as narrated by the bird, describes the destruction of the environment through development and pollution and ends, "And I am the last free bird." There is no applause.

JESSICA: How come he was the last? What happened to the other birds?

EBK: What do you think?

VOICES: They died. They died.

DANIEL: They died. They couldn't breathe because [of] all the smoggy stuff up there. Like in a fire.

EBK: Can you have more birds if only one is left in the whole world?

VOICES: No, no. They can if they have babies. Well, girls have babies.

EBK: Only if there's a boy.

DANIEL: Without a boy they'd really be stuck.

The children are a bit stunned by this story. It is different from the stories they are used to hearing. It ends so abruptly that they really don't have time to interpret its meaning.

Eric recovers enough to ask one of our initiating questions, which helps get the discussion started.

ERIC: What part did you like in the whole book?

EBK: I think I like the beginning best. Because it was when all the land looked pretty and everything. But I didn't like the part when the people made a mess of everything.

SCOTT: How do you feel to read it?

EBK: It makes me sad when I read it.

VOICES: It makes me feel sad too.

EBK: Even if I start out feeling happy, if I read this book I get sad.

VOICES: Me too. Me too.

DANIEL: Then why do you read it?

EBK: That's what books can do sometimes. They can change how you feel. Has that ever happened to you?

CHRISTOPHER: Not a lot.

SCOTT: Like Dr. Suess books make you laugh and some books, they're scary.

TIMOTHY: I like the first part too.

In this portion of the discussion the children deal with the most salient feature of the story for all of us: its emotional impact. The plaintive poetry is haunting and disturbing. Daniel asks the obvious question: "Why read it?" The answer is left to be pondered.

Next, we consider the meaning of extinction and it's consequences.

EBK: Do you think this is a true story?

DANIEL: Half real and half fake.

EBK: What part was true in this story?

DANIEL: Like when a lot of the birds died from the smog and stuff.

EBK: That does happen, doesn't it? There have been some animals that people have killed off so that there aren't any left. Can you think of any—

ERIC: —like deers—

EBK: —animals that are extinct? No, deer get killed, but they're not extinct.

DANIEL: Um, in the Dover library there was a tiger or something like that. He was the last one found in New Hampshire.

SCOTT: There was some people and they saw this thing? It was like a person except he had some prints of his feet too. And you know those bumps on the side of your foot? They're moved up. And he had fur and everything. And they thought Bigfoot was coming back alive.

EBK: So, nobody knows if Bigfoot really did exist, but they think he would be the last of that type of animal?

SCOTT: Yeah.

RICKY: Dinosaurs.

SCOTT: Someone said they're still alive.

TRACEY: Little baby ones.

EBK: Lizards, which are part of the same family, but not huge dinosaurs.

TRACEY: There's one that I heard, he's real long, he lives in the water . . .

EBK: You mean the Loch Ness Monster?

TRACEY: Yeah.

EBK: They're not sure what that is.

SCOTT: Like they were shooting bald eagles out of the sky.

JESSICA: That's why eagles are almost extinct.

ERIC: And cave men too.

RICHIE: Skunks 'stinct.

EBK: Oh, a skunk *stinks*, but a skunk isn't *ex*tinct. This is the word *ex*tinct. It's a different word from stink. Extinct means that it's all gone. There are none left.

There are complex issues represented in this discussion. The children are scratching the surface of ideas as deep as mortality, history, eternity, and responsibility, and, as the last exchange demonstrates, they are grappling with vocabulary too. However, as this discussion has lasted nearly thirty minutes, I need to move on to independent reading. I dismiss the students from the group to get their reading folders, and they head for the bookshelves to choose books they'd like to read.

I help children find books and make selections. Then I go to the conference table to meet with Monday's conference group. As I read with Brad, Timothy and Christopher struggle through *Where the Wild Things Are.* I keep a tape recorder running at the conference table to record these spontaneous conversations. I later listen to the recordings to get a sense of what the children have been working on, where they've gotten stuck, and the strategies they've used for getting unstuck. I also tape my individual reading and writing conferences, as well as class discussions, group conferences, and lessons. The tapes are invaluable. Listening to myself and to the children forces me to really hear what is going on.

When I first listened to myself on tape I was shocked at the discrepancy between the effect my words and actions were actually having and the effect I intended. Soon I was sitting down every night with a notepad when I listened. I divided the paper in half; on the left side I wrote down the issues I heard myself pursuing, on the right what the children were interested in. I was dismayed to see how often I simply didn't listen to the children at all. I had my own agenda. I began to wonder what I might accomplish if I heard what the children needed. I also recognized times when my agenda was valid and necessary to my students' growth. Listening to the tapes has gradually trained me to listen to the children. The tapes have helped me learn when and how to intervene and have allowed me to evaluate the success of that intervention based on the children's response. They keep me honest.

1:30 P.M.   I finish my reading conferences and check the reading sign-up sheet to see who's on the list to read to the class today. Having children read to the class is a practice I initiated to give them an opportunity to demonstrate their reading ability and to share stories they love with their classmates. Don Graves and Jane Hansen (1983) named this event "The Author's Chair." Now there are "author's chairs" in classrooms all across the country. Today Ricky sits in the author's chair to read Robert's book, *I Love God*.

RICKY: *I Love God*, by Robert Lewis. "I love God because he loves us. God is our father in his way. God is the father of the world. Some people think God is not real. I think he is real."

CHRISTINA: I do too. He, he's invisible.

VOICES: No. No. He's just a spirit.

RICKY: "I love God because God is our father. I love God because he is a good spirit. I love God." The end.

DANIEL: Ricky, why are you so interested in Robert's book?

RICKY: Because I love God, I love God like Robbie does.

ROBERT: Which part did you like?

RICKY: "love God" at the end.

ROBERT: Why did you think this is a good book?

RICKY: Because it seems to me that you put in a lot of—over and over—"love Gods."

EBK: Do you like that?

RICKY: Yeah!

VOICES: It's repeated. Repeated. I know he loves God.

EBK: So some people didn't like it because it repeated, but you like it because it emphasized how he felt.

CHRISTINA: God is a good spirit. He loves all of us.

God, his nature and existence, is a fertile and serious topic, and I find at two o'clock that the discussion is still going strong. Reluctantly I bring the talk to an end.

2:00 P.M.   The time after reading period is spent in a variety of ways. Sometimes we do a special art project or a social studies activity; sometimes we work on science. Today I want to spend some time looking at our pumpkins.

The class gathers around and discovers my note to Erin and Becca. Erin and Becca's note and my response provide the foundation for our science lesson. The class wonders why the pumpkins are getting so mushy: "It's like they're melting."

"They are in the sun—ice melts in the sun."

"And snow."

But some of the children are skeptical about this hypothesis. "Ice and snow are water."

"Yeah, frozen, that's why they melt."

"Things don't melt in the sun."

"Do tables and chairs melt?"

"Oh, come on." The melting theory seems ridiculous now. But Richie has an observation: "My mother's records melted when she left them in the car too long." The melting-pumpkin theory gains some plausibility again. "See, some things do melt."

"Do you think they'll stop getting mushy if we move them out of the sun?" I ask.

"Yes."

"Maybe."

"We can try it." The children and I move the pumpkins off the windowsill to another part of the room. Interest in the pumpkins, on the wane because of their disgusting appearance, is high again. I put out clean chart paper and encourage the children to check the pumpkins and write about them tomorrow.

2:45 P.M.   The school day is almost over. The children get out their "work books" and write about some of the things they've done during the day. Catina writes: "I like to play out at recess. It is fun because I was a Mom playing house. I like math too. I was in reading and it was fun because I did work and read a book and drew a picture. And Ms. Blackburn told me to write neater and I did. She is happy."

We won't have time to share the work book entries today. There's never enough time to do it all, but looking back over the day, I think we've accomplished a lot. There have been numerous opportunities to use books for information and pleasure, to write in a variety of situations, and to discuss ideas. Because these activities are a natural part of my daily routine, they happen regularly, with relatively little effort on my part.

Time Management

I arrived at my management system by risking some trial and error, by observing other experienced professionals, and by doing a lot of study, reflection, and evaluation. Intuition played a major role, as well. There are three basic components to the learning that takes place in my classroom:

1. **Independent Learning** (my students use materials I provide to make discoveries, to role-play, to practice skills, and to demonstrate mastery).
2. **Talk** (I schedule large- and small-group conferences and discussions).
3. **Instruction** (I teach skills directly and I encourage the exchange of information between me and my students and between my students as peers).

These three aspects of learning enjoy a symbiotic relationship. As some students invent stories, spellings, and new ways to use materials, they serve as models for others, who then appropriate and expand on the things that have been learned and discovered. Class discussions take these activities a step beyond the concrete, providing public demonstrations of knowledge and an opportunity to share stories and ideas. I, in turn, take my cues from observing the children's activities and from listening to their ideas. I then develop my instructional lessons based on what the children are showing and telling me.

The schedule I have developed balances independent learning, talk, and instruction. The four major group times in the day—the whole-class meeting, math, reading, and the end-of-day meeting—are geared toward talk and instruction. Independent learning takes places primarily during the morning activity period, but there is another significant opportunity during the afternoon reading period. I like the way the day feels with this kind of schedule, because the time flows easily from one subject to another and because it allows both teacher-initiated and -controlled group work and peer-led group discussion and instruction. There's time for each aspect of learning and an opportunity for everyone's voice to be heard.

I spend an average of two hours a day giving formal instruction, either to small groups or to the whole class. My students spend approximately three hours teaching themselves and one another while I act as a facilitator. I think this is a good use of both my time and theirs. My program allows for many points of contact between the established curriculum and the children's natural interests and abilities—interests and abilities that are prompted by and can be developed in the environment I strive to create.

An Enabling Environment

Children begin the school year expecting to be taught. They do not expect to do the teaching. But I believe that literacy and numeracy are, for the most part, learned rather than taught. They are learned in what

Janet Emig (1983) calls an "enabling environment." According to Emig, this environment is "safe, structured, private, unobtrusive, and literate." She also says that adults in this environment have two roles: "they are fellow practitioners and they are providers of possible content, experiences and feedback" (139).

I think the key idea here is that students and teacher are all practitioners, teaching and learning from one another. If this is true, the place in which children learn needs to be supplied with resources and organized in ways that will encourage independent learning. Time management is also critical. Children who are actively involved in teaching themselves need unbroken chunks of time in which to explore and test what they know.

Making my classroom an enabling environment is a constant challenge. I must find ways to present new information and skills and to allow my students to experiment and make their own discoveries, to teach me what they can do and what they need to know. Writing—their own and that which they read and discuss—is the glue that binds the activities and ideas together. The trick is to set up the classroom to support this kind of written expression from day one.

Becoming Storywriters 2

"Have you noticed that everyone who walks into your room ends up telling a story before they leave?" Susan Sowers, a doctoral student at Harvard and a researcher in my classroom during the 1983–84 school year asked me this question one morning.

The answer was no—I hadn't noticed—but now that she'd mentioned it, I began to listen. I heard Marge Dione, the school nurse, telling a small group of children how she collected eggs every morning when she was a child. Joan Graf, our reading consultant, described the mischief her two cats made around the house. Elaine Lauterborn, our principal, told about calling the gas station at seven o'clock in the morning to jump-start her car. Even classroom visitors found themselves telling stories they hadn't told for years, and several of them commented on it with surprise.

"Why do you think it is that people tell stories in your classroom?"

"I guess because it's the thing to do."

A simple answer. I had made telling stories and listening to them the language of communication in my classroom, but until Susan questioned me I hadn't realized how compelling that language had become. It was so powerful that even outsiders were drawn inside and encouraged to speak the common language.

Listening for the Story

Developing the common language of storytelling is an important requisite for storywriting. In *One Writer's Beginnings*, Eudora Welty (1984) makes the point that children are experts at collecting the stories in their landscapes.

> Long before I wrote stories, I listened for stories. Listening *for* them is something more acute than listening *to* them. I suppose it's an early form of participation in what goes on. Listening children know stories

are *there*. When their elders sit and begin, children are just waiting and hoping for one to come out, like a mouse from its hole. (14)

I begin on the first day of school to help children learn to listen *for* the story. They naturally tell many stories spontaneously in conversation and when they do I pounce. "That's such a good story you're telling. You know I heard Amy talking about her cat at recess. Maybe she'd like to hear the story you just told me."

I eavesdrop shamelessly and pair up storytellers with receptive audiences. In this way I model listening for the story so that it becomes a habit for all of us. I think when children learn to listen for stories they develop an attitude of receptivity that alerts them to the stories in their own lives and encourages others to share their stories too.

Learning to Write the Story

Creating an atmosphere where storytelling flourishes is one step in the process of learning to be storywriters, but there is a gap between the telling and the writing. Children have to learn the conventions of print and print production. They need to learn how to organize and focus their stories so that a reader can make sense of them without the teller's being present to interpret or clarify. It's my job as a writing teacher to help the children bridge this gap.

Dictation

Sometimes the stories my students tell are so interesting that I'm tempted to jump the gap, grab a pencil and do the writing for them. But I resist. While taking dictation is one demonstration of the connection between the spoken and written word, it sets an example of print production in terms of length, neatness, spelling, and fluency that the child cannot meet. The dictated text is often too long for a child to decode or memorize without help. This means that the child is no longer in control of the storytelling: it requires the mediation of an adult scribe and interpreter. This loss of control is a high price to pay for getting the story into print.

One day Travis told me a detailed story about the deer his father shot. He described how his father stalked the deer and how he shot it. Travis went along with his father when the animal was skinned and butchered. He knew many interesting facts about the process. Yet when I asked him if he wanted to write about it, Travis shrugged his shoulders and said no. The story was too detailed for him to tackle and so good that my suggestion that he write just one thing wasn't satisfying.

It's hard to watch stories and ideas slip away because a student is unable or unwilling to produce the necessary text, but if I had offered to take Travis's story by dictation, thus forcing him to be responsible for writing he hadn't done himself, I might have interfered with his development in both reading and writing. Instead, we added his deer story to his list of topics on the outside of his writing folder. Later in the year when he became more fluent, he went back to it several times. It was a hard story for him to write because he cared about it so much. He never felt he did it justice and never selected it for publication, but he and I learned a lot from his repeated attempts. I doubt he would have continued to work on it had I done the writing for him that first day.

Of course there may be special times and circumstances when taking dictation makes sense. If there is a handicapping condition that makes writing physically taxing or impossible, then obviously dictation is necessary. I write for my students in group situations when time pressures make my doing so more expedient than having each child come up and write individually. However, I do not make it a practice to write for my students as a way of teaching them to write.

Whether to use dictation as an initial step in the teaching of writing is one of the most controversial issues in my work with teachers. I have described my reasons and reservations. Individual teachers must evaluate their own beliefs and circumstances to determine whether my methods and practices are good ones for them to adopt.

The Writing Center

The first step in becoming a storywriter is for the children to do the writing themselves. I organize a writing center in my classroom by assembling the following materials:

staplers (two standard, 1 long-reach)

staples

colored magic markers (several sizes)

crayons

pencils

erasers

scissors

dictionaries

masking tape

transparent tape

colored file folders

hanging file folders

date stamps, letter stamps, and pads

assorted papers

rubber cement

dental floss (for sewing book bindings)

colored cloth tape

labels

a primary typewriter

books of poetry and poetry anthologies

Much of the furniture in my classroom has a history. Scrounged from stores that are closing, given to me by friends, or constructed by my indulgent father, it is an unusual collection. "First to Last Panty Hose" proclaims a revolving shelf in my writing center. I could cover these words up, but I enjoy my students' reaction when they finally figure out what they say. On this shelf I arrange all the materials the children will need to make books and to take them apart.

The first year I taught writing I made stacks and stacks of little blank books for my students to write in. These were all the same—blank ditto paper folded in half to make ten pages stapled in the middle. These kept my writing center neat, but I discovered that the format of the book affected the content of the children's writing. No matter how often I reassured them that it was O.K. to leave pages blank or to add more pages, their tendency was to try to get the content of their stories to fit the space available. This did not result in the best writing.

Now, I start each of the children off with a large blank writing book that I partially assemble during the summer. At my first open house before school starts the children and their parents decorate the cover and finish putting the book together. The children write in these books until mid-October. Having the writing book for the first month allows the children to develop an understanding of what writing is without worrying about keeping track of a lot of papers and a writing folder. The writing books are also easy for me to carry home and study as I monitor progress. When the students outgrow the writing books, they begin to determine their own format for their writing and to choose their own materials. At this point they begin keeping their writing in folders. This tends to be more chaotic but the benefits outweigh any inconvenience. A student has to think carefully about the topic and decide how much information there is before beginning to write. A simple act of choosing paper becomes an important planning and prewriting activity.

A shelf unit next to the writing center holds all the writing books and folders. Each student has two files for their writing, a colored "in process" folder and a hanging "cumulative" folder. I put all the colored file folders, which contain the writing the students are currently working on, in a dishpan. The hanging folders are kept in milk crates on another shelf. After a student is finished with a piece of writing but has not selected it for publication, I remove it from the in-process folder and put it into the cumulative folder. This keeps the paper manageable and ensures that none of the writing is lost. The cumulative file is the best way to record the history of a child as a writer. I use these files in conjunction with other record-keeping methods to follow and evaluate a student's progress.

In another corner of the room, I set up a publishing area. All the paraphernalia needed for making books is kept on shelves and in a large dishpan. The primary typewriter is set up here too. I make use of whatever extra personnel I can—an aide or a parent volunteer—to help me with the publishing, so I try to make this corner as out of the way as possible. That way my assistants can work there relatively unmolested.

First steps

At the beginning of the school year, I meet with a small group—five or six children—at the writing table each day. I give them each one of the large blank writing books that I make during the summer and ask them to write something on the first page. Typical responses include writing the alphabet or random letters (Figure 2–1), copying letters or words from around the classroom (Figure 2–2), mimicking cursive writing, writing numbers, and drawing (Figure 2–3). In addition to observing the children's initial writing experiences, I also administer a word dictation test Mary Ellen Giacobbe shared during a workshop she gave at the New Hampshire Writing Program in 1983. The words were chosen to represent the variety of possible placements of initial, medial, and final vowels and consonants, so the test gives me a sense of how well

FIGURE 2–1 *Writing the alphabet.*

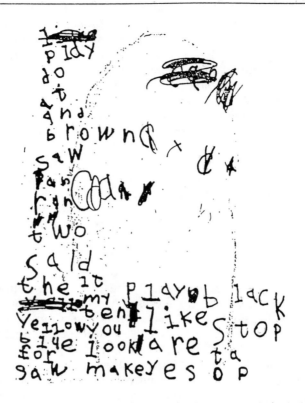

Figure 2–2 *Copying letters or words.*

each child hears and recognizes these sounds. This helps me characterize the spelling patterns each child uses. Figure 2–4 shows how three children—Jay, Craig, and Nina—spelled the first nine words on the dictation test when I gave it in October. Jay has initial and final consonant sounds, Craig is using medial vowels, and Nina, the most sophisticated of the three, is experimenting with silent *e*'s. I readminister this test at the middle and the end of the year. This documentation of a child's spelling progress is very helpful for both parents and future teachers.

I've also developed a checklist (Figure 2–5) that I staple onto the back inside cover of the blank writing books I give my students in September. Every week I take the writing books home and read through them, filling out the checklist as I do so to get a sense of the way the child's writing is developing, both in the use of invented spelling and in terms of topic and content.

FIGURE 2-3 *Drawing.*

	JAY	CRAIG	NINA
rag	RG	RAG	RAG
buzz	BS	BVS	BUES
lid	LT	LID	LEUD
six	SCS	SICS	SECS
game	GA	GAM	GEAM
nice	NS	NPCS	NIES
doctor	DR	DOCDR	DEOCR
view	VU	VEU	VEUE
yellow	UX	EULOI	YALLO

FIGURE 2-4 *A dictation test.*

Drawing

Draws as rehearsal 10-20 _transitional - sketchy drawing_

Draws to add information to text. (What kind? emotional, factual) _Drawings provide characters & settings. Writing tends to describe action._

Drawing is static (active?) 10-20
Note topics _space ships flying, shooting bows & arrows._

Revises drawing. How? _Adds to drawings after conference._

Invented Spelling

Associates consonant sounds with letters:
(b)(c)(d)(f)(g)(h) j (k)(l)(m)(n)(p) q (r)(s)(t)
v (w) x y (z)

initial ⎤
              ⎟ _uses consonants sounds in all of these_
medial ⎬
              ⎟ _positions._
final ⎦

Uses vowels (a)(e)(i)(o)(u) 10-20 _Sometimes substitutes vowels as placeholders if he's not sure which one to use_
(short)
long _Long vowels tend to be "letter/name"_

Type of invention: phonemic 10-20 _Cat, look, I, for, in, the_
letter name/sound spelling, (transitional), correct. _combination of sounding out & correct spelling._

Composition

Labeling   9-18   9-9   9-9
Jat (jet), Rbo (rainbow), Hos (house)

Date of first complete sentence _9-21 I'm going to the Rochester fair. (mgn to the rFr.)_

Date of first piece with story line _10-4_

Date of first publication _10-4 My Cat Was Lost_

Reading the Writing

Can read invented spellings 10-20 _Yes, usually reads inventions easily_
How? _Remembers content & can sound out if he gets stuck_

How long after piece was written is child able to read inventions? _Christopher read his journal 2 months after writing his first page._

Rereads while writing. _Yes 10-20_

Reads journal entries to peers. _Yes, without prompting! 10-20_

FIGURE 2-5 _A writing checklist._

Moving closer to print

Once I've determined how each child interprets the act of writing, I begin the process of moving them closer to using print to tell a story. The next time they come to the writing table I ask the children to write or draw about something that's important to them and I introduce the term *topic*. From then on I listen for their stories and identify them as good topics for writing. In this way the children begin to understand what "having a topic" means. I keep a record (Figure 2–6) of the children's topic choices on my status-of-the-class form (Atwell 1987). This record allows me to see at a glance what the students are writing about and how often I've discussed their writing in conferences. I set this up so I can see two weeks of information at a time. This allows me to identify patterns that develop across the whole class. I can see whether several students are working on the same topic, for example. I also know immediately who might be getting "lost in the shuffle," because the blank spaces are obvious.

The students at the writing table converse, sing, argue, and play while they work. I talk with them individually as they finish. Initially many of their topics are determined by the things they can draw.

Relationship of print to picture

Adults are used to thinking of drawing as illustration produced after the text to enhance or embellish it. But for my first graders, drawing usually precedes the text and is the primary carrier of the message. Most children come into my classroom with a repertoire of drawings that represent familiar objects in their world: people, flowers, houses, trees, rainbows, suns. They fill page after page of their writing books with these drawings. I encourage the children to talk about their drawings and to add some bit of print to these pages. Many times they write one-word labels, as Christopher did in the piece of writing shown in Figure 2–7. Christopher has combined invented spelling and standard spelling in labeling each of these objects.

For many students, this kind of drawing and labeling will be the form their writing will take for several months. I used to be anxious that the children outgrow this stage and get on with "real writing"—which, for me, meant something with a narrative line. But teachers like Judy Hilliker (1988, 14) have taught me to respect and understand a child's need to make meaning pictorially. I treat my students' drawings as "real writing" and help them read their drawings as well as their words.

While valuing their drawing, I watch for signs of print development as the writing expands beyond one-word labels. At first the picture remains prominent, with the writing, though expanded, clearly secondary, as in the two pages from Timothy's writing book shown in Figure

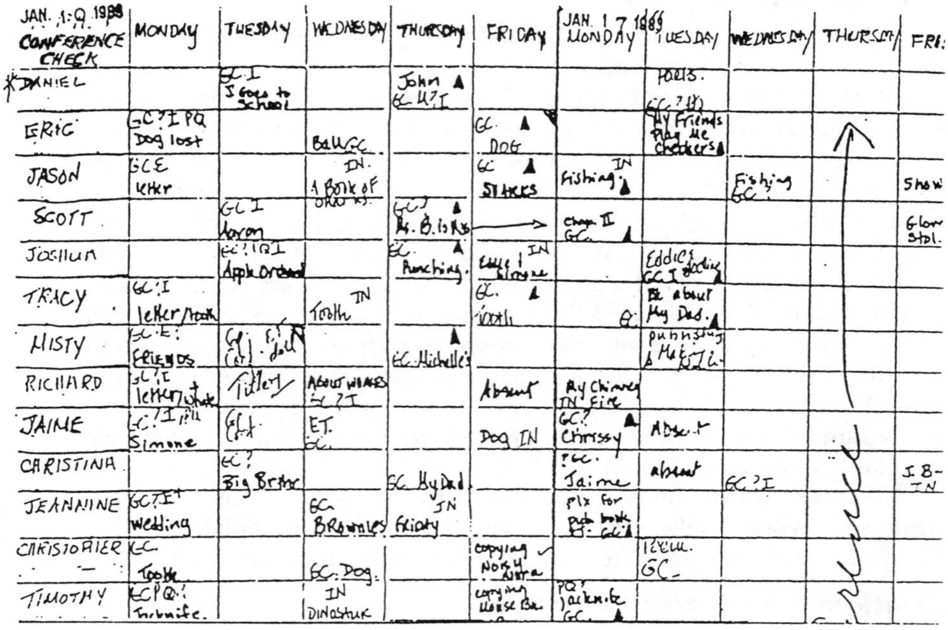

JAN. 1-9 1989 CONFERENCE CHECK	MONDAY	TUESDAY	WEDNESDAY	THURSDAY	FRIDAY	JAN. 17 1989 MONDAY	TUESDAY	WEDNESDAY	THURSDAY	FRI.
✶DANIEL		GC I J goes to School		John ▲ GC I?I		POLLS. GC ?(E)				
ERIC	GC? I PQ Dog lost		BallGC.	GC ▲ DOG		My Friends Play Me Checkers▲			↑	
JASON	GCE letter		IN A Book of Dinos	GC ▲ Stickers	Fishing IN ▲			Fishing GC		Show
SCOTT		GC I Karen		GC I ▲ J. B. lobes →	chap II GC				Glow Stbl.
JOSHUA		GC?I I?I Apple Orch		GC ▲ Punching.	GC I IN Blouse	Eddie's GC I Jacket				
TRACY	GC I letter/tooth		Tooth IN		GC ▲ Tooth	Be about My Dad ▲				
MISTY	GC E FRIENDS	GC E I doll		GC Michelle's ▲		publishing I Mutt I I				
RICHARD	GC I letter/white	Tiller	About Whales GC ?I		Absent	My Chimney IN Fire				
JAIME	GC I I?I Pie Simone	GC E	ET GC.		Dog IN	GC? Chrissy ▲	Absent			
CHRISTINA		GC? Big Brthr		GC My Dad ▲		GC. Jaime	absent	GC ?I		J 8- IN
JEANNINE	GC?I Wedding		GC Brownies	IN Friday		Plx for pub book GC I				
CHRISTOPHER	GC Tooth		GC. Dog.		copying Not 4 Extra ▲	Teen GC				
TIMOTHY	GC PO? Pocketknife.		IN Dinostuk		copying Whale Bk	PO? Jacknife GC.				

Conference Codes

GC = Group Conference
+ = productive
− = unproductive

IN = Individual Conference
▲ = published
▼ = revisions made

? = asked questions in group conference

    I = informational
    E = evaluative
    PO = process question

FIGURE 2-6 *An example of a status-of-the-class record.*

I like Chris.
Sun. Tree. Tree.
House. Pool. Boy.

FIGURE 2–7 *Labeling.*

2–8. All the energy and action in Timothy's writing is contained in his picture; the print on the next page merely captions it.

My students tell elaborate stories about their drawings. Usually these stories do not get written down but I know that if I help the children become good storytellers, they will also become good storywriters when their capacity for print production matures. I ask the children to write one important thing about their picture and I help them sound out the words. If they have difficulty forming the letters or if they don't know the letters they need, I demonstrate on a small slate. My students can also practice on this slate before writing the letters on their page. Children seem to appreciate this opportunity to mess around on an easily erased surface. Many reluctant writers have been encouraged to try because writing with the chalk (especially colored chalk) is fun and less risky that making marks on paper.

As a result of my gentle prompting, more print begins to appear on the page but generally still not until after the picture has been drawn.

This is a pterodactyl story. It is about pterodactyls.

FIGURE 2–8 *Two facing pages in Timothy's writing book.*

Jeff has put tremendous effort into detailing a house, shown in Figure 2–9. The print begins to tell a story but is still sparse and is carefully placed around the house so as not to encroach on it. The next three figures, also by Jeff, demonstrate how picture and print begin to vie with each other for prominence. In his drawing of the hot air balloon (Figure 2–10), Jeff continues to preserve his picture but the words have become important enough that he is willing to squeeze them in around the picture. Jeff's picture of the tractor trailer (Figure 2–11) preceded his story, but for the first time the amount of print begins to match the amount of space and energy in the picture. Finally, in Figure 2–12, the print and picture attain equal importance as Jeff is willing to write over the picture to ensure that his printed message is complete.

I watch for signs like these that show me when children are moving into using print to communicate. Jeff's way of working out the relationship between print and picture manifested itself in a struggle over space—and its organization—on the page.

Danny's moment of realization came when he discovered that his words and picture did not match. Danny drew a standard lollipop tree and wrote a caption beside it (Figure 2–13). During a conference I pointed out that the tree in his picture had leaves, while his words told a different story. Danny thought for a moment, then turned the paper over and drew a second tree, which he labeled "bare" (Figure 2–14). This was an important moment. The next day he wrote "Snow Melt-

Jeff built a house one day. Jeff built a brick house one day.

FIGURE 2-9 *Jeff's house story.*

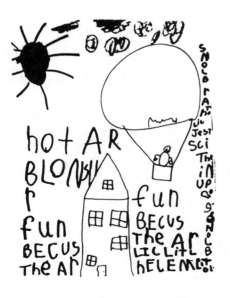

Hot air balloons are fun because they are like little helium balloons [that] go up in the sky just like hot air balloons.

FIGURE 2-10 *Jeff's hot air balloon story.*

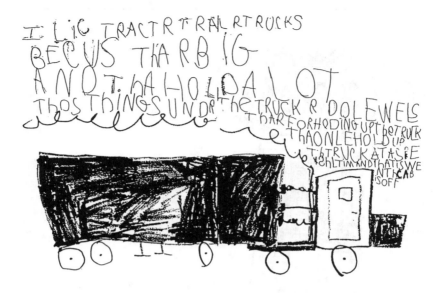

I like tractor trailer trucks because they are big and they hold a lot. Those things under the truck are dolly wheels. They are for holding up the truck. They only hold up the truck at a special time and that is when the cab is off.

FIGURE 2-11 *Jeff's tractor trailer story.*

Boy is it loud when the wood comes down. I help by loading wood. I am happy because we have our wood home to burn for the winter.

FIGURE 2-12 *Jeff's wood-chopping story.*

Tree.
The tree is dead.
The tree is bare.

FIGURE 2–13 *Danny's first tree story.*

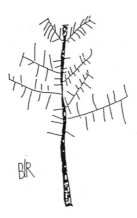

FIGURE 2–14 *Danny's second tree story.*

ing" (Figure 2–15). The print was now clearly dominant, forcing the picture to become an illustration rather than the main source of information for the reader.

As eager as I am for my students to write, I don't want them to stop drawing. I encourage drawing in other ways and have found *Teaching Children to Draw: A Guide for Teachers and Parents,* by Marjorie Wilson and Brent Wilson (1982), to be a helpful resource for developing children's

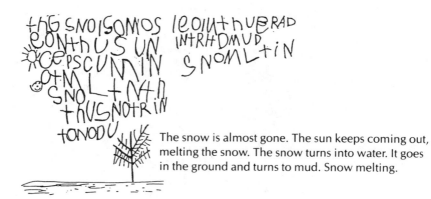

The snow is almost gone. The sun keeps coming out, melting the snow. The snow turns into water. It goes in the ground and turns to mud. Snow melting.

FIGURE 2–15 *"Snow Melting."*

self-expression through drawing. I set out special materials for my students to use in illustrating the books they publish and help them appreciate the artwork in the picture books I read to the class. However, when I am acting as a writing teacher, I need to encourage the children to use words to tell their stories. Once they are fluent they find a balance between what the words express and what the pictures convey. Jeff worked this out for himself. Danny needed some specific intervention from me to help him.

The act of composing

During the months of September and October my students benefit from my presence at the writing table while they are in the act of composing. I help them sound out words, show them how to write letters, teach them that it helps to reread what they've written, and act as their memory while they work their way through a long sentence. These excerpts from a conference with Robert show how my participation sustains him and keeps his interest in the story high:

EBK: What did you write here, Robert? One fish . . . ?

ROBERT: "One fish died."

EBK: "One fish died." So first you have to say . . . one fish— /f/ /i/ /sh/.

ROBERT: (*Writing*) F-i-sh

EBK: How did you write fish on your other page?

ROBERT: (*Turning back*) Let's see . . . (*Looking at word*) f-sh.

EBK: /Sh/, remember, but on this page you didn't know about the /i/ yet.

ROBERT: /i/

EBK: See, /sh/ comes at the end. You know a new letter sound, /i/, so the /i/ would come in the middle of the /f/ and the /sh/. Now you learned this sound so why don't you put it in. (*Robert writes the* i *and turns back to the page he is working on*)

I help get Robert started on his first sentence, since he still needs lots of support for his invented spelling. I also introduce him to the "living off the land" strategy, to quote a term I've heard Don Graves use. There's no point in reinventing the wheel, or the word. Robert has already written the word *fish* on the previous page. I suggest that he look it up to remind himself of the "sh" sound. Robert does a bit of revision by adding the *i* to the word *fsh* that he'd written the day before. Robert now continues with his sentence, "One fish died."

ROBERT: D-I-D (*Spelling out loud*) Died. Too bad, that was a good fish, too.

EBK: (*Immediately reinforcing Robert's spontaneous comment about the fish and encouraging him to add this piece of dialogue to his story*) Well, maybe you should put that: "One fish died. Too bad."

ROBERT: (*Writing*) T-O-B . . .

EBK: O.K. Now you have: "Too bad. We only have one." I wonder how that fish feels being by himself?

ROBERT: He wished he had the other fish.

EBK: "One fish died. Too bad. We only have one." He wishes he had his friend, right? Just like the minnow in *Fish Is Fish* [Lionni 1974] when his friend the tadpole turned into a frog?

ROBERT: Mmmm.

EBK: In fact I might get that book and see what it says. (*Getting book*) Let's read how the fish felt when the frog left. (*Reading*) "The minnow too had grown and become a full-fledged fish." F-I-S-H see, *fish*, just like you wrote. (*Robert looks and smiles broadly*) "He wondered where his four-footed friend had gone but days and weeks went by and his friend did not return." So how did the minnow feel?

ROBERT: Sad.

EBK: He wondered where his friend had gone. Do you think our fish wonders where the other fish is?

ROBERT: Yes, I think I'll write "I wonder where the fish is."

By relating Robert's story to *Fish Is Fish*, I validate his choice of topic. I also reinforce the correct spelling of *fish*. More importantly I connect Robert's story to the larger world of stories. His own simple story suddenly gains dimension from this association. In the process Robert gets an idea about how to continue his story.

Each time Robert adds to his story I read it back to him, making sure that he hears it as a whole. This is important because the production of each word is difficult and it is easy for children to get bogged down with individual words.

In this final segment, Robert's story escapes from the drudgery of invented spelling and enters the realm of fiction and silliness:

EBK: Now: "One fish died. Too bad. We only have one. I wonder where his friend . . ."

ROBERT: Went—/w/ /i/ /n/ /t/.

EBK: Do you think he went to fish heaven?

ROBERT: (*Laughing*) Yeah!

EBK: What do you think fish heaven is like?

ROBERT: Fish heaven is probably flooded. (*Laughs*)

EBK: (*Laughing too*) I guess that's the kind of heaven fish like. Now what? Do you think you'll put in about fish heaven being flooded?

ROBERT: No. But I'm going to *make* fish heaven.

EBK: Do you think the fish wear little halos in fish heaven? (*Robert laughs*) Just like in the book, remember how the minnow kept imagining that people looked like fish, only all dressed up? So we can imagine in your story that the fish in fish heaven have angel wings. They look like this (*Sketching*) and have halos over their heads.

Now the whole writing table is involved, drawing fish heaven and fish with haloes.

BRAD: I wish *I* was a fish.

ROBERT: (*Drawing*) There's a fish . . . Look! What's at the bottom? It's leaking!

EBK: Fish heaven is leaking! Maybe that's why it rains—because fish heaven starts to leak.

There is much laughter. Robert continues to draw fish heaven. His completed story reads:

Fish Is Fish

One fish died. Too bad. We only have one. I wonder where his friend went? He went to fish heaven. Fish heaven is flooded.

Shared participation

The creation of Robert's story is a shared experience. So much has been made of the idea of "ownership" that sometimes teachers are afraid to allow themselves and the other students to get into the story and play around. I think this is a mistake. Inspiration comes from participation and association, not from isolation. I respect the author's authority to make the important decisions about his writing, but *ownership* is a stingy word. Virginia Woolf said, "Literature is no-one's private ground. Literature is common ground. Let us trespass freely and fearlessly . . ." (quoted in Olsen 1965, 264). Fish heaven was my idea but Robert makes it his own through his drawing and his own inventiveness, "Fish heaven is flooded."

I get into the act in other ways, too. Often I will write a short piece in my writing book and share it with the group. Now it's my students' turn to trespass. They enjoy the glimpse I give into my home life, and the writing allows me to model strategies. I wrote this piece during a conference demonstration for teachers but it is typical of the kind of writing I do in my classroom and share with my students:

> This morning Emily finally accomplished the feat of putting on my makeup. She took the cover off the highlighter, stuck her finger in, and smeared it all over her face. She had a glob on each corner of her mouth and stripes on her cheeks. The makeup stick had the imprint of her finger in it and was a mess. She came to me, sticking her chin out proudly so I could admire the smear. I wasn't mad at all, because she looked funny. I told her how beautiful she was and gave her a makeup sponge to perfect the decorations.
>
> I'm sure every baby album in the world has a picture of a baby with Mommy's makeup smeared all over it's face. But it always delights each time.

The children in the conference group all wanted to know whether I was "mad" at Emily. Although I thought my reaction was clear, my young audience, familiar with adult displeasure, needed more reassurance. I added: "I wasn't mad at all, because she looked funny." Even a simple piece of writing like this allowed me to show how to insert information into the body of the story.

Publishing

By the end of September I make sure that every student in my class has "published" a book. Some children, like Robert, are able to develop simple stories through the process of drawing a picture and discussing their ideas with me and with classmates. Other children need me to take the connecting step for them. I have them sit next to me as we read though their writing book, and I try to identify common features.

Often the common feature is subject-related. For example, Joshua's writing book contained several pages of elaborately drawn vehicles (Figure 2–16). I suggested that we collect these pages and create a book titled *Vehicles*. Joshua was thrilled, particularly when I showed him Ann Rockwell's *Cars*(1984). Making this connection to a book written by an adult gave Joshua's book new status.

Sometimes the common thread is a formulaic sentence pattern, as in these pages from Amy's writing book:

> This is a car. It is moving.
> This is a tree. It is in our classroom.
> This is a spider. It is ugly.
> This is a face. It is laughing.
> This is a bunny. It hops.

Amy decided to call this book *All Kinds of Things*.

I "publish" these books by binding them so they can be read and handled by the class. Sometimes I have an assistant type a student's text and ask the author to draw new illustrations. For books that rely heavily on pictures, I xerox the pages from the writing book and bind them together. The authors can color or add text to these pictures if they choose.

FIGURE 2–16 *One of Joshua's vehicle pictures.*

I think it's important that the children publish early and often. A large part of becoming a storywriter depends on being treated like one. The analogy that comes to mind is that of my three-year-old daughter stumping around the kitchen in my boots. She can't fill my shoes yet but she's getting an idea of what it feels like to walk in them. Just as my boots allow Emily to play at being me or Santa Claus, these first published books are the props that allow my students to play at being writers and readers. They are a body of literature far more accessible than any easy "reader" or trade book. And, besides giving the children practice in being authors, these first books also provide the models for organizing strategies the children will adopt in their writing later on.

Record Keeping

I want to keep track of my students' growth from the early stages of labeling on through the twists and turns they take as they learn to organize, sequence, and prioritize their ideas and experiences. Over the years I've experimented with many different record-keeping formats. I ask myself the following questions:

1. What do I want to know?
2. About whom? (Is this information about individuals, groups, or the whole class?)
3. For what purpose and for what audience? (Is this information for my own use, will it be conveyed to other staff members, or is it to be shared with administrators or parents for evaluation purposes?)
4. When do I need to know? (Should this be a periodic check several times a year or is this an ongoing record?)
5. Who is the best person to collect this information? (Am I the best recorder, should the children themselves collect it, or would a specialist or other third party be more appropriate?)
6. What is the best format to use?

Over the years, I've come up with a variety of record-keeping formats—some borrowed from other teachers and some original.

The word dictation test, my writing book checklist, and the status-of-the-class chart, discussed earlier, all help me record specific information and are particularly useful early in the year. They allow me to chart growth in invented spelling, in sound/symbol correspondence, and in basic understanding of story structures. But I need another way to record general observations about each student's individual progress and process and about her participation in writing conferences. One summer I made a checklist that incorporated both reading and writing skills. The original checklist was taller than I am!

This was obviously impractical so I revised it. I had the new checklist (Figure 2–17) printed directly onto folders and used them as the students' writing folders. The process I went through devising this checklist was very useful and the checklist became a helpful reminder of things I needed to be aware of in my students' writing. But it didn't allow enough space to write in depth about what was going on. Now, instead of filling this list out for each child, I keep it at the writing table and use it as a reference when I'm looking at student writing. I then use individual composition books that I keep in each student's writing folder to record my observations. My notes are very eclectic. Sometimes I write descriptive observations:

> Parks is writing his own version of *The Clay Pot Boy* [Jamison 1973]. He is concerned that it not be the same as the one Timothy's writing. "It's okay if they are different but not if they're the same," he told me. Timothy had also expressed concern that Parks's book not be the same.

Often, I list writing issues addressed or skills taught:

> Worked with Parks on punctuation—periods and exclamation points. Discussed it both in reading and writing. Had him add punctuation to haunted house book. He and Timothy went over Timothy's book and punctuated it. Their idea, not mine!

I frequently include bits of dialogue that occur in conferences as well as plans for revision of a piece or for future writing projects:

> Shawn had a group conference on "The Adventures of the Superheroes." Robert said, "For a word here you could say what the lightning men do." Additions: Lightning men and swamp creatures.

These anecdotal records are meant for my eyes only. They are so idiosyncratic that no one else could make sense of them. However, I can go back through these booklets and pull out useful information to report to others.

I like the children to take some of the responsibility for keeping track of their progress. Judy Eagen was my mentor in Project: Write, the first grant-funded training program in writing process to evolve out of Don Graves's work in Atkinson, New Hampshire. She devised a system of record keeping that involved her students and their writing folders. On the front of the folder Judy had the children keep a record of

DRAWING

Note function of drawing
in relation to text.

INVENTED SPELLING

Uses diagraphs sh wh th ch

Associates sounds to 2 letter
blends

st bl pl tr fr fl cl gl gr sp
  sm sn sw br gl

Type of invention: phonemic
letter name/sound spelling
transitional
correct (%)

COMPOSITION

Labeling

Lists, chains

Bed to bed

Personal Narrative

Time sense: past present future

Audience awareness

Takes into consideration:
setting initiating event

internal response
consequence   reaction

Voice; expressive transactional
       poetic   transitional

Endings

REVISION

Date of first revision in text

Type: added on at end
       added in body
       new draft
       deletion

FIGURE 2-17 *A checklist for recording reading and writing skills.*

Motivation for revision
  teacher initiated
  peer conference
  self-initiated

Revision techniques:
  erases   starts over
  crosses out   writes over
  uses arrows/ other symbols
  cuts apart

READING THE WRITING

Can read invented spelling
(How)

Rereads while writing

Can read published pieces

Reads drafts and published
pieces of others

CONCEPT OF WORD

Locates words in own writing

Identifies boundaries of words

Recognizes words from own writing
in other contexts.

Spaces between words

MECHANICS

Uses punctuation appropriately

. ! ? ,

Capitalizes first letter at
beginning of sentence

Uses comma in succession

Adds s to form plurals

adds ed, ing endings

CONFERENCES

Knows when a conference is needed

Types of questions: informational emotional
process

FIGURE 2-17 *(Reading and writing checklist continued.)*

"Things I Can Do in My Writing." Skills were only listed on the folder if the child demonstrated an ability to attend to that skill. It was the child who added the skill to the list, thereby taking responsibility for it. I adopted this method of record keeping the first year I taught writing and have been using it ever since. Figure 2–18 shows the first eleven items on Sam's folder. Starting in November, Sam and I began to evaluate and list specific writing skills that he felt he'd mastered. At first, because of space considerations, he dictated these to me and I wrote them on the front of his folder. Later he took on this task himself.

From time to time every writer hits a slump and the "I Can" list is a powerful reminder of how much a child has accomplished. When students feel discouraged I ask them to read their "I Can" list out loud. As they read, their heads come up and their shoulders straighten. Inevitably they think of a few more items to add and feel much better. I use the "I Can" list as a group motivator, too. Every couple of months I have a whole-class share session and each child reads one item from the list as we go around the circle. It's always impressive to hear what everyone can do and it lets the children know one another's strengths so they know who to turn to as a resource.

Using these methods of record keeping, I observe my students' development during the first two months of the school year. Knowing their strengths helps me decide when and how hard to nudge them.

Organizing the Story

Usually by November all my students are producing writing, with or without accompanying pictures. These stories are often three lines long, as is Robert's story about his new kittens.

Pepper

Pepper is my cat.
She has 4 kittens.
The kittens are cute.

The first line captions the picture, introducing the subject. The next line elaborates slightly, and the last line adds a judgment by the writer. The structure of the stories is a reflection of the conversations I'm having at the writing table. In these conversations I attempt to draw out more details and to get a sense of how the writer feels about the topic.

When the students' fluency in producing text improves, they are able to write down more of the details of the stories they tell me. The writing retains some of the characteristics of the three-line story but the middle gets longer.

THINGS I CAN DO . . .

1. Sam can sound out words and write all by himself   11-84

2. Sam can think of good topics to write about and they don't have to be true.   11-84

3. Sam can read his writing   11-84

4. Sam can think of good titles.   12-84

5. Sam can decide when he's ready to publish   12-84

6. Sam can leave spaces between words   12-84

7. Sam can write better when he uses lined paper.   1-85

8. Sam Car mery is How to speL wros   3-85
(Sam can memorize how to spell words)

9. Sam can PLAn nt to write aßout   3-85
(Sam can plan what to write about)

10. SOme times I get idees from DRoing A piccHR   3-85
(Sometimes I get ideas from drawing a picture)   4-85

11. I can put PERioDs At tHe enD ov a seNtce
(I can put periods at the end of a sentence)

FIGURE 2–18 *Sam's "Things I Can Do" list.*

I Went to the Parade

I went to the parade. It was fun. I saw the mans with horns. I saw the pink panther. It was fun. He dressed in pink. I saw horses. It was fun. I saw the girls with batons. It was fun. I saw a truck with Christmas stuff. It was exciting. It was crowded with people, but it still was still fun.

In this story about the parade, Tara lists the things she saw, with a repeated interpolation about how she felt: "It was fun." When Tara reads the story at the writing table, one of her classmates shifts rest-lessly and after the fourth "It was fun" protests that "It was fun" keeps on "going over and over." Tara changes the next one to "It was excit-ing." This revision to please her audience doesn't ring true, however. Tara ends on a familiar note: "But it still was still fun." I can almost hear her saying "So there."

One of the problems children face as their stories get longer is how to organize the information they have. Tara's story is a list. She is prob-ably remembering the parade in some kind of sequence because the "Christmas stuff" is last, providing the story (and the parade) with its climax. But Tara does not use any structure cues to move us through the time sequence in her story. She does not say "First I saw the mans with the horns" or "The truck with the Christmas stuff came last." Each event is listed separately and could be shuffled around without chang-ing the meaning of the story. Tara's story is an inventory of the things she saw.

Inventories help children to take stock of and report to others what they know about a particular subject. All writers use some form of inventory from time to time as a first draft or a brainstorming exercise, to be focused and developed later. But for the beginning writer, inven-tories *are* the story. When I help my students organize their first books for publication, inventories, attribute books, and "all about—" books are the favorite formats. So it's not surprising that they choose to model much of their later writing on these first books as well.

Attribute books are organized around a common feature such as color. The writer then lists familiar items that have that feature incommon—for example, "A rose is red. A lollipop is red. A heart is red." These books are enjoyable for children because they combine art-work with a simple predictable sentence pattern that's easy to write and to read.

Like the inventory and the attribute book, the "all about—" book gives the students an opportunity to explore and demonstrate their knowledge of a particular subject. Lucas was an animal lover and he wanted to share some of his information about various creatures. In October he wrote *The Pet Book*:

> Lizards are very slimy creatures, but some people like them. They eat turtle food. Guinea Pigs are sensitive creatures. Fish can breathe under water. They eat odoriferous fish food. Birds bite. They eat seeds. Dogs are nice. They eat dog food and drink water. Cats eat cat food. They drink water.

In addition to describing the pets, Lucas was also experimenting with adjectives: *slimy, sensitive, odoriferous*. Even as early as October Lucas had begun to collect words from the books I read to the class and to include them in his writing. The word *odoriferous* comes from *The Amazing Bone* by William Steig (1976).

Because I make it a point to read books with simple repetitive texts at the beginning of the year, my students often pattern their first stories on these predictable books. Shawn was influenced by a Bill Martin book, *The Haunted House* (1970), when he wrote this story.

The Haunted House

I came upon a haunted house. I opened the door. I saw a goblin. A-A-A-A.
I went in the T.V. room. I saw a devil A-A-A-A.
I went in the kitchen. I saw Daddy Frankenstein. A-A-A-A-A.
I went upstairs. I saw a witch. She went E-E-E-E-E.
I thought they were bad, but they were good.

Shawn's longest piece of writing up to this point had been thirteen words. By organizing his writing along the Bill Martin model, Shawn was able to increase his text to fifty-six words. When children hit on an organizing principle that works for them, the content of their writing and the ease with which it is produced can improve dramatically. I try to surround the children with many examples of good writing. We discuss ways that writers organize their writing so that the children begin to develop an ear for the structure of a piece. At the end of the year, I read *The Hobbit* (Tolkein 1966) to the class. Shawn decided to write his own version and at first followed Tolkien's plot (albeit in abbreviated form).

The Hobbit

Bilbo is the name of the hobbit. He has furry feet and chubby cheeks and he is fat.
    Bilbo is going on an adventure with the dwarves. The hobbit is going to fight the three-headed dragon.
    They saw some trolls. They got captured. They escaped. It was thundering because the stone giants kicked the rocks. They finally got to the dragon's cave.

One day while Shawn was reading his story in a group conference, Timmy protested that Shawn had forgotten one of the parts of the story as Tolkien had written it. Shawn thought for a moment and then said, "You know, all that author does is make the hobbit have one 'venture and then another 'venture. I can do that. I can write whatever 'venture I want." Shawn had seen through the content of the story to the structure on which it was built.

Lists, inventories, attribute books, predictable books all are loosely organized around a common feature or sentence pattern. I encourage these forms because they allow the writer to learn to develop a topic and to gain fluency, to become an author. But they do not attempt to sequence events, to order them in time. Imposing sequence on one's experience is a way of gaining control, of beginning to discover cause and effect in daily events. One easy way of ordering events is to sequence them in a bed-to-bed story. The writer begins with getting up in the morning and continues through the day, climbing back into bed at night.

A list of things, not events, the bed-to-bed story is an easy and satisfying book to write because the beginning and ending are already determined, the order takes care of itself. Each event listed is given equal importance, there is no focus on any one event.

Another way to sequence events is the "chain narrative." Like the bed-to-bed story, it is a list of events, but it doesn't necessarily begin and end in bed. Here is an example of chain narrative written by Danny, the author of "Snow Melting."

We Were Late for School

We were late for school because we had to eat breakfast. Then we had to brush teeth. Then we had to comb hair. Then we had to set the table. Then we had to get our jackets. Then we said "Bye" to my brother. Then we went to school. There were all kinds of kids. Then we played. Then the bell rang. Then we lined up. Then she called lines. First graders were last. Then I looked what area I was in. I was in writing. Then I wrote about this. I feel happy writing about it. It is fun writing. I like writing. If you write a lot you get more books.

Danny's story exemplifies the characteristics of chain narrative: a list of events ordered chronologically with little thought about how the story will end. The chain narrative is one of the first formats the writer uses to describe the separate events an experience comprises. It is the logical outcome of the "and then what happened?" question I ask in conference as I try to get the children to describe more about the experience.

Children are not the only ones who write chain narratives. Shortly after my first child, Emily, was born, I sat down to write an account of her birth to put in her baby book. The moment of birth was obviously the climax and I wanted it to be as dramatic in the writing as it was in life. I also wanted to write an accurate description of the events leading up to delivery. I wrote ten pages of text before I finally came to the moment of her arrival. Then I wrote through her arrival and into the morning of the next day—a total of eighteen pages before I stopped.

When I reread the result I realized with disappointment that I had written a chain narrative. The moment of birth was just another event in the series of events I had described. As written, it was not the climax I expected. Somehow I had to resolve the problem: wanting to tell everything exactly the way it happened and also needing to make Emily's birth the focal point. To do this I had to interrupt the chronological sequence. My solution was to begin with Emily's birth and flash back to the events leading up to it. I also tried to cluster the events and interpret their significance to my husband and myself rather than simply list them.

My chain narrative did not satisfy me as a final product, but it was probably a necessary step toward achieving my goal. I had to put everything down so I could see the whole experience. Only then could I be selective and design the piece so it had the impact I wanted.

Because I am an experienced writer with a sense of what my finished product can be, I was immediately dissatisfied with my chain narrative. The children in my class do not react this way at first. Nor should they. They get very involved in writing bed-to-bed stories and chain narratives. There is a momentum that speeds the writing along. The writing gets longer and they have a real sense of satisfaction in being able to produce a long book with a lot of pages. Like me, they have to gain perspective on the events of their lives by learning to order them chronologically. Each event is included because it is next in the sequence—either in actual time or in the sequence of free association in the writer's mind. As yet, the writer is not giving thought to a central focus or to cause and effect.

"Action stories" are favorites with little boys, and in these stories cause and effect make their appearance. Action stories move from one explosion or battle to another. The consequences of action are immediately felt. Their appeal is power and sound effect. Most of the story is in the pictures and in the oral performance. In the example shown in Figure 2–19, Shawn has as his theme "Orcis the Evil Dictator." His drawing teems with activity.

Like the chain narrative there is really no beginning or end to these action stories. When I meet with teachers to discuss their students' writing, action stories are always a source of frustration. I wonder, is this because most elementary teachers are women? Perhaps we don't have an understanding or appreciation of action stories because they aren't a part of our repertoire. Are we uncomfortable with displays of power and dominion? I suspect that these issues underlie some of the concern about action stories. But it's true—when you've seen one explosion, you've seen them all. After the space shuttle tragedy, there were so many explosions all over my classroom that I decided some intervention

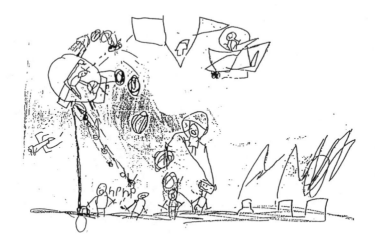

FIGURE 2-19 *Shawn's "Orcas the Evil Dictator."*

was needed or we might not survive. I challenged the children to find a way to save the people in their action stories instead of demolishing them. The solutions were creative. They certainly made the stories more interesting. People landed on clouds or were rescued by visitors from outer space. Sometimes the whole thing turned out to be a dream. Saving the people added the elements of solution and resolution.

I also asked the children other questions: Are you or your friends in this story? Are there any heroes or heroines in this story? These questions prompted the development of characters. Now there were actors as well as action.

Developing Audience Awareness

The children's developing sense of audience can act to interrupt the flow of the chain narrative. From the beginning of the year I encourage my students to be audiences for one another's storytelling, storywriting and storyreading. Learning how to be a good audience involves more that just listening. Being able to respond—to ask good questions, to tell related stories that expand the child's sense of his own story or the story he is reading—is critical. I have to teach the children to be good responders. This is the next step toward developing storywriters.

Developing Storywriters 3

My role at the writing table changes in November or December, depending on the development of the class. At the beginning of the year I spend a lot of time helping my students with the production aspects of composing—learning how to form and sound out letters, how to organize the print on the page. Initially I have to concentrate more on these skills than on writing content. But as my students' production skills improve I can spend more of my time working with them on developing a story. I work with the children individually, helping them verbalize the story and get it onto paper.

By midyear most of the children can decide on a topic, choose materials, and write a draft independently. They no longer need me to be directly involved in the act of composing. When I judge that this transition has occurred I set up a writing table that is separate from the conference table. Now the five or six children who choose or are assigned to write produce their drafts at the writing table one day and then gather another day at the conference table to discuss their writing. My teaching emphasis shifts from individual conferences, in which I am the sole responder, to group conferences, in which the other students in the group also listen to each piece of writing and respond to it. By participating in these group conferences the children develop a sense of audience.

I'll use the transcript of a conference I taped one November to show how I try to help the children with their response skills:

EBK: O.K. Which one are you going to read?

JAMISON: (*Showing a drawing*) "Dirt Bike."

EBK: Well, does anyone have a comment or question for Jamison?

ANDREW: Don't you think you should put more information in it? Other than dirt bike?

MISTY: Why didn't you put more information?

JAMISON: 'Cause I didn't know what to write next.

EBK: O.K. so maybe these people can help you. What do people want to know about this dirt bike?(*Daniel raises his hand*) Daniel?

DANIEL: Should put some more.

EBK: Like what? What do you want to *know*?

DANIEL: Some more information.

EBK: Look, picture in your mind—Jamison riding on his dirt bike. What would you want to know?

MISTY: We want to know what, what happened on it.

EBK: Did something happen? Yes, that's a good question.

I chose this conference as an example because it is typical of early group conferences. It illustrates the students' confusion about how to ask questions and it also shows that the writer's response to these questions can be less than electric. Jamison does not have a clear sense of his story's potential. He has a topic but no story. To help him I guide the children toward asking him questions. At first this is difficult. They want more information but they don't know how to ask Jamison for it. I try to put them closer to the driver's seat by saying, "Look, picture Jamison riding his dirt bike," so they'll be more in touch with the experience. Misty immediately asks the pivotal question that could give the story some focus: "We want to know what happened on it." I reinforce this question but Jamison doesn't seem able to answer right away. In fact it takes the whole conference to get Jamison to finally describe a little about riding the bike.

MISTY: Who was riding it?

EBK: Is it your dirt bike, Jamison?

JAMISON: Yes.

AMANDA: Who drives it? Your father or you?

JAMISON: My mother and my father and me and my sister.

DANIEL: Should go on a dirt road with it.

EBK: Do you mean, where does he ride it?

DANIEL: Yes.

EBK: Where do you ride it?

JAMISON: Portland Glass.

EBK: You ride it in the parking lot at Portland Glass? Why do you ride it there?

JAMISON: 'Cause it's more fun to go over jumps and stuff.

EBK: Oh, you didn't tell us about jumps did you? Hmmm. (*Pausing to see whether Jamison will elaborate*) Now I think you might have some more ideas. You can tell us who rides the bike and where you ride it and you can tell us what happens on it—like going over the jumps.

JAMISON: Yes. "Dirt Bike." "I ride my dirt bike at Portland Glass. I go over jumps."

In the preceding portion of the conference, Daniel makes a statement: "Should go on a dirt road with it." I rephrase this as a question to encourage Jamison to respond. Jamison does give his audience a little more information about riding the dirt bike but he is strangely reticent. As we shall see, he had much more to say about his classmates' writing than he did about his own.

During repeated readings, Jamison's audience coaxes more of the story out of him but this version remains his finished piece. Although Jamison's finished story does not match the story's potential, the process of listening to his classmates' questions teaches Jamison about how his readers approach his text.

The students begin to internalize the *who, where, what, how, why, and when* questions of their audience, and as they do they begin to organize their writing around anticipated reader response. In Noelle's story, "My Class Plays Kiss and Chase," she anticipates the questions of her peers (which I've emphasized below) and includes them in the text as a device for developing her story.

My Class Plays Kiss and Chase

Amanda is my friend. I go outside at recess. We always play kiss and chase. *Who plays?* Kristie, Jason, Andrew, Misty, Jaime, Jacqui, Stephanie, Lynn, and Jeff. The girls chase the boys first. Then the boys chase the girls second. Me and Amanda chase after Jason and Andrew. Stephanie and Kristie chase after Jeff. When the boys kiss the girls, we say "Yuk!" When the girls kiss the boys, they say "Gross!" *How come we play?* We like to say Naa, Naa, Naa, Naa, Naa, you can't catch us. *How come I like to play?* I have long legs to run. They never get me. They always get Amanda and Lynn and Kristie. Jason gets them.

Noelle's story has a completely different feel than the other stories quoted so far. There is a conversational quality to "My Class Plays Kiss and Chase" that is a result of the dialogue Noelle participates in at the writing table. Noelle is not simply describing a series of events, she is also relishing her audience's response to them. As she writes, she shifts back and forth between the writer's and the reader's perspective.

Writing that takes the reader into consideration does more than list or classify. The children's stories have a new purpose: to entertain. When my students discover their audience, the first signs of deliberate humor begin to appear. Ricky, for instance, created a book of "funny stories":

My Pepere Thought the Cake Was a Real Cake

My pepere thought the sponge cake was a real cake, but it was not. My memere laughed. My pepere was sad.

The Duck Who Swallowed the Soap

The little boy catched the duck.
The little boy catched the duck with a net.
The duck flapped his wings and the little boy got wet.
The little boy brang the duck home and put him in the bathtub.
The duck swallowed the soap.
BUBBLE!

The Man Who Is Crazy

The man who is crazy has a crooked bathtub . . .
and a crooked toilet . . .
and a crooked sink . . .
He has a crooked bed . . .
and a crooked toothbrush.
Whatever the man buys, he makes it crooked!

Ricky's little book of stories was a huge success. "The Man Who Is Crazy" is a variation of the nursery rhyme that begins "There was a crooked man" (Baring-Gould and Baring-Gould 1957), but Ricky offers an explanation for how the man's possessions came to be so deformed. His final illustration (Figure 3–1) shows the man banging his latest purchase with a hammer.

Other students often chose Ricky's book to read aloud to the class. By reading these stories they were able to get the class to laugh. It was almost as good as having written it themselves!

When my students write with the audience in mind their writing has a liveliness not present in lists, inventories, or chain narrative. But organizing a story around reader reaction has something in common with these other strategies: the controlling agent is external to the writer. For example, in a chain narrative the sequence controls the writing. In writing that's focused on reader response, the reader controls the writer. I want my storywriters to be considerate of their readers, not controlled by them. I need to help the students learn to be discriminating about the reactions and suggestions of their classmates.

Figure 3–1 *Ricky's final illustration for "The Man Who Is Crazy."*

Andrew had a group conference on his story "I Saw the Puppet Movie." His audience gives him some helpful suggestions.

ANDREW: "I Saw the Puppet Movie." "Yesterday I saw a puppet movie. It was about a little boy who was hurting nature. There was a old turtle. It talked. That turtle was a puppet. It had orange spots. There is no such thing as a turtle that has orange spots. After the puppet movie was over, they showed a real turtle and they showed a skunk, and showed a snake. Then we went to our classroom and finished quiet reading. We get a newspaper. Then we did cleanup jobs. Then we went home. The end."

EBK: O.K. Does somebody have a question for Andrew?

MISTY: How come you put in about up in the classroom?

EBK: That's a good question.

ANDREW: Because it told more information.

JAMISON: I don't think it belongs in the piece of writing.

EBK: Why not?

JAMISON: Because it ain't about the puppet movie.

EBK: If you want to add more information about the puppet movie to make it a longer piece of writing, are there some other things that you could add?

ANDREW: That . . . that we got to feel the snake. And we saw two, um, turtle shells too.

JAMISON: Why didn't you put that stone rock in it?

EBK: Oh.

JAMISON: You forgot about that.

MISTY: You could have put in that we could touch the snake.

EBK: So do you think you could add some other things and maybe take out that part that really doesn't belong?

ANDREW: Yes.

Andrew has a focus, the puppet movie, but his story trails off into a chain narrative at the end. Both Misty and Jamison question him about this. Andrew could improve his story if he heeds the suggestions of his listeners. It's interesting to observe Jamison's role. This conference took place right before the conference on "Dirt Bike." Jamison seemed so lost in dealing with his own writing, yet right on target when listening to Andrew's. Although he recognized the problem in Andrew's story and could suggest ways to expand the information, he was unable to do the same for himself. This is often the case. The children see the flaws first in someone else's writing. After they participate in a conference that helps to find a solution, they begin to identify similar problems in their own writing.

In this next conference, I try to help Amanda maintain her focus even though her audience demands that she be true to her title.

AMANDA: "At the Beach." "I have been making sand castles for five years. It is fun to make sand castles. Why is it so much fun to make sand castles? Because you can get dirty and because I get wet. I am happy at the beach because I make the biggest sand castles that me and my father and my sister and my mother could make. The end."

STACY: How did you think up all about it?

AMANDA: Well, I went to a beach and I wanted to tell what I do at the beach and I, there is some, some funny things I could probably put in there.

JAMISON: You didn't tell about if you go swimming.

AMANDA: I know, because it's so cold—during the winter we made it.

JAMISON: How come all you do is make sand castles? You told us more about the sand castles than you did of the beach. You didn't say anything about the beach. It was all about sand castles.

AMANDA: I wanted to tell about sand castles because I like sand castles more than just sand, I don't just like digging just sand, not putting it back.

EBK: I think one of the reasons that people are confused is your title.

AMANDA: Oh.

EBK: What is your title?

AMANDA: "At the Beach."

JAMISON: You should write "About Sand Castles," something like that.

EBK: How do you feel about that?

AMANDA: I don't know, still kinda funny about it. I'm going to add something about the beach and . . .

EBK: Do you think that would make it better? What did you really want to write about? Do you want to write all about the beach or did you just want to write about sand castles?

AMANDA: I wanted to write about the beach. Like, "We find shells."

EBK: Sometimes when you think of a topic you think you want to write all about something, then it turns out you just write about one part.

AMANDA: Yeah!

At the beginning of the conference Amanda's audience suggests that she has not told all the things she does at the beach. Amanda's story has taken a different focus, which she has developed in an interesting way. I encourage Amanda to stick with her focus, first by reinforcing Jamison's suggestion that she change the title to reflect the true subject of her writing. I explain that it's O.K. for the topic to change after the writer gets started: "Sometimes when you think of a topic you think you want to write all about it, then it turns out you just write about one part."

EBK: Instead of adding more on to it about the beach, what else could you do?

AMANDA: Make another draft?

EBK: Just change the title, like Jamison said.

AMANDA: I can't! I did it in crayon.

EBK: Well cross it off and put down instead "Sand Castles" or "Castles in the Sand," that's a new title.

AMANDA: I want to make a new draft.

EBK: And what will you add to that draft?

AMANDA: I'm gonna copy this and put more down about the beach. I'm gonna call it "At the Beach and Making Sand Castles." "Then we went to Bath and to that big place where we saw all kinds of things and . . ."

Amanda's reaction to the idea of revision is interesting. She resists the idea of changing the title: "I can't. I did it in crayon." Rather than adding more pages to the draft she already has, she wants to start from scratch by recopying her first draft into a new book to make a new draft. Many children have a difficult time changing their original piece of writing. They don't want to "mess it up." This is understandable considering how much effort it takes to get the print on the page in the first place. When my students refuse to add information or to make changes, I accept this decision but always ask, If you *were* going to do it, *how* would you change the story? I want them to tell and to show me what they would do. By getting them to discuss the possibilities I help my students realize the options they have for making revisions. Talking about it eventually leads to action. Once they take that first step, I can teach them various revision techniques.

When Amanda resists the idea of changing the title I try a second tactic: refocusing her attention on the sand castles. I hope to draw out more information to show her that she can make an interesting book just about sand castles. Amanda does elaborate but in the end insists on writing a new draft about sand castles "and about the beach."

EBK: Would you read the first page again?

AMANDA: "I have been making sand castles for five years."

EBK: How come you said how long you've been making them?

AMANDA: Because maybe people would want to know how long I've been making them. Or there won't be many questions, like they won't say, "How long have you been making them?"

EBK: This part was interesting to me because I was wondering how your sand castles have changed. At the end of the book you said that they were better so how did they change?

AMANDA: A first I made little ones and then bigger ones. They were so little when I was first starting and now they are giants . . . so big!

EBK: What did you learn about making sand castles from the time you first started?

AMANDA: I had to use water. The first time I started I just used sand. Then I just used water and then I put them together.

EBK: I see. Do you think that might be interesting information to put in?

AMANDA: Yeah. My father helped us make a giant sand castle like that and we put shells all around it and we made it flat. We put another one and a separate one.

EBK: I think this is very interesting. That's one thing I really like about this piece of writing because I sort of begin to get an idea that you see yourself growing up and getting better at making them. Is this one of the things that you've wanted to say? Is there anything that you'd like to add or do now to this piece of writing?

AMANDA: Make another draft and I might publish it.

EBK: When you start your new draft, what will you write in it?

AMANDA: Like this, and then I'll write some other stuff.

EBK: About sand castles?

AMANDA: And about the beach.

During this conference Amanda's most enthusiastic response has been toward the subject of sand castles, yet she feels duty bound to treat the whole topic, "At the Beach." Her sense of duty derives from her own habit of writing "all about" books and from her audience's initial expectation that she continue to do so. I am teaching two things here: (1) a lesson about how a writer finds a focus and (2) a lesson about maintaining the focus in spite of reader reaction. It doesn't seem as though I've been successful, at least not this time. I'll need to have many conversations before these new ideas about focus are internalized.

Revision

Revision means to look again. Although my young writers are reluctant to make changes, the group writing conferences give them the opportunity to re-vision their experiences; to see them through the eyes of others. This happens because the conferences are not just question-and-answer sessions but are times for the children to tell stories that relate to the writing they listen to. My students come to appreciate the universality or uniqueness of their experiences. They gain a sense of the narrative possibilities. Listen as Brian reads his story to the group:

BRIAN: (*Reading in a monotone*) "Skiing." "I went skiing. It was fun. I went over the jump." (*Brian turns the book so we can see the picture of the jump*)

TIMMY: Like what did it feel like when you were gliding though the air when you jumped off the . . .

BRIAN: Scared!

EBK: That was a good word, *gliding* through the air . . .

TIMMY: My father did that, but one time his strap broke when he was flying and he landed and his skate turned and them the straps broke and came off.

EBK: How did it feel anyway?

BRIAN: Scary.

EBK: How come?

BRIAN: 'Cause, um, there was a jump and when you land there's a hill and then a fence. I thought I was going to hit the fence.

TIMMY: And that reminds me of when me and my father went over a jump on our sleds. That time there was a stump of a tree and we went up. I thought when I was two years old when my father went skiing he, he stayed up in the sky. When you say "Stop!" he stops and then he goes down. (*Makes motion of falling hard*) When I was two years old I thought that.

When Brian came to the writing table for his conference he wasn't excited about his story. He read it in a monotone. But his audience was interested. The story reminded them of so many stories and they began to tell them.

Brian's original draft is passive and motionless. No rush of wind or crunch of snow, just a direct statement of fact. Timmy's stories, however, consistently reinforce the image of flying. Although Brian uses the word *jump* as a noun, Timmy immediately responds to it as a verb: "Like what did it feel like when you were gliding through the air when you jumped off the . . . ." He uses *jump* as a verb and supplies a synonym—*gliding*. He does this again in his story about his father: "My father did that but one time his strap broke when he was flying and he landed . . . ." This time the synonym is *flying*. Timmy's descriptions of skiing allow Brian to relive his experience.

BRIAN: You know, I, I had to lean forward when I was jumping in the sky.

EBK: Mmmm, maybe you could say that: "I had to lean forward when I was jumping in the sky." It does feel like you're jumping into the sky doesn't it? It's almost like flying. Do you think that's why people like to do it, even though it's scary?

BRIAN: Uh-huh. (*Nods yes*)

As he listens to Timmy's stories, Brian assumes the role of spectator in relation to his own text. As a spectator to Timmy's stories as well as his own, Brian is able to contrast and compare. He can qualify his experience to make it more distinctive. His revised draft reads:

Skiing

I went skiing. It was fun. I went over the jump. I had to lean forward when I was jumping in the sky. I fall down when I land.

Brian's revisualization of his skiing experience allows him to describe it more graphically for his audience. When the mime duo Pontine came to our school, Brian's book was chosen for dramatization because of the image he created. As their sense of the options for revision increase, children learn to make sophisticated decisions about including or deleting information. Brian decides to delete his explanation "Pros are bikes" from his story about a bike race (see Figure 3–2) because it interrupts the action. He is counting on the reader to infer this piece of information.

Bike Race

I am racing my bike. Pros are bikes. The Pros are racing against my team. The Pros got stuck in the mud. My team won.

Both Pauline and Noelle decide to reorganize the information in their stories. Pauline uses arrows to redirect the reader (see Figure 3–3). Her original story reads:

Once I knew a little boy that broke his leg. His mommy cried. He cried too and so did his sister. He couldn't walk for a week because he had a cast on his leg. His name was John. His mother's name was Kathy. His sister's name was Kelly.

There are so many questions about how the accident occurred that after the group conference Pauline decides to add: "Because he fell off of a ladder because one of the things on the ladder fell off." The arrows show us that this information belongs after the first sentence and before the family's reaction.

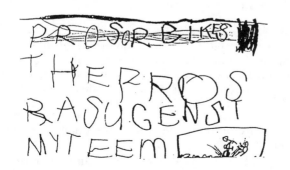

Pros are bikes.
The Pros race against
my team.

FIGURE 3–2 *Brian's revision to his bike race story.*

The child's handwritten story (as drawn):

WWN I hooued I The boy That brack
his teg
his mommy Bee G us
CFID he FELO FF
he cri o Tow HE PLOTOF LHP SS IS TH
AND Soo vp LiThe BeeCus
dil
his sister he Coop hI WoCK Eo
A WeeK Beecu Zhe had a CasT: on

The Boy Got Hurt

Once I knew a little boy that broke his leg because he fell off a ladder [because one of the things on the ladder fell off]. His mommy cried. He cried too and so did his sister. He couldn't walk for a week because he had a cast on his leg. His name was John. His mother's name was Kathy and his sister's name was Kelly.

FIGURE 3–3 *Pauline's story "The Boy Got Hurt."*

Noelle chooses to cut and paste her explanation about the "trick rings" into the middle of her story (see Figure 3–4):

My Dad made me and my sister circus rings because we go to gymnastics and we have to practice. Me and my sister can do frontwards flips and backward flips. And me and my sister was downstairs doing circus [tricks] and we got hot. Then we got a drink. My big sister broke the circus rings and my Dad fixed the circus rings. We made the circus rings out of strong rope.

I suggest that the children write on only one side of the paper to make this kind of revision easier.

Tara practices another kind of re-vision. By maintaining a commitment to a particular topic and trying it out over and over again Tara continues to look again all year long. Tara described her school day six

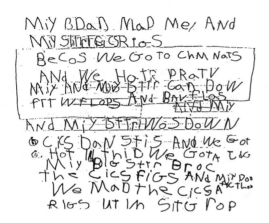

My dad made me and my sister circus rings because we go to gymnastics and we have to practice. Me and my sister can do front flips and back flips. And me and my sister was doing circus [tricks] downstairs and we got hot. Then we got a drink. My big sister broke the circus rings and my dad fixed the circus rings. We made the circus rings out of strong rope.

FIGURE 3-4 *Noelle's story about the circus rings.*

different times. Tara never published any of these stories. I think she had the same problem with her description of her school day that I had with Emily's birth. She seems torn between wanting to document the routine and capturing her feelings about the experience as a whole. Her first four attempts are chain narratives like this one:

I Go to Great Falls School

I go to Great Falls school. I go inside in the morning. I do my workpapers and I do my clean up jobs. Then I play with the toys. Then I go to lunch. I make stuff in the Art area and I play with play dough. Then I have silent rest. I read books and I publish books. Then I go outside for recess. I change names and I listen to the record player. Then I go home. Bye. Bye.

Her last two attempts cluster events and evaluate them. In her final attempt she is successful at giving a feel for the classroom atmosphere and her relationship to me and her friends. Notice that she is still using her favorite phrase, "It was fun."

School

I go to school. It is fun. We go inside in the morning. When we go inside in the morning, we sit down. Then we pay for lunch. In the morning we have recess before we go inside the school. We line up. The quietest line goes first.

Then we go to centers. The centers are: Art, Reading, Math and Writing. In the Art we do fun stuff because we make stuff. In the

Reading we learn reading. In the Math we learn numbers. In the Writing we write stuff and conference with the other kids. They do it too. It is fun.

Then the teacher blinks the lights. Then we clean up for recess. After recess we have snack. On Wednesday, Friday and sometimes Monday we have gym. Our gym teacher's name is Mr. Daigle. Gym is fun. We have trampoline. Sometimes we have gym outside. We come back from gym. We change names from areas.

I play house for recess. I like the kids. I have friends. My friends are Angel, Amy, Kristan, and Buzzy, Debra, and Sherry. I play with them. They like me and I like them. We are nice.

We do workpapers. Then the teacher blinks the lights again. We pick up for lunch recess. We line up to go outside. It is fun at school. We play games. We have parties. At Valentine's we pass out cards.

My teacher's name is Miss Blackburn.

We paint stuff. I read books and publish books.

Then we go home. The teacher says "Good-bye, have a nice day." Then I go home. I take a bus. It is fun.

This kind of long-term revision can only be appreciated if I keep a cumulative file of my students' work and look through it with them periodically. My status-of-the-class chart can also alert me to this kind of commitment to a topic. By color coding I can see patterns in an individual student's topic and I can see patterns across the class as a whole.

Learning to Focus

Amanda's and Andrew's stories, quoted earlier, demonstrate some common issues that young writers have as they begin to juggle organization, focus, and reader response. The writer has to get into the story where it counts. She has to be selective about the information and events she includes. And she has to end the story in a satisfying way. Here is such a story by Kristie:

My Cousin Cindy and Her Friend Lisa

Cindy is eight. Lisa is eleven. Cindy is my cousin. They won't let me play house with them because they think I am too little. I said "Won't you ever let me play with you?" "We'll think about it. We'll tell you in the morning."

Lisa slept over Cindy's house that night. The next day they played with me. I felt proud because they played with me. They played with me. I played with them. I played house with them. Lisa was the baby. Cindy was the Mom. I was the kid that day. Now they let me play with them whenever I want.

Kristie has as her theme the problem of her relationship with her older cousin and her cousin's friend. The information and events she includes all relate to this problem; they help us understand Kristie's feelings and the way in which the problem is resolved. Her story has a focus. Kristie does not tell about what she ate for breakfast, she doesn't list everything that happened during the course of the day. Instead, she sets up the situation for us in the first few lines, then develops and resolves it in the middle. At the end she brings us into the present to describe how things stand now. Kristie's writing demonstrates several points about her development as a storywriter. First, she is in touch with her feelings and with the meaning of her story to herself and to her audience. Secondly, characters rather than events provide the focus for her story.

It's interesting to me that as the people in their audience become more important to my students, the people in their stories also gain dimension. Perhaps the ability to shift viewpoints from writer to reader and back to writer makes the children more insightful about motives and reactions. They begin to see themselves as characters in their own stories, not just as narrators of events.

Me and My Brother Have Make-up

I have make-up. I put my eye shadow on and my lipstick on and my crown I got when I was 3. My eye-shadow is green with sparkles. I was the queen of the world.

My brother puts my lipstick on. He gets it on his nose, on his cheeks, too. He makes a mess. He gets in trouble. When he gets in trouble, sometimes Mom and Dad laugh at him. He really looks funny.

We play dress-up sometimes. I dress up like Snow White. My brother dresses up like a dwarf. We try to dress up like a character.

When we put the make-up on, the longer we keep it on the harder it is to take off. We use hot water sometimes.

When we take off the make-up, I am not the queen of the world anymore. Me and David are plain old Amy and David.

Amy writes about herself with a great deal of self-awareness in this story. I know how Amy feels, how she relates to family members. In Tara's story about the parade I learn what Tara does. In Amy's story I get a sense of who Amy is.

Another way I highlight characters as a central focus is to draw attention to the way adult authors develop characters in their stories. When I read children's literature I discuss the characters. After reading *Little Red Riding Hood*, Harriet Pincus's (1968) version of the Brothers Grimm story, I asked, "What kind of character is the wolf in *Little Red Riding Hood?*"

"Bad!"

"How do you know?"

"Because he eats the grandmother."

"Yes, that wasn't very polite of him, was it? Let me read the first couple of pages again and you raise your hands when you first know about the wolf." On page four I read: "'Since she did not know how wicked he was, she did not feel frightened.'" Hands shot up. "Yes, the author tells us right away that the wolf is wicked."

As we go through the story again I point out the difference between the way the wolf speaks to Little Red Riding Hood—"'Good day Little Red Riding Hood,' said he. 'Where are you going so early?'"—and the way he thinks about her—"The wolf thought to himself: 'This tender young thing would be a delicious meal.'" I explain that the authors tell us what the wolf is thinking so we won't be fooled like Little Red Riding Hood. I also point out that the author uses three methods to give us information about the characters:

1. She tells us certain things as the narrator of the story ("The wolf was wicked").
2. She gives us clues through dialogue, both the dialogue we hear aloud and the internal dialogue.
3. The pictures that accompany the text give us insight into the way the characters feel and think.

We have many discussions like these, first examining the characters and their roles within a story and then moving the characters from one story into another and discussing how this shift would effect the outcome.

"What would happen if the princess in *The Frog Prince* [Tarcov 1974] were Cinderella?"

"Cinderella would be nice to the frog?"

"Why?"

"Yeah, because Cinderella had animal friends, like the mice."

"Yes, and if she was nice, do you think she would've thrown the frog against the wall?"

"No!" Obviously the story would have a very different ending.

"The Ballerina," by Caitlin, is an example of a first attempt to create a story around a made-up character.

The Ballerina

One day a ballerina was walking across the road. She was going to ballet lessons. Now she is at ballet lessons. She is on her toes. Good-bye ballerina lessons. Now she is going home and practicing ballet lessons. And she is on her toes again. And then, Boom! Boom! went the ballet dancer. She is all tired out. Now it is almost bedtime. Now they are eating supper. Now it is time to go to bed.

The story, simple though it is, has a lead and a setting: "One day a ballerina was walking across the road. She was going to ballet lessons." It has action: "She is on her toes" and "practicing ballet lessons." There is even a small crisis: "And then, Boom! Boom! went the ballet dancer"; a response: "She is all tired out"; and a resolution: "Now it is almost bedtime." Caitlin has managed to pull together the basic elements of story and to develop a character other than herself.

When I see my students beginning to work through these story elements, I try to capitalize on it. One way I do this is to identify these elements during whole-group share. I make a chart and label it with the qualities of good writing that I feel are appropriate for the group. Initially I might have only two categories: topic and information (see Figure 3-5). I explain that *topic* means having a focus and sticking to it rather than writing about many different events or subjects, and that *information* refers to the writer's ability to describe the subject with some detail. Each student takes a turn reading a draft to the group. When everyone is finished I ask the children to nominate writers who have successfully fulfilled the requirements of these categories. Since I begin with basic elements, all of the children's names will appear somewhere on the list. As the students nominate their classmates I ask them to explain how the piece of writing satisfies the criteria, thereby identifying the qualities of good writing with specific pieces of writing. The children will then have many models of their classmates' work to build on.

As their writing becomes more sophisticated I add more categories to the chart (Figure 3-6). Now some students' names will appear in more than one category. In Figure 3-6, for example, Caitlin's name appears in every category.

My students notice that the best stories are those that incorporate more of the categories. In fact, this year they are so enthusiastic about

Topic/Focus	Information

FIGURE 3-5 *Basic chart to record qualities of good writing.*

Setting	People/Characters	Action
Caitlin	*Caitlin*	*Caitlin*

Feelings	Humor	What Happened/ Events
Caitlin	*Caitlin*	*Caitlin*

FIGURE 3–6 *Writing chart with expanded categories.*

the chart that they ask me to hang one up in the writing center so they can use it as a reference.

The chart exercise combined with my discussions of the characters in children's literature helps my students improve their stories. Here is Tamar's "fairy tale with a moral":

The Beautiful Queen

There once was a beautiful queen and she lived in a palace. When she was walking everyone said "Look at that beautiful queen!"

After her walk she goes home and tells the princess how everyone told her how beautiful she was. After chatting they ate chocolate cake and chocolate chip cookies.

Then one day the queen was walking. Everyone said "OOOOO Look at that ugly queen!" When the queen heard what the people said, she ran home and ran to see what she looked like. She *was* disgusting! "Oh, dear," the queen said to herself, "I never wanted to look *this* ugly! Now what shall I do? I won't show the princess. Oh, what a sensible mind I have not to show the princess," the queen said to herself.

The queen pretended that she was sick and said to the princess, "Don't come in my room, or you'll get sick too."

When the princess went out to parties the queen snuck out and made her meals and brought them to her room.

Then one day she figured out how she got ugly. She got ugly because she was being too vain. And she decided not to brag again. Suddenly she turned beautiful again! And it was evening and the queen and princess were eating dinner.

And the queen never acted like she was the most beautiful person in the whole world again and so she stayed beautiful forever.

It took Tamar two weeks to write this story. She spent much of this time staring into space. There were many things to figure out, but one problem was giving her the most trouble. When I asked what she was thinking about she said: "I have to figure out why the queen gets ugly and how she's going to turn beautiful again." At first Tamar thought the queen would eat too much and get fat—hence the chocolate cake and chocolate chip cookies. But she wasn't satisfied. "If she gets fat, she'll just have to go on a diet to be beautiful again and that isn't a very interesting story." Finally, she hit on the idea that the queen's bragging and vanity, a common theme in fairy tales, would be her downfall. Once this problem was resolved, the story progressed quickly.

My students' growing awareness of how setting, characters, and events work together to create a story manifests itself in their personal narratives, too. Misty wrote two drafts of "I Love Grandpa" before she settled on this as her final version:

I Love Grandpa

Grandpa lives in an old folks home. Grandpa is old. Grandpa has mumbley hands and face. Misty feels sad because Grandpa is starting to die.

Misty and Tammy went to visit Grandpa. Grandpa gives them candy bars. Misty says "Thank-you." Tammy says "Thank-you." Grandpa walks with a walker. Misty and Tammy feel so sad because Grandpa can't walk that good.

Two days ago Grandpa died. Grandpa was in a casket. The people went to Grandpa's funeral. Misty and Tammy went to his funeral. Misty and Tammy cried at the funeral. Misty cried because she misses her Grandpa. She misses him because she felt good about him. Misty loves Grandpa. Grandpa is up in heaven.

The first two drafts of the story were written in the first person. Then Misty shifted to third person, calling herself "Misty" instead of "I."

EBK: Why did you change "I" to "Misty"?

MISTY: Because I put in about the funeral, that part ain't really true.

EBK: Oh, it isn't. You mean you didn't really go to the funeral?

MISTY: (*Shooting a guilty look at me*) No, I didn't go. I *wanted* to go but my mom wouldn't let me.

EBK: Why, do you think?

MISTY: Because she said people would be crying.

EBK: Yes, funerals are sad sometimes and I'll bet your mom didn't want you to be sad about your grandpa. She probably wants you to remember the good things. But you put it in your story . . .?

MISTY: Yeah, because it's a better story because people would ask, "Did you go the funeral?" and it's more interesting if I say yes.

Misty seems to know that her audience would appreciate the funeral as the climax of her story. I also think adding it was a bit of wish fulfillment on Misty's part. She isn't entirely comfortable about bending the truth, but she does it because suddenly the story is that important. She plays with elements of it, crossing the line between fact and fiction to satisfy her sense of the story's potential. Now telling a good story is more important than telling the absolute truth. This is a far cry from chain narrative, which tells the whole truth and nothing but. Misty is in control of her story and she wants to control her audience's reaction to it, too.

Misty invented the word *mumbley* herself. She explained: "Well, you know how old people talk kinda soft and they have all that skin hanging down from their faces?" Misty had combined the idea of *mumble* with *wrinkly* to get *mumbley.*

In her second paragraph, Misty describes how she and her sister behave when they go to visit their grandpa in the old folks home. When he gives them the small present of the candy bars, both Misty and Tammy say thank-you. Their politeness is a measure of their respect and love for the old man.

There are stories like this, stories that demand to be told well. They draw extraordinary writing from their authors. I can't expect Misty to write like this each time she puts pencil to paper. Everyone in the class sensed that this book was special. They all wanted to read it and to read it aloud to an audience. Hearing her writing read and discussed often by others helped Misty internalize what she'd done, thus increasing the chance that she could do it again. This is one of the benefits of having children read to the class.

The Author's Chair

In the February 1983 issue of *Language Arts,* Don Graves and Jane Hansen published an article called "The Author's Chair." In this article they describe my practice of having my students read to the class and conduct book discussions. A child who signs up to read can read her own writing, the published writing of a classmate, or a trade book written by an adult.

At first I saw the author's chair as a way to spotlight the children's reading and writing accomplishments: reading to the class is a celebration. But it soon became apparent that the author's chair is also a powerful literacy event. When a child chooses to read he is responsible for interpreting that story for an audience. In the discussion period afterward the reader has to answer questions about the author's motives and intentions. He listens and responds to his classmates' reaction to the story.

If the book is one the reader has written himself, it is easier to answer the questions audience members ask: "How did you get the idea for the story?" "Why did you decide to write it?" "What is your favorite part? Why?" "Did you have a hard time writing [or reading] any part of the book?"

But when the class asks similar questions about a piece of literature written by an adult, the reader has to speculate about how the author would answer those questions: "Where did Maurice Sendak get the idea for *Where the Wild Things Are?*" "Why do you think he wanted to write it?" "What is his best part of the story? How can you tell?" "What was the hardest part for him to write?"

To answer questions like these the child uses his knowledge of authorship to go inside the writing. I think my students are able to appropriate writers' strategies more quickly because they sit in the hot seat—the author's chair. They take responsibility as authors of their own writing and they imagine what it would be like to be responsible for the words of others.

Publishing

Another way my students learn to take responsibility is by evaluating their writing in preparation for publication. After a child has completed several pieces of writing, usually about four, it is time to consider one for publication. During this publishing conference the child reads all the writing and chooses the best one. I do the same. Then we compare our choices. Often we agree. Sometimes we don't. The children's choices evolve as their knowledge of the qualities of good writing improve.

Initially many children will chose the most recently completed piece, simply because it's freshest in their mind. Or they choose the topic they like best regardless of the amount of information included or the story's development. It's my job to dispute these choices when I must, but not to veto them. I explain to the author why I agree or disagree, citing the strong points of each piece of writing and pointing out the weak ones. Because the child always has the last word, I'm not afraid to argue in favor of my choice. Sometimes I persuade the writer to change her mind or to revise a piece to strengthen it and make it worthy of publication, but this is not necessarily my goal. My goal is to initiate a dialogue in which the writer and I justify or challenge the writing. I want my writers to be convicted about their work and to learn how to evaluate and to persuade. To do this they have to know why they have chosen the topic, what their intentions are, and the value of the piece to a reader; most importantly, they have to care enough about their writing to defend it. They must know that the power to be a good writer or a bad writer is not mine to confer. It is a voice they must find inside themselves.

So far I've mentioned a number of ways I help my students to become storywriters:

1. I help them listen *for* the stories in their own lives and in the lives of others.
2. I provide opportunities for them to tell their stories and I create audiences for those stories.
3. I model good response and hold individual and group writing conferences regularly to give them practice in giving and receiving responses.
4. I publish their writing to validate it as a body of literature and to make it available as a resource.
5. I discuss literature (the children's own and adult literature) to reveal strategies writers use.
6. I isolate and teach the qualities of good writing.
7. I provide a forum (the author's chair) in which the students lead literature discussions.

My students' writing improves because the items on this list are embedded in the daily activity of the classroom. The writing gains depth as the children develop their abilities to discover topics, find a focus, consider their audience, and organize their information.

I have been in classrooms where the students write and have writing conferences, where published books sit in the bookcases. I pick these books up and read them, but the writing is voiceless. It lacks the depth of involvement and personal feeling that makes Misty's story special. Why? I think this quality of voice depends on the teacher's ability to care deeply about literature and about the life of the mind and to model that caring for the students. I must empower my students to discover their own voices by daring to have a voice myself as a literate person who reads and writes for real. By participating with them, I learn as much as they do, closing the gap between teacher and pupil.

In his article "Learning and Teaching," Michael Oakeshott (1967) says that a child who is the pupil of such a teacher acquires not merely a model for the particular occasion, but the disposition to recognize *everything* as an occasion. *It is a habit of listening for an individual intelligence at work in every utterance that may be acquired by imitating a teacher who has this habit.* And the intellectual virtues may be imparted only by a teacher who really cares about them for their own sake and never stoops to the priggishness of mentioning them. *Not the cry, but the rising of the wild duck impels the flock to follow him in flight.* (176, my emphasis)

This brings me back to the beginning. To teach writing well I must make a habit of "listening for the story," of listening for the "individual intelligence at work" and at play.

Like a Tadpole Growing: Developing Readers

4

Becca stared into space, her writing book open in front of her. I sat down next to her at the writing table and began to fill in the status-of-the-class chart for October 3. When all the other children finished telling me their topics, Becca finally stirred and looked at me. "I'm going to write a book about learning to read," she announced. I smiled, thinking of my bookcase at home filled with books by such notables as Frank Smith (1982), Don Holdaway (1979), Marie Clay (1982), and Louise Rosenblatt (1978) on the same subject. Becca was in good company. "What do you think you'll say about learning to read?" I asked. "You know, Ms. Blackburn, I was thinking, I'm just like a tadpole growing— first I can only read a little bit, but then I just keep growing and practicing and getting better until I'm all grown up to be a real good reader."

As I jotted Becca's comment down on the back of the status-of-the-class record, I was reminded that learning to read does indeed make different creatures of us all. Becoming literate is probably as big a metamorphosis for the young child as adolescence is for the older one. I had a feeling that Becca's comparison of herself to a "tadpole growing" was not just a charming simile. She was experiencing a change and she was aware of it. The page Becca wrote in her writing book that day is shown in Figure 4–1.

Her advice about learning to read is to *try*. And this is exactly the message I give every day, beginning the very first day of school.

The Library

The class library is the heart of my classroom. Everything that happens is somehow connected to that space. When students are independent readers, they plan their own reading agendas. They need to know where to find the books they want to read. The students in my classroom become sophisticated readers with an impressive understanding of their own reading processes. But they are only six-year-olds, after all. They

83

I think I can read if you try.
You may not read today.
I think I can read.

FIGURE 4–1 *Becca's advice about learning to read.*

have a limited tolerance for frustration and like many of us they do not like putting things away. My classroom library has to be set up with all these needs in mind. It has to be well and simply organized so that the children can find the books they want quickly. They must be able to return books to their proper places easily. Storing books in bins rather than on shelves makes good sense. Often young readers are "reading" the pictures on the cover, not the title. With the books facing forward in bins, they can see the covers of the books and make their selection. The bins are organized alphabetically and books can be returned with a minimum of difficulty. Boxes, colored dishpans, and baskets all make good book bins. In addition to the general book bins, I have a separate shelf with bins for multiple copies of books and for the various sets of basal readers and preprimers I keep in the classroom. The kids call these basal sets "level books" and they love to test themselves periodically to see at which level they are reading.

A special forward-facing bookshelf built by my father is the focal point of the library. On this shelf I display library books, new books, and—most importantly—the children's published books. It's significant that the children's books sit shoulder to shoulder with those written by grown-ups. (Message: child authors and adult authors share equal status.) These books are also the first books seen by anyone entering the room. They say "read me." And who can resist?

Although the books live in the library, they do not belong there. Books decorate every shelf and countertop. They are taken outside, taken home, hoarded in the students' cubby buckets. We need to have cubby bucket purges at least once a month to find these books and get them back into circulation. I enjoy these cleaning sessions. Books that have been hidden in someone's cubby are greeted like long-lost friends. Shouts of "So that's where *The Frog Prince* [Tarcov, 1974] is, I've been looking for that!" are heard over and over again. Arguments erupt as indignant readers face one another, each trying to make the best case for taking possession of a favorite book. Books, authors, and characters are valued with much passion. I keep lists of the books my students love too much to share and refer to them when I'm ordering books for the classroom. We also use these lists when we're deciding which book to designate "book of the month" on our monthly book order. And I publish a "best sellers" list in our weekly class newsletters so parents can have it as a resource.

The Reading Center

Next to the class library is the reading center. Here my students have access to a variety of teacher-made and commercial games and activities that allow them to practice reading skills. An old cast-iron bathtub filled with pillows is a cozy spot for listening to tapes and looking at books. On a small table I have a Language Master™ machine. My students can practice letter sounds, sight words, and other specific skills that require a certain amount of rote memorization and drill.

The Reading Period

The centerpiece of my reading program is the reading period, which begins after lunch and lasts approximately an hour and a half. I structure this time so that it is bounded by stories and by images of people reading, enjoying, and talking about books. The reading period begins as I gather my students into the library to listen to me read a book to the class. Often I accept suggestions from the children about the reading material chosen, but this is also a time for me to exercise my prerogative as teacher to introduce books that I'd like the class to hear. After my turn is over and we've had a chance to discuss the book, the children move off to choose their own books and read. Usually about thirty minutes is allotted for this. During this time I meet individually or in groups with the children to discuss and evaluate their reading progress. Finally, the children meet again in the library to listen to and discuss a book read by a classmate.

During the first few weeks of the school year, I help the children expand their definition of reading. I want them to realize that they have been reading many things for a very long time. Over the years I've built up a collection of "environmental print"—cards containing labels from grocery items, pictures from magazines, and signs found in their larger world. We read these together and discuss the children's decoding strategies—picture clues, context clues, letter and word recognition. I help my students see ways to use these same strategies when they pick up a book. And I encourage them to find their own examples of things they can read and to bring these in to share with the class.

When I sit down to read books to the class, I choose simple books that I think they can be successful with immediately. I remind them of the many easy books, board books, wordless books, rhyming books, predictable books, number, color, and alphabet books they can already read. As they leave the library area for their independent reading period, I make sure each student has in mind a book he wants to look at, one she can make meaningful in some way.

At the same time I encourage my students to "play at" reading much harder books with familiar story lines. Fairy tales are especially popular, as are books like *Where the Wild Things Are* (Sendak 1962), *The Very Hungry Caterpillar* (Carle 1969), and *Corduroy* (Freeman 1968). I provide multiple copies of as many books as possible so that the students can form their own reading groups and help one another learn to read a favorite book.

While the class reads independently, I meet with students individually or in small groups for reading conferences. I start the year by circulating during reading time and making notes on my clipboard about each child's behavior. I take note of how a child chooses books to read. Is making a selection easy or difficult? Are the choices realistic? Is he always frustrated by picking out a book that is too difficult? Does she continually chose books that offer no challenge? Who does he choose to read with? Are these companions helpful or distracting? What are her behavior patterns? How long can she work constructively? How does he make the transition from one book to the next?

Here's an excerpt from notes I made during the first week of school one year:

September 6   Today when I dismissed the children for independent reading, Christopher, Timothy, Jessica, and Darcy went over to the art area, got out scissors and paper, and began an art activity. Their reaction to my question about what they were doing: "We can't read so we figured we'd do this." I guess they assumed my instructions didn't apply to them! I asked them which books they liked and they all agreed on *Where the Wild Things Are*. I got four copies and helped them get started "reading" the story. After that they seemed to get the idea and spent a good half hour looking at books together.

Jeanine had a pile of about fifteen books in front of her. She was diligently copying titles into her title book. She obviously enjoyed this more than reading the books! At the same time I discovered Lynn copying the text of *Curious George* [Rey 1941] in her title book. Why? "Because I like this story a real lot." Why do I always forget what September is like? It must be selective amnesia.

Reading Conferences

I study my students' learning styles for about a month. Once I collect enough information, I form conference groups. I group children who work well together. This means the groups are formed along friendship or mentorship lines. They are of mixed abilities.

When I began to teach reading this way, the conference groups were fluid. I gathered students together randomly, as need dictated. The children objected to this. They wanted to have stable conference groups and to know which day of the week they would be meeting with me. To accommodate them, I set up a schedule for the conference groups. Darcy knows that her group will meet on Mondays, Christopher that his is on Tuesdays, and so on. Knowing which day they will meet helps them, because they enjoy preparing for their conferences.

At the beginning of the year, a conference group of five or six children meets at the conference table together. I work individually with each child as the other children read to themselves and wait their turn. There is always a lot of listening in on the individual conferences, so everyone benefits from being together at the table.

The student sets the agenda for the conference. One brings a book she wants to read to me; another brings one he wants help with. I always ask why the child has chosen the book and record the answer on the record sheet (Figure 4–2) I keep in the student's folder. Then the conference begins.

Today Christopher chooses *Where the Wild Things Are* by Maurice Sendak.

Title _Fish is Fish_   Date Oct. 5, 1983

Why did you choose this book?   "Everyone else had a turn to read this book & I didn't."

Words   Had Brad count words on each page & try to identify as he read. No idea of word boundaries

Friend "I know, because its a /f/" could identify this word & some others because of position of word in sentence.

Content

Spent quite a while on the words & didn't discuss content much. Brad said "If there was a bunny rabbit at the beach then I know he'd have fun." I think he was thinking ahead to the next question.

Brad said in order to read this he — "I'll sound out the words then I'll rhyme them together. Then I'll know it then I'll read it to the class." rhyme together? — It's like you sound them out & then you rhyme them together.

What do you think you'll read next? <u>Going to the Beach</u>

Evaluation

Right now Brad's primary strategy is memorization — very interesting that he described sounding out although he doesn't do it!

Don't know how much sense he made of my "word boundary" lesson.

Feels confident about himself as a reader

FIGURE 4–2 *A record sheet for a book conference.*

EBK: Oh, *Where the Wild Things Are*. Why did you decide to read this?

CHRISTOPHER: Because you read it and I like when they roar their terrible roars.

EBK: O.K.

CHRISTOPHER: *Where the Wild Things Are*. "The night, the next ..."

EBK: What did he do that night? "The night Max wore . . ."

CHRISTOPHER: ". . . wore his wolf suit . . ."

EBK: Yes that's right, go ahead.

CHRISTOPHER: *Rereads*)"And . . ."

EBK: Yup, "The night Max wore his wolf suit and . . ."

CHRISTOPHER: "Max . . ."

EBK: "Made."

CHRISTOPHER: "Made . . ."

EBK: What did Max do? What do we call it when someone does naughty things?

CHRISTOPHER: Mischief.

EBK: "Mischief of one kind . . ."

CHRISTOPHER: "Of one kind of . . ."

EBK: *T,h* together says what? (*Christopher and I sound it out together*) 'The night Max wore his wolf suit and made mischief of one kind and . . ."

CHRISTOPHER: "Another."

EBK: Yes.

CHRISTOPHER: "His mother called him the wild thing and Max got sent to bed without eating his supper."

Showing great perseverance, Christopher continues to go through the entire book in this manner. He reads some chunks but gets stuck on many individual words. He uses a variety of strategies to figure out the difficult words. I urge him along by repeating the sections he's already read to help maintain momentum. I ask questions to jog his memory and supply words and phrases. Since Christopher is determined to read this whole book in spite of the difficulties he has with the words, it's important for me to keep the story going so he won't get discouraged. When he finishes, I offer to reread the story to him so he can enjoy it. As I read, Christopher joins me where he can.

EBK: What will you do next in order to become a better reader?

CHRISTOPHER: First I have to practice reading a lot more books. Then maybe I'll sign up to read to the class.

EBK: What will you read next?

CHRISTOPHER: *ABCs,* by Dr. Seuss [1963c].

EBK: Will it be easier for you than *Where the Wild Things Are*?

CHRISTOPHER: Maybe. I'm going to try to read it [*Wild Things*] again.

This conference took ten minutes. I could have discouraged Christopher from reading *Where the Wild Things Are* as soon as it became clear that it was too difficult for him. However, I think it's important, especially at the beginning of the year, to prove to the children that I mean it when I say they can choose their own books. It's my responsibility to let them make inappropriate selections and to channel them gently toward books that *are* appropriate to their reading level. This day Christopher reads very little of the book himself, but I reinforce the words he does know. I check these off on his Dolch word list (adding those that are not on the list at the end) and give him word cards for these words so that he can practice. Christopher leaves the conference feeling successful and with ideas for how he will improve and what he'll read next.

While Christopher has been working with me, Jessica and Darcy, also in the conference group, have been reading *The Ear Book* (Dr. Seuss 1963a) together. Now it's their turn. The two girls alternate reading pages from *The Ear Book,* obviously enjoying their collaboration.

EBK: How did you guys learn to read that book?

DARCY: Well, Jessica taught me how to read it. I heard her and Richie read it and started to read it.

EBK: How did she teach you?

DARCY: She read it to me a couple times and then I tried to read it to her, but I didn't get it right, so next time I read it to her I finally got it right.

JESSICA: When I first started, I had to sound the words in order to learn it, then I got to read it after. (*Jessica points out the words she knew before she started the book*)

Darcy and Jessica continue to talk back and forth about the books they've learned to read together. "Ms. Blackburn, guess how we'll learn to read all these books?" asks Darcy. "Because we're helping each other with the words. If we weren't friends we probably wouldn't be helping each other." They decide to work on another Dr. Seuss book together, *Marvin K. Mooney* (1972).

Darcy and Jessica prove how effective friendly collaboration can be. My job is easy. I check in on them, help them articulate their processes and goals, record their successes, and let them pursue reading on their own. When they need me, I'm available, otherwise I stay out of their way.

I have about twelve minutes left to complete my conferences and two more children to meet with. Joey is next reading *Brown Bear, Brown Bear, What Do You See?* by Bill Martin (1967).

EBK: I wonder if you're gong to read it like Jaime did.

JOEY: Why, did she read it good?

EBK: Well, remember she read it so fast she didn't even look at the words? We had to tell her to read more slowly.

Although Joey has memorized the text, he does read more slowly and pays more attention to the words. Then, halfway through, he invents a guessing game:

JOEY: (*Asking the question of himself*) I wonder what the dog's going to see next? (*He can't remember and tries to cheat by looking ahead*)

EBK: Don't peek. See if you can guess which one comes next.

JOEY: The teacher!

EBK: No, it's a black sheep.

We finish the book in this way, with Joey teasing me by saying "teacher" every time. I suspect that there's an element of face saving in Joey's playfulness. He's only memorized the first part of the book and rather than fail at reading the end, he turns it into a game. I play along with him to allow him to maintain his dignity.

EBK: What will you read next?

JOEY: I might try this again.

EBK: You know, let's go back to that page where we started to play the guessing game and put a bookmark there. That way when you pick up the book you can turn right to the part you don't know and just work on that. Do you know what a bookmark is?

JOEY: No.

Now I take the opportunity to explain the function of bookmarks so Joey understands he has the option of starting or stopping the book wherever he wants. Joey gets paper and scissors and cuts out a bookmark for himself.

Olga is the last person I need to meet with today, and I have almost run out of time. While I've been working with the others, she's read several books and played audience for Jessica and Darcy as they rehearsed. *The Ear Book.* She's gone to the bookcase with them when they went looking for *Marvin K. Mooney* and come back with a Dr. Seuss book herself, *Dr. Seuss's ABC* (1963c). I have only a few minutes left, not enough time to work with Olga on the book she's chosen.

EBK: Olga, you're last today and there's not much time. I'm sorry. Look, I'm writing a big note on my clipboard that I need to meet with you tomorrow morning during activity time. Maybe you can take this book home and practice on it tonight. (*Olga nods, but she's disappointed*) O.K. Let's see, Why did you choose *ABCs?*

OLGA: 'Cause I never read it.

Since Olga isn't familiar with *ABCs,* we quickly read the book together. Joey joins us, reading with lots of expression. He and Olga team up on the first half of the book, Olga reading the first two lines of each page, Joey finishing the rest. A little group gathers as I read the last part to both children. When I finish, Olga is eager to take the book home to practice. The interest of the other children confirms her book choice. I leave the conference table relieved that Olga is so happy with her conference. I know, however, that she needs more time and I will be sure to keep my promise to meet with her in the morning.

This session is typical of the way the conference groups operate at the beginning of the year. I meet once a week with each child. This is quite a switch from the daily reading group, but the students are using reading and writing all day long, every day—I have many opportunities to monitor them, and they get lots of practice. The daily reading group is unnecessary.

My role in the reading conferences is different from a teacher's role in a traditional reading group. My concern is less on What did I teach? and more on What did I learn about Joey, Darcy, Jessica, Christopher, and Olga as readers? I spend more time keeping records of what they do, say, and know than I do on creating lesson plans. Another difference is the kind of talk that goes on. My students and I really converse about the books and about their process of metamorphosis from tadpole to frog. By choosing their own books, the children initiate the topic of conversation. The pace of the conversation is determined by the child's reading ability, interests, and needs. My silences are often as instructive as my suggestions. When I do ask questions, they arise out of the context of the conversation as it develops and they tend to be open-ended. Often they are predictable questions (Why did you choose this book?

What will you read next?) that children have a fair chance of answering since they can anticipate and prepare for them.

One day in October, Ricky reads from his own writing journal:

EBK: Why did you choose to read your journal today?

RICKY: Because I'm happy about what I did on this book.

EBK: Are you going to read your whole journal or just a part of it?

RICKY: The whole book. (*He begins, paraphrasing the pages, except the story about Halloween. He reads this one word for word. He has chosen this story for publication*)

EBK: Now, I notice something about the way you read this story ["Halloween"]. You read this story perfectly, just the way you wrote it. Some of these other stories you didn't actually read every single word, you sort of told what they were about. Why was it that you could read this story so well?

Before Ricky begins, I ask my standard question about book choice. This gives me a feeling for Ricky's mood. If he had answered that he'd chosen to read his journal because he needed help remembering the words, my approach would have been different. Now I know that Ricky is very proud of his work and may not be amenable to "helpful criticism" from me, since he doesn't recognize that he needs any help. When Ricky finishes I make a declarative statement about how he read his journal and I ask him to reflect on why he read his Halloween story differently.

RICKY: I didn't forget this one, and see it has bigger letters and the other ones, I made kind of a little bit small letters and I couldn't see some.

EBK: Do you think that maybe the topic of this story was a little more interesting to you right now than the others?

RICKY: Yeah, because it's almost Halloween!

EBK: So that's important in being able to read, isn't it? You need to really be interested in what you're reading. Now this story has big letters (*Pointing to another story in his book*) I wonder if you'll remember this?

RICKY: Hmmm. I might forget it 'cause on this one ["Halloween"] I didn't erase. (*There are a lot of scratched out places on the other page*)

Ricky then "reads" the other story I've pointed out, but what he's really doing is telling the page. What he says doesn't correspond with the sounds that are there.

Reading is still a mystery to Ricky. He's not quite sure how people go about reading the words on the page. He thinks that maybe making his letters larger or writing more neatly is the key. Of course, both of these strategies do help, but Ricky hasn't prioritized their importance relative to other strategies. By listening to him I get a clearer picture of where Ricky is in his transformation from beginning reader to reader. I try to help him see that being *interested* in the words on the page makes a big difference in being able to read them. That interest is far more important than any physical feature of the print itself.

EBK: Ricky, how are you learning to read?

RICKY: By sounding out the letters and trying to remember them.

EBK: Do you think other people can read this book?

RICKY: If they sound it out, yeah.

EBK: Can you read their books?

RICKY: If I sound them out.

EBK: What's another way that you could learn to read their books besides sounding them out?

RICKY: By seeing the letters and just knowing what they say.

EBK: Pretend you were going to read Robert's book about kittens but you couldn't sound it out, what would you do?

RICKY: Ask Robert.

Now I'm probing a bit to find out what other strategies Ricky is familiar with. He knows about sounding out words and he understands that people can know what a word says just by looking at it. He realizes that other children in the class can be helpful to him in learning to read new books. This information reassures me that Ricky is making progress in his understanding of how learning to read works. I know that what Ricky tries out in talk today, he will begin to put into practice—if not tomorrow, as least in the near future.

Sometimes children mistake strategies that work in writing for the same ones that are helping them in reading. One of the most common is the tendency to see "sounding out" as the dominate strategy for attacking new words. Students often use a variety of strategies for decoding words but when asked, How did you figure that out? they answer, I sounded it out.

Daniel reads a preprimer, *Rhymes and Tales* (1980), to me one day without pausing once to sound out a word.

EBK: Now why is it that you can read this book so fast?

DANIEL: I put the sounds together.

EBK: Do you really, I've never heard you do that. Could you show me on the first page? Pretend that you can't read this, I know you can, but just show me how you would sound that out. (*Daniel tries to sound out the word* sun) Is that the sound those letters make?

DANIEL: Isn't that a *u*?

EBK: Yes, but is doesn't say /oo/. It says /uh/. You know something, Daniel, I'm wondering if you sound out words or if you have another way of figuring out these words.

DANIEL: When you cover them like this. Then you try to figure out the other ones and then you cover the other part and you try to figure that one out. You can sound out that little bit, and then you sound out the other bit, then you get it.

EBK: Oh, why don't you try maybe doing this. Let's try it with this word here [*hot*].

DANIEL: (*Spelling it*) H-O-T.

EBK: Are you saying the sounds?

DANIEL: No.

EBK: You know something, I think it seems hard for you to sound out words. I think you must have an easier way of reading these words. Let's try to figure it out.

Because Daniel sounds out words when he writes, he thinks "sounding out" is the right way to describe his reading. It is not. He uses at least four other methods: picture clues, context clues, memory of the story from previous readings, and visual memory of individual words. He "sounds out" infrequently and is still a bit confused about how to use his knowledge of letter sounds to decode. It's important for me to reveal a student's reading processes to him, to make them more accessible as a set of conscious alternatives so he learns to choose the best strategies for each reading situation. This is an important function of the reading conferences.

Teaching Skills

There are certain things, of course, that I can and do teach directly. Teaching individual letter sounds (long and short vowels, and consonants) as well as diagraphs and blends as group minilessons speeds up the children's encoding and decoding in both reading and writing. Early in the year, my students rely heavily on memorization as a way to gain fluency as readers. It is indeed a useful strategy, but I need to help the children learn to recognize words and to decode them. Whenever a student reads a book that he has memorized, as Joey did when he read *Brown Bear, Brown Bear,* I always go back to the beginning of the book and ask the reader to scan each page for words he knows. When Joey brought *Brown Bear* to me the next day, he knew a few words (the ones in italics) by sight:

> Brown bear, brown bear
> What do you *see*?
> *I* see a red bird
> Looking at *me.*

I suggested that he try sounding out *red* and *at*, because I felt he'd be successful. He was. I checked these words off on the Dolch word list in Joey's reading folder, dated each word, and wrote the title *Brown Bear* next to them. I made cards for Joey with these words on them and dated each of the cards. I put the cards on a metal ring and stuck it into the pocket of Joey's folder. Joey can practice reading these words by himself or with his friends during independent reading.

Once a classroom visitor asked me to characterize my teaching and I surprised us both by answering: "I do everything backwards." Giving Joey words to practice that he already knows is an example of such "backwardness," yet there is some sense to it. Joey had success with these words in the context of this one story. I want to be sure that he recognizes them again in a different context, that he commits them to memory. Because they are his particular words, he has an investment in them and this makes the word cards more meaningful than if I simply drilled words from the Dolch word list at random.

Writing the title of the book next to each word allows me to cue the child when the word appears in a different context. If Joey gets stuck on the word *see* while reading, I can remind him that he learned that word in *Brown Bear.* Often just mentioning the title of the book will help a student recall the word. This is an interesting phenomenon. Sometimes students run through several sections of a book in their minds until they get the right word. And they always know which word is the right one. Instead of just learning to recognize the individual words on the word cards, the children are also learning them in chunks of texts in a variety of syntaxes. I think this allows them to use the words more effectively in their talk and in their writing. If they need to find the word to check its spelling, they know where to look. It is amazing to me how good we all become at remembering which words belong to which story. I have thousands of words stored in my head this way. By the end of the year, the children do, too.

Each time we meet for a reading conference, and often at other times during the day, I have my students run through their word cards. I stamp the date on the cards each time I listen to the child read them and put a check on them each time they read them correctly. After three correct readings, the cards are removed from the ring and taken home. This way, my students build a repertoire of words that they know by sight. Combined with the amount of practice they get applying phonetic skills in their writing, and with the number of words they learn easily by reading their own published books, the children quickly substitute real reading for memorization. By January the word cards are obsolete for most of the class.

The skills normally tackled during reading groups and taught through worksheets and drills can be addressed naturally at the reading conference, as the children's reading development dictates. Darcy comes to me for a conference on *The Nose Book* (Perkins 1970):

EBK: Why did you want to read this book?

DARCY: Because I'm learnin' how to read this book and I know how to read half of it.

EBK: Darcy, do you want to use this reading conference to read the part you already know, or would it be helpful to work on the part you don't know?

DARCY: (*Pausing about thirty seconds to consider*) The part I have trouble with, like this is one page . . .

EBK: Alright, well you read what you can.

DARCY: I'll just skip this page. . . . "I see a nose on—" I have trouble on this word.

EBK: "I see a nose on /eh/ /v/ /er/ . . .

DARCY: Every! "Every face." Now I think I know what this word is. "Everybody grows a nose."

EBK: Right! Now why did you know you could figure out this word [*everybody*]?

DARCY: Because when I got that word over there, this is the only word I have trouble on.

However, as Darcy continues, I see that her troubles are not over. She is having a great deal of difficulty because there are so many words with silent *e*'s and long vowel combinations.

EBK: O.K. You know why you're having trouble with this book?

DARCY: Can't sound it out.

EBK: Right, because there's a rule you don't know yet. When I tell you this rule it will really help you.

Instead of timing my teaching according to a curriculum guide or teacher's manual, I wait to teach the silent *e* and long vowel rule until Darcy really needs it. This rule now takes on a magical quality for Darcy as it miraculously unlocks the mystery of all those words she's been struggling with. Not only does she put it to use immediately but she also rushes off to teach it to her friends. Within several days of this conference everyone is so eager to have this pixie dust sprinkled on them that it is necessary to teach the silent *e* and long vowel rule to the whole class as a minilesson. All the children are not ready or able to use this rule right away, as Darcy is, but the point is that I treat learning these rules as an exciting event. I get to be the fairy godmother.

Many issues of phonics, sentence structure, and syntax that are commonly taught as lessons in reading groups are addressed more easily and appropriately in a writing situation. The students' own writing provides a context for practice and implementation, making worksheets unnecessary. I don't want to diminish the relevance of learning rules for language structure, but I've found that my students deduce and assimilate many of these rules from their experience as readers and writers. They often apply the rules before they know what they are. Moti was excited one day when he made the discovery that *ph* is sounded the same as an *f*. "Guess what, I was reading *Babar and the Wully Wully* [De Brunhoff 1975], and I noticed that in the word *elephant* the ph says /f/, that's just like at my house when I was trying to write the word *phone* and my dad spelled it for me and it started with *ph*. I thought it was *fone*." Naturally, Moti was anxious to tell others of his discovery.

Keeping Track of Progress

It is more difficult to keep track of what the children know about specific word-attack skills in this kind of program. However, I have found some ways that work for me.

I keep my record-keeping system in the student's reading folder—a pocket folder the same color as that student's writing folder. (This color coordination makes them easier to find and file.) Into this folder I put the Dolch word list, a record booklet that I make for each student, and a blank composition book for the student to use as a "title book."

I've already mentioned the Dolch word list and described how I use it. It's one way that I keep a record of the children's sight/word development.

The record book that I make has sheets stapled into it with two guiding questions and a space to write about decoding strategies and content or comprehension. There is also a place for me to write a reflection about the conference. This sheet (see Figure 4–3) allows me to keep notes on specific skills discussed and strategies used. I then transfer a record of the skills onto file cards. The file cards allow me to do a quick inventory of the skills each child has been introduced to so that I can follow up with more individual practice or plan a whole-class minilesson if I feel it will be beneficial.

Finally, my students use the title book to keep their own record of books read (see Figure 4–4). I instruct them to copy the titles of the books they read or look at during the reading period into the title book and to date each entry. (Date stamps make this simple.) If they read the same book several days in a row, I want them to write the title down each time. The title books are a "big deal." The children feel important keeping a record of the books they read. They feel important when they see how many books they can read. It is a way to make them accountable for their time during independent reading. Colleagues often ask me how I motivate my students to read at the beginning of the year, the time when reading is most difficult for them. The title books are a big-help. They are evidence for the children of what they are doing during reading time, evidence they can touch and share with others. Having to write the title forces them to pay attention to their own book choices and helps them remember what they've read. Their work and choices are affirmed by me at school and by their parents when they take the title books home.

The title books are also a significant element of record keeping for me. Here is the list of books from Eleza's title book for the period September 25 to October 15:

Jump, Frog, Jump [Kalin 1989]	predictable book
Gus [1979]	preprimer
Good Morning, Chick [Ginsberg 1980]	easy reader
The School [Burningham 1975]	easy reader
Gus	
Gus	
The Very Hungry Caterpillar [Carle 1969]	predictable book
The Caterpillar [1988]	easy reader
My Friend the Cow	
The Great Big, Especially Beautiful Easter Egg [Stevenson 1983]	trade book
Who Took the Farmer's Hat? [Nodset 1963]	predictable book

	Beginning	Middle	End
I Vocabulary Word Recognition Locates word in own writing.			
Identifies word boundaries and spacing			
Word Analysis Discriminates between words by using initial and final consonant clues.			
Discriminates between words according to position in sentence.			
Uses context clues.			
Associates sounds to diagraphs: sh, wh, th, ch			
Associates sounds to 2 letter blends: st, bl, pl, br, fl, cl, gl, gr, sp, sm, sw, sl, tr, sn.			
Knows that letters aeiou, y and combinations of these represent different sounds.			
Is familar with silent letters			
Knows sounds for oo, ou, ow			
Knows sounds for ir, er, ur,			
Comments:			
II Structural Analysis Knows word endings: ed (wantid), ed (moved), ed (likt)			
Recognizes compound words.			
Understands contractions			

FIGURE 4–3 *A record sheet for tracking reading strategies.*

	Beginning	Middle	End
Knows use of s as plural			
Recognizes and uses past, present and future tense.			
III Mechanics Observes and uses punctuation: . , ! ?			
Observes and uses capitals at the beginning of sentences and proper names.			
Reads expressively to convey meaning.			
Comments:			

FIGURE 4–3 *(Reading strategies record sheet continued.)*

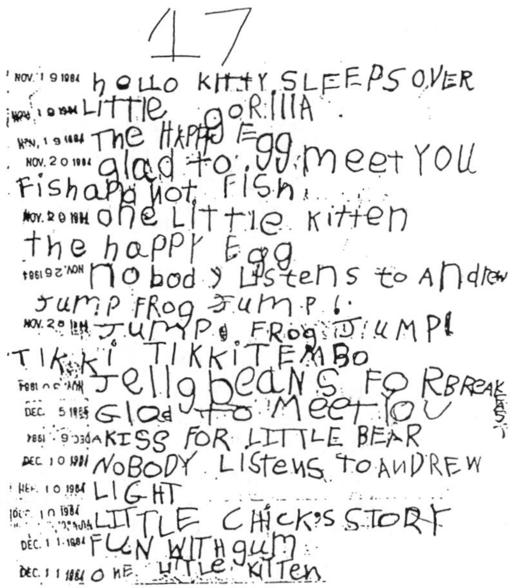

FIGURE 4–4 *A student's record of books read.*

The Three Billy Goats Gruff [Appleby 1985]	easy reader
The Happy Day [Krauss 1949]	trade book
Noisy Nora [Wells 1973]	trade book
When Will I Read? [Cohen 1977]	trade book
Fun With Gum [1979]	preprimer
My Trip to New Hampshire	Eleza's published book
Dinosaurs [Dallinger 1977]	trade book
My Dad Came Home	classmate's published book
Sam and Al [1979]	preprimer
Old Hat, New Hat [Berenstein and Berenstein 1970]	easy reader
One Little Kitten [Hoban 1979]	trade book

I read through these title books several times a week, and in them I write notes to parents to let them know how their child is progressing in reading. I ask the parents to write back to me in the title book to let me know how their child is using books at home. I like to know what books parents are reading to their children and what reading interests the child exhibits at home that may not be evident at school. Here's one such note:

> *October 10* Simon works hard on his reading and is very conscientious during reading time. He has just written and published his own story and I hope he'll read this to the class soon. Simon has made great progress on his letter sounds and visual memory of words. Does he enjoy reading at home? Sincerely, Ellen

Simon's mom responds:

> Yes, Simon is very proud of his reading ability and reads us (sounding out and memory) *Hop on Pop*, and *Old Hat, New Hat*, two Dr. Seuss books. He regularly "reads" to himself—looking at his own or library books—and his older sister and myself read to him. We tend to read chapter books such as: *James and the Giant Peach* [Dahl 1962], *Robin Hood* [Storr 1984], *Bedknobs and Broomsticks* [Norton 1990], *Little Bear* [Minarik 1957], and the Puffin books, fairy tales and poetry.

The next entries, a note to Erin's parents and her dad's response, show how helpful the title books are to all of us in understanding the way a child's approach to reading can change.

November 11 Erin's list of titles has changed quite a bit since she first started recording them. Initially she had no system for selecting books and chose randomly, often trying to read books that were too difficult. Now her list indicates that she's gained a sense of herself as a reader— what she *can* do and what she *wants* to do in the future. She selects books at her reading level, but also tries a variety of books within her reading level. She rereads books to gain fluency in anticipation of reading to the class. Sincerely, Ellen

We can notice her improvement at home with her ability to concentrate on reading words she is not familiar with. She *enjoys* reading something. That, to us, is far more important than any specific reading level she might be at and we can see this is your aim as well.

The parents are encouraged to take note of the books their child is interested in and to follow up on that interest by talking to the child about the books, checking the books out of the library, or purchasing the books as gifts for birthdays.

Later in the school year I suggest that my students include a little note to me about the books they read, how they are feeling about reading, what their plans are, etc.; I respond to them in a note as well. Figure 4–5 is one example of this type of exchange. Below are additional examples from Simon's title book (my responses appear in italics):

December 11 Miss Blackburn, this is easy, very easy. I read *Going to Mystic Seaport* [his own published book]
Simon, that book is easy, because you wrote it, right?

February 11 Miss, Blackburn, I read *I Wish I Was Sick Too* [Brandenberg 1976]. It was hard.
Simon, you did a good job reading it for the first time. I hope you practice on it and read it to the class.
I had trouble on some bits. I will practice on it.

February 13 I read *I Wish I Was Sick Too*. At first it was hard, but it is easy now.
Good, you kept trying.

Simon's mom joins in:

It is most enjoyable reading through this book. It says so much about Simon's progress. He is reading more and more at home and telling me the spelling of words he likes. Thank you.

In the title books the children learn how to use writing to record information. They see examples of note writing between adults and write

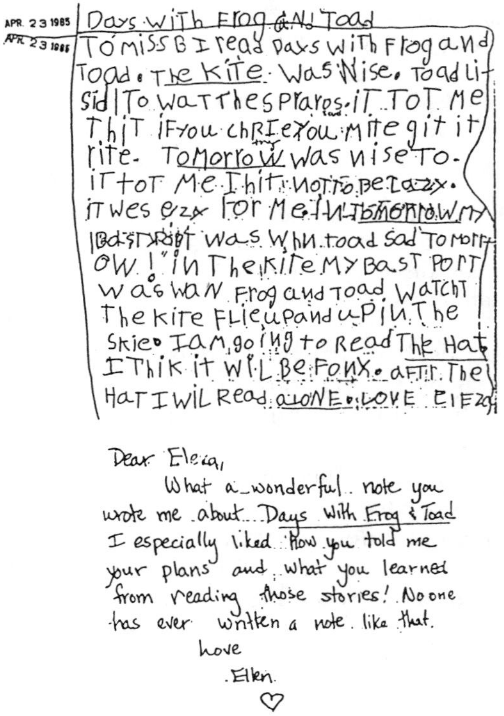

APR 23 1985
APR 23 1985

Days with Frog and Toad

To Miss B I read Days with Frog and
Toad. The Kite. Was Nise. Toad li-
sid to wat the sprares. it tot me
thit if you chrieYou mite git it
rite. Tomorrow was nise to.
it tot me. I hit not to be lazy.
it wes ezy for me. IN tomorrow my
Bd srt prt was whn toad sad tomorrow!" iN The Kite My Bast pprt
was wan Frog and Toad watcht
the Kite Flieup and u piN the
skie. I am going to Read The Hat
I think it wil Be fonx. aftr The
Hat I wil Read aLone. LoVE. EieZa

Dear Eleza,
    What a wonderful note you
wrote me about Days With Frog & Toad
I especially liked How you told me
your plans and what you learned
from reading those stories! No one
has ever written a note like that.
        Love
        .Ellen.

Days with Frog and Toad

To Miss B,
I read *Days with Frog and Toad*. *The Kite*
was nice. Toad listened to what sparrow
[said]. It taught me that if you try you might
get it right. *Tomorrow* was nice too. It taught
me that not to be lazy. It was easy for me. In
Tomorrow my best part was when Toad said
"Tomorrow!" In *The Kite* my best part was
when Frog and Toad watched the kite flies
up and up in the sky. I am going to read *The
Hat*. I think it will be funny. After *The Hat* I
will read *Alone*.
Love, Eleza

FIGURE 4–5 *My exchange of notes with Eleza about the books she is reading.*

notes themselves. Periodically during the year, and especially at the end of the year, my students count up the number of books they've read and reread. On average this will be three hundred and fifty books. What a great sense of achievement they feel! And this is possible because they have kept a record.

The title books are a good anecdotal record for me. By reading through them before each reporting period I get a feeling for the kinds of book choices the student is making. I can see change and improvement in those choices. Rereading my notes to parents and their responses allows me to recall some of the issues we've addressed concerning the child's reading.

Using these methods of record keeping I can give an accurate assessment of a student's reading level at each reporting period and, if necessary, can suggest where the child will fit into a basal program.

When I prepare the child's folder for next year's teacher, I include copies of the Dolch word list, my file cards of individual skills, the title book, and an anecdotal report of the child's reading progress.

"Getting to be a Real Good Reader"

By midyear, the majority of the class is beyond the preprimer stage. The change in the students' reading ability is reflected in their title books. This sampling from Eleza's book for January 7 through January 30 shows that she is reading many trade books with more complicated plots. There are only two easy readers in this list, compared with twelve in her September list.

Strega Nona [De Paola 1975]	trade book
Giant John [Lobel 1964]	trade book
The Stupids Die [Allard 1981]	trade book
Snow White [Littledale 1980]	trade book
My Puppy Is Born [Cole 1981]	nonfiction
Chickens Aren't the Only Ones [Heller 1981]	nonfiction
Nobody Listens to Miss Blackburn	classmate's book
Little Bear [Minarik 1957]	easy reader
The Mitten [Tressalt 1964b]	trade book
Here Comes the Bride [Raabe 1978]	easy reader
Broderick [Ormondroyd 1984]	trade book
The Popcorn Book [De Paola 1978]	nonfiction
Miss Nelson Is Back [Allard and Marshall 1982]	trade book
Spiders [Dallinger 1981]	trade book
Rumpelstiltskin [Tarcov 1974]	trade book

The criteria for book choices also develop. At the beginning of the year, the most frequent response to the question "Why did you choose this book?" is "Because it was easy," or "Because it has big words [large type]." At midyear the answers become "Because I heard Daniel read it and it's a good story"; "I like this story so I wanted to learn how to read it"; or "I want to read this book to the class." There is less concern about the mechanics of reading and more interest in reading for pleasure or to please an audience.

The children evaluate the books they read, and some of their judgments are indicative of the writing they do:

Dear Ellen, I read *The Hating Book* [Zolotow 1969]. It is not good, but the ending was good. Love, Mike

Dear Ellen, I read *The Three Wishes* [Clifton 1976]. I would've written it different because the man should've wished different things, but it was a good book. Love, Mike

Indeed the children bring more and more of their experience as writers to bear on the books they read. They realize that writers make choices about including and excluding information. They know that plot is crafted by real people and they speculate about why authors wrote as they did. Sometimes they become frustrated and do more then speculate, they seek to improve. Simon was disgusted with the ending of a story in one of the preprimers. The story is a version of the old folktale about the mice who put the bell on the cat. However, this version has a defeatist ending. The mice decide none of them is brave enough to put a bell on the cat:

"Can you get the bell on the cat?"
"I cannot get the bell on the cat."
"Can you?"
"Not I."
"Not I."
"It cannot work."
"We cannot get the bell on the cat."

The story ends too blandly for Simon. After discussing possible endings with a group of friends, Simon wrote:

All the mice were sad. One of the mice said, "Wait!" and he told them. They got into the medicine cabinet. They got the sleeping powder and they put it in the cat's food and when the cat ate some, he fell asleep and they put the bell on the cat and now when the cat comes, it rings.

We bound Simon's new ending into the book and added his name to the title page.

Because they are writers, my students demand more of the books they read. They read actively, with a liveliness that results from their relationship with text and their sense of control over the process of learning to be literate.

Reading Partners

Periodically during the year I take a break from my usual conference schedule to circulate and observe during the reading period. One spring I wrote this description:

Today I walked around observing during reading time. I wanted to see who is reading with whom. What groups have developed.

Daniel and Jason sat together in front of the A-frame bookcase. This was after Daniel commented to me "Jason likes me to read to him. Last time I read to him, he stayed with me the whole time. I read *Firefighters* [Johnson 1985] and he sat there the whole time."

Misty and Scott sat together at the round table. At first they read *Why Can't I Fly?* [Gelman 1986] together, but Misty either finished it first or decided to read something else because when I came back Scott was still reading it and Misty was reading *Hansel and Gretel* [Gross 1988]. She was making comments about the story as she went along. These comments were only half directed to Scott because he never answered her and Misty didn't seem to expect him to. Scott read *Where the Wild Things Are* [Sendak 1962] and *Doghouse for Sale* [Pape 1979].

At the art table Joey, Jaime, Rickie, and Joeline were working hard. But, they were all working independently. Even though Rickie and Jaime were both reading *More Spaghetti, I Say!* [Gelman 1977a] neither of them helped the other. At one point Rickie even slammed his fist on the table because he was having difficulty, but wasn't inspired to ask Jaime for help. There was a good atmosphere at the table. A lot of energy focused on reading.

In the math area Jeannine, Simone, and Richie were reading. Jeanine kept getting up and going to the next table to get Misty's help. Simone also occasionally looked over to help Jeanine. Simone has better word-attack skills and can supply more reasonable guesses.

Richie spent quite a bit of time wandering around, as usual. I kept an eye on him and tried to suggest that he choose something more appropriate to work on.

Robert and Chrissy were in the A-frame bookcase. They were taking turns reading *Danny and the Dinosaur* [Hoff 1958]. They worked together well. Robert went to the library to get a reptile book and came back and read it to Chrissy.

Olga and Yudhy sat together in the reading area. Olga seemed to be reading to Yudhy most of the time. They stayed together and had a good period.

Joshua and Eric were both reading in the bathtub. Joshua was looking at the dinosaurs book and Eric was reading *The Ear Book* [Dr. Seuss 1963a] and *The Very Hungry Caterpillar* [Carle 1969].

Everyone seemed to be working fairly well today. I was really interested in the partnerships that did and didn't develop. I am making a chart to show who read together and what they read. I want to share it with the kids and see what they have to say about how they work during reading time.

The children were very interested in this set of observations. Like me, they enjoyed seeing how they were helping each other with their reading. It was from this discussion that the practice of having reading partners came to be. Using my notes and their input I organized the class into pairs of reading partners. We decided to have a "reading partners day" about once every two weeks. On reading partners day I encouraged my students to work with the multiple copies of books that I had in the classroom and to take turns choosing books to read. This did not always go smoothly, since there were disagreements about book choices. Some books were too hard for one of the partners, or too easy, or not interesting. But I thought even these arguments were productive since they encouraged the children to negotiate; to justify their choices and to empathize with another child's point of view and reading level. Reading partners added variety to the reading period. Children were encouraged to read books that they might not have tried on their own and they came to take great pride in their partner's progress.

Book of the Month

During the first two years of the research project with Don Graves and Jane Hansen, I was entirely consumed by the task of establishing a reading/writing classroom. I worked hard to perfect methods of teaching in an individualized reading program. As time passed, I started to relax and feel comfortable with my routine. The children were choosing their own books and they were learning to read. I knew how to work independently with them but I had also managed to create a collaborative community of readers and writers who cared about one another and a shared body of literature. So naturally as things became easier I became restless. Wasn't something missing? I decided there was. The children certainly shared reading. They listened to stories as a class and they read the same books, over and over again. But we never all read the same book at the same time. So I started our class "Book-of-the-Month Club."

For years I had participated in Scholastic Books' See Saw Book Club and every month sent home with my students the newsletter listing paperbacks for sale. Now I designated one book each month as our "book of the month" and asked parents to purchase a copy for their child. In September, for example, I chose *The Very Hungry Caterpillar*, by Eric Carle (1969). When the books arrived, the excitement was infectious. Even Niva, who spoke little English, hugged her book and sniffed the pages as she saw the others doing. She was thrilled when she discovered holes in the pages and stuck her fingers through them. We read the book together, almost like a choral reading. Although children have a similar experience in shared reading with Big Books, there is something extra special about owning the book yourself and about having all those copies everywhere.

During the month I planned many activities related to the book. Since we were using the books nearly everyday, the children kept them at school in their cubby buckets. We did counting and sequencing projects, and made caterpillars out of egg cartons. We captured a monarch butterfly caterpillar and watched its metamorphosis. Because the children owned the books, they could underline words, write numbers underneath the fruits, circle their favorite foods, and draw little caterpillars in the margins. At the end of the month the children took *The Very Hungry Caterpillar* home and the whole process began again with a new book.

The book of the month generated a new feeling of companionship around books and reading. While individualization is important, so is developing commonalities. Every child, regardless of individual reading level, learned to read some if not all of each monthly selection. The class had the books of the month and the activities surrounding them as common experiences.

Book Discussion Groups

As my students' appreciation for the books they read deepens, their needs during reading conferences change. It is probably accurate to say that early reading conferences from September to January focus on what Rosenblatt (1978) labels "efferent" reading. That is, I spend the most time working with the children on the text itself—on its content and on identifying the words. As the children approach greater fluency and the reading material becomes more complex, the subject of the conference switches to "aesthetic" reading. We are able to attend to the experiences, images, ideas, and feelings the books evoke. In this conference, Ricky discusses the differences he feels when he reads funny stories and when he reads sad ones.

EBK: How do you feel when you read a funny story?

RICKY: Happy, because my heart beeps and it's beeping so hard.

EBK: You mean that your heart starts beating so hard? Is that because you're excited? Do you ever have that feeling when you read other kinds of stories?

RICKY: Yeah, like my funny book about the duck that swallowed the soap.

EBK: Yes, that's a funny book too. What kind of feeling would you get if you read a sad story? Have you ever read a sad story?

RICKY: Yeah, Misty's story about "I Love Grampa." My heart beat slow on that one and I didn't get excited.

EBK: Remember when Misty wrote that, I started to cry right in school?

RICKY: Yeah, On that one I'm low down and it just gets my heart beeping slow that I feel like, mm, she must be sorry for him to die . . . I feel like that.

EBK: When you read a sad book it changes how you feel. You can be in a happy mood and read a sad book and all of sudden you feel low down.

RICKY: (*Demonstrating how he looks and sounds reading Misty's story*) Yeah.

EBK: Isn't if funny that a bunch of words on a page written by someone else can make you feel the way she felt?

At this point it is no longer necessary to have individual reading conferences and I switch from these to group book discussions. This change parallels the change from individual to group writing conferences that takes place at the same time of year. For group book discussions my students meet and take turns sharing a book they're currently reading. These discussions focus on my students' response to the story. Sometimes the children will summarize the story first and read a favorite part to get the conversation started. Often, a book is so familiar that the group will plunge right in with reactions and questions. The talk during book discussions typically draws the story into the students' lives and expands on it. Very rarely do I hear any discussion mirroring the kinds of comprehension questions frequently asked in teacher's manuals. The children do not ask for the name of the main character. They don't ask the reader to sequence the events in the story. Instead, Sam shares *Madeline's Rescue* (Bemelmans 1953) and tries out his idea for a new ending: "What if the puppies keep having babies until there are so many dogs that the *children* are the pets!" Madeline's role in such a story is discussed and developed. Basic literacy and comprehension are assumed in these discussions. The children use their creativity to elaborate and extend.

Jessica takes her turn in discussion group and shares *Robert the Rose Horse* (Heilbroner 1962), a current class favorite. First she describes the plot of the story and then reads some of her favorite parts; next she opens the floor to discussion.

TRACEY: Why did you want to read this?

JESSICA: Because I never read this and I want to read it to the class.

JOEY: Guess what? I can't make up my mind which part I like the best, and I like the whole book.

JESSICA: I 'specially like this part. (*Showing the page where Robert smells the roses and sneezes*) "Kachooo!"

SCOTT: (*Looking at the picture*) How come the dogs go up and the birds came down?

JESSICA: Because the birds were flying. And the birds were flying and the dogs weren't. The dogs were walking.

SCOTT: That's strange. That's strange.

TIMOTHY: Let me see.

JOEY: See there's the bird, upside down.

TRACEY: That's funny, where he fell down.

The children are in control of the group. Jessica takes the responsibility of interpreting the picture for Scott. I do not speak at all until about halfway through the discussion. When I do, I make a simple observation that I hope will generate some comparison between two books the children are familiar with. There is no hesitation while the children decide what I might be fishing for: they easily shift direction in response to my comment.

EBK: This week we've read two books about robbers.

JESSICA: There were three robbers in both books.

TRACEY: In *The Three Robbers* [Ungerer 1962] they were nice guys, but in this one they weren't.

SCOTT: Nope, they were all bad.

JESSICA: The whole book is different. The robbers in *Robert and the Rose Horse* didn't throw pepper on the horsey.

EBK: They didn't put pepper in Robert's eyes. What if the robbers in *Robert and the Rose Horse* had the pepper blower from *The Three Robbers* and they put pepper in Robert's eyes?

VOICES: Oh, no!

JESSICA: He still might have sneezed though. He just don't know where. Then he wouldn't know which direction to sneeze in because his eyes would be full of pepper. (*The students all begin to talk at once: "I like the ending." "Yeah." "See!"*)

SCOTT: Can we make a play of this?

JESSICA: We need the robbers . . .

JOEY: I want to be a chicken. (*The group begins to make a list of cast members and to assign parts*)

Although I certainly hold my own as a responsible adult member of the discussion group, my participation allows space for the children to react and to determine the direction of the discussion. Acting out books is a popular way of "owning" the story. I think my question about the pepper blower prompted the decision to act out the story. The children were beginning to feel the plot slipping around and wanted to play out some of the new options my question suggested. They acted out the story with several different endings.

Reading to the Class: The Author's Chair

As a literacy event, reading to the class benefits writing, reading, and speaking. Earlier I wrote about the importance of "the author's chair" for the writer. This event, reading to the class, is also significant in the development of readers. Reading to the class is a privilege the reader achieves when she has mastered a particular book. Each student decides when he is ready to read and signs up. As the year progresses my students come to understand the responsibility they have to their audience when they put their name on the list.

At the beginning of the year many students do not know how to judge their own readiness to read and their own reading ability. Typical is Joey's behavior during the second week of school. Joey signed up to read his writing book to the class. He took his seat in front of his audience and opened his book. Turning it toward the class, with an embarrassed smile, Joey silently showed us four pages of meandering lines and dots.

"He's not saying anything . . ."

"Joey, what is it?"

"There's no words, so how can he read it?"

"That's O.K. There are wordless books," I say. "Maybe when Joey feels more comfortable, he'll tell us about his designs." We applaud Joey's effort. At least he has made a start.

It takes several months for the children to realize that reading to the class is a performance. A performance makes heavy demands on the reader. It is not enough to read the words. The child must give them meaning and expression, must respond to cues and reaction from the audience. The reader has the same relationship to the text that an actor has to a script. Nowhere in a traditional reading program is this demand for excellence made on the reader. More than any test or drill I could possibly devise, reading to the class is an incentive for and a demonstration of the best a child can do. Everywhere around the room during independent reading the children are practicing to read to the class. They read and reread a line or paragraph, trying out different emphases.

They polish their delivery and anticipate where the class will laugh, groan, or applaud. Finally, the reader moderates comments and fields questions from the class at the end of the reading. The whole-class discussions that occur after a reading are so important that I need a separate chapter (Chapter 9) to address them.

Reading/Writing Connections

Virginia Woolf (1950) once described her experience as a reader in this way:

> It seemed as if what I read was laid upon the landscape, not printed, bound, or sewn up, but somehow the product of trees and fields and the hot summer sky. . . . If I looked down at my book I could see Keats and Pope behind him and Sir Thomas Browne—hosts of them merging in a mass of Shakespeare, behind whom if one peered long enough, some shapes of men in pilgrim's dress emerged—Chaucer perhaps. ... (152–53)

Since much of my students' writing is personal narrative, a major part of what they read is literature that is embedded in their landscape. The characters are people in their family, or in their class; the setting is their own neighborhood. Reading is not a vicarious way of experiencing the world. The world described in my students' writing is the world they live in. They read as participants as well. Their reading is qualitatively different as a result of their experience as writers. Like Virginia Woolf they can extend their feeling of connectedness to the trade books they read, fitting them into their landscapes as easily as they do their own writing and the writing of their classmates.

One day I read *Owl at Home*, by Arnold Lobel (1975). The first story, called "Strange Bumps," describes how Owl gets into bed and sees lumps at the foot of his bed. These lumps are his feet, but he doesn't realize this and is terrified. The next morning Amanda stopped by the writing table: "You know that story you read yesterday, about those strange bumps, well, that's just like at my house. My cat saw my feet under my covers and she thought it was a mouse and she kept trying to bite me."

"Your cat didn't know those strange bumps were your feet either, did she? Just like Owl." Lobel's story was quickly assimilated into Amanda's experience.

I don't believe that simply adding writing to the curriculum is enough to develop the relationship between reading and writing. I think this is a relationship that needs nurturing. By now much has been writ-

INVENTION

Invented Spelling

Children develop their own spellings of words based upon knowledge of sound/symbol associations and their internatlization of writing and spelling conventions.

Invented Reading

Children create their own version of a familiar story using picture clues and memorization of words and phrases. They demonstrate their knowledge of reading conventions.

CHOICE

Topic Choice

Children choose their own topics to write about.

Book Choice

Children choose their own books to read.

DISCUSSION

Writing Conferences

Children have writing conferences to improve their written messages. During the conference, questions are asked to find out what the writer knows about the subject and the writing process.

Reading Conferences

Children have reading conferences to improve their fluency and comprehension of reading materials. Questions are asked to reveal what the child knows about the content of the piece and about the reading process. During class discussions of books the reader is asked about his/her interpretation and appreciation of the text.

REVISION

Rewriting

Children revise their writing to change or improve the meaning of the piece. An internalized sense of audience helps to stimulate rethinking and rewriting during the act of composing. Interaction between writer and audience helps to promote new revisions.

Rereading

When children reread books they often change their original interpretation or find new meaning in the text. Audience reaction can prompt a new assessment of a book.

PUBLICATION

Writers publish to make their accomplishments, ideas, and feelings public. Each book that is published adds to the body of literature available to the class.

Children who read a book to the class are making their interpretation and command of the text public. Each book that is read aloud becomes more accessible and adds to the body of literature available to the class.

FIGURE 4–6 *Common principles in my teaching.*

ten about how to enhance and develop the complementary nature of the two processes. But in 1981, when Don Graves, Jane Hansen, and I began our research, this was new territory. I had intuition and experience, and students were reading and writing in my classroom, but I didn't have an articulated theory about how or why reading and writing worked together as they did. I tried to work this out in a paper given in May 1982 at the Canadian Council for the Teachers of English convention. I later published the paper in *Language Arts* (Karelitz 1984). In it I offered an outline (see Figure 4–6) of the common principles that I believed were operating in my teaching and in my classroom.

These principles have been studied and elaborated on by many others over the past ten years, but I think this chart is still an accurate and worthwhile abbreviation of a complicated process. If a teacher encourages and attends to invention, choice, discussion, revision, and publication, I think the common ground between reading and writing will be fertile ground. In such a landscape the children will have a personal and individual encounter with literature, and, like Woolf, they will know the landscape is populated by other authors. At first, instead of Shakespeare, they will see Sendak. Instead of Chaucer, they will see Ricky, Jessica, and Christopher. But they have set their feet on the pathway, that steady stream of stories and storytellers that stretches back through history and reaches forward into their future.

As I read over what I have written in this chapter, I find that teaching reading seems easy. In a way that is true. Of course, it has taken years of experimentation and reflection to develop the various literacy events and the patterns of interaction between them. And, for individual students on any given day, learning to read is hard work. But it is part of the natural activity of the classroom. The children want to read for their own reasons. They want to publish books and read to the class because those are the important rituals of our classroom. If students need resource-room support, I make sure they get that support at a time other than the classroom reading period. I do not want them to miss out on experiences that are so important for building a community of learners and readers. Every child participates. Every child learns to read— some better than others, of course, but I have never had a child leave my classroom a nonreader. The process of reading, writing, and talking about stories and authors has its own momentum. This makes teaching much easier for me.

Batteries and Butterflies: Writing About Science

The ditto sheet prescribed for my first science lesson was neatly ruled into two-inch squares. The assumption was clear: six-year-olds can't write, so any recording would take the form of writing a number or copying a one-word answer chosen from samples at the top of the page. Although it was still only October, my first graders had filled pages and pages of their journals with elaborate drawings, stories, and invented spelling. A two-inch square was too cramped a space to contain their observations and illustrations, the products of their minds. I put the ditto sheet back into the folder. I'd have to find another way for my children to write about science.

It took me two years to develop a "better" way to help my students record their observations about science projects. As with every change in my teaching style, I began with a feeling of discomfort about the pre-scribed methods and worked my way toward practices that felt more comfortable.

Since I wasn't sure how to define the issues involved in teaching children to write in the sciences I began as simply as possible. I wanted to build on the program I had already established.

The Science Center

My students don't *do* math, science, art, and writing; rather, I try to help them become mathematicians, scientists, artists, and authors. I provide my students with the tools and the atmosphere to get "into character." The first-grade curriculum in the life and physical sciences emphasizes four general concepts—matter, energy, organism, and ecosystem—and four process-oriented concepts—property, system, reference frame, and scientific model (SCIS II Elementary Science Program 1978, 6). To accomplish the goal of familiarizing my students with these concepts I set up the science center like a laboratory. One bookshelf holds tools for exploring the physical sciences. I have magnets, magnifying glasses, a microscope, prisms, batteries, wires, light bulbs, clear plastic bottles, a siphon, containers in different sizes and shapes, and balls of many sizes, weights, and "bounciness." I've collected a number of reference charts that are rolled up and stored in a large pail for students' use: maps of the United States, the world, and the solar system; charts categorizing flowers, animals, animal tracks, and dinosaurs; even the periodic tables.

Children can develop their own experiments and make their own discoveries using these materials, but I always have several displays and activities going on in the science center. I may, for example, start displays of leaves and seed pods in the fall and have my students add to them. And I'll have an activity relating to the physical sciences. These are not elaborate. One activity I provided was a basket of pears and the questions, What happens when you roll a pear? Why? Can you find or make something else that does the same thing?

I usually post my questions on a chart pad, inviting my students to investigate, share their knowledge, make a prediction, or formulate a hypothesis: Have you ever tried to break a rock? What happened? What do you know about water? How many different colors can you make with a prism?

I encourage students to write questions for one another, too. Shawn's question is more science fiction than science, but we had fun with it:"What would you do if a space ship landed on earth?"

> I would make friends with them then I would go on their space ship. Timmy.

> I would take off in their spaceship and leave them on earth. "Too bad, I have to leave you behind because there is no room!" Shawn

> I would run. Catina

> I would sneak up and spy on them. Ellen

Since I teach life science as well as physical science, the classroom pets are a big attraction in the science center. A pair of guinea pigs and the fresh water aquarium are the mainstays, but I try to include animals and plants that represent different species. Birds, fish, reptiles, mammals, amphibians, and insects all live in or visit my classroom during the school year. We've played host to box turtles, painted turtles, boa constrictors, garter snakes, mice, hamsters, gerbils, rabbits, a piglet, a lamb, salamanders, chameleons, worms, an ant farm, baby birds, star fish, rock crabs, hermit crabs, and a spider that sucked blood from raw beef. If a creature can be purchased in a pet store or caught outside, it's probably been in my classroom.

My plant collection includes bulbs, sprouted vegetables and seeds, and various potted plants—cactuses, bromeliads, and a Venus flytrap. The students learn about living things by observing birth and growth cycles of the baby guinea pigs. They witness the metamorphosis of caterpillars, mealworms, and tadpoles. They grow seeds, bulbs, and root cuttings and care for the plants and animals in the classroom.

A project in the life sciences may also involve working in small groups with older students to mark off a plot of land outside and observe it through the seasons. An active and interesting science center makes the whole room lively. There is never a dull moment, something is always changing, growing, hatching, or escaping. This was the setting for my experiment with science writing.

My immediate goal relative to developing my students' science writing was to improve their abilities to be good observers and recorders. Therefore, I borrowed an idea from Kathy Matthews (1985, 64). Kathy has what she calls "community books," which she places around her classroom in strategic spots—next to the window, by an animal's cage, or underneath an interesting display. These books are invitations to the students to write down their observations and feelings. I made up several of these books: *Weather and Seasons, Fish Friends, Our Guinea Pigs,* and *Outside Our Window.*

Weather and Seasons ties in with the daily job of doing the calendar. Each week a different student is the calendar/weather person. He or she brings in and discusses seasonal pictures (either hand-drawn or cut from magazines) or some artifacts that are appropriately seasonal. I have many poems and short prose passages related to weather copied onto file cards, and these are kept in envelopes on the bulletin board. The person in charge of the calendar for that week chooses one of these to be read, by me early in the year and later by the student. Because these poems are read over and over, they become part of my students' repertoire and often influence their writing. The calendar person is also responsible for writing in the *Weather and Seasons* book. The pictures brought in are glued into the book and the student writes a short observation about the weather.

My students often sit and watch our fish—mesmerized by the hum of the pump, the sound of the bubbles, and the slow circling of the fish. Besides being an opportunity to learn about fish and their habitat, the tank has a calming effect. The students write in *Fish Friends* whenever they wish—most often noting the fish's appearance:"Swimmy has fat eyes. Parks." "I like the fish with the dotted tail. It is pretty. Caitlin." "I like the fish with the polka dots. Calies."

Our Guinea Pigs, also an invitation to watch and write about animals, is next to the guinea pigs' cage. Two guinea pigs, a male and female, provide many opportunities to observe animal behavior, including mating, giving birth, and nurturing the young. Each pig has its own basket, which the children use to carry the pigs to different places in the room. The guinea pigs play checkers, read books, walk through mazes, and frequently jump out of their baskets to skitter across the floor. They are highly successful and beloved classroom pets. The children especially enjoy writing about their antics and about the baby guinea pigs with which we are frequently blessed: "Our guinea pigs are cute and furry and fluffy. Robert." "The guinea pigs had three baby guinea pigs. They grow very fast. And the baby guinea pigs are very soft and cute. Brian."

Outside Our Window is a place for the children to make note of events that occur outside the classroom. I didn't intend for this to be limited to observations of natural phenomena. I thought it might also be a place in which to describe people and record events. However, my students use this book most often to make notes about plant and animal behavior: "I see grass and it is hot and sunny. Yuvi." "I saw sun and birds on the ground and bees. Those are fun to see and sticks and stones are fun to play with. Maryam." "I saw bushes and I saw small leaves because they are just growing. It's beautiful—spring."

Life Sciences

The community books set the stage for more writing to occur outside the usual format I'd established for narrative writing. I then turned my attention to writing that was specifically focused on the sciences. There are two strands to the science curriculum I use: life sciences and physical sciences. I wasn't sure what form the children's writing would take, nor was I clear on how to incorporate the terminology from the science curriculum into the writing. Instead of using the first life science lesson, I substituted some projects of my own. Once my students had developed their style of writing, I believed I could go back to the curriculum and blend in the concepts and terminology they needed to learn.

One of the basic concepts in the life science curriculum is the idea of change—growth, metamorphosis. Since it was October, I used our Halloween pumpkins to demonstrate one process of change—decomposition.

The carved pumpkins sat on a sunny windowsill. Next to them I placed chart paper and a can of magic markers. At a class meeting I explained that we were going to watch what happened to the pumpkins. I encouraged the children to record their observations on the chart paper; I asked them to sign and circle each contribution. It was early in the school year and there were still many styles of invented spellings and ways of organizing space on the page. I wanted to be sure that the children provided clear boundaries around their work to preserve it from encroachment. I also wanted to be able to check with the author of each observation to ensure we could decode the invented spelling. I did this at the end of every day, bringing the chart paper to the final circle time and having the children who contributed read their observations. I then rewrote their observations in standard spelling next to their writing so we'd all remember it later.

We kept these pumpkins until January. The changes both in them and in the children's writing were impressive. At first the observations were fairly straightforward and limited to what was obvious and visible.

The little pumpkin has spots on it. Oded and Uri

The pumpkin—the top is dry. Oded

The pumpkin is softer and it is drier. Becca

But then students began to explain what they were seeing by comparing it with other familiar phenomena:

The little pumpkin has white fur in it. Becca

The little pumpkin is snowing. Calies

I figured out that the pumpkin has cobwebs in it. It looks disgusting because it looks that the pumpkin is going to grow spiders. Caitlin

The children's natural curiosity and desire to make sense of what was happening prompted them to develop some hypotheses. But I also believe that the writing itself was a catalyst. The children weren't just writing their messages and moving away, they were also reading what others had already written. I often saw groups of children huddled over the chart paper trying to decode a classmate's invented spelling. If they weren't successful, they'd find the author, pull him over and demand a reading. Occasionally I would also be called over for consultation. The writing already on the paper had an impact on what was written afterward. The student contributing next tried to make her statement unique. This desire to add something new put pressure on the writers to be more precise, more descriptive, to search for interesting vocabulary and comparisons.

When I noticed my students' struggle to explain the "furry cobwebs," I wondered what form my intervention should take. Should I tell them it was mold and do a lesson on growing mold—perhaps the standard experiment with growing mold on bread? Because I was curious about what would happen if I intervened in writing, I decided to participate with my students and simply provide the proper terminology in writing. I wanted to see whether the children would adopt the terminology offered and what other questions and observations would develop from such subtle intervention. I wrote: "The pumpkin is collapsing and the lids are shriveling up. In the big pumpkin there are patches of mold, but the little pumpkin is covered with mold."

Not only did the children accept and understand my explanation of the "cobwebs" as mold, they went on to use the term in their own writing. They also found many synonyms for *collapsing*. This once again resulted in an expanded description that combined simile with accurate description:

> The little pumpkin has mold. Calies

> The big pumpkin collapsed. Simon

> The big pumpkin got squished in his house. Uri

> The big pumpkin is sagging. Caitlin

> The big pumpkin is softer and he is shrinking. Moti

> The big pumpkin looks like an old person and inside there are white spots and there are black dots and I think that the outside looks like yellow and I think it looks ugly. Rachel

My students and I continued to write about the pumpkins until January, when their demise was obvious. The process of change we'd observed had been truly amazing. The once round, orange balls were now flat, black plates. Before we threw them away I read *Mouskin's Golden House* by Edna Miller (1964). In this story the collapsing pumpkin serves as a warm cozy shelter for the field mouse, Mouskin. I used the story as an opportunity to discuss the part decomposition plays in the cycle of growth.

I wanted to publish my students' writing. Instead of retyping it, I simply cut the observations out and glued them into a large drawing book. Some of the children chose to illustrate these observations. I covered the front and back of the pad with contact paper and titled the book *Changes*. For me the title signified both the changes the students had observed and the changes that had occurred in their writing. A page from this book is shown in Figure 5–1.

I was eager to show *Changes* to our science coordinator. She supplied materials, conducted workshops on how to use and expand on the curriculum, and observed classrooms regularly. Since Jackie was generally supportive of teacher innovation, I was surprised when her response was not as enthusiastic as I had expected. The writing was certainly better than could have resulted from the ditto sheets, she admitted, but she was concerned that the students weren't getting accurate information or using appropriate terminology. Was I sure they separated the facts (white fur as mold) from fiction (cobwebs growing spiders)? The idea that the white fur was "cobwebs growing spiders" reflected a misconception not only about mold but about the life cycle of spiders as well. Had I dealt with this?

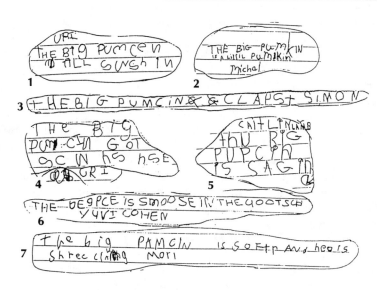

1. The big pumpkin is all squish[ed] in. Uri
2. The big pumpkin is a little pumpkin. Michal
3. The big pumpkin collapsed. Simon
4. The big pumpkin got squished in his house. Uri
5. The big pumpkin is sagging. Caitlin
6. The big pumpkin is smooshed in the outside. Yuvi
7. The big pumpkin is softer and he is shrinking. Moti

FIGURE 5–1 *A page from* Changes.

At first I felt annoyed and unappreciated, but the criticisms had the nagging ring of truth. I realized I had been viewing the writing with the eyes of a poet, not of a scientist. What made writing in the sciences different from other genres? For one thing I had responsibility to the subject matter, not just to the writing. Secondly, the ambiguities and range of interpretation that simile and metaphor allow are intriguing in poetry but can be simply inaccurate or misleading in scientific observations. The chart paper exercise was useful in collecting those first observations, hypotheses, and misconceptions, but I needed to help my students learn to test these first impressions: to look again, rethink their ideas, and record them appropriately.

I thought about this problem for the rest of the year. As I worked my way through the science curriculum, I began to plan for the following September. Over the summer I read through the children's work and made some decisions. I would keep the chart paper for spontaneous, playful writing. These forms gave me insight into the connections children were making between what they already knew about the way the world works and new experiences. They also allowed for a kind of interactive, collective building of hypotheses and pooling of knowledge, since the students were constantly reading and discussing one another's contributions. To this writing I added what I felt was a more reflective component. I would have each child keep a personal science notebook—a "lab" book. Students could choose to write in these whenever they wished, but the notebooks would also be used during formal science lessons—those provided for in the science curriculum or ones I formulated. Each child would write a personal account of the science experience and we'd have a class share of these accounts at the end of the lesson. One requirement for these accounts would be to use the proper vocabulary—terminology that had been used and taught during the lesson. Beyond this I wasn't sure what criteria to apply. I thought I would wait to see what the children did and continue from there—leading from behind.

Once I decided to use the notebooks and had planned how to use them, I gave some thought to what they should be. Having a special place to write for science might help the children make distinctions between their science writing and their narrative writing. I wanted all the students to have the same books, so I arranged for a local stationery store to stock blank, hardcover composition books and to sell them at a reduced price to parents. Then, before school started, I included a note explaining my intentions with my customary "hello" letter to parents, asking them to purchase the books. The parents responded favorably and most of the children arrived with the books on the first day of school. I did have to send reminders to several and I bought books for one or two students myself, but by the third week of September, the whole class had books. We personalized these books by making marbleized paper covers (a science lesson in itself). The books were then stored on a special shelf in the science area.

The first entry in the science notebooks came after a walking field trip to a local park. We had discussed the idea of an animal's *habitat* before we went on the trip. While at the park I used the term many times to describe the places the animals lived. The children tried to incorporate the new word in their writing when they returned (see Figures 5–2 and 5–3).

The first lesson in the life science curriculum involved planting seeds. As the seeds sprouted and began to grow I asked my students to study their plants and to write their observations in their notebooks. Characteristic of these first entries was a tendency to anthropomorphize. The children also tended to convey more about themselves and their feelings than they did about the sprouts. (See Figures 5–4, 5–5, and 5–6.)

This was natural. The students' narrative writing focuses on themselves and they have more practice writing in this mode. Also, much children's literature portrays animals as characters with human qualities and inanimate objects as animate. I saw that some distinctions

I saw the turtle's habitat in the water. The duck said "Quack, quack"

FIGURE 5–2 *A student writing about a field trip.*

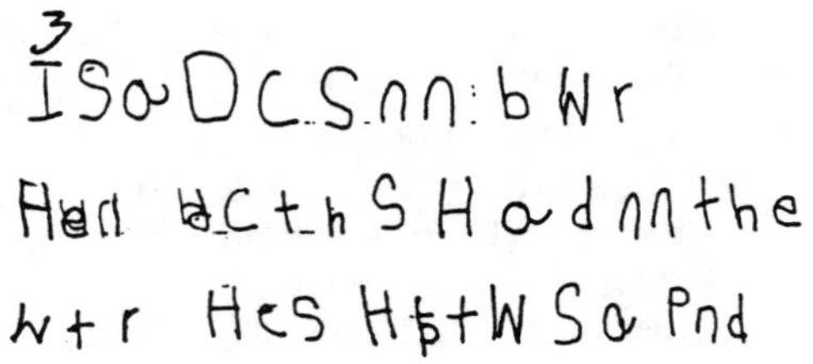

ᶾĪSɑDCSⲚⲚ:bWr
Aⱸⲛ ʙ̣CτⳂSHɑdⲚⲚthe
Wₜr HⲉS Hₛ̄tWSɑPnd

I saw ducks in the water. He ducked his head in the
water. His habitat was a pond.

FIGURE 5–3 *Another student writing about a field trip.*

My PLɑɴⱦ is DeⲚ:I ₜR𝖎y D ᵗᴏᵥ mɑ|ⱪ
:iⱦ ʙeₜⱪ ʙɥⱦ iⱦ Jₑ̃ₜ SⱦɑiD
hɑw iⱦ wɑⳄ

My plant is dead. I tried to
make it better but it just stayed
how it was.

FIGURE 5–4 *A student's observation about his plant.*

My sunflower plant is growing.
I like my plant. I planted it.

FIGURE 5–5 *Another student writes about her plant.*

This is my plant. My plant is alive.
george is my plant. He is doing
pretty good I guess? He is green.
His leaf is one foot. Can you find
the one I mean?

FIGURE 5–6 *Another observation about a plant.*

needed to be made between genres. My students needed to learn the difference between fact and fiction. I decided to demonstrate these differences by reading and discussing them as I read books to the class.

Before I start to read a book I instruct the class to raise their hands as soon as they can tell whether the book is a true animal story or a make-believe one. When I call on a student, I ask what words or statements gave the first clues.

For example, here is a passage from *Fox Eyes*, by Margaret Wise Brown (1977):

> There was once a spy, a red fox who came to spy on opossums. There were five of them and they were supposed to be asleep, but they weren't. They each had one eye open. They were playing possum.
>   The fox noted all this and went on his way. But with their one eye open, the possums had seen the eye of the fox gleaming through the hole. They knew that the fox knew they were playing possum. And that he had caught on to their tricks.

The author is attributing intentionality to the actions of the fox and opossums that isn't really accurate. The act of "playing possum" has survival value for the animal and is instinctive rather than contemplated. The author uses expressions—"spy," "the fox noted," "caught on to their tricks"—that elevate the fox's actions—sniffing a possum hole looking for dinner—beyond instinct and hunger.

A book like this is difficult for the children to evaluate because the language and clues are subtle. In *The Bear on the Doorstep*, by Jane Flory (1980), the animals are clearly out of character:

> No one knew where the bear came from. The Rabbits found him on their doorstep one morning sound asleep.
>   "What a dear little baby!" said Mother Rabbit. "Can we keep him?"
>   Father Rabbit said, "Why not? We have so many, one more won't make any difference."

When I read passages like this my students delight in finding the inaccuracies. Of course, inherent in the success of this story is the author's confidence that the reader really understands the differences in life-style between the rabbits and the bear. To appreciate the humor, the children have to have accurate knowledge of animal behavior. I make sure that my students realize this and understand the extent of the information they bring to the text.

I enjoy helping students compare writing like this with the writing in *Turtle Pond*, by Berniece Freschet (1971). Here the turtle behaves like a turtle.

It was a warm June day at the pond.
White lilies opened wide. Bees buzzed near.
A redheaded woodpecker drummed on a maple tree.
A turtle lay on a rock.
Because of the color of her shell she looked very much like the rock.
She lay in the sun and waited for a mayfly. A mayfly flew down.
The turtle stretched her long neck out. With a quick snap of her jaws—the mayfly was gone.
The turtle laid her head on one foot and waited for another fly to come close.

Finally I read from literature that combines good, poetic writing with substantial information. *Beach Bird*, by Carol Carrick and Donald Carrick (1973), is a good example. The Carricks use powerful imagery—"sand drifted inland, pushed by the shoulder of the wind"; "roots driving deep"; "leaves reaching"—and they use simile to help transport the reader to the scene: "The rocks were overgrown with seaweed like mermaid's hair and hung with chains of shiny mussels."

By discussing literature in this way I train my students' ears to the subtle differences in format, word choices, and cadence of nonfiction versus fiction. As they become better able to distinguish informative texts from fairy tales, the tone of their writing in the science notebooks begins to reflect this awareness.

My routine for science lessons normally begins with a whole-class meeting during which I introduce any new concepts or terminology to the students and answer questions. The children then disperse to tables around the room. In groups of five or six they study their own plants or animals or conduct their own experiments and discuss their discoveries with their friends. I provide each group with sets of word cards containing the relevant terms. The students record their observations in their science notebooks and then bring their books to a whole-class share. The lesson ends with each student in turn reading the entry in the notebook to the group. Because there are twenty-three children in the class, time is always a consideration—there isn't much opportunity for students to comment on one another's writing at these sessions. To compensate, I jot down things I notice on a record sheet with each child's name on it and report them at the end of each child's reading. I try to reinforce the use of proper terminology, accurate description, interesting hypotheses (even when incorrect), and good word choices. Each child's writing is recognized by me in a positive way.

In January we began a unit on mealworms. About once a week the students took their petri dishes to their tables to observe and record the changes the insects were going through. Using materials from the science kit, I introduced terminology such as *egg, larvae, pupae, and beetle*. We discussed the ideas of metamorphosis and life cycle. The children learned that each creature has its own system made up of components necessary to its growth and survival. They performed simple experiments to determine what preferences mealworms have for food, how they respond when given a choice of being in a light or a dark space, and what they do when obstacles are placed in their way. The following examples show how the students incorporated these concepts into their writing. First, Michael's observations:

> *January 30.* I have 7 larvae and they eat a lot of meal and you need apples to keep the cup moist. Larvae are a kind of worm. One of my larvae have molted.

> *February 3.* All of my mealworms are alive and we have had them for 25 days and I have one squiggler.

> *March 6.* One of my larvaes have molted and I have a white one. The white ones are the ones that have molted.

> *March 14.* The mealworm's system: [diagram] When you put these things together you get a system. If you take one of these things away the system would be broken.

> *March 27.* I have 2 pupaes. One of them is starting to change into a beetle and the second one squims around when I touch it. Two of my larvae have gone halfway through their metamorphosis.

> *April 9.* I let my larvae go on April 9th. I watched them to see what they would do. I put my pupae in a bush outside of our window. It was fun having them, but I had to let them go.

Michael's entries are rather businesslike. He keeps an inventory of the mealworms and gives us some useful information. He explains the terminology he is using and tries to use it accurately.

Tamar's entries have a chatty tone, reminiscent of her writing about her seedlings earlier in the year.

> *January 30.* I have a lazy mealworm. All he likes to do is sit on the apple and nibble on it while all the others move. My mealworms move so quickly I don't get a chance to see them. Two of my mealworms molted. I have 2 pupae now. I can't wait until they turn into a beetle.

> *February 3.* The life cycle of my mealworms: [diagram] None of my mealworms are dead. I had 6 mealworms. You're supposed to have 7 so Ellen put one more mealworm in my mealworm container.

March 5. My mealworm's best kind of food is oatmeal. I have one pupae and one beetle. I put a toothpick in front of my mealworm. It went back. I put my mealworm in between apple juice, blue water, and vinegar. My mealworm went to the apple juice.

March 13. Jacob put Ellen's mealworms on the radiator for a few days. Today I took [the container] off and the mealworms were cooked and dead.

March 27. Metamorphosis: I have two beetles. I noticed that beetles carry around lead in their wings. And I also noticed that they can fly with their wings so I have to keep an eye on them while the lid's off. I like my mealworms and I like my pupaes and I like my beetles the best.

I enjoy Tamar's entries because she has so much enthusiasm for the project. Tamar hypothesized that the black in the beetle's wings was lead since it matched the color of her pencil tip. Although I questioned this idea, I was unable to shake her belief in this hypothesis. This was her "discovery" and she was tenacious in defending it.

Jay's writing in his lab book is a combination of Michael's and Tamar's. It is both informative and personal. He gives the most complete description of the "test" we subjected the mealworms to and the best explanation of a system.

January 30. 6 Larvae. One larvae is lazy. The other six are pretty lazy. Larvaes are baby mealworms. They change into a pupae and then they change into a beetle. They need air and one apple and people and, of course, a mealworm. None of my mealworms have molted their skins.

February 3. The mealworms go through a change called metamorphosis.

February 25. One of my mealworms molted. None of my mealworms has changed into a beetle or a pupae. Two of my mealworms went on a test. The test was favorite foods and liquids and dark and light and backing up. My mealworms backed up and on the light and dark my mealworms went to the light. In the food test my mealworms went to the cornmeal.

March 13. People, Air, Apple, Bran are the things that the mealworms need to live. It is called a system. These things are most important. If we take one of these out of the system, the mealworms would die.

March 27. I used to have 2 pupae but now I have 2 beetles and another beetle. I still have 2 pupae. The new beetle is weird. The end.

April 9. Today we let our mealworms go outside. I was sad but I bet they were happy. One of my beetles almost flied. I said "Good bye." That's all.

Although these entries lack the continuity of a "composition," they have the freshness of firsthand accounts. There are some problems. I challenged the use of the word "lazy" by several of the children, since it implies that the mealworms have some business they should be attending to and aren't. We discussed what the mealworms' role is and clarified that their only real responsibility is to change into pupae. As long as they were proceeding toward this goal, lack of activity couldn't be judged "lazy."

These entries are a definite improvement over the ones the children wrote about their seeds. The writers tried to accurately describe the appearance, behavior, and metamorphosis of their mealworms. They also used the proper terminology and attempted to record the new information and concepts they were learning. However, they did not offer explanations of the mealworms' behavior or compare their mealworms with other students'. Jay's mealworms behaved unexpectedly on one of the tests. The prediction was that mealworms would prefer dark rather than light, but Jay doesn't comment on why his mealworms "failed" the test. Later in the school year the children begin to take this next step.

Nina's writing about the mealworms shows an interesting way of dealing with the tension she felt about having to write in this particular genre. Nina has a strong narrative voice that comes through in her illustrations (see Figure 5–7). In the first entry we see the mealworms' house with mealworms peeking out of the windows. One mealworm is eating oatmeal while his friend (who likes apple juice) thinks "he's dumb." Her writing records the actual results of her experiments while the pictures record the "effect." In the second entry we see a baby carriage with several baby mealworms in and around it. They are all saying "Hi!" Finally a mealworm picks apples from a tree and asks, "Which meal is ripe?" (a play on the word *meal*). Another worm asks, "What is he doing?"

Nina's use of cartoons to satisfy her narrative impulse allowed her to comply with the task and with her own sense of story at the same time. I tucked her solution away for future use should I need to help a student who needs this same outlet. So often the children provide me with the answers I need to writing problems.

I felt, after reading the mealworm accounts, that the students had made progress in learning to observe and to describe. It was interesting to compare these with the writing in the community books. While this

Figure 5–7 *Nina's story about mealworms.*

writing also showed an improved ability to notice and record, it continued to be an outlet for more personal expression.

> We have new baby guinea pigs. One's named Gingerbread and Furball
> and we love them and Daddy guinea pig talks to Mommy guinea pig
> and Daddy guinea pig guards the baby guinea pigs and the Mommy
> guinea pig is cute. Erica

> The guinea pigs are playing follow the leader in the math table. It is
> funny. Timmy

> I saw the guinea pig in the food dish like a soldier with a gun [he
> means hunkered down, hiding]. Eric

> I like the fish because they wiggle their tails. They look for food. Erica

> I like the fish with the polka dots. Calies

> Rocky has been going to the top of the water. That means he is sick.
> Eric

> One fish died, too bad. His name was Swimmy. Swimmy is in fish
> heaven. Parks.

By the end of the year, my students' writing in the life sciences showed
its own growth and metamorphosis. The children had learned how to

look at plants and animals and to describe what they saw in terms appropriate to the task of scientific observation. Yet they also incorporated their knowledge of storytelling and writing for an audience.

In addition to greater fluency compared with the beginning of the year, Jamie's writing shows a mind that does not just observe his surroundings, but reasons and makes predictions based on past experiences.

> Today on our trip to Hall's Pond, I saw some ducks, birds and buds. Also I noticed that buds are a sign of spring. I noticed ducks and birds are a sign of spring. The reason why birds are a sign of spring is because they come from the south and they only come when it is warm and when it gets warm that means it is changing seasons and the next season is spring. I saw squirrels also. A rabbit would be underground.

Nina, too, goes beyond reporting to anticipating the appearance of other inhabitants of Hall's Pond: "Today I went to Hall's Pond. It was different. I saw some ducks and birds. I saw signs of spring. In spring you might find other animals like frogs and fish." Nina's drawing (Figure 5–8) has perspective and dimensionality that once again lends a narrative quality to her writing. The path around Hall's Pond is shaded, dark in spots and overgrown. The thick vines and underbrush are reminiscent of a jungle and make a perfect sanctuary for birds and small animals. We are pictured walking down the path, single file, through a tunnel of vines. There is a sense of adventure and suspense about what will be around the next tree trunk. Nina captures this spirit in her drawing.

Michael writes his personal observations of guinea pig behavior. He organizes his writing into sections, each section beginning with a subtitle:

Guinea Pigs

1. Guinea Pigs in Closed in Places
   Guinea pigs like dark closed in places. If you sit Indian style and face the guinea pig toward you he will walk in.

2. Running
   The black and white guinea pig is crazy. When you put her down, she will run all over the place.

3. Taking Out
   When you want to take a guinea pig out, first you take out the father.

Michael also observes the tadpoles: "The tadpoles swim in the water like fish. But they have pointed tails unlike fish. And they swim by wav-

Today I went to Hall's Pond. It was different. I saw some ducks and birds. I saw signs of spring. In spring you might find other animals like frogs and fish.

Figure 5–8 *Nina's report on Hall's Pond.*

ing their tail in the water. When you wave your hand over the water they will swim around."

Maeshan and Mara write about the hamsters. Mara: "Hamsters are rodents and they love to dig! Also the hamster is related to squirrels. Hamsters run through holes that he or she digs with its nails. And that's how some hamsters make their home. In fact, they only weigh about 21 milligrams. The End." Maeshan: "The hamster likes to stay in the tunnel. He or she will peek out of the tunnel. They run in the holes. One of them was digging a hole. They were 20 centemeters long."

These are self-initiated writing projects done while the students worked in the science center during morning activity period and recorded results in their science notebooks. They all make statements about the animals that they support with evidence from personal observation. Mara elaborates further by adding information she has collected from outside reading. Michael goes a step beyond observation. He conducts little experiments, such as waving his hands over the fish tank, to determine how the tadpoles will react. Maeshan and Mara both collect data about the weight and length of the hamsters. Their writing shows the influence of their collaboration. This procedure—observing, reflecting on what has been witnessed, drawing conclusions or formulating hypotheses and testing them, discussing the observations with colleagues and documenting them—is the basis for scientific inquiry and reporting. These steps are present in embryonic form in the children's science notebooks by June.

Physical Sciences

The issues we worked on in writing in the life sciences were:

1. Using proper terminology.
2. Learning the difference between anthropomorphizing and accurate description.
3. Developing hypotheses and making predictions.
4. Developing the ability to write informative descriptions that incorporate personal observation with supporting information obtained from other sources (books, lessons, conversation).

The physical sciences presented a new challenge for writers. Not only were the preceding issues relevant, but an additional one became apparent, the need to learn how to describe causal relationships.

In the physical science curriculum, the students were provided with several ways to learn about and to test the concepts emphasized in the curriculum. Among these were simple experiments involving chemical reactions and interactions and the opportunity to explore electricity, magnets, and pulleys. I added some experiences with less exotic materials: growing yeast and blowing bubbles.

In writing about these experiments, sequence became an important consideration. In Chapter 2, "Developing Storywriters," I mention that in narrative writing chronological sequence can be altered to create an effect. The sequence can be changed to highlight and dramatize certain events and to downplay others. In fictional accounts, order is entirely at the discretion of the writer. But the description of a scientific phenomenon requires an accurate account of the sequence of events, since this plays an important role in determining cause and effect. At a time when my students were beginning to play with order in their other writing, they now had to attend to a strict accounting of the events in their science notebooks.

When children write personal narrative, they are usually recording events that occur over a duration of time—hours, days, or years. By comparison, the time frame for many of the experiments in the science curriculum was short—a matter of minutes. I think this made isolating separate actions and reactions more difficult. Matthew struggled with this problem as he tried to recall and record his experiment with batteries (see Figure 5–9). Matthew played with these materials for twenty to thirty minutes, arranging them in different ways and discussing possible results with others. When he finally succeeded in lighting the bulb, I'm sure it must have been hard for him to remember exactly what steps he'd taken. Even though I encouraged him to recreate the experiment, his writing reflects his confusion about how to make the process clear to an audience. Not only is the sequence fuzzy to begin with, Matthew doesn't orient the reader by using constructions like "first this, then that." Discovering and using writing strategies that move the reader through the sequence was difficult for many of my students. Again, in narrative writing there are often routine events that any reader can relate to—waking up, eating breakfast, going out to recess—that children can rely on to orient their reader in time and place. Since these were not present for science experiments, I realized that I needed to point out and identify ways writers can give a sense of sequence when time is so compressed.

I used my students' own writing to help me help them. During whole-class share sessions I listened carefully for any successes individ-

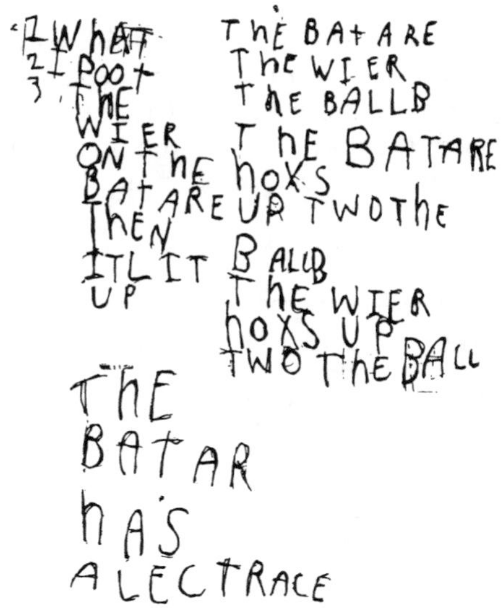

WHAT: I put the wire on the battery, then it lit up. The battery, the wire, the bulb. The battery hooks up to the bulb. The wire hooks up to the bulb. The battery has electricity.

FIGURE 5–9 *Matthew's experiment with batteries.*

ual writers were having with these descriptions. Children began to discover and use "first this, then that." When I brought this to the group's attention I also suggested "if this, then that." As the students experimented with these techniques, they began to use *when* and *because*. The struggle with sequence naturally evolved into the more complicated problem of describing cause and effect. I gradually came to see that we were developing formulas for writing about our work in the physical sciences. At first I was uncomfortable with this, feeling that actively teaching certain sentence structures and strategies was getting in the way of individual development. Then I thought about Bruner's (1986) idea of scaffolding. It seemed to me that a framework was being built that allowed the children to build more stable and accurate accounts. The writing was improving and so was my students' ability to make sense of phenomena.

In our whole-class share sessions we began to use a chart divided into three categories: what, how, and why. After everyone had read their notebook entries we discussed them and the children suggested the names of classmates whom they felt had been particularly successful in describing an event. Some children's names appeared more than once (see Figure 5–10), and it didn't take the class long to realize that entries that contained information in each of these categories were superior to those that omitted one or two. These entries provided models for the other students on how to incorporate all three categories into their writing.

One variation of this exercise was to have two or three children read their accounts and then put them together into one long description taking the best from each. For instance, in January I repeated the seed-growing lesson to see how the children would describe the results now that they'd had more practice writing. After the whole-group share of

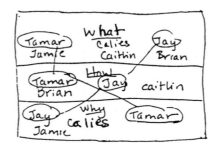

FIGURE 5–10 *A science how-what-why chart.*

these entries, I asked Jamie and Craig to reread theirs. As they did (Jamie: "I have a bean plant. It is not doing well. I think it is dead. This is a picture of it. I have a marigold. It has a flower on it. It is doing well. This is a picture of it." Craig: "My plant is dead because it didn't have any roots. My bean plant is growing and it has roots"), I copied them on chart paper. Cutting the entries apart I rearranged them so they read:

> I have a bean plant.
>
> It is not doing well.
>
> I think it is dead . . . because it doesn't have any roots.
>
> I have a marigold.
>
> It has a flower on it.
>
> It is doing well.
>
> (It is) growing and it has roots.

Jamie's description of his plants did not have any explanation of why his bean plant died or why his marigold was growing well. I borrowed these explanations from Craig's writing to show Jamie how he could improve his descriptions. Craig's accounts had explanations but little physical description of his plants. By attaching Jamie's description of his marigold to Craig's explanation of why his bean plant was growing well, I helped Craig expand his writing to give the reader more information. Later Jay brought his science notebook to me. Turning to his original entry done at the beginning of the year, he showed me how he'd revised it (Figure 5–11).

We also played with changing the order of our descriptions— perhaps putting the hypothesis first and then describing how and what. To do this, I chose entries that reflected different strengths. One child might excel in writing description, for example, and another in formulating hypotheses. I would ask these two children to take turns reading their entries, putting the hypothesis first one time and the description first the next time. The class had a chance to hear how changing the order could effect the meaning. The children enjoyed this kind of play, and I think it gave them many opportunities to see how revision works without requiring a lot of actual rewriting of text. This kind of play kept the formulas I had offered from becoming a strait jacket or a crutch that prevented creativity and experimentation.

One of the lessons in the physical science curriculum was to provide the students with a number of different materials and have them explore possible interactions among these materials. I taught this lesson in March. I set out cups of water, hard candies, magnets, various metal and nonmetal objects, scissors, and paper. The children attempted to describe their experiments using the what-how-why formula as a guide-

My plant died.
The roots were
dried up.

FIGURE 5-11 *Jay's revised science entry.*

line. Jeremy described (see Figure 5-12) how he and Nina turned the water green by dropping a piece of green candy in it and allowing it to dissolve. He was able to organize the sequence of events and to tell what he used and how he and Nina mixed the candy and water. He gave us a sense of the time duration—"after lunch it was green." Telling "why" this occurred proved more difficult. As in the seed examples cited earlier, Jeremy and many other children still took the egocentric point of view that "why" referred to personal motivation rather than scientific explanation.

Jamie gave a similar reason in his description of the same experiment (Figure 5-13). Tamar, however, was able to describe her experiment concisely and to provide a reason (Figure 5-14).

When we read these entries in whole-class share, it was interesting to see the expressions on Jeremy's and Jamie's faces when they heard accounts like Tamar's. Of course they knew why the water changed color. They laughed at their own misunderstanding. Next time they would do better.

And they did. In April we took our cubby buckets outside, filled them with water and detergent, and experimented with blowing bubbles. My students' descriptions of this event clearly show an improvement in their understanding of how to perform an experiment and of developing an hypothesis to explain phenomenon.

In his account (Figure 5-15), Jay describes the system: "We did an experiment with soap, water, and our breath." He tells how he conducted his experiment by blowing through the straw and varying the

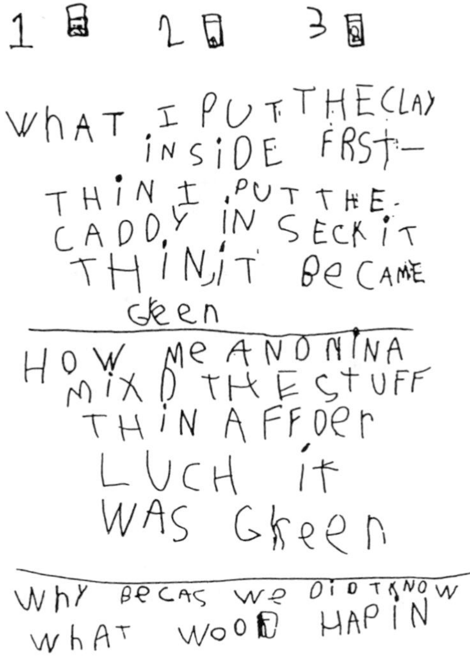

1 🔲 2 🔲 3 🔲

WHAT I PUT THE CLAY
INSIDE FRST—
THIN I PUT THE.
CADDY IN SECK IT
THIN IT BECAME
Green

HOW ME AND NINA
MIXD THE STUFF
THIN AFFOER
LUCH IT
WAS GREEN

WHY BECAS WE DID T KNOW
WHAT WOOD HAPIN

WHAT: I put the clay inside first–then I put the candy in second, then it became green.

HOW: Me and Nina mixed the stuff, then after lunch it was green.

WHY: Because we didn't know what would happen.

FIGURE 5-12 *Jeremy's description of a water experiment.*

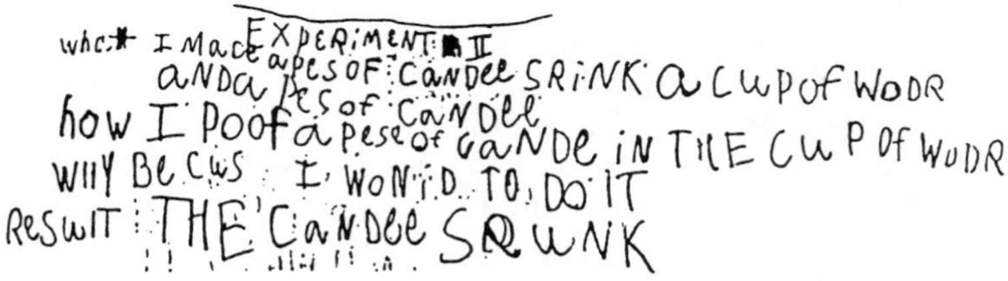

whct I Mad EXPERIMENT II
aNDa pes OF CaNDee SRiNK a CUP OF WODR
how I POOf a pese of CaNDee iN THE CUP OF WUDR
WHY BeCus I WONTD TO DO IT
ReSWIT THE CaNDee SRUNK

EXPERIMENT II
WHAT: I made a piece of candy shrink: a cup of water and a piece of candy
HOW: I put a piece of candy in the cup of water.
WHY: Because I wanted to do it.
RESULT: The candy shrunk.

FIGURE 5-13 *Jamie's description of the same experiment.*

1. I put the candy in the water. 2. The water turned orange because the candy was orange. 3. I took the scissors and stuck some metal thing on the scissors. The magnets stuck on the scissors.

FIGURE 5–14 *Tamar's experiment.*

speed of that blowing. The "why" is implicit in his explanation. Michael and Jamie both add important ideas to Jay's description. Michael (Figure 5–16) goes into more detail about why bending the straw reduces the number of bubbles. Jamie (Figure 5–17) seems a little unclear about the exact nature of the interaction of the air, soap, and water. He believes that the air forces water bubbles into soap bubbles and that the soap covering preserves the bubbles. I discovered that other children had the same misconception. Jamie's description uncovered the misunderstanding and allowed me to lead a discussion to correct it.

What impressed me about the children's writing is that it demonstrates how much they've grown in their understanding of the scientific method: they know how to experiment, and they can describe that experimentation logically and in a form that is interesting to the reader. While Jamie still divides his account into the categories what, how, and why, Jay and Michael have moved away from that. They write prose accounts in which those categories are present but embedded in the text.

A particularly successful lesson was one I devised myself. Since the science curriculum emphasized systems and the interactions between parts of a system, I thought the proofing of yeast would be a good way to demonstrate these concepts in action, with edible results!

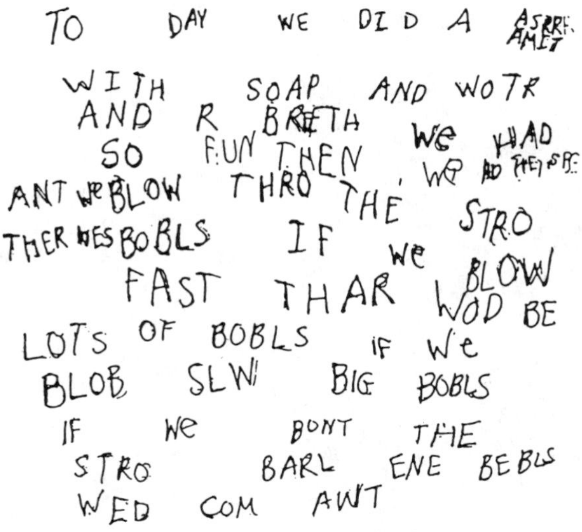

TO DAY WE DID A ASRRE AMET
WITH SOAP AND WOTR
AND R BRETH WE HAD
SO FUN THEN WE AD THE SB:
ANT WE BLOW THRO THE STRO
THER WES BOBLS IF WE STRO
FAST THAR WOD BE
LOTS OF BOBLS IF WE
BLOB SLW BIG BOBLS
IF WE BONT THE
STRO BARL ENE BEBLS
WED COM AWT

Today we did a experiment with soap and water and our
breath. We had so[me] fun. Then we blew through the
straw. There was bubbles. If we blow fast there would be
lots of bubbles. If we blow slow, big bubbles. If we bent
the straw barely any bubbles would come out.

FIGURE 5–15 *Jay's description of the bubble experiment.*

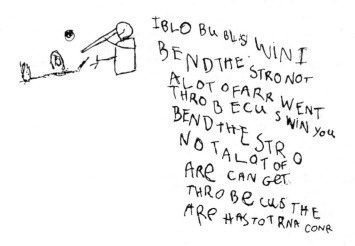

I BLO BU BLS WIN I
BEND THE STRO NOT
A LOT OF ARR WENT
THRO B ECU S WIN you
BEND THE STR O
NO T A LOT OF O
ARE CAN GET
THRO BE CUS THE
ARE HAS TO T RNA CONR

I blow bubbles, when I bend the straw not a lot of air went
through because when you bend the straw, not a lot of air
can get through because the air has to turn a corner.

FIGURE 5–16 *Michael's description of the bubble experiment.*

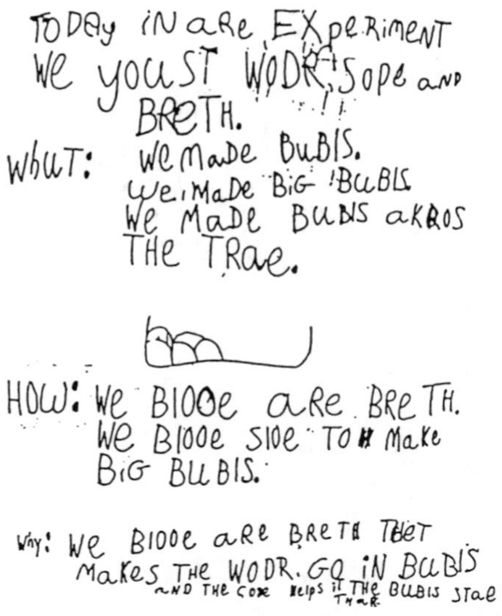

TODAY iN aRe EXpeRimenT
We youST WODR; Sope and
BReTH.

WhuT: We MaDe BuBIS.
We iMaDe BiG BuBIS
We MaDe BuDS akRos
THe TRae.

HOW: We BlOOe aRe BReTH.
We BlOOe Sloe To Make
BiG BuBIS.

Vhy: We BlOOe aRe BReTH ThET
MakeS THe WODR. GO iN BuBIS
aND THe Cox Helps iT THe BuBIS sTae

Today in our experiment we used water, soap and breath.

WHAT: We made bubbles. We made big bubbles. We made bubbles across the tray.

HOW: We blew our breath. We blew slow to make big bubbles.

WHY: We blew out breath, that makes the water go in. Bubbles and the soap helps the bubbles stay there.

FIGURE 5–17 *Jamie's description of the bubble experiment.*

To begin, I divided the class into groups of three or four students. Each group was given several clear plastic cups with a tablespoon of yeast in each cup. They were also given chart paper and markers. My instructions were: "Discover as much as you can about the powder in the cup by smelling, touching, tasting, and listening. Write down what you discover on the chart paper." I gave the class about eight minutes to do this. Then I stopped them and asked each group to read their lists. Here are some of the descriptions.

It looks like sand. Caitlin

It makes a scratchy sound. Jay

It's like little round balls of grain. Nina

It tastes bitter. Tamar

It smells like beer. Jeremy

It feels bumpy. Eric

I recorded their discoveries on a large chart divided into the appropriate sense categories. I then explained that they had just described the "properties" of the powder and invited them to guess what it was. Several of the children knew it was yeast and many of them recognized it once it had been identified.

"So far we have only two parts in our system," I said, "we have a plastic cup and yeast, but now I'm going to add something else. I want you to notice if adding sugar to your system changes anything." As I added the sugar to the cups we noticed an interesting thing—some of the yeast particles "jumped" away from it and clung to the side of the cup. This resulted in a digression as we tried to figure out why this had happened. After offering static electricity as an explanation, I encouraged the class to decide whether the sugar had changed the nature of the yeast in any way. They decided not.

Next, I added a small amount of warm water to each cup. This addition was more dramatic. The students spent about fifteen minutes observing their systems of yeast, sugar, and warm water and noting the interaction of the three elements. I moved from group to group sharing in the noisy reaction I'd created. It was all very exciting, so much so that we forgot about the clock and had to leave for lunch in a hurry. The children returned to find their cups bubbling and foaming over with brew. The room had a strong, pungent odor that some found unpleasant. We decided to dispose of our mess and get out the science notebooks. The students then recorded the elements of their systems and the interaction that occurred between them. Three of these descriptions—Tamar's, Nina's, and Matthew's—are shown in Figures 5–18, 5–19, and 5–20.

The next day we made bread, and in doing so combined the science experiment with literary experience. We read *Strega Nona*, by Tomie DePaola (1975), and, of course, *The Little Red Hen* (Galdone 1973). We had fun with this lesson—it provided physical as well as intellectual nourishment.

By the end of the school year I had learned much about science and about writing. While I felt there was room for improvement, I was satisfied that my students' writing was better and so was their understanding of the scientific method. Some practices I found worth continuing are:

1. Teaching students to hear the differences in tone and emphasis in factual versus fictional writing.

2. Helping students organize their writing by pointing to and demonstrating specific strategies.

I had a cup of yeast. Ellen
put some brown sugar in
and the yeast jumped up.
Then Ellen put some hot
water in the yeast and
the sugar and the cup of
the yeast and the brown
sugar and the hot water
bubbled up and turned
white.

FIGURE 5-18 *Tamar's description of the "systems" experiment.*

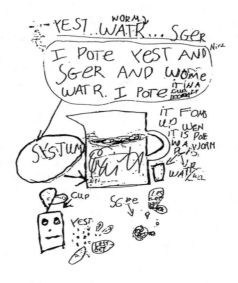

Yeast, warm water, sugar.

I put yeast and sugar and
warm water. I put it in a
cup it foams up. It foams
up when it is put in a
warm place.

FIGURE 5-19 *Nina's description of the "systems" experiment.*

Systems

Some sugar.
Some yeast.
Some medium warm water.
It goes together to make a big
foam lump.

FIGURE 5–20 *Matthew's description of the "systems" experiment.*

3. Playing around with these formulas so that they aren't restrictive.

4. Providing several formats for writing about science interests, one mandatory and the others voluntary.

5. Consistently reading nonnarrative writing to students.

6. Providing many easy-to-read informational texts for them to look at on their own.

Looking back, I think it might be valuable to alternate whole-class shares of the science notebooks with small-group shares. Working in groups at their tables, students can read their entries to one another and discuss them. Since this takes less time than a whole-class share, students will be able to go back and revise, adding or changing their entries to reflect any new ideas they have as a result of their readings and conversation.

I also think occasionally collecting each child's notebook at the end of a life sciences unit and typing the consecutive entries from them (as I did with the mealworm project) is a good idea. Using these notes the children can write a complete text describing the metamorphosis of the mealworm, a text that can be typed and glued into the notebooks when completed. Students are sure to benefit from organizing, explaining, and consolidating the individual entries in this way.

A final reflection: while I feel it's important to help students make distinctions between narrative and nonnarrative writing and even to separate science writing from other nonnarrative forms, the writing I enjoy reading the most blurs the edges of these genres. I am thinking of Annie Dillard's *Tinker at Pilgrim Creek* (1974) or Lewis Thomas's *Lives of a Cell* (1971). Toward the end of the year I found myself helping the children put the "furry cobwebs" back into the writing; to learn to use metaphor and simile responsibly and knowledgeably to inform as well as to delight.

Note Writing: A Neglected Genre

6

> When you write a note, you're doing work in a way. You're asking
> questions and they're answering you. You're practicing like you're a
> grown-up and you write a letter and get a letter back.
>
> Tamar, age six

Tamar and the other students in my first-grade classrooms wrote more
than four hundred notes during the two years I studied their note writing. They wrote notes to me, to my student teachers, to each other, and
to audiences as distant as the Easter Bunny and NASA. This note writing was an excellent way to stimulate writing in general and a wonderful aid to classroom management. But, as I soon realized, the values of
writing notes far exceeded my original intentions. The children were
using notes to accomplish many purposes. Note writing had become a
whole new genre, one that I wanted to study.

I collected notes first in my classroom at the Great Falls School in
Somersworth, New Hampshire, and again at the Edward Devotion
School in Brookline, Massachusetts. The two communities are very different. Somersworth is a predominantly white, working-class community, while Brookline is an affluent, exceptionally literate one, full of
ethnic diversity. Yet, note writing was prolific and similar in both settings.

Note writing began in my Somersworth classroom for pragmatic
reasons. Initially, I saw it as a way to avoid interruptions when I was
busy with conferences and small-group or individual instruction. "Write
me a note," I'd say to the intruders. They would, and I'd write back.

I saved the notes children wrote to me and collected those they
wrote to each other. I picked notes up off the floor, retrieved them from
trash cans, and scavenged them from cubby buckets (asking permission, of course). In this way, I collected about one hundred notes from
my Somersworth classroom.

When I moved to Brookline the following year, I knew note writing would be an important part of my writing program. This time, instead of casually suggesting that the children "write me a note," I introduced note writing at a class meeting. I was prepared with precut scraps of paper in a special container. I read samples of notes my students in Somersworth had written, and I role-played several situations in which note writing could be used. I also supplied an empty dishpan and asked the children to deposit all their notes in this pan when they finished with them. I explained that I was interested not so much in what their notes said but in why and how they wrote them.

About every three weeks, I'd sort through the dishpan, read the notes, and put together those that formed a dialogue. I also talked to the children about the notes, getting background information about why the notes were written and what the outcome had been. These conversations were always nonjudgmental. If I did have a concern about the tenor of a series of notes, I'd write notes myself to the children involved. I would participate with them in the same context rather than operating in the role of authority outside it. I had to negotiate in writing the same way they did.

The children participated in this routine willingly, and I was able to collect over two hundred notes from my classroom at the Devotion School. My manila envelope now bulged with three hundred notes. When I sat down to study them, my living room was soon adrift in odd-sized scraps of paper. I discarded notes that were illegible, incomplete, or written for such routine purposes as asking for tape or for permission to go to the bathroom. I chose 203 notes to analyze.

Immediately two questions emerged: Who writes notes? How do children use notes?

Who Writes Notes?

In my own note-writing days, girls wrote notes and boys stole them. Yet in both of my first-grade classrooms, boys initiated note writing more frequently and wrote more notes than the girls.

Although all the students wrote notes at least once a week, there was a group of "regular note writers" in each class who initiated note writing four or five times a week. In Somersworth, in a class of twenty-one students, five boys and three girls wrote notes regularly. In Brookline I had thirteen "regular note writers" in a class of twenty-two children: eight boys and five girls. And of the 203 notes, twice as many were written by boys (137) than by girls (66).

Not only did the boys write more notes than the girls, but the way they wrote them was different. Boys tended to engage in extended dialogues with each other or to initiate many correspondences at ' time—a sort of scattershot approach. Girls, on the other hand, wrote one note at a time and stopped writing once they got a⟩

I also learned that my "regular note writers" were often who struggled with narrative writing. These children had diffi ing topics and found it hard to sustain interest in a topic once they naɯ decided on one. Because notes are written for a specific purpose, the topic is implicit in the situation that prompts the note. Children did not have to search their memories for experiences to write about. These reluctant writers gained confidence in their writing abilities by writing notes.

How Do Children Use Notes?

My examination of my students' notes uncovered at least twenty different purposes for writing. The children used notes to report, tattle, ask questions, make excuses, ask permission, persuade, seek information, solve problems, develop friendships, gossip, boast, remind, insult, plan activities, acknowledge and thank, apologize, survey, play, celebrate, and console. I have consolidated these twenty purposes into four categories:

1. *Ritual*: Notes written for the purpose of learning and practicing the conventions of note writing. These include polite and impolite correspondence; birthday, Christmas, and celebration cards; condolences; and thank-you notes.
2. *Problem solving:* Notes written to negotiate relationships, settle arguments, and organize and allocate resources.
3. *Reporting and questioning:* Notes written to relay or seek information, gain permission for special privileges, and get materials.
4. *Regulation*: Notes written to regulate oneself or others. These were used to remind, plan, tattle, or persuade.

In my Somersworth classroom, reporting and questioning were initially the most popular reasons for writing notes. This happened because I had encouraged children to use notes to tell or ask me things when I was too busy to answer orally. I was the audience for much of their note writing. In contrast, my class in Brookline started writing ritual notes because I had introduced note writing as a way to communicate with each other as well as with me. They had many audiences for their notes and they learned the conventions more quickly than the children in my first grade in Somersworth. It is interesting, however, that both classes ended the year having gained the same level of proficiency and diversity in their note writing, even though they had started at different points.

Rituals

When my students first started writing notes, they had to learn the conventions and rituals of the genre. This involved much trial and error.

One of Maeshan's first notes was addressed to Jay (Figure 6–1). Although Maeshan was able to construct a piece of writing with a story line and to consider his audience in his other writing, he did not apply this understanding to note writing. Maeshan saw children writing words on paper and giving them to each other. Apparently he thought that was all there was to it. Jay educated him immediately when he responded, "Next send a letter that makes sense" (Figure 6–2).

Jamie T.'s note to Nina was also minimal. Much of her message was contained in the picture (Figure 6–3). Nina was an astute reader of this message. The note she wrote in response (Figure 6–4) provided Jamie with an excellent model of polite correspondence, responding as it does both to Jamie's written message and to the message implied in her picture: friends play together. Although Jamie did not yet have control of the conventions of note writing, she had the satisfaction of demonstrating her feelings and receiving a response. Nina's note helped Jamie to better understand how to write notes in the future.

In the beginning, the children were very patient with each other as they developed an understanding of note writing. The thrill of receiving a note was exciting enough to ensure a response no matter how cryptic the note might be. But this initial excitement was not to last. It soon became necessary for the note to engage the reader in some way; other-

Jay. Up and Down. Love, Maeshan. I love Jay.

FIGURE 6–1 *Maeshan's note to Jay.*

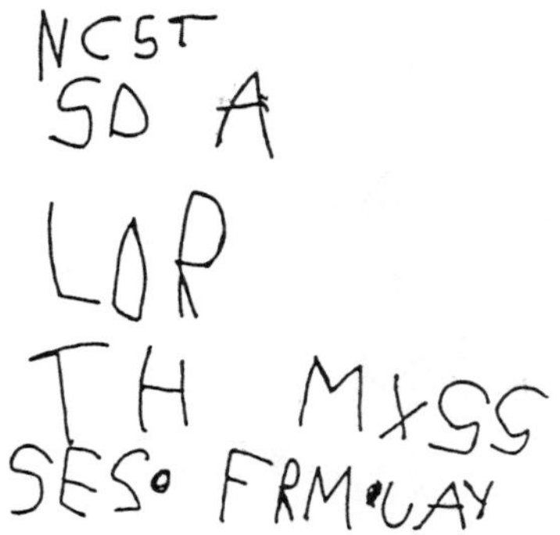

NCST
SO A
LOR
TH MXSS
SES◦ FRM◦JAY

Next, send a letter that makes sense. From Jay.

FIGURE 6-2 *Jay's response to Maeshan.*

MEIDOURFRES

Me and you are friends.

FIGURE 6-3 *Jamie's note to Nina.*

wise, it would be ignored. The children quickly discovered that asking a question was a good way to guarantee a response.

Often the children already knew the answers to the questions they asked. Jamie G. wrote to Jeremy (Figure 6-5) asking whether he was Chinese and received the expected answer (Figure 6-6). Jamie G. certainly knew that Jeremy was Chinese. His Asian heritage was obvious and Jeremy discussed his background often. But the content of the note wasn't as important to Jamie as the action it elicited from Jeremy—a response in writing.

As J. H. Menning and C. W. Wilkinson (1972) observe, "Letter writing is partially a study of probable or estimated human reaction as a

Dear Jamie T.
Thank you for the letter and the things you are doing
and playing with me. I love you.

FIGURE 6–4 *Nina's response to Jamie.*

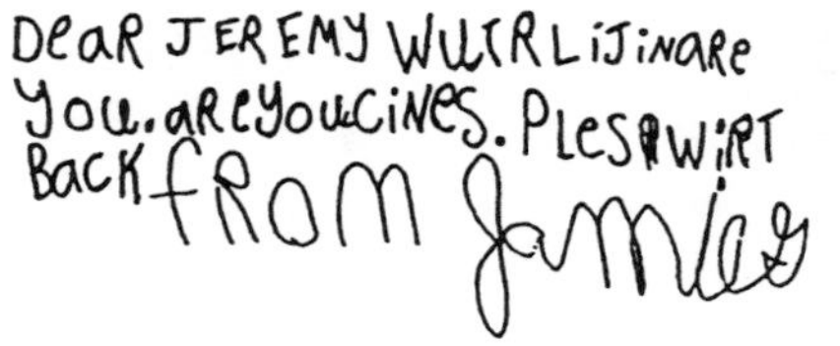

Dear Jeremy. What religion
are you. Are you Chinese.
Please write back. From
Jamie G.

FIGURE 6–5 *Jamie's note to Jeremy.*

basis for securing the desired action." Jamie had tried to ask some
interesting questions. Undoubtedly he had studied "human reaction"
enough to know that race and religion are fairly compelling subjects.
His questions did result in the "desired action"—Jeremy wrote back.

Asking good questions was one way to ensure a response; however,
I tried to expand the options. I wrote many notes to my students during this period. When I wrote I tried to mention something I'd noticed
the child doing or an interest the child had in addition to asking questions. This kind of modeling began to have an effect. Nina wrote me the
letter shown in Figure 6–7. As we have seen from her response to
Jamie, Nina was already aware of the conventions of note writing, prob-

Yes. I am Chinese.
To Jamie G.
From Jeremy.

FIGURE 6-6 *Jeremy's response to Jamie.*

Dear Ms. Blackburn:
I like studying about comets. Comets are very [interesting] and I cried to see Halley's comet. How do I see the comet.
Love, Nina

FIGURE 6-7 *Nina's letter.*

ably having received notes and letters at home. The opportunity to write notes in school accelerated her understanding. In her letter, Nina uses some techniques that I tried to employ in my notes and ones that Menning and Wilkinson describe as good strategies for letter writers.

1. She makes a *positive statement*: "I like studying about comets."

2. She refers to *common experience*: the project the class was doing on Halley's Comet.

3. She uses a *subtle* form of *flattery*: Nina knew that I made the decision to include Halley's Comet in the curriculum and that it is important to me; she reinforces that decision by telling me how much she enjoys studying it.

4. She *asks a question* to ensure a response: "How do you see the comet?"

5. She uses the correct form of *salutation* and *complimentary close*.

Nina has written a letter that maximizes the possibility of a response because it engages the reader on several levels. It does not rely solely on questioning as a device.

I suppose it was inevitable that, having practiced polite correspondence, the children would also try impolite correspondence (see Figures 6–8 and 6–9). These impolite notes were basically good-humored insults. However, the potential for real hurt existed. The children put an end to this kind of note writing themselves (see Jamie G.'s note to Keith in Figure 6–10). If the children had not handled this situation on their own, I certainly would have intervened. A good atmosphere for any kind of writing depends upon trust among the participants. To allow children to use writing as a weapon would have destroyed that atmosphere. I think the children knew this too and did not want to risk losing a good thing.

Problem solving

Another reason the children stopped using notes to cause problems was that they were becoming more aware of the potential for using notes to solve problems. Often the problems they tackled were easy ones, such as the situation Mara and Martina discussed in these notes:

> Martina, I like you alot but sometimes I want my lucky spot. I hope you don't mind. Mara. Answer back.

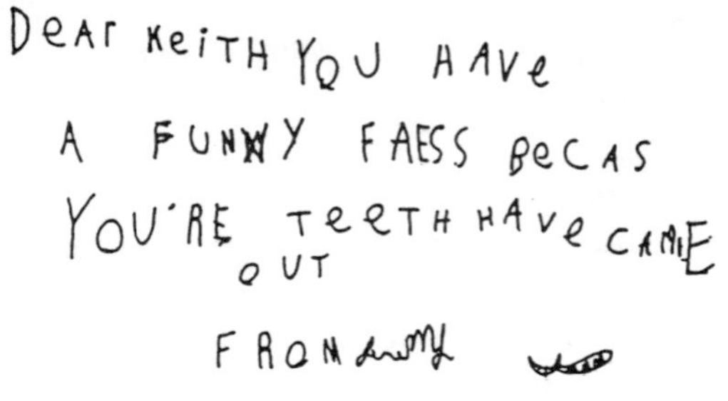

Dear Keith you have a funny face because your teeth have come out.
From Jeremy

FIGURE 6–8 *Jeremy's note to Keith.*

You have a funny face too.

FIGURE 6-9 *Keith's response to Jeremy.*

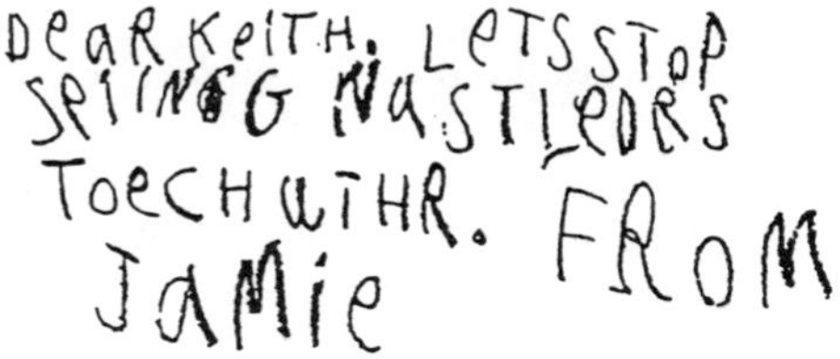

Dear Keith. Let's stop spelling nasty letters to each other. From Jamie

FIGURE 6-10 *Jamie's note to Keith.*

> Mara, One day I could have the lucky place and one day you could have your lucky place and we could share the lucky place. From Martina to Mara. Answer back.

Until I saw these notes, I had no idea there even was a "lucky place" in my classroom. The "lucky place" turned out to be a particular spot in front of the bookshelf where we sat for group meetings and lessons. Knowing about the "lucky place" helped me to understand the puzzling squirming and whispering that always occurred at group time.

Other problems were less concrete: "Dear Maeshan, Why do you tease me? From Jay." Maeshan answered: "Because I love you." I asked Jay what he thought Maeshan's answer meant and he wasn't sure. Jay was too young to be familiar with the adage "You always hurt the one you love." I explained this bit of human psychology to him, but Jay still felt it was a raw deal. He thought he'd be better off if Maeshan liked him less.

Nina's note to Monica had a plaintive tone: "Dear Monica, Why have you been so mean to me, Why? Love, Nina." Although Monica didn't respond in writing, Nina's note did affect her behavior. I learned from both girls that the note initiated a resolution of their differences, which they worked out orally.

Jacob and Jay exchanged a series of notes starting on November 26 and ending just before Valentine's Day. These notes are fascinating landmarks that plot a critical period in their relationship with each other. The first group of notes was initiated by Jay. Jay's family had moved to Brookline just before school started. He had no friends at the beginning of the year and had some difficulty adjusting. By the time their note writing began in November, he and Jacob had discovered each other and become "best friends." The first set of six notes illustrates their friendship.

Dear Jacob, can we have another sleep over or can you come over to my house? Jay

Answer: I would like it if you would always go to my house not yours. Jacob

Jacob, Would you meet at the end of the street to see Halley? Jay

I love you, Jacob. From Jay.

Jacob, It was fun goin to find Halley and can we have another sleep over? From Jay

Jay, I want to have another sleep over if I can. Jacob

Starting with the seventh note a change occurred. Jay, initially very insecure about his social status, had begun to "feel his oats." He began to break away from Jacob. Jacob was very hurt, particularly because Jay asserted his independence from Jacob by picking on him. Jacob tried to maintain some dignity in spite of his hurt feelings by writing Jay this note: "I would like it if you would not tease me." Notice the formal tone in Jacob's use of the construction "I would like it if. . ." Jacob was taking advantage of the written form to avoid an embarrassing face-to-face confrontation (he is likely to cry) and to communicate to Jay that he still had some control over the situation. Jay responded: "I won't tease you."

But Jacob knew Jay very well and he doubted that Jay could keep his promise. He wrote to Jay the next morning to remind him: "Did you remember the letter? From Jacob." "Yes I remember. From Jay to Jacob." Jacob was still not convinced and he tried hard to protect himself from hurt. Later in the day he wrote: "I have a feeling that you won't remember." And sure enough, he was right. The final note in this series read: "Jacob to Jay. You forgot the letter."

For a teacher observing this relationship as it was manifested in the boys' conversation and behavior, these notes provided an interesting counterpoint. Jacob was hopelessly outmatched when he and Jay engaged in spoken battles. Jay was quick-witted and fast with a comeback. He soon had Jacob reverting to tears and temper tantrums. During the period when these notes were being written, Jay and Jacob were fencing orally and Jacob was losing. The note writing allowed Jacob to bounce back—to get the last "I told you so" and to reassert himself.

Although these notes were interrupted by Christmas break, the boys resumed the dialogue when they returned in January. This time Jacob initiated the correspondence: "Jacob to Jay. Why don't you send any letters." He got no response from Jay so he tried again. "Jacob to Jay. Why don't you sit with me?"

I don't have a note from Jay in response. He may have written one that didn't get into the dishpan or he may have talked to Jacob. The gist of his response must have been that Jacob had wrecked something of Jay's so Jay wouldn't sit with him. Jacob wrote, in justification of himself: "You wrecked my jail, so I wrecked yours." And again: "Jacob to Jay. Don't sit with me."

Several days after this bitter exchange, I emptied the dishpan. Finding the notes, I decided to intervene and find out how things were going. I wrote to Jay:

> Dear Jay, Have you and Jacob been getting along better now? I notice that you two don't always play together. I think sometimes Jacob doesn't like it. What do you think? Love, Ellen

> You are right. I sometimes do not get along with Jacob.

> Jay, What do you guys fight about?

> We fight about who gets more things.

After receiving Jay's response, I met with both boys and showed them all their notes. We talked about their friendship. I pointed out what good friends they were and how much they enjoyed each other's company at the beginning of the series of notes. We looked together at how their friendship had deteriorated, but I also emphasized that they must still care about each other to spend so much time writing back and forth. I said, "You guys have written twenty notes and you kept writing them for two months! That's a long time, don't you think?"

They were still feeling stubborn, but they were clearly interested in and impressed by the evidence their own writing presented. They left our meeting looking warily at each other. The next day Jay wrote:

> Jay to Jacob. If you want to be in my team sign your name in this box.
> I won't tease you. [Jacob signed]

Jacob, do you think I can come over to your house?

Dear Jacob, I hope we have a good time when we go to your house.

Jacob to Jay. We are going to my Dad's.

Happy Valentine's Jacob. From Jay

This was not the end of Jacob and Jay's squabbles, but this series of notes, coupled with my intervention did have an impact. The physical evidence of the notes and the messages they conveyed allowed both boys to reflect on their behavior and their feelings in a way that wouldn't have been possible if all their arguments had been spoken. While they continued to bicker, both in speech and in writing, I also observed that they were being selective in how they moved back and forth between oral and written arguments. They were more successful at resolving their problems in writing. Both boys were aware of this now and could choose to write notes when things began to get out of control.

My students' use of note writing to solve problems caused me to ask the question, How is note writing different from conversation? Since the children were free to move around the classroom and talk to each other at any time, I reasoned that the decision to write a note must indicate an awareness of the potential of print. It was obvious to me as an adult observer that note writing allowed children to consider more options about ways to initiate and respond to communication. It seemed clear in the Jacob/Jay exchange that Jacob was using notes to gain some distance and to confront Jay indirectly, so he would have an advantage. Could my students really be conscious of making these kinds of choices? I asked them: "I'm wondering why you write notes when you could just go and talk about these things. What's the difference?"

I say some words [in a note] and that makes people like me more. It's nicer to send a letter. I can't describe it but it's nicer because talking's easier and writing's harder. Matthew

When someone writes a letter to you it feels like someone likes you and if you want to show you like someone you can write them a letter. Nicole

It's special and you haven't had a note for a long time and then you get it and you think—what could it be? Blaize

What we have to say might be secret, or you might want to discuss it alone. Craig

We're in school for reading and writing but talking we already know
how to do so writing notes gives you practice reading and writing.
Mara

Sometimes someone's busy and you don't want to interrupt, so you
write them a note. Jeremy

When you write it you get a nicer answer than when you tell it because
in writing you can't make your words sound mean. Nina

From these answers it is clear my students had a good understanding
of the "options" note writing allowed. They recognized that a note was
"special" because it took more time and effort to write, and that a note
had an element of surprise and secrecy about it. They even mentioned
the more practical considerations—that note writing allowed more practice in reading and writing, and that it was less intrusive.

The most interesting response came from Nina. She seemed to be
articulating the idea that a note writer can plan and choose words, and
that this can maximize the chances that the reader will respond favorably. The experiment with impolite correspondence proved that it was
possible to "make your words sound mean," so I reread Nina's statement to her and asked for clarification.

"Nina, you could write mean notes to people, couldn't you?"

"Yes, but if you don't want to you don't have to."

"Well, you don't have to *say* mean things either, do you?"

"No, but sometimes I do—because I get so . . . so . . . mad and I say
something or . . . or call someone a name without even trying."

Because the children had an opportunity to write notes, they were
able to learn the wonderful flexibility of print. Although the notes were
a more permanent record than conversation, they also gave the children
time to reflect on the impact their words could have and to choose carefully from a number of possible ways of expressing themselves. The
children learned to attend to their own language and to make judgments about how they were using it to affect human behavior. Their
personal narratives and stories also had an impact on their audience,
but the response was broader. The note writer tries to influence very
specific feelings and behaviors, and this prompts more diligent "study
of probable human reaction."

Reporting and questioning

The inability of a teacher to be in three places at once is always a source
of frustration. The notes I received from students reporting their activities were very important to me. My students' notes kept me up to date
and enabled me to share their little triumphs and discoveries. This was
a great comfort to me. Here are some examples.

Jeannine provided me with an inventory of her morning activities:

> Miss B. I listened to *Rumpelstiltskin*
> [Tarcov 1973] two times.
> I wrote a bunch of words.
> I did my workpapers. Jeannine

Catina discussed a writing topic:

> I wrote about "I Have a Boyfriend." Don't tell Parks Do you know who
> is my boyfriend? Catina

> It must be Parks since you don't want him to see. Am I right?

> Yes

> Well, he'll know as soon as you publish the book or read it to the class
> won't he? What about that? You'll still be embarrassed.

> No, I never thought about that. Should I tell him? Catina.

> Well, which is more embarrassing? Telling him or waiting for him to
> hear your story?

> Telling him.

Parks shared an observation from the science area:

> Miss. B. I saw the little egg move. Parks

> Which little egg?

> In the fish tank. It looked like it was getting bigger.

> Wow! Already? You have good eyes! Are the eggs still a little bit gray?

> Yes

> Did you make your observation on the paper over there?

> Yes, I will.

Not only do I have an opportunity to learn what children are doing
through their notes, I can also extend or suggest new possibilities when
I answer them. When Parks wrote about the little eggs, I was able to

draw out specifics from him that would make his observation better. I also reminded him of his responsibility to record his observation on chart paper near the tank. I gave Parks the attention and help he needed without disrupting the group I was working with.

I also wrote notes to elicit reports from children who didn't seem to be as gainfully occupied as I wanted them to be.

> Shawn, what are you writing? Ms. B.

> The rest of my G.I. Joe story.

> Oh, thanks, I'm glad you are working.

At the time I wrote this note Shawn wasn't writing at all. He was crawling under the table to pinch someone's leg. My note quickly reminded him of his duties and let him know I was aware of his indiscretions. Answering me also got him writing again and back "on task."

The children wrote many notes asking questions of me. These, like the notes they wrote to report activities, enabled me to deal with concerns and still maintain the momentum of my teaching. Amanda wrote to ask:

> Miss B. Can we use the tape recorder? Amanda

> Yes.

> How do we set it up?

> I think you just have to unplug the record player earphones and switch them to the tape recorder.

Amanda was able to carry out my instructions for setting up the tape recorder on her own. This prevented me from having to get up and do it, and it also reinforced her own independence. When Shawn was having a dispute with Timmy over the buying power of thirty-five cents, he wrote to me: "How many crackers and peanut butter can you get for $.35?" Catina was ready for a writing conference and was anxious to make sure I'd have time for her: "Can I have a conference on *I Went to my Friend's House?*"

Regulation

The nature of my students' notes changed when they began to report on each other. The children wrote their notes hoping to convince and persuade me to take action on their behalf. I exchanged this correspondence with Ricky:

Anthony and Tommy are making noise.

Are they disturbing you?

Yes.

Did you tell them that?

Yes.

What happened?

They still made noise. When they saw the note, they stopped.

Oh, next time maybe you should write *them* the note and see what happens. What do you think?

O.K.

In this case the situation resolved itself without direct intervention from me. But sometimes the children really lobbied for my attention. I received two notes about Brian. Eric's said, "Brian won't let us trace." Parks complained, "Brian won't share. He's being selfish."

In his note Eric simply reports the situation. He leaves the interpretation to me. Parks, on the other hand, is trying to influence my judgment by using loaded words and by making a judgment for me. Parks knows that sharing is a behavior valued by adults. The failure to share is a sign of a selfish character that Parks believes is wrong. Parks wants to be sure that I see Brian's behavior in the same light.

I do not always insist that everyone share classroom materials. Sometimes it's O.K. for a child to maintain sole possession of an item if sharing is going to disrupt his or her work. I answered Eric and Parks: "Is that because he's using it? If he's using it, he probably can't share. There are other drawing books."

When my students reported the activities and behaviors of others, hoping that I would get involved, I saw these notes as being regulatory in nature. The children were consciously using language to provoke action. This is an important function of writing.

Several years ago I wrote a letter to my Public Works Department complaining about the habit snowplow operators had of dumping snow in my driveway. It was important for me to persuade the city workers to take pity on me. Like Parks, I had to choose my words and tone carefully. There are many such battles to be fought in adult life. My first graders were learning early how to use language to fight them.

As adults we often write notes to ourselves to regulate our own behavior. In fact, this is probably the most frequent use we make of notes. When children use writing as a tool to self-regulate, it marks a significant step in taking responsibility for their own behavior.

The children in Nancy Frane's first-grade classroom began to use notes in just this way. Nancy had a "message board" in her classroom at the Edward Devotion School. She agreed to save these messages for me. Like me, Nancy was interested in encouraging children to use writing in a variety of ways. Her message board was meant to provide a way for children to make announcements and to communicate with each other. Interestingly, many of the children's messages were not addressed to others. Instead, they wrote messages to themselves as reminders.

> Misha, Do not forget about you inside cubby.

> Einat, Finish writing abou the author, To Einat

> Dear Sara, Don't forget to read, Love Sara

> PLAY Don't forget to finish the play.

> Tal, Don't forget to have your writing conference, Tal.

Nancy's message board was like the refrigerator door or the kitchen bulletin board. It elicited a kind of note writing that the children had probably seen at home. Nancy's experience underscores the value in providing different environmental cues for note writing.

In an effort to regulate her own behavior, Nina went beyond the format of a "reminder." One day she was playing with our two guinea pigs in the science area. The pigs were typically oblivious, in their small-brained way, to the tasks Nina prepared for them. She became more and more forceful in her attempts to persuade them, until finally I had to ask her to put them back in the cage. A few minutes later Nina wrote the note in Figure 6–11, addressed to Monica.

On the surface, this is simply another example of the ritual uses to which children put notes. It is set up like a greeting card. But, given the particular context in which it was written, it becomes more than that. Nina was struggling with her difficulty in handling our classroom pets. Nina loved the animals but couldn't accept their limited abilities. Instead of assuming a parental role toward the animals, Nina wanted them to be her friends and peers. Monica, on the other hand, seemed to understand her role as "parent-caretaker." She was nurturing and gentle with the animals.

To Someone We Like

Dear Monica
Thank you for being so nice to us. From Gee Pig.

FIGURE 6–11 *Nina's note to Monica.*

By assuming the persona of a guinea pig, Nina was using the note as a tool to help herself become more empathetic. I think I triggered this by my frequent use of the reasoning: "How would you feel if you were the guinea pigs and. . .?" Nina wanted to change her behavior with the animals. She used note writing as a way of putting herself in their place, of regulating her feelings.

Benefits

The benefits of note writing are implicit in the preceding examples and discussion of my students' notes. Note writing created an extra layer of discourse in my classroom that allowed my students to experiment with argumentation, persuasion, and regulation. Yet most school curricula would not give time to this kind of writing, preferring to emphasize narrative writing almost exclusively. Because notes are so short and limited in their function and because they don't demand as much organization from the writer, they have been given a lowly place in the literary hierarchy, if recognized at all.

Having watched my first graders as they worked to learn both narrative and note writing, I think the hierarchy seems unfair. Note writing is different from, but no less difficult than, narrative. The children had to learn the rituals and conventions of note writing just as they had to learn about narrative writing. The very brevity of notes puts pressure on the writer to choose words with care and to be particularly mindful of audience reaction. When the children wrote notes to solve problems, they had to deal with things as they are in the real world. They couldn't fabricate or use poetic license to get them out of a difficult situation or to make a point.

Shirley Brice Heath has been studying the development of the essay as a literary form. She recently pointed out (1986) that the essay has its roots in letters and journals, but that historically, these literate behaviors were considered leisure activities. Because letters and journals are still seen as "extracurricular," they are neglected in developing curricula for essay writing in schools.

As important as note writing is for its own sake, I also see it evolving into letter writing or even essay writing as the children begin to branch out to reach more distant audiences.

Brian wrote to the Easter Bunny (Figure 6–12). His plea for a three-wheeler included a picture of the Easter Bunny riding one. Brian told me that the rabbit could use the vehicle to deliver the eggs and then could leave it at Brian's house on his last stop. This letter contains, then, two justifications for why the Easter Bunny should grant Brian's wish: Brian has been patient, waiting virtually all his life (he's already waited five years and he's only six), and there will be a benefit to the Easter Bunny, too, whose job would be made easier by riding the three-wheeler on his rounds and then leaving it for Brian.

In another example, Brad wrote the following note to NASA:

Dear NASA, I have a idea. You can take a bucket of air on the space shuttle to the moon. When you get to the moon, let the air out. Then

Dear Rabbit,
I waited 5 years for a three wheeler.
I want one.
Please! Rabbit.
Brian Breton

Figure 6–12 *Brian's note to the Easter Bunny.*

you can try to breathe. Be careful because the air might go down to earth. When you get back, write back and tell me if it worked. Brad Tate

Both boys adapted their experience in writing notes to classmates and used it in a new situation to go beyond the classroom walls. Just as Shirley Brice Heath suggests that letters and journals can evolve into the more formal essay, I observed children evolving new ways to use notes as tools for learning.

Parks wanted to find out how many of the children had pets. Although I suggested that he do a checklist and graph his results, Parks preferred to write notes to all his classmates. He told me he could "find out more things" that way. He ran into difficulty because he had to keep writing notes back and forth to get all the information he wanted. Parks's notes might have been the precursor to a questionnaire. If he hadn't exhausted himself writing all those notes, we could have taken the notes and used them to create a questionnaire. Unfortunately, he lost interest in the project.

The students at the writing table decided one day that they would write each other notes instead of talking about each piece of writing. Blaize wrote a story about walking to school on a cold morning. Here are the notes he received:

Dear Blaize, Why did you like it if it was cold? From Tamar

I like the part when you said you were walking to school by yourself. Michael

Blaize, I don't understand your story. Nina

Blaize, Your story was interesting, but I got worried when you said you forgot the way. Did you get scared? Ellen

When the conference was over, and the children had written notes to all four participants, I asked them how they felt about the experience. They all agreed that it was fun, but that it took much longer than talking. A benefit, they felt, was that they had all the notes to refer to when they went back to revise their writing.

Parks and the other students at the writing table discovered that note writing has its limitations. But they continued to experiment with notes as a tool in academic situations. Jamie G. made an entry (Figure 6–13) in his science notebook. Throughout the year, I had encouraged the children to use their science notebooks to record their observations

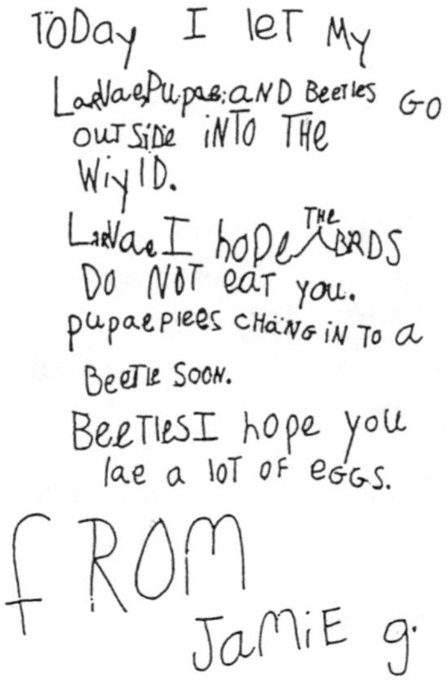

Today I let my
LarvaePupae, and Beetles go
outside into the
Wild.
Larvae I hope the Birds
Do Not eat you.
pupae piees change in to a
Beetle Soon.
BeetlesI hope you
lae a lot of eggs.
FROM
Jamie g.

> Today I let my larvae and beetles
> go outside into the wild. Larvae,
> I hope the birds do not eat you.
> Pupae, please change into a beetle
> soon. Beetles, I hope you lay a lot
> of eggs.
> From Jamie G.

FIGURE 6-13 *Jamie's entry in his science book.*

objectively. I wanted the children to experiment with using different writing voices to avoid having everything they wrote sound like personal narrative. In this case, Jamie switched into a note-writing format when he felt it was an appropriate way to emphasize his feelings about letting his mealworms go. Although the note was a familiar rather than a "scientific" form, he resisted the urge to anthropomorphize. I asked him about his entry and he said, "I wanted to write them a note to wish them through their metamorphosis."

These examples demonstrate the potential notes have for evolving into more formal literary forms and their use as cognitive tools to advance learning. The benefits, then, of adding note writing to the curriculum are numerous. Here, for convenience, is a list:

- Note writing creates an extra layer of discourse.
- It provides students with natural opportunities to practice a variety of written forms.
- The primary purpose of notes is to get something done in the real world.
- Lessons learned in note writing carry over to other forms of writing.

- Beginning writers may have difficulty sustaining narrative, but the brevity of notes allows them to complete a writing project in a satisfying way.
- Students who don't enjoy or excel in narrative writing often enjoy note writing, and this is especially true for boys.
- Note writing gives teachers and students another set of options about the way information can be communicated.
- It allows students to experience the differences between written and spoken communication in solving problems.
- Students become increasingly successful in using the note-writing format to control their own behavior and to influence the behavior of others.
- The classroom teacher is able to remain in contact with the students and their activities even though occupied with a specific group of children.
- The teacher is able to suggest solutions to problems or to extend learning and still remain attentive to the group of students currently being worked with.
- Note writing encourages a collaborative relationship between children and between teacher and student through the use of written dialogue to negotiate the meaning of a particular event or relationship.
- Finally, note writing gives students lots of practice in encoding or decoding written messages.

If notes are to be used profitably in the classroom, the question still remains, What classroom practices make note writing work? From my own experience I've identified some things a teacher can do to stimulate note writing:

- Provide appropriate materials and a time when note writing can happen, legitimizing it as a "literate behavior."
- Model note writing for the students and participate with them.
- Collect the notes and discuss them with the students, both to learn how children are using notes and to help them become aware of their note-writing behaviors.
- Encourage students to use notes to accomplish specific tasks, not just to socialize.

- Collect examples of notes grown-ups write—office memos, reminders, notes to family members—and display them.

- Provide a variety of environmental cues to stimulate note writing and note taking: message boards, mailboxes, observation sheets in activity centers.

- Integrate note writing into the curriculum by encouraging students to write notes about books they've read in reading logs, for example, or to write notes during a writing conference.

Like many good classroom practices, my note-writing experience was more accidental than planned. Teachers are continually inventing new solutions to old problems, but we must document our solutions for each other. It is my hope that other teachers will try note writing in their classrooms and that they will add to, revise, or even discard the insights and conclusions I've come to here so that note writing will no longer be a neglected genre.

Little Pieces

7

As the note-writing chapter demonstrates, a "piece" of writing need not be long to contribute significantly to a writer's ability. There are many small writing projects that can be added to the classroom with minimal effort and maximum reward. Many of these projects have already been described throughout this book, but several more deserve mention.

Lists

As Tom Newkirk observes in his book *More Than Stories* (1989), "Listing and categorizing are powerful tools for gaining dominion over the world" (70). I encourage list making as a writing activity in my classroom. The students make lists individually— the list of books read in their "title books," for example—but we also make class lists. The ideas for these lists generally come from the children. Always popular are lists of books published by classmates, lists of favorite books by adult authors, lists of children who have lost teeth (and how many they have lost), lists of toys, siblings, or junk food. Other lists are more innovative and ambitious. One year, my students decided to make a list of all the jump rope rhymes they knew. Since they wanted to write each rhyme down, this required a lot of work. Another group made a list of "Embarrassing Moments," complete with descriptions. This list was extremely entertaining and even prompted some fiction writing as children attempted to come up with even more outrageous situations. The lists remain hanging as long as there is interest in adding to them or until a new cataloging passion takes over. I save all the lists to use as references and some of them, such as the jump rope rhyme list, actually get published.

Community Books

In Chapter 5, I discuss the way "community books" are used to stimulate written observation and description in the sciences. Other commu-

173

nity books develop around interests of the class. Usually the idea for the book appears in some other kind of writing that's happening in the classroom. For example, *I Had a Dream* . . . began when Parks wrote his dream (Figure 7–1) in the class newspaper. Parks's story stimulated so much writing about dreams that we decided to make a community book to which everyone could contribute.

Some of the dreams were just that, real dreams that the children recorded (Figure 7–2). Others got embellished: "I had a dream about a hand. He was climbing all over me.I woke up. I felt my hand. I was scared of my hand. A-a-a-a-a-a, I was scared." The last line, "A-a-a-a-a-a, I was scared," is patterned after a classmate's book called *The Haunted House,* which was in turn patterned after Bill Martin's book by the same title. The author of this dream is not just reporting her dream, she is telling a story. And some of the dreams *were* stories that the children created using "I had a dream . . ." as the "story starter":

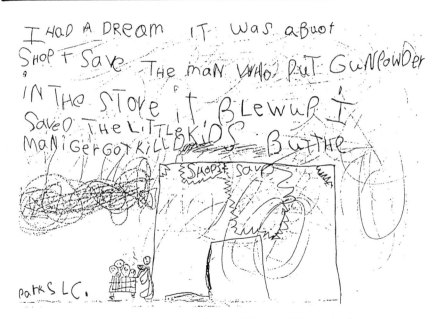

I had a dream. It was about Shop and Save and the man who put gunpowder in the store. It blew up. I saved the little kids, but the manager got killed.

Figure 7–1 *Parks's dream.*

I had a dream that when I had a birthday my mother drove away.

FIGURE 7-2 *Amy's dream.*

I had a dream about dinosaurs going to school. They could write and they could talk. But they had a problem. They had *A Problem!* They could not get in the door!

I had a dream. . . . Once there was a thing from outer space. He shot lightning out of his hands. He looked funny. He was the size of the Empire State Building.

What's Cooking? A Book of Favorite Recipes began as a list of favorite foods. Once the children saw the foods on the list, they became curious about how to prepare them. Writing recipes is hard work, they discovered. The list of ingredients and the description of procedures must be complete. If they are not (see Figure 7-3), confusion and indigestion result. The most mysterious recipe was this one for "Flat Toast" by Nickie: "You take a little pan and you put it on the stove. Then you turn it on for a little time. Then you turn it off. Then, there, you have it!"

When we role-played making some of these foods, the students realized the flaws in the writing. Consequently there was a greater effort to organize and sequence (see Eric's soup recipe in Figure 7-4). And this recipe for "Ice Cream Milk"—"1 cup of ice cream. 1 cup of milk. 1 straw. 1 cherry. Put it in a blender"—would work, although I hope the chef would use some common sense about putting the straw in the blender!

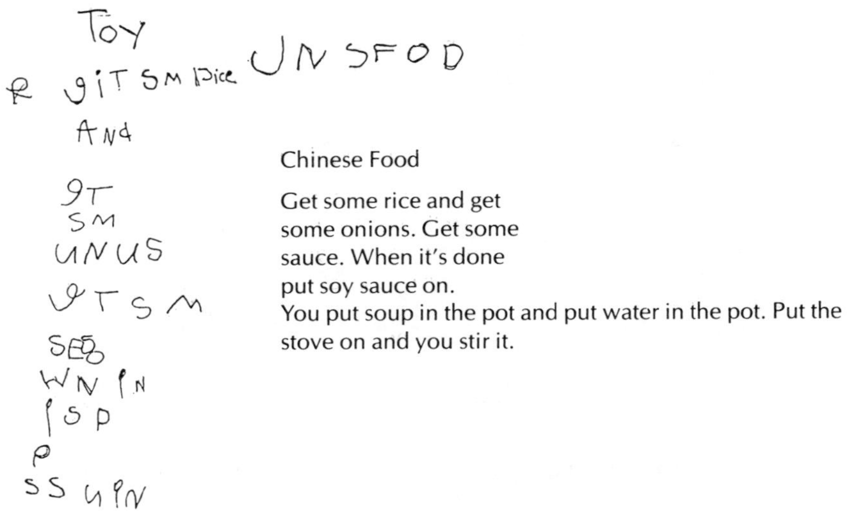
Toy
R gIT SM Rice UN SFOD
And
gT
SM
UNUS
gTSM
SES
WN IN
ISP
P
SS UPN
Chinese Food
Get some rice and get
some onions. Get some
sauce. When it's done
put soy sauce on.
You put soup in the pot and put water in the pot. Put the
stove on and you stir it.

FIGURE 7–3 *Toy's recipe for Chinese food.*

In each of these next recipes, the writers give the complete list of ingredients as well as the correct order and procedure for cooking with them.

Maple Sugar Snow

Take some snow, put it in a glass.
Pour some maple syrup in it.
Now it is ready to eat.

Grilled Cheese

Take some butter and cheese and two pieces of bread.
Put butter on the bread, and put cheese on the bread.
Put it in the pan and cook it.

These community books are kept in a bin in the writing area. When a child is stuck for a topic, I often suggest reading through these books, as well as any of the other community books scattered around the room, to jog loose an idea.

Questions and Answers

I have chart paper and markers set up all around the classroom for the students and me to use. I encourage the children to write questions for

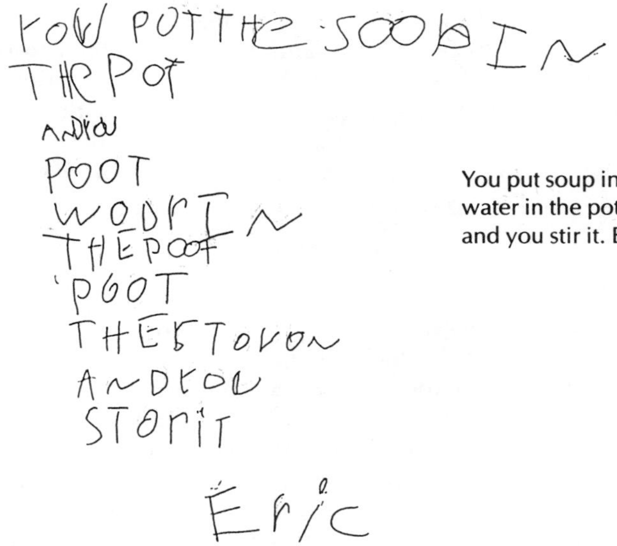

rov POTTHe SOOb IN
THE POT
ANDYOU
POOT
WOOrIN
THEPOOT
'PGOT
THESTOVON
ANDYOU
STORIT

Eric

You put soup in the pot and put
water in the pot. Put the stove on
and you stir it. Eric.

FIGURE 7–4 *Eric's soup recipe.*

each other to answer, and I write questions and answers too. Sometimes my questions relate to a subject we are working on. For example, when we were studying the metamorphosis of the mealworms, I asked the question: "Do fish shed or molt?" One answer: "Yes. It's like when you take a shower and then you walk on the dry floor, you shed water on the floor."

Frequently, the questions are snatched from the dialogue I overhear in the classroom. One day, after a particularly difficult math lesson, Brian announced to his friends that "math is boring, isn't it?"

"Hey, that sounds like a good survey question, Brian. Why don't you write that down and see how many people agree," I suggested. The class was about evenly divided in their opinions about math, but the arguments justifying those opinions were anything but boring.

Questions are posed by authors, too. One day I read *How Far Is Far?* by Alvin Tressalt (1964a), and wrote the title question on chart paper. My students answered rather poetically, I thought: "Far is as deep as the center of the earth." "Far is like when we go to visit Nana and we keep saying 'How far is it?'" "Far never ends."

The children write questions of their own. One particularly tricky question dealt with the existence of Santa Claus: "Do you believe in

Santa Claus? Why or why not?" Some did: "I believe in Santa Claus because I heard his reindeer on the roof." "I believe in Santa Claus because I saw Rudolph's nose when we were coming home on Christmas Eve from my Nana's." "I believe in Santa because I talked to him and I heard his reindeer." The skeptics, however, didn't: "I don't believe in Santa because my Mom goes to the store and buys the toys." "I don't believe in Santa because when I see him he's just a person."

Writing questions and answers stimulates children to consider issues and ideas, to problem solve, and to persuade and justify.

Mystery Pictures

"Mystery pictures" are another way to develop the art of observation and justification. To make these, I tack a magazine picture of a familiar object to a bulletin board and then cover the picture with a piece of construction paper in which I have cut a hole. The students can see only a portion of the picture through the hole and have to guess what the complete picture is. They write their guesses on chart paper with an explanation of why they feel their guess is correct. At the end of the week the picture is uncovered and we discuss their guesses and explanations. I like to have the children volunteer new descriptions that characterize the object without naming it directly. The mystery pictures (which have been laminated to make them durable) can be reused as an oral guessing game. Working in pairs, one child chooses a picture and then tries to describe it so that her partner guesses its identity before the egg timer runs out. Both of these activities are wonderful ways to develop vocabulary and attention to detail.

Many useful writing activities occur spontaneously. Developing these into significant writing opportunities requires vigilance and a commitment to using writing to complement classroom activities. In the first chapter, I described how Sam, at my suggestion, wrote an ad to sell his Cuisenaire™ rod buildings. This suggestion, given off the top of my head, resulted in a spate of ad writing that consumed a major part of class time for several weeks and continued sporadically throughout the year.

When Sam finished his ad, I suggested that he use it as a commercial during morning meeting. Sam read his ad to the class and the children asked him questions about his real estate. Sam had to make up his advertising copy as he went, creating a fictional setting for his buildings. This was so much fun that the rest of the class wanted to write ads and do commercials too. I suggested that they cut pictures out of magazines and write copy to accompany the product. Then they could act out the ad in the form of a commercial for the class at some point during the day. For the next few weeks we were constantly interrupted by sales pitches for everything from cockroach-chasing beetles to real estate schemes for selling entire cities.

Jacob cut pictures of green beetles from an ad for Raid™ and invented a new form of ecological pest control (see Figure 7–5). The beetles threaten, "If you don't buy me I will have a temper tantrum." Thinking this might not be a powerful enough hook to convince a home owner to invest in green beetles, Jacob adds: "He chases cockroaches away. He is twice the size of a cockroach. Buy it at Bradlees! Buy it!" I think this was a case of the cure being worse than the disease, but the kids loved it, especially since, in acting it out, Jacob actually threw a temper tantrum.

> This city costs $200,000,308.99. 80 washing machines and 20 dryers. It is near the ocean. There is 2,000 parks. No pollution. Electricity $.02 a year. Paper delivery $.02 a year. Send money to Box 200.

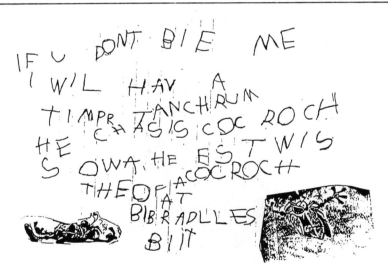

If you don't buy me, I will have a temper tantrum. He chases cockroaches away. He is twice the size of a cockroach. Buy at Bradlees. Buy it!

FIGURE 7–5 *Jacob's approach to pest control.*

Jay's ad for an entire city certainly sounds attractive. Admittedly, it's going to be tough to have clean, dry clothes, but with no pollution and 2,000 parks maybe it's inhabitants won't be very dirty.

The ads were very entertaining but Jamie's writing reminded me that school agendas do not always allow children to demonstrate their true potential. Jamie resisted writing. In November when this ad-writing campaign took place, her writing consisted of single-word labels. Ad writing activated her. Jamie cut flowers from a flower catalog and wrote, laboriously, in invented spelling (see Figure 7–6): "Ths flawr is good bcus it gros 10 tism fastr thn yoo oodne flawr. In srng yoo grdn wl lok luk ths. In smr yoo grdn wl lok luk ths. Tha gro thu bst." ("This flower is good because it grows ten times faster than your ordinary flower. In spring your garden will look like this. In summer your garden will look like this. They grow the best.)

Then Jamie cut out a picture of a kitchen and wrote: "Ths kthn iz $200,230 dlrs. 2 snks, 8 cbords, cums cmplt wth frnuchr." ("This kitchen is $200,230 dollars. 2 sinks, 8 cupboards, comes complete with furniture.") Jamie was not inspired by the language of school or of storywriting, but she certainly has acquired the language of TV commercials. I was humbled by the realization that Jamie's lack of motivation stemmed not from her own resistance, but from my failure to provide a writing task that interested her.

This flower is good because it grows ten times faster
than your ordinary flower.

FIGURE 7–6 *Jamie's ad for flowers.*

Our ad-writing experience paid off. Toward the end of the year, our school sold raffle tickets to raise funds for a grand piano. My class made posters advertising the ticket sales as well as the cause and hung them in stores along the street. Our ticket sales were excellent and I attribute that success to the posters. Many people came in off the street to buy tickets because they were so impressed and convinced by the children's writing.

By adding simple writing activities like these, I multiply the opportunities for children to experiment with writing in different genres. I also give writers a chance to find their own niche. Not every writer is a storywriter. In fact, I think these other writing tasks take the pressure off the storywriting the children do.

When I started to teach writing, I tried to turn everything into a story. This was frustrating for both me and my students. It did not produce good stories. Now when someone looses a tooth or skins a knee, I don't try to draw forth every detail in the proper sequence in the hope that there's "a story in it." I let the student decide how to communicate. Perhaps he does want to write a story, but alternatively he can add his name to the missing tooth list or write a line or two about the accident in the morning newspaper. The students have options about how they want to express their ideas. They make decisions about how much information they have and who their audience should be. Making choices like these improves all the writing they do.

Although I advocate using writing as much as possible, I am also wary about overdoing it. It's important to identify when writing is appropriate and when another approach, perhaps dramatic, artistic, or graphic is better.

Eris Doorneweerd, a first-grade teacher at the Driscoll School in Brookline, Massachusetts, has her class record the colors of the sky each day. In a small book on the windowsill, one child—a different child each day—is responsible for replicating the color of the sky with watercolors. There is no writing in the book to indicate the weather, only the delicate shades to give the "reader" clues. Eris also has her students draw the moon with white chalk on strips of black paper each night. After a month the strips are hung up around the classroom. It is possible to see the phases of the moon evolve along the length of strips.

Each of the activities I've described requires slightly different writing and thinking skills, yet each is easy to provide and to maintain. When I share these ideas with teachers in workshops they want to know, But what do you do with all that writing? Do you publish it, evaluate it? My answer: I pay attention to it. That is, I write along with the children. I read and discuss the writing they do. I take into consideration a student's preferences for certain kinds of writing. I try to make sure that all the children participate in the various forms of writing available. But mostly I just allow it to happen and enjoy it. I don't worry about revising or evaluating. Like the writing about the pumpkins I described in Chapter 5, these activities seem to prompt collective revisions and refinements over time.

Writing, painting, drawing, and discussing are important ways for making connections between observation, experience, and thought. Whenever children are helped to respond in these ways, they make their mark upon their world.

Numbers Tell Stories Too 8

When I started to teach writing I was satisfied with my math program. I used a hands-on approach, acquiring many of the excellent manipulative materials—Cuisenaire™ rods, Unifix™ cubes, attribute blocks, to name a few—available for teaching math concepts. *Mathematics Their Way* (Baratta-Lorton 1976) was a constant resource as were the McDonald Series manuals (1967), an outgrowth of the Nuffield Mathematics Project. But my students demonstrated many abilities in their writing that caused me to question assumptions I had about Piagetian cognitive theory—particularly his theories about young children's abilities to deal intellectually with abstract concepts.

According to Piaget (1965), children between the ages of four and seven are egocentric and bound by perception. They have difficulty going beyond the way things appear and cannot easily take another's point of view into consideration. According to widely accepted interpretation of Piagetian theory, these tendencies make it necessary to handle mathematical concepts in a very concrete way. Yet every day in my classroom, I heard children trying out alternatives in their writing based on the insights of classmates. These insights could not have been realized by egocentric, perceptually bound people. The children readily switched roles from writer to reader to listener to storyteller. In a journal entry I reflected:

> I find I've moved away from my block-building, water-play past. This makes me wonder, a bit guiltily, Why? Why have I moved away? I think because in working with writing I have found children able to do the kind of thinking, problem solving, experimentation with words and numbers that I once only thought possible with concrete materials. I suppose that doesn't make these materials obsolete exactly, but it does change their place of priority.

I became uncomfortable with the gap I felt between the activities using manipulative materials and the eventual need to transfer these understandings to numerical symbols.

During the summer of 1983, I read *Cosmicomics* by Italo Calvino (1965). In this collection of stories, Calvino writes about the evolution of the universe. (Paul West, reviewing the book for *Book World*, called Calvino's characters "mathematical formulae and simple cellular structures.") In the story "All at One Point" Calvino explores the theory, based on "Edwin P. Hubble's calculations on the galaxies' velocity of recession" (43) that all of the matter in the universe is concentrated at a single point. He begins the story:

> Naturally, we were all there—Old Qfwfq said,—where else could we have been? Nobody knew then that there could be space. Or time either: what use did we have for time, packed in there like sardines?
>
> I say "packed like sardines," using a literary image: in reality there wasn't even space to pack us into. Every point of each of us coincided with every point of each of the others in a single point which was where we all were. In fact, we didn't even bother one another, except for personality differences, because when space doesn't exist, having somebody unpleasant like Mr. Pbert Pberd underfoot all the time is the most irritating thing.

Calvino continues to develop his story, creating a humorous narrative out of dry mathematics and physics. I wondered if I could apply the writing of stories to mathematics in my classroom? I'd already been prodded to change my math program by Sarah Dawson, the second-grade teacher across the hall. Sarah was my partner in Project: Write the first summer the program was offered. She and I supported each other through our first year of teaching writing and now she helped me add another dimension to my math program.

Sarah used an interesting math program called the Comprehensive School Mathematics Program (CSMP) (l977). She nagged me for two years, tempting me with testimonials about how well CSMP worked with the writing program. But whenever I went into her classroom to observe, I saw children making strange diagrams using dots and arrows that I couldn't understand. I left shaking my head. I hated to admit it, but I was afraid I couldn't teach something that seemed so complicated. Finally, ashamed of my own cowardice, I asked to borrow the CSMP teacher's manuals for the summer. In the introduction I read:

> We believe that learning takes place when children react to interesting situations . . . whether real life or fantasy, such as in stories or games. These situations involve children personally and allow arithmetic to take the form of "adventures in the world of numbers."

"Adventures in the world of numbers and physics" would certainly be a way to describe *Cosmicomics*. I read on:

> We believe that every child can and does learn something from each situation encountered in the program, sometimes suddenly and dramatically, sometimes latently. For this reason, CSMP teachers do not stick to one topic until it is "mastered." Indeed our experience indicates that true learning often stops when the purpose of a lesson is merely the mastery of a skill. Instead, we believe that learning is more a "spiral" process than a "straight line" process, that intuitive leaps play as big a role as acquiring small successive pieces of information, and that a variety of situations can provide the interrelated experiences through which we learn. (3)

By the time I finished the introduction, I wished I had listened to Sarah earlier. The CSMP program introduces children to mathematical situations through the use of stories and helps children diagram the relationships inherent in these situations using dots, arrows, and string pictures. Parks's math lesson, which I discuss in Chapter 1, is an example of such a story. The lessons are presented in the form of storytelling dialogues between teacher and students.

This idea of using stories and pictures to teach mathematical concepts intrigued me. In addition to the stories presented in the lessons, the CSMP program includes excellent storybooks by Frederique Papys, the mathematician and originator of the dot, arrow, and string diagrams. The storybook set includes one Big Book version to be used by the teacher and standard individual copies for each child. I sensed immediately that children in a classroom that emphasized storytelling and storywriting as much as mine did would be comfortable with the format of the lessons. I knew that eventually they would be able to make up their own stories using the stories in the lessons as a model. I felt the drawing of the dot, arrow, and string diagrams was a "way in" to math—a way to graphically represent ideas before putting them into numerical form in much the same way drawing is a first step toward putting ideas into print when the children write.

CSMP makes use of some manipulative materials as well. Computations are done on a "minicomputer," a kind of abacus similar to a chip-trading game. Attribute blocks and tangram puzzles are also an important part of the program. Addition, subtraction, multiplication, division, and fractions are introduced to first graders. I was impressed that negative numbers were part of the curriculum as well. I did not learn about negative numbers until seventh grade. I remember I felt betrayed and discouraged. I was having enough trouble with the numbers I already knew about and now I discovered there were a whole bunch more! I was glad that my first graders wouldn't be surprised.

As excited as I was about using the CSMP materials, I saw it as an addition to my previous program, not a replacement. So I took the CSMP teacher's manuals apart, punched holes in the pages, and put them into a large loose-leaf notebook. Then, over a period of weeks, I went through all my math books and resources. I made notes of ideas and xeroxed pages. Finally, I reread the CSMP manuals and inserted whatever other material I felt was appropriate. I penciled in the titles of children's literature that seemed relevant. When I was finished I had my own customized math program. The next step was to determine how to schedule and organize the math program.

The Math Center

My new plans for math did not necessitate any changes in the math center. Each center in my classroom has a special activity that serves as a focal point. In the math center, the sorting table invites investigation. The table is a going-out-of-business find: a deep, wooden display table that once held hardware gadgets. It is lined with black felt and filled with an assortment of objects for sorting: marbles, wood turnings, buttons, screws, colored beads, shells, acorns, small blocks (of various shapes), bottle caps, lids, and paper clips. There is enough "junk" in the table so that each of the twenty-three students in my class can generously fill a cup with items to use for sorting, comparing, counting, or classifying and for making patterns in group math lessons. The table accommodates four sorters/builders/designers at a time and is always occupied. In addition to the sorting table I have the math apparatuses I've already mentioned; Cuisenaire™ rods, Unifix™ cubes, attribute blocks. Besides the activities on the math shelves, there is an estimating jar, filled with something different each week. At the end of the week we count the contents in various ways—by ones, twos, tens—to see whose guess of how many the jar contained came closest. I also have a bulletin board and display table where we collect items from our daily lives that involve using math. Measuring cups, egg cartons, sales slips, different kinds of rulers, even parking tickets are on display as a reminder of how numbers help (or hinder) us.

I have always set aside forty-five minutes to an hour for daily math lessons and this did not change with the implementation of my new math program. However, these daily lessons and the ones presented in CSMP were teacher led. I wanted to create an opportunity for the children to compose and teach a lesson that would embody the principles of invention, choice, discussion, revision, and publication. So I set up a bin marked Math Lessons and invited children to submit ideas for teaching their own lessons. Sometimes the lessons take the form of a note telling me of an idea or project. Often a child creates a worksheet or a dot diagram. Joseph put the worksheet shown in Figure 8–1 into the bin one day. He wanted to have the class complete a "counting snake." His worksheet doesn't give a clue about how the dots should be counted—by ones, twos, or tens. He planned to explain this as part of his lesson. Becca submitted a variation on the counting snake (see Figure 8–2). Instead of dots, she is asking the children to count the arrows. Many times children develop a worksheet without really developing a lesson to go with it. The lesson needs to be worked out during a meeting with me. We discuss the concepts inherent in the idea or worksheet and role-play the lesson. Our meeting sometimes results in a revision of the worksheet or of the child's plan. When we are satisfied with the lesson we set a date for the child to "publish" it—that is, to face the class and take on the responsibility of teaching.

As with reading to the class, teaching a math lesson is a performance that requires full mastery of a concept. Children practiced teaching math lessons much as they practiced reading to the class. They were attentive to the content of the lessons I taught, of course, but also to my

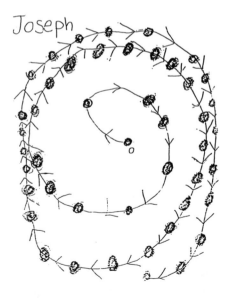

FIGURE 8–1 *Joseph's math worksheet.*

Count the
arrows
and
put the
number here.
By Becca.

FIGURE 8–2 *Becca's math worksheet.*

methods of teaching so that they could emulate them. Developing a math lesson is harder, though, because unlike a book that can be picked from a shelf, teaching a math lesson involves making a lesson plan. For this reason fewer students submitted math lessons than signed up to read to the class. I never had more than one child-led math lesson per week.

The children's lessons—whether they involved using manipulatives or stories and dot diagrams—were modeled on my teacher-led lessons and never broke new ground. This resulted not from my students' lack of inventiveness but from my own inexperience at seeing potential for mathematical connections in our everyday activities. My math program needed time to mature, just as my writing program had.

The student-led math lessons were one new addition to the math program. Math notebooks were another. The math notebooks were used during formal math lessons, when I encouraged my students to draw their own math stories. The children also used them to record work in the math center. They often drew pictures of Cuisenaire™ rod constructions or traced the designs they made and wrote explanations of what they had done. In the past, I provided separate record sheets for this activity, but now I hoped that keeping all this work together in a notebook would stimulate comparison and reflection. The notebooks were also used as scrapbooks in which the students collected samples of "environmental math" and wrote about them.

The notebooks fell short of the expectations I had for them, but I believe I have some solutions. One problem was the notebook itself. I used regular three-ring notebooks with plastic covers and blank paper. The standard-sized paper was too small for first graders to draw on and the rings got in their way. The plastic covers wouldn't stay flat and couldn't be folded back. Because the notebooks were awkward to handle, students didn't use them when they worked on their own math projects. Thus one of my major goals, creating a record of each child's math work that would reach a "critical mass," was not realized. In the future I'll use large rectangular sketch books instead of the notebooks or rig up portfolios similar to the ones I use in my art center. This will allow the children to have larger, more convenient space on which to work.

The second reason the notebooks weren't as useful as I'd hoped relates once again to my status as a novice. I didn't know how to cue my students about when and how they could use the notebooks to draw and play with math concepts. I discovered one way to do this as I drew with my three-year-old daughter, Emily.

Emily did not have the dexterity to draw figures at three years old. She certainly could not draw all of the characters she needed to tell the stories she created nonstop all day long. I got her a two-by-three-foot pad and had her use dots to tell her stories. On her first page, Emily made many groups of different-colored dots with her markers. Some of the groups were accompanied by smiling "Mommy" faces because these dots were the Mommy's children. I introduced the idea of drawing different-colored strings around each group to identify the sets of children belonging to each Mommy. Emily decided these were "play yards" for the children. Since she was already a talented storyteller Emily then created an element of conflict. Picking up a black marker, she began to scribble all over the sets of dots and said, "Suddenly some 'blackness' came and covered up the children so the Mommies couldn't find them." After this catastrophe (which made Emily a little uncomfortable even though she conceived it) we turned the page. Emily drew new colored dots, again inside play yards. Then she made a set of black dots. "They're afraid of the black dots," she said, pointing to the sets of colored dots. "But suddenly [things always happen suddenly in Emily's stories] the black dots have their own play yard!" Emily drew a thick black line around the black dots. "Oh!" Emily worried, "Will they have some friends?" Taking my cue from Emily's question I began to draw lines matching some of the black dots with dots in other sets, introducing the idea of one-to-one correspondence.

Emily continued to play with the dots and the "blackness" off and on for months. She experimented with different alliances between the sets of dots and various ways to contain the "blackness." The dots went on walks and had many adventures, adventures that often gave me an opening to suggest resolutions or plot variations that had mathematical significance.

Watching Emily I realized that I can initiate the same kind of drawing and storytelling in my classroom. The dot, arrow, and string diagrams give me the means for representing mathematical relationships between characters and events. I can use the black dots in a first-grade classroom to teach the concept of negative numbers. If a black dot matches up with a colored dot, they both disappear, so that positive-five colored dots plus negative-five black dots equals zero. Imagine the narrative possibilities in the idea of negative numbers and how exciting this could be when children realize that such numbers do exist and hold such power!

These are the kind of math stories I'd like to work on in the future. If my students can create stories as Emily did, the student-led math lessons will truly be initiating events that will contribute to a new awareness of math concepts.

I particularly enjoy using children's literature to introduce and extend some of the "big" concepts like negative numbers and infinity. Two books that work well are *How Far Is Far?* by Alvin Tresselt (1964a), and *What Is Beyond the Hill?* by Ernest A. Ekker (1986). Both books deal with the idea of infinity. In *How Far Is Far?* the author uses simile to gently lead the reader beyond familiar, concrete realities into the unknown. When the child in the story asks, "How deep is down?" he receives various answers, beginning with a water bug's ("As deep as a rain puddle after an April shower") and concluding with an oak tree's ("Deeper than the water that runs in hidden rivers under the earth"). "That's too deep for me," says the little boy.

When I read this book my students had a big discussion about questions and answers. They went through the book counting how many questions the boy asked and how many answers he received. I wrote more questions on chart paper and the children wrote answers. Jason was intrigued by the idea of deep and far. He tried to define these terms in relation to a globe. Thinking about the old saying "You can dig a hole to China," he argued that deep was more than far. His definition would have to mean that the globe was shaped like an oval. I showed him the globe and discussed the diameter of a circle. Jason revised his answer and decided that "far never ends." I showed the class the symbol for infinity (∞) and related it to the idea that numbers never end either.

During the next week I had several parents stop by to ask what I was teaching, because their children were running around the house making infinity symbols on any likely surface. It didn't take long for active minds to question how the number line could have a beginning if numbers never end. The children's interest naturally led to the introduction of negative numbers.

While the lessons with manipulatives provide important demonstrations of mathematical principles, they are not as portable as diagrams, stories, and symbols. The idea of infinity was exciting in and of itself, but the fact that the children could "write infinity," could carry that symbol with them and reproduce it, certainly added to its interest.

In the first chapter of *The Boy Who Would Be a Helicopter*, Vivian Paley (1990) writes:

> A day without storytelling is a disconnected day. The children at least have their play, but I cannot remember what is real to the children without their stories to anchor fantasy and purpose. . . .
>
> The stories are at the center of this fantasy of mine that one day I will link together all of the things we do and say in the classroom. (3)

This, I realize, is part of what I was striving for in reworking my math program. Number stories give students a way to think and talk about math concepts that is consistent with other work they do in the classroom. And being able to use stories, symbols, and diagrams empowers children to think mathematically in a way that manipulatives alone do not. Paley's words help me articulate more clearly my own goal of connecting all learning in my classroom through the medium of story.

Around the Author's Chair: Whole-Class Book Discussions

"Talk is cheap." "That's easy for you to say." "He's all talk, no action." "Put your money where your mouth is." "Put it in writing." "Speak softly and carry a big stick." "Actions speak louder than words." "Children should be seen and not heard."

All these adages reflect a lack of confidence in the spoken word. In our culture, direct action or the written word are valued, conversation is a poor substitute. Yet dialogue is the glue that binds daily interaction in the classroom. Teachers of young children know that some of the most fascinating and meaningful discussions take place during recess and while the students are eating lunch—times when their conversations aren't supervised and mediated by adults.

I try to bring discussions like these into the classroom. I have made talk about books and writing a daily occurrence. More importantly I treat talk as an end in itself, not simply a vehicle for improving writing or for testing reading comprehension. One of the most significant "talk events" occurs during and after I or one of the children read to the class; when we sit in "the author's chair."

Originally, I saw the author's chair as a form of publication, a way for the children to "go public" with the achievement of learning to read. As the event evolved, however, I realized that its greater value was to provide a forum for talk about books and about the role of reading and writing in our lives. It is significant that the author's chair is also the teacher's chair, the place where I sit to read to the class and to conduct some of the important business of teaching in my classroom. I invite the children in my class to share the teacher's role with me in many ways—by teaching math lessons, making their own worksheets, choosing their own topics for writing, picking the books they read, and conducting book discussions from the author's chair. My author's chair is nothing fancy, just a child-sized classroom chair, but the discussions that take place around it are critical to the learning that takes place in my classroom.

The Reading Process

Each day my students and I take turns reading to the class. I begin the reading period by sharing a book with the class and entertaining comments, questions, and stories after my reading. At the end of the period a student reads to the class and moderates the discussion. The children sign up on a sheet, usually about a week in advance. In fact, once my students are accustomed to the routine, the reading sign-up spot gets stampeded every Monday morning. Reading to the class is a favorite and coveted privilege. It takes about a month for the children to appreciate fully the responsibility they are assuming when they sign up. There are many false starts, times when children sit down to read and realize they have overestimated their own abilities. But by October a standard of competency has been established and the children understand that their reading performance needs to meet that standard. It's not surprising, then, that in the beginning, discussions frequently focus on the *process* of learning to read. This is important to my students— most haven't been to kindergarten, and reading for pleasure is not frequently practiced in their homes.

On October 11, I began the reading period by reading *Bring in the Pumpkins* (Ipcar 1976). When I finished Edward asked me how I learned to read the book.

EBK: How did I learn to read it? Because when I was in first grade, I learned how to read just the way you are—(*thinking better of that*)— Well, no actually when I learned how to read the teacher held up word cards and we had to take turns reading them. Once you learn how to read, Edward, you never forget. You always know how.

VOICES: I know how to read. Yeah, so do I.

EBK: You can read anything you want. You can pick up a book and read it without practicing on it.

DANIEL: If they picked up a book like that, grown-ups can read every book.

JEANNINE: I can't pick up every book, and read every book.

This discussion about learning to read continues after the independent reading period is over when Daniel, a repeating first grader, reads a difficult version of *Rumpelstiltskin* (Tarcov 1973). When he's finished, Richie has a question:

RICHIE: Daniel, this is a hard question. Um—you didn't, last year, you couldn't even read that last year.

DANIEL: 'Cause I wasn't practicing a level. When I really got started into reading, I used to read a lot of levels like this but not all of them, I wouldn't just read four, five, six. I'd read seven and eight, then five and then I'd read something in ten. (*Daniel is referring to testing himself by reading through the basal readers to see what level he can read*)

EBK: You mean you didn't read them in order, you skipped around?

DANIEL: Yeah, 'cause sometimes there's stories in the book you can't read and you want to read one of the bigger books and to start to read one of those, then you start reading one of the little ones. Then you know how to read both of them. Once you start reading big books you can read all of the little ones.

Daniel is teaching the class something important about learning to read—that is, learning to read is his responsibility and it doesn't necessarily proceed sequentially through a set of books of graduated difficulty. The desire to read a particular story is very important. Daniel learned that he could challenge himself by reading books at a variety of levels. Even though it might require incredible effort, that effort was rewarded by the boost it gave him in being able to read easier material.

These talks about learning to read convey very different information from the typical reading lesson. They highlight the joy of being a learner, the personal commitment and sense of achievement possible when you challenge yourself to do what you "can't" do—to read a book you "can't" read. Children enjoy challenges. They do not appreciate having things made easy for them by well-meaning adults. Listen again to Daniel, discussing his reading process with me during a reading conference.

EBK: That's the end of the story. Wow! You figured these words out all by yourself, didn't you? Was it hard to do?

DANIEL: Kind of, a little bit.

EBK: It's harder to read the words than it is to just tell the story isn't it?

DANIEL: Yes it is, because when you look at the pictures it's too easy. It's too easy to go by the pictures. Cinchy. But to go by the words, that's how you learn to read.

EBK: I see. Is it more interesting to go by the words than just by the pictures?

DANIEL: Yes.

EBK: It is, even though it's hard?

DANIEL: Yes, because it's just fun sounding out the letters.

EBK: You mean figuring things out is interesting? You know, some people think kids don't like to figure things out, so they try to make reading easy.

DANIEL: I just try to figure it out for myself. I figure, why not? If grown-ups learned to do it, why shouldn't I know how to do it? I don't wait for grown-ups to tell me. I figure, why should I wait for them?

It's this kind of "take charge" attitude that my students demonstrate and share with their peers in the author's chair. I often feel that these lessons are far more important than any I could devise on skills and word recognition.

Authorship: Connecting Reading and Writing

As reading becomes more automatic, the talk changes. This change reflects the connections the students are making between their writing and their reading. Now instead of worrying about how to produce print, the children are beginning to care about the structure and content of the stories they write at the writing table. The children apply this analytical style to reading trade books as well. They are alert to story structures because of their own experiences as writers. They compare stories with similar plots. On November 15, I read *Mushroom in the Rain*, by Mirra Ginsburg (1987), and *A Good House*, a "basalized" version of the folktale *The Mitten* [Tressalt 1964b], from one of the preprimers. Both stories have similar plots: many animals of impossible size crowd into too small a space. When I finish with *A Good House*, Jessica begins the discussion:

JESSICA: I noticed something [in *A Good House*]. Everybody was crowding in it like in *The Mushroom*.

TIMMY: Yeah, yeah, everybody was crowding in.

EBK: It had a different ending though didn't it?

VOICES: Yeah. Yeah, it did.

DANIEL: (*Pointing to the mouse*) 'Cause he kept telling them to come in.

EBK: Yes, that was different too. The mouse kept telling them, "Sure come on in." What did the ant say?

VOICES: No, no, no.

EBK: Well, the ant always said, "I don't think there's room," and the animals sort of persuaded the ant, didn't they?

The children recognize that the main plot of the stories is similar. I encourage them to notice the differences between the stories. They go beyond listing the differences to making judgments about them.

JOEY: Yeah, but I'm glad the mushroom didn't blow up [like the mitten did].

EBK: You're glad.

JOEY: It would be the same story!

Robert introduces a new criterion for analyzing the stories: realism.

ROBERT: I like the part when the ant said "There's no room, there's no room."

EBK: Why did you like that?

ROBERT: Because it couldn't be a true story like that. (*Points to the mitten picture*)

EBK: You think it seems truer that the ant would say, "There's not enough room," than the mouse saying "Come in, come in?"

ROBERT: Mmm.

The children like even their fairy tales to be convincing.

The discussions often begin with a series of formulaic questions: What part do you like the best? Why did you want to read this book? How does it feel to be an author [reader]? These questions serve the same function discussing the weather does at a cocktail party: they get the discussion going. They are safe, nonthreatening, predictable questions. Anyone can join the discussion by asking questions like these. The value of these questions became clearer to me when I taught in Brookline, Massachusetts, and had a number of bilingual students in my class. Even children with limited English vocabularies learned to ask the questions. This allowed them to participate right away in an important classroom event.

Interestingly, I think predictable questions often result in unpredictable—more thoughtful—responses. This makes sense because the child anticipates the questions and has time to prepare for them. This is a totally different approach from that of *surprising* students with tough questions to see whether they are on their toes. And, the *children* are asking most of the questions, not the teacher.

In December, my students speculated about the effect different endings might have on the reader after I finished reading *The Snow Child* (Littledale 1978), a story with a plot similar to *Frosty the Snowman* (Bedford 1986). We began with a formulaic question that led to comparing the book to similar stories.

CHRISTOPHER: Ms. Blackburn, What part do you like best?

EBK: I guess I like the way the author made it seem like it was going to be a sad story [the snow child melting] and then it had a happy ending [the snow child returns every winter].

DANIEL: (*Always interested in getting a reaction*) She could've changed it and had the kids eat the snow child, 'cause kids like to eat snow.

EBK: Would that have been as good a story? What do you think?

VOICES: No, No, No.

DANIEL: Well it would've been more sad.

EBK: Yes, it would've been very sad. That would be like eating Frosty the Snowman.

RICHIE: (*Teasing the class, hoping to make the more tender-hearted indignant*) Um, they could've, I'm just saying *if* you want to make it sadder or something you could just tell that some of the big kids were wrecking it.

CHRISSY: (*Asking me*) How did you feel when you read the sad part?

EBK: It made me feel sad too. Does anyone know the story of Pinocchio? What happened to him?

JEANINE: At the end he became a real puppet.

EBK: He turned into a real boy. So the author of *The Snow Child* could've written that the little snow child turned into a real child couldn't she? If she'd wanted it to be a real happy ending.

Notice that the children are interviewing me, the reader, about the story; the reader is not questioning the audience. I think my students can speculate about reader reaction to plot changes so insightfully because that reaction has been made visible to them through the discussions about books.

Developing the Art of Discussion

Because my students experience book discussions as reciprocal conversations, reading to the class has also become highly participatory. In fact, it would be more accurate to call it reading *with* the class. Comments and discussion occur all through the reading, not just at the end. Listen as Scott reads *Are You My Mother?* (Eastman 1960):

SCOTT: "A mother bird sat on her egg. . . ." (*Class chuckles*)

VOICES: *A very big* egg! Bigger than her!

SCOTT: (*Continuing*) ". . . the egg jumped. 'Oh, oh,' said the mother bird. 'My baby will be here. He will want to eat.'"

DANIEL: (*Chuckling*) Funny picture.

SCOTT: "'I must get something for my baby bird to eat!' she said. 'I will be back.' So away she went."

ROBERT: So away she went.

SCOTT: "The egg jumped. It jumped and jumped and jumped! Out came the baby bird." (*Laughter*)

VOICE: Cute.

SCOTT: "'Where is my mother?' he asked. He looked for her."

CHRISTOPHER: I thought baby birds can't fly when they first come out of the eggs.

SCOTT: *You'll* see. "He looked up. He did not see her. He looked down. He did not see her." You know why, Ms. Blackburn, I wanted to read this to the class? They haven't heard it yet. "'I will go and look for her. I will go and look for her,' he said. So away he went."

JESSICA: This is the funniest.

EBK: I know, he's going to step right off of there.

VOICES: Oh, oh, oh!

SCOTT: "Down, out of the tree he went. Down, down, down. It was a long way down."

EBK: Guess you were right, Christopher.

CHRISTOPHER: Baby birds don't know how to fly.

DANIEL: No, they don't, see.

VOICES: Hey! Hey!

EBK: I would think he'd be dead by now.

SCOTT: "The baby bird could not fly. He could not fly, but he could walk. 'Now I will go and find my mother,' he said."

ROBERT: If I was that baby bird, I'd be dead.

SCOTT: "He did not know what his mother looked like. He went right by her. He did not see her." (*Laughter*)

EBK: He probably doesn't even know he's a bird.

DANIEL: He doesn't know *what* he is.

JESSICA: He thinks he's something else, like a dog.

CHRISSY: A cat.

SCOTT: I'll tell you at the end.

As the reading continues, the baby bird does attempt to bond with different mothers—everything, in fact, from a dog to a backhoe. And audience reaction becomes more lively, much to Scott's satisfaction. He does not have a captive audience here. His friends are definitely free to participate. The reading is a collaborative effort, different from the usual storytime where the children sit quietly listening, waiting for their turn at the end of the reading. In this case the story counts as one turn in the reading, not the only turn. The children's responses blend with the author's words. I think this accounts for the sense of camaraderie the children have with books and authors. While there are times for silent appreciation (and we have these, too), these more lively readings allow the stories to come into my students' experience in a unique way. Their collaboration with the reader does not interfere with their comprehension. Instead, the enthusiasm seems to encourage attention to story details. The audience comments, questions, and speculates as the story unfolds. Because the children are active listeners, there's no awkward silence at the end of the reading, the discussion simply continues:

DANIEL: I like the part—I like the Snort.

SCOTT: Yeah, I *knew* you guys would like *that* part!

DARIEN: Why'd you want to read this book?

SCOTT: 'Cause no one read it to the class. And Eric said *he* was going to read it, but he didn't. And he asked me when *I* was going to read it. And I walked over here and said, yeah, *Are You My Mother?*

MISTY: Scott, what part do you like the best? I probably like the Snort.

VOICES: Me too, me too.

SCOTT: Just let me find it, and then I'll read it. This part. (*Pages through the book*) I'll read it to you. (*Rereads the part about Snort as other children also "read" in chorus*)

Scott is very pleased at the response and at his own ability to correctly anticipate his friends' reactions.

One day I had a classroom visitor, a woman who had recently completed her Ph.D. in reading. On this day one of the students chose to read *Tikki Tikki Tembo*, by Arlene Mosel (1968), the story of a Chinese boy whose name takes so long to say that he nearly drowns before his brother can alert their mother of the danger her son is in. Once the mother finally understands, she urges the brother to run and get the old man with the ladder. From my adult perspective, I viewed this as literary device to delay the rescue and to increase suspense, but the mother's reaction was puzzling to the class. When the story was over, there was an interesting discussion. Why didn't the mother run to her son's rescue herself? This made makes more sense to a modern child's mind. I could tell from my students' comments that they were truly disturbed by this lapse of maternal energy and intelligence. Would their own mothers be so slow to respond? Now was the time for a brief lesson in Chinese history and culture. I explained about foot binding and the role of women in Chinese society. The children responded with stories about their own mothers. Ricky commented that it was just like at his house. His mother wanted to go to work but his Dad wanted her to stay at home. It was a recurrent sore point in the family.

After the children went to lunch, my visitor and I finally had a chance to discuss the event. Excitedly I asked, "Well, what did you think of that discussion, wasn't it wonderful?"

My visitor hesitated and I knew something was wrong. "Well," she said, "I felt the discussion went on much too long, and when do you ask comprehension questions?" At first I didn't know how to respond. After all, what better demonstration of comprehension at the deepest level could my students have given? They had made the story so much a part of themselves and their experience that it was uncomfortable. Their need to make sense of it was so great they voluntarily discussed it for forty-five minutes. The readings and book discussions often last forty-five minutes, because it takes this long for the ideas and associations to develop. Naturally, every student does not sit with rapt attention the entire time. The children tune in and out of the discussion as their interest dictates. But I see nothing wrong with this. Children learn how to get themselves back into the activity of the group. They learn patience, cooperation, and concern for their classmates' needs and interests. If the discussions ended after fifteen minutes, much of this richness would be lost.

The book discussions provide a dialogue that goes far beyond conveying a few teaching points or answering comprehension questions. They are models of what it means to be a thinking, feeling, literate person. But my visitor was right to be nervous. To quote Courtney Cazden in *Classroom Discourse* (1988):

> For the teacher, this shift from a series of questions is more than a
> change in surface verbal behavior. At the heart of the shift from lesson
> to discussion is a different conception of knowledge and teaching. (59)

While a researcher in my classroom, Susan Sowers interviewed me about the book discussions. "Do you have any guidelines for responding to the children's comments and questions during discussions?" she asked.

"No, I just ad lib!" I said. Then I went on to qualify that answer for two pages of transcript. Since each discussion is different, I do have to ad lib. But I also tape the discussions and listen to them after school while I clean up the room, on my way home in the car, or at home in the evening. Listening to the discussions as an auditor rather than a participant allows me to really hear them. I get a better sense of what issues and concerns are being addressed and by whom. I also listen to my own comments and questions to see whether they are helpful. On my clipboard I have a class list on which, during the discussions, I keep a simple record of the questions asked or comments made by individual children. I make further notes on this list if I need to when I listen to the tapes. Sometimes I talk to students about their participation, suggesting that they try asking different questions if I feel they're getting stuck asking formulaic questions all the time.

If given the floor, young children will talk about anything and everything for as long as possible. They will compete to see who can tell the most or the longest stories. This is the first hurdle to overcome when developing the art of discussion. While I don't mind if the discussion eventually digresses from the text of the book read, I do insist, particularly at the beginning of the year, that when the discussion begins, the comments, questions, and stories be related in some way. Just as students need to learn what a writing topic is, they need to understand that discussions also develop around a central topic. But—and this is the tricky part—discussions often swirl away from the initial focus. I allow this to happen as well. The difference between a discussion and random storytelling is whether the majority of the class is attending to the stories, taking cues from them, and following the thread of the talk as it develops. As long as this is happening, I am comfortable with any direction the talk may take. In this discussion, following my reading of *Snow White* (Littledale 1980), I play an important role in the direction of the discussion without monopolizing it.

ERIC: I was glad she [the queen] died.

EBK: You were glad . . .

VOICES: Yeah, she died.

EBK: They got rid of her. Whatever happened to the magic mirror?

VOICE: Broke.

SIMONE: Yeah, I saw it on TV.

ERIC: What part did you like best?

VOICES: In the whole book, the whole book.

EBK: I like the part where they put her in the glass coffin because that was a different idea. I wonder how the author ever got the idea to put her in a glass coffin?

SCOTT: From the movie. They always put her in a glass case.

EBK: Well, the story came before the movie. The story is very old. Do you know any other fairy tale where they had a glass something that's not usually glass?

DANIEL: Glass slipper!

This discussion begins with the familiar pattern of teacher questioning. What distinguishes it from being a question-answer session is that the children are also interviewing me about the book. The reciprocal questioning is an important feature of our class book discussions. In this next section, I point out some of the troublesome aspects of Snow White's character.

EBK: Robert?

ROBERT: Um, it was a good thing at first when she didn't die.

EBK: You mean in the beginning, the first time the queen tried to poison her?

ROBERT: Yeah.

EBK: What kind of character was Snow White anyway?

DANIEL: She just hangs around . . .

VOICES: She's pretty. She was good.

EBK: She was good. What made her good?

SIMONE: She didn't do the things like, "Mirror, mirror, on the wall, who's the fairest of them all."

EBK: She wasn't vain. I know one thing—to me she wasn't a very smart character because she kept doing the same thing over and over again.

RICHIE: I know it! The dwarves said don't, don't—

EBK: —don't let people in and she kept doing it!

SCOTT: I never let people in my house when I'm alone.

EBK: I know. It's kind of weird. But anyway she ended up with a prince!

Although I ask my students rather standard questions about the characters, I'm not asking them to give me a "right" answer. I have my own ideas about Snow White. Taking my cue from Daniel's response that Snow White "just hangs around," I share my rather subversive opinion. I think my willingness to be critical of conventional opinion gives Scott permission to develop his own ideas later in the discussion.

SIMONE: I like the part where the queen fell down dead.

EBK: Do you think she deserved it?

SIMONE: Yeah.

EBK: What kind of character was the queen?

SCOTT: Mean, she wasn't pretty at all.

EBK: I got the feeling she was pretty, but she wasn't a nice person.

SIMONE: I know, she was mean.

EBK: She was too interested in being pretty.

JESSICA: I liked the part when she strangled herself and fell down to the floor dead.

JASON: She chokes when she sees someone prettier.

DANIEL: My mother knows someone, she calls her Tallullah because her hair looks like an old movie actress and her name was Tallullah. She thinks she's so beautiful. And she has these short purple shorts. She walks around the streets.

The wicked queen is a more complex character than Snow White. She's both beautiful and evil. The children have some difficulty holding both of those characteristics together. Through their talk they begin to work this out. Daniel gives us a perfect little anecdote of vanity gone wrong, but I let his story speak for itself—there are some things better left unexamined!

JAMIE: I think the princess was better than the queen.

EBK: You thought Snow White was better than the queen? I think the author thought so too.

SCOTT: I don't!

EBK: You didn't think Snow White was better than the queen? Why?

SCOTT: The queen owned more money. And she owned a castle. Snow White didn't own that much money.

EBK: No.

SCOTT: She didn't own a castle.

VOICE: No.

EBK: But would you trust someone like the queen?

VOICE: Never!

SCOTT: Sometimes.

EBK: Well, sometimes just doesn't do it. The one time you trust her and she does something bad to you. She will go down to her cellar with the skeletons and make this . . .

Scott: I'd take that skeleton . . .

EBK: You think you can overpower her, huh! You wouldn't be afraid of her?

Scott: (*Even though many of the other children are now protesting as well*) I like the skeleton.

Scott, laughing, shields his face with his arm as the children lean toward him to protest. "You do not! You're just saying that!" Scott is now very pleased to have caused such controversy. From a pragmatic view he does have a point, but the children suspect false bravado when he claims to like skeletons.

This discussion came a long way from the first polite questions about my favorite part of the story. As a matter of fact, at the end, it nearly became downright rude. But one thing is certain, the children weren't just going through the motions; they were invested.

In my interview with Susan I mentioned several other things I look for and try to develop in the book discussions. I wean my students from having to be recognized by me before they can speak. Instead, the children learn to carry on cross-discussion, addressing me or each other directly, taking turns without raising hands, just as they do at their snack tables. This contributes to the feeling that I am a participant not just a moderator or judge of the comments the children make. I set a pattern for this exchange, asking that my students look at each other and address each other by name.

Often discussions consist of parallel stories told in response to the reading. Children are prompted to tell a story because it relates to the text or because their memories are jogged by a comment a classmate has made. But they tell it simply as their story; they don't necessarily realize how it connects. I try to pick out those connections. Often I will ask, What made you think of that? so the train of thought will be made explicit.

The layering of parallel stories can reveal deeper issues that lie beneath the surface of my students' stories. These issues are not yet concrete enough in the children's minds to be discussed directly. The stories are metaphors and the metaphors are clues to me, clues I need to listen for and work with as a participant in the dialogue.

As author of the week, it was Misty's turn to read to the class, but she was absent. I decided to take her place and to read her newest published book to the class.

EBK: *I Love My Cat.* "Me and my sister were outside playing. My father told me and my sister to come in. We came in. I saw the cat on the table. I said, 'Where did you get him?' My Mom said 'From a barn.'

He was shy because he was little. When he got bigger, he protected me. My father made a cabin in my room. We slept in with the cat. I hugged him. We named him Blackie. About two days later we had to give Blackie away. The landlord said, 'You have to give him away.' We gave him away to my neighbor. Before we gave Blackie away, I kissed him six times. My next-door neighbors didn't take care of him and he ran away. I felt sad. The next day we went up to The Pines. We found Blackie. Some girls took him. They said he was theirs."

JESSICA: She should have put in . . . she told me that their next-door neighbor gave all the food to the other cat, and then Blackie ran away.

EBK: You mean the reason why Blackie ran away was that the neighbor didn't feed Blackie enough?

JESSICA: He gave all the food to the others.

SIMONE: What part did you like the best?

EBK: When Misty said, "Before we gave Blackie away, I kissed him six times," and she made six hearts, one for each kiss.

SIMONE: I know it! I know it!

EBK: It's a sad part though.

CHRISSY: When we didn't live here, we lived in the trailer and then I came home from school and then I wanted a cat real bad and I heard this "Meow," and then I said, *"Whose cat?!"*

EBK: You said it just like Misty did? *"Whose cat?!"* And did your mother answer the same thing? Did she say "Yours!"?

CHRISSY: Yeah.

By emphasizing the expression in Chrissy's voice and relating it to the way Misty described her conversation, I make the connection between the emotional moment when Misty discovers her kitten and Chrissy's feelings when a similar event takes place at her house. Darien's story builds off both Jessica's and Chrissy's.

DARIEN: A dog followed me home, then I opened my door, then he ran into my house and my mother let him stay and my father gave him to *me*.

EBK: Do you think that dog belonged to someone?

DARIEN: Yes.

EBK: Well isn't that just like in Misty's story. . . . If the animal belonged to someone else and ran away, wouldn't the owner feel sad if you kept their animal?

DANIEL: And plus, the cat wouldn't really be used to it.

ERIC: Yeah, he would be real sad.

RICHIE: And plus they'd be spending their money for nothing.

EBK: How do you mean?

RICHIE: On the cat, 'cause they bought the cat . . .

JESSICA: They could get their money back.

EBK: You mean that if you lose an animal and it runs away, then you also lose your money? That's true, but I don't think that's the most important thing. I think mostly people feel sad . . .

DANIEL: Yeah 'cause it's a living creature just like us, just like having a baby and it dies on you . . .

Through the use of parallel stories, this section pursues the concept of ownership. The children are dealing with the difficulty in laying owner-ship claims on living things. While it's possible to buy, and thus, tech-nically, to own, an animal's body, the animal may have other ideas depending on how it is treated. My comments and questions help to bring the issue into focus. At the end of the discussion Daniel brings in the fragile nature of life by referring to the death of an infant. Even the strong bond of "ownership" that parenthood presumes cannot protect from this kind of loss.

ERIC: Maybe Misty . . . Misty really missed her cat. She probably thought that the next-door neighbors would feed him enough.

DANIEL: That was kinda sad.

JEANINE: That was sad.

JASON: I think I knew Misty's feelings because when the cop came and told my father to give my dog away because he was barking too much.

ERIC: That reminds me of my own cat—'cause we used to have a cat and he was knocking over everything so we had to give him away.

EBK: I wonder, did you kiss your cat six times? Or did you not feel the way Misty did? Were you glad to give him away?

ERIC: No.

EBK: You weren't glad.

ERIC: 'Cause he used to scratch me this much!

DANIEL: Get a big cage for him.

EBK: Maybe you didn't feel like Misty did.

ERIC: I didn't feel like her. 'Cause it didn't have any kittens.

Jason does something here that the other children haven't done. He makes a connecting statement preceding his story: "I think I know Misty's feelings because. . . ." Eric's story introduces a different reaction to losing a pet. There are times when pets can be a nuisance and we are glad to find new homes for them. Eric seems reluctant to admit to this feeling, finally justifying it by saying that his cat didn't have kittens so it was okay to feel annoyed and angry at it. Because I am listening carefully, I pick up on this subtle shift and help to make the distinction between Eric's and Misty's experience with cats. Tracy continues to follow Eric's direction.

TRACY: That reminds me of my cat because I go upstairs and my mom said if the cat keeps on jumping up on the counter and drinks all the fish's water we'll have to give him away.

EBK: Mmm. Maybe you could get a cover for your fish tank. They do sell covers in the pet stores. Then you wouldn't have to give your cat away.

ERIC: That would be sad.

DANIEL: I also have a kitten.

CHRISSY: Tracy gots a black cat.

EBK: So this book reminds everyone of their own pet, doesn't it?

The children continue to tell pet stories, now diverging widely from the original discussion of cats and ownership. Eric's story provides the opening for this to happen.

In Margaret Mead's autobiography, *Blackberry Winter* (1972), she says that "the enjoyment of the intellect, as mediated by the words in books, was central" (97) to the life of her family. Mead implies that life's experiences can be more fully enjoyed when they are put into print or when they are compared with those already in print. Much of the enjoyment my students get out of being readers and writers comes from the opportunity they have to share their ideas about the books they write and read through discussion.

One summer I was walking on the beach behind a young mother and her preschool-aged daughter. It was a beautiful day. A soft breeze off the water gently blew the little girl's blond hair and tugged at the large straw hat her mother was wearing. The little girl bounced along, chattering, stopping now and then to look intently up at her mother. It was such a nice picture that I turned to look more closely at their faces as I walked past. The bright day dimmed a bit for me when I saw that the mother was wearing a walkman and headphones. She wasn't listening to a word the child was saying.

Now that I have two preschool-aged children, I have more compassion for the mother's need for privacy and peace. However, children can only learn to listen if they are given many opportunities to speak—about things that are important to them and to audiences that care. Discussions should not be tests of what the children know or have learned. As a teacher I need to listen carefully to what the children are saying—all of it—before I impose my agenda.

The book discussions the children have in and around the author's chair resemble gossip more closely than literary criticism. In an interesting article entitled "In Praise of Gossip," published in *The Hudson Review*, Patricia Meyer Spacks (1982) makes the point that gossip has its virtues:

> People discourse *to* one another; they gossip *with*. . . . One discourses from a height, gossips around the kitchen table. Why value platforms to the exclusion of rocking chairs? We need not reject discourse in its concern with large truth, but we might acknowledge also . . . the revelatory power of the small, shared truth. (24)

These small shared truths are the children's lessons about learning to read and about life shared in and around the author's chair.

Beyond the Author's Chair

A school year has passed. A year that began with the first awkward attempts to put letters on the page ends with stories like "The Beautiful Queen" and "I Love Grandpa." During that year the children have discovered important facts and feelings about themselves and their friends. They have learned to express these feelings in words, both written and spoken. They have both confirmed their existing perspectives and realized new ones in the hundreds of books they've written and read, listened to and discussed.

Sometimes when I read the journals published by and for the profession I get the impression that literacy is a grave and serious business. There is talk of "literate occasions," "predictive operations," and "literacy-oriented preschoolers." (What do they look like? I wonder. Is it safe to meet them in a dark alley?) These concepts may be useful and fascinating in a theoretical sense, but they do not help the duck get off the ground. They do not describe the joy, pride, and excitement I witness every day as my students explore themselves and their worlds in stories.

Richard J. Margolis (1969) poses an interesting question:

> Will I remember
> how I looked
> and what I did
> when I was young
> (when I am old?)
> Will I remember what I wondered?
> When I am old
> who will I be?
> Still me? (22)

The children in my classroom will remember. They are writing their own histories, documenting their wonderment. They defy gravity when they write out of love or silliness, for discovery and elation. Their voices soar.

Afterword: And What Is Beyond That Hill?

One of the most powerful images from my teaching career is of the first day of school each year at the Great Falls School in Somersworth, New Hampshire. I walk outside to see the children in their bright new clothes scurrying around the playground like windblown fall leaves. As the bell rings, my first graders reluctantly say good-bye to parents standing, now, behind the chain-link fence surrounding the playground and line up behind me. To enter the building, we must go through the dark doorway that leads from the basement to the classrooms above. I am always amazed that these little ones will follow me, a stranger, into the darkness beyond. Yet, I never had a child turn away. This event symbolizes the tremendous responsibility and privilege I have as a teacher to lead children into a new world of knowledge and accomplishment. I've tried to make my classroom a worthy reward for the trust the children demonstrate when they follow me into that black doorway.

This book brings closure to a very significant decade of my experience as a teacher. But, as Ekker says in *And What Is Beyond the Hill?* (1986), "No, the world does not stop here. What is beyond that hill is another hill, and another hill, and yet another hill" (5,6).

Public education in this country is in crisis. There is great need to reconsider the way we organize time and space and the way we use our resources. Flexibility in the way children are grouped would allow more peer and multiage collaboration. We need to look for ways in which students can engage in authentic activities both within the classroom and outside it in the community.

The Author's Chair and Beyond describes how I worked within the constraints of the traditional school day to provide these experiences for the children in my classroom. Now, I am finding these constraints increasingly uncomfortable. It is no longer enough to lead the children into individual classrooms that support authentic achievement. We need all our schools to become more sensitive, challenging, and cooperative learning environments—for staff as well as students. The future

211

task is to demonstrate and promote a restructuring of that traditional school; to create learning spaces that more adequately and elegantly reflect the needs and the abilities of our children. This is what is beyond the hill.

References

ALLARD, HARRY. 1981. *The Stupids Die*. Boston: Houghton Mifflin.

ALLARD, HARRY, AND JAMES MARSHALL. 1982. *Miss Nelson Is Back*. Boston: Houghton Mifflin.

APPLEBY, ELLEN. 1985. *The Three Billy Goats Gruff*. New York: Scholastic.

BARATTA-LORTON, MARY. 1976. *Mathematics Their Way*. Menlo Park, CA: Addison Wesley.

BARING-GOULD, WILLIAM S., AND CEIL BARING-GOULD. 1957. *The Annotated Mother Goose*. New York: Bramhall House.

BEDFORD, ANNIE N. 1986. *Frosty the Snowman*. New York: Golden Books.

BEMELMANS, LUDWIG. 1953. *Madeline's Rescue*. New York: Viking.

BERENSTEIN, STAN, AND JAN BERENSTEIN. 1970. *Old Hat, New Hat*. New York: Random House.

BRANDENBERG, FRANZ. 1976. *I Wish I Was Sick Too*. New York: William Morrow.

BROWN, MARGARET WISE. 1977. *Fox Eyes*. New York: Pantheon.

BRUNER, JEROME. 1985. *Child's Talk: Learning to Use Language*. New York: Norton.

BURNINGHAM, JOHN. 1975. *The School*. New York: Thomas Crowell.

CALVINO, ITALO. 1965. *Cosmicomics*. New York: Harcourt Brace Jovanovich.

CARLE, ERIC. 1969. *The Very Hungry Caterpillar*. New York: Philomel.

CARRICK, CAROL, AND DONALD CARRICK. 1973. *Beach Bird*. New York: Dial.

CATERPILLAR. 1988. Chicago: Contemporary Books.

CAZDEN, COURTNEY. 1988. *Classroom Discourse: The Language of Teaching and Learning*. Portsmouth, NH: Heinemann.

CLAY, MARIE. 1982. *Observing Young Readers*. Portsmouth, NH: Heinemann.

CLIFTON, LUCILLE. 1976. *The Three Wishes*. New York: Viking.

Cohen, Miriam. 1977. *When Will I Read?* New York: Greenwillow.

Cole, Joanna. 1981. *My Puppy Is Born.* New York: Scholastic.

Comprehensive School Mathematics Program (McREL). 1977. Cemral, Inc.: An Education Laboratory. Scranton, PA: Harper and Row.

Dahl, Roald. 1962. *James and the Giant Peach.* New York: Knopf.

Dallinger, Jane. 1981. *Spiders.* New York: Learner Publications.

Dallinger, Peter. 1977. *Dinosaurs.* New York: Random House.

De Brunhoff, Laurent. 1975. *Babar and the Wully Wully.* New York: Random House.

De Paola, Tomi. 1975. *Strega Nona.* New York: Treehouse, Prentice Hall.

———. 1978. *The Popcorn Book.* New York: Holiday.

Dillard, Annie. 1974. *Pilgrim at Tinker Creek.* New York: Harper and Row.

Dr. Seuss [Theodore Geisel]. 1963a. *The Ear Book.* New York: Random House.

———. 1963b. *Hop on Pop.* New York: Random House.

———. 1963c. *Dr.Seuss's ABC.* New York: Random House.

———. 1972. *Marvin K. Mooney, Will You Please Go Now.* New York: Random House.

Eastman, P.D. 1960. *Are You My Mother?* New York: Random House.

Ekker, Ernest. 1986. *And What Is Beyond the Hill?* New York: Lippincott.

Emig, Janet. 1983. "Non-Magical Thinking: Presenting Writing Developmentally in Schools." In *The Web of Meaning,* edited by Dixie Goswami and Maureen Butler. 135–44. Portsmouth, NH: Boynton-Cook/Heinemann.

Flory, Jane. 1980. *The Bear on the Doorstep.* Boston: Houghton Mifflin.

Freeman, Don. 1968. *Corduroy.* New York: Puffin.

Freschet, Berniece. 1971. *Turtle Pond.* New York: Scribner's.

Furth, Hans G. 1970. *Piaget for Teachers.* Englewood Cliffs, NJ: Prentice Hall.

Fun With Gum. 1979. Cleveland, OH: Modern Curriculum Press.

Galdone, Paul. 1973. *The Little Red Hen.* New York: Salisbury.

Gelman, Rita Golden. 1977. *More Spaghetti, I Say!* New York: Scholastic.

———. 1986. *Why Can't I Fly?* New York: Scholastic.

Ginsberg, Mira. 1987. *Mushroom in the Rain.* New York: Macmillan.

———. 1980. *Good Morning, Chick.* New York: Greenwillow.

"A Good House." 1980. In *Pets and People.* Holt Basic Reading Series.

New York: Holt, Rinehart and Winston.

GRAVES, DONALD, AND JANE HANSEN. 1983. "The Author's Chair." *Language Arts* 60:176–83.

GROSS, RUTH BELOV. 1988. *Hansel and Gretel.* New York: Scholastic.

GUS. 1979. Cleveland, OH: Modern Curriculum Press.

HELLER, RUTH. 1981. *Chickens Aren't the Only Ones.* New York: Putnam's.

HEILBRONER, JOAN. 1962. *Robert the Rose Horse.* New York: Random House.

HILLIKER, JUDITH. 1988. "Labeling to Beginning Narrative: Four Kindergarten Children Learn to Write." In *Understanding Writing: Ways of Observing, Learning, and Teaching K–8,* 2d ed., edited by Thomas Newkirk and Nancie Atwell. 14–22. Portsmouth, NH: Heinemann.

HOBAN, TANA. 1979. *One Little Kitten.* New York: Greenwillow.

HOFF, SYD. 1958. *Danny and the Dinosaur.* New York: Harper.

HOLDAWAY, DON. 1979. *The Foundations of Literacy.* New York: Scholastic.

IPCAR, DAHLOV. 1976. *Hard Scrabble Harvest (Bring in the Pumpkins).* New York: Doubleday.

JAMISON, CYNTHIA. 1973. *The Clay Pot Boy.* New York: Coward.

JOHNSON, JEAN. 1985. *Firefighters.* New York: Walker and Co.

KALIN, ROBERT. 1989. *Jump, Frog, Jump.* New York: Scholastic.

KARELITZ, ELLEN BLACKBURN. 1984. "Common Ground: Developing the Relationship Between Reading and Writing." *Language Arts* 61(4).

KRAUSS, RUTH. 1949. *The Happy Day.* New York: Harper.

LIONNI, LEO. 1974. *Fish Is Fish.* New York: Knopf.

LITTLEDALE, FREYA. 1978. *The Snow Child.* New York: Scholastic.

———. 1980. *Snow White.* New York: Scholastic.

LOBEL, ARNOLD. 1975. *Owl at Home.* New York: Harper.

———. 1964. *Giant John.* New York: Harcourt Brace Jovanovich.

MCDONALD SERIES. 1967. Nuffield Mathematics Project. New York: John Wiley.

MARGOLIS, RICHARD. 1969. *Only the Moon and Me.* Philadelphia: J. B. Lippincott.

MARTIN, BILL, JR. 1970. *The Haunted House.* New York: Holt, Rinehart and Winston.

———. 1967. *Brown Bear, Brown Bear, What Do You See?* New York: Holt, Rinehart and Winston.

MATTHEWS, KATHY. 1985. "Beyond the Writing Table." In *Breaking*

Ground: Teachers Relate Reading and Writing in the Elementary School, edited by Jane Hansen, Thomas Newkirk, and Donald Graves. 63–71. Portsmouth, NH: Heinemann.

MEAD, MARGARET. 1972. *Blackberry Winter: My Earlier Years.* New York: William Morrow.

MILLER, EDNA. 1964. *Mousekin's Golden House.* New York: Prentice Hall.

MINARIK, ELSA. 1957. *Little Bear.* New York: Harper.

MOSEL, ARLENE. 1968. *Tikki Tikki Tembo.* New York: Scholastic.

NEWKIRK, THOMAS. 1989. *More Than Stories: The Range of Children's Writing.* Portsmouth, NH: Heinemann.

NODSET, JOAN L. 1963. *Who Took the Farmer's Hat?* New York: Harper.

NORTON, MARY. 1990. *Bedknobs and Broomsticks.* San Diego, CA: Harcourt Brace Jovanovich.

OAKESHOTT, MICHAEL. 1967. "Learning and Teaching." In *The Concept of Education,* edited by R. S. Peters. New York: The Humanities Press.

OLSEN, TILLIE. 1978. *Silences.* New York: Delacorte.

ORMONDROYD, EDWARD. 1984. *Broderick.* Boston: Houghton Mifflin.

PALEY, VIVIAN GUSSIN. 1990. *The Boy Who Would Be a Helicopter: The Uses of Storytelling in the Classroom.* Cambridge: Harvard University Press.

PAPE, DONNA LUGG. 1979. *Doghouse for Sale.* New York: Garrard.

PERKINS, AL. 1970. *The Nose Book.* New York: Random House.

PIAGET, JEAN. 1965. *The Child's Conception of Number.* New York: Norton.

PIAGET, JEAN, AND BARBEL INHELDER. 1969. *The Psychology of the Child.* New York: Basic Books.

PINCUS, HARRIET. 1968. *Little Red Riding Hood. Based on the story by the Brothers Grimm.* New York: Harcourt, Brace and World.

RAABE, JANIS ASAD. 1978. *Here Comes the Bride.* Cleveland, OH: Modern Curriculum Press.

RABOFF, ERNEST. 1968. *Marc Chagall.* Art for Children. New York: Doubleday.

REY, H. A. 1941. *Curious George.* Boston: Houghton Mifflin.

RHYMES AND TALES. 1980. Holt Basic Reading. New York: Holt, Rinehart and Winston.

ROBIN HOOD. 1984. Retold by Catherine Storr. Milwaukee, WI: Raintree.

ROCKWELL, ANN. 1984. *Cars.* New York: Dutton.

ROSENBLATT, LOUISE. 1978. *The Reader, the Text, the Poem: The Transactional Theory of the Literary Work.* Carbondale, IL: Southern Illinois University Press.

SAM AND AL. 1979. Cleveland OH: Modern Curriculum Press.

SCIENCE CURRICULUM IMPROVEMENT STUDY II: ELEMENTARY SCIENCE PROGRAM. 1978. Boston: American Science and Engineering, Inc.

SENDAK, MAURICE. 1962. *Where the Wild Things Are.* New York: Harper.

SPACKS, PATRICIA. 1982. "In Praise of Gossip." *The Hudson Review* 35: 19–36.

STEIG, WILLIAM. 1976. *The Amazing Bone.* New York: Penguin.

STEVENSON, JAMES. 1983. *The Great Big Especially Beautiful Easter Egg.* New York: Greenwillow.

STONE, HARRIS. 1967. *The Last Free Bird.* Englewood Cliffs, NJ: Prentice Hall.

TARCOV, EDITH. 1974. *The Frog Prince: A Folktale Retold from Grimm.* New York: Scholastic.

——— . 1973. *Rumpelstiltskin.* New York: Scholastic.

THOMAS, LEWIS. 1971. *Lives of a Cell: Notes of a Biology Watcher.* New York: Bantam.

TOLKIEN, J. R. R. 1966. *The Hobbit.* Boston: Houghton Mifflin.

TRESSALT, ALVIN. 1964a. *How Far Is Far?* New York: Parents Magazine.

——— . 1964b. *The Mitten.* New York: Lothrup, Lee and Shepard.

UNGERER, TOMI. 1962. *The Three Robbers.* New York: Aladdin.

WELLS, ROSEMARY. 1973. *Noisy Nora.* New York: Dial.

WELTY, EUDORA. 1984. *One Writer's Beginnings.* Cambridge: Harvard University Press.

WILSON, MARJORIE, AND BRENT WILSON. 1982. *Teaching Children to Draw: A Guide for Teachers and Parents.* Englewood Cliffs, NJ: Prentice Hall.

WOOLF, VIRGINIA. 1950. *The Captain's Deathbed and Other Essays.* New York: Harcourt Brace Jovanovich.

ZOLOTOW, CHARLOTTE. 1969. *The Hating Book.* New York: Harper.

Also available from Heinemann. . .

Two Years
A Teacher's Memoir
Mary Kenner Glover
Foreword by *Georgia Heard*

"Especially in this time, when the basic concept of child-centered learning is being challenged. . . this book is a refreshing antidote, filled with the voices and learning of children."
                    -- From the Foreword by Georgia Heard

This book describes two years with a class in which the chemistry and timing between students and a teacher were extraordinary. In 1977, Mary Kenner Glover and a friend founded a private alternative school in the garage of the author's home. The school, Awakening Seed, grew from a small group of nine preschoolers to its current enrollment of 130 students ranging in age from three to ten. While offering a glimpse into the life of the school, *Two Years* records a remarkable segment of the author's teaching history in a first grade classroom. It provides insight into how classrooms can be organized and operated so that learning and a sense of well-being are fostered for both children and teachers. The book makes a strong statement about the value of children having consecutive years with the same teacher, showing the level of caring that happens when relationships are given time to grow. It offers a look at what classrooms can be like when children -- not mandated curriculums -- come first.

0-435-08738-X   1992   128 pages   Paper

Listening In
Children Talk About Books (and other things)
Thomas Newkirk with *Patricia McLure*

Joyce: *If you had a magic wand* [like one of the characters in the story], *what do you think you would do with it? To get rid of. . .*

Cindy: *I would try to get rid of maybe my brother sometimes. If he's bothering me. But if he's being nice I wouldn't.*
                    --From *Listening In*

In *Listening In,* Thomas Newkirk invites the reader to eavesdrop on the student readers in Patricia McLure's first/second-grade classroom in Lee, New Hampshire. As the children joke, tell stories, and exaggerate during discussions of the books they read, it becomes clear that these "digressions" are an integral part of the learning process, essential for reading groups to work effectively. By examining the rich oral culture of children, *Listening In* challenges the narrow, text-dominated, question-controlled "on-task" model that passes for discussion in most U.S. classrooms. Filled with transcripts of student dialogue, the book asks readers to consider this talk as a meeting of cultures -- the adult culture of the teacher and the oral culture of the children, which must be recognized and validated by the teacher for learning and sharing to begin.

0-435-08713-4   1992   176 pages   Paper

Joyful Learning
A Whole Language Kindergarten
Bobbi Fisher
Foreword by *Don Holdaway*

"A 'must read'. . . Because Bobbi is a superb teacher, the book is practical and real. . . Her whole approach is so well integrated that it doesn't seem like work, but a natural, professional approach to each child."
                    -- Teaching K-8, Aug/Sept. 1991

As a veteran kindergarten teacher, Bobbi Fisher has given workshops to kindergarten teachers around the country to describe what goes on in her whole language classroom through the day and to explain why she does what she does. At Bobbi's workshops teachers often ask her if there is a whole language book especially for their needs -- a practical guide linking theory and practice. *Joyful Learning* is that book. It is written to assist kindergarten and other pre-primary teachers in developing whole language programs to match their own teaching styles and school cultures, to meet the needs of their student and parent populations, and to satisfy the curriculum goals of their school systems. The author discusses whole language theory and offers practical, applicable advice on such topics as shared reading, the reading and writing process, use of math manipulatives, dramatic play environments, assessment, and communication with parents.

0-435-08569-7   1991   243 pages   Paper

Special Voices
Cora Lee Five

Special Voices is a book of stories, the stories of children with special needs and the story of how their teacher learned to create a classroom environment that enabled them to overcome many of their problems. Ms. Five describes how students with various learning needs and emotional and behavioral problems became part of, and flourished within, the classroom community instead of working in isolated settings. Readers will become involved in the struggles and successes of learners whom they will easily recognize. They will hear the voices of Angela, a child with learning disabilities; Tomoko and Yasuo, two ESL children; Andrew, a child at risk, and others. Classroom teachers will be inspired by the stories of these eight children and their dedicated teacher. Through these stories teachers will find answers to many of their own problems related to special learners and they will discover how they too can learn from their students.

0-435-08594-8   1991   192 pages   Paper

Lessons from a Child
Lucy McCormick Calkins

"I can't imagine a more practical guide to implementing a writing workshop in an elementary classroom. . . Most of the current books I have read on the topic of writing are rather dry or theoretical. It is refreshing to read a practical, helpful report on writing methods and to see an author address the issues of great concern to teachers."
-- Early Childhood Education

A story of one child's growth in writing, *Lessons from a Child* follows Susie from Susie's introduction to the writing process through her early efforts at revision and at writing for real audiences to her becoming a committed writer. The story of Susie is part of a larger drama encompassing 150 children, their teachers and classrooms. Lucy Calkins explains how teachers can work with children, helping them to teach themselves and each other. Matters of classroom management, methods for helping children to use the peer conference, and ways mini-lessons can extend children's understanding of good writing are all covered here. Most important, the sequences of writing development and growth are thoroughly discussed.

0-435-08206-X   1983   192 pages   Paper

Order from your favorite supplier or direct.

MATHEMATICAL PHYSICS

MATHEMATICAL PHYSICS

EUGENE BUTKOV
St. John's University, New York

ADDISON-WESLEY PUBLISHING COMPANY

Reading, Massachusetts
Menlo Park, California · London · Amsterdam · Don Mills, Ontario · Sydney

This book is in the

ADDISON-WESLEY SERIES IN ADVANCED PHYSICS

Consulting Editor: MORTON HAMERMESH

ISBN 0-201-00727-4
NOPQRSTUV-MA-8987654321

PREFACE

During the past decade we have witnessed a remarkable increase in the number of students seeking higher education as well as the development of many new colleges and universities. The inevitable nonuniformity of conditions present in different institutions necessitates considerable variety in purpose, general approach, and the level of instruction in any given discipline. This has naturally contributed to the proliferation of texts on almost any topic, and the subject of mathematical physics is no exception. There is a number of texts in this field, and some of them are undoubtedly of outstanding quality.

Nevertheless, many teachers often feel that none of the existing texts is properly suited, for one reason or another, for their particular courses. More important, students sometimes complain that they have difficulties studying the subject from texts of unquestionable merit. This is not as surprising as it sounds: Some texts have an encyclopedic character, with the material arranged in a different order from the way it is usually taught; others become too much involved in complex mathematical analysis, preempting the available space from practical examples; still others cover a very wide variety of topics with utmost brevity, leaving the student to struggle with a number of difficult questions of theoretical nature. True enough, a well-prepared and bright student should be able to find his way through most of such difficulties. A less-gifted student may, however, find it very difficult to grasp and absorb the multitude of new concepts strewn across an advanced text.

Under these circumstances, it seems desirable to give more stress to the pedagogical side of a text to make it more readable to the student and more suitable for independent study. Hopefully, the present work represents a step in this direction. It has several features designed to conform to the path an average student may conceivably follow in acquiring the knowledge of the subject.

First, the inductive approach is used in each chapter throughout the book. Following the fundamentals of modern physics, the text is almost entirely devoted to linear problems, but the unifying concepts of linear space are fully developed rather late in the book after the student is exposed to a number of practical mathematical techniques. Also, almost every chapter starts with an example or discussion of elementary nature, with subject matter that is probably familiar to the reader. The introduction of new concepts is made against a familiar background and is later extended to more sophisticated situations. A typical example is Chapter 8, where the basic aspects of partial differential equations are illustrated using the "elementary functions" exclusively. Another facet of this trend is the repeated use of the harmonic oscillator and the stretched string as physical models: no

v

attempt is made to solve as many problems for the student as possible, but rather to show how various methods can be used to the same end within a familiar physical context.

In the process of learning, students inevitably pose a number of questions necessary to clarify the material under scrutiny. While most of these questions naturally belong to classroom discussion, it is certainly beneficial to attempt to anticipate some of them in a text. The *Remarks* and many footnotes are designed to contribute to this goal. The author hopes they answer some questions in the mind of the student as well as suggest some new ones, stimulating an interest in further inquiry. A number of cross-references serves a similar purpose, inviting the reader to make multiple use of various sections of the book. The absence of numbered formulas is intentional: if the student bothers to look into the indicated section or page, he should not simply check that the quoted formula "is indeed there," but, rather, glance through the text and recall its origin and meaning.

The question of mathematical rigor is quite important in the subject treated here, although it is sometimes controversial. It is the author's opinion that a theoretical physicist should know where he stands, whether he is proving his own deductions, quoting somebody else's proof, or just offering a reasonable conjecture. Consequently, he should be trained in this direction, and the texts should be written in this spirit. On the other hand, it would be unwise to overload every student with mathematics for two main reasons: first, because of the limitations of time in the classroom and the space in a text, and second, because physicists are apt to change their mathematical postulates as soon as experimental physics lends support to such suggestions. The reader can find examples of the latter philosophy in Chapters 4 and 6 of the text. Whether the author was able to follow these principles is left to the judgment of users of this book.

Each chapter is supplied with its share of problems proportional to the time presumed to be allotted to its study. The student may find some of the problems rather difficult since they require more comprehension of the material rather than sheer technique. To balance this, a variety of hints and explanations are often supplied. Answers are not given because many problems contain the answer in their formulation; the remaining ones may be used to test the ability of the student for independent work. The exercises within the text can be used as problems to test the students' manipulative skills.

For many of the methods of instruction of mathematical physics presented in this book, the author is indebted to his own teachers at the University of British Columbia and McGill University. The encouragement of his colleagues and students at St. John's University and Hunter College of the City University of New York is greatly appreciated. Also, the author wishes to thank Mrs. Ludmilla Verenicin and Miss Anne Marie Nowom for their help in the preparation of the manuscript.

Palo Alto, Calif.   E. B.
August 1966

CONTENTS

CHAPTER 1

VECTORS, MATRICES, AND COORDINATES

1.1 INTRODUCTION

To be able to follow this text without undue difficulties, the reader is expected to have adequate preparation in mathematics and physics. This involves a good working knowledge of advanced calculus, a basic course in differential equations, and a basic course in undergraduate algebra. Rudimentary knowledge of complex numbers, matrices, and Fourier series is very desirable but not indispensable. As for the subjects in physics, the reader should have completed the standard undergraduate training in mechanics, thermodynamics, electromagnetism, and atomic physics.

Despite these prerequisites, a need is often recognized for reviewing some of the preparatory material at the beginning of a text. Let us follow this custom and devote some time to the subject of vector analysis which has a bearing, in more than one way, on the material developed in this text. Of course, such a review must be brief and we must omit all the details, in particular those involving mathematical proofs. The reader is referred to standard textbooks in advanced calculus and vector analysis* for a full discussion. On the other hand, we hope to draw attention to some interesting points not always emphasized in commonly used texts.

1.2 VECTORS IN CARTESIAN COORDINATE SYSTEMS

In many elementary textbooks a vector is defined as a quantity characterized by *magnitude and direction*. We shall see in Chapter 10 that vectors are much more general than this, but it is fair to say that the concept of vectors was first introduced into mathematics (by physicists) to represent "quantities with direction," e.g., displacement, velocity, force, etc. Doubtless, they are the simplest and most familiar kinds of vectors.

As we well know, quantities with direction can be graphically represented by arrows and are subject to two basic operations:

a) multiplication by a scalar,†   b) addition.

These operations are illustrated in Fig. 1.1.

---

* For example, A. E. Taylor, *Advanced Calculus;* T. M. Apostol, *Mathematical Analysis;* W. Kaplan, *Advanced Calculus.*

† Until we are ready to discuss complex vectors (Chapter 10) we shall assume that scalars are real numbers.

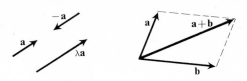

Figure 1.1

In many cases we can plot various vectors from a single point, the origin. Then each vector can be characterized by the coordinates of its "tip." Various coordinate systems are possible but the *cartesian coordinate systems* are the most convenient. The reason is very simple and very deep: The cartesian coordinates of a point can serve as the *components* of the corresponding vector at the same time. This is illustrated in Fig. 1.2, where *orthogonal* cartesian systems, in plane and in space, are selected. Note that the three-dimensional system is "right-handed";* in general, we shall use right-handed systems in this book.

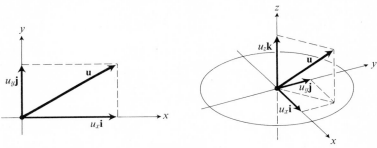

Figure 1.2

We can now associate with a vector **u** (in space) a set of *three scalars* (u_x, u_y, u_z), such that $\lambda\mathbf{u}$ will correspond to $(\lambda u_x, \lambda u_y, \lambda u_z)$ and $\mathbf{u} + \mathbf{v}$ will correspond to $(u_x + v_x, u_y + v_y, u_z + v_z)$. Note that *no such relations* hold, in general, if a vector is characterized by other types of coordinates, e.g., spherical or cylindrical.

In addition, orthogonal cartesian coordinates result in very simple formulas for other common quantities associated with vectors, such as

a) length (magnitude) of a vector:

$$|\mathbf{u}| = u = (u_x^2 + u_y^2 + u_z^2)^{1/2},$$

b) projections of a vector on coordinate axes:†

$$u_x = u \cos (\mathbf{u}, \mathbf{i}), \qquad u_y = u \cos (\mathbf{u}, \mathbf{j}), \qquad u_z = u \cos (\mathbf{u}, \mathbf{k}),$$

---

* Rotation of the x-axis by 90° to coincide with the y-axis appears *counterclockwise* for all observers with $z > 0$.

† Standard notation is used: The symbols **i**, **j**, **k** are unit vectors in x-, y-, and z-directions, respectively. The symbol $(\mathbf{u}, \mathbf{v})$ stands for the angle between the directions given by **u** and **v**.

c) projection of a vector on an arbitrary direction defined by vector **s** (Fig. 1.3):

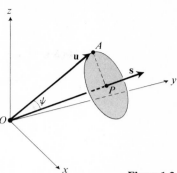

$$OP = u_s = u \cos \psi$$
$$= u_x \cos (\mathbf{s}, \mathbf{i}) + u_y \cos (\mathbf{s}, \mathbf{j}) + u_z \cos (\mathbf{s}, \mathbf{k}),$$

d) scalar product (dot product) of two vectors:

$$(\mathbf{u} \cdot \mathbf{v}) = uv \cos (\mathbf{u}, \mathbf{v}) = u_x v_x + u_y v_y + u_z v_z,$$

e) vector product (cross product):

Figure 1.3

$$[\mathbf{u} \times \mathbf{v}] = (u_y v_z - u_z v_y)\mathbf{i} + (u_z v_x - u_x v_z)\mathbf{j} + (u_x v_y - u_y v_x)\mathbf{k}.$$

The important distinctive feature of the cross product is that $[\mathbf{u} \times \mathbf{v}] \neq [\mathbf{v} \times \mathbf{u}]$, namely, it is not commutative; rather, it is anticommutative:

$$[\mathbf{u} \times \mathbf{v}] = -[\mathbf{v} \times \mathbf{u}].$$

Remark. Apart from its important physical applications, the cross product of two vectors leads us to the concept of "oriented area." The magnitude of $[\mathbf{u} \times \mathbf{v}]$, namely $uv |\sin (\mathbf{u}, \mathbf{v})|$, is equal to the area of the parallelogram formed by **u** and **v**. The *direction* of $[\mathbf{u} \times \mathbf{v}]$ can serve to distinguish the "positive side" of the parallelogram from its "negative side." Figure 1.4 shows two views of the same parallelogram illustrating this idea.

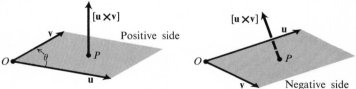

Figure 1.4

Closely related to this property is the concept of a *right-handed triple* of vectors. Any three vectors **u**, **v**, and **w**, *taken in this order*, are said to form a right-handed (or positive) triple if the so-called *triple product*

$$([\mathbf{u} \times \mathbf{v}] \cdot \mathbf{w})$$

is positive.* This happens if **w** is on the same side of the plane defined by the vectors **u** and **v**, as illustrated in Fig. 1.5. It is not hard to verify that $([\mathbf{u} \times \mathbf{v}] \cdot \mathbf{w})$ represents, in this case, the volume V of the parallelepiped formed by the vectors **u**, **v**, and **w**.

---

* These vectors form a left-handed (negative) triple if $([\mathbf{u} \times \mathbf{v}] \cdot \mathbf{w}) < 0$.

Exercise. Show that

$$V = |([\mathbf{u} \times \mathbf{v}] \cdot \mathbf{w})|$$

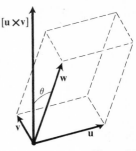

under any circumstances. Show also that the sign of the triple product is unchanged under cyclic permutation of $\mathbf{u}$, $\mathbf{v}$, and $\mathbf{w}$, that is,

$$([\mathbf{u} \times \mathbf{v}] \cdot \mathbf{w}) = ([\mathbf{w} \times \mathbf{u}] \cdot \mathbf{v}) = ([\mathbf{v} \times \mathbf{w}] \cdot \mathbf{u}).$$

Figure 1.5

1.3 CHANGES OF AXES.　ROTATION MATRICES

We have seen that a given vector $\mathbf{u}$ is associated with a set of three numbers, namely its components,* with respect to some orthogonal cartesian system. However, it is clear that if the system of axes is changed, the components change as well. Let us study these changes.

Consider, for vectors in a plane, a change in the system of axes which is produced by a rotation by the angle θ, as illustrated in Fig. 1.6. The old system is (x, y) and the new system is (x', y'). Since $\mathbf{u} = u_x \mathbf{i} + u_y \mathbf{j}$, the x'-component of $\mathbf{u}$ is the sum of projections of vectors $u_x \mathbf{i}$ and $u_y \mathbf{j}$ on the x'-axis, and similarly for the y'-component. From the diagram we see that this yields

$$u_x' = u_x \cos\theta + u_y \sin\theta, \qquad u_y' = -u_x \sin\theta + u_y \cos\theta.$$

It is instructive to note that the angle between the x'- and y-axes is $(\pi/2 - \theta)$ while the angle between the y'- and x-axes is $(\pi/2 + \theta)$. In view of

$$\sin\theta = \cos\left(\frac{\pi}{2} - \theta\right)$$

and

$$-\sin\theta = \cos\left(\frac{\pi}{2} + \theta\right),$$

we see that all four coefficients in the above equations represent *cosines of the angles* between the respective axes.

Let us now turn to the three-dimensional case. Figure 1.7 represents two orthogonal cartesian systems, both *right-handed*, centered at O. It is intuitively clear that the primed system can be obtained from the unprimed one by the motion of a "rigid body about a fixed point." In fact, it is shown in almost any textbook on mechanics† that such a motion can be reduced to a rotation about some axis (Euler's theorem).

---

* Instead of "components," the term "coordinates of a vector" is often used (see also Section 10.3).

† For example, Goldstein, *Classical Mechanics*, Section 4.6.

Write

$$\mathbf{u} = u_x\mathbf{i} + u_y\mathbf{j} + u_z\mathbf{k},$$

collect contributions to u'_x from the three vectors $u_x\mathbf{i}$, $u_y\mathbf{j}$, and $u_z\mathbf{k}$, and obtain

$$u'_x = u_x \cos (\mathbf{i}', \mathbf{i}) + u_y \cos (\mathbf{i}', \mathbf{j}) + u_z \cos (\mathbf{i}', \mathbf{k}),$$

where $\mathbf{i}'$ is, of course, the unit vector in the x'-direction. Note that the cosines involved are the *directional cosines* of the x'-direction with respect to the unprimed system or, for that matter, the *dot products* of $\mathbf{i}'$ with $\mathbf{i}$, $\mathbf{j}$, and $\mathbf{k}$.

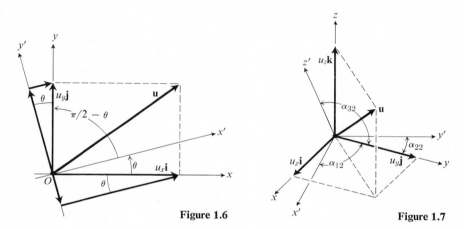

Figure 1.6   Figure 1.7

It is clear that similar formulas can be written for u'_y and u'_z. At this stage, however, it is very convenient to switch to a different notation: Instead of writing (u_x, u_y, u_z), let us write (u_1, u_2, u_3) and similarly (u'_1, u'_2, u'_3) for (u'_x, u'_y, u'_z). Moreover, denote by α_{mn} the angle between the mth primed axis and the nth unprimed axis (three such angles are marked on Fig. 1.6) and by a_{mn} the corresponding cosine (that is, $a_{mn} = \cos \alpha_{mn}$). This new notation permits us to write the transformation formulas in an easily memorized pattern:

$$u'_1 = a_{11}u_1 + a_{12}u_2 + a_{13}u_3,$$
$$u'_2 = a_{21}u_1 + a_{22}u_2 + a_{23}u_3,$$
$$u'_3 = a_{31}u_1 + a_{32}u_2 + a_{33}u_3,$$

or, if desired, in the compact form

$$u'_m = \sum_{n=1}^{3} a_{mn}u_n \qquad (m = 1, 2, 3).$$

From this analysis we conclude that the new components (u'_1, u'_2, u'_3) can be obtained from the old components (u_1, u_2, u_3) with the help of *nine* coefficients.

These nine coefficients, arranged in the self-explanatory pattern below are said to form a *matrix*.* We shall denote matrices by capital letters.

Columns

	1st	2nd	3rd	
	a_{11}	a_{12}	a_{13}	1st
$A =$	a_{21}	a_{22}	a_{23}	2nd $\rangle$ Rows
	a_{31}	a_{32}	a_{33}	3rd

Matrix A has *three rows* and *three columns;* the individual coefficients a_{mn} are referred to as *matrix elements*, or *entries*. It is customary to use the first subscript (m in our case) to label the row and the second one to label the column; thus the matrix element a_{kl} should be located at the intersection of the kth row with the lth column.

The set of elements in a given row is very often called a *row vector* and the set of elements in a column, a *column vector*. This nomenclature is justified by the fact that any three numbers can be treated as components of *some* vector in space. However, at this stage it is worthwhile to make a digression and establish a geometric interpretation for the column vectors of A. The reader should pay particular attention to the argument because of its general significance.

Let us imagine a unit vector **u**. Suppose the unprimed system was oriented in such a way that **u** was along the x-axis. Then the components of **u** are (1, 0, 0) and **u** actually coincides with the vector **i**. If the coordinate system is now rotated, the new components of **u** are given by

$$u_1' = a_{11}1 + a_{12}0 + a_{13}0 = a_{11},$$
$$u_2' = a_{21}1 + a_{22}0 + a_{23}0 = a_{21},$$
$$u_3' = a_{31}1 + a_{32}0 + a_{33}0 = a_{31}.$$

We see that the first column vector of matrix A is composed of the new components of vector **u**. In other words, we can say that the new components of **i** are (a_{11}, a_{21}, a_{31}) and we can write

$$\mathbf{i} = a_{11}\mathbf{i}' + a_{21}\mathbf{j}' + a_{31}\mathbf{k}'.$$

Similar statements relate **j** and **k** to the second and third column vectors of A. Note that in this discussion the unit vectors **i, j, k** assume a role independent of their respective coordinate axes. The axes are rotated but the vectors **i, j, k** stay in place and are then referred to the rotated system of axes.

---

* More precisely, a 3 × 3 matrix is formed. The reader can easily construct an analogous 2 × 2 matrix to account for two-dimensional rotations.

Exercise. Establish the geometrical meaning of the row vectors of matrix A representing a rotation.

The definitions introduced above allow the computation of (u'_1, u'_2, u'_3) from (u_1, u_2, u_3) by the following rule: *To obtain u'_k, take the dot product of the kth row of matrix A with the vector* **u**, *as given by the triple* (u_1, u_2, u_3). Since in this process each row of the matrix is "dotted" with (u_1, u_2, u_3), we may regard it as some kind of multiplication of a vector by a matrix. In fact, this operation is commonly known as *vector-matrix multiplication* and is visually exhibited as shown:

$$
\begin{array}{ccc}
a_{11} & a_{12} & a_{13} \\
a_{21} & a_{22} & a_{23} \\
a_{31} & a_{32} & a_{33}
\end{array}
\cdot
\begin{array}{c}
u_1 \\
u_2 \\
u_3
\end{array}
=
\begin{array}{c}
u'_1 \\
u'_2 \\
u'_3
\end{array}
\cdot
$$

$$
\text{Matrix } A \qquad \text{Column vector } u \qquad \text{Column vector } u'
$$

As we see, the old components are arranged in a *column* which we shall denote by u. This column vector is multiplied by the matrix A and this results in another column vector, denoted by u'. The multiplication means, of course: *Form the dot product of the first row of A with u for the first component of u'; then form the dot product of the second row of A with u to get u'_2, and similarly for u'_3.* The entire procedure is symbolically written as

$$Au = u'.$$

Remark. Note that the set (u_1, u_2, u_3), arranged in a column, has *not* been denoted simply by **u** but rather by a new symbol u.* The point is that in the context of our problem, both u and u' represent the *same vector* **u**, but with respect to different systems of axes. We must think of u and u' as two different *representations* of **u**, and the matrix A shows us how to switch from one representation to another.

Before we discuss further topics involving matrices, let us record the fact that our matrix A is not just a collection of nine arbitrary scalars. Its matrix elements are interdependent and possess the following properties.

a) The columns of A are *orthogonal to each other*, namely,

$$a_{11}a_{12} + a_{21}a_{22} + a_{31}a_{32} = 0,$$
$$a_{12}a_{13} + a_{22}a_{23} + a_{32}a_{33} = 0,$$
$$a_{13}a_{11} + a_{23}a_{21} + a_{33}a_{31} = 0.$$

This property follows from the fact that the columns of A are representations (in the new system) of the vectors **i**, **j**, and **k** and these vectors are mutually orthogonal.

---

* The symbol u should not be confused with $|\mathbf{u}|$, the magnitude of vector **u**, which is also denoted by u (p. 2).

b) The columns of A have unit magnitude, namely,

$$a_{11}^2 + a_{21}^2 + a_{31}^2 = 1,$$
$$a_{12}^2 + a_{22}^2 + a_{32}^2 = 1,$$
$$a_{13}^2 + a_{23}^2 + a_{33}^2 = 1,$$

because $\mathbf{i}$, $\mathbf{j}$, and $\mathbf{k}$ are unit vectors.

c) The rows of A are also mutually orthogonal and have unit magnitude. This is verified by establishing the geometrical meaning of the row vectors of A.*

Matrices satisfying these three properties are called *orthogonal*. We may then conclude that the matrices representing rotations of orthogonal cartesian systems in space are orthogonal matrices.

Remark. There are orthogonal matrices which do not represent rotations. Rotation matrices have an additional property: their *determinant* (i.e., the determinant of the equations on p. 5) is equal to $+1$. Otherwise, orthogonal matrices can have the determinant equal to -1. The point is that a rotation must yield a right-handed triple $(\mathbf{i}', \mathbf{j}', \mathbf{k}')$ of unit vectors since $(\mathbf{i}, \mathbf{j}, \mathbf{k})$ is a right-handed triple.†

1.4 REPEATED ROTATIONS. MATRIX MULTIPLICATION

The matrix notation introduced in the preceding sections is particularly useful when we are faced with repeated changes of coordinate axes. In addition to the primed and unprimed systems related by a matrix A, let there be a third double-primed system of axes (x'', y'', z'') and let it be related to the primed system by a matrix B:

$$B = \begin{vmatrix} b_{11} & b_{12} & b_{13} \\ b_{21} & b_{22} & b_{23} \\ b_{31} & b_{32} & b_{33} \end{vmatrix}.$$

Evidently, the system (x'', y'', z'') can be related directly to the system (x, y, z) through some matrix C and our task is to evaluate the matrix elements c_{mn} in terms of matrix elements a_{mn} and b_{mn}. We have

$$u_1'' = b_{11}u_1' + b_{12}u_2' + b_{13}u_3',$$
$$u_2'' = b_{21}u_1' + b_{22}u_2' + b_{23}u_3',$$
$$u_3'' = b_{31}u_1' + b_{32}u_2' + b_{33}u_3',$$

and

$$u_1' = a_{11}u_1 + a_{12}u_2 + a_{13}u_3,$$
$$u_2' = a_{21}u_1 + a_{22}u_2 + a_{23}u_3,$$
$$u_3' = a_{31}u_1 + a_{32}u_2 + a_{33}u_3,$$

---

* It will be shown in Chapter 10 that any $N \times N$ matrix which satisfies (a) and (b) must also satisfy (c).

† See Problem 4 at the end of this chapter.

from which it follows that

$$u_1'' = (b_{11}a_{11} + b_{12}a_{21} + b_{13}a_{31})u_1 + (b_{11}a_{12} + b_{12}a_{22} + b_{13}a_{32})u_2$$
$$+ (b_{11}a_{13} + b_{12}a_{23} + b_{13}a_{33})u_3,$$
$$u_2'' = (b_{21}a_{11} + b_{22}a_{21} + b_{23}a_{31})u_1 + (b_{21}a_{12} + b_{22}a_{22} + b_{23}a_{32})u_2$$
$$+ (b_{21}a_{13} + b_{22}a_{23} + b_{23}a_{33})u_3,$$
$$u_3'' = (b_{31}a_{11} + b_{32}a_{21} + b_{33}a_{31})u_1 + (b_{31}a_{12} + b_{32}a_{22} + b_{33}a_{32})u_2$$
$$+ (b_{31}a_{13} + b_{32}a_{23} + b_{33}a_{33})u_3.$$

The maze of matrix elements above becomes quite manageable if we observe that every coefficient associated with u_n is a dot product of some row of matrix B and some column of matrix A. A closer look at these relationships leads us to the following statement: *The element c_{mn} of matrix C is obtained by taking the dot product of the mth row of matrix B with the nth column of matrix A.*

Now, if we record our relationship in the vector-matrix symbolic notation

$$u' = Au, \qquad u'' = Bu', \qquad u'' = Cu,$$

then we are naturally led to the relation

$$u'' = Cu = B(Au).$$

It seems reasonable now to *define* the product of two matrices, like B and A, to be equal to a third matrix, say C, so that the above relationship may also be written as*

$$u'' = Cu = (BA)u.$$

In this sense we write

$$
\begin{bmatrix} c_{11} & c_{12} & c_{13} \\ c_{21} & c_{22} & c_{23} \\ c_{31} & c_{32} & c_{33} \end{bmatrix}
=
\begin{bmatrix} b_{11} & b_{12} & b_{13} \\ b_{21} & b_{22} & b_{23} \\ b_{31} & b_{32} & b_{33} \end{bmatrix}
\cdot
\begin{bmatrix} a_{11} & a_{12} & a_{13} \\ a_{21} & a_{22} & a_{23} \\ a_{31} & a_{32} & a_{33} \end{bmatrix}
$$

or, symbolically,
$$C = BA$$

given that the matrix elements of C are defined by the rule quoted above.

Having introduced the notion of matrix multiplication, we are naturally interested in determining whether it has the same properties as the multiplication of ordinary numbers (scalars). A simple check shows that the *associative* law holds: If we multiply three matrices A, B, and C in that order, then this can be done in two ways:

$$ABC = (AB)C = A(BC)$$

(where it is understood that the operation in parentheses is performed first).

---

* The difference is, of course, that in $B(Au)$ the column vector u is first multiplied by A, producing another column vector which is, in turn, multiplied by B. In $(BA)u$ the matrices are being multiplied first, resulting in a new matrix which acts on u.

Exercise. Verify this statement. [*Hint:* If $AB = D$, then the elements of D are given by

$$d_{mn} = \sum_{l=1}^{3} a_{ml} b_{ln}.$$

Develop the matrix elements of $(AB)C$ and $A(BC)$ in this fashion and verify that they are the same.]

On the other hand, matrix multiplication is *not commutative:*

$$AB \neq BA,$$

and, furthermore, there is no simple relation, in general, between AB and BA. This noncommutativity feature precludes the possibility of defining "matrix division."* However, it is possible to talk about the *inverse* of a matrix and this concept arises naturally in our discussion of rotations. Indeed, if we rotate our orthogonal cartesian system of axes, the new coordinates of vector **u** are obtained from the vector-matrix equation

$$u' = Au.$$

Suppose now that we rotate the axes back to their original position. The new components of vector **u** are given by (u_1, u_2, u_3) and the old ones are given by (u'_1, u'_2, u'_3); these components must be related by some matrix B:

$$u = Bu'.$$

Combining these relations we obtain

$$u = B(Au) = (BA)u.$$

Therefore, the matrix BA must transform the components (u_1, u_2, u_3) into themselves. It is easy to see that this task is accomplished by the so-called *unit matrix* ("identity matrix")

$$I = \begin{vmatrix} 1 & 0 & 0 \\ 0 & 1 & 0 \\ 0 & 0 & 1 \end{vmatrix}.$$

Exercise. Show that if $u = (BA)u$ is to hold for an arbitrary vector u, then BA must necessarily be of the above form. In other words, the *identity matrix is unique.*

It is now customary to call B the *inverse* of matrix A and to denote it by symbol A^{-1} so that we have $A^{-1}A = I$. Since we could have performed our rotations in reverse order, it is not hard to see that $AB = I$ as well, that is, $A^{-1}A = AA^{-1}$ and $A = B^{-1}$. While two rotation matrices may not commute, a rotation matrix always commutes with its inverse.†

---

* If we write $A/B = X$ the question would arise whether we imply $A = BX$ or $A = XB$.

† See Section 10.4 for a general statement to that effect.

It may now be of interest to relate the elements of matrix B to those of matrix A. To obtain b_{mn} we should, in principle, solve the equations on p. 5 for u_1, u_2, u_3. However, in the *case of rotations*, we have a much simpler method at our disposal. Let us write the matrix equation $BA = I$ in detail:

$$
\begin{vmatrix}
b_{11} & b_{12} & b_{13} \\
b_{21} & b_{22} & b_{23} \\
b_{31} & b_{32} & b_{33}
\end{vmatrix}
\cdot
\begin{vmatrix}
a_{11} & a_{12} & a_{13} \\
a_{21} & a_{22} & a_{23} \\
a_{31} & a_{32} & a_{33}
\end{vmatrix}
=
\begin{vmatrix}
1 & 0 & 0 \\
0 & 1 & 0 \\
0 & 0 & 1
\end{vmatrix} .
$$

To get the first row of I we must take the dot products of the first row vector of B with each of the column vectors of A. However, we know that the latter are just the vectors $\mathbf{i}, \mathbf{j}, \mathbf{k}$ in new representation. We see that the first row vector of B is orthogonal to $\mathbf{j}$ and $\mathbf{k}$ and its dot product with $\mathbf{i}$ is unity. Consequently, it could be nothing else but the vector $\mathbf{i}$ (in new representation, of course), and we conclude that $b_{11} = a_{11}$, $b_{12} = a_{21}$, and $b_{13} = a_{31}$.

Repeat this argument for the other rows of B and deduce that the rows of B are the columns of A and vice versa. This is also expressed by the formula

$$b_{mn} = a_{nm}.$$

Any two matrices A and B satisfying these conditions are called *transposes* of each other and are denoted by $B = A^T$ and $A = B^T$. While it is *not, in general, true* that the inverse and transpose of a matrix are identical, this rule holds for rotation matrices and is very useful.

1.5 SKEW CARTESIAN SYSTEMS. MATRICES IN GENERAL

If the coordinate axes in a cartesian system form angles other than 90°, we have a skew cartesian system. Figure 1.8 shows two such systems, one in plane and one in space, along with the decomposition of a vector into its respective components.

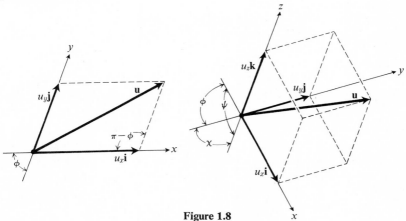

Figure 1.8

Skew systems are specified by the angles between the axes (one in plane, three in space) which may vary between 0° and 180°. As before, **i**, **j**, and **k** will be used to denote unit vectors in the direction of axes. Note that we can still talk about right-handed systems in space, where the vectors **i, j, k** (in that order!) form a right-handed triple.

The vectors are added and multiplied by scalars according to the same rules that were stated before. However, the length of a vector is now given by a different formula. For instance, for a plane vector we have from Fig. 1.8(a), by the cosine theorem,

$$|\mathbf{u}|^2 = u_x^2 + u_y^2 - 2u_xu_y \cos(\pi - \phi) = u_x^2 + u_y^2 + 2u_xu_y \cos \phi$$

so that

$$|\mathbf{u}| = \sqrt{u_x^2 + u_y^2 + 2u_xu_y \cos \phi}.$$

In general, the dot product is no longer given by the sum of the products of components, but by a more complicated formula. As a matter of fact we shall even introduce a new name for it and call it the *inner product* of two vectors which is then defined by

$$(\mathbf{u} \cdot \mathbf{v}) = |\mathbf{u}| \cdot |\mathbf{v}| \cdot \cos(\mathbf{u}, \mathbf{v}).$$

The reason is that we would like to retain the name dot product to mean the sum of the products of components of two vectors, regardless of whether the axes are orthogonal or skew.*

The derivation of a formula for inner product in a skew system is greatly facilitated by its distributive property, namely,

$$(\mathbf{u} \cdot (\mathbf{v} + \mathbf{w})) = (\mathbf{u} \cdot \mathbf{v}) + (\mathbf{u} \cdot \mathbf{w}).$$

Indeed, from Fig. 1.9, no matter which coordinate system is used, we see that

$$(\mathbf{u} \cdot (\mathbf{v} + \mathbf{w})) = |\mathbf{u}| \cdot |\mathbf{v} + \mathbf{w}| \cdot \cos \theta = |\mathbf{u}| \cdot (\overline{MN}).$$

However, $\overline{MN} = \overline{MP} + \overline{PN}$; since $\overline{MP}$ is the projection of **v** on **u**, we have $|\mathbf{u}| \cdot (\overline{MP}) = |\mathbf{u}| \cdot |\mathbf{v}| \cdot \cos(\mathbf{u}, \mathbf{v})$, and similarly for PN, establishing the result. Note that this argument is also valid for vectors in space.

Now we can write† for two vectors in a plane $\mathbf{u} = u_x\mathbf{i} + u_y\mathbf{j}$ and $\mathbf{v} = v_x\mathbf{i} + v_y\mathbf{j}$:

$$(\mathbf{u} \cdot \mathbf{v}) = (u_x\mathbf{i} \cdot v_x\mathbf{i}) + (u_x\mathbf{i} \cdot v_y\mathbf{j}) + (u_y\mathbf{j} \cdot v_x\mathbf{i}) + (u_y\mathbf{j} \cdot v_y\mathbf{j})$$
$$= u_xv_x + u_xv_y \cos \phi + u_yv_x \cos \phi + u_yv_y.$$

Note that this formula reduces to the usual dot product when $\phi = 90°$.

---

* With this distinction, the dot product becomes an *algebraic* concept (referring to the components) while inner product is a *geometrical* concept, independent of the coordinate system. The two are identical provided the system is orthogonal.

† Since $(\mathbf{u} \cdot \mathbf{v}) = (\mathbf{v} \cdot \mathbf{u})$, the second distributive law $((\mathbf{u} + \mathbf{v}) \cdot \mathbf{w}) = (\mathbf{u} \cdot \mathbf{w}) + (\mathbf{v} \cdot \mathbf{w})$ is trivial.

There is no difficulty now in establishing other formulas for skew systems, in plane or in space. We shall not go into these details but rather consider another important question: the transformation of coordinates from an orthogonal to a skew system of axes. Consider, for instance, Fig. 1.10; here a skew $x'y'$-system with unit vectors $\mathbf{i}'$ and $\mathbf{j}'$ is superimposed on an orthogonal xy-system with unit vectors $\mathbf{i}$ and $\mathbf{j}$. A given vector $\mathbf{u}$ can be represented either as $\mathbf{u} = u_x\mathbf{i} + u_y\mathbf{j}$ or as $\mathbf{u} = u_x'\mathbf{i}' + u_y'\mathbf{j}'$.

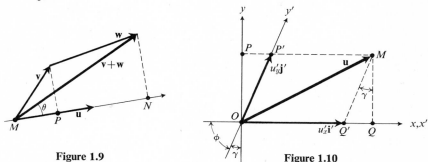

Figure 1.9   Figure 1.10

Although $\mathbf{i}' = \mathbf{i}$, the components u_x' and u_x are not equal; rather, we have

$$u_x' = \overline{OQ'} = \overline{OQ} - \overline{Q'Q} = u_x - u_y \tan \gamma.$$

Also,

$$u_y' = \overline{OP'} = u_y \sec \gamma.$$

We see that the new components (u_x', u_y') are linearly related to the old components (u_x, u_y) and this relationship can be represented by means of vector-matrix multiplication:

$$\begin{vmatrix} u_x' \\ u_y' \end{vmatrix} = \begin{vmatrix} 1 & -\tan \gamma \\ 0 & \sec \gamma \end{vmatrix} \cdot \begin{vmatrix} u_x \\ u_y \end{vmatrix}.$$

This can be written symbolically as

$$u' = Au,$$

where u' stands for the column vector (u_x', u_y'), and u stands for the column vector (u_x, u_y). The obvious difference from the previous cases is that the matrix A is no longer orthogonal. Its inverse A^{-1} is readily calculated by solving for u_x, u_y in terms of u_x', u_y' and it reads

$$A^{-1} = \begin{vmatrix} 1 & \sin \gamma \\ 0 & \cos \gamma \end{vmatrix}.$$

Note that it is no longer the transpose of A.

It is still true that the columns of A are the old unit vectors in new representation (Fig. 1.11), that is,

$$\mathbf{i} = \mathbf{i}' = 1 \cdot \mathbf{i}' + 0 \cdot \mathbf{j}', \qquad \mathbf{j} = -\tan\gamma \cdot \mathbf{i}' + \sec\gamma \cdot \mathbf{j}'.$$

The rows of matrix A do not have a simple geometrical interpretation, but the columns of matrix A^{-1} do have one.*

From the above analysis we may conjecture that, in general, a change from one set of unit vectors to another in a plane or in space involves a *linear relationship* between the old and new components of a vector, expressible by a vector-matrix multiplication $u' = Au$ (A is a 2×2 or a 3×3 matrix). We shall consider this problem in detail in Chapter 10. For the time being we shall mention the fact that *not every matrix A* can represent such a relationship. Consider, for instance, the following hypothetical relation between the new and old coordinates of some vector $\mathbf{u}$:

$$u'_x = 4u_x - 2u_y, \qquad u'_y = 2u_x - u_y.$$

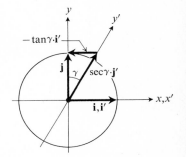

Figure 1.11

If we attempt to solve these two equations for u_x and u_y we find that they have *no solution* if u'_x and u'_y are arbitrary. We say that the matrix

$$A = \begin{bmatrix} 4 & -2 \\ 2 & -1 \end{bmatrix}$$

does not possess an inverse; such matrices are called *singular matrices*. It is not difficult to see that in this example the pair u'_x, u'_y cannot possibly represent an arbitrary vector in plane: Our equations imply $u'_x = 2u'_y$ so that there is only one independent component instead of the two required for a plane.

Remark. It is of interest to note that if $u'_x = 2u'_y$ is actually satisfied, our system of equations has *an infinity* of solutions for u_x and u_y (since two equations reduce to a single one). Furthermore, if an additional requirement $u_x = 2u_y$ is imposed, the system has a *unique solution* ($u_x = \frac{1}{3}u'_x$; $u_y = \frac{1}{3}u'_y$). All these features should be remembered since they are important in physical applications.

1.6 SCALAR AND VECTOR FIELDS

So far we have been discussing constant vectors, but we can also contemplate vectors which depend on one or more variable parameters. The simplest example is, perhaps, a position vector which depends on time t. In a *fixed coordinate system*, this is equivalent to saying that its components are functions of time

---

* If A were orthogonal, the rows of A would be identical with columns of A^{-1} (see pp. 11 and 440).

and we write

$$\mathbf{u} = \mathbf{u}(t) = u_x(t) \cdot \mathbf{i} + u_y(t) \cdot \mathbf{j} + u_z(t) \cdot \mathbf{k}.$$

Such vectors can be differentiated with respect to the variable t according to the definition

$$\frac{d}{dt} \mathbf{u}(t) = \lim_{\Delta t \to 0} \frac{\mathbf{u}(t + \Delta t) - \mathbf{u}(t)}{\Delta t}.$$

With $\mathbf{u}(t)$ and $\mathbf{u}(t + \Delta t)$ expressed in terms of their components, it is trivial to deduce that

$$\frac{d}{dt} \mathbf{u}(t) = \frac{du_x}{dt} \mathbf{i} + \frac{du_y}{dt} \mathbf{j} + \frac{du_z}{dt} \mathbf{k}$$

so that the operation of differentiation of a vector is reduced to differentiation of its components.

While vectors depending on time are widely used in mechanics of particles, we shall be more interested in another type of variable vectors: those depending on space coordinates (x, y, z).* Such vectors are said to form *vector fields* and can be denoted as follows:

$$\mathbf{u} = \mathbf{u}(x, y, z) = u_x(x, y, z)\mathbf{i} + u_y(x, y, z)\mathbf{j} + u_z(x, y, z)\mathbf{k}.$$

Common examples are electric and magnetic fields in space, velocity field of a fluid in motion, and others.

The simplest kind of such a field is probably the so-called *gradient field*† which can be derived from a single scalar function $\varphi(x, y, z)$, usually referred to as a *scalar field*. Familiar cases of scalar fields include the temperature distribution in a solid body, density of a nonhomogeneous medium, electrostatic potential, etc.

A scalar field gives rise to numerous other quantities through its various partial derivatives. In particular, let us concentrate our attention on

a) the total differential

$$d\varphi = \frac{\partial \varphi}{\partial x} dx + \frac{\partial \varphi}{\partial y} dy + \frac{\partial \varphi}{\partial z} dz,$$

and

b) the directional derivative‡

$$\frac{d\varphi}{ds} = \frac{\partial \varphi}{\partial x} \frac{dx}{ds} + \frac{\partial \varphi}{\partial y} \frac{dy}{ds} + \frac{\partial \varphi}{\partial z} \frac{dz}{ds}.$$

---

* These vectors may also depend on time, but we shall be mostly interested in instantaneous relationships, where t has some fixed value.

† This is also called *conservative field* or *potential field*.

‡ Rate of change of φ per unit length in some particular direction characterized, say, by the element of arc ds of some curve. See, e.g., Apostol, p. 104.

The expressions on the right-hand side of the equations in (a) and (b) have the appearance of a dot product. It is convenient to define the *gradient* of a scalar field $\varphi(x, y, z)$ by the vector

$$\operatorname{grad} \varphi = \frac{\partial \varphi}{\partial x} \mathbf{i} + \frac{\partial \varphi}{\partial y} \mathbf{j} + \frac{\partial \varphi}{\partial z} \mathbf{k}.$$

Then we can write

$$d\varphi = (\operatorname{grad} \varphi \cdot d\mathbf{s}) \qquad \text{and} \qquad \frac{d\varphi}{ds} = (\operatorname{grad} \varphi \cdot \mathbf{s}_0),$$

where $d\mathbf{s} = dx\,\mathbf{i} + dy\,\mathbf{j} + dz\,\mathbf{k}$ represents infinitesimal displacement in some direction and

$$\mathbf{s}_0 = \frac{dx}{ds} \mathbf{i} + \frac{dy}{ds} \mathbf{j} + \frac{dz}{ds} \mathbf{k}$$

is the unit vector in the specified direction.*

Since every differentiable scalar field generates a gradient field, it is natural to ask whether any given vector field $\mathbf{u} = \mathbf{u}(x, y, z)$ may not be the gradient of some scalar φ. The answer is negative and this becomes clear as we examine the basic properties of gradient fields. In this survey we shall need certain assumptions regarding the differentiability of various functions and analytic properties of curves and surfaces involved in vector analysis. We shall mention these assumptions as we need them. In many cases they can be relaxed and the results can be generalized, but we shall confine ourselves to the common situations encountered in physics.

A curve in space is called *smooth* if it can be represented by

$$x = x(t), \qquad y = y(t), \qquad z = z(t),$$

where $x(t)$, $y(t)$, and $z(t)$ have continuous derivatives with respect to the parameter t (for a curve in a plane, simply set $z = 0$). Smooth curves possess tangents at all points and a (vector) line element $d\mathbf{s}$ can be defined at any point. The smoothness also guarantees the existence of line integrals.† This last property is trivially extended to *piecewise smooth* curves; i.e., those consisting of a *finite* number of smooth parts. We shall assume that all curves considered by us are piecewise smooth.

Regarding the differentiability of various functions, we must remember the following definitions and statements: the interior of a sphere of arbitrary radius ϵ (usually thought to be small) centered at some point $M(x, y, z)$ is called a *neighborhood*‡ of this point (in a plane, replace "sphere" by "circle"). If a set of points

---

* Observe that $dx/ds = \cos(\mathbf{s}_0, \mathbf{i})$, etc., are the directional cosines of the direction defined by $d\mathbf{s}$ or by $\mathbf{s}_0$.

† We shall assume that all integrals are Riemann integrals which are adequate for our purposes. For example, see Apostol p. 276.

‡ A more precise term is an ϵ-neighborhood.

is such that it contains some neighborhood of every one of its points, then it is called an *open set*. For instance, the *interior* of a cube is an open set; we can always draw a small sphere about each interior point which will lie entirely within the cube. However, the cube with *boundary points included* is no longer an open set.

The reason these concepts are needed is that partial derivatives of a function in space are defined by a limiting process that is tied to a neighborhood. We must make sure a region is an open set before we can say that $f(x, y, z)$ is differentiable in this region.

In addition, we shall be mostly interested in connected open sets, or *domains*. These are open sets any two points of which can be connected by a *polygon*, i.e., a curve which is formed by a finite number of connected straight-line segments. From now on we shall assume that all our piecewise smooth curves lie in domains where the functions under consideration (scalar fields and components of vector fields) possess *continuous first-order partial derivatives*.

Let us now return to the properties of gradient fields. Suppose that

$$\mathbf{u} = \operatorname{grad} \varphi(x, y, z)$$

and consider the following integral between points

$$M(x_0, y_0, z_0) \qquad \text{and} \qquad N(x_1, y_1, z_1),$$

taken along some curve C:

$$\int_M^N (\mathbf{u} \cdot d\mathbf{s}) = \int_M^N \left(\frac{\partial \varphi}{\partial x} dx + \frac{\partial \varphi}{\partial y} dy + \frac{\partial \varphi}{\partial z} dz \right).$$
$$\text{Along } C \qquad\qquad \text{Along } C$$

Using the parameter t as the variable of integration, we have

$$\int_M^N (\mathbf{u} \cdot d\mathbf{s}) = \int_{t_0}^{t_1} \left(\frac{\partial \varphi}{\partial x} \frac{dx}{dt} + \frac{\partial \varphi}{\partial y} \frac{dy}{dt} + \frac{\partial \varphi}{\partial z} \frac{dz}{dt} \right) dt = \int_{t_0}^{t_1} \frac{d\varphi}{dt} dt = \varphi(t_1) - \varphi(t_0),$$
$$\text{Along } C$$

where t_0 and t_1 are the values of the parameter t corresponding to points M and N. We see that the integral is simply the difference of values of $\varphi(x, y, z)$ at points N and M and, therefore, is *independent* of the choice of curve C.

Conversely, if the integral

$$\int_M^N (\mathbf{u} \cdot d\mathbf{s})$$

is independent of path,* then keeping M fixed and treating N as a variable point, we can *define* a function

$$\varphi(x, y, z) = \int_M^{(x,y,z)} (\mathbf{u} \cdot d\mathbf{s}) = \int_M^{(x,y,z)} (u_x\, dx + u_y\, dy + u_z\, dz).$$

---

* From now on, we shall occasionally use the term "path" to indicate a piecewise smooth curve.

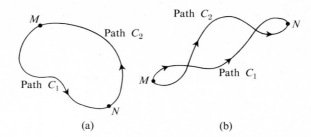

Figure 1.12

It is now simple to show that grad φ = **u**. For instance,

$$\varphi(x + \Delta x, y, z) - \varphi(x, y, z) = \int_{(x,y,z)}^{(x+\Delta x,y,z)} (u_x\, dx + u_y\, dy + u_z\, dz)$$

$$= \int_{(x,y,z)}^{(x+\Delta x,y,z)} u_x\, dx$$

and the statement $u_x = \partial\varphi/\partial z$ follows from the fundamental theorem of integral calculus.

We have then established the following theorem: *The necessary and sufficient condition that* **u** = grad φ *is the independence of path of the integral* $\int(\mathbf{u} \cdot d\mathbf{s})$.

An alternative way of stating this result follows from consideration of the integral

$$\oint (\mathbf{u} \cdot d\mathbf{s})$$

over a *simple closed path* C, called the *circulation* of vector **u** around C. By simple closed path we mean a closed path which does not intersect itself.*

The following theorem holds: *The circulation of* **u** *vanishes for an arbitrary simple closed path* C *(in a domain* D*) if and only if the integral* $\int_M^N (\mathbf{u} \cdot d\mathbf{s})$ *is independent of path (in* D*)*.

Indeed, let C (Fig. 1.12a) be a simple closed path. Choose two arbitrary points M and N on C and write

$$\oint_C (\mathbf{u} \cdot d\mathbf{s}) = \underset{\text{Along } C_1}{\int_M^N (\mathbf{u} \cdot d\mathbf{s})} + \underset{\text{Along } C_2}{\int_N^M (\mathbf{u} \cdot d\mathbf{s})} = \underset{\text{Along } C_1}{\int_M^N (\mathbf{u} \cdot d\mathbf{s})} - \underset{\text{Along } C_2}{\int_M^N (\mathbf{u} \cdot d\mathbf{s})}.$$

If the integral $\int_M^N (\mathbf{u} \cdot d\mathbf{s})$ is independent of path, the right-hand side vanishes and the circulation is zero.

Conversely, if two paths C_1 and C_2 connecting two points (Fig. 1.12b) do not intersect (in space), a simple closed path can be formed from them and the above equation holds. If the left-hand side is zero, so is the right-hand side, yielding the independence of path. If C_1 and C_2 intersect a *finite* number of times, the proof is obtained by splitting the closed path into a finite number of simple

---

* This property permits us to assign the direction of integration around the curve, characterized by the vector $d\mathbf{s}$, in a unique fashion.

closed paths. In the rather exceptional case when C_1 and C_2 cross each other an infinite number of times, a limiting process can be invoked reducing this case to the preceding one.*

Remark. Within the context of the above discussion, it is emphasized that by $\varphi(x, y, z)$ we mean a well-defined *single-valued* function† over the entire domain and nothing short of this requirement will suffice. In many treatments‡ of the magnetostatic field **H**, one introduces the so-called scalar magnetic potential X so that $\mathbf{H} = \operatorname{grad} X$ and yet the circulation of **H** does not vanish over some contours. However, in all such cases it is impossible to define X uniquely over the *entire* contour (for those contours for which it is possible, the circulation of **H** does indeed vanish).

It should now be clear that many vector fields do not fall into the category of gradient fields since it is easy to construct a vector **u** for which the integral $\int (\mathbf{u} \cdot d\mathbf{s})$ will actually depend on path. It is perhaps even easier to sketch some such fields, a task facilitated by the introduction of the concept of *field lines*. These field lines are curves with tangents directed along the vector field **u** at every point. For instance, Fig. 1.13 shows the velocity field (in the plane) of a fluid rotating around a circular obstacle. In this case the field lines are the trajectories along which the particles of fluid actually move.

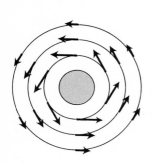

Figure 1.13

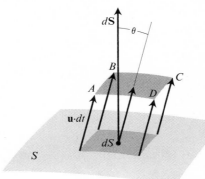

Figure 1.14

It is evident that the circulation of the velocity vector **u** around any one of the circles in Fig. 1.13 cannot be zero (the product $\mathbf{u} \cdot d\mathbf{s}$ has the same sign at each point of the circle). Consequently, the above field cannot be a gradient field.

The velocity field of a fluid is, perhaps, the best starting point for investigation of other types of vector fields because it naturally leads us to another fundamental concept: the *flux of a vector field*.

Consider the element dS of a surface S (Fig. 1.14). Just as in the case of curves, we shall deal only with *piecewise smooth* surfaces, i.e., those consisting of

---

* The details may be found in O. D. Kellogg, *Foundations of Potential Theory*.

† A multivalued function is not *one* function, but a collection of *several* different functions.

‡ For example, Reitz and Milford, *Foundations of Electromagnetic Theory*, Section 8.8.

a finite number of smooth portions.   By a *smooth surface* we mean a surface representable by

$$x = x(p, q), \qquad y = y(p, q), \qquad z = z(p, q),$$

where p and q are independent parameters and the functions x, y, and z have continuous first partials with respect to p and q in the domain under consideration. Smooth surfaces possess tangential planes at all points and can be *oriented;* that is, we can distinguish between the positive side and the negative side of the surface. We shall also assume that our piecewise smooth surfaces are constructed in such a way that they are oriented.*   It is customary to represent surface elements dS by vectors $d\mathbf{S}$ of magnitudes that are directed along the positive normal to the surface, as illustrated in Fig. 1.14.   Suppose that the vector field $\mathbf{u}$ represents the velocity of a moving fluid.   It can be seen that the inner product $(\mathbf{u} \cdot d\mathbf{S})$ represents the amount of fluid passing through dS per unit time.   Indeed, the particles of fluid crossing dS at time t will occupy the face $ABCD$ of the shown parallelepiped at time $t + dt$ and all particles of fluid which have crossed dS between t and $t + dt$ will be located at $t + dt$ inside the parallelepiped.   Consequently, the amount of fluid passing through dS in the interval dt is given by the volume of the parallelepiped, equal to

$$dS \cdot |\mathbf{u}| \cdot dt \cos \theta = (\mathbf{u} \cdot d\mathbf{S}) \, dt.$$

Divide by dt and obtain the desired statement.

By analogy with these observations, we define, in general, the flux of a vector field $\mathbf{u}$ through a surface S by the surface integral

$$\Phi = \iint\limits_{S} (\mathbf{u} \cdot d\mathbf{S}).$$

In this formula, S can be either an open or a closed surface.   A very familiar case of the latter is found in Gauss' theorem in electrostatics.

1.7 VECTOR FIELDS IN PLANE

According to the material of the preceding section, integrals representing circulation and flux are important in the study of vector fields.   For vectors in a plane, the circulation integral has the form†

$$\oint_{C} (\mathbf{u} \cdot d\mathbf{s}) = \oint_{C} (u_x \, dx + u_y \, dy).$$

Integrals of this type can be analyzed by means of *Green's theorem: If C is a (piecewise smooth) simple closed curve in a simply connected domain D and if P(x, y)*

---

* For details, consult, e.g., Kaplan, p. 260 *et seq.*

† Unless stated otherwise, it is conventional to take the direction of integration in such integrals, i.e., the orientation of $d\mathbf{s}$, as *counterclockwise.*

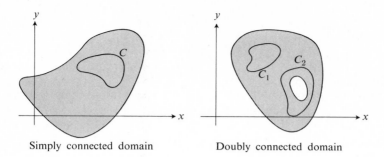

Simply connected domain   Doubly connected domain

Figure 1.15

and $Q(x, y)$ have continuous first partials in D, then

$$\oint_C (P\,dx + Q\,dy) = \iint_S \left(\frac{\partial Q}{\partial x} - \frac{\partial P}{\partial y}\right) dS$$

where S is the area bounded by C.

The importance of the requirement that C is a simple closed curve (see p. 18) lies in the fact that we *can distinguish* the interior of the curve from its exterior by the following rule: As we proceed along the curve in the direction of *d*s we designate the region appearing on our right as the exterior and that on our left as the interior. If the curve crosses itself such a formulation leads to contradiction as should be obvious by considering a curve in the shape of a "figure eight."

A domain in a plane is said to be *simply connected* if every simple closed curve in it has its interior inside the domain as well. Figuratively speaking, a domain is simply connected if it has no "holes" (Fig. 1.15).

Without going into mathematical details we shall sketch a possible method of proving Green's theorem which greatly facilitates its physical interpretations. First of all, note that $P(x, y)$ and $Q(x, y)$ can always be treated as the components $u_x(x, y)$ and $u_y(x, y)$ of some vector field, and we shall adopt, for convenience, this identification. Let us now divide the area S into a network of meshes, as illustrated in Fig. 1.16(a). Taking the integrals $\int (\mathbf{u} \cdot d\mathbf{s})$ around each mesh in

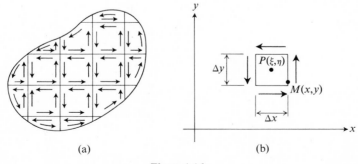

(a)   (b)

Figure 1.16

counterclockwise direction we can easily deduce that

$$\oint_C (\mathbf{u} \cdot d\mathbf{s}) = \sum_{\substack{\text{All} \\ \text{meshes}}} \oint (\mathbf{u} \cdot d\mathbf{s}).$$

(The contribution from a common boundary between two meshes cancels out because of opposite orientations of vectors $d\mathbf{s}$ for each mesh; this leaves only the contributions from the pieces of C.) Furthermore, multiplying and dividing each term in the sum by the area ΔS of each mesh, we obtain

$$\oint_C (\mathbf{u} \cdot d\mathbf{s}) = \sum_{\substack{\text{All} \\ \text{meshes}}} \frac{\oint (\mathbf{u} \cdot d\mathbf{s})}{\Delta S} \Delta S.$$

Suppose now that the number of meshes is increased to infinity and that each mesh "shrinks to a point" so that $\Delta S \to 0$. If the limit

$$\lim_{\Delta S \to 0} \frac{\oint (\mathbf{u} \cdot d\mathbf{s})}{\Delta S} = f(x, y)$$

exists and is independent of the shape of ΔS,* then the sum reduces to an integral and we have

$$\oint_C (\mathbf{u} \cdot d\mathbf{s}) = \iint_S f(x, y) \, dS.$$

Therefore, it remains for us to evaluate the function $f(x, y)$. A typical mesh is shown in Fig. 1.16(b); it need not be rectangular since the arguments presented below are valid for an arbitrary shape. If u_x and u_y have continuous partials, then we can write

$$(u_x)_M \cong (u_x)_P + \left(\frac{\partial u_x}{\partial x}\right)_P (x - \xi) + \left(\frac{\partial u_x}{\partial y}\right)_P (y - \eta)$$

and

$$(u_y)_M \cong (u_y)_P + \left(\frac{\partial u_y}{\partial x}\right)_P (x - \xi) + \left(\frac{\partial u_y}{\partial y}\right)_P (y - \eta)$$

with the approximations being within the first order in $|x - \xi|$ and $|y - \eta|$.† Here $P(\xi, \eta)$ is the fixed point to which ΔS ultimately shrinks and $M(x, y)$ is an arbitrary point on the boundary of the mesh. Writing now

$$\oint (\mathbf{u} \cdot d\mathbf{s}) = \oint u_x \, dx + \oint u_y \, dy,$$

---

* Except that the largest diameter of ΔS must approach zero: the mesh should not become infinitesimally thin while retaining finite length.

† By the theorem on existence of total differential, guaranteed by the continuity of partial derivatives.

we see that the following six integrals will be needed:

$$\oint dx, \qquad \oint dy, \qquad \oint x\,dy, \qquad \oint y\,dx, \qquad \oint x\,dx, \qquad \oint y\,dy.$$

The first two are zero, the second two are $+\Delta S$ and $-\Delta S$, respectively, and the last two are zero. As a result, we have

$$\oint (\mathbf{u} \cdot d\mathbf{s}) \cong \left(\frac{\partial u_y}{\partial x} - \frac{\partial u_x}{\partial y}\right)_P \Delta S.$$

Consequently,

$$f(x, y) = \lim_{\Delta S \to 0} \frac{\oint(\mathbf{u} \cdot d\mathbf{s})}{\Delta S} = \frac{\partial u_y}{\partial x} - \frac{\partial u_x}{\partial y},$$

where the stipulation that the partials are to be calculated at $P(\xi, \eta)$ can be omitted since P is now an arbitrary point within C. We have then the result

$$\oint_C (u_x\,dx + u_y\,dy) = \iint_S \left(\frac{\partial u_y}{\partial x} - \frac{\partial u_x}{\partial y}\right) dS,$$

which is simply Green's theorem in our notation.

    With regard to a vector field $\mathbf{u} = u_x\mathbf{i} + u_y\mathbf{j}$, the function $f(x, y)$ is known as the *curl* of $\mathbf{u}$ so that, by definition,

$$\operatorname{curl} \mathbf{u} = \lim_{\Delta S \to 0} \frac{\oint(\mathbf{u} \cdot d\mathbf{s})}{\Delta S}.$$

We have then evaluated the expression for curl $\mathbf{u}$ in (orthogonal) cartesian coordinates in plane:

$$\operatorname{curl} \mathbf{u} = \frac{\partial u_y}{\partial x} - \frac{\partial u_x}{\partial y}.$$

Remark. Attention is drawn to the fact that, for a vector field *in a plane*, curl $\mathbf{u}$ is essentially a scalar* and *not a vector*. The point is that by vectors we must mean quantities expressible as $a\mathbf{i} + b\mathbf{j}$ and curl $\mathbf{u}$ is definitely not this type, whether or not we introduce the third axis.

    A vector field $\mathbf{u}$ which has zero curl at some point is called an *irrotational field* (at that point). If $\mathbf{u}$ is irrotational in a simply connected domain, then by Green's theorem, it is a conservative field (gradient field) in this domain, i.e., it has zero circulation. The converse has to be worded rather carefully: If $\mathbf{u}$ is a gradient field (namely, $\mathbf{u} = \operatorname{grad} \varphi$), then it is irrotational *provided* φ has continuous second-order partial derivatives.

---

* In a more elaborate nomenclature, curl $\mathbf{u}$ is called pseudoscalar due to its peculiar property of changing sign if the x- and y-axes are interchanged. See Section 16.5.

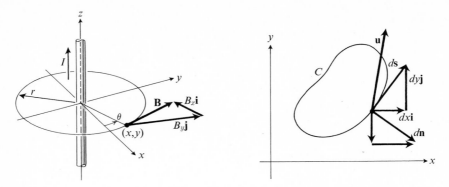

Figure 1.17   **Figure 1.18**

Example. The magnetic induction field (**B**-field) due to an infinite current-carrying wire is known to be (outside the wire)*

$$\mathbf{B} = \frac{\mu_0 I}{2\pi r}\, \mathbf{s}_0 \quad \text{(MKSA units)}.$$

In the xy-plane (as shown in Fig. 1.17),

$$B_x = -B\sin\theta = -\frac{\mu_0 I}{2\pi r}\frac{y}{r} = -\frac{\mu_0 I}{2\pi}\frac{y}{x^2 + y^2},$$

$$B_y = B\cos\theta = \frac{\mu_0 I}{2\pi}\frac{x}{x^2 + y^2}.$$

This field happens to be irrotational everywhere *except at the origin.* Therefore $\oint_C (\mathbf{B} \cdot d\mathbf{s}) = 0$ if C does not encircle the origin, but not otherwise. A function $\chi(x, y)$ may be found such that $\mathbf{B} = \operatorname{grad} \chi$ in a simply connected domain D, but this can be done only if the domain does not contain the origin.

The **B**-field inside the wire is known to be

$$\mathbf{B} = \frac{\mu_0 I}{2\pi R^2}\, r\mathbf{s}_0,$$

where R is the radius of the wire. Here $B_x = -(\mu_0 I/2\pi R^2)y$ and $B_y = (\mu_0 I/2\pi R^2)x$. The field is not irrotational and cannot be represented as $\operatorname{grad} \varphi$ anywhere.

Let us now turn our attention to the concept of flux for vectors in plane. The obvious analog to the three-dimensional case is the integral

$$\Phi = \int_C (\mathbf{u} \cdot \mathbf{n}_0)\, ds = \int_C (\mathbf{u} \cdot d\mathbf{n})$$

taken over a curve C (not necessarily closed) with $\mathbf{n}_0$ being the *unit normal* to the curve and $d\mathbf{n} = \mathbf{n}_0\, ds$. This is illustrated in Fig. 1.18.

---

* $\mathbf{s}_0$ is the unit vector that is tangential to the circle drawn around the axis of the wire.

Exercise. For a flow of fluid in a plane, relate the integral Φ above to the amount of fluid crossing the curve C per unit time. Specify physical units of all the quantities used.

In many applications, the flux through a closed curve is involved. Evidently if $d\mathbf{s} = dx\,\mathbf{i} + dy\,\mathbf{j}$, then*

$$d\mathbf{n} = dy\,\mathbf{i} - dx\,\mathbf{j}$$

and

$$\oint_C (\mathbf{u} \cdot d\mathbf{n}) = \oint_C (u_x\,dy - u_y\,dx).$$

Setting $P = -u_y$, $Q = u_x$, this integral can be transformed by means of Green's theorem so that

$$\oint_C (\mathbf{u} \cdot d\mathbf{n}) = \iint_S \left(\frac{\partial u_x}{\partial x} + \frac{\partial u_y}{\partial y} \right) dx\,dy$$

provided, of course, that the partials are continuous everywhere inside C.

This relationship is usually referred to as the divergence theorem (in a plane) and is written as

$$\oint_C (\mathbf{u} \cdot d\mathbf{n}) = \iint_S \operatorname{div} \mathbf{u} \cdot dS,$$

where

$$\operatorname{div} \mathbf{u} = \frac{\partial u_x}{\partial x} + \frac{\partial u_y}{\partial y}$$

is another function derivable from a vector field and is known as the *divergence* of $\mathbf{u}$.

While the above derivation is straightforward, it does not reveal the geometric (or physical) meaning of div $\mathbf{u}$. It is instructive to invoke the technique used in Green's theorem: Dividing the area S into a network of meshes, we find that it is not hard to establish that

$$\oint_C (\mathbf{u} \cdot d\mathbf{n}) = \sum_{\substack{\text{All} \\ \text{meshes}}} \frac{\oint (\mathbf{u} \cdot d\mathbf{n})}{\Delta S} \Delta S,$$

because the vectors $d\mathbf{n}$ at the common boundary of two adjacent meshes are oppositely directed. This observation permits us to *define* the divergence of $\mathbf{u}$ as flux out of an infinitesimal area (per unit area), namely,

$$\operatorname{div} \mathbf{u} = \lim_{\Delta S \to 0} \frac{\oint (\mathbf{u} \cdot d\mathbf{n})}{\Delta S}.$$

Exercise. Derive the formula div $\mathbf{u} = \partial u_x/\partial x + \partial u_y/\partial y$ starting from the above definition and using the arguments analogous to those for curl $\mathbf{u}$. Spell out the conditions required in the derivation.

---

* It is a standard convention that for closed curves in a plane (and closed surfaces in space) the positive normal is the outward-pointing normal.

Remark. From our definitions of curl **u** and div **u** it is seen that both represent a new kind of derivative, namely, a derivative with respect to infinitesimal area rather than infinitesimal displacement:

$$\text{curl } \mathbf{u} = \lim_{\Delta S \to 0} \frac{\oint (\mathbf{u} \cdot d\mathbf{s})}{\Delta S}, \qquad \text{div } \mathbf{u} = \lim_{\Delta S \to 0} \frac{\oint (\mathbf{u} \cdot d\mathbf{n})}{\Delta S}.$$

It may be of interest to mention that the gradient of a scalar field φ can be represented in a similar fashion; i.e., the following statement holds:

$$\text{grad } \varphi = \lim_{\Delta S \to 0} \frac{\oint \varphi \cdot d\mathbf{n}}{\Delta S}.$$

Another interesting observation is that curl **u** can be related to an integral involving $d\mathbf{n}$ and div **u** to an integral involving $d\mathbf{s}$. Indeed, the identities

$$(\mathbf{u} \cdot d\mathbf{n}) = [\mathbf{u} \times d\mathbf{s}], \qquad (\mathbf{u} \cdot d\mathbf{s}) = [d\mathbf{n} \times \mathbf{u}],$$

are not hard to verify provided we treat the cross product of two vectors in plane as a *scalar*, which is the logical thing to do.* Consequently, the following statements also hold:

$$\text{curl } \mathbf{u} = \lim_{\Delta S \to 0} \frac{\oint [d\mathbf{n} \times \mathbf{u}]}{\Delta S}, \qquad \text{div } \mathbf{u} = \lim_{\Delta S \to 0} \frac{\oint [\mathbf{u} \times d\mathbf{s}]}{\Delta S}.$$

Vector fields which have zero divergence are called *solenoidal fields*. They are very common in physics. For instance, the electrostatic field is solenoidal in the absence of charged matter; the magnetic induction field is solenoidal everywhere.

1.8 VECTOR FIELDS IN SPACE

We would now like to extend the analysis of the last section to vectors in space. We shall start with the flux of a vector field **u** through a closed surface S, because this integral is, perhaps, easiest to handle. It reads

$$\Phi = \oiint_S (\mathbf{u} \cdot d\mathbf{S}) = \oiint_S (u_x \, dS_x + u_y \, dS_y + u_z \, dS_z),$$

where dS_x, dS_y, and dS_z are projections of vector $d\mathbf{S}$ on the coordinate axes.

Integrals of this type can be handled by *Gauss' theorem: If S is a (piecewise smooth) closed orientable surface contained, along with its interior, in a domain D and if L(x, y, z), M(x, y, z), and N(x, y, z) have continuous first partials in D, then*

$$\oiint_S (L \, dS_x + M \, dS_y + N \, dS_z) = \iiint_V \left(\frac{\partial L}{\partial x} + \frac{\partial M}{\partial y} + \frac{\partial N}{\partial z} \right) dV,$$

where V is the volume bounded by S.

---

* A typical cross product of two vectors in physics is the torque $\boldsymbol{\Gamma} = [\mathbf{r} \times \mathbf{F}]$ which, for vectors in a plane, is completely described by magnitude and sign (clockwise or counterclockwise). See the remark on p. 23 which may lead to a conjecture that the cross product in a plane is a pseudoscalar (and, indeed, it is).

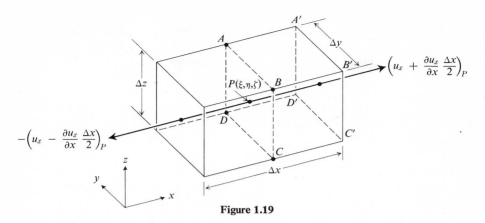

Figure 1.19

Gauss' theorem can be restated in vector notation, by identifying L, M, and N with the components of a vector field $\mathbf{u} = u_x\mathbf{i} + u_y\mathbf{j} + u_z\mathbf{k}$. The concept of divergence of $\mathbf{u}$,

$$\text{div } \mathbf{u} = \frac{\partial u_x}{\partial x} + \frac{\partial u_y}{\partial y} + \frac{\partial u_z}{\partial z},$$

is readily introduced so that Gauss' theorem can be rewritten as

$$\oiint_S (\mathbf{u} \cdot d\mathbf{S}) = \iiint_V \text{div } \mathbf{u} \cdot dV$$

and is often referred to as the *divergence theorem*.

The deduction of this theorem can be done again by a method analogous to that in the preceding section. In this case we cut the volume V into small pieces, say, rectangular blocks, one of which is shown in Fig. 1.19. If we calculate the flux of $\mathbf{u}$ through each block and add all the results, we must obtain the flux through the outer boundary S; just as before, the flux of $\mathbf{u}$ through an interface between two blocks must appear in the sum twice, but with the opposite sign because of the changed direction of the "outward normal" (see the footnote on p. 25). Consequently,

$$\oiint_S (\mathbf{u} \cdot d\mathbf{S}) = \sum_{\substack{\text{All} \\ \text{blocks}}} \frac{\oiint(\mathbf{u} \cdot d\mathbf{S})}{\Delta V} \Delta V$$

introducing, for an obvious purpose, the volume ΔV of each block. We now *define* the divergence of $\mathbf{u}$ by means of

$$\text{div } \mathbf{u} = \lim_{\Delta V \to 0} \frac{\oiint(\mathbf{u} \cdot d\mathbf{S})}{\Delta V}.$$

Gauss' theorem can now be deduced by ironing out the mathematical details and developing the formula for div $\mathbf{u}$ in cartesian coordinates. We shall give a simplified version of this from the consideration of a rectangular block ΔV (Fig. 1.19).

It is not hard to show that the flux of **u** through a rectangle such as $ABCD$, is given* within the first order in Δy and Δz by

$$\Phi_{ABCD} \cong (u_x)_P \, \Delta y \, \Delta z,$$

where $(u_x)_P$, is calculated at the center P of the rectangle. Indeed, for any point within $ABCD$ we have

$$u_x \cong (u_x)_P + \left(\frac{\partial u_x}{\partial y}\right)_P (y - \eta) + \left(\frac{\partial u_x}{\partial z}\right)_P (z - \zeta)$$

and the last two terms yield zero when integrated over the area $ABCD$.

Consequently, the flux of **u** through the face $A'B'C'D'$ is to be determined by the value of u_x at the center of this face and is given by

$$\left[(u_x)_P + \left(\frac{\partial u_x}{\partial x}\right)_P \frac{\Delta x}{2}\right] \Delta y \, \Delta z.$$

Similarly, the flux through the opposite face is

$$-\left[(u_x)_P - \left(\frac{\partial u_x}{\partial x}\right)_P \frac{\Delta x}{2}\right] \Delta y \, \Delta z.$$

There is a minus sign in front because we now want the positive normal in the negative x-direction. Adding these two fluxes we obtain

$$\left(\frac{\partial u}{\partial x}\right)_P \Delta x \, \Delta y \, \Delta z.$$

The fluxes through the other four faces are obtained in a similar way leading to the statement about the flux through a small parallelepiped ΔV:

$$\Phi_{\Delta V} \cong \left(\frac{\partial u_x}{\partial x} + \frac{\partial u_y}{\partial y} + \frac{\partial u_z}{\partial z}\right) \Delta V.$$

The expression for divergence now readily follows and concludes our analysis.

Let us now consider the question of circulation of a vector in space. Such an integral has the form

$$\oint_C (\mathbf{u} \cdot d\mathbf{s}) = \oint_C (u_x \, dx + u_y \, dy + u_z \, dz),$$

and we shall assume that C is a (piecewise smooth) simple closed curve in space. It need not be a plane curve but we shall assume that it can be *spanned* by a (piecewise smooth) orientable surface S; that is, C can serve as the boundary for such a

---

* Assuming a positive normal in the positive x-direction.

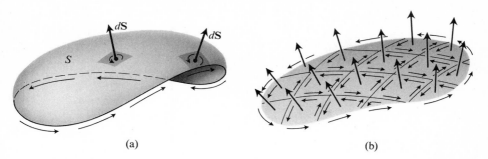

Figure 1.20

surface. This situation is illustrated in Fig. 1.20(a). It is a standard convention to define the positive direction of circulation around a surface element dS so that it forms the "right-hand screw system" with the positive normal to the surface.* The positive direction of circulation around the boundary curve C is now chosen so that it coincides with such direction for the adjacent surface element (Fig. 1.20a). When all this is done, we can quote *Stokes' theorem: If S is a (piecewise smooth) orientable surface spanning a (piecewise smooth) simple closed curve C, mutually oriented as described, then*

$$\oint_C [L(x, y, z)\, dx + M(x, y, z)\, dy + N(x, y, z)\, dz]$$
$$= \iint_S \left[\left(\frac{\partial N}{\partial y} - \frac{\partial M}{\partial z}\right) dy\, dz + \left(\frac{\partial L}{\partial z} - \frac{\partial N}{\partial x}\right) dz\, dx + \left(\frac{\partial M}{\partial x} - \frac{\partial L}{\partial y}\right) dx\, dy \right]$$

provided L, M, and N have continuous partials in a domain containing S and C.

As before, we can treat L, M, and N as the components of a vector field $\mathbf{u}$. By the now familiar technique, we divide S into a network of (curved) meshes (Fig. 1.20b) and claim

$$\oint_C (\mathbf{u} \cdot d\mathbf{s}) = \sum_{\substack{\text{All}\\ \text{meshes}}} \frac{\mathscr{S}(\mathbf{u} \cdot d\mathbf{s})}{\Delta S} \Delta S,$$

where ΔS is the area of a given mesh. As before, we calculate

$$\lim_{\Delta S \to 0} \frac{\mathscr{S}(\mathbf{u} \cdot d\mathbf{s})}{\Delta S} = \lim_{\Delta S \to 0} \frac{\mathscr{S}(u_x\, dx + u_y\, dy + u_z\, dz)}{\Delta S}.$$

Considering a small mesh about a point $P(\xi, \eta, \zeta)$ we have, for each point $M(x, y, z)$ on its boundary Γ (Fig. 1.21a),

$$(u_x)_M \cong (u_x)_P + \left(\frac{\partial u_x}{\partial x}\right)_P (x - \xi) + \left(\frac{\partial u_x}{\partial y}\right)_P (y - \eta) + \left(\frac{\partial u_x}{\partial z}\right)_P (z - \zeta), \quad \text{etc.}$$

---

* A rule well known from the study of magnetic fields.

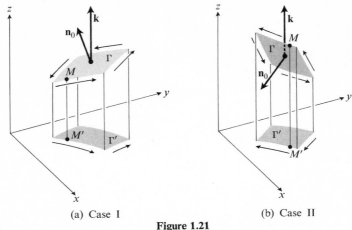

(a) Case I   (b) Case II

Figure 1.21

We shall need integrals like

$$\oint_\Gamma dx, \quad \oint_\Gamma x\,dx, \quad \oint_\Gamma y\,dx, \quad \oint_\Gamma z\,dx,$$

and similar ones. These integrals can be evaluated by projecting our mesh on the coordinate planes.

Suppose that we want to obtain the integrals of the type $\mathscr{J}_\Gamma f(x, y)\,dx$ and $\mathscr{J}_\Gamma f(x, y)\,dy$. Since the points M and M' (see Fig. 1.21) have the same x and y, these integrals reduce to $\mathscr{J}_{\Gamma'} f(x, y)\,dx$ and $\mathscr{J}_{\Gamma'} f(x, y)\,dy$ *except for the sign** which depends on the orientation of the mesh:

$$\oint_\Gamma f(x, y)\,dx = \pm \oint_{\Gamma'} f(x, y)\,dx, \quad \text{etc.}$$

The plus sign is for Case I (Fig. 1.21a), where the point M' describes Γ' in counterclockwise direction, the minus sign is for Case II (Fig. 1.21b), with M' going clockwise.†

In particular, note that

$$\oint_{\Gamma'} dx = \oint_{\Gamma'} x\,dx = 0$$

while

$$\oint_\Gamma y\,dx = \pm \oint_{\Gamma'} y\,dx = \mp \Delta S',$$

where $\Delta S'$ is the area bounded by Γ', i.e., the area of the projection of the mesh

---

* The symbol $\mathscr{J}_{\Gamma'}$ *by itself* is meant to indicate counterclockwise integration (see the footnote on p. 20).

† The motion of M' cannot be chosen at will because it is determined by the motion of M in the *positive direction of circulation* around the mesh.

on the xy-plane. Since the mesh is small, we have (Fig. 1.21)

$$\Delta S' \cong \Delta S \cos (\mathbf{n}_0, \mathbf{k}) \quad \text{in Case I,} \quad \Delta S' \cong -\Delta S \cos (\mathbf{n}_0, \mathbf{k}) \quad \text{in Case II,}$$

(where $\mathbf{n}_0$ is the unit normal to ΔS). In either case,

$$\oint_\Gamma y \, dx = -\Delta S \cos (\mathbf{n}_0, \mathbf{k}).$$

Similarly, we can deduce

$$\oint_\Gamma x \, dy = +\Delta S \cos (\mathbf{n}_0, \mathbf{k})$$

(this integral is also needed). Other integrals are evaluated in an analogous fashion. In particular, $\oint_\Gamma z \, dx$ and $\oint_\Gamma x \, dz$ require projection on the xz-plane, and so on. The net result of this calculation reads

$$\oint_\Gamma (\mathbf{u} \cdot d\mathbf{s}) \cong \Delta S \left[\left(\frac{\partial u_z}{\partial y} - \frac{\partial u_y}{\partial z} \right)_P \cos (\mathbf{n}_0, \mathbf{i}) + \left(\frac{\partial u_x}{\partial z} - \frac{\partial u_z}{\partial x} \right)_P \cos (\mathbf{n}_0, \mathbf{j}) \right.$$
$$\left. + \left(\frac{\partial u_y}{\partial x} - \frac{\partial u_x}{\partial y} \right)_P \cos (\mathbf{n}_0, \mathbf{k}) \right].$$

Introducing the curl of a vector in space (which is now a *vector*, in distinction to the plane case) by means of the relation

$$\lim_{\Delta S \to 0} \frac{\oint (\mathbf{u} \cdot d\mathbf{s})}{\Delta S} = (\text{curl } \mathbf{u} \cdot \mathbf{n}_0),$$

we have the result

$$\text{curl } \mathbf{u} = \left(\frac{\partial u_z}{\partial y} - \frac{\partial u_y}{\partial z} \right) \mathbf{i} + \left(\frac{\partial u_x}{\partial z} - \frac{\partial u_z}{\partial x} \right) \mathbf{j} + \left(\frac{\partial u_y}{\partial x} - \frac{\partial u_x}{\partial y} \right) \mathbf{k},$$

which also gives rise to the statement that circulation of $\mathbf{u}$ around an infinitesimal oriented area described by $d\mathbf{S}$ is equal to $(\text{curl } \mathbf{u} \cdot d\mathbf{S})$. Thus Stokes' theorem can now be written in the compact form:*

$$\oint_C (\mathbf{u} \cdot d\mathbf{s}) = \iint_S (\text{curl } \mathbf{u} \cdot d\mathbf{S}).$$

As in the case of vectors in a plane, the vector fields satisfying div $\mathbf{u} = 0$ are called solenoidal and those satisfying curl $\mathbf{u} = 0$ are called irrotational. The concept of irrotational field is closely related to the concept of conservative field ($\mathbf{u} = \text{grad } \varphi$) but these two fields should not be identified because of topological complications. In particular, if a field is irrotational in a domain D, *it does not*

---

* The shape of the area element is irrelevant; because of this we can identify dS_x in $d\mathbf{S} = dS_x\mathbf{i} + dS_y\mathbf{j} + dS_z\mathbf{k}$ with $dy \, dz$, etc.

follow that its circulation about an arbitrary simple closed curve in D is zero. The point is that we may not be able to invoke Stokes' theorem because we may not be able to construct a suitable spanning surface S which would lie inside D.

Example. Consider a tightly wound coil of current-carrying wire in the shape of a torus. The **B**-field inside the torus is irrotational; indeed, curl **B** satisfies the equation*

$$\text{curl } \mathbf{B} = \mu_0 \mathbf{J} + \epsilon_0 \mu_0 \frac{\partial \mathbf{E}}{\partial t} \quad \text{(MKSA units)}$$

and there is no current density **J** and no displacement current in the interior of the torus; we assume a dc-situation. However, the **B**-field at the center of each turn of the coil is known to be $\mathbf{B} = \mu_0 n I$ yielding a circulation along the central circle C of the torus:

$$\oint_C (\mathbf{B} \cdot d\mathbf{s}) = \mu_0 n I \cdot 2\pi R \neq 0.$$

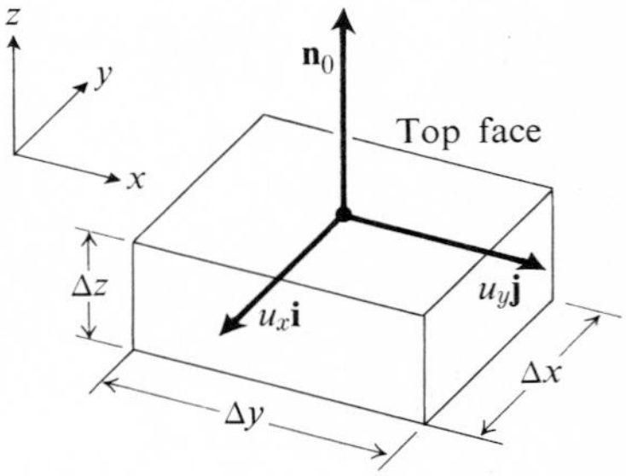

Figure 1.22

It is easy to see that any surface spanning C must necessarily extend outside the torus and cut through the windings where curl $\mathbf{B} \neq 0$.

Since the quantities div **u** and curl **u** in a plane have been defined as *area derivatives* (p. 26) and since div **u** in space has been defined as a *volume derivative* (p. 27), it may be conjectured that curl **u** in space is also reducible to a volume derivative. This is in fact true and the formula reads

$$\text{curl } \mathbf{u} = \lim_{\Delta V \to 0} \frac{\oiint [d\mathbf{S} \times \mathbf{u}]}{\Delta V},$$

where the surface integral is over the boundary enclosing the volume ΔV. We shall sketch the proof of this relation by considering ΔV in the form of a rectangular parallelepiped as shown in Fig. 1.22. The contributions to $\oiint [d\mathbf{S} \times \mathbf{u}]$ from the top face involve only $u_x \mathbf{i}$ and $u_y \mathbf{j}$ and yield, in the usual notation,

$$\iint_{\text{Top face}} [d\mathbf{S} \times \mathbf{u}] \cong \Delta x \, \Delta y \left\{ \left(u_x + \frac{\partial u_x}{\partial z} \frac{\Delta z}{2} \right)_P \mathbf{j} - \left(u_y + \frac{\partial u_y}{\partial z} \frac{\Delta z}{2} \right)_P \mathbf{i} \right\},$$

where P is the center of the parallelepiped. The bottom face will have $d\mathbf{S}$ with the direction reversed and

$$\iint_{\substack{\text{Bottom} \\ \text{face}}} [d\mathbf{S} \times \mathbf{u}] \cong -\Delta x \, \Delta y \left\{ \left(u_x - \frac{\partial u_x}{\partial z} \frac{\Delta z}{2} \right)_P \mathbf{j} - \left(u_y + \frac{\partial u_y}{\partial z} \frac{\Delta z}{2} \right)_P \mathbf{i} \right\}.$$

---

* One of Maxwell's equations; see, e.g., Reitz and Milford, pp. 296–297.

Adding these, we obtain

$$\left\{\left(\frac{\partial u_x}{\partial z}\right)_P \mathbf{j} - \left(\frac{\partial u_y}{\partial z}\right)_P \cdot \mathbf{i}\right\} \Delta x\, \Delta y\, \Delta z.$$

Contributions from the other four faces are treated similarly, establishing the result.

Remark. The gradient of a scalar field φ can also be represented as a volume derivative, namely

$$\operatorname{grad} \varphi = \lim_{\Delta V \to 0} \frac{\oiint \varphi d\mathbf{S}}{\Delta V}.$$

We shall conclude this section by mentioning some quantities obtained from the repeated operations involving gradient, divergence, and curl. First of all observe the identity

$$\operatorname{curl} \operatorname{grad} \varphi \equiv 0$$

representing the statement that a conservative field is always irrotational (provided, of course, that the second-order partials of φ are continuous, as mentioned on p. 23). The second operation of similar type yields the definition of the *Laplace differential operator* ∇^2 or simply the Laplacian,*

$$\nabla^2 \varphi \equiv \operatorname{div} \operatorname{grad} \varphi,$$

with the well-known expression in cartesian coordinates

$$\nabla^2 \varphi = \frac{\partial^2 \varphi}{\partial x^2} + \frac{\partial^2 \varphi}{\partial y^2} + \frac{\partial^2 \varphi}{\partial z^2}.$$

Both of these operations have their counterparts for plane vectors. There are also two operations which are only possible for vectors in space: $\operatorname{div} \operatorname{curl} \mathbf{u}$ and $\operatorname{curl} \operatorname{curl} \mathbf{u}$. Straightforward calculation in cartesian coordinates yields $\operatorname{div} \operatorname{curl} \mathbf{u} \equiv 0$. A more sophisticated argument of some interest is to take a closed surface S in a domain D where $\operatorname{curl} \mathbf{u}$ is defined (and its components have continuous partials). Split S into two parts, S_1 and S_2, by a curve C, as illustrated in Fig. 1.23. By Stokes' theorem,

$$\oint_C (\mathbf{u} \cdot d\mathbf{s}) = \iint_{S_1} (\operatorname{curl} \mathbf{u} \cdot d\mathbf{S}_1) = -\iint_{S_2} (\operatorname{curl} \mathbf{u} \cdot d\mathbf{S}_2);$$

---

* The symbol ∇^2 is related to the so-called "nabla" or "del" operator

$$\nabla \equiv \mathbf{i} \frac{\partial}{\partial x} + \mathbf{j} \frac{\partial}{\partial y} + \mathbf{k} \frac{\partial}{\partial z}$$

capable of representing gradient, divergence, and curl by means of the notations $\operatorname{grad} \varphi \equiv \nabla \varphi$, $\operatorname{div} \mathbf{u} \equiv (\nabla \cdot \mathbf{u})$, and $\operatorname{curl} \mathbf{u} \equiv [\nabla \times \mathbf{u}]$, which are sometimes quite handy.

the minus sign arises from the "wrong" orientation of S_2 with respect to C. Consequently,

$$\iint\limits_{S_1} (\text{curl } \mathbf{u} \cdot d\mathbf{S}_1) + \iint\limits_{S_2} (\text{curl } \mathbf{u} \cdot d\mathbf{S}_2) = \oiint\limits_{S} (\text{curl } \mathbf{u} \cdot d\mathbf{S}) = 0$$

for *any* closed surface in D. Applying the divergence theorem, we obtain,

$$\iiint\limits_{V} \text{div curl } \mathbf{u} \cdot dV = 0.$$

Then, since this is true for an arbitrary volume V in D, it follows that div curl $\mathbf{u} = 0$.

Regarding the operation curl curl $\mathbf{u}$, we can derive the following expression for the cartesian coordinates:

$$\text{curl curl } \mathbf{u} = \text{grad div } \mathbf{u} - \nabla^2 \mathbf{u},$$

where the symbol $\nabla^2 \mathbf{u}$ stands for the operation $\nabla^2 u_x \mathbf{i} + \nabla^2 u_y \mathbf{j} + \nabla^2 u_z \mathbf{k}$. This formula, however, is *not valid* for other coordinate systems.*

Exercise. Verify the above formula using the expressions for divergence, gradient, and curl in cartesian coordinates.

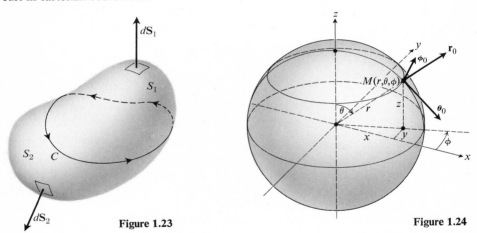

Figure 1.23   Figure 1.24

1.9 CURVILINEAR COORDINATES

Sometimes it is more convenient to use coordinate systems other than cartesian. In general, a point in space can be described by three parameters which we will denote by l, m, n. A well-known example is given by *spherical* coordinates r, θ, ϕ, as shown in Fig. 1.24, along with the usual cartesian coordinates x, y, z

---

* Of course, it is possible to *define* the operation $\nabla^2 \mathbf{u}$ by (grad div $\mathbf{u} - $ curl curl $\mathbf{u}$) in any coordinate system, but this is not done since $\nabla^2 \mathbf{u}$ does not reduce to the operation "div grad" applied to components of $\mathbf{u}$.

which are related to r, θ, ϕ by

$$x = r \sin \theta \cos \phi, \qquad y = r \sin \theta \sin \phi, \qquad z = r \cos \theta.$$

In general, x, y, z can be thought as being functions of l, m, n:

$$x = x(l, m, n), \qquad y = y(l, m, n), \qquad z = z(l, m, n).$$

We shall assume that at least within some domain D in space, these functions have continuous derivatives and can also be solved for l, m, n:

$$l = l(x, y, z),$$

$$m = m(x, y, z),$$

$$n = n(x, y, z).$$

Observe that this implies that the Jacobian

$$J = \frac{\partial(x, y, z)}{\partial(l, m, n)}$$

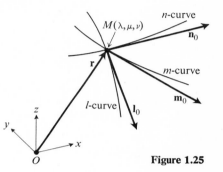

Figure 1.25

does not vanish.* Let us now choose a particular point M with cartesian coordinates (ξ, η, ζ); it can also be denoted as $M(\lambda, \mu, \nu)$, in terms of the coordinates l, m, n. If we keep $m = \mu = $ const and $n = \nu = $ const and change l, then we obtain a (smooth) curve passing through M which may be called the *l-curve*. Similarly, we can define *m-curve* and *n-curve*. This is shown in Fig. 1.25. Furthermore, we can introduce unit vectors l_0, m_0, and n_0 along the tangents to these curves (pointed in the direction of increasing l, m, n). This establishes a *local system of axes*. For convenience, the labels l, m, n are chosen so that (l_0, m_0, n_0) form a right-handed triple.

Our local systems possess, in general, the following features which distinguish them from the system formed by cartesian unit vectors $\mathbf{i}$, $\mathbf{j}$, and $\mathbf{k}$.

1. The axes may not be orthogonal; moreover, the angles between the axes may change from one point to another.

2. The orientation of l_0, m_0, n_0 (with respect to $\mathbf{i}, \mathbf{j}, \mathbf{k}$) may change from one point to another, even if the angles between the axes remain the same.

3. The physical meaning of parameters l, m, n may not be the length, and dl, dm, dn need not be identical with the elements ds of arc in the respective directions.

Let us investigate properties (1), (2), and (3). We can always think of point M as being defined by a *position vector* $\mathbf{r} = x\mathbf{i} + y\mathbf{j} + z\mathbf{k}$. Treating x, y, z as

---

* See, e.g., Kaplan, pp. 31 *et seq.*

functions of l, m, n we can write

$$\mathbf{r} = x(l, m, n)\mathbf{i} + y(l, m, n)\mathbf{j} + z(l, m, n)\mathbf{k}.$$

Changing $\mathbf{r}$ by $d\mathbf{r}$ amounts to changing x, y, z by dx, dy, dz which is, in turn, caused by changing l, m, n by dl, dm, dn. We have the following general relations:

$$dx = \frac{\partial x}{\partial l}\, dl + \frac{\partial x}{\partial m}\, dm + \frac{\partial x}{\partial n}\, dn,$$

$$dy = \frac{\partial y}{\partial l}\, dl + \frac{\partial y}{\partial m}\, dm + \frac{\partial y}{\partial n}\, dn,$$

$$dz = \frac{\partial z}{\partial l}\, dl + \frac{\partial z}{\partial m}\, dm + \frac{\partial z}{\partial n}\, dn.$$

If we move along the l-curve, then $dm = dn = 0$, and $d\mathbf{r}$ becomes*

$$(d\mathbf{r})_{m,n} = (dx \cdot \mathbf{i} + dy \cdot \mathbf{j} + dz \cdot \mathbf{k})_{m,n} = \left(\frac{\partial x}{\partial l}\mathbf{i} + \frac{\partial y}{\partial l}\mathbf{j} + \frac{\partial z}{\partial l}\mathbf{k}\right) dl.$$

This defines the derivative of $\mathbf{r}$ with respect to the parameter l:

$$\frac{\partial \mathbf{r}}{\partial l} \equiv \frac{(d\mathbf{r})_{m,n}}{dl} = \frac{\partial x}{\partial l}\mathbf{i} + \frac{\partial y}{\partial l}\mathbf{j} + \frac{\partial z}{\partial l}\mathbf{k}.$$

By its very meaning, $\partial \mathbf{r}/\partial l$ is a vector along the direction of $\mathbf{l}_0$. Therefore, $\mathbf{l}_0$ can be expressed as

$$\mathbf{l}_0 = \frac{\partial \mathbf{r}/\partial l}{|\partial \mathbf{r}/\partial l|} = \frac{(\partial x/\partial l)\mathbf{i} + (\partial y/\partial l)\mathbf{j} + (\partial z/\partial l)\mathbf{k}}{\sqrt{(\partial x/\partial l)^2 + (\partial y/\partial l)^2 + (\partial z/\partial l)^2}}.$$

The quantity

$$h_l = \sqrt{\left(\frac{\partial x}{\partial l}\right)^2 + \left(\frac{\partial y}{\partial l}\right)^2 + \left(\frac{\partial z}{\partial l}\right)^2}$$

has a simple geometric interpretation: The length of elementary arc ds produced when only l changes is given by $ds = |(d\mathbf{r})_{m,n}| = h_l\, dl$.

In a similar fashion we deduce

$$\mathbf{m}_0 = \frac{(\partial x/\partial m)\mathbf{i} + (\partial y/\partial m)\mathbf{j} + (\partial z/\partial m)\mathbf{k}}{h_m}, \quad h_m = \sqrt{\left(\frac{\partial x}{\partial m}\right)^2 + \left(\frac{\partial y}{\partial m}\right)^2 + \left(\frac{\partial z}{\partial m}\right)^2},$$

$$\mathbf{n}_0 = \frac{(\partial x/\partial n)\mathbf{i} + (\partial y/\partial n)\mathbf{j} + (\partial z/\partial n)\mathbf{k}}{h_n}, \quad h_n = \sqrt{\left(\frac{\partial x}{\partial n}\right)^2 + \left(\frac{\partial y}{\partial n}\right)^2 + \left(\frac{\partial z}{\partial n}\right)^2}.$$

---

* We use the notation familiar from thermodynamics: $(d\mathbf{r})_{m,n}$ means such $d\mathbf{r}$ where m and n are kept constant.

Suppose now that the triple $\mathbf{l}_0$, $\mathbf{m}_0$, $\mathbf{n}_0$ is an *orthogonal triple*. Then we must have the relations

$$\frac{\partial x}{\partial l}\frac{\partial x}{\partial m} + \frac{\partial y}{\partial l}\frac{\partial y}{\partial m} + \frac{\partial z}{\partial l}\frac{\partial z}{\partial m} = 0, \quad \text{etc.}$$

These relations are satisfied for most coordinate systems employed in physics. In particular, this is true for spherical and cylindrical coordinate systems, as can be easily verified.

This analysis clarifies feature (1) of local systems of axes. Regarding the orientation of local axes, note that it does indeed vary from point to point for spherical and cylindrical coordinate systems. In fact, this is the characteristic property of *curvilinear* coordinate systems, as opposed to cartesian ones. Feature (3) is also illustrated by spherical and cylindrical coordinates where some of the parameters l, m, n represent angles rather than lengths. As a general rule, the elementary displacement $d\mathbf{r}$ decomposed along the local system of axes will read

$$d\mathbf{r} = \frac{\partial \mathbf{r}}{\partial l}dl + \frac{\partial \mathbf{r}}{\partial m}dm + \frac{\partial \mathbf{r}}{\partial n}dn = h_l\, dl \cdot \mathbf{l}_0 + h_m\, dm \cdot \mathbf{m}_0 + h_n\, dn \cdot \mathbf{n}_0.$$

Let us assume that the local system is orthogonal;* then the element of arc is given by a simple formula,

$$ds = |d\mathbf{r}| = \sqrt{h_l^2\, dl^2 + h_m^2\, dm^2 + h_n^2\, dn^2}.$$

For instance, for spherical coordinates, $h_r = 1$, $h_\theta = r$, $h_\phi = r\sin\theta$, and

$$ds = \sqrt{dr^2 + r^2\, d\theta^2 + r^2 \sin^2\theta\, d\phi^2}.$$

We shall conclude our survey of curvilinear coordinates by the derivation of formulas for common differential operations in vector calculus. In order to express grad φ in terms of new axes and new variables, we could start with

$$\text{grad } \varphi = \frac{\partial \varphi}{\partial x}\mathbf{i} + \frac{\partial \varphi}{\partial y}\mathbf{j} + \frac{\partial \varphi}{\partial z}\mathbf{k},$$

then use

$$\frac{\partial \varphi}{\partial x} = \frac{\partial \varphi}{\partial l}\frac{\partial l}{\partial x} + \frac{\partial \varphi}{\partial m}\frac{\partial m}{\partial x} + \frac{\partial \varphi}{\partial n}\frac{\partial n}{\partial x} \quad \text{etc.}$$

and also express $\mathbf{i}, \mathbf{j}, \mathbf{k}$ in terms of $\mathbf{l}_0, \mathbf{m}_0, \mathbf{n}_0$. A quicker way is to utilize the statement

$$(\text{grad } \varphi \cdot d\mathbf{r}) \equiv d\varphi \equiv \frac{\partial \varphi}{\partial l}dl + \frac{\partial \varphi}{\partial m}dm + \frac{\partial \varphi}{\partial n}dn$$

---

* The associated coordinates are then called orthogonal coordinates.

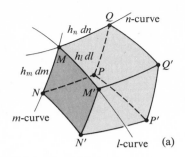

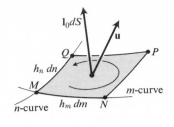

(a)   (b)   **Figure 1.26**

and rewrite it in the form

$$(\text{grad } \varphi \cdot d\mathbf{r}) = \left(\frac{1}{h_l}\frac{\partial\varphi}{\partial l}\right) h_l \, dl + \left(\frac{1}{h_m}\frac{\partial\varphi}{\partial m}\right) h_m \, dm + \left(\frac{1}{h_n}\frac{\partial\varphi}{\partial n}\right) h_n \, dn$$

from which it follows immediately* that

$$\text{grad } \varphi = \frac{1}{h_l}\frac{\partial\varphi}{\partial l}\mathbf{l}_0 + \frac{1}{h_m}\frac{\partial\varphi}{\partial m}\mathbf{m}_0 + \frac{1}{h_n}\frac{\partial\varphi}{\partial n}\mathbf{n}_0.$$

The calculation of divergence can be also carried out starting from the general definition

$$\text{div } \mathbf{u} = \lim_{\Delta V \to 0} \frac{\oiint(\mathbf{u}\cdot d\mathbf{s})}{\Delta V}.$$

Without loss of generality, ΔV can be taken as a volume element with the sides along the l-, m-, and n-curves (Fig. 1.26a). In general, the flux through an elementary area oriented in the $\mathbf{l}_0$-direction is given by

$$u_l \cdot h_m \, dm \cdot h_n \, dn.$$

As we subtract the fluxes through the areas $M'N'P'Q'$ and $MNPQ$ we must not forget that not only u_l, but also h_m and h_n, are functions of l, m, and n.† By an argument similar to that on pp. 27–28 (we give here a simplified version), we deduce that the net outward flux through these two faces is

$$\frac{\partial}{\partial l}(u_l h_m h_n) \, dl \, dm \, dn.$$

Adding the analogous contributions from the other four faces and dividing by the volume of our volume element (which is $h_l \, dl \, h_m \, dm \, h_n \, dn$), we obtain immediately

$$\text{div } \mathbf{u} = \frac{1}{h_l h_m h_n}\left\{\frac{\partial}{\partial l}(u_l h_m h_n) + \frac{\partial}{\partial m}(u_m h_n h_l) + \frac{\partial}{\partial n}(u_n h_l h_m)\right\}.$$

---

* Recall that $d\mathbf{r}$ is arbitrary; therefore, by setting $dm = dn = 0$ we obtain $(\text{grad }\varphi)_l = (1/h_l)(\partial\varphi/\partial l)$, etc. We tacitly assume that the coordinates are orthogonal.

† In cartesian coordinates $h_l = h_m = h_n = 1$.

Example. In spherical coordinates we identify l, m, n with r, θ, ϕ, in that order. Then $h_l = h_r = 1$, $h_m = h_\theta = r$, $h_n = h_\phi = r \sin \theta$, and

$$\operatorname{div} \mathbf{u} = \frac{1}{r^2 \sin \theta} \left\{ \frac{\partial}{\partial r} (r^2 \sin \theta\, u_r) + \frac{\partial}{\partial \theta} (r \sin \theta\, u_\theta) + \frac{\partial}{\partial \phi} (r u_\phi) \right\}.$$

This may be simplified and, if desirable, ultimately reduced to

$$\operatorname{div} \mathbf{u} = \frac{\partial u_r}{\partial r} + \frac{2}{r} u_r + \frac{1}{r} \frac{\partial u_\theta}{\partial \theta} + \frac{\cot \theta}{r} u_\theta + \frac{1}{r \sin \theta} \frac{\partial u_\phi}{\partial \phi}.$$

The curl of $\mathbf{u}$ can be deduced from the circulation of $\mathbf{u}$ around the faces of the very same volume element. For instance, the face $MNPQ$ yields (Fig. 1.26b)

$$\int_N^P (\mathbf{u} \cdot d\mathbf{s}) + \int_Q^M (\mathbf{u} \cdot d\mathbf{s}) = (u_n h_n\, dn)_{NP} - (u_n h_n\, dn)_{MQ} = \frac{\partial}{\partial m} (u_n h_n)\, dn\, dm,$$

$$\int_P^Q (\mathbf{u} \cdot d\mathbf{s}) + \int_M^N (\mathbf{u} \cdot d\mathbf{s}) = -(u_m h_m\, dm)_{PQ} + (u_m h_m\, dm)_{MN}$$

$$= -\frac{\partial}{\partial n} (u_m h_m)\, dm\, dn,$$

which is combined to form

$$(\operatorname{curl} \mathbf{u})_l\, h_m\, dm\, h_n\, dn = \left\{ \frac{\partial}{\partial m} (u_n h_n) - \frac{\partial}{\partial n} (u_m h_m) \right\} dm\, dn.$$

This determines the l-component of curl $\mathbf{u}$. The complete formula reads

$$\operatorname{curl} \mathbf{u} = \frac{1}{h_m h_n} \left\{ \frac{\partial}{\partial m} (u_n h_n) - \frac{\partial}{\partial n} (u_m h_m) \right\} \mathbf{l}_0$$

$$+ \frac{1}{h_n h_l} \left\{ \frac{\partial}{\partial n} (u_l h_l) - \frac{\partial}{\partial l} (u_n h_n) \right\} \mathbf{m}_0$$

$$+ \frac{1}{h_l h_m} \left\{ \frac{\partial}{\partial l} (u_m h_m) - \frac{\partial}{\partial m} (u_l h_l) \right\} \mathbf{n}_0.$$

Finally, the expression for the Laplacian ∇^2 is obtained by combining the formulas for gradient and divergence:

$$\nabla^2 \varphi = \operatorname{div} \operatorname{grad} \mathbf{u} = \frac{1}{h_l h_m h_n} \left\{ \frac{\partial}{\partial l} \left(\frac{h_m h_n}{h_l} \frac{\partial \varphi}{\partial l} \right) + \frac{\partial}{\partial m} \left(\frac{h_n h_l}{h_m} \frac{\partial \varphi}{\partial m} \right) + \frac{\partial}{\partial n} \left(\frac{h_l h_m}{h_n} \frac{\partial \varphi}{\partial n} \right) \right\}.$$

For instance, in the spherical system this reads (after trivial simplification)

$$\nabla^2 \varphi = \frac{1}{r^2} \frac{\partial}{\partial r} \left(r^2 \frac{\partial \varphi}{\partial r} \right) + \frac{1}{r^2 \sin \theta} \frac{\partial}{\partial \theta} \left(\sin \theta \frac{\partial \varphi}{\partial \theta} \right) + \frac{1}{r^2 \sin^2 \theta} \frac{\partial^2 \varphi}{\partial \phi^2}.$$

BIBLIOGRAPHY

APOSTOL, T. M., *Mathematical Analysis*, Reading, Mass.: Addison-Wesley Publishing Co., 1957.

GOLDSTEIN, H., *Classical Mechanics*, Reading, Mass.: Addison-Wesley Publishing Co., 1959.

KAPLAN, W., *Advanced Calculus*, Reading, Mass.: Addison-Wesley Publishing Co., 1957.

KELLOGG, O. D., *Foundation of Potential Theory*, Berlin: Springer Verlag Ohg., 1929.

TAYLOR, A. E., *Advanced Calculus*, Boston: Ginn & Company, 1955.

REITZ, J. R. and F. J. MILFORD, *Foundations of Electromagnetic Theory*, Reading, Mass.: Addison-Wesley Publishing Co., 1960.

PROBLEMS

1. Let two vectors in a plane, u_1 and u_2, be defined by the polar coordinates of their tips: (θ_1, r_1) and (θ_2, r_2). If $u_3 = u_1 + u_2$ is defined by (θ_3, r_3), show how θ_3 and r_3 are related to θ_1, θ_2, r_1, and r_2.

2. A triple vector product of three vectors is defined by the expression $[u \times [v \times w]]$. Show that for any three vectors the following identity holds:

$$[u \times [v \times w]] + [v \times [w \times u]] + [w \times [u \times v]] = 0.$$

Hint: Use the vector identity

$$[a \times [b \times c]] = b(a \cdot c) - c(a \cdot b).$$

The above formula, known as the *Jacobi identity*, appears in a variety of contexts in physics and mathematics.

3. Consider the following three vectors in space given by their coordinates

$$u(\tfrac{6}{7}, -\tfrac{3}{7}, \tfrac{2}{7}), \qquad v(\tfrac{2}{7}, \tfrac{6}{7}, \tfrac{3}{7}), \qquad w(-\tfrac{3}{7}, -\tfrac{2}{7}, \tfrac{6}{7}).$$

a) Verify that these vectors are unit vectors, orthogonal to each other, and form a right-handed triple, if ordered as above.

b) Construct the rotation matrix transforming the old components of a vector (namely those with respect to i, j, k) to the new ones (with respect to u, v, w).

c) Evaluate, by vector-matrix multiplication, the new coordinates of the vectors $a(0, 3, 2)$, $b(-1, 4, -3)$, and $c(2, -2, -2)$. Can you give a geometrical interpretation of the peculiar behavior of vector c?

4. a) Show that the triple product (p. 3) of vectors $u(u_1, u_2, u_3)$, $v(v_1, v_2, v_3)$, and $w(w_1, w_2, w_3)$ can be expressed by the determinant

$$\det \begin{vmatrix} u_1 & v_1 & w_1 \\ u_2 & v_2 & w_2 \\ u_3 & v_3 & w_3 \end{vmatrix} = ([u \times v] \cdot w).$$

b) Using this, prove that if a 3×3 matrix is orthogonal, then its determinant can have only two values, either $+1$ or -1.

c) Consider the matrices

$$
A = \begin{vmatrix} 1 & 0 & 0 \\ 0 & 1 & 0 \\ 0 & 0 & -1 \end{vmatrix}, \quad
B = \begin{vmatrix} \sqrt{3}/2 & \frac{1}{2} & 0 \\ \frac{1}{2} & -\sqrt{3}/2 & 0 \\ 0 & 0 & -1 \end{vmatrix},
$$

$$
C = \begin{vmatrix} -1 & 0 & 0 \\ 0 & -1 & 0 \\ 0 & 0 & 1 \end{vmatrix}, \quad
D = \begin{vmatrix} 2\sqrt{3}/5 & -3\sqrt{3}/10 & \frac{1}{2} \\ \frac{2}{5} & -\frac{3}{10} & \sqrt{3}/2 \\ \frac{3}{5} & \frac{4}{5} & 0 \end{vmatrix},
$$

and indicate which ones represent rotations. Also, describe the geometrical meaning of others.

5. Compare, in general, the ijth matrix element of AB with that of BA, for 3×3 matrices A and B. Construct two noncommuting 3×3 matrices of your choice, i.e., such that $AB \neq BA$.

6. According to the discussion on p. 4, the matrix

$$
A = \begin{vmatrix} \cos \theta & \sin \theta \\ -\sin \theta & \cos \theta \end{vmatrix}
$$

represents a rotation of axes in plane. Show that

$$
A^2 = AA = \begin{vmatrix} \cos 2\theta & \sin 2\theta \\ -\sin 2\theta & \cos 2\theta \end{vmatrix} \quad \text{and} \quad A^3 = AAA = \begin{vmatrix} \cos 3\theta & \sin 3\theta \\ -\sin 3\theta & \cos 3\theta \end{vmatrix}
$$

and give the geometrical interpretation of this result.

7. Show that the matrix

$$
B = \begin{vmatrix} \cos \phi & \sin \phi \\ \sin \phi & -\cos \phi \end{vmatrix}
$$

does not represent a rotation of axes. Give a geometrical interpretation of matrix B. [*Hint:* Draw the old and the new coordinate axes, as well as the straight line $y = x \tan (\phi/2)$.]

8. Find the inverses of the following matrices by solving the equations $B_k A_k = I$ or otherwise:

$$A_1 = \begin{bmatrix} 2 & -1 & 0 \\ 1 & 1 & 1 \\ -3 & 0 & 4 \end{bmatrix}, \quad A_2 = \begin{bmatrix} \frac{1}{3} & \frac{2}{3} & \frac{2}{3} \\ 0 & -1/\sqrt{2} & 1/\sqrt{2} \\ 2\sqrt{2}/3 & -\sqrt{2}/6 & -\sqrt{2}/6 \end{bmatrix},$$

$$A_3 = \begin{bmatrix} -\frac{1}{3} & -\frac{2}{3} & \frac{2}{3} \\ -\frac{2}{3} & \frac{2}{3} & \frac{1}{3} \\ \frac{2}{3} & \frac{1}{3} & \frac{2}{3} \end{bmatrix}, \quad A_4 = \begin{bmatrix} 1 & 3 & 2 \\ 1 & -1 & 0 \\ 2 & 0 & 1 \end{bmatrix},$$

Comment on the cases A_2, A_3, and A_4.

9. Let (x', y') be the coordinates of a point in a skew cartesian system in plane. Let the x'- and y'-axes make angles α and β, respectively, with the x-axis (Fig. 1.27). Show that the equation of a circle with radius R and the center at the origin reads

$$x'^2 + y'^2 + 2x'y' \cos(\beta - \alpha) = R^2.$$

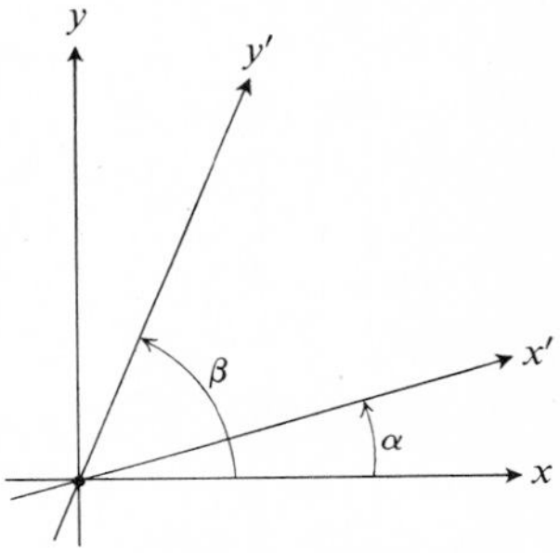

10. Show that the vector $v = 2i + j - 6k$ cannot be expressed as a linear combination of the vectors

$$u_1 = i + j + 2k, \quad u_2 = 3i - j, \quad u_3 = 2i + k.$$

Figure 1.27

Show that the vector $w = -2j - 3k$ can be expressed in this fashion, in more than one way. Give the algebraic explanation of these facts. Also give a geometrical interpretation.

11. Evaluate the following integrals around the circle $x^2 + y^2 = 1$; use Green's theorem if it is convenient:

   a) $\oint (u \cdot ds)$, where $u = (2y^2 - 3x^2 y)i + (4xy - x^3)j$,
   b) $\oint (2x^2 - y^3) \, dx + (x^3 + y^3) \, dy$,
   c) $\oint (v \cdot dn)$, where $v = (x^2 + y^2)i - 2xyj$ (dn is defined on p. 24).

12. Let $F(x, y) = x^2 - y^2$. Evaluate

   a) $\int_{(0,0)}^{(2,8)} (\text{grad } F \cdot ds)$ along the curve $y = x^3$,

   b) $\oint \dfrac{\partial F}{\partial n} \, ds$ around the circle $x^2 + y^2 = 1$. Here $\partial F/\partial n$ is the directional derivative of F along the outer normal and $ds = |ds|$.

13. Show that the vector field $u = yzi + zxj + xyk$ is both irrotational and solenoidal. Find φ such that grad $\varphi = u$. Can you find a vector field A such that curl $A = u$?

14. Prove the following identities for scalar fields f, φ and vector fields u, v in space:

   a) grad $(f\varphi) = f \text{grad } \varphi + \varphi \text{ grad } f$,
   b) curl $(fu) = f \text{curl } u + [\text{grad } f \times u]$,
   c) div $[u \times v] = (v \cdot \text{curl } u) - (u \cdot \text{curl } v)$.

15. Using divergence and Stokes' theorems, if it is convenient, calculate the following integrals.

   a) $\oiint_S (\mathbf{u} \cdot d\mathbf{S})$, where $\mathbf{u} = x^3\mathbf{i} + y^3\mathbf{j} + z^3\mathbf{k}$ and S is the sphere of radius R about the origin,

   b) $\oiint_S (\mathbf{v} \cdot d\mathbf{S})$, where $\mathbf{v} = x^5\mathbf{i} + y^5\mathbf{j} + z^5\mathbf{k}$ and S is the sphere as in (a),

   c) $\oiint_S (x \, dy \, dz + y \, dz \, dx + z \, dx \, dy)$, where S is the sphere as in (a),

   d) $\oint_\Gamma (\mathbf{u} \cdot d\mathbf{s})$, where $\mathbf{u} = -3y\mathbf{i} + 3x\mathbf{j} + \mathbf{k}$ and Γ is the circle $x^2 + y^2 = 1$ lying in the plane $z = 2$.

16. A flat disk rotates about the axis normal to its plane and passing through its center. Show that the velocity vector $\mathbf{v}$ of any point on the disk satisfies the equation

$$\text{curl } \mathbf{v} = 2\boldsymbol{\omega},$$

where $\boldsymbol{\omega}$ is the angular velocity vector.

17. Consider a conducting medium with variable charge density $\rho(x, y, z)$ and variable current density $\mathbf{J}(x, y, z)$. Let V be an arbitrary volume within the medium bounded by a (piecewise smooth) closed surface S. Considering the total amount of charge inside V and the amount entering it per unit time through the surface S, deduce that

$$\frac{d}{dt} \iiint_V \rho(x, y, z) \, dV = - \oiint_S (\mathbf{J}(x, y, z) \cdot d\mathbf{S})$$

With the help of the divergence theorem, deduce the so-called equation of continuity

$$\text{div } \mathbf{J} + \frac{\partial \rho}{\partial t} = 0.$$

18. Using the techniques employed in Sections 1.7 and 1.8, outline the possible proofs of the following statements:

$$\text{grad } \varphi = \lim_{\Delta S \to 0} \frac{\oint \varphi d\mathbf{n}}{\Delta S} \quad \text{(in a plane)}, \qquad \text{grad } \varphi = \lim_{\Delta V \to 0} \frac{\oiint \varphi d\mathbf{S}}{\Delta V} \quad \text{(in space)}.$$

19. Evaluate the quantities h_r, h_θ, h_z (see p. 36) for the cylindrical coordinate system. Using appropriate formulas from Section 1.9, write the expressions for gradient, divergence, curl, and the Laplacian in cylindrical coordinates.

CHAPTER 2

FUNCTIONS OF A COMPLEX VARIABLE

2.1 COMPLEX NUMBERS

In the course of study of roots of algebraic equations and in particular the cubic equation, it has been found convenient to introduce the concept of a number whose square is equal to -1. By a well-established tradition, this number is denoted by i, and we write $i^2 = -1$ and $i = \sqrt{-1}$. If we allow i to be multiplied by real numbers, we obtain the so-called *imaginary numbers** of the form bi (where b is real). If the usual rules of multiplication are extended to imaginary numbers, then we must conclude that the products of imaginary numbers are real numbers; moreover, their squares are negative real numbers. For instance,

$$(3i)(-4i) = (3)(-4)i^2 = (-12)(-1) = 12,$$
$$(-5i)^2 = (-5)^2 i^2 = -25.$$

If imaginary numbers are adjoined to real numbers, we have a system within which we can perform multiplication and division (except by zero, of course). We say that such a system is *closed* under multiplication and division. However, our system is not closed under addition and subtraction.† To eliminate this deficiency, so-called *complex numbers* are introduced. These are numbers which are most often written in the form

$$a + bi \qquad (a, b = \text{real numbers})$$

and are assumed to obey appropriate algebraic rules. As will be shown below, the system of complex numbers is closed under addition, subtraction, multiplication, and division plus the "extraction of roots" operation. In short, it has all the desirable algebraic characteristics and represents an extension of the real number system. The study of complex numbers is invaluable for every physicist because the description of physical laws is much more complicated without them.

---

* Imaginary numbers are also called *pure imaginary numbers* to stress the distinction from the more general case of complex numbers. The name originated from the belief that imaginary numbers, as well as complex numbers, do not represent directly observable quantities in nature. While this point of view is now mostly abandoned, the original nomenclature still exists.

† The system is not closed under the operation of extraction of the square root either; for example, $\sqrt{i}$ is neither real nor (pure) imaginary.

2.2 BASIC ALGEBRA AND GEOMETRY OF COMPLEX NUMBERS

If complex numbers are written in the usual form $a + ib$ (or $a + bi$) then the usual algebraic operations with them are defined as follows.

1. Addition:

$$(a_1 + ib_1) + (a_2 + ib_2) = (a_1 + a_2) + i(b_1 + b_2).$$

2. Multiplication:

$$(a_1 + ib_1) \cdot (a_2 + ib_2) = (a_1 a_2 - b_1 b_2) + i(a_1 b_2 + a_2 b_1).$$

The second rule is easy to follow if we recognize that the expressions $a + ib$ are multiplied in the same manner as binomials, using the distributive and associative laws, and i^2 is replaced by -1.

Complex numbers of the form $a + i0$ are tacitly identified with real numbers since they obey the same algebraic rules and are generally indistinguishable from each other.* Complex numbers of the form $0 + ib$ are then (pure) imaginary numbers. It is customary to write simply $a + i0 = a$ and $0 + ib = ib$. Subtraction of complex numbers can be defined as *inverse addition* so that if

$$(a_1 + ib_1) - (a_2 + ib_2) = x + iy,$$

then

$$a_1 + ib_1 = (x + iy) + (a_2 + ib_2)$$

from which it follows that†

$$x = a_1 - a_2 \quad \text{and} \quad y = b_1 - b_2.$$

An alternative is to form the negative of a complex number,

$$-(a + ib) = (-1)(a + ib) = (-1 + i0)(a + ib) = -a - ib,$$

and reduce the subtraction to addition.

The rule for division can be similarly deduced by inverting the multiplication. A shortcut method is given by the following technique:

$$\frac{a + ib}{c + id} = \frac{a + ib}{c + id} \frac{c - id}{c - id} = \frac{(ac + bd) + i(bc - ad)}{c^2 + d^2}$$

$$= \frac{ac + bd}{c^2 + d^2} + i\frac{bc - ad}{c^2 + d^2} \quad (c^2 + d^2 \neq 0).$$

It is readily seen that the divisor can be any complex number except zero (namely the number $0 + i0$, which is unique and is written simply 0).

---

* In a more rigorous language, "the subset of complex numbers of the form $a + i0$ is *isomorphic* to the set of real numbers under the correspondence $a + i0 \leftrightarrow a$."

† It is tacitly postulated that $x_1 + iy_1 = x_2 + iy_2$ if and only if $x_1 = x_2$ and $y_1 = y_2$.

Remarks

1. The addition of complex numbers obeys the same rule as the addition of vectors in plane, provided a and b are identified with components of a vector. Note, however, that the multiplication of complex numbers differs from the formation of dot and cross products of vectors.

2. The use of the symbol i and the related binomial $a + ib$ is conventional, but not indispensable. It is possible to define a complex number as a pair of real numbers, (a, b), obeying certain peculiar rules, e.g., the multiplication can be defined by

$$(a_1, b_1)(a_2, b_2) = (a_1 a_2 - b_1 b_2, a_1 b_2 + a_2 b_1),$$

and so on. It should be clear that the form $a + ib$ is just a *representation* of a complex number.

It is customary to represent complex numbers by points in the so-called *complex plane*, or Argand diagram (Fig. 2.1). If we denote the complex number $x + iy$ by a single symbol z and write $z = x + iy$, then to each z there corresponds a point in the complex plane with the abscissa x and the ordinate y. This idea also leads us to the *trigonometric representation* of a complex number:

$$z = r\,(\cos\theta + i\sin\theta),$$

where $r = \sqrt{x^2 + y^2}$ and $\tan\theta = y/x$. In this representation r is unique (positive square root) but θ is not. A common convention is to demand that†

$$-\pi < \theta \le \pi,$$

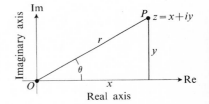

Figure 2.1

along with the standard rule of quadrants, namely, $\theta < 0$ if $y < 0$.

The following nomenclature and notation will be widely used: If

$$z = x + iy = r\,(\cos\theta + i\sin\theta)$$

then

$x = \text{Re } z$ is the *real part* of z,

$y = \text{Im } z$ is the *imaginary part* of z,

$r = |z|$ is the *modulus* of z, also known as the *magnitude* or *absolute value* of z,

θ is the *argument* of z, also called the *polar angle* or *phase*.‡

The number $x - iy$ is called the *complex conjugate* of the number $z = x + iy$ and vice versa. We shall denote it by z^*. We can say that z and z^* represent (on the complex plane) the reflections of each other with respect to the real axis.

---

† Another commonly used convention is $0 \le \theta < 2\pi$.

‡ A more precise name for θ would be the "principal value of the argument of z" (see p. 57).

Remarks

1. The quantity zz^* is always a nonnegative real number equal to $|z|^2$ or to $|z^*|^2$ (which are the same).

2. The quantity $z + z^*$ is always a real number, equal to $2\,\mathrm{Re}\,z$ or to $2\,\mathrm{Re}\,z^*$ (which are the same).

3. The rules $(z_1 + z_2)^* = z_1^* + z_2^*$ and $(z_1 z_2)^* = z_1^* z_2^*$ are evident and should be remembered.

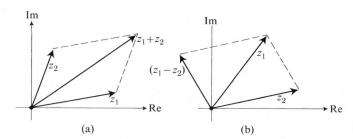

(a)   (b)   **Figure 2.2**

Because complex numbers obey the same addition rule that applies to vectors in a plane, they can be added graphically by the *parallelogram rule* (Fig. 2.2a). Conversely, vectors in a plane can be represented by complex numbers. The scalar product of two such vectors can be obtained by the rule

$$(\mathbf{z}_1 \cdot \mathbf{z}_2) = \mathrm{Re}\,(z_1^* z_2) = \mathrm{Re}\,(z_1 z_2^*),$$

where it is understood that $\mathbf{z}_1$ and $\mathbf{z}_2$ are vectors corresponding to complex numbers z_1 and z_2 respectively. The vector product can be obtained in a similar fashion:

$$[\mathbf{z}_1 \times \mathbf{z}_2] = \mathrm{Im}\,(z_1^* z_2) = -\mathrm{Im}\,(z_1 z_2^*).$$

Exercise. Verify the validity of the above rules for scalar and vector products.

In the theory of complex variables, the expression $|z_1 - z_2|$ is often used. According to Fig. 2.2(b) this quantity (modulus of the complex number $z_1 - z_2$) is equal to the distance between the points z_1 and z_2 in the complex plane. It follows that the statement $|z - z_0| < R$ (which often occurs in proofs of various theorems) means geometrically that point z is within the circle of radius R drawn around the point z_0 as a center (i.e., z is in the R-neighborhood of z_0; see p. 16). The following two inequalities are easily proved from geometrical considerations:

1. $|z_1 + z_2| \le |z_1| + |z_2|.$

(A side of a triangle is less than or equal to the sum of the other two sides.)

2. $|z_1 - z_2| \ge \big||z_1| - |z_2|\big|.$

(The difference of two sides of a triangle is less than or equal to the third side.)

Remark. It should be emphasized that inequalities can exist only among the *moduli* of complex numbers, not among the complex numbers themselves. A complex number cannot be *greater* or *smaller* than another complex number. Also, there are no *positive* or *negative* complex numbers.

2.3 DE MOIVRE FORMULA AND THE CALCULATION OF ROOTS

While addition and subtraction of complex numbers are most easily performed in their cartesian form $z = x + iy$, multiplication and division are easier in trigonometric form. If $z_1 = r_1(\cos \theta_1 + i \sin \theta_1)$ and $z_2 = r_2(\cos \theta_2 + i \sin \theta_2)$, then elementary calculation shows that

$$z_1 z_2 = r_1 r_2 [\cos (\theta_1 + \theta_2) + i \sin (\theta_1 + \theta_2)]$$

with the provision that if $\theta_1 + \theta_2$ happens to be greater than π, or less than or equal to $-\pi$, then the amount 2π should be added or subtracted to fulfill the condition $-\pi < (\theta_1 + \theta_2) \leq \pi$.

Remark. It should be emphasized that even though $\cos (\theta \pm 2\pi) = \cos \theta$ and $\sin (\theta \pm 2\pi) = \sin \theta$, the value of θ is supposed to be uniquely specified. This will become evident when θ is subjected to certain operations, e.g., in the course of evaluation of roots. The convention $-\pi < \theta \leq \pi$ is not the only one possible, but *some* convention must be adopted and ours is just as good as any other.

Using the same trigonometric identities as in the above multiplication rule, we can also obtain the so-called *De Moivre formula:*

$$(\cos \theta + i \sin \theta)^n = \cos n\theta + i \sin n\theta \qquad (n = \text{integer}).$$

Thus we now have the general rule for calculating the nth power of a complex number z. If $z = r(\cos \theta + i \sin \theta)$, then $z^n = R(\cos \phi + i \sin \phi)$, where $R = r^n$ and $\phi = n\theta \pm 2\pi k$ with the integer k chosen in such a way that $-\pi < \phi \leq \pi$.

The rule for calculating the nth root of a complex number can now be derived without much difficulty. If $z = r(\cos \theta + i \sin \theta)$, then the complex number

$$w_0 = \sqrt[n]{r} \left(\cos \frac{\theta}{n} + i \sin \frac{\theta}{n} \right)$$

is definitely the nth root of z because $w_0^n = z$. However, this is not the only nth root of z; the numbers

$$w_k = \sqrt[n]{r} \left(\cos \frac{\theta + 2\pi k}{n} + i \sin \frac{\theta + 2\pi k}{n} \right),$$

where $k = 1, 2, 3, \ldots, (n - 1)$, are also nth roots of z because $w_k^n = z$. It is

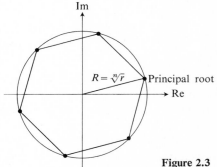

Figure 2.3

customary to call the number w_0 the *principal root* of z. The nth roots of a complex number z are always located at the vertices of a regular polygon of n sides inscribed in a circle of radius $R = \sqrt[n]{r}$ about the origin (Fig. 2.3).

Exercise. Verify that all possible roots of a complex number z are given by the above formulas. Show that all complex numbers except one have exactly n (different) nth-order roots. Which complex number is the exception?

2.4 COMPLEX FUNCTIONS. EULER'S FORMULA

Complex numbers $z = x + iy$ may be considered as variables if x or y (or both) vary. If this is so, then complex functions may be formed. For instance, consider the equation $w = z^2$. If we write $z = x + iy$ and $w = u + iv$, it follows that

$$u = x^2 - y^2, \qquad v = 2xy.$$

From this we conclude that if w is a function of z, then u and v are, in general, functions of both x and y. Thus we are dealing with two (independent) real functions of two (independent) real variables.

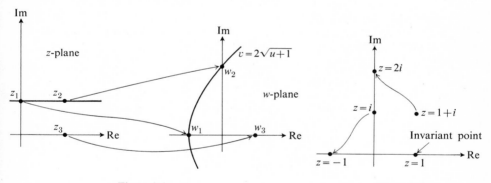

Figure 2.4   Figure 2.5

    Graphical representation of complex functions poses a problem since we must deal with *four* real variables simultaneously. The idea of *mapping* is most commonly used. Two separate complex planes, the z-plane and the w-plane, are considered side by side, and a point z_0 is said to be mapped onto the point $w_0 = f(z_0)$. For instance, formula $w = z^2$ maps $z_1 = i$ onto $w_1 = i^2 = -1$; it also maps $z_2 = 1 + i$ onto $w_2 = 2i$, $z_3 = 1$ onto $w_3 = 1$, and so on. This is illustrated in Fig. 2.4, where it is also indicated that the horizontal line $y = 1$ in the z-plane is mapped onto the parabola $v = 2\sqrt{u + 1}$ in the w-plane. Sometimes it is convenient to superimpose the two planes. Then the images of various points are located on the same plane and the function $w = f(z)$ is said to transform the complex plane into itself (or a part of itself), as in Fig. 2.5, for the same function $w = z^2$.

Exercise. Show that the function $w = iz$ represents counterclockwise rotation of the complex plane by $90°$. How would you describe a rotation by $180°$? How would you describe a clockwise rotation by $90°$?

Algebraic functions of a complex variable are defined by algebraic operations which are directly applicable to complex numbers. Transcendental functions, however, may require special definitions. Consider, for instance, the exponential function e^x (real x). Its basic properties are

$$1. \quad e^{x_1+x_2} = e^{x_1}e^{x_2}, \qquad 2. \quad (e^x)^a = e^{ax}.$$

It is desired to define a complex exponential function e^z with the same properties. Write $z = x + iy$; then

$$e^z = e^{x+iy} = e^x e^{iy}.$$

The quantity e^x is a well-defined real number, but how shall we define e^{iy}? One possible method is as follows: *Assume* that e^{iy} can be represented by the usual power series

$$e^{iy} = 1 + (iy) + \frac{(iy)^2}{2!} + \frac{(iy)^3}{3!} + \cdots$$

Then, rearranging the terms, we have

$$e^{iy} = \left(1 - \frac{y^2}{2!} + \frac{y^4}{4!} - \cdots\right) + i\left(y - \frac{y^3}{3!} + \frac{y^5}{5!} - \cdots\right)$$

$$= \cos y + i \sin y.$$

The validity of this procedure can be established after the development of the theory of convergence for complex series. However, at this stage we may simply *define* the function e^{iy} by means of

$$e^{iy} = \cos y + i \sin y.$$

This is *Euler's formula*. The desired properties,

$$e^{i(y_1+y_2)} = e^{iy_1}e^{iy_2}, \qquad (e^{iy})^n = e^{iny} \qquad (n = \text{integer}),$$

follow from the identities

$$(\cos y_1 + i \sin y_1)(\cos y_2 + i \sin y_2) = \cos(y_1 + y_2) + i \sin(y_1 + y_2)$$

and

$$(\cos y + i \sin y)^n = \cos ny + i \sin ny.$$

The definition of a complex exponential function is then given by the formula

$$e^z = e^x(\cos y + i \sin y)$$

which has the desired properties and reduces to the real exponential function if $\text{Im } z = 0$.

2.5 APPLICATIONS OF EULER'S FORMULA

Euler's formula leads to the compact *polar representation* of complex numbers,

$$z = x + iy = r(\cos \theta + i \sin \theta) = re^{i\theta}.$$

Suppose that a complex number z is multiplied by $e^{i\alpha}$, where α is a real constant. Then

$$e^{i\alpha}z = re^{i(\theta+\alpha)}.$$

The new number can be obtained by rotating the point z about the origin by an angle α. This fact has many important applications.

Euler's formula also permits the description of sinusoidally varying real quantities by means of complex exponentials. A general form of such quantity is

$$f(t) = a \cos (\omega t - \theta),$$

where a (amplitude), ω (angular frequency), and θ (phase) are constants, and t is a real variable (usually time). Consider the *complex* function of the *real* variable

$$g(t) = Be^{-i\omega t}$$

where B is a complex constant. Set $B = ae^{i\theta}$; then

$$g(t) = ae^{i\theta}e^{-i\omega t} = a \cos (\theta - \omega t) + ia \sin (\theta - \omega t)$$
$$= a \cos (\omega t - \theta) - ia \sin (\omega t - \theta).$$

In other words, $f(t) = \mathrm{Re}\ \{g(t)\}$.

Complex functions of a real variable can be treated by the methods of calculus of real variables. For instance, if

$$g(t) = u(t) + iv(t) \qquad (u, v = \text{real functions}),$$

then

$$\frac{dg}{dt} = \frac{du}{dt} + i \frac{dv}{dt},$$

and so on. Differentiation of $Be^{-i\omega t}$ is very simple:

$$\frac{d}{dt} (Be^{-i\omega t}) = -i\omega Be^{-i\omega t}.$$

The use of complex exponentials is illustrated in the following example. Consider a (damped) harmonic oscillator subject to a harmonically varying external force. The differential equation to be solved reads

$$\ddot{x} + 2\alpha\dot{x} + \omega_0^2 x = F \cos (\omega t - \phi) \qquad (\dot{x} = (dx/dt) \text{ etc.}),$$

where the constants α, ω_0, F, ω, and ϕ are real, and both variables x and t are real.

Now, introduce a *complex function*

$$f(t) = \tilde{F}e^{-i\omega t},$$

where ω is real but $\tilde{F}$ may be complex. Let $\tilde{F} = Fe^{i\phi}$; then

$$\text{Re } f(t) = \text{Re } \{Fe^{-i(\omega t - \phi)}\} = F\cos(\omega t - \phi).$$

Consider the differential equation

$$\ddot{x} + 2\alpha\dot{x} + \omega_0^2 x = f(t),$$

where $x = x(t)$ is evidently complex. The point now is that the *real part* of this complex function $x(t)$ is just the solution of the original (real) differential equation. This can be verified directly by substitution:

$$x(t) = \text{Re } x(t) + i\,\text{Im } x(t).$$

Exercise. Prove the general theorem: If a complex function $x(t)$ satisfies a *linear* differential equation, say of second order,

$$\ddot{x} + p(t)x + q(t)x = f(t),$$

where p and q are *real* but $f(t)$ may be complex, then the real part of x satisfies the same equation with $f(t)$ replaced by $\text{Re } f(t)$ and the imaginary part of x satisfies the same equation with $f(t)$ replaced by $\text{Im } f(t)$. [*Hint:* Quote the footnote on p. 45 in your proof.]

Suppose that a steady-state solution is sought for our harmonic oscillator problem. Our physical intuition suggests* that it should be a harmonic function of frequency ω, namely, of the form $A\cos(\omega t - \psi)$. This, in turn, suggests that we seek the solution of our complex equation in the form

$$x(t) = \tilde{A}e^{-i\omega t},$$

where $\tilde{A} = Ae^{i\psi}$ is a complex constant. Substitute this into the equation and obtain

$$-\omega^2\tilde{A} - 2\alpha i\omega\tilde{A} + \omega_0^2\tilde{A} = \tilde{F}$$

so that

$$\tilde{A} = \frac{\tilde{F}}{-\omega^2 - 2\alpha i\omega + \omega_0^2}.$$

This essentially solves the problem. The explicit solution of the physical (real) problem is

$$\text{Re } \{x(t)\} = \text{Re } \{\tilde{A}e^{-i\omega t}\} = \text{Re } \left\{\frac{Fe^{-i(\omega t - \phi)}}{(\omega_0^2 - \omega^2) - i2\alpha\omega}\right\}.$$

---

* This is rigorously proved in many textbooks on differential equations. However, no harm is done if we just conjecture such a solution.

The final evaluation of this expression is straightforward; for instance, we may write (see p. 45)

$$\frac{Fe^{-i(\omega t - \phi)}}{(\omega_0^2 - \omega^2) - i2\alpha\omega} = \frac{Fe^{-i(\omega t - \phi)}[(\omega_0^2 - \omega^2) + i2\alpha\omega]}{(\omega_0^2 - \omega^2)^2 + 4\alpha^2\omega^2}.$$

Now the rule

$$\text{Re}\,(z_1 z_2) = \text{Re}\,z_1\,\text{Re}\,z_2 - \text{Im}\,z_1\,\text{Im}\,z_2$$

yields

$$\text{Re}\left\{\frac{Fe^{-i(\omega t - \phi)}[(\omega_0^2 - \omega^2) + i2\alpha\omega]}{(\omega_0^2 - \omega^2)^2 + 4\alpha^2\omega^2}\right\} = \frac{F(\omega_0^2 - \omega^2)}{(\omega_0^2 - \omega^2)^2 + 4\alpha^2\omega^2}\cos{(\omega t - \phi)}$$

$$+ \frac{F2\alpha\omega}{(\omega_0^2 - \omega^2)^2 + 4\alpha^2\omega^2}\sin{(\omega t - \phi)}.$$

Of course, this result can be obtained without any recourse to complex numbers: The solution of the original (real) differential equation can be sought in the form

$$x = a\cos\omega t + b\sin\omega t.$$

Differentiate and substitute into the equation. On separation of the terms with $\cos\omega t$ and $\sin\omega t$, obtain the simultaneous algebraic equations

$$a(\omega_0^2 - \omega^2) + b2\alpha\omega = F\cos\phi t,$$
$$b(\omega_0^2 - \omega^2) - a2\alpha\omega = -F\sin\phi t.$$

The relevant determinants are

$$\Delta = \det\begin{vmatrix} \omega_0^2 - \omega^2 & 2\alpha\omega \\ -2\alpha\omega & \omega_0^2 - \omega^2 \end{vmatrix} = (\omega_0^2 - \omega^2)^2 + 4\alpha^2\omega^2,$$

$$\Delta_a = \det\begin{vmatrix} F\cos\phi t & 2\alpha\omega \\ -F\sin\phi t & \omega_0^2 - \omega^2 \end{vmatrix} = F(\omega_0^2 - \omega^2)\cos\phi t + 2F\alpha\omega\sin\phi t,$$

$$\Delta_b = \det\begin{vmatrix} \omega_0^2 - \omega^2 & F\cos\phi t \\ -2\alpha\omega & -F\sin\phi t \end{vmatrix} = -F(\omega_0^2 - \omega^2)\sin\phi t + 2F\alpha\omega\cos\phi t.$$

The solution ($a = \Delta_a/\Delta$, $b = \Delta_b/\Delta$) is easily reducible to that given before.

The advantage of the complex method may be appreciated from the fact that the actual process of solving the equation is in this case very brief; the remainder of the calculation (separation of the real part) is a procedure common to all such problems and, therefore, can be reduced to triviality.

2.6 MULTIVALUED FUNCTIONS AND RIEMANN SURFACES

Certain complex functions are multivalued and they are usually considered as consisting of *branches*, each branch being a single-valued function of z. For instance, $f(z) = \sqrt{z}$ can be split into two branches according to the usual formula for the roots ($z = re^{i\theta}$):

1. *Principal branch,* $f_1(z) = \sqrt{r}\, e^{i(\theta/2)}$,
2. *Second branch,* $f_2(z) = \sqrt{r}\, e^{i[(\theta+2\pi)/2]}$.

Strictly speaking, $f_1(z)$ and $f_2(z)$ are two separate functions but they are intimately connected and for this reason they are treated together as two branches of a (double-valued) function $f(z) = \sqrt{z}$.

Note that the principal branch does not map the z-plane onto the entire w-plane, but rather onto the right half-plane (Re $w > 0$) to which the positive imaginary semiaxis is added. The negative imaginary semiaxis is not included. The second branch, which has no special name, maps the z-plane onto the left half-plane (Re $w < 0$) plus the negative imaginary semiaxis. Except for $z = 0$, no other point on the w-plane (*image plane*) is duplicated by both mappings.

Also observe another important feature of the two branches. Each branch taken separately is *discontinuous* on the negative real semiaxis. The meaning of this is as follows: The points

$$z_1 = e^{i(\pi-\delta)} \quad \text{and} \quad z_2 = e^{i(-\pi+\delta)},$$

where δ is a small positive number, are very close to each other. However, their images under the principal branch mapping, namely

$$f_1(z_1) = e^{i(\pi/2-\delta/2)} \quad \text{and} \quad f_1(z_2) = e^{-i(\pi/2-\delta/2)},$$

are very far from each other. On the other hand, note that the image of z_2 under the mapping $f_2(z)$, namely,

$$f_2(z_2) = e^{i(\pi/2+\delta/2)},$$

is very close to the point $f_1(z_1)$. It appears that the continuity of mapping can be preserved if we switch branches as we cross the negative real semiaxis.

To give this idea a more precise meaning we must define the concept of *continuous function* of a complex variable. Let $w = f(z)$ be defined in some neighborhood (see pp. 47 and 16) of point z_0 and let $f(z_0) = w_0$. We say that $f(z)$ is continuous at z_0 if* $f(z) \to w_0$ whenever $z \to z_0$ in the sense that given $\delta > 0$ (arbitrarily small), the inequality $|f(z) - w_0| < \delta$ holds whenever $|z - z_0| < \epsilon$ holds, for sufficiently small ϵ. It is readily shown† that if $w = u(x, y) + iv(x, y)$, then the continuity of w implies the continuity of $u(x, y)$ and $v(x, y)$ and vice versa.

---

* Also written as $\lim_{z \to z_0} f(z) = f(z_0)$.
† For example, see Kaplan, p. 495.

Riemann proposed an ingenious device to represent both branches by means of a single continuous mapping: Imagine two separate *z*-planes cut along the negative real semiaxis from "minus infinity" to zero. Imagine that the planes are superimposed on each other but retain their separate identity in the manner of two sheets of paper laid on top of each other. Now suppose that the second quadrant of the upper sheet is joined along the cut to the fourth quadrant of the lower sheet to form a continuous surface (Fig. 2.6). It is now possible to start a curve *C* in the third quadrant of the upper sheet, go around the origin, and cross the negative real semiaxis into the third quadrant of the lower sheet in a continuous motion (remaining on the surface). The curve can be continued on the lower sheet around the origin into the second quadrant of the lower sheet.

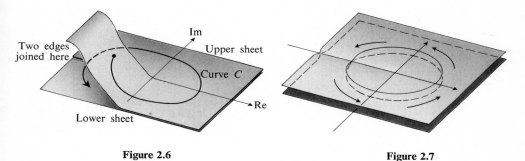

Figure 2.6   Figure 2.7

Now imagine the second quadrant of the lower sheet joined to the third quadrant of the upper sheet *along the same* cut (independently of the first joint and actually disregarding its existence). The curve *C* can then be continued onto the upper sheet and may *return to the starting point*. This process of cutting and cross-joining two planes leads to the formation of a *Riemann surface* which is *thought of* as a single continuous surface formed of two *Riemann sheets* (Fig. 2.7).

An important remark is now in order: The line between the second quadrant of the upper sheet and the third quadrant of the lower sheet is to be considered as *distinct* from the line between the second quadrant of the lower sheet and the third quadrant of the upper one. This is where the paper model fails us. According to this model the negative real semiaxis appears as the line where all four edges of our cuts meet. However, the Riemann surface has no such property; there are *two* real negative semiaxes on the Riemann surface just as there are two real positive semiaxes. The mapping $f(z) = \sqrt{z}$ may help to visualize this: The principal branch maps the upper Riemann sheet (negative real semiaxis excluded) onto the region Re $w > 0$ of the *w*-plane. The line joining the second upper with the third lower quadrants is also mapped by the principal branch onto the positive imaginary semiaxis. The lower Riemann sheet (negative real semiaxis excluded) is mapped by the second branch onto the region Re $w < 0$. The line joining the second lower with the third upper quadrants is mapped (by the second branch) onto the negative imaginary semiaxis. In this fashion the entire Riemann surface is mapped one-to-one onto the w-plane ($z = 0$ is mapped onto $w = 0$; this particular correspondence, strictly speaking, belongs to neither branch since the polar angle θ is not defined for $z = 0$).

The splitting of a multivalued function into branches is arbitrary to a great extent. For instance, define the following two functions which also may be treated as branches of $f(z) = \sqrt{z}$:

$$\text{Branch } A: \quad f_A(z) = \begin{cases} \sqrt{r}\, e^{i(\theta/2)} & \text{for } 0 < \theta \leq \pi, \\ \sqrt{r}\, e^{i[(\theta+2\pi)/2]} & \text{for } -\pi < \theta \leq 0. \end{cases}$$

$$\text{Branch } B: \quad f_B(z) = \begin{cases} \sqrt{r}\, e^{i[(\theta+2\pi)/2]} & \text{for } 0 < \theta \leq \pi, \\ \sqrt{r}\, e^{i(\theta/2)} & \text{for } -\pi < \theta \leq 0. \end{cases}$$

Note that branch A is continuous on the negative real semiaxis but is discontinuous on the positive real semiaxis (so is branch B). These two branches constitute, together, the double-valued function $f(z) = \sqrt{z}$, and this representation is no better and no worse than the previous one. Also observe that the Riemann surface built up by these two branches is the same as the one described before.

It is not difficult to see that the function $f(z) = \sqrt{z}$ can be split in two branches in many other ways. In all of them, however, there will be a *branch line* (or *branch cut*) extending from $z = 0$ to infinity. This line may be a curve. The Riemann surface can be obtained by joining two Riemann sheets across the cut, and this surface is unique. The point $z = 0$ where any branch line must start (or end) is called a *branch point*. The position of the branch point is determined by the nature of the multivalued function and is independent of the choice of branches.

This technique can be extended to other multivalued functions. Some require more than two Riemann sheets (for instance $f(z) = \sqrt[3]{z}$ requires three). Some require two Riemann sheets but two branch points* ($f(z) = \sqrt{(z - 1)(z + 1)}$), etc. There are functions requiring an infinite number of Riemann sheets such as $f(z) = z^\alpha$ with irrational α and some of transcendental functions which we shall briefly consider below.

Using the definition of exponential function,

$$e^z = e^x(\cos y + i \sin y),$$

we may define trigonometric and hyperbolic functions:

$$\cos z = \tfrac{1}{2}(e^{iz} + e^{-iz}), \qquad \sin z = \frac{1}{2i}(e^{iz} - e^{-iz}),$$

$$\tan z = \frac{\sin z}{\cos z}, \qquad \cot z = \frac{1}{\tan z},$$

$$\cosh z = \tfrac{1}{2}(e^z + e^{-z}), \qquad \sinh z = \tfrac{1}{2}(e^z - e^{-z}),$$

$$\tanh z = \frac{\sinh z}{\cosh z}, \qquad \coth z = \frac{1}{\tanh z}.$$

---

* If the so-called *point at infinity* (Section 2.14) is taken into account, then the mapping $f(z) = \sqrt{z}$ also has two branch points.

All these functions are periodic: $\sin z$ and $\cos z$ have a (primitive) period 2π, $\tan z$ has a (primitive) period π, e^z, $\sinh z$, and $\cosh z$ have a (primitive) period $2\pi i$. A score of familiar formulas can be established, for instance,

$$\sin (z_1 + z_2) = \sin z_1 \cos z_2 + \cos z_1 \sin z_2,$$

$$\sin z_1 - \sin z_2 = 2 \cos \frac{z_1 + z_2}{2} \sin \frac{z_1 + z_2}{2}, \quad \text{etc.}$$

Also note that

$$\cosh z = \cos (iz) \qquad \sinh z = -i \sin (iz).$$

It is worthwhile to mention that $|\sin z|$ and $|\cos z|$ are by no means bounded by unity, for instance,

$$|\sin 2i| \cong 3.24.$$

The logarithmic function is defined as the inverse of exponential function. Solving $e^w = z = re^{i\theta}$ for w, we obtain the general solution

$$w = \log r + i\theta + i2n\pi \qquad (n = \text{integer}).$$

This function is multivalued: Its principal branch is usually denoted by $w = \log z$ and is defined as

$$\log z = \log r + i\theta \qquad (-\pi < \theta \le \pi).$$

The entire multivalued function is referred to as

$$w = \text{Log } z = \log z + i2n\pi.$$

These formulas are often written with the help of the *argument of z* function which is also multivalued, the principal branch being

$$\arg z = \theta \qquad (-\pi < \theta \le \pi)$$

and the entire function reading $\text{Arg } z = \arg z + 2n\pi$. Thus we may write

$$\log z = \log |z| + i \arg z, \qquad \text{Log } z = \log |z| + i \, \text{Arg } z.$$

The functions $\text{Arg } z$ and $\text{Log } z$ require a Riemann surface consisting of infinitely many Riemann sheets.

The definition of inverse trigonometric and hyperbolic functions now easily follows. All are multivalued:

$$\text{Arc cos } z = i \, \text{Log} (z + \sqrt{z^2 - 1}),$$

$$\text{Arc sin } z = \frac{\pi}{2} - \text{Arc cos } z,$$

$$\text{Arc tan } z = \frac{1}{2i} \text{Log} \frac{i - z}{i + z},$$

$$\text{Arsinh } z = \text{Log} (z + \sqrt{z^2 + 1}),$$

$$\text{Arcosh } z = \text{Log} (z + \sqrt{z^2 - 1}),$$

$$\text{Artanh } z = \tfrac{1}{2} \text{Log} \frac{1 + z}{1 - z}.$$

Their principal branches are denoted by arc cos z, etc.* The general *power function* z^α is defined by

$$z^\alpha = e^{\alpha \, \text{Log} \, z}.$$

For rational $\alpha(\alpha = p/q$, where p, q are integers and $q \neq 0)$ this function coincides with $\sqrt[q]{z^p}$ $(q > 0)$ or with $(\sqrt[-q]{z^p})^{-1}$ $(q < 0)$ and has q branches. For irrational α the power function is infinitely multivalued.

2.7 ANALYTIC FUNCTIONS. CAUCHY THEOREM

In this section we shall discuss the subject of calculus of functions of a complex variable. The basic concept of the continuity of a complex function has already been presented, and it is not difficult to verify that the sum, product, and quotient (except for division by zero) of two continuous functions is continuous. A continuous function of a continuous function is also continuous.†

Let C be a piecewise smooth curve in a complex plane. If $f(z)$ is continuous on C, then *the complex integral*

$$\int_C f(z) \, dz$$

can be defined and expressed in terms of real integrals by putting

$$f(z) = u(x, y) + iv(x, y) \qquad \text{and} \qquad dz = dx + i \, dy;$$

this yields

$$\int_C f(z) \, dz = \int_C (u \, dx - v \, dy) + i \int_C (v \, dx + u \, dy),$$

where the real integrals $\int_C (u \, dx - v \, dy)$ and $\int_C (v \, dx + u \, dy)$ are known to exist.‡ Curve C may be open or closed but the direction of integration must be specified in either case. The reversal of this direction results in the change of sign of the integral. Complex integrals are, therefore, reducible to curvilinear real integrals and possess the following properties:

$$\int_C (f(z) + g(z)) \, dz = \int_C f(z) \, dz + \int_C g(z) \, dz, \qquad (1)$$

$$\int_C k f(z) \, dz = k \int_C f(z) \, dz \qquad (k = \text{complex constant}), \qquad (2)$$

$$\int_C f(z) \, dz = \int_{C_1} f(z) \, dz + \int_{C_2} f(z) \, dz, \qquad (3)$$

where C is decomposed into two curves, C_1 and C_2. The absolute value of an integral can be estimated by the formula

$$\left| \int_C f(z) \, dz \right| \leq ML,$$

where $M = \max |f(z)|$ on C, and L is the length of C.

---

* Another widespread notation is arc sin $z = \sin^{-1} z$, arsinh $z = \sinh^{-1} z$, and so on.

† For example, Kaplan, p. 496.

‡ In the sense of Riemann; see, e.g., Courant, Vol. 1, p. 133, and Kaplan, p. 299.

As our next concept we shall define the *derivative* of a complex function: Changing z into $z + \Delta z$ (with complex Δz), we obtain $f(z + \Delta z)$ and we can write*

$$f'(z) = \frac{d}{dz} f(z) = \lim_{\Delta z \to 0} \frac{f(z + \Delta z) - f(z)}{\Delta z}.$$

As in the case of real functions, this limit may or may not exist. It may be emphasized that in the above formula Δz may approach zero in an arbitrary fashion, that is, $z + \Delta z$ may approach z along any curve or by any sequence. This rather stringent requirement implies that $f(z)$ must indeed be "well behaved" at point z in order to be differentiable.

Function $f(z)$ is said to be *analytic* (*regular*, or *holomorphic*) at point z if it possesses a derivative at z and at all points of some *neighborhood of z* (small but finite). This additional requirement results in many desirable properties of analytic functions, such as the existence of derivatives of all orders. The theory of functions of a complex variable deals essentially with analytic functions.

Mere existence of a derivative at all points of a neighborhood may be shown to imply that the derivative is continuous.† Also, it is a simple matter to verify (by the same technique as for real variables) that the derivatives of complex functions obey the usual rules:

$$\frac{d}{dz} (w_1 + w_2) = \frac{dw_1}{dz} + \frac{dw_2}{dz}, \tag{1}$$

$$\frac{d}{dz} (w_1 w_2) = w_1 \frac{dw_2}{dz} + \frac{dw_1}{dz} w_2, \tag{2}$$

$$\frac{dw}{dz} = \frac{dw}{d\zeta} \frac{d\zeta}{dz}, \quad \text{where } w = w(\zeta) \quad \text{and} \quad \zeta = \zeta(z), \tag{3}$$

$$\frac{d}{dz} (z^n) = nz^{n-1} \quad (n = \text{integer}), \tag{4}$$

and so on. The differentials of complex functions are defined in the same way as for real functions: If $w = f(z)$, then $dw = f'(z)\, dz$.

If we set $f(z) = w = u(x, y) + iv(x, y)$, then the definition of the derivative can be rewritten as

$$f'(z) = \lim_{\substack{\Delta x \to 0 \\ \Delta y \to 0}} \frac{[u(x + \Delta x, y + \Delta y) - u(x, y)] + i[v(x + \Delta x, y + \Delta y) - v(x, y)]}{\Delta x + i\,\Delta y}.$$

The limiting value on the right-hand side must be the same for the arbitrary approach $\Delta z \to 0$. In particular, set $\Delta z = \Delta x$ (approach along the real axis); then

$$f'(z) = \frac{\partial u}{\partial x} + i \frac{\partial v}{\partial x}.$$

---

* See p. 54 (including the footnote) for the definition of a limit.
† See, e.g., Knopp, *Theory of Functions*, Vol. 1, p. 65.

Alternatively, set $\Delta z = i\,\Delta y$ (approach along the imaginary axis); then

$$f'(z) = \frac{\partial v}{\partial y} - i\frac{\partial u}{\partial y}.$$

It follows that for a differentiable function $w = u + iv$ we must have

$$\frac{\partial u}{\partial x} = \frac{\partial v}{\partial y}, \qquad \frac{\partial u}{\partial y} = -\frac{\partial v}{\partial x}.$$

These are the *Cauchy-Riemann conditions;* they follow directly from the definition of the derivative. If, further, $f(z)$ is analytic, then $f'(z)$ must be continuous which, in turn,* implies that the partial derivatives of u and v are continuous.

The inverse theorem also holds: If $u(x, y)$ and $v(x, y)$ have continuous first partial derivatives satisfying Cauchy-Riemann conditions in some neighborhood of z, then $f(z) = u + iv$ is analytic at z.

Integrals of analytic functions possess some very important properties. Perhaps the most fundamental one is expressed by the *Cauchy theorem: If $f(z)$ is analytic in a simply connected domain D, and C is a (piecewise smooth) simple closed curve in D, then*

$$\oint_C f(z)\,dz = 0.$$

Proof. Write the integral as

$$\oint_C f(z)\,dz = \oint_C (u\,dx - v\,dy) + i\oint_C (v\,dx + u\,dy).$$

Analyticity of $f(z)$ implies continuity of partial derivatives of u and v and Green's theorem (p. 20) is applicable. However, then the Cauchy-Riemann conditions imply

$$\oint_C (u\,dx - v\,dy) = \iint_S \left(-\frac{\partial v}{\partial x} + \frac{\partial u}{\partial y}\right) dx\,dy = 0,$$

$$\oint_C (v\,dx + u\,dy) = \iint_S \left(\frac{\partial u}{\partial x} - \frac{\partial v}{\partial y}\right) dx\,dy = 0,$$

and the theorem follows.

There is a converse of the Cauchy theorem, known as the

Morera theorem:† If $f(z)$ is continuous in a domain D and if $\oint f(z)\,dz = 0$ for every simple closed path in D with its interior also in D, then $f(z)$ is analytic in D.

It is not difficult to see that the Cauchy theorem is true for multiply connected domains provided the interior of the simple closed path C is also inside the domain

---

* See, e.g., Kaplan, p. 510.
† Knopp, *Theory of Functions*, Vol. 1, p. 66.

(i.e., the path does not encircle a hole; see Fig. 1.15). Similar extensions hold for related integral theorems that will be quoted later.

The vanishing of a contour integral (an integral around a simple closed path) is closely related to the *independence of path* of an integral. In fact, the considerations of Section 1.6 can be applied easily to complex integrals, leading to the statement: If $\oint f(z)\,dz = 0$ for every simple closed path, then the integral

$$\int_{z_0}^{z} f(\zeta)\,d\zeta$$

is independent of path (between z_0 and z).

Suppose now that the point z_0 is fixed. If the integral $\int_{z_0}^{z} f(\zeta)\,d\zeta$ is independent of path, then it must represent a function of z. This function is then a primitive function of $f(z)$ (or an indefinite integral of $f(z)$) as follows from the *fundamental theorem of integral calculus: If $f(z)$ is analytic in a simply connected domain D, then the function*

$$F(z) = \int_{z_0}^{z} f(\zeta)\,d\zeta$$

is also analytic in D and $f(z) = (d/dz)F(z)$.

Proof. Since $f(z)$ is analytic, the integral is independent of path and is therefore a function of z. In the expression

$$F(z) = U + iV = \int_{(x_0,y_0)}^{(x,y)} (u\,dx - v\,dy) + i\int_{(x_0,y_0)}^{(x,y)} (v\,dx + u\,dy),$$

both integrals are independent of path (by Green's theorem and the Cauchy-Riemann conditions). It also follows that*

$$\frac{\partial U}{\partial x} = u, \qquad \frac{\partial U}{\partial y} = -v,$$

$$\frac{\partial V}{\partial x} = v, \qquad \frac{\partial V}{\partial y} = u,$$

so that u and v satisfy the Cauchy-Riemann conditions as well. Therefore $F(z)$ is analytic. Moreover,

$$\frac{dF}{dz} = \frac{\partial U}{\partial x} + i\frac{\partial V}{\partial x} = u + iv = f(z),$$

and the theorem follows.

Any two primitive functions must differ by a (complex) constant; this follows from the fact that $f'(z) = 0$ implies $f(z) = $ const (integrate $\partial u/\partial x = 0$, $\partial u/\partial y = 0$, etc.).

----

* For example, Kaplan, p. 244.

2.8 OTHER INTEGRAL THEOREMS.   CAUCHY INTEGRAL FORMULA

It should be emphasized that all conditions stated in the Cauchy theorem must be checked before applications. Consider, for instance, the integral

$$I = \oint_C \frac{1}{z - a}\,dz \qquad (a = \text{const}).$$

Is this integral zero or not?   Generally speaking, $f(z) = 1/(z - a)$ is an analytic function but it fails to be analytic at one (and only one) point, namely, $z = a$. The function is not even defined at this point and thus cannot possess a derivative.

Let the curve C involved in the definition of I be a simple closed curve. Then, if the point $z = a$ is outside the curve, the Cauchy theorem holds and $I = 0$. If it is inside, the Cauchy theorem cannot be applied. In fact, the integral is not equal to zero, as demonstrated by the following considerations: If C is a circle of radius R centered at $z = a$, then the integral is easily evaluated by setting $z = a + Re^{i\theta}$. In this case $dz = iRe^{i\theta}\,d\theta$ and

$$I = \int_{-\pi}^{+\pi} i\,d\theta = 2\pi i.$$

It is not difficult to show that the same result is true for any simple closed path C_1, which encircles point $z = a$. Suppose that C_1 is entirely inside the circle C (Fig. 2.8). Then a thin channel made up of curves B_1 and B_2 can be constructed to connect the interior of C_1 with the exterior of C and the Cauchy theorem can be applied to the shaded region; a domain D can be constructed so that the shaded region is within it.   The integral over C_1 is clockwise. As the sides B_1 and B_2 of the channel are allowed to approach each other, the integrals of $f(z) = 1/(z - a)$ along B_1 and B_2 will (in the limit) cancel out, leaving us with the statement

$$\underset{\text{Counterclockwise}}{\oint_C f(z)\,dz} + \underset{\text{Clockwise}}{\oint_{C_1} f(z)\,dz} = 0.$$

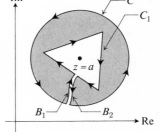

Figure 2.8

Reversing the direction of the second integration to counterclockwise, we obtain

$$\oint_C f(z)\,dz = \oint_{C_1} f(z)\,dz$$

(with both directions counterclockwise).

If C is entirely within C_1, the proof is similar. If C and C_1 intersect, the proof is even simpler.

Exercise. Produce a proof of the discussed statement given that C and C_1 intersect at two points.

If the integral I is evaluated around a closed path which is not simple, its value is not necessarily $2\pi i$. In cases of practical interest it will be equal to $n2\pi i$, where n is the number of times the path encircles the point $z = a$ counterclockwise less the number of times it encircles the point $z = a$ clockwise.

Of course, it should be understood that the integral $\oint f(z)\,dz$ may happen to be zero even if the Cauchy theorem does not apply. For instance, calculate the integral

$$J = \oint \frac{1}{(z-a)^n}\,dz,$$

where n is a positive integer not equal to unity and the contour is a circle of radius R around $z = a$. Using $z = a + Re^{i\theta}$, obtain

$$J = \int_{-\pi}^{+\pi} iR^{1-n}e^{i(1-n)\theta}\,d\theta = \frac{R^{1-n}}{1-n}e^{i(1-n)\theta}\Big|_{-\pi}^{+\pi} = 0.$$

This result evidently holds for any closed path encircling $z = a$.

In both of these examples, the possibility of the point $z = a$ being exactly on the path of integration has been avoided, and for a good reason; such integrals cannot actually be defined. Whenever this situation occurs in practical problems, the path must be deformed to avoid the troublesome point. How this is to be done depends on the nature of the problem.*

Function $f(z)$ in the Cauchy theorem must, of course, be single valued. It may be a particular branch of a multiple-valued function, but then care should be taken that this particular branch is analytic. Consider, for instance, the integral

$$\oint_{|z|=1} \sqrt{z}\,dz$$

along the *unit circle* about the origin. First of all, the branch of the (double-valued) function $\sqrt{z}$ must be specified. Suppose it is the principal branch. Then

$$\oint \sqrt{z}\,dz = \int_{-\pi}^{+\pi} e^{i(\theta/2)}ie^{i\theta}\,d\theta = -\tfrac{4}{3}i.$$

The Cauchy theorem is not applicable because $f(z)$ is not analytic within the circle $|z| = 1$. The points where it fails to be analytic are along the real axis from $x = -1$ to $x = 0$ where $f(z)$ is not even continuous. Note also that although $f(z)$ is continuous at $z = 0$, it is not analytic at that point either.

Consider now the same integral

$$\oint_{|z+2|=1} \sqrt{z}\,dz$$

* One such example is given in Section 12.9.

taken around the point $z = -2$ (Fig. 2.9). If the principal branch is involved in the integration, the Cauchy theorem is not applicable. However, split $\sqrt{z}$ into the following two branches (as on p. 56):

$$\text{Branch } A: \begin{cases} \sqrt{z} = \sqrt{r}\, e^{i(\theta/2)} & \text{if } 0 < \theta \le \pi, \\ \sqrt{z} = \sqrt{r}\, e^{i[(\theta+2\pi)/2]} & \text{if } -\pi < \theta \le 0. \end{cases}$$

$$\text{Branch } B: \begin{cases} \sqrt{z} = \sqrt{r}\, e^{i[(\theta+2\pi)/2]} & \text{if } 0 < \theta \le \pi, \\ \sqrt{z} = \sqrt{r}\, e^{i(\theta/2)} & \text{if } -\pi < \theta \le 0. \end{cases}$$

Now the branch cut is along the positive real semiaxis, and each branch is analytic within (and on) the circle $|z + 2| = 1$ and the Cauchy theorem may be applied.

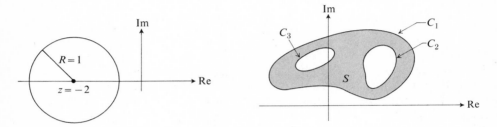

Figure 2.9   Figure 2.10

The Cauchy theorem can be generalized in more than one way. Observe that the interior of a simple closed path is evidently a simply connected domain with the path serving as its boundary. A (finite) collection of nonintersecting simple closed paths may form a *multiply connected domain*, as illustrated in Fig. 2.10: The paths C_1, C_2, and C_3 form the boundary of the (triply connected) domain S. With respect to this domain S, the contours C_1, C_2, and C_3 are oriented in the following sense (see p. 21): The positive direction of circulation around C_1, C_2, and C_3 is such that the domain S appears *to the left*. This implies, in our example, a counterclockwise direction for C_1 but a clockwise direction for C_2 and C_3.

These concepts lead to the so-called *Cauchy theorem for multiply connected domains: If S is a multiply-connected domain whose boundary B consists of a finite number of simple closed paths, then*

$$\oint_B f(z)\, dz = 0,$$

provided $f(z)$ is analytic in S and on B and the integration is carried out in a positive direction over all parts of B. The proof is constructed without difficulty by using the technique of channels (p. 62).

In this (and other) integral theorems the analyticity of $f(z)$ on a contour (as well as in its interior) is demanded. This is because the Cauchy theorem requires the contour to be located *within* some simply connected domain *D*. Actually, this condition can be relaxed and the following *boundary integral theorem* holds: If $f(z)$ is analytic in the interior S of a simple closed path C and $f(z)$ is continuous on C,* then $\oint_C f(z) \, dz = 0$. The proof is based on the construction of a contour C' which is in S and arbitrarily close to C; the Cauchy theorem is valid for C'. The continuity of $f(z)$ is then used to show that the integral over C' must approach the integral over C as C' approaches C.

The Cauchy theorem can be used to deduce many other properties of integrals, the basic one being the *Cauchy integral formula: If $f(z)$ is analytic inside and on C and if the point $z = a$ is in the interior of C, then*

$$\oint \frac{f(z) \, dz}{z - a} = 2\pi i f(a).$$

Proof. Construct a circle C' about $z = a$ with an arbitrarily small radius R such that the circle is within C (Fig. 2.11). The integral over C is evidently the same as the integral over C' (use the channel technique). Rewrite this integral:

$$\oint_{C'} \frac{f(z) \, dz}{z - a} = \oint_{C'} \frac{f(z) - f(a)}{z - a} \, dz + f(a) \oint_{C'} \frac{1}{z - a} \, dz$$

$$= \oint_{C'} \frac{f(z) - f(a)}{z - a} \, dz + f(a) 2\pi i$$

by a previous result. The remaining integral on the right-hand side must be independent of the radius R (because other terms are independent of R).

It can also be estimated that

$$\left| \oint_{C'} \frac{f(z) - f(a)}{z - a} \, dz \right| \le \oint_{C'} \frac{|f(z) - f(a)|}{|z - a|} \, ds \le \frac{M}{R} 2\pi R = 2\pi M,$$

where $M = \max |f(z) - f(a)|$ on the circle C'. If R is chosen sufficiently small, then M can be made arbitrarily small [by continuity of $f(z)$ at the point $z == a$]. Therefore the quantity

$$\left| \oint_{C'} \frac{f(z) - f(a)}{z - a} \, dz \right|$$

can be shown to be less than any positive number, no matter how small. This is possible only if

$$\oint_{C'} \frac{f(z) - f(a)}{z - a} \, dz = 0,$$

and the theorem follows.

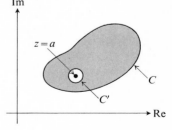

Figure 2.11

---

* To be precise, provided a point on C is approached from the interior.

The Cauchy integral formula reveals a remarkable property of analytic functions: If the values of a function are specified along a closed contour, then its value at an arbitrary point inside the contour is already predetermined. To emphasize this, replace a in the formula by z (variable) and denote the dummy variable by ζ:

$$f(z) = \frac{1}{2\pi i} \oint \frac{f(\zeta)\, d\zeta}{\zeta - z}.$$

In this formula, the integral is a function of the (variable) parameter z and can be differentiated with respect to z. The following theorem (*Leibnitz rule*) follows from the corresponding properties of real integrals:*

$$\frac{d}{dz} \oint_C f(\zeta, z)\, d\zeta = \oint_C \frac{\partial f(\zeta, z)}{\partial z}\, d\zeta$$

(contour C must be a simple closed curve in the usual sense, namely, it should not extend to infinity, otherwise the convergence questions must be considered).

Application of the Leibnitz rule to the Cauchy integral theorem yields an integral expression for the derivative:

$$\frac{df(z)}{dz} = \frac{1}{2\pi i} \oint \frac{f(\zeta)\, d\zeta}{(\zeta - z)^2}.$$

Repetition of this process gives us the nth derivative

$$\frac{d^n f(z)}{dz^n} = \frac{n!}{2\pi i} \oint \frac{f(\zeta)\, d\zeta}{(\zeta - z)^{n+1}}.$$

2.9 COMPLEX SEQUENCES AND SERIES

No serious study of analytic functions is possible without their representation in the form of series, and we now turn our attention to consideration of this aspect of the theory. Our first task would be to consider complex sequences.

An infinite sequence of complex numbers $\{z_n\} = \{z_1, z_2, \ldots\}$ is said to converge to the (complex) limit z, provided

$$|z_n - z| < \epsilon$$

for sufficiently large n; ϵ is, of course, an arbitrarily small positive number. Convergence of complex sequences is reducible to that of real sequences by the following fundamental theorem: *The sequence $\{z_n\}$ converges to $z = x + iy$ if and only if* $\mathrm{Re}\, z_n$ *converges to* x *and* $\mathrm{Im}\, z_n$ *converges to* y.

Proof. If $\mathrm{Re}\, z_n = x_n \to x$ and $\mathrm{Im}\, z_n = y_n \to y$, then

$$|z_n - z| = |(x_n - x) + i(y_n - y)| \le |x_n - x| + |y_n - y| < (\epsilon/2) + (\epsilon/2) = \epsilon$$

---

* See Kaplan, p. 219.

for sufficiently large n. Conversely, if $|z_n - z| < \epsilon$, then z_n is within the circle of radius ϵ about the point z. This implies

$$|x_n - x| < \epsilon \quad \text{and} \quad |y_n - y| < \epsilon,$$

and the theorem follows.

It should now be clear that many of the theorems on real sequences hold for complex sequences as well, for instance the *Cauchy convergence principle: The sequence $\{z_n\}$ converges if and only if $|z_m - z_n| < \epsilon$ for all m and n larger than some integer N.*

Proof. If $|z_m - z_n| < \epsilon$, then $|x_m - x_n| < \epsilon$ and the sequence $|x_n\}$ must be bounded. By the *Bolzano-Weierstrass principle** an infinite bounded (real) sequence must possess *points of accumulation.* Let us take any two of them, ξ_1 and ξ_2 (not necessarily distinct). Then

$$|\xi_1 - \xi_2| = |(\xi_1 - x_m) + (x_m - x_n) + (x_n - \xi_2)|$$
$$\leq |\xi_1 - x_m| + |x_m - x_n| + |x_n - \xi_2|.$$

From the Bolzano-Weierstrass principle it follows that

$$|\xi_1 - x_m| < \epsilon/3, \qquad |x_n - \xi_2| < \epsilon/3,$$

while from the Cauchy condition it follows that $|x_m - x_n| < \epsilon/3$. Therefore $|\xi_1 - \xi_2| < \epsilon$, which implies (since ϵ is arbitrary) that $\xi_1 = \xi_2$. A similar argument holds for $y_n = \text{Im } z_n$ so that the point of accumulation is unique and therefore the sequence converges.

Conversely, if $|z_n - z| < \epsilon$, then

$$|z_m - z_n| \leq |z_m - z| + |z - z_n| < \epsilon/2 + \epsilon/2 = \epsilon,$$

and the second part of the theorem follows as well.

Convergent sequences can be added, subtracted, multiplied, and divided (term by term), and the usual theorems on limits hold:

$$\lim (z_n \pm \zeta_n) = \lim z_n \pm \lim \zeta_n,$$
$$\lim (z_n \zeta_n) = \lim z_n \lim \zeta_n, \quad \text{etc.}$$

Let us now turn to the consideration of complex series. An infinite series of complex numbers $\sum_{n=1}^{\infty} z_n$ is said to be convergent if the sequence $\{S_n\}$ of its partial sums,

$$S_n = \sum_{k=1}^{n} z_k,$$

---

* See, e.g., Knopp, *Theory and Application of Infinite Series*, Section 10.

is a convergent sequence. Denoting $S = \lim S_n$, we customarily write

$$S = \sum_{n=1}^{\infty} z_n.$$

If the sequence of partial sums does not converge, then the series is said to be divergent. It is to be emphasized that, under certain circumstances, divergent series can be given definite meanings and such series are widely used in applications.* However, the theorems derived for convergent sequences should not be indiscriminately applied to divergent sequences.

A series is said to be *absolutely convergent* if the (real) series of moduli

$$\sum_{n=1}^{\infty} |z_n|$$

is a convergent series. An absolutely convergent series is convergent (the proof is trivial). In most cases one proves convergence of a complex series by establishing that it is absolutely convergent. The following tests are most common.

Comparison test. If $|z_n| \leq a_n$ and $\sum a_n$ converges, then $\sum z_n$ converges absolutely.

Ratio test. If $|z_{n+1}/z_n| \leq k$ for all n sufficiently large and $k < 1$, then $\sum z_n$ converges absolutely. If $|z_{n+1}/z| \geq k$ for all n sufficiently large, and $k > 1$, then $\sum z_n$ diverges.

Root test. If $\sqrt[n]{|z_n|} \leq k < 1$ for all n sufficiently large, then $\sum z_n$ converges absolutely, and if $\sqrt[n]{|z_n|} \geq k > 1$ for all n sufficiently large, then $\sum z_n$ diverges.

Proofs of these theorems are similar to those for real series; they are based on the inequalities for absolute values which are also true for complex numbers.

Divergence of a series can often be quickly established by the nth *term test:* If z_n fails to converge to zero then the series $\sum z_n$ diverges.

If necessary, the question of convergence of a complex series can always be reduced to that of two real series by the basic theorem: The series $\sum z_n = \sum (x_n + iy_n)$ converges to $S = P + iQ$ if and only if $\sum x_n$ converges to P and $\sum y_n$ converges to Q. For instance, series which are convergent but not absolutely convergent can be treated in this fashion.

Complex series can be added and subtracted provided they are convergent. They can be multiplied only if they are absolutely convergent, the product being also an absolutely convergent series; if the series are not absolutely convergent, then we are faced with the problem of arranging the product series.†

---

* For example, see Section 6.4.

† See Knopp, *Theory and Application of Infinite Series*, Section 45.

Terms of a complex series may depend on a complex variable z. Most common series are power series, for instance,

$$\sum_{n=0}^{\infty} z^n = 1 + z + z^2 + z^3 + \cdots$$

In many cases such series will converge only if z is confined to a certain region. The above series converges absolutely, by ratio test, provided $|z| < 1$. This series diverges, by ratio test, if $|z| > 1$. The ratio test is inconclusive if $|z| = 1$, but then the nth-term test shows that the series diverges. It is seen that the above power series converges absolutely for all points inside a circle of radius $R = 1$ called the *radius of convergence*.

The concept of the radius of convergence can be applied to every power series. Indeed, if a power series is convergent on a circle of some radius r, then it is absolutely convergent everywhere inside this circle* (by comparison test). The problem is then to find the upper bound of r which is the sought radius of convergence.

Exercise. Show that the series

$$1 - 3z + 9z^2 - 27z^3 + 81z^4 - \cdots$$

has a radius of convergence equal to $\frac{1}{3}$, while the series

$$1 + z + 2!z^2 + 3!z^3 + 4!z^4 + \cdots$$

has a radius of convergence equal to zero; the point $z = 0$ is the only value for which the series converges.

If the upper bound described above does not exist, then the series converges absolutely for all values of z and is said to have an *infinite radius of convergence*. For example,

$$1 + z + \frac{z^2}{2!} + \frac{z^3}{3!} + \frac{z^4}{4!} + \cdots$$

Partial sums of a power series represent a sequence of polynomials in z. Sequences of other functions can also be considered. The sequence $\{f_n(z)\}$ of functions defined in a region R (z belongs to R) is said to converge to a limit function $f(z)$ in R, provided

$$\lim_{n \to \infty} f_n(z) = f(z)$$

for each z in R. For instance, the partial sums of the series

$$\sum_{n=0}^{\infty} z^n = 1 + z + z^2 + z^3 + \cdots$$

---

* This statement is known as Abel's theorem. See Kaplan, p. 350.

form a sequence of functions (polynomials)

$$f_n(z) = \sum_{k=0}^{n} z^k,$$

and this sequence converges to the function $f(z) = 1/(1 - z)$ in the (open) region $|z| < 1$ because

$$f_n(z) = 1 + z + z^2 + \cdots + z^n = \frac{1 - z^{n+1}}{1 - z} = \frac{1}{1 - z} - \frac{z^{n+1}}{1 - z}$$

and

$$\lim_{n \to \infty} \frac{z^{n+1}}{1 - z} = 0 \qquad \text{for } |z| < 1.$$

For this reason the function $f(z) = 1/(1 - z)$ is said to be the sum of the above series (for $|z| < 1$ only!):

$$\sum_{n=0}^{\infty} z^n = 1/(1 - z) \qquad (|z| < 1).$$

When representing a function by a sequence of other functions, it is necessary to know how well a certain function $f(z)$ is approximated by the nth term of a sequence $\{f_n(z)\}$. This question leads to the definition of a *uniform convergence:* The sequence $\{f_n(z)\}$ is said to converge uniformly to $f(z)$ in a region R provided that the inequality

$$|f_n(z) - f(z)| < \epsilon,$$

which is satisfied if $n > N$, holds simultaneously for all z in R.

In plain terms: Let us suppose we desire a certain accuracy ϵ for our approximation. For some particular z, the tenth function in the sequence may suffice (ten terms of a series, if we are talking about partial sums). But for another z, the tenth function may be inadequate because the speed of convergence is slower. In general, we may need to go farther and farther along the sequence as we proceed to points where the convergence gets increasingly worse. Uniform convergence sets the end to this process. The convergence can be no worse than a certain specified degree and the Nth term will guarantee a certain accuracy for the entire region.

Example. The sequence of partial sums of the series

$$\sum_{n=0}^{\infty} z^n$$

is convergent for $|z| < 1$ but it is not uniformly convergent; the convergence becomes increasingly worse as $|z| \to 1$. However, in the region $|z| \leq k$ where $k < 1$, the convergence is uniform. It may be "bad" at $z = k$, but once N is found such that

$$\left| \sum_{m=0}^{n} z^m - \frac{1}{1-z} \right| < \epsilon$$

for all $n > N$ and $z = k$, then the same value of N will hold for all other z with $|z| \le k$.

The series of functions is called *uniformly convergent* (in a region R) if the sequence of its partial sums is uniformly convergent (in that region). Uniform convergence of series is most commonly established by the *Weierstrass M-test:* The series $\sum f_n(z)$ of functions is uniformly convergent in a region R if there exists a series of positive constants M_n such that

$$|f_n(z)| \le M_n \qquad \text{for all } z \text{ in } R$$

and the series $\sum M_n$ is convergent. The proof follows from the comparison test and the fact that the M_n are independent of z.

Several important theorems can be established for a uniformly convergent series as follows.

Continuity theorem. The sum of a uniformly convergent series of continuous functions is a continuous function.

Integrability theorem. A uniformly convergent series of continuous functions can be integrated term by term.

Differentiability theorem. A uniformly convergent series can be differentiated term by term, provided all terms have continuous derivatives and the resulting series is uniformly convergent.

All these theorems can be proved by the same methods as those used for real variables.* One can also show that the sums and products of uniformly convergent series are uniformly convergent (within the same region, of course).

From the above results one can deduce the

Weierstrass theorem. If the terms of the series $\sum f_n(z)$ are analytic inside and on a simple closed curve C and the series converges uniformly on C, then its sum is an analytic function (inside and on C) and the series may be differentiated or integrated any number of times.

2.10 TAYLOR AND LAURENT SERIES

Consider a power series of powers $(z - a)^n$ where a is a fixed complex number:

$$c_0 + c_1(z - a) + c_2(z - a)^2 + c_3(z - a)^3 + \cdots$$

If this series converges for some value $z_0 \ne a$ (for $z_0 = a$ the series always converges), then it is absolutely convergent everywhere in the interior of the circle

---

* For these methods see Kaplan, pp. 345–348.

of radius $|z_0 - a| = R_0$ about the point a (by comparison test). Moreover, it will be uniformly convergent within a circle of radius R *less* than R_0 (by the Weierstrass M-test). It follows that the above power series represents, within a circle R (at least), a complex function

$$f(z) = \sum_{n=0}^{\infty} c_n(z - a)^n.$$

By the Weierstrass theorem, this function must be analytic within the circle. Summarizing these results, we can state that every power series with a *nonzero radius of convergence* represents a regular function in some neighborhood of the point $z = a$. Such series may be added and multiplied (where the neighborhoods overlap) and differentiated and integrated any number of times.

The converse statement is also true: *Every function $f(z)$ analytic at $z = a$ can be expanded in a power series*

$$f(z) = \sum_{n=0}^{\infty} c_n(z - a)^n$$

valid in some neighborhood of point a. This series, known as the *Taylor series*, is unique, and the coefficients c_n can be obtained from the formula

$$c_n = \frac{1}{n!} \left. \frac{d^n f(z)}{dz^n} \right|_{z=a}.$$

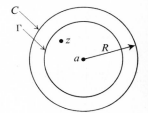

Figure 2.12

Proof. Let $f(z)$ be analytic within a circle C about the point a and let z be inside C (Fig. 2.12). It is then always possible to construct a circle Γ such that Γ is inside C and the point z is inside Γ. This is necessary to ensure that $f(z)$ is analytic on Γ and the Cauchy formula can be applied:

$$f(z) = \frac{1}{2\pi i} \oint_{\Gamma} \frac{f(\zeta)}{\zeta - z} \, d\zeta.$$

The quantity $1/(\zeta - z)$ may now be expanded by means of a geometric series:

$$\frac{1}{\zeta - z} = \frac{1}{\zeta - a} \cdot \frac{1}{1 - (z - a)/(\zeta - a)}$$

$$= \frac{1}{\zeta - a} \sum_{n=0}^{\infty} \left(\frac{z - a}{\zeta - a} \right)^n.$$

This is allowable because the series converges (by ratio test). Then

$$f(z) = \frac{1}{2\pi i} \oint_{\Gamma} \frac{f(\zeta)}{\zeta - z} \, d\zeta = \frac{1}{2\pi i} \oint_{\Gamma} \sum_{n=0}^{\infty} \frac{f(\zeta)(z - a)^n}{(\zeta - a)^{n+1}} \, d\zeta.$$

The series appearing in the integrand, viewed as a function of ζ, is uniformly convergent on Γ and, by the Weierstrass theorem, can be integrated term by term:

$$f(z) = \frac{1}{2\pi i} \sum_{n=0}^{\infty} (z - a)^n \oint_{\Gamma} \frac{f(\zeta)}{(\zeta - a)^{n+1}} \, d\zeta.$$

In view of the formula (p. 66)

$$f^{(n)}(a) = \frac{d^n f(z)}{dz^n}\bigg|_{z=a} = \frac{n!}{2\pi i} \oint \frac{f(\zeta)}{(\zeta - a)^{n+1}} \, d\zeta,$$

we obtain

$$f(z) = \sum_{n=0}^{\infty} \frac{1}{n!} f^{(n)}(a)(z - a)^n.$$

It remains for us to show that this power series is unique. Indeed, if there is a series with undetermined coefficients c_n,

$$f(z) = \sum_{n=0}^{\infty} c_n(z - a)^n,$$

which represents an analytic function in some neighborhood of point a, then it is uniformly convergent within and on a circle Γ inside the neighborhood. Differentiating the series n times and setting $z = a$, we obtain

$$c_n = \frac{1}{n!} f^{(n)}(a),$$

which completes the proof.

Power series can be generalized to contain negative powers of $(z - a)$ to read

$$\sum_{n=-\infty}^{+\infty} c_n(z - a)^n.$$

Such series may be split into two parts:

$$\sum_{n=0}^{\infty} c_n(z - a)^n \quad \text{and} \quad \sum_{m=1}^{\infty} \frac{c_{-m}}{(z - a)^m},$$

and the original series will converge provided *both* parts converge.

The series of positive powers converges inside a circle of some radius R_1 about the point $z = a$. The series of negative powers will, in general, converge outside a circle of some radius R_2 about $z = a$. To see this, denote

$$\frac{1}{z - a} = \zeta$$

so that the series of negative powers of $(z - a)$ becomes

$$\sum_{m=1}^{\infty} c_{-m} \zeta^m.$$

Unless this series happens to have zero radius of convergence it will, in general, converge within a circle of radius R' about the origin. But $|\zeta| < R'$ implies

$$|z - a| > 1/R' = R_2,$$

and the statement follows. Therefore we conclude that if $R_2 > R_1$, then the series

$$\sum_{n=-\infty}^{+\infty} c_n(z - a)^n$$

will converge within the annulus

$$R_1 < |z - a| < R_2.$$

It can, of course, happen that $R_2 < R_1$, in which case our series will diverge everywhere.

The following theorem can now be derived: *Every function $f(z)$ analytic in an annulus*

$$R_1 < |z - a| < R_2$$

can be expanded in a series of positive and negative powers of $(z - a)$, namely

$$f(z) = \sum_{n=-\infty}^{+\infty} c_n(z - a)^n.$$

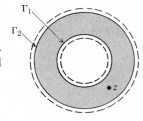

This series, known as the *Laurent series*, is unique for a given annulus, and the coefficients c_n can be obtained from

$$c_n = \frac{1}{2\pi i} \oint_\Gamma \frac{f(z)\,dz}{(z - a)^{n+1}},$$

where Γ is a circle of radius R such that $R_1 < R < R_2$.

Figure 2.13

Proof. Contract the radius R_2 slightly and expand the radius R_1 slightly to obtain an annular region, with point z inside, to which the generalized Cauchy formula is applicable (Fig. 2.13):*

$$f(z) = \frac{1}{2\pi i} \oint_{\Gamma_2} \frac{f(\zeta)\,d\zeta}{\zeta - z} + \frac{1}{2\pi i} \oint_{\Gamma_1} \frac{f(\zeta)\,d\zeta}{\zeta - z}.$$

The first integral can be treated as in the derivation of the Taylor series:

$$\frac{1}{2\pi i} \oint_{\Gamma_2} \frac{f(\zeta)\,d\zeta}{\zeta - z} = \frac{1}{2\pi i} \oint_{\Gamma_2} \frac{f(\zeta)(z - a)^n}{(\zeta - a)^{n+1}}\,d\zeta = \sum_{n=0}^{\infty} (z - a)^n \frac{1}{2\pi i} \oint_{\Gamma_2} \frac{f(\zeta)\,d\zeta}{(\zeta - a)^{n+1}}.$$

Term-by-term integration is permissible by uniform convergence.

---

* We shall occasionally use the convenient symbols $\oint$ and $\oint$ to indicate clockwise or counterclockwise direction of integration.

The second integral is treated by expanding $1/(\zeta - z)$ in a somewhat different geometric series:

$$\frac{1}{\zeta - z} = -\frac{1}{z - a} \cdot \frac{1}{1 - (\zeta - a)/(z - a)} = -\sum_{m=0}^{\infty} \frac{(\zeta - a)^m}{(z - a)^{m+1}}$$

which is convergent by ratio test. Then

$$\frac{1}{2\pi i} \oint_{\Gamma_1} \frac{f(\zeta)\, d\zeta}{\zeta - z} = -\frac{1}{2\pi i} \oint_{\Gamma_1} \frac{f(\zeta)\, d\zeta}{\zeta - z}$$

$$= \sum_{m=0}^{\infty} \frac{1}{(z - a)^{m+1}} \frac{1}{2\pi i} \oint_{\Gamma_1} f(\zeta)(\zeta - a)^m \, d\zeta.$$

Replace m by $-(n + 1)$ (n must be negative) and rewrite the above as

$$\frac{1}{2\pi i} \oint_{\Gamma_1} \frac{f(\zeta)\, d\zeta}{\zeta - z} = \sum_{n=-1}^{-\infty} (z - a)^n \frac{1}{2\pi i} \oint_{\Gamma_1} \frac{f(\zeta)\, d\zeta}{(\zeta - a)^{n+1}}.$$

Finally, note that the integrals

$$\oint_{\Gamma_2} \frac{f(\zeta)\, d\zeta}{(\zeta - a)^{n+1}} \qquad (n = 0, 1, 2, \dots)$$

and

$$\oint_{\Gamma_1} \frac{f(\zeta)\, d\zeta}{(\zeta - a)^{n+1}} \qquad (n = -1, -2, -3, \dots)$$

may be just as well evaluated over a common circle Γ, concentric with Γ_1 and Γ_2, and lying within the annulus $R_1 < R < R_2$.

To prove the uniqueness, assume that an expansion

$$f(z) = \sum_{n=-\infty}^{+\infty} c_n(z - a)^n$$

exists and is valid in the annulus $R_1 < |z - a| < R_2$. Choose an arbitrary integer k, multiply both sides of this expression by $(z - a)^{-k-1}$, and integrate around a circle Γ about $z = a$, lying within the annulus. Then

$$\oint_{\Gamma} \frac{f(z)\, dz}{(z - a)^{k+1}} = \sum_{n=-\infty}^{+\infty} c_n \oint_{\Gamma} \frac{dz}{(z - a)^{k+1-n}}.$$

All integrals on the right-hand side will vanish except one, for which $n = k$, and whose value is $2\pi i$. Therefore

$$\oint_{\Gamma} \frac{f(z)\, dz}{(z - a)^{k+1}} = c_k 2\pi i,$$

which completes the proof.

The part of the Laurent series consisting of positive powers of $(z - a)$ is called the *regular part*. It resembles the Taylor series but it should be emphasized that the nth coefficient cannot be associated, in general, with $f^{(n)}(a)$ because the latter may not exist. In most applications, $f(z)$ is not analytic at $z = a$. The other part, consisting of negative powers, is called the *principal part*. Either part (or both) may terminate or be identically zero. Of course, if the principal part is identically zero, then $f(z)$ is analytic at $z = a$, and the Laurent series is identical with the Taylor series.

Remark. The Laurent series is unique only for a specified annulus. In general, a function $f(z)$ may possess two or more entirely different Laurent series about a given point, valid for different (nonoverlapping) regions. For instance,

$$\frac{1}{z(1 - z)} = \frac{1}{z} + 1 + z + z^2 + z^3 + \cdots, \qquad 0 < |z| < 1,$$

$$\frac{1}{z(1 - z)} = -\frac{1}{z^2} - \frac{1}{z^3} - \frac{1}{z^4} - \cdots, \qquad 1 < |z| < \infty$$

(the notation $0 < |z| < 1$ is to be understood as $\epsilon < |z| < 1$ with ϵ arbitrarily small; similarly, $1 < |z| < \infty$ means $1 < |z| < M$ with M arbitrarily large).

In the following examples, several very common techniques for the construction of Taylor and Laurent series are illustrated.

Example 1. *Use of Geometric series.* $f(z) = 1/(z - a)$ ($a = $ nonzero complex constant).

It is known that

$$1 + z + z^2 + z^3 + \cdots = \sum_{n=0}^{\infty} z^n = \frac{1}{1 - z} \qquad (|z| < 1).$$

Therefore

$$f(z) = \frac{1}{z - a} = -\frac{1}{a}\frac{1}{1 - z/a} = -\frac{1}{a}\sum_{n=0}^{\infty}\left(\frac{z}{a}\right)^n \qquad (|z| < |a|).$$

This is the Taylor series of $f(z)$ about the point $z = 0$. Its radius of convergence is $R = |a|$ because at the distance R from the origin there is a point $z = a$ where $f(z)$ fails to be analytic. This is the only point where $f(z)$ is not analytic. Therefore $f(z)$ should possess a Laurent series about $z = 0$ which would be valid for $|z| > |a|$. Write

$$f(z) = \frac{1}{z - a} = \frac{1}{z}\frac{1}{1 - a/z}.$$

If $|z| > |a|$, then $|a/z| < 1$, and we can expand

$$\frac{1}{1 - a/z} = \sum_{n=0}^{\infty}\left(\frac{a}{z}\right)^n \qquad (|z| > |a|).$$

Therefore

$$f(z) = \frac{1}{z-a} = \frac{1}{z} \sum_{n=0}^{\infty} \left(\frac{a}{z}\right)^n = \sum_{n=0}^{\infty} \frac{a^n}{z^{n+1}} \qquad (|z| > |a|).$$

This is the desired Laurent series.

The function $f(z)$ can be expanded by this method about any point $z = b$: Indeed, write

$$f(z) = \frac{1}{z-a} = \frac{1}{(z-b)-(a-b)} = \frac{1}{\zeta - (a-b)} \qquad (b \neq a).$$

Then, either

$$f(z) = -\frac{1}{(a-b)} \sum_{n=0}^{\infty} \frac{\zeta^n}{(a-b)^n} = -\frac{1}{(a-b)} \sum_{n=0}^{\infty} \frac{(z-b)^n}{(a-b)^n}$$

$$(|z-b| < |a-b|),$$

or

$$f(z) = \sum_{n=0}^{\infty} \frac{(a-b)^n}{(z-b)^{n+1}} \qquad (|z-b| > |a-b|).$$

Example 2. *Rational fraction decomposition.*

$$f(z) = \frac{1}{z^2 - (2+i)z + 2i}.$$

The roots of the denominator are $a = i$, $b = 2$ (simple and distinct). Therefore $f(z)$ fails to be analytic only at $z = i$ and $z = 2$ and should possess a Taylor series about $z = 0$ valid for $|z| < 1$ ($|i| = 1$) and two Laurent series about $z = 0$ valid for $1 < |z| < 2$ and $|z| > 2$. To obtain these three series, we use the identities

$$z^2 - (2+i)z + 2i = (z-i)(z-2)$$

and

$$f(z) = \frac{1}{(z-i)(z-2)} = \frac{1}{2-i} \left(\frac{1}{z-2} - \frac{1}{z-i} \right).$$

Suppose that the Laurent series valid for $1 < |z| < 2$ is desired. The function $1/(z-2)$ should then be expanded in Taylor series about $z = 0$ (Example 1). This series is, in particular, valid for $1 < |z| < 2$. The function $1/(z-i)$ should be expanded in the Laurent series about $z = 0$ valid for $|z| > 1$ (Example 1). This series is also valid for $1 < |z| < 2$. If these two series are subtracted, we may obtain (multiplying by $1/(2-i)$) a series for $f(z)$ valid for $1 < |z| < 2$ which is the desired Laurent series.

Example 3. *Differentiation.* $f(z) = 1/(z-1)^2$.

The method applied in Example 2 fails here because of the double root of the denominator. Among the alternative methods the simplest one is, perhaps, to observe that

$$\frac{1}{(z-1)^2} = \frac{d}{dz} \left(\frac{1}{1-z} \right).$$

The series
$$\frac{1}{1-z} = 1 + z + z^2 + \cdots = \sum_{n=0}^{\infty} z^n \qquad (|z| < 1)$$

can be differentiated term by term within the circle of convergence. Therefore

$$\frac{1}{(z-1)^2} = 1 + 2z + 3z^2 + \cdots = \sum_{n=0}^{\infty} (n+1)z^n \qquad (|z| < 1).$$

Example 4. *Integration.* $f(z) = \log(1 + z) = \log|1 + z| + i \arg(1 + z)$.

This is the principal branch of the (multivalued) logarithmic function. The branch line extends from "minus infinity" to minus one and $\log(1 + z)$ is analytic within the circle $|z| = 1$.

We know that
$$\frac{d}{dz} \log(1 + z) = \frac{1}{1+z}.$$

Therefore we may expand

$$1/(1+z) = 1 - z + z^2 - z^3 + z^4 - \cdots = \sum_{n=0}^{\infty} (-1)^n z^n \qquad (|z| < 1)$$

and integrate term by term:

$$\int^z \frac{d\zeta}{1+\zeta} = z - \frac{z^2}{2} + \frac{z^3}{3} - \frac{z^4}{4} + \cdots + C \qquad (|z| < 1),$$

where C is the constant of integration. Since $\log 1 = 0$, it follows that $C = 0$ and

$$\log(1+z) = z - \frac{z^2}{2} + \frac{z^3}{3} - \cdots = \sum_{n=1}^{\infty} (-1)^{n+1} \frac{z^n}{n} \qquad (|z| < 1).$$

Other branches of $\text{Log}(1 + z)$ will have the same series except for different values of the constant C.

2.11 ZEROS AND SINGULARITIES

Point $z = a$ is called a *zero* (or a *root*) of the function $f(z)$ if $f(a) = 0$. If $f(z)$ is analytic at $z = a$, then its Taylor series

$$f(z) = \sum_{n=0}^{\infty} c_n(z - a)^n$$

must have $c_0 = 0$. If $c_1 \neq 0$, the point $z = a$ is called a *simple zero* (or a zero of order one). It may happen that c_1 and, perhaps, several other next coefficients vanish. Let c_m be the first nonvanishing coefficient (unless $f(z) \equiv 0$ such coefficient must exist). Then the zero is said to be *of order m*. The order of a zero may be evaluated (without the knowledge of Taylor series) by calculating

$$\lim_{z \to a} \frac{f(z)}{(z - a)^n}$$

for $n = 1, 2, 3, \ldots$; the lowest value of n for which this limit will not vanish is equal to the order of the zero.

If a function $f(z)$ is analytic in the neighborhood of some point $z = a$ with the exception of the point $z = a$ itself, then it is said to have an *isolated singularity* (or an isolated singular point) at $z = a$.

It is customary to distinguish isolated singularities by the following types of behavior of $f(z)$ as $z \to a$ in an arbitrary fashion:

1. $f(z)$ remains bounded, that is, $|f(z)| \leq B$ for a fixed B.

2. $f(z)$ is not bounded and $|f(z)|$ approaches infinity, namely, $|f(z)| > M$ (any M) for $|z - a| < \epsilon$ (some ϵ).

3. Neither of the two cases above; in plain terms, $f(z)$ oscillates in a "wild" manner.

Examples of these three types of singularities (at $z = 0$) are

Case 1, $f(z) = \sin z/z,$

Case 2, $f(z) = 1/\sin z,$

Case 3, $f(z) = e^{1/z}.$

The first case turns out to be trivial because then the limit $\lim_{z \to a} f(z)$ must exist, and if the function $f(z)$ is defined at $z = a$ by $f(a) = \lim_{z \to a} f(z)$, then it must be regular at $z = a$ as well.

Remark. The formula $f(z) = \sin z/z$ *does not define*, in a rigorous sense, the value of the function at $z = 0$. The extended formula

$$f(z) = \begin{cases} \sin z/z, & z \neq 0, \\ 1, & z = 0, \end{cases}$$

does define the function $f(z)$ at $z = 0$ (and elsewhere).

To prove the above statement concerning Case 1, observe that $f(z)$ is analytic in an annulus $\rho < |z - a| < R$ within a neighborhood of $z = a$. By the Cauchy theorem, for any point z within this annulus (Fig. 2.14), we have

$$f(z) = \frac{1}{2\pi i} \oint_\Gamma \frac{f(\zeta)\,d\zeta}{\zeta - z} + \frac{1}{2\pi i} \oint_\gamma \frac{f(\zeta)\,d\zeta}{\zeta - z}.$$

We shall show that the second integral must be zero for all ρ. If this is so, then $f(z)$ must approach the limit

$$\lim_{z \to a} f(z) = \frac{1}{2\pi i} \oint \frac{f(\zeta)\,d\zeta}{\zeta - a},$$

which will prove two things at once: (a) $\lim_{z \to a} f(z)$ exists, (b) if $f(a)$ is defined by this limit then the redefined function $f(z)$ is analytic at $z = a$ as well.

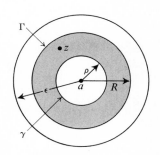

Figure 2.14

To achieve this result, write $\zeta - z = (\zeta - a) - (z - a)$ and observe that

$$|(\zeta - a) - (z - a)| \geq |z - a| - |\zeta - a| = |z - a| - \rho.$$

Then, for a *fixed z*,

$$\left| \frac{1}{2\pi i} \oint_\gamma \frac{f(\zeta)\, d\zeta}{\zeta - z} \right| \leq \frac{1}{2\pi} \frac{B}{|z - a| - \rho} 2\pi\rho = \frac{B\rho}{|z - a| - \rho}.$$

The integral must be independent of ρ because of the analyticity of the integrand. Since it is less than an arbitrary positive number (for sufficiently small ρ) it must be equal to zero. The proof is now complete.

Because of the described property, isolated singularities of the first type are called *removable singularities*. In practice, if a function is defined by a formula which fails for some isolated point $z = a$, then the formula is tacitly replaced by the corresponding limit. In this sense, the functions

$$f(z) = \sin z/z, \qquad g(z) = e^{\sin z/z}, \qquad h(z) = 1/z - \cot z$$

are analytic at $z = 0$.

The second type of isolated singularity, when $|f(z)| \to \infty$ as $z \to a$, is called a *pole*. Since the singularity is isolated, there must exist a Laurent series

$$f(z) = \sum_{n=-\infty}^{+\infty} c_n(z - a)^n$$

valid for $0 < |z - a| < R$ (for some R). If the principal part terminates, i.e., if the Laurent series is of the form

$$f(z) = \sum_{n=-m}^{+\infty} c_n(z - a)^n,$$

then $f(z)$ has a pole *of order m* at $z = a$. Conversely, if $f(z)$ has a pole at $z = a$, it must have the Laurent series (for $0 < |z - a| < R$) of the above form as seen from the following argument: Consider the function

$$g(z) = 1/f(z).$$

Unless $f(z) \equiv 0$ there must exist a neighborhood of $z = a$ where $f(z)$ has no zeros. In this neighborhood, $g(z)$ is analytic and

$$|g(z)| \to 0 \qquad \text{as} \qquad z \to a$$

(because $|f(z)| \to \infty$). Therefore $g(z)$ has a zero at $z = a$. This zero must be of some definite order m, namely,

$$g(z) = \sum_{n=m}^{\infty} b_n(z - a)^n \qquad (0 \leq |z - a| < R).$$

Rewrite this as

$$g(z) = (z - a)^m \sum_{k=0}^{\infty} b'_k(z - a)^k = (z - a)^m \psi(z),$$

where $b'_k = b_{m+k}$ and $b'_0 \neq 0$. Now

$$f(z) = \frac{1}{g(z)} = \frac{1}{(z - a)^m} \frac{1}{\psi(z)}.$$

Since $\psi(z)$ is analytic at $z = a$ and does not vanish there, it follows that $1/\psi(z)$ must be analytic as well and possess a Taylor series at $z = a$. Then

$$f(z) = \frac{1}{(z - a)^m} \sum_{k=0}^{\infty} c'_k(z - a)^k.$$

However, this is evidently a Laurent series with a terminating principal part so that the argument is complete.

Example. The function $f(z) = \csc z = 1/\sin z$ has the Laurent series valid for $0 < |z| < \pi$:

$$\csc z = \frac{1}{z} + \frac{1}{6}z + \frac{7}{360}z^3 + \frac{31}{15120}z^5 + \cdots,$$

from which it follows that it has a *simple* pole at the origin.

The order of a pole may be obtained without knowledge of the Laurent series. This is done by evaluating

$$\lim_{z \to a} (z - a)^n f(z)$$

for $n = 1, 2, 3, \ldots$; the lowest value of n for which this limit exists will yield the order of the pole. Note that this particular limit cannot be zero.

The third type of isolated singularity is known as *essential singularity*. The Laurent series valid for $0 < |z - a| < R$ (for some R) must have an infinite principal part.

Example. The function $f(z) = e^{1/z}$ possesses the following Laurent series valid for $0 < |z| < R$ (R can be arbitrary):

$$e^{1/z} = 1 + \frac{1}{z} + \frac{1}{2!} \cdot \frac{1}{z^2} + \frac{1}{3!} \cdot \frac{1}{z^3} + \cdots$$

Since the principal part is infinite, the function has essential singularity at $z = 0$. Note that $|f(z)|$ neither remains bounded as $z \to 0$ nor approaches infinity, for an arbitrary manner of approach: For instance, if z approaches zero along the negative real semiaxis, then $|f(z)| \to 0$; if it approaches zero along the positive real semiaxis, then $|f(z)| \to \infty$; if it approaches zero along the imaginary axis, then $|f(z)|$ remains constant but arg $f(z)$ oscillates, and so on.

In fact it is not difficult to show that even in an arbitrarily small neighborhood of an essential singularity, a function $f(z)$ assumes values arbitrarily close to any desired complex number (Weierstrass-Casorati theorem). Also, an even more explicit statement can be proved, known as

Picard's theorem. In an arbitrarily small neighborhood of an essential singularity, a function $f(z)$ assumes infinitely many times every complex value except, perhaps, one particular value.

Remark. It should be emphasized that an infinite principal part in the Laurent series implies essential singularity only if the series is valid "up to the singular point":*

$$f(z) = \frac{1}{(z-1)^2} + \frac{1}{(z-1)^3} + \frac{1}{(z-1)^4} + \cdots$$

does not mean that $f(z)$ has essential singularity at $z = 1$. The point is that the above series converges only if $|z - 1| > 1$. It actually represents the function

$$f(z) = \frac{1}{z^2 - 3z + 2}$$

in the annulus $1 < |z - 1| < R$ (for any R). This function evidently has a simple pole at $z = 1$.

Apart from isolated singularities, complex functions can have other types of breakdown of analyticity. The most common case is that of a *branch point*. Consider, for instance, the function $f(z) = \sqrt{z}$. For every point except the origin it is possible to construct a neighborhood and find a branch of $\sqrt{z}$ that will be analytic in this neighborhood. This branch may not be the principal one or its complementary, called the second branch in Section 2.6; rather, it may be something like branch A in the terminology on p. 56. For the origin, this is not possible because any neighborhood of $z = 0$ will contain a portion of the branch line (whatever it may be) where the selected branch is discontinuous. Similar statements can be made about other multivalued functions and their branches.

It is evident that there can be no Taylor or Laurent series valid for the region $0 < |z - a| < R$ (for some R) about a branch point $z = a$. However, Laurent series valid for $R_1 < |z - a| < R_2$ are sometimes possible.

Example

$$\sqrt{z^2 - 1} = z - \frac{1}{2}\frac{1}{z} - \frac{1}{8}\frac{1}{z^3} - \frac{1}{16}\frac{1}{z^5} - \frac{5}{128}\frac{1}{z^7} - \cdots$$

This series is valid for $|z| > 1$ and represents a branch of the function $\sqrt{z^2 - 1}$ which is analytic in this region. The branch line joins, in this case, two branch points $z = +1$ and $z = -1$ and does not extend to infinity (Fig. 2.15). Replacing

---

* Namely, for all points in a neighborhood $|z - a| < \epsilon$ except $z = a$.

z by $(z - 1)$, we obtain a Laurent series centered about the branch point $z = 1$. The latter will converge for $|z - 1| > 2$.

Another type of singular behavior of an analytic function occurs when it possesses an infinite number of isolated singularities converging to some limit point. Consider, for instance,

$$f(z) = \csc \frac{1}{z} = \frac{1}{\sin (1/z)}.$$

The denominator has simple zeros whenever

$$z = \frac{1}{n\pi} \qquad (n = \pm 1, \pm 2, \ldots).$$

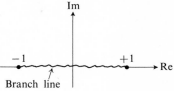

Figure 2.15

The function $f(z)$ has simple poles at these points and the sequence of these poles converges toward the origin. The origin cannot be called an isolated singularity because every neighborhood of it contains at least one pole (actually an infinite number of them).

2.12 THE RESIDUE THEOREM AND ITS APPLICATIONS

Let $f(z)$ be analytic in some neighborhood of $z = a$ except, perhaps, at $z = a$ itself [in other words $f(z)$ is either analytic at $z = a$ or has an isolated singularity there]. Let C be a simple closed path lying in this neighborhood and surrounding $z = a$. Then the integral

$$\text{Res } f(a) = \frac{1}{2\pi i} \oint_C f(z)\, dz$$

is independent of the choice of C and is called the *residue* of function at the point $z = a$. Evidently, if $f(z)$ is analytic at $z = a$ (the point $z = a$ is then called a *regular point*), the residue is zero. If $z = a$ is an isolated singularity, then the residue may or may not be zero.

Examples

1. $f(z) = 1/z$; the residue at $z = 0$ is equal to unity.
2. $f(z) = 1/z^2$; the residue at $z = 0$ is equal to zero.

According to the formula on p. 74, the residue is seen to be identical with the coefficient c_{-1} in the Laurent series

$$f(z) = \sum_{n=-\infty}^{+\infty} c_n (z - a)^n,$$

which is valid for $0 < |z - a| < R$ (for some R).

The residues of a function at its isolated singularities find their application in the evaluation of integrals, complex or real. The basis for these applications is the *residue theorem: If $f(z)$ is analytic on and inside a closed contour C except for a finite number of isolated singularities at $z = a_1, a_2, \ldots, a_n$, which are all located inside C, then*

$$\oint_C f(z)\, dz = 2\pi i \sum_{k=1}^{n} \text{Res } f(a_k).$$

This theorem is proved by the technique of cutting the channels between the contour C and small circles $C_1, C_2, \ldots$ around each singularity (Fig. 2.16).

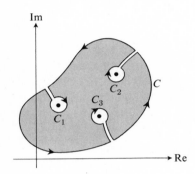

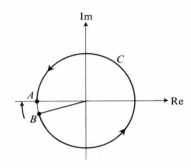

Figure 2.16   Figure 2.17

There is a variety of practical methods for quick evaluation of residues:

FIRST METHOD. From the definition,

$$\text{Res } f(a) = \frac{1}{2\pi i} \oint_C f(z)\, dz$$

(using a suitably chosen contour C). This method is rarely used, but may be valuable if the primitive function of $f(z)$ is known and has a branch point at $z = a$.

Example. $f(z) = 1/z$, $F(z) = \text{Log } z$. Any branch of Log z may be chosen, but in order to preserve the relationship

$$f(z) = F'(z) = \frac{dF(z)}{dz},$$

the closed contour must be disconnected and the appropriate limiting process must be applied. For instance (Fig. 2.17),

$$\oint_C \frac{1}{z}\, dz = \lim_{B \to A} \int_B^A \frac{dz}{z} = \lim_{B \to A} \{\log (A) - \log (B)\} = 2\pi i.$$

Here the principal branch was used, which possesses a discontinuity $2\pi i$ on the negative real semiaxis.

SECOND METHOD. For a *simple* pole at $z = a$ the following formula holds:

$$\operatorname{Res} f(a) = \lim_{z \to a} (z - a)f(z).$$

The limit involved is often obtained by simple substitution or the use of well-known limiting values.

Example. $f(z) = \tan z / z^2$. Then

$$\operatorname{Res} f(0) = \lim_{z \to 0} z \frac{\tan z}{z^2} = \lim_{z \to 0} \frac{\sin z}{z} \frac{1}{\cos z} = 1.$$

THIRD METHOD. For a pole of order m at $z = a$ the following formula holds:

$$\operatorname{Res} f(a) = \frac{1}{(m - 1)!} \lim_{z \to a} \left\{ \frac{d^{m-1}}{dz^{m-1}} [(z - a)^m f(z)] \right\}.$$

Example. $f(z) = e^z / z^4$. Then

$$\operatorname{Res} f(0) = \frac{1}{3!} \lim_{z \to 0} \left\{ \frac{d^3}{dz^3} \left(z^4 \frac{e^z}{z^4} \right) \right\} = \frac{1}{6} \lim_{z \to 0} e^z = \frac{1}{6}.$$

FOURTH METHOD. A common case of a simple pole is when $f(z)$ has the form

$$f(z) = \frac{\varphi(z)}{\psi(z)},$$

where $\varphi(a) \neq 0$ and $\psi(z)$ has a simple zero at $z = a$. In this case

$$\operatorname{Res} f(a) = \frac{\varphi(a)}{\psi'(a)}.$$

Note that if $z = a$ is a simple zero of $\psi(z)$, then $\psi'(a)$ cannot vanish.

Example. $f(z) = e^z / \sin z$. Then

$$\operatorname{Res} f(0) = \left. \frac{e^z}{\cos z} \right|_{z=0} = 1.$$

FIFTH METHOD. Expand $f(z)$ in the Laurent series and pick out the residue. This method is valuable if $f(z)$ is a product of functions with known Laurent series. The series for $f(z)$ is then obtained by multiplication. In practice, the coefficient c_{-1} can be picked out by inspection.

Example. $f(z) = e^{tz} / (z + 2)(z - 1)^4$.

The residue at $z = 1$ is desired. In the first step, transfer the pole to the origin:

$$z - 1 = \omega, \qquad z = \omega + 1.$$

Then

$$f(z) = e^t \frac{e^{t\omega}}{(\omega + 3)\omega^4}.$$

In the second step, expand $e^{t\omega}$ and $1/(3 + \omega)$:

$$e^{t\omega} = 1 + t\omega + \frac{t^2}{2!}\omega^2 + \frac{t^3}{3!}\omega^3 + \cdots \qquad \text{(all } \omega\text{)},$$

$$\frac{1}{3 + \omega} = \frac{1}{3}\frac{1}{1 + \omega/3} = \frac{1}{3}\left\{1 - \frac{\omega}{3} + \frac{\omega^2}{3^2} - \frac{\omega^3}{3^3} + \cdots\right\} \qquad (|\omega| < 3).$$

In the third step, evaluate (by inspection) the coefficient with ω^3 from the product of the above two series:

$$\frac{1}{3}\left\{-\frac{1}{3^3} + \frac{t^3}{3!} - \frac{t}{3^2} - \frac{t^2}{3\cdot 2!}\right\}.$$

In the fourth step, evaluate the residue:

$$\text{Res } f(1) = e^t\left(\frac{t^3}{18} - \frac{t^2}{18} - \frac{t}{27} + \frac{1}{81}\right).$$

Exercise. Prove the validity of the third method given above. [*Hint:* Represent $f(z)$ as

$$f(z) = \varphi(z)/(z - a)^m$$

and use the formula from p. 66.]

The residue theorem can be applied to the evaluation of a wide variety of definite integrals, real or complex. Some of the most frequently used procedures are shown in the several examples which follow.

Example 1. Consider the real integral

$$I = \int_0^{2\pi} \frac{1}{1 - 2p\cos\theta + p^2} \qquad (|p| \neq 1).$$

This integral can be converted into a contour integral in complex plane by setting $z = e^{i\theta}$. Then

$$d\theta = \frac{dz}{iz} \qquad \cos\theta = \frac{1}{2}\left(z + \frac{1}{z}\right)$$

and

$$I = \oint_C \frac{dz}{i(z - p)(1 - pz)},$$

where C is the unit circle in the z-plane. The integrand has two poles: at $z = p$ and $z = 1/p$. If $|p| < 1$, the pole $z = p$ is inside the contour, while the pole $z = 1/p$ is outside. Only the residue at $z = p$ is needed; it is equal to

$$\frac{1}{i}\frac{1}{1 - p^2};$$

therefore

$$I = 2\pi i\frac{1}{i}\frac{1}{1 - p^2} = \frac{2\pi}{1 - p^2} \qquad (|p| < 1).$$

If $|p| > 1$, the needed residue is at $z = 1/p$ and it is equal to

$$\frac{1}{i} \frac{1}{p^2 - 1},$$

yielding

$$I = 2\pi i \frac{1}{i} \frac{1}{p^2 - 1} = \frac{2\pi}{p^2 - 1} \qquad (|p| > 1).$$

Note that both results can be combined into

$$I = \frac{2\pi}{|p^2 - 1|} \qquad (|p| \neq 1),$$

while the integral is not defined for $|p| = 1$.

This method can be used for integrals of the type $\int_0^{2\pi} R(\cos\theta, \sin\theta)\, d\theta$, where $R(\cos\theta, \sin\theta)$ is a *rational* function of $\cos\theta$ and $\sin\theta$.

Example 2. Consider the real integral

$$I = \int_{-\infty}^{+\infty} \frac{dx}{x^2 + a^2} = \lim_{R \to \infty} \int_{-R}^{+R} \frac{dx}{x^2 + a^2} \qquad (a > 0).$$

The integral $\int_{-R}^{+R} dx/(x^2 + a^2)$ can be treated as a portion of the complex integral $\oint_C dz/(z^2 + a^2)$ evaluated over the contour C shown in Fig. 2.18. Indeed (set $z = x$ on the real axis):

$$\oint_C \frac{dz}{z^2 + a^2} = \int_{-R}^{+R} \frac{dx}{x^2 + a^2} + \int_{C_R} \frac{dz}{z^2 + a^2}.$$

Let us *estimate* the integral over the semicircle C_R when R is very large: Write

$$\frac{1}{z^2 + a^2} = \frac{1}{z^2} \frac{1}{1 + a^2/z^2}.$$

If $|z| = R$ is very large, then $|a^2/z^2| = a^2/R^2$ is small and $|1 + a^2/z^2|$ is *almost* equal to unity (Fig. 2.19). To be precise, observe that $|1 + a^2/z^2| > \frac{1}{2}$ for

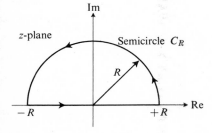

Figure 2.18

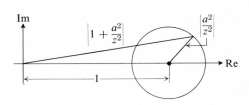

Figure 2.19

$R > a\sqrt{2}$, and consequently

$$\frac{1}{|1 + a^2/z^2|} < 2 \qquad \text{(for } R > a\sqrt{2}\text{)}.$$

This implies

$$\frac{1}{|a^2 + z^2|} < \frac{2}{R^2} \qquad \text{(for } R > a\sqrt{2}\text{)}.$$

Now, employ the estimate (p. 58)

$$\left| \int_{C_R} \frac{dz}{z^2 + a^2} \right| \leq \pi R \max \frac{1}{|z^2 + a^2|} < \pi R \frac{2}{R^2} = \frac{2\pi}{R}.$$

Then

$$\lim_{R \to \infty} \int_{C_R} \frac{dz}{z^2 + a^2} = 0.$$

Observe now that the integral $\oint_C dz/(z^2 + a^2)$ is independent of the radius R (so long as R is greater than a) because the only singularity of the integrand *within C* is at $z = ai$ and, by the residue theorem,

$$\oint_C \frac{dz}{z^2 + a^2} = 2\pi i \text{ Res } f(ai) = 2\pi i \frac{1}{2ai} = \frac{\pi}{a}$$

(for all C such that $R > a$). Consequently, if we let $R \to \infty$, we have

$$\oint_C \frac{dz}{z^2 + a^2} = \lim_{R \to \infty} \int_{-R}^{+R} \frac{dx}{x^2 + a^2} + \lim_{R \to \infty} \int_{C_R} \frac{dz}{z^2 + a^2},$$

which reduces to

$$\frac{\pi}{a} = \int_{-\infty}^{+\infty} \frac{dx}{x^2 + a^2} \qquad (a > 0).$$

Exercise. Show that if $a < 0$, then

$$\int_{-\infty}^{+\infty} \frac{dx}{x^2 + a^2} = -\frac{\pi}{a}.$$

[*Hint:* No new calculations need be done, just some logical deductions.]

The above procedure can be applied to integrals of the type

$$\int_{-\infty}^{+\infty} \frac{P(x)}{Q(x)} dx,$$

where $P(x)$ and $Q(x)$ are polynomials in x and (a) $Q(x)$ should have no real zeros*

---

* If $Q(x)$ has real zeros, then the integral is not defined (see p. 63), unless particular modifications are made (e.g., p. 111).

and (b) the degree of $Q(x)$ must exceed the degree of $P(x)$ by at least 2 (otherwise the integral over the semicircle C_R may not tend to zero). For such integrals it is true that

$$\int_{-\infty}^{+\infty} \frac{P(x)}{Q(x)}\, dx = 2\pi i \sum_{+} \text{Res},$$

where $\sum_+ \text{Res}$ is the sum of the residues of the integrand in the upper half-plane. This statement is a special case of the following theorem: *If $f(z)$ is continuous for $|z| > R_0$ (some R_0) and $|zf(z)| \to 0$ uniformly as $|z| \to \infty$, then*

$$\lim_{R \to \infty} \oint_{|z|=R} f(z)\, dz = 0.$$

Proof

$$\left| \oint_{|z|=R} f(z)\, dz \right| = \left| \oint_{|z|=R} zf(z) \frac{dz}{z} \right| \le \max_{|z|=R} |zf(z)| \frac{2\pi R}{R}.$$

Uniform convergence of $|zf(z)|$ means that $|zf(z)| < \epsilon$ (for arbitrarily small ϵ) whenever $|z| \ge R$ (that is, independently of the manner in which z approaches infinity). Then

$$\left| \oint_{|z|=R} f(z)\, dz \right| \le 2\pi\epsilon,$$

and the theorem follows. The conditions of the theorem are satisfied by the function

$$f(z) = \frac{P(z)}{Q(z)} \qquad (\text{with deg } Q \ge \text{deg } P + 2)$$

because (a) all zeros of Q must be within some fixed circle about the origin and (b) the condition $|zf(z)| < \epsilon$ for $|z| \ge k$ (for some k) can be satisfied.

Remark. The method described above can be extended to certain integrals of the type

$$\int_0^\infty f(x)\, dx,$$

where $f(x)$ is an even function of x.

Example 3. Consider the real integral

$$I = \int_0^\infty \frac{\cos x\, dx}{x^2 + a^2} \qquad (a > 0).$$

Note, first of all, that

$$I = \frac{1}{2} \int_{-\infty}^{+\infty} \frac{\cos x\, dx}{x^2 + a^2}.$$

The replacement of x by z will not help in this case because $\cos z$ is not "well behaved" in the upper half-plane; it is not bounded. However, the function e^{iz} *is bounded* in the upper half-plane because $e^{iz} = e^{-y}e^{ix}$ and $|e^{ix}| = 1$ (all real x)

while $|e^{-y}| \leq 1$ (all nonnegative y). For this reason, consider the complex integral

$$J = \oint_C \frac{e^{iz} \, dz}{z^2 + a^2} = \int_{-R}^{+R} \frac{e^{ix} \, dx}{x^2 + a^2} + \int_{C_R} \frac{e^{iz} \, dz}{z^2 + a^2}$$

evaluated over the contour shown in Fig. 2.20. Observe that

$$\lim_{R \to \infty} \int_{C_R} \frac{e^{iz} \, dz}{z^2 + a^2} = 0$$

(as in Example 2). Also,

$$J = 2\pi i \operatorname{Res} f(ai) = 2\pi i \frac{e^{-a}}{2ai} = \frac{\pi}{a} e^{-a},$$

so that

$$\int_{-\infty}^{+\infty} \frac{e^{ix} \, dx}{x^2 + a^2} \equiv \int_{-\infty}^{+\infty} \frac{\cos x \, dx}{x^2 + a^2} + i \int_{-\infty}^{+\infty} \frac{\sin x \, dx}{x^2 + a^2} = \frac{\pi}{a} e^{-a} \qquad (a > 0).$$

Since the right-hand side is real, it follows that

$$I = \int_0^{+\infty} \frac{\cos x \, dx}{x^2 + a^2} = \frac{1}{2} \frac{\pi}{a} e^{-a} \qquad (a > 0).$$

Remark. The statement

$$\int_{-\infty}^{+\infty} \frac{\sin x \, dx}{x^2 + a^2} = 0$$

could have been made immediately on the grounds of symmetry. However, if it were not true, we would have obtained the value of this integral as well from the imaginary part of $2\pi i \sum_+ \operatorname{Res}$.

Example 4. Consider the real integral

$$I = \int_0^\infty \frac{\sin x}{x} \, dx.$$

As before, observe that

$$I = \frac{1}{2} \int_{-\infty}^{+\infty} \frac{\sin x}{x} \, dx.$$

Since $\sin z$ is not "well behaved" on the upper half-plane, we shall try to evaluate the complex integral

$$\oint \frac{e^{iz}}{z} \, dz.$$

A new problem now arises: the integrand has a pole on the real axis. Note that this pole is not caused by $\sin x$ but rather by $\cos x$, which has been added to form the complex integral.

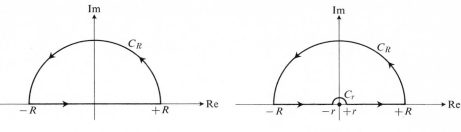

Figure 2.20   **Figure 2.21**

To be able to apply the residue theorem we must avoid the pole at the origin in some fashion. Let us suppose we do this by means of a semicircle of a small radius r in the upper half-plane, as shown in Fig. 2.21. Then we can write

$$\oint_C \frac{e^{iz}}{z}\,dz = \int_{-R}^{-r} \frac{e^{ix}}{x}\,dx + \int_{C_r} \frac{e^{iz}}{z}\,dz + \int_{+r}^{+R} \frac{e^{ix}}{x}\,dx + \int_{C_R} \frac{e^{iz}}{z}\,dz.$$

The reason the chosen contour C is helpful in the evaluation of our real integral is as follows. Note that (by continuity of $\sin x / x$)

$$\int_{-\infty}^{+\infty} \frac{\sin x}{x}\,dx = \lim_{r \to 0}\int_{-\infty}^{-r} \frac{\sin x}{x}\,dx + \lim_{r \to 0}\int_{-r}^{+r} \frac{\sin x}{x}\,dx + \lim_{r \to 0}\int_{+r}^{+\infty} \frac{\sin x}{x}\,dx.$$

Now, since evidently

$$\lim_{r \to 0}\int_{-r}^{+r} (\sin x / x)\,dx = 0,$$

it follows that

$$\int_{-\infty}^{+\infty} \frac{\sin x}{x}\,dx = \lim_{r \to 0}\int_{-\infty}^{-r} \frac{\sin x}{x}\,dx + \lim_{r \to 0}\int_{+r}^{+\infty} \frac{\sin x}{x}\,dx.$$

We can now see that the *imaginary parts* of the first and the third integrals on the right-hand side of the relation

$$\oint_C \frac{e^{iz}}{z} = \int_{-R}^{-r} \frac{e^{ix}}{x}\,dx + \int_{C_r} \frac{e^{iz}}{z}\,dz + \int_{+r}^{+R} \frac{e^{ix}}{x}\,dx + \int_{C_R} \frac{e^{iz}}{z}\,dz$$

will give us the desired result in the limit where $r \to 0$ and $R \to \infty$, *provided* we manage to calculate the other three integrals in the formula.

Let us estimate the integral over C_R. The method of Example 2 fails here; however, we can perform integration by parts:*

$$\int_{C_R} \frac{e^{iz}}{z}\,dz = \frac{e^{iz}}{iz}\Big|_{z=-R}^{z=+R} + \int_{C_R} \frac{e^{iz}}{iz^2}\,dz = \frac{2\cos R}{iR} + \int_{C_R} \frac{e^{iz}}{iz^2}\,dz.$$

---

* From the results of Section 2.7 it is trivial to verify that integration by parts applies to complex integrals as well as to real ones.

If $R \to \infty$, both terms on the right-hand side approach zero ($\cos R$ is bounded because R is real).

Next, we evaluate the integral over C_r:

$$\int_{C_r} \frac{e^{iz}}{z}\, dz = \int_{C_r} \frac{1 + e^{iz} - 1}{z}\, dz = \int_{C_r} \frac{dz}{z} + \int_{C_r} \frac{e^{iz} - 1}{z}\, dz.$$

Since e^{iz} is continuous at $z = 0$ and is equal to unity there, it follows that

$$|e^{iz} - 1| < \epsilon$$

for $r = |z|$ sufficiently small, say $r < \delta$ (for some δ). Therefore

$$\left| \int_{C_r} \frac{e^{iz} - 1}{z}\, dz \right| = \left| \int_{C_r} (e^{iz} - 1) i\, d\theta \right| \leq \pi\epsilon \qquad (r < \delta)$$

and

$$\lim_{r \to 0} \int_{C_r} \frac{e^{iz} - 1}{z}\, dz = 0.$$

Also,

$$\int_{C_r} \frac{dz}{z} = -i \int_0^\pi d\theta = -\pi i$$

so that

$$\lim_{r \to 0} \int_{C_r} \frac{e^{iz}}{z}\, dz = -\pi i.$$

Returning now to our equation, setting $e^{ix} = \cos x + i \sin x$ and using the fact that

$$\int_{-R}^{-r} \frac{\cos x}{x}\, dx + \int_{+r}^{+R} \frac{\cos x}{x}\, dx = 0$$

for *any* r and R, we deduce that

$$\oint_C \frac{e^{iz}}{z}\, dz = i \int_{-R}^{-r} \frac{\sin x}{x}\, dx + i \int_{+r}^{+R} \frac{\sin x}{x}\, dx + \int_{C_r} \frac{e^{iz}}{z}\, dz + \int_{C_R} \frac{e^{iz}}{z}\, dz.$$

The left-hand side is zero (no poles of e^{iz}/z within the contour). Taking the limits $r \to 0$, $R \to \infty$ (in either order), we obtain

$$0 = i \int_{-\infty}^{+\infty} \frac{\sin x}{x}\, dx - \pi i.$$

Therefore*

$$I = \int_0^\infty \frac{\sin x}{x}\, dx = \frac{\pi}{2}.$$

---

* Of course, this integral can be evaluated by much more elementary methods. The purpose of the above analysis is to illustrate the techniques of the residue calculus on a simple example rather than to obtain this particular result.

Example 5. We shall now evaluate the integral of Example 4 by a somewhat different method. We write

$$I = \int_0^\infty \frac{\sin x}{x}\, dx = \frac{1}{2} \int_{-\infty}^{+\infty} \frac{\sin x}{x}\, dx = \frac{1}{2} \int_{-\infty}^{+\infty} \frac{\sin z}{z}\, dz.$$

Here we treat our integral as a complex integral over a path (real axis) which is *open* (so far). Since $\sin z/z$ is continuous at $z = 0$, we may *deform the contour* as shown in Fig. 2.22 and claim that

$$I = \lim_{r \to 0} \int_{C'} \frac{\sin z}{z}\, dz.$$

Now set

$$\sin z = \frac{1}{2i}(e^{iz} - e^{-iz}).$$

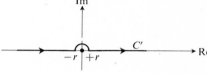

Figure 2.22

The problem is to evaluate

$$I_1 = \lim_{r \to 0} \int_{C'} \frac{e^{iz}}{z}\, dz \quad \text{and} \quad I_2 = \lim_{r \to 0} \int_{C'} \frac{e^{-iz}}{z}\, dz.$$

For I_1, close the contour as usual (Fig. 2.23a). Show that the integral over C_R approaches zero, and deduce that

$$\int_{C'} \frac{e^{iz}}{z}\, dz = 0.$$

For I_2, close the contour through the *lower half-plane* as shown in Fig. 2.23(b). Now $|e^{-iz}|$ is bounded in the lower half-plane and the integral over C'_R approaches zero. On the other hand, note that (a) there is a contribution from the pole at the origin and (b) the clockwise integration introduces a change in the sign. When this is taken into account, we obtain

$$\int_{C'} \frac{e^{-iz}}{z}\, dz = -2\pi i \operatorname{Res} f(0) = -2\pi i.$$

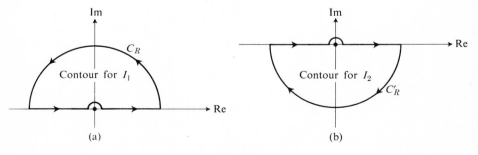

Figure 2.23

Combining these results, we deduce that

$$\int_{-\infty}^{+\infty} \frac{\sin x}{x}\, dx = \frac{1}{2i}(I_1 - I_2) = \frac{1}{2i}(0 + 2\pi i) = \pi$$

in conformity with the previous result.

Remark 1. The integral over the semicircle C_r in Example 4 has been shown to yield the value $-\pi i$ in the limit $r \to 0$. This is just one-half the value obtained by integration over the full circle. One may prove a general theorem to this effect: Let $f(z)$ be analytic at $z = a$. Consider the integral

$$I_\alpha = \int_{z_1}^{z_2} \frac{f(z)\, dz}{z - a}$$

taken from $z_1 = a + re^{i\theta_1}$ to $z_2 = a + re^{i\theta_2}$ along the circle $|z - a| = r$ (Fig. 2.24). Then

$$\lim_{r \to 0} I_\alpha = \alpha i f(a)$$

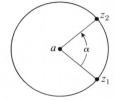

Figure 2.24

where $\alpha = \theta_2 - \theta_1 + 2n\pi$ (choose n so that $|\alpha| \le 2\pi$).

Exercise. Prove this theorem using a technique similar to that in Example 4.

Remark 2. The statement that the integral of e^{iz}/z over C_R in Example 4 vanishes in the limit $R \to \infty$ is also a special case of a more general result, known as

Jordan's lemma: *If $f(z)$ converges uniformly to zero whenever z approaches infinity, then*

$$\lim_{R \to \infty} \int_{C_R} f(z) e^{i\lambda z}\, dz = 0,$$

where λ is any positive number and C_R is the upper half of the circle $|z| = R$.

The term "uniform convergence" as $z \to \infty$ means that $|f(z)| < \epsilon$ whenever $|z| > M$ (for some M) no matter what the phase of z is.

Example 6. The integral reads

$$I = \int_{-\infty}^{+\infty} \frac{e^{ax}\, dx}{\cosh \pi x} \qquad (-\pi < a < \pi).$$

Observe that for large positive x, $\cosh \pi x$ behaves like $\frac{1}{2}e^{\pi x}$. Consequently, the integrand behaves like $2e^{(-\pi + a)x}$, and the integral converges. For large $|x|$ but negative x, $\cosh \pi x$ behaves like $\frac{1}{2}e^{-\pi x} = \frac{1}{2}e^{\pi |x|}$ and the integral converges again.

Closing the contour by a semicircle will not help in this case since the integrand is not diminishing (in modulus) as we go up or down along the imaginary axis. However, let us try the rectangular contour shown in Figure 2.25. The poles of the integrand are at

$$z = \frac{2k+1}{2}\, i,$$

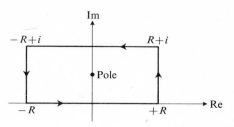

where k is an integer. Within our contour there is only one pole, namely, at $z = i/2$. The residue is

$$\left.\frac{e^{az}}{(\cosh \pi z)'}\right|_{z=i/2} = \frac{e^{ai/2}}{\pi i}.$$

Figure 2.25

Write

$$I_R = \int_{-R}^{+R} \frac{e^{ax}\, dx}{\cosh \pi x}$$

and consider the integral

$$I'_R = \int_{R+i}^{-R+i} \frac{e^{az}\, dz}{\cosh \pi z} = \int_{+R}^{-R} \frac{e^{a(x+i)}\, dx}{\cosh \pi(x+i)}.$$

Observe that

$$\cosh \pi(x+i) = \tfrac{1}{2}(e^{\pi x} e^{\pi i} + e^{-\pi x} e^{-\pi i}) = \tfrac{1}{2}(-e^{\pi x} - e^{-\pi x}) = -\cosh \pi x.$$

Therefore

$$I'_R = -\int_{+R}^{-R} \frac{e^{ai} e^{ax}\, dx}{\cosh \pi x} = +e^{ai} I_R.$$

It remains for us to consider

$$J_1 = \int_0^1 \frac{e^{a(R+iy)} i\, dy}{\cosh \pi(R+iy)} \quad \text{and} \quad J_2 = \int_1^0 \frac{e^{a(-R+iy)} i\, dy}{\cosh \pi(-R+iy)}.$$

In the limit $R \to \infty$, which is what interests us,

$$|\cosh \pi(R+iy)| \sim e^{\pi R}.$$

The details are easily worked out: Show that $|\cosh \pi(R+iy)|$ is *greater* than, say $\tfrac{1}{2} e^{\pi R}$, for $R \to \infty$. It follows that J_1 is bounded by, say $2e^{(-\pi+a)R}$, and this approaches zero since $|a| < \pi$. A similar argument holds for J_2. Collecting our results, we obtain

$$2\pi i\, \frac{e^{ai/2}}{\pi i} = I_R + I'_R + J_1 + J_2 = (1 + e^{ai})I$$

so that

$$I = \frac{1}{\cos (a/2)} = \sec \frac{a}{2}.$$

Example 7. This example deals with the extension of previous techniques to contours involving branch lines of multivalued functions.   Consider the real integral

$$I = \int_0^\infty \frac{x^{\alpha-1}}{1+x}\, dx \qquad (0 < \alpha < 1).$$

Note again that the integral is well defined (convergent) at both limits $x \to 0$ and $x \to \infty$.

In the field of complex numbers the general power function $z^{\alpha-1}$ implies (p. 58)

$$z^{\alpha-1} = e^{(\alpha-1)\operatorname{Log} z} = |z|^{\alpha-1} e^{i(\alpha-1)\operatorname{Arg} z} = |z|^{\alpha-1} e^{i(\alpha-1)(\theta + 2k\pi)}.$$

The branch which reduces to the real function $x^{\alpha-1}$ (for $x > 0$) is the principal branch, with $k = 0$.   It is convenient to work with the branch for which

$$0 \leq \operatorname{Arg} z < 2\pi.$$

This branch coincides with the principal branch for $\operatorname{Im} z > 0$ and with the branch $k = 1$ for $\operatorname{Im} z < 0$.   Then our real integral I coincides* with the integral of this branch along the upper edge of the branch cut (see Fig. 2.26).   Close the contour as shown in the figure.   The integral over the lower edge of the branch cut is then

$$\int_\infty^0 \frac{|z|^{\alpha-1} e^{i(\alpha-1)2\pi}}{1+z}\, dz = -e^{2\pi(\alpha-1)i} \int_0^\infty \frac{x^{\alpha-1}\, dx}{1+x}.$$

Therefore,

$$2\pi i \operatorname{Res} f(-1) = [1 - e^{2\pi(\alpha-1)i}]I + \int_{C_r} \frac{z^{\alpha-1}\, dz}{1+z} + \int_{C_R} \frac{z^{\alpha-1}\, dz}{1+z}.$$

Now, for $|z| = R$,

$$\left| \int_{C_R} \frac{z^{\alpha-1}\, dz}{1+z} \right| \sim 2\pi R \cdot R^{\alpha-2} \to 0 \qquad (\text{as } R \to \infty)$$

and for $|z| = r$,

$$\left| \int_{C_r} \frac{z^{\alpha-1}\, dz}{1+z} \right| \sim 2\pi r \cdot r^{\alpha-1} = 2\pi r^\alpha \to 0 \qquad (\text{as } r \to 0).$$

The residue at $z = -1$ is $e^{i(\alpha-1)\pi}$; therefore

$$I = \frac{2\pi i e^{i(\alpha-1)\pi}}{1 - e^{i(\alpha-1)2\pi}} = \frac{\pi}{\sin \alpha \pi}.$$

---

* In the limit $\epsilon \to 0$, $r \to 0$, and $R \to \infty$, of course.

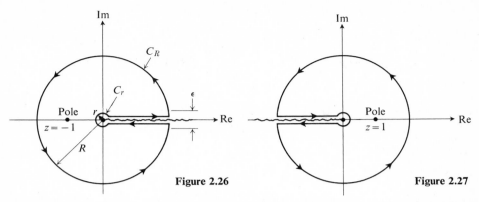

Figure 2.26   Figure 2.27

Remark. It is also possible to operate with the standard principal branch $-\pi < \operatorname{Arg} z \leq \pi$ by setting $x = -x'$ in I to get

$$I = -\int_0^\infty \frac{(-x')^{\alpha-1}}{1 - x'} \, dx' = \int_\infty^0 \frac{|x'|^{\alpha-1}}{1 - x'} \, dx'$$

using $-x' = |x'|$ for $x' \leq 0$. The contour is then chosen as in Fig. 2.27. The integral of the principal branch along the upper edge of the cut is now

$$\int_{-\infty}^0 \frac{|z|^{\alpha-1} e^{(\alpha-1)\pi i}}{1 - z} \, dz = e^{(\alpha-1)\pi i} I.$$

The integral over the lower edge is

$$\int_0^{-\infty} \frac{|z|^{\alpha-1} e^{-(\alpha-1)\pi i}}{1 - z} = -e^{-(\alpha-1)\pi i} I,$$

and the residue at the pole $z = 1$ is simply unity. The final result is the same as before. This method is applicable to integrals of the type

$$\int_0^\infty x^{\alpha-1} f(x) \, dx,$$

where α is not an integer and $f(x)$ is a rational function.

2.13 CONFORMAL MAPPING BY ANALYTIC FUNCTIONS

If the function $f(z) = u(x, y) + iv(x, y)$ is analytic in a certain region R, then u and v are known to satisfy the Cauchy-Riemann conditions

$$\frac{\partial u}{\partial x} = \frac{\partial v}{\partial y}, \qquad \frac{\partial u}{\partial y} = -\frac{\partial v}{\partial x}.$$

Differentiate the first equation with respect to x and the second one with respect to y. Observe that the second-order partials must be continuous (u and v are differentiable any number of times) and therefore

$$\frac{\partial^2 v}{\partial x\, \partial y} = \frac{\partial^2 v}{\partial y\, \partial x}.$$

It follows that

$$\frac{\partial^2 u}{\partial x^2} + \frac{\partial^2 u}{\partial y^2} = 0$$

which is the *Laplace equation* for u. In a similar fashion, show that v also satisfies the Laplace equation

$$\frac{\partial^2 v}{\partial x^2} + \frac{\partial^2 v}{\partial y^2} = 0.$$

Remark. Functions satisfying the Laplace equation are called *harmonic functions*. We have shown that real and imaginary parts of an analytic function are harmonic.

If a given function $u(x, y)$ is harmonic in a simply connected region R, then it is possible to construct another harmonic function $v(x, y)$, called the *conjugate function* to u such that u and v form real and imaginary parts of a complex analytic function $f(z)$. This can be done by the integral

$$v(x, y) = \int_{(x_0, y_0)}^{(x, y)} \left[\left(-\frac{\partial u}{\partial y} \right) dx + \left(\frac{\partial u}{\partial x} \right) dy \right] + \text{const},$$

where the path (so long as it is within R) is arbitrary. Since u is harmonic, we have

$$\frac{\partial}{\partial y} \left(-\frac{\partial u}{\partial y} \right) = \frac{\partial}{\partial x} \left(\frac{\partial u}{\partial x} \right),$$

and the integral is independent of path. The harmonic properties of complex analytic functions are widely used in physics.

Example. The electrostatic potential φ is known to satisfy the three-dimensional Laplace equation

$$\frac{\partial^2 \varphi}{\partial x^2} + \frac{\partial^2 \varphi}{\partial y^2} + \frac{\partial^2 \varphi}{\partial z^2} = 0,$$

where z is a third real variable. In many cases, however, the potential is independent of z. Then

$$\frac{\partial^2 \varphi}{\partial x^2} + \frac{\partial^2 \varphi}{\partial y^2} = 0.$$

The real part of any analytic function can serve as a solution for the potential in *some region R*. For instance, consider

$$f(z) = \log z = \log |z| + i \arg z.$$

The function

$$\text{Re} (\log z) = \log \sqrt{x^2 + y^2} = u(x, y)$$

satisfies the Laplace equation.   It happens to be constant along the circles
$x^2 + y^2 = $ const (cylinders in three-dimensional space).   It follows that it represents the unique solution of the electrostatic problem in the space between two
coaxial conducting cylinders (Fig. 2.28).

This remarkable property of analytic functions serves as a basis for many
important methods used in electrostatics, fluid dynamics, and other branches of
physics.   We shall not enter into the study of these methods, usually known as
conformal mapping methods, and the interested reader is referred to a variety
of other texts.*   Despite their power and elegance, conformal mapping methods
are limited in scope since they are applicable only to a particular partial differential
equation (the Laplace equation) and even then only to problems reducible to
plane problems.   However, we shall mention a closely related *geometric* property
of analytic functions of profound significance.

If the curves $u(x, y) = $ const and $v(x, y) = $ const are plotted in the complex
plane, it is seen that they make a system of orthogonal trajectories, i.e., at each
point z the two curves $u = $ const and $v = $ const passing through it are normal
to each other [excluding the trivial case $f(z) = $ const].   This follows from the
Cauchy-Riemann equations: The vector

$$\text{grad } u = \frac{\partial u}{\partial x}\mathbf{i} + \frac{\partial u}{\partial y}\mathbf{j}$$

is known to be normal to the curve $u(x, y) = $
const.   Similarly,

$$\text{grad } v = \frac{\partial v}{\partial x}\mathbf{i} + \frac{\partial v}{\partial y}\mathbf{j} = -\frac{\partial u}{\partial y}\mathbf{i} + \frac{\partial u}{\partial x}\mathbf{j}$$

is normal to the curve $v(x, y) = $ const.   Now
the dot product

$$(\text{grad } u \cdot \text{grad } v) = \frac{\partial u}{\partial x}\left(-\frac{\partial u}{\partial y}\right) + \frac{\partial u}{\partial y}\left(\frac{\partial u}{\partial x}\right) = 0$$

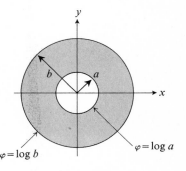

Figure 2.28

shows that grad u is normal to grad v and the statement follows.

In the electrostatic interpretation, in which $u(x, y) = $ const represents an
equipotential surface, the curve $v(x, y) = $ const (in the z-plane) represents a
line of force.

The geometrical meaning of this property is that the function $w = f(z)$ maps
the orthogonal network of curves $u(x, y) = $ const and $v(x, y) = $ const in the
z-plane onto the orthogonal network of straight lines $u = $ const and $v = $ const
in the w-plane.   An example, with $w = z^2$ and $u(x, y) = x^2 - y^2$, $v(x, y) = 2xy$,
is shown in Fig. 2.29.

---

* For example, Nehari, *Conformal Mapping;* Kober, *Dictionary of Conformal Representations;* Bieberbach, *Conformal Mapping.*

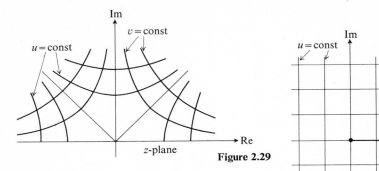

Figure 2.29

Note that the function $f(z) = z^2$ maps half the z-plane onto the entire w-plane. If the points on the real z-axis are included then the real positive semiaxis in the w-plane serves as a *double image* (for a *single image* it is necessary to exclude either the real negative or the real positive semiaxis in the z-plane).

It is, perhaps, most convenient to say that $w = z^2$ maps the *open* upper half-plane (the region $\text{Im } z > 0$) onto the *open region* consisting of the w-plane with the real positive semiaxis *removed*. This is usually referred to as the "w-plane with a cut along the positive real semiaxis."

Now consider a point $z = z_0$ in the z-plane and a smooth curve C passing through it. Let $f(z)$ be analytic at $z = z_0$ and let $f(z)$ map point z_0 onto w_0 and the curve C onto curve Γ passing through it (Fig. 2.30).

Also consider a point z_1 on C, close to z_0, and its image w_1 on Γ. Denote $z - z_0 = \Delta z$, $w_1 - w_0 = \Delta w$. By definition of the derivative,

$$\lim_{z_1 \to z_0} \frac{\Delta w}{\Delta z} = f'(z_0).$$

Therefore

$$\lim_{z_1 \to z_0} \frac{|\Delta w|}{|\Delta z|} = |f'(z_0)|.$$

Geometrically, the left-hand side can be interpreted as the *magnification* of an (infinitesimal) arc of curve C as the curve C is transformed into the curve Γ. This magnification is the *same* for all curves passing through z_0.

Now consider the angles θ_0 and ϕ_0 which the curves C and Γ make with the real axis. We have

$$\phi_0 - \theta_0 = \lim_{z_1 \to z_0} [\arg \Delta w - \arg \Delta z] = \lim_{z_1 \to z_0} \left(\arg \frac{\Delta w}{\Delta z} \right) = \arg f'(z_0) = \alpha.$$

Geometrically, this means that the curve C is *rotated* through an angle α when it is transformed into Γ. This angle of rotation is the *same* for all curves passing through z_0. Observe, however, that these two geometrical statements lose their meaning at the points z_0 where $f'(z_0) = 0$.

The properties described above are usually referred to as the *conformal mapping properties*. Customarily the term "conformal mapping" is defined by:

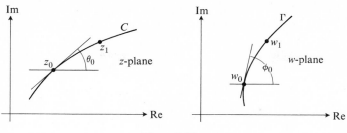

Figure 2.30

a) *Invariance of angles:* An angle at z_0 formed by two curves remains unchanged (in magnitude and orientation).

b) *Invariance of infinitesimal circles:* An infinitesimal circle around z_0 retains its shape; it differs from a circle by higher order infinitesimals than its radius.

Our analysis leads then to the following theorem: *If a function $f(z)$ is analytic at z_0 and the derivative $f'(z_0)$ does not vanish, then the mapping $z \to f(z)$ is conformal at z_0.*

Remarks

1. The statement $f'(z_0) \neq 0$ guarantees the existence of the inverse mapping because if $w = f(z)$ and $z = g(w)$, then $g'(w_0) = 1/f'(z_0)$ provided $f'(z_0) \neq 0$.

2. The mapping $f(z) = z^*$, which reflects the z-plane in the real axis, preserves the angles and maps circles into circles but it is not considered conformal because the orientation of the angles is reversed (Fig. 2.31).

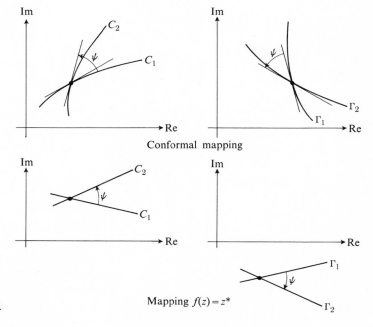

Figure 2.31   Mapping $f(z) = z^*$

2.14 COMPLEX SPHERE AND POINT AT INFINITY

Many concepts of the theory of complex variables are greatly simplified through the introduction of the so-called *point at infinity*. This is done with the help of the stereographic projection between the complex plane and the *complex sphere* which is defined as follows: Construct a sphere of radius R (for convenience, R may be taken as $\frac{1}{2}$) such that the complex plane is tangential to it at the origin, as shown in Fig. 2.32. The point P on the sphere opposite to the origin (called the *north pole* for convenience) is used as the "eye" of stereographic projection.

Lines through P are drawn which intersect both the sphere and the plane permitting a mapping of point z on the plane onto the point ζ on the sphere (Fig. 2.32). In this fashion the entire complex plane is mapped onto the complex sphere (or *Riemann sphere*). Curves and regions in the z-plane are mapped onto curves and regions on the ζ-sphere.

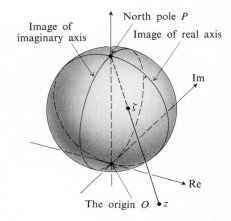

Note that the point P itself has no counterpart on the z-plane. Nevertheless, it has been found convenient to adjoin to the z-plane an extra point, known as the *point at infinity*, in such a way that a curve passing through P on the ζ-sphere is defined as *approaching the point at infinity* in the z-plane.

Figure 2.32

The concept of the point at infinity is very useful, particularly in the analysis of mappings. The following statements of properties can be verified without much difficulty.

1. Circles in plane are mapped onto circles on the sphere which *do not pass through P*.

2. Straight lines in plane are mapped onto circles on the sphere which *do pass through P*.

3. Maps of intersecting straight lines have two common points on the ζ-sphere, one of which is P.

4. Maps of parallel straight lines have only the point P in common and they have a common tangent at P.

5. The exterior of a circle $|z| = R$ with $R \gg 1$ is mapped onto the interior of a small spherical cap around point P. As $R \to \infty$ the cap "shrinks to P."

These and similar properties give rise to a series of definitions applied to the so-called *extended complex plane*, i.e., a complex plane to which the point at infinity is adjoined.

Examples

a) The mapping $w = 1/z$ maps $z_0 = 0$ onto $w_0 = \infty$ (point at infinity adjoined to w-plane) and vice versa. The rigorous meaning of this is, of course, that if a sequence of points in the z-plane converges to $z_0 = 0$, then a corresponding sequence of points on the w-*sphere* converges to its north pole.

b) The region $|z| > R$ is a neighborhood of the point at infinity.

The importance of the complex sphere is greatly enhanced by the fact that if two curves intersect in the z-plane at an angle γ, then their images on the sphere will intersect at the same angle. In fact, the stereographic projection is *conformal*. (The proof is not difficult, but will be omitted here.) This permits the definition of the *angle at infinity* which two curves make if they *recede to infinity* in the z-plane. This angle is *defined to be* the angle that their images on the sphere make at the point P.

Now the following theorem can be stated.

Theorem. *The mapping $w = 1/z$ is conformal at the origin $z = 0$.*

Observe that the *function* $f(z) = 1/z$ is not defined at $z = 0$ but the *mapping* $w = 1/z$ is defined (by the subterfuge of the sphere). The conformality does not follow from the analyticity, but rather from the relationships on the complex sphere.

Corollary. The mapping $w = 1/z$ is conformal at infinity (despite the fact that $f'(z)$ approaches zero as z recedes to infinity).

The concept of the point at infinity is closely interwoven with the study of singularities of analytic functions. The very notion of analyticity can be extended to the point at infinity by the following device: A function $f(z)$ is *defined* to be *analytic at infinity* if the function

$$g(z) = f(1/z)$$

is analytic at $z = 0$. Moreover, it is possible to introduce the concept of a *pole at infinity*, *branch point at infinity*, etc., through the corresponding behavior of $g(z)$ at the origin. In this connection, the function $f(z) = e^z$, which has no zeros and no singularities in the entire complex plane, turns out to possess an essential singularity at infinity. Other functions which have no singularities (e.g., all polynomials in z) are also found to have a breakdown of analyticity at infinity.

Exercise. Show that a polynomial $P(z)$ of degree n has a pole of nth order at infinity.

In fact, a survey of familiar functions reveals the fact that functions which are analytic at infinity possess at least one singularity elsewhere, i.e., for some finite value of z. The natural conjecture is that there may not be a "perfectly analytic" function. This problem has actually been resolved and is embodied in the

Liouville theorem. The only function $f(z)$ which is analytic in the entire complex plane *and* the point at infinity is the constant function $f(z) = \text{const}$.

In conclusion, it may be mentioned that in some texts the term *complex plane* is tacitly assumed to mean the *extended complex plane*, with the point at infinity included. Certain theorems may then be more conveniently stated. However, one should never forget that while there is a point at infinity, there is still no such thing as a complex number "infinity," in the sense that it should possess the *algebraic* properties shared by other complex numbers.

2.15 INTEGRAL REPRESENTATIONS

It is a very common occurrence that certain functions are represented and even defined by integrals, with constant or variable limits. For instance, consider the real function, the derivative of which is equal to $\sin x/x$. It is known that the indefinite integral of $\sin x/x$ is not expressible in terms of elementary functions* in finite form. Therefore, there is no other alternative but to *define* such functions by means of an integral and it is customary to write

$$\text{Si}\,(x) = \int_0^x \frac{\sin \xi}{\xi}\,d\xi,$$

where $\text{Si}\,(x)$ is a new function, called the *sine-integral*. It is, of course, but one of many primitive functions of $\sin x/x$ (i.e., the one which vanishes at the origin) the others being obtainable by adding an arbitrary constant to $\text{Si}\,(x)$.

If we want to extend the definition of $\text{Si}\,(x)$ to complex variables, it can be done in a trivial way. We write

$$\text{Si}\,(z) = \int_0^z \frac{\sin \zeta}{\zeta}\,d\zeta,$$

where ζ is a complex variable and the integral is now a *curvilinear* integral in the complex ζ-plane over some path connecting the points $\zeta = 0$ and $\zeta = z$. It does not matter which particular path is chosen since the function $f(\zeta) = \sin \zeta/\zeta$ is analytic for all (finite) values† of ζ and the integral is independent of path.

A different situation is encountered in the so-called *cosine integral*, defined by

$$\text{Ci}\,(x) = -\int_x^{+\infty} \frac{\cos \xi}{\xi}\,d\xi.$$

This function is easily seen to be a primitive function of $\cos x/x$. The choice of limits is conventional but the main feature is that the integral diverges at $x = 0$. While it is still possible to extend the definition to complex variables by writing

$$\text{Ci}\,(z) = -\int_z^{+\infty} \frac{\cos \zeta}{\zeta}\,d\zeta,$$

---

* That is, algebraic, exponential, trigonometric, and their inverse functions.
† See the discussion on pp. 79–80.

the question arises as to the specification of the path of integration. Presumably, the upper limit implies an *asymptotic approach* to the real axis.* Three such paths are illustrated in Fig. 2.33. The integrals taken along C_1 and C_2 are easily shown to be identical, but the integral along C_3 will differ by $2\pi i$ times the residue of the integrand at $\zeta = 0$. This means essentially that Ci (z) is a *multivalued* function, the integrals along different paths yielding different branches. Two of these branches are characterized by the paths C_1 and C_3 (or other paths equivalent to them). Other branches can be obtained by circling the origin n times before proceeding to "plus infinity."

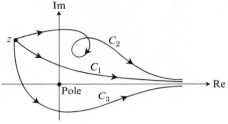

Figure 2.33

Remark. The above analysis reveals that Ci (x) for real negative x should be defined by one of the branches of complex function Ci (z) because the real integral

$$\int_x^{+\infty} \frac{\cos \xi}{\xi}\, d\xi$$

is divergent for $x < 0$ due to the behavior of the integrand at $\xi = 0$. It has been found, however, that this divergent integral (like many similar others) can be given a definite meaning by the prescription

$$\lim_{\epsilon \to 0} \left\{ \int_x^{-\epsilon} \frac{\cos \xi}{\xi}\, d\xi + \int_{+\epsilon}^{+\infty} \frac{\cos \xi}{\xi}\, d\xi \right\}$$

known as the *Cauchy principal value* (or simply the *principal value*) and is often denoted by

$$\fint_x^{+\infty} \frac{\cos \xi}{\xi}\, d\xi.$$

Because of this result, it is customary to define Ci (x) for $x < 0$ by

$$\text{Ci }(x) = -\fint_x^{+\infty} \frac{\cos \xi}{\xi}\, d\xi \qquad (x < 0).$$

Principal values of integrals occur very often in physical applications; the complex version of this definition† will be given shortly.

---

* As usual, we require Ci (z) to reduce to Ci (x) as z becomes real and positive. The method of *approaching infinity* cannot be modified because cos z has essential singularity at infinity (see p. 109).

† The integral $-\fint_x^{+\infty} (\cos \xi / \xi)\, d\xi$ is still a branch of Ci (z), although not one of those described previously.

A second type of representation of functions by integrals occurs when the limits of integration are fixed but the integrand depends on a parameter. A well-known example of this kind is the integral

$$\int_0^\infty e^{-\lambda x^2}\, dx = \frac{\sqrt{\pi}}{2}\lambda^{-1/2}$$

occurring in the kinetic theory of gases and many other branches of physics.* It may be viewed as an integral representation of the function $I(\lambda) = (\sqrt{\pi}/2)\lambda^{-1/2}$. This point of view is, as a matter of fact, utilized in practice when the function $I(\lambda)$ is differentiated† to yield other important integrals, like

$$\frac{dI(\lambda)}{d\lambda} = -\frac{\sqrt{\pi}}{4}\lambda^{-3/2} = -\int_0^\infty x^2 e^{-\lambda x^2}\, dx,$$

$$\frac{d^2 I(\lambda)}{d\lambda^2} = \frac{3\sqrt{\pi}}{8}\lambda^{-5/2} = \int_0^\infty x^4 e^{-\lambda x^2}\, dx,\quad \text{etc.}$$

In this particular example the function $I(\lambda)$ represented by the integral is a familiar one, but the same idea can be used to generate a variety of new functions. Consider, for instance, the integral

$$f(n) = \int_0^\infty t^n e^{-t}\, dt \qquad (n = 1, 2, 3, \ldots),$$

which is equal to $n!$ as is not difficult to prove.

The above *integral representation* of $n!$ suggests the extension of the notion of factorial. We may define the *factorial function* $\Pi(x)$ by the integral

$$\Pi(x) = \int_0^\infty t^x e^{-t}\, dt,$$

where x is not necessarily a positive integer. The integral converges at infinity for all values of x, but we must demand that $x > -1$ for the integral to converge at $t = 0$. Consequently, the function $\Pi(x)$ is defined for all (real) $x > -1$ by the above integral representation.

Since $\Pi(n) = n!$, we have

$$\Pi(n + 1) = (n + 1)\Pi(n) \qquad (n = 1, 2, 3, \ldots).$$

This formula holds for all values of x $(x > -1)$. Indeed, integrating by parts, we obtain

$$\int_0^\infty t^{x+1} e^{-t}\, dt = -t^{x+1} e^{-t}\Big|_0^\infty + \int_0^\infty (x + 1)t^x e^{-t}\, dt.$$

---

* For the evaluation of this integral, see Kaplan, p. 218.

† Differentiation of improper integrals should be justified by appropriate theorems. See e.g., Kaplan, p. 379.

Since

$$\lim_{t \to \infty} t^{x+1}e^{-t} = 0 \qquad \text{(all } x\text{)},$$

$$\lim_{t \to 0} t^{x+1}e^{-t} = 0 \qquad (x > -1),$$

it follows that

$$\int_0^\infty t^{x+1}e^{-t}\,dt = (x+1)\int_0^\infty t^x e^{-t}\,dt$$

or

$$\Pi(x+1) = (x+1)\Pi(x) \qquad (x > -1).$$

In particular, $\Pi(0) = 1$. This is the actual reason for the commonly used convention

$$0! = 1.$$

The recursion formula $\Pi(x+1) = (x+1)\Pi(x)$ permits calculation of $\Pi(x)$ for any x ($x > -1$) provided a table of $\Pi(x)$ is compiled for the interval $0 \le x \le 1$. Moreover, it permits an *extension* of the definition of $\Pi(x)$ into the region $x < -1$.

Example. Calculate $\Pi(\tfrac{1}{2})$, $\Pi(-\tfrac{1}{2})$, $\Pi(-\tfrac{3}{2})$.

The first value can be obtained directly from the definition

$$\Pi(\tfrac{1}{2}) = \int_0^\infty t^{1/2}e^{-t}\,dt$$

by the substitution $t = x^2$. Then

$$\Pi(\tfrac{1}{2}) = 2\int_0^\infty x^2 e^{-x^2}\,dx = 2\frac{\sqrt{\pi}}{4} = \frac{\sqrt{\pi}}{2}$$

by a previous result. The value of $\Pi(-\tfrac{1}{2})$ can also be obtained directly in the same manner. But it can be, alternatively, obtained from the recursion formula. If we set $x = -\tfrac{1}{2}$, then

$$\Pi(\tfrac{1}{2}) = \tfrac{1}{2}\Pi(-\tfrac{1}{2});$$

therefore

$$\Pi(-\tfrac{1}{2}) = \sqrt{\pi}.$$

The value of $\Pi(-\tfrac{3}{2})$ *cannot* be obtained directly (the integral diverges) but it may be *defined* via the recursion formula. If we set $x = -\tfrac{3}{2}$, then

$$\Pi(-\tfrac{1}{2}) = (-\tfrac{1}{2})\Pi(-\tfrac{3}{2}),$$

yielding

$$\Pi(-\tfrac{3}{2}) = -2\sqrt{\pi}.$$

An important feature of $\Pi(x)$ is that it approaches infinity as x approaches -1 from the right. The conclusion that $\Pi(x)$ has infinite discontinuities at x equal to a negative integer follows from this fact and the recursion formula. The graph of $\Pi(x)$ is sketched in Fig. 2.34.

While the extension of the concept of the factorial is widely used in applied mathematics, it is not usually accomplished by means of the factorial function $\Pi(x)$ but rather by means of the related *gamma function* defined by

$$\Gamma(x) = \Pi(x - 1).$$

Evidently $\Gamma(x)$ satisfies the relations

$$\Gamma(x + 1) = x\Gamma(x) \qquad \text{(real } x),$$
$$\Gamma(x) = (x - 1)! \qquad (x = \text{positive integer}),$$

and has the integral representation

$$\Gamma(x) = \int_0^\infty t^{x-1} e^{-t}\, dt \qquad (x > 0).$$

The behavior of $\Gamma(x)$ as a function of x is easily obtained from Fig. 2.34 just by shifting the origin to the point $x = -1, y = 0$.

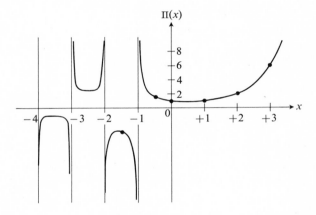

Figure 2.34

Integral representations of the type given for factorial and gamma functions can be extended to complex integrals as well. A complex function $g(z)$ may be defined by a definite integral

$$g(z) = \int_{\substack{s_1 \\ \text{Along } C}}^{s_2} f(z, s)\, ds,$$

where the endpoints s_1 and s_2 as well as the *path C* between them is prescribed. In many cases the points s_1 and s_2 coincide and the path is a closed contour.

From the theory of analytic functions, it follows that the path of integration can be *deformed* within certain limits (as much as the Cauchy theorem and its consequences permit this).

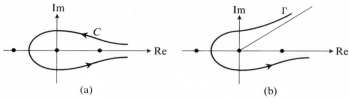

Figure 2.35

Example 1. Function $f(x, t)$ is analytic in the t-plane except for isolated singularities at $s = 0$, $s = 1$, and $s = -1$. Define

$$g(x) = \int_C f(x, t) \, dt,$$

where C is the contour shown on Fig. 2.35(a) and both limits are at infinity. Is it correct to deform the contour into another contour Γ shown on Fig. 2.35(b)? Although the new contour does not enclose any new singularities, it is to be remembered that the Cauchy theorem has been derived for finite contours only. This case calls for caution.

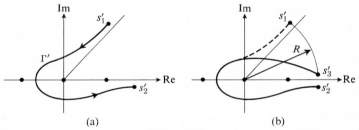

Figure 2.36

Consider the contour Γ' (Fig. 2.36a) with the finite endpoints. It can be deformed as shown on Fig. 2.36(b). If the contribution from the arc $s_1's_3'$ of the circle of radius R approaches zero as $R \to \infty$, then the equivalence between C and Γ holds. Otherwise, it does not.

Example 2. Suppose we desire to extend the integral representation of the gamma function to complex variables. The integrand

$$f(z, t) = t^{z-1}e^{-t}$$

is a multivalued function, where both z and t are treated as complex, with a branch point at $t = 0$. The branches are given explicitly by

$$f(z, t) = e^{(z-1)\,\text{Log}\,t}\,e^{-t}.$$

Let us select the branch of $\text{Log}\,t$ for which $0 \leq \text{Arg}\,t < 2\pi$, with a branch line along the real positive semiaxis and construct a contour like the one shown in

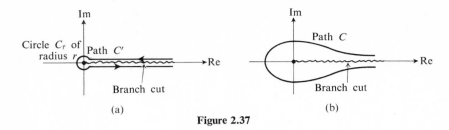

Figure 2.37

Fig. 2.37(a). It is not hard to see that the contribution to the integral

$$\int_{C'} t^{z-1} e^{-t}\, dt$$

from the (incomplete) circle C_r vanishes in the limit when $r \to 0$ and the integral over the upper edge of the branch cut reduces to $-\Gamma(z)$ if z is real.* The integral over the *lower edge* reduces to $\Gamma(z)e^{(z-1)2\pi i}$ or, what is the same, to $\Gamma(z)e^{z2\pi i}$. Consequently, the entire integral is equal to $(e^{z2\pi i} - 1)\Gamma(z)$ for real z. It is now evident that we may deform the path C' to path C (Fig. 2.37b) without affecting the value of the integral in any way. Moreover, the integral is well defined not only for real but also for complex values of z. This permits us to define the complex function $\Gamma(z)$ by means of the integral representation

$$\Gamma(z) = \frac{1}{e^{z2\pi i} - 1} \int_C t^{z-1} e^{-t}\, dt$$

with the path C and the branch of the integrand prescribed above.

Remark. This formula seems to suggest that $\Gamma(z)$ has poles for z equal to an integer. This is actually true only if z is a nonpositive integer: If $z = 1, 2, 3, \ldots$, then the integrand becomes a single-valued function analytic at $t = 0$ and on the real t-axis. This causes the integral to vanish; the gamma function is then defined by a limiting process which does indeed yield $(n - 1)!$.

A great number of complex integral representations used in physics have the peculiar feature that the path of integration appears to be passing through the poles of the integrand. We shall briefly discuss the associated questions.

Example 3. Let the function† $f(x, k)$ be analytic in the k-plane except for the *simple poles* at $k = k_0$ and $k = -k_0$ (k_0 is a real positive number). Consider

$$g(x) = \int_C f(x, k)\, dk,$$

where C is the real axis (traversed from left to right).

---

* The technique is very similar to that employed in Example 7 of Section 2.12. Note, however, that here we *do not* close the contour C' via the large circle C_R (why?).
† For example, $f(x, k) = e^{ikx}/(k_0^2 - k^2)$ (a similar one is used in Section 12.9).

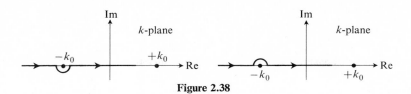

Figure 2.38

As it stands, the function $g(x)$ is not properly defined because the path of integration traverses (two) singularities. However, we can give $g(x)$ a definite meaning by deforming the path so that the *poles are avoided*. For a given pole, this can be done in two obvious ways:

1. avoid the pole counterclockwise,

2. avoid the pole clockwise,

by "stopping the integration" a short distance in front of the pole and going around it in a semicircle of "small" radius. In this case, which is most common in physics, this implies "going below" or "going above" the pole (Fig. 2.38).

In either of the two interpretations the value of radius γ does not matter so long as $f(x, k)$ is analytic for $0 < |k + k_0| \leq r$. It is not difficult to see that the difference between the two values for $g(x)$ will amount to the quantity

$$2\pi i \operatorname{Res} f(x, -k_0).$$

In fact, the path going below the pole will have a contribution

$$+\pi i \operatorname{Res} f(x, -k_0)$$

from the small semicircle (in the limit $r \to 0$). The path going above the pole will have a contribution

$$-\pi i \operatorname{Res} f(x, -k_0)$$

from its semicircle.

Remark. In physical literature, the following notation is widely used for these two cases: Let

$$h(x, k) = f(x, k)(k + k_0).$$

Then the integral avoiding the pole from below is written as

$$g_1(x) = \int_{-\infty}^{+\infty} \frac{h(x, k)}{k - (k_0 + i\epsilon)} \, dk \qquad (k \text{ is real}),$$

implying that, instead of the path going below the pole, the pole itself is displaced upward by an infinitesimal amount ϵ. Similarly, the integral avoiding the pole from above is written as

$$g_2(x) = \int_{-\infty}^{+\infty} \frac{h(x, k)}{k - (k_0 - i\epsilon)} \, dk \qquad (k \text{ is real}).$$

If the ideas behind this notation are clearly understood, no confusion should arise.

Remarks

1. In the example considered, there is another simple pole at $k = +k_0$. It may be treated in the same way as the pole $k = -k_0$ but independently of it. In other words, paths which avoid one pole from below and the other one from above are widely used in practice.

2. If the poles are not simple, the above analysis does not apply and the problem becomes more complicated.

3. The above considerations are easily generalized for the case of a simple pole not on the real axis, provided the path has a tangent at the pole.

In problems arising from physical considerations the choice between avoiding a pole clockwise or counterclockwise (or "from above" and "from below") is dictated by *additional* requirements or assumptions, not contained in the formal derivation of the integral representation (see, e.g., Section 12.9).

Sometimes the physical considerations demand that the residue at the pole should not contribute to the integral at all. In this case, the integral of Example 3 may be defined to mean (as far as the pole at $k = -k_0$ is concerned)

$$g_3(x) = \lim_{\epsilon \to 0} \left\{ \int_{-\infty}^{-k_0-\epsilon} f(x, k) \, dk + \int_{-k_0+\epsilon}^{+\infty} f(x, k) \, dk \right\},$$

where $\epsilon > 0$; note that ϵ must be the same in both integrals. This definition is the complex version of the concept of the Cauchy principal value. It is not difficult to verify that the above definition implies

$$g_3(x) = \tfrac{1}{2}[g_1(x) + g_2(x)].$$

As our last example of integral representations we shall consider an important case of a rather simple real function expressed through a complex integral.

Example 4. *The step function.* Let t be real and let s be complex. Consider the integral in the s-plane

$$\lim_{h \to \infty} \frac{1}{2\pi i} \int_{\gamma-ih}^{\gamma+ih} \frac{e^{ts}}{s} \, ds \qquad (\gamma > 0, h > 0)$$

taken along the vertical line $x = \gamma$ as shown in Fig. 2.39(a). This particular path, often called the *Bromwich contour* is important in the theory of Laplace transforms (see Section 5.9).

The above integral, if convergent, defines a real function $f(t)$ which we will now proceed to evaluate. Draw a circle about the origin with a large radius R and close the contour as shown in Fig. 2.39(b). First of all, integrate by parts:*

$$\int_{N}^{M} \frac{e^{ts}}{s} \, ds = \frac{1}{s} \frac{e^{ts}}{t} \bigg|_{\gamma-ih}^{\gamma+ih} + \frac{1}{t} \int_{N}^{M} \frac{e^{ts}}{s^2} \, ds.$$
$$\text{Along } C_R \qquad\qquad\qquad\qquad\qquad\qquad \text{Along } C_R$$

---

* Compare with p. 91.

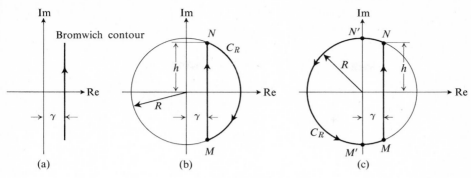

Figure 2.39

The integrated term

$$\frac{1}{t}\frac{e^{ts}}{s}\bigg|_{\gamma-ih}^{\gamma+ih} = \frac{e^{\gamma t}}{t}\left[\frac{e^{iht}}{\gamma+ih} - \frac{e^{-iht}}{\gamma-ih}\right]$$

will approach zero as $R \to \infty$ because $|e^{\gamma t}/t|$ is independent of R while

$$\left|\frac{e^{iht}}{\gamma+ih} - \frac{e^{-iht}}{\gamma-ih}\right| \leq \left|\frac{e^{iht}}{\gamma+ih}\right| + \left|\frac{e^{-iht}}{\gamma-ih}\right| = \frac{1}{R} + \frac{1}{R} = \frac{2}{R}.$$

In the remaining integral, estimate

$$\left|\frac{1}{t}\int_N^M \frac{e^{ts}}{s^2}\,ds\right| \leq \frac{1}{|t|}\frac{|e^{tx}|}{R^2}\pi R \qquad (x = \text{Re } s).$$

The quantity $|e^{tx}|$ will be bounded if $t < 0$ (since $x > 0$ on C_R) and then this term will also approach zero as $R \to \infty$.

Since the integrand e^{ts}/s is analytic within the whole closed contour, the contour integral vanishes; this implies

$$\lim_{h\to\infty}\frac{1}{2\pi i}\int_{\gamma-ih}^{\gamma+ih}\frac{e^{ts}}{s}\,ds = 0 \qquad (\text{if } t < 0).$$

In other words, our function $f(t)$ is zero for *all negative values* of t.

For $t > 0$, the contour of Fig. 2.39(b) is not very useful since the contribution from C_R is difficult to evaluate. However, since it is the magnitude of e^{tx} which seems to govern the estimate of the integral, it is reasonable to close the contour "to the left" for $t > 0$ as in Fig. 2.39(c). As before, integrate by parts and argue that the integrated part yields no contribution (in the limit), being unaffected by the sign of t. The remaining integral,

$$\frac{1}{t}\int_N^M \frac{e^{ts}}{s^2}\,ds,$$

$$\text{Along } C_R$$

is estimated as follows: For the semicircle from N' to M' we have

$$\left|\frac{e^{ts}}{s^2}\right| \leq \frac{1}{R^2}$$

precisely because now $t > 0$ while $\operatorname{Re} s \leq 0$. The length of the semicircle is πR so that the contribution vanishes. For the portions from N to N' and from M' to M we can at least say that

$$\left|\frac{e^{ts}}{s^2}\right| \leq \frac{e^{t\gamma}}{R^2},$$

and there is no contribution either.

Within the contour, however, there is now a pole at the origin with the residue unity. Therefore

$$\lim_{h\to\infty} \frac{1}{2\pi i} \int_{\gamma-ih}^{\gamma+ih} \frac{e^{ts}}{s}\, ds = 1 \qquad \text{(if } t > 0\text{)}.$$

In other words, $f(t)$ is unity *for all positive t*. It remains to evaluate $f(t)$ for $t = 0$. This may be done without recourse to residues:

$$f(0) = \lim_{h\to\infty} \frac{1}{2\pi i} \int_{\gamma-ih}^{\gamma+ih} \frac{ds}{s} = \frac{1}{2\pi i} \lim_{h\to\infty} \log\frac{\gamma + ih}{\gamma - ih} = \frac{1}{2\pi i} \log(-1) = \frac{1}{2}.$$

Observe that it is essential that in order to obtain the value $\frac{1}{2}$, the points N and M must remain symmetrical with respect to the real axis as they recede to infinity. This is somewhat analogous to the process of defining the principal value of an integral.

The function $f(t)$ defined by

$$f(t) = \frac{1}{2\pi i} \int_{\gamma-i\infty}^{\gamma+i\infty} \frac{e^{ts}}{s}\, ds,$$

(a convenient notation for the limits) is called the *step function* (or the *unit function*) and is denoted by $S(t)$:

$$S(t) = \begin{cases} 0 & (t < 0), \\ \frac{1}{2} & (t = 0), \\ 1 & (t > 0). \end{cases}$$

Remark. The term "step function" is more descriptive and avoids confusion with the function $f(t) = 1$, which is unity *everywhere*. In many books the value $S(0) = \frac{1}{2}$ is not specified and the following definition is used:

$$S(t) = \begin{cases} 0 & (t < 0), \\ 1 & (t > 0). \end{cases}$$

Except in the notation used in proofs of certain theorems, this distinction is usually irrelevant in applied mathematics.

The function $S(t - a)$ which is defined by

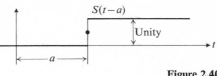

$$S(t - a) = \begin{cases} 0 & (t < a), \\ \frac{1}{2} & (t = a), \\ 1 & (t > 0), \end{cases}$$

Figure 2.40

represents a step function which has been shifted by an amount a. It is shifted to the right if $a > 0$ as shown in Fig. 2.40. This function is called a step function in a general sense and is widely used in physical applications. It is evident that

$$S(t - a) = \frac{1}{2\pi i} \int_{\gamma-i\infty}^{\gamma+i\infty} \frac{1}{s} e^{(t-a)s} \, ds.$$

Functions given by complex integral representations are often subject to differentiation and integration *under the integral sign*. The validity of such procedures is elucidated by the following two theorems which we quote without proofs.

Theorem on integration. Let Γ and C be finite paths (open or closed) and let $h(z)$ and $f(z, s)$ be analytic, with respect to z and s, on Γ and C. Then

$$\int_{\alpha}^{\beta} h(z) \, dz \int_{a}^{b} f(z, s) \, ds = \int_{a}^{b} ds \int_{\alpha}^{\beta} h(z)f(z, s) \, dz.$$
$$\text{\small Along } \Gamma \qquad \text{\small Along } C \qquad \qquad \text{\small Along } C \text{ Along } \Gamma$$

Remark. If Γ or C (or both) involve the point at infinity, then the uniform convergence of $h(z)f(z, s)$ is usually required for the generalization of the theorem.

Theorem on differentiation (Weierstrass). Let

$$g(z) = \int_{a}^{b} f(z, s) \, ds.$$
$$\text{\small Along } C$$

If C is a finite path in the s-plane and $f(z, s)$ is analytic with respect to z in some *closed* region D (in the z-plane) for all s on C, then

a) $g(z)$ is analytic in the *interior* of D,
b) $dg(z)/dz = \int_{a}^{b} (\partial f(z, s)/\partial z) \, ds$ (for all z in the interior of D).
   $\text{\small Along } C$

Again, if the path C involves the point at infinity, then uniform convergence of the *differentiated integral* is usually required for an extension of this theorem. For instance, the integral

$$S(t) = \frac{1}{2\pi i} \int_{\gamma-i\infty}^{\gamma+i\infty} \frac{e^{ts}}{s} \, ds$$

should not be differentiated under the integral sign. Indeed, the "differentiated integral" $1/2\pi i \int_{\gamma-i\infty}^{\gamma+i\infty} e^{ts} \, ds$ *does not converge at all*, much less uniformly, for *any* value of t. Note that this is true despite the fact that the derivative $dS(t)/dt$ exists for all t except $t = 0$.

BIBLIOGRAPHY

BIEBERBACH, L., *Conformal Mapping*. New York: Chelsea Publishing Co., 1953.

CHURCHILL, R. V., *Complex Variables and Applications*. New York: McGraw-Hill Book Co., 1960.

DETTMAN, J. W., *Applied Complex Variables*. New York: Macmillan Co., 1965.

KNOPP, K., *Theory and Applications of Infinite Series*. Glasgow: Blackie & Son Ltd., 1963.

KNOPP, K., *Theory of Functions*. New York: Dover Publications Inc., 1945.

KOBER, H., *Dictionary of Conformal Representations*. New York: Dover Publications Inc., 1952.

NEHARI, Z., *Conformal Mapping*. New York: McGraw-Hill Book Co., 1952.

TITCHMARSH, E. C., *The Theory of Functions*. New York: Oxford University Press, 1950.

PROBLEMS

1. Show that $\operatorname{Re} z_1 \operatorname{Re} z_2 = \frac{1}{2} \operatorname{Re}(z_1 z_2) + \frac{1}{2} \operatorname{Re}(z_1 z_2^*)$.

2. Prove that if $z(i - 1) = -z^*(i + 1)$, then arg z is either $\pi/4$ or $-3\pi/4$.

3. If a and b are two complex numbers and t is a real parameter, then the expression $z = a + t(b - a)$ represents a curve in complex plane. Set $z = x + iy$ and determine the parametric equations $x = x(t)$ and $y = y(t)$ of this curve. What kind of curve is it?

4. Show that the equation $z = Ae^{it} + Be^{-it}$, where A and B are complex constants, and t is a real parameter, represents an ellipse. Describe this ellipse (its semiaxes, center, orientation, etc.) in terms of A and B.

5. Show that the transformation

$$z + a = \zeta \qquad (a = \text{complex constant})$$

represents a translation in the complex plane. Show that the equation

$$(z + 1 - i)(z^* + 1 + i) = 1$$

represents a circle in the complex plane. [*Hint:* Set $z + 1 - i = \zeta$.]

6. Show that the equations

a) $|z - 1| - |z + 1| = 1$,   b) $\operatorname{Re}(1 - z) = |z|$

represent, respectively, a hyperbola and a parabola in the complex plane. Can these conclusions be drawn just by inspection of the equations without any algebraic work? [*Hint:* Recall certain fundamental properties of hyperbola and parabola.]

7. Prove the inequalities on p. 47 by purely algebraic methods (without recourse to the Argand diagram). [*Suggestion:* First prove the inequalities

a') $|1 + z| \leq 1 + |z|$,   b') $|1 - z| \geq |1 - |z||$

and then generalize them by setting $z = z_2/z_1$. (What if $z_1 = 0$?)]

8. Use DeMoivre formula to show that

$$\sin 4\theta = 4 \cos^3 \theta \sin \theta - 4 \cos \theta \sin^3 \theta.$$

What is the corresponding expression for $\cos 4\theta$?

9. Express the following complex numbers in trigonometric form:

a) $z = \sqrt[3]{i - 1}$,   b) $z = (-1 - i)^{4/5}$.

10. Show that $i^i = e^{-(\pi/2 + 2n\pi)}$ (n = integer). [*Hint:* Calculate Log i.]

11. Using the definitions of complex functions $\sin z$ and $\sinh z$, show that

a) $\sin (z_1 \pm z_2) = \sin z_1 \cos z_2 \pm \cos z_1 \sin z_2$,
b) $\sinh (z_1 \pm z_2) = \sinh z_1 \cosh z_2 \pm \cosh z_1 \sinh z_2$.

What are the corresponding relations for $\cos z$ and $\cosh z$?

12. Show that the *complex* function $\sin z$ can vanish only on the real axis and, in particular, at points $x = n\pi$ (n = integer). At what points does the function $\sinh z$ vanish?

13. Along which curves in the complex plane do the functions $\sinh z$ and $\cosh z$ assume real values?

14. Show that all solutions of the equation

$$\sin z = 1000$$

are given, approximately, by the formula

$$z = (n + \tfrac{1}{2})\pi \pm i \cdot 7.601,$$

where n is an even integer. [*Hint:* Decompose $\sin z$ into real and imaginary parts and solve the resulting equations.]

15. If $z = x + iy$, show that

$$\tanh z = \frac{\sinh 2x + i \sin 2y}{\cosh 2x + \cos 2y}.$$

16. There is no difficulty in calculating the sums

a) $\displaystyle\sum_{n=0}^{N} e^{nx}$ b) $\displaystyle\sum_{n=0}^{N} e^{inx}$ (x = real)

because both of them represent a geometric progression. Apply Euler's formula to deduce that

$$\sum_{n=0}^{N} \cos nx = \frac{\sin \tfrac{1}{2}(N + 1)x}{\sin \tfrac{1}{2}x} \cos \frac{Nx}{2}   (x = \text{real}).$$

What is the corresponding sum involving $\sin nx$?

17. Apply the idea of the preceding problem to calculate the infinite sums (consult Section 2.9)

$$\sum_{n=0}^{\infty} a^n \cos nx,   \sum_{n=0}^{\infty} a^n \sin nx,   (a = \text{real const}).$$

For what values of a will the results be valid?

18. Figure 2.41 represents a portion of an AC-circuit with the potential difference (voltage) between points A and B given by

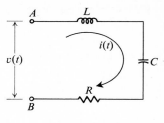

$$v(t) = V_A - V_B = V_0 \cos \omega t.$$

Consult a textbook of your choice and show that the current $i(t)$ (as shown) must obey the differential equation

Figure 2.41

$$L\frac{d^2 i(t)}{dt^2} + R\frac{di(t)}{dt} + \frac{i(t)}{C} = \frac{dv(t)}{dt}.$$

Show how the method of complex exponentials can be used to find a complex solution $i(t)$ which varies harmonically in time. Perform the transition to real variables, show that

$$i(t) = I_0 \cos(\omega t + \phi),$$

and evaluate I_0 and ϕ in terms of L, R, C, and V_0.

19. Do the functions

$$u(x, y) = \frac{x(1 + x) + y^2}{(1 + x)^2 + y^2}, \qquad v(x, y) = \frac{y}{(1 + x)^2 + y^2}$$

satisfy the Cauchy-Riemann conditions? Can u and v serve as real and imaginary parts of some analytic function of $z = x + iy$ or not?

20. Consider the function

$$f(z) = (3y^2 - x^3) + i(6xy^2 - 3yx^2).$$

a) Are the Cauchy-Riemann conditions satisfied at each point of the real axis?
b) Are the partial derivatives

$$\frac{\partial u}{\partial x}, \frac{\partial u}{\partial y}, \frac{\partial v}{\partial x}, \quad \text{and} \quad \frac{\partial v}{\partial y}$$

continuous at each point of the real axis?
c) Is the function $f(z)$ analytic at each point of the real axis?

21. Show that the function $f(z) = x^2 + iy$ is not analytic for any z. Consequently, the integral $\int_0^{2+i} f(z)\,dz$ is expected to depend on the path. Illustrate this by calculating the integral along three *smooth* paths of your choice connecting the points $z_1 = 0$ and $z_2 = 2 + i$.

22. Is the integral

$$I = \int_0^i \frac{dz}{1 - z^2}$$

independent of path? If so, state clearly under what conditions. How would you calculate I for any given path C in the most convenient way?

23. Let $z^{1/2}$ denote the principal value of the square root. Compute the integral $\int_{+1}^{-1} dz/z^{1/2}$

    a) along the upper half of the unit circle ($|z| = 1$),
    b) along the lower half of the unit circle ($|z| = 1$).

24. Using the Cauchy theorem, Cauchy integral formula, or their consequences, evaluate the following integrals, all taken around the circle $|z| = 2$:

    a) $\oint \dfrac{\cos z}{z}\, dz,$ b) $\oint \dfrac{\sin z}{z}\, dz,$ c) $\oint \dfrac{e^z}{z - 1}\, dz,$

    d) $\oint \dfrac{2z^2 + 3z - 1}{z - 1 + i}\, dz,$ e) $\oint \dfrac{2z}{z^2 - 9}\, dz,$ f) $\oint \dfrac{\sin z}{z^2}\, dz,$

    g) $\oint \dfrac{e^z}{(z - 1)^2}\, dz,$ h) $\oint \dfrac{\sin z}{z^n}\, dz.$

25. Evaluate the integral

$$\oint_C \frac{e^z}{z^2 - 1}\, dz$$

    a) given that C is the circle $|z - 1| = 1$,
    b) given that C is the circle $|z - i| = 1$,
    c) given that C is the ellipse $x^2/4 + y^2/9 = 1$, $x + iy = z$,
    d) given that C is the curve $x^4 + y^4 = \frac{1}{2}$. [*Hint:* Describe the curve C in polar coordinates and observe that the problem hinges on the investigation of maxima and minima of the function $f(\theta) = \cos^4 \theta + \sin^4 \theta$).]

26. Consider the multivalued function

$$F(z) = \operatorname{Log} \frac{z + 1}{z - 1}.$$

Construct a branch $f_1(z)$ of $F(z)$ which is continuous everywhere except for a cut along the real axis from $z = -1$ to $z = +1$. Specify the branch carefully, i.e., give exact formulas for calculation of the values of $f_1(z)$ for all values of z. Determine the values of

$$\lim_{\epsilon \to 0} \tfrac{1}{2}[f_1(x - i\epsilon) + f_1(x + i\epsilon)].$$

27. Construct another branch $f_2(z)$ of $F(z)$ given in the preceding problem which is continuous everywhere except for two cuts along the real axis, from $-\infty$ to -1, and from $+1$ to $+\infty$. Again, specify $f_2(z)$ with utmost care.

28. Show that among the following complex series of constants,

    a) $\displaystyle\sum_{n=1}^{\infty} \frac{i^n}{n\sqrt{n}},$ b) $\displaystyle\sum_{n=1}^{\infty} e^{-n(1+i)},$

    c) $\displaystyle\sum_{n=2}^{\infty} \frac{i^n}{\log n},$ d) $\displaystyle\sum_{n=1}^{\infty} \frac{(1 + i)^n}{n},$

the series (a) and (b) converge absolutely, the series (c) converges, but not absolutely, and the series (d) diverges.

29. Show that the following complex power series are absolutely and uniformly convergent for $|z| \leq 1$:

a) $\sum_{n=1}^{\infty} \left(\frac{z-1}{3} \right)^n$,   b) $\sum_{n=1}^{\infty} \frac{1}{n^2} (\cos nx + i \sin ny)$.

30. Show that the series $\sum_{n=1}^{\infty} (z^n/n!)$ is absolutely convergent for all z. Show that it is uniformly convergent for $|z| \leq R$ for arbitrary R. Despite the fact that R is arbitrary, why would it be incorrect to say that the series converges uniformly for all z?

31. Show that the function $f(z) = \arctan z$ must possess a Taylor series about the point $z = 1$. Without evaluating the series, show that its radius of convergence must be equal to $\sqrt{2}$.

32. Expand the following functions in a Taylor or a Laurent series valid in the immediate neighborhood of the specified points. Determine the regions in which the expansions are valid.

a) $f(z) = \cos z$ $(z = 0)$.   b) $f(z) = \dfrac{1}{z(z^2 + 1)}$ $(z = 0)$.

c) $f(z) = \dfrac{z}{z^2 - 1}$ $(z = 2)$.   d) $f(z) = \dfrac{1}{z^2 + 1}$ $(z = 1)$.

e) $f(z) = \dfrac{e^z}{z(z^2 + 1)}$ $(z = 0)$. [*Hint:* Multiply the series for e^z and $1/(z^2 + 1)$.]

f) $f(z) = \cosh z$ $(z = i\pi)$.

33. Find *all* Laurent (or Taylor) expansions of the following functions about the indicated points:

a) $f(z) = \dfrac{1}{z(z - 2)}$ $(z = 1)$,   b) $f(z) = \dfrac{1}{(z + 1)^3}$ $(z = 0)$,

c) $f(z) = \dfrac{z}{z^2 - 1}$ $(z = 2)$,   d) $f(z) = \dfrac{1}{\sqrt{1 + z}}$ $(z = 0)$,

e) $f(z) = \log (1 + z)$ $(z = 0)$,   f) $f(z) = \text{Log} \dfrac{z + 1}{z - 1}$ $(z = 0)$.

Since the last three examples involve branch lines and (possibly) multivaluedness, *state clearly* which branch you use in each particular expansion.

34. Determine points where the following functions are not analytic. If the singularities are isolated, determine their character (if a pole, state the order) and calculate the residues:

a) $f(z) = \dfrac{z + 1}{z^2 - 2z}$,   b) $f(z) = \dfrac{z^2 - 2z}{(z + 1)^2(z^2 + 4)}$,   c) $f(z) = \dfrac{1 - e^{2z}}{z^4}$,

d) $f(z) = \dfrac{z}{\cos z}$,   e) $f(z) = \tanh z$,   f) $f(z) = \dfrac{e^{az}}{\cosh \pi z}$,

g) $f(z) = \left(\dfrac{3}{z^3} - \dfrac{1}{z} \right) \sin z - \dfrac{3}{z^2} \cos z$,   h) $f(z) = \left(\dfrac{3}{z^3} - \dfrac{1}{z} \right) \cos z - \dfrac{3}{z^2} \sin z$.

35. Show that

$$f(z) = \sin \frac{1}{1-z}$$

has an essential singularity at $z = 1$.

36. Using the residue theorem, evaluate the following integrals around the indicated contours:

a) $\oint_C \dfrac{dz}{z^2 + 4}$,   where C is the circle $|z - 2i| = 1$,

b) $\oint_C \dfrac{\cosh \pi z}{z(z^2 + 1)}\, dz$,   where C is the circle $|z| = 2$,

c) $\oint_C ze^{1/z}\, dz$,   where C is the circle $|z| = 2$,

d) $\oint_C \dfrac{z - 1}{z^2 + iz + 2}\, dz$,   where C is the curve $x^4 + y^4 = 4$.

[See Problem 25(d) above.]

37. Illustrate the use of the residue theorem in evaluation of the following real integrals:

a) $\displaystyle\int_0^{2\pi} \frac{d\theta}{1 + \epsilon \cos \theta} = \frac{2\pi}{\sqrt{1 - \epsilon^2}}$ $(|\epsilon| < 1)$,

b) $\displaystyle\int_0^{2\pi} \frac{\cos 3\theta}{5 - 4\cos \theta}\, d\theta = \frac{\pi}{12}$,   c) $\displaystyle\int_0^{\pi} \frac{d\theta}{1 + \sin^2 \theta} = \frac{\pi}{\sqrt{2}}$,

d) $\displaystyle\int_0^{2\pi} \frac{d\theta}{(a + b\sin \theta)^2} = \frac{2\pi a}{(a^2 - b^2)^{3/2}}$ $(a > |b|)$,

e) $\displaystyle\int_0^{2\pi} \cos^n \theta\, d\theta = \frac{1 \cdot 3 \cdot 5 \cdots (n - 1)}{2 \cdot 4 \cdot 6 \cdots n}\, 2\pi = \frac{n!\pi}{2^{n-1}(n/2!)^2}$ $(n = \text{even integer})$.

38. Establish the following results on the basis of the techniques of Section 2.12:

a) $\displaystyle\int_{-\infty}^{+\infty} \frac{dx}{x^4 + a^4} = \frac{\pi}{a^3\sqrt{2}}$,   b) $\displaystyle\int_0^{\infty} \frac{x^2}{x^6 + 1}\, dx = \frac{\pi}{6}$,   c) $\displaystyle\int_{-\infty}^{+\infty} \frac{dx}{(x^2 + 1)^3} = \frac{3\pi}{8}$,

d) $\displaystyle\int_{-\infty}^{+\infty} \frac{\cos kx\, dx}{(x - a)^2 + b^2} = \frac{\pi}{b} e^{-kb} \cos ka$ $(k > 0;\ b > 0)$,

e) $\displaystyle\int_0^{\infty} \frac{x \sin x\, dx}{x^2 + 1} = \frac{\pi}{2e}$,

f) $\displaystyle\int_{-\infty}^{\infty} \frac{\cos x\, dx}{(x^2 + a^2)(x^2 + b^2)} = \frac{\pi}{a^2 - b^2}\left(\frac{e^{-b}}{b} - \frac{e^{-a}}{a}\right)$ $(a \neq b)$.

[What is the result of (f) if $a = b$?] Quote all theorems needed to justify the validity of your procedure.

39. Prove the following statements:

a) $\displaystyle\int_{-\infty}^{+\infty} \frac{\cosh ax}{\cosh \pi x}\, dx = \sec \frac{a}{2}$ $(|a| < \pi)$.

[*Hint:* Reduce to Example 6 in the text.]

b) $\displaystyle\int_{-\infty}^{+\infty} \frac{e^{ax}}{1 + e^x}\, dx = \frac{\pi}{\sin a\pi}$ $(|a| < 1)$.

[*Hint:* Use the rectangle with sides $y = 0$, $y = 2\pi$, $x = -R$, and $x = +R$ for the contour.]

c) $\displaystyle\int_0^\infty \frac{x^{a-1}}{1 + x^2}\, dx = \frac{\pi}{2} \csc \frac{a\pi}{2}$ $(0 < a < 2)$.

[*Hint:* Use the contour shown in Fig. 2.26.]

d) $\displaystyle\int_{-\infty}^{+\infty} \frac{x^2 e^x}{1 + e^{2x}}\, dx = \frac{\pi^3}{8}$.

[*Hint:* Use the rectangle with the sides $y = 0$, $y = \pi$, $x = -R$, and $x = +R$.]

40. Show that the function

$$u(x, y) = \frac{\sin 2x}{\cosh 2y + \cos 2x}$$

can serve as a real part of some analytic function $f(z)$. Evaluate $v(x, y) = \mathrm{Im}\, f(z)$ by a method of your choice. Express $f(z)$ explicitly in terms of z.

41. The complex transformation $w = be^{z-a}$, where a, $b =$ complex const, maps the isosceles triangle T with the vertices at $z_1 = b$, $z_2 = b + 1$, and $z_3 = b + 1 + i$ into some curvilinear triangle T' in the w-plane. Illustrate the invariance of angles property of this mapping by explicitly calculating the interior angles of T' to be $90°$, $45°$, and $45°$.

42. Show that the image of the circle $(x - 1)^2 + y^2 = 1$ under the mapping $w = z^2$ is a cardioid $\rho = 2(1 - \cos \phi)$, where $w = \rho e^{i\phi}$. Sketch the cardioid and locate the point where the invariance of angles breaks down. Explain. [*Hint:* Express the equation of the circle in polar coordinates in the z-plane.]

43. Show that the integral

$$\int_{-1}^{+1} \frac{dx}{x}$$ $(x$ is real$)$

does not exist. Show that the integral

$$\int_{-1}^{+1} \frac{dx}{x}$$

does exist and is equal to zero. [*Hint:* Show that the primitive function of $1/x$ is $\log |x|$, which is valid for both positive and negative x.]

CHAPTER 3

LINEAR DIFFERENTIAL
EQUATIONS OF SECOND ORDER

3.1 GENERAL INTRODUCTION. THE WRONSKIAN

A great variety of physical problems is reducible to linear differential equations, in particular, to those of second order. These also occur in the treatment of partial differential equations. The general form of such an equation is

$$A(x)\frac{d^2y}{dx^2} + B(x)\frac{dy}{dx} + C(x)y = D(x).$$

All variables are, in general, complex but special emphasis is put on real equations. It is customary to divide the equation by $A(x)$ [points where $A(x)$ vanishes must be given special treatment]:

$$y'' + P(x)y' + Q(x)y = R(x).$$

If $R(x) \equiv 0$, the equation is homogeneous. Otherwise it is nonhomogeneous.

During the discussion of basic properties of the solutions, it will be tacitly assumed that the functions P, Q, and R are *analytic* within the region (of variable x) under consideration. However, P, Q, or R may fail to be analytic at some particular points, e.g., when $A(x) = 0$. Whenever this occurs, special attention will be given to this fact.

Let us first consider the homogeneous equation

$$y'' + P(x)y' + Q(x)y = 0.$$

A fundamental property of its solutions stems from the linearity of the equation: *A linear combination of two solutions is also a solution*, namely,

$$y = C_1y_1(x) + C_2y_2(x)$$

is a solution provided y_1 and y_2 are solutions. Function $y(x) \equiv 0$ is always a solution and is known as the *trivial* solution.

Two solutions are called *linearly independent* provided that neither of them is a multiple of the other, i.e., that the condition

$$C_1y_1(x) + C_2y_2(x) = 0$$

can be satisfied *for all x* only if $C_1 = C_2 = 0$. It is obvious that neither y_1 nor y_2 can be trivial if they are linearly independent.

Linear dependence or independence of solutions can be established from the knowledge of their values and the values of their first derivatives at some particular point $x = x_0$. If

$$y_1(x_0) = ky_2(x_0) \quad \text{and} \quad y_1'(x_0) = ky_2'(x_0) \quad (k = \text{const}),$$

then y_1 and y_2 are linearly dependent. One way to see this is to note that the DE* yields

$$y_1''(x_0) = ky_2''(x_0).$$

Now differentiate the DE and deduce that† $y_1'''(x_0) = ky_2'''(x_0)$, and so on. It follows that the functions y_1 and y_2 must be multiples of each other.

Conversely, if

$$y_1(x_0)/y_2(x_0) \neq y_1'(x_0)/y_2'(x_0),$$

then the functions must be linearly independent. To demonstrate this, let us introduce the function

$$W[y_1(x), y_2(x)] = y_1(x)y_2'(x) - y_2(x)y_1'(x)$$

which is called the *Wronskian* of the two solutions y_1 and y_2. If the two solutions are linearly dependent, then their Wronskian vanishes identically. The Wronskian has a remarkable property: Either it is identically zero or it is never zero; it cannot vanish for any particular value of x. To show this, calculate the derivative

$$\frac{dW}{dx} = y_1y_2'' + y_1'y_2' - y_2y_1'' - y_2'y_1' = y_1y_2'' - y_2y_1''.$$

From the fact that y_1 and y_2 are solutions of the DE, namely,

$$y_1'' + P(x)y_1' + Q(x)y_1 = 0,$$
$$y_2'' + P(x)y_2' + Q(x)y_2 = 0,$$

it follows that

$$y_1y_2'' - y_2y_1'' + P(x)[y_1y_2' - y_2y_1'] = 0$$

if we multiply the first equation by $-y_2$, the second one by y_1 and add. Therefore

$$\frac{dW}{dx} + P(x)W = 0$$

and

$$W(x) = W(x_0) \exp\left\{-\int_{x_0}^{x} P(\xi)\, d\xi\right\},$$

where $W(x_0)$ is a constant, equal to the value of W at some particular point x_0.

---

* We shall use the abbreviation DE for *differential equation*.
† We assume that $y(x)$ is analytic at $x = x_1$, see pp. 129 and 146.

Since the exponential function never vanishes, $W(x)$ is either identically zero (if $W(x_0) = 0$) or it is never zero (if $W(x_0) \neq 0$), as stated.

Returning to the condition $y_1(x_0)/y_2(x_0) \neq y_1'(x_0)/y_2'(x_0)$, we see that, in this case $W(x_0) \neq 0$ so that the Wronskian can never vanish, much less be identically zero. Then y_1 and y_2 cannot be linearly dependent. It follows that they are linearly independent.

Remark. The Wronskian is often represented in the form of a determinant:

$$W[y_1(x), y_2(x)] = \det \begin{vmatrix} y_1(x) & y_2(x) \\ y_1'(x) & y_2'(x) \end{vmatrix}.$$

3.2 GENERAL SOLUTION OF THE HOMOGENEOUS EQUATION

From the previous discussion it is evident that a solution of our DE is completely specified if its value and the value of its derivative are specified at a certain point $x = x_0$. From this, in turn, it follows that the formula

$$y(x) = C_1 y_1(x) + C_2 y_2(x),$$

where y_1 and y_2 are two linearly independent solutions and C_1 and C_2 are suitably chosen constants, represents the *general solution* of the homogeneous equation. Indeed, let $y(x)$ be a solution with specified values

$$y(x_0) = a, \qquad y'(x_0) = b.$$

Substitute these values into the above formula and into the formula for $y'(x)$ (obtained by differentiation):

$$a = C_1 y_1(x_0) + C_2 y_2(x_0),$$
$$b = C_1 y_1'(x_0) + C_2 y_2'(x_0).$$

This system can be solved for C_1 and C_2 and it definitely possesses a unique solution because the determinant

$$\det \begin{vmatrix} y_1(x_0) & y_2(x_0) \\ y_1'(x_0) & y_2'(x_0) \end{vmatrix} = W(x_0)$$

cannot be zero (y_1 and y_2 are linearly independent).

If one solution $y_1(x)$ of the DE is known, then a second one, linearly independent of y_1, can be found by the following straightforward procedure: Observe that

$$\frac{d}{dx}\left(\frac{y_2}{y_1}\right) = \frac{y_1 y_2' - y_2 y_1'}{y_1^2} = \frac{W(x)}{[y_1(x)]^2}.$$

The Wronskian is a known function:

$$W(x) = W(x_0) \exp\left\{-\int_{x_0}^{x} P(\xi)\, d\xi\right\}$$

except for the constant $W(x_0)$ (x_0 may be chosen arbitrarily). Consequently, the ratio y_2/y_1 can be evaluated *up to a constant factor*

$$\frac{y_2(x)}{y_1(x)} = W(x_0) \int_{x_1}^{x} \exp\left\{-\int_{x_0}^{\xi} P(\eta)\, d\eta\right\} \frac{d\xi}{[y_1(\xi)]^2},$$

where both x_0 and x_1 are arbitrary. This implies that $y_2(x)$ is determined: Since any (linearly independent of y_1) solution will suffice, the constant $W(x_0)$ may be chosen arbitrarily.

The above result can also be obtained by the so-called *method of variation of constants*,* due to Lagrange: If $y_1(x)$ is a solution, then $Cy_1(x)$ (C = const) is also a solution, but linearly dependent of y_1; now try to find a linearly independent solution by making C a variable, i.e., assume that

$$y_2(x) = C(x)y_1(x).$$

Substituting this formula into the DE obtain a DE for $C(x)$, which can be solved in a straightforward fashion. The result reads

$$C(x) = A \int_{x_1}^{x} \exp\left\{-\int_{x_0}^{\xi} P(\eta)\, d\eta\right\} \frac{d\xi}{[y_1(\xi)]^2},$$

where all three constants x_0, x_1, and A may be chosen arbitrarily.

Exercise. Give all the details in the derivation of the above formula for $C(x)$.

3.3 THE NONHOMOGENEOUS EQUATION. VARIATION OF CONSTANTS

The linearity of the nonhomogeneous equation allows us to state the following important theorem: If u_1 is a solution of the nonhomogeneous equation and y is a solution of the corresponding homogeneous equation [obtained by setting $R(x) = 0$], then the function

$$u(x) = u_1(x) + y(x)$$

is also a solution of the nonhomogeneous equation. The proof is trivial (by substitution into the DE).

This theorem is the basis for the most common method of solving nonhomogeneous equations known as the *method of complementary function:* Let u_1 be an arbitrary solution of the nonhomogeneous equation (known as the *particular integral*) and let y be the general solution of the homogeneous equation (known

---

* Also widely known as the *method of variation of parameters.*

as *the complementary function*). Then $u = u_1 + y$ represents the *general solution* of the nonhomogeneous equation.

Indeed, u must be a solution by the preceding theorem. To show that it is a general solution, let us represent the complementary function as a linear combination of two linearly independent solutions of the homogeneous equation. Then

$$u(x) = u_1(x) + C_1 y_1(x) + C_2 y_2(x).$$

If we set $u(x_0) = a$, and $u'(x_0) = b$, then the following equations must hold for C_1 and C_2:

$$C_1 y_1(x_0) + C_2 y_2(x_0) = a - u_1(x_0),$$
$$C_1 y_1'(x_0) + C_2 y_2'(x_0) = b - u_1'(x_0).$$

Since $W(y_1, y_2) \neq 0$, this system has a unique solution for C_1 and C_2, and the theorem follows.

A particular integral (or the general solution, for that matter) of a nonhomogeneous equation can be obtained in a straightforward fashion if the complementary function is known. The particular integral is sought in the form

$$u(x) = v_1(x)y_1(x) + v_2(x)y_2(x),$$

which can be obtained from the complementary function by replacing the constants C_1 and C_2 by the functions v_1 and v_2; hence we have the name *variation of constants*.

Note that the above relation does not define $v_1(x)$ and $v_2(x)$ uniquely, even if $u(x)$ is specified. For instance, it is possible to add to $v_1(x)$ an arbitrary function $g(x)$ and at the same time subtract from $v_2(x)$ the function $g(x)y_1(x)/y_2(x)$ because

$$(v_1 + g)y_1 + [v_2 - gy_1/y_2]y_2 = v_1 y_1 + v_2 y_2.$$

We can profit from this arbitrariness by imposing certain additional requirements on v_1 and v_2 to facilitate their determination. Let us calculate $u'(x)$:

$$u' = v_1 y_1' + v_2 y_2' + v_1' y_1 + v_2' y_2.$$

If we make the additional requirement that

$$v_1' y_1 + v_2' y_2 = 0,$$

we simplify the determination of v_1 and v_2, as seen below. This also has an interesting practical meaning: If the value $u(x_0)$ and the slope $u'(x_0)$ are fixed at some point x_0 and if $u(x)$ were to be *approximated* near x_0 by a linear combination $C_1 y_1 + C_2 y_2$, then the *constants* C_1 and C_2 would be determined from the equations

$$u(x_0) = C_1 y_1(x_0) + C_2 y_2(x_0),$$
$$u'(x_0) = C_1 y_1'(x_0) + C_2 y_2'(x_0).$$

These values of C_1 and C_2 are known as *osculating parameters* of the solution $u(x)$ at the point x_0. The condition imposed on v'_1 and v'_2 implies that

$$u(x) = v_1(x)y_1(x) + v_2(x)y_2(x),$$
$$u'(x) = v_1(x)y'_1(x) + v_2(x)y'_2(x).$$

In other words, $v_1(x)$ and $v_2(x)$ are just the (variable) osculating parameters of the solution $u(x)$.

Now calculate u'' and substitute u'', u', and u into the DE. Utilize the fact that y_1 and y_2 are solutions of the homogeneous equation. The result reads

$$v'_1 y'_1 + v'_2 y'_2 = R.$$

This relation, along with the requirement that

$$v'_1 y_1 + v'_2 y_2 = 0,$$

yields

$$v'_1 = -y_2 R/W, \qquad v'_2 = y_1 R/W,$$

where $W =$ Wronskian of y_1 and y_2. Now obtain, by direct integration,

$$v_1(x) = -\int_{x_1}^{x} \frac{y_2(\xi)R(\xi)}{W(\xi)} \, d\xi, \qquad v_2(x) = \int_{x_2}^{x} \frac{y_1(\xi)R(\xi)}{W(\xi)} \, d\xi.$$

Here x_1 and x_2 can be arbitrary if an arbitrary particular solution $u(x)$ is sought. In fact, a different choice of x_1 and x_2 changes v_1 and v_2 by additive constants so that the resulting solution $u(x)$ is the *general solution* of the nonhomogeneous equation.

The results of the last three sections may be summarized in a conclusion: To find a general solution of the nonhomogeneous equation

$$y'' + Py' + Qy = R,$$

it is necessary to find *only one* solution y_1 of the homogeneous equation

$$y'' + Py' + Qy = 0.$$

Then the second solution y_2 (linearly independent of y_1) of the homogeneous equation can be found by direct integration and, after that, the general solution of the nonhomogeneous equation can also be found by straight integration.

3.4 POWER SERIES SOLUTIONS

Many linear differential equations of second order have solutions which are not expressible in a simple form in terms of well-known functions, such as algebraic, trigonometric, and logarithmic functions. Some seemingly "simple" equations like $y'' + xy = 0$ fall into this class. We may obtain, however, a valid representation of many such functions in terms of power series.

From the very nature of the second-order linear DE it follows that if P, Q, and R are analytic at *some point* $x = a$, then the solution y, if it exists at all, must be analytic at that point. Indeed, the DE implies that $y(x)$ possesses first and second derivatives in some neighborhood of $x = a$ (a neighborhood over which P, Q, and R are still analytic). Therefore, the solution can be expressed by a Taylor series:

$$y(x) = c_0 + c_1(x - a) + c_2(x - a)^2 + c_3(x - a)^3 + \cdots$$

The most familiar series of this type is the Maclaurin series (or power series in x) which is, of course, a Taylor series for the special choice $a = 0$. Many differential equations will have a solution analytic at the origin which is then expressible as

$$y(x) = c_0 + c_1 x + c_2 x^2 + c_3 x^3 + \cdots$$

Of course, this is true only within a certain radius of convergence R. But, within this radius of convergence, the series can be differentiated any number of times, so that y' and y'' are expressed by similar series.

This forms the basis for the *power series method*, illustrated by the following example: Consider $y'' - k^2 y = 0$ (k = real const). (The general solution of this equation is $C_1 e^{kx} + C_2 e^{-kx}$, so that the result can be checked.) Assume the solution in the form

$$y(x) = c_0 + c_1 x + c_2 x^2 + c_3 x^3 + \cdots$$

Then

$$y'(x) = c_1 + 2c_2 x + 3c_3 x^2 + 4c_4 x^3 + \cdots,$$
$$y''(x) = 2c_2 + 3 \cdot 2c_3 x + 4 \cdot 3c_4 x^2 + \cdots$$

The series for y'' and y are now substituted into the DE and the coefficients with all powers are set equal to zero [on the basis of the theorem that all Taylor coefficients of the function $f(z) \equiv 0$ must vanish]. It follows that

$$2c_2 - k^2 c_0 = 0, \quad 3 \cdot 2c_3 - k^2 c_1 = 0, \quad 4 \cdot 3c_4 - k^2 c_2 = 0, \quad \text{and so on.}$$

This yields

$$c_2 = \frac{k^2}{2} c_0, \qquad c_3 = \frac{k^2}{3 \cdot 2} c_1, \qquad c_4 = \frac{k^2}{4 \cdot 3} c_2, \quad \text{etc.}$$

In general, it is seen that

$$c_n = \frac{k^2}{n(n - 1)} c_{n-2} \qquad \text{(all } n \geq 2\text{)}.$$

Such a formula is called a *recursion formula* (or *recurrence formula*) for the coefficients. If c_0 is known, then all even coefficients can be determined. Odd coefficients can be determined if c_1 is known. The entire solution splits into even and odd parts and can be written as

$$y(x) = c_0(1 + k^2 x^2/2! + k^4 x^4/4! + \cdots) + c_1(x + k^2 x^3/3! + k^4 x^5/5! + \cdots)$$

Both series appearing above converge absolutely for all values of x (e.g., by ratio test) and uniformly within an arbitrary radius of convergence (by Weierstrass M-test). Consequently each one of them represents an analytic function over the entire complex x-plane, and both functions evidently satisfy the DE. Therefore, we have obtained the solution in the form

$$y(x) = c_0 y_1(x) + c_1 y_2(x),$$

where $y_1(x)$ and $y_2(x)$ are solutions, and c_0 and c_1 are arbitrary constants. The solutions y_1 and y_2 are obviously linearly independent since one of them is even and the other is odd. We conclude that we have obtained the general solution of the DE.

In our particular example the series are recognized as hyperbolic functions:

$$y_1(x) = 1 + k^2 x^2/2! + k^4 x^4/4! + \cdots = \cosh kx,$$
$$y_2(x) = x + k^2 x^3/3! + k^4 x^5/5! + \cdots = (1/k) \sinh kx.$$

The general solution $y(x) = c_0 \cosh kx + (c_1/k) \sinh kx$ is, of course, equivalent to $y(x) = C_1 e^{kx} + C_2 e^{-kx}$.

Remark. The solution $y_1(x)$, being an even series, implies that $y_1'(0) = 0$, while the solution $y_2(x)$, being an odd series, implies that $y_2(0) = 0$.

3.5 THE FROBENIUS METHOD

The power series $\sum_{n=0}^{\infty} c_n x^n$ is a Taylor series about the point $x = 0$. It will represent a solution provided the solution is analytic at $x = 0$. If the solution is not analytic at $x = 0$, we may, of course, switch to some other point $x = a$ where it is analytic. However, there is another approach: If the solution is not analytic at $x = 0$ because it has a pole there, then it will possess a Laurent series of a similar form:

$$y(x) = \sum_{n}^{\infty} c_n x^n$$

except that it will not begin with $n = 0$ but rather with $n = -m$, where $m = $ order of the pole.

The method of Frobenius utilizes this idea: We seek a solution of the DE in the form

$$y(x) = x^s \sum_{n=0}^{\infty} c_n x^n = \sum_{n=0}^{\infty} c_n x^{s+n} \qquad (c_0 \neq 0),$$

where s is left completely undetermined. This *generalized power series* is capable of describing

a) analytic functions that do not vanish at the origin ($s = 0$),
b) analytic functions with a zero of order m at the origin ($s = m = $ positive integer),
c) functions with a pole of order m at the origin ($s = -m = $ negative integer),
d) functions with certain types of branch points at the origin ($s = $ noninteger).

An example of (d) is the function $f(x) = \sqrt{x}/\sin x$ which is expressible by the series

$$f(x) = x^{1/2}(1/x + x/6 + \tfrac{7}{360}x^3 + \tfrac{31}{15120}x^5 + \cdots)$$
$$= x^{-1/2}(1 + \tfrac{1}{6}x^2 + \tfrac{7}{360}x^4 + \cdots).$$

If the solution of a DE is expressible by the series

$$y(x) = x^s \sum_{n=0}^{\infty} c_n x^n \qquad (c_0 \neq 0),$$

then, in general, such a series can be differentiated term by term. Indeed:

1. If s is zero or a positive integer, the series is a Taylor series and can be differentiated any number of times within its radius of convergence.

2. If s is a negative integer, the series is a Laurent series and can be differentiated any number of times within the annulus for which it holds.

3. If s is not an integer, then $y'(x)$ is expressible as

$$y'(x) = (x^s)' \sum_{n=0}^{\infty} c_n x^n + x^s \left(\sum_{n=0}^{\infty} c_n x^n \right)'.$$

The expression x^s means, of course, some particular branch of x^s (recall the definition $x^s = e^{s\,\text{Log}\,x}$). It is not difficult to show that, for *any branch*,

$$\frac{d}{dx} x^s = s x^{s-1}$$

except at the branch line for this particular branch. More precisely,

$$\frac{d}{dx}(e^{s\,\text{Log}\,x}) = e^{(s-1)\,\text{Log}\,x}$$

with the *same branch* of Log x on both sides of the equation. In short, x^s can be differentiated by the same rule as x^n (n = positive integer). This implies that the whole *Frobenius series*

$$y(x) = \sum_{n=0}^{\infty} c_n x^{s+n}$$

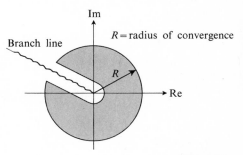

Figure 3.1

can be differentiated term by term. At worst, the results will be valid in a region like the one shown in Fig. 3.1. The same statement is true for $y''(x)$ and $y'(x)$.

The series for $y'(x)$ and $y''(x)$ are now substituted into the DE and the coefficients of equal powers of x are equated to zero by similar considerations as for power series. The resulting relationship often permits the evaluation of one or two solutions of the DE. Applications of this method and the new problems raised by it are illustrated by the following examples.

Example 1. *Pole at the origin.* The DE reads

$$x^2 y'' + 2xy' + (x^2 - 2)y = 0.$$

A solution is sought in the form

$$y(x) = \sum_{n=0}^{\infty} c_n x^{s+n}.$$

Then

$$y'(x) = \sum_{n=0}^{\infty} c_n(s + n)x^{s+n-1},$$

$$y''(x) = \sum_{n=0}^{\infty} c_n(s + n)(s + n - 1)x^{s+n-2}.$$

Substitute into the DE, and obtain

$$\sum_{n=0}^{\infty} [c_n(s + n)(s + n - 1) + 2c_n(s + n) - 2c_n]x^{s+n} + \sum_{n=0}^{\infty} c_n x^{s+n+2} = 0.$$

To compare the coefficients with various powers of x it is convenient to standardize the notation so that the powers of x have the form x^{s+n} in the second sum, as well as in the first one. For this purpose, set $n + 2 = n'$ in the second sum and obtain

$$\sum_{n=0}^{\infty} c_n x^{s+n+2} = \sum_{n'=2}^{\infty} c_{n'-2} x^{s+n'}.$$

Since n' is a "dummy index," it may be "unprimed" and this sum may just as well be written as

$$\sum_{n=2}^{\infty} c_{n-2} x^{s+n}.$$

The DE then assumes the form

$$\sum_{n=0}^{\infty} c_n[(s + n)(s + n - 1) - 2]x^{s+n} + \sum_{n=2}^{\infty} c_{n-2} x^{s+n} = 0.$$

Write separately the powers of x which appear in the first but not in the second sum, namely, the terms with $n = 0$ and $n = 1$:

$$c_0[s(s + 1) - 2]x^s + c_1[(s + 1)(s + 2) - 2]x^{s+1}$$

$$+ \sum_{n=2}^{\infty} \{c_n[(s + n)(s + n + 1) - 2] + c_{n-2}\} x^{s+n} = 0.$$

It is necessary, first of all, that

$$c_0[s(s + 1) - 2] = 0.$$

Since $c_0 \neq 0$ (x^s is assumed to be the lowest power of x appearing in the series), it follows that

$$s(s + 1) - 2 = 0.$$

Such an equation, arising from the lowest power of x on the left-hand side of the DE, is called the *indicial equation;* it determines possible values of s. In this particular case these values are $s_1 = 1$, $s_2 = -2$.

The second condition to be satisfied is

$$c_1[(s + 1)(s + 2) - 2] = 0.$$

Whether $s = 1$ or $s = -2$, it follows from this equation that c_1 must be zero.

The next condition, valid for all values of n greater than or equal to 2, reads

$$c_n[(s + n)(s + n + 1) - 2] + c_{n-2} = 0$$

or

$$c_n = \frac{1}{2 - (s + n)(s + n + 1)} c_{n-2} \qquad (n \geq 2).$$

This recursion formula determines all other coefficients (note that the denominator cannot vanish if $n \geq 2$).

For $s = 1$ we have

$$c_2 = \frac{1}{2 - 3 \cdot 4} c_0 = -\frac{1}{10} c_0,$$

$$c_4 = \frac{1}{2 - 5 \cdot 6} c_2 = \frac{1}{280} c_0, \quad \text{etc.,}$$

and, evidently, $c_3 = c_5 = \cdots = 0$. This yields the series

$$y_1(x) = c_0(x - x^3/10 + x^5/280 - \cdots)$$

This series is absolutely convergent (by ratio test) for all values of x in the complex x-plane and defines, therefore, a function which is analytic for all (finite) values of x. This function has a simple zero at the origin.

Now take $s = -2$. Then

$$c_2' = \frac{1}{2 - 0} c_0' = \frac{1}{2} c_0',$$

$$c_4' = \frac{1}{2 - 2 \cdot 3} c_2' = -\frac{1}{8} c_0', \quad \text{etc.}$$

Again, $c_3' = c_5' = \cdots = 0$. The series is

$$y_2(x) = c_0'(1/x^2 + \tfrac{1}{2} - x^2/8 + \cdots).$$

This series is absolutely convergent (by ratio test) for $|x| > 0$. It is a Laurent series and defines a function that is analytic for all x except $x = 0$ where $y_2(x)$

has a pole of second order. In this case the method of Frobenius has led us directly to the general solution of the DE.

Remark. If we set $c_0 = \frac{1}{3}$, then the function $y_1(x)$ actually becomes

$$j_1(x) = \sin x/x^2 - \cos x/x,$$

and is known as the spherical Bessel function of order one. Similarly, if $c_0' = -1$, then $y_2(x)$ becomes

$$n_1(x) = -\cos x/x^2 - \sin x/x$$

and is known as the spherical Neumann function of order one. Both of them, along with other related functions, are of great importance in physics.

Example 2. *Branch point at the origin.* The DE reads

$$x^2 y'' + xy' + (x^2 - \tfrac{1}{4})y = 0.$$

Write, as before,

$$y = \sum_{n=0}^{\infty} c_n x^{s+n},$$

$$y' = \sum_{n=0}^{\infty} c_n(s + n)x^{s+n-1},$$

$$y'' = \sum_{n=0}^{\infty} c_n(s + n)(s + n - 1)x^{s+n-2},$$

and obtain

$$\sum_{n=0}^{\infty} c_n[(s + n)(s + n - 1) + (s + n) - \tfrac{1}{4}]x^{s+n} + \sum_{n=0}^{\infty} c_n x^{s+n+2} = 0.$$

The indicial equation (coefficient with x^s) is $s(s - 1) + s - \frac{1}{4} = 0$, yielding the roots $s_1 = \frac{1}{2}$, $s_2 = -\frac{1}{2}$.

Consider $s = \frac{1}{2}$; then $c_1[\frac{3}{2} \cdot \frac{1}{2} + \frac{3}{2} - \frac{1}{4}] = 0$, so that $c_1 = 0$.

Use $n + 2 = n'$ in the sum $\sum_{n=0}^{\infty} c_n x^{s+n+2}$, combine this with the first sum, and deduce the recursion relation

$$c_n[(n + \tfrac{1}{2})(n - \tfrac{1}{2}) + (n + \tfrac{1}{2}) - \tfrac{1}{4}] + c_{n-2} = 0,$$

or

$$c_n = -\frac{1}{n(n + 1)} c_{n-2} \qquad (n \geq 2).$$

It follows that all odd coefficients vanish and the series reads

$$y_1(x) = c_0 x^{1/2}\left[1 - \frac{x^2}{2 \cdot 3} + \frac{x^4}{2 \cdot 3 \cdot 4 \cdot 5} - \cdots\right].$$

This series converges for all x (by ratio test) and yields a solution that is analytic in the whole plane except for the branch cut of $x^{1/2}$.

Now consider the second case, $s = -\frac{1}{2}$. The equation for c_1' now reads

$$c_1'[\tfrac{1}{2}(-\tfrac{1}{2}) + \tfrac{1}{2} - \tfrac{1}{4}] = 0$$

and is satisfied by all values of c_1'. In other words, c_1' remains arbitrary. The recursion formula is

$$c_n' = -\frac{1}{n(n-1)} c_{n-2}' \qquad (n \geq 2).$$

Since c_1' need not be zero, it is no longer true that all odd coefficients vanish. The series will, in general, contain both even and odd powers of x and can be written as

$$y_2(x) = c_0'x^{-1/2}[1 - x^2/2 + x^4/(2 \cdot 3 \cdot 4) - \cdots]$$
$$+ c_1'x^{-1/2}[x - x^3/(2 \cdot 3) + x^5/(2 \cdot 3 \cdot 4 \cdot 5) - \cdots].$$

This series also converges for all x. The branch line for $x^{-1/2}$ can be chosen to be the same as in $y_1(x)$ so that both solutions are analytic in the same region.

It now appears that $y_2(x)$ alone represents the general solution since it has two arbitrary constants multiplying two linearly independent parts. (Note that one series is even and the other is odd, so they must be linearly independent.) Therefore, the solution $y_1(x)$ must be a special case of $y_2(x)$, and indeed it is: Set $c_0' = 0$, $c_1' = c_0$ in $y_2(x)$ and obtain $y_1(x)$.

Remark. It is not difficult to see that this phenomenon (one root of the indicial equation determining the general solution) can happen only if the roots of the indicial equation differ by an integer. It is then the smaller root which yields the general solution.

The solution $y_2(x)$ obtained above can be written in a more compact form as

$$y_2(x) = c_0'x^{-1/2} \cos x + c_1'x^{-1/2} \sin x.$$

The functions

$$J_{-1/2}(x) = \sqrt{2/\pi}\, x^{-1/2} \cos x$$

and

$$J_{1/2}(x) = \sqrt{2/\pi}\, x^{-1/2} \sin x$$

are known as the Bessel functions (of the first kind) of order $-\frac{1}{2}$ and $\frac{1}{2}$, respectively. The solution can be written as

$$y_2(x) = AJ_{1/2}(x) + BJ_{-1/2}(x).$$

Remark. The DE $x^2y'' + xy' + (x^2 - \nu^2)y = 0$ (ν = nonnegative real number) is known as the *Bessel differential equation of order ν.* Its solutions, known as *cylindrical functions* (or Bessel functions of various kinds), occur in many physical problems.

Example 3. *Convergence questions.* Consider the DE

$$(1 - x^2)y'' - 2xy' + \lambda y = 0 \qquad (\lambda = \text{real constant}).$$

The Frobenius series
$$y = \sum_{n=0}^{\infty} c_n x^{s+n}$$

leads to

$$\sum_{n=0}^{\infty} c_n(s + n)(s + n - 1)x^{s+n-2}$$

$$- \sum_{n=0}^{\infty} c_n[(s + n)(s + n - 1) - 2(s + n) + \lambda]x^{s+n} = 0.$$

The indicial equation stems from the lowest power x^{s-2} and reads $s(s - 1) = 0$ yielding the roots $s_1 = 0$, $s_2 = 1$.

The equation for c_1 (power x^{s-1}) reads $c_1(s + 1)s = 0$ and yields $c_1 = 0$ if $s = 1$, and arbitrary c_1 if $s = 0$: the case discussed in Example 2. The recursion formula is

$$c_n = \frac{(n - 2)(n - 1) - \lambda}{n(n - 1)} c_{n-2} \qquad (n \geq 2).$$

The root $s = 0$ gives rise, therefore, to the general solution in the form

$$y(x) = c_0 \sum_{n=\text{even}}^{\infty} c_n' x^n + c_1 \sum_{n=\text{odd}}^{\infty} c_n' x^n.$$

The root $s = 1$ yields, evidently, the odd part of this solution.

Now consider the convergence of the series. By ratio test,

$$R_n = \left| \frac{c_n' x^n}{c_{n-2}' x^{n-2}} \right| = \left| \frac{(n - 2)(n - 1) - \lambda}{n(n - 1)} \right| \cdot |x|^2.$$

Both series converge for $|x| < 1$, whatever the value of λ may be. For $|x| = 1$, the ratio test is inconclusive. However, the integral test yields

$$\int^M \frac{(t - 2)(t - 1) - \lambda}{t(t - 1)} dt = \int^M \frac{(t - 2)}{t} dt - \int^M \frac{\lambda}{t(t - 1)} dt$$

and since

$$\int^M \frac{t - 2}{t} dt \to \infty \quad \text{as } M \to \infty,$$

both series, in general, diverge* for $|x| = 1$. There is, however, an exception: If λ happens to be of the form $\lambda = l(l + 1)$, where l is a nonnegative integer, then

---

* This is not unexpected: Our equation, when written in the form $y'' + Py' + Qy = 0$, reveals that the coefficients $P(x)$ and $Q(x)$ *are not analytic* at $x = \pm 1$. It is not unreasonable to suspect that the solutions *may* also fail to be analytic at these points. In this case our series (both are Taylor series) will indeed have a radius of convergence equal to unity.

one of the series will terminate giving rise to a polynomial. The other series will be divergent. A similar statement holds for $|x| > 1$.

In conclusion, the Frobenius method yields a *general solution* of the DE only for the region $|x| < 1$. However, if $\lambda = l(l + 1)$, then there is a *particular solution* of Frobenius type (namely, a polynomial) which is valid for all values of x.

The DE considered above is known as the *Legendre DE* and is one of the most important ones in physics. In particular, physical conditions usually require that the solution be analytic at $|x| = 1$. Such solutions are possible if $\lambda = l(l + 1)$ and are obtained from the general solution

$$y(x) = c_0 \sum_{n=\text{even}}^{\infty} c_n' x^n + c_1 \sum_{n=\text{odd}}^{\infty} c_n' x^n$$

by setting $c_1 = 0$ (if l is even), or $c_0 = 0$ (if l is odd). It is, furthermore, customary to standardize the solutions by the following choice of the coefficients with the lowest powers of x:

$$c_0 c_0' = (-1)^{l/2} \frac{l!}{2^l \left[\left(\frac{l}{2} \right)! \right]^2} \qquad (l = \text{even}),$$

$$c_1 c_1' = (-1)^{(l-1)/2} \frac{l!}{2^{l-1} \left[\left(\frac{l-1}{2} \right)! \right]^2} \qquad (l = \text{odd}).$$

These standardized solutions are denoted by $P_l(x)$ and are called *Legendre polynomials* (or Legendre functions of the first kind). The lowest ones are

$$P_0(x) = 1,$$
$$P_1(x) = x,$$
$$P_2(x) = \tfrac{1}{2}(3x^2 - 1),$$
$$P_3(x) = \tfrac{1}{2}(5x^3 - 3x),$$
$$P_4(x) = \tfrac{1}{8}(35x^4 - 30x^2 + 3), \quad \text{etc.}$$

The second solution of the Legendre equation, linearly independent of $P_l(x)$ and appropriately standardized, is denoted by $Q_l(x)$ and is called the *Legendre function of the second kind*. Functions $Q_l(x)$ $(l = 0, 1, 2, \ldots)$ are multivalued and have branch points at $x = \pm 1$.

For $|x| < 1$, we customarily select the following definition for the lowest function:

$$Q_0(x) = -1 + x^2 + x^4/3 + x^6/5 + x^8/7 + \cdots \qquad (|x| < 1),$$

or, in a compact form,

$$Q_0(x) = \operatorname{artanh} x = \frac{1}{2} \log \frac{1 + x}{1 - x} \qquad (|x| < 1).$$

The other Legendre functions of the second kind are then expressed in terms of $Q_0(x)$ as follows:

$$Q_1(x) = P_1(x)Q_0(x) - 1,$$
$$Q_2(x) = P_2(x)Q_0(x) - \tfrac{3}{2}x,$$
$$Q_3(x) = P_3(x)Q_0(x) - \tfrac{5}{2}x^2 + \tfrac{2}{3}, \quad \text{etc.}$$

The functions $Q_l(x)$ are also used in physical applications but to a far lesser extent than Legendre polynomials.

Example 4. *Logarithmic singularity.* The DE reads $xy'' + y' = 0$. The Frobenius series $y(x) = \sum_{n=0}^{\infty} c_n x^{s+n}$ yields

$$\sum_{n=0}^{\infty} [c_n(s+n)(s+n-1) + c_n(s+n)]x^{s+n-1} = 0$$

and

$$c_n(s+n)^2 = 0 \quad \text{(all } n\text{)}.$$

The indicial equation is $c_0 s^2 = 0$ and has the *double root* $s = 0$.

It is seen that there is no recursion formula (in the proper sense of the word). Rather, c_0 may be chosen arbitrarily, but all other coefficients vanish. This results in *only one* solution of Frobenius type, namely,

$$y_1(x) = c_0 = \text{const.}$$

It is reasonable to conclude that the second solution cannot be represented by a series of Frobenius type. Possible causes of such a failure may be that the second solution $y_2(x)$ possesses at the origin (a) an essential singularity, or (b) a branch point of a special type, not covered by Frobenius series.

Whatever the nature of the difficulty at the origin, the second solution must be analytic *somewhere* and a Taylor expansion about another point may be attempted. An alternative procedure is to utilize the Lagrange method (of variation of constants) mentioned in Section 3.2. In this particular case we have $P(x) = 1/x$, so that (set $y_1(x) = c_0$ and choose $x_0 = x_1 = 1$, $A = c_0$)

$$y_2(x) = C(x)c_0 = Ac_0 \int_{x_1}^{x} \exp\left\{-\int_{x_0}^{\xi} \frac{d\eta}{\eta}\right\} \frac{d\xi}{c_0^2}$$

$$= \frac{A}{c_0} \int_{x_1}^{x} \frac{d\xi}{\xi} = \frac{A}{c_0} \text{Log } x = \text{Log } x.$$

This solution is, of course, a multivalued function, but it is sufficient to select some (arbitrary) branch, say the principal branch $y_2 = \log x$, to serve as our second solution: All other branches of Log x can be represented as linear combinations of the two basic solutions $y_1(x) = 1$ (we have chosen $c_0 = 1$) and $y_2(x) = \log x$.

Our conclusion is that branch points of *logarithmic type* may be encountered when solving some simple linear DE of second order. This may suggest that we try, in general, series of the type

$$\log x \sum_{n=0}^{\infty} c_n x^{s+n} \qquad (c_0 \neq 0),$$

or perhaps, the combination

$$y(x) = \log x \sum_{n=0}^{\infty} c_n x^{s+n} + \sum_{m=0}^{\infty} a_m x^{r+m} \qquad (c_0 \neq 0, a_0 \neq 0).$$

This type of expression may be called a *generalized Frobenius series* and may be used to extend the Frobenius method. It is very common in physical applications.

Example 5. *Double root of the indicial equation.* Consider the DE

$$xy'' + y' + xy = 0$$

which is known as the Bessel DE of order zero. The Frobenius series

$$y(x) = \sum_{n=0}^{\infty} c_n x^{s+n} \qquad (c_0 \neq 0)$$

results in the indicial equation, $c_0 s^2 = 0$, the equation for c_1, $c_1(s + 1)^2 = 0$, and the recursion formula,

$$c_n = -\frac{1}{(s + n)^2} c_{n-2} \qquad (n \geq 0).$$

Analysis shows that there is only one solution of the Frobenius type, i.e., the series of even powers of x:

$$y_1(x) = c_0 \sum_{n=0,2,4,\ldots}^{\infty} (-1)^{n/2} \frac{1}{2^n \left(\dfrac{n}{2}!\right)^2} x^n \qquad \text{(with } 0! = 1\text{)}.$$

Exercise. Spell out the detailed arguments leading to this conclusion.

The series converges for all values of x. If the standard choice $c_0 = 1$ is made, then the solution is known as the Bessel function of order zero:

$$J_0(x) = \sum_{n=\text{even}}^{\infty} (-1)^{n/2} \frac{x^n}{2^n \left(\dfrac{n}{2}!\right)^2} .$$

An attempt will now be made to find a second solution in the generalized Frobenius form:

$$y(x) = \log x \sum_{n=0}^{\infty} c_n x^{s+n} + \sum_{m=0}^{\infty} a_m x^{r+m} \qquad (c_0 \neq 0, a_0 \neq 0).$$

Before $y(x)$ is differentiated and substituted into the differential equation, observe that the series

$$\sum_{n=0}^{\infty} c_n x^{s+n}$$

cannot possibly be anything but $J_0(x)$ (or a multiple of it). Indeed, write

$$y(x) = \log x \cdot u(x) + v(x),$$

where $u(x)$ and $v(x)$ are Frobenius series. Then

$$y' = u' \log x + (1/x)u + v',$$

$$y'' = u'' \log x + (2/x)u' - (1/x^2)u + v''.$$

Substitute into the DE:

$$\log x(xu'' + u' + xu) + (2u' + xv'' + v' + xv) = 0.$$

All terms in parentheses are Frobenius series and since $\log x$ is not expressible as a Frobenius series, it is not difficult to conclude that

$$xu'' + u' + xu = 0,$$

which proves the statement since $J_0(x)$ (or a multiple of it) is the only Frobenius-type solution of the DE under consideration.

This simplifies the problem: It is now necessary to find

$$v(x) = \sum_{m=0}^{\infty} a_m x^{r+m} \qquad (a_0 \neq 0)$$

satisfying $xv'' + v' + xv = -2J_0'$. Write

$$J_0(x) = \sum_{n=0}^{\infty} b_n x^n,$$

where the coefficients b_n are known. Then

$$J_0'(x) = \sum_{n=0}^{\infty} b_n n x^{n-1}.$$

Substitute this expression, along with the Frobenius series for v, v', and v'', into the above equation. Obtain, in the usual fashion,

$$a_0 r^2 x^{r-1} + a_1(r+1)^2 x^r + \sum_{m=2}^{\infty} [a_m(r+m)^2 + a_{m-2}]x^{r+m-1} = \sum_{n=0}^{\infty} (-2nb_n)x^{n-1}.$$

Recall that

$$b_n = \begin{cases} (-1)^{n/2} \dfrac{1}{2^n \left(\dfrac{n}{2}!\right)^2} & (n = \text{even}), \\ \\ 0 & (n = \text{odd}). \end{cases}$$

The lowest power of x on the right is, therefore, the first power. Consequently, the choice $r = 2$ may be tried. Then

$$a_0 = -(2 \cdot 2 \cdot b_2)/2^2 = -b_2 = \tfrac{1}{4}.$$

Also, $a_1 = 0$, and

$$a_m(m + 2)^2 + a_{m-2} = -2(m + 2)b_{m+2} \quad (m \geq 2).$$

The last relation yields the recursion formula

$$a_m = -\frac{1}{(m + 2)^2} a_{m-2} - \frac{2}{m + 2} b_{m+2} \quad (m \geq 2),$$

from which all other coefficients a_m may be calculated (in particular, all odd coefficients vanish). This yields

$$v(x) = \sum_{m=0}^{\infty} a_m x^{m+2} = \frac{1}{4} x^2 - \frac{3}{2^7} x^4 + \frac{11}{2^9 \cdot 3^3} x^6 - \cdots$$

and establishes the second solution as

$$y_2(x) = \log x \cdot J_0(x) + v(x).$$

This function is denoted by many authors by $Y_0(x)$ and is called the Bessel function of the second kind of order zero.

Remark. In modern literature it is customary to select a different function to represent the second solution, namely, the following linear combination of $J_0(x)$ and $Y_0(x)$:

$$N_0(x) = (\pi/2)Y_0(x) + (\gamma - \log 2)J_0(x),$$

where γ is the so-called *Euler-Mascheroni constant:*

$$\gamma = \lim_{N\to\infty} \left(\sum_{p=1}^{N} \frac{1}{p} - \log N \right) = \lim_{N\to\infty} \left(1 + \frac{1}{2} + \frac{1}{3} + \cdots + \frac{1}{N} - \log N \right) = 0.5772 \ldots$$

The function $N_0(x)$ is usually called the Neumann function of order zero. However, there are authors who denote this function by $Y_0(x)$ and call it the Bessel function of the second kind of order zero. In general, the nomenclature and standardization of special functions like these are far from being settled.

Example 6. *Complex roots of the indicial equation.* Consider the *Euler* DE:

$$x^2 y'' + xy' + y = 0.$$

The Frobenius series
$$y(x) = \sum_{n=0}^{\infty} c_n x^{s+n}$$

yields the relation $c_n[(s + n)^2 + 1] = 0$. The indicial equation (set $n = 0$) $c_0(s^2 + 1) = 0$ has the *complex* roots $s = \pm i$. For either of these two values, all coefficients c_n (except c_0) must vanish. If c_0 is chosen to be unity, two solutions are obtained:
$$y_1(x) = x^i, \qquad y_2(x) = x^{-i}.$$

Both functions are multivalued. Select the principal branches:
$$y_1(x) = e^{i \log x}, \qquad y_2(x) = e^{-i \log x}.$$

The Wronskian of these two solutions reads
$$W(y_1, y_2) = e^{i \log x} e^{-i \log x}(-i/x) - e^{-i \log x} e^{i \log x}(i/x)$$
$$= -i/x - i/x = -2i/x.$$

Since the Wronskian never vanishes (for finite x) the solutions are linearly independent and the general solution is obtained:
$$y(x) = A e^{i \log x} + B e^{-i \log x},$$

where A and B are complex constants.

If a real solution is desired, write
$$e^{i \log x} = e^{i(\log |x| + i \arg x)}.$$

For real and positive x, $\arg x = 0$, and $\log |x| = \log x$ so that
$$e^{i \log x} = \cos(\log x) + i \sin(\log x).$$

The real functions $\cos(\log x)$ and $\sin(\log x)$ are linearly independent, and each must satisfy the DE (see the Exercise on p. 52). The general real solution may be taken as
$$y(x) = c_1 \cos(\log x) + c_2 \sin(\log x) \qquad (x > 0).$$

This solution is meaningless for $x < 0$. However, a different branch of x^i may be selected to produce the general solution in this case as well.

Observe that both solutions have a branch point of logarithmic type although they are formally represented by a (terminating) Frobenius series.

Example 7. *Roots differing by an integer.* Consider the Bessel differential equation of order one
$$x^2 y'' + x y' + (x^2 - 1)y = 0.$$

The Frobenius series
$$y(x) = \sum_{n=1}^{\infty} c_n x^{s+n}$$

yields the indicial equation, $c_0(s^2 - 1) = 0$, the equation for c_1, $c_1 s(s + 2) = 0$, and the recursion formula,

$$c_n = - \frac{1}{(s + n + 1)(s + n - 1)} c_{n-2} \qquad (n \geq 2).$$

The roots are $s = \pm 1$. In either case, $c_1 = 0$. However, an attempt to construct the Frobenius series with $s = -1$ fails because c_2 is not defined by the recursion formula. Colloquially speaking, c_2 "blows up" (or "becomes infinite").

The second root, $s = +1$, transforms the recursion formula into

$$c_n = - \frac{1}{n(n + 2)} c_{n-2} \qquad (n \geq 2),$$

which readily determines all coefficients. The choice $c_0 = \frac{1}{2}$ yields the Bessel function of order one:

$$J_1(x) = \sum_{n=\text{even}}^{\infty} (-1)^{n/2} \frac{1}{2^n \left(\frac{n}{2}!\right)^2 (n + 2)} x^{n+1} = \frac{1}{2} x - \frac{1}{2^4} x^3 + \frac{1}{3 \cdot 2^7} x^5 - \cdots$$

The second solution can be attempted in the form (as in Example 5)

$$y_2(x) = \log x \cdot J_1(x) + v(x)$$

and leads to the DE for $v(x)$:

$$x^2 v'' + xv + (x^2 - 1)v = -2x J_1'.$$

Since $J_1(x)$ has a simple zero at the origin, it is convenient to write

$$J_1(x) = \sum_{n=0}^{\infty} b_n x^{n+1}.$$

Then

$$- 2x J_1'(x) = \sum_{n=0}^{\infty} [-2b_n(n + 1)] x^{n+1}.$$

Assuming $v(x)$ to be a Frobenius series,

$$v(x) = \sum_{m=0}^{\infty} a_m x^{r+m} \qquad (a_0 \neq 0),$$

and substituting into the DE, we obtain

$$a_0(r + 1)(r - 1)x^r + a_1 r(r + 2)x^{r+1}$$

$$+ \sum_{m=2}^{\infty} [a_m(r + m + 1)(r + m - 1) + a_{m-2}]x^{r+m}$$

$$= \sum_{n=0}^{\infty} [-2b_n(n + 1)]x^{n+1}.$$

Recall that

$$b_n = \begin{cases} (-1)^{n/2} \dfrac{1}{2^n \left(\dfrac{n}{2}!\right)^2 (n+2)} & (n = \text{even}), \\ 0 & (n = \text{odd}). \end{cases}$$

so that the series on the right-hand side has only odd powers and starts with the first power. A value for r should be chosen so that the series on the left-hand side has the same form. A little reflection indicates the likely choice: $r = -1$, $a_1 = 0$. It would appear, at the first glance, that a_0 is arbitrary. This is not so, however. The equation now becomes

$$\sum_{m=2}^{\infty} [a_m m(m-2) + a_{m-2}]x^{m-1} = \sum_{n=0}^{\infty} [-2b_n(n+1)]x^{n+1}.$$

Equate the coefficients with the first power of x on both sides ($m = 2, n = 0$):

$$a_0 = -2b_0 = -2(\tfrac{1}{2}) = -1.$$

Observe that a_2 is not involved in this equation and *remains arbitrary*. To find other coefficients, set $m = n + 2$ and obtain the general recursion formula

$$a_{n+2}n(n+2) + a_n = -2b_n(n+1).$$

The case $n = 0$ has already been considered. For $n > 0$ this relation can be solved for a_{n+2}:

$$a_{n+2} = -\frac{1}{n(n+2)} a_n - \frac{2(n+1)}{n(n+2)} b_n \qquad (n > 0).$$

It follows that all odd coefficients vanish, since $a_1 = 0$ and all odd b_n vanish. If a_2 is selected, then all other even coefficients can be calculated.

It is not difficult to see that different choices of a_2 amount to adding to $v(x)$ a multiple of $J_1(x)$. This is not surprising since if the function

$$u(x) = \log x \cdot J_1(x) + v(x)$$

is a second solution (linearly independent of J_1), then

$$u(x) + cJ_1(x)$$

is still a solution, linearly independent of $J_1(x)$ and having the same generalized Frobenius form. One customary choice is $a_2 = -\tfrac{1}{4}$, which leads to the function

$$Y_1(x) = \log x \cdot J_1(x) - \frac{1}{x} - \frac{1}{4}x + \frac{5}{2^6}x^3 - \frac{5}{2^7 \cdot 3^2}x^3 + \cdots.$$

(known as the Bessel function of the second kind of order one).

Another choice of the second solution is the Neumann function of order one:

$$N_1(x) = (2/\pi)[Y_1(x) + (\gamma - \log 2)J_1(x)].$$

Example 8. *Three-term recursion formula.* Consider the DE $y'' + (1 - x^2)y = 0$.

If $y(x) = \sum_{n=0}^{\infty} c_n x^{s+n}$, then

$$\sum_{n=0}^{\infty} (s + n)(s + n - 1)c_n x^{s+n-2} + \sum_{n=0}^{\infty} c_n x^{s+n} - \sum_{n=0}^{\infty} c_n x^{s+n+2} = 0.$$

The indicial equation $c_0 s(s - 1) = 0$ has two roots, $s = 0$ and $s = 1$. Consider the root $s = 0$. The equation for c_1 reads $c_1(s + 1)s = 0$ and leaves c_1 arbitrary. For the next two coefficients ($n = 2$ and $n = 3$), the second sum is involved leading to

$$n(n - 1)c_n + c_{n-2} = 0$$

or

$$c_n = -\frac{c_{n-2}}{n(n - 1)} \qquad (n = 2, 3).$$

For $n \geq 4$ the third sum becomes involved, and we have

$$n(n - 1)c_n + c_{n-2} - c_{n-4} = 0$$

or

$$c_n = \frac{c_{n-4} - c_{n-2}}{n(n - 1)} \qquad (n \geq 4).$$

Observe that the general recursion formula involves three terms. It is seen that if c_0 is chosen, then $c_2 = -c_0/(2 \cdot 1) = -\frac{1}{2}c_0$ and c_4 is now calculated from c_0 and c_2. All other even coefficients are obtained in a similar fashion and are independent of the selection of odd coefficients.

It is possible then to set $c_1 = 0$ and to construct an *even* series solution since from $c_1 = 0$ it follows that $c_3 = 0$, and then $c_5 = c_7 = c_9 = \cdots = 0$. The series reads (with $c_0 = 1$)

$$y_1(x) = 1 - \tfrac{1}{2}x^2 + \tfrac{1}{8}x^4 - \tfrac{1}{48}x^6 + \cdots$$

and is easily recognized as

$$e^{-x^2/2} = 1 - \left(\frac{x^2}{2}\right) + \frac{1}{2!}\left(\frac{x^2}{2}\right)^2 - \frac{1}{3!}\left(\frac{x^2}{2}\right)^3 + \cdots = y_1(x).$$

The second solution may be obtained as the odd series, generated by the coefficient c_1. We set $c_0 = 0$ and $c_1 = 1$ (this is somewhat unorthodox since c_0 is, as a rule, assumed not to vanish; however, the ultimate results are not affected by this departure from the usual technique). Then the following series emerges:

$$y_2(x) = x - \tfrac{1}{6}x^3 + \tfrac{7}{120}x^5 - \tfrac{3}{560}x^7 + \cdots$$

Each of the series, $y_1(x)$ and $y_2(x)$, is a solution of the DE, and they are linearly independent (one is odd, the other is even). The general solution

$$y(x) = c_1 y_1(x) + c_2 y_2(x)$$

is, therefore, obtained. As for the root, $s = 1$, it is easy to verify that it will generate, basically, the solution $y_2(x)$.

Remark. This DE occurs in quantum mechanics where it is used to represent the ground state of a harmonic oscillator. Physical principles demand selection of the solution which approaches zero as $x \to \pm\infty$. The solution $y_1(x)$ satisfies this condition, whereas the solution $y_2(x)$ does not. This may not be evident from the series for $y_2(x)$, but by the method of variation of constants it is not difficult to show that

$$y_2(x) = y_1(x) \int_0^x \frac{d\xi}{[y_1(\xi)]^2} = e^{-x^2/2} \int_0^x e^{\xi^2} d\xi.$$

The integral $\int_0^x e^{\xi^2} d\xi$ represents the area between the curve $y = e^{x^2}$ and the x-axis. Bearing this in mind, it is almost trivial to show that, for instance,

$$\int_0^x e^{\xi^2} d\xi \geq \frac{x}{2} e^{x^2} \qquad (x > 0),$$

which implies that $|y_2(x)| \geq \frac{|x|}{2} e^{x^2/2} \to \infty$ as $|x| \to \infty$.

The examples presented above show that the Frobenius method, when successful, leads to the solution of a second-order linear DE provided this solution is either (a) regular at the origin, or (b) possesses a pole or branch point of *power* or *logarithmic* type at the origin. Obviously, it is desirable to determine in advance whether a given DE will have solutions with these properties. Two basic theorems to that effect are given below. They involve the following definitions.

Definition 1. If the functions $P(x)$ and $Q(x)$ in the DE

$$y'' + P(x)y' + Q(x)y = 0$$

are analytic at the origin, then the origin is called *ordinary point* of the DE. Otherwise, the origin is called a *singular point*.

Definition 2. If $P(x)$ and $Q(x)$ are not both analytic, but are of the form

$$P(x) = \frac{\varphi(x)}{x}, \qquad Q(x) = \frac{\psi(x)}{x^2},$$

where $\varphi(x)$ and $\psi(x)$ are analytic at $x = 0$, then the origin is called the *regular singular point*. Otherwise, it is called an *irregular singular point*.

Theorem 1. If the origin is an ordinary point, then any solution of the DE is analytic at $x = 0$.

Theorem 2. *Theorem of Fuchs.* If the origin is a regular singular point, then any solution of the DE is either (a) analytic at the origin, or (b) possesses a pole or branch point of power or "logarithmic" type. (In other words, it is expressible as a generalized Frobenius series.)

Proofs of these theorems can be found in advanced texts on differential equations or complex variables.

Remarks

1. If the origin is an irregular singular point, there is still a possibility of a solution of the Frobenius type. If one such solution is found, the other may be obtained, for instance, by the method of variation of constants.

2. The entire theory outlined above can be applied to any other finite point by a trivial argument.

Finally, here is a brief summary of possible situations encountered in the use of the Frobenius method: If the initial attempt to find a solution is made in terms of a Frobenius series,

$$y(x) = \sum_{n=0}^{\infty} c_n x^{s+n} \qquad (c_0 \neq 0),$$

then the lowest power of x gives rise to the indicial equation which is a quadratic equation in s (with real coefficients for a real DE). The following cases arise, according to the nature of the roots (which may be complex, even for a real DE).

CASE 1. Two distinct roots *not differing by an integer*. There are two linearly independent solutions of power type. Each solution contains one arbitrary parameter (Example 6).

CASE 2. *A double root*. There is one power-type solution and one logarithmic-type solution (Examples 4 and 5).

CASE 3. Two distinct roots *differing by an integer* (two subcases are possible):

a) Two solutions of power type, each corresponding to one root. The lower root yields a two-parameter solution. The higher root yields a one-parameter solution and is a special case of the first solution (Examples 1, 2, 3, and 8).

b) One solution of power type, given by the higher root. The lower root fails to give a solution (infinite coefficients), but a logarithmic-type solution exists (Example 7).

3.6 SOME OTHER METHODS OF SOLUTION

Power series of ascending powers of x are convenient in the vicinity of the origin. For "far-away" points it is much better to use power series of descending powers of x (as in the principal part of a Laurent series). For instance, if a function $f(x)$ is analytic at infinity, then it must be representable by a series

$$f(x) = \sum_{m=0}^{\infty} a_m(1/x^m)$$

valid for $|x| > R$, where R is some nonnegative constant. Such expansions are usually called *expansions about the point at infinity*.

Expansions of this type may be attempted directly in the process of a solution of the linear DE of second order. However, it is advisable to proceed in an indirect way by making the substitution $x = 1/z$. Then

$$\frac{dy}{dx} = \frac{dy}{dz}\frac{dz}{dx} = \frac{dy}{dz}(-z^2),$$

$$\frac{d^2y}{dx^2} = \frac{d^2y}{dz^2}\left(\frac{dz}{dx}\right)^2 + \frac{dy}{dz}\frac{d^2z}{dx^2} = z^4\frac{d^2y}{dz^2} + 2z^3\frac{dy}{dz},$$

and the DE becomes

$$\frac{d^2y}{dz^2} + \left[\frac{2}{z} - \frac{1}{z^2}P\left(\frac{1}{z}\right)\right]\frac{dy}{dz} + \frac{1}{z^4}Q\left(\frac{1}{z}\right)y = 0.$$

The desired expansion in descending powers of x is now a Taylor expansion about $z = 0$. If the coefficients

$$F(z) = \frac{2}{z} - \frac{1}{z^2}P\left(\frac{1}{z}\right), \qquad G(z) = \frac{1}{z^4}Q\left(\frac{1}{z}\right)$$

are analytic at $z = 0$, then such an expansion exists and can be found by standard methods.

Example 1. The DE reads $x^4y'' + 2x^3y' - y = 0$. On division by x^4, we obtain

$$y'' + \frac{2}{x}y' - \frac{1}{x^4}y = 0.$$

The expansion $y(x) = \sum_{m=0}^{\infty} a_m x^{-m}$ is desired. After the transformation $x = 1/z$, we obtain

$$F(z) = \frac{2}{z} - \frac{1}{z^2}2z = 0, \qquad G(z) = -\frac{1}{z^4}z^4 = -1.$$

Both $F(z)$ and $G(z)$ are analytic at $z = 0$, and the new DE reads

$$\frac{d^2y}{dz^2} - y = 0.$$

The desired series are

$$y_1(z) = e^z = \sum_{n=0}^{\infty}\frac{z^n}{n!}, \qquad y_2(z) = e^{-z} = \sum_{n=0}^{\infty}(-1)^n\frac{z^n}{n!},$$

or

$$y_1(x) = \sum_{n=0}^{\infty}\frac{x^{-n}}{n!} = 1 + \frac{1}{x} + \frac{1}{2!}\frac{1}{x^2} + \frac{1}{3!}\frac{1}{x^3} + \cdots,$$

$$y_2(x) = \sum_{n=0}^{\infty}(-1)^n\frac{x^{-n}}{n!} = 1 - \frac{1}{x} + \frac{1}{2!}\frac{1}{x^2} - \frac{1}{3!}\frac{1}{x^3} + \cdots$$

Both series converge for $|x| > 0$ and represent the expansions about the point at infinity of the functions $y_1(x) = e^{1/x}$, $y_2(x) = e^{-1/x}$.

Example 2. Consider the zero-order Legendre differential equation

$$(1 - x^2)y'' - 2xy' = 0.$$

It is desired to obtain the expansion of $Q_0(x)$ about the point at infinity. Divide by $(1 - x^2)$ to obtain

$$y'' - \frac{2x}{1 - x^2} y = 0.$$

Here $P(x) = 2x/(x^2 - 1)$, $Q(x) = 0$, and

$$F(z) = \frac{2}{z} - \frac{1}{z^2} P\left(\frac{1}{z}\right) = \frac{2z}{z^2 - 1}, \qquad G(z) = 0.$$

The new DE reads

$$\frac{d^2 y}{dz^2} + \frac{2z}{z^2 - 1} y = 0$$

and has exactly the same form as the original one. It is known to possess the solutions

$$y_1(z) = 1, \qquad y_2(z) = z + \frac{z^3}{3} + \frac{z^5}{5} + \frac{z^7}{7} + \cdots \qquad (|z| < 1).$$

Therefore the original zero-order Legendre equation possesses the solutions

$$y_1(x) = 1, \qquad y_2(x) = \frac{1}{x} + \frac{1}{3x^3} + \frac{1}{5x^5} + \frac{1}{7x^7} + \cdots \qquad (|x| > 1).$$

The first solution is $P_0(x)$. The second solution *may be called* $Q_0(x)$; it can be written in compact form as

$$Q_0(x) = \text{arcoth } x = \tfrac{1}{2} \log \left[(x + 1)/(x - 1) \right] \qquad (|x| > 1).$$

Remark. The function $Q_0(x)$ is multivalued. The choice of branches

$$Q_0(x) = \begin{cases} \tfrac{1}{2} \log \dfrac{1 + x}{1 - x}, & |x| < 1, \\[2ex] \tfrac{1}{2} \log \dfrac{x + 1}{x - 1}, & |x| > 1 \end{cases}$$

is, of course, arbitrary, but it is the standard choice. If a problem warrants it, another selection of branches can be made.

The above discussion deals with expansions in integral powers of x. It may evidently be extended to generalized Frobenius expansions about the point at infinity.

Linear differential equations of second order are often transformed, for various reasons, by a change of variable. The *dependent variable y* is usually changed by

$$y(x) = y_1(x)v(x),$$

where $y_1(x)$ is known or determined by certain conditions; the result is a DE for $v(x)$. An example of this technique has been found in the method of variation of constants: here $y_1(x)$ is one of the solutions of the DE. Other applications include (a) the elimination of the first-derivative term, and (b) the factorization of the behavior at infinity.

If the above substitution is made, then the DE becomes

$$y_1v'' + (2y_1' + Py_1)v' + (y_1'' + Py_1' + Qy_1)v = 0.$$

Instead of eliminating the third term by choosing y_1 to be a particular integral, we may require that

$$2y_1' + Py_1 = 0$$

and eliminate the first-derivative term. This means that

$$y_1(x) = \exp\left\{-\tfrac{1}{2}\int^x P(\xi)\,d\xi\right\}$$

and the DE for v reads

$$v'' - (Q - \tfrac{1}{2}P' - \tfrac{1}{4}P^2)v = 0.$$

This technique finds its applications in estimating the behavior of the solutions "at infinity" and various approximation methods.

Example 3. Consider the DE $x^2y'' + 2xy' + (x^2 - 2)y = 0$ (spherical Bessel equation of order two).

Divide by x^2: $y'' + (2/x)y' + (1 - 2/x^2)y = 0$. Let $y = y_1v$, where

$$y_1 = \exp\left\{-\frac{1}{2}\int_1^x \frac{2}{\xi}\,d\xi\right\} = \exp\{-\log x\} = \frac{1}{x}.$$

Then v satisfies

$$v'' + (1 - 2/x^2)v = 0.$$

Suppose that x is *real* and $|x|$ is large. Then x^2 is large and v is *expected* to be similar to the solution of the approximate equation $u'' + u = 0$. In other words, v is *expected* to behave like sin x or cos x for large values of $|x|$, implying that the solutions of the original DE will behave like sin x/x and cos x/x as $|x| \to \infty$. The conditions under which such statements are true, and the degree of approximation must, of course, be analyzed and proved (consult books and articles on *asymptotic behavior* of solutions). In this case it may suffice to point out that the *exact* solutions for v may be taken as

$$v_1(x) = \cos x - \sin x/x, \qquad v_2(x) = \sin x + \cos x/x,$$

and for large $|x|$ (real x), they indeed behave like $\cos x$ and $\sin x$.

Example 4. The differential equation

$$y'' + (2n + 1 - x^2)y = 0 \qquad (n = 0, 1, 2, \ldots)$$

is used in quantum mechanics to describe the motion of a harmonic oscillator.*

It is known (Example 8, Section 3.5) that one of the solutions for the case $n = 0$, the ground state of the harmonic oscillator, reads $y(x) = e^{-x^2/2}$. It has been found advantageous to "factor out" $e^{-x^2/2}$ for the cases $n \neq 0$ as well. Set

$$y(x) = e^{-x^2/2}v(x).$$

Then the DE for $v(x)$ reads $v'' - 2xv' + 2nv = 0$. This is the *Hermite* DE.

The acceptable solutions in quantum mechanics are Hermite polynomials (because y must vanish at infinity). This leads to the solution for $y(x)$ in the form

$$y(x) = H_n(x)e^{-x^2/2},$$

where $H_n(x)$ is the nth Hermite polynomial.

Changes of the *independent variable* are also useful. If, in the DE

$$y'' + P(x)y' + Q(x)y = 0,$$

the change of variable $t = f(x)$ is made, then

$$y' = \frac{dy}{dx} = \frac{dy}{dt}\frac{dt}{dx} = \frac{dy}{dt}f'(x),$$

$$y'' = \frac{d^2y}{dx^2} = \frac{d^2y}{dt^2}[f'(x)]^2 + \frac{dy}{dt}f''(x),$$

and the equation becomes

$$\frac{d^2y}{dt^2}[f'(x)]^2 + \frac{dy}{dt}[f''(x) + P(x)f'(x)] + Q(x)y = 0.$$

If x is expressed in terms of t [by solving $t = f(x)$], then the DE will have t as the new independent variable. A judicious choice of the function $f(x)$ may simplify the new equation.

In particular, if we require that $f''(x) + P(x)f'(x) = 0$, which implies that $f'(x) = \exp\{-\int^x P(\xi)\,d\xi\}$, then the new DE will have no first-derivative term.

Example 5. The Euler differential equation $x^2y'' + xy' + y = 0$ can be simplified by the transformation $x = e^t, t = \log x$ (for $x > 0$).

---

* See Section 11.3.

The transformed equation reduces to

$$\frac{d^2y}{dt^2} + y = 0$$

and has solutions $y_1(t) = \cos t$ and $y_2(t) = \sin t$. This leads to the general solution of the Euler DE

$$y(x) = c_1 \cos (\log x) + c_2 \sin (\log x)$$

(as on p. 142).

BIBLIOGRAPHY

CODDINGTON, E. A., *An Introduction to Ordinary Differential Equations*, Englewood Cliffs, N.J.: Prentice-Hall, Inc., 1961.

CODDINGTON, E. A., and N. LEVINSON, *Theory of Ordinary Differential Equations*, New York: McGraw-Hill Book Co., 1955.

INCE, E. L., *Ordinary Differential Equations*, New York: Dover Publications Inc., 1926.

RAINVILLE, E. D., *Intermediate Course in Differential Equations*, New York: John Wiley & Sons, 1943.

PROBLEMS

1. Observe that the DE $x^2y'' + xy' - y = 0$ has a solution $y_1(x) = x$. Use the method of variation of constants to find a second solution and then proceed to solve $x^2y'' + xy' - y = 1/(1 - x)$.

2. From our experience with the preceding problem, it should not be difficult to find a solution of $(1 - x)y'' + xy' - y = 0$ by inspection. Using this, solve

$$(1 - x)y'' + xy' - y = (1 - x)^2.$$

3. Using the method of variation of constants, show that the general solution of $\ddot{x} + \omega^2 x = f(t)$ can be expressed as

$$x(t) = A \cos \omega t + B \sin \omega t + \frac{1}{\omega} \int_0^t \sin \omega(t - \tau) f(\tau) \, d\tau.$$

4. Consider the Bessel equation of order zero: $xy'' + y' + xy = 0$. Show that the Wronskian of *any* two solutions is $W(x) = C/x$ where C is a constant, dependent on the particular choice of the solutions. What is the Wronskian of two solutions of the Legendre equation? of the Bessel equation of order ν?

5. Show that the Wronskian of $J_0(x)$ and $Y_0(x)$ is $1/x$. [*Hint:* Since $W = C/x$ for *all* values of x, one may choose an x so small that only the leading terms need to be considered.] What is the Wronskian of $J_0(x)$ and $N_0(x)$? of $P_0(x)$ and $Q_0(x)$?

6. Show that the Airy DE $y'' - xy = 0$ possesses two linearly independent solutions that are analytic at the origin. Evaluate them by the power series method.

7. Solve the DE $x^2y'' + (x^2 + x)y' + y = 0$ by the Frobenius method. Can you express the obtained series in a closed form?

8. Solve the DE $x^2y'' + x^2y' - 2y = 0$ by the Frobenius method. Show that one of the series terminates. Express the second solution in a closed form (using a method of your choice).

9. Show that the DE $(x^4 + 2x^2)y'' + 3xy' - 6x^2y = 0$ possesses the following series solutions:

$$y_1(x) = 1 + \tfrac{3}{5}x^2 + \tfrac{1}{15}x^4 - \tfrac{1}{195}x^6 + \tfrac{1}{1105}x^8 - \cdots,$$
$$y_2(x) = (1/\sqrt{x})\,(1 + \tfrac{7}{8}x^2 + \tfrac{21}{128}x^4 - \tfrac{7}{1024}x^6 + \tfrac{35}{32768}x^8 - \cdots).$$

What is the radius of convergence of the series?

10. Solve completely by the (generalized) Frobenius method the following differential equations:

a) $xy'' + (1 + x)y' + 2y = 0$,
b) $xy'' + 2y' + y = 0$,
c) $x^2y'' + 4xy' + xy = 0$.

11. Show that the DE $xy'' + (1 - x)y' + \lambda y = 0$ possesses polynomial solutions if λ is a nonnegative integer. Evaluate these polynomials for $\lambda \leq 4$, standardizing them by the condition $y(0) = 1$.

12. Consider the DE $(1 - x^2)y'' - xy' + \lambda y = 0$.

a) What are the singular points of this equation?
b) Solve the equation by the Frobenius method and deduce the values of λ such that one of the solutions will be analytic at the singular points. Show that this solution is a polynomial.
c) Develop explicitly several such polynomials standardizing them by the condition $y(1) = 1$.

13. Show that the DE $y'' + (\cosh 2x - 4)y = 0$ possesses the solution

$$y(x) = x + \tfrac{1}{2}x^3 - \tfrac{1}{40}x^5 - \tfrac{209}{5040}x^7 - \cdots$$

[*Hint:* Expand $\cosh 2x$ in a power series before applying the Frobenius method.]

14. Show that the equation $x^4y'' - y = 0$ has no solutions of Frobenius type. Try, however, expansions about the point at infinity and show that

$$y(x) = Ax \cosh(1/x) + Bx \sinh(1/x).$$

15. In the DE $y'' + 2y' + (1 - 2/x^2)y = 0$, conjecture the behavior of $y(x)$ for large x (see p. 148). Denote this function by $y_\infty(x)$ and proceed to solve the DE by substitution $y(x) = y_\infty(x)v(x)$.

16. A number of DE's can be reduced to the Bessel equation. For instance, show that the DE $y'' + x^py = 0$ can be reduced to the Bessel equation of order $\nu = 1/(p + 2)$ (see p. 135) by the change of the dependent variable $y(x) = \sqrt{x}\,u(x)$, followed by the change of the independent variable

$$z = \frac{2}{2 + p}\,x^{(2+p)/2}.$$

CHAPTER 4

FOURIER SERIES

4.1 TRIGONOMETRIC SERIES

A series of sines and cosines of the type

$$\frac{a_0}{2} + \sum_{n=1}^{\infty} (a_n \cos nx + b_n \sin nx)$$

is known as a *trigonometric series*. In most applications the variable x is *real*. Then $\sin nx$ and $\cos nx$ are bounded and the series will converge if some rather mild conditions are imposed on a_n and b_n.

Examples

1. $$a_n = b_n = 1/n^2 \quad (n \neq 0), \qquad a_0 = 0.$$

   The series reads

$$\cos x + \sin x + \tfrac{1}{4} \cos 2x + \tfrac{1}{4} \sin 2x + \tfrac{1}{9} \cos 3x + \cdots$$

and converges absolutely and uniformly for all (real) values of x (e.g., by the ratio test and the Weierstrass M-test).

2. $$a_n = 0 \quad (\text{all } n), \qquad b_n = 1/n.$$

   The series reads

$$\sin x + \tfrac{1}{2} \sin 2x + \tfrac{1}{3} \sin 3x + \cdots$$

and converges for all x, e.g., by integral test since the integral $\int^{\infty} (\sin tx/t)\, dt$ converges for all x. However, the convergence is not absolute; for instance, take the point $x = \pi/2$; it is not uniform either (for the entire x-axis).

3. $$a_n = 1, \qquad b_n = 0 \qquad (\text{all } n).$$

   The series reads

$$\tfrac{1}{2} + \cos x + \cos 2x + \cos 3x + \cdots$$

and diverges (by the nth-term test) for almost all values of x (the exceptions are points like $x = \pi/2$).

If the trigonometric series converges (whether uniformly or not), then it represents some function $f(x)$, and we can write

$$f(x) = \frac{a_0}{2} + \sum_{n=1}^{\infty} (a_n \cos nx + b_n \sin nx).$$

What kind of functions are representable in such a manner? For a representation by a power series the conditions are (for real x):

1. The function is differentiable any number of times.

2. The remainder in Taylor's formula approaches zero.

These conditions are fairly restrictive. The remarkable property of trigonometric series (discovered by Fourier) is that they can represent functions from a much wider class, including discontinuous functions.

One property of trigonometric series should never be lost from sight: By their very nature these series can represent only *periodic functions** with period 2π [this need not be the primitive period, that is, $f(x)$ may have a smaller period T, but 2π must be an integral multiple of T].

4.2 DEFINITION OF FOURIER SERIES

Let us assume that a certain function is represented by

$$f(x) = \frac{a_0}{2} + \sum_{n=1}^{\infty} (a_n \cos nx + b_n \sin nx),$$

and the series converges *uniformly* in the interval $-\pi \leq x \leq \pi$. (If this is so, then the series converges uniformly for all values of x as well.) We multiply the series by $\cos mx$, where m is a positive integer:

$$f(x) \cos mx = \frac{a_0}{2} \cos mx + \sum_{n=1}^{\infty} a_n \cos nx \cos mx + \sum_{n=1}^{\infty} b_n \sin nx \cos mx.$$

This series is still uniformly convergent and can be integrated term by term:

$$\int_{-\pi}^{+\pi} f(x) \cos mx \, dx = \frac{a_0}{2} \int_{-\pi}^{+\pi} \cos mx \, dx + \sum_{n=1}^{\infty} a_n \int_{-\pi}^{+\pi} \cos nx \cos mx \, dx$$

$$+ \sum_{n=1}^{\infty} b_n \int_{-\pi}^{+\pi} \sin nx \cos mx \, dx.$$

This procedure allows the determination of coefficients a_n if $f(x)$ is known and is based on the important property of sines and cosines known as the *orthogonality property:*

a) $\displaystyle \int_{-\pi}^{+\pi} \sin nx \cos mx \, dx = 0$ (all $n, m > 0$),

b) $\displaystyle \int_{-\pi}^{+\pi} \cos nx \cos mx \, dx = \begin{cases} 0 & (\text{if } n \neq m) \\ \pi & (\text{if } n = m) \end{cases}$,

c) $\displaystyle \int_{-\pi}^{+\pi} \sin nx \sin mx \, dx = \begin{cases} 0 & (\text{if } n \neq m) \\ \pi & (\text{if } n = m) \end{cases}$.

---

* So far as the interval $(-\infty < x < +\infty)$ is concerned, of course.

These formulas can be derived directly, using the well-known properties of sines and cosines. For instance,

$$\sin nx \sin mx = \tfrac{1}{2} \cos (n - m)x - \tfrac{1}{2} \cos (n + m)x.$$

Therefore

$$\int_{-\pi}^{+\pi} \sin nx \sin mx \, dx = \tfrac{1}{2} \int_{-\pi}^{+\pi} \cos (n - m)x \, dx - \tfrac{1}{2} \int_{-\pi}^{+\pi} \cos (n + m)x \, dx.$$

If $n \neq m$, then

$$\int_{-\pi}^{+\pi} \cos (n - m)x \, dx = \frac{\sin (n - m)x}{(n - m)} \Big|_{-\pi}^{+\pi} = 0.$$

If $n = m$, then

$$\int_{-\pi}^{+\pi} \cos (n - n)x \, dx = \int_{-\pi}^{+\pi} dx = 2\pi.$$

Also,

$$\int_{-\pi}^{+\pi} \cos (n + m)x \, dx = 0 \qquad \text{(for all } n, m > 0)$$

and formula (c) is established. Formulas (a) and (b) are proved in a similar fashion.

Returning now to our series, we see that all terms in the infinite sums *except one* will vanish. Moreover,

$$\int_{-\pi}^{+\pi} \cos mx \, dx = 0 \qquad (m > 0)$$

so that

$$\int_{-\pi}^{+\pi} f(x) \cos mx \, dx = a_m \pi.$$

This relation permits us to calculate any desired coefficient a_m when the function $f(x)$ is known.

The coefficients b_n are treated similarly: The expansion is multiplied by $\sin mx$ and is integrated. Orthogonality relations yield

$$\int_{-\pi}^{+\pi} f(x) \sin mx \, dx = b_m \pi.$$

Finally, to obtain a_0, we integrate the expansion

$$f(x) = a_0/2 + \sum_{n=1}^{\infty} (a_n \cos nx + b_n \sin nx)$$

as it stands. This results in

$$\int_{-\pi}^{+\pi} f(x) \, dx = a_0 \pi.$$

It follows that the coefficients a_0, a_n, and b_n can be evaluated from the following formulas:

$$a_n = (1/\pi)\int_{-\pi}^{+\pi} f(x) \cos nx \, dx \qquad (n \geq 0),$$

$$b_n = (1/\pi)\int_{-\pi}^{+\pi} f(x) \sin nx \, dx \qquad (n > 0).$$

The coefficients a_n and b_n calculated from a given function $f(x)$ by means of these formulas are known as the *Fourier coefficients* of $f(x)$. The trigonometric series constructed by means of these coefficients,

$$\frac{a_0}{2} + \sum_{n=1}^{\infty} (a_n \cos nx + b_n \sin nx),$$

is called the *Fourier series* of $f(x)$.

It is important to note that Fourier coefficients can be constructed for a wide class of functions, including some discontinuous functions.

4.3 EXAMPLES OF FOURIER SERIES

Example 1. Consider the function $f(x) = x^2$. Its Fourier coefficients are readily calculated:

$$a_0 = (1/\pi)\int_{-\pi}^{+\pi} x^2 \, dx = \tfrac{2}{3}\pi^2,$$

$$a_n = (1/\pi)\int_{-\pi}^{+\pi} x^2 \cos nx \, dx = (-1)^n(4/n^2) \qquad (n > 0),$$

$$b_n = (1/\pi)\int_{-\pi}^{+\pi} x^2 \sin nx \, dx = 0.$$

The Fourier series is easily seen to be uniformly convergent for all values of x and represents a function

$$g(x) = \pi^2/3 + \sum_{n=1}^{\infty} (-1)^n(4/n^2) \cos nx.$$

The graph of $g(x)$ is shown in Fig. 4.1. It is clear that the Fourier series of $f(x) = x^2$ represents a *periodic extension* of the values of $f(x)$ in the interval $(-\pi, +\pi)$.

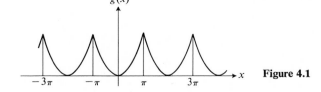

Figure 4.1

Example 2. Now consider a discontinuous function

$$f(x) = \begin{cases} -1 & (x < 0), \\ +1 & (x \geq 0). \end{cases}$$

The Fourier coefficients are

$$a_0 = \frac{1}{\pi} \int_{-\pi}^{0} (-1)\, dx + \frac{1}{\pi} \int_{0}^{+\pi} (+1)\, dx = -1 + 1 = 0,$$

$$a_n = \frac{1}{\pi} \int_{-\pi}^{0} (-\cos nx)\, dx + \frac{1}{\pi} \int_{0}^{+\pi} (+\cos nx)\, dx = 0,$$

$$b_n = \frac{1}{\pi} \int_{-\pi}^{0} (-\sin nx)\, dx + \frac{1}{\pi} \int_{0}^{+\pi} (+\sin nx)\, dx$$

$$= \frac{2}{\pi} \int_{0}^{\pi} \sin nx\, dx = \begin{cases} 4/n\pi & (n = \text{odd}), \\ 0 & (n = \text{even}), \end{cases}$$

and the Fourier series reads

$$g(x) = \frac{4}{\pi} \sum_{n=\text{odd}}^{\infty} \frac{1}{n} \sin nx.$$

The series is convergent in the interval $(-\pi, +\pi)$ and therefore $g(x)$ is well defined. The graph of $g(x)$ is shown in Fig. 4.2. Explicitly, the Fourier series converges to $+1$ for $0 < x < \pi$, to -1 for $-\pi < x < 0$, and to zero for $x = -\pi$, $x = 0$, and $x = +\pi$. It "almost" reproduces $f(x)$ in the interval $-\pi \leq x \leq +\pi$, the exceptions occurring (1) at the ends of the interval and (2) at the point of discontinuity of $f(x)$.

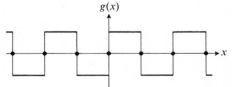

$g(x)$

Figure 4.2

This feature is a general property of Fourier series: If the function $f(x)$ has a jump discontinuity at some point x_0, then its Fourier series converges to the "midpoint of the jump." More precisely, consider the following rather common notation for the two limits of $f(x)$ when $x \to x_0$:

$$f(x_0 + 0) \equiv \lim_{\substack{x \to x_0 \\ x > x_0}} f(x),$$

$$f(x_0 - 0) \equiv \lim_{\substack{x \to x_0 \\ x < x_0}} f(x),$$

(the so-called limits *from the right* and *from the left*). Then the Fourier series converges to

$$\tfrac{1}{2}[f(x_0 + 0) + f(x_0 - 0)].$$

Because of the periodicity of Fourier series, the points $x = \pi$ and $x = -\pi$ often become points of discontinuity for the sum of the series. For this reason, for $x = \pm\pi$, the series converges to

$$\tfrac{1}{2}[f(-\pi + 0) + f(\pi - 0)].$$

Remark. These two statements remain in force when the two limits $f(x_0 + 0)$ and $f(x_0 - 0)$, or the limits $f(-\pi + 0)$ and $f(\pi - 0)$, are identical. For instance, if $f(x)$ is continuous at $x = x_0$, then

$$f(x_0 + 0) = f(x_0 - 0) = f(x_0),$$

and the Fourier series simply converges to $f(x_0)$, namely, the actual value of the function. The other interesting example arises when $f(x)$ is discontinuous at $x = x_0$ because some point is "removed from the curve" as in

$$f_1(x) = \begin{cases} x^2 & (x \neq 0), \\ 1 & (x = 0). \end{cases}$$

This rather artificially constructed function will possess the same Fourier coefficients and, therefore, the same Fourier series as the function

$$f(x) = x^2 \qquad \text{(all } x\text{)}.$$

This Fourier series will converge to the function $g(x)$ of Example 1. Observe that

$$f_1(0 + 0) = f_1(0 - 0) = 0 \qquad \text{and} \qquad g(0) = \tfrac{1}{2}[f_1(0 + 0) + f_1(0 - 0)] = 0,$$

but that

$$g(0) \neq f_1(0).$$

Let us summarize the conclusions obtained so far:

1. If a trigonometric series converges *uniformly* to a certain function $f(x)$ (necessarily periodic), then the coefficients a_n and b_n are necessarily given by the formulas

$$a_n = (1/\pi)\int_{-\pi}^{+\pi} f(x)\cos nx\, dx, \qquad b_n = (1/\pi)\int_{-\pi}^{+\pi} f(x)\sin nx\, dx,$$

and the given trigonometric series is a Fourier series for $f(x)$.

2. If a function $f(x)$ is given and its Fourier coefficients do exist, then the Fourier series is *expected* to reproduce the *periodic extension* of $f(x)$ except, perhaps, for some minor changes (as in Example 2).

It is needless to point out that the second conclusion is not precise and requires elaboration. In fact, it raises the fundamental question of the theory of Fourier series: "What conditions must a function $f(x)$ satisfy in order that its Fourier series converges to $f(x)$ in the interval $-\pi \leq x \leq \pi$?"

It may be pointed out that the period 2π is not mandatory in the theory of Fourier series. Replacement of x by $(2\pi/T)x$ yields a series with period T:

$$f(x) = \frac{a_0}{2} + \sum_{n=1}^{\infty} \left(a_n \cos \frac{2\pi nx}{T} + b_n \sin \frac{2\pi nx}{T} \right).$$

Here $f(x)$ is a periodic function with period T. [The trigonometric series is tacitly assumed to converge to $f(x)$.]

Conversely, if $f(x)$ is given, it will give rise to the Fourier coefficients

$$a_n = \frac{2}{T} \int_{-T/2}^{+T/2} f(x) \cos \frac{2\pi nx}{T} \, dx, \qquad b_n = \frac{2}{T} \int_{-T/2}^{+T/2} f(x) \sin \frac{2\pi nx}{T} \, dx,$$

and the resulting Fourier series will be expected to reproduce $f(x)$ in the interval $-T/2 \leq x \leq T/2$.

This form of Fourier series is most often used in the treatment of phenomena that are *periodic in time:* The symbol x represents the time variable (usually replaced by t while $2\pi/T$ is replaced by ω).

In this connection, Fourier series are often expressed in a form involving amplitudes and phases. For example, if we write

$$A_n = \sqrt{a_n^2 + b_n^2} \qquad (n > 0),$$

and

$$\phi_n = \arctan \frac{b_n}{a_n} \qquad (n > 0),$$

then the Fourier series reads

$$f(x) = \frac{a_0}{2} + \sum_{n=1}^{\infty} A_n \cos \left(\frac{2\pi nx}{T} - \phi_n \right).$$

In many applications, where x represents distance, the period $2L$ is most convenient. The formulas read

$$f(x) = a_0/2 + \sum_{n=1}^{\infty} [a_n \cos (n\pi x/L) + b_n \sin (n\pi x/L)],$$

$$a_n = 1/L \int_{-L}^{+L} f(x) \cos (n\pi x/L) \, dx,$$

$$b_n = 1/L \int_{-L}^{+L} f(x) \sin (n\pi x/L) \, dx.$$

4.4 PARITY PROPERTIES. SINE AND COSINE SERIES

Suppose that a function $f(x)$ is to be expanded into a Fourier series in the interval $(-L, +L)$. If $f(x)$ is even, then all coefficients b_n must vanish while the coefficients a_n are obtained by integrating from 0 to L only and multiplying the result by 2:

$$f(x) = \frac{a_0}{2} + \sum_{n=1}^{\infty} a_n \cos \frac{n\pi x}{L},$$

$$a_n = \frac{2}{L} \int_0^L f(x) \cos \frac{n\pi x}{L} \, dx \qquad (f(x) = \text{even}).$$

Similarly, if $f(x)$ is odd, then all a_n are zero and

$$f(x) = \sum_{n=1}^{\infty} b_n \sin \frac{n\pi x}{L}$$

$$b_n = \frac{2}{L} \int_0^L f(x) \sin \frac{n\pi x}{L} \, dx \qquad (f(x) = \text{odd}).$$

These two results give rise to two other types of trigonometric expansions, known as the *Fourier cosine series* and the *Fourier sine series*. Suppose that an *arbitrary* (not necessarily even or odd) function $f(x)$ is given. If we calculate the "half-range integrals" and *define*

$$a_n = \frac{2}{L} \int_0^L f(x) \cos \frac{n\pi x}{L} \, dx,$$

and form the series

$$\frac{a_0}{2} + \sum_{n=1}^{\infty} a_n \cos \frac{n\pi x}{L},$$

then this series will reproduce the function

$$g(x) = \begin{cases} f(x) & (0 < x < L), \\ f(-x) & (-L < x < 0), \end{cases}$$

which may be called the *symmetric extension* of $f(x)$ into the interval $(-L, 0)$. We say that we have expanded $f(x)$ into a *Fourier cosine series* over the interval $(0, L)$.
      Similarly, we may define

$$b_n = \frac{2}{L} \int_0^L f(x) \sin \frac{n\pi x}{L} \, dx$$

and construct the series

$$\sum_{n=1}^{\infty} b_n \sin \frac{n\pi x}{L},$$

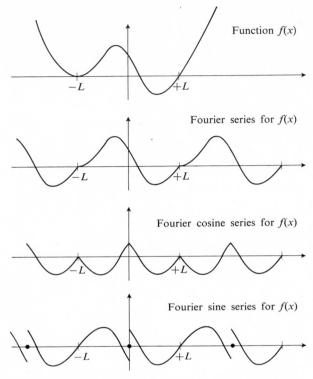

Function $f(x)$

Fourier series for $f(x)$

Fourier cosine series for $f(x)$

Fourier sine series for $f(x)$

Figure 4.3

which should represent the *antisymmetric extension* of $f(x)$:

$$g(x) = \begin{cases} f(x) & (0 < x < L), \\ -f(-x) & (-L < x < 0). \end{cases}$$

We say that we have expanded $f(x)$ into a *Fourier sine series* over the interval $(0, L)$.

The three different trigonometric series for a given function are represented in Fig. 4.3.

Example. $f(x) = x/2L + \frac{1}{2}$.

The Fourier (full range) coefficients are

$$a_0 = 1, \qquad a_n = \frac{1}{L} \int_{-L}^{+L} \left(\frac{x}{2L} + \frac{1}{2} \right) \cos \frac{n\pi x}{L}\, dx = 0,$$

$$b_n = \frac{1}{L} \int_{-L}^{+L} \left(\frac{x}{2L} + \frac{1}{2} \right) \sin \frac{n\pi x}{L}\, dx = \frac{(-1)^{n+1}}{n\pi},$$

and the Fourier series reads

$$g(x) = \frac{1}{2} + \sum_{n=1}^{\infty} \frac{(-1)^{n+1}}{n\pi} \sin \frac{n\pi x}{L}.$$

The Fourier sine (half-range) coefficients are

$$b_n = \frac{2}{L} \int_0^L \left(\frac{x}{2L} + \frac{1}{2}\right) \sin \frac{n\pi x}{L} dx = \frac{1 - 2\cos n\pi}{n\pi},$$

and the Fourier sine series reads

$$g_1(x) = \frac{3}{\pi} \sum_{n=1,3,5,\dots}^{\infty} \frac{1}{n} \sin \frac{n\pi x}{L} - \frac{1}{\pi} \sum_{n=2,4,6,\dots}^{\infty} \frac{1}{n} \sin \frac{n\pi x}{L}.$$

Finally, the Fourier cosine (half-range) coefficients are

$$a_0 = \frac{3}{2}, \qquad a_n = \frac{2}{L} \int_0^L \left(\frac{x}{2L} + \frac{1}{2}\right) \cos \frac{n\pi x}{L} dx = \frac{\cos n\pi - 1}{n^2\pi^2},$$

and the Fourier cosine series reads

$$g_2(x) = \frac{3}{4} - \frac{2}{\pi^2} \sum_{n=1,3,5}^{\infty} \frac{1}{n^2} \cos \frac{n\pi x}{L}.$$

All three series are shown in Fig. 4.4.

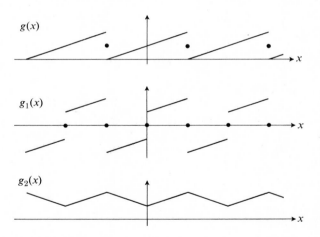

Figure 4.4

The formulas for the Fourier sine and cosine series for "half the range" are related to the fact that the functions $\sin nx$ are orthogonal over the interval $(0, \pi)$:

$$\int_0^\pi \sin nx \sin mx \, dx = 0 \qquad (n \neq m),$$

and the same is true for the functions $\cos nx$:

$$\int_0^\pi \cos nx \cos mx \, dx = 0 \qquad (n \neq m).$$

However, they are not orthogonal to each other, namely, the integral

$$\int_0^\pi \sin nx \cos mx \, dx$$

is not necessarily zero.

There is a remarkable proof of the orthogonality of sines based on the knowledge of two facts:

1. The functions $\sin nx$ satisfy the DE $y'' + n^2 y = 0$.
2. The functions $\sin nx$ vanish at $x = 0$ and $x = \pi$.

The method is as follows: Write

$$y_n = \sin nx, \qquad y_m = \sin mx \qquad (n \neq m).$$

Then

$$y_n'' + n^2 y_n = 0, \qquad y_m'' + m^2 y_m = 0.$$

Multiply the first equation by y_m, multiply the second one by y_n, subtract, and integrate from $x = 0$ to $x = \pi$:

$$\int_0^\pi (y_n'' y_m - y_m'' y_n) \, dx + (n^2 - m^2) \int_0^\pi y_n y_m \, dx = 0.$$

In the first integral, use integration by parts:

$$\int_0^\pi y_n'' y_m \, dx - \int_0^\pi y_m'' y_n \, dx = y_n' y_m \Big|_0^\pi - \int_0^\pi y_n' y_m' \, dx$$

$$- y_m' y_n \Big|_0^\pi + \int_0^\pi y_n' y_m' \, dx = (y_n' y_m - y_m' y_n) \Big|_0^\pi.$$

Since y_m and y_n vanish at $x = 0$ and $x = \pi$, it follows that this expression is zero. Therefore

$$(n^2 - m^2) \int_0^\pi y_m y_n \, dx = 0.$$

Since $n \neq m$, it follows that

$$\int_0^\pi y_m y_n \, dx = 0.$$

A similar proof can be developed for the cosines: The function $\cos nx$ has the following properties:

1. It satisfies the DE $y'' + n^2 y = 0$.
2. Its derivative vanishes at $x = 0$ and $x = \pi$. The proof is essentially the same except that now the expression

$$(y_n' y_m - y_m' y_n) \Big|_0^\pi$$

vanishes because the derivatives y_m' and y_n' vanish.

Finally, consider a similar proof for both sines and cosines over the interval $(-\pi, +\pi)$. Let y_n denote either $\sin nx$ or $\cos nx$.

We make use of two facts:

1. y_n satisfies the DE $y_n'' + n^2 y_n = 0$.
2. y_n is periodic: $y_n(x + 2\pi) = y_n(x)$.

In this case, the integration is from $-\pi$ to $+\pi$, and the statement

$$(y_n' y_m - y_m' y_n)\big|_{-\pi}^{\pi} = 0$$

is made on the basis of periodicity. The result, namely

$$\int_{-\pi}^{+\pi} y_m y_n \, dx = 0 \qquad (\text{for } n \neq m),$$

establishes, at once, the three orthogonality relations:

$$\int_{-\pi}^{+\pi} \sin nx \sin mx \, dx = 0 \qquad (n \neq m),$$

$$\int_{-\pi}^{+\pi} \cos nx \cos mx \, dx = 0 \qquad (n \neq m),$$

$$\int_{-\pi}^{+\pi} \sin nx \cos mx \, dx = 0 \qquad (n \neq m).$$

Observe, however, that the method employed *does not prove* the orthogonality of $\sin nx$ and $\cos nx$, namely,

$$\int_{-\pi}^{+\pi} \sin nx \cos nx \, dx = 0,$$

which must be established separately.

4.5 COMPLEX FORM OF FOURIER SERIES

The Fourier expansion

$$f(x) = \frac{a_0}{2} + \sum_{n=1}^{\infty} \left(a_n \cos \frac{n\pi x}{L} + b_n \sin \frac{n\pi x}{L} \right) \qquad (-L \leq x \leq L)$$

can be cast into complex form. Write

$$\cos \frac{n\pi x}{L} = \frac{1}{2} \left(e^{i(n\pi x/L)} + e^{-i(n\pi x/L)} \right)$$

$$\sin \frac{n\pi x}{L} = \frac{1}{2i} \left(e^{i(n\pi x/L)} - e^{-i(n\pi x/L)} \right)$$

and insert these expressions into the series. It is convenient to define

$$c_n = \begin{cases} \frac{1}{2}(a_n - ib_n) & (n > 0), \\ \frac{1}{2}(a_n + ib_n) & (n < 0), \\ \frac{1}{2}a_0 & (n = 0). \end{cases}$$

Then the Fourier series can be written in its complex form:

$$f(x) = \sum_{n=-\infty}^{+\infty} c_n e^{i(n\pi x/L)} \qquad (-L \le x \le L).$$

The convenience of this form is obvious.

From the formulas for a_n and b_n follows the formula for c_n:

$$c_n = (1/2L)\int_{-L}^{+L} f(x)e^{-i(n\pi x/L)}\, dx.$$

Exercise. Deduce this statement by a detailed argument.

Alternatively, the above formula may be derived by multiplying the series by $e^{-i(n\pi x/L)}$ and integrating. The complex exponentials are readily shown to be orthogonal in the sense† that

$$\int_{-L}^{+L} e^{i(n\pi x/L)} e^{-i(m\pi x/L)}\, dx = \begin{cases} 0 & (n \ne m), \\ 2L & (n = m), \end{cases}$$

and the formula for c_n follows.

Remark. Although the Fourier series now appears in complex form, its sum $f(x)$ is still assumed to be real. In this case the following properties are easily verified:

1. c_0 is real; $c_{-n} = c_n^*$,
2. If $f(x)$ is even, all c_n are real,
3. If $f(x)$ is odd, $c_0 = 0$ and all c_n are pure imaginary.

Now consider the complex functions of the real variable x. They can also be expanded into Fourier series and the complex form of the series is now a natural one. The formula for c_n does not change, but the above three properties of the coefficients no longer hold.

One may show, however, that

a) if $f(x)$ is even, then $c_{-n} = c_n$, and
b) if $f(x)$ is odd, then $c_{-n} = -c_n$ (and $c_0 = 0$).

Example. The function

$$f(x) = \begin{cases} 0 & (-\pi < x \le 0), \\ 1 & (0 < x \le \pi) \end{cases}$$

can be represented by a complex Fourier series. We calculate

$$c_0 = \frac{1}{2\pi}\int_0^\pi dx = \frac{1}{2},$$

$$c_n = \frac{1}{2\pi}\int_0^\pi e^{-inx}\, dx = \frac{1 - e^{-in\pi}}{2\pi n i} = \begin{cases} 0 & (n = \text{even}), \\ \dfrac{1}{\pi n i} & (n = \text{odd}). \end{cases}$$

---

† For complex functions, orthogonality is defined by $\int f_n(x)f_m^*(x)\, dx = 0\ (m \ne n)$ (See Section 9.4).

Therefore

$$f(x) = \frac{1}{2} + \frac{1}{\pi i} \sum_{\substack{n=-\infty \\ n=\text{odd}}}^{+\infty} \frac{1}{n} e^{inx}.$$

4.6 POINTWISE CONVERGENCE OF FOURIER SERIES

Before Fourier series are applied to the solution of physical problems, it is desirable to know whether the Fourier series of a given function $f(x)$ will actually converge to $f(x)$. Common examples seem to indicate that, as a rule, the Fourier series converges to

$$\tfrac{1}{2}[f(x + 0) + f(x - 0)]$$

at all points inside the interval $(-L, +L)$, and to

$$\tfrac{1}{2}[f(-L + 0) + f(L - 0)]$$

at the endpoints of the interval.

The determination of exact conditions under which this result can be expected has been a subject of intense research for more than a century. A variety of sufficient conditions has been found. The two theorems given below are probably sufficient for most physical applications.

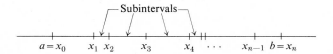

Figure 4.5

Definition 1. A function defined in a closed interval $a \leq x \leq b$ is called *piecewise continuous* if the interval can be split into a *finite number* of subintervals such that in each subinterval (see Fig. 4.5)

a) $f(x)$ is continuous,

b) $f(x)$ possesses (finite) limits at the left and right ends of each subinterval.

Condition (b) means that $f(x_i - 0)$ and $f(x_i + 0)$ exist for all $i = 1, 2, \ldots, n$, and also that $f(a + 0)$ and $f(b - 0)$ must exist.

The function $f(x)$ is called *piecewise smooth* if it is piecewise continuous and its *derivative* $f'(x)$ is piecewise continuous in each subinterval. The function $f(x)$ is called *piecewise very smooth* if it is piecewise smooth, and its *second derivative* $f''(x)$ is piecewise continuous [in each subinterval of continuity of $f'(x)$].

Definition 2. A function defined in a closed interval $a \leq x \leq b$ is said to satisfy the *Dirichlet conditions* if

a) $f(x)$ is piecewise continuous, and

b) the interval (a, b) can be split into a *finite number* of subintervals where $f(x)$ is monotone.

Theorem 1. If $f(x)$ is piecewise very smooth in the interval $(-L, +L)$, then its Fourier series converges to

$$\tfrac{1}{2}[f(x - 0) + f(x + 0)] \quad (-L < x < +L),$$
$$\tfrac{1}{2}[f(-L + 0) + f(L - 0)] \quad (x = \pm L).$$

The convergence is uniform in any closed subinterval where $f(x)$ is continuous.

Theorem 2. The statement of Theorem 1 holds if instead of being a piecewise very smooth function, $f(x)$ satisfies the Dirichlet conditions for $-L \leq x \leq L$.

The proof of Theorem 1 is much easier than that of Theorem 2. Both can be found in treatises on Fourier series and many other textbooks.

Remark. Theorems 1 and 2 do not, by any means, exhaust the theory of Fourier series. This may be appreciated by the following example.

Example. The function

$$f(x) = \log\left(\cos\frac{x}{2}\right) \quad (-\pi < x < \pi)$$

possesses the Fourier series

$$g(x) = -\log 2 - \sum_{n=1}^{\infty} \frac{(-1)^n}{n} \cos nx.$$

For all values of x such that $-\pi < x < \pi$, the series uniformly converges to $f(x)$ in any interval $x_1 \leq x \leq x_2$ with $x_1 > -\pi$, $x_2 < \pi$. It diverges for $x = \pm\pi$: It may be said to approach "minus infinity" as $x \to \pm\pi$, but so does $f(x)$. Evidently the Fourier series represents $f(x)$ in a most faithful manner, and yet $f(x)$ is neither piecewise very smooth nor does it satisfy the Dirichlet conditions.

Most of the difficulties in the theory of Fourier series can be traced to the concept of *pointwise convergence*. There are, however, other types of convergence, like *convergence in the mean* which is, perhaps, better suited for physical applications.

4.7 CONVERGENCE IN THE MEAN

When a certain fixed quantity x is being measured, then a set of n (equivalent) measurements yields n values

$$x_1, x_2, x_3, \ldots, x_n,$$

which are, in general, different. The best estimate of x is then taken to be the average:

$$\langle x \rangle \equiv (1/n) \sum_{i=1}^{n} x_i.$$

It is common practice to describe the precision of the measurements by the *mean square deviation* d^2:

$$d^2 \equiv (1/n) \sum_{i=1}^{n} [x_i - \langle x \rangle]^2$$

(or, equivalently, by the *root mean square deviation d*).

This idea can be applied to the problem: How well does a given set of measurements fit a given theoretical curve? For instance, the set of measurements shown in Fig. 4.6 seems to confirm the linear relationship shown by the straight line. But how good is the fit?

A common procedure is to calculate the deviations between the actual values y_i of the measurements, and the theoretical predictions $\bar{y}_i$ (from the equation of the straight line $\bar{y}_i = mx_i + b$), and to form the mean square deviation

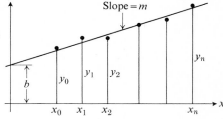

$$D = (1/n) \sum_{i=0}^{n} (y_i - \bar{y}_i)^2,$$

Figure 4.6

which then serves as the measure of the precision of the fit.

Conversely, if the theoretical relationship is not known, one may construct one on the basis of the measurements. A common method is to choose the parameters m and b in the equation $y = mx + b$ in such a manner that D is *minimized*. This is known as the *method of least squares* in the theory of measurements and the idea can be extended to the fitting of two functions, both of which are defined for all points within a certain interval.

If the measurements y_i were taken at equal intervals Δx, then $\Delta x \cdot n = L$, where $L = x_n - x_0$ is the length of the interval. In this case

$$D = (1/L) \sum_{i=0}^{n} (y_i - \bar{y}_i)^2 \, \Delta x.$$

As n is now increased, the sum assumes, more and more the appearance of an integral. It seems logical, then, to measure the "extent of fit" of two functions $y(x)$ and $\bar{y}(x)$ by the integral $D = (1/L) \int_a^b [y(x) - \bar{y}(x)]^2 \, dx \; (L = |b - a|)$.

If one of the functions, say $y(x)$, has a number of undetermined parameters, then one may determine these parameters by requiring that D be minimized. Note that if the interval $a \le x \le b$ is fixed, the factor $1/L$ is irrelevant.

Definition. The integral

$$\int_a^b [f(x) - g(x)]^2 \, dx$$

for two functions $f(x)$ and $g(x)$ defined over the interval $a \le x \le b$ is called the *total square deviation* of $f(x)$ and $g(x)$.

This concept will be applied to trigonometric series. Let us suppose that a piecewise continuous function $f(x)$ is given in the interval $-\pi \le x \le \pi$, and that $f(x)$ is to be approximated by a trigonometric polynomial

$$g_n(x) = A_0/2 + \sum_{k=1}^{n} (A_k \cos kx + B_k \sin kx),$$

where the coefficients A_k $(k = 0, 1, \ldots, n)$ and B_k $(k = 1, 2, 3, \ldots, n)$ are undetermined.

Let us define A_k and B_k by requiring that the total square deviation

$$D_n = \int_{-\pi}^{+\pi} [f(x) - g_n(x)]^2 \, dx$$

be minimized. Straightforward calculation yields

$$D_n = \int_{-\pi}^{+\pi} [f(x)]^2 \, dx + \left\{ A_0^2 \pi/2 - A_0 \int_{-\pi}^{+\pi} f(x) \, dx \right\}$$

$$+ \sum_{k=1}^{n} \left\{ \pi A_k^2 - 2A_k \int_{-\pi}^{+\pi} f(x) \cos kx \, dx \right\}$$

$$+ \sum_{k=1}^{n} \left\{ \pi B_k^2 - 2B_k \int_{-\pi}^{+\pi} f(x) \sin kx \, dx \right\} \cdot$$

Exercise. Using the orthogonality relations, give all the details leading to this formula.

The whole expression is minimized if each term in { } is minimized. For instance, the quantity

$$\delta_k = \pi A_k^2 - 2A_k \int_{-\pi}^{+\pi} f(x) \cos kx \, dx \qquad (k = 1, 2, \ldots, n)$$

has an extremum if

$$\frac{d\delta_k}{dA_k} = 2\pi A_k - 2 \int_{-\pi}^{+\pi} f(x) \cos kx \, dx = 0,$$

or

$$A_k = \frac{1}{\pi} \int_{-\pi}^{+\pi} f(x) \cos kx \, dx \qquad (k = 1, 2, \ldots, n).$$

This extremum is a minimum since $d^2 \delta_k/dA_k^2 = 2\pi > 0$. In this fashion we also obtain

$$B_k = (1/\pi) \int_{-\pi}^{+\pi} f(x) \sin kx \, dx \qquad (k = 1, 2, \ldots, n),$$

$$A_0 = (1/\pi) \int_{-\pi}^{+\pi} f(x) \, dx.$$

It is seen that the total square deviation is minimized if A_k and B_k are chosen as the *Fourier coefficients* of the function $f(x)$.

Now substitute these optimal values (denoting them as a_k and b_k) of the coefficients into the expression for D_n to obtain the minimum total square deviation:

$$[D_n]_{\min} = \int_{-\pi}^{+\pi} [f(x)]^2 \, dx - \left\{ (\pi/2)a_0^2 + \pi \sum_{k=1}^{n} (a_k^2 + b_k^2) \right\}.$$

Since D_n cannot be negative, the following inequality holds:

$$a_0^2/2 + \sum_{k=1}^{n} (a_k^2 + b_k^2) \leq (1/\pi) \int_{-\pi}^{+\pi} [f(x)]^2 \, dx.$$

This holds for any n. Let $n \to \infty$ (transition to the Fourier series). The sequence on the left is bounded (by the integral on the right) and is monotone nondecreasing. Therefore, it possesses a limit and this limit satisfies the inequality

$$a_0^2/2 + \sum_{k=1}^{\infty} (a_k^2 + b_k^2) \leq (1/\pi) \int_{-\pi}^{+\pi} [f(x)]^2 \, dx,$$

known as *Bessel's inequality*.

In the spirit of this approach, the Fourier series of a function $f(x)$ is considered to be a satisfactory representation of $f(x)$ provided the total square deviation approaches zero:

$$\lim_{n \to \infty} [D_n]_{\min} = 0.$$

In general, a sequence of functions $\{f_n(x)\}$ is said to *converge in the mean* to a function $f(x)$ if

$$\lim_{n \to \infty} \int_a^b [f(x) - f_n(x)]^2 \, dx = 0.$$

Note that $f(x)$ is not unique since the "removal of one point" will not change the value of the integral.

If the Fourier series of a certain function $f(x)$ converges in the mean to $f(x)$, then Bessel's inequality becomes

$$a_0^2/2 + \sum_{k=1}^{\infty} (a_k^2 + b_k^2) = (1/\pi) \int_{-\pi}^{+\pi} [f(x)]^2 \, dx,$$

and is known as *Parseval's equation*.

The fundamental question of the theory of Fourier series now becomes, "For what class of functions does the Fourier series converge in the mean (to its function)?"

Remark. Whenever Parseval's equation holds for a certain class of functions, then the set of sines and cosines,

$$\{\sin nx, \cos nx\} \qquad (n = 0, 1, 2, \ldots),$$

is called *complete* with respect to that class of functions and Parseval's equation is usually referred to as the *completeness relation*. Then the above question may be restated as, "For what class of functions is the set {sin nx, cos nx} complete?" The following theorem gives at least a partial answer to this question.

Theorem. The system {sin nx, cos nx} is complete with respect to all piece-wise continuous functions in the interval $-\pi \leq x \leq \pi$.

Observe that the conditions are weaker than those demanded by Theorems 1 and 2 for pointwise convergence. The proof of this theorem can be found in a variety of textbooks.*

Remarks

1. In some texts the term "complete" already implies *complete with respect to all piece-wise continuous functions.*

2. The conditions of the theorem are sufficient but not necessary. For instance, $f(x) = \log [\cos (x/2)]$ does not fall into the above class.

3. Pointwise convergence does not imply convergence in the mean. The former means

$$\lim_{n \to \infty} f_n(x) = f(x) \qquad (a \leq x \leq b),$$

and the latter means

$$\lim_{n \to \infty} \int_a^b [f(x) - f_n(x)]^2 \, dx = 0.$$

If the processes of integration and "taking the limit" were interchangeable, then the second statement would follow from the first. Unfortunately, they are not always interchangeable.

4.8 APPLICATIONS OF FOURIER SERIES

Fourier series can be applied to an extremely wide variety of physical problems. As an introduction we shall confine ourselves to the following examples.

Example 1. The electrical circuit shown in Fig. 4.7 is driven by a variable electromotive force $E(t)$ which is periodic (but not necessarily sinusoidal). The *response* of the system, namely the current $I(t)$, is to be found. The function $I(t)$ is known to satisfy the differential equation

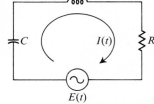

Figure 4.7

$$L\frac{d^2I}{dt^2} + R\frac{dI}{dt} + \frac{1}{C}I = \frac{dE}{dt}.$$

---

* For example, Tolstov, *Fourier Series*, Section 5.2; Kaplan, *Advanced Calculus*, Section 7.12.

Under steady-state conditions the function $I(t)$ is also periodic, with the same period T as for $E(t)$. Let us assume that $E(t)$ and $I(t)$ possess Fourier expansions (written in their complex form):

$$E(t) = \sum_{n=-\infty}^{+\infty} E_n e^{in\omega t}, \qquad I(t) = \sum_{n=-\infty}^{+\infty} c_n e^{in\omega t} \qquad (\omega = 2\pi/T).$$

Furthermore, let us assume that the series can be differentiated term by term the necessary number of times:

$$\frac{dE}{dt} = \sum_{n=-\infty}^{+\infty} in\omega E_n e^{in\omega t},$$

$$\frac{dI}{dt} = \sum_{n=-\infty}^{+\infty} in\omega c_n e^{in\omega t},$$

$$\frac{d^2 I}{dt^2} = \sum_{n=-\infty}^{+\infty} (-n^2\omega^2) c_n e^{in\omega t}.$$

Substitute into the DE and equate the coefficients with the same exponential $e^{in\omega t}$ on both sides (on the basis of the orthogonality property). Then

$$(-n^2\omega^2 L + in\omega R + 1/C)c_n = in\omega E_n.$$

Therefore

$$c_n = \frac{i(n\omega/L)}{(\omega_0^2 - n^2\omega^2) + 2\alpha n\omega i} E_n,$$

where $\omega_0^2 = 1/CL$ is the natural frequency of the circuit, and $2\alpha = R/L$ is the attenuation factor of the circuit. Thus the problem is essentially solved, since the Fourier coefficients for $I(t)$ are obtained in terms of the Fourier coefficients for $E(t)$ which read

$$E_n = (1/T) \int_{-T/2}^{+T/2} E(t) e^{-in\omega t} \, dt.$$

Remark. In the course of determining the solution, the term-by-term differentiation was *assumed* to be valid. If the series for E' and I'' converge uniformly, the validity of such a procedure is guaranteed. However, it is possible to relax this requirement and to demonstrate the validity of the result under much weaker conditions. In particular, the result can be shown to be valid provided the Fourier series for $E(t)$ exists, regardless of the uniform convergence of the series for the derivative.

Example 2. A simply supported beam is shown in Fig. 4.8; note the direction of the y-axis, which was chosen to make $y(x)$ positive. It is uniformly loaded by a load q per unit length. The deflection $y(x)$ of the beam is sought. The function $y(x)$ is known to satisfy* the DE

$$\frac{d^4 y}{dx^4} = \frac{1}{EI} q(x),$$

---

* See, e.g., Salvadori and Schwartz, *Differential Equations in Engineering Problems*, Section 2.10.

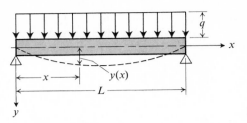

Figure 4.8

where $q(x)$ is the load per unit length at point x (in our case $q = $ const) and $1/EI$ is the rigidity of the beam.

Since the function $y(x)$ must vanish at the points $x = 0$ and $x = L$, it may be conveniently expanded into a Fourier sine series

$$y(x) = \sum_{n=1}^{\infty} b_n \sin \frac{n\pi x}{L}.$$

Assuming the validity of the fourfold term-by-term differentiation, obtain

$$\frac{d^4 y(x)}{dx^4} = \sum_{n=1}^{\infty} \left(\frac{n\pi}{L}\right)^4 b_n \sin \frac{n\pi x}{L}.$$

Also expand $q(x) = q = $ const into the Fourier sine series

$$q = \sum_{n=1}^{\infty} q_n \sin \frac{n\pi x}{L},$$

where

$$q_n = \frac{2}{L} \int_0^L q \sin \frac{n\pi x}{L} dx = \begin{cases} \dfrac{4q}{n\pi} & (n = \text{odd}) \\ 0 & (n = \text{even}) \end{cases}.$$

Substitute both series into the DE and equate the coefficients (on the basis of orthogonality of $\sin (n\pi x/L)$. This yields

$$b_n = \frac{1}{EI} \frac{L^4}{n^4 \pi^4} q_n = \begin{cases} \dfrac{4qL^4}{EI\pi^5} \dfrac{1}{n^5} & (n = \text{odd}) \\ 0 & (n = \text{even}) \end{cases}$$

so that

$$y(x) = \frac{4qL^4}{EI\pi^5} \sum_{n=1,3,5,\ldots}^{\infty} \frac{1}{n^5} \sin \frac{n\pi x}{L}.$$

One practical advantage of this form for $y(x)$ is the rapid convergence of the series (due to the fifth power of n in the denominator). For $x = L/2$ (maximum deflection) the second term in the series represents only $1/3^5 \cong 0.00412 \cong 0.4\%$ of the leading term.

Remark. Since the series for $q(x)$ [and, therefore, for d^4y/dx^4] is not uniformly convergent, the validity of the procedure remains in doubt. However, it may be justified most easily by means of the theory of distributions (see Chapter 6).

BIBLIOGRAPHY

CHURCHILL, R. V., *Fourier Series and Boundary-Value Problems*, New York: McGraw-Hill Book Co., 1941.

ROGOSINSKI, W. R., *Fourier Series*, New York: Chelsea Publishing Co., 1959.

SALVADORI, M. G., and R. J. SCHWARTZ, *Differential Equations in Engineering Problems*, Englewood Cliffs, New Jersey: Prentice-Hall, Inc., 1954.

SNEDDON, I. N., *Fourier Series*, Glenco, Illinois: The Free Press, 1961.

TOLSTOV, G. P., *Fourier Series*, Englewood Cliffs, New Jersey: Prentice-Hall, Inc., 1962.

PROBLEMS

1. a) Prove that if $f(x)$ is even and possesses the property $f(x + L) = -f(x)$, then its Fourier series in $(-L, +L)$ has only cosine terms of odd order and the following formula holds:

$$a_{2m+1} = \frac{4}{L} \int_0^{L/2} f(x) \cos \frac{(2m + 1)\pi x}{L} \, dx \qquad (m = 0, 1, 2, \ldots).$$

   b) What is the condition that has to be imposed on $f(x)$ to ensure that its Fourier series in $(-L, +L)$ has only even-order cosine terms?

   c) Establish a theorem similar to (a) for odd functions.

2. Show that if a function $f(x)$ vanishes at $x = 0$ and its derivative $f'(x)$ vanishes at $x = L$, then it can be represented *in the range* $0 \leq x \leq L$ by a sine series

$$f(x) = \sum_{n=1,3,5,\ldots}^{\infty} b_n \sin (n\pi x/2L)$$

containing only odd terms.

3. a) Show that the *sawtooth function* (Fig. 4.9) has the Fourier series

$$f(t) = \frac{a}{2} - a \sum_{n=1}^{\infty} b_n \sin \frac{2\pi nt}{T},$$

and develop the formula for b_n.

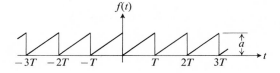

Figure 4.9

b) Make a precise plot of the partial sums

$$\varphi_N(t) = \frac{a}{2} - a \sum_{n=1}^{N} b_n \sin \frac{2\pi nt}{T},$$

for $N = 1, 2, 3$ in the interval $(0, T)$. Superimpose all three graphs on a plot of $f(t)$ to illustrate the process of convergence of the Fourier series.

4. Develop the Fourier series in the interval $(0, T)$ for the following *triangular wave*:

$$f(t) = \begin{cases} 2at/T & (0 \le t \le T/2), \\ 2a(1 - t/T) & (T/2 \le t \le T). \end{cases}$$

5. An alternating current $i(t) = A \sin \omega t$ has been passed through

   a) a *half-wave* rectifier, which transmits the current when it is flowing in the positive direction only, and

   b) a *full-wave* rectifier, which transmits the (instantaneous) absolute value of the current.

   Show that in the first case, the output current is

$$\frac{A}{\pi} + \frac{A}{2} \sin \omega t - \frac{2A}{\pi} \sum_{n=1,3,5,\ldots}^{\infty} \frac{\cos (n + 1)\omega t}{n(n + 2)},$$

and in the second case, it is

$$\frac{2A}{\pi} - \frac{4A}{\pi} \sum_{n=2,4,6,\ldots}^{\infty} \frac{\cos n\omega t}{n^2 - 1}.$$

6. By expanding $f(x) = \cosh ax$ into a Fourier series, show that

$$\cosh ax = \frac{\sinh a\pi}{a\pi} + \frac{2a \sinh a\pi}{\pi} \sum_{n=1}^{\infty} \frac{(-1)^n}{n^2 + a^2} \cos nx \qquad (-\pi < x < \pi).$$

7. Expand $f(x) = \cos kx$, where k is *not* an integer, into a Fourier series in the interval $(-\pi, +\pi)$.

8. Show that

$$\sinh \frac{m\pi x}{b} = \frac{2}{\pi} \sum_{n=1}^{\infty} \frac{(-1)^n b^2 n}{b^2 n^2 + a^2 m^2} \sinh \frac{m\pi a}{b} \sin \frac{n\pi x}{a} \qquad (-\pi < x < \pi).$$

9. Expand the function

$$f(t) = \begin{cases} 1 & (0 \le t < h) \\ 0 & (h < t < 2\pi) \end{cases} \qquad (h = \text{const})$$

into a complex Fourier series in $(0, 2\pi)$. Having done this, convert the series into real form and show that

$$f(t) = \frac{h}{2\pi} + \frac{1}{\pi} \sum_{n=1}^{\infty} \frac{1}{n} \left[\sin n(h - t) + \frac{1}{n} \sin nt \right].$$

10. Show that the function

$$f(x) = \begin{cases} 1 - x/2h & (0 \le x \le 2h), \\ 0 & (2h < x \le 2\pi) \end{cases}$$

can be represented on the interval $(0, \pi)$ by the Fourier cosine series

$$f(x) = \frac{2h}{\pi} \left[\frac{1}{2} + \sum_{n=1}^{\infty} \left(\frac{\sin nh}{nh} \right)^2 \cos nx \right].$$

What is the corresponding Fourier sine series for the same interval?

11. The Fourier series can be employed to evaluate certain important sums. For instance:

a) Establish that

$$f_1(x) = \frac{\pi - x}{2} = \sum_{n=1}^{\infty} \frac{1}{n} \sin nx.$$

b) Integrate both sides and evaluate the constant of integration to obtain the function $f_2(x)$ such that

$$f_2(x) = \sum_{n=1}^{\infty} (\cos nx/n^2).$$

Can you justify the validity of term-by-term integration?

c) Set $x = 0$, and show that $\sum_{n=1}^{\infty} (1/n^2) = \pi^2/6$.

d) Develop this idea further to establish the result

$$\sum_{n=1}^{\infty} (1/n^4) = \pi^4/90.$$

e) Verify your result in (d) by means of Parseval's equation applied to the function $f_2(x)$ obtained in (b).

12. A damped harmonic oscillator under the influence of an external periodic force $f(t)$ obeys the differential equation

$$m\ddot{x} + \lambda\dot{x} + kx = f(t).$$

Assuming a steady-state solution, solve the problem by the Fourier series method. In particular, develop the explicit series for $x(t)$ if $f(x)$ is the triangular wave of Problem 4 above.

13. A simply supported beam like that shown in Fig. 4.8 is loaded by a variable load (per unit length) $q(x) = (a/L)x$.

a) Show that the deflection is given by

$$y(x) = \frac{2aL^4}{\pi^4 EI} \sum_{n=1}^{\infty} \frac{(-1)^{n+1}}{n^5} \sin \frac{n\pi x}{L}.$$

b) Solve the problem in closed form (integrating the DE) and show that the error for the deflection at the midpoint is only 0.387%, provided only the first Fourier term is used.

14. A periodic (but not harmonic) electromotive force

$$E(t) = \begin{cases} E_0(1 + 4t/T) & (-T/2 \leq t < 0), \\ E_0(1 - 4t/T) & (0 \leq t < T/2) \end{cases}$$

[with $E(t + T) = E(t)$] is applied to the LRC-circuit in Fig. 4.7.

a) Develop the solution for the current $I(t)$ in the following Fourier Series form:

$$I(t) = c_0 + \sum_{n=1}^{\infty} c_n \sin (n\omega t + \phi_n),$$

where $\omega = 2\pi/T$; note the use of sine functions.

b) Let $R = 1.6\,\Omega$, $L = 6.35$ mh, $c = 4\,\mu$f, $E_0 = 12$ V, and $T = 5 \times 10^{-3}$ sec. Prepare your expressions for c_n and $\tan \phi_n$ for rapid numerical calculation, and calculate c_n and $\tan \phi_n$ up to $n = 13$.

c) Explain the physical reason why the amplitude c_5 dominates all the others. Comment on the behavior of ϕ_n.

CHAPTER 5

THE LAPLACE TRANSFORMATION

5.1 OPERATIONAL CALCULUS

The relationship

$$\frac{d}{dx} F(x) = f(x)$$

can be described by the following statement: A certain operation, called differentiation and denoted by d/dx is to be performed on the function $F(x)$; the result of this operation is another function, $f(x)$. To emphasize the treatment of d/dx as an *operator*, it is denoted by D.

After the rules,

$$Dx^n = nx^{n-1},$$

$$D(Ax^n + Bx^m) = AD(x^n) + BD(x^m) \qquad (A, B = \text{const}),$$

are established, one can obtain a derivative of an arbitrary polynomial. In this approach no reference is made to any infinitesimals or limits and the calculation of derivatives is done by formal manipulations.

It has been suggested, notably by Heaviside, that the operator D can be treated in many respects like an ordinary number. Consider the following example: A particular integral of the DE $y'' - 3y' + 2y = x^2$ is sought. The equation is rewritten in operational form as

$$(D^2 - 3D + 2)y = x^2.$$

The quadratic expression in D is factorized,

$$(D - 1)(D - 2)y = x^2,$$

and the equation is "divided" by $(D - 1)(D - 2)$:

$$y = \frac{x^2}{(D - 1)(D - 2)}.$$

Furthermore, the right-hand side of the equation is split into rational fractions,

$$y = \frac{x^2}{D - 2} - \frac{x^2}{D - 1},$$

and the factors $1/(D - 2)$ and $1/(D - 1)$ are "expanded":

$$\frac{1}{D - 1} = -\frac{1}{1 - D} = -1 - D - D^2 - D^3 - \cdots,$$

$$\frac{1}{D - 2} = -\frac{1}{2}\frac{1}{1 - D/2} = -\frac{1}{2} - \frac{D}{4} - \frac{D^2}{8} - \frac{D^3}{16} - \cdots.$$

The function x^2 is operated upon by these "operational series":

$$(-1 - D - D^2 - \cdots)x^2 = -x^2 - 2x - 2,$$

$$\left(-\frac{1}{2} - \frac{D}{4} - \frac{D^2}{8} - \cdots\right)x^2 = -\frac{x^2}{2} - \frac{x}{2} - \frac{1}{4},$$

and the "solution" is obtained:

$$y = \left(-\frac{x^2}{2} - \frac{x}{2} - \frac{1}{4}\right) - (-x^2 - 2x - 2) = \frac{x^2}{2} + \frac{3}{2}x + \frac{7}{4}.$$

The remarkable result of these liberties taken with the operation of obtaining the derivative is that the function $y(x) = \frac{1}{2}x^2 + \frac{3}{2}x + \frac{7}{4}$ is *indeed* a particular integral of $y'' - 3y' + 2y = x^2$, as can be verified by substitution. It is not difficult to find many other examples where such an astonishing procedure will work. On the other hand, it is evidently meaningless as a *general theory* of differential calculus.

It has been found that the operations employed above are closely related to the properties of the so-called Laplace integral,

$$\int_0^\infty e^{-sx} f(x)\, dx,$$

and the theory of this integral may provide a basis for the understanding of operational calculus.

5.2 THE LAPLACE INTEGRAL

If a function $f(t)$ is defined in the region $0 \le t < \infty$, where t and $f(t)$ are real, then the function $F(s)$, defined by the *Laplace integral*

$$F(s) = \int_0^\infty e^{-st} f(t)\, dt \qquad (s = \text{complex}),$$

is known as the *Laplace transform* of $f(t)$. Symbolically,

$$F(s) = \mathcal{L}\{f(t)\},$$

emphasizing the point of view that $F(s)$ is a result of a certain operation (as defined above) performed on a function $f(t)$.

Remark. In many applications the variable s may be restricted to real values. However, it is convenient to work with the general case of complex s.

Examples

1. $f(t) = t$, $F(s) = \int_0^\infty te^{-st}\,dt = 1/s^2$ (Re $s > 0$).

Observe that if s is complex and $s = \sigma + i\omega$, then

$$F(s) = \int_0^\infty te^{-\sigma t}e^{-i\omega t}\,dt$$

$$= \int_0^\infty te^{-\sigma t}\cos \omega t\,dt - i\int_0^\infty te^{-\sigma t}\sin \omega t\,dt.$$

Both integrals converge if $\sigma > 0$ and diverge if $\sigma \leq 0$. For $\sigma > 0$, the actual evaluation is conveniently done in the complex form (using integration by parts).

2. $f(t) = 1$, $F(s) = \int_0^\infty e^{-st}\,dt = 1/s$ (Re $s > 0$),

Using integration by parts and induction,

3. $f(t) = t^n$ ($n =$ integer), $F(s) = \int_0^\infty t^n e^{-st}\,dt = n!/s^{n+1}$ (Re $s > 0$).

Using the definition of gamma function,

4. $f(t) = t^\alpha$ ($\alpha > -1$), $F(s) = \dfrac{\Gamma(\alpha + 1)}{s^{\alpha+1}}$ (Re $s > 0$).

5. $f(t) = e^{at}$, $F(s) = \dfrac{1}{s - a}$ (Re $s > a$),

6. $f(t) = \sin kt$, $F(s) = \dfrac{k}{s^2 + k^2}$ (Re $s > 0$),

7. $f(t) = \cos kt$, $F(s) = \dfrac{s}{s^2 + k^2}$ (Re $s > 0$).

From these examples, it is evident that the Laplace integral converges, as a rule, for a restricted region of s (in the complex s-plane). It is a general feature of the Laplace integral that this region can be characterized by Re $s > \alpha$, where α is some real constant. In other words, the Laplace integral converges to the right of some vertical line in the s-plane (Fig. 5.1).

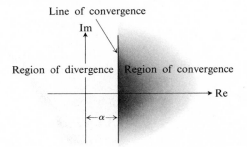

Figure 5.1

Of course, there are functions for which the Laplace integral diverges for all values of s; in other words, these functions do not possess a Laplace transform. For instance, $f(t) = e^{t^2}$. The integral $\int_0^\infty e^{t^2-st}\, dt$ diverges for all (complex) s. Thus the first problem in the theory of Laplace transforms is to determine the class of functions and the values of s for which the transform exists.

Definition 1. A function defined on the (infinite) interval $a \leq t < \infty$ is called *piecewise continuous* on (a, ∞) if for every *finite* interval $a \leq t \leq b$ the function has a *finite* number of discontinuities such that at each discontinuity $t = t_0$ the limits $f(t_0 + 0)$ and $f(t_0 - 0)$ exist.

Remark. This is an extension of the definition of piecewise continuity in the finite interval employed in Section 4.6.

Definition 2. A function $f(t)$, defined on the interval $a \leq t < \infty$, is said to be of *exponential order* σ_0 if

$$|e^{-\sigma_0 t} f(t)| \leq M \qquad (\sigma_0 = \text{real}),$$

where M is a (real positive) constant. In plain terms, $f(t)$ does not increase faster than $e^{\sigma_0 t}$ (for some σ_0) as $t \to \infty$.

Existence theorem. If $f(t)$ is piecewise continuous for $0 \leq t < \infty$ and is of exponential order σ_0, then the Laplace integral

$$F(s) = \mathcal{L}\{f(t)\} = \int_0^\infty e^{-st} f(t)\, dt$$

converges for $\text{Re } s > \sigma_0$. Moreover, the integral is absolutely and uniformly convergent for $\text{Re } s \geq \sigma_1$ ($\sigma_1 = $ real), where $\sigma_1 > \sigma_0$.

Proof. Let $s = \sigma + i\omega$ and consider

$$G_R(s) = \int_0^R e^{-\sigma t} |f(t)|\, dt = \int_0^R |e^{-st}|\, |f(t)|\, dt.$$

There is a finite number of discontinuities (say, m) within $0 \leq t \leq R$; denote them by $t_1, t_2, \ldots, t_m$, and, furthermore, let $t_0 = 0$. Then

$$G_R(s) = \int_0^R e^{-\sigma t} |f(t)|\, dt = \sum_{i=0}^m \int_{t_i}^{t_{i+1}} e^{-\sigma t} |f(t)|\, dt + \int_{t_m}^R e^{-\sigma t} |f(t)|\, dt$$

$$\leq \sum_{i=0}^m M \int_{t_i}^{t_{i+1}} e^{-(\sigma-\sigma_0)t}\, dt + M \int_{t_m}^R e^{-(\sigma-\sigma_0)t}\, dt$$

using Definition 2. Integration yields

$$G_R(s) \leq \frac{M}{\sigma - \sigma_0} \sum_{i=0}^m e^{-(\sigma-\sigma_0)t} \Big|_{t_i}^{t_{i+1}} + \frac{M}{\sigma - \sigma_0} e^{-(\sigma-\sigma_0)t} \Big|_{t_m}^R$$

$$= \frac{M}{\sigma - \sigma_0} [1 - e^{-(\sigma-\sigma_0)R}] \leq \frac{M}{\sigma - \sigma_0},$$

since the terms in the sum cancel by pairs. The bound $M/(\sigma - \sigma_0)$ is independent of R. Therefore, the function $G_R(s)$ is bounded as $R \to \infty$. Since it is monotone nondecreasing (a nonnegative integrand), it must approach a limit:

$$\lim_{R \to \infty} G_R(s) = \lim_{R \to \infty} \int_0^R |e^{-st} f(t)| \, dt$$

$$= \int_0^\infty |e^{-st} f(t)| \, dt = G(s).$$

The existence of $G(s)$ implies absolute convergence of the Laplace integral and, therefore, the existence of the Laplace transform

$$\mathcal{L}\{f(t)\} = \int_0^\infty e^{-st} f(t) \, dt \qquad (\text{Re } s > \sigma_0).$$

The uniform convergence for $\text{Re } s \geq \sigma_1$ (with $\sigma_1 > \sigma_0$) is established by the Weierstrass M-test for the integrals:

$$\int_0^R |e^{-st} f(t)| \, dt \leq \int_0^R |e^{-\sigma_1 t} f(t)| \, dt \qquad (\text{for all } R).$$

Observe that the Laplace integral is convergent in the *open* region $\text{Re } s > \sigma_0$, but uniformly convergent in the *closed* region $\text{Re } s \geq \sigma_1$ (where $\sigma_1 > \sigma_0$).

Remark. The property of piecewise continuity ensures the existence of finite integrals (extensions are possible); the property of exponential order ensures the convergence at infinity.

The conditions on $f(t)$ prescribed in the existence theorem are sufficient but not necessary. There exist functions which are not of exponential order but, nevertheless, possess the Laplace transform, for example,

$$f(t) = 2te^{t^2} \cos e^{t^2}.$$

This function is not of exponential order because $e^{t^2} > Me^{\sigma t}$ for sufficiently large t, no matter how large M and σ may be. However, the Laplace integral

$$\int_0^\infty e^{-st} 2te^{t^2} \cos e^{t^2} \, dt$$

does exist for $\text{Re } s > 0$. Indeed, integrating by parts, we have

$$\int_0^\infty e^{-st} 2te^{t^2} \cos e^{t^2} = e^{-st} \sin e^{t^2} \Big|_0^\infty + s \int_0^\infty e^{-st} \sin e^{t^2} \, dt$$

$$= -\sin 1 + s \int_0^\infty e^{-st} \sin e^{t^2} \, dt.$$

Since $|\sin e^{t^2}|$ is bounded the last integral exists for $\text{Re } s > 0$. Therefore $f(t)$ possesses a Laplace transform.

It is fair to say, however, that functions like this are extremely unlikely to appear in physical problems.

5.3 BASIC PROPERTIES OF LAPLACE TRANSFORM

The fundamental feature of the Laplace transform, implied by the very nature of the Laplace integral, is that two functions which are identical in the range $0 \le t < \infty$ but different otherwise have the same Laplace transform.

For instance, the step function

$$S(t) = \begin{cases} 0 & (t < 0), \\ 1 & (t > 0) \end{cases}$$

has the Laplace transform

$$\mathcal{L}\{S(t)\} = \int_0^\infty e^{-st}\, dt = 1/s \qquad (\text{Re } s > 0),$$

which is identical with the Laplace transform of the function $f(t) = 1$ (all t).

In general, the two functions (see Fig. 5.2) $f_1(t) = f(t)$ and $f_2(t) = f(t)S(t)$ will possess the same Laplace transform.

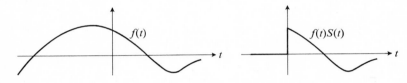

Figure 5.2

Remark. A similar situation occurs in Fourier series: Two functions, $f_1(x)$ and $f_2(x)$, which are identical in the interval $-\pi \le x \le \pi$ but different otherwise will possess the same Fourier series (of period 2π).

As a matter of fact, if a certain function $f(t)$ has Laplace transform $F(s)$, it is *more convenient* to treat $F(s)$ as the Laplace transform of $f(t)S(t)$ rather than of $f(t)$. The reason for this may become clear from the following example:

Suppose that the function $f(t)S(t)$ is "shifted" by a length a *to the right* (Fig. 5.3). The Laplace transform of $f(t - a)S(t - a)$ is

$$\mathcal{L}\{f(t - a)S(t - a)\} = \int_a^\infty e^{-st} f(t - a)S(t - a)\, dt \qquad (a > 0).$$

We make a change of variable, $t = \tau + a$, and obtain

$$\int_a^\infty e^{-st} f(t - a)S(t - a)\, dt = \int_0^\infty e^{-s(\tau+a)} f(\tau)S(\tau)\, d\tau = e^{-as} \int_0^\infty e^{-s\tau} f(\tau)S(\tau)\, d\tau,$$

or

$$\mathcal{L}\{f(t - a)S(t - a)\} = e^{-as}\mathcal{L}\{f(t)\} \qquad (a > 0).$$

This relation is often called the *shifting property* (or the *translation property*): If a function $f(t)$ is "chopped" by multiplication by $S(t)$ and the resulting function $f(t)S(t)$ is translated to the right by an amount a, then the Laplace transform is

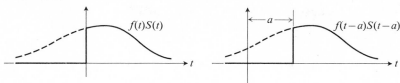

Original $f(t)$ for $t < 0$

Figure 5.3

multiplied by e^{-as}. The reference to "chopping" is then avoided if the above formula is rewritten in the form

$$\mathcal{L}\{f(t - a)S(t - a)\} = e^{-as}\mathcal{L}\{f(t)S(t)\} \qquad (a > 0).$$

It is worthwhile to emphasize the condition $a > 0$. The shifting property *does not hold* for $a < 0$. Whether or not the function $f(t)$ is "chopped," if it is translated to the left, the new transform bears, in general, no relationship to the original one.

Armed with the knowledge of shifting property and observing that

$$\mathcal{L}\{1\} = 1/s, \qquad \mathcal{L}\{e^{at}\} = 1/(s - a) \qquad (\text{Re } s > a),$$

it seems logical to inquire whether an analogous property will exist if $f(t)$ is multiplied by an exponential function. Indeed,

$$\mathcal{L}\{e^{-at}f(t)\} = \int_0^\infty e^{-st}e^{-at}f(t)\, dt = \int_0^\infty e^{-(s+a)t}f(t)\, dt.$$

Setting $s + a = r$, we obtain

$$\int_0^\infty e^{-(s+a)t}f(t)\, dt = F(r) = F(s + a)$$

so that

$$\mathcal{L}\{e^{-at}f(t)\} = F(s + a),$$

where $F(s) = \mathcal{L}\{f(t)\}$. This result may be called the *attenuation property* (or the *substitution property*): If $f(t)$ is "attenuated" by the exponential factor e^{-at}, then the transform is shifted (to the left!) with respect to the variable s. Observe that the attenuation property is valid whether a is positive or negative. However, the transform usually has a different region of existence [as Re $s > a$ for $1/(s - a)$ versus Re $s > 0$ for $1/s$].

Remark. The term "attenuation," borrowed from electrical engineering, ordinarily means multiplication by e^{-at}, where $a > 0$. This is the case in most practical applications, and therefore the name attenuation property is more descriptive than the name substitution property, implying that $s + a$ is substituted for s.

The most important property of the Laplace transform is, perhaps, the simple relationship between $\mathcal{L}\{f(t)\}$ and $\mathcal{L}\{f'(t)\}$. Suppose that $f(t)$ is continuous, and integrate the Laplace integral by parts:

$$\int_0^\infty e^{-st} f(t)\, dt = -\left. (1/s) e^{-st} f(t) \right|_0^\infty + 1/s \int_0^\infty e^{-st} f'(t)\, dt$$

or

$$s \int_0^\infty e^{-st} f(t)\, dt = f(0) + \int_0^\infty e^{-st} f'(t)\, dt.$$

Assuming that $\mathcal{L}\{f'(t)\}$ exists, this may be written as

$$\mathcal{L}\{f'(t)\} = s\mathcal{L}\{f(t)\} - f(0)$$

and is known as the *derivative property*.

Remark. Integration by parts is not permissible unless $f(t)$ is continuous. On the other hand, $f'(t)$ may be piecewise continuous. For an extension of this formula when $f(t)$ is piecewise continuous, see Section 5.7.

The derivative property forms the basis for most applications of the Laplace transform and sheds light on Heaviside's operational calculus.

Example. A particular integral of the DE $y' - y = e^{-x}$ is sought.

Multiply the equation by e^{-sx} and integrate from 0 to ∞. Let

$$\mathcal{L}\{y(x)\} = Y(s).$$

Then, employing the derivative property, deduce

$$[s Y(s) - y(0)] - Y(s) = 1/(s + 1).$$

Suppose that $y(0) = 0$. If an arbitrary particular integral is sought, this choice is just a matter of convenience. Then $(s - 1)Y(s) = 1/(s + 1)$, and

$$Y(s) = \frac{1}{(s + 1)(s - 1)} = \frac{1}{2} \frac{1}{s - 1} - \frac{1}{2} \frac{1}{s + 1}.$$

It is known from the preceding examples that

$$\mathcal{L}\{e^x\} = 1/(s - 1), \quad \text{and} \quad \mathcal{L}\{e^{-x}\} = 1/(s + 1).$$

It follows that $Y(s)$ is the Laplace transform of the function $y(x) = \frac{1}{2} e^x - \frac{1}{2} e^{-x}$, which is, indeed, a particular integral of the given DE.

It is not difficult now to derive a formula for the Laplace transform of the second derivative and, for that matter, of the derivative of any order. Replace $f(t)$ by $f'(t)$ and $f'(t)$ by $f''(t)$ in the derivative property and obtain

$$\mathcal{L}\{f''(t)\} = s\mathcal{L}\{f'(t)\} - f'(0)$$

or

$$\mathcal{L}\{f''(t)\} = s^2 \mathcal{L}\{f(t)\} - sf(0) - f'(0).$$

This formula is valid, of course, provided $f'(t)$ is continuous (and f, f', and f'' have a Laplace transform).

The general formula for the nth derivative, established by induction, reads

$$\mathcal{L}\{f^{(n)}(t)\} = s^n \mathcal{L}\{f(t)\} - \sum_{k=1}^{n} s^{k-1} f^{(n-k)}(0),$$

where $f^{(m)}(t)$ is the mth derivative of $f(t)$ and $f^{(m)}(0)$ is its value at $t = 0$.

5.4 THE INVERSION PROBLEM

The example of the preceding section involving a DE provides a blueprint for the use of the Laplace transform in solving similar problems: The relation satisfied by the unknown function $f(t)$ is subjected to the Laplace transform. The result is a relation satisfied by $F(s) = \mathcal{L}\{f(t)\}$. From this relation $F(s)$ can (in principle) be determined. The third step is to find the unknown function $f(t)$ from its Laplace transform $F(s)$. This last problem involves performing the so-called *inverse Laplace transformation*.

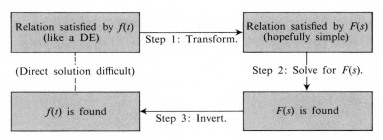

Figure 5.4

The entire idea is very conveniently expressed in the following "flow diagram" (Fig. 5.4). The first step in this scheme is straightforward: Laplace integrals have to be evaluated. The second step, finding $F(s)$, should be rather simple (if it is not, then there is little point in using the Laplace transform at all). The third step is, perhaps, the most difficult one and a variety of methods is used to perform it.

The inversion problem is greatly facilitated by the fact that the Laplace transformation represents a *linear operation*, that is, it has the following two fundamental properties:

a) $\mathcal{L}\{af(t)\} = a\mathcal{L}\{f(t)\}$ ($a = $ const),

b) $\mathcal{L}\{f_1(t) + f_2(t)\} = \mathcal{L}\{f_1(t)\} + \mathcal{L}\{f_2(t)\}$.

These two properties stem from the fact that the operator $\mathcal{L}$ which transforms $f(t)$ into $F(s)$ is an *integral operator*.*

_____

* Properties (a) and (b) are general properties of integrals.

Bearing this in mind, we expect that if a transform $F(s)$ can be split into two parts,

$$F(s) = F_1(s) + F_2(s),$$

then it can be inverted term by term, writing

$$f(t) = f_1(t) + f_2(t),$$

where

$$F_1(s) = \mathcal{L}\{f_1(t)\}, \quad \text{and} \quad F_2(s) = \mathcal{L}\{f_2(t)\}.$$

Symbolically, this is written as

$$\mathcal{L}^{-1}\{F_1(s) + F_2(s)\} = \mathcal{L}^{-1}\{F_1(s)\} + \mathcal{L}^{-1}\{F_2(s)\},$$

where the *inverse operator* $\mathcal{L}^{-1}$ transforms the function $F(s)$ into the corresponding function $f(t)$. Similarly, we expect that

$$\mathcal{L}^{-1}\{aF(s)\} = a\mathcal{L}^{-1}\{F(s)\} \quad (a = \text{const}).$$

These relations mean that $\mathcal{L}^{-1}$ is, presumably, also a linear operator.

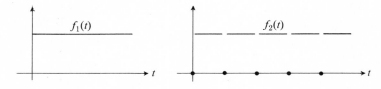

Figure 5.5

Remark. The linearity of $\mathcal{L}$ alone is not sufficient *to prove* that $\mathcal{L}^{-1}$ is linear as well. What it actually implies is that the two functions

$$f(t) = \mathcal{L}^{-1}\{F_1(s) + F_2(s)\} \quad \text{and} \quad \bar{f}(t) = \mathcal{L}^{-1}\{F_1(s)\} + \mathcal{L}^{-1}\{F_2(s)\}$$

have the *same Laplace transform*. However, does it mean that $f(t)$ and $\bar{f}(t)$ are the same? Not necessarily so, even if only the values for $0 \leq t < \infty$ are taken into consideration. For instance, the two functions (Fig. 5.5)

$$f_1(t) = 1 \quad (\text{all } t \geq 0),$$

$$f_2(t) = \begin{cases} 0 & (t = \text{integer}), \\ 1 & (t = \text{not an integer}) \end{cases}$$

are not identical but have the same Laplace transform. The difficulty would disappear if the inverse transform were *unique* (no two different functions can have the same Laplace transform).

From a certain point of view, e.g., a physicist's, functions like $f_2(t)$ are "abnormal" and should not be taken into consideration. Then, perhaps, $f_1(t)$ can be regarded as *the* inverse transform of $F(s) = 1/s$.

To put this idea on a firm basis, various theorems have been proposed. For instance, it can be shown* that if we confine ourselves to (real) functions which are

   a) piecewise continuous and piecewise smooth (i.e., have a piecewise continuous derivative) on $(0, \infty)$,
   b) of exponential order,
   c) defined by $\frac{1}{2}[f(x_0 + 0) + f(x_0 - 0)]$ at each jump discontinuity x_0,

then two such functions possessing the same Laplace transform $F(s)$ must be identical. In other words, the inverse transform is unique within the class of such functions. This theorem is adequate for a great majority of physical problems.

5.5 THE RATIONAL FRACTION DECOMPOSITION

In a large number of practical problems, the function $F(s)$ to be "inverted"† is a rational function of s. In this case, a very general and efficient method can be developed for the solution of the problem, as illustrated below by a series of examples.

Example 1. Find $f(t)$ if $F(s) = 1/(s^2 - 5s + 6)$.

It is easily checked that this function can be decomposed into elementary rational fractions:

$$F(s) = \frac{1}{(s - 2)(s - 3)} = \frac{1}{s - 3} - \frac{1}{s - 2}.$$

In the spirit of the discussion of the preceding section, we can conclude that

$$f(t) = \mathscr{L}^{-1}\left\{\frac{1}{s - 3}\right\} - \mathscr{L}^{-1}\left\{\frac{1}{s - 2}\right\} = e^{3t} - e^{2t}.$$

The idea used above can be applied to all rational functions $F(s)$, namely, functions of the type $F(s) = P(s)/Q(s)$, where $P(s)$ and $Q(s)$ are polynomials in s. Without loss of generality, we may assume that $Q(s)$ is of higher degree than $P(s)$. Indeed, if this were not so, then we could divide $P(s)$ by $Q(s)$ until a remainder of the desired form is obtained, namely,

$$F(s) = R(s) + P_1(s)/Q(s),$$

where $R(s)$ and $P_1(s)$ are polynomials and $Q(s)$ is of higher degree than $P_1(s)$.

---

* See, e.g., Churchill, *Operational Mathematics*, Chapter 6.
† That is, subjected to the inverse Laplace transformation.

Remark. The case deg $P(s) \geq$ deg $Q(s)$ is, actually, not likely to occur in practice since a polynomial $R(s)$ does not possess an inverse Laplace transform.*

The decomposition of a rational function is based on the knowledge of roots of the denominator $Q(s)$. If the coefficients of $Q(s)$ are real, then it is known from algebra that $Q(s)$ can be factorized (apart from a constant factor) into factors of two types:

1. $(s - r)^m$ for each real root r of multiplicity m;
2. $(s^2 + as + b)^n$ for each pair of complex conjugate roots (satisfying $s^2 + as + b = 0$) of multiplicity n.

Corresponding to each real root r there is a set of m terms in the decomposition of $P(s)/Q(s)$, of the type

$$\frac{A_1}{(s - r)} + \frac{A_2}{(s - r)^2} + \frac{A_3}{(s - r)^3} + \cdots + \frac{A_m}{(s - r)^m} \qquad (A_i = \text{const}).$$

Corresponding to each pair of complex conjugate roots, there is a set of terms of the type

$$\frac{B_1 s + C_1}{(s^2 + as + b)} + \frac{B_2 s + C_2}{(s^2 + as + b)^2} + \cdots + \frac{B_n s + C_n}{(s^2 + as + b)^n} \qquad (B_i, C_i = \text{const}).$$

Each of these elementary fractions can be inverted in a straightforward manner, using the attenuation rule and the transforms of the powers of t and trigonometric functions. In particular,

$$\mathcal{L}^{-1}\left\{\frac{A}{(s - r)^k}\right\} = A \frac{t^{k-1}}{(k - 1)!} e^{rt}$$

by the result of Example 3 of Section 5.2 and the attenuation property.

For quadratic factors it is convenient to *complete the square:*

$$s^2 + as + b = (s + a/2)^2 + (b - a^2/4) = (s + a/2)^2 + c^2.$$

[Note that $b - a^2/4 > 0$; otherwise, the roots would not be complex. Therefore c is real.] Then we can write

$$\frac{Bs + C}{s^2 + as + b} = \frac{B(s + a/2) + (C - (a/2)B)}{(s + a/2)^2 + c^2}$$

$$= B \frac{s + a/2}{(s + a/2)^2 + c^2} + \frac{[C - (a/2)B]}{(s + a/2)^2 + c^2}.$$

From the results of Examples 6 and 7 of Section 5.2 and the attenuation rule, we can deduce that

$$\mathcal{L}^{-1}\left\{B \frac{(s + a/2)}{(s + a/2)^2 + c^2}\right\} = Be^{-(a/2)t} \cos ct$$

---

* See, however, the discussion of the delta function in Chapter 6, in particular, p. 232.

and

$$\mathcal{L}^{-1}\left\{\frac{C - (a/2)B}{(s + a/2)^2 + c^2}\right\} = \frac{C - (a/2)B}{c} e^{-(a/2)t} \sin ct.$$

A general inversion formula for

$$\frac{B(s + a/2) + [C - (a/2)B]}{[(s + a/2)^2 + c^2]^k} \qquad (k > 1),$$

can also be derived. However, in the case of multiple complex roots it is probably more convenient to employ the general complex technique used when $Q(s)$ has complex coefficients. In this case there is no need to introduce factors of type 2 in the factorization of $Q(s)$: The polynomial $Q(s)$ can be represented as a product of factors of type 1 with complex roots, and the inversion can be carried out in complex form. If necessary, the final result $f(t)$ can be split into real and imaginary parts at the very end.

Exercise. Show that the attenuation rule is valid even if α in $F(s + \alpha)$ is complex (this is necessary for inversion in the complex form described above).

Example 2. Find $f(t)$ if

$$F(s) = \frac{3s^2 - 2s + 16}{(s - 1)(s + 2)(s - 6)}.$$

The factorization of the denominator is already performed and the decomposition is of the form

$$F(s) = \frac{A}{s - 1} + \frac{B}{s + 2} + \frac{C}{s - 6}.$$

Therefore

$$\frac{A(s + 2)(s - 6) + B(s - 1)(s - 6) + C(s - 1)(s + 2)}{(s - 1)(s + 2)(s - 6)}$$
$$= \frac{3s^2 - 2s + 16}{(s - 1)(s + 2)(s - 6)}.$$

This implies the identity that is valid for *all* s:

$$A(s + 2)(s - 6) + B(s - 1)(s - 6) + C(s - 1)(s + 2) = 3s^2 - 2s + 16.$$

In principle, we could obtain A, B, and C by equating the coefficients of powers of s. However, this is not the quickest method:* It is more profitable to observe that since the above equation holds for all values of s, we may set s equal to any number we please.

If we set $s = 1$, we immediately obtain

$$A(1 + 2)(1 - 6) = 3 - 2 + 16, \qquad \text{or} \qquad A = -\tfrac{17}{15}.$$

---

* It leads to three equations with three unknowns. For more complicated rational functions, this method is quite cumbersome.

Similarly, with $s = -2$, we obtain $B = \frac{8}{9}$, and with $s = 6$, we obtain $C = \frac{19}{10}$. The remainder of the problem (inversion) is straightforward:

$$f(t) = -\tfrac{17}{15}e^t + \tfrac{8}{9}e^{-2t} + \tfrac{19}{10}e^{6t}.$$

It is not difficult to see that this method will produce quick results whenever $Q(s)$ has simple roots. In fact, this situation can be disposed of once and for all by the following formulas:

$$Q(s) = A \prod_{i=1}^{n} (s - r_i) \qquad (A = \text{const}), \tag{1}$$

where the symbol $\prod$ designates the product of n factors,

$$\prod_{i=1}^{n} (s - r_i) = (s - r_1)(s - r_2) \cdots (s - r_n),$$

with $r_i(i = 1, 2, 3, \ldots n)$ being the n (simple) roots of $Q(s)$;

$$F(s) = P(s)/Q(s) = 1/A \sum_{i=1}^{n} A_i/(s - r_i); \tag{2}$$

$$A_j = P(r_j)/\prod_{i \neq j}^{n} (r_j - r_i) \qquad (j = 1, 2, \ldots, n), \tag{3}$$

where the symbol

$$\prod_{i \neq j}^{n}$$

means that the product is taken from $i = 1$ to $i = n$, but with the factor corresponding to $i = j$ omitted. Furthermore,

$$f(t) = (1/A) \sum_{i=1}^{n} A_i e^{r_i t}. \tag{4}$$

This extremely helpful result is sometimes called the *Heaviside expansion theorem*. An alternative form of this theorem reads: If all roots r_i of $Q(s)$ are simple, and if the degree of $P(s)$ is less than the degree of $Q(s)$, then

$$\mathcal{L}^{-1} \left\{ \frac{P(s)}{Q(s)} \right\} = \sum_{i=1}^{n} \frac{P(r_i)}{Q'(r_i)} e^{r_i t},$$

where $Q'(r_i)$ is the derivative of $Q(s)$ evaluated at $s = r_i$.

This form of the theorem follows from the fact that if

$$Q(s) = A \prod_{i=1}^{n} (s - r_i),$$

then

$$Q'(r_j) = A \prod_{i \neq j}^{n} (r_j - r_i)$$

(as verified by elementary calculus).

Example 3. Find $f(t)$ if $F(s) = 1/(s^3 + s^2 + s + 1)$.

Although $Q(s)$ is not written in factorized form, our knowledge of algebra should tell us that if $Q(s)$ is multiplied by $s - 1$, then

$$(s - 1)(s^3 + s^2 + s + 1) = s^4 - 1.$$

Therefore

$$F(s) = \frac{s - 1}{s^4 - 1} = \frac{s - 1}{(s^2 + 1)(s + 1)(s - 1)} = \frac{1}{(s^2 + 1)(s + 1)}.$$

Although the real decomposition

$$F(s) = \frac{A'}{s + 1} + \frac{B's + C'}{s^2 + 1}$$

is available, we shall employ the complex decomposition

$$F(s) = \frac{A}{s + 1} + \frac{B}{s + i} + \frac{C}{s - i}.$$

By using the Heaviside expansion theorem, we find that

$$A = \frac{1}{(-1 + i)(-1 - i)} = \frac{1}{2},$$

$$B = \frac{1}{(-i + 1)(-i - i)} = \frac{1}{4}(-1 + i),$$

$$C = \frac{1}{(i + 1)(i + i)} = \frac{1}{4}(-1 - i),$$

so that

$$f(t) = \frac{1}{2} e^{-t} + \frac{(-1 + i)}{4} e^{-it} + \frac{(-1 - i)}{4} e^{it}.$$

This expression is easily brought to real form:

$$f(t) = \tfrac{1}{2}e^{-t} - \tfrac{1}{2}\cos t + \tfrac{1}{2}\sin t.$$

Example 4. Find $f(t)$, given that $F(s) = s^2/(s - 1)^3$.

According to the rules of algebra, $F(s)$ can be decomposed into elementary fractions:

$$F(s) = \frac{A}{(s - 1)} + \frac{B}{(s - 1)^2} + \frac{C}{(s - 1)^3}.$$

Then

$$F(s) = \frac{A(s - 1)^2 + B(s - 1) + C}{(s - 1)^3} = \frac{s^2}{(s - 1)^3}$$

implies that

$$A(s - 1)^2 + B(s - 1) + C = s^2.$$

According to the idea of Example 2, we can obtain C easily by setting $s = 1$; then $C = 1$.

However, any other value of s will yield a system of equations for A and B. Can we obtain A and B by an easier method? Our experience in calculus may suggest that we *differentiate* our relation with respect to s: If it holds for all s, then

$$2A(s - 1) + B = 2s$$

must also hold for all s. If we set $s = 1$ *now* we immediately obtain $B = 2$. In the same spirit, we can differentiate once more and obtain $2A = 2$, so that $A = 1$. Our result is then

$$F(s) = \frac{s^2}{(s - 1)^3} = \frac{1}{(s - 1)} + \frac{2}{(s - 1)^2} + \frac{1}{(s - 1)^3},$$

so that

$$f(t) = e^t + e^t 2t + e^t \tfrac{1}{2} t^2 = e^t (1 + 2t + t^2/2).$$

The idea employed in this example may be generalized and expressed in terms of the following theorem:

General Heaviside theorem. Let $F(s) = P(s)/Q(s)$, where $P(s)$ and $Q(s)$ are polynomials and the degree of $Q(s)$ is greater than the degree of $P(s)$, and let $s = r$ be a root of $Q(s)$ of multiplicity m ($m \geq 1$). Then $F(s)$ can be decomposed as follows:

$$F(s) = H(s) + \sum_{k=1}^{m} \frac{A_k}{(s - r)^k},$$

where $H(s)$ is finite at $s = r$ (it may be zero) and

$$A_k = \frac{1}{(m - k)!} \frac{d^{m-k}}{ds^{m-k}} G(s),$$

with $G(s)$ defined by $G(s) = F(s)(s - r)^m$.

Observe the similarity of the expression for A_k with the formula for the residue (if $k = 1$) of a function having a pole of order m.

Exercise. Prove the general Heaviside theorem. [*Hint:* Consider $F(s)$ as a function of the complex variable s. Show that it can have only isolated singularities and consider a Laurent expansion about one of them.]

5.6 THE CONVOLUTION THEOREM

Consider the problem of forced oscillations of a (damped) harmonic oscillator. It is described by the DE

$$\ddot{x} + 2\lambda \dot{x} + \omega_0^2 x = f(t) \qquad (\dot{x} = dx/dt, \text{ etc.})$$

and initial conditions such as $x(0) = x_0$ and $\dot{x}(0) = v_0$. The Laplace transform method calls for taking the transform of the DE,

$$s^2 X(s) - sx_0 - v_0 + 2\lambda s X(s) - 2\lambda x_0 + \omega_0^2 X(s) = F(s),$$

where $F(s) = \mathcal{L}\{f(t)\}$ is known, and $X(s) = \mathcal{L}\{x(t)\}$ is sought.
This equation is now solved for $X(s)$:

$$X(s) = \frac{2\lambda x_0 + v_0 + sx_0}{s^2 + 2\lambda s + \omega_0^2} + \frac{F(s)}{s^2 + 2\lambda s + \omega_0^2} = X_1(s) + X_2(s).$$

The first term may be inverted once and for all. It is logical to expect, and easy to verify, that it gives rise to the solution of the *homogeneous equation* with the given initial conditions $x(0) = x_0$, $\dot{x}(0) = v_0$. Indeed, use the technique of rational fractions:

$$\frac{2\lambda x_0 + v_0 + sx_0}{s^2 + 2\lambda s + \omega_0^2} = \frac{x_0(s + \lambda)}{(s + \lambda)^2 + (\omega_0^2 - \lambda^2)} + \frac{v_0 + \lambda x_0}{(s + \lambda)^2 + (\omega_0^2 - \lambda^2)},$$

tacitly assuming, just to be specific, that $\omega_0^2 > \lambda^2$ so that the roots are complex; this is the more common case in practice. The right-hand side of this equation is the transform of

$$x_1(t) = x_0 e^{-\lambda t} \cos \omega t + \frac{v_0 + \lambda x_0}{\omega} e^{-\lambda t} \sin \omega t \qquad (\omega = \sqrt{\omega_0^2 - \lambda^2}),$$

and this function does indeed satisfy the homogeneous equation and the stated initial conditions.

The entire problem, then, reduces to the inversion of

$$X_2(s) = \frac{F(s)}{s^2 + 2\lambda s + \omega_0^2}.$$

We have seen that the function $x_2(t) = \mathcal{L}^{-1}\{X_2(s)\}$ represents the *response* of the harmonic oscillator to the external influence characterized by the function $f(t)$ [or its transform $F(s)$]. Moreover, the function $x_2(t)$ is expected to satisfy the initial conditions $x_2(0) = 0$, $\dot{x}_2(0) = 0$, in order that the entire solution will satisfy the given initial conditions. In other words, it represents the response to the function $f(t)$ of a harmonic oscillator *initially at rest*.

From the point of view of the general theory of differential equations, the function $x_2(t)$ is then a *particular integral* of the nonhomogeneous equation, while $x_1(t)$ is a complementary function.

Remark. A subtle difference between the decomposition of $x(t)$ into two parts in the Laplace transform method and the complementary function method is that in the former case both parts have specified initial conditions. In the latter case this is not so and the adjustment of arbitrary constants is made at the very end.

Now we turn to the general problem of inverting

$$X_2(s) = \frac{F(s)}{s^2 + 2\lambda s + \omega_0^2}.$$

The structure of $X_2(s)$ is always the same: It is a *product* of two functions of s, namely,

$$F(s) \quad \text{and} \quad G(s) = \frac{1}{s^2 + 2\lambda s + \omega_0^2}.$$

The inverses of these two functions are known: One is $f(t)$ and the other is

$$g(t) = \mathcal{L}^{-1}\left\{\frac{1}{s^2 + 2\lambda s + \omega_0^2}\right\} = \frac{1}{\omega} e^{-\lambda t} \sin \omega t \qquad (\omega = \sqrt{\omega_0^2 - \lambda^2}).$$

Remark. The function on the right-hand side vanishes at $t = 0$, but its derivative does not. This may seem like a contradiction of a previous statement if we set $F(s) = 1$. However, such a conclusion is premature because $F(s)$ is not an *arbitrary* function of s, but rather a transform of some $f(t)$. This actually *rules out* the possibility $F(s) = 1$ because a function such that $\mathcal{L}\{f(t)\} = 1$ *does not exist.*†

The fundamental problem now is to find $\mathcal{L}^{-1}\{F(s)G(s)\}$ if $\mathcal{L}^{-1}\{F(s)\} = f(t)$ and $\mathcal{L}^{-1}\{G(s)\} = g(t)$ are known. The answer lies in the so-called *convolution theorem.*‡

Definition. *A convolution of the two functions $f(t)$ and $g(t)$ is denoted by $(f * g)$ and is defined by*

$$(f * g) \equiv \int_0^t f(\tau)g(t - \tau)\, d\tau.$$

Note that $(f * g) = (g * f)$ which is easily verified by the change of variable $u = t - \tau$. The geometrical illustration of this concept is as follows: Suppose that two functions $f(\tau)$ and $g(\tau)$ are given (Fig. 5.6a). The curve $g(\tau)$ is imagined

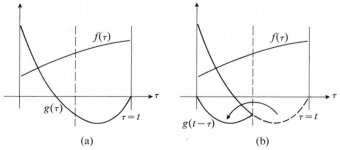

(a)   (b)

Figure 5.6

---

† See, however, p. 232.

‡ Or *Faltung theorem*, based on the German word *faltung*, meaning "folding" in English.

to be drawn on a separate sheet of paper which is folded to the left, along the line $\tau = t/2$ (Fig. 5.6b) yielding the curve $g(t - \tau)$ for $0 \le \tau \le t/2$. Similar folding to the right will produce $g(t - \tau)$ for $t/2 \le \tau \le t$ (Fig. 5.7). A better description of this process would be, perhaps, a *reflection of* $g(\tau)$ *with respect to the line* $\tau = t/2$.

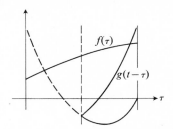

Figure 5.7

Theorem 1. If $f(t)$ and $g(t)$ are piecewise continuous and of exponential orders α and β, then their convolution $(f * g)$ is continuous and of exponential order $\gamma = \max(\alpha, \beta) + \epsilon$, where ϵ is positive but arbitrarily small.

Proof. Evidently, $f(\tau)g(t - \tau)$ is piecewise continuous for $0 \le \tau \le t$. Therefore, the convolution integral $\int_0^t f(\tau)g(t - \tau)\,d\tau$ is a continuous function of t.† Moreover, from

$$|f(\tau)| \le M_1 e^{\alpha\tau} \qquad (|g(\tau)| \le M_2 e^{\beta\tau}),$$

it follows that

$$\left| \int_0^t f(\tau)g(t - \tau)\,d\tau \right| \le \int_0^t M_1 e^{\alpha\tau} M_2 e^{\beta(t-\tau)}\,d\tau$$

$$= M_1 M_2 e^{\beta t}\, \frac{e^{(\alpha-\beta)t} - 1}{\alpha - \beta} \qquad (\alpha \ne \beta).$$

If $\alpha > \beta$, then

$$\frac{e^{(\alpha-\beta)t} - 1}{\alpha - \beta} < \frac{e^{(\alpha-\beta)t}}{\alpha - \beta},$$

so that

$$|(f * g)| \le \frac{M_1 M_2}{(\alpha - \beta)} e^{\alpha t} \quad \text{(as desired)}.$$

If $\alpha < \beta$, then

$$\frac{e^{(\alpha-\beta)t} - 1}{\alpha - \beta} = \frac{1 - e^{-(\beta-\alpha)t}}{\beta - \alpha} \le \frac{1}{\beta - \alpha},$$

so that

$$|(f * g)| \le \frac{M_1 M_2}{\beta - \alpha} e^{\beta t} \quad \text{(as desired)}.$$

Finally, if $\alpha = \beta$, then

$$\left| \int_0^t f(\tau)g(t - \tau)\,d\tau \right| \le t M_1 M_2 e^{\alpha t}.$$

---

† Consult the theory of the Riemann integral in texts on advanced calculus.

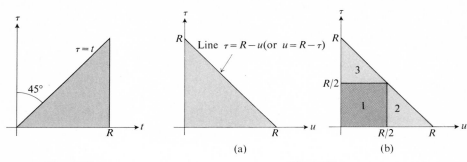

Figure 5.8   **Figure 5.9**

However, $t < M_3 e^{\epsilon t}$ for arbitrary $\epsilon > 0$ and some M_3 (depending on ϵ, but not on t). Therefore

$$|(f * g)| \le M_1 M_2 M_3 e^{(\alpha + \epsilon)t} \quad \text{(as desired)}.$$

Theorem 2 (*Convolution Theorem*). If $f(t)$ and $g(t)$ are piecewise continuous and of exponential orders α and β, then

$$\mathcal{L}\{(f * g)\} = F(s)G(s) \qquad [\text{Re } s > \max(\alpha, \beta)],$$

where $F(s) = \mathcal{L}\{f(t)\}$ and $G(s) = \mathcal{L}\{g(t)\}$.

Proof. By Theorem 1, $\mathcal{L}\{(f * g)\}$ exists and is defined by

$$\mathcal{L}\{(f * g)\} = \lim_{R \to \infty} \int_0^R e^{-st}\, dt \int_0^t f(\tau) g(t - \tau)\, d\tau = \lim_{R \to \infty} I_R.$$

Consider the (finite) integral I_R and transform it as follows: I_R is a double integral over the shaded triangle in Fig. 5.8. Interchange the order of integration:

$$I_R = \int_0^R d\tau \int_\tau^R e^{-st} f(\tau) g(t - \tau)\, dt = \int_0^R f(\tau)\, d\tau \int_\tau^R e^{-st} g(t - \tau)\, dt.$$

Perform the change of variable $t - \tau = u$, $dt = du$, to show that

$$I_R = \int_0^R f(\tau)\, d\tau \int_0^{R-\tau} e^{-s(u+\tau)} g(u)\, du.$$

The region of integration in the $u\tau$-plane is shown in Fig. 5.9(a). Split this region into three parts as in Fig. 5.9(b) and write

$$I_R = I_{R1} + I_{R2} + I_{R3} = \int_0^{R/2} e^{-st} f(\tau)\, d\tau \int_0^{R/2} e^{-su} g(u)\, du$$

$$+ \int_0^{R/2} e^{-s\tau} f(\tau)\, d\tau \int_{R/2}^{R-\tau} e^{-su} g(u)\, du + \int_{R/2}^R e^{-s\tau} f(\tau) \int_0^{R-\tau} e^{-su} g(u)\, du.$$

Let $R \to \infty$ and observe that

$$\lim_{R \to \infty} I_{R1} = \lim_{R/2 \to \infty} \int_0^{R/2} e^{-s\tau} f(\tau)\, d\tau \lim_{R/2 \to \infty} \int_0^{R/2} e^{-su} g(u)\, du = F(s)G(s).$$

It remains for us to show that $\lim_{R \to \infty} I_{R2} = 0$ and $\lim_{R \to \infty} I_{R3} = 0$. Indeed,

$$|I_{R2}| \leq \int_0^{R/2} e^{-s\tau} |f(\tau)|\, d\tau \int_{R/2}^{R-\tau} e^{-su} |g(u)|\, du$$

$$\leq \int_0^{R/2} e^{-s\tau} |f(\tau)|\, d\tau \int_{R/2}^{R} e^{-su} |g(u)|\, du.$$

Since the integral

$$\int_0^{\infty} e^{-su} |g(u)|\, du$$

converges (by the existence theorem), the Cauchy criterion for improper integrals implies that

$$\int_{R/2}^{R} e^{-su} |g(u)|\, du < \epsilon \qquad \text{(for any } \epsilon > 0\text{)}$$

for $R = $ sufficiently large, and

$$|I_{R2}| \leq \epsilon \int_0^{R/2} e^{-st} |f(\tau)|\, d\tau.$$

Since the integral on the right-hand side converges, it is bounded,

$$\int_0^{R/2} e^{-s\tau} |f(\tau)|\, d\tau \leq B \qquad \text{(all } R\text{)}$$

so that $|I_{R2}| \leq \epsilon B$, where B is independent of R, and ϵ is arbitrarily small for sufficiently large R. Therefore

$$\lim_{R \to \infty} I_{R2} = 0.$$

A similar argument holds for I_{R3}, and this completes the derivation.

Example 1. We can now complete the solution of the harmonic oscillator problem. Knowing that

$$\mathcal{L}^{-1}\{F(s)\} = f(t), \qquad \mathcal{L}^{-1}\left\{\frac{1}{s^2 + 2\lambda s + \omega_0^2}\right\} = \frac{1}{\omega} e^{-\lambda t} \sin \omega t \quad (\omega = \sqrt{\omega_0^2 - \lambda^2}),$$

and using the convolution theorem

$$\mathcal{L}^{-1}\{F(s)G(s)\} = \int_0^t f(\tau) g(t - \tau)\, d\tau,$$

we can write

$$\mathcal{L}^{-1}\left\{\frac{F(s)}{s^2 + 2\lambda s + \omega_0^2}\right\} = \int_0^t \frac{1}{\omega} e^{-\lambda(t-\tau)} \sin \omega(t - \tau) f(\tau)\, d\tau,$$

so that the complete solution reads

$$x(t) = x_0 e^{-\lambda t} \cos \omega t + \frac{v_0 + \lambda x_0}{\omega} e^{-\lambda t} \sin \omega t$$

$$+ \frac{1}{\omega} \int_0^t e^{-\lambda(t-\tau)} \sin \omega(t - \tau) f(\tau) \, d\tau.$$

This function satisfies the nonhomogeneous DE and the conditions $x(0) = x_0$, and $\dot{x}(0) = v_0$.

Example 2. Find the inverse transform of $F(s) = 1/(s^2 + c^2)^2$ ($c = $ const).

Since the inverse transform of $(s^2 + c^2)^{-1}$ is known,

$$\mathcal{L}^{-1}\left\{\frac{1}{s^2 + c^2}\right\} = \frac{1}{c} \sin ct,$$

we can find the inverse of $F(s)$ by the convolution theorem:

$$\mathcal{L}^{-1}\left\{\frac{1}{s^2 + c^2} \frac{1}{s^2 + c^2}\right\} = \int_0^t \frac{1}{c} \sin c\tau \frac{1}{c} \sin c(t - \tau) \, d\tau.$$

Evaluating the integral

$$\int_0^t \sin c\tau \sin c(t - \tau) \, d\tau = \sin ct \int_0^t \sin c\tau \cos c\tau \, d\tau - \cos c\tau \int_0^t \sin^2 c\tau \, d\tau$$

$$= \sin ct \frac{1 - \cos 2ct}{4c} - \cos ct \frac{2ct - \sin 2ct}{4c},$$

we can obtain

$$\mathcal{L}^{-1}\left\{\frac{1}{(s^2 + c^2)^2}\right\} = \frac{1}{2c^3} (\sin ct - ct \cos ct).$$

5.7 ADDITIONAL PROPERTIES OF LAPLACE TRANSFORM

Since $\mathcal{L}\{f'(t)\}$ is simply related to $\mathcal{L}\{f(t)\}$, it follows that $\mathcal{L}\{\int^t f(\tau) \, d\tau\}$ should be simply related to $\mathcal{L}\{f(t)\}$.

The primitive function theorem. If the function $f(t)$ is piecewise continuous and of exponential order α, then

$$\mathcal{L}\left\{\int_0^t f(\tau) \, d\tau\right\} = \frac{1}{s} F(s) \qquad \left[\text{Re } s > \frac{1}{2} (\alpha + |\alpha|)\right],$$

where $F(s) = \mathcal{L}\{f(t)\}$. This theorem follows readily from the convolution theorem by treating $1/s$ as $G(s)$.

Example. Find $f(t)$ if $F(s) = 1/(s^2 + as)$.

Instead of using the rational fraction decomposition, we can write

$$F(s) = (1/s)[1/(s + a)]$$

and deduce that

$$f(t) = \int_0^t e^{-a\tau} d\tau = \frac{1 - e^{-at}}{a}.$$

If the Laplace transform of a general *indefinite integral* of $f(t)$,

$$g(t) = \int_a^t f(\tau) d\tau \qquad (t > a \geq 0),$$

is desired and written as $G(s) = \mathcal{L}\{g(t)\}$, then integrating by parts, we obtain

$$\int_0^\infty e^{-st} f(t) dt = e^{-st} g(t) \Big|_0^\infty + s \int_0^\infty e^{-st} g(t) dt.$$

If $g(t)$ is of exponential order, then for Re $s > \beta$ (some β),

$$\lim_{t \to \infty} e^{-st} g(t) = 0.$$

Therefore

$$F(s) = -g(0) + sG(s),$$

or

$$G(s) = \frac{F(s)}{s} - \frac{1}{s} \int_0^a f(t) dt \qquad (t > a \geq 0).$$

It now remains for us to inquire when $g(t)$ is of exponential order. If $f(t)$ is of exponential order α, then

$$|g(t)| = \left| \int_a^t f(\tau) d\tau \right| \leq M \int_a^t e^{\alpha\tau} d\tau = M \frac{e^{\alpha t} - e^{\alpha a}}{\alpha},$$

so that $g(t)$ is of exponential order α if $\alpha > 0$, and of exponential order zero if $\alpha < 0$, and of exponential order ϵ (any $\epsilon > 0$) if $\alpha = 0$.

Example. Suppose that we wish to find the Laplace transform of

$$g(t) = \text{erf} (t\sqrt{a}) = \frac{2}{\sqrt{\pi}} \int_0^{t\sqrt{a}} e^{-u^2} du = \frac{2\sqrt{a}}{\sqrt{\pi}} \int_0^t e^{-av^2} dv.$$

As a first step, we find, by direct integration, the transform of $f(t) = e^{-at^2} (a > 0)$:

$$\mathcal{L}\{e^{-at^2}\} = \int_0^\infty e^{-st} e^{-at^2} dt = \int_0^\infty e^{-(at^2 + st)} dt.$$

In cases like this the technique of *completing the square* is found to be convenient:

$$at^2 + st = (t\sqrt{a} + s/2\sqrt{a})^2 - s^2/4a.$$

Therefore

$$\mathcal{L}\{e^{-at^2}\} = e^{s^2/4a} \int_0^\infty e^{-(t\sqrt{a}+s/2\sqrt{a})^2} \, dt.$$

Now, set $(t\sqrt{a} + s/2\sqrt{a}) = u$, and obtain

$$\mathcal{L}\{e^{-at^2}\} = e^{s^2/4a} \frac{1}{\sqrt{a}} \int_{s/2\sqrt{a}}^\infty e^{-u^2} \, du = \frac{\sqrt{\pi}}{2\sqrt{a}} e^{s^2/4a} \operatorname{erfc} \frac{s}{2\sqrt{a}}.$$

Since

$$\int_0^t e^{-a\tau^2} \, d\tau = \frac{\sqrt{\pi}}{2\sqrt{a}} \operatorname{erf}(t\sqrt{a}),$$

the primitive function theorem can be applied and we can deduce that

$$\mathcal{L}\{\operatorname{erf}(t\sqrt{a})\} = \frac{2\sqrt{a}}{\sqrt{\pi}} \mathcal{L}\left\{\int_0^t e^{-a\tau^2} \, d\tau\right\} = \frac{2\sqrt{a}}{\sqrt{\pi}} \frac{1}{s} \mathcal{L}\{e^{-at^2}\}$$

so that

$$\mathcal{L}\{\operatorname{erf}(t\sqrt{a})\} = \frac{1}{s} e^{s^2/4a} \operatorname{erfc} \frac{s}{2\sqrt{a}}.$$

Sometimes an occasion arises for us to employ the differentiation or integration of transforms: The expression

$$F(s) = \int_0^\infty e^{-st} f(t) \, dt$$

is a uniformly convergent integral for a suitable range of values of s (see the existence theorem). Therefore

$$\frac{dF(s)}{ds} = -\int_0^\infty t e^{-st} f(t) \, dt \quad \text{or} \quad \frac{dF}{ds} = -\mathcal{L}\{tf(t)\}.$$

This formula can be generalized:

$$\frac{d^n F}{ds^n} = (-1)^n \mathcal{L}\{t^n f(t)\}.$$

Let us suppose now that $F(s) = \mathcal{L}\{f(t)\}$ and we wish to integrate $F(s)$. In particular, consider

$$G(s) = \int_s^\infty F(\sigma) \, d\sigma.$$

By definition,

$$G(s) = \int_s^\infty d\sigma \int_0^\infty e^{-\sigma t} f(t) \, dt.$$

By uniform convergence, the order of integration can be interchanged and

$$G(s) = \int_0^\infty f(t)\, dt \int_s^\infty e^{-\sigma t}\, d\sigma = \int_0^\infty f(t)\, \frac{e^{-st}}{t}\, dt.$$

In other words,

$$\int_s^\infty F(\sigma)\, d\sigma = \mathcal{L}\left\{ \frac{1}{t}\, f(t) \right\}.$$

Example. Evaluate $\mathcal{L}\{\sin \omega t/t\}$ and $\mathcal{L}\{\mathrm{Si}\,(t)\}$.

We know that $\mathcal{L}\{\sin \omega t\} = \omega/(s^2 + \omega^2)$. Therefore

$$\mathcal{L}\left\{ \frac{\sin \omega t}{t} \right\} = \int_s^\infty \frac{\omega}{\sigma^2 + \omega^2}\, d\sigma = \left. \arctan \frac{\sigma}{\omega} \right|_s^\infty$$

$$= \frac{\pi}{2} - \arctan \frac{s}{\omega} = \operatorname{arccot} \frac{s}{\omega}.$$

Also, since

$$\mathrm{Si}\,(t) = \int^t \frac{\sin u}{u}\, du,$$

it follows that

$$\mathcal{L}\{\mathrm{Si}\,(t)\} = \frac{1}{s}\, \mathcal{L}\left\{ \frac{\sin t}{t} \right\} = \frac{1}{s} \operatorname{arccot} s.$$

As the last topic of this section, consider the extension of the theorem on the transform of the derivative for the case of discontinuous functions.

Suppose that $f(t)$ is continuous for $0 \leq t < \infty$ except for a jump discontinuity at $t = t_1$. Then $f'(t)$ is not defined at all at $t = t_1$, but we may define the Laplace integral of $f'(t)$ by means of the following equation:

$$\int_0^\infty e^{-st} f'(t)\, dt = \lim_{\substack{u \to t_1 \\ u < t_1}} \int_0^u e^{-st} f'(t)\, dt + \lim_{\substack{v \to t_1 \\ v > t_1}} \int_v^\infty e^{-st} f'(t)\, dt.$$

(We have tacitly assumed that $f'(t)$ is piecewise continuous.)

Now the integration by parts can be justified for each integral separately and we have

$$\mathcal{L}\{f'(t)\} = \lim_{\substack{u \to t_1 \\ u < t_1}} \left. e^{-st} f(t) \right|_0^u + \lim_{\substack{v \to t_1 \\ v > t_1}} \left. e^{-st} f(t) \right|_v^\infty + s \int_0^\infty e^{-st} f(t)\, dt,$$

where the integrals involving $f(t)$ are combined. This yields

$$\mathcal{L}\{f'(t)\} = e^{-st_1}[f(t_1 + 0) - f(t_1 - 0)] - f(0) + s\mathcal{L}\{f(t)\}.$$

Remark. Since for the purposes of the Laplace transformation function $f(t)$ is identified with $f(t)S(t)$, the term $f(0)$ should be actually written as $f(0 + 0)$. This reflects the fact that $f(t)$ has, at $t = 0$, a jump discontinuity as well (in general).

The above argument can be trivially extended to a *finite* number of jump discontinuities of $f(t)$.

The generalized derivative theorem. If $f(t)$ is piecewise continuous with, at most, a finite number of jump discontinuities in $(0, \infty)$, if $f(t)$ is of exponential order α, and if $f'(t)$ is piecewise continuous for $0 \le t < \infty$, then

$$\mathcal{L}\{f'(t)\} = sF(s) - f(0 + 0) - \sum_{i=1}^{n} e^{-st_i}[f(t_i + 0) - f(t_i - 0)].$$

Example. Find $\mathcal{L}\{f'(t)\}$ if

$$f(t) = e^{t-1}S(t - 1) = \begin{cases} 0 & (0 < t < 1), \\ e^{t-1} & (t > 1). \end{cases}$$

Since $f(t)$ has a jump discontinuity at $t = 1$, we use the generalized derivative theorem

$$\mathcal{L}\{f'(t)\} = s\mathcal{L}\{f(t)\} - f(0 + 0) - e^{-s}[f(1 + 0) - f(1 - 0)].$$

Thus we have

$$\mathcal{L}\{f(t)\} = \int_1^\infty e^{-st}e^{t-1}\, dt = \frac{e^{-s}}{s - 1} \qquad (\text{Re } s > 1),$$

where $f(t)$ is of exponential order unity. Also, $f(0 + 0) = 0$, $f(1 + 0) = 1$, and $f(1 - 0) = 0$. Therefore

$$\mathcal{L}\{f'(t)\} = \frac{se^{-s}}{s - 1} - e^{-s} = \frac{e^{-s}}{s - 1}.$$

Remark. In this case it happens that $f'(t) = f(t)$.

5.8 PERIODIC FUNCTIONS. RECTIFICATION

Suppose that the Laplace transform of a periodic function $f(t)$ (with the period T) is sought. It often happens that $f(t)$ can be expressed by a simple analytic formula in the interval $0 \le t \le T$, but not in the interval $0 \le t < \infty$: For example, the *saw-tooth function* illustrated in Fig. 5.10. For such functions it is not difficult to evaluate the integral

$$\int_0^T e^{-st}f(t)\, dt$$

as opposed to the direct evaluation of the Laplace integral

$$\int_0^\infty e^{-st}f(t)\, dt.$$

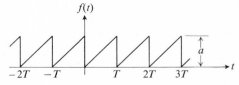

Figure 5.10

To find $\mathcal{L}\{f(t)\}$, introduce a new function

$$g(t) = \begin{cases} f(t) & (0 \leq t \leq T), \\ 0 & (t > T). \end{cases}$$

Let $\mathcal{L}\{g(t)\} = G(s)$. Suppose that $g(t)$ is shifted by an amount T to the right along the t-axis. The new transform is then $G(s)e^{-sT}$ (by the *shifting property*). The transform of the sum, which represents "two waves" of the original $f(t)$, is then $G(s) + G(s)e^{-sT}$. Continue this process and obtain the transform $F(s)$ of the periodic function $f(t)$ as the sum of the infinite series

$$F(s) = G(s) \sum_{n=0}^{\infty} e^{-nsT}.$$

The series can be summed (geometric series),

$$\sum_{n=0}^{\infty} e^{-nsT} = \frac{1}{1 - e^{-sT}},$$

resulting in $F(s) = G(s)/(1 - e^{-sT})$.

An alternative proof is to shift the function $f(t)S(t)$ to the right by an amount T and obtain the new transform $F(s)e^{-sT}$. Subtract this from $F(s)$ which will result in $F(s)(1 - e^{-sT})$. This is nothing other than

$$\int_0^T e^{-st}f(t)\,dt = G(s),$$

and the formula follows (this process repeats the method used in summing the geometric series).

Certain periodic functions have their values in the second half of the period related to those in the first half of the period. For instance, $\sin t$ has a certain behavior in $0 \leq t \leq \pi$ and repeats it with an inverted sign in $\pi \leq t \leq 2\pi$, namely, $\sin (t + \pi) = -\sin t$.

Suppose that a function $f(t)$ possesses the property

$$f(t + T/2) = -f(t)$$

(from which it also automatically follows that $f(t)$ is periodic with period T).

We define

$$G(s) = \int_0^{T/2} e^{-st}f(t)\,dt.$$

Then it is readily seen that $F(s) = G(s)/(1 + e^{-sT/2})$.

Exercise. Perform the derivation of the above formula.

Remark. Functions satisfying $f(t + T/2) = -f(t)$ are sometimes called *antiperiodic*.

In many physical applications, antiperiodic functions are "rectified" by defining

$$f_R(t) = f(t) \qquad (0 \le t \le T/2),$$
$$f_R(t + T/2) = f_R(t).$$

This is usually called the *full-wave rectification* and the new function is periodic with period $T/2$. An example is the *rectified sine wave* in Fig. 5.11.

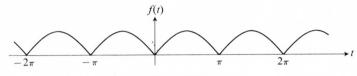

Figure 5.11

It is not difficult to show that

$$\mathcal{L}\{f_R(t)\} = \coth \frac{sT}{4} G(s),$$

where

$$G(s) = \int_0^{T/2} e^{-st} f(t)\, dt.$$

5.9 THE MELLIN INVERSION INTEGRAL

The problem of finding $\mathcal{L}^{-1}\{F(s)\}$ can be approached, in a general fashion, by the integral representation of the step function discussed in Section 5.9.

It is known that $\mathcal{L}\{S(t - \tau)\} = e^{-\tau s}/s$, and

$$S(t - \tau) = \frac{1}{2\pi i} \int_{\gamma-i\infty}^{\gamma+i\infty} e^{ts} \frac{e^{-\tau s}}{s}\, ds.$$

From this it is easy to construct the Laplace transform and an integral representation of a *rectangular pulse*, defined by

$$\beta(t) = \begin{cases} 0 & (0 \le t < \tau), \\ b & (\tau < t < \tau + \lambda), \\ 0 & (\tau + \lambda < t), \end{cases}$$

as shown in Fig. 5.12.

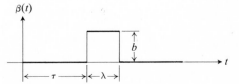

Figure 5.12

The rectangular pulse can be treated as the difference of two step functions,

$$\beta(t) = bS(t - \tau) - bS(t - \tau - \lambda),$$

and then $\beta(t)$ can be represented by

$$\beta(t) = \frac{1}{2\pi i} \int_{\gamma-i\infty}^{\gamma+i\infty} e^{ts} e^{-\tau s} \frac{1 - e^{-\lambda s}}{s} b \, ds.$$

Remark. $\beta(t)$ has not been defined for $t = \tau$ and for $t = \tau + \lambda$, but the integral representation implies that $\beta(\tau) = \beta(\tau + \lambda) = b/2$ (see p. 114).

Observe that the Laplace transform of $\beta(t)$ is

$$B(s) = e^{-\tau s} \frac{1 - e^{-\lambda s}}{s} b,$$

so that the above formula actually performs the inverse Laplace transform on $B(s)$.

Bearing this in mind, let us approximate an arbitrary (continuous or piecewise continuous) function $f(t)$ by a series of rectangular pulses of different heights stacked side by side (Fig. 5.13). Call this approximation $\varphi(t)$ and assume that the number of pulses is finite (which is possible if $f(t) \to 0$ as $t \to \infty$).

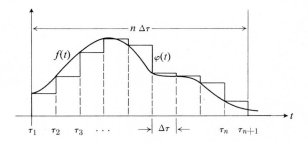

Figure 5.13

The integral representation for $\varphi(t)$ can be obtained by combining the integral representations of individual pulses, namely,

$$\varphi(t) = \frac{1}{2\pi i} \sum_{k=1}^{n} \int_{\gamma-i\infty}^{\gamma+i\infty} e^{ts} e^{-s\tau_k} \frac{1 - e^{-s\,\Delta t}}{s} f(\tau_k) \, ds$$

$$= \frac{1}{2\pi i} \int_{\gamma-i\infty}^{\gamma+i\infty} e^{ts} \, ds \sum_{k=1}^{n} e^{-s\tau_k} f(\tau_k) \frac{1 - e^{-s\,\Delta\tau}}{s}.$$

Now let us suppose that we increase n indefinitely while simultaneously decreasing $\Delta\tau$ and extending the range (where $\varphi(t)$ is nonvanishing) to infinity. If $\Delta\tau$ is very small, then $(1/s)(1 - e^{-s\,\Delta\tau})$ will not differ much from $\Delta\tau$. It is true that this will be increasingly less valid in the regions where $|s|$ is large; however, the quantity $|e^{-s\tau_k}(1 - e^{-s\,\Delta\tau})|$ is in any case bounded (recall that Re $s = \gamma = \text{const}$)

while the presence of s in the denominator will make the entire sum "small," contributing little to the integral. We may *expect* that in this process the sum

$$\sum_{k=1}^{n} e^{-s\tau_k} f(\tau_k) \frac{1 - e^{-s\,\Delta\tau}}{s}$$

can be replaced by the integral

$$\int_0^{\infty} e^{-s\tau} f(\tau)\, d\tau = \mathcal{L}\{f(t)\}.$$

On the other hand, $\varphi(t)$ would approach $f(t)$ in such a process, and it appears as though the following formula would hold:

$$f(t) = \frac{1}{2\pi i} \int_{\gamma-i\infty}^{\gamma+i\infty} e^{ts} F(s)\, ds,$$

where $F(s) = \int_0^{\infty} e^{-st} f(t)\, dt$. It is needless to emphasize that we have not proved the above formula, but have merely established some reasons why it may be valid.

Now consider the problem from another point of view. Define the function

$$g(t) = \frac{1}{2\pi i} \int_{\gamma-i\infty}^{\gamma+i\infty} e^{tz} F(z)\, dz,$$

provided the integral converges, where $F(s) = \mathcal{L}\{f(t)\}$ and γ is as yet undetermined. Subject $g(t)$ to the Laplace transformation:

$$\mathcal{L}\{g(t)\} = \int_0^{\infty} e^{-st} g(t)\, dt = \frac{1}{2\pi i} \int_0^{\infty} e^{-st}\, dt \int_{\gamma-i\infty}^{\gamma+i\infty} e^{tz} F(z)\, dz.$$

If the order of integration is interchangeable (uniform convergence required), then

$$\mathcal{L}\{g(t)\} = \frac{1}{2\pi i} \int_{\gamma-i\infty}^{\gamma+i\infty} F(z)\, dz \int_0^{\infty} e^{(z-s)t}\, dt.$$

Evidently, $\operatorname{Re} z = \gamma < \operatorname{Re} s$, otherwise the second integral will not converge at all. Under this condition,

$$\mathcal{L}\{g(t)\} = \frac{1}{2\pi i} \int_{\gamma-i\infty}^{\gamma+i\infty} F(z) \frac{1}{s - z}\, dz.$$

To evaluate this integral, close the contour by an arc C_R "to the right" (Fig. 5.14) to enclose the point S within. If $F(z)$ has no singularities to the right of the line $\operatorname{Re} z = \gamma$, and if the integral over C_R gives no contribution, then, by the Cauchy integral formula,

$$\frac{1}{2\pi i} \int_{\gamma-i\infty}^{\gamma+i\infty} F(z) \frac{1}{s - z}\, dz = F(s),$$

so that the functions $g(t)$ and $f(t)$ possess the same Laplace transform $F(s)$.

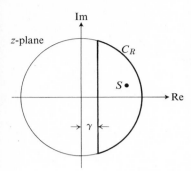

Figure 5.14   **Figure 5.15**

According to the remarks in Section 5.4, the integral formula

$$f(t) = \frac{1}{2\pi i} \int_{\gamma-i\infty}^{\gamma+i\infty} e^{ts}F(s)\, ds,$$

known as the *Mellin inversion integral,* may be considered as an adequate inversion formula provided that γ is chosen in such a way as to leave all singularities of $F(s)$ *to the left* of the line Re $s = \gamma$. This is implied by the result of the Cauchy integral formula used above.

Remark. The above discussion yields a sketch of the proof of a general inversion formula employing the Mellin integral. The complete proof imposes certain conditions on $f(t)$ and $F(s)$. In most practical cases these conditions can be verified directly.

We shall illustrate the use of the Mellin integral to find the inverse transform of the function $F(s) = (1/s)e^{-k\sqrt{s}}$, where $k \geq 0$. In order to evaluate the integral

$$f(t) = \frac{1}{2\pi i} \int_{\gamma-i\infty}^{\gamma+i\infty} \frac{1}{s} e^{-k\sqrt{s}} e^{ts}\, ds,$$

we close the contour (for $t > 0$) as shown in Fig. 5.15, with the cut along $(-\infty, 0)$ because of the branch line of function $\sqrt{s}$ [and, therefore, of function $F(s)$]. Employing the technique of Section 2.15, Example 4, it is possible to show that the contributions from the arcs MP and $P'N$ of the circle C_R vanish in the limit $R \to \infty$.

On the segment PQ we have* $s = re^{i\pi} = -r$ and $\sqrt{s} = \sqrt{r}\, e^{i(\pi/2)} = i\sqrt{r}$, while on the segment $P'Q'$, $s = re^{-i\pi} = -r$ and $\sqrt{s} = \sqrt{r}\, e^{-i(\pi/2)} = -i\sqrt{r}$. We find that the contributions from these segments are

$$\frac{1}{2\pi i} \int_R^\rho \frac{1}{(-r)} e^{-ik\sqrt{r}} e^{-tr} (-dr) + \frac{1}{2\pi i} \int_\rho^R \frac{1}{(-r)} e^{ik\sqrt{r}}\, e^{-tr} (-dr)$$

$$= \frac{1}{\pi} \int_\rho^R \frac{\sin k\sqrt{r}}{r} e^{-tr}\, dr \to \frac{2}{\pi} \int_0^\infty \frac{\sin u}{u} e^{-(tu^2/k^2)}\, du$$

---

* In the limit $\epsilon \to 0$. See Section 2.12, Example 7.

(setting $k\sqrt{r} = u$ and taking the limits $\rho \to 0$, $R \to \infty$). It remains for us to consider the integral over the "small circle" C_ρ. Because of the *polelike* behavior of $F(s)$ at $s = 0$, we expect a contribution from C_ρ that is analogous to a residue.* Indeed, using $s = \rho e^{i\theta}$,

$$\lim_{\substack{\epsilon \to \infty \\ \rho \to 0}} \frac{1}{2\pi i} \int_Q^{Q'} \frac{1}{s} e^{-k\sqrt{s}} e^{ts}\, ds = \frac{1}{2\pi} \int_{-\pi}^{+\pi} d\theta = -1.$$

Consequently, by use of the residue theorem (no singularities of $F(s)$ inside our contour),

$$\frac{1}{2\pi i} \int_{\gamma - i\infty}^{\gamma + i\infty} \frac{1}{s} e^{-k\sqrt{s}} e^{ts}\, ds = 1 - \frac{2}{\pi} \int_0^\infty \frac{\sin u}{u} e^{-tu^2/k^2}\, du.$$

The integral can be evaluated without much trouble and reads

$$\frac{2}{\pi} \int_0^\infty \frac{\sin u}{u} e^{-tu^2/k^2}\, du = \operatorname{erf} \frac{k}{2\sqrt{t}}.$$

Consequently,

$$\mathscr{L}^{-1}\left\{\frac{1}{s} e^{-k\sqrt{s}}\right\} = \operatorname{erfc} \frac{k}{2\sqrt{t}}.$$

Exercise. Evaluate the above integral. [*Hint:* First evaluate $\int_0^\infty \cos xu \cdot e^{-\lambda u^2}\, du$ and then integrate both sides with respect to x.]

5.10 APPLICATIONS OF LAPLACE TRANSFORMS

Example 1. In the *LRC*-series circuit shown in Fig. 5.16, the switch S is closed at $t = 0$ and opened at $t = T$. We want to find the current $i(t)$ if $q(0) = 0$ and $i(0) = 0$.

Kirchhoff's law requires that

$$L\frac{di(t)}{dt} + Ri(t) + \frac{q(t)}{C} = e(t),$$

where

$$e(t) = \begin{cases} e_0 & (0 < t < T), \\ 0 & (t > T). \end{cases}$$

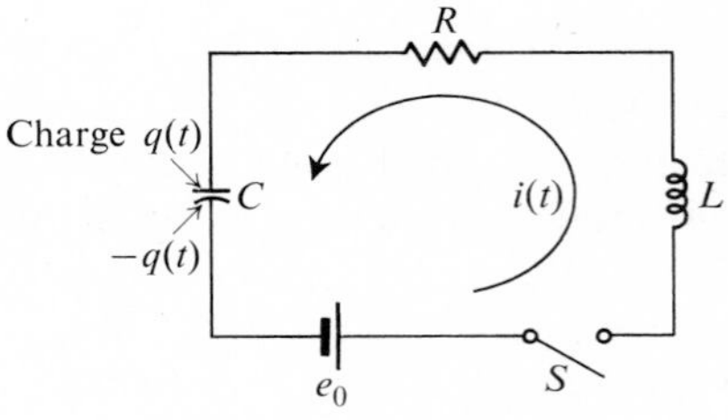

Moreover, from the definition of current, we find that

$$i(t) = \frac{dq(t)}{dt}.$$

Figure 5.16

---

* It should be emphasized, however, that $s = 0$ is *not a pole* of $F(s)$, but a branch point. (Compare with p. 96.)

Apply the Laplace transform to *both* differential equations, i.e., multiply by e^{-st} and integrate from 0 to ∞:

$$LsI(s) - Li(0) + (1/C)Q(s) = E(s),$$
$$I(s) = sQ(s) - q(0).$$

Use initial conditions and eliminate $Q(s)$: $(Ls + R + 1/Cs)I(s) = E(s)$, where

$$E(s) = e_0 \int_0^T e^{-st}\, dt = e_0 \frac{1 - e^{-sT}}{s}.$$

Therefore

$$I(s) = \frac{e_0}{L} \frac{1 - e^{-sT}}{s^2 + (R/L)s + 1/LC}.$$

Let $\alpha = R/2L$, and $\omega^2 = 1/LC - R^2/4L^2$. Three different cases arise:

a) *The oscillatory case,* $\omega^2 > 0$. Inversion of $I(s)$ yields

$$i(t) = \frac{e_0}{\omega L} e^{-\alpha t} \sin \omega t - \frac{e_0}{\omega L} e^{-\alpha(t-T)} \sin \omega(t - T)S(t - T).$$

b) *The overdamped case,* $\omega^2 < 0$. Let $\omega^2 = -\beta^2$ and replace ω by $i\beta$ in the above formula:

$$i(t) = \frac{e_0}{\beta L} e^{-\alpha t} \sinh \beta t - \frac{e_0}{\beta L} e^{-\alpha(t-T)} \sinh \beta(t - T)S(t - T).$$

c) *The critically damped case,* $\omega^2 = 0$. The transform reads

$$I(s) = \frac{e_0}{L} \frac{1 - e^{-sT}}{(s + R/2L)^2},$$

so that

$$i(t) = \frac{e_0}{L} te^{-\alpha t} - \frac{e_0}{L} (t - T)e^{-\alpha(t-T)}S(t - T).$$

Example 2. A beam of rigidity EI is clamped at one end and is loaded as shown in Fig. 5.17; the weight of the beam is neglected. The deflection $y(x)$ is sought. For the coordinate system shown, the following differential relations are known to hold.*

a) $\dfrac{d^2y(x)}{dx^2} = -\dfrac{1}{EI} m(x),$

where $y(x)$ is the deflection of the beam at point x, and $m(x)$ is the bending moment [counterclockwise

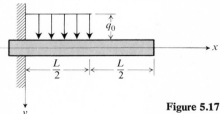

Figure 5.17

---

* For example, Salvadori and Schwartz, *Differential Equations in Engineering Problems,* Section 2.10.

torque of all (external) forces to the *right* of point x],

b) $\dfrac{dm(x)}{dx} = t(x),$

where $t(x)$ is the shearing force (resultant of all vertical forces to the *right* of point x),

c) $\dfrac{dt(x)}{dx} = -q(x),$

where $q(x)$ is the load per unit length at point x.

From these relations it follows that (as on p. 174)

$$EI\frac{d^4y(x)}{dx^4} = q(x).$$

Since the beam is clamped, we have $y(0) = 0$, $y'(0) = 0$. Also, $t(0) = q_0(L/2)$, as well as

$$m(0) = -\frac{q_0L}{2}\frac{L}{4} = -\frac{q_0L^2}{8}.$$

From these last two conditions, it follows that

$$y''(0) = q_0L^2/8EI, \qquad y'''(0) = -q_0L/2EI.$$

We now transform the DE and use all four initial conditions to obtain

$$s^4\,Y(s) - s\frac{q_0L^2}{8EI} + \frac{q_0L}{2EI} = \frac{q_0}{EI}\frac{1 - e^{-sL/2}}{s},$$

so that

$$Y(s) = \frac{q_0}{EI}\frac{1}{s^5} - \frac{q_0}{EI}\frac{e^{-sL/2}}{s^5} + \frac{q_0L^2}{8EI}\frac{1}{s^3} - \frac{q_0L}{2EI}\frac{1}{s^4}.$$

Inversion yields

$$y(x) = \frac{q_0}{24EI}x^4 - \frac{q_0}{24EI}\left(x - \frac{L}{2}\right)^4 S\left(x - \frac{L}{2}\right) + \frac{q_0L^2}{16EI}x^2 - \frac{q_0L}{12EI}x^3.$$

It is more convenient to rewrite this solution in the form

$$y(x) = \begin{cases} \dfrac{q_0}{EI}\left(\dfrac{x^4}{24} - \dfrac{Lx^3}{12} + \dfrac{L^2x^2}{16}\right) & \left(0 \le x < \dfrac{L}{2}\right), \\[2ex] \dfrac{q_0}{EI}\left(\dfrac{L^3x}{48} - \dfrac{L^4}{384}\right) & \left(\dfrac{L}{2} < x \le L\right), \end{cases}$$

from which, for instance, it is clearly seen that the right half of the beam will remain straight, a fact anticipated on physical grounds.

Remark. Point $x = L/2$ is not mentioned in the above formula, but the values of y and its first *three* derivatives can be calculated at $x = L/2$ from either of the two lines with the same result. They are continuous at $x = L/2$. The *fourth* derivative, however, is discontinuous at $x = L/2$ [because $q(x)$ is]. Rigorously speaking, this implies that the fourth derivative *does not exist* at $x = L/2$ and the DE actually breaks down.

We can eliminate this difficulty by giving our physical problem a better mathematical formulation, namely, by requiring that the DE

$$\frac{d^4y}{dx^4} = \frac{q(x)}{EI}$$

hold *separately* for left and right halves of the beam, and matching the *limiting values* of $y(x)$ and its first three derivatives as $x \to L/2$ from the left and from the right. In practice, however, a short cut is taken with the help of the step function, as above. Note that the widespread definition $S(0) = 1/2$ is completely irrelevant in this case since it is devoid of any physical meaning.

Example 3. Two circuits are coupled magnetically, as shown in Fig. 5.18. We wish to find the currents $i_1(t)$ and $i_2(t)$ after the switch S is closed.

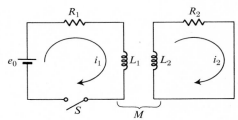

Figure 5.18

Kirchhoff's laws state that

$$L \frac{di_1}{dt} + M \frac{di_2}{dt} + R_1 i_1 = e_0 S(t),$$

$$M \frac{di_1}{dt} + L_2 \frac{di_2}{dt} + R_2 i_2 = 0.$$

Assuming the initial currents to be zero, we transform both equations to obtain

$$(L_1 s + R_1)I_1 + MsI_2 = e_0/s, \qquad MsI_1 + (L_2 s + R_2)I_2 = 0.$$

The determinant of the system is

$$\Delta = \det \begin{vmatrix} L_1 s + R_1 & Ms \\ Ms & L_2 s + R_2 \end{vmatrix}$$

$$= (L_1 L_2 - M^2)s^2 + (L_1 R_2 + L_2 R_1)s + R_1 R_2.$$

It is known from electromagnetic theory that $L_1 L_2 \geq M^2$. The usual condition in practice is $L_1 L_2 > M^2$. Thus we have

$$I_1(s) = \frac{e_0}{(L_1 L_2 - M^2)} \frac{L_2 s + R_2}{s(s - r_1)(s - r_2)},$$

$$I_2(s) = -\frac{Me_0}{(L_1 L_2 - M^2)} \frac{1}{(s - r_1)(s - r_2)},$$

where r_1 and r_2 are the roots of

$$(L_1L_2 - M^2)s^2 + (L_1R_2 + L_2R_1)s + R_1R_2 = 0.$$

Since

$$(L_1R_2 + L_2R_1)^2 - 4R_1R_2(L_1L_2 - M^2) = (L_1R_2 - R_1L_2)^2 + 4R_1R_2M^2 > 0,$$

both roots are real. Moreover, they are both negative since

$$\frac{L_1R_2 + L_2R_1}{L_1L_2 - M^2} > 0 \quad \text{and} \quad \frac{R_1R_2}{L_1L_2 - M^2} > 0.$$

Rational fraction decomposition yields

$$I_1(s) = \frac{e_0}{L_1L_2 - M^2}\left\{\frac{R_2}{r_1r_2s} + \frac{L_2r_1 + R_2}{r_1(r_1 - r_2)(s - r_1)} + \frac{L_2r_2 + R_2}{r_2(r_2 - r_1)(s - r_2)}\right\},$$

$$I_2(s) = -\frac{Me_0}{L_1L_2 - M^2} \cdot \frac{1}{r_1 - r_2}\left\{\frac{1}{s - r_1} - \frac{1}{s - r_2}\right\}.$$

Inverting [using $r_1r_2 = R_1R_2/(L_1L_2 - M^2)$], we find that

$$i_1(t) = \frac{e_0}{R_1} + \frac{e_0}{L_1L_2 - M^2}\left\{\frac{L_2r_1 + R_2}{r_1(r_1 - r_2)}e^{r_1t} - \frac{L_2r_2 + R_2}{r_2(r_1 - r_2)}e^{r_2t}\right\},$$

$$i_2(t) = -\frac{Me_0}{(L_1L_2 - M^2)}\frac{1}{(r_1 - r_2)}(e^{r_1t} - e^{r_2t}).$$

It is seen that $i_1 \to e_0/R_1$ and $i_2 \to 0$ as $t \to \infty$ as expected on physical grounds. Also, $i_1(0) = 0$ and $i_2(0) = 0$.

The case of $L_1L_2 = M^2$, although an idealization, reveals an interesting point of theoretical importance. The determinant of the system is now a linear function of s,

$$\Delta = (L_1R_2 + L_2R_1)s + R_1R_2,$$

and the transforms of the currents are

$$I_1(s) = \frac{e_0/s(L_2s + R_2)}{(L_1R_2 + L_2R_1)s + R_1R_2}, \qquad I_2(s) = -\frac{Me_0}{(L_1R_2 + L_2R_1)s + R_1R_2},$$

yielding

$$i_1(t) = \frac{e_0}{R_1} - \frac{e_0L_1R_2}{R_1(L_1R_2 + L_2R_1)}\exp\left(-\frac{R_1R_2}{L_1R_2 + L_2R_1}t\right),$$

$$i_2(t) = -\frac{e_0M}{L_1R_2 + L_2R_1}\exp\left(-\frac{R_1R_2}{L_1R_2 + L_2R_1}t\right).$$

Note that these two functions *do not satisfy* the initial conditions $i_1(0) = i_2(0) = 0$. Instead, we have

$$i_1(0) = \frac{e_0L_2}{L_1R_2 + L_2R_1}, \qquad i_2(0) = -\frac{e_0M}{L_1R_2 + L_2R_1}.$$

Before we inquire into the causes of this discrepancy, we may convince ourselves that our results constitute the *true solution of the physical problem*. In fact, the conditions $i_1(0) = 0$, $i_2(0) = 0$ are inconsistent with our system of differential equations:

$$L_1 \frac{di_1}{dt} + M \frac{di_2}{dt} + R_1 i_1 = e_0 S(t),$$

$$M \frac{di_1}{dt} + L_2 \frac{di_2}{dt} + R_2 i_2 = 0.$$

Indeed, let us multiply the first equation by M, the second one by L_1, subtract, and use the condition $L_1 L_2 = M^2$. The result is

$$MR_1 i_1(t) - L_1 R_2 i_2(t) = Me_0 \qquad \text{(for } t > 0\text{)},$$

from which it follows that $i_1(t)$ and $i_2(t)$ cannot simultaneously approach zero as $t \to 0$ (but $t > 0$).

Our physical intuition then tells us that at the moment the switch was closed, the currents i_1 and i_2 have *instantaneously jumped* to certain "initial" values, from their previous values $i_1 = i_2 = 0$ (which are certainly valid for $t < 0$). To find what these values can be, we integrate either of the differential equations from $-\epsilon$ to $+\epsilon$, where ϵ is a small positive number. Then, since $i_1(-\epsilon) = 0$ and $i_2(-\epsilon) = 0$,

$$Mi_1(\epsilon) + L_2 i_2(\epsilon) = 0.$$

As $\epsilon \to 0$, the values $i_1(\epsilon)$ and $i_2(\epsilon)$ approach the "adjusted" initial values of the currents:

$$\lim_{\substack{\epsilon \to 0 \\ \epsilon > 0}} i_1(\epsilon) = i_1(0 + 0), \qquad \lim_{\substack{\epsilon \to 0 \\ \epsilon > 0}} i_2(\epsilon) = i_2(0 + 0).$$

Therefore the adjusted initial values must satisfy the simultaneous equations

$$Mi_1(0 + 0) + L_2 i_2(0 + 0) = 0,$$
$$MR_1 i_1(0 + 0) - L_1 R_2 i_2(0 + 0) = Me_0.$$

Solving these, we obtain

$$i_1(0 + 0) = \frac{e_0 L_2}{L_1 R_2 + L_2 R_1}, \qquad i_2(0 + 0) = -\frac{e_0 M}{L_1 R_2 + L_2 R_1}$$

exactly as in our solution.

This analysis helps to explain why we have obtained the correct solution with the incorrect initial conditions: The adjusted conditions are effectively *built in* within the differential system describing the state of affairs for $t > 0$.

This phenomenon of "instantaneous" adjustment of currents occurs quite often in switching problems in electrical networks if certain idealizations are made (like the assumption $L_1 L_2 = M^2$ which is, strictly speaking, unattainable in physical systems). Similar phenomena occur in mechanical systems, subject to sudden blows which change their state of motion.

Example 4. Consider the DE $xy'' + y' + xy = 0$ with the initial conditions $y(0) = 1$, $y'(0) = 0$.

In this problem, the formula

$$\mathcal{L}\{xy(x)\} = -\frac{dY(s)}{ds}, \qquad Y(s) = \mathcal{L}\{y(x)\}$$

can be put to use. Using the initial conditions, obtain

$$\mathcal{L}\{y''(x)\} = s^2 Y(s) - s,$$

so that

$$\mathcal{L}\{xy''\} = -2s\, Y(s) - s^2 \frac{dY(s)}{ds} + 1.$$

The transformed equation reads

$$-2s Y - s^2 Y' + 1 + sY - 1 - Y' = 0,$$

or

$$Y'(1 + s^2) + sY = 0.$$

The solution of this DE is elementary:

$$Y(s) = C/\sqrt{1 + s^2},$$

where C is a constant of integration. To find $y(x)$, expand $Y(s)$ in inverse powers of s:

$$Y(s) = \frac{C}{s}\left(1 + \frac{1}{s^2}\right)^{-1/2} = \frac{C}{s}\left[1 + \frac{(-\frac{1}{2})}{s^2} + \frac{(-\frac{1}{2})(-\frac{3}{2})}{1 \cdot 2} \frac{1}{s^4} + \cdots\right]$$

$$= \frac{C}{s}\sum_{n=0}^{\infty} (-1)^n \frac{1 \cdot 3 \cdot 5 \cdots (2n-1)}{2^n n!} \frac{1}{s^{2n}} = C\sum_{n=0}^{\infty} (-1)^n \frac{(2n)!}{2^{2n}(n!)^2} \frac{1}{s^{2n+1}}$$

(Laurent series converging for $|s| > 1$). Assume that this expression can be inverted term by term. Then

$$y(x) = C\sum_{n=0}^{\infty} \frac{(-1)^n x^{2n}}{2^{2n}(n!)^2}.$$

To justify the procedure, observe that the series for $y(x)$ converges uniformly for $0 \le x \le R$ with an arbitrary R. Therefore, it may be multiplied by e^{-st} and integrated term by term, yielding the series for $Y(s)$. In other words, it follows that $Y(s)$ is indeed the Laplace transform of $y(x)$.

Adjusting the constant C so that $y(0) = 1$, we obtain the desired solution which is the Bessel function of order zero:

$$J_0(x) = \sum_{n=0}^{\infty} (-1)^n \frac{1}{2^{2n}(n!)^2} x^{2n}.$$

Remark. This method may be helpful in solving some other differential equations of second order, but it may turn out to be useless if the transformed equation is more complicated than the original one. Also, if the solution has a singularity at $x = 0$, the initial values $y(0)$ and $y'(0)$ cannot be specified (for instance, $Y_0(x)$, the second solution of the above equation, cannot be obtained by our method).

BIBLIOGRAPHY

CARSLAW, H. S. and J. C. JAEGER, *Operational Methods in Applied Mathematics.* New York: Oxford University Press, 1947.

CHURCHILL, R. V., *Operational Mathematics.* New York: McGraw-Hill Book Co., 1958.

SCOTT, E. J., *Transform Calculus with an Introduction to Complex Variables.* New York: Harper, 1955.

VAN DER POL, B. and H. BREMMER, *Operational Calculus Based on the Two-sided Laplace Integral.* New York: Cambridge University Press, 1955.

PROBLEMS

1. Show that the functions $\cosh at$ and $\sinh at$ are of exponential order and evaluate their Laplace transforms.

2. Evaluate $\mathcal{L}\{\sqrt{t}\, e^t\}$. For what values of s will the transform exist?

3. By performing the rational fraction decomposition, establish the results given below.

a) $\mathcal{L}^{-1}\left\{\dfrac{s+1}{s(s^2+1)}\right\} = 1 + \sin t - \cos t$

b) $\mathcal{L}^{-1}\left\{\dfrac{s+1}{s^2(s^2+s+1)}\right\} = t - \dfrac{2}{\sqrt{3}}\, e^{-(t/2)} \sin \dfrac{\sqrt{3}}{2}\, t$

c) $\mathcal{L}^{-1}\left\{\dfrac{s^4 + 2s^3 + 2}{s^3(s^2 - s - 2)}\right\} = \dfrac{17}{12}\, e^{2t} + \dfrac{1}{3}\, e^{-t} - \dfrac{t^2}{2} + \dfrac{t}{2} - \dfrac{3}{4}$

4. Solve the following differential equations by subjecting them to a Laplace transformation, as in the flow diagram in Section 5.4.

a) $y' + y = e^{2t}$, $y(0) = 0$

b) $y'' - 4y' + 4y = 0$, $y(0) = 0$, $y'(0) = 1$

c) $y'' - y' - 2y = t^2$, $y(0) = 1$, $y'(0) = 3$

d) $y'' + 4y = 0$, $y(0) = 1$, $y(\pi/4) = -1$

[*Hint:* Treat $y'(0)$ in (d) as an unknown parameter and determine it at the very end.]

5. Show that the following systems of differential equations have the solutions indicated:

a) $\begin{cases} \dfrac{dx}{dt} + \dfrac{dy}{dt} - 4y = 1, & x(0) = 0 \\[2mm] x + \dfrac{dy}{dt} - 3y = t^2, & y(0) = 0 \end{cases}$ $\begin{aligned} x(t) &= \dfrac{1 + 6t + 4t^2 - e^{2t}}{4} \\[2mm] y(t) &= \dfrac{1 + 2t - e^{2t}}{4} \end{aligned}$

b) $\begin{cases} \dfrac{d^2x}{dt^2} - 8x + \dfrac{dy}{dt}\sqrt{6} = 0, & x(0) = 1, \quad \dot{x}(0) = 0 \\[2mm] \dfrac{d^2y}{dt^2} + 2y - \dfrac{dx}{dt}\sqrt{6} = 0, & y(0) = 0, \quad \dot{y}(0) = 0 \end{cases}$

$$x(t) = \tfrac{3}{2}\cosh 2t - \tfrac{1}{2}\cos 2t$$

$$y(t) = \frac{\sqrt{6}}{2}\sinh 2t - \frac{\sqrt{6}}{2}\sin 2t$$

[*Hint:* Apply the Laplace transform simultaneously to both differential equations and solve the resulting equations for the transforms $x(s) = \mathcal{L}\{x(t)\}$ and $Y(s) = \mathcal{L}\{y(t)\}$.]

6. Consider the DE $y'' - 3y' + 2y = x^2$ with $y(0) = \tfrac{7}{4}$, $y'(0) = \tfrac{3}{2}$. Show that

$$Y(s) = \left(\frac{1}{s-2} - \frac{1}{s-1}\right)\left(\frac{2}{s^3} + \frac{7}{4}s - \frac{15}{4}\right).$$

Observe what would happen if the expressions $1/(s-2)$ and $1/(s-1)$ are expanded as in Section 5.1 and comment on the significance of the initial condition chosen above.

7. Let $N_A(t)$, $N_B(t)$, and $N_C(t)$ represent the number of nuclei of three radioactive substances which decay according to the scheme

$$A \xrightarrow{\lambda_A} B \xrightarrow{\lambda_B} C,$$

with decay constants λ_A and λ_B (the substance C is considered stable). Then the functions N_A, N_B, and N_C are known to obey the system of differential equations

$$\frac{dN_A}{dt} = -\lambda_A N_A, \qquad \frac{dN_B}{dt} = -\lambda_B N_B + \lambda_A N_A, \qquad \frac{dN_C}{dt} = \lambda_B N_B.$$

Assuming that $N_A(0) = N_0$, and $N_B(0) = N_C(0) = 0$, solve the problem by Laplace transform methods and show that

$$N_C(t) = N_0\left(1 - \frac{\lambda_B}{\lambda_B - \lambda_A}e^{-\lambda_A t} + \frac{\lambda_A}{\lambda_B - \lambda_A}e^{-\lambda_B t}\right).$$

Also calculate $N_A(t)$ and $N_B(t)$.

8. Show how the convolution theorem can be used to establish the following result:

$$\mathcal{L}^{-1}\left\{\frac{s^2}{(s^2 + a^2)^2}\right\} = \frac{1}{2}\left(t\cos at + \frac{1}{a}\sin at\right).$$

9. Solve the problem of a damped harmonic oscillator (as in Section 5.6):

$$\ddot{x} + 2\lambda\dot{x} + \omega_0^2 x = f(t), \qquad x(0) = x_0, \quad \dot{x}(0) = v_0,$$

by means of the convolution theorem for

a) $\omega_0^2 < \lambda^2$ (overdamped case)

b) $\omega_n^2 = \lambda^2$ (critically damped case)

10. Establish the following results:

$$\mathcal{L}\{\text{Ci}\,(t)\} = -(1/2s)\log(1 + s^2),$$
$$\mathcal{L}\{\text{Ei}\,(-t)\} = -(1/s)\log(1 + s),$$

where

$$\text{Ci}\,(t) = -\int_t^\infty \frac{\cos u}{u}\,du \quad \text{(the } cosine\ integral\text{)},$$

$$\text{Ei}\,(t) = \int_{-\infty}^t \frac{e^u}{u}\,du \quad (t < 0) \quad \text{(the } exponential\ integral\text{)}.$$

11. Use the theorem on integration of transforms to establish the formula

$$\mathcal{L}\left\{\frac{1 - \cos at}{t}\right\} = \frac{1}{2}\log\left(1 + \frac{a^2}{s^2}\right).$$

12. Starting from the formula $\mathcal{L}\{\text{erfc}\,(k/2\sqrt{t})\} = (1/s)e^{-k\sqrt{s}}$, develop the inverse transform of $e^{-k\sqrt{s}}$. [*Hint:* Use the differentiation rule.]

13. Using the result of Problem 12 and employing the rule of differentiation of transforms, develop the inverse transform of $(1/\sqrt{s})e^{-k\sqrt{s}}$.

14. Using the *primitive function theorem* and the result of Problem 13, develop the inverse transform of $(1/s\sqrt{s})e^{-k\sqrt{s}}$.

15. To find $\mathcal{L}^{-1}\{F(s)\}$, the function $F(s)$ is sometimes expanded in a series of suitable functions and inverted term by term. For instance, show that

$$\mathcal{L}^{-1}\left\{\frac{\sinh k\sqrt{s}}{\sinh \sqrt{s}}\right\} = \sum_{n=0}^\infty \left[\text{erfc}\,\frac{2n + 1 - k}{2\sqrt{t}} - \text{erfc}\,\frac{2n + 1 + k}{2\sqrt{t}}\right]$$

by expressing $F(s)$ in terms of exponential functions, using the expansion

$$\frac{1}{e^\alpha - e^{-\alpha}} = \frac{e^{-\alpha}}{1 - e^{-2\alpha}} = e^{-\alpha}\sum_{n=0}^\infty e^{-2n\alpha}$$

and inverting term by term. This idea is widely used in heat-conduction problems.

16. Illustrate the Mellin inversion integral by applying it to the following inversion problems:

$$\mathcal{L}^{-1}\{1/(s^2 + a^2)\}, \quad \mathcal{L}^{-1}\{1/\sqrt{s}\}.$$

Specify the contour in each case and produce the necessary mathematical details to develop the results.

17. In the circuit shown (Fig. 5.19), the switch S is closed at $t = 0$ when the charge on the capacitor is $q(0) = q_0 = $ const. Set up the equation satisfied by $q(t)$ for $t > 0$ and show that

$$q(t) = q_0 e^{-\alpha t}[\cos \omega t + (\alpha/\omega) \sin \omega t],$$

where $\alpha = R/2L$ and $\omega^2 = 1/LC - R^2/4L^2$.

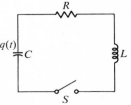

Figure 5.19

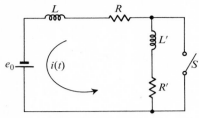

Figure 5.20

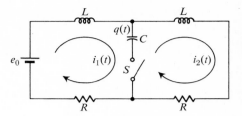

Figure 5.21

18. In the circuit shown (Fig. 5.20), the switch S is kept closed for $t < 0$ and is opened at $t = 0$. Assuming a steady DC-current prior to $t = 0$ (e_0 is a constant EMF), set up the equation satisfied by $i(t)$ for $t > 0$ and solve it by methods of the Laplace transform to show

$$i(t) = \frac{e_0}{R + R'} + \frac{e_0 R'}{R(R + R')} e^{-[(R+R')/(L+L')]t}.$$

19. Consider the simply supported beam of Section 4.8, Example 2. In accordance with the statements on pp. 174 and 212, one must solve

$$EI\frac{d^4 y(x)}{dx^4} = q(x) = q = \text{const,}$$

subject to $y(0) = y(L) = 0$ and $y''(0) = y''(L) = 0$. Observe that these conditions are more suited to the Fourier series method than to the Laplace transform method. Nevertheless, the problem is manageable if we use the Laplace transform [see the hint in Problem 4(d) above]. Find $y(x)$ by the Laplace transform method and show that it possesses the Fourier sine series displayed on p. 174.

20. The switch S in the circuit shown in Fig. 5.21 is kept open for $t < 0$, the capacitor is kept uncharged and a DC-current (due to $e_0 = \text{const}$) is present. If the switch is closed at $t = 0$, show that the *loop currents* $i_1(t)$ and $i_2(t)$ and the charge $q(t)$ on the capacitor obey the following relations:

$$L\frac{di_1}{dt} + Ri_1 + \frac{q}{C} = e_0, \qquad L\frac{di_2}{dt} + Ri_2 - \frac{q}{C} = 0,$$

where $dq/dt = i_1 - i_2$, $i_1(0) = i_2(0) = e_0/2R$. Solve this system by Laplace transform methods and show that

$$q(t) = \frac{e_0 c}{2}\left(1 - e^{-\alpha t}\cos \omega t - \frac{\alpha}{\omega}e^{-\alpha t}\sin \omega t\right),$$

$$i_1(t) = \frac{e_0}{2R} + \frac{e_0}{2L\omega}e^{-\alpha t}\sin \omega t,$$

$$i_2(t) = \frac{e_0}{2R} - \frac{e_0}{2L\omega}e^{-\alpha t}\sin \omega t,$$

where $\alpha = R/2L$ and $\omega^2 = 2/LC - \alpha^2$. *Caution:* Before inverting, *simplify* the transforms $Q(s)$, $I_1(s)$, and $I_2(s)$ to the utmost degree.

CHAPTER 6

CONCEPTS OF THE THEORY OF DISTRIBUTIONS

6.1 STRONGLY PEAKED FUNCTIONS AND THE DIRAC DELTA FUNCTION

In physics, we often encounter the concept of a pulse of "infinitely short" duration. For instance, a body set in motion (from rest) by a sudden blow attains a momentum equal to the impulse of the blow, namely,

$$mv = I = \int_{t_0}^{t_0+\tau} F(t)\, dt,$$

where $F(t)$ is the force and τ is the duration of the action of the force. The term "blow" implies that τ is so small that the change in momentum occurs instantaneously. However, since such a change in momentum is a finite number, it follows that $F(t)$ should have been infinite during the blow and zero otherwise.

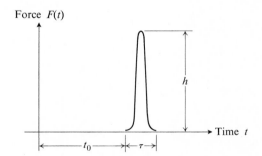

Figure 6.1

This kind of description is not proper in terms of common mathematical concepts. For that matter, it may not even be physically rigorous. Indeed, the actual graph of force is more likely to be a strongly peaked function, as in Fig. 6.1, where h is very large while τ is very small such that the area under the curve is equal to a given value of I. In many cases, a great majority, as a matter of fact, the exact shape of the strongly peaked function [$F(t)$ in this case] is not known. However, insofar as the observable physical effects of such functions are concerned, this lack of information does not usually matter. What is significant, though, is the intensity of the impulse, namely, the value of the integral

$$\int_{t_0}^{t_0+\tau} F(t)\, dt,$$

221

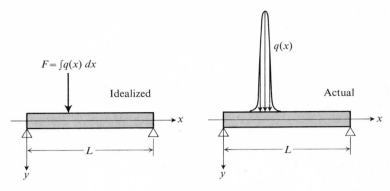

Figure 6.2

and the time when the impulse occurred, namely t_0 (or, perhaps, $t_0 + \tau/2$, but that hardly matters if τ is sufficiently small).

Strongly peaked functions are common to all branches of physics. For instance, a concentrated force acting on a beam is actually a strongly peaked distribution of load (Fig. 6.2). In electrical circuits, strongly peaked currents of extremely short duration often occur in switching processes, like the redistribution of charges between the two capacitors shown in Fig. 6.3 when the switch S is closed. Initially, the voltages $V_1 = Q_1/C_1$ and $V_2 = Q_2/C_2$ are assumed to be different. When the switch is closed, there is a rush of current through it until the charges Q_1 and Q_2 are redistributed into

$$Q_1' = \frac{C_1(Q_1 + Q_2)}{C_1 + C_2}, \qquad Q_2' = \frac{C_2(Q_1 + Q_2)}{C_1 + C_2}.$$

If the resistance of the leads is negligible, then this current pulse is of infinitely short duration and the current is infinitely large. Needless to say, this cannot be rigorously true; apart from the inevitable resistance (small, but never zero), there will also be a self-inductance L of the loop which will tend to moderate the steep rise of the current to its peak value after the switch is closed. In short, the current pulse will be a strongly peaked function of time.

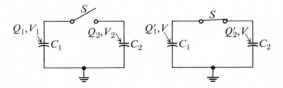

Figure 6.3

In order to facilitate a variety of operations in mathematical physics, and particularly in quantum mechanics, Dirac proposed the introduction of the so-called *delta function* $\delta(x)$ which will be a representative of an infinitely sharply peaked function given symbolically by

$$\delta(x) = \begin{cases} 0 & (x \neq 0), \\ \infty & (x = 0), \end{cases}$$

but such that the integral of $\delta(x)$ is *normalized to unity:*

$$\int_{-\infty}^{+\infty} \delta(x)\,dx = 1.$$

The first and basic operation to which Dirac sought to subject $\delta(x)$ is the integral

$$\int_{-\infty}^{+\infty} \delta(x) f(x)\,dx,$$

where $f(x)$ is any continuous function. This integral can be "evaluated" by the following argument: Since $\delta(x)$ is zero for $x \neq 0$, the limits of integration may be changed to $-\epsilon$ and $+\epsilon$, where ϵ is a small positive number. Moreover, since $f(x)$ is continuous at $x = 0$, its values within the interval $(-\epsilon, +\epsilon)$ will not differ much from $f(0)$ and we can claim, approximately, that

$$\int_{-\infty}^{+\infty} \delta(x) f(x)\,dx = \int_{-\epsilon}^{+\epsilon} \delta(x) f(x)\,dx \cong f(0) \int_{-\epsilon}^{+\epsilon} \delta(x)\,dx,$$

with the approximation improving as ϵ approaches zero. However,

$$\int_{-\epsilon}^{+\epsilon} \delta(x)\,dx = 1$$

for all values of ϵ, because $\delta(x) = 0$ for $x \neq 0$, and $\delta(x)$ is normalized. It appears then that letting $\epsilon \to 0$, we have exactly

$$\int_{-\infty}^{+\infty} \delta(x) f(x)\,dx = f(0).$$

Remark. The limits $-\infty$ and $+\infty$ may be replaced by any two numbers a and b provided $a < 0 < b$.

The above integral is sometimes referred to as the *sifting property* of the delta function: $\delta(x)$ acts as a sieve, selecting from all possible values of $f(x)$ its value at the point $x = 0$.

6.2 DELTA SEQUENCES

The statement that

$$\delta(x) = \begin{cases} 0 & (x \neq 0), \\ \infty & (x = 0) \end{cases}$$

is not a proper statement and cannot be used to define a function, much less an integrable function. An alternative attempt may be to define $\delta(x)$ as the function which satisfies the property

$$\int_{-\infty}^{+\infty} \delta(x)f(x)\,dx = f(0)$$

for all continuous $f(x)$. However, this attempt also fails. It is possible to show that there can be no function with this property.

What remains to be true, however, is that there exist sequences of strongly peaked functions which *approach* the sifting property; e.g., the following may hold for a sequence $\phi_n(x)$ ($n = 1, 2, 3, \ldots$):

$$\lim_{n \to \infty} \int_{-\infty}^{+\infty} \phi_n(x)f(x)\,dx = f(0).$$

Sequences with this property will be called *delta sequences*. For instance, the functions

$$\phi_n(x) = \begin{cases} 0 & (|x| \geq 1/n) \\ n/2 & (|x| < 1/n) \end{cases} \quad (n = 1, 2, 3, \ldots)$$

form a delta sequence. Indeed, consider the integral

$$\int_{-\infty}^{+\infty} \phi_n(x)f(x)\,dx$$

for any continuous $f(x)$. By definition of $\phi_n(x)$, we have

$$\int_{-\infty}^{+\infty} \phi_n(x)f(x)\,dx = \int_{-1/n}^{+1/n} (n/2)f(x)\,dx = (n/2)\int_{-1/n}^{+1/n} f(x)\,dx.$$

Now, using the mean value theorem for integrals, we can deduce that

$$(n/2)\int_{-1/n}^{+1/n} f(x)\,dx = (n/2)(2/n)f(\xi) = f(\xi) \qquad (-1/n \leq \xi \leq +1/n).$$

If $n \to \infty$, then $\xi \to 0$. From the continuity of $f(x)$, it follows that $f(\xi) \to f(0)$, establishing the result

$$\lim_{n \to \infty} \int_{-\infty}^{+\infty} \phi_n(x)f(x)\,dx = f(0),$$

which qualifies $\phi_n(x)$ as a delta sequence.

For many purposes it may be desirable to construct delta sequences from functions which are continuous and differentiable (this was not the case with the above sequence). For instance, some such sequences are

a) $\qquad \phi_n(x) = \dfrac{n}{\pi}\,\dfrac{1}{1 + n^2x^2},$

b) $\qquad \phi_n(x) = \dfrac{n}{\sqrt{\pi}}\,e^{-n^2x^2},$

c) $\qquad \phi_n(x) = \dfrac{1}{n\pi}\,\dfrac{\sin^2 nx}{x^2}.$

All these functions are *normalized to unity* in the sense* that

$$\int_{-\infty}^{+\infty} \phi_n(x)\,dx = 1,$$

and each sequence possesses the desired property [provided $f(x)$ is continuous and the integral converges]:

$$\lim_{n\to\infty} \int_{-\infty}^{+\infty} \phi_n(x)f(x)\,dx = f(0).$$

But again, it is incorrect to say that these sequences converge to the delta function: The limits of these sequences *do not exist* (according to common definitions of convergence).

Remark. The normalization of the ϕ_n is not mandatory for a delta sequence; it should only be required that

$$\lim_{n\to\infty} \int_{-\infty}^{+\infty} \phi_n(x)\,dx = 1,$$

as follows from the sifting property by setting $f(x) = 1$.

Exercise. Show that $\lim_{n\to\infty} \phi_n(x)$ does not exist for any of the three sequences listed above.

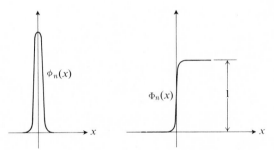

$\phi_n(x)$

$\Phi_n(x)$

1

Figure 6.4

It is instructive to investigate the indefinite integrals of functions $\phi_n(x)$, namely, the functions

$$\Phi_n(x) = \int_{-\infty}^{x} \phi_n(\xi)\,d\xi.$$

For instance, for the sequence (a) given above, the graphs of $\phi_n(x)$ and $\Phi_n(x)$ for rather large values of n would look like those shown in Fig. 6.4.

Also, it is not difficult to verify that

$$\lim_{n\to\infty} \Phi_n(x) = S(x),$$

---

* There are two commonly used definitions of this term. For the second definition, see p. 468. The integral need not be over $(-\infty, +\infty)$ but rather over an interval appropriate for the problem under consideration.

and we may be tempted to say that $\delta(x)$ is the derivative of the step function $S(x)$. Again, however, $dS(x)/dx = 0$ for all $x \neq 0$ (which is all right), but the derivative does not exist at $x = 0$, exactly where the peak of the delta function is expected to be.

6.3 THE δ-CALCULUS

The use of delta sequences made of differentiable functions has a very important consequence; for instance (Fig. 6.5), let $\phi_n(x) = (n/\sqrt{\pi})e^{-n^2x^2}$; then

$$\frac{d\phi_n(x)}{dx} = -\frac{2n^3}{\sqrt{\pi}} xe^{-n^2x^2}.$$

Consider the integral

$$\int_{-\infty}^{+\infty} \frac{d\phi_n(x)}{dx} f(x)\, dx,$$

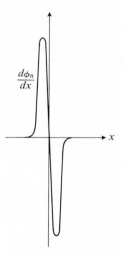

where $f(x)$ is differentiable. Integrating by parts, we obtain

$$\int_{-\infty}^{+\infty} \frac{d\phi_n(x)}{dx} f(x)\, dx = \phi_n(x)f(x)\Big|_{-\infty}^{+\infty} - \int_{-\infty}^{+\infty} \phi_n(x) \frac{df(x)}{dx}\, dx.$$

Assume that

$$\lim_{x \to \pm\infty} (n/\sqrt{\pi})e^{-n^2x^2} f(x) = 0.$$

Figure 6.5

(This is usually true since we are dealing with functions for which the integral $\int_{-\infty}^{+\infty} \phi_n(x)f(x)\, dx$ converges.) Then, letting $n \to \infty$, we have

$$\lim_{n \to \infty} \int_{-\infty}^{+\infty} \frac{d\phi_n(x)}{dx} f(x)\, dx = -\lim_{n \to \infty} \int_{-\infty}^{+\infty} \phi_n(x)f'(x)\, dx = -f'(0).$$

It appears that the sequence $\phi_n'(x)$ is associated with the *derivative-sifting property*. This gives rise to the symbol $\delta'(x)$, the so-called derivative of the delta function, such that

$$\int_{-\infty}^{+\infty} \delta'(x)f(x)\, dx = -f'(0).$$

This idea can be developed further, giving rise to higher-order derivatives of $\delta(x)$ possessing the property

$$\int_{-\infty}^{+\infty} \frac{d^m \delta(x)}{dx^m} f(x)\, dx = (-1)^m \frac{d^m f(0)}{dx^m}.$$

It is needless to emphasize that the only meaning that can be assigned to the above statement is that

$$\lim_{n \to \infty} \int_{-\infty}^{+\infty} \frac{d^m \phi_n(x)}{dx^m} f(x) \, dx = (-1)^m \frac{d^m f(0)}{dx^m},$$

and it is tacitly assumed that the functions involved are differentiable m times and that the integrals

$$\int_{-\infty}^{+\infty} \frac{d^k \phi_n(x)}{dx^k} f(x) \, dx$$

converge for all n and for all k from 0 to m.

It should now be clear that the treatment of $\delta(x)$ and its derivatives as functions in the ordinary sense (which they cannot be) is a shortcut method for obtaining results depending on certain limiting processes. This procedure may be called δ-*calculus* and it is widely employed in physical literature. As in the case of Heaviside's operational calculus, it will yield valid results provided its limitations are recognized and observed.

We may develop the various rules of δ-calculus by formal analytic operations starting from the properties

a) $\int_{-\infty}^{+\infty} \delta(x) f(x) \, dx = f(0),$

b) $\delta(x) = \dfrac{d}{dx} S(x),$

c) $\delta(x) = \begin{cases} 0 & (x \neq 0), \\ \infty & (x = 0) \end{cases}$ with $\int_{-\infty}^{+\infty} \delta(x) \, dx = 1$

and ignoring, for the time being, their mathematical justification.

Example 1. Verify the rule that $x \, \delta(x) = 0$.

Consider $\int_{-\infty}^{+\infty} x \, \delta(x) f(x) \, dx$, where $f(x)$ is continuous at $x = 0$. Write $x f(x) = g(x)$; then $g(0) = 0$. Consequently,

$$\int_{-\infty}^{+\infty} x \, \delta(x) f(x) \, dx = 0$$

for *all* continuous (at $x = 0$) functions $f(x)$. This justifies the equivalence of $x \, \delta(x)$ and the zero function.

Example 2. Determine the meaning of $\delta(x - a)$.

Consider $\int_{-\infty}^{+\infty} \delta(x - a) f(x) \, dx$. Set $x - a = \xi$ and write $f(\xi + a) = g(\xi)$; then

$$\int_{-\infty}^{+\infty} \delta(x - a) f(x) \, dx = \int_{-\infty}^{+\infty} \delta(\xi) g(\xi) \, d\xi = g(0) = f(a).$$

Remark. In the spirit of δ-calculus it may be said that

$$\delta(x - a) = \frac{d}{dx} S(x - a).$$

Example 3. Verify the rule

$$\delta(ax) = (1/|a|) \,\delta(x), \, a \neq 0.$$

Assume that $a > 0$ and write, using $ax = \xi$, $dx = (1/a) \, d\xi$:

$$\int_{-\infty}^{+\infty} \delta(ax)f(x) \, dx = \int_{-\infty}^{+\infty} \delta(\xi)f(\xi/a)(1/a) \, d\xi = (1/a)f(0).$$

If $a < 0$, use $ax = \xi$, $dx = (1/a) \, d\xi$ again; now, however, the limits of integration are interchanged and

$$\int_{-\infty}^{+\infty} \delta(ax)f(x) \, dx = \int_{+\infty}^{-\infty} \delta(\xi)f(\xi/a)(1/a) \, d\xi = -(1/a)f(0).$$

In either case, the result is $(1/|a|)f(0)$, thus establishing the rule.

Remark: From this it follows that $\delta(x)$ is an even function (set $a = -1$).

Example 4. Verify the rule

$$\delta(x^2 - a^2) = (1/2a)[\delta(x + a) + \delta(x - a)]   (a > 0).$$

Observe that $\delta(x^2 - a^2) = \delta[(x + a)(x - a)]$. Since $\delta(\xi) = 0$ unless $\xi = 0$, it follows that $\delta(x^2 - a^2) = 0$ except at the points $x = \pm a$. Therefore, we can write

$$\int_{-\infty}^{+\infty} \delta(x^2 - a^2)f(x) \, dx = \int_{-a-\epsilon}^{-a+\epsilon} \delta[(x + a)(x - a)]f(x) \, dx$$

$$+ \int_{a-\epsilon}^{a+\epsilon} \delta[(x + a)(x - a)]f(x) \, dx   (a > 0),$$

where $0 < \epsilon < 2a$ and ϵ can be arbitrarily small. Now, in the neighborhood of $x = -a$, the factor $(x - a)$ may be replaced by $-2a$. Then

$$\int_{-a-\epsilon}^{-a+\epsilon} \delta[(x + a)(x - a)]f(x) \, dx = \int_{-a-\epsilon}^{-a+\epsilon} \delta[(-2a)(x + a)]f(x) \, dx$$

$$= \int_{-a-\epsilon}^{-a+\epsilon} \frac{1}{|-2a|} \delta(x + a)f(x) \, dx$$

$$= \int_{-\infty}^{+\infty} \frac{1}{2a} \delta(x + a)f(x) \, dx.$$

The infinite limits can be used again because $\delta(x + a) = 0$ except at $x = -a$.

In a similar manner,

$$\int_{a-\epsilon}^{a+\epsilon} \delta[(x + a)(x - a)]f(x)\, dx = \int_{-\infty}^{+\infty} \frac{1}{2a} \delta(x - a)f(x)\, dx,$$

and the rule is established.

Remark. This rule breaks down for $a = 0$. There is apparently no way of interpreting the expression $\delta(x^2)$.

6.4 REPRESENTATIONS OF DELTA FUNCTIONS

For the purpose of formal operations employed in the δ-calculus it is convenient to establish for $\delta(x)$ such expressions as Fourier series, the Laplace transform, and integral representations.

Consider the pulse $\phi_a(x)$ shown in Fig. 6.6. Its Fourier coefficients are $b_n = 0$ (the function is even), $a_0 = 1/L$, $a_n = (1/n\pi a) \sin(n\pi a/L)$ ($n \geq 1$). Therefore the Fourier series reads

$$\phi_a(x) = \frac{1}{2L} + \sum_{n=1}^{\infty} \frac{1}{n\pi a} \sin \frac{n\pi a}{L} \cos \frac{n\pi x}{L}.$$

Letting $a \to 0$, we obtain the Fourier series for $\delta(x)$:

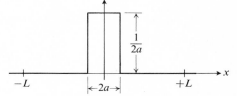

$$\delta(x) = \frac{1}{2L} + \frac{1}{L} \sum_{n=1}^{\infty} \cos \frac{n\pi x}{L}.$$

Figure 6.6

Observe that this series is divergent; this should not come as a surprise because if it were convergent, then $\delta(x)$ would exist as a *bona fide* function, which as we know, is not the case.

Despite this drawback it should not be concluded that this series is absolutely useless. For instance, multiply it by a "well-behaved" function $f(x)$ and integrate term by term from $x = -L$ to $x = +L$:

$$\frac{1}{2L} \int_{-L}^{+L} f(x)\, dx + \sum_{n=1}^{\infty} \frac{1}{L} \int_{-L}^{+L} f(x) \cos \frac{n\pi x}{L}\, dx = \frac{a_0}{2} + \sum_{n=1}^{\infty} a_n,$$

where a_n ($n = 0, 1, 2, \ldots$) are Fourier coefficients of $f(x)$. If $f(x)$ is represented by a Fourier series

$$f(x) = \frac{a_0}{2} + \sum_{n=1}^{\infty} \left(a_n \cos \frac{n\pi x}{L} + b_n \sin \frac{n\pi x}{L} \right),$$

then, if $f(x)$ is continuous at $x = 0$,

$$f(0) = \frac{a_0}{2} + \sum_{n=1}^{\infty} a_n.$$

It follows that the divergent series

$$\frac{1}{2L} + \frac{1}{L} \sum_{n=1}^{\infty} \cos \frac{n\pi x}{L}$$

does possess the sifting property and may be treated as a representative of the delta function.

In a similar fashion we may develop various other series for delta function. For instance, the Fourier sine series for $\delta(x - \xi)$ reads

$$\delta(x - \xi) = \frac{2}{L} \sum_{n=1}^{\infty} \sin \frac{n\pi\xi}{L} \sin \frac{n\pi x}{L} \qquad (0 < \xi < L).$$

We may also develop integral representations of $\delta(x)$. Recall the integral for the step function (Section 2.15):

$$S(x) = \frac{1}{2\pi i} \int_{\gamma - i\infty}^{\gamma + i\infty} \frac{1}{z} e^{xz} \, dz.$$

Differentiating formally under the integral sign, we obtain

$$\delta(x) = \frac{dS(x)}{dx} = \frac{1}{2\pi i} \int_{\gamma - i\infty}^{\gamma + i\infty} e^{xz} \, dz.$$

The number γ in the integral for $S(x)$ may be arbitrary but positive because of the pole at $z = 0$. However, there is no pole of the integrand for $\delta(x)$ so that we may set (for convenience) $\gamma = 0$, yielding

$$\delta(x) = \frac{1}{2\pi i} \int_{-i\infty}^{+i\infty} e^{xz} \, dz.$$

This integral representation can be cast in a slightly different form by a change of variables, $k = -iz$ (this corresponds to a rotation of the plane by 90° clockwise). Then

$$\delta(x) = \frac{1}{2\pi} \int_{-\infty}^{+\infty} e^{ikx} \, dk.$$

This remarkable integral (divergent, of course)* is extremely common in physical applications of the δ-calculus. Its sifting property may be established in a variety of ways. As an illustration, consider the function

$$\phi_a(x) = \frac{1}{2\pi} \int_{-\infty}^{+\infty} e^{-a^2 k^2} e^{ikx} \, dk \qquad (a \neq 0).$$

---

* See p. 115.

Here the so-called *convergence factor* $e^{-a^2k^2}$ makes the integral convergent. Formally, we would be inclined to say that

$$\frac{1}{2\pi} \int_{-\infty}^{+\infty} e^{ikx}\, dk = \lim_{a \to 0} \phi_a(x)$$

provided the operations of integration and taking the limit $a \to 0$ could be interchanged.

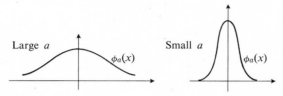

Figure 6.7

Now, the integral defining $\phi_a(x)$ can be easily evaluated: Complete the square,

$$-a^2k^2 + ikx = -(ak + x/2ai)^2 - x^2/4a^2.$$

Then

$$\phi_a(x) = (1/2\pi)e^{-x^2/4a^2} \int_{-\infty}^{+\infty} e^{-(ak+x/2ai)^2}\, dk.$$

Set $ak + x/2ai = u$ and use* $\int_{-\infty}^{+\infty} e^{-u^2}\, du = \sqrt{\pi}$ to obtain

$$\phi_a(x) = (1/2a\sqrt{\pi})e^{-x^2/4a^2}.$$

This function, known as the Gaussian (or *normal*) probability function, is strongly peaked when a is small (Fig. 6.7). Moreover, $\phi_a(x)$ is normalized:

$$\int_{-\infty}^{+\infty} \phi_a(x)\, dx = 1 \qquad \text{(all } a\text{).}$$

It is then expected, and can be rigorously proved, that

$$\lim_{a \to 0} \int_{-\infty}^{+\infty} \phi_a(x)f(x)\, dx = f(0)$$

for any "reasonably behaving" function $f(x)$; for instance, differentiability at $x = 0$ will suffice. This analysis suggests that the following formula will hold:

$$(1/2\pi) \int_{-\infty}^{+\infty} \int_{-\infty}^{+\infty} e^{ikx} f(x)\, dk\, dx = f(0).$$

In fact (see Chapter 7), this formula does hold, in the usual rigorous sense, for a wide class of functions $f(x)$, provided that the integration over x is carried out first.

---

* The integral over u is now a complex integral along the line Im $u = -x/2a$. Use, however, the Cauchy theorem and show that the integration along the real axis (in the u-plane) must yield the same result.

We shall conclude this section by evaluating the Laplace transform of the delta function. Consider again the (normalized) rectangular pulse (Fig. 6.8). Its Laplace transform is

$$\int_{t_0}^{t_0+\tau} \frac{1}{\tau} e^{-st}\, dt = e^{-st_0} \frac{1 - e^{-s\tau}}{s\tau}.$$

Now let $\tau \to 0$; since

$$\lim_{\tau \to 0} \frac{1 - e^{-s\tau}}{s\tau} = 1,$$

we can write $\mathcal{L}\{\delta(t - t_0)\} = e^{-st_0}.$

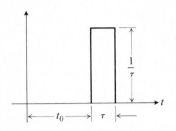

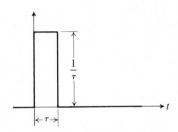

Figure 6.8   Figure 6.9

Remark. Although the formula $\mathcal{L}\{\delta(t)\} = 1$ can be established by setting $t_0 = 0$, it should be pointed out that this delta function is not quite the same as the one defined for the interval $(-\infty, +\infty)$. For instance, we could not say that $\delta(t)$ (as constructed above) is an even function since in the Laplace transform theory all functions are assumed to be zero for $t < 0$, and the rectangular pulse used to construct the delta function has the appearance of the graph shown in Fig. 6.9, rather than that of the curve in Fig. 6.6. A practical consequence of this fact is that the sifting property is now going to read

$$\int_0^\infty \delta(t) f(t)\, dt = f(0 + 0),$$

rather than $\int_{-\infty}^{+\infty} \delta(t) f(t)\, dt = f(0)$. This fact is worth remembering since in many problems using the Laplace transform, the value $f(0)$ can hardly be defined at all (e.g., Example 3 in Section 5.10).

6.5 APPLICATIONS OF THE δ-CALCULUS

Consider the motion of a damped harmonic oscillator under the action of an external force $f(t)$. The DE reads

$$m\ddot{x} + \rho\dot{x} + kx = f(t).$$

Suppose that the force $f(t)$ represents a sudden blow at time t_0. The exact form of the force is not known, but it is known that its impulse is I:

$$\int_{t_0-\epsilon}^{t_0+\epsilon} f(t)\, dt = I \qquad (\epsilon > 0),$$

where ϵ may be taken to be arbitrarily small. Such a force $f(t)$ can be approximated by the function

$$I\,\delta(t - t_0)$$

so that the differential equation to be solved reads

$$\ddot{x} + 2\lambda\dot{x} + \omega_0^2 x = (I/m)\,\delta(t - t_0) \qquad (\lambda = \rho/2m,\ \omega_0 = \sqrt{k/m}).$$

Suppose that the oscillator is at rest at $t = 0$; we tacitly assume that $t_0 > 0$. Then

$$x(0) = 0, \qquad \dot{x}(0) = 0.$$

We shall solve this equation by means of Laplace transforms. The transformed equation reads

$$s^2 X(s) + 2\lambda s\, X(s) + \omega_0^2 X(s) = (I/m)e^{-st_0}$$

so that

$$X(s) = \frac{I}{m}\,\frac{e^{-st_0}}{s^2 + 2\lambda s + \omega_0^2}\,.$$

The roots of the denominator are $r = -\lambda \pm \sqrt{\lambda^2 - \omega_0^2}$. To be specific, assume that $\omega_0^2 > \lambda^2$ and set $\omega^2 = \omega_0^2 - \lambda^2$. Furthermore, write

$$X(s) = \frac{I}{m}\,\frac{1}{(s - r_1)(s - r_2)}\,e^{-st_0}$$

and invert by use of the Heaviside theorem:

$$x(t) = \frac{I}{m}\left\{\frac{e^{r_1(t-t_0)}}{r_1 - r_2} + \frac{e^{r_2(t-t_0)}}{r_2 - r_1}\right\}.$$

Now use $r_1 = -\lambda + i\omega$, $r_2 = -\lambda - i\omega$ and reduce this to

$$x(t) = (I/m)e^{-\lambda(t-t_0)} \sin \omega(t - t_0)S(t - t_0)$$

or

$$x(t) = \begin{cases} 0 & (t < t_0), \\ (I/m)e^{-\lambda(t-t_0)} \sin \omega(t - t_0) & (t > t_0). \end{cases}$$

It is instructive to obtain this solution by conventional methods. Since the force $f(t)$ supposedly acts instantaneously at $t = t_0$, the oscillator obeys the homogeneous equation for both $t < t_0$ and $t > t_0$:

$$\ddot{x} + 2\lambda\dot{x} + \omega_0^2 x = 0 \qquad (t \neq t_0).$$

Also

$$\left.\begin{array}{l} x(t) = 0 \\ \dot{x}(t) = 0 \end{array}\right\} \quad (\text{for } t < t_0).$$

For $t > t_0$, the general solution may be written as $x(t) = Ae^{-\lambda t} \sin(\omega t + \phi)$.

To find A and ϕ, note that physical conditions imply that $x(t)$ is continuous everywhere (including $t = t_0$). Also observe that this cannot be said about $\dot{x}(t)$. With this in mind, integrate the DE from $t_0 - \epsilon$ to $t_0 + \epsilon$:

$$\int_{t_0-\epsilon}^{t_0+\epsilon} \ddot{x}\, dt + 2\lambda \int_{t_0-\epsilon}^{t_0+\epsilon} \dot{x}\, dt + \omega_0^2 \int_{t_0-\epsilon}^{t_0+\epsilon} x\, dt = I/m$$

or

$$\dot{x}(t_0 + \epsilon) - \dot{x}_0(t - \epsilon_0) + 2\lambda x(t_0 + \epsilon) - 2\lambda x(t_0 - \epsilon) + \omega_0^2 \int_{t_0-\epsilon}^{t_0+\epsilon} x\, dt = I/m.$$

This is valid for an arbitrary ϵ. Let $\epsilon \to 0$ and use the continuity of $x(t)$; then

$$\lim_{\epsilon \to 0} \int_{t_0-\epsilon}^{t_0+\epsilon} x(t)\, dt = 0, \quad \text{and} \quad \lim_{\epsilon \to 0} [x(t_0 + \epsilon) - x(t_0 - \epsilon)] = 0.$$

Note also that $\dot{x}(t_0 - \epsilon) = 0$ (both x and $\dot{x}$ vanish for $t < t_0$). Consequently,

$$\lim_{\epsilon \to 0} \dot{x}(t_0 + \epsilon) = \dot{x}(t_0 + 0) = I/m.$$

Since

$$\dot{x}(t) = -\lambda e^{-\lambda t} A \sin(\omega t + \phi) + \omega e^{-\lambda t} \cos(\omega t + \phi) \qquad (t > t_0),$$

we can obtain, letting $t \to t_0$ *from the right*,

$$I/m = \omega e^{-\lambda t_0} A \cos(\omega t_0 + \phi).$$

On the other hand, letting $t \to t_0$ in the expression for $x(t)$, we can obtain

$$0 = e^{-\lambda t_0} A \sin(\omega t_0 + \phi).$$

Thus, $\sin(\omega t_0 + \phi) = 0$, or $\omega t_0 + \phi = n\pi$ ($n = $ integer). Then

$$\cos(\omega t_0 + \phi) = (-1)^n \quad \text{and} \quad A = (-1)^n (I/\omega m) e^{\lambda t_0}.$$

The solution reads

$$x(t) = (-1)^n (I/\omega m) e^{-\lambda(t-t_0)} \sin[\omega(t - t_0) + n\pi] \qquad (t > t_0).$$

Whatever n may be, the above result is identical with

$$x(t) = (I/\omega m) e^{-\lambda(t-t_0)} \sin \omega(t - t_0) \qquad (t > t_0).$$

It is seen that the solution obtained through δ-calculus is a correct one, and that we arrived at it with less effort than by using conventional methods.

As another example, consider a simply supported beam loaded by a concentrated force P at the center (Fig. 6.10). In the DE*

$$\frac{d^4 y(x)}{dx^4} = \frac{1}{EI}\, q(x),$$

---

* See p. 174.

we can now set $q(x) = P \, \delta(x - L/2)$ on the grounds that P actually represents an infinitely sharply peaked distribution of load with

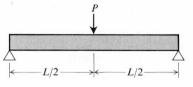

$$\int_{L/2-\epsilon}^{L/2+\epsilon} q(x)\, dx = P, \qquad (\epsilon > 0),$$

Figure 6.10

where ϵ is arbitrarily small.

This problem can be solved efficiently by the Fourier sine series expansions. Assume that

$$y(x) = \sum_{n=1}^{\infty} b_n \sin (n\pi x/L),$$

and use the (divergent) series

$$\delta\left(x - \frac{L}{2}\right) = \frac{2}{L} \sum_{n=1}^{\infty} \sin \frac{n\pi}{2} \sin \frac{n\pi x}{L} = \frac{2}{L} \sum_{n=1,3,5,\dots}^{\infty} (-1)^{(n-1)/2} \sin \frac{n\pi x}{L}.$$

Substitute this into the DE,

$$\sum_{n=1}^{\infty} \left(\frac{n\pi}{L}\right)^4 b_n \sin \frac{n\pi x}{L} = \frac{2P}{EIL} \sum_{n=1,3,5,\dots}^{\infty} (-1)^{(n-1)/2} \sin \frac{n\pi x}{L}.$$

Consequently,

$$b_n = \begin{cases} (-1)^{(n-1)/2} \dfrac{2PL^3}{EI\pi^4} \dfrac{1}{n^4} & (n = \text{odd}), \\[2mm] 0 & (n = \text{even}) \end{cases}$$

and

$$y(x) = \frac{2PL^3}{EI\pi^4} \sum_{n=1,3,5,\dots}^{\infty} \frac{(-1)^{(n-1)/2}}{n^4} \sin \frac{n\pi x}{L}.$$

It is not difficult to verify (by methods similar to those used in the first example) that this is indeed the Fourier sine series of the correct solution $y(x)$. Observe, however, that a direct attempt to verify this will fail; we will hit a snag after differentiating the series three times, at which time uniform convergence will cease to be valid.

Remark. As in Example 2 of Section 4.8, we find that the series is rapidly convergent. For instance, if $x = L/2$, the leading term alone yields the approximate deflection

$$y\left(\frac{L}{2}\right) \cong \frac{2}{\pi^4} \frac{PL^3}{EI}$$

which is only about 1% off the exact result

$$y\left(\frac{L}{2}\right) = \frac{1}{48} \frac{PL^3}{EI}.$$

6.6 WEAK CONVERGENCE

The ideas mentioned in the preceding sections which lead to the concept of the delta function can be systemized into what is known as the *theory of distributions*, or *generalized functions*.

As the name suggests, the theory is concerned with the problem of *extending the definition* of a function so that concepts such as $\delta(x)$ can be put on a firm mathematical basis. There are various ways to achieve this. We shall pursue the idea expressed in Section 6.2, namely, the approach to distributions through integrals of sequences of functions of the type

$$\int f_n(x)g(x)\,dx \qquad (n = 1, 2, 3, \ldots)$$

A sequence of functions $f_n(x)$ (such as a delta sequence) leads to a new mathematical concept (such as delta function), provided such a sequence of integrals converges for *any* suitable function $g(x)$. Now, what shall we call "suitable?" From Section 9.3 we know that if we wish to define concepts like $\delta'(x)$, $\delta''(x)$, etc., then $g(x)$ should be *infinitely differentiable*.* Also, we shall assume that the limits of integration (unless stated otherwise) will be $-\infty$ and $+\infty$. Therefore, $g(x)$ must have "proper behavior" at infinity. We shall insist on a very strong requirement of this type, namely, that $g(x)$ must be *identically zero* outside some finite interval (a, b) (a different one for different $g(x)$, in general).†

Functions $g(x)$ that satisfy these requirements will be called *test functions*. This name is appropriate, since the sifting property of delta sequences, for instance, is *tested* on these functions.

Example. The function

$$g(x) = \begin{cases} e^{-a^2/(a^2-x^2)} & (|x| < a) \\ 0 & (|x| \geq a) \end{cases} \quad (a > 0)$$

is a test function. Indeed, it is evidently infinitely differentiable for $|x| \neq a$. As for the points $x = \pm a$, one can show, using the basic definitions of the derivative, that all derivatives exist and are equal to zero. As an illustration, let us demonstrate that $g'(x) = 0$ at $x = -a$. For convenience, we set $a + x = \xi$ and express g as a function of ξ. In the immediate vicinity of the point $\xi = 0$ (that is, $x = -a$) we have

$$g(\xi) = \begin{cases} 0 & (\xi \leq 0), \\ e^{-a^2/\xi(2a-\xi)} & (\xi > 0). \end{cases}$$

By definition of the derivative,

$$\frac{dg(x)}{dx}\bigg|_{x=-a} = \frac{dg(\xi)}{d\xi}\bigg|_{\xi=0} = \lim_{\xi \to 0} \frac{g(\xi) - g(0)}{\xi} = \lim_{\xi \to 0} \frac{g(\xi)}{\xi}.$$

---

* That is, differentiable any number of times.

† Less restrictive conditions can be adopted, requiring only that $g(x)$ approaches zero "sufficiently fast" as $x \to \pm\infty$ (e.g., Lighthill, *Fourier Analysis and Generalized Functions*).

If $\xi < 0$, then $g(\xi) = 0$ and the limit on the right-hand side of the equation is zero. If $\xi > 0$, we use $\eta = 1/\xi$ and write

$$\lim_{\xi \to 0} (1/\xi)e^{-a^2/\xi(2a-\xi)} = \lim_{\eta \to \infty} \eta e^{-[a^2/(2a-1/\eta)]\eta}.$$

Since $e^{-a^2\eta/(2a-1/\eta)} < e^{-(a/2)\eta}$ and since $\lim_{\eta \to \infty} \eta e^{-(a/2)\eta} = 0$, it follows that the proof is complete.

Having defined the test functions, we can now proceed to define the class of *core functions** from which the functions $f_n(x)$ will be selected. There is a variety of choices.† Unless stated otherwise, we shall require the core functions to be infinitely differentiable over the entire range $(-\infty, +\infty)$. Their behavior at infinity may be arbitrary. The term core functions is related to the fact that it is this *class of functions* which is being *extended* to encompass other (not infinitely differentiable) functions as well as bona fide distributions, such as the delta function.

Now consider a sequence of core functions $f_n(x)$ $(n = 1, 2, 3, \ldots)$. It will be called a *weakly convergent sequence* provided that the limit

$$\lim_{n \to \infty} \int_{-\infty}^{+\infty} f_n(x)g(x)\, dx$$

exists for *all test functions* $g(x)$. A weakly convergent sequence may or may not be convergent in any of the conventional definitions, like *pointwise convergent, uniformly convergent, convergent in the mean*, etc. The concept of weak convergence is a special one designed to extend the class of core functions in a peculiar fashion. Such extensions are possible by means of other types of convergence, but, in a sense, extension by weak convergence is more powerful. Consider, for instance, the sequence of core functions

$$f_n(x) = \tfrac{1}{2} + (1/\pi) \arctan nx.$$

It is not difficult to verify that this sequence converges (pointwise) to the step function $S(x)$. However, the core consists of functions infinitely differentiable over $(-\infty, +\infty)$ and $S(x)$ is *not a core function*. Therefore, the sequence $f_n(x)$ cannot be said to converge "within the core." Nevertheless, it converges weakly: One can show that

$$\lim_{n \to \infty} \int_{-\infty}^{+\infty} f_n(x)g(x)\, dx = \int_{-\infty}^{+\infty} S(x)g(x)\, dx = \int_{0}^{\infty} g(x)\, dx$$

for all test functions $g(x)$.

We are now in a position to *define artificially* the discontinuous function $S(x)$ by adjoining to the core functions the "limit" of $f_n(x)$ defined *only inside an integral*

---

* There is no uniform nomenclature in the theory of distributions. Most authors will call these functions *admissible functions*.

† There is no unique theory of distributions, but rather there are several, based on similar principles but differing in details.

by means of

$$\lim_{n \to \infty} \int_{-\infty}^{+\infty} (\tfrac{1}{2} + (1/\pi) \arctan nx) g(x)\, dx = \int_{-\infty}^{+\infty} S(x) g(x)\, dx.$$

Why do we try to define the step function $S(x)$ in such a complicated way? Is it not much simpler to define it pointwise as follows?*

$$S(x) = \begin{cases} 0 & (x < 0), \\ \tfrac{1}{2} & (x = 0), \\ 1 & (x > 0). \end{cases}$$

The answer is obvious because, with exactly the same ease, we can define the delta function which *defies* any pointwise definition. Consider, for instance, the sequence of core functions quoted on p. 224:

$$f_n(x) = \frac{n}{\pi} \frac{1}{1 + n^2 x^2}.$$

As $n \to \infty$, this sequence does not converge to any function (within the core or otherwise). Nevertheless, it converges weakly and

$$\lim_{n \to \infty} \int_{-\infty}^{+\infty} f_n(x) g(x)\, dx = g(0)$$

for any test function $g(x)$. The proof is as follows:

$$\int_{-\infty}^{+\infty} \frac{n}{\pi} \frac{1}{1 + n^2 x^2} g(x)\, dx = \int_{-\infty}^{-1/\sqrt{n}} \frac{n}{\pi} \frac{1}{1 + n^2 x^2} g(x)\, dx$$

$$+ \int_{-1/\sqrt{n}}^{+1/\sqrt{n}} \frac{n}{\pi} \frac{1}{1 + n^2 x^2} g(x)\, dx + \int_{+1/\sqrt{n}}^{+\infty} \frac{n}{\pi} \frac{1}{1 + n^2 x^2} g(x)\, dx.$$

Let B be the bound for $g(x)$, namely, $|g(x)| \le B$ for all x. Then

$$\left| \int_{1/\sqrt{n}}^{\infty} \frac{n}{\pi} \frac{1}{1 + n^2 x^2} g(x)\, dx \right| \le B \int_{1/\sqrt{n}}^{\infty} \frac{n}{\pi} \frac{1}{1 + n^2 x^2}\, dx = B \left(\frac{1}{2} - \frac{1}{\pi} \arctan \sqrt{n} \right).$$

Since

$$\lim_{n \to \infty} \left(\frac{1}{2} - \frac{1}{\pi} \arctan \sqrt{n} \right) = 0,$$

it follows that

$$\lim_{n \to \infty} \int_{1/\sqrt{n}}^{\infty} \frac{n}{\pi} \frac{1}{1 + n^2 x^2} g(x)\, dx = 0.$$

* Thereby extending the core by pointwise convergence.

Similarly,

$$\lim_{n\to\infty} \int_{-\infty}^{-1/\sqrt{n}} \frac{n}{\pi} \frac{1}{1 + n^2 x^2} g(x)\,dx = 0.$$

Finally, using the mean value theorem ($f_n(x) > 0$),

$$\int_{-1/\sqrt{n}}^{+1/\sqrt{n}} \frac{n}{\pi} \frac{1}{1 + n^2 x^2} g(x)\,dx = g(\xi) \int_{-1/\sqrt{n}}^{+1/\sqrt{n}} \frac{n}{\pi} \frac{1}{1 + n^2 x^2}\,dx$$

$$= g(\xi) \frac{2}{\pi} \arctan \sqrt{n} \qquad (-1/\sqrt{n} \le \xi \le +1/\sqrt{n}),$$

so that

$$\lim_{n\to\infty} \int_{-1/\sqrt{n}}^{+1/\sqrt{n}} \frac{n}{\pi} \frac{1}{1 + n^2 x^2} g(x)\,dx = g(0),$$

completing the proof.

We can now give a rigorous definition of a *distribution* as follows: A distribution $\phi(x)$ is a mathematical concept associated with a weakly convergent sequence of core functions* for which the symbolic integral

$$\int_{-\infty}^{+\infty} \phi(x) g(x)\,dx$$

has a meaning, by means of the prescription†

$$\int_{-\infty}^{+\infty} \phi(x) g(x)\,dx = \lim_{n\to\infty} \int_{-\infty}^{+\infty} f_n(x) g(x)\,dx.$$

Remarks

1. Each core function corresponds to some distribution since we can construct a sequence consisting of only a single core function $f(x)$.

2. A great variety of different weakly convergent sequences will yield the same values of

$$\lim_{n\to\infty} \int_{-\infty}^{+\infty} f_n(x) g(x)\,dx$$

for all test functions $g(x)$ (e.g., various kinds of delta sequences). Such *equivalent* sequences correspond to the same distribution.

---

* There is another, more abstract, but also more general, approach to the theory of distributions which defines a distribution as a *linear continuous functional over the space of test functions* (e.g., Gelfand and Shilov, *Generalized Functions*, Academic Press, 1965). This definition dispenses with core functions altogether, along with the integrals.

† For convenience in describing the relationship between a distribution $\phi(x)$ and the weakly convergent sequence $\{f_n(x)\}$, we shall use the expression "the *sequence* $\{f_n(x)\}$ *weakly converges to* (a distribution) $\phi(x)$." The precise meaning of this statement is given by our definition.

Example 1. The following sequences are equivalent, all corresponding to the distribution denoted by $\theta(x)$:

a) $f_n(x) = \frac{1}{2}\,\text{erfc}\,(-nx) = (1/\sqrt{\pi})\int_{-nx}^{\infty} e^{-u^2}\,du,$

b) $f_n(x) = \frac{1}{2} + (1/\pi)\,\text{Si}\,(nx) = (1/\pi)\int_{-\infty}^{nx} (\sin u/u)\,du,$

c) $f_n(x) = e^{-e^{-nx}}.$

Note: Sequences (a) and (b) also converge pointwise to the conventional step function $S(x)$ (as given on p. 114); sequence (c) converges pointwise to the function

$$\overline{S}(x) = \begin{cases} 0 & (x < 0), \\ 1/e & (x = 0), \\ 1 & (x > 0). \end{cases}$$

From the point of view of classical theory of functions, $S(x)$ and $\overline{S}(x)$ are *different functions*. From the point of view of the theory of distributions, $S(x)$ and $\overline{S}(x)$ correspond to the *same distribution* $\theta(x)$ which is not even defined by a formula like that for $S(x)$ and $\overline{S}(x)$, but rather through the limiting process described in weak convergence.

Example 2. The sequences

a) $f_n(x) = \dfrac{n}{\pi}\dfrac{1}{1 + n^2x^2},$ b) $f_n(x) = \dfrac{n}{\sqrt{\pi}}\,e^{-n^2x^2},$

c) $f_n(x) = \dfrac{1 - \cos nx}{n\pi x^2},$ d) $f_n(x) = \dfrac{1}{n\pi}\dfrac{\sin^2 nx}{x^2},$

are equivalent, yielding the result

$$\lim_{n\to\infty} \int_{-\infty}^{+\infty} f_n(x)g(x)\,dx = g(0) \qquad (\text{all } g(x)).$$

The distribution defined by any of these sequences is called *delta function** and is denoted by $\delta(x)$.

6.7 CORRESPONDENCE OF FUNCTIONS AND DISTRIBUTIONS

Let $\phi(x)$ be a distribution. In this case the expression

$$\int_{-\infty}^{+\infty} \phi(x)g(x)\,dx$$

is *not* an integral (in the Riemann sense), but rather the limit of a sequence of

---

* Of course, we should call it *delta distribution* instead, but the name *delta function* is now part of a long tradition.

Riemann integrals. However, it may be *equivalent* to a Riemann integral if a *function* $f(x)$ can be found (not necessarily a core function) such that

$$\int_{-\infty}^{+\infty} f(x)g(x)\,dx = \int_{-\infty}^{+\infty} \phi(x)g(x)\,dx = \lim_{n\to\infty}\int_{-\infty}^{+\infty} f_n(x)g(x)\,dx$$

for all test functions $g(x)$. As a rule, this will happen if the sequence $f_n(x)$ converges pointwise to some function $\overline{f}(x)$ which can be taken as $f(x)$.* However, surprisingly enough, there are exceptions to this "obvious" rule.

Example. The functions

$$F_n(x) = \begin{cases} e^{-1/[1-4(nx-1)^2]} & (|x - 1/n| < 1/2n), \\ 0 & (|x - 1/n| \geq 1/2n) \end{cases}$$

are evidently core functions.† They are infinitely differentiable everywhere and vanish outside the interval $(1/2n, 3/2n)$. Let us normalize them:

$$f_n(x) = \frac{F_n(x)}{\int_{1/2n}^{3/2n} F_n(x)\,dx}$$

(so that now $\int_{1/2n}^{3/2n} f_n(x)\,dx = 1$). The sequence of functions $f_n(x)$ *converges pointwise to zero*. Indeed, if $x \leq 0$, then $f_n(x) = 0$ (for all n). If $x > 0$, choose N large enough so that $N > 3/2x$. Then $f_n(x) = 0$ for all $n \geq N$ and the statement follows. Observe, however, that the convergence is *not uniform*.

The sequence $f_n(x)$ also *converges weakly*. For any test function $g(x)$ we have, by the mean value theorem (note that $f_n(x) \geq 0$),

$$\int_{-\infty}^{+\infty} f_n(x)g(x)\,dx = \int_{1/2n}^{3/2n} f_n(x)g(x)\,dx$$

$$= g(\xi)\int_{1/2n}^{3/2n} f_n(x)\,dx = g(\xi) \qquad (1/2n \leq \xi \leq 3/2n).$$

Now, if $n \to \infty$, then ξ must approach zero (from the right). By continuity of test functions,

$$\lim_{\xi\to 0} g(\xi) = g(0).‡$$

---

* Clearly, $f(x)$ is not unique, as the case with $S(x)$ and $\overline{S}(x)$ shows (Section 6.6). We have

$$\int_{-\infty}^{+\infty} S(x)g(x)\,dx = \int_{-\infty}^{+\infty} \overline{S}(x)g(x)\,dx$$

for all test functions $g(x)$.
† These functions are of the same kind as $g(x)$ on p. 236, with $a = 1/2n$, and centered about the point $x = 1/n$ (rather than $x = 0$); that is, x has been replaced by $(x - 1/n)$.
‡ This means that $\{f_n(x)\}$ is a delta sequence. However, while previous delta sequences were divergent, this one is convergent (to zero); convergence has been achieved by shifting the peak of $f_n(x)$ while making it higher and narrower.

We have, therefore, shown that

$$\lim_{n \to \infty} f_n(x) = \overline{f}(x) = 0$$

so that

$$\int_{-\infty}^{+\infty} \lim_{n \to \infty} f_n(x)g(x)\, dx = 0 \qquad [\text{all } g(x)],$$

but

$$\lim_{n \to \infty} \int_{-\infty}^{+\infty} f_n(x)g(x)\, dx = g(0) \qquad [\text{all } g(x)].$$

This example illustrates that the concept of pointwise convergence may have very little meaning from the point of view of a physicist. Indeed, if functions $f_n(x)$ represent successive approximations to a certain physical quantity and the formula

$$\int_{-\infty}^{+\infty} f_n(x)\, dx = 1$$

remains true at all times, how is it possible to reconcile physical intuition with the statement that $f_n(x)$ "converges to zero?" It is reasonable to conjecture that, at least for certain purposes, distributions are more suitable for description of physical quantities than conventional functions.

Let us look into some problems created by this proposal. First of all, it should be firmly remembered that we cannot talk about the value of a distribution at any given point.* For instance, $\delta(x)$ cannot be assigned any value at $x = 0$. By itself, this would not be so bad, but the fact that the entire contribution to the integral

$$\int_{-\infty}^{+\infty} \delta(x)\, dx = 1$$

comes exactly from $x = 0$ is rather embarrassing. As another example, the distribution $\theta(x)$ [corresponding to the step function $S(x)$] is defined by the sequences of the integrals

$$\lim_{n \to \infty} \int_{-\infty}^{+\infty} f_n(x)g(x)\, dx = \int_{0}^{\infty} g(x)\, dx,$$

and does not distinguish between $S(x)$ and $\overline{S}(x)$ of Section 6.6. It is equivalent to either of them. Evidently, $\theta(x)$ cannot be assigned a definite value at $x = 0$.

Does not this property of distributions contradict the commonly assumed properties of physical quantities as functions? Perhaps not. For instance, consider the measurement of an electric current $I(t)$ varying in time. The current is measured by an ammeter possessing a certain inertia: It cannot respond to *in-*

---

* From that point of view, the notation $\phi(x)$ for a distribution is misleading. The symbol $\phi(x)$ is meant to indicate that there is a number y [$y = \phi(x)$] corresponding to the number x. We follow, however, this traditional notation which has its obvious advantages.

stantaneous changes in current. What is being measured is not really a function $I(t)$ but rather some sort of *average current*, more like the expression

$$1/\epsilon \int_t^{t+\epsilon} I(\tau)\, d\tau$$

for some finite ϵ (however small it may be). From this point of view physical quantities hardly possess the mathematical properties of classical functions.

Nevertheless, since classical functions certainly approximate physical quantities, it is necessary to show that distributions can perform the same task. In other words, we must show that there exist distributions virtually indistinguishable from ordinary functions, at least of the types used in physics. The major step in this direction is accomplished by the following theorem.

The smudging theorem. For every continuous function $f(x)$ one can construct a sequence $\{f_n(x)\}$ of core functions so that

$$|f_n(x) - f(x)| < \epsilon$$

for arbitrarily small ϵ, *uniformly in x* within any finite interval.

Proof. Consider the sequence of the core functions*

$$U_n(x, \xi) = \begin{cases} e^{-1/[1-n^2(x-\xi)^2]} & (|x - \xi| < 1/n), \\ 0 & (|x - \xi| \geq 1/n). \end{cases}$$

They will be normalized if we divide them by the normalization *integral*

$$N_n = \int_{x-1/n}^{x+1/n} \exp\left[-\frac{1}{1 - n^2(x - \xi)^2}\right] d\xi = \int_{-1/n}^{+1/n} \exp\left(-\frac{1}{1 - n^2\xi'^2}\right) d\xi'$$

(by a change of variables $\xi' = x - \xi$); note that N_n is independent of x. Now define a sequence

$$f_n(x) = \frac{1}{N_n} \int_{x-1/n}^{x+1/n} f(\xi) U_n(x, \xi)\, d\xi,$$

which is a sequence of core functions. Indeed, $f_n(x)$ is infinitely differentiable itself and vanishes at $x = \pm 1/n$, along with all its derivatives.†

---

* See the footnote on p. 241.

† The formula

$$\frac{d}{dx}\int_{a(x)}^{b(x)} f(x, t)\, dx = \int_{a(x)}^{b(x)} \frac{\partial f(x, t)}{\partial x}\, dt + f[x, b(x)]\frac{db(x)}{dt} - f[x, a(x)]\frac{da(x)}{dx}$$

is being invoked. It is valid in a finite interval $[a(x), b(x)]$ if $\partial f/\partial x$ is continuous.

Remark. What is being done is the *averaging* (or *smudging**) of the function $f(x)$ over the interval $(x - 1/n, x + 1/n)$ by means of the function U_n. This creates an infinitely differentiable function $f_n(x)$ out of $f(x)$ (which may lack such a property) in such a way that $f_n(x)$ is a very good approximation to $f(x)$ for large values of n.

We can also write

$$f(x) = f(x) \frac{\int_{x-1/n}^{x+1/n} U_n(x, \xi)\, d\xi}{N_n} = \frac{1}{N_n} \int_{x-1/n}^{x+1/n} f(x) U_n(x, \xi)\, d\xi$$

and construct the expression (since $U_n \geq 0$)

$$|f_n(x) - f(x)| = 1/N_n \int_{x-1/n}^{x+1/n} |f(\xi) - f(x)| U_n(x, \xi)\, d\xi.$$

Since $|x - \xi| \leq 1/n$, one can always choose n large enough to make $|x - \xi|$ arbitrarily small which implies, by continuity of $f(x)$,

$$|f(\xi) - f(x)| < \epsilon$$

valid for all x in an arbitrary finite interval, with ϵ being arbitrarily small. Then

$$|f_n(x) - f(x)| \leq \epsilon/N_n \int_{x-1/n}^{x+1/n} U_n(x, \xi)\, d\xi = \epsilon$$

as required.

The *uniform convergence* provision in the smudging theorem permits us to formulate the following corollary.

Corollary. For every continuous function $f(x)$ an *equivalent* distribution $\phi(x)$ can be found such that

$$\int_{-\infty}^{+\infty} \phi(x) g(x)\, dx = \int_{-\infty}^{+\infty} f(x) g(x)\, dx$$

for any test function $g(x)$.

Indeed, let $f_n(x)$ be a sequence of core functions as described in the smudging theorem. Let $g(x)$ be a test function; by definition, it must vanish outside a certain interval (a, b). Therefore

$$\left| \int_{-\infty}^{+\infty} f_n(x) g(x)\, dx - \int_{-\infty}^{+\infty} f(x) g(x)\, dx \right| = \left| \int_a^b [f_n(x) - f(x)] g(x)\, dx \right|$$

$$\leq \int_a^b |f_n(x) - f(x)| |g(x)|\, dx.$$

By the smudging theorem, $|f_n(x) - f(x)|$ can be made arbitrarily small for *all* x inside the interval (a, b). Therefore

$$\left| \int_{-\infty}^{+\infty} f_n(x) g(x)\, dx - \int_{-\infty}^{+\infty} f(x) g(x)\, dx \right| \leq \epsilon \int_a^b |g(x)|\, dx = \epsilon B(b - a),$$

---

* See Lighthill, *Fourier Analysis and Generalized Functions*, p. 22.

where B is the bound on $|g(x)|$. Since we can make the right-hand side arbitrarily small by choosing n sufficiently large for any given test function $g(x)$, it follows that

$$\lim_{n\to\infty} \int_{-\infty}^{+\infty} f_n(x)g(x)\,dx = \int_{-\infty}^{+\infty} f(x)g(x)\,dx,$$

establishing the equivalence between a distribution $\phi(x)$ defined by the left-hand side of the above formula and a continuous function $f(x)$.

Remark. The equivalence of $f(x)$ and $\phi(x)$ can be extended to piecewise continuous functions. However, it is simpler to treat these functions as derivatives of piecewise smooth functions* and employ the differentiability property of distributions (see the discussion in Section 6.8).

6.8 PROPERTIES OF DISTRIBUTIONS

Distributions can be subjected to various *linear* operations common to ordinary functions. First of all, distributions can be added and multiplied by constants (in other words, linear combinations of distributions are also distributions). This follows from the consideration of sequences of integrals

$$\int_{-\infty}^{+\infty} [f_n(x) + h_n(x)]g(x)\,dx$$

and

$$\int_{-\infty}^{+\infty} [Cf_n(x)]g(x)\,dx \qquad (C = \text{const}).$$

If $f_n(x)$ and $h_n(x)$ are core functions, so are the functions

$$s_n(x) = f_n(x) + h_n(x)$$

and

$$z_n(x) = Cf_n(x).$$

Moreover, sequences $s_n(x)$ and $z_n(x)$ must be weakly convergent if the sequences $f_n(x)$ and $h_n(x)$ are weakly convergent. Therefore, the above sequences of integrals *define* the distributions

$$\sigma(x) = \phi(x) + \chi(x), \qquad \zeta(x) = C\phi(x),$$

where $\phi(x)$ and $\chi(x)$ are distributions corresponding to $f_n(x)$ and $h_n(x)$.

Distributions can also be multiplied by *infinitely differentiable* functions. Indeed, let $h(x)$ be an infinitely differentiable function and let the sequence $f_n(x)$ be weakly convergent. Consider the sequence

$$\int_{-\infty}^{+\infty} [h(x)f_n(x)]g(x)\,dx.$$

* See p. 167.

The functions $y_n(x) = h(x)f_n(x)$ are core functions. Also, the above integral must converge as $n \to \infty$, because it may be written as

$$\int_{-\infty}^{+\infty} f_n(x)[h(x)g(x)]\, dx,$$

and $\overline{g}(x) = h(x)g(x)$ clearly is a test function. We can therefore *define* a new distribution

$$\psi(x) = h(x)\phi(x)$$

corresponding to the sequence $y_n(x)$.

Remark. It is not possible to define a product of two distributions in a general fashion (i.e., it is not possible to define a product of two *arbitrary* distributions*). The reason is that if a sequence of functions $p_n(x) = f_n(x)h_n(x)$ is formed, it may not be weakly convergent and does not define a distribution. For instance, let†

$$f_n(x) = h_n(x) = (n/\sqrt{\pi})e^{-n^2 x^2}.$$

It is not difficult to find a test function $g(x)$ for which the integral

$$\int_{-\infty}^{+\infty} f_n(x)h_n(x)g(x)\, dx$$

will fail to converge [e.g., $g(x) = 1$ for $|x| < a$ and arbitrary otherwise].

Distributions also permit linear transformation of an independent variable, namely, if $\phi(x)$ is a distribution, then $\phi(x - a)$ and $\phi(Cx)$ are also distributions (where a and C are constants). They are defined by the sequences of core functions $f_n(x - a)$ and $f_n(Cx)$ which are weakly convergent because one can write

$$\int_{-\infty}^{+\infty} f_n(x - a)g(x)\, dx = \int_{-\infty}^{+\infty} f_n(x)g(x + a)\, dx$$

and

$$\int_{-\infty}^{+\infty} f_n(Cx)g(x)\, dx = 1/|C| \int_{-\infty}^{+\infty} f_n(x)g(x/C)\, dx \qquad (C \neq 0).$$

Since $g(x + a)$ and $g(x/C)$ are test functions and $f_n(x)$ is weakly convergent, the statement follows.

One of the most important properties of distributions is their *infinite differentiability*. The *derivative* of a distribution $\phi(x)$ is associated with a sequence of derivatives of core functions $f_n(x)$, which converges weakly to $\phi(x)$. To verify that this is possible, note that $f_n'(x)$ is a core function if $f_n(x)$ is one. Furthermore, integrating

---

* Some particular distributions can form a product; e.g., the above example $\psi = h\phi$ can be treated as such a product since $h(x)$ is equivalent to a distribution.

† We are attempting here to construct $[\delta(x)]^2$; this turns out to be impossible within the framework of the theory.

by parts, we obtain

$$\int_{-\infty}^{+\infty} f_n'(x)g(x)\, dx = f_n(x)g(x)\Big|_{-\infty}^{+\infty} - \int_{-\infty}^{+\infty} f_n(x)g'(x)\, dx$$
$$= -\int_{-\infty}^{+\infty} f_n(x)g'(x)\, dx,$$

because $g(x)$ vanishes outside some finite interval. Since $g'(x)$ is a test function (if $g(x)$ is one), the limit (as $n \to \infty$) of the right-hand side exists. Then the limit of the left-hand side must exist as well. Therefore $f_n'(x)$ is weakly convergent to some distribution which we *define* to be the derivative of $\phi(x)$ and denote by $\phi'(x)$. The distributions $\phi(x)$ and $\phi'(x)$ are related by the formula

$$\int_{-\infty}^{+\infty} \phi'(x)g(x)\, dx = -\int_{-\infty}^{+\infty} \phi(x)g'(x)\, dx$$

for any test function $g(x)$.

If $\phi(x)$ is equivalent to some differentiable function $f(x)$ (see p. 244), then $\phi'(x)$ can be shown to be equivalent to $f'(x)$.* Suppose, however, that $\phi'(x)$ is not differentiable everywhere. To be specific, assume that $f(x)$ is continuous and piecewise smooth. Let us investigate in what sense $\phi'(x)$ extends the definition of the derivative $f'(x)$ to those points where it does not exist in the classical sense. First of all, $\phi'(x)$ does not really define $f'(x)$ at any *point:* A distribution has no value at a point. What is still true for a distribution is that it can be equivalent to a function in the *neighborhood* of some point, say $x = \xi$. This is shown as follows: Let $\bar{g}(x)$ be a test function, different from zero *only within* some neighborhood of point ξ, namely, the interval $(\xi - \epsilon, \xi + \epsilon)$. Now, if for a function $f(x)$ and a distribution $\phi(x)$ it is true that

$$\int_{\xi-\epsilon}^{\xi+\epsilon} \phi(x)\bar{g}(x)\, dx = \int_{\xi-\epsilon}^{\xi+\epsilon} f(x)\bar{g}(x)\, dx$$

for *all* functions $\bar{g}(x)$ of the described type, then we say that $\phi(x)$ is equivalent to $f(x)$ in the neighborhood of point ξ. If $f(x)$ is continuous in $(\xi - \epsilon, \xi + \epsilon)$, then $\phi(x)$ can be constructed, e.g., by the method used on p. 244 (corollary to the smudging theorem).

We can now show that if $\phi(x)$ and $f(x)$ are equivalent at $x = \xi$† and $f'(\xi)$ exists, then $\phi'(x)$ and $f'(x)$ are equivalent at $x = \xi$. Indeed, if $\bar{g}(x)$ vanishes outside $(\xi - \epsilon, \xi + \epsilon)$, so does $\bar{g}'(x)$, and we have, for *all* such $\bar{g}(x)$,

$$\int_{\xi-\epsilon}^{\xi+\epsilon} \phi'(x)\bar{g}(x)\, dx = \int_{-\infty}^{+\infty} \phi'(x)\bar{g}(x)\, dx = -\int_{-\infty}^{+\infty} \phi(x)\bar{g}'(x)\, dx$$
$$= -\int_{\xi-\epsilon}^{\xi+\epsilon} \phi(x)\bar{g}'(x)\, dx.$$

---

* By a technique similar to that used in proving the smudging theorem.

† For brevity, if $\phi(x)$ is equivalent to $f(x)$ in a neighborhood of ξ, then we shall simply say that $\phi(x)$ is equivalent to $f(x)$ at ξ.

However, exactly the same relation applies to $f'(x)$, yielding

$$\int_{\xi-\epsilon}^{\xi+\epsilon} f'(x)\overline{g}(x)\,dx = -\int_{\xi-\epsilon}^{\xi+\epsilon} f(x)\overline{g}'(x)\,dx.$$

Therefore

$$\int_{\xi-\epsilon}^{\xi+\epsilon} \phi'(x)\overline{g}(x)\,dx = \int_{\xi-\epsilon}^{\xi+\epsilon} f'(x)\overline{g}(x)\,dx,$$

establishing the equivalence of $\phi'(x)$ and $f'(x)$ at $x = \xi$.

What about those points ξ where $f'(\xi)$ does not exist? Since $f(x)$ is piecewise smooth, $f'(x)$ must suffer a jump discontinuity at $x = \xi$, and be expressible (in a sufficiently small neighborhood of ξ) by

$$f'(x) = f_1(x) + hS(x - \xi) \qquad (x \neq \xi),$$

where $f_1(x)$ is continuous and h is a constant. Since $\phi'(x)$ must "faithfully" follow $f'(x)$ for $x \neq \xi$, it must satisfy the relation

$$\int_{\xi-\epsilon}^{\xi+\epsilon} \phi'(x)\overline{g}(x)\,dx = \int_{\xi-\epsilon}^{\xi+\epsilon} [f_1(x) + hS(x - \xi)]\overline{g}(x)\,dx,$$

for all appropriate $\overline{g}(x)$. This relation uniquely defines $\phi'(x)$ and makes it equivalent to the discontinuous function

$$f_1(x) + hS(x - \xi).$$

Note that it makes no difference whatever how $S(x - \xi)$ is defined at $x = \xi$ (see p. 240) because this fact does not affect the value of the integral

$$\int_{\xi-\epsilon}^{\xi+\epsilon} [f_1(x) + hS(x - \xi)]\overline{g}(x)\,dx.$$

From this analysis we see that distributions can represent discontinuous functions (at least those with jump discontinuities).*

Since the derivative of a distribution is well defined without any restrictions,† it follows that a "distribution with jump discontinuities," as $\phi'(x)$ above, can be differentiated as well. Let $\psi(x)$ be equivalent, in the neighborhood of the point ξ, to a discontinuous function of the type

$$y(x) = u(x) + hS(x - \xi),$$

where $u(x)$ is differentiable in $(\xi - \epsilon,$ $\xi + \epsilon)$ except, perhaps, at the point $x = \xi$ itself. A typical such function is shown in Fig. 6.11.

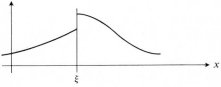

Figure 6.11

---

* Many other types of discontinuities can be accommodated as well; see, e.g., Gelfand and Shilov, *Generalized Functions*, Vol. I.

† From this it follows, of course, that distributions are infinitely differentiable.

Let $\theta(x - \xi)$ be the distribution corresponding to $S(x - \xi)$. Then

$$\int_{-\infty}^{+\infty} \theta'(x - \xi)g(x)\, dx = -\int_{-\infty}^{+\infty} \theta(x - \xi)g'(x)\, dx$$

$$= -\int_{-\infty}^{+\infty} S(x - \xi)g'(x)\, dx$$

$$= -\int_{\xi}^{\infty} g'(x)\, dx = -g(x)\big|_{\xi}^{\infty} = g(\xi).$$

From Section 6.6 it follows that $\theta'(x - \xi)$ corresponds to a delta sequence, and therefore $\theta'(x - \xi) = \delta(x - \xi)$. It easily follows that the distribution $\psi'(x)$ must have the form*

$$\psi'(x) = u'(x) + h\, \delta(x - \xi),$$

where $u'(x)$, in turn, is of the general form

$$u'(x) = u_1(x) + kS(x - \xi) \qquad (k = \text{const}),$$

$u_1(x)$ being some function continuous in $(\xi - \epsilon, \xi + \epsilon)$.

This analysis establishes the rule: When a distribution with jump discontinuities is differentiated, each discontinuity at $x = \xi$ of magnitude h (height of the jump) results in a term $h\, \delta(x - \xi)$ in the expression for the derivative.

Since distributions can be differentiated, they can be required to satisfy differential equations. Because of the linear character of the theory of distributions, the differential equations satisfied by them should, as a rule, be linear, namely, of the form $\mathcal{L}y = f$, where $\mathcal{L}$ is a linear differential operator with infinitely differentiable coefficients.†

Suppose that f is a bona fide function. Then the above DE can be viewed as a "classical" DE (for functions) or as a DE for distributions. Without going into details, we shall illustrate some of the features of the second point of view.

If the DE has no finite singular points,‡ then it can be shown that it has no other solutions (in the space of distributions) except "classical" ones, i.e., those with a counterpart in the space of functions. In particular, the DE

$$\frac{dy}{dx} = 0$$

has, in the space of distributions, the general solution

$$y(x) = C = \text{const}.$$

The presence of singularities in the DE can create, however, some peculiar situations.

---

* The rule $[a\phi(x) + b\chi(x)]' = a\phi'(x) + b\chi'(x)$ is taken for granted. The proof is trivial.

† See p. 245 on multiplication of distributions by functions.

‡ For second-order differential equations, see Chapter 3. For other cases, consult any advanced textbook on differential equations.

Example 1. Consider the DE

$$x \frac{dy}{dx} = 0;$$

for $x > 0$, $y(x)$ must coincide with a constant. The same is true for $x < 0$. However, the constant *need not be the same*. Indeed, the "step-function" distribution $y(x) = \theta(x)$ satisfies the DE because $\theta'(x) = \delta(x)$ and* $x\,\delta(x) = 0$. So far as the distributions are concerned, our DE has *two* linearly independent solutions, say $y_1(x) = 1$ and $y_2(x) = \theta(x)$, and the general solution reads $y(x) = C_1 + C_2\theta(x)$. Note that the classical counterpart of $\theta(x)$, namely $S(x)$, cannot possibly satisfy the DE because it has *no derivative* at $x = 0$. Such a deficiency cannot happen to a distribution.

Example 2. Consider the DE $x^2\,(dy/dx) = -y$.

It has a classical solution $y(x) = 0$ which is also a distribution. It also has a classical solution

$$y(x) = Ce^{1/x} \qquad (C \neq 0).$$

However, this solution does not qualify as a distribution: No sequence of core functions can be found to be equivalent to $Ce^{1/x}$ for $x \neq 0$ and to be weakly convergent.† Finally, differential equations satisfied by distributions may not be applicable to ordinary functions. The most common and most important of these are of the type

$$\mathcal{L}y = \delta(x - \xi),$$

giving rise to the so-called Green's functions (see Chapter 12).

6.9 SEQUENCES AND SERIES OF DISTRIBUTIONS

In many applications we have to deal with sequences of distributions $\phi_m(x)$ ($m = 1, 2, \ldots$) or, more generally, with distributions $\phi_\mu(x)$ depending on an arbitrary parameter μ. A sequence $\{\phi_m(x)\}$ of distributions is said to be *convergent* if there is a distribution $\phi(x)$ such that‡

$$\lim_{m \to \infty} \int_{-\infty}^{+\infty} \phi_m(x)g(x)\,dx = \int_{-\infty}^{+\infty} \phi(x)g(x)\,dx,$$

or, more generally,

$$\lim_{\mu \to \mu_0} \int_{-\infty}^{+\infty} \phi_\mu(x)g(x)\,dx = \int_{-\infty}^{+\infty} \phi(x)g(x)\,dx$$

---

* $\int_{-\infty}^{+\infty} x\,\delta(x)g(x)\,dx = 0$ (all g).

† This is not because the integral $\int_{-\infty}^{+\infty} e^{1/x}g(x)\,dx$ is divergent (some divergent integrals possess valid interpretation in the theory of distributions); it is rather because it is *badly* divergent.

‡ It may be shown that if $\lim_{m \to \infty} \int_{-\infty}^{+\infty} \phi_m(x)g(x)\,dx$ exists, then $\phi(x)$ must exist as well.

for all test functions $g(x)$. We write then, *by definition*,

$$\phi(x) = \lim_{\mu \to \mu_0} \phi_\mu(x)$$

and call $\phi(x)$ the *limit* of the sequence $\{\phi_\mu(x)\}$.

Example. The functions $\{\cos mx\}$ may also be looked on as distributions. In this sense they form a *convergent* sequence as $m \to \infty$. Indeed, let $g(x)$ be an arbitrary test function. Then it must vanish outside some interval (a, b) and be bounded inside this interval:

$$|g(x)| \leq B \qquad (a \leq x \leq b).$$

Then

$$\int_{-\infty}^{+\infty} \cos mx \cdot g(x)\, dx = \int_a^b \cos mx \cdot g(x)\, dx$$

$$= \frac{\sin mx}{m} g(x)\Big|_a^b - \frac{1}{m} \int_a^b \sin mx \cdot g'(x)\, dx.$$

Now, $g(a) = g(b) = 0$, while

$$\left| \int_a^b \sin mx \cdot g'(x)\, dx \right| \leq B(b - a).$$

As we let $m \to \infty$, the right-hand side of our equation approaches zero. Therefore, the sequence of *distributions* $\{\cos mx\}$ converges to zero.* Note that the sequence of *functions* $\{\cos mx\}$ does not converge to anything: it is a divergent sequence. We have here, evidently, a different definition of convergence: For distributions, this concept is an extension of *weak convergence* of functions (as opposed to *pointwise convergence*). For that matter, the sequence of functions $\{\cos mx\}$ converges weakly (to zero, of course).

    Theorem. If $\phi(x) = \lim_{\mu \to \mu_0} \phi_\mu(x)$, then

$$\phi'(x) = \lim_{\mu \to \mu_0} \phi_\mu'(x).$$

Proof. Recall that

$$\int_{-\infty}^{+\infty} \phi'(x) g(x)\, dx = -\int_{-\infty}^{+\infty} \phi(x) g'(x)\, dx.$$

Therefore

$$\lim_{\mu \to \mu_0} \int_{-\infty}^{+\infty} \phi_\mu'(x) g(x)\, dx = -\lim_{\mu \to \mu_0} \int_{-\infty}^{+\infty} \phi_\mu(x) g'(x)\, dx$$

$$= -\int_{-\infty}^{+\infty} \phi(x) g'(x)\, dx = \int_{-\infty}^{+\infty} \phi'(x) g(x)\, dx,$$

and the theorem is established.

---

* By *zero* we mean the (unique) distribution called *zero distribution*, equivalent to the function $f(x) \equiv 0$ in the neighborhood of any point x.

This property of distributions greatly facilitates various analytic operations with them. It does not hold, in general, for ordinary functions. For instance, the sequence of functions $f_m(x) = \sin mx/m$ converges to the *zero function* as $m \to \infty$, namely,

$$\lim_{m \to \infty} f_m(x) = f(x), \qquad \text{where } f(x) \equiv 0.$$

Now, each function $f_m(x)$ is differentiable, but the sequence of derivatives, $f'_m(x) = \cos mx$, is a divergent sequence. Note, however, that $f(x)$ possesses a derivative, namely, the zero function again.

The convergence of a *series* of distributions can be defined, in a customary fashion, by the convergence of a sequence of the partial sums. For example, given a set of distributions $\psi_k(x)$, $k = 1, 2, 3, \ldots$, we form a sequence of partial sums:

$$\sigma_m(x) = \sum_{k=1}^{m} \psi_k(x) \qquad (m = 1, 2, 3, \ldots).$$

If this sequence converges to some distribution $\sigma(x)$, we say that

$$\sigma(x) = \lim_{m \to \infty} \sigma_m(x) = \sum_{k=1}^{\infty} \psi_k(x).$$

Such a series can be differentiated *term by term*. Indeed, from

$$\lim_{m \to \infty} \sigma_m(x) = \sigma(x),$$

it follows that

$$\lim_{m \to \infty} \sigma'_m(x) = \sigma'(x).$$

However,

$$\sigma'_m(x) = \sum_{k=1}^{m} \psi'_k(x).$$

Therefore

$$\sigma(x) = \lim_{m \to \infty} \sum_{k=1}^{m} \psi'_k(x) = \sum_{k=1}^{\infty} \psi'_k(x)$$

as stated.

Example. We wish to demonstrate that the formal series $\sum_{k=1,3,5,\ldots}^{\infty} \cos kx$, which is divergent in the usual sense, can be regarded as a distribution.

Consider the series $\sum_{k=1,3,5,\ldots}^{\infty} (1/k^2) \cos kx$. This series converges uniformly in the conventional sense and represents the periodic function

$$f(x) = \begin{cases} \pi^2/8 + \pi x/4 & (-\pi \le x < 0), \\ \pi^2/8 - \pi x/4 & (0 \le x < \pi), \\ f(x + 2n\pi) & \text{otherwise} \quad (n = \text{integer}). \end{cases}$$

We can associate with $f(x)$ a distribution $\phi(x)$ equivalent to $f(x)$ everywhere (in a neighborhood of any point x) which may be considered as the sum of the above series within the space of distributions.*

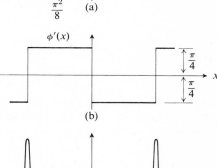

$$\phi(x) = \sum_{k=1,3,5,\ldots}^{\infty} (1/k^2)\cos kx.$$

Figure 6.12(a) represents graphically either $\phi(x)$ or $f(x)$.

The series for $\phi(x)$ can be differentiated term by term and yields

$$\phi'(x) = -\sum_{k=1,3,5,\ldots}^{\infty} (1/k)\sin kx,$$

representing the distribution

$$\phi'(x) = \begin{cases} +\pi/4 & (-\pi \leq x < 0), \\ -\pi/4 & (0 \leq x < \pi), \\ \phi'(x+2n\pi) & \text{(otherwise)} \end{cases}$$

shown in Fig. 6.12(b).

Figure 6.12

Note that $\phi'(x)$ corresponds to $f'(x)$ as well, although the term-by-term differentiation is not easy to justify since the series for $f'(x)$ does not converge uniformly. Differentiating once again, we obtain

$$\phi''(x) = -\sum_{k=1,3,5,\ldots}^{\infty} \cos kx,$$

which makes sense only within the framework of the distribution. We can say that

$$\phi''(x) = \begin{cases} (\pi/2)[\delta(x+\pi) - \delta(x)] & (-\pi/2 \leq x < 3\pi/2), \\ \phi''(x+2n\pi) & \text{(otherwise).} \end{cases}$$

This distribution is shown schematically in Fig. 6.12(c).

From this example it should be clear that any trigonometric series

$$a_0/2 + \sum_{k=1}^{\infty} (a_k \cos kx + b_k \sin kx),$$

whether convergent or divergent, can be viewed as a distribution *provided* that as $k \to \infty$, the coefficients a_k and b_k do not increase faster than some power k^N (where N is arbitrary, but fixed), namely,

$$|a_k| \leq Ak^N \qquad |b_k| \leq Bk^N \qquad (A, B = \text{const}).$$

---

* We treat $\cos kx$ as a distribution.

Indeed, apart from the term $a_0/2$, such a series can be obtained by differentiating the series

$$\sum_{k=1}^{\infty} \left(\frac{a_k}{k^{N+2}} \cos kx + \frac{b_k}{k^{N+2}} \sin kx \right)$$

$N + 2$ times.* However, this latter series evidently converges (even uniformly) to some function $f(x)$, which then gives rise to the corresponding distribution $\phi(x)$. The original series is essentially (that is, apart from $a_0/2$) the $(N + 2)$-derivative of $\phi(x)$.

From these considerations, it follows that practically every Fourier series occurring in physical applications may be interpreted as a distribution. Of some theoretical interest is the inverse problem, namely, how to expand a given distribution $\phi(x)$ into a Fourier series. Of course, if $\phi(x)$ is equivalent to some, say, piecewise smooth, function $f(x)$, this can be done by the usual formula (in complex form, see Section 4.5): If

$$f(x) = \sum_{m=-\infty}^{+\infty} c_m e^{i(m\pi x/L)} \qquad (-L \le x \le L),$$

then

$$c_m = (1/2L)\int_{-L}^{+L} f(x)e^{-i(m\pi x/L)}\, dx.$$

To adapt this approach to other kinds of distributions, we must bear in mind that a Fourier series can truly represent only *periodic functions*, in which case the integral for c_m can be evaluated over an arbitrary interval of length $2L$. We should expect, therefore, that only periodic distributions can be expanded into Fourier series. By such distributions we shall mean distributions which can be constructed by sequences of periodic core functions,† that is, functions satisfying

$$f_n(x) = f_n(x + 2kL) \qquad (k = \text{integer}).$$

We are now tempted to form a sequence of integrals

$$c_{mn} = (1/2L)\int_{-L}^{+L} f_n(x)e^{-i(m\pi x/L)}\, dx$$

and to seek the limit as $n \to \infty$ to obtain c_m. However, it is not obvious that such a limit exists, even if $\{f_n(x)\}$ is weakly convergent. Note that the limits of integration are not $\pm\infty$ any longer and $e^{-i(m\pi x/L)}$ is not a test function.

---

* Without loss of generality, $N + 2$ may be considered to be divisible by 4.

† If an arbitrary (nonperiodic) distribution is given, we can, in most cases, extend it periodically. For instance, $\delta(x)$ can be turned into a distribution consisting of a delta function at each point $x = 2kL$ ($k = $ integer).

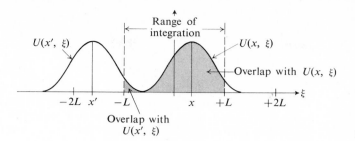

Figure 6.13

This difficulty is solved in the following manner: Consider the function*

$$u(x) = (1/N)\int_{-L}^{+L} U(x, \xi)\, d\xi,$$

where

$$U(x, \xi) = \begin{cases} e^{-L^2/[L^2-(x-\xi)^2]} & (|x - \xi| < L), \\ 0 & (|x - \xi| > L), \end{cases}$$

and

$$N = \int_{x-L}^{x+L} U(x, \xi)\, d\xi = \int_{-L}^{+L} U(0, \xi)\, d\xi.$$

The function $u(x)$ is identically zero for $x < -2L$ and for $x > 2L$ because the region where $U(x, \xi)$ is different from zero *does not overlap* with the range of integration $(-L, L)$. For $-2L \leq x \leq 2L$ there is a partial overlapping† as shown in Fig. 6.13; from this figure it is clear that $u(x)$ can be calculated for $0 \leq x \leq 2L$ by the formula

$$u(x) = (1/N)\int_{x-L}^{L} e^{-L^2/[L^2-(x-\xi)^2]}\, d\xi \qquad (0 \leq x \leq 2L)$$

and for $-2L \leq x \leq 0$ by the formula

$$u(x) = (1/N)\int_{-L}^{x+L} e^{-L^2/[L^2-(x-\xi)^2]}\, d\xi \qquad (-2L \leq x \leq 0).$$

The function $u(x)$ is represented schematically in Fig. 6.14 and possesses the important property $u(x) + u(x - 2L) = 1$, for $0 \leq x \leq 2L$. To see this, let $x' = x - 2L$ so that $-2L \leq x' \leq 0$ and

$$u(x') = (1/N)\int_{-L}^{x'+L} e^{-L^2/[L^2-(x'-\xi)^2]}\, d\xi.$$

---

* Similar functions have been used in the smudging theorem.

† Complete overlapping occurs only for $x = 0$.

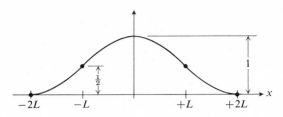

Figure 6.14

Replace x' by $x - 2L$, and get

$$u(x - 2L) = (1/N)\int_{-L}^{x-L} e^{-L^2/[L^2-(x-2L-\xi)^2]}\,d\xi.$$

Next make a change of variable, $\xi = \xi' - 2L$, and drop the primes to obtain

$$u(x - 2L) = (1/N)\int_{L}^{x+L} e^{-L^2/[L^2-(x-\xi)^2]}\,d\xi$$

$$= (1/N)\int_{x-L}^{x+L} e^{-L^2/[L^2-(x-\xi)^2]}\,d\xi - (1/N)\int_{x-L}^{L} e^{-L^2/[L^2-(x-\xi)^2]}\,d\xi$$

$$= 1 - u(x),$$

as stated.

The function $u(x)$ permits us to represent the integral

$$(1/2L)\int_{-L}^{+L} f_n(x)e^{-i(m\pi x/L)}\,dx$$

in such a form that its convergence is easily established. Indeed, consider the integral

$$(1/2L)\int_{-\infty}^{+\infty} f_n(x)u(x)e^{-i(m\pi x/L)}\,dx.$$

This integral *must* possess a limit when $n \to \infty$ if $\{f_n(x)\}$ is a weakly convergent sequence, since $u(x)e^{-i(m\pi x/L)}$ is evidently a test function. Because of the properties of $u(x)$, this integral can be confined to the interval $(-2L, +2L)$, and we can write

$$(1/2L)\int_{-2L}^{+2L} f_n(x)u(x)e^{-i(m\pi x/L)}\,dx$$

$$= (1/2L)\int_{-2L}^{0} f_n(x)u(x)e^{-i(m\pi x/L)} + (1/2L)\int_{0}^{2L} f_n(x)u(x)e^{-i(m\pi x/L)}\,dx.$$

Now set $x = \xi - 2L$ in the first integral; if $f_n(x)$ is periodic, then

$$(1/2L)\int_{-2L}^{0} f_n(x)u(x)e^{-i(m\pi x/L)}\,dx = (1/2L)\int_{0}^{2L} f_n(\xi)u(\xi - 2L)e^{-i(m\pi \xi/L)}\,d\xi.$$

Combining this with the second integral and using $u(x - 2L) + u(x) = 1$, we obtain

$$(1/2L)\int_{-2L}^{+2L} f_n(x)u(x)e^{-i(m\pi x/L)}\,dx = (1/2L)\int_{0}^{2L} f_n(x)e^{-i(m\pi x/L)}\,dx.$$

However, by periodicity of $f_n(x)$, this is just the integral c_{mn} defined before. We have, therefore, proved that

$$\lim_{n \to \infty} c_{mn} = \lim_{n \to \infty} (1/2L) \int_{-L}^{+L} f_n(x) e^{-i(m\pi x/L)} \, dx$$

exists for weakly convergent sequences of *periodic* core functions, and have extended the definition of Fourier coefficients to the space of distributions.

6.10 DISTRIBUTIONS IN N DIMENSIONS

The concept of a distribution can be extended to two and more dimensions. We shall only briefly outline the necessary modifications and, to be specific, confine ourselves to distributions in a plane (two-dimensional case). For test functions, one should choose functions vanishing outside some finite region Ω in the plane and possessing partial derivatives of all orders. Core functions should have only the second property.

Example. The function

$$g(x, y) = \begin{cases} e^{-a^2/(a^2 - r^2)} & (|r| < a), \\ 0 & (|r| \geq a), \end{cases}$$

where $r^2 = x^2 + y^2$, is a test function (also a core function). As its one dimensional counterpart, it can be extensively used in theoretical considerations. The distributions are defined by means of the limit

$$\lim_{n \to \infty} \int_{-\infty}^{+\infty} \int_{-\infty}^{+\infty} f_n(x, y) g(x, y) \, dx \, dy.$$

The delta function can be defined, for instance, by the sequence

$$f_n(x, y) = (n^2/\pi) e^{-n^2(x^2 + y^2)}$$

and is usually denoted by $\delta(\mathbf{r})$, $\delta(x, y)$, or sometimes by $\delta(x) \, \delta(y)$;* this latter form is very convenient if the test function can be factorized:

$$\int_{-\infty}^{+\infty} \int_{-\infty}^{+\infty} \delta(\mathbf{r}) g_1(x) g_2(y) \, dx \, dy = \int_{-\infty}^{+\infty} \delta(x) g_1(x) \, dx \int_{-\infty}^{+\infty} \delta(y) g_2(y) \, dy$$

$$= g_1(0) g_2(0).$$

Note, however, that $\delta(\mathbf{r})$ is axially symmetric (invariant under rotations).

The partial derivatives of a distribution $\phi(x, y)$ can be defined in a similar fashion as for one dimension. The following formula holds:

$$\int_{-\infty}^{+\infty} \int_{-\infty}^{+\infty} \frac{\partial \phi(x, y)}{\partial x} g(x, y) \, dx \, dy = -\int_{-\infty}^{+\infty} \int_{-\infty}^{+\infty} \phi(x, y) \frac{\partial g(x, y)}{\partial x} \, dx \, dy.$$

---

* There is no difficulty in interpreting a product of distributions in this case because the distributions refer to independent variables.

Of particular interest in practice is the result of the application of the Laplace differential operator

$$\nabla^2 = \frac{\partial^2}{\partial x^2} + \frac{\partial^2}{\partial y^2}$$

to a distribution $\phi(x, y)$. For instance, it is possible to show that

$$\delta(\mathbf{r}) = -(1/2\pi)\nabla^2 \log(1/r) \qquad r = \sqrt{x^2 + y^2},$$

where $\log(1/r)$ is regarded as a distribution.

BIBLIOGRAPHY

ERDELYI, A., *Operational Calculus and Generalized Functions*. New York: Holt, Rinehart, and Winston, 1962.

GELFAND, I. M., and G. E. SHILOV, *Generalized Functions*, Vol. I. New York: Academic Press Inc., 1964.

LIGHTHILL, M. J., *Introduction to Fourier Analysis and Generalized Functions*. New York: Cambridge University Press, 1960.

ZEMANIAN, A. H., *Distribution Theory and Transform Analysis*. New York: McGraw-Hill Book Co., 1965.

PROBLEMS

1. Let $f(z)$ be an arbitrary function analytic in the upper half-plane. Show that

$$\lim_{n\to\infty} \int_{-\infty}^{+\infty} \phi_n(x)f(x)\, dx = f(0),$$

where

$$\phi_n(x) = \frac{n}{\pi} \frac{1}{1 + n^2x^2}.$$

In other words, $\phi_n(x)$ is a delta sequence for such functions $f(x)$. [*Hint:* Set $1/n = a$ and evaluate the integral by residue calculus; then let $a \to 0$.]

2. Show that

$$\lim_{n\to\infty} \int_{-\infty}^{x} \phi_n(\xi)\, d\xi = S(x)$$

for the functions

a) $\phi_n = \dfrac{n}{\pi} \dfrac{1}{1 + n^2x^2}$ b) $\phi_n = \dfrac{n}{\sqrt{\pi}} e^{-n^2x^2}.$

3. Using the sequence of rectangular pulses (as in Section 6.4), develop the Fourier series for $\delta(x - \xi)$ in the interval $(-L, +L)$.

4. If the step function $S(x)$ is developed in a Fourier series in $(-L, +L)$, the result is

$$S(x) = \frac{1}{2} + \frac{2}{\pi} \sum_{n=\text{odd}}^{\infty} \frac{1}{n} \sin \frac{n\pi x}{L}.$$

Differentiating term by term, we can obtain the series $(2/L) \sum_{n=\text{odd}}^{\infty} \cos (n\pi x/L)$. However, this differs from the Fourier series for $\delta(x)$ given on p. 229. Can you trace the reason for this discrepancy?

5. Show that the step function admits an integral representation

$$S(t) = \frac{1}{2\pi i} \int_{-\infty}^{+\infty} \frac{e^{i\omega t}}{\omega} d\omega$$

and specify the treatment of the path of integration at the pole.

6. Give an argument in support of the formula $\delta(x)/x = -\delta'(x)$. What kind of *rigorous* statement can you produce in relation to this formula?

7. Consider the problem of the bending of the beam shown in Fig. 6.15. With the help of the discussion in Section 5.10 (Example 2) and Section 6.5, formulate the problem using the delta function. In particular, show that

$$y''(0) = P\xi/EI, \qquad y'''(0) = -P/EI.$$

Solve the problem by a method of your own choice and show that the deflection is given by

$$y(x) = \begin{cases} \dfrac{Px^2}{2EI}\left(\xi - \dfrac{x}{3}\right) & (0 \le x < \xi), \\[2ex] \dfrac{P\xi^2}{2EI}\left(x - \dfrac{\xi}{3}\right) & (\xi \le x \le L). \end{cases}$$

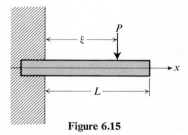

Figure 6.15

8. Consider the circuit problem of Section 4.8, Example 1 (Fig. 4.7). Suppose that the periodic electromotive force $E(t)$ has the form of the *square wave* shown in Fig. 6.16. Show that the problem may be formulated by means of the delta functions. Solve the problem for the steady-state current $I(t)$.

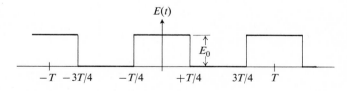

Figure 6.16

CHAPTER 7

FOURIER TRANSFORMS

7.1 REPRESENTATIONS OF A FUNCTION

A function $f(x)$ may be represented, e.g., by a power series

$$f(x) = \sum_{n=0}^{\infty} a_n x^n$$

provided it satisfies the necessary conditions for this expansion. If the set of coefficients $\{a_n\}$ is given, then the function $f(x)$ can be constructed, at least within the radius of convergence. In other words, a function can be *defined* by means of the coefficients a_n.

Similarly, if a function $f(x)$ is representable by a Fourier series

$$f(x) = \sum_{n=-\infty}^{+\infty} c_n e^{i(n\pi x/L)} \qquad (-L < x < L),$$

we may say that the set of coefficients $\{c_n\}$ also defines $f(x)$. Evidently, the same function can be represented by either the a_n set or the c_n set; of course, we must know what each set is supposed to mean.

The set of numbers c_n or a_n can be regarded as a *function* of the variable n, written as $c(n)$. Truly, this function is defined for a discrete set of values of the independent variable (instead of a continuous interval) but this is not fundamental. As a matter of fact, we are already familiar with a case where the representation is over a continuous variable; this is the Laplace transform of a function $f(t)$:

$$F(s) = \mathcal{L}\{f(t)\}.$$

We can say that $F(s)$ *represents* $f(t)$ since $f(t)$ can be defined (uniquely if it is continuous) by $F(s)$:

$$f(t) = \frac{1}{2\pi i} \int_{\gamma-i\infty}^{\gamma+i\infty} F(s)e^{ts} \, ds.$$

In this spirit, we do not regard $F(s)$ as a *different* function from $f(t)$, but rather, we say that $F(s)$ *is $f(t)$ in the Laplace transform representation*.

In the Fourier series case, the function $c(n)$ is often called the *Fourier spectrum* of $f(x)$. It may be plotted as shown in Fig. 7.1.*

---

* For convenience, assume that $f(x)$ is real and even; then $c(n)$ is real.

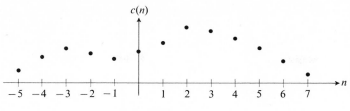

Figure 7.1

Instead of plotting c vs. "wave number" n we may plot c vs. "frequency"

$$k = n\pi/L.$$

If L is large, then the frequencies are closely spaced because $\Delta k = (\pi/L)\,\Delta n = \pi/L$ (for adjacent points on the graph). If L is large, Δk is small. With this change of scale, the Fourier spectrum may appear as shown in Fig. 7.2. It is natural to speculate about the possibility of a *continuous spectrum* as L approaches infinity and all frequencies are present.* It may be instructive to consider the following, purely heuristic approach: We know that

$$f(x) = \sum_{n=-\infty}^{+\infty} c_n e^{i(n\pi x/L)} \qquad (-L < x < L),$$

where

$$c_n = (1/2L)\int_{-L}^{+L} f(x)e^{-i(n\pi x/L)}\,dx.$$

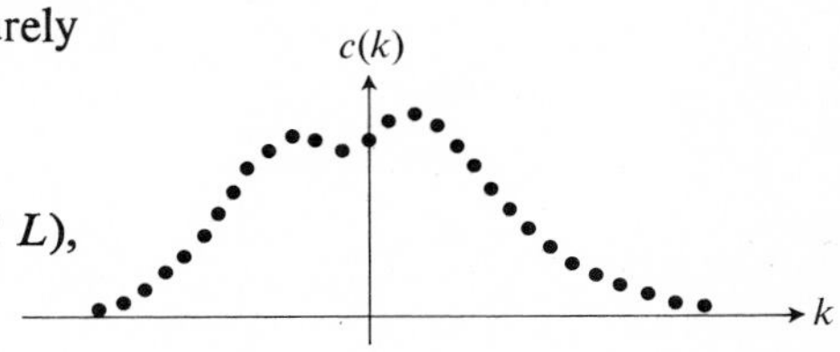

Figure 7.2

The transition $L \to \infty$ is difficult to perform directly since c_n apparently approaches zero. We follow the idea of using the frequencies. We set $n\pi/L = k$; then $\Delta k = (\pi/L)\,\Delta n$. The "adjacent" values of k are obtained by putting $\Delta n = 1$, which corresponds to $(L/\pi)\,\Delta k = 1$. Then we can multiply each term of the Fourier series by $(L/\pi)\,\Delta k$ with impunity and write

$$f(x) = \sum_{n=-\infty}^{+\infty} \left(\frac{L}{\pi}c_n\right)e^{i(n\pi x/L)}\,\Delta k,$$

where

$$\frac{L}{\pi}c_n = \frac{1}{2\pi}\int_{-L}^{+L} f(x)e^{-i(n\pi x/L)}\,dx.$$

Switching completely to the k-notation and writing $(L/\pi)c_n = c_L(k)$, we can obtain

$$c_L(k) = \frac{1}{2\pi}\int_{-L}^{+L} f(x)e^{-ikx}\,dx \qquad \text{and} \qquad f(x) = \sum_{Lk/\pi=-\infty}^{+\infty} c_L(k)e^{ikx}\,\Delta k.$$

---

* The nomenclature employed here is borrowed from optics and is self-explanatory.

If we now let $L \to \infty$ we expect the second sum to "go over" into an integral and we obtain

$$c(k) = \lim_{L \to \infty} c_L(k) = \frac{1}{2\pi} \int_{-\infty}^{+\infty} f(x)e^{-ikx}\,dx$$

and

$$f(x) = \int_{-\infty}^{+\infty} c(k)e^{ikx}\,dk.$$

This set of formulas (in a somewhat different form) is known as the *Fourier transformation*. We shall adopt a modern version,* defining a function

$$F(k) = \sqrt{2\pi}\,c(-k),$$

so that the formulas now read

$$F(k) = \frac{1}{\sqrt{2\pi}} \int_{-\infty}^{+\infty} f(x)e^{ikx}\,dx,$$

$$f(x) = \frac{1}{\sqrt{2\pi}} \int_{-\infty}^{+\infty} F(k)e^{-ikx}\,dx.$$

The function $F(k)$ is known as the *Fourier transform* of the function $f(x)$. The concept of the Fourier transform of a function $f(x)$ is analogous to the concept of its Laplace transform. Conversely, $f(x)$ is called the *inverse Fourier transform* of $F(k)$ so that the transformation and inversion formulas are obtained at the same time. Note that the only difference between direct and inverse Fourier transforms is the sign in the exponential function.

7.2 EXAMPLES OF FOURIER TRANSFORMATIONS

In the preceding section we have conjectured the validity of the formulas

$$F(k) = \frac{1}{\sqrt{2\pi}} \int_{-\infty}^{+\infty} f(x)e^{ikx}\,dx,$$

$$f(x) = \frac{1}{\sqrt{2\pi}} \int_{-\infty}^{+\infty} F(k)e^{-ikx}\,dx.$$

Strictly speaking, there is no question about the validity of the first formula. If $f(x)$ is an integrable function and if the integral converges, $F(k)$ is simply *defined* by the above integral. The question, however, is whether the original function $f(x)$

---

* There are several ways of defining Fourier transformation; the differences between them are trivial.

can be retrieved by the second formula. We shall illustrate the validity of the second formula by considering some particular examples.

Example 1. Consider the *Gaussian probability function**

$$f(x) = Ne^{-\alpha x^2} \qquad (N, \alpha = \text{const}).$$

Its Fourier transform $F(k)$ will be denoted by $\mathcal{F}\{f(x)\}$ and will be calculated from

$$F(k) = \mathcal{F}\{f(x)\} = \frac{1}{\sqrt{2\pi}} \int_{-\infty}^{+\infty} f(x)e^{ikx} \, dx = \frac{N}{\sqrt{2\pi}} \int_{-\infty}^{+\infty} e^{-\alpha x^2} e^{ikx} \, dx.$$

The technique used for the calculation of this integral was given in Section 6.4. We complete the square,

$$-\alpha x^2 + ikx = -(x\sqrt{\alpha} - ik/2\sqrt{\alpha})^2 - k^2/4\alpha,$$

and make the change of variables $x\sqrt{\alpha} - ik/2\sqrt{\alpha} = u$ to obtain

$$F(k) = \frac{N}{\sqrt{2\pi\alpha}} e^{-k^2/4\alpha} \int_{-\infty}^{+\infty} e^{-u^2} \, du = N\sqrt{\frac{1}{2\alpha}} e^{-k^2/4\alpha}.$$

It is of interest to observe that $F(k)$ is also a Gaussian probability function with a peak at the origin, monotone decreasing as $k \to \pm\infty$. Note, however, that if $f(x)$ is sharply peaked (large α), then $F(k)$ is flattened, and vice versa (Fig. 7.3). This is a general feature in the theory of Fourier transforms. In quantum-mechanical applications it is related to the Heisenberg uncertainty principle.

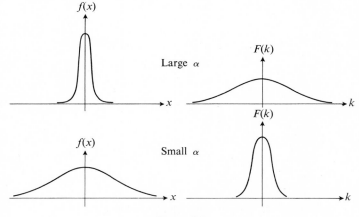

Figure 7.3

---

* See Section 6.4; the constant N is often chosen to be the *normalization constant*, yielding $\int_{-\infty}^{+\infty} f(x) \, dx = 1$.

The inverse integral

$$\frac{1}{\sqrt{2\pi}} \int_{-\infty}^{+\infty} F(k)e^{-ikx}\,dx = \frac{1}{\sqrt{2\pi}} \frac{N}{\sqrt{2\alpha}} \int_{-\infty}^{+\infty} e^{-k^2/4\alpha}e^{-ikx}\,dk$$

can be calculated by the same technique; as a short-cut, one may set

$$\alpha' = 1/4\alpha \quad \text{and} \quad x' = -x;$$

then

$$\frac{1}{\sqrt{2\pi}} \int_{-\infty}^{+\infty} e^{-\alpha'k^2}e^{ix'k}\,dk = \frac{1}{\sqrt{2\alpha'}} e^{-x'^2/4\alpha'} = \sqrt{2\alpha}\,e^{-\alpha x^2}$$

so that

$$\frac{1}{\sqrt{2\pi}} \int_{-\infty}^{+\infty} F(k)e^{-ikx}\,dk = \frac{N}{\sqrt{2\alpha}} \sqrt{2\alpha}\,e^{-\alpha x^2} = f(x),$$

and the conjecture is verified.

Example 2. Consider the function $f(x) = a/(x^2 + a^2)$ $(a > 0)$.

Its Fourier transform is given by

$$F(k) = \mathcal{F}\{f(x)\} = \frac{a}{\sqrt{2\pi}} \int_{-\infty}^{+\infty} \frac{e^{ikx}}{x^2 + a^2}\,dx.$$

This integral is just "tailored" for the calculus of residues.* Note that the contour has to be closed differently for $k > 0$ and for $k < 0$. Let us write

$$F(k) = \int_{-\infty}^{+\infty} \frac{a}{\sqrt{2\pi}} \frac{e^{ikx}}{(x + ai)(x - ai)}\,dx.$$

If $k > 0$, the contour is closed "up"; the pole $z = ai$ yields the residue

$$\frac{a}{\sqrt{2\pi}} \frac{e^{-ka}}{2ai}$$

so that

$$F(k) = \sqrt{\pi/2}\,e^{-ka} \qquad (k > 0).$$

If $k < 0$, the contour is closed "down"; the pole $z = -ai$ yields the residue

$$\frac{a}{\sqrt{2\pi}} \frac{e^{ka}}{(-2ai)}$$

(there is an extra minus sign because of the clockwise integration) so that

$$F(k) = \sqrt{\pi/2}\,e^{ka} \qquad (k < 0).$$

_____

* A similar problem was solved on p. 90.

For $k = 0$ it is possible to close the contour either way. Alternatively, using

$$\frac{a^2}{x^2 + a^2} = \frac{d}{dx}\left(\arctan\frac{x}{a}\right),$$

we directly obtain

$$F(0) = \frac{1}{\sqrt{2\pi}} \int_{-\infty}^{+\infty} \frac{a}{x^2 + a^2}\, dx = \frac{1}{\sqrt{2\pi}} \arctan\frac{x}{a}\bigg|_{-\infty}^{+\infty} = \sqrt{\frac{\pi}{2}}.$$

The final result can be written as

$$F(k) = \sqrt{\pi/2}\ e^{-|k|a} \qquad \text{(all } k\text{)}$$

and is shown in Fig. 7.4.

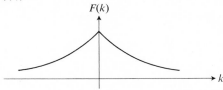

Figure 7.4

Again, if $f(x)$ has a fairly sharp peak (small a), then $F(k)$ is rather spread and conversely. Of some interest is the discontinuous derivative of $F(k)$, which is related to the fact that $f(x)$ does not approach zero sufficiently fast as $x \to \pm\infty$ [e.g., the Fourier transform for the function $xf(x)$ is not defined for $k = 0$ and the Fourier transform of $x^2 f(x)$ is not defined for any k].

Example 3. Consider now the *box function*

$$f(x) = \begin{cases} 1 & (|x| \le a) \\ 0 & (|x| > a) \end{cases} (a > 0).$$

Its Fourier transform reads

$$F(k) = \frac{1}{\sqrt{2\pi}} \int_{-a}^{+a} e^{ikx}\, dx = \frac{1}{\sqrt{2\pi}} \frac{e^{ika} - e^{-ika}}{ik} = \sqrt{\frac{2}{\pi}} \frac{\sin ak}{k}.$$

The functions $f(x)$ and $F(k)$ are shown in Fig. 7.5.

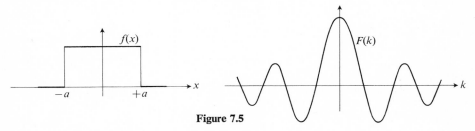

Figure 7.5

7.3 PROPERTIES OF FOURIER TRANSFORMS

Let us investigate the properties of the function $F(k) = \mathfrak{F}\{f(x)\}$ defined by the integral

$$F(k) = \frac{1}{\sqrt{2\pi}} \int_{-\infty}^{+\infty} f(x)e^{ikx}\, dx.$$

First of all, it is clear that $F(k)$ is defined only if $f(x)$ satisfies certain restrictions. For instance, $f(x)$ should be *integrable* in any finite region. In physical practice, this means that $f(x)$ has, at worst, jump discontinuities or mild infinite discontinuities.† Also, the integral should converge at infinity. As a general rule, this would require that $f(x) \to 0$ as $x \to \pm\infty$.

A very common *sufficient* (but not necessary) condition is the requirement that $f(x)$ is *absolutely integrable*, meaning that the integral

$$\int_{-\infty}^{+\infty} |f(x)|\, dx$$

exists. Since $|f(x)e^{ikx}| = |f(x)|$, it follows that the integral for $F(k)$ is absolutely convergent; therefore it is convergent.

Because of the presence of the complex factor e^{ikx}, it is evident that $F(k)$ is, in general, a complex function.‡ Let us assume, on the other hand, that $f(x)$ is real. Then we have the so-called *conjugation property*

$$F(-k) = F^*(k).$$

The proof is trivial: take the complex conjugate of the integral defining $F(k)$. There are two immediate corollaries to this property.§

a) If $f(x)$ is even, $F(k)$ is real,
b) If $f(x)$ is odd, $F(k)$ is purely imaginary.

Exercise. Establish these two properties.

The appearance of the exponential function e^{ikx} (sometimes called the *kernel of transform*) suggests that there should be similarities between Fourier transforms and Laplace transforms.

Indeed, it is not difficult to establish the *attenuation property* and the *shifting property* for Fourier transforms:

$$\mathfrak{F}\{f(x)e^{ax}\} = F(k - ai), \qquad \mathfrak{F}\{f(x - a)\} = e^{ika}F(k).$$

---

† For example, the function $f(x) = |x|^{-\alpha}e^{-x^2}$ is integrable for $0 < \alpha < 1$, although it is infinite at $x = 0$.

‡ A complex function of the real variable k, since we tacitly assume that k is real. However, extensions to complex k are possible.

§ All examples in Section 7.2 involve even functions.

The proofs are easily obtained by obvious changes of variables (k or x) in the integral for $F(k)$. Note that the first property is valid for all a (provided that the relevant transforms exist). The second property is also true for all a and is assured if $F(k)$ exists.*

Exercise. Establish the above formulas and statements.

We should also expect some kind of *differentiation property*. Let us suppose that $\mathfrak{F}\{f'(x)\}$ exists. In this case, integrating by parts, we have

$$\frac{1}{\sqrt{2\pi}} \int_{-\infty}^{+\infty} f'(x)e^{ikx}\, dx = \frac{1}{\sqrt{2\pi}} f(x)e^{ikx}\Big|_{-\infty}^{+\infty} - \frac{ik}{\sqrt{2\pi}} \int_{-\infty}^{+\infty} f(x)e^{ikx}\, dx.$$

If the Fourier transform of $f(x)$ exists, this usually means† that $f(x) \to 0$ as $x \to \pm\infty$. Then we have

$$\mathfrak{F}\{f'(x)\} = -ik\mathfrak{F}\{f(x)\}.$$

The extension to higher derivatives is obvious; in particular, the one most often used in physics is the relation

$$\mathfrak{F}\{f''(x)\} = -k^2 F(k).$$

It is evident that Fourier transforms should possess many properties analogous to those of Fourier series.‡ For instance, the conditions of existence of the Fourier transform are analogous to the conditions of existence of the Fourier coefficients. The problem of inversion of the Fourier transform is analogous to the problem of convergence of the Fourier series to the original function $f(x)$. We have seen (Section 4.7) that this latter problem can be dealt with in the sense of convergence in the mean. If this is true for the inverse Fourier transform, then we should expect an analog of Parseval's formula (p. 171). A bit of reflection (e.g., by a heuristic argument like the one in Section 7.1) tells us that we should expect that the formula

$$\int_{-\infty}^{+\infty} |F(k)|^2\, dk = \int_{-\infty}^{+\infty} |f(x)|^2\, dx,$$

known as the (first) *Parseval theorem* in Fourier transform theory, will hold.

As a matter of fact, one may propose a more general formula:

$$\int_{-\infty}^{+\infty} F(k)G(-k)\, dk = \int_{-\infty}^{+\infty} f(x)g(x)\, dx,$$

known as the *second Parseval theorem* in the Fourier transform theory.

---

* Compare this with similar properties of the Laplace transform in Section 5.3.

† If this does not hold, then $f(x)$ can be treated as a distribution (see Section 7.5) and the differentiation property is still valid (p. 277).

‡ For example, the conjugation property for Fourier series is given on p. 166.

To establish this result, we use the definition

$$G(-k) = \frac{1}{\sqrt{2\pi}} \int_{-\infty}^{+\infty} g(x)e^{-ikx}\, dx;$$

then

$$\int_{-\infty}^{+\infty} F(k)G(-k)\, dk = \int_{-\infty}^{+\infty} F(k)\, dk \int_{-\infty}^{+\infty} \frac{1}{\sqrt{2\pi}} g(x)e^{-ikx}\, dx.$$

Suppose we can interchange the order of integration. Then

$$\int_{-\infty}^{+\infty} F(k)G(-k)\, dk = \int_{-\infty}^{+\infty} g(x)\, dx \frac{1}{\sqrt{2\pi}} \int_{-\infty}^{+\infty} F(k)e^{-ikx}\, dk.$$

Suppose further that the Fourier inversion integral is valid:

$$\frac{1}{\sqrt{2\pi}} \int_{-\infty}^{+\infty} F(k)e^{-ikx}\, dk = f(x).$$

In this case, the second Parseval theorem follows. The first Parseval theorem is then a mere consequence: Set $f(x) = g(x)$ (real functions) and recall that $G(-k) = G^*(k)$ to obtain

$$\int_{-\infty}^{+\infty} G(k)G^*(k)\, dk = \int_{-\infty}^{+\infty} [g(x)]^2\, dx$$

or

$$\int_{-\infty}^{+\infty} |G(k)|^2\, dk = \int_{-\infty}^{+\infty} |g(x)|^2\, dx,$$

as stated.

Remarks

1. A sufficient condition for the interchange of the order of integration in the above proof is the absolute convergence of the integrals

$$\int_{-\infty}^{+\infty} F(k)e^{-ikx}\, dx \qquad \text{and} \qquad \int_{-\infty}^{+\infty} g(x)e^{-ikx}\, dx,$$

or, in other words, the convergence of

$$\int_{-\infty}^{+\infty} |F(k)|\, dk \qquad \text{and} \qquad \int_{-\infty}^{+\infty} |g(x)|\, dx.$$

2. The *pointwise* validity of the Fourier inversion integral is not really necessary: For instance, the values of the integral

$$\frac{1}{\sqrt{2\pi}} \int_{-\infty}^{+\infty} F(k)e^{-ikx}\, dk$$

may differ from the values of the original function $f(x)$ at some isolated points† provided this discrepancy does not affect the value of the integral

$$\int_{-\infty}^{+\infty} g(x)f(x)\, dx.$$

Exactly the same assumptions are sufficient to establish the *convolution theorem* for Fourier transforms.

Theorem. If $\mathfrak{F}\{h(x)\} = F(k)G(k)$, then

$$h(x) = (f * g) = (g * f) = (1/\sqrt{2\pi}) \int_{-\infty}^{+\infty} f(\xi)g(x - \xi)\, d\xi,$$

where $F(k) = \mathfrak{F}\{f(x)\}$ and $G(k) = \mathfrak{F}\{g(x)\}$.

Indeed (denote the inverse Fourier transform by $\mathfrak{F}^{-1}$),

$$\mathfrak{F}^{-1}\{F(k)G(k)\} = \frac{1}{\sqrt{2\pi}} \int_{-\infty}^{+\infty} F(k)G(k)e^{-ikx}\, dk$$

$$= \frac{1}{2\pi} \int_{-\infty}^{+\infty} F(k)e^{-ikx}\, dk \int_{-\infty}^{+\infty} g(\xi)e^{ik\xi}\, d\xi.$$

If the interchanging of the order of integrations is permissible, then

$$\mathfrak{F}^{-1}\{F(k)G(k)\} = \frac{1}{2\pi} \int_{-\infty}^{+\infty} g(\xi)\, d\xi \int_{-\infty}^{+\infty} F(k)e^{-ik(x-\xi)}\, dk$$

$$= \frac{1}{\sqrt{2\pi}} \int_{-\infty}^{+\infty} g(\xi)f(x - \xi)\, d\xi,$$

as stated.

7.4 FOURIER INTEGRAL THEOREM

For those functions $f(x)$ for which the inverse transformation is valid, we can write the integral identity, known as the Fourier integral theorem:

$$f(x) = \frac{1}{2\pi} \int_{-\infty}^{+\infty} e^{-ikx}\, dk \int_{-\infty}^{+\infty} f(\xi)e^{ik\xi}\, d\xi.$$

If $f(x)$ is a real function it may be convenient to recast this identity into real form. We write

$$f(x) = \frac{1}{\sqrt{2\pi}} \int_{-\infty}^{0} F(k)e^{-ikx}\, dk + \frac{1}{\sqrt{2\pi}} \int_{0}^{\infty} F(k)e^{-ikx}\, dk.$$

---

† This will actually happen (in general) if $f(x)$ is piecewise smooth.

Making a change of variable, $k' = -k$, in the first integral (and dropping the prime) and using the conjugation property $F(-k) = F^*(k)$, we obtain

$$f(x) = \frac{1}{\sqrt{2\pi}} \int_0^\infty [F(k)e^{-ikx} + F^*(k)e^{ikx}]\, dk.$$

However,

$$F(k)e^{-ikx} = \frac{1}{\sqrt{2\pi}} \int_{-\infty}^{+\infty} f(\xi)e^{ik(\xi-x)}\, d\xi.$$

Now, we take the complex conjugate of this formula to obtain $F^*(k)e^{ikx}$ and add:

$$F(k)e^{-ikx} + F^*(k)e^{ikx} = \frac{1}{\sqrt{2\pi}} \int_{-\infty}^{+\infty} f(\xi)2\cos k(\xi - x)\, d\xi,$$

yielding the real form of the Fourier integral theorem:

$$f(x) = \frac{1}{\pi} \int_0^\infty dk \int_{-\infty}^{+\infty} f(\xi)\cos k(\xi - x)\, d\xi.$$

One of the basic mathematical problems in the theory of Fourier transforms is to establish the class of functions $f(x)$ for which this theorem is valid. The question is analogous to that in the theory of Fourier series: What are the functions $f(x)$ for which the Fourier series will actually converge to $f(x)$?

It is hardly surprising that the answer is similar: For instance, the following two theorems provide *sufficient* conditions for the validity of the Fourier integral theorem.†

Theorem 1. If $f(x)$ is absolutely integrable in $(-\infty, +\infty)$ and is piecewise very smooth in every finite interval, then the Fourier integral theorem is valid in the sense that

$$\frac{1}{\pi} \int_0^\infty dk \int_{-\infty}^{+\infty} f(\xi)\cos k(\xi - x)\, d\xi = \tfrac{1}{2}[f(x + 0) + f(x - 0)].$$

Theorem 2. The result of Theorem 1 remains valid if the statement "... is piecewise very smooth in every finite interval ..." is replaced by "... satisfies Dirichlet conditions in every finite interval ..."

We shall omit the proofs of these theorems. As mentioned before (Section 6.7), the concept of pointwise convergence (involved in the above theorems) is not only unnecessary in physics but may be even meaningless. The idea of convergence in the mean (Section 4.7) or, perhaps, that of weak convergence (Section 6.6) is certainly more suitable.

---

† Compare with the theorems in Section 4.6. Again, the above conditions are by no means necessary: For instance, functions with certain "mild" infinite discontinuities also conform to the Fourier integral theorem.

7.5 FOURIER TRANSFORMS OF DISTRIBUTIONS

Among functions possessing Fourier transforms (and satisfying the Fourier integral theorem) we can find those used in the construction of the delta sequences of Sections 6.2 and 6.6. For instance, the sequence of functions

$$f_n(x) = (n/\sqrt{\pi})e^{-n^2x^2}$$

generates the sequence of Fourier transforms*

$$F_n(k) = (1/\sqrt{2\pi})e^{-k^2/4n^2}.$$

We know that the sequence $\{f_n(x)\}$ converges weakly to $\delta(x)$. It would be natural to *define* the Fourier transform of the delta function by the limit

$$\lim_{n\to\infty} F_n(k) = \frac{1}{\sqrt{2\pi}} \lim_{n\to\infty} e^{-k^2/4n^2}.$$

Of course, one should prescribe what kind of convergence is implied in the above limiting process. In this particular case it makes no difference because $e^{-k^2/4n^2}$ converges to unity, both pointwise and weakly:

$$\lim_{n\to\infty} e^{-k^2/4n^2} = 1$$

and

$$\lim_{n\to\infty} \int_{-\infty}^{+\infty} e^{-k^2/4n^2} g(k)\, dk = \int_{-\infty}^{+\infty} g(k)\, dk$$

for all test functions $g(k)$.

From this point of view we are inclined to claim that $\mathfrak{F}\{\delta(x)\} = 1/\sqrt{2\pi}$. Naturally, we are also interested in the possibility of inverting the Fourier transforms of distributions. This means that we will require

$$\delta(x) = \mathfrak{F}^{-1}\left\{\frac{1}{\sqrt{2\pi}}\right\} = \frac{1}{\sqrt{2\pi}} \int_{-\infty}^{+\infty} \frac{1}{\sqrt{2\pi}} e^{-ikx}\, dk = \frac{1}{2\pi} \int_{-\infty}^{+\infty} e^{-ikx}\, dk.$$

This formula has already been obtained on p. 230.† Its obvious interpretation is that the sequence of functions

$$\frac{1}{2\pi} \int_{-\infty}^{+\infty} e^{-k^2/4n^2} e^{-ikx}\, dk$$

converges weakly to the delta function as $n \to \infty$. This is of course true, since these functions obviously are the $f_n(x)$ defined in the beginning.

---

* See Example 1 in Section 7.2.

† The sign of the exponent makes no difference. Make a change of variable $k' = -k$ and drop the primes.

If we want to provide this idea with a general basis, we must make sure that, given a weakly convergent sequence $\{f_n(x)\}$, the sequence of corresponding Fourier transforms $\{F_n(k)\}$ is also weakly convergent. The immediate snag in this requirement is that many core functions $f_n(x)$, as defined in Section 6.6, will *not possess Fourier transforms at all.* For instance, $f(x) = x^2$ is a core function, but the integral

$$\int_{-\infty}^{+\infty} x^2 e^{ikx}\, dx$$

diverges.

If we have grasped the fundamental idea of the theory of distributions, we see that the way out of this difficulty is to *restrict the core* in such a fashion that the core functions are sufficiently "well behaved." This will cause no difficulties because such a restriction is not really a restriction at all. Just as we were able to generate discontinuous functions out of infinitely differentiable core functions (see p. 237), we should also be able to generate functions like $f(x) = x^2$ out of our restricted core. The only difference is that such functions will now become distributions, but this is hardly a disadvantage (see p. 242).

The core can be restricted in various ways. Perhaps the most convenient restriction for our purposes is as follows: The core functions $f(x)$ should be infinitely differentiable over $(-\infty, +\infty)$ and, *along with all their derivatives,* should vanish at infinity faster than any power of x. In other words,

$$\lim_{x \to \pm\infty} |x^n[d^m f(x)/dx^m]| = 0$$

for all m and all n.*

The advantage of this particular restriction is that not only the Fourier transform of each core function exists, but that it is *also a core function.*

To establish this, observe that

$$\frac{dF(k)}{dk} = \frac{1}{\sqrt{2\pi}} \int_{-\infty}^{+\infty} ixf(x)e^{ikx}\, dx.$$

The differentiation under the integral sign is valid because the integral

$$\int_{-\infty}^{+\infty} |xf(x)|\, dx$$

converges according to the properties of $f(x)$,† thereby establishing an absolute and uniform convergence of dF/dk.

These arguments can be repeated any number of times, yielding

$$\frac{d^m F(k)}{dk^m} = \frac{(i)^m}{\sqrt{2\pi}} \int_{-\infty}^{+\infty} x^m f(x)e^{ikx}\, dx.$$

---

* These are the "good functions" of Lighthill.

† Note that $xf(x)$ is a core function; for instance, $|xf(x)| < B/x^2$ as $x \to \pm\infty$.

Therefore $F(k)$ is infinitely differentiable. Now, integrate by parts and obtain

$$\frac{d^m F(k)}{dk^m} = \frac{(i)^m}{\sqrt{2\pi}} x^m f(x) \frac{e^{ikx}}{ik}\Big|_{-\infty}^{+\infty} - \frac{(i)^m}{\sqrt{2\pi}} \frac{1}{(ik)} \int_{-\infty}^{+\infty} \frac{d}{dx} [x^m f(x)] e^{ikx}\, dx.$$

The term which was integrated out is evidently zero. Again, this operation can be repeated any number of times, say $n + 1$ times, to yield

$$\frac{d^m F(k)}{dk^m} = (-1)^{n+1} \frac{(i)^m}{\sqrt{2\pi}} \frac{1}{(ik)^{n+1}} \int_{-\infty}^{+\infty} \frac{d^{n+1}}{dx^{n+1}} [x^m f(x)] e^{ikx}\, dx.$$

Since $x^m f(x)$ must be a core function, its $(n + 1)$-derivative must be one too, and the integral on the right converges. From this, it follows immediately that

$$\left| k^n \frac{d^m F(k)}{dk^m} \right| < \frac{A}{k}$$

for some constant A. Therefore

$$\lim_{k \to \infty} \left| k^n \frac{d^m F(k)}{dk^m} \right| = 0 \qquad \text{(all } m, n),$$

completing the proof.

With this definition of core functions, the base is laid for the development of a theory of distributions incorporating Fourier transforms. It is not difficult to establish the Fourier and Parseval theorems for core functions and to transplant these (along with other) properties of core functions onto distributions generated by weakly convergent sequences.*

The distributions generated by this core include many functions that are nonvanishing at infinity, such as polynomials of all orders. Although more restricted than distributions generated by the core of Chapter 6, they are adequate for physical purposes.

7.6 FOURIER SINE AND COSINE TRANSFORMS

Let the function $f(x)$ be an even real function. Using the real form of the Fourier integral theorem, we can write

$$f(x) = \frac{1}{\pi} \int_0^\infty dk \int_{-\infty}^{+\infty} f(\xi)[\cos kx \cos k\xi + \sin kx \sin k\xi]\, dx$$

$$= \frac{1}{\pi} \int_0^\infty \cos kx\, dk \int_{-\infty}^{+\infty} f(\xi) \sin k\xi\, d\xi + \frac{1}{\pi} \int_0^\infty \sin kx\, dk \int_{-\infty}^{+\infty} f(\xi) \sin k\xi\, d\xi.$$

---

* Lighthill, *Fourier Analysis and Generalized Functions*. Lighthill uses test functions of the same type as core functions, calling them "good functions."

Since $f(\xi)$ is even, the second integral vanishes and the first one can be modified to yield

$$f(x) = \frac{2}{\pi} \int_0^\infty \cos kx \, dk \int_0^\infty f(\xi) \cos k\xi \, d\xi.$$

This formula suggests the following idea, analogous to that in Section 4.4 for Fourier series: Suppose that a function $f(x)$ is defined *only* in the interval $(0, \infty)$. If we extend its definition over the entire interval $(-\infty, +\infty)$ in an *even* manner defining

$$f^{(+)}(x) = \begin{cases} f(x) & (x > 0), \\ f(-x) & (x < 0), \end{cases}$$

then the above formula should be applicable to $f^{(+)}(x)$. In this spirit, we define the *Fourier cosine transform* by*

$$F_C(k) = \mathfrak{F}_C\{f(x)\} = \sqrt{\frac{2}{\pi}} \int_0^\infty f(x) \cos kx \, dx$$

with the inverse

$$\mathfrak{F}_C^{-1}\{F(k)\} = \sqrt{\frac{2}{\pi}} \int_0^\infty F_C(k) \cos kx \, dx = f(x).$$

Remark. In these formulas there is no mention of the function $f^{(+)}(x)$. However, if we choose x to be negative in the inversion integral (in the first integral, x is a dummy variable) we automatically obtain an even extension of $f(x)$, namely, $f^{(+)}(x)$. Of course, if we are interested *exclusively* in the region $0 \le x < \infty$, this remark is irrelevant.†

Needless to say, the Fourier cosine transform should have its odd counterpart, the *Fourier sine transform*. If $f(x)$ is odd, then the Fourier integral theorem yields

$$f(x) = \frac{2}{\pi} \int_0^\infty \sin kx \, dk \int_0^\infty f(\xi) \sin k\xi \, d\xi.$$

Consequently, if $f(x)$ is given *only* over $(0, \infty)$, we can define

$$F_S(k) = \mathfrak{F}_S\{f(x)\} = \sqrt{\frac{2}{\pi}} \int_0^\infty f(x) \sin kx \, dx$$

with the inverse

$$\mathfrak{F}_S^{-1}\{F_S(k)\} = \sqrt{2/\pi} \int_0^\infty F_S(k) \sin kx \, dk = f(x).$$

Evidently, the inversion integral reproduces $f(x)$ in the "odd fashion" for $(-\infty, 0)$.

---

* Since only the region $x > 0$ is involved, we can revert to the symbol $f(x)$ instead of $f^{(+)}(x)$.

† See, however, the convolution theorems on pp. 275–276.

Fourier sine and cosine transforms are expected to possess properties similar to those of Fourier transforms. For instance, integrating by parts, we have

$$\mathfrak{F}_C\{f'(x)\} = \sqrt{2/\pi} \int_0^\infty f'(x) \cos dx\, dx$$
$$= \sqrt{2/\pi}\, f(x) \cos kx \Big|_0^\infty + \sqrt{2/\pi}\, k \int_0^\infty f(x) \sin kx\, dx.$$

In most cases of practical interest, $f(\infty) = 0$.*

Then

$$\mathfrak{F}_C\{f'(x)\} = -\sqrt{2/\pi}\, f(0) + kF_S(k).$$

Note the "interference" of the Fourier sine and cosine transforms. However, let us calculate $\mathfrak{F}_C\{f''(x)\}$, integrating by parts twice (assuming $f'(\infty) = f(\infty) = 0$); the result reads

$$\mathfrak{F}_C\{f''(x)\} = -\sqrt{2/\pi}\, f'(0) - k^2 F_C(k)$$

and involves only Fourier cosine transforms. Similar results are obtained for Fourier sine transforms.

Our experience with Laplace transforms and Fourier series should tell us that Fourier transforms, Fourier sine transforms, and Fourier cosine transforms can be employed in much the same fashion, for instance, in solving differential equations. The above result then indicates that the Fourier cosine and sine transforms are convenient under certain special conditions, such as in the absence of the derivatives of odd or even order in the differential equations and when relevant functions and their derivatives vanish at infinity.†

The interrelation between Fourier sine and cosine transforms is also exhibited in the convolution theorems. For the cosine transform we have

$$\mathfrak{F}_C^{-1}\{F_C(k)G_C(k)\} = \sqrt{2/\pi} \int_0^\infty F_C(k)G_C(k) \cos kx\, dk$$
$$= (2/\pi) \int_0^\infty F_C(k) \cos kx\, dk \int_0^\infty g(\xi) \cos k\xi\, d\xi.$$

We now use

$$\cos kx \cos k\xi = \tfrac{1}{2}[\cos k(x - \xi) + \cos k(x + \xi)]$$

to obtain (interchanging the order of integration)

$$\mathfrak{F}_C^{-1}\{F_C(k)G_C(k)\} = (1/\pi) \int_0^\infty g(\xi)\, d\xi \int_0^\infty F_C(k)\,[\cos k(x - \xi) + \cos k(x + \xi)]\, dk$$
$$= (1/\sqrt{2\pi}) \int_0^\infty g(\xi)[f^{(+)}(x - \xi) + f(x + \xi)]\, d\xi.$$

Note: The appearance of $f^{(+)}$ (even extension of f) is due to the fact that in the range $x \le \xi < \infty$, we have $(x - \xi) < 0$ and the inversion of $F_C(k)$ must yield $f^{(+)}$.

---

* See also p. 277 for a related comment in the theory of distributions.

† The last requirement can be relaxed if distributions are used (see Section 7.5).

If we perform the same operations for the Fourier sine transform, then we will use

$$\sin kx \sin k\xi = \tfrac{1}{2}[\cos k(x - \xi) - \cos k(x + \xi)]$$

and deduce that

$$\mathfrak{F}_S^{-1}\{F_S(k)G_S(k)\} = (1/\pi)\int_0^\infty g(\xi)\,d\xi\int_0^\infty F_S(k)\,[\cos k(x - \xi) - \cos k(x + \xi)]\,dk.$$

Note that the sine transform $F_S(k)$ is now "mismatched" with cosine functions. We can define a new function*

$$\tilde{f}(x) = \mathfrak{F}_C^{-1}\{F_S(k)\}$$

and state that

$$\mathfrak{F}_S^{-1}\{F_S(k)G_S(k)\} = 1/\sqrt{2\pi}\int_0^\infty g(\xi)[\tilde{f}(x - \xi) - \tilde{f}(x + \xi)]\,d\xi.$$

Observe that $\tilde{f}(x)$ is, by definition, an even function.

7.7 APPLICATIONS OF FOURIER TRANSFORMS. THE PRINCIPLE OF CAUSALITY

Example 1. Consider a damped harmonic oscillator acted on by an external force $g(t)$. The motion of the oscillator is then governed by the differential equation

$$\ddot{x}(t) + 2\alpha\dot{x}(t) + \omega_0^2 x(t) = f(t),$$

where $f(t) = (1/m)g(t)$. This problem has been treated in Section 2.5 for the case where $f(t)$ is a sinusoidally varying function of frequency ω. By means of Fourier transforms, we can extend this result to an arbitrary function $f(t)$. In all cases of practical interest, $f(t)$ will possess a Fourier transform;† then

$$f(t) = (1/\sqrt{2\pi})\int_{-\infty}^{+\infty} F(\omega)e^{-i\omega t}\,d\omega,$$

where

$$F(\omega) = (1/\sqrt{2\pi})\int_{-\infty}^{+\infty} f(t)e^{i\omega t}\,dt.$$

The solution $x(t)$ is also expected, on physical grounds, to possess a Fourier transform [which we shall denote by $A(\omega)$] so that

$$x(t) = (1/\sqrt{2\pi})\int_{-\infty}^{+\infty} A(\omega)e^{-i\omega t}\,d\omega.$$

---

* We transform $f(x)$ by a sine transform and invert by a cosine transform.

† At least as a distribution; for instance, any bounded piecewise continuous $f(t)$ can be treated as a distribution according to the results of Section 7.5.

We can easily find $A(\omega)$ by subjecting the differential equation to a Fourier transformation and using $\mathcal{F}\{\dot{x}\} = -i\omega\mathcal{F}\{x\}$, and $\mathcal{F}\{\ddot{x}\} = -\omega^2\mathcal{F}\{x\}$. *Note:* These formulas assume that $x(\pm\infty) = \dot{x}(\pm\infty) = 0$. In many cases this will be true. However, if $x(t)$ is treated as a *distribution*, no such restriction is needed. We have, *by definition,**

$$\int_{-\infty}^{+\infty} \frac{d}{dt} x(t) e^{i\omega t} \, dt = -\int_{-\infty}^{+\infty} x(t) \frac{d}{dt} e^{i\omega t} \, dt.$$

The transformed differential equation reads

$$-\omega^2 A(\omega) - 2\alpha\omega i A(\omega) + \omega_0^2 A(\omega) = F(\omega)$$

and yields

$$A(\omega) = \frac{F(\omega)}{(\omega_0^2 - \omega^2) - 2\alpha\omega i}.$$

The solution of the problem is then

$$x(t) = \frac{1}{\sqrt{2\pi}} \int_{-\infty}^{+\infty} \frac{F(\omega) e^{-i\omega t}}{(\omega_0^2 - \omega^2) - 2\alpha\omega i} \, d\omega.$$

In most cases this integral can be evaluated by the calculus of residues. For this purpose it is necessary to know the zeros of the denominator,†

$$Z(\omega) = (\omega_0^2 - \omega^2) - 2\alpha\omega i,$$

because they will create the poles of the integrand.‡ If $\alpha > 0$, as is usually the case, the poles are in the lower half-plane and are located at

$$\omega_{1,2} = \pm\sqrt{\omega_0^2 - \alpha^2} - \alpha i \qquad \text{if } \omega_0 > \alpha \quad \text{(Case 1)},$$

$$\omega_{1,2} = (-\alpha \pm \sqrt{\alpha^2 - \omega_0^2})i \qquad \text{if } \omega_0 < \alpha \quad \text{(Case 2)},$$

$$\omega_1 = \omega_2 = -\alpha i \text{ (double root)} \quad \text{if } \omega_0 = \alpha \quad \text{(Case 3)},$$

as shown in Fig. 7.6. In Cases 1 and 2 there are two simple poles while in Case 3 there is one pole of second order.

We shall confine ourselves to Case 1, that of a weakly damped oscillator.§ Write $Z(\omega)$ in the form $Z(\omega) = -(\omega - \omega_1)(\omega - \omega_2)$ and evaluate the residues

---

* This is so because the sequences of core functions weakly converging to $\dot{x}(t)$ will possess this property. The idea is the same as that on p. 247, with appropriate changes according to Section 7.5.

† $Z(\omega)$ is sometimes referred to as the *impedance* by analogy with the *LRC*-circuit described by the same differential equation.

‡ Unless $F(\omega)$ has a zero at the same spot (an unlikely event).

§ The other two cases are treated similarly and present no difficulties.

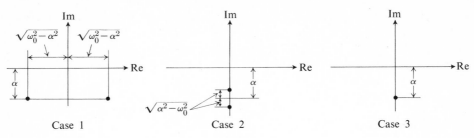

Figure 7.6

of the integrand:

The residue at $\omega = \omega_1$ is

$$\frac{1}{\sqrt{2\pi}} \frac{F(\omega_1)e^{-i\omega_1 t}}{(\omega_1 - \omega_2)}.$$

The residue at $\omega = \omega_2$ is

$$-\frac{1}{\sqrt{2\pi}} \frac{F(\omega_2)e^{-i\omega_2 t}}{(\omega_1 - \omega_2)},$$

where $\omega_1 - \omega_2 = 2\sqrt{\omega_0^2 - \alpha^2} = 2p$.

As a particular example, assume that $f(t)$ has the form (Fig. 7.7)

$$f(t) = \begin{cases} f_0 & |t| < \tau), \\ 0 & |t| \geq \tau). \end{cases}$$

The Fourier transform of $f(t)$ reads

$$F(\omega) = \frac{f_0}{\sqrt{2\pi}} \int_{-\tau}^{+\tau} e^{i\omega t}\, dt = f_0 \sqrt{\frac{2}{\pi}} \frac{\sin \omega\tau}{\omega};$$

then

$$x(t) = -\frac{f_0}{\pi} \int_{-\infty}^{+\infty} \frac{\sin \omega\tau \cdot e^{-i\omega t}}{\omega(\omega - \omega_1)(\omega - \omega_2)}\, d\omega,$$

where $\omega_1 = p - \alpha i$, $\omega_2 = -p - \alpha i$ $(p = \sqrt{\omega_0^2 - \alpha^2})$.

The only singularities of the integrand are those at $\omega = \omega_1$ and $\omega = \omega_2$. In order to find how the contour can be closed we must investigate the boundedness of the integrand. We write

$$\sin \omega\tau = (1/2i)(e^{i\omega\tau} - e^{-i\omega\tau}).$$

It is clear that if $t > \tau$, the function

$$\frac{\sin \omega\tau \cdot e^{-i\omega t}}{\omega}$$

is bounded in the lower half-plane and the

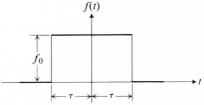

Figure 7.7

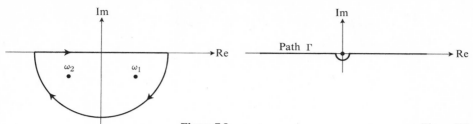

Figure 7.8   **Figure 7.9**

contour may be closed "down" as shown in Fig. 7.8. This yields

$$x(t) = + \frac{f_0}{\pi} 2\pi i \left[\frac{\sin \omega_1 \tau \cdot e^{-i\omega_1 t}}{\omega_1(\omega_1 - \omega_2)} - \frac{\sin \omega_2 \tau \cdot e^{-i\omega_2 t}}{\omega_2(\omega_1 - \omega_2)} \right]$$

$$= \frac{2 f_0 i}{\omega_1 \omega_2 (\omega_1 - \omega_2)} (\omega_2 \sin \omega_1 \tau \cdot e^{-i\omega_1 t} - \omega_1 \sin \omega_2 \tau \cdot e^{-i\omega_2 t}).$$

If a real form is desired, set

$$\omega_1 = p - \alpha i, \qquad \omega_2 = -p - \alpha i \qquad (\omega_1 \omega_2 = -\omega_0^2)$$

and express $\sin \omega_1 \tau$ and $\sin \omega_2 \tau$ in terms of exponential functions:

$$x(t) = (f_0/2\omega_0^2)[e^{(\alpha+ip)(\tau-t)} + e^{(\alpha-ip)(\tau-t)} - e^{-(\alpha+ip)(\tau+t)} - e^{-(\alpha-ip)(\tau+t)}$$

$$+ (\alpha i/p)(e^{(\alpha+ip)(\tau-t)} - e^{(\alpha-ip)(\tau-t)} - e^{-(\alpha+ip)(\tau+t)} + e^{-(\alpha-ip)(\tau+t)})].$$

This expression reduces to

$$x(t) = (f_0/\omega_0^2)[\cos p(t - \tau) + (\alpha/p) \sin p(t - \tau)]e^{-\alpha(t-\tau)}$$

$$- (f_0/\omega_0^2)[\cos p(t + \tau) + (\alpha/p) \sin p(t + \tau)]e^{-\alpha(t+\tau)} \qquad (t > \tau).$$

For $t < -\tau$, the contour may be closed "up" and yields zero. This is expected:
Before the external force has begun to act, a *damped** oscillator could have
been only in the state of rest.

If $|t| < \tau$, matters are somewhat more complicated. It is evidently convenient
to split the integral for $x(t)$ into two parts, according to the decomposition

$$\sin \omega \tau = (1/2i)(e^{i\omega\tau} - e^{-i\omega\tau}).$$

The part containing $e^{-i\omega(t+\tau)}$ may be evaluated by a contour closed "down"
and the part containing $e^{-i\omega(t-\tau)}$ by a contour closed "up." However, each integrand will then have an extra pole at $\omega = 0$.

Since the "combined integrand" appearing in the original expression for
$x(t)$ has no pole at $\omega = 0$, it is clear that the path of integration may be deformed
into the one shown in Fig. 7.9, without affecting the (overall) result in any way.†

---

* That is, "positively" damped (case $\alpha > 0$).

† One can circumvent the pole from "above" just as well, or take the principal value.
This will change nothing.

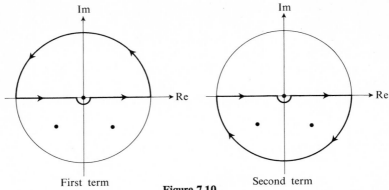

First term   **Figure 7.10**   Second term

After this is done, the combined integrand can be split as stated, with both parts assumed to be evaluated along the path given in Fig. 7.9:

$$x(t) = -\frac{f_0}{2\pi i}\int_\Gamma \frac{e^{-i\omega(t-\tau)}}{\omega(\omega - \omega_1)(\omega - \omega_2)}\,d\omega + \frac{f_0}{2\pi i}\int_\Gamma \frac{e^{-i\omega(t+\tau)}}{\omega(\omega - \omega_1)(\omega - \omega_2)}\,d\omega.$$

Now the contours can be closed as planned (Fig. 7.10), resulting in

$$x(t) = -\frac{f_0}{\omega_1\omega_2} - f_0\frac{e^{-i\omega_1(t+\tau)}}{\omega_1(\omega_1 - \omega_2)} + f_0\frac{e^{-i\omega_2(t+\tau)}}{\omega_2(\omega_1 - \omega_2)}.$$

After some algebraic manipulations, this result reduces to

$$x(t) = f_0/\omega_0^2 - f_0/\omega_0^2[\cos p(t + \tau) + (\alpha/p)\sin p(t + \tau)]e^{-\alpha(t+\tau)}$$
$$(-\tau < t < \tau).$$

Remark. This formula also solves a different problem, namely, that of an external force beginning to act at $t = -\tau$ (with $f(t) = f_0 = $ const) and *never ceasing to act.* Indeed, in the above formula the oscillator "does not know" that the force will stop acting at time $t = \tau$, and cannot distinguish between the two situations. Of course, in the case of a permanent external force, this formula is valid for all $t > -\tau$ and illustrates how the oscillator will approach the steady state of a fixed displacement as t increases:

$$x(\infty) = \frac{f_0}{\omega_0^2} = \text{const.}$$

Example 2. *Nondamped Oscillator.* The use of the Fourier transform and contour integration has some special features when the oscillator is not damped and obeys the DE $\ddot{x} + \omega_0^2 x = f(t)$.

The procedure of the preceding example remains the same until we reach the expression

$$x(t) = \frac{1}{\sqrt{2\pi}}\int_{-\infty}^{+\infty}\frac{F(\omega)e^{-i\omega t}}{\omega_0^2 - \omega^2}\,d\omega.$$

The difference is that now the poles of the integrand are on the real axis, namely, at $\omega_1 = \omega_0$ and $\omega_2 = -\omega_0$. Because of this, the integral for $x(t)$ is not even defined until a way of circumventing these poles is prescribed.

At this point an additional insight into the physical nature of the problem is desirable. For instance, the original DE may describe an actual mechanical or electrical oscillator. Such an oscillator inevitably has some degree of damping and the damping term has been omitted from the DE only because it was deemed to be small. If this is so, then the poles should not actually be on the real axis, but slightly below it. This suggests the rule: Replace ω_0 by $\omega_0 - i\epsilon$, where ϵ is an arbitrarily small positive number. This will depress the poles below the real axis and properly define the integral for $x(t)$. After all calculations are performed, one may let $\epsilon \to 0$ and evaluate the limit, which is then the desired result. This can be written as follows:*

$$x(t) = -\frac{1}{\sqrt{2\pi}} \int_{-\infty}^{+\infty} \frac{F(\omega)e^{-i\omega t}}{[\omega - (\omega_0 - i\epsilon)][\omega - (-\omega_0 - i\epsilon)]} \, d\omega,$$

or, alternatively, as†

$$x(t) = +\frac{1}{\sqrt{2\pi}} \int_{-\infty}^{+\infty} \frac{F(\omega)e^{-i\omega t}}{\omega_0^2 - (\omega + i\epsilon)^2} \, d\omega.$$

This result is, of course, equivalent to the requirement that the integral for $x(t)$ should be taken along the path Γ, as shown in Fig. 7.11 (rather than along the real axis in the rigorous sense).

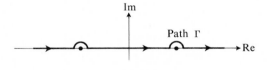

Figure 7.11

If the problem at hand falls within the stated category, the solution is straight-forward. Sometimes, however, our DE represents some rather abstract physical oscillator and very little, if anything, is known about any conceivable damping.‡ In this case the following argument may be helpful: Suppose that the oscillator is at rest when $t = -\infty$, a situation expressed by $x(-\infty) = 0$. Suppose, further, that the oscillator is disturbed by a rectangular pulse

$$f(t) = \begin{cases} 1/\tau & \text{(for } 0 < t < \tau\text{)}, \\ 0 & \text{(otherwise)}. \end{cases}$$

---

* Read the remark on p. 111.
† These two expressions are identical for any ϵ.
‡ Such problems occur in quantum mechanics and in quantum field theory.

In this case

$$F(\omega) = \frac{1}{\sqrt{2\pi}} \int_0^\tau \frac{1}{\tau} e^{i\omega t}\, dt = \frac{i}{\sqrt{2\pi}} \frac{1 - e^{i\omega\tau}}{\omega\tau}$$

and

$$f(x) = -\frac{i}{2\pi\tau} \int_{-\infty}^{+\infty} \frac{(1 - e^{i\omega\tau})e^{-i\omega t}}{\omega(\omega - \omega_0)(\omega + \omega_0)}\, d\omega,$$

with the path of integration as yet undetermined. The integrand has two poles, at $\omega = \omega_0$ and $\omega = -\omega_0$, with the residues

$$-\frac{i}{2\pi\tau} \frac{(1 - e^{i\omega_0\tau})e^{-i\omega_0 t}}{2\omega_0^2},$$

and

$$-\frac{i}{2\pi\tau} \frac{(1 - e^{-i\omega_0\tau})e^{i\omega_0 t}}{2\omega_0^2}.$$

To simplify the argument, assume that τ is very small, which implies a very short pulse. Note, however, that the height of the pulse is then very large. In this case the expression

$$\frac{i}{\tau} \frac{1 - e^{i\omega_0 t}}{\omega_0}$$

approaches unity and the residues become*

$$-\frac{e^{-i\omega_0 t}}{4\pi\omega_0} \quad \text{and} \quad +\frac{e^{i\omega_0 t}}{4\pi\omega_0}.$$

Now consider the case $t < 0$. Whatever the treatment of the poles, the integral for $x(t)$ may be evaluated by closing the contour "up." Now, from the *physical point of view*, the oscillator is originally at rest and is not expected to be set into motion before the pulse occurs. Therefore, we *require* that $x(t) = 0$ for $t < 0$. If one or both poles were to be circumvented "from below," their residues would contribute, and the above requirement could not be fulfilled. Evidently no other treatment of the poles except to circumvent them "from above" can be accepted. It follows then that the path of integration must again be chosen as shown in Fig. 7.11.

Note: For $t > 0$ the contour cannot be closed "up" but must be closed "down." Both poles contribute, and the final result yields

$$x(t) = (\sin \omega_0 t)/\omega_0 \qquad (t > 0)$$

and represents the response of the oscillator to an instantaneous impulse.

---

* The replacement of residues by their limiting values as $\tau \to 0$ is equivalent to replacing $f(t)$ by the delta function $\delta(t)$.

Remarks

1. The approach outlined above may be said to be based on the *principle of causality:* If one physical phenomenon causes another one, then the effect cannot be felt before the cause has occurred. If there is any reason to believe that our oscillator should obey the principle of causality,* then the above argument yields the desired result without a recourse to any damping.

2. The treatment of poles explicitly derived for an instantaneous impulse can be shown to be valid for other types of functions $f(t)$ which vanish identically prior to some time t_0 (not necessarily zero) and even some others, namely those which admit solutions $x(-\infty) = 0$.

Example 3. *A Beam on Elastic Foundation.* Consider a beam of length L resting on an elastic foundation (Fig. 7.12); this term implies that the foundation is capable of exerting a force of reaction (per unit length) that is proportional to the displacement $y(x)$ (Fig. 7.13).† The DE satisfied by the function is then

$$EI\frac{d^4y}{dx^4} = q(x) - Cy(x) \qquad (C = \text{const}),$$

where $q(x)$ is the external force per unit length.

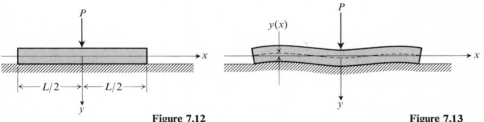

Figure 7.12   **Figure 7.13**

If the beam is very long and loaded by a concentrated force (Fig. 7.12), in which case the function $q(x)$ is reducible to $P\,\delta(x)$, then it may be replaced by an infinite beam, because its deflections $y(x)$ are going to be very small for large values of $|x|$. If this approximation is accepted, then the solution can be obtained by Fourier transform methods. Using

$$\mathcal{F}\left\{\frac{d^4y}{dx^4}\right\} = k^4 Y(k) \quad \text{if } \mathcal{F}\{y\} = Y(k),$$

---

* Except for some scientific speculations, the principle of causality is commonly accepted as a universal law of nature. However, the history of physics has witnessed many revolutionary changes and we must always bear in mind that a speculation today may be a theory tomorrow.

† We assume that the beam is "glued" to the foundation so that the reaction can result in either pressure or tension. This approximates the more common case in civil engineering where the reaction can only be in an upward direction (transverse pressure on the beam).

we obtain $(EIk^4 + C)Y(k) = Q(k)$, where $Q(k) = \mathfrak{F}\{q(x)\}$. Therefore

$$y(x) = \mathfrak{F}^{-1}\{Y(k)\} = \frac{1}{\sqrt{2\pi}} \int_{-\infty}^{+\infty} \frac{Q(x)e^{-ikx}}{EIk^4 + C} dk.$$

If we take* $q(x) = P\,\delta(x)$, then $Q(k) = P/\sqrt{2\pi}$ and

$$y(x) = \frac{P}{2\pi} \int_{-\infty}^{+\infty} \frac{e^{-ikx}}{EIk^4 + C} dk.$$

Writing $EI/C = \alpha^4$ and using $\alpha k = z$, we obtain

$$y(x) = \frac{P}{2\pi C\alpha} \int_{-\infty}^{+\infty} \frac{e^{-i(x/\alpha)z}}{z^4 + 1} dz.$$

The integrand has four simple poles:

$$z_1 = e^{i(\pi/4)}, \qquad z_2 = e^{i(3\pi/4)}, \qquad z_3 = e^{-i(\pi/4)}, \qquad z_4 = e^{-i(3\pi/4)}.$$

For $x > 0$, the contour for $y(x)$ can be closed down and only the poles z_3 and z_4 contribute. For $x < 0$, the contour is closed up and only the poles z_1 and z_2 contribute. The calculation is straightforward and yields:

$$y(x) = \frac{P}{\alpha C 2\sqrt{2}} \left(\cos \frac{x}{\alpha\sqrt{2}} + \sin \frac{x}{\alpha\sqrt{2}} \right) e^{-x/\alpha\sqrt{2}} \qquad (x > 0),$$

$$y(x) = \frac{P}{\alpha C 2\sqrt{2}} \left(\cos \frac{x}{\alpha\sqrt{2}} - \sin \frac{x}{\alpha\sqrt{2}} \right) e^{x/\alpha\sqrt{2}} \qquad (x < 0).$$

These two expressions can be combined into a single one:

$$y(x) = \frac{P}{\alpha C 2\sqrt{2}} \left(\cos \frac{|x|}{\alpha\sqrt{2}} + \sin \frac{|x|}{\alpha\sqrt{2}} \right) e^{-|x|/\alpha\sqrt{2}} \qquad \text{(all } x\text{)}.$$

BIBLIOGRAPHY

CARSLAW, H. S., *Introduction to the Theory of Fourier's Series and Integrals*. London: Macmillan Co., 1930.

SNEDDON, I. N., *Fourier Transforms*. New York: McGraw-Hill Book Co., 1951.

TITCHMARSH, E. C., *Introduction to the Theory of Fourier Integrals*. New York: Oxford University Press, 1948.

TRANTER, C. J., *Integral Transforms in Mathematical Physics*. London: Methuen & Co. Ltd., 1956.

---

* We shall work within the space of distributions.

PROBLEMS

1. Verify the (first) Parseval theorem for each of the three functions $f(x)$ used in the examples of Section 7.2.

2. Find the Fourier transforms of the following functions:

a) $f(x) = e^{-\lambda x^2} \cos \beta x \quad (\lambda > 0)$,   b) $f(x) = \dfrac{\cos \beta x}{a^4 + x^4}$,

c) $f(x) = \begin{cases} \cos k_0 x & (|x| < N\pi/k_0), \\ 0 & (|x| > N\pi/k_0), \end{cases}$ N is a positive integer.

3. Establish the following result (using the technique of Example 6, Section 2.12):

$$\mathfrak{F}\left\{\frac{\sinh ax}{\sinh \pi x}\right\} = \frac{1}{\sqrt{2\pi}} \frac{\cos a}{\cosh k + \cos a} \qquad (|a| < \pi).$$

4. a) Obtain the analog of conjugation property (Section 7.3) for the case of purely imaginary $f(x)$.

b) Do the same for the case of complex $f(x)$.

5. Establish the following formulas:

a) $\mathfrak{F}_S\{e^{-x} \cos x\} = \sqrt{\dfrac{2}{\pi}} \dfrac{k^3}{k^4 + 4}$,

b) $\mathfrak{F}_S\left\{f(x) = \begin{cases} \sin x & (0 \le x \le \pi) \\ 0 & (x > \pi) \end{cases}\right\} = \sqrt{\dfrac{2}{\pi}} \dfrac{\sin k\pi}{1 - k^2}$,

c) $\mathfrak{F}_S\{xe^{-ax}\} = \sqrt{\dfrac{2}{\pi}} \dfrac{a^2 - k^2}{(a^2 + k^2)^2}$,

d) $\mathfrak{F}_C\{x^{\alpha-1}\} = \sqrt{\dfrac{2}{\pi}} \Gamma(\alpha) \dfrac{\cos (\alpha\pi/2)}{k^\alpha} \quad (0 < \alpha < 1)$.

6. Develop the formulas for

a) $\mathfrak{F}_S\left\{\dfrac{d^2 f(x)}{dx^2}\right\}$,   b) $\mathfrak{F}_S\left\{\dfrac{d^4 f(x)}{dx^4}\right\}$,   c) $\mathfrak{F}_C\left\{\dfrac{d^4 f(x)}{dx^4}\right\}$

similar to that for $\mathfrak{F}_C\{d^2 f(x)/dx^2\}$ quoted on p. 275.

7. Deduce the following convolution theorems:

a) $\mathfrak{F}_C^{-1}\{F_S(k)G_S(k)\} = \dfrac{1}{\sqrt{2\pi}} \displaystyle\int_0^\infty g(\xi)[f(x + \xi) - f^{(-)}(x - \xi)]\, d\xi$

(where $f^{(-)}(x)$ is the "odd extension" of $f(x)$),

b) $\mathfrak{F}_S^{-1}\{F_S(k)G_C(k)\} = \dfrac{1}{\sqrt{2\pi}} \displaystyle\int_0^\infty g(\xi)[f(x + \xi) + f^{(-)}(x - \xi)]\, d\xi$,

c) $\mathfrak{F}_S^{-1}\{F_S(k)G_C(k)\} = \dfrac{1}{\sqrt{2\pi}} \displaystyle\int_0^\infty f(\xi)[g^{(+)}(x - \xi) - g(x + \xi)]\, d\xi$.

8. Using the symmetry of the integrand, show that

$$\mathcal{F}_C\{e^{-\alpha x^2}\} = \frac{1}{\sqrt{2\alpha}} e^{-k^2/4\alpha}.$$

Let $f(x) = \text{erfc}(\lambda x) = (2/\sqrt{\pi}) \int_{\lambda x}^{\infty} e^{-t^2}\, dt$. Using the formula connecting $\mathcal{F}_C\{f'(x)\}$ with $\mathcal{F}_S\{f(x)\}$ and the above result, show that

$$\mathcal{F}_S\{\text{erfc}(\lambda x)\} = \sqrt{\frac{2}{\pi}} \frac{1 - e^{-k^2/4\lambda^2}}{k}.$$

9. Solve the problem discussed in Example 1, Section 7.7, for the following cases:
   a) overdamped oscillator, $\omega_0 < \alpha$,
   b) critically damped oscillator, $\omega_0 = \alpha$.

10. A damped harmonic oscillator is subjected to an external force

$$g(t) = \sin \lambda t/t.$$

On physical grounds, it may be assumed that the displacement of the oscillator vanishes at $t = \pm\infty$. Formulate the problem in mathematical terms. Can the Laplace transform methods be used for its solution? Solve the problem by Fourier transform methods (use Example 3 of Section 7.2).

11. Consider the equation

$$\ddot{x} - \alpha^2 x = 0 \qquad (0 \le t < \infty)$$

with the boundary conditions: (1) $\dot{x}(0) = b = \text{const}$, (2) $x(\infty) < \infty$, that is, $x(t)$ is bounded at infinity. Show how this problem can be solved by the Fourier cosine transform method. Verify the solution by the Laplace transform method.

12. Consider the equation

$$\ddot{x} - \alpha^2 x = f(t) \qquad (0 \le t < \infty)$$

with the boundary conditions $\dot{x}(0) = b$ and $x(\infty) < \infty$. Apply the Fourier cosine transform method to show that

$$x(t) = -\frac{b}{\alpha} e^{-\alpha t} - \frac{1}{2\alpha} \int_0^{\infty} f(\xi)[e^{-\alpha|x-\xi|} + e^{-\alpha(x+\xi)}]\, d\xi.$$

Now treat the problem by the Laplace transform method and comment on the difficulties involved. What is the factor determining the choice of transform?

13. Consider the problem

$$\ddot{x} - \alpha^2 x = f(t) \qquad (0 \le t < \infty)$$

with the boundary conditions $x(0) = a$ and $x(\infty) < \infty$. Solve for $x(t)$ by a method of your choice.

CHAPTER 8

PARTIAL DIFFERENTIAL EQUATIONS

8.1 THE STRETCHED STRING. WAVE EQUATION

A vast number of physical problems can be formulated by differential equations involving functions of more than one variable, known as *partial differential equations*. In this chapter we shall consider several relatively simple examples which will serve as an introduction to the formulation of such problems and methods of their solution.

Consider a thin wire or a string stretched horizontally by a force T.* If the tension T in the string is very large compared to its weight, the string will be, to a high degree of accuracy, straight and horizontal in its equilibrium position. We shall assume that such a string offers no resistance to bending. For instance, a steel wire 1 m long and 1 mm in diameter stretched by $T = 200$ lb will behave like a rope (Fig. 8.1a) rather than like a bar (Fig. 8.1b) when it is loaded in the middle by a force $P = 0.1$ lb (note that the weight of the wire is about 0.013 lb). The truth of this statement can be verified experimentally and can be inferred theoretically. By the customary theory of bending, the deflection at the midpoint† is

$$\delta = \frac{PL^3}{48EI} \quad \text{with} \quad I = \frac{\pi d^4}{64},$$

where E = Young's modulus and d = diameter of the wire. For our wire, this formula results in such a large deflection (about 94 cm) that the theory becomes inapplicable. Actually, the resistance of the wire to pure extension will check the process of deformation, and the equilibrium shape of the wire will essentially be determined by the condition of smallest extension (about 0.7 cm), leading to Fig. 8.1(a).

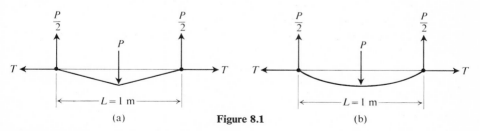

(a)   **Figure 8.1**   (b)

---

* More precisely by a pair of such forces.
† See Example 2 in Section 6.5.

Now suppose that the wire can be deformed from its original, almost straight, shape by some moderate (small with respect to T) forces which are either acting permanently or are used to produce an initial displacement or initial transverse motion of the wire. It is then reasonable to expect that the slope of the deformed wire will be small everywhere during the motion (for instance, the maximum slope should not exceed 0.05). Suppose further that the wire is never subject to any other horizontal forces except the tension T, or to any initial horizontal displacements or velocities of its points.

From all these fairly restrictive conditions we can derive certain consequences:

a) The elements of the wire can have only transverse displacements, since there are no initial longitudinal displacements or motions and no subsequent net longitudinal forces.

b) The tangential force in the wire is at all times and at all points constant (to a high degree of accuracy) and equal to T. Indeed, for an arbitrary piece AB of the deformed wire the equation (see Fig. 8.2)

$$T_1 \cos \alpha = T_2 \cos \beta$$

must hold at all times. However,

$$\cos \alpha = \frac{1}{\sqrt{1 + \tan^2 \alpha}} \cong 1 - \tfrac{1}{2} \tan^2 \alpha \cong 1$$

(to an accuracy of 0.5% or better if $|\tan \alpha| < 0.05$). The same argument holds for $\cos \beta$, leading to

$$T_1 = T_2 = T.$$

We can now derive the equation which must be satisfied by the deflection u of the wire at any point x and any instant of time t. Considering an element dx (Fig. 8.3), we obtain, noting that $dx \cong ds$ within our approximations,

$$T (\sin \beta - \sin \alpha) + F \, dx - \rho g \, dx = \rho \, dx \, \frac{\partial^2 u}{\partial t^2},$$

where ρ is the density of the string (so that $\rho \, dx$ is the mass of the element), F is the external force per unit length at point x, and $\partial^2 u / \partial t^2$ is the acceleration of the element in the transverse direction.

The above equation represents Newton's second law applied to the element dx. Within our approximations we can set

$$\sin \alpha = \frac{\tan \alpha}{\sqrt{1 + \tan^2 \alpha}} \cong \tan \alpha = \frac{\partial u}{\partial x} \left(x - \frac{dx}{2} \right)$$

and, similarly,

$$\sin \beta \cong \frac{\partial u}{\partial x} \left(x + \frac{dx}{2} \right).$$

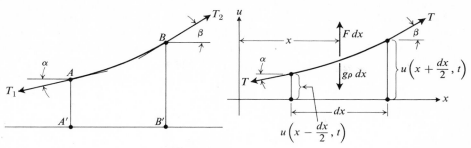

Figure 8.2   Figure 8.3

It is then reasonable to replace

$$\frac{\sin \beta - \sin \alpha}{dx} \cong \frac{\partial u/\partial x(x + dx/2) - \partial u/\partial x(x - dx/2)}{dx}$$

by the second derivative $\partial^2 u/\partial x^2$, and the equation becomes

$$T\frac{\partial^2 u}{\partial x^2} + F(x, t) - \rho(x)g = \rho(x)\frac{\partial^2 u}{\partial t^2},$$

where we have taken into account that the string may not be homogeneous (so that ρ may vary with x) and the external force F may vary with x and t.

This general equation for $u(x, t)$ can be simplified in many cases. For instance, if $\rho(x)g$ is small compared to $F(x, t)$, it may be neglected and the equation reduces to

$$T\frac{\partial^2 u}{\partial x^2} + F(x, t) = \rho(x)\frac{\partial^2 u}{\partial t^2}.$$

(Note that the term $\rho(\partial^2 u/\partial t^2)$ should not be neglected, because $\partial^2 u/\partial t^2$ may be large due to fast vibrations; the term $T(\partial^2 u/\partial x^2)$ is, in general, appreciable because T is large.) If there are no transverse forces acting on the string, then the equation assumes the form

$$T\frac{\partial^2 u}{\partial x^2} = \rho(x)\frac{\partial^2 u}{\partial t^2}.$$

Finally, if ρ is constant, as in the case of a homogeneous string, then the equation can be written in the form

$$\frac{\partial^2 u}{\partial x^2} = \frac{1}{c^2}\frac{\partial^2 u}{\partial t^2},$$

where $c^2 = T/\rho = \text{const}$ (note that c is real because ρ and T are positive). This equation is known as the (one-dimensional) *wave equation;* it is a linear partial differential equation of the second order in two variables (x and t), with constant coefficients.

Although partial differential equations are, generally speaking, more difficult to solve than ordinary differential equations, some of them have fairly simple solutions. Such is the case with the above wave equation. Consider the function

$$u(x, t) = f(x - ct),$$

where f is an *arbitrary* twice differentiable function. It is simple to verify that $u(x, t)$ is a solution of our wave equation.

Exercise. Produce a proof of the above statement by setting $z = x - ct$, using

$$\frac{\partial u}{\partial x} = \frac{\partial u}{\partial z} \frac{\partial z}{\partial x}, \quad \text{etc.}$$

A simple reflection will show that the function

$$u(x, t) = g(x + ct)$$

is also a solution of the wave equation no matter what g is.* As a matter of fact, it is possible to prove that the expression

$$u(x, t) = f(x - ct) + g(x + ct)$$

represents the *general solution* of our PDE;† i.e., any solution can be expressed in this form.

Despite all this, physical problems leading to the one-dimensional wave equation do not become trivial just because the general solution is known. Physical problems impose certain conditions on the solution $u(x, t)$. For instance, since a typical stretched-string problem usually implies that the string, of a given length L, is *fixed* at the ends which may be placed at $x = 0$ and $x = L$, it follows that the solution must satisfy the conditions

$$u(0, t) = 0 \quad \text{and} \quad u(L, t) = 0$$

for all values of the variable t. Such conditions are appropriately called the *boundary conditions*.

Moreover, the physical problem begins at a certain instant of time, usually selected to be $t = 0$, and it is often assumed that the initial shape and the distribution of initial velocities‡ of the string are given. These so-called *initial conditions* are functions of the variable x and can be expressed by the statements

$$u(x, 0) = u_0(x), \qquad \frac{\partial u}{\partial t}(x, 0) = v_0(x),$$

---

* So long as it is differentiable twice.

† PDE will be used as the abbreviation for "partial differential equation."

‡ These correspond to the familiar notions of initial position and initial velocity in particle mechanics.

where $u_0(x)$ and $v_0(x)$ are given functions, representing the displacements and velocities of *all points* of the string at the time $t = 0$.

When various such conditions are imposed on $u(x, t)$, then it is by no means easy (in general) to determine the functions f and g in the general solution. In many cases it is convenient to abandon altogether the form

$$u(x, t) = f(x - ct) + g(x + ct),$$

and to approach the problem from an entirely different angle.* In particular, we shall discuss the methods which favor compliance with *boundary conditions* from the very start.

8.2 THE METHOD OF SEPARATION OF VARIABLES

Since the additional conditions imposed on $u(x, t)$ in our string problem fall into two groups, (a) those involving x (boundary conditions) and (b) those involving t (initial conditions), it may be reasonable to seek solutions of the PDE in the form

$$u(x, t) = X(x)T(t),$$

where X is a function of x only and T is a function of t only. If $X(x)$ is chosen to satisfy the conditions
$$X(0) = 0, \qquad X(L) = 0,$$

then the function $u(x, t)$ will satisfy the same conditions. Then $T(t)$ may, perhaps, be chosen to satisfy the initial conditions.

We now require that $u(x, t)$ satisfy the PDE. We have

$$\frac{\partial^2 u(x, t)}{\partial x^2} = \frac{d^2 X(x)}{dx^2} T(t), \qquad \frac{\partial^2 u(x, t)}{\partial t^2} = X(x) \frac{d^2 T(t)}{dt^2}.$$

Therefore

$$\frac{d^2 X}{dx^2} T = \frac{1}{c^2} X \frac{d^2 T}{dt^2}.$$

Dividing both sides by $X(x)T(t)$, we obtain

$$\frac{1}{X} \frac{d^2 X}{dx^2} = \frac{1}{c^2} \frac{1}{T} \frac{d^2 T}{dt^2}.$$

The left-hand side of this equation depends on x alone; the right-hand side depends on t alone. If this equality is to hold for all x and t, it is evident that either side must be a constant (same for both sides):

$$\frac{1}{X} \frac{d^2 X}{dx^2} = \lambda, \qquad \frac{1}{c^2} \frac{1}{T} \frac{d^2 T}{dt^2} = \lambda.$$

---

* For some problems, however, this form is very suitable.

The constant λ is known as a *separation constant*. The equation for $X(x)$ can be written as

$$\frac{d^2 X}{dx^2} = \lambda X$$

and will lead to exponential functions if $\lambda > 0$, to trigonometric functions if $\lambda < 0$, and to a linear function if $\lambda = 0$:

$$X(x) = \begin{cases} Ae^{x\sqrt{\lambda}} + Be^{-x\sqrt{\lambda}} & (\lambda > 0), \\ A' \cos(x\sqrt{-\lambda}) + B' \sin(x\sqrt{-\lambda}) & (\lambda < 0), \\ A''x + B'' & (\lambda = 0). \end{cases}$$

It is not difficult to verify that the boundary conditions $X(0) = 0$, $X(L) = 0$ can be satisfied *only* if $\lambda < 0$ and, moreover, *only* if A' is set equal to zero and the values of λ satisfy the condition

$$\sqrt{-\lambda} = n\pi/L \qquad (n = 1, 2, 3, \ldots).$$

Exercise. Show, in detail, that it is possible to satisfy either $X(0) = 0$ or $X(L) = 0$, but not both, if $\lambda \geq 0$. Also, prove the statement made for the case $\lambda < 0$.

These "allowed" values of the separation constant λ,

$$\lambda_n = -n^2\pi^2/L^2 \qquad (n = 1, 2, 3, \ldots),$$

are usually called the *eigenvalues*, or *characteristic values*, of the problem under consideration.* By this we mean the problem of finding functions satisfying the given DE *and* the given boundary conditions. In our case there is an infinity of such functions, called *eigenfunctions*, and they read

$$X_n(x) = B'_n \sin(n\pi x/L) \qquad (n = 1, 2, 3, \ldots),$$

where B'_n is an arbitrary (nonzero) constant which may, in general, be different for different eigenfunctions.

In our problem of the stretched string the function $T(t)$ which is multiplied by $X(x)$ must satisfy the DE with the same separation constant as $X(x)$. Therefore, to each eigenfunction $X_n(x)$ there corresponds a function $T_n(t)$ satisfying

$$\frac{1}{c^2} \frac{1}{T_n} \frac{d^2 T_n}{dt^2} = \lambda_n = -\frac{n^2\pi^2}{L^2}.$$

This yields

$$T_n(t) = C_n \cos\frac{n\pi ct}{L} + D_n \sin\frac{n\pi ct}{L},$$

where C_n and D_n are arbitrary constants.

---

* The word *eigenvalue* is an adaptation of the German term *eigenwert* derived from *eigen* = proper and *wert* = value.

Summarizing our results we may say that the attempt to find the solution of our PDE with given boundary conditions and initial conditions in the form

$$u(x, t) = X(x)T(t)$$

leads us, so far, to an *infinite number* of such functions which may be written as

$$u_n(x, t) = \left(A_n \cos \frac{n\pi ct}{L} + B_n \sin \frac{n\pi ct}{L} \right) \sin \frac{n\pi x}{L},$$

where $A_n = B'_n C_n$ and $B_n = B'_n D_n$ are arbitrary constants. Each of these functions $u_n(x, t)$ satisfies the PDE and the boundary conditions. It remains for us to select from among these functions, adjusting the constants A_n and B_n, those functions that will also satisfy the desired initial conditions. Before we do this, however, note that each function $u_n(x, t)$ represents, on its own, *some* kind of possible motion of the stretched string (corresponding to some special initial conditions). These types of motion are known as the *characteristic modes* (or *normal modes*) of vibration of the string. Each one represents a harmonic motion (vibration) with the characteristic frequency (or "eigenfrequency")

$$\omega_n = n\pi c/L \qquad (n = 1, 2, 3, \ldots).$$

A bit of reflection will show that it is not possible to satisfy *arbitrary* initial conditions

$$u(x, 0) = u_0(x), \qquad \frac{\partial u}{\partial t}(x, 0) = v_0(x)$$

by any *single* function $u_n(x, t)$. Indeed, any particular function $u_n(x, t)$ will satisfy initial conditions of the form

$$u_0(x) = A_n \sin \frac{n\pi x}{L}, \qquad v_0(x) = B_n \frac{cn\pi}{L} \sin \frac{n\pi x}{L}$$

and *no others*. To overcome this difficulty we can lean back on the powerful *principle of superposition*. Our PDE is *linear homogeneous*, and so are our boundary conditions. It is trivial to verify that if two functions $u_n(x, t)$ and $u_m(x, t)$ satisfy the PDE and the boundary conditions, then their linear combination

$$f(x, t) = C_1 u_n(x, t) + C_2 u_m(x, t)$$

will also satisfy the PDE and the boundary conditions. By induction this will also be true for a linear combination of a *finite* number of functions $u_n(x, t)$. It is not unreasonable to conjecture that the same properties will hold for an *infinite series* formed by the functions $u_n(x, t)$:

$$y(x, t) = \sum_{n=1}^{\infty} \left(A_n \cos \frac{n\pi ct}{L} + B_n \sin \frac{n\pi ct}{L} \right) \sin \frac{n\pi x}{L},$$

provided the series converges (or if not, provided it can be treated as a distribution, in conformity with the principles stated in Chapter 6).

To be more precise, the function defined above certainly satisfies the boundary conditions

$$y(0, t) = y(L, t) = 0$$

(since each term satisfies them). It will also satisfy the PDE, *provided* it can be differentiated twice term by term with respect to both x and t. From the point of view of the classical theory of functions, this may impose considerable restrictions on A_n and B_n; e.g., the twice differentiated series $y(x, t)$ must be uniformly convergent. On the other hand, from the point of view of the theory of distributions it is sufficient* that A_n and B_n are of the order of some power of n:

$$|A_n| < An^N, \qquad |B_n| < Bn^N \qquad \text{(some } N\text{)},$$

and this point of view may be adequate for physical applications.

In any case, however, the justification of the method depends on the properties of A_n and B_n, and it is usually convenient to *assume* its validity and *justify it later*, after the solution has been developed.

It is needless to emphasize that the function $y(x, t)$ is a Fourier sine series in x (it is also a Fourier series in t, but this fact is of much less importance). Setting $t = 0$ and using the first initial condition, we obtain

$$u_0(x) = \sum_{n=1}^{\infty} A_n \sin \frac{n\pi x}{L}.$$

If the function $u_0(x)$ can be expanded into a Fourier sine series, the coefficients A_n can be determined. In physical problems $u_0(x)$ is invariably continuous, piecewise very smooth, and vanishes at $x = 0$ and $x = L$. Therefore, it can be represented as above.

Similarly, calculating $(\partial u/\partial t)(x, t)$ and using the second initial condition, we can obtain

$$v_0(x) = \sum_{n=1}^{\infty} B_n \frac{cn\pi}{L} \sin \frac{n\pi x}{L}.$$

In physical problems $v_0(x)$ is sometimes assumed to be discontinuous. However, it is invariably piecewise continuous and piecewise very smooth, and the coefficients B_n can be determined as well.

Consequently, we have constructed a solution to our problem in the form of a series

$$y(x, t) = \sum_{n=1}^{\infty} \left(A_n \cos \frac{n\pi ct}{L} + B_n \sin \frac{n\pi ct}{L} \right) \sin \frac{n\pi x}{L},$$

which satisfies the boundary conditions and initial conditions for all physically reasonable functions $u_0(x)$ and $v_0(x)$.

---

* See p. 253.

8.3 LAPLACE AND POISSON EQUATIONS

Many problems in electricity and magnetism are also reducible to partial differential equations. For instance, one of Maxwell's equations reads (in MKSA units)

$$\operatorname{curl} \mathbf{E} + \mu_0 \frac{\partial \mathbf{H}}{\partial t} = 0.$$

In the so-called *electrostatic case*, where the magnetic field **H** is absent (**H** constant in time leads to the same situation), this equation reduces to

$$\operatorname{curl} \mathbf{E} = 0.$$

Since this holds *everywhere* in space it is possible to derive the electrostatic field from a scalar φ (the electrostatic potential),*

$$\mathbf{E} = -\operatorname{grad} \varphi.$$

If this property is combined with Maxwell's first equation (for vacuum),

$$\operatorname{div} \mathbf{E} = \rho/\epsilon_0,$$

then we obtain

$$\operatorname{div} \operatorname{grad} \varphi = \nabla^2 \varphi = -\rho/\epsilon_0,$$

where ρ is the charge density (assumed to be given as a function of coordinates) and ϵ_0 is constant (electric permittivity of free space).

An equation of the type ($\mathbf{r}$ = position vector)

$$\nabla^2 \varphi = f(\mathbf{r})$$

is known as the *Poisson equation*. Its particular case, when $f(\mathbf{r}) = 0$,

$$\nabla^2 \varphi = 0$$

is known as the *Laplace equation*. As follows from the above, it must be satisfied by the electrostatic potential $\varphi(\mathbf{r})$ in a charge-free region.

Example. A very long, hollow, metal cylinder of radius a is split lengthwise into two halves, insulated from each other. The halves of the cylinder are kept at potentials $+V$ and $-V$, respectively. It is desired to find the electrostatic field **E** inside the cylinder. This problem may be solved (approximately) by an idealized infinitely long and infinitely thin split cylinder (Fig. 8.4). It is convenient (see the boundary conditions below) to treat the problem in cylindrical coordinates, as shown.

---

* Minus sign is conventional.

The field **E** is easily found from the electrostatic potential φ which must satisfy the Laplace equation written in cylindrical coordinates

$$\frac{1}{r}\frac{\partial}{\partial r}\left(r\frac{\partial\varphi}{\partial r}\right) + \frac{1}{r^2}\frac{\partial^2\varphi}{\partial\theta^2} + \frac{\partial^2\varphi}{\partial z^2} = 0.$$

From symmetry considerations it is evident that φ must be independent of z, so that

$$\varphi = \varphi(r, \theta).$$

The following boundary conditions are imposed on φ:

$$\varphi(a, \theta) = +V \qquad (0 < \theta < \pi),$$
$$\varphi(a, \theta) = -V \qquad (-\pi < \theta < 0).$$

Moreover, it is understood that φ must be periodic in θ with period 2π and must possess a gradient everywhere inside the cylinder ($r < a$). It is expected that this condition will break down at the points $r = a$, $\theta = 0$, or π (where the "insulation" is) since **E** will be expected to be infinite at these points, by virtue of our idealization of the problem.

The method of separation of variables can be used again. Set

$$\varphi(r, \theta) = R(r)\Theta(\theta).$$

Then

$$\frac{d^2\Theta}{d\theta^2} = \lambda\Theta, \qquad (1)$$

$$\frac{1}{r}\frac{d}{dr}\left(r\frac{dR}{dr}\right) + \frac{\lambda}{r^2}R = 0. \qquad (2)$$

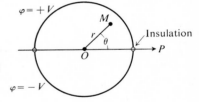

Figure 8.4

Since φ is periodic in θ, Θ must be also, which immediately implies that $\lambda = -m^2$ ($m = 0, 1, 2, 3, \ldots$) and Θ is then a linear combination of $\sin m\theta$ and $\cos m\theta$. The *radial equation* (2) becomes

$$\frac{d^2R}{dr^2} + \frac{1}{r}\frac{dR}{dr} - \frac{m^2}{r^2}R = 0,$$

which is the Euler equation, with the solutions r^m, and r^{-m} (for $m > 0$), and $C = \text{const}$ and $\log r$ (for $m = 0$). Since $\varphi(r, \theta)$ must possess a gradient at $r = 0$, the solutions r^{-m} and $\log r$ are not admissible.

According to the general principle, we form a linear (infinite) superposition of solutions:

$$\varphi(r, \theta) = A_0 + \sum_{m=1}^{\infty} r^m(A_m \cos m\theta + B_m \sin m\theta).$$

To satisfy the boundary condition

$$\varphi(a, \theta) = f(\theta) = \begin{cases} +V & (0 < \theta < \pi), \\ -V & (-\pi < \theta < 0), \end{cases}$$

we set

$$A_0 + \sum_{m=1}^{\infty} a^m(A_m \cos m\theta + B_m \sin m\theta) = f(\theta)$$

so that the constants A_m and B_m are related to the Fourier coefficients of $f(\theta)$.

Evidently, $A_0 = A_m = 0$ (all m) because of antisymmetry of $f(\theta)$ under the interchange $\theta \to -\theta$. This property could have been inferred for $\varphi(r, \theta)$ as well. Such facts often considerably simplify the process of solution in more complicated problems.

Direct calculation yields

$$B_m = \frac{2V}{\pi a^m} \int_0^\pi \sin m\theta \, d\theta = \begin{cases} 0 & (m = \text{even}), \\ \dfrac{4V}{a^m \pi m} & (m = \text{odd}). \end{cases}$$

Then

$$\varphi(r, \theta) = \frac{4V}{\pi} \sum_{m=1,3,5,\dots}^{\infty} \frac{1}{m} \left(\frac{r}{a}\right)^m \sin m\theta.$$

It is not difficult to verify that this function satisfies the conditions of the problem. In particular, if $r \leq r_1$, where r_1 is any positive number less than a, the series can be differentiated term by term twice with respect to both r and θ (the factor r/a will cause uniform convergence of the twice-differentiated series). Thus the PDE is easily verified.

Remark. From a physicist's point of view, $\varphi(r, \theta)$ does not have to satisfy the PDE at $r = a$, so long as it approaches the prescribed boundary conditions [which it does since at $r = a$ it reduces to the Fourier series for $f(\theta)$].

8.4 THE DIFFUSION EQUATION

Another type of PDE arises in the study of diffusion of some substances through a continuous medium, such as diffusion of smoke through the air, diffusion of neutrons in a nuclear reactor, or diffusion of a dissolving chemical through the solvent.

Let ρ denote the density of the substance (often called the *concentration*) measured in units: "stuff"/cm^3, where "stuff" is the appropriate unit for the substance, such as the number of neutrons or the number of atoms in the solute. Let $\mathbf{j}$ denote the current density measured in "stuff"/cm$^2 \cdot$ sec (amount of substance passing per unit time through a unit area normal to the direction of flow).

Then most diffusion phenomena obey the following linear law, sometimes called *Fick's law:*

$$\mathbf{j} = -D \operatorname{grad} \rho,$$

where $D = \text{const}$ is the *diffusion coefficient*, which depends on the properties of the medium (D is measured in cm^2/sec).

Suppose, furthermore, that the diffusing substance is neither absorbed nor emitted by the medium. Then the equation of continuity (*conservation law* for the substance)

$$\frac{\partial \rho}{\partial t} + \operatorname{div} \mathbf{j} = 0$$

must hold. Combining the above two equations, we obtain

$$\frac{\partial \rho}{\partial t} = D\nabla^2 \rho.$$

This result is known as the *diffusion equation*.

An immediate modification is possible if the substance is capable of being absorbed (destroyed) or emitted (created) as is the case of a chemical compound or neutrons (absorption and emission by the nuclei). In this case, the equation of continuity reads

$$\frac{\partial \rho}{\partial t} + \operatorname{div} \mathbf{j} = s,$$

where s is the *source density*, i.e., the amount of substance created (or destroyed, if $s < 0$) per unit volume per unit time. The expression above gives rise to the nonhomogeneous diffusion equation

$$\frac{\partial \rho}{\partial t} = D\nabla^2 \rho + s.$$

Remark. In some problems, one encounters the steady state of diffusion processes. Then ρ is independent of time and the equation reduces to the Poisson ($s \neq 0$) or the Laplace ($s = 0$) equation.

Some other physical phenomena, such as conduction of heat, lead to the same type of equation. Conduction of heat is usually assumed to obey the linear heat flow equation (first established by Fourier)

$$\mathbf{q} = -k \operatorname{grad} u,$$

where $\mathbf{q}$ is the heat current density ($\text{cal/cm}^2 \cdot \text{sec}$), u is the temperature (deg), and k is the thermal conductivity ($\text{cal/cm} \cdot \text{sec} \cdot \text{deg}$). For an arbitrary volume V enclosed by a surface S the heat influx per unit time is $-\oiint_S (\mathbf{q} \cdot d\mathbf{S})$ (the minus sign is traced to the conventional definition of $d\mathbf{S}$ to be directed outward).

If, in addition, heat is generated (e.g., by an exothermal chemical reaction) at a rate given by $s(x, y, z)$ per unit time and unit volume, then the total heat received by V in a time interval Δt is

$$Q = \left[-\oint_S (\mathbf{q} \cdot d\mathbf{S}) + \iiint_V s \, dV \right] \Delta t.$$

According to the basic formula of calorimetry, this amount of heat will raise the temperature within V by an amount Δu so that

$$Q = \iiint_V c\rho \, \Delta u \, dV,$$

where ρ is the mass density (gm/cm^3), c is the heat capacity (cal/gm $\cdot$ deg). (It is tacitly assumed that V is sufficiently small and a unique temperature u may be assigned to the entire volume.) Thus we are led to the statement

$$-\oint_S (\mathbf{q} \cdot d\mathbf{S}) = \iiint_V \left[c\rho \frac{\Delta u}{\Delta t} - s \right] dV.$$

If Δt is very small then $\Delta u/\Delta t$ may be replaced by $\partial u/\partial t$. Applying the divergence theorem,* we deduce that

$$- \operatorname{div} \mathbf{q} = c\rho \frac{\partial u}{\partial t} - s.$$

Combining this with the heat flow equation, we obtain

$$\frac{\partial u}{\partial t} = a^2 \nabla^2 u + bs,$$

where

$$a^2 = \frac{k}{c\rho} \left(\frac{\text{cm}^2}{\text{sec}} \right), \qquad b = \frac{1}{c\rho} \left(\frac{\text{cm}^3 \cdot \text{deg}}{\text{cal}} \right).$$

In particular, if no heat sources are present, this result reduces to

$$\frac{\partial u}{\partial t} = a^2 \nabla^2 u,$$

which is often called the *heat-conduction equation*.

8.5 USE OF FOURIER AND LAPLACE TRANSFORMS

Example 1. A very long and narrow pipe is filled with water. At time $t = 0$ a quantity of salt (M gm) is introduced into the pipe at some point x_0 (remote from both ends of the pipe). We wish to find the concentration of salt at any later time.

---

* See Section 1.8.

We can idealize this physical problem by assuming an infinitely long pipe (Fig. 8.5). Moreover, since the pipe is narrow, the variations of concentration of salt over a cross section of the pipe may be neglected and the concentration can be treated as a function of two variables only, x and t:

$$\rho = \rho(x, t) \qquad \text{(in gm/cm}^3\text{)}.$$

This function satisfies the one-dimensional diffusion equation

$$\frac{\partial \rho}{\partial t} = D \frac{\partial^2 \rho}{\partial x^2}.$$

The initial conditions can be idealized by the statement that $\rho(x, 0)$ is zero everywhere except at the cross section $x = x_0$, where M gm of salt have been introduced. This statement can be expressed by means of the Dirac delta function

$$\rho(x, 0) = (M/A)\, \delta(x - x_0),$$

where A is the cross-sectional area of the pipe.

The boundary conditions for this problem may be formulated by the statement

$$\lim_{x \to \pm\infty} \rho(x, t) = \rho(\pm\infty, t) = 0 \qquad \text{(all } t\text{)},$$

reflecting the physical law of conservation of the total amount of salt.

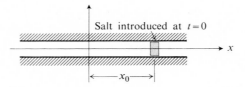

Salt introduced at $t=0$

Figure 8.5

Exercise. Show that if $\rho(x, t) > \rho_0 > 0$ for all $x > N$ and some t (some fixed ρ_0 and N), then the total amount of salt cannot be finite.

The boundary conditions of this problem bear a certain resemblance to the problem of the vibrating string in Section 8.2. The basic difference is, however, that the sought function $\rho(x, t)$ must now vanish at the ends of an *infinite* interval (rather than at points $x = 0$ and $x = L$). This fact suggests that the solution is more likely to be expressible by means of a Fourier transform than by a Fourier series. As a matter of fact, since $\rho(x, t)$ must be *very smooth* with respect to x, that is, it must possess a second derivative, and since it is absolutely integrable (bear in mind that $\rho(x, t) \geq 0$),

$$\int_{-\infty}^{+\infty} \rho(x, t)A\, dx = M,$$

it follows that it must possess the Fourier transform.

Let

$$R(k, t) = \mathcal{F}\{\rho(x, t)\} = \frac{1}{\sqrt{2\pi}} \int_{-\infty}^{+\infty} \rho(x, t)e^{ikx}\, dx.$$

We shall assume the validity of differentiation under the integral sign,* namely,

$$\frac{dR(k, t)}{dt} = \frac{1}{\sqrt{2\pi}} \int_{-\infty}^{+\infty} \frac{\partial\rho(x, t)}{\partial t} e^{ikx}\, dx$$

as well as the usual property $\mathcal{F}\{\partial^2\rho/\partial x^2\} = -k^2 R(k, t)$. Then $R(k, t)$ satisfies the ordinary DE

$$\frac{dR(k, t)}{dt} = -Dk^2 R(k, t),$$

and is given by

$$R(k, t) = R(k, 0)e^{-Dk^2 t}.$$

Given the initial condition, it now follows that

$$R(k, 0) = \mathcal{F}\left\{\frac{M}{A}\delta(x - x_0)\right\} = \frac{M}{A}\frac{1}{\sqrt{2\pi}}e^{ikx_0}$$

(in the sense of the theory of distributions). Therefore

$$R(k, t) = \frac{M}{A\sqrt{2\pi}}e^{ikx_0}e^{-Dk^2 t}.$$

The inversion is not difficult (see, for example, p. 231), and the result is

$$\rho(x, t) = \frac{M}{A}\frac{1}{\sqrt{4\pi\, Dt}}e^{-(x-x_0)^2/4Dt}.$$

This should then be the solution to our problem. It is easy to verify that it satisfies the PDE and the boundary conditions (either as a distribution or as a "classical" function). Also,

$$\lim_{t\to 0} \rho(x, t) = (M/A)\,\delta(x - x_0),$$

in the sense of distributions, of course. This is all that is required to adopt $\rho(x, t)$ as the solution of the physical problem. If desired, the steps taken in the Fourier transform technique can also be justified.

---

* If we postulate that $\rho(x, t)$ is a distribution (see p. 242) with respect to both x and t, then this procedure can be shown to be automatically valid (by methods similar to those in Section 6.9). Otherwise, the idea mentioned on p. 294 can be invoked. A justification a posteriori will be possible after $\rho(x, t)$ is found.

Exercise. Show that (in the sense of classical functions) for any $t \neq 0$, $\rho(x, t)$ is expressible by

$$\rho(x, t) = \frac{1}{\sqrt{2\pi}} \int_{-\infty}^{+\infty} R(k, t) e^{-ikx} \, dk$$

and that it can be differentiated twice under the integral sign with respect to x, and once with respect to t.

The sketch of the obtained solution is given in Fig. 8.6.*

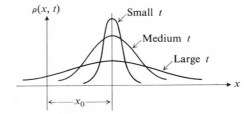

Figure 8.6

Example 2. A very long and narrow cylindrical rod thermally insulated over its lateral surface is kept at zero temperature up to $t = 0$ at which time one of its ends is placed in thermal contact with a heat reservoir at the temperature u_0. It is desired to find the temperature in the rod at any later time.

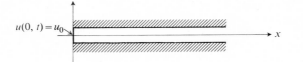

Figure 8.7

As in the preceding example, the temperature in the rod can be treated as a function of only two variables,

$$u = u(x, t),$$

and the rod can be considered to be semi-infinite (Fig. 8.7). The problem may be mathematically formulated as follows: $u(x, t)$ must satisfy the PDE

$$\frac{\partial u}{\partial t} = a^2 \frac{\partial^2 u}{\partial x^2}$$

with the initial condition $u(x, 0) = 0$ and the boundary conditions

$$u(0, t) = u_0, \qquad u(\infty, t) \equiv \lim_{x \to \infty} u(x, t) = 0.$$

---

* Different scales are used for the ordinates; otherwise, the area under each curve should be the same.

This problem can be conveniently solved by the method of Laplace transforms. Indeed, from the second law of thermodynamics, it follows that

$$u(x, t) \leq u_0;$$

therefore $u(x, t)$ must possess a Laplace transform. It is reasonable to assume that its time derivatives also possess a Laplace transform (except at $t = 0$) so that if

$$U(x, s) = \mathcal{L}\{u(x, t)\},$$

then

$$\frac{d^2 U(x, s)}{dx^2} = \frac{s}{a^2} U(x, s),$$

which is obtained by taking the Laplace transform of the PDE and using the initial condition. Solving (with boundary conditions applied), we find that

$$U(x, s) = U(0, s)e^{-x\sqrt{s}/a} = \frac{u_0}{s} e^{-x\sqrt{s}/a}.$$

If the available table of Laplace transforms does not list this function directly, then the rule

$$\mathcal{L}\left\{ \int_0^t f(\tau)\, d\tau \right\} = \frac{1}{s} F(s),$$

where $F(s) = \mathcal{L}\{f(t)\}$, may, perhaps, be used. If even this is not possible, that is, $F(s) = e^{-x\sqrt{s}/a}$ is not listed, then we may employ Mellin's inversion formula

$$u(x, t) = \frac{u_0}{2\pi i} \int_{\gamma-i\infty}^{\gamma+i\infty} \frac{1}{s} e^{st} e^{-x\sqrt{s}/a}\, ds.$$

Bearing in mind the branch cut created by $\sqrt{s}$ as well as the contribution from the origin, we close the contour as shown in Fig. 8.8.

Employing an argument similar to that in Example 4, Section 2.15 or, alternatively, setting $s = i\omega$ and making use of Jordan's lemma, we see that the contribution from C_R vanishes in the limit $R \to \infty$. In the contribution from A to B we may set

$$s = \sigma e^{i\theta} \to \sigma e^{i\pi},$$

and in the contribution from C to D, we may set

$$s = \sigma e^{i\theta} \to \sigma e^{-i\pi},$$

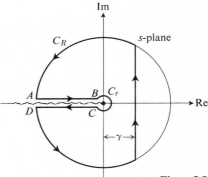

Figure 8.8

where σ is real and where the limits $\theta \to \pm\pi$ are anticipated. The sum of these contributions reduces to

$$\frac{u_0}{\pi} \int_0^\infty e^{-\sigma t} \sin \frac{x\sqrt{\sigma}}{a} \frac{d\sigma}{\sigma}.$$

Write $\sqrt{\sigma}/a = k$ and reduce this to

$$\frac{2u_0}{\pi} \int_0^\infty e^{-a^2 k^2 t} \frac{\sin kx}{k} dk.$$

This integral may be evaluated, e.g., from the formula

$$\int_0^\infty e^{-\lambda u^2} \cos \omega u \, du = \frac{1}{2}\sqrt{\frac{\pi}{\lambda}} e^{-\omega^2/4\lambda} \qquad (\lambda > 0)$$

by integration over ω from 0 to x:

$$\int_0^x d\omega \int_0^\infty e^{-\lambda u^2} \cos \omega u \, du = \int_0^\infty e^{-\lambda u^2} \frac{\sin xu}{u} du = \frac{1}{2}\sqrt{\frac{\pi}{\lambda}} \int_0^x e^{-\omega^2/4\lambda} d\omega$$

$$= \frac{\pi}{2} \operatorname{erf} \frac{x}{2\sqrt{\lambda}}.$$

Therefore

$$\frac{2u_0}{\pi} \int_0^\infty e^{-a^2 k^2 t} \frac{\sin kx}{k} dk = u_0 \operatorname{erf} \frac{x}{2a\sqrt{t}}.$$

The contribution from C_r yields $-u_0$. Therefore

$$u(x, t) = \frac{u_0}{2\pi i} \int_{\gamma-i\infty}^{\gamma+i\infty} e^{st-x\sqrt{s}/a} \frac{ds}{s}$$

$$= -\left(-u_0 + u_0 \operatorname{erf} \frac{x}{2a\sqrt{t}}\right) = u_0 \operatorname{erfc} \frac{x}{2a\sqrt{t}}.$$

8.6 THE METHOD OF EIGENFUNCTION EXPANSIONS AND FINITE TRANSFORMS

The selection of methods used to solve physical problems involving partial differential equations is based on the geometry of the problem and the character of the boundary conditions. For instance, the choice between Fourier transforms and Fourier series (arising from the separation of variables) can be traced to the fact that in one case the range of variation of x is infinite, that is from $-\infty$ to $+\infty$, and in the second case it is finite, from 0 to L.

In many respects, however, the method of separation of variables and the method of transforms are closely related. To illustrate this, let us consider again the problem of the vibrating string solved in Section 8.2.

This problem consists of finding a solution $u(x, t)$ of the one-dimensional wave equation

$$\frac{\partial^2 u}{\partial x^2} = \frac{1}{c^2} \frac{\partial^2 u}{\partial t^2}$$

satisfying the boundary conditions

$$u(0, t) = u(L, t) = 0,$$

and the initial conditions

$$u(x, 0) = u_0(x), \qquad \frac{\partial u}{\partial t}(x, 0) = v_0(x).$$

Instead of looking for solutions of the PDE as we have done in Section 8.2, let us focus our attention on the boundary conditions. Our solution $u(x, t)$ is evidently a very smooth function with respect to x and vanishes at the ends of the interval $(0, L)$. Therefore, it *must be expressible* in a Fourier sine series appropriate for this interval:

$$u(x, t) = \sum_{n=1}^{\infty} b_n(t) \sin \frac{n\pi x}{L}.$$

It is worthwhile to emphasize that this statement is completely independent of the fact that the functions $\sin(n\pi x/L)$ "have something to do" with the solutions of the wave equation vanishing at $x = 0, L$. True enough, this fact is of great help later, but, in principle, the above formula must be valid *no matter what kind* of PDE the function $u(x, t)$ satisfies.

Let us now differentiate $u(x, t)$:

$$\frac{\partial^2 u}{\partial x^2} = -\sum_{n=1}^{\infty} \frac{n^2 \pi^2}{L^2} b_n(t) \sin \frac{n\pi x}{L},$$

$$\frac{\partial^2 u}{\partial t^2} = \sum_{n=1}^{\infty} \frac{d^2 b_n}{dt^2} \sin \frac{n\pi x}{L}.$$

Substituting into the PDE, we obtain

$$\sum_{n=1}^{\infty} \left(\frac{1}{c^2} \frac{d^2 b_n}{dt^2} - \frac{n^2 \pi^2}{L^2} b_n \right) \sin \frac{n\pi x}{L} = 0.$$

This equation must be valid for all x, implying that the coefficients with each $\sin(n\pi x/L)$ ($n = 1, 2, 3, \ldots$) must vanish:

$$\frac{1}{c^2} \frac{d^2 b_n}{dt^2} - \frac{n^2 \pi^2}{L^2} b_n = 0.$$

In case this conclusion does not sound rigorous, the following argument may be invoked: Multiply the series by $\sin(m\pi x/L)$ (fixed m) and integrate over $(0, L)$.

Assuming the validity of term-by-term integration* and using the orthogonality property

$$\int_0^L \sin \frac{n\pi x}{L} \sin \frac{m\pi x}{L} \, dx = 0 \qquad (n \neq m),$$

we conclude that only the term with $n = m$ survives and the DE for $b_n(t)$ follows. It is now a simple matter to solve the DE for b_n and obtain

$$b_n(t) = A_n \cos \frac{n\pi c t}{L} + B_n \sin \frac{n\pi c t}{L}.$$

The sought solution $u(x, t)$ is therefore

$$u(x, t) = \sum_{n=1}^{\infty} \left(A_n \cos \frac{n\pi c t}{L} + B_n \sin \frac{n\pi c t}{L} \right) \sin \frac{n\pi x}{L},$$

and the coefficients A_n and B_n are obtained from $u_0(x)$ and $v_0(x)$ in the usual way:

$$A_n = \frac{2}{L} \int_0^L u_0(x) \sin \frac{n\pi x}{L} \, dx,$$

$$B_n = \frac{2}{n\pi c} \int_0^L v_0(x) \sin \frac{n\pi x}{L} \, dx.$$

This type of approach may be called *the method of eigenfunction expansions*, since we start by expanding $u(x, t)$ in a series of *some suitable eigenfunctions*. It can be cast in a form similar to that of the Fourier transform approach: This time we again start with the PDE

$$\frac{\partial^2 u}{\partial x^2} = \frac{1}{c^2} \frac{\partial^2 u}{\partial t^2}.$$

Let us multiply this equation by $\sin (n\pi x/L)$ and integrate over x from 0 to L:

$$\int_0^L \frac{\partial^2 u}{\partial x^2} \sin \frac{n\pi x}{L} \, dx = \frac{1}{c^2} \int_0^L \frac{\partial^2 u}{\partial t^2} \sin \frac{n\pi x}{L} \, dx \qquad (n = 1, 2, 3, \ldots).$$

This procedure is analogous to the method of taking the Fourier sine transform with one difference: the "wave number" k in $\sin kx$ is not arbitrary but restricted to discrete values $k = n\pi/L$, and the range of integration is a finite interval (these two facts are intimately related). It is from this point of view that we may talk about applying the *finite sine transform* to the PDE.

---

* From now on we shall tend to omit mathematical details of this type; see p. 294 for a general approach to such problems.

The right-hand side of our equation can be written as

$$\frac{1}{c^2} \frac{d^2}{dt^2} \int_0^L u(x, t) \sin \frac{n\pi x}{L} \, dx$$

[with appropriate assumptions about $u(x, t)$]. As for the left-hand side, we integrate by parts:

$$\int_0^L \frac{\partial^2 u}{\partial x^2} \sin \frac{n\pi x}{L} \, dx = \frac{\partial u}{\partial x} \sin \frac{n\pi x}{L} \Big|_0^L + \frac{n\pi}{L} \int_0^L \frac{\partial u}{\partial x} \cos \frac{n\pi x}{L} \, dx$$

$$= \frac{n\pi}{L} \int_0^L \frac{\partial u}{\partial x} \cos \frac{n\pi x}{L} \, dx$$

[by virtue of the properties of $\sin (n\pi x/L)$ at the boundary]. It is at this point that the choice of the "transform by $\sin (n\pi x/L)$" is to be appreciated. Let us integrate by parts once more:

$$\frac{n\pi}{L} \int_0^L \frac{\partial u}{\partial x} \cos \frac{n\pi x}{L} \, dx = \frac{n\pi}{L} u \cos \frac{n\pi x}{L} \Big|_0^L - \frac{n^2 \pi^2}{L^2} \int_0^L u \sin \frac{n\pi x}{L} \, dx$$

$$= - \frac{n^2 \pi^2}{L^2} \int_0^L u \sin \frac{n\pi x}{L} \, dx.$$

The net result of these derivations is the ordinary DE

$$\frac{1}{c^2} \frac{d^2}{dt^2} \int_0^L u(x, t) \sin \frac{n\pi x}{L} \, dx = - \frac{n^2 \pi^2}{L^2} \int_0^L u(x, t) \sin \frac{n\pi x}{L} \, dx$$

for the function

$$f(n, t) = \int_0^L u(x, t) \sin \frac{n\pi x}{L} \, dx \qquad (n = 1, 2, 3, \ldots).$$

In accordance with the previous notation this function will be denoted by

$$f(n, t) = \frac{L}{2} b_n(t)$$

so that $b_n(t)$ satisfies

$$\frac{d^2 b_n(t)}{dt^2} = - \frac{n^2 \pi^2 c^2}{L^2} b_n(t) \qquad (n = 1, 2, 3, \ldots)$$

and the remainder of the problem is as before.

Remarks

1. It is to be firmly remembered that the function $b_n(t)$ can be considered as a *representation* of the function $u(x, t)$: If $b_n(t)$ is given, then $u(x, t)$ is determined (by summing the Fourier sine series); the function b_n is a function of *two* variables; one *continuous* (t) and the other *discrete* (n).

2. The function $b_n(t)$ is a representation of $u(x, t)$ *with respect to* a particular set of functions $\{\sin (n\pi x/L)\}$. The success of the method is based on three facts: (a) the functions $\sin (n\pi x/L)$ satisfy the same boundary conditions as $u(x, t)$, (b) the functions $\sin (n\pi x/L)$ are orthogonal to each other, and (c) the PDE is significantly simplified for the chosen representation: it becomes an ordinary DE and of a simple type.*

3. The method of eigenfunction expansion and the method of finite transform are essentially identical. They are similar to the method of infinite transform. Which particular approach is more useful in a given problem depends on the geometry and the nature of the boundary conditions. The method of separation of variables is then a general technique which leads us to the particular eigenfunction expansion or transform appropriate for the problem at hand.

8.7 CONTINUOUS EIGENVALUE SPECTRUM

The method of separation of variables applied in Section 8.2 to the PDE

$$\frac{\partial^2 u}{\partial x^2} = \frac{1}{c^2} \frac{\partial^2 u}{\partial t^2},$$

along with the boundary conditions $u(0, t) = u(L, t) = 0$, has led us to a set of eigenvalues

$$\lambda_n = -\frac{n^2 \pi^2}{L^2} \qquad (n = 1, 2, 3, \ldots)$$

corresponding to the eigenfunctions

$$X_n(x) = B_n' \sin (n\pi x/L) \qquad (n = 1, 2, 3, \ldots)$$

of the *separated equation*

$$\frac{d^2 X}{dx^2} = \lambda X.$$

This set of eigenvalues is commonly called the *spectrum* of the *differential operator*

$$\mathcal{O} \equiv \frac{d^2}{dx^2}$$

which is regarded as being applied to the functions $f(x)$ satisfying the boundary conditions

$$f(0) = f(L) = 0.$$

Among all possible functions satisfying these boundary conditions, the particular functions

$$X_n(x) = \sin (n\pi x/L) \qquad (n = 1, 2, 3, \ldots),$$

satisfying $X'' = \lambda X$, are called the eigenfunctions of the differential operator $\mathcal{O}$.

---

* Compare the above with the idea described on p. 187.

From the preceding section, it follows that these functions play an important part in the problem of construction of solutions of the wave equation.

This spectrum happens to be discrete as is usually the case with the boundary conditions on a finite interval. However, if the interval is infinite, the eigenvalue spectrum (of the same operator $\mathcal{O}$) is usually continuous.

Remark. The term spectrum is, of course, borrowed from optics (so is the symbol λ). The quantum-mechanical description of an atom involves an eigenvalue problem and the resulting eigenvalues are related to the wavelengths of light waves emitted by the atom.

Example. Four large conducting plates are arranged as shown in Fig. 8.9 with their respective electrostatic potentials. Since the size of the plates is much larger than the separation $2a$, they can be treated as though they were extended to infinity in the x- and z-directions. We wish to find the electrostatic potential in the region between the plates.

We find that the mathematical formulation of the problem requires the electrostatic potential $\varphi(x, y)$ to satisfy

$$\frac{\partial^2 \varphi}{\partial x^2} + \frac{\partial^2 \varphi}{\partial y^2} = 0$$

and the boundary conditions

$$\varphi(x, a) = \varphi(x, -a) = +V \qquad (x > 0),$$
$$\varphi(x, a) = \varphi(x, -a) = -V \qquad (x < 0)$$

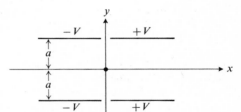

Figure 8.9

or, more compactly, $\varphi(x, \pm a) = V[2S(x) - 1]$, where $S(x)$ is the step function.

Let us apply the method of separation of variables: If $\varphi(x, y) = X(x)Y(y)$, then

$$\frac{d^2 X}{dx^2} = \lambda X, \qquad \frac{d^2 Y}{dy^2} = -\lambda Y.$$

In order to determine the eigenvalues, we should use the boundary conditions. The boundary conditions apparently involve the variable y, but they do not seem to favor any particular choice of λ. It appears that all three possible forms

$$Y(y) = A_1 \cos (\sqrt{\lambda}\, y) + B_1 \sin (\sqrt{\lambda}\, y) \qquad (\lambda > 0), \tag{1}$$

$$Y(y) = A_2 + B_2 y \qquad (\lambda = 0), \tag{2}$$

$$Y(y) = A_3 e^{y \sqrt{-\lambda}} + B_3 e^{-y \sqrt{-\lambda}} \qquad (\lambda < 0) \tag{3}$$

could, conceivably, form a linear combination satisfying the boundary conditions.

The reason for this indeterminacy is not hard to find: The boundary conditions with respect to y are *nonhomogeneous*, namely, they do not demand that $\varphi(x, a)$ and $\varphi(x, -a)$ *vanish* but rather that they reduce to a *function of x*, namely,

$f(x) = V[2S(x) - 1]$. Compare this with the vibrating string problem of Section 8.2. The requirement that $\varphi(x, \pm a) = 0$ (this is a *homogeneous* boundary condition) could have been satisfied by requiring that $Y_\lambda(\pm a) = 0$ [for each eigenfunction $Y_\lambda(y)$ corresponding to an eigenvalue λ]. However, there is no simple condition for $Y_\lambda(y)$ such that $\varphi(x, \pm a)$ will be made equal to some $f(x)$. A way out of this difficulty may be found if we recognize that there are also certain boundary conditions *involving* x which we have missed so far.

An important property of the boundary conditions is that they are *antisymmetric* (odd) with respect to x:

$$\varphi(-x, \pm a) = -\varphi(x, \pm a).$$

This fact suggests the possibility that the entire solution is antisymmetric with respect to x:

$$\varphi(-x, y) = -\varphi(x, y).$$

That this must indeed be true follows from physical considerations.*

In particular, the antisymmetry implies that

$$\varphi(0, y) = 0 \qquad (-a \le y \le a).$$

This is a *homogeneous* boundary condition with respect to x. It seems, therefore, that one should start the investigation of the equation for $X(x)$, rather than that for $Y(y)$. Before we do this, however, it is useful to recognize another boundary condition with respect to x which is quite valuable. Physical intuition tells us that $\varphi(x, y)$ must be bounded, in particular, when $x \to \pm\infty$. As a matter of fact, we can *require* that

$$\varphi(-\infty, y) \equiv \lim_{x \to -\infty} \varphi(x, y) = -V,$$

$$\varphi(+\infty, y) \equiv \lim_{x \to +\infty} \varphi(x, y) = +V.$$

(A solution violating these conditions should be discarded on physical grounds.)

Now consider the equation

$$\frac{d^2 X}{dx^2} = \lambda X.$$

It is not hard to verify that the condition

$$\varphi(\pm\infty, y) < \infty \qquad \text{(boundedness)}$$

can be satisfied only if $\lambda < 0$. Set, for convenience, $\lambda = -k^2 (k > 0)$. Furthermore, the condition $\varphi(0, y) = 0$ rules out the function $\cos kx$. Therefore

$$X_k(x) = A_k \sin kx \qquad (k > 0).$$

---

* Compare with Section 8.3.

There is no further restriction on k and we conclude that the eigenvalues λ of the problem,

$$X'' = \lambda X, \qquad X(0) = 0, \qquad X(\pm\infty) < \infty,$$

form a *continuous spectrum* $(-\infty < \lambda < 0)$. There is a nondenumerable set of eigenfunctions $X_k(x)$.

Now consider the equation for $Y(y)$. Since λ is bound to be negative $(\lambda = -k^2)$, we obtain

$$Y_k(y) = B_k e^{ky} + C_k e^{-ky}.$$

Having learned the importance of symmetry considerations, we can also recognize the fact that the solution $\varphi(x, y)$ must be symmetric (even) with respect to y:

$$\varphi(x, -y) = \varphi(x, y) \qquad \text{(all } x).$$

We shall impose this condition on each $Y_k(y)$ which implies that $B_k = C_k$, or, in other words,

$$Y_k(y) = D_k \cosh ky.$$

Remark. This requirement would, in any event, follow from further analysis, but this step simplifies our task.

We shall now attempt to solve the problem by constructing a "linear combination" of functions

$$\varphi_k(x, y) = A_k \cosh ky \sin kx \qquad (k > 0),$$

(where the constant D_k has been absorbed into A_k). Instead of an infinite series, as was the case with the discrete spectrum (infinite but denumerable), it is reasonable to expect that $\varphi(x, y)$ should be expressible as an integral over a continuous (infinite nondenumerable) spectrum of eigenvalues. Indeed, an integral can be regarded as a form of linear superposition, and the analogy between the Fourier series and the Fourier transform strongly indicates such a possibility.

Thus we conjecture that

$$\varphi(x, y) = \int_0^\infty A_k \cosh ky \sin kx \, dk.$$

This is, of course, equivalent to the statement that $\varphi(x, y)$ is expressible in terms of its Fourier sine transform, namely,

$$\varphi(x, y) = \sqrt{2/\pi} \int_0^\infty \Phi(k, y) \sin kx \, dk,$$

where

$$\Phi(k, y) = \sqrt{\pi/2} \, A_k \cosh ky.$$

It remains for us to evaluate A_k. Since k is a continuous variable, it is more appropriate to replace A_k by $A(k)$. This function can be determined from the requirement

$$\varphi(x, a) = V = \int_0^\infty A(k) \cosh ky \sin kx \, dk \qquad (k > 0).$$

Note that once this is satisfied, all other three original boundary conditions will be satisfied because of the symmetry properties of the functions $\sin kx$ and $\cosh ky$.

According to the inversion formula for the Fourier sine transform, we have

$$\Phi(k, y) = \sqrt{2/\pi} \int_0^\infty \varphi(x, y) \sin kx \, dx.$$

In particular, for $y = a$,

$$\Phi(k, a) = \sqrt{\pi/2} \, A(k) \cosh ka = \sqrt{2/\pi} \int_0^\infty V \sin kx \, dx.$$

The needed integral

$$\int_0^\infty \sin kx \, dx$$

is divergent. Nevertheless, it can be treated as a distribution, in which case,*

$$\int_0^\infty \sin kx \, dx = 1/k \qquad (k > 0).$$

Therefore

$$A(k) = \frac{2V}{\pi} \frac{1}{k} \frac{1}{\cosh ka}$$

and

$$\varphi(x, y) = \frac{2V}{\pi} \int_0^\infty \frac{\cosh ky}{\cosh ka} \frac{\sin kx}{k} \, dk.$$

It is not hard to see that we could have arrived at the same result by applying the Fourier sine transform directly to the PDE. Indeed, let us assume that $\varphi(x, y)$ possesses the Fourier sine transform with respect to x, along with its derivatives $\partial\varphi/\partial x$ and $\partial^2\varphi/\partial x^2$. Then

$$\mathcal{F}_S\{\varphi(x, y)\} = \Phi(k, y),$$

and

$$\mathcal{F}_S\left\{\frac{\partial^2\varphi(x, y)}{\partial x^2}\right\} = -k^2\Phi(k, y).$$

Therefore, the transformed PDE reads

$$-k^2\Phi(k, y) + \frac{d^2\Phi(k, y)}{dy^2} = 0.$$

Solving and applying the requirement that $\Phi(k, y)$ is symmetric with respect to y [because $\varphi(x, y)$ is so], we obtain

$$\Phi(k, y) = C(k) \cosh ky.$$

---

* The sequence $f_N(k) = \int_0^N \sin kx \, dx = (1 - \cos kN)/k$ diverges as $N \to \infty$, but it is weakly convergent for a suitably chosen set of test functions $g(k)$ defined for $0 \le k < \infty$.

The function $C(k)$ can be obtained from the condition

$$\Phi(k, a) = \mathfrak{F}_S\{V\} = \sqrt{2/\pi} \ (V/k)$$

and the remaining procedure is the same as before.

It is still necessary to prove that the obtained function

$$\varphi(x, y) = \frac{2V}{\pi} \int_0^\infty \frac{\cosh ky}{\cosh ka} \frac{\sin kx}{k} \, dk$$

is indeed a solution of our problem (we have employed some conjectures and assumptions).

First of all, note that the integral converges: For $|y| \leq a$, we have

$$\left| \frac{\cosh ky}{\cosh ka} \right| \leq 1,$$

and the integral

$$\int_0^\infty \frac{\sin kx}{k} \, dx$$

certainly exists (it is equal to $\pi/2$). Next, it is evident that $\varphi(x, y)$ is symmetric in y, antisymmetric in x and reduces to V for $y = a$ and $x > 0$. Finally, we must prove that $\varphi(x, y)$ satisfies the Laplace DE. If $\varphi(x, y)$ can be differentiated under the integral sign, this becomes obvious. Differentiation is possible, provided $|y| < a$, since one can easily prove that

$$\lim_{k \to \infty} k^n \frac{\cosh ky}{\cosh ka} = 0$$

for any n and $|y| < a$ (uniformly for $|y| \leq a_0 < a$).

Remark. The integral

$$\int_0^\infty \frac{\cosh ky}{\cosh ka} \frac{\sin kx}{k} \, dk$$

can be evaluated explicitly (by the calculus of residues). Then the verification of the result becomes straightforward.

8.8 VIBRATIONS OF A MEMBRANE. DEGENERACY

Consider a horizontal membrane stretched equally with a tension T (per unit length) in all directions. The membrane can be of any shape, but we shall treat here a rectangular membrane (Fig. 8.10).

Apart from the tension T we shall assume that there are no horizontal forces acting on the membrane and that the points on the membrane can have only transverse (vertical) displacements. As in the case of the stretched string (as opposed to a beam), the membrane is assumed to offer no resistance to shearing

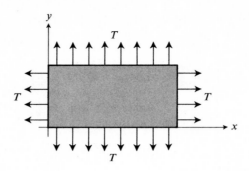

Figure 8.10

forces or bending moments (as opposed to a plate), and its deformations are controlled only by its resistance to further stretching.

If the tension T is large compared to possible transverse forces, the (vertical) displacements and the slope of the membrane will be small. To develop the equation of motion for the membrane, consider an element $dx\,dy$ (Fig. 8.11a). This element is subject to tension on all four sides (only horizontal forces are shown). Evidently, $T_1 = T_2$ and $T_3 = T_4$. Moreover, from Fig. 8.11(b), which illustrates a triangular element in equilibrium, it follows that

$$T_5\,ds\cos\alpha = T_1\,dx \qquad T_5\,ds\sin\alpha = T_3\,dy$$

so that ($ds\cos\alpha = dx$, $ds\sin\alpha = dy$ by geometry)

$$T_1 = T_5 = T_3.$$

Therefore

$$T_1 = T_2 = \cdots = T_5 = T$$

demonstrating that the tension is the same in all directions.

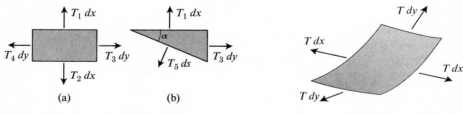

(a)   (b)

Figure 8.11   **Figure 8.12**

If the element $dx\,dy$ is deformed, then it is subject to forces of tension slightly inclined to the horizontal (Fig. 8.12). However, since the deformations are small, these forces are virtually equal to their horizontal components and may be replaced by T.

Now consider the vertical forces. Arguing as in the case of the stretched string (p. 288), we may conclude that the pair of $T\,dx$-forces will produce a small vertical component

$$T\,dx\left\{\frac{\partial u}{\partial y}\left(y+\frac{dy}{2}\right)-\frac{\partial u}{\partial y}\left(y-\frac{dy}{2}\right)\right\}\cong T\,dx\,\frac{\partial^2 u}{\partial y^2}\,dy,$$

where $u=u(x,y;t)$ is the displacement of the membrane. A similar statement holds for the pair of $T\,dy$-forces. Newton's second law yields, then,

$$T\,dx\,dy\left(\frac{\partial^2 u}{\partial x^2}+\frac{\partial^2 u}{\partial y^2}\right)+F\,dx\,dy=\mu\,dx\,dy\,\frac{\partial^2 u}{\partial t^2},$$

where μ is the mass per unit area of the membrane, and F is the external vertical force (if any) per unit area. This leads to the equation

$$\frac{\partial^2 u}{\partial x^2}+\frac{\partial^2 u}{\partial y^2}+\frac{F}{T}=\frac{\mu}{T}\frac{\partial^2 u}{\partial t^2}.$$

If there are no external forces (free vibrations of the membrane) and if μ is constant, this expression reduces to the two-dimensional wave equation

$$\frac{\partial^2 u}{\partial x^2}+\frac{\partial^2 u}{\partial y^2}=\frac{1}{c^2}\frac{\partial^2 u}{\partial t^2}\qquad c^2=\frac{T}{\mu}.$$

The function $u=u(x,y;t)$ must satisfy certain boundary conditions. Usually the edges of the membrane are fixed. Then the boundary conditions read $u=0$ at the boundary (all t). However, sometimes the boundary (or part of it) is left "free," meaning that it can move in the vertical direction and there is no external transverse* force acting on it. This is equivalent to the boundary condition $\partial u/\partial n=0$ at the boundary (all t), where $\partial u/\partial n$ is the *normal gradient* of u, or the directional derivative along the normal.

An intermediate case is also possible: the boundary may be elastically supported and capable of producing a transverse force proportional to the displacement. This situation is equivalent to the boundary condition

$$\frac{\partial u}{\partial n}+\alpha u=0\qquad\text{at the boundary (all }t\text{)},$$

where α is a constant.

Finally, the motion of the membrane is to be determined by the initial conditions prescribing the initial displacement and the initial velocity of the membrane:

$$u(x,y;0)=u_0(x,y),\qquad\frac{\partial u}{\partial t}(x,y;0)=v_0(x,y).$$

---

* Note that the "free boundary" must still be able to exert a horizontal tension T.

Example. A rectangular membrane with sides a and b is clamped at the boundary. It is desired to analyze the motion $u = u(x, y; t)$ in terms of the *characteristic modes of vibration*.

Set up a cartesian coordinate system with the axes along two edges of the membrane. The boundary conditions assume the form

$$u(0, y; t) = u(a, y; t) = 0, \qquad u(x, 0; t) = u(x, b; t) = 0.$$

Set $u(x, y; t) = X(x)Y(y)T(t)$ and, separating the variables in the wave equation, obtain

a) $\qquad \dfrac{d^2 T}{dt^2} = \lambda c^2 T$

b) $\qquad \dfrac{d^2 X}{dx^2} = \lambda_1 X$

c) $\qquad \dfrac{d^2 Y}{dy^2} = \lambda_2 Y$ $\qquad$ (with the provision that $\lambda_1 + \lambda_2 = \lambda$).

From the boundary conditions it follows* that

$$\lambda_1 = -\frac{m^2 \pi^2}{a^2} \quad (m = 1, 2, 3, \ldots), \qquad \lambda_2 = -\frac{n^2 \pi^2}{b^2} \quad (n = 1, 2, 3, \ldots),$$

leading to a double-labeled set of eigenfunctions

$$\psi_{mn}(x, y) = X_m(x) Y_n(y) = \sin \frac{m\pi x}{a} \sin \frac{n\pi y}{b},$$

with the corresponding "time factors"

$$T_{mn}(t) = A_{mn} \cos \omega_{mn} t + B_{mn} \sin \omega_{mn} t,$$

where

$$\omega_{mn} = \pi c \sqrt{m^2/a^2 + n^2/b^2} \qquad (m, n = 1, 2, 3, \ldots).$$

Each pair of integers (m, n) corresponds to a particular characteristic mode of vibration of the membrane.

A particular solution $u(x, y; t)$ is then sought as a superposition of all modes:

$$u(x, y; t) = \sum_{m=1}^{\infty} \sum_{n=1}^{\infty} (A_{mn} \cos \omega_{mn} t + B_{mn} \sin \omega_{mn} t) \sin \frac{m\pi x}{a} \sin \frac{n\pi y}{b}.$$

The right-hand side represents, of course, a *double Fourier sine series*. The coefficients A_{mn} and B_{mn} can be obtained in the usual fashion (see Chapter 4). Set $t = 0$; then

$$u_0(x, y) = \sum_{m=1}^{\infty} \sum_{n=1}^{\infty} A_{mn} \sin \frac{m\pi x}{a} \sin \frac{n\pi y}{b}.$$

---

* Compare with Section 8.2.

Multiply by sin $(m'\pi x/a)$ sin $(n'\pi y/b)$ and integrate over x from 0 to a and over y from 0 to b (in other words, take the double integral over the area of the membrane). Assuming the validity of term-by-term integration, conclude that the only term on the right-hand side which will yield a nonvanishing integral is the term with $m = m'$ and $n = n'$, due to the orthogonality of our eigenfunctions. This leads to the formula

$$A_{mn} = \frac{4}{ab} \int_0^a \int_0^b u_0(x, y) \sin \frac{m\pi x}{a} \sin \frac{n\pi y}{b} \, dx \, dy.$$

In the same fashion, evaluating the series for $\partial u/\partial t$ and using $v_0(x, y)$, obtain

$$B_{mn} = \frac{4}{ab\omega_{mn}} \int_0^a \int_0^b v_0(x, y) \sin \frac{m\pi x}{a} \sin \frac{n\pi y}{b} \, dx \, dy.$$

The assumptions necessary for the validity of all these operations are invariably satisfied (at least in the sense of the theory of distributions) in all physical problems. Our solution is, therefore, complete.

Let us now look into some of the features of characteristic (or *normal*) modes. If the membrane vibrates in one of its normal modes, then all its points will execute harmonic motion with frequency ω_{mn}:

$$u(x, y; t) = C_{mn} \sin \frac{m\pi x}{a} \sin \frac{n\pi y}{b} \cos (\omega_{mn}t + \delta_{mn})$$

(for convenience, we have set $A_{mn} = C_{mn} \cos \delta_{mn}$ and $B_{mn} = -C_{mn} \sin \delta_{mn}$). In this motion some points (x, y) of the membrane will *remain at rest at all times t*, for instance, the points with $x = a/m$ (and arbitrary y). Evidently, such points will lie along certain curves, called *nodal curves* (in analogy to the *nodal points* for a stretched string).

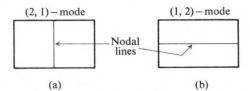

(a)   (b)

Figure 8.13

As a particular example, consider the (2, 1)-mode (that is, $m = 2$, $n = 1$). The eigenfunction reads

$$\psi_{21}(x, y) = \sin \frac{2\pi x}{a} \sin \frac{\pi y}{b} .$$

The only nodal curve is the straight line $x = a/2$ (Fig. 8.13a). Similarly, the (1, 2)-mode ($m = 1$, $n = 2$) has the nodal line $y = b/2$ (Fig. 8.13b).

Generally speaking, each mode vibrates with its own frequency ω_{mn} given by

$$\omega_{mn} = c\pi\sqrt{m^2/a^2 + n^2/b^2}.$$

However, sometimes two or more modes possess the same frequency. This is possible only if a/b is a rational number. As an example, consider the case of a *square membrane* ($a = b$). The (2, 1)- and (1, 2)-modes will vibrate with the same frequency [namely $(c\pi\sqrt{5}/a)$]. It is then said that this frequency exhibits *degeneracy* (one may regard ω_{mn} as an eigenvalue of our problem; the eigenvalue is degenerate if there is more than one eigenfunction corresponding to it).

Furthermore, it is evident that *any linear combination* of (2, 1)- and (1, 2)-modes will represent a harmonic motion of the membrane (of the same frequency). For instance, the motions given by

$$u_1(x, y; t) = \left(A \sin \frac{2\pi x}{a} \sin \frac{\pi y}{a} + A \sin \frac{\pi x}{a} \sin \frac{2\pi y}{a} \right) \cos \frac{c\pi\sqrt{5}}{a} t,$$

$$u_2(x, y; t) = \left(A \sin \frac{2\pi x}{a} \sin \frac{\pi y}{a} - A \sin \frac{\pi x}{a} \sin \frac{2\pi y}{a} \right) \cos \frac{c\pi\sqrt{5}}{a} t$$

represent harmonic vibrations of the membrane with nodal lines as shown in Fig. 8.14. These solutions are often called *hybrid modes*. From the physical point of view they must be regarded as characteristic modes in their own right and may be treated as basic solutions for this particular frequency [the original (2, 1)- and (1, 2)-modes are linear combinations of u_1 and u_2].

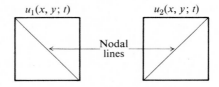

Figure 8.14

Generally speaking, if a frequency is degenerate, there is an *infinite number* of associated modes, formed by all possible linear combinations of basic (linearly independent) modes. Some of these modes possess nodal curves which are not straight lines.

Remark. In general, hybrid modes are not orthogonal to each other. In most cases it is convenient to work with orthogonal modes, and because of this some may be preferable to others.

Exercise. Show that the modes u_1 and u_2 given above are orthogonal to each other. Construct a pair of nonorthogonal hybrid modes.

8.9 PROPAGATION OF SOUND. HELMHOLTZ EQUATION

Experiments indicate that the phenomenon of sound in air is related to rapid oscillations of air density and pressure about some average values ρ_0 and p_0. These changes are caused by the so-called *collective* oscillatory motion of air molecules described by their *macroscopic velocities.**

Consider a small quantity of air within a volume V (at some particular instant t) and let $\mathbf{v} = \mathbf{v}(r, t)$ be the macroscopic velocity of air at point $\mathbf{r}$ and time t. If $\rho = \rho(\mathbf{r}, t)$ is the density of air, then the force per unit volume is given by Newton's second law:

$$\mathbf{f}(\mathbf{r}, t) = \rho \frac{d\mathbf{v}}{dt}.$$

The total force on volume V is then

$$\mathbf{F} = \iiint\limits_V \rho \frac{d\mathbf{v}}{dt} \, dV.$$

If the weight and other *body forces*, namely, those depending on the volume, are negligible, then this total force is equal to the surface integral of pressure (viscosity is neglected as well):

$$\iiint\limits_V \rho \frac{d\mathbf{v}}{dt} \, dV = - \oiint \rho \, d\mathbf{S}.$$

Transform the surface integral by means of the formula from vector calculus,[†]

$$\oiint\limits_S p \, d\mathbf{S} = \iiint\limits_V \operatorname{grad} p \, dV,$$

and use the fact that V is arbitrary to obtain the equation of motion in differential form:

$$\rho \frac{d\mathbf{v}}{dt} + \operatorname{grad} p = 0.$$

To this formula we may add the equation of continuity (conservation of matter):

$$\frac{\partial}{\partial t} \iiint\limits_V \rho \, dV = - \oiint\limits_S \rho(\mathbf{v} \, d\mathbf{S}).$$

---

* As distinct from their random thermal motion. Usually, the thermal motions almost "cancel out" on the average. The statistical net velocity of a macroscopically small (but still containing millions of molecules) group of adjacent molecules is called the macroscopic velocity.

† This formula follows from the representation of the gradient on p. 33.

By use of the divergence theorem and the arbitrariness of V, we deduce that

$$\frac{\partial \rho}{\partial t} + \text{div} \, (\rho \mathbf{v}) = 0.$$

Finally, the pressure $p = p(\mathbf{r}, t)$ and the density $\rho = \rho(\mathbf{r}, t)$ can be related by thermodynamical formulas. For the frequencies involved in sound waves (20–20,000 cps), the oscillations of p and ρ take place so rapidly that there is no time for an appreciable amount of heat to be exchanged between two adjacent volumes of air during an oscillation. In other words, the expansion and contraction of air are adiabatic and

$$\frac{p}{p_0} = \left(\frac{V}{V_0}\right)^{-\gamma} = \left(\frac{\rho}{\rho_0}\right)^{\gamma} \qquad \gamma = \frac{c_p}{c_v},$$

where c_p is the specific heat at constant pressure and c_v is the specific heat at constant volume. The propagation of sound is governed, therefore, by the following equations:

$$\rho \frac{d\mathbf{v}}{dt} + \text{grad} \, p = 0, \qquad \frac{\partial \rho}{\partial t} + \text{div} \, (\rho \mathbf{v}) = 0, \qquad p = p_0 \left(\frac{\rho}{\rho_0}\right)^{\gamma}.$$

Remark. Since $\mathbf{v}$ is a function of both position and time, the derivative $d\mathbf{v}/dt$ is the total or *hydrodynamic* derivative*

$$\frac{d\mathbf{v}}{dt} = \frac{\partial \mathbf{v}}{\partial t} + (\mathbf{v} \cdot \text{grad}) \, \mathbf{v}.$$

A considerable simplification of these equations is possible for a typical acoustic wave of moderate intensity. Consider, for instance, a sound wave of frequency $500 \, \text{sec}^{-1}$, where the air particles vibrate with an amplitude of the order of 10^{-6} cm. The wavelength† is approximately

$$\lambda = \frac{c}{f} \cong \frac{3.3 \times 10^4 \, \text{cm/sec}}{500 \, \text{sec}^{-1}} \sim 60 \, \text{cm},$$

where c is the speed of sound and f is the frequency. The speed v of air particles is of the order of

$$v \sim 2\pi f a = 2\pi \times 500 \times 10^{-6} \sim 3 \times 10^{-4} \, \text{sec}^{-1}.$$

---

* Consult any textbook on fluid mechanics;

$$(\mathbf{v} \cdot \text{grad}) \, \mathbf{v} \equiv \left(v_x \frac{\partial}{\partial x} + v_y \frac{\partial}{\partial y} + v_z \frac{\partial}{\partial x}\right)(v_x \mathbf{i} + v_y \mathbf{j} + v_z \mathbf{k}).$$

† For the purpose of general orientation, take the example of a plane harmonic wave with $u_x = a \cos 2\pi(x/\lambda - ft)$, where u_x is the displacement of air particles.

The velocity gradient is of the order of

$$\left|\frac{\partial v_x}{\partial x}\right| \sim \frac{2\pi}{\lambda} v \cong \frac{2\pi \times 3 \times 10^{-3}}{60} \sim 3 \times 10^{-4} \, \text{sec}^{-1},$$

while the rate of change of v at a given point is of the order of

$$\left|\frac{\partial \mathbf{v}}{\partial t}\right| \sim 2\pi f v \cong 2\pi \times 500 \times 3 \times 10^{-3} \sim 10 \, \text{cm/sec}^2.$$

The term $\partial \mathbf{v}/\partial t$ is clearly much larger than the term $(\mathbf{v} \cdot \text{grad}) \, \mathbf{v}$, the latter being of the order of

$$|(\mathbf{v} \cdot \text{grad}) \, \mathbf{v}| \sim v \left|\frac{\partial v_x}{\partial x}\right| \sim 3 \times 10^{-3} \times 3 \times 10^{-4} \sim 10^{-6} \, \text{cm/sec}^2$$

so that $d\mathbf{v}/dt$ can be replaced by $\partial \mathbf{v}/\partial t$.

Moreover, the relative changes in density are quite small: If a column of air $\lambda/4$ in length is compressed by an amount $a = 10^{-6}$ cm, the increase in density is of the order of

$$\delta = \frac{\rho - \rho_0}{\rho_0} \cong \frac{a}{\lambda/4} = \frac{10^{-6} \, \text{cm}}{15 \, \text{cm}} \lesssim 10^{-7}.$$

It follows that

$$\left(\frac{\rho}{\rho_0}\right)^\gamma = (1 + \delta)^\gamma \cong 1 + \gamma\delta$$

and $p \cong p_0(1 + \gamma\delta)$, implying that the relative changes in pressure are also small.

Finally, in the expression

$$\text{div} \, (\rho \mathbf{v}) = \mathbf{v} \cdot \text{grad} \, \rho + \rho \, \text{div} \, \mathbf{v},$$

the first term on the right-hand side of the equation is smaller than the second one by something like a factor of 10^7 (since $\rho \sim 10^{-3}$ gm/cm^3, $|\text{div} \, \mathbf{v}| \sim 3 \times 10^{-4}$ sec^{-1}, $|\text{grad} \, \rho| \lesssim 10^{-11}$ gm/cm^4).

Therefore we are left with a simplified (but still quite accurate) system of equations:

$$\rho_0 \frac{\partial \mathbf{v}}{\partial t} + \text{grad} \, p = 0, \qquad \frac{\partial \rho}{\partial t} + \rho_0 \, \text{div} \, \mathbf{v} = 0,$$

$$p = p_0(1 + \gamma\delta), \qquad \delta = \frac{\rho - \rho_0}{\rho_0},$$

where ρ has been replaced by ρ_0, in accordance with $\delta \sim 10^{-7}$. From the last equation it follows that

$$\text{grad} \, p = p_0 \gamma \, \text{grad} \, \delta$$

so that [also use $\partial \rho/\partial t = \rho_0 \, (\partial \delta/\partial t)$]

$$\frac{\partial \mathbf{v}}{\partial t} + \frac{p_0 \gamma}{\rho_0} \text{grad} \, \delta = 0, \qquad \frac{\partial \delta}{\partial t} + \text{div} \, \mathbf{v} = 0.$$

Taking the divergence of the first equation and the time derivative of the second and combining, we obtain

$$\frac{\partial^2 \delta}{\partial t^2} = c^2 \nabla^2 \delta,$$

where

$$c^2 = p_0 \gamma / \rho_0.$$

The relative change in density δ obeys, therefore, a homogeneous wave equation. Evidently, the same wave equation is satisfied by the density ρ itself and the pressure p:

$$\frac{\partial^2 \rho}{\partial t^2} = c^2 \nabla^2 \rho,$$

$$\frac{\partial^2 p}{\partial t^2} = c^2 \nabla^2 p.$$

Usually an additional function, known as the *velocity potential* φ, is introduced by means of

$$\mathbf{v} = -\operatorname{grad} \varphi.$$

This is always possible if the initial distribution of velocities is irrotational. From

$$\frac{\partial \mathbf{v}}{\partial t} = -c^2 \operatorname{grad} \delta,$$

it follows that

$$\mathbf{v}(\mathbf{r}, t) = \mathbf{v}(\mathbf{r}, 0) - c^2 \operatorname{grad} \int_0^t \delta(\mathbf{r}, \tau) \, d\tau.$$

Therefore, if curl $\mathbf{v}(\mathbf{r}, 0) = 0$, then $\mathbf{v}(\mathbf{r}, 0) = -\operatorname{grad} \psi$ and*

$$\mathbf{v}(\mathbf{r}, t) = -\operatorname{grad} \left[\psi + c^2 \int_0^t \delta \, d\tau \right] = -\operatorname{grad} \varphi.$$

The velocity potential also satisfies the wave equation. Indeed,

$$\frac{\partial \varphi}{\partial t} = c^2 \delta.$$

Substituting this equation into $\partial \delta / \partial t + \operatorname{div} \mathbf{v} = 0$, we obtain

$$\frac{\partial^2 \varphi}{\partial t^2} = c^2 \nabla^2 \varphi.$$

Example. Sound waves are generated at one end of a long straight rectangular tube of cross section $a \times b$. We wish to investigate the patterns of these waves inside the tube for various frequencies.

---

* This statement defines φ as $\psi + c^2 \int_0^t \delta \, d\tau$.

For this purpose we seek a solution $\varphi(\mathbf{r}, t)$ which varies harmonically with time:

$$\varphi(\mathbf{r}, t) = \psi(\mathbf{r})e^{-i\omega t} \qquad (\omega = \text{real}),$$

where ω is the frequency (presumably arbitrary).

Note that the complex form is chosen for convenience. The real or imaginary part of φ can be used for a real solution. It follows that $\psi(\mathbf{r})$ must satisfy the PDE

$$\nabla^2 \psi + k^2 \psi = 0, \qquad k = \omega/c,$$

known as the *Helmholtz equation*. Physical requirements also demand that $\psi(\mathbf{r})$ satisfy the following boundary condition at the walls of the tube:

$$\frac{\partial \psi}{\partial n} = 0,$$

where $\partial \psi/\partial n = (\text{grad } \psi \cdot \mathbf{n}_0)$ is the normal gradient of ψ, $\mathbf{n}_0$ being the unit vector normal to the surface. This condition is due to the fact that, at the boundary, the air particles can move only in a direction tangential to the (rigid) walls of the tube.

Remarks

1. The problem is essentially an eigenvalue problem in three dimensions since the Helmholtz equation can be rewritten in the form

$$\nabla^2 \psi = \lambda \psi \qquad (\lambda = -k^2)$$

with *undetermined* λ. It is analogous to the equation for $X(x)$ in the case of the vibrating string (p. 292).

2. There are *no initial conditions* for the function $\varphi(\mathbf{r}, t)$ because we have *specified* the time dependence. We are only looking for suitable eigenfunctions in terms of which we can (hopefully) expand a particular physically realizable solution $\varphi(\mathbf{r}, t)$.

3. Experimental evidence has led us to assume that the time factor is $e^{-i\omega t}$. Actually, we could have invoked the method of separation of variables. Assume that

$$\varphi(\mathbf{r}, t) = \psi(\mathbf{r})T(t).$$

Then

$$\text{a)} \quad \nabla^2 \psi = \lambda \psi, \qquad \text{b)} \quad \frac{d^2 T}{dt^2} = \lambda c^2 T.$$

Tackling equation (b) first, we see that the possibility that $\lambda > 0$ will lead to exponential functions which are not acceptable on physical grounds: If the source of sound maintains a steady output, then the velocity potential φ cannot increase or decrease steadily *at all points* $\mathbf{r}$, because this would cause the intensity of the sound to increase (decrease) everywhere and contradict the conservation of energy. The possibility that $\lambda = 0$ would allow only $T(t) = \text{const}$ (same reasoning); this is of no physical interest, since $\delta = \partial \varphi/\partial t = 0$. Consequently, the only possibility is $\lambda < 0$, leading to the form assumed in the beginning.

We solve the Helmholtz equation by separation of variables. Let the coordinate system be chosen as in Fig. 8.15, with the tube extending in the z-direction. Set

$$\psi(\mathbf{r}) = X(x)\,Y(y)Z(z);$$

then

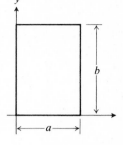

a) $\dfrac{d^2 X}{dx^2} = \lambda_1 X,$ b) $\dfrac{d^2 Y}{dy^2} = \lambda_2 X,$ c) $\dfrac{d^2 Z}{dz^2} = \lambda_3 Z,$

with the provision that $\lambda_1 + \lambda_2 + \lambda_3 = -k^2$. The condition $\partial\psi/\partial n = 0$ at the walls leads to the statements

$$\left.\frac{dX}{dx}\right|_{x=0,a} = 0, \qquad \left.\frac{dY}{dy}\right|_{y=0,b} = 0.$$

Figure 8.15

The condition on X implies that either $\lambda_1 = 0$ and $X = $ const, or $\lambda_1 < 0$ (set $\lambda_1 = -k_1^2$) and $X = \cos(m\pi x/a)$, where m is a positive integer.

Similar conclusions are drawn for Y. It is convenient, then, to introduce the following functions of x and y:

$$\chi_{mn}(x, y) = \cos\frac{m\pi x}{a}\cos\frac{n\pi y}{b} \qquad (m, n = 0, 1, 2, 3, \ldots),$$

which are labeled by a pair of indices involving all possible combinations of the two nonnegative integers m and n. In this, they are similar to the functions ψ_{mn} of the preceding section; note, however, that the values $m = 0$ and $n = 0$ are now permissible. These functions are related (see below) to different *modes of propagation* of the sound along the tube. Turning now to the equation

$$\frac{d^2 Z}{dz^2} = \lambda_3 Z,$$

we see that the constant λ_3 must satisfy

$$\lambda_3 = -(k^2 + \lambda_1 + \lambda_2) = -\left(\frac{\omega^2}{c^2} - \frac{m^2\pi^2}{a^2} - \frac{n^2\pi^2}{b^2}\right).$$

Thus for a fixed frequency ω, the constant λ_3 will be positive or negative depending on the selection of integers m and n, i.e., on the choice of the mode of propagation. If λ_3 is positive, Z will be proportional to $e^{-z\sqrt{\lambda_3}}$. (If sound is generated at $z = 0$ and the tube extends along the positive z-axis, the increasing exponential solution is unphysical and must be discarded.) We say that the sound wave is *attenuated*.

If, on the other hand, λ_3 is negative, then, setting $\lambda_3 = -k_3^2$, we have

$$Z = A\cos k_3 z + B\sin k_3 z.$$

Note that $k_3 = \sqrt{\omega^2/c^2 - m^2\pi^2/a^2 - n^2\pi^2/b^2}$. In this case we say that the sound wave is *propagated*.

It is seen that if the frequency ω is fixed, only a certain (finite) number of modes will be propagated, namely, those modes for which m and n are sufficiently small to allow

$$\omega^2/c^2 > m^2\pi^2/a^2 + n^2\pi^2/b^2.$$

The $(0, 0)$-mode is always propagated. It represents a *plane wave* in the z-direction (φ is independent of x, y and is constant over a plane $z = $ const at a given instant of time). Low frequencies can be propagated only by means of a few (lowest) modes, high frequencies allow a large number of modes. For a given mode ($m, n = $ fixed), the frequency given by

$$\omega_{mn} = \pi c\sqrt{m^2/a^2 + n^2/b^2}$$

is called the *cutoff frequency*. If $\omega > \omega_{mn}$, the mode is propagated; if $\omega < \omega_{mn}$, it is attenuated.

Remarks

1. In this problem we have investigated only the *background* for representation of an arbitrary acoustic wave propagating down the tube. It is now reasonable to conjecture that such a wave can be decomposed into waves of all frequencies (by means of a Fourier spectrum) and, moreover, a given frequency component can be decomposed into a number of allowed modes. If the frequency ω is considered as an eigenvalue, then it exhibits degeneracy reflected in the number of modes.

2. There is a possibility of further degeneracy (if a/b is rational), as in the membrane problem.

BIBLIOGRAPHY

CARSLAW, H. S., and J. C. JAEGER, *Conduction of Heat in Solids*. New York: Oxford University Press, 1959.

FRANKLIN, P., *An Introduction to Fourier Methods and the Laplace Transformation*. New York: Dover Publications, Inc., 1949.

MORSE, P. M., *Vibration and Sound*, New York: McGraw-Hill Book Co., 1948.

SOMMERFELD, A., *Partial Differential Equations in Physics*. New York: Academic Press, Inc., 1949.

PROBLEMS

1. A stretched string of length L is "plucked" at the point and its initial shape is given by

$$u(x, 0) = \begin{cases} \dfrac{hx}{\xi} & (x < \xi), \\[2mm] \dfrac{h(L - x)}{L - \xi} & (x \geq \xi). \end{cases}$$

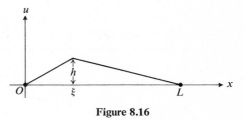

Figure 8.16

The initial distribution of velocities is zero, that is, $\partial u/\partial t(x, 0) = 0$. Show that the motion of the string can be represented by

$$u(x, t) = \frac{2hL^2}{\pi^2\xi(L - \xi)} \sum_{n=1}^{\infty} \frac{1}{n^2} \sin \frac{n\pi\xi}{L} \sin \frac{n\pi x}{L} \cos \frac{n\pi ct}{L}.$$

2. When a piano string of length L is struck by the piano hammer near the point $x = \xi$, it is assumed that the initial distribution of velocities is given by

$$v_0(x) = \begin{cases} v_0 \cos \dfrac{\pi(x - \xi)}{d} & \left(\text{for } |x - \xi| < \dfrac{d}{2}\right), \\ 0 & \left(\text{for } |x - \xi| > \dfrac{d}{2}\right). \end{cases}$$

Assume no initial displacement and show that the motion of the string is given by

$$u(x, t) = \frac{4v_0 d}{\pi^2 c} \sum_{n=1}^{\infty} \frac{1}{n} \frac{\sin (n\pi\xi/L) \cos (n\pi d/2L)}{1 - (nd/L)^2} \sin \frac{n\pi x}{L} \cos \frac{n\pi ct}{L}.$$

3. A heat-conducting cylindrical rod of length L is thermally insulated over its lateral surface and its ends are kept at zero temperature. If the initial temperature of the rod is $u_0 = $ const, show that the temperature $u(x, t)$ at any later time must satisfy

$$\frac{\partial u}{\partial t} = a^2 \frac{\partial^2 u}{\partial x^2}, \qquad u(0, t) = u(L, t) = 0, \qquad u(x, 0) = u_0.$$

Show that *exactly the same* mathematical formulation is applicable to the problem of cooling an infinite slab of thickness L, initially at temperature u_0 and with its surfaces maintained at zero temperature. Solve this problem by separating the variables and show that

$$u(x, t) = \frac{4u_0}{\pi} \sum_{n=1,3,5,\ldots}^{\infty} \frac{1}{n} e^{-(n^2\pi^2 a^2/L^2)t} \sin \frac{n\pi x}{L}.$$

Does this series converge rapidly for small or for large values of t?

4. Suppose that in the preceding problem the initial temperature distribution is an arbitrary function of x: $u(x, 0) = f(x)$. Show why the method of Fourier finite sine transforms can be used immediately. Use this technique to develop the formula

$$u(x, t) = \frac{2}{L} \sum_{n=1}^{\infty} e^{-(n^2\pi^2 a^2/L^2)t} \sin \frac{n\pi x}{L} \int_0^L f(\xi) \sin \frac{n\pi\xi}{L} d\xi.$$

5. Attempt to solve Problems 3 and 4 by application of the Laplace transform with respect to t and avoiding the Fourier series altogether. Comment on the difficulties. If you cannot find a way out, take the special case $f(x) = x$ in Problem 4 and show that

$$U(x, s) = \frac{x}{s} - \frac{L}{s} \frac{\sinh (x\sqrt{s}/a)}{\sinh (L\sqrt{s}/a)}.$$

Now apply the technique of Problem 15, Chapter 5, to complete the solution. Does the obtained series converge rapidly for small or large values of t? Solve Problem 3 by this method.

6. Suppose that the rod (or the slab) of Problem 4 is *insulated* at $x = 0$ and $x = L$. Set up the new boundary conditions and establish a suitable set of eigenfunctions. Show that the solution is now

$$u(x, t) = \frac{1}{L} \int_0^L f(\xi)\, d\xi + \frac{2}{L} \sum_{n=1}^{\infty} e^{-(n^2 \pi^2 a^2/L^2)t} \cos\frac{n\pi x}{L} \int_0^L f(\xi) \cos\frac{n\pi\xi}{L}\, d\xi.$$

7. Consider an infinite heat-conducting rod stretching in the x-direction ($-\infty < x < \infty$) and insulated over the lateral surface. It is desired to find the temperature at time $t > 0$ if the initial temperature at $t = 0$ is prescribed: $u(x, 0) = f(x)$. Formulate the problem (PDE, initial condition, boundary conditions). Which method of solution would you select and why? Using an appropriate convolution theorem, show that

$$u(x, t) = \frac{1}{2a\sqrt{\pi t}} \int_{-\infty}^{+\infty} f(\xi) e^{-(x-\xi)^2/4a^2 t}\, d\xi.$$

8. Consider the following two problems:

a) Determine the steady-state (independent of time) temperature distribution in an infinite rod with the cross section shown in Fig. 8.17(a) and the lateral surfaces maintained at the temperature given.

b) Determine the electrostatic potential in an infinite cylinder split lengthwise into four parts and charged as shown (Fig. 8.17b).

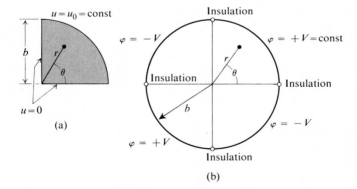

(a)

(b)   **Figure 8.17**

State the mathematical formulation of both problems. Produce a rigorous proof (by symmetry considerations) that the solution of the second problem provides us automatically with the solution to the first one. Show, in the most efficient manner, that the solution of the second problem can be given by

$$\varphi(r, \theta) = \frac{8u_0}{\pi} \sum_{n=2,6,10,\dots}^{\infty} \frac{1}{n} \left(\frac{r}{b}\right)^n \sin n\theta.$$

9. Show that the problem discussed in Example 2, Section 8.5, can be solved by applying the Fourier sine transform with respect to x. [Consult, if necessary, the solutions of Problems 6 and 8 in Chapter 7.]

10. Consider the semi-infinite heat-conducting medium defined by the region $x \geq 0$ and arbitrary y and z. Let it be initially at zero temperature and let its surface $x = 0$ have a prescribed variation of temperature $u(0, t) = f(t)$ (for $t \geq 0$). Use a method of your choice to show that

$$u(x, t) = \frac{x}{2a\sqrt{\pi}} \int_0^t \frac{e^{-x^2/4a^2(t-\tau)}}{(t-\tau)^{3/2}} f(\tau)\, d\tau.$$

[Hint: The result of Problem 12, Chapter 5, may be helpful.]

11. The principle of superposition (Section 8.2) can be used in a variety of situations not mentioned so far. Suppose that in Problem 3 above, only the end $x = L$ is kept at zero temperature, while at the end $x = 0$ a *prescribed heat current density* $\mathbf{q}$ (p. 298) enters the rod.

a) Show that the problem may be formulated by

$$\frac{\partial u}{\partial t} = a^2 \frac{\partial^2 u}{\partial x^2}, \qquad u(L, t) = 0, \qquad \frac{\partial u}{\partial x}\bigg|_{x=0} = b = \text{const}, \qquad u(x, 0) = u_0.$$

b) Instead of imposing the initial condition $u(x, 0) = u_0$, find a steady-state (time-independent) solution $u_1(x)$ of the above problem.

c) Show that the sum of $u_1(x)$ and the solution of Problem 3 yields the solution sought in (a).

12. Consider a very long (infinite) heat-conducting bar of rectangular cross section, such as the one shown in Fig. 8.18.

a) If the face $x = a$ is kept at a constant temperature u_0 and the other three faces are kept at zero temperature, show that the steady-state solution can be expressed by

$$u(x, y) = \frac{4u_0}{\pi} \sum_{n=1,3,5,\ldots}^{\infty} \frac{1}{n} \frac{\sinh(n\pi x/b)}{\sinh(n\pi a/b)} \sin \frac{n\pi y}{b}.$$

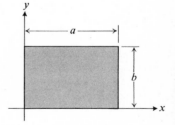

Figure 8.18

b) Write (without solving the PDE) the steady-state solution for the case in which the face $y = b$ is kept at the temperature u_0 and the remaining three faces are at zero temperature.

c) Suppose that both faces $x = a$ and $y = b$ are kept at temperature u_0, and the faces $x = 0$ and $y = 0$ at zero temperature. Can you write the solution immediately?

d) State clearly what features of the PDE, boundary conditions, etc., permit the use of the techniques hinted at above.

13. For some additional applications of the superposition principle, consider Problem 12(c) again.

a) Observe that the function $u_1(x, y) = u_0 x/a$ satisfies the PDE; state also the boundary conditions satisfied by u_1.

b) Suppose the solution to Problem 12(c) is sought in the form

$$u(x, y) = \frac{u_0 x}{a} + u_2(x, y).$$

What boundary conditions should $u_2(x, y)$ satisfy?

c) If $u_2(x, y)$ is sought in the form of a Fourier sine series, show that

$$u(x, y) = \frac{u_0 x}{a} + \frac{2u_0}{\pi} \sum_{n=1}^{\infty} \frac{\sinh (n\pi y/a) + (-1)^n \sinh [n\pi(b - y)/a]}{n \sinh (n\pi b/a)} \sin \frac{n\pi x}{a}.$$

d) Show that the function $u(x, y)$ given above satisfies

$$u(x, 0) = u(x, b) = 0.$$

[*Hint:* Develop the function $u_0 x/a$ in a Fourier sine series for $0 \le x < a$.]

14. A radioactive gas is diffusing into the atmosphere from contaminated ground so that μ μgm/cm$^2 \cdot$ sec escape into the air. Assume the ground and the atmosphere to be semi-infinite media with $x = 0$ as the boundary.

a) Show that the density of the radioactive gas in the air is governed by the relations

$$\frac{\partial \rho(x, t)}{\partial t} = D \frac{\partial^2 \rho(x, t)}{\partial x^2} - \lambda \rho(x, t) \qquad (D, \lambda = \text{const}),$$

$$\frac{\partial \rho}{\partial x}\bigg|_{x=0} = -X = \text{const} \qquad (\rho(\infty, t) < \infty).$$

b) Assume that $\rho(x, 0) = 0$ $(x \ge 0)$ and solve the problem by the Fourier cosine transform method to show that

$$\rho(x, t) = \frac{2X}{\pi} \int_0^{\infty} \frac{1 - e^{-(Dk^2+\lambda)t}}{k^2 + \lambda/D} \cos kx \, dk.$$

c) Solve the problem by the Laplace transform method and show that

$$\rho(x, t) = X \sqrt{\frac{D}{\pi}} \int_0^t \frac{1}{\sqrt{\tau}} e^{-\lambda\tau} e^{-x^2/4D\tau} \, d\tau.$$

[*Hint:* Obtain the inverse transform of $(1/\sqrt{s})e^{-a\sqrt{s}}$ from Problem 12, Chapter 5, and use the convolution theorem.]

d) Show that the solutions found under (b) and (c) are equivalent. *Hint:* Recall that

$$\int_0^t e^{-(Dk^2+\lambda)\tau} \, d\tau = \frac{1 - e^{-(Dk^2+\lambda)\tau}}{Dk^2 + \lambda}.$$

15. A stretched string of length L is initially at rest. For $t > 0$, it is subject to forced vibrations described by the PDE

$$\frac{\partial^2 u}{\partial x^2} - \frac{1}{c^2} \frac{\partial^2 u}{\partial t^2} = -kx.$$

Find the motion of the string by the following *method of complementary function:* Seek a solution $u = u_1 + u_2$, where u_1 is a general solution of the *homogeneous* PDE (as above, with the right-hand side of the equation being zero) and satisfies the boundary conditions but not the initial conditions, while u_2 is a particular solution of the nonhomogeneous PDE and the boundary conditions but is *independent of time.* Complete this idea; show its consistency and solve the problem.

16. A rectangular membrane $0 \leq x \leq a$, $0 \leq y \leq b$ is clamped on all sides and is loaded by a uniformly distributed external force q (per unit area).

    a) Show that the static (time-independent) deflection $u(x, y)$ satisfies a nonhomogeneous PDE and homogeneous boundary conditions.

    b) Show that the function

    $$u_1(x, y) = \frac{qx(a - x)}{2T}$$

    satisfies the PDE, but not all the boundary conditions.

    c) If the overall solution is sought in the form $u_1(x, y) + u_2(x, y)$ (see Problem 15), determine the PDE and the boundary conditions which should be satisfied by u_2.

    d) Complete the solution, simplify it, and show that

    $$u(x, y) = \frac{qx(a - x)}{2T} - \frac{4qa^2}{T\pi^3} \sum_{n=1,3,5,\ldots}^{\infty} \frac{1}{n^3} \frac{\cosh [n\pi(2y - b)/2a]}{\cosh (n\pi b/2a)} \sin \frac{n\pi x}{a}.$$

17. The stretched string of length L undergoes forced vibrations according to

    $$\frac{\partial^2 u}{\partial t^2} = c^2 \frac{\partial^2 u}{\partial x^2} + A \sin \omega t \qquad (A = \text{const}).$$

    a) Seek a steady-state solution in the form $u(x, t) = y(x) \sin \omega t$ and show that it can be written as

    $$u(x, t) = \frac{2A}{\omega^2} \frac{\sin (kx/2) \sin [k(L - x)/2]}{\cos (kL/2)} \sin \omega t \qquad \left(k = \frac{\omega}{c}\right). \tag{i}$$

    b) Let the string be at rest prior to $t = 0$. Solve the problem by the finite transform method and show that

    $$u(x, t) = \frac{4A}{\pi} \sin \omega t \sum_{n=\text{odd}}^{\infty} \frac{\sin (n\pi x/L)}{n(\omega_n^2 - \omega^2)} - \frac{4A}{\pi} \frac{L\omega}{c\pi} \sum_{n=\text{odd}}^{\infty} \frac{\sin (n\pi x/L) \sin \omega_n t}{n^2(\omega_n^2 - \omega^2)}, \tag{ii}$$

    where $\omega_n = n\pi c/L$; assume that $\omega \neq \omega_n$. Comment on the physical meaning of each sum.

    c) Should the first sum in (b) be identical with the solution (i) in (a)? Verify your answer by expansion of (i) into a Fourier sine series.

    d) Suppose that $\omega = m\pi c/L$ for some m. What modifications are needed in part (b)? Solve this problem and comment on the validity of the solution.

18. Consider a parallelepiped $a \times b \times c$ made of solid material. One of the $(a \times b)$-faces is maintained at the temperature $u = u_0 = \text{const}$, and the other five faces are kept at zero temperature. Suppose that we wish to obtain a time-independent temperature distribution.

a) Formulate the problem in cartesian coordinates with one vertex of the parallelepiped at the origin.

b) Solve the problem and show that your solution is equivalent to (or identical with)

$$u(x, y, z) = \frac{16u_0}{\pi^2} \sum_{m=\text{odd}}^{\infty} \sum_{n=\text{odd}}^{\infty} \frac{1}{mn} \frac{\sinh \alpha_{mn}(c - z)}{\sinh \alpha_{mn}c} \sin \frac{m\pi x}{a} \sin \frac{n\pi y}{b},$$

where $\alpha_{mn} = \pi\sqrt{m^2/a^2 + n^2/b^2}$.

c) Evaluate $\bar{u}(x, y, z) = \lim_{c \to \infty} u(x, y, z)$.

d) The function $\bar{u}(x, y, z)$ can be used to solve a certain problem in electrostatics. Formulate this problem.

19. A rectangular membrane with dimensions $(a \times b)$ is at rest for $t < 0$. For $t > 0$, it is subject to external forces (per unit area)

$$F(x, y; t) = A(x, y)e^{-i\omega t}.$$

a) Formulate the problem.

b) Solve the problem for the general (no resonance) case if $\omega \neq \pi c\sqrt{m^2/a^2 + n^2/b^2}$ with $m, n = $ integers.

c) Solve the problem for the case of resonance: $\omega = \pi c\sqrt{m_0^2/a^2 + n_0^2/b^2}$ (for some particular m_0 and n_0).

d) Comment on the validity of the solution found in (c).

e) Discuss the resonance case if the frequency is degenerate.

20. We wish to investigate the characteristic modes of vibration of air in an enclosure of the shape of a rectangular parallelepiped $(-a/2 \leq x \leq a/2, -b/2 \leq y \leq b/2, -c/2 \leq z \leq c/2)$.

a) Set up the PDE and the boundary conditions satisfied by the velocity potential.

b) Seeking solutions varying in time as $e^{-i\omega t}$, determine the characteristic frequencies and the characteristic modes of vibration.

c) Let $a = b = 2$ m and $c = 3$ m. Show that the lowest triple-degenerate mode has frequency $\omega = \pi c\sqrt{2}$ (c in m/sec). What are the lowest fourfold and fivefold degenerate modes?

CHAPTER 9

SPECIAL FUNCTIONS

9.1 CYLINDRICAL AND SPHERICAL COORDINATES

In many physical problems the boundary conditions are such that the values of a function (or its derivative) are specified on curved surfaces (spheres, cylinders, etc.). In cases of this sort the cartesian coordinate system is not suitable for the formulation of boundary-value problems.

Indeed, the successful solution of the problems in Chapter 8 did depend, to a great extent, on the fact that the boundaries were usually mutually perpendicular straight lines or planes and could have been represented by statements such as $x = $ const, $y = $ const, and $z = $ const.

If the boundaries are curved surfaces, then it is, in general, convenient to use a coordinate system in which the required surfaces* are represented by

$$u = \text{const}, \qquad v = \text{const}, \quad \text{etc.,}$$

where $u, v, \ldots$ are the coordinates (this has actually been done in Section 8.3).

The majority of common physical boundary-value problems involve boundaries in the shape of planes, spheres, and circular cylinders (or their portions). In these cases the choice of spherical or cylindrical coordinate systems is natural.

We shall now consider the application of the method of separation of variables to the three-dimensional wave equation

$$\nabla^2 \varphi = \frac{1}{c^2} \frac{\partial^2 \varphi}{\partial t^2}$$

in cylindrical and spherical coordinate systems. Other partial differential equations mentioned in Chapter 8 can be treated similarly, leading to much the same "separated-out" ordinary differential equations.

First, we separate out the time factor by setting

$$\varphi(\mathbf{r}, t) = \psi(\mathbf{r})T(t).$$

This leads to the equations

$$\text{a)} \quad \frac{d^2 T}{dt^2} = \lambda c^2 T, \qquad \text{b)} \quad \nabla^2 \psi = \lambda \psi,$$

where (b) is still a PDE.

---

* Or curves in the case of two-dimensional problems.

In most cases we are interested in a solution which varies harmonically in time; this implies negative values of λ. It is customary to set

$$\lambda = -k^2, \qquad k/c = \omega$$

and write, as a possible solution, the expression

$$\varphi_k(\mathbf{r}, t) = \psi_k(\mathbf{r})e^{-i\omega t}.$$

Remark. The choice $e^{-i\omega t}$, instead of $e^{+i\omega t}$, is customary and convenient. If necessary, we may allow k and ω to take on negative values. A superposition of such solutions may be made real, if desired. Alternatively, real (or imaginary) parts of φ_k may be used.

Whether or not ω is allowed to take on arbitrary values depends on the boundary conditions imposed on $\psi_k(\mathbf{r})$. This question will be resolved by the study of the Helmholtz equation

$$\nabla^2\psi + k^2\psi = 0.$$

In the cylindrical system, this equation reads*

$$\frac{1}{r}\frac{\partial}{\partial r}\left(r\frac{\partial\psi}{\partial r}\right) + \frac{1}{r^2}\frac{\partial^2\psi}{\partial\theta^2} + \frac{\partial^2\psi}{\partial z^2} + k^2\psi = 0.$$

If we set $\psi(r, \theta, z) = R(r)\Theta(\theta)Z(z)$, substitute into the equation, and divide the equation by ψ, we obtain

$$\frac{1}{rR}\frac{d}{dr}\left(r\frac{dR}{dr}\right) + \frac{1}{r^2\Theta}\frac{d^2\Theta}{d\theta^2} + \frac{1}{Z}\frac{d^2Z}{dz^2} + k^2 = 0.$$

The first two terms depend on r and θ only; the last two are independent of r and θ. This is possible only if

$$\frac{1}{Z}\frac{d^2Z}{dz^2} + k^2 = \text{const},$$

leading to

$$\frac{d^2Z}{dz^2} - \lambda_1 Z = 0 \qquad (\lambda_1 = \text{const}). \tag{a}$$

Using this and multiplying the original equation by r^2, we obtain

$$\frac{r}{R}\frac{d}{dr}\left(r\frac{dR}{dr}\right) + \frac{1}{\Theta}\frac{d^2\Theta}{d\theta^2} + (k^2 + \lambda_1)r^2 = 0.$$

Arguing as before, we conclude that

$$\frac{d^2\Theta}{d\theta^2} - \lambda_2\Theta = 0 \qquad (\lambda_2 = \text{const}). \tag{b}$$

---

* See Section 1.9 for the general treatment of curvilinear coordinates.

Then the remainder can be written as

$$\frac{d}{dr}\left(r\frac{dR}{dr}\right) + \left[r(k^2 + \lambda_1) + \frac{\lambda_2}{r}\right]R = 0. \qquad \text{(c)}$$

Thus we can say that the Helmholtz equation is (completely) separable in the cylindrical coordinate system.

In the spherical system, the Helmholtz equation reads (see p. 39)

$$\frac{1}{r^2}\frac{\partial}{\partial r}\left(r^2\frac{\partial\psi}{\partial r}\right) + \frac{1}{r^2\sin\theta}\frac{\partial}{\partial\theta}\left(\sin\theta\frac{\partial\psi}{\partial\theta}\right) + \frac{1}{r^2\sin^2\theta}\frac{\partial^2\psi}{\partial\phi^2} + k^2\psi = 0.$$

We set $\psi(r,\theta,\phi) = R(r)\Theta(\theta)\Phi(\phi)$, and proceed as before. After the necessary manipulations, it can be seen that the Helmholtz equation is also separable in spherical coordinates and the separated equations read:

$$\frac{d^2\Phi}{d\phi^2} - \lambda_1\Phi = 0, \qquad \text{(a)}$$

$$\frac{d}{d\theta}\left(\sin\theta\frac{d\Theta}{d\theta}\right) + \left[-\sin\theta\cdot\lambda_2 + \frac{\lambda_1}{\sin\theta}\right]\Theta = 0, \qquad \text{(b)}$$

$$\frac{d}{dr}\left(r^2\frac{dR}{dr}\right) + [r^2k^2 + \lambda_2]R = 0. \qquad \text{(c)}$$

Exercise. Supply the necessary details and produce an explicit derivation of the above three equations.

9.2 THE COMMON BOUNDARY-VALUE PROBLEMS

The separated equations derived in the preceding section contain undetermined separation constants λ_1 and λ_2. These separation constants usually become eigenvalues in the context of appropriate boundary conditions.

Example 1. It is commonly required that solutions ψ of the Helmholtz equation in a cylindrical system are periodic in θ. This property makes the equation

$$\frac{d^2\Theta}{d\theta^2} - \lambda_2\Theta = 0$$

an *eigenvalue equation* since it restricts possible choices of λ_2. It requires that

$$\lambda_2 = -m^2 \qquad (m = 0, 1, 2, \ldots)$$

and leads to trigonometric (or complex exponential) functions which serve as eigenfunctions.

The second separation constant λ_1 (for a problem in cylindrical coordinates) is determined from additional boundary conditions. If these boundary conditions involve z, then the equation

$$\frac{d^2Z}{dz^2} - \lambda_1 Z = 0$$

becomes an eigenvalue equation. For instance, suppose that $\psi(r, \theta, z)$ must vanish at $z = 0$ and $z = L$. We require that $Z(z)$ satisfies these conditions. This leads to $\lambda_1 = -n^2\pi^2/L^2$ $(n = 1, 2, 3, \ldots)$, and

$$Z_n(z) = \sin\frac{n\pi z}{L}.$$

In this case the equation for $R(r)$ reads

$$\frac{d}{dr}\left(r\frac{dR}{dr}\right) + \left[r\left(k^2 + \frac{n^2\pi^2}{L^2}\right) - \frac{m^2}{r}\right]R = 0.$$

If k^2 is still undetermined (and suitable boundary conditions are imposed on R), then this equation is an eigenvalue equation for k^2.

It is customary to transform this equation by a *change of scale* in the independent variable,

$$x = r\sqrt{k^2 + \frac{n^2\pi^2}{L^2}};$$

then

$$\frac{d}{dr} = \sqrt{k^2 + \frac{n^2\pi^2}{L^2}}\frac{d}{dx},$$

and, setting $R(r) = R(x/\sqrt{k^2 + n^2\pi^2/L^2} = y(x)$, we find that the equation becomes

$$\frac{d}{dx}\left(x\frac{dy}{dx}\right) + \left(x - \frac{m^2}{x}\right)y = 0.$$

This is the Bessel DE* of order m. It is often rewritten as

$$\frac{d^2y}{dx^2} + \frac{1}{x}\frac{dy}{dx} + \left(1 - \frac{m^2}{x^2}\right)y = 0,$$

and will be treated in detail later in this chapter. (The cases $m = 0$ and $m = 1$ have been solved in Section 3.5, Examples 5 and 7.)

Example 2. In the spherical coordinate system, it is also commonly required that $\psi(r, \theta, \phi)$ be periodic in ϕ. This leads to the result that in

$$\frac{d^2\Phi}{d\phi^2} - \lambda_1\Phi = 0,$$

the separation constant has the allowed values

$$\lambda_1 = -m^2 \qquad (m = 0, 1, 2, 3, \ldots).$$

---

* See the Remark on p. 135.

Consider the simple case when the entire solution $\psi(r, \theta, \phi)$ is known to be independent of ϕ. Then, evidently, we must set $m = 0$, and $\Phi(\phi)$ must be equal to a constant (the other solution, $\Phi = C\phi$, is not periodic).

The equation for Θ reads

$$\frac{d}{d\theta}\left(\sin\theta\,\frac{d\Theta}{d\theta}\right) - \lambda_2\sin\theta\,\Theta = 0.$$

It is customary (and convenient) to make a change of independent variable in this equation by setting $\cos\theta = x$. Then

$$\frac{d}{d\theta} = \frac{dx}{d\theta}\frac{d}{dx} = -\sin\theta\,\frac{d}{dx},$$

and, setting $\Theta(\theta) = \Theta\,(\arccos x) = y(x)$, we obtain the equation

$$\frac{d}{dx}\left[(1 - x^2)\frac{dy}{dx}\right] - \lambda_2 y = 0.$$

This is the Legendre DE.* Within the context of our problem, the range of x for which the solutions are of physical interest is the interval $-1 \le x \le +1$ (this corresponds to the range $0 \le \theta \le \pi$). It is usually required that the solution $\psi(r, \theta, \phi)$ of the Helmholtz equation be everywhere bounded. If this requirement is applied to $\Theta(\theta)$, then the Legendre equation becomes an eigenvalue equation. In Section 3.5, we demonstrated that the points $x = \pm 1$ are the critical ones; hence a solution bounded at $x = \pm 1$ can be obtained only if

$$\lambda_2 = -l(l + 1) \qquad (l = 0, 1, 2, \ldots).$$

The corresponding eigenfunctions are the Legendre polynomials $P_l(x)$. In terms of θ,

$$\Theta_l(\theta) = P_l(\cos\theta) \qquad (l = 0, 1, 2, 3, \ldots).$$

If the solution $\psi(r, \theta, \phi)$ is not expected to be independent of ϕ, then the equation for Θ reads

$$\frac{d}{d\theta}\left(\sin\theta\,\frac{d\Theta}{d\theta}\right) - \left(\sin\theta\cdot\lambda_2 + \frac{m^2}{\sin\theta}\right)\Theta = 0.$$

It is again convenient to set $\cos\theta = x$, resulting in

$$\frac{d}{dx}\left[(1 - x^2)\frac{dy}{dx}\right] - \left(\lambda_2 + \frac{m^2}{1 - x^2}\right)y = 0 \qquad (m = 0, 1, 2, 3, \ldots),$$

which is known as the *associated Legendre equation*. It will be studied in Section 9.8 and it will be shown that for a solution bounded at $x = \pm 1$ to exist,

---

* See Section 3.5, Example 3.

it is again necessary that

$$\lambda_2 = -l(l+1) \qquad (l = 0, 1, 2, \ldots).$$

Moreover, it will also be required that $l \geq m$.

The *radial equation* in the spherical system now reads

$$\frac{d}{dr}\left(r^2 \frac{dR}{dr}\right) + [r^2 k^2 - l(l+1)]R = 0;$$

it may be an eigenvalue equation for k^2 if suitable boundary conditions are imposed on R.

It is customary to set $kr = x$, transforming the equation into

$$\frac{d}{dx}\left(x^2 \frac{dy}{dx}\right) + [x^2 - l(l+1)]y = 0.$$

Solutions of this equation are known as *spherical Bessel and Neumann functions* (the case $l = 1$ has been solved in Section 3.5, Example 1). The reason for these names is that the above equation is related to the Bessel equation: Setting

$$y(x) = \frac{u(x)}{\sqrt{x}},$$

substituting this into the equation for y, and performing the necessary manipulations, we can show that $u(x)$ must satisfy

$$x^2 \frac{d^2u}{dx^2} + x \frac{du}{dx} + [x^2 - (l + \tfrac{1}{2})^2]u = 0,$$

which can be recognized as the Bessel equation of order $l + \tfrac{1}{2}$. (Compare this result with Section 3.5, Example 2.) We shall investigate this equation later in this chapter.

9.3 THE STURM-LIOUVILLE PROBLEM

Each of the equations arising from the separation of the Helmholtz PDE in the last section has the form

$$\frac{d}{dx}\left[p(x)\frac{dy}{dx}\right] - s(x)y + \lambda r(x)y = 0,$$

which is known as the *Sturm-Liouville equation*. It is assumed that all other separation constants except λ have already been determined. The above equation is then assumed to be the eigenvalue equation for λ. Since its solutions will be required to satisfy certain boundary conditions, we are actually confronted with a *boundary-value problem* and the boundary conditions are of as much importance as the DE.

The Sturm-Liouville problem is associated with the Sturm-Liouville differential operator

$$\mathcal{L} \equiv \frac{d}{dx}\left[p(x)\frac{d}{dx} \right] - s(x),$$

which is a *linear differential operator* of the second order. In terms of $\mathcal{L}$, the Sturm-Liouville DE is conveniently written as

$$\mathcal{L}\{y(x)\} = -\lambda r(x)y(x).$$

The operator $\mathcal{L}$ is called linear because it possesses the property*

$$\mathcal{L}\{C_1 y_1 + C_2 y_2\} = C_1\mathcal{L}\{y_1\} + C_2\mathcal{L}\{y_2\},$$

which is also one of the key properties of the operator d^2/dx^2 used extensively in Chapter 8. As a matter of fact, the operator d^2/dx^2 is nothing but a special case of the Sturm-Liouville operator; i.e., it occurs when $p(x) = 1$ and $s(x) = 0.$†

Following the ideas of the preceding chapter, we may ask whether it might be possible to represent a solution of a PDE (with boundary conditions and initial conditions) by means of a series of eigenfunctions of an appropriate Sturm-Liouville operator, as we did by means of a Fourier series. This turns out to be the case, at least for the vast majority of problems encountered in physics.

In order to arrive at such a conclusion we shall need to employ the *orthogonality* of eigenfunctions of the operator $\mathcal{L}$. Let the interval under consideration be denoted by (a, b), where one or both limits may be at infinity. Consider any two nontrivial‡ eigenfunctions $y_m(x)$ and $y_n(x)$ corresponding to the eigenvalues λ_m and λ_n; then

$$\frac{d}{dx}\left[p(x)\frac{dy_m}{dx} \right] - s(x)y_m + \lambda_m r(x)y_m = 0,$$

$$\frac{d}{dx}\left[p(x)\frac{dy_n}{dx} \right] - s(x)y_n + \lambda_n r(x)y_n = 0.$$

Multiply the first equation by y_n, the second one by y_m, subtract, and integrate from a to b (compare with Section 4.4). The terms containing $s(x)$ will cancel out while the terms containing the derivatives can be simplified by integration by parts:

$$\int_a^b y_n \frac{d}{dx}\left[p\frac{dy_m}{dx} \right] dx = y_n p \frac{dy_m}{dx}\bigg|_a^b - \int_a^b p\frac{dy_m}{dx}\frac{dy_n}{dx}\, dx.$$

---

* Compare with p. 187. Of course, the Laplace transform operator is not to be confused with the Sturm-Liouville operator despite the use of the same letter $\mathcal{L}$.

† In the eigenvalue problems of Chapter 8 we also had $r(x) = 1$, a situation which is, in general, quite common.

‡ The function $y(x) \equiv 0$ may satisfy the DE and the boundary conditions and is known as the *trivial solution*. Obviously, it is of no interest in the above context.

When two such terms are subtracted, the integrals on the right-hand side of the equation cancel out.

The net result of this manipulation is

$$p(x)\left[y_n(x)\frac{dy_m(x)}{dx} - y_m(x)\frac{dy_n(x)}{dx}\right]\Bigg|_a^b = (\lambda_n - \lambda_m)\int_a^b r(x)y_m(x)y_n(x)\,dx.$$

The left-hand side depends on the boundary conditions imposed on the eigenfunctions and their derivatives [and the properties of $p(x)$]. If it happens to vanish, then

$$(\lambda_n - \lambda_m)\int_a^b r(x)y_m(x)y_n(x)\,dx = 0,$$

which leads to the (self-explanatory) statement that eigenfunctions corresponding to *different* eigenvalues ($\lambda_m \neq \lambda_n$) are orthogonal to each other *with respect to the weight function r(x)*.

The appearance of $r(x)$ does not interfere with the evaluation of coefficients in a series of eigenfunctions. Indeed, let us *assume* that

a) there is an infinite number of eigenfunctions $y_m(x)$,
b) the eigenfunctions are all orthogonal to each other with respect to $r(x)$,
c) a function $f(x)$ can be represented by an infinite series

$$f(x) = \sum_m a_m y_m(x).$$

We multiply both sides by $r(x)y_n(x)$ and integrate from a to b, assuming that term-by-term integration is permissible. By employing orthogonality, we find that only the term with $n = m$ will survive on the right-hand side, so that

$$\int_a^b f(x)r(x)y_n(x)\,dx = a_n\int_a^b [y_n(x)]^2 r(x)\,dx,$$

yielding the nth coefficient in the series:

$$a_n = \frac{\int_a^b f(x)r(x)y_n(x)\,dx}{\int_a^b r(x)[y_n(x)]^2\,dx}.$$

We are now faced with the question: What kind of boundary conditions will result in orthogonal eigenfunctions? The relation

$$p(x)\left[y_n(x)\frac{dy_m(x)}{dx} - y_m(x)\frac{dy_n(x)}{dx}\right]\Bigg|_a^b = 0$$

may be satisfied by a variety of conditions, some of which are listed below.

a) The functions $y_m(x)$ and $y_n(x)$ vanish at $x = a$ and $x = b$. These boundary conditions are usually called the (homogeneous) *Dirichlet conditions* (e.g., the stretched string problem of Section 8.2).

b) The derivatives $dy_m(x)/dx$ and $dy_n(x)/dx$ vanish at $x = a$ and $x = b$. These boundary conditions are usually called the (homogeneous) *Neumann conditions* (e.g., the acoustical problem in Section 8.9).

c) A linear combination of $y_m(x)$ and its derivative vanishes at $x = a$ and $x = b$:

$$y_m(a) + \alpha \frac{dy_m(a)}{dx} = 0, \qquad y_m(b) + \beta \frac{dy_m(b)}{dx} = 0 \qquad (\alpha, \beta = \text{const}),$$

where α and β are, of course, the same for all eigenfunctions. We may call them the *intermediate* (homogeneous) conditions (e.g., recall the elastically supported membrane mentioned on p. 315).

d) One of the above conditions at $x = a$ and another one at $x = b$.

All these conditions are said to be "nonmixed" because the values of $y_m(x)$ and $y'_m(x)$ at $x = a$ are unrelated to those at $x = b$.

Mixed conditions are also possible. Perhaps the most common one is the requirement that

$$y_m(a) = y_m(b), \qquad \frac{dy_m(a)}{dx} = \frac{dy_m(b)}{dx},$$

coupled with $p(a) = p(b)$. The condition of periodicity (e.g., the split-cylinder problem of Section 8.3) is of this form.

Another possible boundary condition arises when

$$p(a) = 0 \qquad \text{or} \qquad p(b) = 0 \quad \text{(or both)}.$$

At first sight this appears to impose no restrictions on the eigenfunctions and their derivatives. However, note that the DE can be written as

$$p(x)\frac{d^2y}{dx^2} + p'(x)\frac{dy}{dx} - s(x)y - \lambda r(x)y = 0,$$

and the zeros of $p(x)$ such as points a and b, are singular points of the equation. The solutions $y(x)$ may, and usually do, possess singularities at these points (see Chapter 3). Such is the case, for instance, with the Legendre DE (Section 3.5, Example 3), where the boundedness of eigenfunctions is required at both zeros of $p(x) = 1 - x^2$. It is possible to construct even more complicated boundary conditions, but the above list includes the most frequent types.

9.4 SELF-ADJOINT OPERATORS

The procedure employed in the last section may be compactly written as

$$\int_a^b y_n(\mathcal{L}y_m)\,dx - \int_a^b y_m(\mathcal{L}y_n)\,dx = (\lambda_n - \lambda_m)\int_a^b ry_my_n\,dx.$$

Thus, requiring that $y_m(x)$ and $y_n(x)$ satisfy the boundary conditions of one of the types described, we have actually proved the relation

$$\int_a^b y_n(\mathfrak{L}y_m)\,dx = \int_a^b y_m(\mathfrak{L}y_n)\,dx.$$

A bit of reflection shows us that this formula must hold for *any two functions* $f(x)$ and $g(x)$ which satisfy the appropriate boundary conditions, namely,

$$\int_a^b f(\mathfrak{L}g)\,dx = \int_a^b g(\mathfrak{L}f)\,dx.$$

(The proof is exactly as before: integration by parts and application of the boundary conditions; note that the terms with $r(x)$ do not appear here at all.)

A linear differential operator $\mathfrak{D}$ is said to be *self-adjoint* if it satisfies the relation†

$$\int_a^b f(\mathfrak{D}g)\,dx = \int_a^b g(\mathfrak{D}f)\,dx$$

for any two functions f and g satisfying the appropriate boundary conditions (of course, f and g must be suitably differentiable so that $\mathfrak{D}f$ and $\mathfrak{D}g$ have meaning). Therefore we have shown that the operators of the Sturm-Liouville type are self-adjoint.

It is also evident that the eigenfunctions of any self-adjoint operator, namely, those satisfying

$$\mathfrak{D}y = -\lambda r(x)y,$$

are mutually orthogonal with respect to $r(x)$, provided they belong to different eigenvalues λ.

Remarks

1. It is, perhaps, more appropriate to call the functions $y(x)$ the *generalized eigenfunctions* (as opposed to functions satisfying $\mathfrak{D}y = \lambda y$) but the term *eigenfunction* will be used for brevity.

2. If the functions under consideration are, in general, complex and the operators are also complex, then the following modifications are made: The operator $\mathfrak{D}$ is said to be self-adjoint if

$$\int_a^b f^*(\mathfrak{D}g)\,dx = \int_a^b g^*(\mathfrak{D}^*f)\,dx$$

and the following properties can be proved:

a) Eigenvalues of self-adjoint operators are always real.

b) Eigenfunctions corresponding to different eigenvalues are orthogonal in the sense that

$$\int_a^b r(x)y_m^*(x)y_n(x)\,dx = 0 \qquad (m \neq n),$$

where $r(x)$ is assumed to be real. Complex self-adjoint operators are usually called *Hermitian operators*.

---

† This is true for real functions only; for complex functions see below.

9.5 LEGENDRE POLYNOMIALS

The Legendre DE

$$\frac{d}{dx}\left[(1 - x^2)\frac{dy}{dx}\right] - \lambda y = 0$$

becomes an eigenvalue equation if we impose the condition that the solution $y(x)$ is bounded at $x = -1$ and $x = +1$. Application of the Frobenius method reveals (see Section 3.5, Example 3) that both solutions can be represented by a Maclaurin series about the origin, but the series, in general, diverge for $|x| = 1$. Therefore, the solutions must possess singularities on the unit circle. It is not difficult to verify (using theorems of Section 3.5) that these singularities must be at one of the points $x = \pm 1$ (other points on the unit circle are ordinary points).*

The exception to this behavior is the case

$$\lambda = -l(l + 1) \qquad (l = 0, 1, 2, 3, \ldots),$$

where one of the solutions reduces to a polynomial (the second solution has been shown to possess branch points at $x = -1$ and $x = +1$). These polynomials are then the eigenfunctions of our problem.

However, an eigenfunction can be multiplied by an *arbitrary constant* and still remain an eigenfunction (of the same eigenvalue) as follows from the fact that the Legendre DE, like other Sturm-Liouville equations, is homogeneous. It is convenient to *standardize* the eigenfunctions in some fashion. This can be done, for instance, by choosing the leading term of a Frobenius series to be unity. It is customary, however, to adopt a different standardization, choosing the leading term to be as indicated in Section 3.5. The eigenfunctions standardized in this way are called Legendre polynomials and are denoted by $P_l(x)$, $l = 0, 1, 2, 3, \ldots$. Some of the merits of this standardization are exhibited below.

The idea behind the Sturm-Liouville problem is the possibility of expanding a solution of the PDE in terms of eigenfunctions. Keeping this in mind, consider the electrostatic potential in empty space produced by a point charge q at the origin. It is given by

$$\varphi = \frac{q}{4\pi\epsilon_0}\frac{1}{|\mathbf{r}|} \qquad \text{(MKSA units)}.$$

If the charge is displaced a unit distance along the z-axis, the solution is

$$\varphi = \frac{q}{4\pi\epsilon_0}\frac{1}{|\mathbf{r} - \mathbf{k}|},$$

---

* It turns out that one solution is regular at $x = -1$ and has a branch point at $x = +1$ while the other exhibits the opposite behavior.

where **k** is the unit vector in the z-direction. In spherical coordinates this reads

$$\varphi(r, \theta, \phi) = \frac{q}{4\pi\epsilon_0} \frac{1}{\sqrt{1 - 2r\cos\theta + r^2}}.$$

Suppose that we now want to establish this solution by the method of separation of variables applied to the Laplace equation $\nabla^2\varphi = 0$ which φ must satisfy (p. 295). Set $\varphi = R(r)\Theta(\theta)\Phi(\phi)$. Recognizing that the solution is independent of ϕ, we set $\Phi(\phi) = $ const. Thus the function $\Theta(\theta)$ must satisfy

$$\frac{d}{d\theta}\left(\sin\theta\,\frac{d\Theta}{d\theta}\right) - \lambda\sin\theta\,\Theta = 0,$$

leading to the Legendre equation and the Legendre polynomials. The equation for $R(r)$ reads

$$\frac{d}{dr}\left(r^2\frac{dR}{dr}\right) - l(l+1)R = 0$$

and yields the solutions $R = r^l$ or $R = 1/r^{l+1}$. If we seek a series expansion valid near the origin, then the form $R = 1/r^{l+1}$ is discarded, and we have

$$\varphi(r, \theta, \phi) = \frac{q}{4\pi\epsilon_0} \frac{1}{\sqrt{1 - 2r\cos\theta + r^2}}$$

$$= \sum_{l=0}^{\infty} A_l r^l P_l(\cos\theta).$$

Is such an expansion legitimate? The answer is yes, because $\varphi(r, \theta, \phi)$ regarded as a function of r is analytic at the origin* so that there is a (unique) Maclaurin series

$$\varphi = \sum_{l=0}^{\infty} a_l(\cos\theta)r^l.$$

On the other hand, $\varphi(r, \theta, \phi)$ regarded as a function of $\cos\theta \equiv x$ is analytic in x for any fixed $r < 1$ so that there is a (unique) expansion

$$\varphi = \sum_{l=0}^{\infty} c_l(r)P_l(x).$$

These two statements can be reconciled only by the conclusion that $\varphi(r, \theta, \phi)$ has a (unique) expansion of the type

$$\varphi(r, \theta, \phi) = \sum_{l=0}^{\infty} A_l r^l P_l(\cos\theta) \qquad (r < 1).$$

---

* More precisely, $f(r) = (1 - 2r\cos\theta + r^2)^{-1/2}$ has a *regular branch* at $r = 0$ (a branch analytic at $r = 0$).

The standardization of Legendre polynomials can now be expressed by the requirement that all the coefficients A_l should be equal to $q/4\pi\epsilon_0$ so that the following relation holds:*

$$\frac{1}{\sqrt{1 - 2r\cos\theta + r^2}} = \sum_{l=0}^{\infty} r^l P_l(\cos\theta) \qquad (r < 1).$$

This formula *determines* the Legendre polynomials, yielding the leading term of the Frobenius series quoted in Section 3.5. Indeed, the left-hand side can be expanded by the binomial formula ($\cos\theta = x$):

$$(1 - 2xr + r^2)^{-1/2} = [1 - r(2x - r)]^{-1/2}$$

$$= 1 + \tfrac{1}{2}r(2x - r) + \frac{1 \cdot 3}{2^2 \cdot 2!} r^2(2x - r)^2 + \cdots$$

$$+ \frac{1 \cdot 3 \cdot 5 \cdots (2n - 1)}{2^n n!} r^n(2x - r)^n + \cdots,$$

which is valid for $|x| \leq 1$ and $|r| < 1$. Collecting the terms proportional to r^l, $l = 0, 1, 2, 3, \ldots$, we obtain the coefficient with r^l which is, by definition, the Legendre polynomial $P_l(x)$. In this fashion we can obtain

$$P_0(x) = 1, \qquad P_1(x) = x, \qquad P_2(x) = \tfrac{1}{2}(3x^2 - 1), \quad \text{etc.}$$

or, in general (after some algebraic manipulations),

$$P_l(x) = \frac{1 \cdot 3 \cdot 5 \cdots (2l - 1)}{l!}$$

$$\times \left[x^l - \frac{l(l - 1)}{2(2l - 1)} x^{l-2} + \frac{l(l - 1)(l - 2)(l - 3)}{2 \cdot 4 \cdot (2l - 1)(2l - 3)} x^{l-4} - \cdots \right]$$

Exercise. Produce the algebraic details leading to this formula.

From the same binomial expansion we can verify that the leading Frobenius term is

$$c_0 = \begin{cases} (-1)^{l/2} \dfrac{l!}{2^l \left(\dfrac{l}{2}!\right)^2} & (l = \text{even}), \\[3em] (-1)^{(l-1)/2} \dfrac{l!}{2^l \left(\dfrac{l-1}{2}!\right)^2} & (l = \text{odd}), \end{cases}$$

and the entire polynomial can be represented explicitly as

$$P_l(x) = \sum_{k=0}^{[l/2]} (-1)^k \frac{(2l - 2k)!}{2^l \cdot k!(l - 2k)!(l - k)!} x^{l-2k},$$

---

* Known as the *Poisson formula*.

where the symbol $[l/2]$ means *the greatest integer contained in* $l/2$; in other words, $[l/2] = l/2$ if l is even and $[l/2] = (l - 1)/2$ if l is odd.*

Legendre polynomials possess many important and useful properties which can, in principle, be derived from the above explicit formula. However, most of these properties are more easily derived by other methods which can be also applied to other types of eigenfunctions arising from Sturm-Liouville problems.

In this respect, the function (p. 344)

$$G(x, t) = \frac{1}{\sqrt{1 - 2xt + t^2}}$$

is most helpful. It is called the *generating function* for Legendre polynomials. We differentiate $G(x, t)$ with respect to the parameter t:

$$\frac{\partial G}{\partial t} = \frac{x - t}{(1 - 2xt + t^2)^{3/2}}.$$

This can be rewritten as

$$(1 - 2xt + t^2)\frac{\partial G}{\partial t} + (t - x)G = 0.$$

Substituting the series for $G(x, t)$, we conclude that

$$\sum_{l=0}^{\infty} l t^{l-1} P_l(x) - \sum_{m=0}^{\infty} 2m t^m x P_m(x) + \sum_{n=0}^{\infty} n t^{n+1} P_n(x)$$

$$+ \sum_{p=0}^{\infty} t^{p+1} P_p(x) - \sum_{q=0}^{\infty} x t^q P_q(x) = 0.$$

Equating the coefficients with equal powers of t we can obtain the so-called *pure recursion relation*†

$$(2l + 1)x P_l(x) = (l + 1)P_{l+1}(x) + l P_{l-1}(x) \qquad (l = 1, 2, 3, \ldots).$$

This formula allows us to calculate $P_{l+1}(x)$ if $P_l(x)$ and $P_{l-1}(x)$ are known and can be used to calculate all Legendre polynomials one by one, starting from

$$P_0(x) = 1 \quad \text{and} \quad P_1(x) = x.$$

Remark. If $l = 0$, the above formula is still valid provided the last term is *omitted.*‡ All subsequent formulas (unless stated otherwise) will be assumed to hold for $l = 0$ with the provision that terms containing $P_{l-1}(x)$ are omitted.

---

* This is a very common notation in mathematical literature.

† The term "pure" refers to the fact that this formula contains no derivatives of $P_l(x)$. See below for other recursion formulas.

‡ The argument that the last term is zero since it is multiplied by l is not rigorous because P_{l-1} is not defined.

If we now differentiate $G(x, t)$ with respect to x, we obtain

$$t(1 - 2xt + t^2)^{3/2} = \sum_{l=0}^{\infty} t^l \frac{dP_l(x)}{dx}.$$

This can be rewritten as

$$tG(x, t) = (1 - 2xt + t^2) \sum_{l=0}^{\infty} t^l \frac{dP_l(x)}{dx},$$

or

$$t \sum_{l=0}^{\infty} t^l P_l(x) = (1 - 2xt + t^2) \sum_{l=0}^{\infty} t^l \frac{dP_l(x)}{dx}.$$

Comparing the coefficients with t^{l+1}, we obtain

$$P_l(x) = P'_{l+1}(x) - 2xP'_l(x) + P'_{l-1}(x) \qquad (l \geq 1).$$

A variety of similar formulas known as the *recursion formulas* can be developed. For instance, differentiate the pure recursion formula

$$(2l + 1)P_l(x) + (2l + 1)xP'_l(x) = (l + 1)P'_{l+1}(x) + lP'_{l-1}(x).$$

If $P'_{l+1}(x)$ is eliminated from the last two relations, then the relation

$$lP_l(x) + P'_{l-1}(x) - xP'_l(x) = 0 \qquad (l \geq 1) \tag{a}$$

is obtained; if, on the other hand, $P'_{l-1}(x)$ is eliminated, then the result is

$$P'_{l+1}(x) = xP'_l(x) + (l + 1)P_l(x) \qquad (l \geq 0). \tag{b}$$

Furthermore, we replace l by $(l - 1)$ in (b) and combine with (a) to eliminate $P'_{l-1}(x)$ and obtain the so-called differentiation formula

$$(x^2 - 1)P'_l(x) = lxP_l(x) - lP_{l-1}(x) \qquad (l \geq 1),$$

which expresses the derivative of the Legendre polynomial in terms of other P_l.

Of special interest are the so-called *ladder operations* (also called *step-up* and *step-down* operations, or *l-raising* and *l-lowering* operations)

$$P_{l-1}(x) = xP_l(x) + \frac{1 - x^2}{l} P'_l(x) \qquad (l \geq 1),$$

$$P_{l+1}(x) = xP_l(x) - \frac{1 - x^2}{l + 1} P'_l(x) \qquad (l \geq 0).$$

Ladder operations can be combined to establish the second-order DE satisfied by P_l, namely, the Legendre DE. Indeed, replacing l by $l - 1$ in the second ladder relation and expressing P_{l-1} and P'_{l-1} in terms of P_l, P'_l, and P''_l as deduced (by differentiation) from the first relation, we obtain

$$(1 - x^2)P''_l - 2xP'_l + (l^2 + l)P_l = 0 \qquad \text{(all } l\text{)},$$

as required.

The generating function can be used to evaluate Legendre polynomials for particular values of x. For instance, setting $x = 1$, we obtain

$$G(1, t) = \frac{1}{\sqrt{1 - 2xt + t^2}}\bigg|_{x=1}$$

$$= \frac{1}{\sqrt{1 - 2t + t^2}} = \frac{1}{1 - t}$$

$$= 1 + t + t^2 + \cdots = \sum_{l=0}^{\infty} t^l.$$

However,

$$G(1, t) = \sum_{l=0}^{\infty} t^l P_l(1).$$

It follows that $P_l(1) = 1$ (all l). Similarly, expanding $G(-1, t)$ and $G(0, t)$ in powers of t, we obtain

$$P_l(-1) = (-1)^l,$$

$$P_l(0) = \begin{cases} 0 & (l = \text{odd}), \\ (-1)^{l/2} \dfrac{l!}{2^l \left(\dfrac{l}{2}!\right)^2} & (l = \text{even}). \end{cases}$$

Besides the generating function, a very useful tool in studying the properties of Legendre polynomials is the *Rodrigues formula*

$$P_l(x) = \frac{1}{2^l l!} \frac{d^l}{dx^l} (x^2 - 1)^l.$$

To verify this relation, expand $(x^2 - 1)^l$ by means of the binomial theorem

$$(x^2 - 1)^l = \sum_{k=0}^{l} (-1)^k \frac{l!}{k!(l - k)!} x^{2l-2k}.$$

Differentiate l times,

$$\frac{d^l}{dx^l} (x^2 - 1)^l = \sum_{k=0}^{[l/2]} (-1)^k \frac{l!}{k!(l - k)!} \frac{(2l - 2k)!}{(l - 2k)!} x^{l-2k},$$

and the result checks with the explicit formula for $P_l(x)$ on p. 344.

Also, the Rodrigues formula can be used to demonstrate the orthogonality of Legendre polynomials by direct integration. Let us consider

$$\int_{-1}^{+1} P_l(x) P_m(x) \, dx = \frac{1}{2^{l+m} l! \, m!} \int_{-1}^{+1} \frac{d^l}{dx^l} (x^2 - 1)^l \frac{d^m}{dx^m} (x^2 - 1)^m \, dx.$$

We may assume that $m \leq l$. (If $m > l$, we merely interchange l and m in the derivation below.) Integrating by parts, we obtain

$$\int_{-1}^{+1} \frac{d^l}{dx^l} (x^2 - 1)^l \frac{d^m}{dx^m} (x^2 - 1)^m \, dx = \frac{d^{l-1}}{dx^{l-1}} (x^2 - 1)^l \frac{d^m}{dx^m} (x^2 - 1)^m \Big|_{-1}^{+1}$$

$$- \int_{-1}^{+1} \frac{d^{l-1}}{dx^{l-1}} (x^2 - 1)^l \frac{d^{m+1}}{dx^{m+1}} (x^2 - 1)^m \, dx.$$

The function $(x^2 - 1)^l = (x + 1)^l (x - 1)^l$ has zeros of the lth order at $x = 1$ and $x = +1$; when it is differentiated $(l - 1)$ times it still has zeros (simple zeros) at $x = \pm 1$. Therefore, the integrated term vanishes.

Now repeat the integration by parts $(l - 1)$ more times. Each time the term which was integrated out will vanish, just as above. The result is

$$(-1)^l \int_{-1}^{+1} (x^2 - 1)^l \frac{d^{l+m}}{dx^{l+m}} (x^2 - 1)^m \, dx.$$

The function $(x^2 - 1)^m$ is a polynomial of order $2m$. If $m < l$, it follows that the polynomial has been differentiated more than $2m$ times. Consequently,

$$\frac{d^{l+m}}{dx^{l+m}} (x^2 - 1)^m = 0 \qquad (m < l),$$

and hence

$$\int_{-1}^{+1} P_l(x) P_m(x) \, dx = 0 \qquad (l \neq m).$$

The advantage of this method of proving the orthogonality is that the so-called *normalization integral*

$$N_l = \int_{-1}^{+1} P_l(x) P_l(x) \, dx$$

can also be evaluated. Indeed, if $m = l$ in the above derivation, then

$$\frac{d^{2l}}{dx^{2l}} (x^2 - 1)^l = (2l)!$$

so that

$$N_l = \int_{-1}^{+1} P_l(x) P_l(x) \, dx = \frac{(2l)!}{2^{2l}(l!)^2} \int_{-1}^{+1} (x^2 - 1)^l \, dx.$$

The integral is not difficult to evaluate:

$$I_l = \int_{-1}^{+1} (x^2 - 1)^l \, dx = (-1)^l \frac{2^{l+1} l!}{1 \cdot 3 \cdot 5 \cdots (2l + 1)}.$$

This yields

$$\int_{-1}^{+1} P_l(x) P_l(x) \, dx = \frac{2}{2l + 1}.$$

Exercise. Evaluate I_l by a method of your choice. (One such method is to establish the relation $I_l = -[2l/(2l + 1)]I_{l-1}$, using integration by parts. Can you suggest any others?)

The normalization integral can also be derived from the generating function. Write

$$\frac{1}{\sqrt{1 - 2xt + t^2}} = \sum_{l=0}^{\infty} t^l P_l(x)$$

and square both sides:

$$\frac{1}{1 - 2xt + t^2} = \sum_{m=0}^{\infty} \sum_{l=0}^{\infty} t^{l+m} P_l(x) P_m(x).$$

Integrate both sides with respect to x from -1 to $+1$. Because of the orthogonality of Legendre polynomials only the terms with $m = l$ on the right-hand side of the equation will survive, reducing the double series to a simple one:

$$\int_{-1}^{+1} \frac{1}{1 - 2xt + t^2} = \sum_{l=0}^{\infty} t^{2l} \int_{-1}^{+1} [P_l(x)]^2 \, dx.$$

Now evaluate the left-hand side of the equation:

$$\int_{-1}^{+1} \frac{1}{1 - 2xt + t^2} = \frac{1}{t} \log \frac{1 + t}{1 - t} \qquad (t < 1).$$

Expand this function in powers of t by utilizing the Maclaurin series for $\log (1 + t)$, and obtain

$$\frac{1}{t} \log \frac{1 + t}{1 - t} = 2 \sum_{n=0}^{\infty} \frac{1}{(2n + 1)} t^{2n},$$

and the normalization integral $N_l = 2/(2l + 1)$ follows.

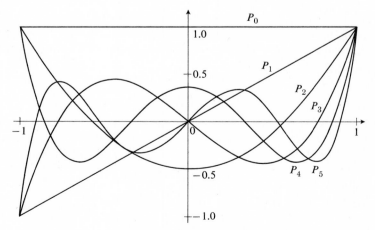

Legendre polynomials   **Figure 9.1**

A few of the lowest Legendre polynomials are listed below and are represented in Fig. 9.1:

$$P_0(x) = 1, \quad P_1(x) = x, \quad P_2(x) = \tfrac{1}{2}(3x^2 - 1),$$
$$P_3(x) = \tfrac{1}{2}(5x^3 - 3x), \quad P_4(x) = \tfrac{1}{8}(35x^4 - 30x^2 + 3),$$
$$P_5(x) = \tfrac{1}{8}(63x^5 - 70x^3 + 15x).$$

9.6 FOURIER-LEGENDRE SERIES

One of the major reasons for studying Legendre polynomials is the expectation that they will provide a basis for an *eigenfunction expansion* analogous to the Fourier series, namely,

$$f(x) = \sum_{l=0}^{\infty} a_l P_l(x).$$

If a function $f(x)$ is representable in this fashion and if the series converges uniformly, then the coefficients a_l can be obtained by the same technique as that used to derive Fourier coefficients. Multiply both sides by $P_m(x)$ and integrate from -1 to $+1$. Use the orthogonality property and the normalization integral to deduce

$$\int_{-1}^{+1} f(x) P_m(x)\, dx = \frac{2}{2l+1}\, a_m$$

so that

$$a_l = \frac{2l+1}{2} \int_{-1}^{+1} f(x) P_l(x)\, dx \qquad (l = 0, 1, 2, \ldots),$$

as quoted in Section 9.3, p. 339. The series obtained in this way is called the *Fourier-Legendre series* and the coefficients a_l are known as the *Fourier-Legendre coefficients*. Evidently, we can obtain the Fourier-Legendre coefficients for any function $f(x)$ for which the appropriate integrals exist (e.g., for any piecewise continuous function) and ask the same questions as in the theory of Fourier series:

a) Will the series converge?

b) Will it converge to $f(x)$?

The answers to these questions are the same as for Fourier series, for instance:

1. If $f(x)$ is piecewise very smooth in the interval $(-1, +1)$, then its Fourier-Legendre series converges to $f(x)$ for the points at which $f(x)$ is continuous and to $\tfrac{1}{2}[f(x + 0) + f(x - 0)]$ for the points at which $f(x)$ has jump discontinuities; the convergence is uniform over any closed interval containing no discontinuities.

2. The statement that $f(x)$ *is piecewise very smooth* in (1) may be replaced by the statement that $f(x)$ *satisfies the Dirichlet conditions.*

3. If $f(x)$ is piecewise continuous, then its Fourier-Legendre series converges in the mean to $f(x)$.

These results can be established from the general analysis of the Sturm-Liouville problem.*

Remark. To establish the last result we may use directly the properties of P_l, in particular, the very helpful fact that the P_l are *polynomials*. Then the following theorem, due to Weierstrass, can be fruitfully employed:

Weierstrass' theorem. If $f(x)$ is continuous in a finite interval $a \leq x \leq b$, then a sequence of polynomials $F_1(x)$, $F_2(x)$, ... can be constructed which converges uniformly to $f(x)$ in (a, b).

Since any polynomial of the Nth degree is a linear combination of Legendre polynomials with $l = 0, 1, 2, \ldots, N$, it follows that $f(x)$ can be approximated uniformly in (a, b), to any desired degree of accuracy by a *finite sum* composed of the $P_l(x)$.

One should not think that this conclusion proves uniform convergence of Fourier-Legendre series to *any* continuous $f(x)$; for this to happen, Dirichlet conditions may still be needed. The point is that the Weierstrass polynomial $F_N(x)$ is not necessarily constructed by adding a multiple of $P_N(x)$ to already existing $F_{N-1}(x)$. However, from the Weierstrass theorem one can establish the *convergence in the mean* of the Fourier-Legendre series. Indeed, from the Weierstrass theorem, it follows that for arbitrarily small ϵ, a polynomial $F_N(x)$ can be found such that

$$\left| f(x) - F_N(x) \right| < \epsilon \qquad (a \leq x \leq b).$$

Therefore

$$\int_{-1}^{+1} [f(x) - F_N(x)]^2 \, dx \leq 2\epsilon^2.$$

However, it can be shown, by the same technique as for Fourier series, that among all polynomials of degree N, the partial Fourier-Legendre sum gives a *minimum total square deviation* $(D_N)_{\min}$ (see Section 4.7) so that

$$(D_N)_{\min} \leq 2\epsilon^2.$$

If N is allowed to increase, then $(D_N)_{\min}$ must remain bounded (Bessel's inequality). Since ϵ is arbitrarily small, it follows that (note that if ϵ is very small, N must be chosen sufficiently large)

$$\lim_{N \to \infty} (D_N)_{\min} = 0,$$

and the convergence in the mean is established for all continuous functions $f(x)$.

---

* See, e.g., Titchmarsh, *Eigenfunction Expansions.* New York: Oxford University Press, 1946; Coddington and Levinson, *Theory of Ordinary Differential Equations.* New York: McGraw-Hill, 1955.

The above result implies that Legendre polynomials form a *complete set* with respect to functions $f(x)$ continuous in (a, b). The extension to piecewise continuous functions is not difficult. Since the number of discontinuities is finite, we can enclose them by a finite number of arbitrarily narrow subintervals which will give an infinitesimal contribution to the integral

$$\int_{-1}^{+1} \left[f(x) - \sum_{l=1}^{N} a_l P_l(x) \right]^2 dx,$$

and the statement follows.

As in the case of Fourier series, the problems of convergence can be approached by the methods developed in Chapter 6. It is not difficult to prove (by the technique of integration by parts, as for the Fourier series) that Fourier-Legendre series will converge uniformly for *very smooth* functions. By the smudging theorem of Chapter 6, any function $f(x)$ continuous in $(-1, +1)$ can be approximated uniformly by an infinitely differentiable (hence very smooth) function $g(x)$. It follows, by the same argument as above, that Fourier-Legendre series converge in the mean for all continuous functions.

Moreover, as in the case of Fourier series, it is not difficult to show that any Fourier-Legendre series with* $a_l \sim \Theta(l^n)$, where n is fixed, can be treated as a distribution. This is adequate for most physical applications.

From the point of view of the theory of distributions, the following formula holds:

$$\sum_{l=0}^{\infty} \frac{2l + 1}{2} P_l(x)P_l(x_0) = \delta(x - x_0).$$

Indeed, if both sides are multiplied by a test function $f(x)$ and integrated (with respect to x) from -1 to $+1$, the right-hand side reduces to $f(x_0)$. The left-hand side must be integrated term by term (according to the properties of distributions) and yields

$$\sum_{l=0}^{\infty} \frac{2l + 1}{2} P_l(x_0) \int_{-1}^{+1} f(x)P_l(x)\, dx = \sum_{l=0}^{\infty} a_l P_l(x_0).$$

Therefore, the left-hand side reduces to the Fourier-Legendre series for f which converges, in the usual sense, to $f(x_0)$. This establishes the quoted formula.

Example. Two conducting hemispherical shells of radius a are fitted together, but are insulated around their circle of contact. The hemispheres are kept at electrostatic potentials $+V$ and $-V$, respectively. Find the potential φ inside the sphere.†

Solution. Because of the geometry of conducting surfaces, the use of the spherical system is indicated. The distribution of potential φ possesses axial symmetry, and

---

* The notation $a_l \sim \Theta(l^n)$ means $|a_l| \leq Al^n$, where A is some constant, and is universally used in mathematical literature. For clarification of the statement, see p. 253.
† Compare this problem with the one in Section 8.3.

therefore, φ is a function of r and θ only. It must satisfy the Laplace PDE $\nabla^2\varphi = 0$ subject to the conditions that

$$\varphi(a,\theta) = \begin{cases} +V & (0 \le \theta < \pi/2), \\ -V & (\pi/2 < \theta \le \pi), \end{cases}$$

as well as the condition that it possess the gradient $(\mathbf{E} = -\mathrm{grad}\ \varphi)$ everywhere *in the interior* of the sphere.

Setting $\varphi(r,\theta) = R(r)\Theta(\theta)$ and separating the variables, we have

$$\frac{d}{d\theta}\left(\sin\theta\,\frac{d\Theta}{d\theta}\right) - \lambda\sin\theta\Theta = 0, \qquad \frac{d}{dr}\left(r^2\frac{dR}{dr}\right) + \lambda R = 0.$$

After setting $\cos\theta = x$, we find that the first equation becomes the Legendre DE and leads to Legendre polynomials as its solutions:

$$\Theta_l(\theta) = P_l(\cos\theta) \qquad (l = 0, 1, 2, \ldots).$$

The second equation, with $\lambda = -l(l+1)$, is the Euler DE

$$r^2\frac{d^2R}{dr^2} + 2r\frac{dR}{dr} - l(l+1)R = 0,$$

and the relevant solution (finite at $r = 0$) is $R_l(r) = r^l$. In this fashion we have particular solutions of the PDE of the form

$$\varphi_l(r_1\theta) = r^lP_l(\cos\theta) \qquad (l = 0, 1, 2, 3, \ldots).$$

We form an infinite series of these solutions,

$$\varphi(r_1\theta) = \sum_{l=0}^{\infty} A_l r^l P_l(\cos\theta),$$

and try to determine the coefficients A_l in such a way that $\varphi(r,\theta)$ satisfies the remaining boundary condition

$$\varphi(a,\theta) = \sum_{l=0}^{\infty} A_l a^l P_l(\cos\theta).$$

Obviously, this is a Fourier-Legendre series (with $\cos\theta$ replacing x). Instead of switching to the x-variable we may develop the necessary formulas directly in terms of the θ-variable.

Upon substituting $x = \cos\theta$,* we find that the orthogonality relation

$$\int_{-1}^{+1} P_l(x)P_{l'}(x)\,dx = \frac{2}{2l+1}\,\delta_{ll'}$$

---

* Note that we may say that functions $\Theta_l(\theta)$ are orthogonal with respect to the weight function $\sin\theta$; this, of course, follows from the Sturm-Liouville equation for $\Theta(\theta)$.

becomes

$$\int_0^\pi P_l(\cos \theta) P_{l'}(\cos \theta) \sin \theta \, d\theta = \frac{2}{2l + 1} \delta_{ll'}.$$

Consequently, if we multiply our series by $P_{l'}(\cos \theta) \sin \theta$ and integrate over θ from 0 to π, we obtain the desired Fourier-Legendre coefficients

$$A_l = \frac{1}{a^l} \frac{2l + 1}{2} \int_0^\pi \varphi(a, \theta) P_l(\cos \theta) \sin \theta \, d\theta.$$

For our particular function

$$\varphi(a, \theta) = \begin{cases} +V & (0 \le \theta < \pi/2), \\ -V & (\pi/2 < \theta \le \pi), \end{cases}$$

a symmetry argument is helpful: $\varphi(a, \theta)$ is antisymmetric with respect to the interchange*

$$\theta \leftrightarrow (\pi - \theta).$$

On the other hand, $\sin (\pi - \theta) = \sin \theta$ and $\cos (\pi - \theta) = -\cos \theta$, and since $P_l(\cos \theta)$ contains only odd powers of $\cos \theta$ if $l = $ odd, and only even powers of $\cos \theta$ if $l = $ even, it follows that

$$\int_0^\pi \varphi(a, \theta) P_l(\cos \theta) \sin \theta \, d\theta = 0 \quad \text{(for } l = \text{even)}$$

so that only odd polynomials will be present (compare with the example in Section 8.3). For odd values of l,

$$\int_0^\pi \varphi(a, \theta) P_l(\cos \theta) \sin \theta \, d\theta = 2V \int_0^{\pi/2} P_l(\cos \theta) \sin \theta \, d\theta.$$

We now need the integral

$$\int_0^{\pi/2} P_l(\cos \theta) \sin \theta \, d\theta = \int_0^1 P_l(x) \, dx.$$

Using the generating function

$$\frac{1}{\sqrt{1 - 2xt + t^2}} = \sum_{l=0}^\infty t^l P_l(x) \quad (|t| < 1)$$

and integrating both sides, we obtain

$$\int_0^1 \frac{dx}{\sqrt{1 - 2xt + t^2}} = \sum_{l=0}^\infty t^l \int_0^1 P_l(x) \, dx.$$

---

* This corresponds to the interchange $\cos \theta \leftrightarrow -\cos \theta$ which is, geometrically speaking, a reflection in the equatorial plane of the sphere.

Evaluating the left-hand side explicitly as

$$\int_0^1 \frac{dx}{\sqrt{1 - 2xt + t^2}} = 1 - \frac{1}{t} + \frac{\sqrt{1 + t^2}}{t},$$

utilizing the binomial formula

$$\sqrt{1 + t^2} = \sum_{k=0}^{\infty} \binom{\frac{1}{2}}{k} t^{2k} = \sum_{k=0}^{\infty} \frac{\Gamma(\frac{3}{2})}{\Gamma(k+1)\Gamma(\frac{3}{2} - k)} t^{2k},$$

and setting $2k - 1 = l$, we obtain

$$1 - \frac{1}{t} + \frac{\sqrt{1 + t^2}}{t} = 1 + \sum_{l=\text{odd}}^{\infty} \frac{\Gamma(\frac{3}{2})}{\Gamma(l/2 + \frac{3}{2})\Gamma(1 - l/2)} t^l,$$

so that

$$\int_0^1 P_l(x)\, dx = \frac{\Gamma(\frac{3}{2})}{\Gamma(\frac{3}{2} + l/2)\Gamma(1 - l/2)} \qquad (l = 1, 3, 5, \ldots)$$

and

$$A_l = \frac{1}{a^l} (2l + 1) V \frac{\Gamma(\frac{3}{2})}{\Gamma(\frac{3}{2} + l/2)\Gamma(1 - l/2)} \qquad (l = 1, 3, 5, \ldots).$$

The resulting series

$$\varphi(r, \theta) = V \sum_{l=1,3,5,\ldots}^{\infty} \left(\frac{r}{a}\right)^l \frac{(2l + 1)(\sqrt{\pi}/2)}{\Gamma[(3 + l)/2]\Gamma[(2 - l)/2]} P_l(\cos \theta)$$

is uniformly convergent for all $r \le r_1 < a$ (although if r_1 is close to a, the convergence is slow) and satisfies all conditions of the problem.

9.7 BESSEL FUNCTIONS

The study of the Helmholtz PDE in the cylindrical coordinate system led us to the Bessel DE

$$\frac{d^2y}{dx^2} + \frac{1}{x}\frac{dy}{dx} + \left(1 - \frac{m^2}{x^2}\right) y = 0.$$

The parameter m is very often an integer (see Section 8.2, Example 1) but sometimes this is not so. We shall study the general case where m is an arbitrary real number which can be considered to be nonnegative. To emphasize this, we shall adopt the label μ instead of m:*

$$\frac{d^2y}{dx^2} + \frac{1}{x}\frac{dy}{dx} + \left(1 - \frac{\mu^2}{x^2}\right) y = 0.$$

---

* We adopt the convention to denote arbitrary scalars by Greek letters, and (nonnegative) integers by Latin letters.

This is the Bessel DE of order μ. Its solutions are known as *cylindrical functions;* among these the best known ones are the Bessel functions.

Remark. If μ is fixed, then the Bessel DE does not appear to be an eigenvalue equation. Recall, however, that it may have arisen from (Section 9.2)

$$\frac{d^2R}{dr^2} + \frac{1}{r}\frac{dR}{dr} + \left(k^2 - \frac{\mu^2}{r^2}\right)R = 0,$$

which *is* an eigenvalue equation if k^2 is to be determined from the boundary conditions imposed on R. The eigenvalue has been "suppressed" by the substitution $x = kr$. We shall first study the cylindrical functions as functions of x and later return to the eigenvalue problem for the function $R(r)$.

Consider the solution of the Bessel DE in the form of a Frobenius series,

$$y(x) = \sum_{n=0}^{\infty} a_n x^{s+n}.$$

Rewrite the equation in the form

$$x^2 y'' + xy' + (x^2 - \mu^2)y = 0,$$

and substitute the series. The indicial equation reads

$$a_0(s^2 - \mu^2) = 0$$

and yields the roots $s = +\mu$ and $s = -\mu$. The recursion formula

$$a_n = -\frac{1}{(s + \mu + n)(s - \mu + n)} a_{n-2} \qquad (n \geq 2)$$

reduces for $s = \mu$ to the formula

$$a_n = -\frac{1}{(2\mu + n)n} a_{n-2} \qquad (n \geq 2),$$

and all even coefficients follow from a_0. For odd coefficients, the equation for a_1 is

$$a_1[(s + 1)^2 - \mu^2] = a_1(2\mu + 1) = 0;$$

this requires that $a_1 = 0$, which, in turn, implies that all odd coefficients vanish. The solution is an even function of x, multiplied by x^μ. For convenience, set $n = 2k$; then

$$a_{2k} = -\frac{1}{2^2 k(\mu + k)} a_{2k-2} \qquad (k \geq 1).$$

Apply this formula k times to express a_{2k} in terms of a_0:

$$a_{2k} = (-1)^k \frac{1}{2^{2k}k!(\mu + 1)(\mu + 2)\cdots(\mu + k)} a_0.$$

It is customary (and convenient) to standardize the solutions by choosing

$$a_0 = \frac{1}{2^\mu \Gamma(1 + \mu)}.$$

Now, use $\Gamma(\mu + 1)(\mu + 1)(\mu + 2) \cdots (\mu + k) = \Gamma(\mu + k + 1)$, and obtain an explicit series for the solution $y_1(x)$ which is denoted by $J_\mu(x)$ and called the *Bessel function of order* μ (of the first kind):

$$J_\mu(x) = \sum_{k=0}^{\infty} (-1)^k \frac{1}{k!\Gamma(\mu + k + 1)2^{\mu+2k}} x^{\mu+2k}.$$

The series converges for all values of x whatever μ happens to be (ratio test). If μ is an integer ($\mu = m$), then $J_m(x)$ is single valued, and the above series is a Maclaurin series. If μ is not an integer, then $J_\mu(x)$ has a branch point at the origin. The branches of $J_\mu(x)$ are determined by the branches of x^μ and their number may be finite (μ is rational) or infinite (μ is irrational). It is of interest to note that if μ is allowed to vary continuously, then $J_\mu(x)$ is a *continuous function of* μ for any fixed $x \neq 0$* (uniformly convergent series of continuous functions).

Now consider the second solution of the Bessel equation. The root $s = -\mu$ yields

$$a_1[(s + 1)^2 - \mu^2] = a_1(1 - 2\mu) = 0,$$

as well as

$$a_n = -\frac{1}{n(n - 2\mu)} a_{n-2} \qquad (n \geq 2).$$

It is immediately seen that some difficulties arise when (a) μ is an integer, and (b) μ is a *half-integer*.† However, let us first consider the case where μ is neither of the above. It then follows that $a_1 = 0$ and all odd coefficients vanish, while all even coefficients are well defined by the recurrence relation, giving rise to a solution which has the same form as $J_\mu(x)$ except that μ is replaced by $-\mu$. This solution is called the Bessel function (of the first kind) of order $-\mu$:

$$J_{-\mu}(x) = \sum_{k=0}^{\infty} (-1)^k \frac{1}{k!\Gamma(k - \mu + 1)2^{2k-\mu}} x^{2k-\mu}.$$

It can be seen that $J_{-\mu}(x)$ is linearly independent of $J_\mu(x)$ (the leading terms are x^μ and $x^{-\mu}$, respectively) and the general solution of the Bessel equation reads

$$y(x) = c_1 J_\mu(x) + c_2 J_{-\mu}(x) \qquad (\mu \neq \text{integer}, \ \mu \neq \text{half-integer}).$$

Consider now the case when μ is a half-integer. Then 2μ is an odd integer. The recurrence formula defines all even coefficients in terms of a_0, exactly as before.

---

* We could have written $J(\mu, x)$ but $J_\mu(x)$ is traditional.
† Namely $\frac{1}{2}, \frac{3}{2}, \frac{5}{2}, \ldots$ Rigorously speaking, we should say "one-half of an odd integer," but the above terminology is widespread among physicists.

However, it will break down for odd coefficients: While $a_1, a_3, a_5, \ldots, a_{2\mu-2}$ must be zero, this is not necessarily true for $a_{2\mu}$ (if $\mu = \frac{1}{2}$, this phenomenon arises immediately for a_1). However, there is nothing to prevent us from setting $a_{2\mu} = 0$ by *our own choice*. If this is done, then all subsequent odd coefficients must be zero and we can define $J_{-\mu}(x)$ by exactly the same formula as before. The obvious advantage of this choice is that $J_{-\mu}(x)$ remains a continuous function of μ as μ passes through a half-integer value. It is still true that $J_{-\mu}(x)$ is linearly independent of $J_\mu(x)$ and we still have the general solution

$$y(x) = c_1 J_\mu(x) + c_2 J_{-\mu}(x) \qquad (\mu = \text{half-integer}).$$

Finally, suppose that μ is an integer. We try again to preserve the continuity of $J_{-\mu}(x)$ with respect to μ. We can get rid of all odd coefficients as above, but we run into a difficulty defining the coefficient a_0. The reason is that $\Gamma(-\mu + 1) = \infty$ whenever μ is a positive integer.*

Of course, we could still abide by the formula for a_0 which implies

$$a_{2k} = (-1)^k \frac{1}{k!\Gamma(k - \mu + 1)2^{2k-\mu}},$$

provided we adopt the logical convention that $a_{2k} = 0$ for $k < \mu$ [because $\Gamma(k - \mu + 1)$ has a pole]. This device will preserve the formula for $J_{-\mu}(x)$, as well as the continuity of $J_{-\mu}(x)$ with respect to μ, but the summation will now in effect start from $k = m$:†

$$J_{-m}(x) = \sum_{k=m}^{\infty} (-1)^k \frac{1}{k!\Gamma(k - m + 1)2^{2k-m}} x^{-m+2k}.$$

Changing the dummy index by $k = k' + m$, we obtain

$$J_{-m}(x) = \sum_{k'=0}^{\infty} (-1)^{m+k'} \frac{1}{k'!\Gamma(k' + m + 1)2^{2k'+m}} x^{m+2k'}.$$

However, this is nothing else but $(-1)^m J_m(x)$. We conclude that in our attempt to preserve the continuity of $J_{-\mu}(x)$ we have unfortunately lost the linear independence of the solutions $J_\mu(x)$ and $J_{-\mu}(x)$.

This feature is due to the fact that when the roots of the indicial equation differ by an integer, one of the solutions of the Bessel DE may have logarithmic singularity (see Section 3.5, Example 4). Indeed, for the case of $\mu = m = \text{integer}$, the second solution may be sought (and obtained) in the form

$$y_2(x) = \log x \sum_{n=0}^{\infty} c_n x^{s+n} + \sum_{p=0}^{\infty} a_p x^{r+p}.$$

---

* If $\mu = 0$, then $J_\mu(x)$ is identical with $J_{-\mu}(x)$, and we must look for the second solution elsewhere.

† We now set $\mu = m$ in accord with our convention about Greek and Latin letters.

Depending on the standardization, such solutions are known as the Bessel functions of the second kind, denoted by $Y_m(x)$, or *Neumann functions*, denoted by $N_m(x)$.* We shall defer the treatment of these solutions to a later section; for the time being we shall develop some of the properties of $J_\mu(x)$-functions.

From the Frobenius series for $J_\mu(x)$, it follows that

$$J_\mu(x) = x^\mu f(x),$$

where $f(x)$ is an even function, analytic and nonvanishing at the origin. Therefore, $J_\mu(0) = 0$ except if $\mu = 0$, in which case, $J_0(0) = 1$.

The derivative of $f(x)$ reads

$$f'(x) = \left(\frac{J_\mu(x)}{x^\mu}\right)' = \sum_{k=1}^\infty (-1)^k \frac{1}{(k-1)!\Gamma(k+\mu+1)2^{2k+\mu}} x^{2k-1}$$

and can be related to $J_{\mu+1}(x)$: Replace k by $k+1$ and verify that

$$f'(x) = -\frac{J_{\mu+1}(x)}{x^\mu},$$

which establishes a useful formula:

$$\frac{d}{dx}\left[\frac{J_\mu(x)}{x^\mu}\right] = -\frac{J_{\mu+1}(x)}{x^\mu} \qquad (\mu \geq 0).$$

Similarly, it is not difficult to verify that

$$\frac{d}{dx}[x^\mu J_\mu(x)] = x^\mu J_{\mu-1}(x) \qquad (\mu \geq 1).$$

Combining these two relations, we establish the recurrence formulas

$$J_{\mu+1}(x) + J_{\mu-1}(x) = \frac{2\mu}{x} J_\mu(x)$$

$$J_{\mu+1}(x) - J_{\mu-1}(x) = -2\frac{dJ_\mu(x)}{dx} \qquad (\mu \geq 1).$$

It is now clear that many other recurrence relations, including the differentiation formula and ladder operations, can be established for Bessel functions.† The relationship

$$\frac{J_{\mu+1}(x)}{x^\mu} = -\frac{d}{dx}\left[\frac{J_\mu(x)}{x^\mu}\right] \qquad (\mu \geq 0)$$

---

* Some authors, however, use the symbol $Y_m(x)$ for Neumann functions.

† Note that they are valid for *all values of* μ and are not connected with any eigenvalue problems. The same is true for the solutions of the Legendre equation, although the proofs in Section 8.5 were applicable only for $l =$ integer (because of reliance on the generating function).

permits us to establish an interesting formula expressing $J_m(x)$ in terms of $J_0(x)$ [or, in general, $J_\mu(x)$ in terms of $J_{\mu-k}(x)$]. Dividing the above equation by x, we obtain

$$\frac{J_{\mu+1}(x)}{x^{\mu+1}} = -\frac{1}{x}\frac{d}{dx}\left[\frac{J_\mu(x)}{x^\mu}\right],$$

which shows "what to do" with $J_\mu(x)/x^\mu$ in order to obtain a similar ratio "one order higher," namely, $J_{\mu+1}(x)/x^{\mu+1}$. Starting with $\mu = 0$ and applying this rule m times, we obtain

$$\frac{J_m(x)}{x^m} = \left(-\frac{1}{x}\frac{d}{dx}\right)^m [J_0(x)], \quad \text{or} \quad J_m(x) = x^m\left(-\frac{1}{x}\frac{d}{dx}\right)^m J_0(x),$$

which means that the differential operator $-(1/x)(d/dx)$ is to be applied m times to $J_0(x)$, and the result is multiplied by x^m to yield $J_m(x)$. Observe the similarity to Rodrigues formula for $P_l(x)$, where a simpler differential operator, d/dx, is applied l times.

For Bessel functions of integral order there also exists a generating function of the form

$$e^{x(t-1/t)/2} = \sum_{m=-\infty}^{+\infty} t^m J_m(x) \qquad (t \neq 0).$$

Note that in this case the series on the right is not a Maclaurin series but rather a Laurent series in t. The above formula is often written in the form (set $t = e^{i\theta}$)

$$e^{ix\sin\theta} = \sum_{m=-\infty}^{+\infty} e^{im\theta} J_m(x),$$

where the series on the right is now a (complex) Fourier series for the function $e^{ix\sin\theta}$.

To discuss the orthogonality property of Bessel functions, we shall go back to the separation of the Helmholtz equation in cylindrical coordinates (Section 9.2). For simplicity, suppose that $\varphi(r, \theta, z)$ is independent of z. Then $\nabla^2\varphi + k^2\varphi = 0$ separates into

$$\frac{d^2\Theta}{d\theta^2} - \lambda_2\Theta = 0$$

and

$$\frac{d}{dr}\left(r\frac{dR}{dr}\right) + \left(k^2 r + \frac{\lambda_2}{r}\right) R = 0.$$

In most cases, $\lambda_2 = -m^2$ $(m = 0, 1, 2, \ldots)$ so that $R(r)$ satisfies

$$\frac{d}{dr}\left(r\frac{dR}{dr}\right) + \left(k^2 r - \frac{m^2}{r}\right) R = 0.$$

If the boundary conditions are imposed on $R(r)$, then this equation becomes an eigenvalue equation with the eigenvalue k^2 (note that m^2 is understood to be already determined). This is an equation of the Sturm-Liouville type. Some of the most common physical conditions will demand that

a) at $r = 0$, $R(r)$ must be finite, and
b) at $r = a$, $R(r)$ must satisfy

$$R(a) = 0 \quad \text{(Dirichlet)} \qquad \text{or} \qquad \left.\frac{dR}{dr}\right|_{r=a} = 0 \quad \text{(Neumann)},$$

or

$$AR + B\frac{dR}{dr}\bigg|_{r=a} = 0 \quad \text{(intermediate boundary conditions)}.$$

From the discussion in Section 9.3, it follows that conditions (a) and (b) guarantee the orthogonality of the functions $R_k(r)$ (with respect to the weight function r) over the interval $0 \leq r \leq a$.

In terms of Bessel functions, the above boundary conditions imply that only the $J_m(kr)$-solution is admissible [$N_m(kr)$ is not finite at $r = 0$] and the parameter k must be obtained from

$$J_m(ka) = 0,$$

$$kJ'_m(ka) = 0, \qquad \text{where } J'_m(x) = (d/dx)J_m(x),$$

or

$$AJ_m(ka) + BkJ'_m(ka) = 0.$$

All Bessel functions (of the first kind) have oscillatory character and possess an infinite number of roots. Let the nontrivial* roots of $J_m(x)$ be denoted by α_{mn} ($n = 1, 2, 3, \ldots$). They are listed in tables of Bessel functions. The appropriate values of k for Dirichlet conditions are then

$$k_{mn} = \alpha_{mn}/a \qquad (m = 0, 1, 2, \ldots, n = 1, 2, 3, \ldots).$$

For Neumann conditions we must solve the equation (note that $k \neq 0$)

$$\frac{d}{dx}J_m(x)\bigg|_{x=ka} = 0.$$

The roots of $J'_m(x)$ are also tabulated. Denoting them by β_{mn}, we obtain

$$k_{mn} = \beta_{mn}/a \qquad (m = 0, 1, 2, \ldots, n = 1, 2, \ldots).$$

For the intermediate boundary conditions, the roots of the equation

$$AJ_m(ka) + BkJ'_m(ka) = 0$$

cannot be expected to be, in general, listed, since A and B are arbitrary, but they can be calculated, if necessary, by numerical analysis.

---

* $x = 0$ is always a root of $J_m(x)$ [except for $m = 0$ where $J_0(0) = 1$]. This root is of no interest in the case of Dirichlet conditions.

In this fashion, in all three considered cases, we obtain an infinite set of mutually orthogonal eigenfunctions

$$R_k(r) = J_m(k_{mn}r)$$

and we expect to be able* to expand any (reasonably well-behaved) function $f(r)$ in terms of the series

$$f(r) = \sum_{n=1}^{\infty} a_n J_m(k_{mn}r),$$

known as the *Fourier-Bessel series of order m*. To obtain the coefficients a_n, we may multiply both sides by $rJ_m(k_{mn'}r)$ and integrate over r from 0 to a; by orthogonality

$$\int_0^a f(r)rJ_m(k_{mn'}r)\, dr = a_{n'} \int_0^a r[J_m(k_{mn'}r)]^2\, dr,$$

so that

$$a_{n'} = \frac{\int_0^a f(r)rJ_m(k_{mn'}r)\, dr}{\int_0^a r[J_m(k_{mn'}r)]^2\, dr}.$$

It is desirable to evaluate, once and for all, the normalization integral

$$N_{n'} = \int_0^a r[J_m(k_{mn'}r)]^2\, dr.$$

For this purpose, let us recall the equation

$$\frac{d}{dr}\left(r\frac{dR}{dr}\right) - \frac{m^2}{r}R = -k^2 rR.$$

We replace $R(r)$ by $J_m(kr)$ and write it twice, once for $k = k_{mn}$, so that $J_m(k_{mn}r)$ *does satisfy* the boundary conditions, and the second time for *arbitrary k*, so that $J_m(kr)$ *does not need to satisfy* the boundary conditions:

$$\frac{d}{dr}\left[r\frac{d}{dr}J_m(k_{mn}r)\right] - \frac{m^2}{r}J_m(k_{mn}r) = -k_{mn}^2 rJ_m(k_{mn}r),$$

$$\frac{d}{dr}\left[r\frac{d}{dr}J_m(kr)\right] - \frac{m^2}{r}J_m(kr) = -k^2 rJ_m(kr).$$

We now multiply the equations by $J_m(kr)$ and $J_m(k_{mn}r)$, respectively, subtract, and integrate over $(0, a)$. Employing integration by parts on the left-hand side, we obtain

$$rJ_m(kr)\frac{d}{dr}J_m(k_{mn}r) - rJ_m(k_{mn}r)\frac{d}{dr}J_m(kr)\bigg|_0^a = (k^2 - k_{mn}^2)\int_0^a rJ_m(k_{mn}r)J_m(kr)\, dr.$$

---

* By analogy with the case of Fourier and Fourier-Legendre series.

Now suppose that the boundary conditions are Dirichlet conditions. Then this relation reduces to

$$aJ_m(ka)k_{mn}J_m'(k_{mn}a) = (k^2 - k_{mn}^2)\int_0^a rJ_m(k_{mn}r)J_m(kr)\, dr.$$

This is still *valid for all* k. Differentiating this expression with respect to k,* we obtain

$$aaJ_m'(ka)k_{mn}J_m'(k_{mn}a) = 2k\int_0^a rJ_m(k_{mn}r)J_m(kr)\, dr$$

$$+ (k^2 - k_{mn}^2)\int_0^a rJ_m(k_{mn}r)rJ_m'(kr)\, dr.$$

Let *now* $k \to k_{mn}$. The last term vanishes and we obtain

$$\int_0^a r[J_m(k_{mn}r)]^2\, dr = \frac{a^2}{2}[J_m'(k_{mn}a)]^2,$$

which is the desired normalization integral for the Dirichlet conditions. Other boundary conditions can be treated in a similar fashion.

The above normalization integral (for Dirichlet conditions) can be cast into a form more suitable for actual calculations. [Tables of Bessel functions do not usually list the derivatives of $J_m(x)$.] From the recursion relations on p. 359, it also follows that†

$$\left.\begin{array}{l} \dfrac{dJ_\mu(x)}{dx} = J_{\mu-1}(x) - \dfrac{\mu}{x}J_\mu(x) \\[3mm] \dfrac{dJ_\mu(x)}{dx} = -J_{\mu+1}(x) + \dfrac{\mu}{x}J_\mu(x) \end{array}\right\}\quad (\mu \geq 1).$$

Consequently, if α is a root of $J_\mu(x)$, we have

$$\frac{dJ_\mu(\alpha)}{dx} = J_{\mu-1}(\alpha) = -J_{\mu+1}(\alpha)$$

so that the normalization integral can be written as

$$\int_0^a r[J_m(k_{mn}r)]^2\, dr = \frac{a^2}{2}[J_{m+1}(k_{mn}a)]^2,$$

where k_{mn} is a root of $J_m(ka) = 0$.

Several Bessel functions of integral orders are represented in Fig. 9.2.

Example 1. *Free vibrations of a circular membrane.* It has been shown in Section 8.8 that the free vibrations of a rectangular membrane are described by the

---

* The functions $J_m(kr)$ are analytic with respect to the parameter k.

† These are the differentiation formulas for Bessel functions.

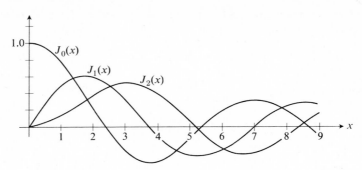

Bessel functions   **Figure 9.2**

wave equation

$$\frac{\partial^2 u}{\partial x^2} + \frac{\partial^2 u}{\partial y^2} = \frac{1}{c^2} \frac{\partial^2 u}{\partial t^2} \qquad \left(c^2 = \frac{T}{\mu} \right).$$

The derivation is valid for a membrane of any shape, but for a circular membrane the polar coordinate system should be used so that the equation becomes

$$\frac{1}{r} \frac{\partial}{\partial r} \left(r \frac{\partial u}{\partial r} \right) + \frac{1}{r^2} \frac{\partial^2 u}{\partial \theta^2} = \frac{1}{c^2} \frac{\partial^2 u}{\partial t^2}.$$

We shall consider a membrane clamped at the boundary, so that $u(r, \theta; t)$ satisfies the Dirichlet boundary conditions:

$$u(a, \theta; t) = 0,$$

where a is the radius of the membrane. The initial conditions consist in the specification of the (transverse) displacements and velocities at $t = 0$:

$$u(r, \theta; 0) = u_0(r, \theta), \qquad \frac{\partial u}{\partial t}(r, \theta; 0) = v_0(r, \theta).$$

We set $u = R\Theta T$ and separate the variables:

$$\frac{d^2 T}{dt^2} = \lambda c^2 T, \qquad \frac{d^2 \Theta}{d\theta^2} = \lambda_1 \Theta,$$

$$\frac{d^2 R}{dr^2} + \frac{1}{r} \frac{dR}{dr} + \left(-\lambda + \frac{\lambda_1}{r^2} \right) R = 0.$$

The functions $T(t)$ are trigonometric or exponential. We reject the latter on physical grounds, so that $\lambda \leq 0$.* We set $\lambda = -k^2$ and $kc = \omega$. Instead of using real trigonometric functions, we may represent $T(t)$ in the form

$$T_\omega(t) = e^{-i\omega t}$$

---

* One can show that the boundary conditions cannot be satisfied anyway if $\lambda > 0$.

with the provision that ω may be either positive or negative. This form is very compact and incorporates both cos ωt and sin ωt. Moreover, the usual periodicity argument requires that

$$\lambda_1 = -m^2 \qquad (m = 0, 1, 2, \ldots),$$

leading to the functions*

$$\Theta_m(\theta) = A_m \cos m\theta + B_m \sin m\theta.$$

The radial equation now reads

$$\frac{d^2R}{dr^2} + \frac{1}{r}\frac{dR}{dr} + \left(k^2 - \frac{m^2}{r^2}\right)R = 0 \qquad (m = 0, 1, 2, \ldots).$$

Its general solution is†

$$R(r) = C_1 J_m(kr) + C_2 N_m(kr).$$

Since Neumann functions $N_m(x)$ are not finite at $x = 0$, they must be rejected (by choosing $C_2 = 0$). The boundary condition at $r = a$ requires that

$$J_m(ka) = 0 \qquad (m = 0, 1, 2, \ldots).$$

This equation determines the eigenvalues k of the problem. In terms of zeros of Bessel functions, we have

$$k_{mn} = \alpha_{mn}/a \qquad (m = 0, 1, 2, \ldots, n = 1, 2, 3, \ldots).$$

The first four roots of the first five Bessel functions are given in Table 9.1.

We can now write the entire solution of our problem in the form of a double series. Because the solution must be real, the coefficients with $e^{i\omega t}$ and $e^{-i\omega t}$

Table 9.1

	$n = 1$	$n = 2$	$n = 3$	$n = 4$
$m = 0$	2.404	5.520	8.654	11.792
$m = 1$	3.832	7.016	10.173	13.323
$m = 2$	5.135	8.417	11.620	14.796
$m = 3$	6.379	9.760	13.017	16.224
$m = 4$	7.586	11.064	14.373	17.616

---

* There appears to be no advantage in the complex representation $e^{\pm im\theta}$ because some problems with the notation arise later.

† Neumann functions $N_m(x)$ were mentioned on p. 359.

must be complex conjugates of each other, and we have

$$u(r, \theta; t) = \sum_{m=0}^{\infty} \sum_{n=1}^{\infty} J_m\left(\alpha_{mn}\frac{r}{a}\right)[(A_{mn}e^{i\omega_{mn}t} + A_{mn}^*e^{-i\omega_{mn}t})\cos m\theta$$
$$+ (B_{mn}e^{i\omega_{mn}t} + B_{mn}^*e^{-i\omega_{mn}t})\sin m\theta],$$

where $\omega_{mn} = ck_{mn} = \alpha_{mn}(c/a)$. The coefficients A_{mn} and B_{mn} now follow from the initial conditions: Set $t = 0$; then

$$u_0(r, \theta) = \sum_{m=0}^{\infty} \sum_{n=1}^{\infty} J_m\left(\alpha_{mn}\frac{r}{a}\right)[(A_{mn} + A_{mn}^*)\cos m\theta + (B_{mn} + B_{mn}^*)\sin m\theta].$$

This expression is evidently a Fourier-Bessel series in r, as well as a Fourier series in θ. To determine $A_{m'n'}$, we multiply both sides by

$$r J_{m'}\left(\alpha_{m'n'}\frac{r}{a}\right)\cos m'\theta$$

and integrate over r from 0 to a, and over θ from 0 to 2π. Because of orthogonality of trigonometric functions, only the cosine terms with $m = m'$ will survive on the right-hand side, with the normalization constant

$$\int_0^{2\pi} \cos^2 m'\theta \, d\theta = \begin{cases} \pi & \text{if } m' \neq 0, \\ 2\pi & \text{if } m' = 0. \end{cases}$$

Furthermore, because of the orthogonality of Bessel functions, only the terms with $n = n'$ will survive on the right-hand side, with the normalization constant

$$\int_0^a r\left[J_{m'}\left(\alpha_{m'n'}\frac{r}{a}\right)\right]^2 dr = \frac{a^2}{2}[J_{m'+1}(\alpha_{m'n'})]^2.$$

Consequently, we obtain the expression

$$\int_0^a \int_0^{2\pi} u_0(r, \theta)\cos m\theta \cdot rJ_m\left(\alpha_{mn}\frac{r}{a}\right) dr \, d\theta = \frac{\pi a^2}{2}[J_{m+1}(\alpha_{mn})]^2(A_{mn} + A_{mn}^*)$$
$$(\text{if } m \neq 0)$$

and a similar expression with an additional factor of 2 on the right if $m = 0$.

It is seen that A_{mn} is not yet completely determined (only its real part follows from the above formula). This is not unexpected since we have not used the second initial condition. Differentiating $u(r, \theta; t)$ with respect to t and then setting $t = 0$, we obtain

$$v_0(r, \theta) = \sum_{m=0}^{\infty} \sum_{n=1}^{\infty} J_m\left(\alpha_{mn}\frac{r}{a}\right)i\omega_{mn}[(A_{mn} - A_{mn}^*)\cos m\theta + (B_{mn} - B_{mn}^*)\sin m\theta].$$

By the same technique as before, we can deduce that

$$\int_0^a \int_0^{2\pi} v_0(r, \theta) \cos m\theta \cdot rJ_m\left(\alpha_{mn}\frac{r}{a}\right) dr\, d\theta = i\frac{\pi a^2}{2} \omega_{mn}[J_{m+1}(\alpha_{mn})]^2(A_{mn} - A_{mn}^*)$$

$$\text{(if } m \neq 0\text{),}$$

and similarly for $m = 0$ (with the factor 2). Now the coefficients A_{mn} can be calculated and expressed by the formulas

$$A_{mn} = \frac{\int_0^a \int_0^{2\pi} \left[u_0(r, \theta) - \frac{i}{\omega_{mn}} v_0(r, \theta)\right] \cos m\theta \cdot rJ_m\left(\alpha_{mn}\frac{r}{a}\right) dr\, d\theta}{\pi a^2[J_{m+1}(\alpha_{mn})]^2} \qquad (m \neq 0),$$

$$A_{0n} = \frac{\int_0^a \int_0^{2\pi} \left[u_0(r, \theta) - \frac{i}{\omega_{0n}} v_0(r, \theta)\right] rJ_0\left(\alpha_{0n}\frac{r}{a}\right) dr\, d\theta}{2\pi a^2[J_1(\alpha_{0n})]^2} \qquad (m = 0),$$

where $\omega_{mn} = ck_{mn} = \alpha_{mn}(c/a)$, all m.

The coefficients B_{mn} are evaluated in a similar fashion. It is easy to check that we need only to replace $\cos m\theta$ by $\sin n\theta$ in the formula for A_{mn} (note that the case $m = 0$ is now absent).

A few words may now be in order regarding the physical interpretation of the results. The frequencies

$$\omega_{mn} = \alpha_{mn}(c/a) \qquad (m = 0, 1, 2, \ldots, n = 1, 2, \ldots)$$

are the *natural frequencies* of the membrane and each term in the double series represents a *natural mode of vibration*.† Each frequency has two corresponding modes, one with $\cos m\theta$ and the other with $\sin m\theta$, exhibiting a *twofold* degeneracy. The exceptions are the cases where $m = 0$, representing the modes possessing radial symmetry. They are *nondegenerate*.‡

The natural modes possess their characteristic patterns of nodal lines (compare with Section 8.8, pp. 317–318). Some of these patterns are sketched below (Fig. 9.3), and their frequencies are given in terms of the fundamental frequency $\omega_{01} \cong 2.40(c/a)$.

The natural modes of vibration create a very convenient tool for the analysis of an arbitrary motion of the membrane. Suppose, for instance, that the initial distribution of displacements and velocities exhibits radial symmetry,§

$$u_0 = u_0(r), \qquad v_0 = v_0(r).$$

Then it follows from the formula for A_{mn} and B_{mn} that only the terms with $m = 0$

---

† Very often called *normal mode of vibration*.

‡ More rigorously speaking, the *frequencies* (eigenvalues) ω_{0n} are nondegenerate.

§ Or *invariance with respect to rotations* in a more sophisticated language.

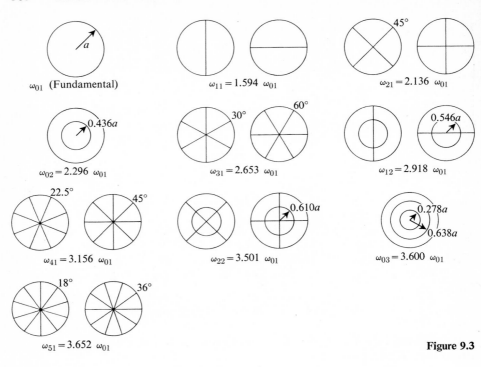

ω_{01} (Fundamental) $\omega_{11} = 1.594\ \omega_{01}$ $\omega_{21} = 2.136\ \omega_{01}$

$\omega_{02} = 2.296\ \omega_{01}$ $\omega_{31} = 2.653\ \omega_{01}$ $\omega_{12} = 2.918\ \omega_{01}$

$\omega_{41} = 3.156\ \omega_{01}$ $\omega_{22} = 3.501\ \omega_{01}$ $\omega_{03} = 3.600\ \omega_{01}$

$\omega_{51} = 3.652\ \omega_{01}$

Figure 9.3

will be present in the solution, which can now be represented by a single (Fourier-Bessel) series:

$$u(r,\ t) = \sum_{n=1}^{\infty} J_0\left(\alpha_{0n}\frac{r}{a}\right)[A_{0n}e^{i\omega_{0n}t} + A_{0n}^{*}e^{-i\omega_{0n}t}].$$

In general, a given mode will be absent from the (double) series for $u(r,\ \theta;\ t)$ provided the initial distributions $u_0(r,\ \theta)$ and $v_0(r,\ \theta)$ are *orthogonal* to the corresponding mode. In other words, the modes which are not present in the initial state of motion (given by u_0 and v_0) are not "excited" at any later time. In the language of physics, the modes are "independent of each other" in the sense that there is no exchange of energy between individual modes.

Example 2. The lateral surface of a very long steel cylinder of radius $b = 10\ \mathrm{cm}$ is kept at constant temperature $u_1 = 100°\mathrm{C}$. Initially the cylinder is at a uniform temperature, $u_0 = 500°\mathrm{C}$. It is desired to calculate the temperature at the center of the cylinder and the rate at which the cylinder loses heat in cal/cm · sec (per unit length) at the time $t = 4\ \mathrm{min}$.

Solution. Approximate the solution by considering an infinite cylinder. The temperature u inside will be a function of r and t only† and must satisfy the PDE

---

† The initial temperature distribution has axial symmetry.

(in cylindrical coordinates)

$$\frac{1}{r} \frac{\partial}{\partial r} \left(r \frac{\partial u}{\partial r} \right) = \frac{1}{a^2} \frac{\partial u}{\partial t}$$

subject to the boundary condition $u(b, t) = u_1$, and to the initial condition $u(r, 0) = u_0$.

For steel, $a^2 = k/cp = 0.126 \text{ cm}^2/\text{sec}$ (see Section 8.4). According to the method of separation of variables, we seek solutions of the PDE of the form

$$u(r, t) = R(r)T(t).$$

Then

$$\frac{d}{dr} \left(r \frac{dR}{dr} \right) + \lambda r R = 0, \qquad \frac{dT}{dt} = -a^2 \lambda T.$$

The separation constant λ should be determined from the boundary conditions applied to the function $R(r)$. A complication arises from the fact that the boundary condition is *nonhomogeneous*. We expect to build up our solution in the form of a series,

$$u(r, t) = \sum_{\lambda} A_\lambda R_\lambda(r) T_\lambda(t)$$

(over allowed values λ), but it is not clear what condition we should impose on *each individual* function $R_\lambda(r)$.

Fortunately, the problem resolves itself by the fact that $u_1 = \text{const}$ is *also a solution* of the PDE, and we can write

$$u(r, t) = u_1 + \sum_{\lambda} A_\lambda R_\lambda(r) T_\lambda(t),$$

demanding now that *all $R_\lambda(r)$ vanish* at $r = b$. This ensures that the entire series will vanish at $r = b$ and the solution $u(r, t)$ will satisfy the BC

$$u(b, t) = u_1.$$

Having fixed the boundary conditions, we may expect to be able to determine the A_λ so that the initial condition is satisfied and the problem will be solved.

Remark. Another way of looking at this idea is to realize that we can shift the origin of the temperature scale without affecting the validity of the heat conduction equations. Instead of using the centigrade scale, we can employ a new scale with "zero" at 100°C. Then we can solve the problem in the new scale and at the end we can switch back to the centigrade scale.

The equation for $T(t)$, coupled with the second law of thermodynamics, requires that λ be nonnegative. For $\lambda = 0$, the radial equation

$$\frac{d^2 R}{dr^2} + \frac{1}{r} \frac{dR}{dr} + \lambda R = 0$$

has the solution $R_0 = A_0 + B_0 \log r$, which is not acceptable since $B_0 \log r$ is not finite at $r = 0$, and A_0 does not vanish at $r = b$.* Consequently, $\lambda > 0$. Setting $\lambda = k^2$, $x = kr$, and reducing the radial equation to the Bessel DE of order zero, we have

$$\frac{d^2y}{dx^2} + \frac{1}{x}\frac{dy}{dx} + y = 0,$$

where $y(x) = R(r)$. The relevant solution is $J_0(x)$ [$N_0(x)$ is not finite at $r = 0$], and the eigenvalues λ_n follow from the Dirichlet condition

$$J_0(kb) = 0,$$

yielding

$$\lambda_n = k_{0n}^2 = \frac{\alpha_{0n}^2}{b^2} \quad (n = 1, 2, 3, \ldots).$$

Solving the equation for $T(t)$ we obtain the series

$$u(r, t) = u_1 + \sum_{n=1}^{\infty} A_n J_0\left(\alpha_{0n}\frac{r}{b}\right) e^{-(\alpha_{0n}^2 a^2/b^2)t}.$$

It remains for us to satisfy the initial condition

$$u_0 = u_1 + \sum_{n=1}^{\infty} A_n J_0\left(\alpha_{0n}\frac{r}{b}\right).$$

This is a Fourier-Bessel series (of order zero) for the function

$$f(r) = u_0 - u_1 = \text{const.}$$

Therefore

$$A_n = \frac{2(u_0 - u_1)\displaystyle\int_0^b J_0\left(\alpha_{0n}\frac{r}{b}\right) r\, dr}{b^2[J_1(\alpha_{0n})]^2}.$$

The integral

$$\int_0^b J_0\left(\alpha_{0n}\frac{r}{b}\right) r\, dr = \frac{b^2}{\alpha_{0n}^2}\int_0^{\alpha_{0n}} J_0(z)z\, dz$$

can be evaluated explicitly. One way of evaluating it is to utilize the formula (see p. 359)

$$\frac{d}{dx}[xJ_1(x)] = xJ_0(x).$$

This immediately yields $\int_0^x J_0(z)z\, dz = xJ_1(x)$, so that

$$A_n = \frac{2(u_0 - u_1)}{\alpha_{0n}J_1(\alpha_{0n})},$$

---

* The solution $R(r) = $ const, which multiplies $T(t) = $ const, yields the constant solution of the PDE. We already have one, $u = u_1 = $ const, and we do not need any more.

and the solution reads

$$u(r, t) = u_1 + 2(u_0 - u_1) \sum_{n=1}^{\infty} \frac{J_0(\alpha_{0n} r/b) e^{-(\alpha_{0n}^2 a^2/b^2)t}}{\alpha_{0n} J_1(\alpha_{0n})}.$$

Using $J_0(0) = 1$, we find that the temperature at the center of the cylinder is given by

$$u(0, t) = u_1 + 2(u_0 - u_1) = \sum_{n=1}^{\infty} \frac{e^{-(\alpha_{0n}^2 a^2/b^2)t}}{\alpha_{0n} J_1(\alpha_{0n})}.$$

This series converges very rapidly for large t. The tables of Bessel functions* yield

$$\alpha_{01} \cong 2.40, \qquad \alpha_{02} \cong 5.52,$$

and

$$J_1(2.40) \cong 0.52, \qquad J_1(5.52) \cong -0.34.$$

Evidently, the ratio of the first two terms in the series is determined by the factor

$$\exp\left[-\frac{(\alpha_{02}^2 - \alpha_{01}^2)a^2}{b^2} t\right].$$

The exponent is

$$\frac{(5.52^2 - 2.40^2) \times 0.126 \times 4 \times 60}{10^2} \cong 7.5.$$

Since $e^{-7.5} \cong 0.0005$, it follows that the second term can be neglected. For $t = 4$ min, the first term yields

$$\frac{\alpha_{01}^2 a^2 t}{b^2} = \frac{2.40^2 \times 0.126 \times 4 \times 60}{100} \cong 1.75,$$

so that the sought temperature is

$$u = 100 + 2 \times 400 \times \frac{e^{-1.75}}{2.4 \times 0.52} = 212°C.$$

The rate of flow of heat at any given point (per unit area and unit time) is given by the heat current density (see p. 298)

$$\mathbf{q} = -k \operatorname{grad} u,$$

where k = heat conductivity = 0.11 cal/cm · sec · deg for steel.

In our case, grad u at $r = b$ is normal to the surface and $|\operatorname{grad} u| = \partial u/\partial r$. Using $J_0'(x) = -J_1(x)$, we obtain from the series for u:

$$q\big|_{r=b} = \frac{2k(u_0 - u_1)}{b} \sum_{n=1}^{\infty} e^{-(\alpha_{0n}^2 a^2/b^2)t}.$$

---

* For example, Jahnke and Emde, *Tables of Higher Functions*.

Multiplying by $2\pi b$, we obtain the desired loss of heat per unit length of the cylinder:

$$Q = 4\pi k(u_0 - u_1) \sum_{n=1}^{\infty} e^{-(\alpha_{0n}^2 a^2/b^2)t}.$$

It is again obvious that only the first term of the series needs to be considered, yielding

$$Q = 4\pi \times 0.11 \times 400 \times e^{-1.75} = 96 \text{ cal/cm} \cdot \text{sec}.$$

9.8 ASSOCIATED LEGENDRE FUNCTIONS AND SPHERICAL HARMONICS

The wave equation

$$\nabla^2 \varphi = \frac{1}{c^2} \frac{\partial^2 \varphi}{\partial t^2}$$

can be separated out in the spherical coordinate system, giving rise to the following four ordinary differential equations (see Section 9.1):

$$\frac{d^2 T}{dt^2} - \lambda c^2 T = 0, \qquad \frac{d^2 \Phi}{d\phi^2} - \lambda_1 \Phi = 0,$$

$$\frac{d}{d\theta}\left(\sin\theta \frac{d\Theta}{d\theta}\right) + \left(-\sin\theta\lambda_2 + \frac{\lambda_1}{\sin\theta}\right)\Theta = 0,$$

$$\frac{d}{dr}\left(r^2 \frac{dR}{dr}\right) + (-\lambda r^2 + \lambda_2)R = 0.$$

In most practical cases the solution is expected to vary harmonically in time. This implies

$$T(t) = e^{-i\omega t}$$

so that $\lambda = -\omega^2/c^2 = -k^2$. Also, if periodicity over the angle ϕ is required, we have

$$\lambda_1 = -m^2 \qquad (m = 0, 1, 2, \ldots),$$

and the functions $\Phi(\phi)$ are trigonometric (or complex exponential). Then the equation for $\Theta(\theta)$ becomes

$$\frac{d}{d\theta}\left(\sin\theta \frac{d\Theta}{d\theta}\right) + \left(-\lambda_2 \sin\theta - \frac{m^2}{\sin\theta}\right)\Theta = 0.$$

We shall again make the customary change of variables (see Section 9.2), $x = \cos\theta$, and reduce this equation to the form [setting $y(x) \equiv \Theta(\theta)$]

$$\frac{d}{dx}\left[(1 - x^2)\frac{dy}{dx}\right] + \left(-\lambda_2 - \frac{m^2}{1 - x^2}\right)y = 0.$$

This equation is known as the *associated Legendre equation*. It becomes an eigenvalue equation for λ_2 if we require that the solution be finite at the singular points*
$x = \pm 1$. A convenient method of investigating the eigenfunctions is to determine, first, their behavior at these points. For this purpose, we translate the origin to $x = 1$ by introducing a new independent variable

$$z = 1 - x.$$

Then the DE transforms into

$$z(2 - z)\frac{d^2y}{dz^2} + 2(1 - z)\frac{dy}{dz} + \left[-\lambda_2 - \frac{m^2}{z(2 - z)}\right]y = 0.$$

Now try a Frobenius series,

$$y(z) = z^s \sum_{k=0}^{\infty} a_k z^k.$$

Actually we can simply set $y(z) = z^s u(z)$, where $u(z)$ is a function which is analytic and does not vanish at $z = 0$. Substitution yields the roots of the indicial equation as $s = \pm m/2$. For our present purposes we can treat m as a nonnegative integer (since only m^2 enters the DE). Only the root $s = +m/2$ is acceptable, and we conclude that our eigenfunctions must be of the form

$$y(x) = (1 - x)^{m/2} f(x),$$

where $f(x)$ is a function analytic and nonvanishing at $x = 1$.
   The investigation of the behavior of $y(x)$ near $x = -1$ can be carried out by means of the substitution $z = 1 + x$ and reveals that

$$y(x) = (1 + x)^{m/2} g(x),$$

where $g(x)$ is a function which is analytic and does not vanish at $x = -1$. Consequently, the acceptable solution $y(x)$ must be of the form

$$y(x) = (1 - x^2)^{m/2} u(x),$$

where $u(x)$ should be analytic over the entire complex x-plane (excluding the point at infinity, of course).†
   The advantage of this technique (compare with Section 3.6) is that the DE satisfied by $u(x)$ is somewhat simpler. It reads

$$(1 - x^2)\frac{d^2u}{dx^2} - 2(m + 1)x\frac{du}{dx} - (\lambda_2 + m + m^2)u = 0 \qquad (m \geq 0).$$

---

* See Fuchs' theorem on p. 146.
† This follows from the fact that $y(x)$ can have no other singularities except at $x = \pm 1$ (and, possibly, at $x = \infty$).

A Frobenius series (about the origin),

$$u(x) = \sum_{n=0}^{\infty} a_n x^{s+n},$$

leads to the recursion formula

$$a_{n+2} = \frac{n(n-1) + 2(m+1)n + \lambda_2 + m(m+1)}{(n+1)(n+2)} a_n \qquad (n \geq 0).$$

As in the case of the Legendre equation,* an analysis of this formula (Section 3.5, Example 3) shows that the series for $u(x)$ will diverge at $|x| = 1$ unless the series terminates; this happens if

$$n(n-1) + 2(m+1)n + \lambda_2 + m(m+1) = 0.$$

Solving for λ_2, we obtain

$$\lambda_2 = -(m+n)(m+n+1),$$

which means that (1) λ_2 is of the form $-l(l+1)$, where l is an integer *not smaller than* m, and (2) the series will terminate after the $(l-m)$-term.

The solutions $u(x)$ are, therefore, polynomials in x. Their explicit form can be obtained from the recursion formula. It turns out that they are multiples of the derivatives of the Legendre polynomials $P_l(x)$. Indeed, let us write down the Legendre DE

$$(1 - x^2)y'' - 2xy' + l(l+1)y = 0$$

and differentiate it m times. A bit of reflection shows us that, in general,

$$\frac{d^m}{dx^m}[xf(x)] = x\frac{d^m f}{dx^m} + m\frac{d^{m-1}f}{dx^{m-1}},$$

and

$$\frac{d^m}{dx^m}[(1 - x^2)g(x)] = (1 - x^2)\frac{d^m g}{dx^m} - 2mx\frac{d^{m-1}g}{dx^{m-1}} - m(m-1)\frac{d^{m-2}g}{dx^{m-2}},$$

so that the equation becomes [identify $y'' = g$; $y' = f$]

$$(1 - x^2)\left(\frac{d^m y}{dx^m}\right)'' - 2(m+1)x\left(\frac{d^m y}{dx^m}\right)'$$

$$+ [l(l+1) - 2m - m(m-1)]\left(\frac{d^m y}{dx^m}\right) = 0.$$

However, this is exactly the equation for $u(x)$. Therefore

$$u(x) = C\frac{d^m P_l(x)}{dx^m},$$

---

* The Legendre equation is, of course, a special case of the associated Legendre equation, namely, when $m = 0$.

where C is an arbitrary constant.* It is customary to standardize the solutions by choosing $C = 1$. This leads to the eigenfunctions of the associated Legendre equation in the form

$$P_l^m(x) = (1 - x^2)^{m/2} \frac{d^m P_l(x)}{dx^m} \qquad (0 \le m \le l),$$

which are known as the *associated Legendre functions* (of the first kind). Employing Rodrigues formula for $P_l(x)$, we obtain the corresponding Rodrigues formula for $P_l^m(x)$:

$$P_l^m(x) = \frac{(1 - x^2)^{m/2}}{2^l l!} \frac{d^{l+m}}{dx^{l+m}} (x^2 - 1)^l \qquad (0 \le m \le l).$$

Remarks

1. If m is odd, then P_l^m has branch points at $x = \pm 1$, and the usual choice of positive square root for $|x| < 1$ implies that the branch cuts are taken to be from $-\infty$ to -1 and from $+1$ to $+\infty$.†

2. Although the Rodrigues formula is designed to be used for nonnegative values of m, it yields meaningful function even if m is negative so long as $|m| \le l$. In fact, many authors define the functions

$$P_l^{-m}(x) = \frac{(1 - x^2)^{-m/2}}{2^l l!} \frac{d^{l-m}}{dx^{l-m}} (x^2 - 1)^l \qquad (m > 0, m \le l).$$

These functions happen to be, however, multiples of functions P_l^m; that is, one can establish the formula

$$P_l^{-m}(x) = (-1)^m \frac{(l - m)!}{(l + m)!} P_l^m(x) \qquad (|m| \le l).$$

Associated Legendre functions with negative m are useful in defining spherical harmonics (see later) but they are not indispensable. Some authors do not use them at all, while others define them arbitrarily, e.g., by

$$P_l^{-m} = (-1)^m P_l^m \qquad \text{or} \qquad P_l^{-m} = P_l^m.$$

Unless stated otherwise, we shall assume that in the symbol $P_l^m(x)$, m is *nonnegative*.

The formula

$$P_l^m(x) = (1 - x^2)^{m/2} \frac{d^m P_l(x)}{dx^m} \qquad (0 \le m \le l)$$

---

* Evidently, $u(x)$ cannot be proportional to $d^m Q_l(x)/dx^m$ because the latter is not analytic at $x = \pm 1$.

† There are some (not very common) physical problems where the region $|x| > 1$, rather than $|x| < 1$ as in our case, is of interest. Then another branch is obtained by changing $(1 - x^2)^{m/2}$ to $(x^2 - 1)^{m/2}$ in Rodrigues formula and still using the positive square root.

allows rapid development of many properties of the P_l^m. In Section 9.5 (p. 345), we had the following relations for Legendre polynomials:

$$(2l + 1)xP_l = (l + 1)P_{l+1} + lP_{l-1}. \tag{I}$$

Also (p. 346),

$$lP_l + P'_{l-1} = xP'_l, \tag{II}$$

$$P'_{l+1} = (l + 1)P_l + xP'_l. \tag{III}$$

Differentiating (I) m times and multiplying by $(1 - x^2)^{m/2}$ we obtain

$$(2l + 1)xP_l^m + (2l + 1)m\sqrt{1 - x^2}\,P_l^{m-1} = (l + 1)P_{l+1}^m + lP_{l-1}^m. \tag{1}$$

Differentiating (II) and (III) $(m - 1)$ times and multiplying by $(1 - x^2)^{m/2}$, we have

$$(l - m + 1)\sqrt{1 - x^2}\,P_l^{m-1} + P_{l-1}^m = xP_l^m, \tag{2}$$

$$P_{l+1}^m = (l + m)\sqrt{1 - x^2}\,P_l^{m-1} + xP_l^m. \tag{3}$$

Eliminating $\sqrt{1 - x^2}\,P_l^{m-1}$ from (1) and (2), we obtain the *pure recurrence relation* (in l):

$$(l - m + 1)P_{l+1}^m - (2l + 1)xP_l^m + (l + m)P_{l-1}^m = 0. \tag{4}$$

A second such pure recurrence relation (in m) can also be derived. Recall the DE for $u(x) = d^m P_l/dx^m$:

$$(1 - x^2)u'' - 2(m + 1)xu' + [l(l + 1) - m(m + 1)]u = 0.$$

We replace m by $m - 1$ and multiply by $(1 - x^2)^{m/2}$ to obtain

$$\sqrt{1 - x^2}\,P_l^{m+1} - 2mxP_l^m + (l + m)(l - m + 1)\sqrt{1 - x^2}\,P_l^{m-1} = 0. \tag{5}$$

The ladder operations are also available. We differentiate

$$P_l^m = (1 - x^2)^{m/2}(d^m/dx^m)P_l$$

and multiply by $(1 - x^2)$:

$$(1 - x^2)\frac{dP_l^m}{dx} = \sqrt{1 - x^2}\,P_l^{m+1} - mxP_l^m \qquad \text{(m-raising)}. \tag{6}$$

From (5) and (6),

$$(1 - x^2)\frac{dP_l^m}{dx} = mxP_l^m - (l + m)(l - m + 1)\sqrt{1 - x^2}\,P_l^{m-1} \qquad \text{(m-lowering)}. \tag{7}$$

From (7) and (2),

$$(1 - x^2)\frac{dP_l^m}{dx} = (l + m)P_{l-1}^m - lxP_l^m \qquad \text{(l-lowering)}. \tag{8}$$

From (8) and (4),

$$(1 - x^2)\frac{dP_l^m}{dx} = (l + 1)xP_l^m - (l - m + 1)P_{l+1}^m \qquad (l\text{-raising}). \qquad (9)$$

Associated Legendre functions with the same index m but with different index l are orthogonal to each other, since they are eigenfunctions of a Sturm-Liouville problem:

$$\int_{-1}^{+1} P_l^m(x)P_{l'}^m(x)\, dx = 0 \qquad (l \neq l').$$

The normalization integral can be derived as follows: Integrating by parts, obtain

$$\int_{-1}^{+1} [P_l^m(x)]^2\, dx = \int_{-1}^{+1} (1 - x^2)^m \frac{d^m P_l}{dx^m}\frac{d^m P_l}{dx^m}\, dx$$

$$= -\int_{-1}^{+1} \frac{d^{m-1}P_l}{dx^{m-1}}\frac{d}{dx}\left[(1 - x^2)^m \frac{d^m P_l}{dx^m}\right] dx.$$

Observe that

$$\frac{d}{dx}\left[(1 - x^2)^m \frac{d^m P_l}{dx^m}\right] = (1 - x^2)^m \frac{d^{m+1}P_l}{dx^{m+1}} - 2mx(1 - x^2)^{m-1}\frac{d^m P_l}{dx^m}.$$

Next, recall that the function $d^{m-1}P_l/dx^{m-1} = u_{m-1}(x)$ must satisfy the DE

$$(1 - x^2)u''_{m-1} - 2mxu'_{m-1} + [l(l + 1) - (m - 1)m]u_{m-1} = 0.$$

Multiply by $(1 - x^2)^{m-1}$, and deduce that

$$\frac{d}{dx}\left[(1 - x^2)^m \frac{d^m P_l}{dx^m}\right] \equiv (1 - x^2)^m \frac{d^{m+1}P_l}{dx^{m+1}} - 2mx(1 - x^2)^{m-1}\frac{d^m P_l}{dx^m}$$

$$= (1 - x^2)^{m-1}[(1 - x^2)u''_{m-1} - 2mxu'_{m-1}]$$

$$= -(1 - x^2)^{m-1}[l(l + 1) - m(m - 1)]u_{m-1}$$

$$= -(1 - x^2)^{m-1}[(l + m)(l - m + 1)]\frac{d^{m-1}P_l}{dx^{m-1}}.$$

This establishes the reduction formula

$$\int_{-1}^{+1} [P_l^m(x)]^2\, dx = (l + m)(l - m + 1)\int_{-1}^{+1} [P_l^{m-1}(x)]^2\, dx.$$

Apply this formula m times, to obtain

$$\int_{-1}^{+1} [P_l^m(x)]^2\, dx = \frac{(l + m)!}{(l - m)!}\int_{-1}^{+1} [P_l(x)]^2\, dx,$$

so that (see p. 348)

$$\int_{-1}^{+1} [P_l^m(x)]^2\, dx = \frac{2}{2l + 1}\frac{(l + m)!}{(l - m)!}.$$

The major use of the associated Legendre functions is in the expansion of functions defined on the *surface of a sphere*. To see this, let us return to our original wave equation.

To each fixed frequency* $\omega = kc$ there corresponds a mode

$$\varphi_k(\mathbf{r}, t) = \psi_k(\mathbf{r})e^{-i\omega t},$$

where $\psi_k(\mathbf{r})$ satisfies the Helmholtz equation (see Section 9.1)

$$\nabla^2 \psi_k + k^2 \psi_k = 0.$$

Instead of setting $\psi_k = R\Theta\Phi$, let us just separate off the radial part by means of

$$\psi_k(r, \theta, \phi) = R(r)Y(\theta, \phi).$$

This leads to

$$\frac{d}{dr}\left(r^2 \frac{dR}{dr}\right) + (k^2 r^2 + \lambda)R = 0,$$

$$\frac{1}{\sin\theta}\frac{\partial}{\partial\theta}\left(\sin\theta\frac{\partial Y}{\partial\theta}\right) + \frac{1}{\sin^2\theta}\frac{\partial^2 Y}{\partial\phi^2} + \lambda Y = 0.$$

The eigenvalue λ will be determined from the second equation [$Y(\theta, \phi)$ must be finite for $0 \le \theta \le \pi$ and $0 \le \phi \le 2\pi$], and we shall have eigenfunctions $Y_\lambda(\theta, \phi)$ corresponding to these eigenvalues. Then the entire function $\psi_k(\mathbf{r})$ can be expressed by a superposition of the type

$$\psi_k(\mathbf{r}) = \sum_\lambda C_\lambda R_\lambda(r) Y_\lambda(\theta, \phi).$$

Remark. The "summation" over λ is to be regarded as symbolic since we have not yet explored the structure of the spectrum of λ: whether it is continuous or discrete, and whether or not there are degeneracies.

To determine the allowed values of λ, we complete the separation of variables by setting $Y(\theta, \phi) = \Theta(\theta)\Phi(\phi)$. This leads to the equations

$$\frac{d}{d\theta}\left(\sin\theta\frac{d\Theta}{d\theta}\right) + \left(-\sin\theta\lambda + \frac{\lambda_1}{\sin\theta}\right)\Theta = 0, \qquad \frac{d^2\Phi}{d\phi^2} - \lambda_1\Phi = 0,$$

which we have already solved. We know that the spectrum of λ_1 is discrete, namely, $\lambda_1 = -m^2$ ($m = 0, 1, 2, \ldots$), and the eigenfunctions can be defined as follows.

For $m = 0$,

$$\Phi_0(\phi) = 1,$$

and for $m \ne 0$,

$$\Phi_m(\phi) = \begin{cases} \text{either} & \cos m\phi, \\ \text{or} & \sin m\phi. \end{cases}$$

---

* It may be an eigenfrequency determined from the radial equation.

These functions are orthogonal to each other and their normalization integrals read

$$\int_0^{2\pi} [\Phi_0(\phi)]^2 \, d\phi = 2\pi, \qquad \int_0^{2\pi} \cos^2 m\phi \, d\phi = \int_0^{2\pi} \sin^2 m\phi \, d\phi = \pi.$$

It is now convenient to have these eigenfunctions *normalized to unity* by multiplying them by appropriate constants so that all normalization integrals are equal to unity. This condition defines the normalized functions

$$\Phi_0(\phi) = \frac{1}{\sqrt{2\pi}} \qquad (m = 0),$$

$$\left. \begin{array}{l} \Phi_m^{(+)}(\phi) = \dfrac{1}{\sqrt{\pi}} \cos m\phi \\[2mm] \Phi_m^{(-)}(\phi) = \dfrac{1}{\sqrt{\pi}} \sin m\phi \end{array} \right\} \quad (m \neq 0),$$

where the symbol $(+)$ or $(-)$ reminds us that these functions are even or odd with respect to the interchange $\phi \leftrightarrow -\phi$. So far as the Θ-functions are concerned, we know that the spectrum of λ is also discrete, with

$$\lambda = -l(l + 1) \qquad (l = 0, 1, 2, 3, \ldots),$$

but that for any given m we must have $l \geq m$. The solutions of the Θ-equation are the associated Legendre functions $P_l^m(\cos \theta)$. It is convenient to normalize them to unity as well, by defining

$$\Theta_l^m(\cos \theta) = \sqrt{\frac{2l + 1}{2} \frac{(l - m)!}{(l + m)!}} \, P_l^m(\cos \theta),$$

so that

$$\int_0^{\pi} [\Theta_l^m(\cos \theta)]^2 \sin \theta \, d\theta = \frac{2l + 1}{2} \frac{(l - m)!}{(l + m)!} \int_{-1}^{+1} [P_l^m(x)]^2 \, dx = 1.$$

It should now be clear that the eigenvalue equation

$$\frac{1}{\sin \theta} \frac{\partial}{\partial \theta} \left(\sin \theta \frac{\partial Y}{\partial \theta} \right) + \frac{1}{\sin^2 \theta} \frac{\partial^2 Y}{\partial \phi^2} + \lambda Y = 0$$

possesses the eigenvalues

$$\lambda = -l(l + 1) \qquad (l = 0, 1, 2, \ldots),$$

which are, however, *degenerate* (except if $l = 0$) because for each fixed value of l we have several eigenfunctions, namely,

$$\Theta_l^0(\cos \theta)\Phi_0(\phi),$$

$$\Theta_l^1(\cos \theta)\Phi_1^{(+)}(\phi) \qquad \text{and} \qquad \Theta_l^1(\cos \theta)\Phi_1^{(-)}(\phi),$$

$$\Theta_l^2(\cos \theta)\Phi_2^{(+)}(\phi) \qquad \text{and} \qquad \Theta_l^2(\cos \theta)\Phi_2^{(-)}(\phi),$$

and so on, up to

$$\Theta_l^l(\cos\theta)\Phi_l^{(+)}(\phi) \qquad \text{and} \qquad \Theta_l^l(\cos\theta)\Phi_l^{(-)}(\phi).$$

Thus each value of l corresponds to $(2l + 1)$ separate eigenfunctions, and hence exhibits a $(2l + 1)$-fold degeneracy.

We now define the fundamental solutions of the PDE (subject to the appropriate boundary conditions)

$$\frac{1}{\sin\theta}\frac{\partial}{\partial\theta}\left(\sin\theta\frac{\partial Y}{\partial\theta}\right) + \frac{1}{\sin^2\theta}\frac{\partial^2 Y}{\partial\phi^2} - l(l+1)Y = 0$$

by means of the formulas

$$Y_{l0}(\theta,\phi) = \sqrt{\frac{2l+1}{4\pi}}\,P_l(\cos\theta) \qquad (m = 0),$$

$$\left.\begin{aligned}
Y_{lm}^{(+)}(\theta,\phi) &= \Theta_l^m(\cos\theta)\Phi_m^{(+)}(\phi) \\
&= \sqrt{\frac{2l+1}{2\pi}\frac{(l-m)!}{(l+m)!}}\,P_l^m(\cos\theta)\cos m\phi \\
Y_{lm}^{(-)}(\theta,\phi) &= \Theta_l^m(\cos\theta)\Phi_m^{(-)}(\phi) \\
&= \sqrt{\frac{2l+1}{2\pi}\frac{(l-m)!}{(l+m)!}}\,P_l^m(\cos\theta)\sin m\phi
\end{aligned}\right\} \quad (m \neq 0).$$

These solutions may be called *spherical harmonics* (in the classical definition*). It follows that the series expression for $\psi_k(\mathbf{r})$ of the type

$$\psi_k(\mathbf{r}) = \sum_\lambda C_\lambda R_\lambda(r)Y_\lambda(\theta,\phi)$$

should actually have the form

$$\psi_k(\mathbf{r}) = \sum_{l=0}^{\infty} R_l(r)\left\{C_{l0}Y_{l0}(\theta,\phi) + \sum_{m=1}^{l}[C_{lm}^{(+)}Y_{lm}^{(+)}(\theta,\phi) + C_{lm}^{(-)}Y_{lm}^{(-)}(\theta,\phi)]\right\}.$$

Suppose that r is fixed; then $\psi_k(\mathbf{r})$ becomes a function of θ and ϕ only and we are dealing with an expression of the type

$$f(\theta,\phi) = \sum_{l=0}^{\infty}\left\{A_{l0}Y_{l0}(\theta,\phi) + \sum_{m=1}^{l}[A_{lm}^{(+)}Y_{lm}^{(+)}(\theta,\phi) + A_{lm}^{(-)}Y_{lm}^{(-)}(\theta,\phi)]\right\}.$$

This series expansion is valid for an arbitrary function $f(\theta,\phi)$,† subject to the usual conditions similar to those for Fourier series, Fourier-Legendre series,

---

* As opposed to the quantum-mechanical definition of spherical harmonics, in which $\cos m\phi$ and $\sin m\phi$ are discarded in favor of $e^{im\phi}$ and $e^{-im\phi}$ and the appropriate definition is made (see Section 14.6).

† It is evident that $f(\theta,\phi)$ can be regarded as a function defined on the surface of a sphere (ϕ = longitude, θ = colatitude).

Fourier-Bessel series, and others.* The expansion coefficients are obtained by multiplying $f(\theta, \phi)$ by the corresponding spherical harmonic and by the factor $\sin \theta$, and integrating over all angles:

$$A_{l0} = \int_0^\pi \int_0^{2\pi} f(\theta, \phi) Y_{l0}(\theta, \phi) \sin \theta \, d\theta \, d\phi \qquad (m = 0),$$

$$A_{lm}^{(\pm)} = \int_0^\pi \int_0^{2\pi} f(\theta, \phi) Y_{lm}^{(\pm)}(\theta, \phi) \sin \theta \, d\theta \, d\phi \qquad (m \neq 0).$$

Remark. The factor $\sin \theta$ which is required for the orthogonality of P_l^m-functions has the following geometrical interpretation. An elementary solid angle is defined by

$$d\Omega = dS/r^2,$$

where dS is an area element of a sphere of radius r. In the spherical system,

$$dS = r \, d\theta \, r \sin \theta \, d\phi,$$

so that

$$d\Omega = \sin \theta \, d\theta \, d\phi$$

and the integrals quoted above can be regarded as the integrals over the solid angle and written symbolically as

$$A_{l0} = \int_\Omega f(\Omega) Y_{l0}(\Omega) \, d\Omega \qquad (m = 0),$$

$$A_{lm}^{(\pm)} = \int_\Omega f(\Omega) Y_{lm}^{(\pm)}(\Omega) \, d\Omega \qquad (m \neq 0).$$

9.9 SPHERICAL BESSEL FUNCTIONS

Let us continue the investigation of the wave and Helmholtz partial differential equations in the spherical coordinate system. According to the results of Section 9.8, the radial equation must have the form

$$\frac{d}{dr}\left(r^2 \frac{dR}{dr}\right) + [k^2 r^2 - l(l + 1)]R = 0 \qquad (l = 0, 1, 2, \ldots).$$

If we make the substitution $x = kr$ [$y(x) \equiv R(r)$], this equation will reduce to

$$x^2 \frac{d^2 y}{dx^2} + 2x \frac{dy}{dx} + [x^2 - l(l + 1)]y = 0.$$

The solutions of this DE are known as the *spherical Bessel* and the *spherical Neumann functions* of order l, denoted respectively by $j_l(x)$ and $n_l(x)$.† The reason for these names is that a substitution

$$y(x) = u(x)/\sqrt{x}$$

---

* See, e.g., Webster, *PDE of Mathematical Physics.*
† See Section 3.5, Example 1 for a Frobenius solution for the case $l = 1$.

reduces our equation to the form

$$\frac{d^2u}{dx^2} + \frac{1}{x}\frac{du}{dx} + \left[1 - \frac{(l + \frac{1}{2})^2}{x^2}\right]u = 0 \qquad (l = 0, 1, 2, \ldots),$$

which is recognized as the Bessel DE of order $l + \frac{1}{2}$. It follows that the solutions of the original DE can be expressed in the form

$$y(x) = C_1 \frac{J_{l+1/2}(x)}{\sqrt{x}} + C_2 \frac{J_{-l-1/2}(x)}{\sqrt{x}},$$

and if the *spherical Bessel function* $j_l(x)$ is defined to be a solution finite at $x = 0$, it follows that it must be a multiple of $J_{l+1/2}(x)/\sqrt{x}$. The factor of proportionality is usually chosen to be $\sqrt{\pi/2}$ (for the reason, see below) so that

$$j_l(x) = \sqrt{\pi/2x}\, J_{l+1/2}(x).$$

The relation of $j_l(x)$ to the Bessel functions permits us to express $j_l(x)$ in terms of $j_0(x)$. From the formula (see p. 359)

$$J_{\mu+1}(x) = -x^\mu \frac{d}{dx}\left[\frac{J_\mu(x)}{x^\mu}\right],$$

it follows if we set $\mu = l + \frac{1}{2}$ and divide by $x^{l+3/2}$, that

$$\frac{J_{l+3/2}(x)}{x^{l+3/2}} = -\frac{1}{x}\frac{d}{dx}\left[\frac{J_{l+1/2}(x)}{x^{l+1/2}}\right], \qquad \text{or} \qquad \frac{j_{l+1}(x)}{x^{l+1}} = -\frac{1}{x}\frac{d}{dx}\left[\frac{j_l(x)}{x^l}\right].$$

Starting with $l = 0$ and applying this formula l times, we obtain*

$$j_l(x) = x^l \left(-\frac{1}{x}\frac{d}{dx}\right)^l j_0(x) \qquad (l = 1, 2, 3, \ldots).$$

This formula uniquely defines all j_l-functions once j_0 is chosen. Our equation for $l = 0$ reads

$$\frac{d^2y}{dx^2} + \frac{2}{x}\frac{dy}{dx} + y = 0.$$

Solving this equation (by the Frobenius or some other method), we find that the functions $\sin x/x$ and $\cos x/x$ are among the solutions. It is customary to define

$$j_0(x) = \sin x/x,$$

and comparison with $J_{1/2}(x)$ shows that

$$j_0(x) = \sqrt{\pi/2x}\, J_{1/2}(x),$$

which explains the factor $\sqrt{\pi/2}$ mentioned earlier.

---

* Compare with a similar formula for $J_m(x)$ on p. 360.

The *spherical Neumann functions* $n_l(x)$ are similarly generated from $n_0(x)$ by means of

$$n_l(x) = x^l \left(-\frac{1}{x}\frac{d}{dx} \right)^l n_0(x) \qquad (l = 1, 2, 3, \ldots),$$

and it is customary to define

$$n_0(x) = -\cos x/x = -\sqrt{\pi/2x}\, J_{-1/2}(x).$$

A few lowest functions $j_l(x)$ and $n_l(x)$ are:

$$j_0(x) = \frac{\sin x}{x},$$

$$j_1(x) = \frac{\sin x}{x^2} - \frac{\cos x}{x},$$

$$j_2(x) = \left(\frac{3}{x^3} - \frac{1}{x}\right)\sin x - \frac{3}{x^2}\cos x,$$

$$j_3(x) = \left(\frac{15}{x^4} - \frac{6}{x^2}\right)\sin x - \left(\frac{15}{x^3} - \frac{1}{x}\right)\cos x,$$

$$n_0(x) = -\frac{\cos x}{x},$$

$$n_1(x) = -\frac{\cos x}{x^2} - \frac{\sin x}{x},$$

$$n_2(x) = -\left(\frac{3}{x^2} - \frac{1}{x}\right)\cos x - \frac{3}{x^2}\sin x,$$

$$n_3(x) = -\left(\frac{15}{x^4} - \frac{6}{x^2}\right)\cos x - \left(\frac{15}{x^3} - \frac{1}{x}\right)\sin x.$$

Remark. The spherical Neumann functions are related to the Neumann functions defined in Section 9.10 by the formula $n_l(x) = \sqrt{\pi/2x}\, N_{l+1/2}(x)$.*

Example 1. Sound waves are generated inside a spherical cavity of radius a. It is desired to investigate the patterns of standing waves inside the cavity and their frequencies.

Solution. The problem can be formulated in terms of the velocity potential (see Section 8.9) which must satisfy the wave equation†

$$\nabla^2\varphi - \frac{1}{c^2}\frac{\partial^2\varphi}{\partial t^2} = 0$$

---

* It is not difficult to verify that $N_{l+1/2}(x)$ is proportional to $J_{-l-1/2}(x)$. However, this is true only if l is an integer (see the footnote on p. 391).

† It is assumed that the source of the sound is removed at $t = 0$ and the air in the cavity is left to vibrate freely.

subject to the boundary condition

$$\frac{\partial \varphi}{\partial r}\bigg|_{r=a} = 0.$$

We are seeking solutions of the form

$$\varphi_k(\mathbf{r}, t) = \psi_k(\mathbf{r})e^{-i\omega t} \qquad (\omega = kc),$$

so that $\psi_k(\mathbf{r})$ must satisfy

$$\nabla^2 \psi_k + k^2 \psi_k = 0 \qquad \text{and} \qquad \frac{\partial \psi_k}{\partial r}\bigg|_{r=a} = 0.$$

From the results of Section 9.9, it follows that (p. 380)

$$\psi_k(\mathbf{r}) = \sum_{l=0}^{\infty} R_l(r) \left\{ C_{l0} Y_{l0}(\theta, \phi) + \sum_{m=0}^{l} [C_{lm}^{(+)} Y_{lm}^{(+)}(\theta, \phi) + C_{lm}^{(-)} Y_{lm}^{(-)}(\theta, \phi)] \right\},$$

where Y_{lm}-functions are spherical harmonics and the functions $R_l(r)$ must satisfy the DE

$$\frac{d}{dr}\left(r^2 \frac{dR_l}{dr}\right) + [k^2 r^2 - l(l+1)]R_l = 0 \qquad (l = 0, 1, 2, \ldots).$$

The general solution of this equation reads

$$R_l(r) = A_l j_l(kr) + B_l n_l(kr).$$

Since the function $n_l(kr)$ is not finite at $r = 0$, it must be discarded by setting $B_l = 0$. The allowed values of k are determined from the boundary condition which now reduces to

$$\frac{d}{dr} j_l(kr)\bigg|_{r=a} = 0.$$

The roots of $(d/dx)j_l(x)$ can be found in tables. For instance, the roots of $(d/d\alpha)j_l(\pi\alpha)$ are given by Table 9.2 (n labels nth root). The corresponding values of k for our problem are then given by

$$k_{ln} = \frac{\pi\alpha_{ln}}{a}$$

and the corresponding frequencies are given by

$$\omega_{ln} = \frac{c\pi\alpha_{ln}}{a}.$$

The mode with the lowest frequency is for $l = 1, n = 1$.* It has a triple degeneracy

---

* The case $l = 0, n = 1$, leads to $\varphi(\mathbf{r}, t) = $ const, which may be kept in the solution but corresponds to no physical sound wave (recall that $\mathbf{v} = -\text{grad } \varphi$).

Table 9.2

l	n	α_{ln}
0	1	0.0000
1	1	0.6626
2	1	1.0638
0	2	1.4303
3	1	1.4369

with angular distributions

$$Y_{10} = \sqrt{\frac{3}{4\pi}}\cos\theta, \qquad Y_{11}^{(+)} = \sqrt{\frac{3}{8\pi}}\sin\theta\cos\phi, \qquad Y_{11}^{(-)} = \sqrt{\frac{3}{8\pi}}\sin\theta\sin\phi$$

and the radial function $j_1(k_{11}r)$. The next mode is for $l = 2$, $n = 1$; it has a five-fold degeneracy (Y_{20}, $Y_{21}^{(+)}$, $Y_{21}^{(-)}$, $Y_{22}^{(+)}$, and $Y_{22}^{(-)}$) and the radial function $j_2(k_{21}r)$. Then there is a nondegenerate mode ($l = 0$, $n = 2$) with $j_0(k_{02}r)$, and so on.

The overall solution of the problem is given by the expansion (some of the details of labeling are omitted for brevity)

$$\varphi(\mathbf{r}, t) = \sum_n \sum_l \sum_m j_l(kr) Y_{lm}(\theta, \phi)(C_{nlm}e^{-i\omega t} + C_{nlm}^* e^{i\omega t}).$$

The coefficients C_{nlm} (actually C_{nl0}, $C_{nlm}^{(+)}$, $C_{nlm}^{(-)}$, etc.) could be determined from the initial conditions which should specify the initial distribution of velocity potential $\varphi(\mathbf{r}, 0)$ and its time derivative $\partial\varphi/\partial t(\mathbf{r}, 0)$ (which is proportional to the fractional change in density).

Example 2. A solid sphere of radius b has an initial temperature distribution $u = u_0(r)$ and cools its surface according to *Newton's law of cooling* (by convection)[†]

$$\frac{\partial u}{\partial r} + h(u - u_1)\Big|_{r=b} = 0 \qquad (h = \text{const}),$$

where u_1 is the temperature of the surrounding medium. It is desired to determine the temperature inside the sphere.

Solution. The temperature distribution $u(r, \theta, \phi; t)$ satisfies the heat conduction equation

$$\nabla^2 u = \frac{1}{a^2}\frac{\partial u}{\partial t}.$$

---

† See, e.g., Carslaw and Jaeger, *Conduction of Heat in Solids*, Section 1.9.

Since u must possess* spherical symmetry at all times, we have $u = u(r, t)$. Separation of the variables $u = RT$ in the spherical system yields

$$\frac{dT}{dt} = -a^2 \lambda T, \qquad \frac{1}{r^2} \frac{d}{dr}\left(r^2 \frac{dR}{dr}\right) + \lambda R = 0.$$

On physical grounds, λ cannot be negative. If $\lambda = 0$, then both $T(t)$ and $R(r)$ are constants (R must be finite at $r = 0$). If $\lambda > 0$, then

$$T(t) = e^{-a^2 k^2 t}, \qquad R(r) = j_0(kr) = \sin kr / kr \qquad (k = \sqrt{\lambda}).$$

The allowed values of k are to be determined from the boundary condition. Here we have a minor problem stemming from the fact that the boundary condition is *nonhomogeneous;* it actually reads

$$\frac{\partial u}{\partial r} + hu = hu_1 = \text{const.}$$

However, from our experience in Example 2, Section 9.7, we can handle this difficulty by changing the temperature scale by $u - u_1 = v$ (new temperature), utilizing the fact that the new variable v will satisfy the same PDE and the homogeneous boundary condition

$$\frac{\partial v}{\partial r} + hv\Big|_{r=b} = 0.$$

Consequently, we require that each eigenfunction $j_0(kr)$ satisfy the boundary condition for v. We have

$$\frac{d}{dr} j_0(kr) = \frac{d}{dr}\left(\frac{\sin kr}{kr}\right) = -\frac{\sin kr}{kr^2} + \frac{k \cos kr}{kr}.$$

The boundary condition yields

$$-\frac{\sin kb}{kb^2} + \frac{\cos kb}{b} + h\frac{\sin kb}{kb} = 0.$$

In the general case, i.e. when $hb \neq 1$, this equation can be rewritten in the form

$$\tan kb / kb = 1/(1 - hb)$$

and must be solved numerically. The special case, $hb = 1$, can be handled explicitly. It implies that $\cos kb = 0$ and, therefore $k = n\pi/2b$, where $n = 1, 3, 5, \ldots$

The nature of the spectrum in the general case is easily revealed by a graphical solution of the eigenvalue equation. Let us set $kb = x$, $1/(1 - hb) = \alpha$, and plot the curves $y = \tan x$ and $y = \alpha x$. The intersections of these curves (Fig. 9.4)†

---

* We shall take this for granted. See also p. 619.

† We have assumed that $\alpha < 0$.

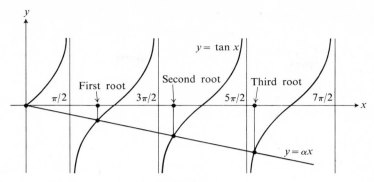

Figure 9.4

yield the desired roots (only positive roots need to be considered). From this graphic construction it is clear that there is one and only one eigenvalue in the interval between $n\pi/2b$ and $(n/2 + 1)(\pi/b)$, where $n = 1, 3, 5, \ldots$ Also, higher-order eigenvalues appear to be almost equal to $(n/2 + 1)(\pi/b)$, $n = $ odd, expressed by the asymptotic formula

$$k_n \sim (n/2 + 1)(\pi/b) \qquad \text{as } n \to \infty \quad (n = \text{odd integer}).$$

The solution to our problem is now written in the form of the series

$$v(r, t) = \sum_{n=1}^{\infty} A_n \frac{\sin k_n r}{k_n r} e^{-a^2 k_n^2 t}.$$

To determine the coefficients A_n, we use the initial condition which yields

$$u_0(r) - u_1 = \sum_{n=1}^{\infty} A_n \frac{\sin k_n r}{k_n r} = \sum_{n=1}^{\infty} A_n j_0(k_n r).$$

From the DE satisfied by $j_0(k_n r)$ it follows that these functions are orthogonal in the interval $(0, b)$ with the weight function r^2. Consequently, we can multiply both sides by $r^2 j_0(k_m r)$ and integrate over $(0, b)$ with the result

$$\int_0^b [u_0(r) - u_1] r^2 j_0(k_m r) \, dr = A_m \int_0^b r^2 [j_0(k_m r)]^2 \, dr.$$

The normalization integral can be deduced by standard techniques, e.g., from the DE as in Section 9.7 (for Bessel functions). In this particular case it is perhaps simpler to utilize the trigonometric functions

$$\int_0^b r^2 [j_0(k_m r)]^2 \, dr = \int_0^b r^2 \frac{\sin^2 k_m r}{k_m^2 r^2} \, dr = \frac{1}{k_m^2} \int_0^b \sin^2 k_m r \, dr$$

$$= \frac{1}{k_m^2} \left[\frac{r}{2} - \frac{\sin 2k_m r}{4k_m} \right]_0^b = \frac{1}{4k_m^3} [2k_m b - \sin 2k_m b].$$

This yields the coefficients A_n and the entire solution in the form

$$u(r, t) = u_1 + \sum_{n=1}^{\infty} A_n \frac{\sin k_n r}{k_n r} e^{-a^2 k_n^2 t},$$

where

$$A_n = \frac{4 k_n^3 \int_0^b [u_0(r) - u_1] r^2 j_0(k_n r)\, dr}{2 k_n b - \sin 2 k_n b}.$$

9.10 NEUMANN FUNCTIONS

Consider the free vibrations of a membrane of the shape of a circular ring ($a \leq r \leq b$) clamped over the entire boundary. The displacement $u(r, \theta; t)$ must satisfy the PDE

$$\frac{1}{r} \frac{\partial}{\partial r} \left(r \frac{\partial u}{\partial r} \right) + \frac{1}{r^2} \frac{\partial^2 u}{\partial \theta^2} = \frac{1}{c^2} \frac{\partial^2 u}{\partial t^2},$$

and the boundary conditions

$$u(a, \theta; t) = 0, \qquad u(b, \theta; t) = 0,$$

where a is the inner radius and b is the outer radius of the membrane. The treatment of the problem by the method of separation of variables follows closely Example 1, Section 9.7 (circular membrane). A characteristic mode given by

$$u_\omega(r, \theta; t) = e^{-i\omega t} \Theta(\theta) R(r)$$

must have the Θ-factor of the form

$$\Theta(\theta) = A_m \cos m\theta + B_m \sin m\theta \qquad (m = 0, 1, 2, \ldots)$$

and the R-factor

$$R(r) = C_1 J_m(kr) + C_2 N_m(kr) \qquad (k = \omega/c),$$

where J_m and N_m are the Bessel and Neumann functions* of order m. Since the point $r = 0$, where N_m has a singularity, is *not on the membrane*, there is no reason now to reject the Neumann function. As a matter of fact we definitely need the N_m-term because we have to satisfy *two* boundary conditions:

$$C_1 J_m(ka) + C_2 N_m(ka) = 0,$$
$$C_1 J_m(kb) + C_2 N_m(kb) = 0$$

and this would be, in general, impossible with $C_2 = 0$.

Exercise. Prove this statement.

---

* See p. 359.

Our problem requires therefore the study of Neumann functions or, more generally, the study of the solutions of the Bessel DE

$$\frac{d^2y}{dx^2} + \frac{1}{x}\frac{dy}{dx} + \left(1 - \frac{m^2}{x^2}\right)y = 0 \qquad (m = 0, 1, 2, \ldots),$$

which are linearly independent of $J_m(x)$.

In our study of the Bessel DE in Section 9.7, we have confined ourselves to $J_\mu(x)$- and $J_{-\mu}(x)$-functions which are linearly independent provided μ is not an integer. If $\mu = m$ is an integer, we have

$$J_{-m}(x) = (-1)^m J_m(x)$$

and we must seek the second solution in the form*

$$y(x) = \log x \sum_{n=0}^{\infty} c_n x^{s+n} + \sum_{p=0}^{\infty} a_p x^{r+p}.$$

In Section 3.5, Example 5, we marked out a special case ($m = 0$) of such a calculation. We showed that the series

$$\sum_{n=0}^{\infty} c_n x^{s+n}$$

must be a multiple of $J_0(x)$. Taking it to be equal to $J_0(x)$, we determined the second series

$$\sum_{p=0}^{\infty} a_p x^{r+p} = v(x) = \frac{1}{2^2}x^2 - \frac{3}{2^7}x^4 + \frac{11}{2^9 \cdot 3^3}x^6 - \cdots$$

and defined the Bessel function of the second kind of order zero as

$$Y_0(x) = \log x J_0(x) - v(x).$$

This is not the only choice of a second solution. A function

$$y(x) = C_1 Y_0(x) + C_2 J_0(x),$$

with $C_1 \neq 0$ would satisfy the DE and be linearly independent of $J_0(x)$. Experience has shown that it is very convenient to choose the second solution to be

$$N_0(x) = (\pi/2)Y_0(x) + (\gamma - \log 2)J_0(x),$$

known as the Neumann function of order zero. The number γ is the Euler-Mascheroni constant (p. 141). Once $N_0(x)$ is defined, Neumann functions of higher order can be generated from it. Indeed, we can *define* $N_m(x)$ by the same formula

---

* See Section 3.5, Example 4.

(of Rodrigues type) as was used to generate spherical Neumann functions (Section 9.9):

$$N_m(x) = x^m \left(-\frac{1}{x}\frac{d}{dx} \right)^m N_0(x).$$

We can now *verify* that N_m-functions satisfy the Bessel DE of order m and are linearly independent of the functions $J_m(x)$.

Exercise. Show that the function $N_m(x)$ satisfies the Bessel DE of order m. [*Hint:* Deduce first the recursion relations on p. 392.]

The advantage of N_m-functions over other possible solutions of the Bessel DE stems from the considerations of their *asymptotic behavior*, namely, their approximate form for large values of x.

Looking over the first few spherical Bessel functions $j_l(x)$ (see p. 383), we may note that for large values of x these functions behave like

$$\pm \sin x/x \qquad \text{or} \qquad \pm \cos x/x$$

(since the other terms contain higher negative powers of x). Since

$$j_l(x) = \sqrt{\pi/2x}\, J_{l+1/2}(x),$$

it follows that the functions $J_{l+1/2}(x)$ behave asymptotically like

$$\pm \sqrt{\frac{2}{\pi}}\frac{\sin x}{\sqrt{x}}, \qquad \text{or} \qquad \pm \sqrt{\frac{2}{\pi}}\frac{\cos x}{\sqrt{x}}.$$

Let us inquire whether the Bessel functions of other orders possess similar properties. For this purpose, we set $y = u(x)/\sqrt{x}$ in the Bessel DE and obtain the equation for $u(x)$:

$$\frac{d^2u}{dx^2} + \left(1 - \frac{\mu^2 - \frac{1}{4}}{x^2} \right) u = 0.$$

Now the first derivative term is eliminated (see Section 3.6) and it is seen that if x is sufficiently large (μ is fixed), then the term $(\mu^2 - \frac{1}{4})/x^2$ can be neglected compared to unity and the equation for u can be approximated by

$$d^2u/dx^2 + u = 0,$$

from which it follows that $u(x)$ must behave like some linear combination of $\sin x$ and $\cos x$ or, what is the same, as $\cos (x + \delta)$. The phase δ defines a particular solution of the Bessel equation. A rigorous analysis (omitted here) shows that functions $J_\mu(x)$ and $J_{-\mu}(x)$ have the following *asymptotic forms:*[*]

$$J_{\pm\mu}(x) \sim \sqrt{\frac{2}{\pi x}} \cos\left(x \mp \frac{\pi\mu}{2} - \frac{\pi}{4} \right) + \mathcal{O}\left(\frac{1}{x^{3/2}} \right) \qquad (x = \text{real}),$$

---

[*] *Caution:* This formula is not (in general) valid if x is complex.

where $\Theta(1/x^{3/2})$ means a quantity less than $C/x^{3/2}$, where C is a positive constant (see footnote on p. 352).*

The asymptotic formula reveals that the difference in phase δ between $J_\mu(x)$ and $J_{-\mu}(x)$ is equal to $\pi\mu$, and when $\mu \to m$ (an integer) this difference reduces to a multiple of π making their asymptotic forms equal up to a factor ± 1. This reflects the relation $J_{-m}(x) = (-1)^m J_m(x)$ (p. 389).

The analysis of asymptotic forms suggests a natural idea of constructing a solution of the Bessel DE which would behave asymptotically as

$$\sqrt{\frac{2}{\pi x}} \sin\left(x - \frac{\pi\mu}{2} - \frac{\pi}{4}\right) \qquad \text{(for real } x\text{)}.$$

Since $\sin(x - \pi\mu/2 - \pi/4)$ is linearly independent of $\cos(x - \pi\mu/2 - \pi/4)$ for *all values of* μ, this solution should be free from the difficulty we have with $J_{-\mu}(x)$ when μ is an integer. Moreover, this solution will have a fixed asymptotic relationship with $J_\mu(x)$, always being 90° out of phase with it. The desired solution is then constructed as follows. We write

$$\sin(t - \alpha) = A \cos(t - \alpha) + B \cos(t + \alpha),$$

and require that A and B may depend on α but not on t, obtaining

$$A = \cot 2\alpha, \qquad B = -\csc 2\alpha.$$

We now identify

$$t = x - \pi/4 \qquad \text{and} \qquad \alpha = \pi\mu/2$$

and conclude that if the Neumann function $N_\mu(x)$ *is defined by*†

$$N_\mu(x) = \cot \mu\pi J_\mu(x) - \csc \mu\pi J_{-\mu}(x) \qquad (\mu \neq \text{integer}),$$

then it will follow that

$$N_\mu(x) \sim \sqrt{\frac{2}{\pi x}} \sin\left(x - \frac{\pi\mu}{2} - \frac{\pi}{4}\right) + \Theta\left(\frac{1}{x^{3/2}}\right)$$

and that $N_\mu(x)$ is linearly independent of $J_\mu(x)$, at least if μ is not an integer. If μ is an integer, the above formula for $N_\mu(x)$ becomes indeterminate. The logical step then is to define $N_m(x)$ by

$$N_m(x) = \lim_{\mu \to m} N_\mu(x) = \lim_{\mu \to m} \frac{\cos \pi\mu J_\mu(x) - J_{-\mu}(x)}{\sin \pi\mu}.$$

---

* In other words, replacing $J_\mu(x)$ by its asymptotic form, we make an error that is less than $C/x^{3/2}$. The constant C is actually no greater than unity.

† Observe that if μ is a half-integer ($\mu = l + 1/2$), then

$$N_{l+1/2}(x) = (-1)^{l+1} J_{-l-1/2}(x).$$

Evaluating the limit by L'Hôpital's rule, we obtain

$$N_m(x) = \frac{1}{\pi}\left[\frac{\partial J_\mu(x)}{\partial \mu} - (-1)^\mu \frac{\partial J_{-\mu}(x)}{\partial \mu}\right]_{\mu=m}.$$

Differentiating the Frobenius series for $J_\mu(x)$ and $J_{-\mu}(x)$ with respect to μ, we can obtain the Frobenius series for $N_m(x)$. The calculation is straightforward (though slightly tedious) and yields*

$$N_m(x) = \frac{1}{\pi}\left[2\log\frac{x}{2} + 2\gamma - \sum_{k=1}^{m}\frac{1}{k}\right]J_m(x) - \frac{1}{\pi}\sum_{n=0}^{m-1}\frac{(m-n-1)!}{n!}\left(\frac{x}{2}\right)^{-m+2n}$$

$$- \frac{1}{\pi}\sum_{n=1}^{\infty}\frac{(-1)^n}{(n+m)!n!}\left\{\sum_{k=1}^{n}\left(\frac{1}{k} + \frac{1}{m+k}\right)\right\}\left(\frac{x}{2}\right)^{m+2n}.$$

From this expression it is seen that $N_m(x)$ possesses a branch point at the origin (because of the presence of $\log x$), and for small values of x behaves like

$$N_m(x) \sim -\frac{2^m}{\pi(m-1)!}\frac{1}{x^m} \qquad (x \to 0).$$

The exception is the function $N_0(x)$ which has no negative powers of x, and which, for small values of x, behaves like

$$N_0(x) \sim \frac{2}{\pi}\log x \qquad (x \to 0).$$

It is also straightforward to verify that N_m-functions, as defined above, satisfy the Rodrigues type formula quoted earlier, so that both definitions are equivalent.

Neumann functions satisfy various recursion relations such as†

$$N_{\mu+1}(x) + N_{\mu-1}(x) = \frac{2\mu}{x}N_\mu(x),$$

$$N_{\mu+1}(x) = \frac{\mu}{x}N_\mu(x) - \frac{dN_\mu(x)}{dx},$$

$$N_{\mu-1}(x) = \frac{\mu}{x}N_\mu(x) + \frac{dN_m(x)}{dx},$$

$$\frac{d}{dx}[x^\mu N_\mu(x)] = x^\mu N_{\mu-1}(x), \qquad \frac{d}{dx}[x^{-\mu}N_\mu(x)] = -\frac{N_{\mu+1}(x)}{x^\mu}.$$

---

* The Euler-Mascheroni constant γ arises in the differentiation of $1/\Gamma(n + \mu + 1)$. The logarithmic derivative of the gamma function reads

$$\psi(x) = \frac{\Gamma'(x)}{\Gamma(x)} = -\gamma - \frac{1}{x} - \sum_{k=1}^{\infty}\left(\frac{1}{k} + \frac{1}{k+x}\right).$$

† These are exactly the same as the recursion relations for $J_\mu(x)$-functions.

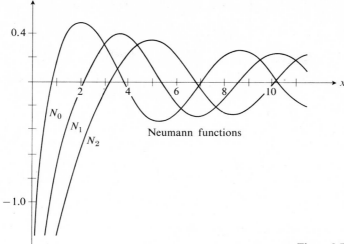

Figure 9.5

Some of the most important indefinite integrals are

$$\int [N_0(x)]^2 x \, dx = \frac{x^2}{2} \{[N_0(x)]^2 + [N_1(x)]^2\},$$

$$\int [N_m(x)]^2 x \, dx = \frac{x^2}{2} \{[N_m(x)]^2 + N_{m+1}(x)N_{m-1}(x)\} \qquad (m \neq 0),$$

$$\int N_0(x) x \, dx = x N_1(x), \qquad \int N_1(x) \, dx = -N_0(x).$$

The three lowest (integral) order Neumann functions are illustrated in Fig. 9.5.

Let us now return to the problem of the ringlike membrane from which we digressed to the study of Neumann functions. The characteristic frequencies $\omega = kc$ are determined by the boundary conditions which require that

$$C_1 J_m(ka) + C_2 N_m(ka) = 0, \qquad C_1 J_m(kb) + C_2 N_m(kb) = 0.$$

These equations have a nontrivial solution for C_1 and C_2 only if the determinant of the system vanishes:

$$J_m(ka)N_m(kb) - J_m(kb)N_m(ka) = 0.$$

The (positive) roots of this transcendental equation determine the eigenvalues. As expected, there is an infinite number of such roots, and they can be labeled by the integers $n = 1, 2, 3, \ldots$, yielding a "double infinity" of eigenvalues k_{mn} ($m = 0, 1, 2, \ldots, n = 1, 2, 3, \ldots$). From the equations for C_1 and C_2, it follows that

$$\frac{C_2}{C_1} = -\frac{J_m(ka)}{N_m(ka)} = -\frac{J_m(kb)}{N_m(kb)},$$

so that the radial eigenfunctions can be chosen, for instance, as

$$R_{mn}(r) = N_m(k_{mn}a)J_m(k_{mn}r) - J_m(k_{mn}a)N_m(k_{mn}r).$$

These functions are not normalized, but they are orthogonal (on the basis of the general Sturm-Liouville theory). Arbitrary motion of the ringlike membrane can be represented in the form of a series over the characteristic modes:

$$u(r, \theta; t) = \sum_{m=0}^{\infty} \sum_{n=1}^{\infty} R_{mn}(r) \cdot e^{-ik_{mn}ct}(A_{mn}\cos m\theta + B_{mn}\sin m\theta) + CC,$$

where CC means complex conjugate. The (complex) coefficients A_{mn} and B_{mn} can be obtained by a method similar to the one used for the circular membrane (Section 9.7).

9.11 MODIFIED BESSEL FUNCTIONS

Example. Consider a solid circular cylinder of radius b and length L. The bases of the cylinder are maintained at zero temperature while its lateral surface is maintained at a constant (positive) temperature u_1. It is desired to find the steady-state distribution of temperature inside the cylinder.

Solution. The usual heat conduction equation

$$\nabla^2 u = \frac{1}{a^2}\frac{\partial u}{\partial t}$$

is now simplified by the requirement that the temperature be independent of time,* and thus reduces to the Laplace equation $\nabla^2 u = 0$. Using cylindrical coordinates, we may formulate the problem for the function $u(r, \theta, z)$ by the following conditions:

$$\frac{1}{r}\frac{\partial}{\partial r}\left(r\frac{\partial u}{\partial r}\right) + \frac{1}{r^2}\frac{\partial^2 u}{\partial \theta^2} + \frac{\partial^2 u}{\partial z^2} = 0,$$

$$u(b, \theta, z) = u_1, \qquad u(r, \theta, 0) = u(r, \theta, L) = 0,$$

$$u(r, \theta, z) \quad \text{has period } 2\pi \text{ in } \theta.$$

Separating the variables ($u = R\Theta Z$), we obtain

$$\frac{d^2 Z}{dz^2} = \lambda_1 Z, \qquad \frac{d^2\Theta}{d\theta^2} = \lambda_2\Theta,$$

$$\frac{d}{dr}\left(r\frac{dR}{dr}\right) + \left[r\lambda_1 + \frac{\lambda_2}{r}\right]R = 0.$$

---

* This state of affairs is achieved in practice if the cylinder is left exposed to the stated boundary conditions for a sufficiently long time.

In the usual fashion, we can conclude that

$$\lambda_1 = -n^2\pi^2/L^2 \qquad (n = 1, 2, 3, \ldots)$$

and

$$\lambda_2 = -m^2 \qquad (m = 0, 1, 2, 3, \ldots).$$

Then the equation for R becomes

$$\frac{d}{dr}\left(r\,\frac{dR}{dr}\right) + \left[-\frac{n^2\pi^2}{L^2}r - \frac{m^2}{r}\right]R = 0.$$

Set $n\pi r/L = x$ and $R(r) = y(x)$. Then $y(x)$ must satisfy

$$\frac{d^2y}{dx^2} + \frac{1}{x}\frac{dy}{dx} + \left(-1 - \frac{m^2}{x^2}\right)y = 0.$$

This equation differs from the Bessel DE of order m,

$$\frac{d^2y}{dx^2} + \frac{1}{x}\frac{dy}{dx} + \left(1 - \frac{m^2}{x^2}\right)y = 0,$$

only by the change in sign of one term. As a matter of fact, if we had made the "complex" substitution $n\pi r/L = -iz$, we would have obtained the actual Bessel DE with respect to z [$y(x) \equiv w(z)$]

$$\frac{d^2w}{dz^2} + \frac{1}{z}\frac{dw}{dz} + \left(1 - \frac{m^2}{z^2}\right)w = 0.$$

It follows immediately that the solutions of our equation for $y(x)$ are

$$J_m(ix) \qquad \text{and} \qquad N_m(ix).$$

As they stand, these functions are not always real. To remedy this it is customary to define the modified Bessel function of the first kind* by means of the formula

$$I_\mu(x) = \frac{1}{i^\mu}J_\mu(ix).$$

This function is always real (even if μ is not an integer). The power series for $J_\mu(x)$ (p. 357) immediately yields the power series for $I_\mu(x)$:

$$I_\mu(x) = \sum_{k=0}^{\infty} \frac{1}{k!\,\Gamma(\mu + k + 1)2^{\mu+2k}}x^{\mu+2k}.$$

The functions $I_\mu(x)$ possess their own slate of recursion formulas, the most im-

---

* Some authors use the term *Bessel functions of imaginary argument* for I_μ and K_μ (see below). The name *hyperbolic Bessel functions* is also used frequently.

portant of which are

$$I_{\mu-1}(x) - I_{\mu+1}(x) = \frac{2\mu}{x} I_\mu(x),$$

$$I_{\mu+1}(x) = -\frac{\mu}{x} I_\mu(x) + \frac{dI_\mu(x)}{dx},$$

$$I_{\mu-1}(x) = \frac{\mu}{x} I_\mu(x) + \frac{dI_\mu(x)}{dx},$$

$$\frac{d}{dx}[x^\mu I_\mu(x)] = x^\mu I_{\mu-1}(x), \qquad \frac{d}{dx}\left[\frac{I_\mu(x)}{x^\mu}\right] = \frac{I_{\mu+1}(x)}{x^\mu}.$$

The asymptotic form (see p. 390) reads

$$I_\mu(x) \sim \frac{1}{\sqrt{2\pi x}} e^x + \mathcal{O}\left(\frac{1}{x^{3/2}}\right) \qquad (x = \text{real}).$$

The second solution of our DE is not finite at the origin. As in the case of Neumann functions, it is desirable for many purposes to have a solution behaving asymptotically like $e^{-x}/\sqrt{x}$. The most common choice is the modified Bessel function of the second kind defined by*

$$K_\mu(x) = \frac{\pi}{2} \frac{I_{-\mu}(x) - I_\mu(x)}{\sin \pi\mu} \qquad (\mu \neq \text{integer}).$$

If μ is an integer, then the usual limiting procedure is employed (see p. 392), yielding

$$K_m(x) = \frac{(-1)^m}{2}\left[\frac{\partial I_{-\mu}(x)}{\partial \mu} - \frac{\partial I_\mu(x)}{\partial \mu}\right]_{\mu=m}.$$

Using the power series for $I_\mu(x)$, we can obtain the Frobenius series for $K_m(x)$:

$$K_m(x) = (-1)^{m+1}\left[\log\frac{x}{2} - \frac{1}{2}\sum_{k=1}^{m}\frac{1}{k}\right]I_m(x)$$

$$+ \frac{1}{2}\sum_{n=0}^{m-1}(-1)^n \frac{(m-n-1)!}{n!}\left(\frac{x}{2}\right)^{2n-m}$$

$$+ \frac{(-1)^m}{2}\sum_{n=0}^{\infty}\frac{\left\{\sum_{k=1}^{n}\left(\frac{1}{k} + \frac{1}{m+k}\right)\right\}}{n!(m+n)!}\left(\frac{x}{2}\right)^{m+2n} \qquad (m \neq 0)$$

and

$$K_0(x) = -\log\frac{x}{2} I_0(x).$$

---

* $I_{-\mu}(x)$ is defined by $i^\mu J_{-\mu}(ix)$. If $\mu = m$ (integer), then $I_{-m}(x) = I_m(x)$.

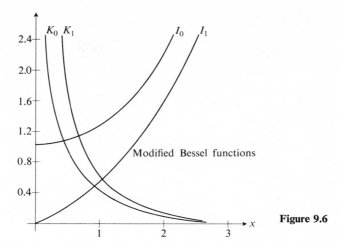

Figure 9.6

The recursion formulas for K_μ-functions differ slightly from those for I_μ:

$$K_{\mu-1}(x) - K_{\mu+1}(x) = -\frac{2\mu}{x} K_\mu(x),$$

$$K_{\mu+1}(x) = \frac{\mu}{x} K_\mu(x) - \frac{dK_\mu(x)}{dx},$$

$$K_{\mu-1}(x) = -\frac{\mu}{x} K_\mu(x) - \frac{dK_\mu(x)}{dx},$$

$$\frac{d}{dx}[x^\mu K_\mu(x)] = -x^\mu K_{\mu-1}(x),$$

$$\frac{d}{dx}\left[\frac{K_\mu(x)}{x^\mu}\right] = -\frac{K_{\mu+1}(x)}{x^\mu}.$$

The asymptotic form is

$$K_\mu(x) \sim \sqrt{\pi/2x}\, e^{-x} + \Theta(1/x^{3/2}).$$

The lowest I_m- and K_m-functions are sketched in Fig. 9.6.

Returning to our problem of heat conduction through a cylinder, we may represent the radial functions* in the form

$$R_{mn} = A_{mn}I_m\left(\frac{n\pi r}{L}\right) + B_{mn}K_m\left(\frac{n\pi r}{L}\right) \qquad (m = 0, 1, 2, \ldots, n = 1, 2, 3, \ldots).$$

---

* Note that the radial equation is *not* an eigenvalue equation; the separation constants are already determined.

Since the K_m-functions are not finite at $r = 0$, they must be dropped. Moreover, since the boundary condition $u(b, \theta, z) = u_1 = \text{const}$ possesses axial symmetry, it is clear that the solution will also be axially symmetric, which means that only the $(m = 0)$-eigenfunctions will enter the solution.* Then

$$\Theta_0(\theta) = \text{const}, \qquad Z_n(z) = \sin \frac{n\pi z}{L},$$

and

$$u(r, \theta, z) = \sum_{n=1}^{\infty} A_n \sin \frac{n\pi z}{L} I_0 \left(\frac{n\pi r}{L} \right).$$

The coefficients A_n are obtained by using the boundary condition which yields

$$u_1 = \sum_{n=1}^{\infty} A_n \sin \frac{n\pi z}{L} I_0 \left(\frac{n\pi b}{L} \right),$$

representing the Fourier sine series for the function $u_1 = \text{const}$. Consequently,

$$A_n I_0 \left(\frac{n\pi b}{L} \right) = \frac{2}{L} \int_0^L u_1 \sin \frac{n\pi z}{L} \, dz = \begin{cases} 4u_1/n\pi & (n = \text{odd}), \\ 0 & (n = \text{even}), \end{cases}$$

and

$$u(r, \theta, z) = \frac{4u_1}{\pi} \sum_{n=1,3,5,\ldots}^{\infty} \frac{1}{n} \frac{I_0(n\pi r/L) \sin (n\pi z/L)}{I_0(n\pi b/L)}.$$

BIBLIOGRAPHY

HOCHSTADT, H., *Special Functions of Mathematical Physics*. New York: Holt, Rinehart and Winston, 1961.

JAHNKE, E., and F. EMDE, *Tables of Higher Functions*. New York: McGraw-Hill Book Co., 1960.

LEBEDEV, N. N., *Special Functions and Their Applications*. Englewood Cliffs, N.J.: Prentice-Hall Inc., 1965.

MAGNUS, W., and F. OBERHETTINGER, *Formulas and Theorems for the Special Functions of Mathematical Physics*. New York: Chelsea Publishing Co., 1949.

RAINVILLE, E. D., *Special Functions*. New York: Macmillan Co., 1960.

SAGAN, H., *Boundary and Eigenvalue Problems in Mathematical Physics*. New York: John Wiley and Sons, Inc., 1961.

WEBSTER, A. G., *Partial Differential Equations of Mathematical Physics*. New York: Hafner Publishing Co., 1950.

---

* This observation saves us the trouble of writing a double series in m and n, using the boundary condition, integrating over θ, and concluding anyway that $A_{mn} = 0$ unless $m = 0$.

PROBLEMS

1. Consider the following Sturm-Liouville problem:

$$\frac{d^2y(x)}{dx^2} + \lambda y(x) = 0 \qquad (a \le x \le b),$$

$$a_1 y(a) + a_2 y'(a) = 0,$$
$$b_1 y(b) + b_2 y'(b) = 0,$$

and distinguish three cases:

$$a_1 = b_1 = 0, \qquad a_2 \ne 0, \qquad b_2 \ne 0, \qquad\qquad \text{(I)}$$
$$a_2 = b_2 = 0, \qquad a_1 \ne 0, \qquad b_1 \ne 0, \qquad\qquad \text{(II)}$$
$$a_1 \ne 0, \qquad a_2 \ne 0, \qquad b_1 \ne 0, \qquad b_2 \ne 0. \qquad \text{(III)}$$

a) Without determining the actual eigenvalues and eigenfunctions, prove, in detail, the orthogonality of nondegenerate eigenfunctions in all three cases.

b) In case III, determine the form of eigenfunctions and show that the eigenvalues λ must be solutions of the following transcendental equation:

$$\tan (b - a)\sqrt{\lambda} = \frac{(b_1 a_2 - b_2 a_1)\sqrt{\lambda}}{a_1 b_1 + a_2 b_2 \lambda}.$$

[*Hint:* Write the solution as $Ay_1(x) + By_2(x)$, apply the boundary conditions, and impose the condition that a nontrivial solution exist for the constants A and B.]

2. Consider the following set of functions:

$$\varphi_n(x) = \begin{cases} N_n \sin (n\pi x/a) & (n = 2, 4, 6, \ldots), \\ N_n \cos (n\pi x/a) & (n = 1, 3, 5, \ldots). \end{cases}$$

Formulate the Sturm-Liouville problem for which these functions serve as eigenfunctions. Determine the normalization constants N_n. Expand a function $f(x)$ of your choice in a series

$$f(x) = \sum_{n=1}^{\infty} c_n \varphi_n(x).$$

3. Certain integrals involving Legendre polynomials can be obtained from various recursion formulas. For instance:

a) Integrate the relation (a) on p. 346 by parts to show that

$$\int_0^1 P_l(x)\, dx = \frac{P_{l-1}(0)}{l+1} \qquad (l \ge 1).$$

b) Deduce the relation $P'_{l+1} - P'_{l-1} = (2l + 1)P_l$, integrate, and show that

$$\int_0^1 P_l(x)\, dx = \frac{P_{l-1}(0) - P_{l+1}(0)}{2l + 1} \qquad (l \ge 1).$$

c) Demonstrate the equivalence of these two results and show explicitly that

$$\int_0^1 P_l(x)\,dx = \begin{cases} 1 & (l = 0), \\ 0 & (l = 2, 4, 6, \ldots), \\ (-1)^{(l-1)/2} \dfrac{(l-1)!}{2^l \left(\dfrac{l+1}{2}\right)! \left(\dfrac{l-1}{2}\right)!} & (l = 1, 3, 5, \ldots). \end{cases}$$

d) Can you show that this is also equivalent to the form given on p. 355?

4. Using a suitable method (e.g., integrating the pure recursion formula on p. 345), evaluate the integral $\int_0^1 x P_l(x)\,dx$. Using this result, show that the Fourier-Legendre expansion of $f(x) = |x|$ reads

$$|x| = \frac{1}{2} - \sum_{l=2,4,6,\ldots}^{\infty} (-1)^{l/2} \frac{(2l+1)(l-2)!}{2^l \left(\dfrac{l-2}{2}\right)! \left(\dfrac{l+2}{2}\right)!} P_l(x).$$

5. The integrals

$$I_{ml} = \int_0^1 x^m P_l(x)\,dx \qquad (m \geq l)$$

occur in many applications of Legendre polynomials.

a) Multiply formula (b) on p. 346 by x^m and, integrating by parts, deduce the relation

$$I_{m-1,l+1} = \frac{m-l}{m} I_{ml} \qquad (m \geq l, l \geq 0).$$

b) Perform similar operations with the pure recursion formula (p. 345) and use the above result to show that

$$I_{ml} = \frac{m}{m+l+1} I_{m-1,l-1} \qquad (m \geq l, l \geq 1).$$

c) Evaluate the integrals I_{m0} and I_{m1} by elementary integration and use the above formula to establish the result

$$I_{ml} = \int_0^1 x^m P_l(x)\,dx = \frac{m(m-1)\cdots(m-l+2)}{(m+l+1)(m+l-1)\cdots(m-l+3)}$$

$$(m \geq l, l \geq 2).$$

d) The product $1 \cdot 3 \cdot 5 \cdot 7 \cdots (2n-1)(2n+1)$ is very often denoted by $(2n+1)!!$. Employing this notation, show that

$$I_{ml} = \frac{m!}{(m-l+1)!} \frac{(m-l+1)!!}{(m+l+1)!!} \qquad (m \geq l, l \geq 2).$$

6. The set of polynomials $U_n(x)$ is defined by the generating function

$$G(x, t) = \frac{1}{1 - 2xt + t^2} = \sum_{n=0}^{\infty} t^n U_n(x).$$

Establish the pure recursion relation, relating U_{n+1}, U_n, and U_{n-1}; distinguish carefully the following cases

(I) $n \geq 2$,   (II) $n = 1$,   and   (III) $n = 0$.

7. In the preceding problem, show that $U_0(x) = 1$. Using the recursion formula, write the first six polynomials ($n \leq 5$). For *all* values of n, prove that

$$U_n(1) = n + 1, \qquad U_n(-1) = (-1)^n(n + 1),$$

$$U_n(0) = \begin{cases} 0 & \text{(odd } n\text{)}, \\ (-1)^{n/2} & \text{(even } n\text{)}. \end{cases}$$

8. Solve the problem treated in Section 9.6 given that the electrostatic potential *outside* the sphere is required. Show how a similar problem can be solved if the function $\varphi(a, \theta)$ (p. 353) is an arbitrary function of θ.

9. From the compiex Fourier series on p. 360, develop the following integral representation of Bessel functions of integral order:

$$J_m(x) = \frac{1}{2\pi} \int_{-\pi}^{+\pi} e^{ix \sin \theta} e^{-im\theta} \, d\theta.$$

Since $J_m(x)$ is a real function, conclude also that

$$J_m(x) = \frac{1}{\pi} \int_0^\pi \cos (x \sin \theta) \cos m\theta \, d\theta + \frac{1}{\pi} \int_0^\pi \sin (x \sin \theta) \sin m\theta \, d\theta.$$

Furthermore, show that $J_m(x)$ is even or odd according to whether m is even or odd and from this fact finally deduce that

$$J_m(x) = \begin{cases} \dfrac{1}{\pi} \displaystyle\int_0^\pi \cos (x \sin \theta) \cos m\theta \, d\theta & (m = \text{even}), \\ \dfrac{1}{\pi} \displaystyle\int_0^\pi \sin (x \sin \theta) \sin m\theta \, d\theta & (m = \text{odd}). \end{cases}$$

10. The normalization integral for Fourier-Bessel series with Dirichlet conditions has been developed on pp. 362–363. Obtain a similar integral for Neumann conditions and show that in the expansion

$$f(r) = \sum_{n=1}^{\infty} b_n J_m \left(\beta_{mn} \frac{r}{a} \right) \qquad (m \geq 1),$$

where β_{mn} is the nth root of $J_m'(x)$, the coefficients b_n are given by

$$b_n = \frac{2 \int_0^a f(r) r J_m[\beta_{mn}(r/a)] \, dr}{a^2[1 - (m^2/\beta_{mn}^2)][J_m(\beta_{mn})]^2} \qquad (m \geq 1).$$

11. Observe that a difficulty arises in the formula of the preceding problem when $m = 0$, because one of the roots of $J_0'(x)$ is $x = 0$.

a) Show that for the case $k = 0$ and $\mu = 0$, the original radial equation (p. 356)

$$\frac{d^2R}{dr^2} + \frac{1}{r}\frac{dR}{dr} + \left(k^2 - \frac{\mu^2}{r^2}\right)R = 0$$

admits a *nontrivial* solution satisfying Neumann conditions. Find this solution.

b) Show that the solution found under (a) is orthogonal with respect to weight r to *all* Bessel functions $J_0[\beta_{0n}(r/a)]$ with $\beta_{0n} \neq 0$.

c) Adjoining this solution to the set $J_0[\beta_{0n}(r/a)]$ and assuming the augmented set to be complete, formulate, in detail, the Fourier-Bessel expansion technique in this case.

12. A very long (infinite) cylinder of radius b has an initial temperature distribution with radial symmetry: $u(r, \theta; 0) = u_0(r)$. Given that the lateral surface of the cylinder is insulated, show that

$$u(r, t) = \frac{2}{b^2}\int_0^b u_0(r)r\,dr + \sum_{n=1}^{\infty} C_n J_0\left(\beta_{0n}\frac{r}{b}\right)e^{-\beta_{0n}^2 a^2 t/b^2},$$

where

$$C_n = \frac{2}{b^2}\frac{\int_0^b f(r)rJ_0[\beta_{0n}(r/b)]\,dr}{[J_0(\beta_{0n})]^2}.$$

[*Hint:* Consult the developments in Problems 10 and 11 above.]

13. Investigate the modes of propagation of sound waves along a cylindrical tube of radius b (this problem is analogous to the Example in Section 8.9). In particular,

a) show that the plane wave is always propagated;

b) show that the cutoff frequency for the next mode is

$$\omega = \alpha_{11}c/b,$$

where $\alpha_{11} = 3.832\ldots$ is the lowest nontrivial root of $J_1(x)$.

14. Show that a general solution of the Laplace equation $\nabla^2\varphi = 0$ in spherical coordinates, valid inside the sphere $r \leq a$ can be expressed in the form

$$\varphi(r, \theta, \phi) = \sum_{l=0}^{\infty}\sum_{m=0}^{l}(A_{lm}\cos m\phi + B_{lm}\sin m\phi)r^l P_l(\cos\theta).$$

a) Assuming that the boundary condition $\varphi(a, \theta, \phi) = f(\theta, \phi)$ is given, write formulas for A_{lm} and B_{lm}, paying special attention to the case $m = 0$.

b) What is the analogous solution of $\nabla^2\varphi = 0$, valid outside the sphere?

15. A dry porous solid sphere of radius a is immersed in a liquid which may diffuse into the sphere according to the PDE developed in Section 8.4. The rate at which the liquid enters the sphere at the boundary (the current density) is equal to $\alpha(C_0 - C)$, where C is the concentration of the liquid just inside the sphere, C_0 is the saturation concentration, and α is a constant. Show that the concentration C is given by

$$C(r, t) = C_0 - \frac{2C_0\alpha}{Dr}\sum_{n=1}^{\infty}\frac{\sin\mu_n a}{\mu_n^2}\sin\mu_n r \cdot e^{-\mu_n^2 Dt},$$

where μ_n are the roots of the equation $\mu a \cot \mu a = 1 - \alpha a/D$.

16. Establish the power series for the spherical Bessel functions

$$j_l(x) = \sum_{k=0}^{\infty} (-1)^k \frac{x^{l+2k}}{k!2^k(2l + 2k + 1)!!},$$

where $(2n + 1)!! = 1 \cdot 3 \cdot 5 \cdot 7 \cdots (2n - 1)(2n + 1)$. [*Hint:* If the power series for $J_{l+1/2}(x)$ is to be used, then you should establish the handy formula

$$\Gamma(n + \tfrac{1}{2}) = \frac{\sqrt{\pi}(2n - 1)!!}{2^n} \qquad (n = 0, 1, 2, \ldots),$$

using $\Gamma(x + 1) = x\Gamma(x)$ n times.]

17. The spherical Bessel functions occur as the Fourier-Legendre coefficients of $e^{i\xi x}$, namely,

$$e^{i\xi x} = \sum_{l=0}^{\infty} i^l(2l + 1)j_l(\xi)P_l(x).$$

Prove this relation by calculating the integral

$$\int_{-1}^{+1} e^{i\xi x}P_l(x)\, dx$$

as follows:

a) Expand $e^{i\xi x}$ in a power series and show that the integrals

$$\int_{-1}^{+1} x^m P_l(x)\, dx$$

vanish unless $m \geq l$ and unless m and l are either both even or both odd.

b) Use the result of Problem 5 above to calculate the integrals and relate the obtained power series in ξ to that for $j_l(\xi)$ given in the preceding problem.

18. Two halves of an infinite conducting cylinder of radius a are maintained at potentials $+V$ and $-V$, respectively (Fig. 9.7). (Compare with the Example in Section 8.7.)

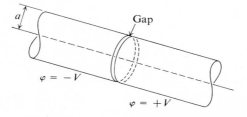

Figure 9.7

a) Treat the problem by separation of variables. What kind of symmetry arguments can be made immediately? Discuss the character of the eigenvalue spectrum and deduce from it the method of solution.

b) Solve the problem and show that

$$\varphi(r, z) = \frac{2V}{\pi} \int_0^{\infty} \frac{I_0(kr)}{I_0(ka)} \frac{\sin kz}{k}\, dk.$$

19. The lateral surface of a cylinder of length L and radius b is maintained at temperature $u_1 = \text{const}$; its bases are cooling according to Newton's law,

$$\frac{\partial u}{\partial n} + h(u - u_0) = 0 \qquad \text{(on the bases)},$$

where u_0 is the temperature of the surrounding medium, and $\partial u/\partial n$ is the outward normal gradient. We wish to find the steady-state temperature distribution inside the cylinder.

a) Show why it may be convenient to make a certain change in the temperature scale and choose the bases of the cylinder to be at $z = \pm L/2$ (rather than at $z = 0$ and $z = L$).

b) Formulate the problem and show that

$$u(r, z) = 2(u_1 - u_0) \sum_{n=1}^{\infty} \frac{\sin \gamma_n}{\gamma_n + \sin \gamma_n \cos \gamma_n} \frac{I_0(2\gamma_n r/L)}{I_0(2\gamma_n b/L)} \cos \frac{2\gamma_n z}{L},$$

where γ_n are the roots of $\tan \gamma = hL/2\gamma$.

CHAPTER 10

FINITE-DIMENSIONAL LINEAR SPACES

10.1 OSCILLATIONS OF SYSTEMS WITH TWO DEGREES OF FREEDOM

The rectilinear motion of a mass m attached to a spring of constant k is governed by the DE

$$\frac{d^2x}{dt^2} + \omega^2 x = 0 \qquad (\omega^2 = k/m).$$

If the mass is released with nontrivial initial conditions, that is $x(0)$ and $\dot{x}(0)$ are not simultaneously zero, it will perform harmonic oscillations with angular frequency ω given by

$$x = A \cos \omega t + B \sin \omega t \qquad (A, B = \text{real constants})$$

or, alternatively, by

$$x = Ce^{-i\omega t} \qquad (C = \text{complex constant})$$

(with the tacit understanding that the real part of x is identified with the real solution). This is an example of oscillations of a system with *one degree of freedom*. The state of the system can be described by a single function:

$$x = x(t)$$

representing the coordinate of the mass m.

Similar oscillatory motion is also observed with systems of *many degrees of freedom*. Let us study a few examples.

Example 1. Two Statically Coupled Masses

Consider two masses m_1 and m_2 connected by springs and moving with negligible friction (Fig. 10.1). The instantaneous positions of the masses are denoted by x_1 and x_2 and their equilibrium positions are denoted by x_{10} and x_{20}. It is convenient to describe the motion in terms of the displacements

$$u_1(t) = x_1(t) - x_{10}, \qquad u_2(t) = x_2(t) - x_{20}.$$

The mass m_1 is acted on by two horizontal forces (Fig. 10.2) given by

$$F_{11} = k_1 e_1, \qquad F_{12} = ke,$$

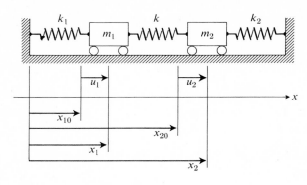

Figure 10.1

Figure 10.2

where e_1 and e are the elongations of the corresponding springs.   Evidently, $e_1 = u_1$ and $e = u_2 - u_1$. The net force in the x-direction is then

$$F_{12} - F_{11} = k(u_2 - u_1) - k_1 u_1,$$

and the equation of motion, $F = ma$, reads

$$m_1 \ddot{u}_1 + (k_1 + k)u_1 - ku_2 = 0.$$

Similarly, for the second mass,

$$m_2 \ddot{u}_2 + (k_2 + k)u_2 - ku_1 = 0.$$

We are now dealing with a system having two degrees of freedom. The state of the system (configuration) is described by *two functions*, $u_1(t)$ and $u_2(t)$, which satisfy a system of *coupled* differential equations.

Experiments indicate that this system is capable of executing harmonic oscillations with certain characteristic frequencies. Therefore, we shall seek the solutions in the form*

$$u_1(t) = U_1 e^{-i\omega t}, \qquad u_2(t) = U_2 e^{-i\omega t} \qquad (U_1, U_2 = \text{complex constants}).$$

Substitution into the system and cancellation of the factor $e^{-i\omega t}$ lead us to a system of two homogeneous linear equations:

$$[-m_1 \omega^2 + (k_1 + k)]U_1 - kU_2 = 0,$$
$$[-m_2 \omega^2 + (k_2 + k)]U_2 - kU_1 = 0.$$

---

* The general theory of coupled differential equations would actually guarantee the existence of such solutions in our case, but we omit the analysis here.

For a nontrivial solution we demand that the determinant of the system vanish:

$$\det \begin{vmatrix} (k_1 + k) - m_1\omega^2 & -k \\ -k & (k_2 + k) - m_2\omega^2 \end{vmatrix} = 0.$$

For the sake of brevity in algebraic manipulations, consider the special case $m_1 = m_2 = m$ and $k_1 = k_2 = k$. Then we have

$$\det \begin{vmatrix} 2k - m\omega^2 & -k \\ -k & 2k - m\omega^2 \end{vmatrix} = 0.$$

The roots of this equation are

$$\omega_1 = \sqrt{k/m}, \qquad \omega_2 = \sqrt{3}\sqrt{k/m}.$$

These are the *characteristic frequencies* of the system. The masses can vibrate (in simple harmonic motion) only with these frequencies and no others.

To find the actual motion of the system we substitute the allowed values of ω into the equations for U_1 and U_2. In this fashion we obtain

$$U_1 = U_2 \quad (\omega = \omega_1) \qquad \text{or} \qquad U_1 = -U_2 \quad (\omega = \omega_2).$$

One of the coefficients remains undetermined, because the equations are homogeneous. Physically this means that the system can vibrate with arbitrary amplitude for either characteristic frequency. The relations between U_1 and U_2 are essentially the *phase relationships* for vibrating masses. The first frequency gives rise to the solution

$$u_1^{(1)}(t) = C_1 e^{-i\omega_1 t}, \qquad u_2^{(1)}(t) = C_1 e^{-i\omega_1 t}.$$

Whatever the value of the complex constant C_1, the two masses will vibrate *in phase* (zero phase difference). To see this clearly, we write

$$C_1 = A_1 e^{i\phi_1} \qquad (A_1, \phi_1 = \text{real}).$$

Then the *real* solutions are

$$u_1^{(1)}(t) = A_1 \cos(\omega_1 t - \phi_1), \qquad u_2^{(1)}(t) = A_1 \cos(\omega_1 t - \phi_1).$$

Similarly, for the second frequency, $u_1^{(2)}(t) = C_2 e^{-i\omega_2 t}$, $u_2^{(2)}(t) = -C_2 e^{-i\omega_2 t}$, or, with $C_2 = A_2 e^{i\phi_2}$,

$$u_1^{(2)}(t) = A_2 \cos(\omega_2 t - \phi_2),$$
$$u_2^{(2)}(t) = -A_2 \cos(\omega_2 t - \phi_2) = A_2 \cos(\omega_2 t - \phi_2 + \pi).$$

In this case the masses vibrate *180° out of phase*.

Each of the two solutions, represented by the pair of functions (u_1, u_2), is called a *characteristic mode* of vibration, or *normal mode* of vibration.* The system may also have a solution which is a superposition of both normal modes:

$$u_1(t) = A_1 \cos(\omega_1 t - \phi_1) + A_2 \cos(\omega_2 t - \phi_2),$$
$$u_2(t) = A_1 \cos(\omega_1 t - \phi_1) - A_2 \cos(\omega_2 t - \phi_2).$$

That this is indeed a solution is evident from the homogeneity of the system of coupled differential equations. It is not too difficult to verify that the above form represents the *general solution* of the problem. An arbitrary motion of the masses can be characterized by four initial conditions:

$$u_1(0), \qquad \dot{u}_1(0), \qquad u_2(0), \qquad \dot{u}_2(0).$$

From these four values, the four parameters A_1, A_2, ϕ_1, and ϕ_2 can be obtained.

Example 2. Coupled Pendula

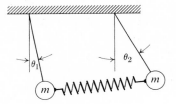

Figure 10.3

Consider two pendula made up of light rods (weight is neglected) of length L and two masses m, connected by a spring (Fig. 10.3). Convenient coordinates to describe the configuration of the system are the angles θ_1 and θ_2. The equation of motion for each pendulum reads

$$I\ddot{\theta} = N,$$

where I is the moment of inertia $(I = mL^2)$, and N is the applied torque about the point of suspension. If the angular displacements θ_1 and θ_2 are small and the usual approximations

$$\sin\theta \cong \theta, \qquad \cos\theta \cong 1$$

are made, then

$$N_1 = -mgL\theta_1 + kL^2(\theta_2 - \theta_1), \qquad N_2 = -mgL\theta_2 + kL^2(\theta_1 - \theta_2),$$

leading to the system of coupled differential equations

$$mL\ddot{\theta}_1 = -(mg + kL)\theta_1 + kL\theta_2, \qquad mL\ddot{\theta}_2 = -(mg + kL)\theta_2 + kL\theta_1.$$

---

* Analogous to normal modes of vibrating string (p. 293). The string can be considered as composed of an infinite number of particles *all of which* vibrate with the same frequency in a normal mode.

It is instructive to derive these equations of motion by a more sophisticated method, using the Lagrangian equations of motion.* If $q_i (i = 1, 2, \ldots, n)$ are the generalized coordinates describing the configuration of a system (with n degrees of freedom), then its motion is given by n equations

$$\frac{d}{dt}\left(\frac{\partial \mathcal{L}}{\partial \dot{q}_i}\right) - \frac{\partial \mathcal{L}}{\partial q_i} = 0 \qquad (i = 1, 2, 3, \ldots, n),$$

where $\mathcal{L}$ is the Lagrangian of the system. For conservative systems the Lagrangian can be taken as the difference between kinetic and potential energies:

$$\mathcal{L} = T - V.$$

In our example ($n = 2$) the generalized coordinates can be chosen as θ_1 and θ_2. The kinetic energy is then

$$T = \tfrac{1}{2}I_1\dot{\theta}_1^2 + \tfrac{1}{2}I_2\dot{\theta}_2^2 = \tfrac{1}{2}mL^2\dot{\theta}_1^2 + \tfrac{1}{2}mL^2\dot{\theta}_2^2,$$

and the potential energy is

$$V = \frac{mgL}{2}\,\theta_1^2 + \frac{mgL}{2}\,\theta_2^2 + \frac{k}{2}[L(\theta_2 - \theta_1)]^2.$$

The first two terms represent the gravitational potential energies of the two masses (with respect to the earth) and the third term represents the elastic potential energy of the spring.

By elementary algebra, the above expression can be brought to the conventional form

$$V = \tfrac{1}{2}\{(mgL + kL^2)\theta_1^2 + (mgL + kL^2)\theta_2^2 - 2kL^2\theta_1\theta_2\}.$$

This is an example of the so-called *quadratic form*. A general quadratic form in n variables q_i is an expression of the type

$$\sum_{i=1}^{n}\sum_{j=1}^{n} a_{ij}q_iq_j,$$

where a_{ij} are coefficients independent of q_i. If a quadratic form contains only terms with squares of q_i, namely, $a_{11}q_1^2, a_{22}q_2^2$, etc., but no cross terms like $a_{12}q_1q_2$, then it is called *diagonal*.†

Observe that the kinetic energy T is also represented by a quadratic form in the variables $\dot{\theta}_1$ and $\dot{\theta}_2$ and it happens to be diagonal. The potential energy V is not a diagonal form because of the presence of the term $-kL^2\theta_1\theta_2$. This term is responsible for the *coupling* between the two pendula because if it were absent,

---

* See, e.g., Goldstein, *Classical Mechanics*, Chapter 1.

† The coefficients a_{ij} may be arranged in a matrix. Diagonal quadratic forms correspond to diagonal matrices (see p. 443).

the resulting system (see below) would reduce to two independent differential equations. Thus we have the case of so-called *static coupling*, where the coupling terms appear in V but not in T.

Let us deduce the equations of motion. We have

$$\frac{\partial \mathfrak{L}}{\partial \dot{\theta}_1} = \frac{\partial T}{\partial \dot{\theta}_1} = mL^2\dot{\theta}_1, \qquad \frac{\partial \mathfrak{L}}{\partial \dot{\theta}_2} = \frac{\partial T}{\partial \dot{\theta}_2} = mL^2\dot{\theta}_2,$$

$$\frac{\partial \mathfrak{L}}{\partial \theta_1} = -\frac{\partial V}{\partial \theta_1} = -(mgL + kL^2)\theta_1 + kL^2\theta_2,$$

$$\frac{\partial \mathfrak{L}}{\partial \theta_2} = -\frac{\partial V}{\partial \theta_2} = -(mgL + kL^2)\theta_2 + kL^2\theta_1.$$

Substituting into the Lagrange equations, we obtain the equations of motion (after canceling L) in the same form as before:

$$mL\ddot{\theta}_1 + (mg + kL)\theta_1 - kL\theta_2 = 0,$$
$$mL\ddot{\theta}_2 + (mg + kL)\theta_2 - kL\theta_1 = 0.$$

It is not difficult to trace the effect of the cross term in the quadratic form for V on the coupling of the two differential equations.

As in the preceding example, we seek the simple harmonic solutions

$$\theta_1 = \Theta_1 e^{-i\omega t}, \qquad \theta_2 = \Theta_2 e^{-i\omega t},$$

which lead to a 2×2 linear algebraic system:

$$[(mg + kL) - mL\omega^2]\Theta_1 - kL\Theta_2 = 0,$$
$$[(mg + kL) - mL\omega^2]\Theta_2 - kL\Theta_1 = 0.$$

As before, the determinant must vanish,

$$\det \begin{vmatrix} (mg + kL) - mL\omega^2 & -kL \\ -kL & (mg + kL) - mL\omega^2 \end{vmatrix} = 0,$$

yielding the characteristic frequencies

$$\omega_1 = \sqrt{g/L}, \qquad \omega_2 = \sqrt{1 + 2kL/mg}\,\sqrt{g/L}.$$

The corresponding phase relationships are

$$\Theta_1 = \Theta_2 \quad (\omega = \omega_1) \qquad \text{or} \qquad \Theta_1 = -\Theta_2 \quad (\omega = \omega_2).$$

The two normal modes are illustrated in Fig. 10.4. It is seen that in the first mode the spring never suffers any elongation and both pendula swing as though they were free. In the second mode the spring suffers maximum deformation (for a given amplitude of vibrations).

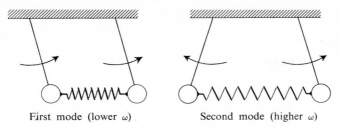

First mode (lower ω)   Second mode (higher ω)

Figure 10.4

Again, an arbitrary motion (due to arbitrary initial conditions) of the pendula can be represented as a superposition of the two characteristic modes. In order to set the pendula in motion in only one of the modes we must choose appropriate initial conditions (e.g., no initial displacement, and equal and oppositely directed initial velocities will "excite" only the second mode).

10.2 NORMAL COORDINATES AND LINEAR TRANSFORMATIONS

When we talk about a system of coupled pendula we imply the physical fact that, in general, the motion of one pendulum is bound to influence the motion of another. This is reflected in mathematical formulation: The DE satisfied by θ_1 depends on θ_2 and vice versa. Or, on a more sophisticated level, the quadratic expression for potential energy contains cross terms.

While it is true that if one pendulum is set in motion, the other will start moving as well, this coupling property does not hold for the normal modes. We can "excite" one normal mode *without affecting the other*. We are led toward the statement that normal modes are not coupled to each other. It is not difficult to find a mathematical formulation of this notion. Let us write the statement that an arbitrary motion of coupled pendula can be represented as a superposition of two normal modes of vibration. Complex notation is particularly simple:

$$\theta_1 = Ae^{-i\omega_1 t} + Be^{-i\omega_2 t}, \qquad \theta_2 = Ae^{-i\omega_1 t} - Be^{-i\omega_2 t},$$

where A and B are complex constants (representing four parameters which can be determined from four initial conditions).

Adding and subtracting these equations, we obtain

$$2Ae^{-i\omega_1 t} = \theta_1 + \theta_2, \qquad 2Be^{-i\omega_2 t} = \theta_1 - \theta_2.$$

When the system vibrates in the first normal mode, then $B = 0$ or $\theta_1 - \theta_2 = 0$ at all times t (Fig. 10.4) is implied; at the same time the quantity $\theta_1 + \theta_2$ exhibits harmonic variations in time. For the second normal mode, $\theta_1 + \theta_2 = 0$ for all t.

It appears, then, that variations in the quantity $\psi_1 = \theta_1 + \theta_2$ are independent of variations in the quantity $\psi_2 = \theta_1 - \theta_2$. This suggests that we try to make a change in generalized coordinates and write the equations of motion in terms of

ψ_1 and ψ_2. We have

$$\theta_1 = \tfrac{1}{2}(\psi_1 + \psi_2), \qquad \theta_2 = \tfrac{1}{2}(\psi_1 - \psi_2).$$

We substitute into the equations of motion:

$$\tfrac{1}{2}mL(\ddot{\psi}_1 + \ddot{\psi}_2) + \tfrac{1}{2}(mg + kL)(\psi_1 + \psi_2) - \tfrac{1}{2}kL(\psi_1 - \psi_2) = 0,$$
$$\tfrac{1}{2}mL(\ddot{\psi}_1 - \ddot{\psi}_2) + \tfrac{1}{2}(mg + kL)(\psi_1 - \psi_2) - \tfrac{1}{2}kL(\psi_1 + \psi_2) = 0.$$

Adding and subtracting, we obtain

$$mL\ddot{\psi}_1 + mg\psi_1 = 0, \qquad mL\ddot{\psi}_2 + (mg + 2kL)\psi_2 = 0.$$

We see that the equations of motion are *decoupled*, and it is a trivial task to evaluate the characteristic frequencies

$$\omega_1 = \sqrt{g/L}, \qquad \omega_2 = \sqrt{g/L + 2k/m}.$$

The generalized coordinates ψ_1 and ψ_2 are known as *normal coordinates*. If we had known how to select them from the beginning (and expressed the Lagrangian in terms of them), then the solution of the problem would have been greatly simplified.

While it is not, in general, possible to "guess" the normal coordinates outright, it is not necessary to go through the process of solving the differential equations of motion. Indeed, let us return to the expression for the potential energy for coupled pendula:

$$V = \tfrac{1}{2}(mgL + kL^2)\theta_1^2 + \tfrac{1}{2}(mgL + kL^2)\theta_2^2 - kL^2\theta_1\theta_2.$$

Let us consider a plane in which θ_1 and θ_2 are cartesian coordinates.* Then the so-called *equipotential curve* $V = $ const is an ellipse with the center at the origin:

$$A\theta_1^2 + 2B\theta_1\theta_2 + C\theta_2^2 = D,$$

where $A = C = \tfrac{1}{2}(mgL + kL^2)$, $B = -\tfrac{1}{2}kL^2$, $D = V = $ const. The axes of the ellipse do not coincide with the θ_1- and θ_2-axes, but it is known from elementary analytic geometry that a rotation of coordinate axes by an angle α (Fig. 10.5),

$$\psi_1 = OA + AB = \theta_1 \cos\alpha + \theta_2 \sin\alpha,$$
$$\psi_2 = MB = CD - AD = \theta_2 \cos\alpha - \theta_1 \sin\alpha,$$

will reduce the ellipse to the standard form (Fig. 10.6)

$$\frac{\psi_1^2}{a^2} + \frac{\psi_2^2}{b^2} = 1,$$

where a and b are the semiaxes of the ellipse. Indeed, we have

$$\theta_1 = \psi_1 \cos\alpha - \psi_2 \sin\alpha, \qquad \theta_2 = \psi_1 \sin\alpha + \psi_2 \cos\alpha.$$

---

* Such a plane may be called the *configuration space* for our system.

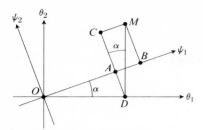

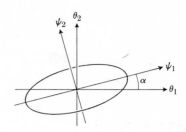

$\psi_1 = OA + AB = \theta_1 \cos \alpha + \theta_2 \sin \alpha$
$\psi_2 = MB = CD - AD = \theta_2 \cos \alpha - \theta_1 \sin \alpha$ **Figure 10.5**   **Figure 10.6**

Substituting into the equation of the ellipse and requiring that the cross term containing $\psi_1\psi_2$ vanish, we obtain

$$\tan 2\alpha = 2B/(A - C).$$

In our case, $A = C$, yielding $\tan 2\alpha = \pm\infty$ and $\alpha = \pm 45°$. The choice $\alpha = +45°$ gives*

$$\theta_1 = (1/\sqrt{2})(\psi_1 - \psi_2), \qquad \theta_2 = (1/\sqrt{2})(\psi_1 + \psi_2),$$

thereby defining the normal coordinates†

$$\psi_1 = (1/\sqrt{2})(\theta_1 + \theta_2), \qquad \psi_2 = (1/\sqrt{2})(-\theta_1 + \theta_2).$$

Substituting this into the expression for V, we obtain

$$V = \tfrac{1}{2}mgL\psi_1^2 + \tfrac{1}{2}(mgL + 2kL^2)\psi_2^2.$$

We have, therefore, *diagonalized* the quadratic expression for V. The linear transformation (from θ_1, θ_2 to ψ_1, ψ_2) which diagonalizes V is seen to be a rotation in the (abstract) plane in which the generalized coordinates θ_1 and θ_2 are treated as cartesian coordinates.

As mentioned previously, the equations of motion are decoupled provided the Lagrangian is a diagonal quadratic form. The kinetic energy T was diagonal in terms of $\dot\theta_1$ and $\dot\theta_2$, but now it must be expressed in terms of $\dot\psi_1$ and $\dot\psi_2$. Fortunately, T remains diagonal after the transformation and reads

$$T = \tfrac{1}{2}mL^2\dot\psi_1^2 + \tfrac{1}{2}mL^2\dot\psi_2^2.$$

It is easy to check that the Lagrangian equations of motion in terms of ψ_1 and ψ_2 are decoupled and read

$$\ddot\psi_1 + \frac{g}{L}\psi_1 = 0, \qquad \ddot\psi_2 + \left(\frac{g}{L} + \frac{2k}{m}\right)\psi_2 = 0$$

(as already given).

---

* The choice $\alpha = -45°$ yields the same normal coordinates, only differently labeled.
† Same as on p. 411 except for the factor $1/\sqrt{2}$, which is not really relevant.

Remark. While the introduction of normal coordinates formally decouples the system of differential equations, it does not change its physical nature which is still that of *coupled pendula.* Normal coordinates do not separate the system into two physical parts which are mutually noninteracting; what is decoupled are just certain configurations of the system which appear to be quite abstract.

It is, however, of some interest to note that we may distinguish the two normal modes in physical terms if we concentrate our attention not to the pendula themselves, but to *the spring* which connects them. In the first (lower frequency) normal mode the spring undergoes *translatory motion* and is not deformed. In the second mode it undergoes *pure deformation*, with its center of gravity remaining at rest.

We shall now proceed to explore further properties of characteristic oscillations of systems with many degrees of freedom.

Example 1. The Double Pendulum

Consider a pendulum of length L_2 and mass m_2 capable of swinging freely from the end of another pendulum of length L_1 and mass m_1, attached to the point O (Fig. 10.7). The equations of motion for the masses m_1 and m_2 are complicated by the presence of constraints; e.g., mass m_2 must always move in such a way that it keeps its distance L_2 from the mass m_1 (the position of which is variable).

We shall proceed by the technique of Lagrangian equations. To find the potential energy, note that if the upper pendulum is displaced by an angle θ_1, the mass m_1 is raised by an amount $L_1 - L_1 \cos \theta_1$ contributing a term $m_1 g L_1 (1 - \cos \theta_1)$ to the potential energy. At the same time, if $\theta_2 = 0$, the mass m_2 is raised by the *same amount* contributing a term $m_2 g L_1 (1 - \cos \theta_1)$.

Additional displacement of the lower pendulum by the angle θ_2 evidently contributes a term $m_2 g L_2 (1 - \cos \theta_2)$. The total potential energy is then

$$V = (m_1 + m_2) g L_1 (1 - \cos \theta_1) + m_2 g L_2 (1 - \cos \theta_2).$$

The kinetic energy is, of course, $T = (m_1/2) v_1^2 + (m_2/2) v_2^2$, but we must express it in terms of our generalized coordinates and their derivatives. Consider an infinitesimal displacement of the double pendulum characterized by the increments $d\theta_1$ and $d\theta_2$ in generalized coordinates (Fig. 10.8). The bob of the upper pendulum moves from A to A' and undergoes the displacement $ds_1 = L_1 d\theta_1$. Therefore

$$v_1^2 = \left(\frac{ds_1}{dt}\right)^2 = \left(L_1 \frac{d\theta_1}{dt}\right)^2 = L_1^2 \dot{\theta}_1^2.$$

The bob of the lower pendulum moves from B to B'' and this displacement $ds_2 = BB''$ may be visualized as follows.

1. The whole system is given an increment $d\theta_1$, with point A going into point A' and point B going into point B'. Evidently,

$$BB' = AA' = L_1 d\theta_1.$$

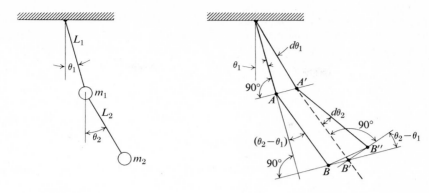

Figure 10.7   **Figure 10.8**

2. The lower pendulum is further moved through an angle $d\theta_2$, causing point B' to go into point B'' with $B'B'' = L_2\, d\theta_2$.

The entire displacement BB'' of the second bob is then given by the cosine theorem:

$$(BB'')^2 = (BB')^2 + (B'B'')^2 = 2(BB')(B'B'') \cos(\theta_2 - \theta_1).$$

Dividing by $(dt)^2$, we obtain

$$v_2^2 = L_1^2\dot{\theta}_1^2 + L_2^2\dot{\theta}_2^2 + 2L_1L_2 \cos(\theta_2 - \theta_1)\dot{\theta}_1\dot{\theta}_2.$$

The total kinetic energy is then

$$T = \tfrac{1}{2}(m_1 + m_2)L_1^2\dot{\theta}_1^2 + \tfrac{1}{2}m_2L_2^2\dot{\theta}_2^2 + m_2L_1L_2 \cos(\theta_2 - \theta_1)\dot{\theta}_1\dot{\theta}_2.$$

Constructing the Lagrangian, we shall adopt the usual approximations valid for small oscillations:

$$1 - \cos\theta_1 \cong \tfrac{1}{2}\theta_1^2, \qquad 1 - \cos\theta_2 \cong \tfrac{1}{2}\theta_2^2, \qquad \cos(\theta_2 - \theta_1) \cong 1.$$

Furthermore, for the sake of simplicity, we shall treat the special case

$$m_1 = m_2 = m, \qquad L_1 = L_2 = L.$$

The Lagrangian reads

$$\mathcal{L} = mL^2\dot{\theta}_1^2 + \tfrac{1}{2}mL^2\dot{\theta}_2^2 + mL^2\dot{\theta}_1\dot{\theta}_2 - mgL\theta_1^2 - \tfrac{1}{2}mgL\theta_2^2.$$

Note that the coupling term now originates from the expression of kinetic energy, rather than from the expression of potential energy. This is called *dynamic coupling*.

The Lagrangian equations of motion read

$$2\ddot{\theta}_1 + 2(g/L)\theta_1 + \ddot{\theta}_2 = 0, \qquad \ddot{\theta}_1 + \ddot{\theta}_2 + (g/L)\theta_2 = 0$$

and represent a system of coupled differential equations.* At this point it is

---

* The differential equations can be solved for $\ddot{\theta}_1$ and $\ddot{\theta}_2$, but there is no particular advantage in this.

natural to inquire whether it is possible to diagonalize the quadratic form for kinetic energy by some linear transformation. This is indeed possible; for instance, the choice of new variables

$$\phi_1 = \theta_1, \qquad \phi_2 = \theta_1 + \theta_2$$

will result in $T = \frac{1}{2}mL^2(\dot{\phi}_1^2 + \dot{\phi}_2^2)$, which is diagonal. However, the potential energy in the new system will read

$$V = \frac{1}{2}mgL(3\phi_1^2 + \phi_2^2 - 2\phi_1\phi_2),$$

which means that the system is now coupled statically, rather than dynamically.

From this example we see that the decoupling of the system of differential equations is not as simple as in the problem of coupled pendula. We have also learned that there is no fundamental difference between static and dynamic coupling.

To find characteristic frequencies, we seek solutions in the form

$$\theta_1 = \Theta_1 e^{-i\omega t}, \qquad \theta_2 = \Theta_2 e^{-i\omega t}.$$

The differential system yields

$$\Theta_1(2g/L - 2\omega^2) - \omega^2\Theta_2 = 0, \qquad -\omega^2\Theta_1 + (g/L - \omega^2)\Theta_2 = 0$$

so that

$$\det \begin{vmatrix} 2g/L - 2\omega^2 & -\omega^2 \\ -\omega^2 & g/L - \omega^2 \end{vmatrix} = 0.$$

Solving, we obtain

$$\omega_1 = \sqrt{(2 + \sqrt{2})g/L}, \qquad \omega_2 = \sqrt{(2 - \sqrt{2})g/L}.$$

The root ω_1 leads to the relationship $\Theta_2 = -\Theta_1\sqrt{2}$, while the root ω_2 yields $\Theta_2 = \Theta_1\sqrt{2}$.

We may set up normal coordinates by employing the method used before. The general solution of the problem reads

$$\theta_1 = Ae^{-i\omega_1 t} + Be^{-i\omega_2 t}, \qquad \theta_2 = -A\sqrt{2}\,e^{-i\omega_1 t} + B\sqrt{2}\,e^{-i\omega_2 t},$$

where A and B specify *how much of each normal mode* is present in the solution. From these equations it follows that

$$2A\sqrt{2}\,e^{-i\omega_1 t} = \theta_1\sqrt{2} - \theta_2, \qquad 2B\sqrt{2}\,e^{-i\omega_2 t} = \theta_1\sqrt{2} + \theta_2.$$

The relationships between θ_1 and θ_2 appearing on the right are characteristic of the configurations pertaining to the corresponding normal modes. Therefore we can introduce the new coordinates*

$$\psi_1 = \theta_1\sqrt{2} - \theta_2, \qquad \psi_2 = \theta_1\sqrt{2} + \theta_2;$$

then

$$\theta_1 = (1/2\sqrt{2})(\psi_1 + \psi_2), \qquad \theta_2 = (1/2)(-\psi_1 + \psi_2).$$

This transformation diagonalizes the Lagrangian:

$$\mathcal{L} = \frac{1}{4}\left\{mL^2 \frac{2-\sqrt{2}}{2}\dot{\psi}_1^2 + mL^2\frac{2+\sqrt{2}}{2}\dot{\psi}_2^2 - mgL\psi_1^2 - mgL\psi_2^2\right\}.$$

In this example we have succeeded in diagonalizing the quadratic form T without perturbing the already existing diagonal form V. In other words, we have performed the simultaneous diagonalization of two quadratic forms. In distinction to the previous example, however, the diagonalizing transformation (from θ- to ψ-coordinates) is *not a rotation*.

Example 2. The problem of the two statically coupled masses solved in Section 10.1 can be easily extended to N masses, as shown in Fig. 10.9 (for convenience, all masses and all springs are chosen to be identical).

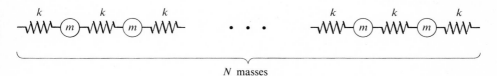

N masses

Figure 10.9

There are two common types of end conditions for such a string of masses. We may assume that the first and the last springs are attached to rigid supports (as in Section 10.1). Alternatively, we may identify the first and the last spring thereby forming a ring.† Both problems are used as prototypes for the study of vibrations of crystalline lattices.‡

We shall now analyze the second type of structure with three masses which may be pictured as moving in a frictionless circular groove, as shown in Fig. 10.10. In terms of displacements x_1, x_2, x_3 (from some fixed equilibrium configuration), the equations of motion can be easily shown to read

$$\ddot{x}_1 = \omega_0^2(x_2 - 2x_1 + x_3),$$
$$\ddot{x}_2 = \omega_0^2(x_3 - 2x_2 + x_1),$$
$$\ddot{x}_3 = \omega_0^2(x_1 - 2x_3 + x_2),$$

---

* Scalar multiples $k_1\psi_1$ and $k_2\psi_2$ will do equally well.

† The ring may be assumed to be circular. Here, we are studying only the longitudinal vibrations.

‡ See, e.g., Kittel, *Introduction to Solid State Physics*, p. 60 et seq.

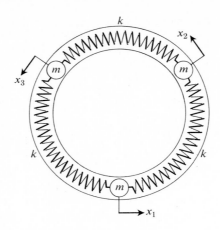

Figure 10.10

where $\omega_0^2 = k/m$. We seek solutions of the form

$$x_k = X_k e^{-i\omega t} \qquad (k = 1, 2, 3).$$

Substituting this into the equations of motion and requiring a nontrivial solution for X_k, we obtain

$$\det \begin{vmatrix} 2 - \omega^2/\omega_0^2 & -1 & -1 \\ -1 & 2 - \omega^2/\omega_0^2 & -1 \\ -1 & -1 & 2 - \omega^2/\omega_0^2 \end{vmatrix} = 0,$$

reducing to $z^3 - 2z - 2 = 0$, where $z = 2 - \omega^2/\omega_0^2$. The roots of this equation are

$$z_1 = 2,$$
$$\left.\begin{matrix} z_2 = -1, \\ z_3 = -1, \end{matrix}\right\} \text{ Double root}$$

corresponding to

$$\omega_1 = 0, \qquad \omega_2 = \omega_3 = \omega_0\sqrt{3}.$$

The first root (zero frequency) is not really an oscillation. We can formally solve the equations for the X_k and find

$$X_1 = X_2 = X_3 = \text{const} = A,$$

which leads to $x_1 = x_2 = x_3 = A$. This is clearly a solution. However, this is not the most general nonoscillatory solution. It is obvious that the functions

$$x_1(t) = A + Bt, \qquad x_2(t) = A + Bt,$$
$$x_3(t) = A + Bt \qquad (A, B = \text{const})$$

satisfy the equations of motion.* They represent a *translatory motion*† of all three masses. If $B = 0$, we have simply a static equilibrium.

The double root $\omega = \omega_0\sqrt{3}$ gives us bona fide vibrations. At first glance it would appear that we have only one normal mode of vibration. Actually there are two modes, both with frequency $\omega = \omega_0\sqrt{3}$. To see this, write the algebraic equations for the amplitudes X_1, X_2, and X_3:

$$(2 - \omega^2/\omega_0^2)X_1 - X_2 - X_3 = 0,$$
$$-X_1 + (2 - \omega^2/\omega_0^2)X_2 - X_3 = 0,$$
$$-X_1 - X_2 + (2 - \omega^2/\omega_0^2)X_3 = 0.$$

If $\omega^2 = 3\omega_0^2$, all three equations reduce to a single one:

$$X_1 + X_2 + X_3 = 0.$$

There are *two* linearly independent solutions of this equation, for instance:

First solution: $X_1 = -X_3$, $X_2 = 0$.
Second solution: $X_1 = 0$, $X_2 = -X_3$.

Any other solution can be expressed as a linear combination of these two solutions which can be regarded as normal modes corresponding to the characteristic frequency $\omega_0\sqrt{3}$. Of course, the above choice is arbitrary and any two other linearly independent modes can be considered as normal modes. We now have a case of (twofold) degeneracy of the characteristic frequency $\omega = \omega_0\sqrt{3}$ (compare with a similar phenomenon in Section 8.8).

Each normal mode gives us a solution with two arbitrary constants.‡ Along with the "translatory solution," this yields six arbitrary constants, sufficient for the description of the motion of three masses with arbitrary initial conditions.

10.3 VECTOR SPACES, BASES, COORDINATES

The solutions of a system of homogeneous differential equations analyzed in the preceding two sections possess the property that linear combinations of such solutions are also solutions. This characterizes the sets of solution functions as

---

* The form $x_k = X_k e^{-i\omega t}$ gives us a two-parameter solution only if $\omega \neq 0$. If $\omega = 0$, other forms for $x_k(t)$ must be sought.

† This may be a misnomer in the sense that masses do not move along a straight line. However, we consider motion in *one dimension*, and the concept of a curved path is out of place.

‡ Recall that the X_k constants are complex and that the physical solutions are given by

$$\text{Re}\,(X_k e^{-i\omega t}) = \text{Re}\,X_k \cos \omega t - \text{Im}\,X_k \sin \omega t$$

involving two constants, $\text{Re}\,X_k$ and $\text{Im}\,X_k$.

elements of a *linear space*, or *vector space*. This space can be of an arbitrary number of *dimensions*, characterized by the number of linearly independent elements (also called *vectors**) in the space. For instance, the solutions of the coupled-pendula problem form a two-dimensional vector space.

We find that similar properties are encountered in solutions of other homogeneous systems, for instance, a second-order DE (two-dimensional vector space) or a PDE (infinite-dimensional vector space). We shall briefly outline some of the most important (for physical applications) properties of vector spaces in general.

A vector space can be characterized by the following ten properties satisfied by its elements (vectors):†

1. Vectors can be added and their sum is also a vector:

$$\mathbf{x} + \mathbf{y} = \mathbf{z} \qquad (\mathbf{x}, \mathbf{y}, \mathbf{z} \text{ are vectors}).$$

2. The addition is commutative:

$$\mathbf{x} + \mathbf{y} = \mathbf{y} + \mathbf{x}.$$

3. The addition is associative:

$$(\mathbf{x} + \mathbf{y}) + \mathbf{z} = \mathbf{x} + (\mathbf{y} + \mathbf{z}).$$

4. There is a *zero vector* **0** such that

$$\mathbf{x} + \mathbf{0} = \mathbf{x}, \quad \text{for } \textit{all} \text{ vectors } \mathbf{x}.$$

5. For each vector **x** there is a *negative vector* **y** such that $\mathbf{x} + \mathbf{y} = \mathbf{0}$.

Remark. Properties 1, 3, 4, and 5 establish a vector space as a *group* under the operation of addition.‡ Property 2 states that this group is commutative (or Abelian).

6. Vectors can be multiplied by scalars, the result also being a vector. If **x** is a vector, then $a\mathbf{x}$ is also a vector (a = scalar).

Remark. By scalars we shall mean either real or complex numbers, thereby introducing real or complex vector spaces. More generally, scalars can be elements of a field.§

7. Multiplication by scalars is associative:

$$a(b\mathbf{x}) = (ab)\mathbf{x} \qquad (a, b = \text{scalars}).$$

---

* The name vector refers to the similarity with the "arrowlike quantities" in a physical space or plane.

† We usually denote vectors (in an abstract sense) by bold face letters (e.g., **x**).

‡ For the definition of a group, consult any textbook in advanced algebra, e.g., Birkhoff and McLane, *A Survey of Modern Algebra*, Chapter 6.

§ Birkhoff and McLane, Chapter 2.

8. First distributive law:

$$(a + b)\mathbf{x} = a\mathbf{x} + b\mathbf{x}.$$

9. Second distributive law:

$$a(\mathbf{x} + \mathbf{y}) = a\mathbf{x} + a\mathbf{y}.$$

10. Invariance under multiplication by unity*

$$1 \cdot \mathbf{x} = \mathbf{x}.$$

Remark. It is now possible to derive (as consequences of these ten postulates) such common properties of vector space as

a) $0 \cdot \mathbf{x} = \mathbf{0}$

or

b) if $\mathbf{x} + \mathbf{y} = \mathbf{0}$, then $\mathbf{y} = (-1) \cdot \mathbf{x}$, etc.

Vector spaces used in physics also possess certain properties related to the notion of *inner product* (analogous to the notion of dot product, or scalar product for vectors in actual physical space, or a plane†). However, it may be instructive to consider first some basic properties of vector spaces regardless of whether or not an inner product is defined.

A *linear combination* of a *finite* number of vectors is the expression

$$a_1\mathbf{x}_1 + a_2\mathbf{x}_2 + \cdots + a_n\mathbf{x}_n = \sum_{i=1}^{n} a_i\mathbf{x}_i,$$

where $a_1, a_2, \ldots, a_n$ are arbitrary scalars. A linear combination can always be made to be equal to the zero vector $\mathbf{0}$ by choosing all a_i to be zero (known as the *trivial set* of the a_i). For some sets of n vectors, this would be the only possibility. Such a set is called *linearly independent*. For some sets of n vectors a *nontrivial set* of the a_i may exist (i.e., *at least one* a_i is not zero). Such a set is called *linearly dependent*.

Example. Solutions of the Bessel DE of order μ form a vector space. The set of the two solutions $J_\mu(x)$ and $J_{-\mu}(x)$ is linearly independent, provided μ is not an integer; if $\mu = m$ is an integer, then the set is linearly dependent because

$$J_m(x) + (-1)^{m+1}J_{-m}(x) = 0$$

---

* This property may appear to be obvious. However, it should be kept in mind that we are describing a *completely abstract* vector space and hence must postulate its properties; we cannot take them for granted. Property 10 cannot be derived from the first nine, so it must be postulated.

† See, however, the footnote on p. 12.

[a nontrivial set of coefficients: 1 and $(-1)^{m+1}$]. On the other hand, the set of the solutions $J_\mu(x)$ and $N_\mu(x)$ is always linearly independent. The set of *three* solutions $J_\mu(x)$, $J_{-\mu}(x)$, and $N_\mu(x)$ is always linearly dependent. As a matter of fact, any three (nontrivial) solutions of the Bessel DE must be linearly dependent.

This last remark leads us to the definition of *dimension* of a vector space. Some vector spaces possess a *maximum* (finite) number N of linearly independent vectors. *Any* $N + 1$ vectors will necessarily be linearly dependent. Such spaces are said to be N-dimensional. Sometimes this is not so. Whatever integer n we choose, we can always find a set of more than n linearly independent vectors in the space. We are then dealing with the case of an infinite-dimensional space.

Example. The set of functions satisfying the PDE

$$\frac{\partial^2 u}{\partial x^2} = \frac{1}{c^2} \frac{\partial^2 u}{\partial t^2}$$

plus the boundary conditions

$$u(0) = u(L) = 0$$

forms a vector space. It is infinite dimensional because, in particular, the functions

$$\left. \begin{aligned} u_m^{(+)}(x, t) &= \sin\frac{m\pi x}{L} \cos\frac{m\pi ct}{L} \\ u_m^{(-)}(x, t) &= \sin\frac{m\pi x}{L} \sin\frac{m\pi ct}{L} \end{aligned} \right\} \quad m = 1, 2, 3, \ldots$$

are vectors in this vector space and any finite number of them is linearly independent. For the time being, we shall concentrate our attention to finite-dimensional spaces.*

Consider an arbitrary finite set of n vectors $\mathbf{x}_1, \mathbf{x}_2, \ldots, \mathbf{x}_n$ in N-dimensional space. They need not be linearly independent. Consider all linear combinations of these vectors, namely, the vectors of the form

$$\mathbf{y} = \sum_{i=1}^{n} a_i \mathbf{x}_i.$$

The vectors $\mathbf{y}$ can be easily shown to form a vector space by themselves. This space need not be the entire N-dimensional space. In fact, if $n < N$, the space of $\mathbf{y}$-vectors could not possibly be N-dimensional. However, even if $n \geq N$, the space of $\mathbf{y}$-vectors need not be the entire N-dimensional space because the $\mathbf{x}_i$-vectors may be linearly dependent. Nevertheless, all $\mathbf{y}$-vectors are members of the original N-space. Therefore we call the space of $\mathbf{y}$-vectors a *subspace* of our N-space. The set of $\mathbf{x}_i$-vectors is said to be a *generating* set (or *spanning* set) for this subspace.

---

* The study of infinite-dimensional spaces is greatly complicated by the questions of convergence of "infinite linear combinations."

Exercise. Show that all vectors **y** (as given above) form a vector space.

Let m be the maximum number of linearly independent vectors among the x_i. Then the subspace of **y**-vectors has dimension m (easily verified). If $m < N$, the subspace is a *proper subspace.** If $m = N$, the subspace coincides with the entire N-space.

In general, if a set of n vectors $x_1, x_2, \ldots, x_n$ contains only m linearly independent vectors $(m < n)$, then one can discard $n - m$ vectors, so that the remaining (linearly independent) set of m vectors is just as effective as the original set in generating a subspace (or the entire N-space).

We say that a set of m *linearly independent* vectors forms a *basis* for the (m-dimensional) subspace generated by this set. If $m = N$, then we have a basis for the entire N-space.†

Example 1. If a cartesian coordinate system is set up in a physical three-dimensional space, then the unit vectors **i**, **j**, and **k** along the x-, y-, and z-axes form a basis. An alternative basis can be chosen as

$$\mathbf{u}_1 = \mathbf{i} + \mathbf{j}, \qquad \mathbf{u}_2 = \mathbf{i} - \mathbf{j}, \qquad \mathbf{u}_3 = \mathbf{i} + \mathbf{j} + \mathbf{k}.$$

That this is indeed a basis for the entire space follows from the facts that $\mathbf{u}_1$, $\mathbf{u}_2$, and $\mathbf{u}_3$ are linearly independent and that there are three of them. Any vector $\mathbf{r} = x\mathbf{i} + y\mathbf{j} + z\mathbf{k}$ can be expressed as a linear combination

$$\mathbf{r} = \sum_{i=1}^{3} q_i \mathbf{u}_i.$$

Exercise. Prove this statement.

Example 2. Consider the plane (passing through the origin)

$$2x - 3y + 7z = 0.$$

The vectors $\mathbf{u}_1 = \mathbf{i} + \frac{2}{3}\mathbf{j}$, $\mathbf{u}_2 = \frac{7}{2}\mathbf{i} - \mathbf{k}$ obviously lie in this plane. All linear combinations of $\mathbf{u}_1$ and $\mathbf{u}_2$ also lie in the plane. We may say that the plane forms a (two-dimensional) subspace for which the vectors $\mathbf{u}_1$ and $\mathbf{u}_2$ (which are linearly independent) form a basis.

Let the set $\{e_1, e_2, \ldots, e_N\}$ be a basis of an N-dimensional space. By definition, any vector **x** can be represented as

$$\mathbf{x} = \sum_{i=1}^{N} x_i \mathbf{e}_i.$$

---

* The set of vectors consisting of *only one* vector **0** can be shown to satisfy all ten postulates and must be admitted as a vector space in its own right. Note, however, that **0** is linearly dependent on itself and the subspace generated by it is considered to be improper.
† A basis can be defined for infinite-dimensional spaces by requiring that each vector be represented by an infinite (in general) linear combination of the basis vectors.

Evidently, the set of scalars $\{x_1, x_2, \ldots, x_N\}$ is unique, because if

$$\mathbf{x} = \sum_{i=1}^{N} x'_i \mathbf{e}_i,$$

is also true, then subtracting, we obtain

$$\mathbf{0} = \sum_{i=1}^{N} (x_i - x'_i)\mathbf{e}_i.$$

Since the $\mathbf{e}_i$ are linearly independent, it follows that $x_i - x'_i = 0$ for all i, which establishes the stated property.

The set of N scalars $\{x_1, x_2, \ldots, x_N\}$ is known as the set of *coordinates* of the vector $\mathbf{x}$ *with respect to* the basis $\{\mathbf{e}_1, \mathbf{e}_2, \ldots, \mathbf{e}_N\}$. This set is ordered and is sometimes referred to as an N-tuple. Provided the basis is specified, it characterizes a vector $\mathbf{x}$ completely and may be called the *representation* of $\mathbf{x}$ *with respect to* a given basis. In most cases vectors are specified by their coordinates.

It is both customary and convenient to arrange the N-tuple of coordinates of a vector in a horizontal pattern:

$$x^T = \boxed{\begin{array}{cccccc} x_1 & x_2 & x_3 & x_4 & \cdots & x_N \end{array}}$$

often called a row vector, or a vertical pattern

$$x = \boxed{\begin{array}{c} x_1 \\ x_2 \\ x_3 \\ \vdots \\ x_N \end{array}}$$

called a column vector.* It is hardly necessary to emphasize that the row vector x^T and the column vector x represent the same object, namely, the abstract vector $\mathbf{x}$. More than that, an entirely different N-tuple (either in row or column form) may represent the same $\mathbf{x}$. This occurs if the basis is changed (see Section 10.5).

10.4 LINEAR OPERATORS, MATRICES, INVERSES

Just as a scalar y may depend on another scalar x and we write $y = f(x)$, a vector $\mathbf{y}$ may depend on vector $\mathbf{x}$ and we write

$$\mathbf{y} = \mathfrak{F}(\mathbf{x}).$$

---

* The notation x and x^T will be explained later.

The symbol $\mathcal{F}$ stands for an *operator* in vector space. It is said to *map* or *transform* vector $\mathbf{x}$ into another vector $\mathbf{y}$ (by some specified procedure). The most important operators are, perhaps, the *linear operators* defined as follows: If $\mathcal{C}$ is a linear operator, then*

$$\left.\begin{aligned}\mathcal{C}(\alpha\mathbf{x}) &= \alpha\mathcal{C}(\mathbf{x}), \\ \mathcal{C}(\mathbf{x} + \mathbf{y}) &= \mathcal{C}(\mathbf{x}) + \mathcal{C}(\mathbf{y})\end{aligned}\right\} \quad (\alpha = \text{scalar}).$$

These fundamental properties of linear operators imply that the effect of operation $\mathcal{C}$ on any vector $\mathbf{x}$ is completely specified by the effect of $\mathcal{C}$ on the basis vectors. Indeed, suppose that $\mathcal{C}$ transforms a basis vector $\mathbf{e}_i$ into some vector $\mathbf{a}_i$; that is, we have

$$\mathcal{C}(\mathbf{e}_i) = \mathbf{a}_i.$$

Now, the vector $\mathbf{a}_i$ can be represented by its coordinates with respect to the basis $\{\mathbf{e}_1, \mathbf{e}_2, \ldots, \mathbf{e}_N\}$:

$$\mathbf{a}_i = \sum_{j=1}^{N} a_{ji}\mathbf{e}_j \quad (i = 1, 2, 3, \ldots, N).$$

We see that the operator $\mathcal{C}$ involves N^2 numbers a_{ji} which can be arranged in an $N \times N$ matrix. It is customary to use the first label (j) to designate the rows, and the second label (i) to designate the columns† so that we have the arrangement

$$A = \begin{matrix} a_{11} & a_{12} & a_{13} & \cdots & a_{1i} & \cdots & a_{1N} \\ a_{21} & a_{22} & a_{23} & \cdots & a_{2i} & \cdots & a_{2N} \\ a_{31} & a_{32} & \cdots & & a_{3i} & \cdots & a_{3N} \\ \vdots & & & & & & \vdots \\ a_{i1} & a_{i2} & \cdots & & a_{ii} & \cdots & a_{iN} \\ \vdots & & & & & & \vdots \\ a_{N1} & a_{N2} & \cdots & & a_{Ni} & \cdots & a_{NN} \end{matrix}.$$

$$\uparrow$$
$$\text{vector } \mathbf{a}_i = \mathcal{C}(\mathbf{e}_i)$$

Just as the N-tuple $x = \{x_i\}$ is a representation of an abstract vector $\mathbf{x}$ with respect to the chosen basis, so the matrix $A = \{a_{kl}\}$ is called the *representation* of the abstract operator $\mathcal{C}$ with respect to the same basis. The numbers a_{kl} are then the matrix elements (or entries) of A.

With the help of matrix A, we can obtain the coordinates of $\mathbf{y} = \mathcal{C}(\mathbf{x})$ from the coordinates of $\mathbf{x}$ as follows.‡

---

* Compare with p. 187.

† As has already been stated on p. 6 for 3×3 matrices.

‡ From now on we shall write $\mathcal{C}\mathbf{x}$ instead of $\mathcal{C}(\mathbf{x})$ whenever it is clear that $\mathcal{C}$ must operate on $\mathbf{x}$.

By linearity properties,

$$\mathbf{y} = \alpha\mathbf{x} = \alpha\left(\sum_i x_i\mathbf{e}_i\right) = \sum_i x_i\mathbf{a}_i.$$

Employing the definition of $\mathbf{a}_i$, we obtain

$$\mathbf{y} = \sum_i x_i \sum_j a_{ji}\mathbf{e}_j = \sum_j \left(\sum_i a_{ji}x_i\right)\mathbf{e}_j.$$

By uniqueness of the set of coordinates, we have

$$y_j = \sum_i a_{ji}x_i \qquad (j = 1, 2, \ldots, N).$$

Explicitly,

$$y_j = a_{j1}x_1 + a_{j2}x_2 + a_{j3}x_3 + \cdots + a_{jN}x_N.$$

The expression on the right-hand side resembles the dot product of two vectors in a three-dimensional physical space. In view of this, we introduce the definition of a *dot product of two N-tuples*, $(\alpha_1, \alpha_2, \ldots, \alpha_N)$ and $(\beta_1, \beta_2, \ldots, \beta_N)$,

$$\sum_i \alpha_i\beta_i.$$

Therefore we can say that y_j is given by the dot product of the jth row of matrix A and the set of coordinates of vector $\mathbf{x}$.

Remark. In many texts the term dot product is used interchangeably with inner product or scalar product. As already mentioned in Section 1.5, we prefer to make a distinction between the two terms and mean by dot product *an algebraic operation between two N-tuples* (and not between two *vectors*), *completely independent of the nature of the basis involved.* On the other hand, the *inner product* for vectors in our physical space of three dimensions is defined by the formula

$$(\mathbf{a} \cdot \mathbf{b}) = |\mathbf{a}| \cdot |\mathbf{b}| \cdot \cos(\mathbf{a}, \mathbf{b})$$

and is equal to the dot product of the triples (a_x, a_y, a_z) and (b_x, b_y, b_z) only if the co-ordinate system is orthogonal (and the basis vectors are unit vectors). A similar situation occurs in N-dimensional spaces (see p. 443). The term "scalar product" is, perhaps, best to avoid altogether, lest it may be confused with multiplication of a vector by a scalar.

It is customary to arrange $(x_1, x_2, \ldots, x_N)$ into a column x and $(y_1, y_2, \ldots, y_N)$ into a column y. Then we have the widespread convention for matrix-vector multiplication,

$$y = Ax,$$

by postulating that* the element in the jth row of y is obtained by "dotting" the jth row of A by the column x. The formula $y = Ax$, involving specific representations of $\mathbf{y}$, $\mathbf{x}$, and α, conveniently reflects the abstract relationship $\mathbf{y} = \alpha\mathbf{x}$.

---

* As on p. 9.

There is an alternative (also used, if convenient): Arrange the coordinates of $\mathbf{x}$ and $\mathbf{y}$ into row vectors and call them x^T and y^T. Also, interchange all the a_{ij} with the a_{ji} viz. perform the reflection of matrix A about its *main diagonal*, the diagonal formed by $a_{11}, a_{22}, a_{33}, \ldots, a_{NN}$. The new matrix, denoted by A^T is the *transpose** of A; denote its elements by a_{mn}^T. By definition, $a_{mn}^T = a_{nm}$ for any given m and n. Then we may write

$$y_j = \sum_i a_{ij}^T x_i,$$

symbolically expressed as

$$y^T = x^T A^T$$

and described by the following rule: To obtain the jth component of y^T, "dot" the row x^T by the jth column of A^T.

Remark. According to the more general theory, a matrix is a rectangular array of $M \times N$ numbers, arranged in M rows and N columns. The product PQ of two matrices, P and Q (in that order), is defined as follows: To obtain the element of the ith row and the jth column of PQ, "dot" the ith row of P by the jth column of Q. This rule, applied to 3×3 matrices, has already been quoted in Section 1.4. The vector-matrix multiplication given by $y = Ax$ or by $y^T = x^T A^T$ is then just a special case of the matrix-matrix multiplication given above (y and x are regarded as matrices with N rows and one column, while y^T and x^T are matrices with one row and N columns).

Suppose that we now wish to apply two linear operators, $\mathcal{C}$ and $\mathcal{D}$, in succession,

$$\mathbf{y} = \mathcal{C}\mathbf{x} \quad \text{and} \quad \mathbf{z} = \mathcal{D}\mathbf{y}.$$

We define a new operator $\mathcal{H}$ by the "product" $\mathcal{H} = \mathcal{D}\mathcal{C}$ (in that order) to designate the overall transformation of $\mathbf{x}$ into $\mathbf{z}$: $\mathbf{z} = \mathcal{H}\mathbf{x} = \mathcal{D}\mathcal{C}\mathbf{x}$. If $\mathcal{C}$ and $\mathcal{D}$ are linear, so is $\mathcal{H}$.

Exercise. Establish the validity of this last statement.

Therefore $\mathcal{H}$ must have a matrix representation H (with respect to the same basis which yields matrices A and D for $\mathcal{C}$ and $\mathcal{D}$). Suppose that we want to construct H from A and D. By definition,

$$y_i = \sum_j a_{ij}x_j, \qquad z_k = \sum_i d_{ki}y_i$$

so that

$$z_k = \sum_i \sum_j a_{ij}\, d_{ki} x_j.$$

Define matrix H by its elements

$$h_{kj} = \sum_i d_{ki} a_{ij}.$$

Then $z_k = \sum_j h_{kj} x_j$ as desired.

---

* See p. 11.

We see that the element in the kth row and the jth column of H is obtained by dotting the kth row of D by the jth column of A. Symbolically, this is written as

$$H = DA,$$

or, according to the rule quoted before, matrix H is the *product* of matrices D and A (in that order!). Evidently, we can write, in a consistent fashion,

$$z = Hx = DAx = Dy.$$

If we want to represent vectors **x**, **y**, and **z** in row notation, we proceed as follows. We transpose the matrices A, D, and H so that $a_{ji}^T = a_{ij}$, etc. Then we can write

$$z_k = \sum_i \sum_j a_{ji}^T d_{ik}^T x_j, \qquad \text{or} \qquad z_k = \sum_j h_{jk}^T x_j$$

with

$$h_{jk}^T = \sum_i a_{ji}^T d_{ik}^T.$$

In symbolic form $z^T = x^T H^T$, where $H^T = A^T D^T$. Note the reverse order of transposed matrices forming the product. This result establishes the rule prescribing how the product of two matrices is to be transposed. The equations $y = Ax$ and $y^T = x^T A^T$ conform to this rule.

Remark 1. Matrices, generally speaking, do not commute, that is, $DA \neq AD$, in general. In other words,

$$\sum_j a_{ij} d_{jk} \neq \sum_j d_{ij} a_{jk}.$$

This statement can be verified by examples. Its origin lies in the fact that linear transformations (or operators) do not commute. (Matrices faithfully follow linear transformations.)

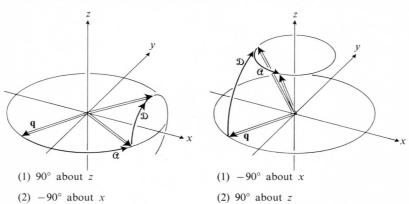

(1) 90° about z

(2) −90° about x

Final result: vector in xz-plane

(1) −90° about x

(2) 90° about z

Final result: vector in yz-plane

Figure 10.11

Example. Operator $\mathcal{C}$ is defined in three-dimensional physical space by the statement that it rotates all vectors by 90° about the z-axis. (By the right-hand screw rule, the direction of rotation is taken to mean the positive direction of the z-axis.) Similarly, $\mathcal{D}$ rotates vectors by $-90°$ about the x-axis.

In Fig. 10.11 the operators $\mathcal{C}$ and $\mathcal{D}$ are applied successively to the vector $\mathbf{q}$, once in order "first $\mathcal{C}$, then $\mathcal{D}$," and once in reverse order. It is evident that the net results are different.

Remark 2. A very important characteristic of a matrix is its determinant. In the theory of determinants it is proved that the product of determinants of matrix $\{a_{ij}\}$ and matrix $\{b_{ij}\}$ is equal to the determinant of matrix $\{c_{ij}\}$, where the elements c_{ij} can be calculated by any of the following four formulas:*

1. $c_{ij} = \sum_k a_{ik}b_{kj},$ 　　　2. $c_{ij} = \sum_k a_{ik}b_{jk},$

3. $c_{ij} = \sum_k a_{ki}b_{kj},$ 　　　4. $c_{ij} = \sum_k a_{ki}b_{jk}.$

In the language of matrix algebra the first of these statements is equivalent to

$$\det (AB) = \det A \det B.$$

The other three statements stem from the property of determinants,

$$\det A^T = \det A.$$

Remark 3. Not only can matrices be multiplied by each other, but they can be added and can be multiplied by scalars according to the following two rules:
　　If

$$F = \{f_{ij}\}, \qquad D = \{d_{ij}\}, \qquad A = \{a_{ij}\},$$

then

$$F = A + D = D + A \qquad \text{means} \qquad f_{ij} = d_{ij} + a_{ij},$$

while αA is a matrix whose elements are αa_{ij}. It is to be noted that

$$\det (\alpha A) = \alpha^N \det A. \qquad \text{(for } N \times N \text{ matrices)}$$

There is a zero matrix O with all elements equal to zero and a unit matrix of the form

$$I = \begin{vmatrix} 1 & 0 & 0 & \cdots & & 0 \\ 0 & 1 & 0 & & & \cdot \\ 0 & 0 & 1 & & & \cdot \\ \vdots & & & \ddots & 1 & 0 \\ 0 & & \cdots & & 0 & 1 \end{vmatrix}$$

---

* The four matrices composed of the elements c_{ij} are, in general, different in all four cases, but their determinants are the same.

The elements of I can be conveniently described by the so-called *Kronecker delta* symbol δ_{ij}, defined by

$$\delta_{ij} = \begin{cases} 0 & (\text{if } i \neq j), \\ 1 & (\text{if } i = j), \end{cases}$$

so that $I = \{\delta_{ij}\}$. Thus $IA = AI = A$ and $OA = AO = O$ for all matrices A. *Caution: $AB = O$* does not imply that either A or B is a zero matrix.

The linear relationship $\mathbf{y} = \alpha\mathbf{x}$ may be described in various ways, such as

a) $\mathbf{y}$ is linearly related to $\mathbf{x}$,
b) $\mathbf{x}$ is transformed into $\mathbf{y}$,
c) $\mathbf{x}$ is mapped into $\mathbf{y}$, etc.

Whatever the statement, the relationship $\mathbf{y} = \alpha\mathbf{x}$ is formally described by the algebraic statement

$$y_i = \sum_j a_{ij}x_j \qquad (i = 1, 2, 3, \ldots, N)$$

referred to a certain basis.

Example 1. Let $\mathbf{y} = \mathbf{L}$ be the angular momentum of a rigid body rotating about a point and $\mathbf{x} = \boldsymbol{\omega}$ be its angular velocity;[*] then

$$L_x = I_{xx}\omega_x + I_{xy}\omega_y + I_{xz}\omega_z,$$
$$L_y = I_{yx}\omega_x + I_{yy}\omega_y + I_{yz}\omega_z,$$
$$L_z = I_{zx}\omega_x + I_{zy}\omega_y + I_{zz}\omega_z.$$

We can say that the *inertia matrix* I[†] represents a linear operator and transforms $\boldsymbol{\omega}$ into $\mathbf{L}$ (labels x, y, z are chosen here instead of 1, 2, 3). Note that from a physical point of view, $\boldsymbol{\omega}$ and $\mathbf{L}$ are two entirely *different* kinds of vectors.

Example 2. Suppose that $\mathbf{y}$ is the position vector at time t of a particle rotating about the origin in the $\xi\eta$-plane with an angular speed ω. Suppose that $\mathbf{x}$ is its initial position (coordinates ξ_0 and η_0). From Fig. 10.12 we can see that $\mathbf{y}$ and $\mathbf{x}$ are linearly related.

Draw a line at an angle ωt to the ξ-axis and construct points M', P, Q, S, and T as shown. Note that

$$OM' = OT = \xi_0, \qquad NM' = MT = \eta_0.$$

Also,

$$\xi(t) = OP = OQ - SM' = \xi_0 \cos \omega t - \eta_0 \sin \omega t,$$
$$\eta(t) = NP = M'Q + NS = \xi_0 \sin \omega t + \eta_0 \cos \omega t.$$

We can say that there exists a (linear) rotation operator $\mathcal{R}$, depending on t as a parameter, which rotates vector $\mathbf{x}$, thus transforming it into $\mathbf{y}$. In the $\xi\eta$-

---

[*] See, e.g., Goldstein, *Classical Mechanics*, Chapter 5, p. 145.

[†] It should not be confused with identity matrix, despite the same symbol I.

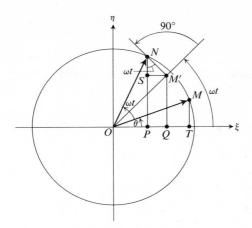

Figure 10.12

coordinate system (a fixed basis) the operator $\mathcal{R}$ is represented by the matrix

$$R = \begin{array}{|cc|} \cos \omega t & -\sin \omega t \\ \sin \omega t & \cos \omega t \end{array}$$

so that $y = Rx$, where y and x are column vectors composed of $\{\xi(t), \eta(t)\}$ and $\{\xi_0, \eta_0\}$, respectively.

Note that, in a physical sense, **x** and **y** are not vectors of different kinds. Both of them represent the same physical concept, a position vector. However, because the distinction in time is involved, it would be incorrect to view **y** and **x** as the *same vector*.

Therefore, in this case as in the preceding one, we view the equations

$$y_i = \sum_j a_{ij} x_j$$

as transforming *one vector into another* within the framework of a fixed basis. This remark will be invoked later when we consider the changes in basis of a vector space.

Now consider the problem of determining **x** in the relation $y = \mathcal{C}x$ when **y** is known. We must solve the equations

$$y_j = \sum_k a_{jk} x_k \qquad (j = 1, 2, 3, \ldots, N)$$

for the unknown quantities x_k. Is this always possible? If not, when is it possible? The answer is provided by the following three theorems from the theory of linear algebraic equations.*

---

* See, e.g., Murdoch, *Linear Algebra for Undergraduates*, Theorems 2.2, 2.6, and 2.8.

Theorem 1. A system of N nonhomogeneous equations in N unknowns *has a solution* if and only if the column vector y is a linear combination of column vectors of matrix A.

Theorem 2. A system of N nonhomogeneous equations in N unknowns *has a unique solution* if and only if det $A \neq 0$.

Theorem 3. A matrix A has det $A = 0$ (such matrices are called *singular*) if and only if its columns (or rows, for that matter) are linearly dependent.

With the help of these three theorems, we now distinguish two cases.

CASE 1. The set of vectors $\mathbf{a}_i = \mathfrak{A}\mathbf{e}_i$ is linearly independent.

The columns of A are linearly independent and det $A \neq 0$. There is a unique solution of our equations for an arbitrary vector $\mathbf{y}$. Therefore we may write

$$\mathbf{x} = \mathfrak{B}\mathbf{y},$$

where $\mathfrak{B}$ is an operator (defined uniquely over the entire vector space). From the fact that $\mathbf{x}$ exists and is unique, it is shown that $\mathfrak{B}$ must be a linear operator (e.g., multiply the equations for the x_k by α to prove the first property on p. 425, etc.). Therefore

$$x_m = \sum_n b_{mn} y_n \qquad (m = 1, 2, 3, \ldots, N)$$

or, symbolically, $x = By$, where B is some matrix. Now apply to vector $\mathbf{x}$, first the operator $\mathfrak{A}$, and then the operator $\mathfrak{B}$ to obtain

$$\mathbf{x} = \mathfrak{B}\mathfrak{A}\mathbf{x}.$$

In matrix language, $x = BAx$. Since B is unique, BA is also unique. Thus BA must be the unit matrix I (and the operator $\mathfrak{B}\mathfrak{A}$ is the identity operator) with the elements given by the Kronecker delta symbol δ_{ij}. It is customary to denote B by the symbol A^{-1} and call it the *inverse* of matrix A. The elements b_{ij} of A^{-1*} must satisfy

$$\sum_j b_{ij} a_{jk} = \delta_{ik}.$$

The operators $\mathfrak{A}$ and $\mathfrak{B}$ can be applied in reverse order, yielding

$$\mathbf{y} = \mathfrak{A}\mathfrak{B}\mathbf{y}, \quad \text{or} \quad y = ABy.$$

Thus, $AB = I$ also holds, so that $A = B^{-1}$. In explicit notation,

$$\sum_k a_{jk} b_{ki} = \delta_{ji}.$$

---

* The symbol a_{ij}^{-1} should be avoided for fear of confusion with the reciprocals of a_{ij}.

The elements b_{ij} of B can be found, e.g., by Cramer's rule*

$$b_{ij} = \frac{\det A_{ji}}{\det A}$$

where A_{ij} is the cofactor of a_{ij} [namely the determinant of the $(N - 1) \times (N - 1)$ matrix, obtained by omitting from A the ith row and the jth columns, multiplied by $(-1)^{i+j}$].

Remark. The elements b_{ij} *do not have* to be found by Cramer's rule. In practice, Cramer's rule is seldom used.

CASE 2. The set of vectors $\mathbf{a}_i = \mathfrak{a}\mathbf{e}_i$ is linearly dependent.

The system $y_j = \sum_k a_{jk} x_k$ will have a solution if and only if $\mathbf{y}$ is a linear combination of the $\mathbf{a}_i$. Moreover, such a solution will not be unique. In short, operator $\mathfrak{B}$ cannot be defined, and the matrix A does not possess an inverse. Note that nonexistence of the inverse is characterized by the fact that $\det A = 0$.

Evidently, this is what happens: Operator $\mathfrak{a}$ maps all vectors onto a subspace spanned by the $\mathbf{a}_i$. This is a proper subspace, having dimension less than N. Therefore, if $\mathbf{y}$ is given outside this subspace, the statement $\mathbf{y} = \mathfrak{a}\mathbf{x}$ is self-contradicting, and this is reflected in the fact that our equations have no solution. If $\mathbf{y}$ belongs to the subspace, a solution exists but is not unique. In order to specify a particular solution in the latter case, some restrictions on $\mathbf{x}$ are needed. For instance, if one requires that $\mathbf{x}$ be also within the subspace spanned by the $\mathbf{a}_i$, one can show that a unique solution is possible.†

10.5 CHANGES OF BASIS

A given vector $\mathbf{x}$ can be represented by two different sets of coordinates with respect to two different bases:

$$\mathbf{x} = \sum_i x_i \mathbf{e}_i, \qquad \mathbf{x} = \sum_i x'_i \mathbf{g}_i.$$

We shall call the set of vectors $\mathbf{e}_i$ the E-basis, and the set of vectors $\mathbf{g}_i$ the G-basis. The problem is how to obtain the n-tuple x' from the n-tuple x if both bases are specified.

Evidently, each $\mathbf{g}_i$-vector can be expressed in terms of $\mathbf{e}_i$-vectors:

$$\mathbf{g}_i = \sum_j g_{ji} \mathbf{e}_j,$$

where the numbers g_{ji} are arranged in a matrix G so that its columns are repre-

---

* See, e.g., Birkhoff and MacLane, p. 306.

† Case 2 is illustrated by a very simple example in two dimensions given on p. 14, although in a somewhat different context (see Section 10.5). However, the algebra is the same.

sentations of $\mathbf{g}_i$-vectors with respect to the E-basis. Conversely,

$$\mathbf{e}_j = \sum_i t_{ij}\mathbf{g}_i,$$

defining an analogous matrix T. It is not difficult to show that

$$GT = TG = I.$$

Exercise. Give the details which establish this statement.

Now write

$$\mathbf{x} = \sum_j x_j\mathbf{e}_j = \sum_j x_j \sum_i t_{ij}\mathbf{g}_i = \sum_i \mathbf{g}_i \sum_j t_{ij}x_j.$$

By the uniqueness of coordinates,

$$x_i' = \sum_j t_{ij}x_j,$$

or, in matrix notation, $x' = Tx$ (or $x'^T = x^T T^T$). The matrix T is called the *transformation matrix* from the E-basis to the G-basis. Its columns are N-tuples of the E-basis with respect to the G-basis. Matrix T is the inverse of matrix G, defining the "new" G-basis in terms of the "old" E-basis.

Remark. The relationships $y = Ax$ and $x' = Tx$ are formally the same but we attach different meanings to them. In the first case, y and x belong to *different vectors;* in the second case, x' and x belong to the *same vector.*

The formal similarity of these operations may be illustrated by the following example: If a vector $\mathbf{x}$ is allowed to rotate in the $\xi\eta$-plane by an angle ϕ (see p. 430), its coordinates will change from (ξ_0, η_0) to (ξ, η) according to*

$$\xi = \xi_0 \cos \phi - \eta_0 \sin \phi,$$

$$\eta = \xi_0 \sin \phi + \eta_0 \cos \phi.$$

However, suppose that now a vector $\mathbf{x}$ is allowed to remain still while the *coordinate system is rotated* through an angle $-\phi$. The coordinates (ξ_0, η_0) will change into (ξ_0', η_0'). It is an easy matter to show that

$$\xi_0' = \xi_0 \cos \phi - \eta_0 \sin \phi, \qquad \eta_0' = \xi_0 \sin \phi + \eta_0 \cos \phi.$$

Note that the matrix involved in both operations is exactly the same but we interpret the results differently.†

---

* The angle of rotation is, as usual, positive for counterclockwise motion.

† A keen observer will not fail to note that the two interpretations are possible because we are pivoting ourselves to the original set of axes as a fixed feature. Otherwise, the terms "rotates" or "remains still" have no meaning.

Example. Let the G-basis in a 2×2 space be defined in terms of the E-basis by the equations $\mathbf{g}_1 = 2\mathbf{e}_1 + 3\mathbf{e}_2$, $\mathbf{g}_2 = 4\mathbf{e}_1 - 5\mathbf{e}_2$, or

$$g_1 = \begin{vmatrix} 2 \\ 3 \end{vmatrix}, \qquad g_2 = \begin{vmatrix} 4 \\ -5 \end{vmatrix}$$

The matrix G is

$$G = \begin{vmatrix} 2 & 4 \\ 3 & -5 \end{vmatrix}$$

Its inverse matrix T can be found by solving the above vector equations for $\mathbf{e}_1$ and $\mathbf{e}_2$:*

$$\mathbf{e}_1 = \tfrac{5}{22}\mathbf{g}_1 + \tfrac{3}{22}\mathbf{g}_2,$$
$$\mathbf{e}_2 = \tfrac{2}{11}\mathbf{g}_1 - \tfrac{1}{11}\mathbf{g}_2.$$

The matrix T is now obtained by arranging the coordinates of the $\mathbf{e}_i$ in columns:

$$T = G^{-1} = \begin{vmatrix} \frac{5}{22} & \frac{2}{11} \\ \frac{3}{22} & -\frac{1}{11} \end{vmatrix}$$

Let $\mathbf{x}$ be a vector given by

$$x = \begin{vmatrix} -1 \\ 2 \end{vmatrix}$$

with respect to the E-basis, and by

$$x' = \begin{vmatrix} x'_1 \\ x'_2 \end{vmatrix}$$

with respect to the G-basis; then

$$\begin{vmatrix} x'_1 \\ x'_2 \end{vmatrix} = \begin{vmatrix} \frac{5}{22} & \frac{2}{11} \\ \frac{3}{22} & -\frac{1}{11} \end{vmatrix} \cdot \begin{vmatrix} -1 \\ 2 \end{vmatrix} = \begin{vmatrix} \frac{3}{22} \\ -\frac{7}{22} \end{vmatrix}$$

---

* The matrix T can be written almost immediately by Cramer's rule. For many-dimensional matrices it is much simpler to solve the equations for the $\mathbf{e}_i$ by other methods (e.g., Gauss' rule) and pick out the matrix T as above.

We now combine the ideas of linear operators and the change of basis. Let **y** and **x** be two *different vectors* related by a linear operator: $\mathbf{y} = \alpha\mathbf{x}$.

With respect to some E-basis, **x** and **y** are given by their N-tuples x and y while α is given by its matrix A, and we have

$$y = Ax \qquad \text{or} \qquad y_i = \sum_j a_{ij}x_j.$$

Suppose that we want to switch from the E-basis to the G-basis. Vectors **x** and **y** will be given by completely different N-tuples, x' and y'. We expect α to be represented by a different matrix A' and wish to find this matrix. We know that

$$y' = Ty \qquad \text{and} \qquad x' = Tx$$

so that $x = T^{-1}x'$. Then

$$y = Ax = AT^{-1}x' \qquad \text{and} \qquad y' = Ty = TAT^{-1}x'.$$

Our conclusion is that $A' = TAT^{-1} = G^{-1}AG$.

This relationship between A' and A is called the *similarity transformation*. It permits us to find a new matrix representation for the operator α when the basis is changed.

We can now appreciate the difference between the linear relationship and the change of basis, both of which are reducible to a matrix-vector multiplication. Suppose that the E-basis is changed to the G-basis. Then $x' = Tx$. This is a linear relationship between two N-tuples, but not between two vectors (the vector remains the same, namely, **x**).

Suppose that we now wish to find what effect a change of basis (an additional one, of course) will have on this equation. Let the G-basis be changed into the F-basis so that

$$\mathbf{f}_i = \sum_j f_{ji}\mathbf{g}_j, \qquad \text{or} \qquad \mathbf{g}_j = \sum_i s_{ij}\mathbf{f}_i$$

(meaning $F = S^{-1}$ and vice versa). Let

$$\mathbf{x} = \sum_i x_i''\mathbf{f}_i$$

be the *new* representation of **x** (with respect to the F-basis). Starting from

$$\mathbf{x} = \sum_j x_j'\mathbf{g}_j,$$

we obtain

$$\mathbf{x} = \sum_j x_j' \sum_i s_{ij}\mathbf{f}_i = \sum_i \mathbf{f}_i \left(\sum_j s_{ij}x_j' \right)$$

so that

$$x_i'' = \sum_j s_{ij}x_j', \qquad \text{or} \qquad x'' = Sx'.$$

The ultimate result is $x'' = STx$. In other words, the matrix T does not undergo any similarity transformation but is simply multiplied by the matrix S on the left.

10.6 INNER PRODUCT, ORTHOGONALITY, UNITARY OPERATORS

Vector spaces used in physics almost invariably possess a property known as the *inner product*. An inner product (or *scalar product*†) is a *scalar* $(\mathbf{x}, \mathbf{y})$ formed by two vectors satisfying the properties given below. They are somewhat different for real and for complex spaces.

REAL SPACES	COMPLEX SPACES
1. The inner product is symmetric:	1. The inner product has *hermitian symmetry:*
$$(\mathbf{x}, \mathbf{y}) = (\mathbf{y}, \mathbf{x}).$$	$$(\mathbf{x}, \mathbf{y}) = (\mathbf{y}, \mathbf{x})^*.$$
2. The inner product is linear with respect to the second factor:	2. (Same as for real spaces.)
$$(\mathbf{x}, \mathbf{y} + \mathbf{z}) = (\mathbf{x}, \mathbf{y}) + (\mathbf{x}, \mathbf{z}),$$ $$(\mathbf{x}, \alpha\mathbf{y}) = \alpha(\mathbf{x}, \mathbf{y}).$$	

Important note: Using property 1 we can check that for *real spaces* the inner product is also linear with respect to the first factor, namely,

$$(\mathbf{x} + \mathbf{y}, \mathbf{z}) = (\mathbf{x}, \mathbf{z}) + (\mathbf{y}, \mathbf{z}),$$
$$(\alpha\mathbf{x}, \mathbf{y}) = \alpha(\mathbf{x}, \mathbf{y}).$$

A similar check for *complex spaces* reveals that the first line above still holds, but that the second one must be replaced by $(\alpha\mathbf{x}, \mathbf{y}) = \alpha^*(\mathbf{x}, \mathbf{y})$.

It is usually said that the inner product in complex space is *antilinear* with respect to the first factor.

Note: Some authors define the inner product to be linear with respect to the first factor and antilinear with respect to the second one. The content of the theory is not changed by either convention so long as one is consistent about it.

REAL SPACES	COMPLEX SPACES
3. The inner product produces a "positive definite norm":	3. (Same as for real spaces.)
$$(\mathbf{x}, \mathbf{x}) \geq 0,$$	
where $(\mathbf{x}, \mathbf{x}) = 0$ if and only if $\mathbf{x} = \mathbf{0}$.	

(*Note:* $\|\mathbf{x}\| = \sqrt{(\mathbf{x}, \mathbf{x})}$ is usually called the *norm*‡ of the vector $\mathbf{x}$.)

---

† Although the term scalar product is very common, we prefer to use the term inner product. See the remark on p. 426.

‡ The term *norm* is also used with a different meaning in mathematical literature, and is not related to inner product.

Remark. The last property may be omitted in some vector spaces used in physics (for instance, the Minkowski space in special relativity). Some modifications are also used.

If the vector space is finite dimensional, an inner product can always be *imposed* on it. Moreover, this can be done in a great variety of ways.

Taking the cue from the definition of scalar product in three-dimensional physical space, we may *define* the inner product in abstract n-dimensional *real* space by the expression

$$(\mathbf{x}, \mathbf{y}) = \sum_i x_i y_i,$$

where x_i and y_i are coordinates of $\mathbf{x}$ and $\mathbf{y}$ with respect to some *specified basis*. This procedure can be made more fundamental if we define the inner products between the basis vectors by

$$(\mathbf{e}_i, \mathbf{e}_j) = \delta_{ij}.$$

Then, by linearity properties (for real space),

$$(\mathbf{x}, \mathbf{y}) = \left(\sum_i x_i \mathbf{e}_i, \sum_j y_j \mathbf{e}_j \right)$$
$$= \sum_i \sum_j x_i y_j (\mathbf{e}_i, \mathbf{e}_j) = \sum_i \sum_j x_i y_j \, \delta_{ij} = \sum_i x_i y_i.$$

If we adopt the same definition for n-dimensional complex space, then we must use antilinearity with respect to the first factor and obtain

$$(\mathbf{x}, \mathbf{y}) = \left(\sum_i x_i \mathbf{e}_i, \sum_j y_j \mathbf{e}_j \right) = \sum_i \sum_j x_i^* y_j (\mathbf{e}_i, \mathbf{e}_j) = \sum_i x_i^* y_i.$$

The inner product imposed in this fashion evidently satisfies property 3 as well.

Remark. With this definition, the rule for forming the inner product can be formulated as follows.

1. In real space, $(\mathbf{x}, \mathbf{y})$ is obtained by "dotting" the n-tuples x and y. Using the language of matrix multiplication,

$$(\mathbf{x}, \mathbf{y}) = x^T y = y^T x.$$

2. In complex space, we must take the complex conjugate of the first n-tuple before "dotting." Writing $(x^T)^* = x^\dagger$, we have $(\mathbf{x}, \mathbf{y}) = x^\dagger y = (y^\dagger x)^*$.

If the inner product of two vectors, real or complex, is zero, they are called *orthogonal*:

$$(\mathbf{x}, \mathbf{y}) = 0 \qquad \text{implies} \qquad \text{``}\mathbf{x} \perp \mathbf{y}\text{''}.$$

A vector (real or complex) is called a *unit vector* if its norm

$$\|\mathbf{x}\| = \sqrt{(\mathbf{x}, \mathbf{x})}$$

is equal to unity. In view of these concepts, the condition *imposed* on the E-basis,

$$(\mathbf{e}_i, \mathbf{e}_j) = \delta_{ij},$$

states that all basis vectors are unit vectors and are mutually orthogonal. Such a basis is called an *orthogonal basis.*‡ There are many different orthogonal bases in any vector space (of dimension greater than one). In addition to some E-basis, let another, say the G-basis, be orthogonal as well:

$$(\mathbf{g}_i, \mathbf{g}_j) = \delta_{ij}.$$

If $\mathbf{x} = \sum_i x_i' \mathbf{g}_i$ and $\mathbf{y} = \sum_i y_i' \mathbf{g}_i$, then (for complex space)

$$(\mathbf{x}, \mathbf{y}) = \sum_i x_i'^* y_i'.$$

For real spaces this reduces to $(\mathbf{x}, \mathbf{y}) = \sum_i x_i' y_i'$.

Suppose that we make a transformation from the E-basis to the G-basis. Then

$$\mathbf{g}_i = \sum_j g_{ji} \mathbf{e}_j.$$

Therefore

$$(\mathbf{g}_i, \mathbf{g}_k) = \left(\sum_j g_{ji} \mathbf{e}_j, \sum_l g_{lk} \mathbf{e}_l \right) = \sum_j \sum_l g_{ji}^* g_{lk} (\mathbf{e}_j, \mathbf{e}_l).$$

If the E-basis is orthogonal, then

$$(\mathbf{g}_i, \mathbf{g}_k) = \sum_j \sum_l g_{ji}^* g_{lk} \delta_{jl} = \sum_j g_{ji}^* g_{jk}.$$

If the G-basis is also orthogonal, then

$$(\mathbf{g}_i, \mathbf{g}_k) = \sum_j g_{ji}^* g_{jk} = \delta_{ik}.$$

This equation is interpreted by the statement that the columns of the G-matrix are mutually orthogonal.§

To obtain a conventional matrix equation, we write $g_{ji} = g_{ij}^T$ and

$$g_{ji}^* = (g_{ij}^T)^* = g_{ij}^\dagger,$$

thereby defining the matrix $G^\dagger$ obtained from the matrix G by transposing it and taking the complex conjugate (in either order); matrix $G^\dagger$ is called the *hermitian adjoint* (*hermitian conjugate*, or simply *adjoint*) of matrix G. The explicit equations relating the elements of matrix G,

$$\sum_j g_{ji}^* g_{jk} = \delta_{ik},$$

can then be written in the symbolic matrix form

$$G^\dagger G = I,$$

---

‡ In this context the term "orthogonal" tacitly implies that the basis vectors are normalized, i.e., made to be unit vectors. Some authors use the term "orthonormal" which is actually more precise.

§ In the sense that their dot product is zero (or unity).

implying that $G^\dagger = G^{-1}$. Matrices satisfying this relation are called *unitary*. In real spaces we have $G^\dagger = G^T$, and the above statement reduces to $G^T G = I$, implying that $G^T = G^{-1}$. Such matrices are called *orthogonal*.‡

Remark. The rows of a unitary (or orthogonal) matrix are also mutually orthogonal. Indeed, consider

$$\sum_j g_{ij}^* g_{kj} = f_{ik},$$

representing the process of "dotting the rows."

Let us rewrite the above as

$$f_{ik} = \sum_j (g_{ji}^\dagger) g_{jk}^T = \sum_j g_{kj} g_{ji}^\dagger.$$

The matrix F with elements f_{ik} satisfies therefore the relation $F = GG^\dagger$. However, we know that if $G^\dagger G = I$, then $GG^\dagger = I$ as well, so that $F = I$ or $f_{ik} = \delta_{ik}$. This means that

$$\sum_j g_{ij}^* g_{kj} = \delta_{ik},$$

representing the orthogonality of rows.

We may now state that the transformation matrix T (figuring in $x' = Tx$) from one orthogonal basis to another must be unitary (or orthogonal). Indeed, if G is unitary (orthogonal), so is $T = G^{-1}$. Bearing in mind the similarity of equations $y = Ax$ and $x' = Tx$ (Section 10.5), we can formulate and prove the following facts about linear operators $\mathcal{Q}$.

Definition. A linear operator $\mathcal{Q}$ is called unitary (orthogonal) if it *preserves the inner products*.

Theorem. If matrix A represents a unitary operator $\mathcal{Q}$ with respect to some orthogonal basis, then A is a unitary (or orthogonal) matrix and vice versa.

Proof. Let the vectors $\mathbf{x}$, $\boldsymbol{\xi}$, $\mathbf{y} = \mathcal{Q}\mathbf{x}$, and $\boldsymbol{\eta} = \mathcal{Q}\boldsymbol{\xi}$ be represented by x, ξ, y, and η with respect to the E-basis. Then

$$(\mathbf{x}, \boldsymbol{\xi}) = \sum_i x_i^* \xi_i \quad \text{and} \quad (\mathbf{y}, \boldsymbol{\eta}) = \sum_j y_j^* \eta_j.$$

Also,

$$y_j = \sum_k a_{ik} x_k \quad \text{so that} \quad y_j^* = \sum_k a_{jk}^* x_k^*$$

as well as

$$\eta_j = \sum_l a_{jl} \xi_l.$$

Then

$$(\mathbf{y}, \boldsymbol{\eta}) = \sum_k \sum_l x_k^* \xi_l \left(\sum_j a_{jk}^* a_{jl} \right) \cdot$$

---

‡ The term orthonormal is more precise (see the footnote on p. 439).

If A is unitary, the expression in parentheses is δ_{kl}, and the theorem follows. Conversely, since the x_k and ξ_l are arbitrary scalars, we can deduce that

$$\sum_j a_{jk}^* a_{jl} = \delta_{kl},$$

and the proof is complete.

10.7 THE METRIC. GENERALIZED ORTHOGONALITY

Sometimes the inner product is defined in a manner that makes a given E-basis nonorthogonal. This means that the inner products of basis vectors do not form a unit matrix but rather some other matrix M with the elements

$$(\mathbf{e}_i, \mathbf{e}_j) = m_{ij}.$$

Because of the hermitian symmetry of the inner product, the elements m_{ij} of M must satisfy the relation

$$m_{ij} = m_{ji}^*.$$

In other words, $M = M.^\dagger$ Such matrices are called *hermitian* or *self-adjoint*. For real spaces, the matrix M must satisfy $M = M^T$. Such matrices are called *symmetric*. The matrix M is sometimes called the *metric*‡ of the vector space (with respect to a given E-basis).

With the matrix M defined, we may calculate the inner products of any two vectors as follows:

$$(\mathbf{x}, \mathbf{y}) = \left(\sum_i x_i \mathbf{e}_i, \sum_j y_j \mathbf{e}_j \right) = \sum_i \sum_j x_i^* y_j (\mathbf{e}_i, \mathbf{e}_j)$$
$$= \sum_i \sum_j x_i^* m_{ij} y_j.$$

In this analysis we have not used, so far, Postulate 3 for the inner product. If this postulate is applied, then we must have

$$(\mathbf{x}, \mathbf{x}) = \sum_i \sum_j x_i^* m_{ij} x_j \geq 0,$$

where the equality sign implies $x_i = 0$ for all i. In matrix notation this statement is expressed by

$$x^\dagger M x \geq 0, \qquad (x^\dagger M x = 0 \text{ implies } x = 0).$$

Hermitian (or real symmetric) matrices M which possess this property are called *positive-definite*.

Let us now consider again a change of basis (transformation of coordinates). We are interested how the metric is going to change. It is instructive to derive the result by matrix algebra, showing the advantages of matrix notation.

---

‡ In mathematical literature the term "metric" is used for a somewhat different concept, without explicit reference to the inner product.

First of all, observe that the inner product can be written in the form

$$(\mathbf{x}, \mathbf{y}) = x^\dagger M y.$$

Let the new basis be given, as usual, by matrix G (its columns are now basis vectors). Then the new coordinates of $\mathbf{x}$ and $\mathbf{y}$ are given by

$$x' = Tx, \qquad y' = Ty,$$

where $T = G^{-1}$. Multiply these equations by G from the left:

$$Gx' = x, \qquad Gy' = y.$$

Now transpose the first equation and take its complex conjugate (in other words, take the hermitian adjoint of the first equation)‡

$$x'^\dagger G^\dagger = x^\dagger.$$

Substitute these results into $x^\dagger M y$ and obtain

$$(\mathbf{x}, \mathbf{y}) = x'^\dagger G^\dagger M G y'.$$

It follows that, with respect to the new basis, the metric is given by the matrix

$$M' = G^\dagger M G.$$

We say that the matrix M has undergone a *congruence transformation*. Note the difference between the congruence transformation and the similarity transformation (p. 436) $A' = TAT^{-1} = G^{-1}AG$ governing the transformation of a matrix representation of a linear operator $\mathcal{Q}$ in an analogous case. Note also that the two types of transformation coincide if G is a unitary matrix (or orthogonal matrix in the case of real space).

Remark 1. The results of Section 10.6 arise as a special case from the formula $M' = G^\dagger M G$. If the original basis is orthogonal, then $M = I$ and $M' = G^\dagger G$. If G is unitary, then $M' = I$ as well (and vice versa). This means that the new basis is orthogonal as well.

Remark 2. For real spaces we can simply replace all hermitian adjoints by transposes (or even leave all formulas intact and employ the property $A^* = A$ for any real matrix A).

The problem of linear operators $\mathcal{Q}$ which preserve inner products is also easily solved. Suppose that

$$(\xi, \eta) = (\mathcal{Q}\mathbf{x}, \mathcal{Q}\mathbf{y}) = (\mathbf{x}, \mathbf{y}).$$

In the usual notation, $\xi = Ax$, $\eta = Ay$, and

$$(\xi, \eta) = \xi^\dagger M \eta = x^\dagger A^\dagger M A y.$$

---

‡ The hermitian adjoint of a product of two matrices is given by $(AB)^\dagger = B^\dagger A^\dagger$, as follows immediately from a similar rule for $(AB)^T$ (see p. 428).

If this is to be equal to $(\mathbf{x}, \mathbf{y}) = x^{\dagger} M y$ for all $\mathbf{x}$ and $\mathbf{y}$, it is necessary and sufficient that

$$A^{\dagger} M A = M,$$

which is the desired condition on A. If the basis is orthogonal, then $M = I$, and this reduces to the result that A must be unitary: $A^{\dagger} A = I$.

We have applied the term *orthogonality* to both abstract vectors and to various n-tuples such as rows or columns of a matrix. It is customary to say that two n-tuples $(x_1, x_2, x_3, \ldots, x_n)$ and $(y_1, y_2, y_3, \ldots, y_n)$, whatever their nature or meaning, are orthogonal if, in real space, their dot product vanishes:

$$x_1 y_1 + x_2 y_2 + x_3 y_3 + \cdots + x_n y_n = 0,$$

or, in complex space,

$$x_1^* y_1 + x_2^* y_2 + x_3^* y_3 + \cdots + x_n^* y_n = 0.$$

So far as two abstract vectors are concerned, they are orthogonal if $(\mathbf{x}, \mathbf{y}) = 0$. This is equivalent to saying that their n-tuples are orthogonal *only if* the basis involved is an orthogonal basis. Otherwise, the n-tuples would satisfy

$$x_1^* m_{11} y_1 + x_1^* m_{12} y_2 + \cdots = \sum_i \sum_j x_i^* m_{ij} y_j = 0.$$

It is sometimes said that the n-tuples x and y are now *orthogonal in a generalized sense* or *orthogonal with respect to matrix M*. The abstract vectors themselves ($\mathbf{x}$ and $\mathbf{y}$) are, of course, simply orthogonal.‡

10.8 EIGENVALUE PROBLEMS. DIAGONALIZATION

In physics, the simplest linear relationship between two vectors $\mathbf{x}$ and $\mathbf{y}$ is such that $\mathbf{y}$ is a scalar multiple of $\mathbf{x}$, for example, $\mathbf{D} = \epsilon \mathbf{E}$ in electrostatics. The general linear relationship

$$\mathbf{y} = \alpha \mathbf{x}$$

is more complicated. However, there may exist special vectors for which this relationship reduces to the simple one, $\mathbf{y} = \lambda \mathbf{x}$ ($\lambda = $ scalar).

For instance, suppose that in some representation, the matrix A of α is *diagonal*, meaning that $a_{ij} \neq 0$ only if $i = j$. Then, for the basis vectors $\mathbf{e}_i$, we have

$$\alpha \mathbf{e}_i = \mathbf{a}_i = \sum_j a_{ji} \mathbf{e}_i = a_{ii} \mathbf{e}_i.$$

In other words, the operator α simply multiplies the vector $\mathbf{e}_i$ by a constant a_{ii}. Note that this constant is, in general, different for different basis vectors $\mathbf{e}_i$.

---

‡ The terms "orthogonal" and "orthogonal in a generalized sense" have already been applied to functions (p. 155, p. 339). These definitions are in close analogy with the material of this section and will be further discussed in Chapter 11.

If the matrix A is not diagonal, the problem reduces to finding certain N-tuples satisfying

$$Ax = \lambda x.$$

These N-tuples are usually called the *eigenvectors* of A.* It is tacitly assumed that an eigenvector should not be trivial (zero vector). The matrix equation $Ax = \lambda x$ corresponds to a set of algebraic equations

$$\sum_j a_{ij}x_j = \lambda x_i \qquad (i = 1, 2, 3, \ldots, N),$$

or

$$\sum_j (a_{ij} - \lambda\delta_{ij})x_j = 0.$$

Written more explicitly, these are N homogeneous equations in N unknowns:

$$
\begin{aligned}
(a_{11} - \lambda)x_1 + a_{12}x_2 + \quad \cdots \quad + a_{1N}x_N &= 0, \\
a_{21}x_1 + (a_{22} - \lambda)x_2 + \cdots + a_{2N}x_N &= 0, \\
\vdots \qquad\qquad\qquad\qquad\qquad & \\
a_{N1}x_1 + \qquad\quad \cdots \qquad\quad + (a_{NN} - \lambda)x_N &= 0.
\end{aligned}
$$

The necessary and sufficient condition for these equations to possess a non-trivial solution is that the determinant of the matrix of coefficients vanish. This matrix can be written as $A - \lambda I$ (I = unit matrix) so that

$$\det (A - \lambda I) = 0,$$

which is known as the *characteristic equation* (or *secular equation*). It is an Nth degree algebraic equation in λ (which is the unknown) and has N roots or less. (Some roots may be multiple; also, even for a real matrix A, some roots may be complex.) These roots are called *eigenvalues* (*characteristic roots* or *latent roots*)† of the matrix A. Note that a scalar multiple of an eigenvector is also an eigenvector.

As mentioned before, it is trivial to find the eigenvalues and eigenvectors of a diagonal matrix. The eigenvalues are simply the diagonal elements a_{ii}, and the eigenvectors are basis vectors. Consequently, it would be profitable to make a transformation of coordinates (i.e., change of basis) so that the transformed matrix A' is diagonal. Since we are dealing with a fixed linear relationship between two vectors ($\lambda\mathbf{x}$ is proportional to $\mathbf{x}$), matrix A must change according to the similarity transformation (p. 436)

$$A' = TAT^{-1} = G^{-1}AG.$$

---

* Actually, they are "eigen-N-tuples" of A. They correspond to (abstract) vectors $\mathbf{x}$ which are eigenvectors of the (abstract) operator $\mathcal{Q}$.

† Eigenvectors are also called *characteristic vectors*. See the footnote on p. 292 and observe the formal similarity between the vector-matrix equation $Ax = \lambda x$ and the differential equation $(d^2/dx^2)X = \lambda X$, which can be found on p. 292.

Matrices A' and A are called *similar*. Similar matrices have the same eigenvalues. Indeed, the characteristic equation for A' reads*

$$\det (G^{-1}AG - \lambda I) = \det (G^{-1}AG - G^{-1}\lambda IG)$$
$$= \det [G^{-1}(A - \lambda I)G] = \det G^{-1} \cdot \det (A - \lambda I) \cdot \det G = 0.$$

However, $\det G^{-1} \det G = \det G^{-1}G = 1$. We see that the characteristic equation is the same for A and A'; therefore A and A' must have the same eigenvalues.

If A' is diagonal, then its elements a'_{ii} are the eigenvalues of A. The problem is to find the matrix G which diagonalizes A. Since we know that the basis vectors are the eigenvectors of a diagonal matrix, it follows that G must have columns equal to eigenvectors of A (because these are the N-tuples of the new basis vectors). Consequently, we need N *linearly independent eigenvectors* of matrix A to be able to diagonalize it. This statement gives the clue for the success or failure of the diagonalization process: Matrix A may happen to have less than N linearly independent eigenvectors.

We shall now describe some important cases for which diagonalization is possible.

Theorem 1. If a matrix A has m *different* eigenvalues, then it has m linearly independent eigenvectors (at least one for each eigenvalue).

Proof. Suppose the contrary, namely, there are only $n < m$ linearly independent eigenvectors, say $x^{(1)}, x^{(2)}, \ldots, x^{(n)}$,† corresponding to the (different) eigenvalues $\lambda_1, \lambda_2, \ldots, \lambda_n$. The eigenvector $x^{(n+1)}$ corresponding to λ_{n+1} must form a (nontrivial) linear combination with them,

$$\sum_{i=1}^{n+1} a_i x^{(i)} = 0,$$

with at least one nonzero a_i.

Multiply this equation on the left by matrix A and use $Ax^{(i)} = \lambda_i x^{(i)}$ to obtain

$$\sum_{i=1}^{n+1} a_i \lambda_i x^{(i)} = 0.$$

Also, multiply by λ_{n+1} (instead of A) and subtract:

$$\sum_{i=1}^{n} a_i(\lambda_i - \lambda_{n+1})x^{(i)} = 0.$$

Note that $x^{(n+1)}$ has been eliminated from the equation. Now all the $x^{(i)}$ are

---

* It is easy to check that $N \times N$ matrices obey the distributive law employed here.

† Recall that by eigenvectors we mean here "eigen-N-tuples." In the equation which follows they are arranged in columns. The zero on the right is a zero column (all elements are zero).

linearly independent; therefore

$$a_i(\lambda_i - \lambda_{n+1}) = 0 \qquad (\text{all } i \leq n).$$

Since $\lambda_i \neq \lambda_{n+1}$, it follows that $a_i = 0$ $(i = 1, 2, 3, \ldots, n)$. However, the original equation then reads $a_{n+1}x^{(n+1)} = 0$ and implies that $a_{n+1} = 0$. This contradicts the assumption that $x^{(n+1)}$ is linearly dependent on $x^{(1)}, x^{(2)}, \ldots, x^{(n)}$; in other words, $n < m$ is impossible, and we conclude that $n \geq m$.

Corollary. If all roots of the characteristic equation are different, there are N linearly independent eigenvectors.

Remark. If λ is complex, then the eigenvectors corresponding to it are, in general, complex. In this case, a matrix is not diagonalizable *within the framework of real space* even if it has N linearly independent eigenvectors.

Many physical problems involve eigenvalues and eigenvectors of real symmetric matrices (in real space) or hermitian matrices (in complex space) and the following theorems are of fundamental importance.

Theorem 2. The eigenvalues of a hermitian (or real symmetric) matrix are all real.

Proof. Let A be hermitian and let $Ax = \lambda x$. Take complex conjugates and then transpose:

$$x^\dagger A^\dagger = \lambda^* x^\dagger.$$

(Note that λ, being a scalar, is not affected by the operation of transposing.) Multiply the first equation by $x^\dagger$ from the left:

$$x^\dagger A x = \lambda x^\dagger x.$$

Multiply the second equation by x from the right, use $A^\dagger = A$, and subtract it from the preceding one:

$$(\lambda - \lambda^*)x^\dagger x = 0.$$

Since $x^\dagger x \neq 0$, it follows that $\lambda = \lambda^*$, that is, λ is real. For real symmetric matrices, the proof is identical, since a real symmetric matrix is a special case of the hermitian matrix.

Theorem 3. If two eigenvalues of a hermitian (or real symmetric) matrix are different, the corresponding eigenvectors are orthogonal.

Proof. Let $Ax^{(1)} = \lambda_1 x^{(1)}$ and $Ax^{(2)} = \lambda_2 x^{(2)}$. Multiply the first equation by $x^{(2)\dagger}$ from the left:

$$x^{(2)\dagger} A x^{(1)} = \lambda_1 x^{(2)\dagger} x^{(1)}.$$

Take the hermitian conjugate of the second equation and multiply by $x^{(1)}$ from the right; use $A^\dagger = A$ (and $\lambda_2^* = \lambda_2$):

$$x^{(2)\dagger}Ax^{(1)} = \lambda_2 x^{(2)\dagger}x^{(1)}.$$

Subtract, obtaining $(\lambda_1 - \lambda_2)x^{(2)\dagger}x^{(1)} = 0$. Since $\lambda_1 \neq \lambda_2$, it follows that

$$x^{(2)\dagger}x^{(1)} = 0.$$

For real symmetric matrices, the proof is the same. Note that the eigenvectors are necessarily real. Observe that the orthogonality stated here refers to N-tuples, reflected in the dot product $x^{(2)\dagger}x^{(1)}$.

Remark. The technique involved in this proof is analogous to that employed in Sections 4.4 (p. 164) and 9.3 (p. 338) because the problems are basically the same.‡

Theorem 4. *Gram-Schmidt Process.* Given any n linearly independent vectors, one can construct from their linear combinations a set of n mutually orthogonal unit vectors (orthonormal set of n vectors).

Proof. Let the given vectors be $\mathbf{x}_1, \mathbf{x}_2, \ldots, \mathbf{x}_n$. Define

$$\mathbf{u}_1 = \frac{\mathbf{x}_1}{\|\mathbf{x}_1\|}$$

to be the first unit vector. Now define

$$\mathbf{u}_2' = \mathbf{x}_2 - (\mathbf{x}_2 \cdot \mathbf{u}_1)\mathbf{u}_1.$$

Taking the inner product of vector $\mathbf{u}_2'$ with $\mathbf{u}_1$, we deduce that it is orthogonal to $\mathbf{u}_1$,

$$(\mathbf{u}_2', \mathbf{u}_1) = (\mathbf{x}_2, \mathbf{u}_1) - (\mathbf{x}_2, \mathbf{u}_1)(\mathbf{u}_1, \mathbf{u}_1) = 0,$$

because $(\mathbf{u}_1, \mathbf{u}_1) = 1$.
    We next normalize $\mathbf{u}_2'$ by defining

$$\mathbf{u}_2 = \frac{\mathbf{u}_2'}{\|\mathbf{u}_2\|}.$$

This is our second unit vector. It is orthogonal to $\mathbf{u}_1$ since $\mathbf{u}_2'$ is so.
    We continue this process by defining

$$\mathbf{u}_k' = \mathbf{x}_k - \sum_{j=1}^{k-1} (\mathbf{x}_k, \mathbf{u}_j)\mathbf{u}_j$$

and

$$\mathbf{u}_k = \frac{\mathbf{u}_k'}{\|\mathbf{u}_k'\|}.$$

---

‡ Observe that the differential operators used in Sections 4.4 and 9.3 were hermitian operators (p. 341). See also Section 11.1.

Note that we can never run into trouble with $\mathbf{u}'_k = \mathbf{0}$ because this would contradict the linear independence of the $\mathbf{x}_i$-vectors. The process is terminated only when the supply of $\mathbf{x}_i$-vectors is exhausted.

Theorem 5. A hermitian matrix can be diagonalized (via similarity transformation‡) by a unitary matrix. A real symmetric matrix can be diagonalized by a real orthogonal matrix.

Proof. Let $\xi = \{\xi_1, \xi_2, \ldots, \xi_N\}$ represent an eigenvector of a hermitian matrix A. Without loss of generality it may be assumed to be a unit vector (it can always be normalized). Let us take from the space *any other* $N - 1$ vectors which, with ξ adjoined to them, form a linearly independent set. By use of the Gram-Schmidt process we can construct an orthonormal basis containing ξ as the first basis vector. We construct a matrix U_1 whose columns are equal to these basis vectors. Then U_1 is unitary and $U_1^{-1} = U_1^\dagger$. Forming the matrix AU_1, we find that the first column of AU_1 will be $\lambda_1\xi$, because ξ is an eigenvector of A, and λ_1 is the corresponding eigenvalue. Now let us form the matrix $U_1^{-1}AU_1$. The rows of $U_1^{-1} = U_1^\dagger$ are orthogonal to ξ (except the first row, which is equal to ξ^*). Therefore the first column of $U_1^{-1}AU_1$ will be of the form

$$\begin{bmatrix} \lambda_1 \\ 0 \\ 0 \\ \vdots \\ 0 \end{bmatrix}$$

Now the matrix $U_1^{-1}AU_1$ is hermitian because

$$(U_1^{-1}AU_1)^\dagger = U_1^\dagger A^\dagger (U_1^{-1})^\dagger = U_1^{-1}AU_1.$$

Therefore it must be of the form

$$U_1^{-1}AU_1 = \left[\begin{array}{c|ccc} \lambda_1 & 0 & 0 & \cdots & 0 \\ \hline 0 & & & & \\ 0 & & & & \\ 0 & & A' & & \\ \vdots & & \text{(hermitian)} & & \\ 0 & & & & \end{array}\right]$$

---

‡ Which also is a congruence transformation (see p. 442) and is commonly known as *unitary transformation.*

where the submatrix A' is hermitian. The crucial feature is the appearance of zeros in the first row.

Consider the $(N - 1) \times (N - 1)$ matrix A'. All its eigenvalues are evidently eigenvalues of A (this is easily checked). Let $\eta = \{\eta_2, \eta_3, \ldots, \eta_N\}$ be its normalized eigenvector corresponding to the eigenvalue λ_2 (it may or may not be equal to λ_1). Construct (by the Gram-Schmidt process) additional $N - 2$ vectors in the $(N - 1)$-space which are orthogonal to η. Extend all these vectors to the entire N-space by assigning zero as their first component and construct a unitary matrix:

$$
U_2 = \begin{array}{|c|c|c|}
\hline
1 & 0 & 0 \ \cdots \ 0 \\
\hline
0 & \eta_2 & \\
0 & \eta_3 & \text{(unitary)} \\
\vdots & \vdots & \\
0 & \eta_N & \\
\hline
\end{array} \ .
$$

If the matrix $U_2^{-1}(U_1^{-1}AU_1)U_2$ is now formed, it is easily checked that it will have the form

$$
\begin{array}{|c|c|c|}
\hline
\lambda_1 & 0 & 0 \ \cdots \ 0 \\
\hline
0 & \lambda_2 & 0 \ \cdots \ 0 \\
\hline
0 & 0 & A'' \\
\vdots & \vdots & \text{(hermitian)} \\
0 & 0 & \\
\hline
\end{array}
$$

with the submatrix A'' being hermitian again.

Now repeat this process until the entire matrix is diagonalized, namely, until the matrix

$$
U_N^{-1} U_{N-1}^{-1} \ldots U_2^{-1} U_1^{-1} A U_1 U_2 \ldots U_{N-1} U_N
$$

is diagonal. Define $U = U_1 U_2 \ldots U_{N-1} U_N$. Evidently U is unitary if all the U_i are unitary. Consequently the matrix $U^{-1}AU$ is diagonal and the theorem is established. For real symmetric matrices the proof is similar.

Remark. From this construction it follows that every hermitian (or real symmetric) matrix possesses the full slate of N linearly independent eigenvectors, even if some of its eigenvalues may be multiple (the case of degeneracy). Eigenvectors corresponding to a degenerate eigenvalue need not be orthogonal. However, there are m of them (linearly independent) in the case of an m-fold degeneracy, and any linear combination of these will still be an eigenvector corresponding to the *same eigenvalue*. Then, by the Gram-Schmidt process, a set of mutually orthogonal eigenvectors can be found. This has actually been done in the proof of the theorem.

Example. The problem of coupled pendula from Section 10.1 has been seen to reduce to the solution of an algebraic system:

$$(g/L + k/m)\Theta_1 - (k/m)\Theta_2 = \omega^2\Theta_1,$$
$$-(k/m)\Theta_1 + (g/L + k/m)\Theta_2 = \omega^2\Theta_2$$

(equations from p. 410, divided by mL for convenience). This is an eigenvalue problem for the matrix

$$A = \begin{vmatrix} (g/L + k/m) & -k/m \\ -k/m & (g/L + k/m) \end{vmatrix}.$$

The eigenvalues λ are obtained from the characteristic equation

$$\det (A - \lambda I) = 0$$

and are

$$\lambda_1 = g/L, \qquad \lambda_2 = g/L + 2(k/m).$$

These are, of course, the squares of characteristic frequencies. The eigenvectors can be obtained by substituting λ_1 and λ_2 into the algebraic system. For $\lambda = \lambda_1$, the system reduces to a single equation

$$(k/m)\Theta_1 - (k/m)\Theta_2 = 0.$$

The normalized solution can be represented by a column vector

$$\begin{vmatrix} \dfrac{1}{\sqrt{2}} \\ \dfrac{1}{\sqrt{2}} \end{vmatrix}.$$

Similarly, for $\lambda = \lambda_2$, the normalized eigenvector is

$$\begin{vmatrix} \dfrac{1}{\sqrt{2}} \\ -\dfrac{1}{\sqrt{2}} \end{vmatrix}.$$

The matrix A is real symmetric and can be diagonalized by the similarity transformation $A' = G^{-1}AG$, where G is an orthogonal matrix having eigenvectors of A as its columns. Since the eigenvalues are distinct, the eigenvectors are automatically orthogonal and

$$G = \begin{bmatrix} \dfrac{1}{\sqrt{2}} & \dfrac{1}{\sqrt{2}} \\[2ex] \dfrac{1}{\sqrt{2}} & -\dfrac{1}{\sqrt{2}} \end{bmatrix}.$$

Since G is orthogonal, it follows that $G^{-1} = G^T$. We find, in this case, that G is symmetric as well so that $G^{-1} = G$. It is easily checked that

$$\begin{bmatrix} \dfrac{1}{\sqrt{2}} & \dfrac{1}{\sqrt{2}} \\[2ex] \dfrac{1}{\sqrt{2}} & -\dfrac{1}{\sqrt{2}} \end{bmatrix} \cdot \begin{bmatrix} \dfrac{g}{L}+\dfrac{k}{m} & -\dfrac{k}{m} \\[2ex] -\dfrac{k}{m} & \dfrac{g}{L}+\dfrac{k}{m} \end{bmatrix} \cdot \begin{bmatrix} \dfrac{1}{\sqrt{2}} & \dfrac{1}{\sqrt{2}} \\[2ex] \dfrac{1}{\sqrt{2}} & -\dfrac{1}{\sqrt{2}} \end{bmatrix} = \begin{bmatrix} \dfrac{g}{L} & 0 \\[2ex] 0 & \dfrac{g}{L}+2\dfrac{k}{m} \end{bmatrix}.$$

A similarity transformation performed on a matrix can be associated with a linear transformation of coordinates in a vector space. In our problem this transformation is relating the "old" coordinates Θ_1, Θ_2 to some "new" coordinates Ψ_1, Ψ_2 by means of the matrix T or its inverse G (in our case these are identical). For instance, the transformation

$$\begin{bmatrix} \Theta_1 \\ \Theta_2 \end{bmatrix} = \begin{bmatrix} g_{11} & g_{12} \\ g_{21} & g_{22} \end{bmatrix} \cdot \begin{bmatrix} \Psi_1 \\ \Psi_2 \end{bmatrix}$$

is explicitly written as

$$\Theta_1 = (1/\sqrt{2})(\Psi_1 + \Psi_2), \qquad \Theta_2 = (1/\sqrt{2})(\Psi_1 - \Psi_2).$$

This corresponds to the transformation to normal coordinates discussed in Section 10.2 (p. 413).

10.9 SIMULTANEOUS DIAGONALIZATION

The eigenvalue problem for coupled pendula (Sections 10.1 and 10.8) can be approached from the point of view of *diagonalizing the Lagrangian*. Indeed, the equations of motion arise from the Lagrangian

$$\mathcal{L} = \tfrac{1}{2}mL^2 \left\{ [\dot{\theta}_1^2 + \dot{\theta}_2^2] - \left[\left(\frac{g}{L}+\frac{k}{m}\right)\theta_1^2 + \left(\frac{g}{L}+\frac{k}{m}\right)\theta_2^2 - 2\frac{k}{m}\theta_1\theta_2 \right] \right\}.$$

The Lagrangian consists of the difference between two quadratic forms (p. 409), one in the variables $\dot{\theta}_1$ and $\dot{\theta}_2$, and the other in the variables θ_1 and θ_2.

A (real) quadratic form (in variables q_i)

$$\sum_{i=1}^{n} \sum_{j=1}^{n} a_{ij} q_i q_j$$

is completely defined by the matrix of its coefficients a_{ij}. This matrix is essentially a *symmetric matrix* because the term containing the product $q_i q_j$ ($i \neq j$) can always be split into two equal parts, one of them denoted by $a_{ij} q_i q_j$ and the other by $a_{ji} q_j q_i$. For instance, the potential energy part of the above Lagrangian can be written as

$$V = \tfrac{1}{2} m L^2 \left[\left(\frac{g}{L} + \frac{k}{m} \right) \theta_1^2 - \frac{k}{m} \theta_1 \theta_2 - \frac{k}{m} \theta_2 \theta_1 + \left(\frac{g}{L} + \frac{k}{m} \right) \theta_2^2 \right],$$

which (apart from the factor $\tfrac{1}{2} m L^2$) gives rise to a real symmetric matrix

$$A = \begin{vmatrix} (g/L + k/m) & -k/m \\ -k/m & (g/L + k/m) \end{vmatrix}.$$

It is essentially this matrix which is diagonalized by means of a transition to normal coordinates. The diagonalization is performed by a linear transformation involving the orthogonal matrix G:

$$\begin{vmatrix} \theta_1 \\ \theta_2 \end{vmatrix} = \begin{vmatrix} \dfrac{1}{\sqrt{2}} & \dfrac{1}{\sqrt{2}} \\ \dfrac{1}{\sqrt{2}} & -\dfrac{1}{\sqrt{2}} \end{vmatrix} \cdot \begin{vmatrix} \psi_1 \\ \psi_2 \end{vmatrix} \qquad \text{or} \qquad \theta = G\psi.$$

The kinetic energy part of the Lagrangian is a quadratic form in $\dot\theta_1$ and $\dot\theta_2$ corresponding to a multiple of the unit matrix (the factor being $\tfrac{1}{2} m L^2$). The (mandatory) transformation of the derivatives

$$\begin{vmatrix} \dot\theta_1 \\ \dot\theta_2 \end{vmatrix} = \begin{vmatrix} \dfrac{1}{\sqrt{2}} & \dfrac{1}{\sqrt{2}} \\ \dfrac{1}{\sqrt{2}} & -\dfrac{1}{\sqrt{2}} \end{vmatrix} \cdot \begin{vmatrix} \dot\psi_1 \\ \dot\psi_2 \end{vmatrix} \qquad \text{or} \qquad \dot\theta = G\dot\psi$$

does not disrupt its diagonal form.* We see that the entire Lagrangian is diagonal-

---

* The unit matrix I commutes with any matrix and so does any multiple of I. We have $G^T cIG = cIG^T G$, where $c = \text{const}$. Moreover, in our case, $G^T G = I$, so the kinetic energy matrix remains unchanged.

ized by the linear transformation $\theta = G\psi$. Indeed, if we use K and V to denote the matrices corresponding to quadratic forms for kinetic and potential energy, then, in matrix language,

$$\mathcal{L} = \dot{\theta}^T K \dot{\theta} - \theta^T V \theta,$$

where $K = (\tfrac{1}{2}mL^2)I$ and $V = (\tfrac{1}{2}mL^2)A$. After the transformation, the Lagrangian is expressed in the form

$$\mathcal{L} = \dot{\psi}^T G^T K G \dot{\psi} - \psi^T G^T V G \psi.$$

Now $K' = G^T K G$ and $V' = G^T V G$ are diagonal matrices, and the statement follows. Note that from this point of view the matrices K and V undergo a congruence transformation and not a similarity transformation (see p. 442). The distinction is, however, lost since G is an orthogonal matrix and $G^T = G^{-1}$.

Let us now consider the similar problem for the double pendulum described in Section 10.2. The Lagrangian reads (p. 415).

$$\mathcal{L} = \tfrac{1}{2}mL^2 \left[(2\dot{\theta}_1^2 + \dot{\theta}_2^2 + 2\dot{\theta}_1\dot{\theta}_2) - \left(2\frac{g}{L}\theta_1^2 + \frac{g}{L}\theta_2^2 \right) \right].$$

If we want a system of decoupled equations of motion we must diagonalize this Lagrangian by a linear transformation*

$$\theta = G\psi.$$

This will result in a new quadratic form,

$$\mathcal{L} = \dot{\psi}^T K' \dot{\psi} - \psi^T V' \psi,$$

where $K' = G^T K G$ and $V' = G^T V G$, while

$$K = \begin{vmatrix} mL^2 & \tfrac{1}{2}mL^2 \\ \tfrac{1}{2}mL^2 & \tfrac{1}{2}mL^2 \end{vmatrix}, \qquad V = \begin{vmatrix} mgL & 0 \\ 0 & \tfrac{1}{2}mgL \end{vmatrix}.$$

The problem is, therefore, to *diagonalize simultaneously* both matrices K and V. The rather accidental fact that V is already diagonal does not make much difference, since $G^T V G$ is not necessarily diagonal if V is diagonal.†

We note that both matrices K and V are real symmetric matrices. Moreover, matrix K is a positive-definite matrix (see p. 441).‡ These facts are sufficient to ensure the possibility of simultaneous diagonalization, as shown below.

---

* A linear transformation preserves the quadratic form of the Lagrangian which produces the equations of motion of the desirable type.

† A diagonal matrix will not even commute, in general, with the matrix G (as was the case for the coupled-pendula problem).

‡ This must always be the case for the K-matrix since it represents kinetic energy which is always nonnegative.

Theorem 1. Two real symmetric matrices, K and V, are *simultaneously diago-nalizable* by a transformation $K' = G^TKG$ and $V' = G^TVG$, provided one of them, say K, is *positive-definite*.

Proof. We find from Theorem 5 of Section 10.8 that there exists an orthog-onal transformation U such that U^TKU is diagonal, with diagonal elements μ_i ($i = 1, 2, \ldots, N$). The matrix U^TKU is also positive-definite. (Replace x in $x^TKx > 0$ by Uy and use the fact that x is arbitrary.) Therefore all the μ_i are *positive*. Now construct a diagonal matrix M with the elements $1/\sqrt{\mu_i}$ along the main diagonal (in the same order as they appear in U^TKU). Verify that the matrix

$$K'' = M^TU^TKUM$$

is a unit matrix. Under the combined transformation by UM, the matrix V will go over into

$$V'' = M^TU^TVUM,$$

which is still real symmetric, as is readily verified. Finally, diagonalize V'' by means of an orthogonal matrix S:

$$V' = S^TV''S.$$

This transformation will not change the matrix $K'' = I$. Now define the overall transformation matrix G by

$$G = UMS.$$

Then both matrices $G^TKG = I$ and $G^TVG = V'$ are diagonal and the theorem is proved. Note that, in general, the matrix G *is not* an orthogonal matrix.

In practice, we can construct the matrix G in a different way, following the cue from the double-pendulum problem. The Lagrangian, written out in terms of the old coordinates θ, reads

$$\mathcal{L} = \dot{\theta}^TK\dot{\theta} - \theta^TV\theta$$

and gives rise to a system of Lagrangian equations of motion which can be written as

$$K\ddot{\theta} + V\theta = 0.$$

Exercise. Deduce this result by writing out $\mathcal{L}$ in double-summation form and performing the necessary operations.

We have been seeking harmonic solutions, with θ being proportional to $e^{-i\omega t}$. For such solutions, $\ddot{\theta}$ is equivalent to $-\omega^2\theta$, so that

$$(V - \omega^2K)\theta = 0.$$

This is a set of N linear homogeneous equations in N unknowns. For a nontrivial solution, we require that

$$\det (V - \omega^2 K) = 0,$$

yielding the characteristic values for ω^2. It is easy to see that these values are merely the diagonal elements of the diagonalized matrix $V' = G^T V G$. Indeed, the transformation by matrix G cannot change the characteristic equation because

$$\det (G^T V G - \omega^2 G^T K G) = \det G^T \cdot \det (V - \omega^2 K) \cdot \det G$$
$$= (\det G)^2 \cdot \det (V - \omega^2 K).$$

On the other hand, the roots of $\det (V' - \omega^2 I) = 0$ are evidently the diagonal elements of V'.

Having determined the characteristic frequencies, we can solve the equations $(V - \omega^2 K)\theta = 0$ and find the N-tuples θ which give the solution in terms of normal coordinates (see p. 416).

We may summarize the results in the language of matrix algebra as follows: Given two matrices V and K, we call the roots of the equation $\det (V - \lambda K) = 0$ the *generalized eigenvalues* of the matrix V *with respect to the matrix K*. The solutions of $(V - \lambda K)x = 0$ may be called *generalized eigenvectors* of the matrix V with respect to the matrix K. The matrices V and K can be simultaneously diagonalized by a nonsingular matrix G, whose columns are the generalized eigenvectors.*

Example. In the double-pendulum problem, the generalized eigenvalues have been found to be

$$\lambda_1 = \omega_1^2 = (2 + \sqrt{2})g/L, \qquad \lambda_2 = \omega_2^2 = (2 - \sqrt{2})g/L,$$

and the generalized eigenvectors can be taken to be (p. 417)†

$$\theta^{(1)} = \begin{bmatrix} \dfrac{1}{2\sqrt{2}} \\[2mm] -\tfrac{1}{2} \end{bmatrix}, \qquad \theta^{(2)} = \begin{bmatrix} \dfrac{1}{2\sqrt{2}} \\[2mm] \tfrac{1}{2} \end{bmatrix}.$$

The matrix

$$G = \begin{bmatrix} \dfrac{1}{2\sqrt{2}} & \dfrac{1}{2\sqrt{2}} \\[2mm] -\tfrac{1}{2} & \tfrac{1}{2} \end{bmatrix}$$

---

* Note that the diagonal form of K need not be the unit matrix. A multiplication of an eigenvector by a scalar k will cause the corresponding diagonal elements of $G^T V G$ and $G^T K G$ to be multiplied by k^2. It is only the *ratios* of diagonal elements that are fixed (they are the generalized eigenvalues).

† We use $\theta^{(1)} = \tfrac{1}{2}\psi_1$ and $\theta^{(2)} = \tfrac{1}{2}\psi_2$.

diagonalizes both K and V matrices:

$$G^T K G = \begin{bmatrix} \dfrac{1}{2\sqrt{2}} & -\tfrac{1}{2} \\[2ex] \dfrac{1}{2\sqrt{2}} & \tfrac{1}{2} \end{bmatrix} \cdot \begin{bmatrix} mL^2 & \tfrac{1}{2}mL^2 \\[2ex] \tfrac{1}{2}mL^2 & \tfrac{1}{2}mL^2 \end{bmatrix} \cdot \begin{bmatrix} \dfrac{1}{2\sqrt{2}} & \dfrac{1}{2\sqrt{2}} \\[2ex] -\tfrac{1}{2} & \tfrac{1}{2} \end{bmatrix}$$

$$= \begin{bmatrix} \dfrac{2-\sqrt{2}}{8}mL^2 & 0 \\[3ex] 0 & \dfrac{2+\sqrt{2}}{8}mL^2 \end{bmatrix},$$

$$G^T V G = \begin{bmatrix} \dfrac{1}{2\sqrt{2}} & -\tfrac{1}{2} \\[2ex] \dfrac{1}{2\sqrt{2}} & \tfrac{1}{2} \end{bmatrix} \cdot \begin{bmatrix} mgL & 0 \\[2ex] 0 & \tfrac{1}{2}mgL \end{bmatrix} \cdot \begin{bmatrix} \dfrac{1}{2\sqrt{2}} & \dfrac{1}{2\sqrt{2}} \\[2ex] -\tfrac{1}{2} & \tfrac{1}{2} \end{bmatrix}$$

$$= \begin{bmatrix} \tfrac{1}{4}mgL & 0 \\[2ex] 0 & \tfrac{1}{4}mgL \end{bmatrix}.$$

The generalized eigenvalues are now the ratios of corresponding diagonal elements:

$$\omega_1^2 = \frac{\tfrac{1}{4}mgL}{[(2-\sqrt{2})/8]mL^2} = (2+\sqrt{2})(g/L),$$

$$\omega_2^2 = \frac{\tfrac{1}{4}mgL}{[(2+\sqrt{2})/8]mL^2} = (2-\sqrt{2})(g/L).$$

BIBLIOGRAPHY

BIRKHOFF, G., and S. MACLANE, *A Survey of Modern Algebra*. New York: Macmillan Co., 1953.

HALMOS, P. R., *Finite-Dimensional Vector Spaces*. Princeton, N.J.: Princeton University Press, 1942.

HOHN, F. E., *Elementary Matrix Algebra*. New York: Macmillan Co., 1958.

MARCUS, M., and H. MINC, *Introduction to Linear Algebra*. New York: Macmillan Co., 1965.

MURDOCH, D. C., *Linear Algebra for Undergraduates*. New York: John Wiley and Sons, 1957.

PROBLEMS

1. Consider the system of coupled differential equations treated in Section 10.1, Example 1 (with $m_1 = m_2$ and $k_1 = k_2$):

$$m\ddot{u}_1 + 2ku_1 - ku_2 = 0, \qquad m\ddot{u}_2 + 2ku_2 - ku_2 = 0.$$

Solve this system by the Laplace-transform method, using the initial conditions

$$u_1(0) = u_2(0) = 0, \qquad \dot{u}_1(0) = v, \qquad \dot{u}_2(0) = 0,$$

and display the solution as a superposition of normal modes (as on p. 408).

2. The equation $2x^2 + 4xy + 5y^2 = 1$ represents an ellipse in the xy-plane. Show that it can be brought to either one of the two "diagonal forms"

a) $x'^2 + 6y'^2 = 1,$ b) $6x'^2 + y'^2 = 1$

by rotations of coordinate axes. Display the matrix of rotation for both cases.

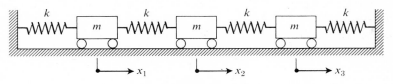

Figure 10.13

3. Consider the problem of three statically coupled masses (Fig. 10.13) analogous to those in Section 10.1, Example 1. Let x_1, x_2, and x_3 be their displacements from equilibrium positions.

a) Set up the equations of motion on the basis of Newton's second law.

b) Evaluate the potential energy of the system and show that it reduces to

$$V = kx_1^2 + kx_2^2 + kx_3^2 - kx_1x_2 - kx_2x_3.$$

c) Check the result under (a) by deducing the Lagrange equations of motion.

d) Show that the characteristic frequencies can be obtained by solving

$$\det \begin{vmatrix} 2-\lambda & -1 & 0 \\ -1 & 2-\lambda & -1 \\ 0 & -1 & 2-\lambda \end{vmatrix} = 0.$$

e) Find the characteristic frequencies and the normal modes.

4. Show that all polynomials of degree less than or equal to N (a positive integer) form a vector space $\mathcal{S}$. What is the dimension of this space? Produce a basis for this space.

5. Consider the set $\mathcal{S}_+$ of all even polynomials from the space of the preceding problem. Is this set a subspace of $\mathcal{S}$? If it is, what is its dimension? Answer the same question for the set $\mathcal{S}_-$ of all odd polynomials. Do the sets $\mathcal{S}_+$ and $\mathcal{S}_-$ have common vectors?

6. Consider the following two sets of polynomials.

Set A:

$$L_0(x) = 1, \qquad L_1(x) = 1 - x,$$

$$L_2(x) = 2 - 4x - x^2, \qquad L_3(x) = 6 - 18x + 9x^2 - x^3.$$

Set B:

$$T_0(x) = 1, \qquad T_1(x) = x,$$

$$T_2(x) = 2x^2 - 1, \qquad T_3(x) = 4x^3 - 3x.$$

Show that both sets span the same vector space and that either set can be regarded as a basis. Show that the first four Legendre polynomials (p. 350) belong to this space. Express P_0, P_1, P_2, and P_3 as linear combinations of the vectors of set A; do the same for set B.

7. Show that all 2×2 matrices form a linear space. Is the multiplication of matrices related to this statement? What is the dimension of this space? Display a basis for such a space.

8. Show that the matrix

$$A = \begin{array}{|ccc|} \hline 1 & 0 & 0 \\ 0 & \cos\theta & -\sin\theta \\ 0 & \sin\theta & \cos\theta \\ \hline \end{array}$$

represents a linear operator which *rotates* all vectors by the angle θ about some axis. (What is this axis and what is the direction of rotation?) Show that the same matrix A represents a rotation of coordinate axes (discussed in Section 1.3). Indicate the axis, the angle and the direction of rotation, and comment.

9. Show that the matrix

$$B = \begin{array}{|ccc|} \hline -1 & 0 & 0 \\ 0 & \cos\phi & \sin\phi \\ 0 & \sin\phi & -\cos\phi \\ \hline \end{array}$$

can represent either rotation of axes or rotation of vectors. Is the angle of rotation related to ϕ? What is the axis of rotation? [*Hint:* Seek a vector which will be unaffected by the rotation.] Calculate B^2; can the angle of rotation be deduced from this result?

10. Suppose that a vector (x, y, z) has been rotated by an angle $\pi/6$ about the z-axis. Display the matrix A transforming (x, y, z) into new coordinates (x', y', z'). Suppose this transformation has been followed by another rotation, this time about the y-axis, through an angle $\pi/4$. (*Note:* Both rotations appear clockwise if viewed along the positive direction of the axis of rotation.) Display the matrix B transforming (x', y', z') into the new coordinates (x'', y'', z''). Show that the overall transformation from (x, y, z) to (x'', y'', z'') is achieved by use of the matrix

$$\begin{bmatrix} \sqrt{\tfrac{3}{8}} & -1/\sqrt{8} & 1/\sqrt{2} \\ \tfrac{1}{2} & \sqrt{3}/2 & 0 \\ -\sqrt{\tfrac{3}{8}} & 1/\sqrt{8} & 1/\sqrt{2} \end{bmatrix}.$$

11. Establish the following properties of $N \times N$ matrices:

a) $(ABC)^T = C^T B^T A^T$. Can this property be extended to more than three matrices?
b) $\det (A^{-1}) = 1/\det A$ (for nonsingular matrices).
c) $(AB)^{-1} = B^{-1}A^{-1}$. Can this property be extended to more than two matrices?

12. Construct two 2×2 matrices, A and B, with *all* matrix elements differing from zero, but such that the product AB is a zero matrix.

13. Define the *commutator* of two matrices, A and B, by $[A, B] \equiv AB - BA$. Verify the Jacobi identity

$$[A, [B, C]] + [B, [C, A]] + [C, [A, B]] = 0.$$

Where else does such an identity occur?

14. The matrix of a certain linear operator with respect to the basis $\mathbf{u}_1(1, 0, 0)$, $\mathbf{u}_2(0, 1, 0)$, $\mathbf{u}_3(0, 0, 1)$ reads

$$A = \begin{bmatrix} 1 & -1 & 0 \\ 2 & 1 & 1 \\ -2 & 0 & 1 \end{bmatrix}.$$

Show that the matrix of the same operator with respect to the basis $\mathbf{v}_1(-\tfrac{2}{3}, \tfrac{1}{3}, \tfrac{2}{3})$, $\mathbf{v}_2(-\tfrac{1}{3}, \tfrac{2}{3}, -\tfrac{2}{3})$, $\mathbf{v}_3(\tfrac{2}{3}, \tfrac{2}{3}, \tfrac{1}{3})$ reads

$$A' = \begin{bmatrix} \tfrac{17}{9} & \tfrac{4}{9} & \tfrac{1}{9} \\ -\tfrac{11}{9} & -\tfrac{1}{9} & \tfrac{20}{9} \\ -\tfrac{2}{9} & -\tfrac{10}{9} & \tfrac{11}{9} \end{bmatrix}.$$

[*Hint:* Note that the new basis is orthogonal; this simplifies the calculations.]

15. Given two bases in space,

U-basis: $\mathbf{u}_1(1, 0, 0)$, $\mathbf{u}_2(0, 1, 0)$, $\mathbf{u}_3(0, 0, 1)$,

V-basis: $\mathbf{v}_1(2, -1, 0)$, $\mathbf{v}_2(1, 1, 1)$, $\mathbf{v}_3(-3, 0, 4)$, find the following four matrices:

a) the matrix which transforms $\mathbf{u}_1$ into $\mathbf{v}_1$, $\mathbf{u}_2$ into $\mathbf{v}_2$, $\mathbf{u}_3$ into $\mathbf{v}_3$;
b) the matrix which transforms $\mathbf{v}_1$ into $\mathbf{u}_1$, $\mathbf{v}_2$ into $\mathbf{u}_2$, $\mathbf{v}_3$ into $\mathbf{u}_3$;
c) the matrix which transforms (for an arbitrary vector) the coordinates x, y, z with respect to the U-basis into the coordinates x', y', z' with respect to the V-basis;
d) the matrix which transforms x', y', z' into x, y, z.

16. Show that for the space of functions discussed in Problem 6, the integral

$$(f, g) = \int_{-1}^{+1} f(x)g(x)\, dx$$

can serve as the inner product of the two functions $f(x)$ and $g(x)$ from the space. Show that the set of Legendre polynomials P_0, P_1, P_2, and P_3 forms an orthogonal (but not normalized) basis in this space.

17. Show that $\mathfrak{D} \equiv d/dx$ is a linear operator in the space discussed in Problem 6. Display the matrices representing this operator with respect to the following bases:

a) the set of polynomials

$$F_0(x) = 1, \ F_1(x) = x, \ F_2(x) = x^2, \ F_3(x) = x^3;$$

b) the set of Legendre polynomials P_0, P_1, P_2, P_3;
c) the set A in Problem 6.

Are any of these matrices nonsingular? Explain.

18. Prove the following statements:

a) The inverse of an orthogonal (unitary) matrix is an orthogonal (unitary) matrix.
b) The product of two orthogonal (unitary) matrices is an orthogonal (unitary) matrix.
c) The product of two symmetric (hermitian) matrices is a symmetric (hermitian) matrix if and only if they commute.

[*Hint:* These and many other statements about matrices can be proved very quickly by matrix algebra.]

19. Prove the following statements:

a) A symmetric matrix remains symmetric after a similarity transformation by an orthogonal matrix.
b) A unitary matrix remains unitary after a unitary transformation (see p. 448, footnote).

20. Define the following special types of matrices:

a) A is antisymmetric (or skew-symmetric) if $A^T = -A$.
b) A is antihermitian if $A^\dagger = -A$.
c) A is antiunitary if $A^\dagger = -A^{-1}$.

Formulate and prove the properties of such matrices that are analogous to those stated in Problems 18 and 19 for symmetric, hermitian, and unitary matrices.

21. Show that:

a) If A is hermitian, then iA is antihermitian.
b) If A and B are hermitian, then $i(AB - BA)$ is also hermitian.

c) For an arbitrary matrix A, show that $\frac{1}{2}(A + A^\dagger)$ is hermitian; hence show that A can be uniquely decomposed into a sum of a hermitian and an antihermitian matrix.

22. Show that all eigenvalues λ_i (which may be complex) of a unitary matrix have unit magnitude (that is, $|\lambda_i| = 1$). Show that eigenvectors of a unitary matrix corresponding to distinct eigenvalues are orthogonal.

23. The sum of elements on the main diagonal (p. 427) of a matrix A is called the *trace* of matrix A, and we define

$$\text{tr } A = \sum_{i=1}^{N} a_{ii}.$$

Establish the following properties of a trace:

a) tr $(A + B) = $ tr $A + $ tr B,
b) tr $(\alpha A) = \alpha$ tr A ($\alpha = $ scalar),
c) tr $(AB) = $ tr (BA).

From the last property, deduce the following statements:

d) The trace of a matrix is unchanged under a similarity transformation.
e) The commutator (see Problem 13) of two matrices must have a zero trace.
f) The relationship $AB - BA = I$ is impossible for $N \times N$ matrices.

24. The vector space discussed in Problem 6 is spanned by the linearly independent set B. Subject this set to the Gram-Schmidt process and develop an orthonormal basis for the space.

25. Diagonalize the following matrices by means of an orthogonal or a unitary matrix:

$$A = \begin{vmatrix} 4 & 0 & -2 \\ 0 & 5 & 0 \\ -2 & 0 & 4 \end{vmatrix}, \quad B = \begin{vmatrix} \frac{3}{2} & \frac{\sqrt{3}}{2}(1 - i) & -\frac{\sqrt{3}(1 + i)}{2\sqrt{2}} \\ \frac{\sqrt{3}}{2}(1 + i) & \frac{5}{3} & \frac{i}{3\sqrt{2}} \\ -\frac{\sqrt{3}(1 - i)}{2\sqrt{2}} & -\frac{i}{3\sqrt{2}} & \frac{11}{6} \end{vmatrix},$$

$$C = \begin{vmatrix} 0 & 0 & -1 & 0 \\ 0 & 0 & 0 & -\sqrt{2}(1 - i) \\ -1 & 0 & 0 & 0 \\ 0 & -\sqrt{2}(1 + i) & 0 & 0 \end{vmatrix}.$$

26. Consider the equation of a surface in space:

$$5x^2 + 3y^2 + 3z^2 + 2xy - 2xz - 2yz = 1.$$

Display the matrix associated with the quadratic form on the left. By finding its eigenvalues, show that the surface must be an ellipsoid. Find the eigenvectors. What are the principal semiaxes of the ellipsoid?

27. Prove the following statements:

   a) If a matrix is positive-definite (see p. 441), then it is necessarily nonsingular.
   b) A (hermitian) matrix is positive-definite if and only if all its eigenvalues are positive.
   c) If A is a nonsingular matrix, then $A^\dagger A$ is positive-definite.

28. Let A be hermitian and R positive-definite. Show that in the eigenproblem $Ax = \lambda Rx$, all (generalized) eigenvalues must be real. [*Hint:* This can be done in two ways: (a) using the technique from p. 446, (b) utilizing the ideas given on p. 444–5.]

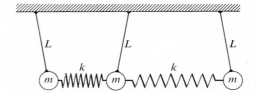

Figure 10.14

29. Find the characteristic frequencies and describe the normal modes of the system of three coupled pendula shown in Fig. 10.14, *without even setting-up* the equations of motion. [*Hint:* Calculate the Lagrangian and employ the matrix methods explained in Section 10.9.]

30. Find the characteristic frequencies and the normal modes of the system shown in Fig. 10.1, given that $m_2 = 2m_1$ and $k_1 = 3k = 3k_2$.

CHAPTER 11

INFINITE-DIMENSIONAL VECTOR SPACES

11.1 SPACES OF FUNCTIONS

The ten postulates defining a vector space (Section 10.3) allow the possibility of infinite-dimensional spaces, which happens when the number of linearly independent vectors in the space is unlimited. However, this feature creates certain difficulties in developing such concepts as basis, coordinates, representations, etc.

It is logical to define a basis in such a space by an *infinite set* of vectors with the following properties: (a) they are linearly independent, and (b) each vector in the space can be represented by a "linear combination" of basis vectors.

So far, the concept of linear independence has been defined (p. 421) for finite sets only. However, it is not difficult to extend it: A set of vectors (finite or infinite) is linearly independent if every finite subset of it is linearly independent. This settles point (a). Point (b) is more troublesome because we evidently need infinite linear combinations.* This poses the question: What kind of interpretation shall we impose on an expression like

$$\mathbf{x} = \sum_{i=1}^{\infty} x_i \mathbf{e}_i ?$$

Evidently, it is necessary to define, in some fashion, the *concept of convergence* in a vector space.

It is instructive, however, to consider first a space in which the basis is automatically defined. Let $\{f(x)\}$ be a set of functions which can be represented by a Fourier series,

$$f(x) = \sum_{n=-\infty}^{+\infty} c_n e^{i(n\pi x/L)}.$$

To be specific, let us assume that the convergence implied here is pointwise. For instance, let $\{f(x)\}$ be the set of continuous, periodic, piecewise smooth functions; the functions with jump discontinuities are excluded.† This set of functions satis-

---

* Otherwise the basis would become untractable.

† They are, at best, represented in the sense

$$\sum_{n=-\infty}^{+\infty} c_n e^{i(n\pi x/L)} = \tfrac{1}{2}[f(x+0) + f(x-0)],$$

which is "not quite" pointwise.

463

fies all postulates of a vector space, as can be verified without difficulty. It follows that this vector space is infinite dimensional and possesses a basis in the sense outlined above, namely, the set of functions

$$\varphi_n(x) = e^{i(n\pi x/L)} \qquad (n = \text{integer}),$$

and the convergence implied by the statement

$$f(x) = \sum_{n=-\infty}^{+\infty} c_n\varphi_n(x)$$

is pointwise convergence.

Though well defined, this vector space has the disadvantage that it is "tied up" to the stated basis, and it is not clear how one can transform the coordinates from one basis to another.† To avoid this restriction, we consider the set of absolutely integrable functions $f(x)$ which are also *square integrable* over an interval (a, b),‡ namely, functions for which the integral

$$\int_a^b |f(x)|^2 \, dx$$

exists.§ There is no mention of any basis, but this set can be shown to be a vector space.

Let us try to verify all ten postulates. The first postulate requires that the function

$$h(x) = f(x) + g(x)$$

is square integrable if $f(x)$ and $g(x)$ are so. To prove this, write

$$\begin{aligned}
|h(x)|^2 &= [f(x) + g(x)][f^*(x) + g^*(x)] \\
&= |f(x)|^2 + |g(x)|^2 + 2\,\text{Re}\,[f^*(x)g(x)] \\
&\leq |f(x)|^2 + |g(x)|^2 + 2|f(x)|\,|g(x)|.
\end{aligned}$$

The integrability of $|h(x)|^2$ now hinges on the integrability of $|f(x)|\,|g(x)|$. To clear this obstacle, note that

$$[|f(x)| - |g(x)|]^2 = |f(x)|^2 + |g(x)|^2 - 2|f(x)|\,|g(x)|.$$

Since the left-hand side is greater than or equal to zero, so is the right-hand side; deduce that

$$2|f(x)|\,|g(x)| \leq |f(x)|^2 + |g(x)|^2.$$

---

† As has been done in Section 10.5 for finite-dimensional spaces.

‡ In modern mathematical literature the term "integrable" is supposed to mean "integrable in the Lebesgue sense," as opposed to the classical meaning "integrable in the Riemann sense." For our present purposes (rather illustrative) the concept of the Riemann integral is adequate.

§ The term "square-integrable" is a misnomer in the case of complex functions because $|f(x)|^2$, rather than $[f(x)]^2$, is implied. For real functions this evidently makes no difference.

Therefore

$$|h(x)|^2 \leq 2[|f(x)|^2 + |g(x)|^2],$$

which ensures the square integrability of $h(x)$ and verifies the first property of vector spaces. The other properties are trivial. Note that it has not been mentioned anywhere that the interval (a, b) must be finite. It follows then that the functions $f(x)$ for which the integral

$$\int_{-\infty}^{+\infty} |f(x)|^2 \, dx$$

converges also form a vector space.

A very important consequence of square integrability is the existence of an *inner product* in this space. Indeed, given two functions (vectors) $f(x)$ and $g(x)$, we can form a scalar†

$$(f, g) = \int_a^b f^*(x)g(x) \, dx.$$

The existence of this integral follows immediately from

$$|f^*g| = |f| \, |g| \leq \tfrac{1}{2}|f|^2 + \tfrac{1}{2}|g|^2,$$

established before. Now verify that (f, g) possesses the three properties of the inner product.‡

1. It has hermitian symmetry:

$$(f, g) = (g, f)^*.$$

2. It is linear with respect to the second factor (and antilinear with respect to the first one):

$$(f, g + h) = (f, g) + (f, h), \qquad (f, ag) = a(f, g) \qquad (a = \text{scalar}).$$

3. It is positive-definite:

$$(f, f) = \int_a^b |f(x)|^2 \, dx \geq 0.$$

A slight problem arises in proving that

$$(f, f) = 0 \qquad \text{implies} \qquad f(x) \equiv 0.$$

A function $f_1(x)$ which is zero for $x \neq 0$ and unity for $x = 0$ satisfies $(f_1, f_1) = 0$ but it is not identically equal to zero. This difficulty is usually resolved by the statement that $(f, f) = 0$ implies that $f(x) = 0$ *except on a set of points which does*

† From now on, we shall bear in mind that (a, b) may mean $(-\infty, +\infty)$.
‡ Defined in Section 10.6.

not contribute to the integral (f, f).* For *continuous* functions, this modification is not necessary. This may be seen from the following theorem.

Theorem. If $p(x)$ is continuous and nonnegative in the interval (a, b) and if $\int_a^b p(x)\,dx = 0$, then $p(x)$ is identically equal to zero in (a, b).

Proof. Suppose that $p(x) \equiv 0$ is not true. Then there exists a point x_0 such that $p(x_0) > 0$. By continuity of $p(x)$, we must have $p(x) > 0$ within some interval $(x_0 - \epsilon, x_0 + \epsilon)$.† Let c be the minimum value of $p(x)$ within this interval: $p(x) \geq c$ in $(x_0 - \epsilon, x_0 + \epsilon)$. Then‡

$$\int_a^b p(x)\,dx \geq \int_{x_0 - \epsilon}^{x_0 + \epsilon} p(x)\,dx \geq 2\epsilon c > 0$$

[using nonnegativity of $p(x)$]. This contradicts

$$\int_a^b p(x)\,dx = 0$$

and establishes the result.

We conclude from the above analysis that we have defined an infinite-dimensional vector space without any reference to a basis.

It may be reasonable to conjecture at this stage that if the interval (a, b) is finite, then one of the orthogonal systems of functions such as trigonometric functions or Legendre polynomials may provide a suitable basis. This can be proved under certain additional assumptions. For instance, if we restrict ourselves to piecewise continuous functions in the interval $(-L, +L)$, then each such function can be represented by a Fourier series

$$f(x) = \sum_{n=-\infty}^{+\infty} c_n e^{i(n\pi x/L)}$$

provided the convergence is interpreted as convergence in the mean:§

$$\lim_{N \to \infty} \int_{-L}^{+L} \left| f(x) - \sum_{n=-N}^{+N} c_n e^{i(n\pi x/L)} \right|^2 dx = 0.$$

What will happen in the case of an infinite interval? From Chapter 7 we know that (under similar restrictions as above) a function will be representable by means of its Fourier transform:

$$f(x) = \frac{1}{\sqrt{2\pi}} \int_{-\infty}^{+\infty} F(k) e^{-ikx}\,dk.$$

---

* Sometimes expressed by saying $f(x)$ is zero *almost everywhere*.

† Or, at least, within $(x_0 - \epsilon, x_0)$ if x_0 happens to be equal to b. Similarly for the case $x_0 = a$.

‡ If $x_0 = a$ or $x_0 = b$, we can obtain $\epsilon c > 0$.

§ See p. 171.

It is logical to regard this expression as a (further) generalization of the idea of basis vectors and coordinates (Section 10.3). Here we should treat the functions

$$\frac{1}{\sqrt{2\pi}}\, e^{-ikx}$$

as basis vectors† and the function $F(k)$ as the set of coordinates.‡ The summation is replaced by an integral.

We cannot enter here into the theoretical questions (many of which are still unexplored) regarding these notions. Instead, let us turn to physical applications of infinite-dimensional spaces.

11.2 THE POSTULATES OF QUANTUM MECHANICS

Quantum mechanics represents a branch of physics where the concept of infinite-dimensional vector spaces§ finds one of its widest applications. Originated in 1926 by Schrödinger and Heisenberg and extensively developed ever since, quantum mechanics can be formulated in a variety of ways. We shall confine ourselves to a simplified (and limited) version which should be adequate for the illustration of basic mathematical concepts. It is based on the description of motion of particles in terms of notions usually associated with waves.

We shall take for granted the following postulates.‖

Postulate A. The state of motion of a particle can be described by a (generally complex) *wave function*

$$\psi(x, y, z; t)$$

which has continuous derivatives throughout the range of the variables involved. The quantity

$$\psi^*\psi\, dV$$

represents the *probability* of finding the particle in a volume element dV at a point (x, y, z) and time t.

Remarks

1. Since the probability of finding a particle *somewhere* must be equal to unity (a certainty), we must have

$$\iiint_{\text{Space}} \psi^*\psi\, dV = 1 \qquad \text{(all } t\text{)},$$

---

† The basis is now *noncountable*, as opposed to the *countable* basis in the Fourier series case.

‡ A function $F(k)$ can be regarded as an infinite set of values of $F(k)$, for each value of k.

§ As well as finite-dimensional spaces.

‖ Like most other fundamental principles of physics, these postulates have been conjectured through experiments and intuition. They cannot be derived (neither can Newton's laws, for that matter).

where *space* means the range of variables x, y, z (usually the entire physical space). We say that ψ is normalized to unity.†

2. The requirement that ψ is normalized to unity is often modified to read ψ *is everywhere bounded*. In this case ψ is interpreted to represent not a single particle but a *beam* of particles (infinite number of them). This interpretation sheds some light on the possibility of observing particles with a definite value of kinetic energy or momentum (see Postulate E below).

3. It is immediately clear that quantum mechanics is a *statistical* theory. It does not predict where a particle is located,‡ but rather, what the chances are of finding it here or there.

> **Postulate B.** Every *measurable* (observable) quantity (e.g., energy, momentum, angular momentum) is represented by a *linear hermitian operator*§ α acting on ψ such that the *average result* of (many) measurements of this quantity in a state $\psi(x, y, z; t)$ is given by
>
> $$\langle \alpha \rangle = \iiint\limits_{\text{Space}} \psi^* (\alpha\psi) \, dV.$$

Remark. The quantity $\langle \alpha \rangle$ is also called the *expectation value* of operator α for the state ψ. It is a *real* quantity [take the complex conjugate of $\langle \alpha \rangle$ and use the fact that α is hermitian (p. 341)], the property necessary for the consistency of the theory.

> **Postulate C.** The operators corresponding to basic measurable quantities are listed below.
>
> a) Operator $\mathcal{X}$ corresponding to the x-coordinate of the particle is given by the scalar x, and similarly for the other two coordinates.
>
> b) Operator $\mathcal{P}_x$ corresponding to the x-component of the momentum **p** of the particle is given by $-i\hbar(\partial/\partial x)$, where $\hbar$ is Planck's constant, and similarly for the other two components.

All other dynamical operators are, in general, obtained from their relations to those given above and such relations are the same as in classical mechanics.‖ If the operator corresponds to a measurable quantity, it must be checked to be hermitian.

Examples

1. For the potential energy of an electron in a Coulomb field of a point charge Q, we have the classical expression (in CGS units)

$$E_{\text{pot}} = -Qe/r \qquad (r = \sqrt{x^2 + y^2 + z^2}).$$

---

† Compare with p. 225.

‡ It is widely believed that such a prediction is, in general, impossible (see the discussion of the Heisenberg uncertainty principle in any textbook on quantum mechanics).

§ The definition given on p. 341 is trivially extended to three-dimensional space.

‖ In a few cases ambiguities do arise but we shall not encounter them here (see Dicke and Wittke, *Introduction to Quantum Mechanics*, p. 103, for an example).

The same expression is valid in quantum mechanics. The operator $\mathcal{E}_{\text{pot}} = -Qe/r$ is hermitian and the expectation value for a state ψ is given by†

$$\langle \mathcal{E}_{\text{pot}} \rangle = -Qe \iiint\limits_{\text{Space}} \frac{\psi^*\psi}{\sqrt{x^2 + y^2 + z^2}} \, dV.$$

2. For the kinetic energy of a particle of mass M, we have the classical expression

$$E_{\text{kin}} = \tfrac{1}{2}Mv^2 = \frac{p^2}{2M} = \frac{1}{2M}(p_x^2 + p_y^2 + p_z^2).$$

The corresponding quantum-mechanical operator is

$$\mathcal{E}_{\text{kin}} = \frac{1}{2M}\left(\frac{\hbar}{i}\right)^2\left(\frac{\partial^2}{\partial x^2} + \frac{\partial^2}{\partial y^2} + \frac{\partial^2}{\partial z^2}\right) = -\frac{\hbar^2}{2M}\nabla^2;$$

it is hermitian.

3. For the z-component of the angular momentum, we have the classical expression

$$L_z = xp_y - yp_x.$$

The corresponding quantum-mechanical operator is

$$\mathcal{L}_z = \frac{\hbar}{i}\left(x\frac{\partial}{\partial y} - y\frac{\partial}{\partial x}\right),$$

which is also hermitian.

Postulate D. The wave function $\psi(x, y, z; t)$ must satisfy the fundamental law of motion expressed by the *Schrödinger equation*

$$\mathcal{H}\psi = i\hbar\frac{\partial\psi}{\partial t},$$

where $\mathcal{H}$ is the operator corresponding to the classical *Hamiltonian function*‡ for the particle, constructed in accordance with Postulate C.

Example. The equation of motion of a free particle reads

$$-\frac{\hbar}{2M}\nabla^2\psi = i\hbar\frac{\partial\psi}{\partial t}$$

because the Hamiltonian function is given in this case by the kinetic energy $p^2/2M$ which corresponds to the operator $-(\hbar^2/2M)\nabla^2$.

---

† Since $1/r$ is a scalar (not a differential) operator, the expression $\psi^*(1/r)\psi$ may also be written as $\psi^*\psi/r$.

‡ See, e.g., Goldstein, Section 7.1.

Postulate E. Every *individual measurement* of a (measurable) quantity corresponding to an (hermitian) operator $\mathcal{Q}$ can yield *only* an *eigenvalue* of $\mathcal{Q}$, namely, a scalar λ for which the equation

$$\mathcal{Q}\psi_\lambda = \lambda\psi_\lambda$$

possesses a nontrivial solution ψ_λ, in accordance with Postulate A.

Remarks

1. This postulate may appear trivial if the spectrum of λ is continuous and coincides with the range of values expected from classical mechanics (as in the examples below). However, in a variety of cases (like the one treated in Section 11.3) the spectrum of λ is discrete, leading to physical results unheard of in classical mechanics.

2. The deep significance of this postulate is implied by the logical conclusion that an *act of measurement* of some quantity may *drastically change* the state of motion. Indeed, the wave function ψ, obeying the Schrödinger equation, may be entirely different from any of the eigenfunctions ψ_λ of an operator $\mathcal{Q}$ and the quantity $\iiint \psi^*(\mathcal{Q}\psi)\, dV$ (see Postulate B) may be entirely different from any of the eigenvalues λ of $\mathcal{Q}$. Nevertheless, if a *given* (not average) measurement of $\mathcal{Q}$ at time $t = t_0$ results in some value (eigenvalue) λ, then it stands to reason that an *immediate repetition* of the measurement of $\mathcal{Q}$ must yield the same result λ with a certainty.* This implies $\iiint \tilde{\psi}^*(A\tilde{\psi})\, dV = \lambda$ at a time t immediately after t_0. Evidently, the new wave function $\tilde{\psi}$ (valid for $t > t_0$) may be entirely different from the old wave function ψ. As a matter of fact, it can be shown that $\tilde{\psi}$ must be equal to the eigenfunction ψ_λ (corresponding to the eigenvalue λ)† of operator $\mathcal{Q}$.

3. If the measurable quantity given by $\mathcal{Q}$ is *conserved*‡ and is known to be a particular eigenvalue λ (e.g., by a performed measurement), then the wave function must satisfy the eigenvalue equation $\mathcal{Q}\psi_\lambda = \lambda\psi_\lambda$ *at all times*.

Examples

1. For the kinetic energy of a free particle moving in the x-direction, the eigenvalue equation reads

$$-\frac{\hbar^2}{2M}\frac{\partial^2 \psi}{\partial x^2} = \lambda\psi.$$

While there are no normalizable solutions of this equation, there is a possibility of bounded solutions (see Remark 2, p. 468), namely, complex exponential (or real trigonometric) functions. As in classical mechanics, the

---

* If this requirement were not satisfied, then the whole concept of a measurement would lose its accepted meaning.

† Or to *one* of the eigenfunctions ψ_λ, in the case of degeneracy.

‡ Whether a given measurable quantity will be conserved or not depends on the nature of the Hamiltonian operator $\mathcal{H}$ governing the motion. The most important case is the one on which the *total energy* is conserved, which happens when $\mathcal{H}$ is independent (explicitly) of the time variable t. In this case, it is the operator $\mathcal{H}$ itself which corresponds to the total energy.

conclusion is that a measurement of kinetic energy cannot yield a negative value.

2. For a particle moving in a conservative field of force with a definite total energy E, the so-called *stationary states* of a particle, the wave function must at all times satisfy the equation

$$-(\hbar^2/2M)\nabla^2\psi + U(x, y, z)\psi = E\psi,$$

and E can only be one of the eigenvalues of this equation.* In this case the Hamiltonian operator $\mathcal{3C}$ consists of a kinetic energy operator $-(\hbar^2/2M)\nabla^2$ and a potential energy operator $U(x, y, z)$, constructed in accordance with Postulate C. Note that ψ must also satisfy $\mathcal{3C}\psi = i\hbar(\partial\psi/\partial t)$, and therefore $i\hbar(\partial\psi/\partial t) = E\psi$. It follows that $\psi(x, y, z; t) = \varphi(x, y, z)e^{-i(E/\hbar)t}$ and it is actually the function $\varphi(x, y, z)$ which we obtain by solving the above equation (the exponential factor cancels out).

11.3 THE HARMONIC OSCILLATOR

A particle of mass M attracted to a fixed point by a force $F = -k\xi$, where ξ is the displacement† has potential energy

$$U(\xi) = (k/2)\xi^2 \qquad (k = \text{positive constant}).$$

Such systems are quite common in classical mechanics: for instance, a mass M tied to a fixed point by an elastic spring or a pendulum. More than that, a particle moving in a *conservative* field near a point of *stable equilibrium* approximates these conditions. Indeed, expanding the potential energy about the point of equilibrium (which may be chosen as the origin) we have

$$U(\xi) = U(0) + \frac{dU}{d\xi}\bigg|_{\xi=0}\xi + \frac{1}{2}\frac{d^2U}{d\xi^2}\bigg|_{\xi=0}\xi^2 + \cdots$$

The value $U(0)$ is an additive constant and may be ignored. The first derivative $dU/d\xi$, evaluated at $\xi = 0$, is proportional to the force and must vanish at the equilibrium point. Barring rather rare cases, the first nonvanishing term is

$$\frac{1}{2}\frac{d^2U}{d\xi^2}\bigg|_{\xi=0}\xi^2,$$

which is of the form $(k/2)\xi^2$.‡ For small displacements, this is the only relevant term.

---

* This equation is usually called the *time-independent Schrödinger equation*.

† We shall confine ourselves to one-dimensional motion.

‡ It is possible to show that $k > 0$ for stable equilibrium.

On an atomic scale, small displacements of particles from their equilibrium positions must be treated by the principles of quantum mechanics.* This implies that we must solve the time-independent Schrödinger equation

$$-\frac{\hbar^2}{2M}\frac{d^2\psi}{dx^2} + \frac{k}{2}\xi^2\psi = E\psi.$$

This equation can be simplified by a change of scale of the independent variable. Set $\xi = \alpha x$, where $\alpha = (\hbar^2/Mk)^{1/4}$. Then the equation becomes

$$d^2\psi/dx^2 - x^2\psi = -\lambda\psi,$$

where $\lambda = (2E/\hbar)\sqrt{M/k} = 2E/\hbar\omega$, ω being the classical frequency of the harmonic oscillator.

We are now faced with an equation of the Sturm-Liouville type, and it appears that the function will have to satisfy the boundary conditions $\psi(\pm\infty) = 0$.† Our experience with similar problems in Chapter 9 suggests that the parameter λ is likely to be restricted to a certain set of allowed values. Since the total energy E of the oscillator is dependent on λ, it follows that the spectrum of λ determines the possible values of E. As we shall see shortly, the spectrum of λ happens to be *discrete*, accounting for the quantization of energy discovered empirically by Planck in 1901.‡

It is possible to treat our DE by the Frobenius method. The customary procedure is, however, to factor out the behavior of (relevant) solutions at infinity (Section 3.6) by setting

$$\psi(x) = e^{-x^2/2}y(x),$$

which results in a DE for $y(x)$,

$$\frac{d^2y}{dx^2} - 2x\frac{dy}{dx} - (1 - \lambda)y = 0,$$

known as the *Hermite DE*.§ To investigate this DE, we shall employ the Frobenius method. Setting

$$y(x) = \sum_{m=0}^{\infty} c_m x^{s+m}$$

---

* On a macroscopic scale, classical and quantum mechanics lead to the same results. The methods of classical mechanics are usually simpler.

† We shall see later that this condition is, in this case, equivalent to the requirement that ψ is normalizable.

‡ This was long before modern quantum mechanics was formulated. On the basis of Planck's discovery, a set of semiempirical rules has been developed, known as the "old quantum theory," which served as a forerunner of present-day concepts. The Bohr theory of the hydrogen atom falls into this category.

§ This example has already been mentioned on p. 151. The behavior of solutions at infinity may be conjectured from a special case treated on pp. 145–146.

and employing the techniques of Chapter 3, we obtain the indicial equation

$$s(s - 1) = 0$$

and the recursion formula

$$c_{m+2} = \frac{2(m + s) + 1 - \lambda}{(m + s + 1)(m + s + 2)} c_m.$$

Evidently, we have a two-parameter Frobenius series (actually a Maclaurin series), and it is convenient to split it into "even" and "odd" parts by choosing*

1. $s = 0$, $c_1 = 0$, $c_0 = $ arbitrary   (for even series),
2. $s = 0$, $c_0 = 0$, $c_1 = $ arbitrary   (for odd series).

Consider the even series; then

$$c_{m+2} = \frac{2m + 1 - \lambda}{(m + 1)(m + 2)} c_m \qquad (m = 0, 2, 4, \ldots).$$

The ratio test

$$\lim_{m \to \infty} \frac{c_{m+2}}{c_m} = \lim_{m \to \infty} \frac{2}{m} = 0$$

reveals that the series will converge for all values of x. This is, of course, expected since all points in the (finite) x-plane are ordinary points for the Hermite DE.† What is, perhaps, more interesting is the observation that the ratio of two adjacent coefficients behaves, for large values of m, like that for the function e^{x^2}. Indeed,

$$e^{x^2} = 1 + x^2 + \frac{x^4}{2!} + \frac{x^6}{3!} + \cdots = \sum_{m=0,2,4,\ldots}^{\infty} \frac{x^m}{(m/2)!} = \sum_{m=0,2,4,\ldots}^{\infty} c'_m x^m$$

so that

$$\frac{c'_{m+2}}{c'_m} = \frac{2}{m}.$$

This means that, apart from a certain finite number N of terms,‡ the tail of the series for $y(x)$ will be almost proportional to the tail of the series for e^{x^2}. Although we shall omit the rigorous proof, this argument *suggests* that $y(x)$ will behave asymptotically like e^{x^2}, thereby causing $\psi(x)$ to behave like $e^{x^2/2}$ and violate the boundary conditions. The only exception to this statement is if the (even) series for $y(x)$ *terminates*, creating an *even polynomial*. This will happen if

$$\lambda = 2n + 1,$$

---

* If $s = 1$, then c_1 must be zero while c_0 is arbitrary. However, the (odd) series generated by this choice is the same as the series arising from $s = 0$ and $c_0 = 0$. The Legendre equation (p. 136) gives rise to a similar situation.

† See p. 146.

‡ This will be true for any (fixed) λ, although N will be large if $|\lambda|$ is large.

where n is an *even nonnegative integer*. In this case the factor $e^{-x^2/2}$ will make the solution $\psi(x)$ satisfy the boundary conditions.

Turning now to the odd solution of the Hermite DE, we can repeat these arguments. The recursion formula remains the same but it now connects odd coefficients:

$$c_{m+2} = \frac{2m+1-\lambda}{(m+1)(m+2)} c_m \qquad (m = 1, 3, 5, \ldots).$$

The series terminates if $\lambda = 2n + 1$, with n now being an *odd positive integer*.*

Summarizing, we may say that the eigenvalues of our problem are determined by the formula

$$\lambda = 2n + 1 \qquad (n = 0, 1, 2, 3, \ldots).$$

If n is even (odd), then the relevant solution† of the Hermite equation is an even (odd) polynomial. When appropriately standardized, these polynomials are known as *Hermite polynomials* and are usually denoted by $H_n(x)$. They possess the usual set of formulas associated with the Sturm-Liouville problems. Although the Hermite DE is not of the Sturm-Liouville type, it can be made so if we multiply it by e^{-x^2}. Then we may write it as

$$\frac{d}{dx}\left[e^{-x^2} \frac{dy}{dx}\right] - e^{-x^2}y + \lambda e^{-x^2}y = 0.$$

It follows immediately (Section 9.3) that Hermite polynomials are orthogonal over the interval $(-\infty, +\infty)$ with respect to the weight function e^{-x^2}:‡

$$\int_{-\infty}^{+\infty} e^{-x^2} H_n(x)H_m(x)\, dx = 0 \qquad (m \neq n).$$

The normalization integral depends on the standardization of solutions of the Hermite DE (choice of c_0 or c_1 in the Frobenius series). It is customary to set the coefficient with the *highest* (that is, nth) power of x to be 2^n. Such a choice results in a simple generating function for Hermite polynomials of the form

$$G(x, t) = e^{-t^2 + 2tx} = \sum_{n=0}^{\infty} \frac{1}{n!} H_n(x)t^n.$$

This relation is verified as follows: Expand e^{-t^2} and e^{2tx} in a power series:

$$e^{-t^2} = 1 - t^2 + \frac{t^4}{2!} - \frac{t^6}{3!} + \cdots,$$

$$e^{2tx} = 1 + (2x)t + \frac{(2x)^2}{2!} t^2 + \frac{(2x)^3}{3!} t^3 + \cdots.$$

---

* Otherwise the function $\psi(x)$ will violate the boundary conditions. This can be inferred, say, by comparing the odd series with the series for xe^{x^2}.

† The second solution behaves like e^{x^2} or xe^{x^2} and is discarded.

‡ This property also follows from the fact that the DE for a harmonic oscillator is a Sturm-Liouville equation [with $r(x) = 1$] and $\psi(x) = e^{-x^2/2}H(x)$.

Suppose that, after multiplying these two series, we are interested in the co-efficient a_{mn} multiplying the mth power of x and the nth power of t. This coefficient should be equal to the coefficient c_m of $H_n(x)$ divided by $n!$.

First of all, note that the powers of x can come only from the expansion for e^{2tx}. For $m = n$, the coefficient is $2^n/n!$, which checks. For $m < n$, we multiply $2^m/m!$ by the coefficient with t^{n-m} from the expansion for e^{-t^2}, yielding

$$a_{mn} = \frac{2^m}{m!} \frac{(-1)^{n-m}}{[(n-m)/2]!}.$$

Note that n and m are either both even or both odd so that $(n - m)/2$ is an integer. Consequently,

$$\frac{a_{m+2,n}}{a_{mn}} = \frac{2^{m+2}}{(m+2)!} \frac{(-1)^{n-m-2}}{[(n-m-2)/2]!} \frac{m!}{2^m} \frac{[(n-m)/2]!}{(-1)^{n-m}} = \frac{2n-2m}{(m+1)(m+2)}.$$

This is simply the recursion formula for the solutions of the Hermite DE with $\lambda = 2n + 1$. Since the coefficients a_{mn} terminate with $m = 0$ (for even n) or $m = 1$ (for odd n), the generating function for Hermite polynomials is estab-lished. We write the few lowest polynomials:

$$H_0(x) = 1, \qquad H_1(x) = 2x, \qquad H_2(x) = 4x^2 - 2,$$
$$H_3(x) = 8x^3 - 12x, \qquad H_4(x) = 16x^4 - 48x^2 + 12.$$

As in the case of Legendre polynomials, we can obtain from the generating function (considering $\partial G/\partial t$) the pure recursion relation

$$2xH_n(x) = 2nH_{n-1}(x) + H_{n+1}(x) \qquad (n \geq 1),$$

and (considering $\partial G/\partial x$) the differentiation formula

$$\frac{dH_n(x)}{dx} = 2nH_{n-1}(x) \qquad (n \geq 1).$$

If we write the generating function in the form

$$G(t, x) = e^{x^2}e^{-(t-x)^2},$$

then it is clear that

$$\frac{\partial^n G}{\partial t^n} = e^{x^2}(-1)^n \frac{\partial^n}{\partial x^n} e^{-(t-x)^2}.$$

However, $(\partial^n G/\partial t^n)_{t=0}$ must be equal to $H_n(x)$; consequently,

$$H_n(x) = (-1)^n e^{x^2} \frac{d^n}{dx^n} e^{-x^2}$$

which is the Rodrigues formula for Hermite polynomials. It can be used to evaluate the normalization integral:* Integrating by parts, we get

$$\int_{-\infty}^{+\infty} e^{-x^2}[H_n(x)]^2\, dx = \int_{-\infty}^{+\infty} H_n(x)(-1)^n \frac{d^n}{dx^n} e^{-x^2}\, dx$$

$$= (-1)^n H_n(x) \frac{d^{n-1}}{dx^{n-1}} e^{-x^2}\Big|_{-\infty}^{+\infty}$$

$$+ (-1)^{n-1}\int_{-\infty}^{+\infty} \frac{dH_n(x)}{dx} \frac{d^{n-1}}{dx^{n-1}} e^{-x^2}\, dx.$$

The first term vanishes.† One can use the differentiation formula to replace dH_n/dx by $2nH_{n-1}(x)$ and repeat the integration by parts $n-1$ more times, obtaining

$$\int_{-\infty}^{+\infty} e^{-x^2}[H_n(x)]^2\, dx = 2^n n! \int_{-\infty}^{+\infty} e^{-x^2}\, dx = 2^n n!\sqrt{\pi}.$$

With this result, we can now write the normalized eigenfunctions of our original equation for a harmonic oscillator‡

$$\psi_n(x) = \frac{e^{-x^2/2} H_n(x)}{(\sqrt{\pi}\, 2^n n!)^{1/2}}.$$

These functions are sometimes called (normalized) Hermite functions.

Remark. Some authors define Hermite polynomials in a somewhat different way, namely, by employing Rodrigues formula:

$$\overline{H}_n(x) = \frac{1}{n!} e^{x^2/2} \frac{d^n}{dx^n} e^{-x^2/2}.$$

Evidently, the functions $\overline{H}_n(x)$ are reducible to the functions $H_n(x)$ by a change of scale for the independent variable and a different choice of normalization constant.

11.4 MATRIX REPRESENTATIONS OF LINEAR OPERATORS

We have seen on several occasions that eigenfunctions of a boundary-value problem of Sturm-Liouville type may be used to expand a "well-behaved" function

---

* Compare with p. 348.

† Because $(d^{n-1}/dx^{n-1})e^{-x^2} = -H_{n-1}(x)e^{-x^2}$.

‡ This is the standard form. For a particular physical oscillator of mass M and spring constant k, the eigenfunctions normalized with respect to variable ξ (see p. 471) read

$$\psi_n(\xi) = \left(\frac{M\omega}{\hbar}\right)^{1/4} \frac{1}{(\sqrt{\pi}\, 2^n n!)^{1/2}} H_n\left(\xi\sqrt{\frac{M\omega}{\hbar}}\right) e^{-M\omega\xi^2/2\hbar},$$

and the allowed values of energy are $E_n = \hbar\omega(n + \tfrac{1}{2})$, $n = 0, 1, 2, \ldots$ $\omega = \sqrt{k/M}$.

$f(x)$ in a series of such eigenfunctions. For instance, Fourier series, Fourier-Legendre series, and Fourier-Bessel series arise in this fashion.

It is reasonable to conjecture that the Hermite functions defined in the preceding section can be used in a similar way; namely, an arbitrary "well-behaved" function $f(x)$ can be represented by a series

$$f(x) = \sum_{n=0}^{\infty} c_n \psi_n(x).$$

Naturally, the questions which remain to be answered are: (1) What shall we mean by "well behaved?" (2) What kind of convergence is implied?

For quantum-mechanical applications, it is sufficient that $f(x)$ is square integrable and continuously differentiable everywhere. It is possible to show (we shall omit the proof) that such functions can be expanded in series of ψ_n, the convergence being simultaneously pointwise, in the mean, and weak. In other words, the set $\{\psi_n(x)\}$ is a *complete set* with respect to this class of functions.*

It is not difficult to check that this class of functions is a linear space for which the set $\{\psi_n(x)\}$ may serve as a basis. Each function $f(x)$ is then represented by its (infinite) set of coordinates

$$\{c_0, c_1, c_2, \ldots\}$$

which are the Fourier-Hermite coefficients involved in its expansion. The functions $\psi_n(x)$ are also representable by such sets of coordinates, namely,

$$\psi_0 = (1, 0, 0, 0, \ldots),$$
$$\psi_1 = (0, 1, 0, 0, \ldots),$$
$$\psi_2 = (0, 0, 1, 0, \ldots), \quad \text{etc.}$$

Let us now consider the representation of various linear operators in our space by means of *matrices*. Since the number of basis vectors is infinite, these matrices will contain an infinite number of rows and columns. They can be defined by formulating a law which describes their matrix elements a_{mn} in terms of the row index m and the column index n. A comprehensive way to do this is to display the upper left corner of such a matrix, namely, a block of elements formed by the intersection of the few first rows and columns. This is analogous to representing an infinite series by displaying the first few terms.

Linear operators transform a vector $f(x)$ from our linear space into another vector $g(x)$. According to Section 10.4, we can construct their matrices by determining their effect on the basis vectors. We shall begin by considering the operator of differentiation (which is a linear operation) in our vector space.

---

* The set $\{\psi_n(x)\}$ is a complete set with respect to certain wider classes of functions, especially if convergence in the mean or weak convergence is implied.

Using the differentiation formula for Hermite polynomials, we can write

$$\frac{d}{dx}\psi_n(x) = \frac{e^{-x^2/2}(dH_n(x)/dx)}{(\sqrt{\pi}\,2^n n!)^{1/2}} - x\frac{e^{-x^2/2}H_n(x)}{(\sqrt{\pi}\,2^n n!)^{1/2}}$$

$$= \sqrt{2n}\,\psi_{n-1}(x) - x\psi_n(x) \qquad (n \neq 0),$$

and

$$\frac{d}{dx}\psi_0(x) = -x\psi_0(x).$$

These relations can be rewritten in the form

$$\left(x + \frac{d}{dx}\right)\psi_n(x) = \begin{cases} \sqrt{2n}\,\psi_{n-1}(x) & (n \neq 0), \\ 0 & (n = 0). \end{cases}$$

We give this formula the following interpretation: Like the symbol d/dx, the symbol x is regarded as a (linear) *operator** within the space spanned by functions $\psi_n(x)$. Viewed as a function, x does not belong to our linear space. On the other hand, if $f(x)$ belongs to our space, then $g(x) = xf(x)$ *may* also belong: While $g(x)$ is certainly (continuously) differentiable if $f(x)$ is, it may not be square integrable. For the moment, assume that $xf(x)$ is square integrable as well. Then multiplication by x transforms the vector $f(x)$ from our vector space into another vector, $g(x)$. We can write this relation in abstract form as $\mathfrak{X}f = g$. The abstract operator $\mathfrak{X}$ means multiplication by x *provided* the abstract vectors f and g are written as functions of x. However, the very same operator $\mathfrak{X}$ will assume the form of a *matrix* if the vectors f and g are given by their Fourier-Hermite coefficients. Similarly, we introduce the abstract notation $\mathfrak{D}$ for the differentiation operator. Now define a new operator

$$\mathcal{G}_- = \mathfrak{X} + \mathfrak{D},$$

so that

$$\mathcal{G}_-\psi_n = \begin{cases} \sqrt{2n}\,\psi_{n-1} & (n \neq 0), \\ 0 & (n = 0). \end{cases}$$

Except for the factor $\sqrt{2n}$, the operator $\mathcal{G}_-$ is essentially a *step-down operator*,† transforming the function $\psi_n(x)$ into the function $\psi_{n-1}(x)$. It is now a simple matter to construct the matrix $\mathcal{G}_-$ corresponding to the operator $\mathcal{G}_-$:

$$G_- = \begin{vmatrix} 0 & \sqrt{2\cdot 1} & 0 & 0 & \cdots \\ 0 & 0 & \sqrt{2\cdot 2} & 0 & \cdots \\ 0 & 0 & 0 & \sqrt{2\cdot 3} & \cdots \\ & & \cdots & & \end{vmatrix}$$

---

* This idea has its origin in quantum mechanics (p. 468).

† Compare with p. 346.

Indeed, multiplication (from the left) of the column vector

$$\psi_n = \begin{bmatrix} 0 \\ 0 \\ \vdots \\ 1 \\ \vdots \\ 0 \\ \vdots \end{bmatrix} \quad \leftarrow n\text{th row}$$

yields the column vector for ψ_{n-1} multiplied by $\sqrt{2n}$ (or zero vector in the case of ψ_0). The actual step-down operator $\mathcal{S}_-$ defined by

$$\mathcal{S}_-\psi_n = \begin{cases} \psi_{n-1} & (n \neq 0), \\ 0 & (n = 0) \end{cases}$$

is represented by the matrix

$$S_- = \begin{bmatrix} 0 & 1 & 0 & 0 & \ldots \\ 0 & 0 & 1 & 0 & \ldots \\ 0 & 0 & 0 & 1 & \ldots \\ & & \ldots & & \end{bmatrix}$$

It is not difficult now to establish the formula

$$\left(x - \frac{d}{dx}\right)\psi_n(x) = \sqrt{2(n+1)}\,\psi_{n+1}(x) \qquad (\text{all } n),$$

and to define the abstract operators $\mathcal{G}_+$ and $\mathcal{S}_+$ such that

$$\mathcal{G}_+\psi_n = (\mathfrak{X} - \mathfrak{D})\psi_n = \sqrt{2(n+1)}\,\psi_{n+1}, \qquad \mathcal{S}_+\psi_n = \psi_{n+1},$$

the second one being the step-up operator. The respective matrices are

$$G_+ = \begin{bmatrix} 0 & 0 & 0 & \ldots \\ \sqrt{2 \cdot 1} & 0 & 0 & \ldots \\ 0 & \sqrt{2 \cdot 2} & 0 & \ldots \\ 0 & 0 & \sqrt{2 \cdot 3} & \ldots \\ & \ldots & & \end{bmatrix}, \quad \text{and} \quad S_+ = \begin{bmatrix} 0 & 0 & 0 & 0 & \ldots \\ 1 & 0 & 0 & 0 & \ldots \\ 0 & 1 & 0 & 0 & \ldots \\ 0 & 0 & 1 & 0 & \ldots \\ & & \ldots & & \end{bmatrix}$$

It is instructive to operate on ψ_n by $\mathcal{G}_+$ and subject the result to $\mathcal{G}_-$. The final result should be a multiple of ψ_n. We write

$$\mathcal{G}_-\mathcal{G}_+\psi_n = (\mathfrak{X} + \mathfrak{D})(\mathfrak{X} - \mathfrak{D})\psi_n$$

and develop the product*

$$\mathcal{G}_-\mathcal{G}_+ = \mathfrak{X}^2 + \mathfrak{D}\mathfrak{X} - \mathfrak{X}\mathfrak{D} - \mathfrak{D}^2,$$

where $\mathfrak{D}\mathfrak{X}$, when applied to a function $f(x)$ means, "multiply $f(x)$ by x and then differentiate the result," and $\mathfrak{X}\mathfrak{D}$ means "differentiate $f(x)$ and multiply the result by x." Write†

$$\frac{d}{dx}[xf(x)] = x\frac{d}{dx}f(x) + f(x).$$

In the language of operators this means

$$\mathfrak{D}\mathfrak{X} = \mathfrak{X}\mathfrak{D} + \mathcal{I},$$

where $\mathcal{I}$ is the identity operator, such that

$$\mathcal{I}f = f$$

for all vectors f from our space.

In this fashion we obtain the relation

$$\mathcal{G}_-\mathcal{G}_+\psi_n = (\mathfrak{X}^2 - \mathfrak{D}^2 + \mathcal{I})\psi_n.$$

However, if we apply $\mathcal{G}_+$ to ψ_n, we must obtain $\sqrt{2(n + 1)}\,\psi_{n+1}$. If we further apply $\mathcal{G}_-$, we must obtain $\sqrt{2(n + 1)}$ times‡ the vector $\sqrt{2(n + 1)}\,\psi_n$, or $2(n + 1)\psi_n$. It then follows that

$$(\mathfrak{X}^2 - \mathfrak{D}^2 + \mathcal{I})\psi_n = (2n + 2)\psi_n \quad \text{or} \quad (\mathfrak{X}^2 - \mathfrak{D}^2)\psi_n = (2n + 1)\psi_n.$$

This is, of course, just the DE for ψ_n-functions. The decomposition of the second-order DE for $\psi_n(x)$ into two first-order relations by means of two ladder operations,

$$\left(x - \frac{d}{dx}\right)\psi_n = \sqrt{2(n + 1)}\,\psi_{n+1}, \qquad \left(x + \frac{d}{dx}\right)\psi_n = \sqrt{2n}\,\psi_{n-1},$$

represents a convenient tool for the analysis of the Sturm-Liouville equations and the calculation of eigenfunctions.§

---

* This algebra of operators follows from the tacit definition $(\mathfrak{X} - \mathfrak{D})\psi_n = \mathfrak{X}\psi_n - \mathfrak{D}\psi_n$ and the linear properties of $\mathfrak{X}$ and $\mathfrak{D}$, that is, $\mathfrak{X}(f_1 + f_2) = \mathfrak{X}f_1 + \mathfrak{X}f_2$, etc.

† The symbols x and d/dx are said to be *x-representations* of $\mathfrak{X}$ and $\mathfrak{D}$.

‡ Note that we apply $\mathcal{G}_-$ to ψ_{n+1} and not to ψ_n; consequently, the factor $\sqrt{2(n + 1)}$ will appear instead of $\sqrt{2n}$.

§ This technique is described in detail in the article by Infeld and Hull, *Rev. Mod. Phys.* **23**, (1951).

Returning to the algebraic aspect of our problem, note that the operators S_- and S_+ satisfy the relation $S_-S_+ = \mathcal{I}$, which is reflected by their matrix representations, $S_-S_+ = I$, where I is the infinite unit matrix

$$I = \begin{vmatrix} 1 & 0 & 0 & 0 & \cdots \\ 0 & 1 & 0 & 0 & \cdots \\ 0 & 0 & 1 & 0 & \cdots \\ 0 & 0 & 0 & 1 & \cdots \\ & & \cdots & & \end{vmatrix}$$

However, it would not be correct to say that S_+ is the inverse matrix of S_- because the product S_+S_- is *not equal* to I. In fact, the matrix S_- is said to be *singular* because there exists a nontrivial vector, namely, ψ_0, such that* $S_-\psi_0 = 0$. This illustrates the peculiar situations that are possible in infinite-dimensional spaces: If the space were finite dimensional, then the statement $S_-S_+ = I$ would imply that S_- is nonsingular, and S_+S_- would be equal to I.†

The matrices X and D corresponding to the operators $\mathfrak{X}$ and $\mathfrak{D}$ are obtained by taking half the sum and half the difference of matrices G_- and G_+:

$$X = \begin{vmatrix} 0 & \sqrt{\tfrac{1}{2}} & 0 & 0 & \cdots \\ \sqrt{\tfrac{1}{2}} & 0 & 1 & 0 & \cdots \\ 0 & 1 & 0 & \sqrt{\tfrac{3}{2}} & \cdots \\ 0 & 0 & \sqrt{\tfrac{3}{2}} & 0 & \cdots \\ & & \cdots & & \end{vmatrix}$$

$$D = \begin{vmatrix} 0 & \sqrt{\tfrac{1}{2}} & 0 & 0 & \cdots \\ -\sqrt{\tfrac{1}{2}} & 0 & 1 & 0 & \cdots \\ 0 & -1 & 0 & \sqrt{\tfrac{3}{2}} & \cdots \\ 0 & 0 & -\sqrt{\tfrac{3}{2}} & 0 & \cdots \\ & & \cdots & & \end{vmatrix}$$

* In finite-dimensional spaces, a matrix A is said to be singular if $\det A = 0$ (p. 432); this is equivalent to saying that the equation $Ax = 0$ has a nontrivial solution. Because of the difficulty in defining the determmniant of an infinite-dimensional matrix, the second criterion is used for the definition of the singular character of S_-.

† The matrix S_+ may be called the *right inverse* of S_-. Note, however, that it is not unique.

It is seen that the X-matrix is hermitian (it is real symmetric) while the D-matrix is not (it is real skew-symmetric). This reflects the fact that the operator $\mathfrak{X}$ corresponds to a measurable dynamical quantity in quantum mechanics while the operator $\mathfrak{D}$ does not.* Multiplying the matrices X and D, we obtain

$$
DX = \begin{vmatrix}
\frac{1}{2} & 0 & \sqrt{\frac{1}{2}} & 0 & \cdots \\
0 & \frac{1}{2} & 0 & \sqrt{\frac{3}{2}} & \cdots \\
-\sqrt{\frac{1}{2}} & 0 & \frac{1}{2} & 0 & \cdots \\
0 & -\sqrt{\frac{3}{2}} & 0 & \frac{1}{2} & \cdots \\
& & \cdots & &
\end{vmatrix}
$$

$$
XD = \begin{vmatrix}
-\frac{1}{2} & 0 & \sqrt{\frac{1}{2}} & 0 & \cdots \\
0 & -\frac{1}{2} & 0 & \sqrt{\frac{3}{2}} & \cdots \\
-\sqrt{\frac{1}{2}} & 0 & -\frac{1}{2} & 0 & \cdots \\
0 & -\sqrt{\frac{3}{2}} & 0 & -\frac{1}{2} & \cdots \\
& & \cdots & &
\end{vmatrix}
$$

and it is seen that $DX - XD = I$. In a similar fashion, we obtain

$$
X^2 - D^2 = \begin{vmatrix}
1 & 0 & 0 & 0 & \cdots \\
0 & 3 & 0 & 0 & \cdots \\
0 & 0 & 5 & 0 & \cdots \\
0 & 0 & 0 & 7 & \cdots \\
& & \cdots & &
\end{vmatrix}
$$

which exhibits the fact that the eigenvalues of the operator $\mathfrak{X}^2 - \mathfrak{D}^2$ are of the form $2n + 1$. The matrix $X^2 - D^2$ is, of course, diagonal because we have chosen its eigenvectors for our basis.

Matrix representations of common operators are possible for other Sturm-Liouville systems as well. As mentioned before, however, we must make sure that the result of the operation is still a vector within our vector space and the operation can be performed term by term on the appropriate series of eigenfunctions.†

---

* The operator $-i\hbar\mathfrak{D}$ represents a measurable quantity (momentum) and its matrix is indeed hermitian.

† Such as, for instance, the term by term differentiation. One may have to further restrict the vector space so that such operations will become valid in general.

11.5 ALGEBRAIC METHODS OF SOLUTION

The results of the preceding section suggest that it may be possible to solve the DE for a harmonic oscillator by purely algebraic methods. This is indeed the case and the details are reasonably simple.

Spelled out in abstract language, our problem is to solve the eigenvalue equation

$$(\mathfrak{X}^2 - \mathfrak{D}^2)\psi = \lambda\psi$$

for the operator $\mathfrak{H} = \mathfrak{X}^2 - \mathfrak{D}^2$ in a certain linear space of ψ-vectors. We shall now represent the ψ-vectors in terms of the set of eigenvectors* of the operator $\mathfrak{H}$.

Our task is to develop matrices H, X, and D which will represent the operators $\mathfrak{H}$, $\mathfrak{X}$, and $\mathfrak{D}$ with respect to the chosen basis. We can make the following statements about these matrices.

a) The matrix X should be hermitian (real symmetric, if we consider real spaces only) while matrix D should be antihermitian (real antisymmetric). This follows from the fact that x and $-ih(d/dx)$ are hermitian operators (p. 468). Note that it follows that the matrix $H = X^2 - D^2$ is hermitian.

b) Matrices X and D must satisfy the commutation relation

$$DX - XD = I,$$

where I is the unit matrix. This follows from the formula†

$$\frac{d}{dx}[xf(x)] = x\frac{d}{dx}f(x) + f(x),$$

or

$$\left[\frac{d}{dx}x - x\frac{d}{dx}\right]f(x) = f(x).$$

The fundamental step in constructing the matrices X and D is to develop their commutation relations with H, since the matrix H is particularly simple (it must be diagonal). From $H = X^2 - D^2$ it follows, on multiplication by X from the right, that $HX = X^3 - D^2X$. Now $D^2X = DDX$ and since $DX = XD + I$, we have

$$D^2X = DXD + D = DXD + D.$$

Using once more $DX = XD + I$, we obtain

$$D^2X = XD^2 + 2D$$

so that

$$HX = X^3 - XD^2 - 2D.$$

---

* We are, therefore, confining ourselves to the space spanned by the eigenvectors of $\mathfrak{H}$. Actually, this space is very wide; it includes, for instance, all square-integrable well-behaved functions.

† A more abstract formulation of quantum mechanics *postulates* the abstract relationship $\mathfrak{X}\mathcal{P}_x - \mathcal{P}_x\mathfrak{X} = ih\mathfrak{I}$, where $\mathcal{P}_x$ is the x-component of the momentum of the particle.

However,

$$X^3 - XD^2 = X(X^2 - D^2) = XH.$$

Therefore

$$HX - XH = -2D.$$

In a similar fashion we can obtain

$$HD - DH = -2X.$$

The widespread notation for a *commutator* of two matrices (or operators) is

$$[A, B] \equiv AB - BA.$$

The above relations are then written as

$$[H, X] = -2D, \qquad [H, D] = -2X.$$

The evident "cross symmetry" which the matrices X and D display with respect to their commutators with H permits easy construction of the even more interesting matrices

$$G_+ = X - D \qquad \text{and} \qquad G_- = X + D,$$

which have the following commutation properties with H:

$$[H, G_+] = [H, X] - [H, D] = -2D + 2X = 2G_+,$$
$$[H, G_-] = [H, X] + [H, D] = -2D - 2X = -2G_-.$$

The reason for introducing G_+ and G_- lies in their priceless property that if ψ_λ is an eigenvector of H corresponding to the eigenvalue λ, then $\psi_\lambda' = G_+\psi_\lambda$ is either the zero vector or an eigenvector of H corresponding to the eigenvalue $\lambda + 2$. Similarly, $\psi_\lambda'' = G_-\psi_\lambda$ is either the zero vector or an eigenvector of H corresponding to the eigenvalue $\lambda - 2$. Indeed,

$$H\psi_\lambda' = HG_+\psi_\lambda = [H, G_+]\psi_\lambda + G_+H\psi_\lambda$$
$$= 2G_+\psi_\lambda + G_+\lambda\psi_\lambda = (\lambda + 2)G_+\psi_\lambda = (\lambda + 2)\psi_\lambda'.$$

Similarly,

$$H\psi_\lambda'' = HG_-\psi_\lambda = [H, G_-]\psi_\lambda + G_-H\psi_\lambda$$
$$= -2G_-\psi_\lambda + \lambda G_-\psi_\lambda = (\lambda - 2)\psi_\lambda''.$$

These facts provide essential information about the spectrum of operator $\mathcal{H}$. In order to construct the entire spectrum, we need one more fact: that all eigenvalues are nonnegative.

Indeed, if $(X^2 - D^2)\psi = \lambda\psi$, then taking the inner product of both sides with ψ, we have in vector-matrix notation (see p. 438),

$$\psi^\dagger X^2 \psi - \psi^\dagger D^2 \psi = \lambda\psi^\dagger\psi.$$

Now, since X is a hermitian matrix, we have

$$\psi^\dagger X^2 \psi = \psi^\dagger X^\dagger X \psi = (X\psi, X\psi) \geq 0.$$

Similarly, since D is antihermitian,

$$-\psi^\dagger D^2 \psi = \psi^\dagger D^\dagger D\psi = (D\psi, D\psi) \geq 0.$$

Since ψ is not the zero vector, we have $(\psi, \psi) > 0$, resulting in

$$\lambda = \frac{(\psi, X^2\psi) - (\psi, D^2\psi)}{(\psi, \psi)} \geq 0,$$

as claimed.

If this algebraic argument seems too sophisticated, one can always retreat to the familiar ground of functions of x: If $[x^2 - (d^2/dx^2)]\psi(x) = \lambda\psi(x)$, then, multiplying by $\psi^*(x)$ and integrating (inner product of p. 465), we obtain

$$\int_{-\infty}^{+\infty} \psi^*(x)x^2\psi(x)\,dx - \int_{-\infty}^{+\infty} \psi^*(x)\frac{d^2}{dx^2}\psi(x)\,dx = \lambda \int_{-\infty}^{+\infty} |\psi(x)|^2\,dx.$$

However, integrating by parts and using the boundary conditions, we have

$$\int_{-\infty}^{+\infty} \psi^*(x)\frac{d^2}{dx^2}\psi(x)\,dx = -\int_{-\infty}^{+\infty} \left|\frac{d\psi}{dx}\right|^2 dx$$

so that

$$\lambda = \frac{\int_{-\infty}^{+\infty} x^2|\psi(x)|^2\,dx + \int_{-\infty}^{+\infty} |d\psi/dx|^2\,dx}{\int_{-\infty}^{+\infty} |\psi|^2\,dx},$$

and it is evident that $\lambda \geq 0$. This proof is just the analog of the algebraic derivation produced above.

Now we can deduce that there *must exist* a nonzero eigenvector ψ_0 of H such that

$$G_-\psi_0 = (X + D)\psi_0 = 0,$$

and this eigenvector corresponds to the eigenvalue $\lambda_0 = 1$ which is the *smallest* eigenvalue of H. Indeed, let λ and ψ_λ be *any* "eigenpair" (eigenvalue and the corresponding eigenvector) of H. Applying operator G_-, we obtain a (nonzero) eigenvector with the eigenvalue $\lambda - 2$ unless we get the zero vector immediately. If the former is the case, we apply operator G_- repeatedly until we obtain the zero vector. This must happen sooner or later because we cannot indefinitely subtract 2 from the original λ without getting a negative eigenvalue, which is impossible.

Let the last nonzero eigenvector be ψ_0, and we have

$$G_-\psi_0 = (X + D)\psi_0 = 0.$$

This means that $X\psi_0 = -D\psi_0$. Then from $DX - XD = I$, it follows that $DX\psi_0 - XD\psi_0 = \psi_0$, $-DD\psi_0 + XX\psi_0 = \psi_0$, or $(X^2 - D^2)\psi_0 = \psi_0$, which means that $\lambda_0 = 1$. Since the original eigenvalue λ was arbitrary, it follows that *all* eigenvalues of H must be of the form

$$\lambda = 1 + 2n \qquad (n = 0, 1, 2, \ldots).$$

Is this sequence finite or infinite? It is infinite because we can show that there *cannot exist* an eigenvector (nonzero, of course) ψ_λ such that $G_+\psi_\lambda = 0$. Indeed, if $G_+\psi_\lambda = (X - D)\psi_\lambda = 0$, then $X\psi_\lambda = D\psi_\lambda$. From $DX - XD = I$, it then follows easily that

$$(X^2 - D^2)\psi_\lambda = -\psi_\lambda,$$

which is impossible since H cannot have negative eigenvalues.

So far, we have deduced the eigenvalues of H and the fact that our linear space is infinite dimensional. In our basis the H-matrix must then have the form

$$H = \begin{vmatrix} \lambda_0 & 0 & 0 & 0 & \cdots \\ 0 & \lambda_1 & 0 & 0 & \cdots \\ 0 & 0 & \lambda_2 & 0 & \cdots \\ 0 & 0 & 0 & \lambda_3 & \cdots \\ & & \cdots & & \end{vmatrix},$$

where $\lambda_n = 1 + 2n$.

The matrices X and D are not necessarily diagonal and we can write*

$$X = \begin{vmatrix} x_{00} & x_{01} & x_{02} \\ x_{10} & x_{11} & x_{12} \\ x_{20} & x_{21} & \cdots \\ & \cdots & \end{vmatrix}, \qquad D = \begin{vmatrix} d_{00} & d_{01} & d_{02} \\ d_{10} & d_{11} & d_{12} \\ d_{20} & d_{21} & \cdots \\ & \cdots & \end{vmatrix}.$$

To make use of $HX - XH = -2D$, we can form the matrices

$$HX = \begin{vmatrix} \lambda_0 x_{00} & \lambda_0 x_{01} & \lambda_0 x_{02} \\ \lambda_1 x_{10} & \lambda_1 x_{11} & \lambda_1 x_{12} \\ \lambda_2 x_{20} & \lambda_2 x_{21} & \cdots \\ & \cdots & \end{vmatrix}, \qquad XH = \begin{vmatrix} \lambda_0 x_{00} & \lambda_1 x_{01} & \lambda_2 x_{02} \\ \lambda_0 x_{10} & \lambda_1 x_{11} & \lambda_2 x_{12} \\ \lambda_0 x_{20} & \lambda_1 x_{21} & \cdots \\ & \cdots & \end{vmatrix}.$$

---

* To conform to the notation employed for ψ_n-functions, we label the rows and columns starting with zero rather than unity.

Subtracting, we have the ijth element in the form $x_{ij}(\lambda_i - \lambda_j)$, and equating this with $-2\,d_{ij}$, we obtain

$$x_{ij}(\lambda_i - \lambda_j) = -2\,d_{ij}.$$

Performing the same operations with the equation $HD - DH = -2X$, we deduce

$$d_{ij}(\lambda_i - \lambda_j) = -2x_{ij}.$$

Eliminating d_{ij} from these two equations, we obtain

$$x_{ij} = \frac{(\lambda_i - \lambda_j)^2}{4}\, x_{ij}.$$

This is satisfied by either $\lambda_i - \lambda_j = \pm 2$ (in which case x_{ij} remains undetermined) or $x_{ij} = 0$. Now, since $\lambda_i = \lambda_j = \pm 2$ only for $i = j + 1$ and $i = j - 1$ (adjacent eigenvalues), it follows that all matrix elements of X are zero except those for which the row index and the column index differ by unity, namely, the elements "just off" the main diagonal.

Therefore, the X-matrix has the form

$$X = \begin{vmatrix} 0 & x_{01} & 0 & 0 & \dots \\ x_{10} & 0 & x_{12} & 0 & \dots \\ 0 & x_{21} & 0 & x_{23} & \dots \\ 0 & 0 & x_{32} & 0 & \dots \\ & & \dots & & \end{vmatrix}.$$

From the relation $d_{ij}(\lambda_i - \lambda_j) = -2x_{ij}$, it follows that the D-matrix also has $d_{ij} = 0$ unless $i = j + 1$ or $i = j - 1$, in which case

$$d_{ij} = -x_{ij} \qquad (\text{for } i = j + 1),$$

and

$$d_{ij} = x_{ij} \qquad (\text{for } i = j - 1).$$

Therefore, the D-matrix looks like

$$D = \begin{vmatrix} 0 & x_{01} & 0 & 0 & \dots \\ -x_{10} & 0 & x_{12} & 0 & \dots \\ 0 & -x_{21} & 0 & x_{23} & \dots \\ 0 & 0 & -x_{32} & 0 & \dots \\ & & \dots & & \end{vmatrix}.$$

It is not difficult to multiply X and D:

$$
DX = \begin{vmatrix}
x_{10}x_{01} & 0 & x_{01}x_{12} & 0 & \cdots \\
0 & -x_{10}x_{01} + x_{21}x_{12} & 0 & x_{12}x_{23} & \cdots \\
-x_{21}x_{10} & 0 & -x_{12}x_{21} + x_{23}x_{32} & 0 & \cdots \\
& & \cdots & &
\end{vmatrix}
$$

In a similar fashion we can construct XD. Subtracting, we obtain a diagonal matrix which must be the unit matrix. This fact yields the following relations:

$$
1 = 2x_{01}x_{10},
$$
$$
1 = -2x_{01}x_{10} + 2x_{21}x_{12}, \quad \text{etc.}
$$

Remembering that X is symmetric, we obtain from the first equation

$$
x_{01} = x_{10} = \sqrt{\tfrac{1}{2}}.
$$

Then, from the second one, $x_{12} = x_{21} = 1$, and so on. In this fashion, step by step, we can build up the matrices X and D (already displayed in the preceding section).

In this approach we have never used the fact that our vectors are actually functions of the variable x. More than that, if we were now given a function $f(x)$ within our vector space, by which we mean, of course, an infinite sequence $(c_0, c_1, c_2, \ldots)$, we could perform a variety of operations with it, including differentiation (by means of the D-matrix), without any knowledge of calculus.

For a physicist, the above approach illustrates the possibility of a more abstract formulation of quantum mechanics. It is possible to dispose of the Schrödinger PDE and use the algebra of operators as the basis of the theory.

11.6 BASES WITH GENERALIZED ORTHOGONALITY

The problem of a harmonic oscillator in quantum mechanics led us to the construction of a set of functions

$$
\psi_n = \frac{e^{-x^2/2}H_n(x)}{(\sqrt{\pi}\,2^n n!)^{1/2}},
$$

which form a basis for the appropriate infinite-dimensional vector space.* This basis is an orthogonal basis,† namely,

$$
\int_{-\infty}^{+\infty} \psi_n(x)\psi_m(x)\,dx = \delta_{nm}.
$$

---

* The space of continuously differentiable and square-integrable functions on $(-\infty, +\infty)$.
† More precisely, an orthonormal basis; compare with the remark on p. 439.

In certain physical problems a similar procedure results in a basis for which the above relationship is somewhat modified. One of the simplest examples may be that of a stretched string of variable density. The PDE for free vibrations for such a string has already been derived in Section 8.1 and reads

$$T\frac{\partial^2 u}{\partial x^2} = \rho(x)\frac{\partial^2 u}{\partial t^2},$$

where T is the tension and $\rho(x)$ is the mass per unit length, or (linear) density.

Let us consider a finite string, extending from $x = 0$ to $x = L$. Our physical intuition suggests, as in the case of $\rho = \text{const}$, the existence of discrete natural modes of vibration. This leads us to seek solutions of the type*

$$u(x, t) = y(x)e^{-i\omega t}.$$

Substituting into the PDE, we obtain the DE for $y(x)$:

$$\frac{d^2 y}{dx^2} = -\lambda\rho(x)y \qquad (\lambda = \omega^2/T).$$

To this we must add, of course, the boundary conditions

$$y(0) = y(L) = 0.$$

Our DE is of the Sturm-Liouville form, already discussed in Section 9.3:

$$\frac{d}{dx}\left[p(x)\frac{dy}{dx}\right] - s(x)y = -\lambda r(x)y.$$

In our case, $p(x) = 1$, $s(x) = 0$, $r(x) = \rho(x)$. The theory of the Sturm-Liouville problem is rather well developed under the assumption that the functions p, s, and r are nonnegative (within the interval under consideration):

$$p(x) \geq 0, \qquad s(x) \geq 0, \qquad r(x) \geq 0.$$

These conditions are almost invariably met in physical applications and we are already familiar with some special cases.†

The eigenfunctions satisfying the Sturm-Liouville equation and appropriate boundary conditions possess certain important properties. First of all, they are orthogonal with respect to $r(x)$ as a weight function, provided they correspond to distinct eigenvalues (i.e., barring the degeneracy),

$$\int_0^L r(x)\psi_m(x)\psi_n(x)\,dx = 0,$$

---

* Instead of relying on physical intuition, we can arrive at the same result by the method of separation of variables. We take the shortcut.

† For example, Legendre polynomials (Section 9.5), Bessel functions (Section 9.7), Fourier sine series (Section 4.4), and others.

where $\psi_m(x)$ and $\psi_n(x)$ satisfy the boundary conditions and the DE with $\lambda = \lambda_m$ and $\lambda = \lambda_n$, respectively, provided $\lambda_m \neq \lambda_n$. The proof has already been given in Section 9.3 along with some sufficient boundary conditions.

The second property concerns the sign of the eigenvalues. Write the Sturm-Liouville equation for some particular eigenfunction $\psi_n(x)$ and the corresponding eigenvalue λ_n:

$$\frac{d}{dx}\left[p(x)\frac{d\psi_n}{dx}\right] - s(x)\psi_n = -\lambda_n r(x)\psi_n.$$

Multiply by ψ_n and integrate over the interval under consideration [such as $(0, L)$, for instance]:

$$\int_0^L \psi_n \frac{d}{dx}\left[p(x)\frac{d\psi_n}{dx}\right] dx - \int_0^L s(x)[\psi_n(x)]^2 \, dx = -\lambda_n \int_0^L r(x)[\psi_n(x)]^2 \, dx.$$

Integrating by parts and applying the boundary conditions, we have

$$\int_0^L \psi_n \frac{d}{dx}\left[p\frac{d\psi_n}{dx}\right] dx = \psi_n p \frac{d\psi_n}{dx}\Big|_0^L - \int_0^L p\left(\frac{d\psi_n}{dx}\right)^2 dx = -\int_0^L p\left(\frac{d\psi_n}{dx}\right)^2 dx.$$

Consequently,

$$\lambda_n \int_0^L r\psi_n^2 \, dx = \int_0^L \left[p\left(\frac{d\psi_n}{dx}\right)^2 + s\psi_n^2\right] dx.$$

Since the case $r(x) \equiv 0$ or $\psi_n(x) \equiv 0$ is evidently excluded, we have

$$\int_0^L r\psi_n^2 \, dx > 0,$$

and it follows immediately that $\lambda_n \geq 0$; that is, the spectrum of eigenvalues is nonnegative. In many cases this result can be sharpened to read $\lambda_n > 0$, as, for instance, in our problem of the stretched string: We have $s(x) \equiv 0$ and $p(x) \equiv 1$; the integral

$$\int_0^L p\left(\frac{d\psi_n}{dx}\right)^2 dx$$

can be zero only if $d\psi_n/dx$ is zero,* that is, $\psi_n = $ const. However, the boundary conditions then demand that $\psi_n(x)$ is zero which is excluded. Therefore the eigenvalues must be positive.†

---

* See the theorem on p. 466.

† The simplest case of $\lambda = 0$ occurring as an eigenvalue is the equation

$$\frac{d^2 y}{dx^2} = -\lambda y$$

subject to $dy/dx = 0$ at $x = 0$ and $x = L$. The eigenfunction $y = 1/\sqrt{L} = $ const corresponds to $\lambda = 0$.

We shall state here, without proof, two additional properties of the Sturm-Liouville problem for the finite interval $(0, L)$:

a) There is a countable infinity of discrete eigenvalues which can be arranged in the sequence

$$0 \leq \lambda_1 \leq \lambda_2 \leq \lambda_3 \leq \cdots$$

b) The set of eigenfunctions is complete,* that is, an arbitrary well-behaved function $f(x)$ can be represented by a Fourier-type series

$$f(x) = \sum_n F_n \psi_n(x),$$

where the coefficients F_n are determined by

$$F_n = \frac{\int_0^L r(x) f(x) \psi_n(x)\, dx}{\int_0^L r(x) [\psi_n(x)]^2\, dx}.$$

Remarks

1. In many cases property (a) can be sharpened to $0 \leq \lambda_1 < \lambda_2 < \lambda_3 < \cdots$, implying that the eigenvalues are nondegenerate. However, even in the case of degeneracy there can be at most two (linearly independent) eigenfunctions corresponding to the same eigenvalue, for the simple reason that the DE is of second order.

2. The restriction on "good behavior" of the functions $f(x)$ depends on the character of convergence desired for the series. Uniform pointwise convergence is ensured if $f(x)$ is continuous, piecewise very smooth, and satisfies the appropriate boundary conditions. Convergence in the mean holds if $f(x)$ is only piecewise smooth.† For the purpose of physical applications it is usually sufficient for the series to converge weakly, in which case $f(x)$ may even be a distribution, such as the delta function.

3. In the case of an infinite $(-\infty < x < +\infty)$ or a semi-infinite $(0 \leq x < \infty)$ interval, the analysis of the spectrum and the properties of eigenfunctions is considerably more complicated.‡ However, in a variety of such cases, the above properties still hold (as in the case of a harmonic oscillator).

From the above statements, it follows that the eigenfunctions of a Sturm-Liouville problem can be used as a basis for an appropriate linear space. It is customary to normalize the eigenfunctions with respect to the weight function $r(x)$, namely, to require that

$$\int_0^L r(x) [\psi_n(x)]^2\, dx = 1.$$

It follows then that the eigenfunctions of our problem form a basis which is orthog-

---

* See p. 352; also pp. 171–172.

† In this case, the boundary conditions can be relaxed. Recall how the function $y(x) \equiv 1$ can be expanded in Fourier sine series in $(0, L)$ despite the fact that $y(x)$ does not vanish at $x = 0$ and $x = L$.

‡ See, e.g., Titchmarsh, *Eigenfunction Expansions Associated with Second-Order Differential Equations*.

onal in the generalized sense, namely, with respect to the weight function $r(x)$:*

$$\int_0^L r(x)\psi_m(x)\psi_n(x)\,dx = \delta_{mn}.$$

We may also say that the functions $\psi_n(x)$ are generalized eigenfunctions of the operator

$$\frac{d}{dx}\left[p(x)\frac{d}{dx}\right] - s(x)$$

with respect to the function $r(x)$.†

11.7 STRETCHED STRING WITH A DISCRETE MASS IN THE MIDDLE

Consider a stretched string of length L and uniform density ρ with a particle of mass m attached in the middle. For future convenience in using symmetry properties of eigenfunctions we shall place the ends of the string at points $x = -L/2$ and $x = +L/2$. It is possible to regard such a string as having variable density $\rho(x)$ given by

$$\rho(x) = \rho + m\,\delta(x).$$

As usual, we seek normal modes in the form $u(x, t) = y(x)e^{-i\omega t}$, which yields an equation of the Sturm-Liouville type for $y(x)$:

$$\frac{d^2y}{dx^2} = -k^2\left[1 + \frac{m}{\rho}\,\delta(x)\right]y \qquad (k^2 = \omega^2\rho/T).$$

In the notation of the preceding section we have $k^2 = \lambda$ and $1 + (m/\rho)\,\delta(x) = r(x)$.

An obvious way of attacking this problem is to solve the equation

$$\frac{d^2y}{dx^2} = -k^2y$$

separately for the interval $(-L/2, 0)$ and for the interval $(0, L/2)$ and connect, in proper fashion, these solutions at the point $x = 0$. Let $y^{(-)}(x)$ be the solution for $(-L/2, 0)$ and let $y^{(+)}(x)$ be the solution for $(0, L/2)$.

Clearly, we must have $y^{(-)}(0) = y^{(+)}(0)$; that is, the overall solution is continuous at $x = 0$. This is not necessarily true, however, for its derivative. The inertia of mass m may produce a concentrated force‡ at $x = 0$ and the string may have a cusp at this point. A simple method of determining the discontinuity of the derivative is to integrate the DE from $x = -\epsilon$ to $x = +\epsilon$ for some arbi-

---

* The integral $\int_0^L r(x)f(x)g(x)\,dx$ is now treated as an inner product of the functions $f(x)$ and $g(x)$ (instead of $\int_0^L f(x)g(x)\,dx$ as on p. 465). This is analogous to the situation in n-dimensional space discussed in Section 10.8.

† The function $r(x)$ is also regarded as an operator (compare with p. 478).

‡ The *weight* of mass m is, however, neglected. (The same is true for the weight of the entire string.)

trarily small but finite ϵ:

$$\frac{dy}{dx}\bigg|_{-\epsilon}^{+\epsilon} = -k^2 \int_{-\epsilon}^{+\epsilon} y\, dx - k^2\frac{m}{\rho}y(0).$$

If we now let $\epsilon \to 0$, the integral on the right will vanish because of the continuity of $y(x)$ at $x = 0$, and we obtain

$$\frac{dy}{dx}(0+0) - \frac{dy}{dx}(0-0) = -k^2\frac{m}{\rho}y(0),$$

or, in our notation,

$$y^{(+)\prime}(0) - y^{(-)\prime}(0) = -k^2\frac{m}{\rho}y(0).$$

We proceed to determine $y^{(-)}(x)$ and $y^{(+)}(x)$ so that they satisfy the appropriate DE and boundary conditions, namely,

$$\frac{d^2y^{(-)}}{dx^2} + k^2y^{(-)} = 0, \qquad y^{(-)}(-L/2) = 0,$$

$$\frac{d^2y^{(+)}}{dx^2} + k^2y^{(+)} = 0, \qquad y^{(+)}(+L/2) = 0.$$

Evidently, such solutions are

$$y^{(-)}(x) = N^{(-)}\sin k(x + L/2), \qquad y^{(+)}(x) = N^{(+)}\sin k(x - L/2)$$

with k, $N^{(-)}$ and $N^{(+)}$ still undetermined. Continuity at $x = 0$ requires that

$$N^{(-)}\sin(kL/2) = N^{(+)}\sin(-kL/2).$$

This condition can be met in two distinct ways:

a) either $N^{(-)} = -N^{(+)}$ (and arbitrary k),
b) or $kL/2 = n\pi$, $n = 1, 2, 3, \ldots$ (and arbitrary $N^{(-)}, N^{(+)}$).

The condition imposed on the derivatives at $x = 0$ requires that

$$kN^{(+)}\cos\frac{kL}{2} - kN^{(-)}\cos\frac{kL}{2} = -k^2\frac{m}{\rho}N^{(-)}\sin\frac{kL}{2}.$$

If $kL/2 = n\pi$, the above result reduces to $N^{(-)} = N^{(+)}$. On the other hand, if $N^{(-)} = -N^{(+)}$, then k must satisfy the equation

$$2\cos\frac{kL}{2} = \frac{mk}{\rho}\sin\frac{kL}{2}.$$

Using $kL/2 = \gamma$, we can rewrite this transcendental equation as

$$\tan\gamma = \frac{\rho L}{m}\frac{1}{\gamma}.$$

It follows that there are two types of eigenvalues:

1. *Integral eigenvalues*, with $k = 2n\pi/L$ and eigenfunctions

$$\psi_n(x) = \begin{cases} N_n \sin \dfrac{2\pi n(x + L/2)}{L} & (-L/2 \leq x \leq 0), \\[2mm] N_n \sin \dfrac{2\pi n(x - L/2)}{L} & (0 \leq x \leq L/2). \end{cases}$$

2. *Transcendental eigenvalues*, with $k = 2\gamma_m/L$, where γ_m is a root of

$$\tan \gamma = (\rho L/m\gamma)$$

and eigenfunctions

$$\psi_m(x) = \begin{cases} N_m \sin \dfrac{2\gamma_m(x + L/2)}{L} & (-L/2 \leq x \leq 0), \\[2mm] -N_m \sin \dfrac{2\gamma_m(x - L/2)}{L} & (0 \leq x \leq L/2). \end{cases}$$

The transcendental eigenvalues can be obtained (or estimated) graphically, as shown in Fig. 11.1.

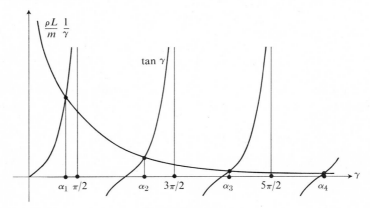

Figure 11.1

We have seen that the lowest eigenvalue is of transcendental type and from there on the two types alternate. The eigenfunctions of type 1 are *even modes** of a homogeneous string of density ρ; the presence of mass m does not affect them at all. On the other hand, the *odd modes* give way to eigenfunctions of type 2. This transition (in reverse direction) can be continuously retraced if we let $m \to 0$.

An interesting situation arises at the other extreme, if we let $m \to \infty$. The transcendental eigenvalues approach the integral ones but the corresponding

* The number of half-wavelengths is even. Otherwise eigenfunctions of type 1 are antisymmetric (or odd) with respect to reflections about the origin in our setup.

wave functions *do not*, because the cusp remains. The limiting shape is that of two separate pieces of the corresponding "integral eigenfunctions" joined at the origin. The physical meaning of the limiting case $m \to \infty$ is that the string is broken into two homogeneous strings, each of length $L/2$.

It is needless to mention that the constants N_n or N_m can be determined from the normalization condition. Adopting some suitable common labeling for eigenfunctions, we can write the condition of generalized orthogonality in the form

$$\int_{-L/2}^{+L/2} \psi_\mu(x)\psi_\nu(x)\, dx + \frac{m}{\rho} \psi_\mu(0)\psi_\nu(0) = \delta_{\mu\nu},$$

where $\psi_\mu(x)$ and $\psi_\nu(x)$ are two eigenfunctions of either type.

11.8 APPLICATIONS OF EIGENFUNCTIONS

In the preceding sections we have shown how to build from the eigenfunctions of a self-adjoint differential operator an orthogonal* basis for the appropriate space of functions. This basis may then be used for solving various related problems such as, first of all, the nonhomogeneous differential equations involving the same differential operator.

Consider the uniform stretched string of length L. Its motion is governed by the PDE (see p. 289)

$$T\frac{\partial^2 u}{\partial x^2} - \rho \frac{\partial^2 u}{\partial t^2} = -F(x, t),$$

where $F(x, t)$ is the externally applied force (per unit length). Let us discuss the case in which the external force varies harmonically with some fixed frequency ω. Then we may set

$$F(x, t) = f(x)e^{-i\omega t}.$$

Physical intuition (and experience) tells us that the string will, in general, respond with harmonic oscillations of the same frequency. This suggests that we seek a solution in the form

$$u(x, t) = y(x)e^{-i\omega t}.$$

Substituting these expressions into the PDE, we obtain the DE for $y(x)$:

$$\frac{d^2 y}{dx^2} + k^2 y = -\frac{1}{T} f(x) \qquad (k^2 = \rho\omega^2/T).$$

To this we must add the boundary conditions $y(0) = y(L) = 0$.

The importance of these particular forms of $F(x, t)$ and $y(x, t)$ is not confined to the fact that they are very common in practice. If $F(x, t)$ were an *arbitrary function* of time, we could subject the entire PDE to a Fourier transformation with

---

* Perhaps in the generalized sense.

respect to t; writing

$$\mathcal{F}\{F(x, t)\} = \varphi(x, \omega), \qquad \mathcal{F}\{u(x, t)\} = \psi(x, \omega),$$

we could obtain a DE for $\psi(x, \omega)$,

$$\frac{d^2\psi}{dx^2} + k^2\psi = -\frac{1}{T}\varphi(x, \omega) \qquad (k^2 = \rho\omega^2/T),$$

plus the boundary conditions $\psi(0, \omega) = \psi(L, \omega) = 0$. Apart from the final task of inverting $\psi(x, \omega)$, and the more complicated dependence on the parameter ω, the problem is essentially the same as for $y(x)$.

Returning to our problem, we realize that we may, in principle, represent $y(x)$ in terms of any basis within the appropriate linear space of functions.* A bit of reflection tells us that the most convenient basis would be that of eigenfunctions of the differential operator

$$\mathcal{L}' = \frac{d^2}{dx^2} + k^2,$$

or, perhaps, the differential operator

$$\mathcal{L} = \frac{d^2}{dx^2}.$$

There is no essential difference between the two choices since the eigenvalue spectrum of $\mathcal{L}'$ is the same as that of $\mathcal{L}$ except for the additive constant k^2. Let us choose the operator $\mathcal{L}$ as the more familiar one. Its normalized eigenfunctions† are

$$\psi_n(x) = \sqrt{\frac{2}{L}} \sin\frac{n\pi x}{L} \qquad (n = 1, 2, 3, \ldots).$$

Choosing this set as the basis, we write

$$y(x) = \sum_{n=1}^{\infty} Y_n\psi_n(x) \qquad f(x) = \sum_{n=1}^{\infty} F_n\psi_n(x).$$

Substitution into the DE yields

$$\sum_{n=1}^{\infty}\left(k^2 - \frac{n^2\pi^2}{L^2}\right) Y_n\psi_n(x) = -\frac{1}{T}\sum_{n=1}^{\infty} F_n\psi_n(x).$$

Multiplying this equation by $\psi_m(x)$, integrating over $(0, L)$, and using the orthogonality of ψ_n, we obtain

$$\left(k^2 - \frac{m^2\pi^2}{L^2}\right) Y_m = -\frac{F_m}{T}.$$

---

* The space of, say, twice differentiable functions, vanishing at $x = 0$ and $x = L$.
† Satisfying the boundary conditions, of course.

The whole process is already familiar to us as the application of Fourier sine series. It should now be evident why the sine functions (and not any other orthogonal basis) are used. If ψ_n were not eigenfunctions of $\mathcal{L}$, we would have

$$\mathcal{L}\psi_n(x) = \chi_n(x),$$

where $\chi_n(x)$ is not proportional to $\psi_n(x)$ and should be expressed by its own series

$$\chi_n(x) = \sum_{n=1}^{\infty} X_n \psi_n(x).$$

Despite the fact that the coefficients X_n should be known, the problem of determining the Y_n would be much more difficult since the algebraic equations involving them would be *coupled*. The use of a basis which makes the operator $\mathcal{L}$ diagonal decouples these equations and the solution becomes almost trivial. We have

$$Y_n = \frac{1}{T} \frac{F_n}{(n^2\pi^2/L^2) - k^2}$$

and

$$y(x) = \frac{1}{T} \sqrt{\frac{2}{L}} \sum_{n=1}^{\infty} \frac{F_n}{(n^2\pi^2/L^2) - k^2} \sin \frac{n\pi x}{L},$$

where

$$F_n = \sqrt{\frac{2}{L}} \int_0^L f(x) \sin \frac{n\pi x}{L} \, dx.$$

Remark. All coefficients Y_n are well defined unless it happens that $k^2 = m^2\pi^2/L^2$ for some integer m; in other words, the external frequency ω matches one of the characteristic frequencies of the string. This is the case of *resonance* and two possibilities arise: Either $F_m = 0$ and Y_m is arbitrary, leaving a certain indeterminacy in the solution,* or $F_m \neq 0$ when the method breaks down. In the latter case the PDE does not possess solutions of the form $y(x)e^{-i\omega t}$.

Once the concept of diagonalization of a differential operator is grasped, various generalizations of the above problem present no intrinsic difficulties. As an example, consider the longitudinal vibrations of a solid rod of length L and variable cross section.

Suppose that the rod is placed horizontally,† with the origin at one end (Fig. 11.2). The longitudinal displacement u of any given cross section is a function of position and time: $u = u(x, t)$. The extension (or contraction) of an element of length dx is evidently

$$u(x + dx, t) - u(x, t)$$

---

* Note that all other coefficients Y_n are still well defined.

† This is only to emphasize that we want to exclude the influence of gravity. If the rod is light, it may just as well be hung vertically.

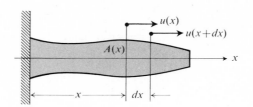

Figure 11.2

so that the strain at any position x is given by

$$\epsilon = \lim_{dx \to 0} \frac{u(x + dx, t) - u(x, t)}{dx} = \frac{\partial u}{\partial x}(x, t).$$

The stress is then*

$$\sigma = E\epsilon = E\frac{\partial u}{\partial x}.$$

Consider the dynamics of an element of length dx. At the left end there is a force $A(x)E\, \partial u(x, t)/\partial x$ acting to the left if $\partial u/\partial x > 0$; at the right end there is a force $A(x + dx)E\, \partial u(x + dx, t)/\partial x$ acting to the right if $\partial u/\partial x > 0$. The net force due to stresses is then

$$A(x + dx)E\frac{\partial u}{\partial x}(x + dx, t) - A(x)E\frac{\partial u}{\partial x}(x, t) \cong \frac{\partial}{\partial x}\left[A(x)E\frac{\partial u}{\partial x}\right]dx.$$

Apart from this there may be external forces (in the x-direction) acting on the rod. If $F(x, t)$ is the sum of these forces per unit length, then the element dx is subject to an additional force $F(x, t)\, dx$.

Since the mass of our element is $\rho A(x)\, dx$ (ρ is the volume density) and its acceleration is $\partial^2 u/\partial t^2$, Newton's second law yields

$$\frac{\partial}{\partial x}\left[A(x)E\frac{\partial u}{\partial x}\right]dx + F(x, t)\, dx = A(x)\rho\frac{\partial^2 u}{\partial t^2}\, dx,$$

and it follows that the unknown function $u(x, t)$ satisfies the PDE

$$\frac{\partial}{\partial x}\left[EA(x)\frac{\partial u}{\partial x}\right] = \rho A(x)\frac{\partial^2 u}{\partial t^2} - F(x, t).$$

This equation is of the general form

$$\frac{\partial}{\partial x}\left[p(x)\frac{\partial u}{\partial x}\right] - s(x)u = r(x)\frac{\partial^2 u}{\partial t^2} - F(x, t)$$

with $p(x) = EA(x) \geq 0$, $s(x) = 0$, and $r(x) = \rho A(x) \geq 0$. Note that the mathematical problem would be no more difficult if the density of the rod ρ and its Young's modulus E were functions of x, rather than constants.

---

* Note that we assume the validity of Hooke's law for (rather rapid) vibrations.

Regarding the boundary conditions, let us assume that the end $x = 0$ of the rod is rigidly fixed and the end $x = L$ is free. This implies $u(0, t) = 0$ and $\partial u(L, t)/\partial x = 0$ at all times t; the latter is implied because there is no stress at the free end.

As in the case of the stretched string, if $F(x, t) = f(x)e^{-i\omega t}$, then we expect a solution $u(x, t) = y(x)e^{-i\omega t}$. This yields

$$\frac{d}{dx}\left[EA(x)\frac{dy}{dx}\right] + \omega^2 \rho A(x)y = -f(x)$$

and $y(0) = 0$, $\partial y(L)/\partial x = 0$. It is now logical to seek nontrivial solutions of the homogeneous DE

$$\frac{d}{dx}\left[EA(x)\frac{d\psi}{dx}\right] + \lambda \rho A(x)\psi = 0$$

satisfying our boundary conditions. These nontrivial solutions are often some well-known special functions (Chapter 9) or some related ones.* At worst, they are calculable by the Frobenius technique (Chapter 3). The important fact is that the set of such functions $\psi_n(x)$, $n = 1, 2, 3, \ldots$, is a basis for the appropriate linear space. This basis can be normalized in the sense that

$$\int_0^L \rho A(x)\psi_m(x)\psi_n(x)\, dx = \delta_{mn}.$$

Bearing these features in mind, multiply the DE for $y(x)$ by $\psi_n(x)$ and integrate over $(0, L)$:

$$\int_0^L \psi_n(x)\frac{d}{dx}\left[EA(x)\frac{dy}{dx}\right]dx + \omega^2 \int_0^L \rho A(x)\psi_n(x)y(x)\, dx = -\int_0^L f(x)\psi_n(x)\, dx.$$

Because of the hermiticity of the operator

$$\mathcal{L} = \frac{d}{dx}\left[EA(x)\frac{d}{dx}\right],$$

we have†

$$\int_0^L \psi_n(x)\frac{d}{dx}\left[EA(x)\frac{dy(x)}{dx}\right]dx = \int_0^L y(x)\frac{d}{dx}\left[EA(x)\frac{d\psi_n(x)}{dx}\right]dx.$$

Now use the fact that $\psi_n(x)$ is a (generalized) eigenfunction of $\mathcal{L}$ corresponding to the eigenvalue λ_n to obtain

$$(\omega^2 - \lambda_n)\int_0^L \rho A(x)\psi_n(x)y(x)\, dx = -\int_0^L f(x)\psi_n(x)\, dx.$$

---

* For example, as in Section 11.7.

† In plain language, integrate twice by parts and use the boundary conditions.

Define

$$F'_n = \int_0^L f(x)\psi_n(x)\, dx.$$

These coefficients are calculable once the functions $\psi_n(x)$ are known. Define also

$$Y_n = \int_0^L \rho A(x) y(x)\psi_n(x)\, dx.$$

These numbers are just the coefficients of expansion of $y(x)$ in terms of the $\psi_n(x)$:

$$y(x) = \sum_{n=1}^{\infty} Y_n \psi_n(x).$$

If the Y_n are found, the problem is solved. This is done via the formula connecting Y_n with F'_n:

$$Y_n = \frac{F'_n}{\lambda_n - \omega^2} \qquad (\lambda_n \neq \omega^2).$$

Again, the resonance phenomena ($\omega^2 = \lambda_n$) are possible and must be treated separately. It is interesting to note that the coefficients F'_n *are not* the coefficients of expansion of $f(x)$ in terms of the ψ_n-basis. Rather, they are the coefficients of expansion of the function

$$g(x) = \frac{f(x)}{\rho A(x)}.$$

BIBLIOGRAPHY

BERBERIAN, S. K., *Introduction to Hilbert Space*. London: Oxford University Press, 1961.

DICKE, R. H., and J. P. WITTKE, *Introduction to Quantum Mechanics*. Reading, Mass.: Addison-Wesley Publishing Co., 1960.

FONG, P., *Elementary Quantum Mechanics*. Reading, Mass.: Addison-Wesley Publishing Co., 1962.

TITCHMARSH, E. C., *Eigenfunction Expansions Associated with Second-Order Differential Equations*. London: Oxford University Press, 1946 and 1958.

PROBLEMS

1. The inner product for the complex space of square-integrable functions defined on p. 465 satisfies the following *Schwarz inequality:*

$$\left| \int_a^b f^*(x) g(x)\, dx \right| \le \sqrt{\int_a^b f^*(x) f(x)\, dx \int_a^b g^*(x) g(x)\, dx}.$$

Observe that

$$\int_a^b \int_a^b |f(x)g(y) - f(y)g(x)|^2\, dx\, dy \ge 0,$$

and deduce from this the Schwarz inequality. [*Hint:* Expand the integrand and simplify the resulting expression.]

2. The Schwarz inequality holds in an arbitrary vector space (with an inner product) and reads (see p. 437)

(see p. 437)

$$|(\mathbf{x}, \mathbf{y})| \leq \sqrt{(\mathbf{x}, \mathbf{x})}\sqrt{(\mathbf{y}, \mathbf{y})} = \|\mathbf{x}\|\,\|\mathbf{y}\|.$$

Prove this statement, starting with the obvious inequality

$$(\mathbf{z}, \mathbf{z}) = \left(\mathbf{x} - \frac{(\mathbf{x}, \mathbf{y})}{(\mathbf{y}, \mathbf{y})}\mathbf{y}, \ \mathbf{x} - \frac{(\mathbf{x}, \mathbf{y})}{(\mathbf{y}, \mathbf{y})}\mathbf{y}\right) \geq 0$$

and expanding the inner product according to the rules of Section 10.6.

3. Another important inequality of general validity is the so-called *triangle inequality*

$$\|\mathbf{x} + \mathbf{y}\| \leq \|\mathbf{x}\| + \|\mathbf{y}\|.$$

Prove this inequality by considering

$$\|\mathbf{x} + \mathbf{y}\|^2 = (\mathbf{x} + \mathbf{y}, \mathbf{x} + \mathbf{y}) \geq 0$$

and using the Schwarz inequality.

4. Using the pure recursion relation for Hermite polynomials, develop the formulas

$$x^2 H_n = n(n-1)H_{n-2} + (n + \tfrac{1}{2})H_n + \tfrac{1}{4}H_{n+2} \qquad (n \geq 2),$$

$$x^3 H_n = n(n-1)(n-2)H_{n-3} + \frac{3n^2}{2}H_{n-1} + \frac{3(n+1)}{4}H_{n+1} + \tfrac{1}{8}H_{n+3} \qquad (n \geq 3).$$

How do these formulas change if $n < 2$ or $n < 3$? Multiply these formulas by appropriate functions and integrate to show that

a) $\displaystyle\int_{-\infty}^{+\infty} \psi_n(x)x^2\psi_n(x)\, dx = n + \tfrac{1}{2}$ (all n),

b) $\displaystyle\int_{-\infty}^{+\infty} \psi_{n-3}(x)x^3\psi_n(x)\, dx = \sqrt{\frac{n(n-1)(n-2)}{8}}$ $(n \geq 3)$.

5. The integrals $\int_{-\infty}^{+\infty} \psi_m(x)x^3\psi_n(x)\, dx$ are called the matrix elements of the operator $\mathfrak{X}^3$ and are very often written as $\langle m|\mathfrak{X}^3|n\rangle$, following a notation introduced by Dirac (similar expressions are written for other linear operators).

a) Show that $\langle m|\mathfrak{X}^3|n\rangle = 0$ unless $m = n - 3$, $m = n - 1$, $m = n + 1$, or $m = n + 3$. Calculate the matrix elements in the last three cases.

b) Using the matrix X in the text, calculate the matrices X^2 and X^3 (display a 6×6 upper left corner) and verify that the elements of the matrix X^3 are indeed equal to the integrals

$$\langle m|\mathfrak{X}^3|n\rangle = \int_{-\infty}^{+\infty} \psi_m x^3 \psi_n\, dx,$$

where m is the row index and n is the column index. Give a clear argument why this should be so in general.

6. Construct the matrices X and D by the following method, representing a modification of the technique used in Section 14.5:

a) Assume that $H = X^2 - D^2$ is an infinite diagonal matrix with eigenvalues $\lambda_n = 1 + 2n$ and that X is a symmetric while D is an antisymmetric matrix. Both are unknown but $[D, X] = I$.

b) Let $G_+ = X - D$ and $G_- = X + D$. Show that G_- must be the transpose of G_+.

c) Using the appropriate commutator, show that the elements $g_{ij}^{(+)}$ of G_+ must vanish unless $i = j + 1$. Develop a similar statement about the elements $g_{ij}^{(-)}$ of G_-.

d) From the expression for $[G_+, G_-]$, show that $g_{ij}^{(+)} = \sqrt{2j}\, \delta_{i,j+1}$.

e) Calculate x_{ij} and d_{ij} from $g_{ij}^{(+)}$ and $g_{ij}^{(-)}$.

7. The stretched string with a discrete mass in the middle described in Section 11.7 is subjected to an external force (per unit length) $F(x, t) = F_0 e^{-i\omega_0 t}$ ($F_0 = $ const). Show that there exists a solution in the form

$$u(x, t) = e^{-i\omega_0 t} \sum_\nu U_\nu \psi_\nu(x),$$

where $\psi_\nu(x)$ are the eigenfunctions described in the text (see p. 495). Evaluate explicitly the coefficients U_ν. Assume the nonresonant case.

8. The solid rod described in Section 11.8 extends from $x = L$ to $x = 2L$ and has a variable circular cross section of radius $r = a\sqrt{x}$ ($a = $ const). The end at $x = 2L$ is rigidly fixed and the end at $x = L$ is free.

a) Set up the boundary-value problem describing the normal modes of free vibrations of the rod.

b) Show that the solutions can be expressed in terms of Bessel and Neumann functions. Display the transcendental equation determining the eigenvalues and construct the eigenfunctions normalized with respect to the appropriate weight function.

CHAPTER 12

GREEN'S FUNCTIONS

12.1 INTRODUCTION

Example 1. Suppose that we wish to solve the ordinary DE

$$m \frac{dv}{dt} = -Rv + f(t)$$

which may represent the motion of a particle of mass m in a resistive medium (coefficient R) under the influence of an external force $f(t)$, where $v(t)$ is the velocity of the particle.

Let us first consider the special problem that occurs when the particle is at rest up to the time $t = \tau$ and then set in motion by a sudden "blow." This implies that the external force $f(t)$ exists only during a small interval, say from τ to $\tau + \Delta\tau$. After the time $\tau + \Delta\tau$ the motion of the particle is governed by the homogeneous equation

$$m \frac{dv}{dt} = -Rv \qquad (t > \tau + \Delta\tau),$$

which, evidently, has the solution

$$v(t) = Ae^{-(R/m)t} \qquad (t > \tau + \Delta\tau).$$

We are not so much interested in what happens between τ and $\tau + \Delta\tau$, but we are certainly interested in the value of A. In other words, we want to know the effect of the blow on the particle. This can be answered by multiplying the DE by dt and integrating between τ and $\tau + \Delta\tau$:

$$m[v(\tau + \Delta\tau) - v(\tau)] = -R \int_{\tau}^{\tau+\Delta\tau} v(t)\, dt + \int_{\tau}^{\tau+\Delta\tau} f(t)\, dt.$$

If the blow had an impulse I, then

$$\int_{\tau}^{\tau+\Delta\tau} f(t)\, dt = I.$$

Assuming $\Delta\tau$ to be very small, we would expect the velocity $v(t)$ to behave essentially as shown by the graph in Fig. 12.1 so that $v(t)$ during the blow could not have been exceedingly large.* If this is so, we can neglect the term $R\int_{\tau}^{\tau+\Delta\tau} v(t)dt$.

---

* This is not true for the force $f(t)$ which must have been large.

503

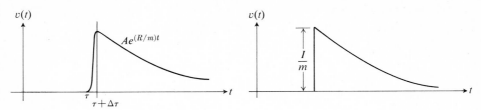

Figure 12.1

Figure 12.2

Now we use

$$v(\tau) = 0, \qquad v(\tau + \Delta\tau) = Ae^{-(R/m)(\tau+\Delta\tau)} \cong Ae^{-(R/m)\tau}.$$

Then $mAe^{-(R/m)\tau} = I$, which yields the idealized solution

$$v(t) = \begin{cases} 0 & (t < \tau), \\ (I/m)e^{-(R/m)(t-\tau)} & (t > \tau) \end{cases}$$

illustrated in Fig. 12.2. The physical meaning of our approach is that we have assumed that the impulse I of the blow had imparted to the particle a momentum $p = mv = I$ so that the velocity immediately after the blow was I/m, and from there on the particle was slowed down by the resistance of the medium. We have neglected the loss of momentum *during the blow*, contained in the integral $R\int_{\tau}^{\tau+\Delta\tau} v(t)\, dt$, which is very reasonable if $\Delta\tau$ is small.

Now suppose that the particle suffered two blows, of impulses I_1 and I_2 at respective times τ_1 and τ_2. Evidently, we can superimpose the corresponding solutions into the overall result

$$v(t) = \begin{cases} 0 & (t < \tau_1), \\ \dfrac{I_1}{m}e^{-(R/m)(t-\tau_1)} & (\tau_1 < t < \tau_2), \\ \dfrac{I_1}{m}e^{-(R/m)(t-\tau_1)} + \dfrac{I_2}{m}e^{-(R/m)(t-\tau_2)} & (t > \tau_2). \end{cases}$$

Generalizing the problem to an arbitrary number of blows, we have

$$v(t) = \sum_{k=1}^{n} \frac{I_k}{m} e^{-(R/m)(t-\tau_k)}$$

with n such that $\tau_n < t < \tau_{n+1}$.

Finally, suppose that a *continuous* force has been acting on the particle. A force $f(t)$ acting at time τ would produce in the interval $d\tau$ an impulse

$$dI = f(\tau)\, d\tau,$$

which would resemble a blow because of its short duration. The continuous action of the force should then have the *cumulative effect* of countless impulses *dI* delivered to the particle. It is not unreasonable to expect the formula for $v(t)$ to "go over" into an integral

$$v(t) = \int_{\tau_0}^{t} \frac{f(\tau)\,d\tau}{m} e^{-(R/m)(t-\tau)} \qquad (t > \tau_0),$$

assuming $v(t) = 0$ and $f(t) = 0$ prior to τ_0.

The above reasoning is, of course, no proof that this formula is valid. However, we may take it as an informed guess, and once it has been written we can verify that it is really a solution of the differential equation

$$m\frac{dv}{dt} = -Rv + f(t) \qquad (t > \tau_0)$$

subject to the condition $v(t) = 0$ for $t = \tau_0$. Indeed, differentiate $v(t)$ as given by the above integral (according to the formula in the footnote on p. 243):

$$\frac{dv(t)}{dt} = -\frac{R}{m}\int_{\tau_0}^{t} \frac{f(\tau)\,d\tau}{m} e^{-(R/m)(t-\tau)} + \frac{f(t)}{m},$$

or

$$\frac{dv(t)}{dt} = -\frac{R}{m}v(t) + \frac{f(t)}{m},$$

which means that $v(t)$ satisfies the DE. The condition $v(\tau_0) = 0$ is self-evident.

Remark. The proper way of writing the obtained solution is

$$v(t) = \begin{cases} 0 & (t < \tau_0), \\ \int_{\tau_0}^{t} \dfrac{1}{m} e^{-(R/m)(t-\tau)} f(\tau)\,d\tau & (t > \tau_0), \end{cases}$$

or, alternatively,

$$v(t) = \int_{-\infty}^{t} G(t,\tau) f(\tau)\,d\tau \qquad (\text{all } t),$$

where

$$G(t,\tau) = \begin{cases} 0 & (t < \tau), \\ \dfrac{1}{m} e^{-(R/m)(t-\tau)} & (t > \tau). \end{cases}$$

The function $G(t,\tau)$ represents physically the *response* (in this case, the velocity) at time t to a *unit impulse* delivered at time τ. It is known as the influence function or, more customarily, as *Green's function*.

Example 2. Now consider a second-order differential equation

$$\frac{d^2x}{dt^2} + 2\lambda\frac{dx}{dt} + \omega_0^2 x = \frac{f(t)}{m},$$

which may represent the motion of a damped harmonic oscillator under the influence of an external force $f(t)$. Assume again that $f(t) = 0$, except for an

impulse I delivered "instantaneously" to the oscillator at time τ while it was still
at rest.

The motion for $t > \tau$ is given by the solution of the *homogeneous equation*

$$x(t) = C_1 e^{-\lambda t} \cos \omega t + C_2 e^{-\lambda t} \sin \omega t,$$

where $\omega = \sqrt{\omega_0^2 - \lambda^2}$ (small damping assumed). As a result of the blow at
$t = \tau$, we expect that $x(t)$ is *still zero* immediately after $t = \tau$, but the velocity
$v(t) = dx/dt$ is given by $v(\tau + 0) = I/m$. These conditions determine the constants C_1 and C_2 and lead to

$$x(t) = \frac{I}{m\omega} e^{-\lambda(t-\tau)} \sin \omega(t - \tau) \qquad (t > \tau).$$

Evidently, we have evaluated Green's function. To find the solution in the general
case, replace I by $f(\tau)\,d\tau$ and integrate over τ:*

$$x(t) = \int_{\tau_0}^{t} \frac{1}{m\omega} e^{-\lambda(t-\tau)} \sin \omega(t - \tau) f(\tau)\,d\tau,$$

and we can now check that this expression does indeed solve the problem.

Remark. Green's function

$$G(t, \tau) = \frac{1}{\omega} e^{-\lambda(t-\tau)} \sin \omega(t - \tau)$$

represents the solution (for $t > \tau$) for the case of a unit impulse delivered within an
infinitely short interval near τ. Evidently, the force needed for this must be "infinite."
It cannot be represented by a conventional function $f(t)$, but we may set

$$f(t) = \delta(t - \tau)$$

and treat the problem from the point of view of the theory of distributions. In this sense,
Green's function $G(t, \tau)$ can be said to satisfy the DE

$$\frac{d^2 G(t, \tau)}{dt^2} + 2\lambda \frac{dG(t, \tau)}{dt} + \omega_0^2 G(t, \tau) = \frac{1}{m} \delta(t - \tau),$$

where $G(t, \tau)$ is also regarded as a distribution.

Example 3. Consider the stretched string at rest under an external distributed
load given by $F(x)$ (force per unit length). The displacement u of the string is a
function of x only and satisfies the differential equation†

$$T\frac{d^2 u(x)}{dx^2} = F(x) \qquad \text{or} \qquad \frac{d^2 u}{dx^2} = \frac{F(x)}{T} = f(x).$$

The boundary conditions are, as usual, $u(0) = u(L) = 0$.

---

* We assume that $f(\tau)$ vanishes for $\tau < \tau_0$, otherwise we replace τ_0 by $-\infty$.
† See Section 8.1; for convenience, $F(x)$ is assumed to act "down," hence the difference
in sign.

Let us solve the problem for a *concentrated load* F_0 at the point $x = \xi$. Evidently, this implies

$$f(x) = \frac{F_0}{T}\,\delta(x - \xi)$$

and we shall seek the solution of the equation

$$\frac{d^2 G(x \mid \xi)}{dx^2} = \delta(x - \xi),$$

which we shall call the Green's function for our problem.* Of course, we require that

$$G(0 \mid \xi) = G(L \mid \xi) = 0.$$

Note that $G(x \mid \xi)$ satisfies the homogeneous DE for all x *except* $x = \xi$. Therefore it must have the form

$$G(x \mid \xi) = Ax + B \qquad \text{for } 0 \le x < \xi,$$

and the boundary condition at $x = 0$ implies $B = 0$ while A remains undetermined. Similarly,

$$G(x \mid \xi) = A'x + B' \qquad (\text{for } \xi < x \le L),$$

and the boundary condition at $x = L$ implies that

$$B' = -A'L$$

while it leaves A' undetermined. Since $G(x \mid \xi)$ physically represents a possible, although somewhat idealized, shape of the string, it must be continuous at $x = \xi$, which implies

$$A\xi = A'(\xi - L),$$

determining A' in terms of A. Now note that we should not require dG/dx to be continuous at $x = \xi$. As a matter of fact, we expect the string to look like the one shown in Fig. 12.3; there should be a jump discontinuity in the slope. To find the magnitude of this jump, we integrate the DE (the true DE for G)

$$\frac{d^2 G}{dx^2} = \delta(x - \xi)$$

between $\xi - \epsilon$ and $\xi + \epsilon$ and then set $\epsilon \to 0$. This yields

$$\frac{dG}{dx}(\xi + 0 \mid \xi) - \frac{dG}{dx}(\xi - 0 \mid \xi) = 1.$$

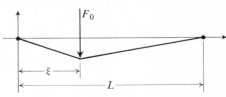

Figure 12.3

---

* The widely used notation $G(x \mid \xi)$, instead of $G(x, \xi)$, will be adopted from now on.

We now obtain $\partial G(\xi + 0 \mid \xi)/\partial x$ from

$$G(x \mid \xi) = \frac{A\xi}{(\xi - L)} (x - L) \qquad (x > \xi),$$

which yields

$$\frac{dG}{dx}(\xi + 0 \mid \xi) = \frac{A\xi}{\xi - L} \cdot$$

Similarly, from $G(x \mid \xi) = Ax$ $(x < \xi)$, we obtain

$$\frac{dG}{dx}(\xi - 0 \mid \xi) = A.$$

Then, from $A\xi/(\xi - L) - A = 1$, we obtain $A = (\xi - L)/L$. Our result is then

$$G(x \mid \xi) = \begin{cases} -\dfrac{x(L - \xi)}{L} & (0 \leq x \leq \xi), \\[2mm] -\dfrac{\xi(L - x)}{L} & (\xi \leq x \leq L). \end{cases}$$

Remark. Note that Green's function is *symmetric* in the variables x and ξ:

$$G(x \mid \xi) = G(\xi \mid x).*$$

This property is very important in many applications. Note that $G(t, \tau)$ in Examples 1 and 2 is not symmetric.

According to the general principles, we now expect that the solution of a non-homogeneous equation $d^2u/dx^2 = F(x)/T$, plus boundary conditions, will be given by

$$u(x) = \int_0^L G(x \mid \xi) \frac{F(\xi)}{T} d\xi.$$

This property may indeed be verified.

12.2 GREEN'S FUNCTION FOR THE STURM-LIOUVILLE OPERATOR

Consider the nonhomogeneous differential equation

$$\frac{d}{dx}\left[p(x) \frac{dy}{dx} \right] - s(x)y = f(x).$$

The left-hand side of this equation is written in the Sturm-Liouville form (see Section 9.3). However, it should be noted that *any* nonhomogeneous linear DE of the second order, namely,

$$A(x)\frac{d^2y}{dx^2} + B(x)\frac{dy}{dx} + C(x)y = D(x),$$

---

* When we interchange x and ξ, we must also change $x < \xi$ to $x > \xi$.

can be brought to the above form as a result of multiplication by

$$H(x) = \frac{1}{A(x)} \exp\left[\int^x \frac{B(\xi)}{A(\xi)} d\xi\right],$$

so that there is no loss of generality.

Exercise. Demonstrate the validity of the above assertion.

On the other hand, note that the above equation does not contain the term $\lambda r(x)y$ present in the Sturm-Liouville equation. However, the function $s(x)$ can often be written as

$$s(x) = s_0(x) - \lambda r_0(x)$$

with some *fixed* λ and with $s_0(x) \geq 0$ and $r_0(x) \geq 0$ (see p. 489). In this case our equation will be *related* to the Sturm-Liouville eigenvalue problem

$$\frac{d}{dx}\left[p(x) \frac{dy}{dx}\right] - s_0(x)y + \lambda_0 r_0(x)y = 0,$$

where λ_0 is an *eigenvalue*, created by certain boundary conditions. From this point of view we are simultaneously treating the equations $\mathcal{L}y = f$ and $(\mathcal{L} + \lambda r)y = f$, where $\mathcal{L}$ is the self-adjoint Sturm-Liouville operator

$$\mathcal{L} = \frac{d}{dx}\left[p(x) \frac{d}{dx}\right] - s(x),$$

and λ is not necessarily an eigenvalue of $\mathcal{L}$ within the framework of the boundary conditions which will be imposed on $y(x)$.

Let us proceed to determine Green's function which satisfies the equation

$$\frac{d}{dx}\left[p(x) \frac{dG}{dx}\right] - s(x)G = \delta(x - \xi)$$

subject to certain boundary conditions. We know that such a function exists for the special case

$$p(x) = 1, \qquad s(x) = 0,$$

and we shall show that this is *almost always* true in the general case. In this discussion we shall discover that the existence of $G(x \mid \xi)$ implies something about the *homogeneous* equation

$$\frac{d}{dx}\left[p(x) \frac{dy}{dx}\right] - s(x)y = 0.$$

We shall build up Green's function by the method used in the case of a stretched string; i.e., we shall require that

a) $G(x \mid \xi)$ satisfies the *homogeneous* equation *except* at $x = \xi$,
b) $G(x \mid \xi)$ satisfies certain *homogeneous* boundary conditions,
c) $G(x \mid \xi)$ is continuous at $x = \xi$.

We expect dG/dx to have a jump discontinuity at $x = \xi$. To arrive at that conclusion exactly, we integrate the differential equation

$$\frac{d}{dx}\left[p(x)\frac{dG}{dx}\right] - s(x)G = \delta(x - \xi)$$

between $\xi - \epsilon$ and $\xi + \epsilon$; this yields

$$p(x)\left.\frac{dG(x \mid \xi)}{dx}\right|_{\xi-\epsilon}^{\xi+\epsilon} - \int_{\xi-\epsilon}^{\xi+\epsilon} s(x)G(x \mid \xi)\,dx = 1.$$

Since $G(x \mid \xi)$ and $s(x)$* are both continuous at $x = \xi$, it follows that

$$\lim_{\epsilon \to 0} \int_{\xi-\epsilon}^{\xi+\epsilon} s(x)G(x \mid \xi)\,dx = 0,$$

and we obtain, in the limit $\epsilon \to 0$,

$$p(\xi)\left[\frac{dG}{dx}(\xi + 0 \mid \xi) - \frac{dG}{dx}(\xi - 0 \mid \xi)\right] = 1$$

so that our last requirement of $G(x \mid \xi)$ will be that

d) dG/dx must have a jump discontinuity of magnitude $1/p(\xi)$ at $x = \xi$.

A few words about the boundary conditions: We shall confine ourselves to the standard boundary conditions for a finite interval (a, b), namely,

$$\alpha_1 G(a \mid \xi) + \alpha_2 G'(a \mid \xi) = 0, \qquad \beta_1 G(b \mid \xi) + \beta_2 G'(b \mid \xi) = 0,$$

where G' means dG/dx, where $\xi \neq a$, $\xi \neq b$, and where α_1 and α_2 should not *both* be zero; similarly for β_1 and β_2. This encompasses Dirichlet, Neumann, and intermediate boundary conditions.

Consider the region $a \leq x < \xi$. We let $y_1(x)$ be a nontrivial solution of the *homogeneous* DE satisfying the boundary conditions at $x = a$:

$$\alpha_1 y_1(a) + \alpha_2 y_1'(a) = 0.$$

Since $G(x \mid \xi)$ must satisfy the same boundary conditions, we have

$$\alpha_1 G(a \mid \xi) + \alpha_2 G'(a \mid \xi) = 0.$$

The set α_1, α_2 is *nontrivial*.† It follows that the Wronskian of y_1 and G must vanish at $x = a$:

$$y_1(a)G'(a \mid \xi) - y_1'(a)G(a \mid \xi) = 0.$$

However, for $a \leq x < \xi$, both $y_1(x)$ and $G(x \mid \xi)$ satisfy the *same DE*, the homogeneous one. Therefore their Wronskian is zero at all points and

$$G(x \mid \xi) = C_1 y_1(x) \qquad (0 \leq x < \xi),$$

---

* The functions $p(x)$ and $s(x)$ are usually assumed to be analytic (Section 3.1).

† At least one of the numbers α_1, α_2 is nonzero.

where C_1 is a constant. By the same token, if a nontrivial function $y_2(x)$ satisfies the homogeneous equation and the boundary conditions at $x = b$, then we have

$$G(x \mid \xi) = C_2 y_2(x) \qquad (\xi < x \le b).$$

The continuity of G and the jump discontinuity of G' at $x = \xi$ imply

$$C_1 y_1(\xi) - C_2 y_2(\xi) = 0, \qquad C_1 y_1'(\xi) - C_2 y_2'(\xi) = -1/p(\xi).$$

This system must now be solved for C_1 and C_2 and it will have a solution *provided* the Wronskian of y_1 and y_2 does not vanish at ξ:

$$y_1(\xi) y_2'(\xi) - y_2(\xi) y_1'(\xi) = 0.$$

In other words, $y_1(x)$ must not be a multiple of $y_2(x)$. Is this always going to be so? The answer is "almost always." If the homogeneous equation admits *no nontrivial solution* satisfying *both boundary conditions at the same time*, then $y_1(x)$ and $y_2(x)$ must be linearly independent.

If, however, the homogeneous equation possesses such a solution $y_0(x)$, namely, with

$$\alpha_1 y_0(a) + \alpha_2 y_0'(a) = 0, \qquad \beta_1 y_0(b) + \beta_2 y_0'(b) = 0,$$

then $y_1(x)$ is necessarily a multiple of $y_0(x)$ and so is $y_2(x)$. Then they are multiples of each other and their Wronskian vanishes. Green's function *does not exist* in this case.

If our original DE has the form

$$(\mathscr{L} + \lambda r) y = f,$$

we see that it will possess Green's function for all values of λ except those which are the *eigenvalues of the homogeneous problem*, namely, for which the nontrivial solutions of

$$(\mathscr{L} + \lambda r) y = 0$$

do exist. We have here an analogy with a system of linear equations (or a vector-matrix equation). The nonhomogeneous problem $Ay = f$ has a solution* only if the matrix A is nonsingular (A^{-1} exists). If it is singular, there is no solution and this happens exactly when the homogeneous system $Ay = 0$ has a nontrivial solution. The reason for this analogy is as follows: From the formula which solves the nonhomogeneous equation

$$y(x) = \int G(x \mid \xi) f(\xi) \, d\xi,$$

it follows that Green's function is used to obtain the function $y(x)$ from the function $f(x)$. Comparing this with $y = A^{-1} f$, we see that $G(x \mid \xi)$ is the analog of the *inverse* of the operator $\mathscr{L} + \lambda r$. Whenever λ is equal to an eigenvalue, the operator

---

* For *arbitrary* (nontrivial) column vector f.

$\mathcal{L} + \lambda r$ becomes *singular* and loses its inverse. We then expect that the equation

$$(\mathcal{L} + \lambda r)y = f$$

will have no solution in this case. This is indeed so for arbitrary f.*

Let us now proceed to find $G(x \mid \xi)$ when it does exist. The system

$$C_1 y_1(\xi) - C_2 y_2(\xi) = 0, \qquad C_1 y_1'(\xi) - C_2 y_2'(\xi) = -1/p(\xi)$$

has in this case a unique solution

$$C_1 = \frac{y_2(\xi)}{p(\xi)W(\xi)}, \qquad C_2 = \frac{y_1(\xi)}{p(\xi)W(\xi)},$$

where $W(\xi)$ is the Wronskian of y_1 and y_2 at $x = \xi$. Explicitly,

$$G(x \mid \xi) = \begin{cases} \dfrac{y_1(x)y_2(\xi)}{p(\xi)W(\xi)} & (a \leq x \leq \xi), \\[3mm] \dfrac{y_2(x)y_1(\xi)}{p(\xi)W(\xi)} & (\xi \leq x \leq b). \end{cases}$$

Exercise. Show that the denominator $p(\xi)W(\xi)$ is actually independent of ξ and must be a constant.

Evidently, $G(x \mid \xi)$ is symmetric in x and ξ. It is also easy to see that $G(x \mid \xi)$ is *unique*. We can always choose a different $y_1(x)$, but it will be a multiple of the "old" y_1, and the Wronskian will be multiplied by the same factor, leaving $G(x \mid \xi)$ the same. This is also true for the choice of $y_2(x)$.

Remark. The boundary conditions considered above were of a nonmixed type.† For mixed boundary conditions Green's function is not always symmetric, although it often is. One can prove, e.g., that $G(x \mid \xi)$ is symmetric for conditions of periodicity:

$$y(a) = y(b) \qquad y'(a) = y'(b), \text{ provided } p(a) = p(b).$$

We shall now prove that the Green's function given above possesses the solving property, that is, the function

$$y(x) = \int_a^b G(x \mid \xi)f(\xi)\,d\xi$$

does indeed satisfy the nonhomogeneous DE and the homogeneous boundary conditions.

In the above expression, x is considered to be a parameter, while ξ is the dummy variable. As we perform the integration, we must switch from the first form for $G(x \mid \xi)$, namely that for $x < \xi$ to the second one (for $x > \xi$) when ξ becomes

---

* For some special functions $f(x)$ the solutions still exist, just as in the case of matrices.
† See p. 340.

equal to x. For this purpose we split the integral as follows:

$$y(x) = \int_a^x G(x \mid \xi) f(\xi) \, d\xi + \int_x^b G(x \mid \xi) f(\xi) \, d\xi.$$

The differentiation yields (footnote on p. 243)

$$\frac{d}{dx} \int_a^x G(x \mid \xi) f(\xi) \, d\xi = \int_a^x \frac{dG(x \mid \xi)}{dx} f(\xi) \, d\xi + G(x \mid x - 0) f(x),$$

$$\frac{d}{dx} \int_x^b G(x \mid \xi) f(\xi) \, d\xi = \int_x^b \frac{dG(x \mid \xi)}{dx} f(\xi) \, d\xi - G(x \mid x + 0) f(x).$$

Since $G(x \mid \xi)$ is continuous everywhere, we have

$$G(x \mid x + 0) = G(x \mid x - 0)$$

so that

$$\frac{dy}{dx} = \int_a^x \frac{dG(x \mid \xi)}{dx} f(\xi) \, d\xi + \int_x^b \frac{dG(x \mid \xi)}{dx} f(\xi) \, d\xi.$$

We differentiate once more to obtain

$$\frac{d^2 y}{dx^2} = \int_a^x \frac{d^2 G(x \mid \xi)}{dx^2} f(\xi) \, d\xi + \frac{dG}{dx} (x \mid x - 0) f(x)$$

$$+ \int_x^b \frac{d^2 G(x \mid \xi)}{dx^2} f(\xi) \, d\xi - \frac{dG}{dx} (x \mid x + 0) f(x).$$

The second and fourth terms on the right will not cancel in this case. Their sum yields

$$\frac{dG}{dx} (x \mid x - 0) - \frac{dG}{dx} (x \mid x + 0) = \frac{1}{p(x)}.$$

The notation may be confusing, but observe that $dG(x \mid x - 0)/dx$ means that we should "differentiate G with respect to the first variable using the $(x > \xi)$-form, and then let $\xi \to x$." Explicitly,

$$\frac{dG}{dx} (x \mid x - 0) = \lim_{\substack{\xi \to x \\ \xi < x}} \frac{y_2'(x) y_1(\xi)}{p(\xi) W(\xi)} = \frac{y_2'(x) y_1(x)}{p(x) W(x)}.$$

For $dG(x \mid x + 0)/dx$, we must use the $(x < \xi)$-form:

$$\frac{dG}{dx} (x \mid x + 0) = \lim_{\substack{\xi \to x \\ \xi > x}} \frac{y_1'(x) y_2(\xi)}{p(\xi) W(\xi)} = \frac{y_1'(x) y_2(x)}{p(x) W(x)}.$$

Introducing all these results into the differential equation

$$p(x) \frac{d^2 y}{dx^2} + p'(x) \frac{dy}{dx} - s(x) y = f(x),$$

we obtain

$$\int_a^x [p(x)G''(x \mid \xi) + p'(x)G'(x \mid \xi) - s(x)G(x \mid \xi)]f(\xi)\,d\xi$$

$$+ \int_x^b [p(x)G''(x \mid \xi) + p'(x)G'(x \mid \xi) - s(x)G(x \mid \xi)]f(\xi)\,d\xi$$

$$+ p(x)\frac{f(x)}{p(x)} = f(x).$$

Since

$$p(x)G''(x \mid \xi) + p'(x)G'(x \mid \xi) - s(x)G(x \mid \xi) = 0,$$

(except for $x = \xi$ which does not affect the values of the integrals) we see that the DE is satisfied. As for the boundary conditions, we observe that

$$y(a) = \int_a^b G(a \mid \xi)f(\xi)\,d\xi, \qquad \frac{d}{dx}y(a) = \int_a^b \frac{d}{dx} G(a \mid \xi)f(\xi)\,d\xi,$$

and $\alpha_1 y(a) + \alpha_2 y'(a) = 0$ because this relation is satisfied by $G(a \mid \xi)$.

12.3 SERIES EXPANSIONS FOR $G(x \mid \xi)$

The explicit formula developed in the preceding section can be used only if we know the solutions of the homogeneous equation. Whether or not this is the case, there are other methods of constructing $G(x \mid \xi)$, for instance, by determining its expansion in a series of suitably chosen orthogonal functions.

Example 1. We desire to construct the Green's function for the nonhomogeneous problem*

$$\frac{d^2 u}{dx^2} = f(x) \qquad \text{with} \qquad u(0) = u(L) = 0.$$

Green's Function $G(x \mid \xi)$ must therefore satisfy

$$\frac{d^2 G}{dx^2} = \delta(x - \xi), \qquad \text{and} \qquad G(0 \mid \xi) = G(L \mid \xi) = 0.$$

Since $G(x \mid \xi)$ vanishes at the ends of the interval $(0, L)$, it follows that it can be expanded in a series of suitably chosen orthogonal functions such as, for instance, the Fourier sine series

$$G(x \mid \xi) = \sum_{n=1}^{\infty} \gamma_n(\xi) \sin \frac{n\pi x}{L},$$

where the expansion coefficients γ_n are expected to depend on the parameter ξ.†

---

* We have already solved this problem in Section 12.1, but it is instructive to try a different method and compare the results.

† Other systems of orthogonal functions could have been chosen. The functions $\sin (n\pi x/L)$ provide an easy solution—for obvious reasons.

It follows that*

$$\frac{d^2 G(x \mid \xi)}{dx^2} = \sum_{n=1}^{\infty} \left(-\frac{n^2 \pi^2}{L^2}\right) \gamma_n(\xi) \sin \frac{n\pi x}{L} \cdot$$

Also, if

$$\delta(x - \xi) = \sum_{n=1}^{\infty} \Delta_n(\xi) \sin \frac{n\pi x}{L},$$

then

$$\Delta_n(\xi) = \frac{2}{L} \int_0^L \delta(x - \xi) \sin \frac{n\pi x}{L} dx = \frac{2}{L} \sin \frac{n\pi \xi}{L} \cdot$$

Substituting the series into the DE for $G(x \mid \xi)$ and equating the coefficients, we obtain

$$\left(-\frac{n^2 \pi^2}{L^2}\right) \gamma_n(\xi) = \frac{2}{L} \sin \frac{n\pi \xi}{L}$$

so that

$$G(x \mid \xi) = -\frac{2L}{\pi^2} \sum_{n=1}^{\infty} \frac{1}{n^2} \sin \frac{n\pi \xi}{L} \sin \frac{n\pi x}{L} \cdot$$

This formula actually represents the same Green function that we had before,

$$G(x \mid \xi) = \begin{cases} -\dfrac{x(L - \xi)}{L} & (0 \leq x \leq \xi), \\ -\dfrac{\xi(L - x)}{L} & (\xi \leq x \leq L), \end{cases}$$

which can be verified directly by expanding the latter expression in a Fourier sine series.

Exercise. Perform the expansion and verify this statement.

We can now use the series for $G(x \mid \xi)$ to construct the solution of the non-homogeneous equation according to the formula

$$y(x) = \int_0^L G(x \mid \xi) f(\xi) \, d\xi,$$

which leads to

$$y(x) = -\frac{2L}{\pi^2} \sum_{n=1}^{\infty} \frac{1}{n^2} \sin \frac{n\pi x}{L} \int_0^L f(\xi) \sin \frac{n\pi \xi}{L} \, d\xi,$$

or

$$y(x) = -\frac{L^2}{\pi^2} \sum_{n=1}^{\infty} \frac{1}{n^2} a_n \sin \frac{n\pi x}{L},$$

where a_n are the Fourier sine coefficients of $f(x)$.

---

* Treat $G(x \mid \xi)$ as a distribution.

This result gives us the solution in the form of a Fourier sine series, a direct consequence of the choice of expansion for $G(x \mid \xi)$. Of course, it could have been obtained by other methods, e.g., by direct expansion of $f(x)$ and $y(x)$ into Fourier sine series (compare with Section 4.8, Example 2) or by the finite transform method (Section 8.6), which amount to the same thing.

Viewed in this light, Green's function may be more valuable for computations if it is known in "closed form." For instance, the expression

$$y(x) = \int_0^x \frac{x(\xi - L)}{L} f(\xi)\, d\xi + \int_x^L \frac{\xi(x - L)}{L} f(\xi)\, d\xi$$

is usually considered to be simpler than the Fourier series for $y(x)$.*

Example 2. A stretched string is subjected to forced vibrations by an external force $F(x, t)$ per unit length which varies harmonically with time.

The equation to be solved is now

$$T\frac{\partial^2 u}{\partial x^2} - \rho\frac{\partial^2 u}{\partial t^2} = F(x, t),$$

where $F(x, t)$ can be represented in the form

$$F(x, t) = f(x)e^{-i\omega t}.$$

We expect the solution $u(x, t)$ to possess the same time dependence†

$$u(x, t) = y(x)e^{-i\omega t}.$$

This implies that $y(x)$ satisfies the differential equation

$$\frac{d^2 y}{dx^2} + k^2 y = \frac{f(x)}{T} \qquad \left(k^2 = \frac{\omega^2}{c^2} = \frac{\omega^2 T}{\rho}\right),$$

as well as the boundary conditions $y(0) = y(L) = 0$.

We shall now seek the Green's function satisfying

$$\frac{d^2 G}{dx^2} + k^2 G = \delta(x - \xi), \qquad G(0 \mid \xi) = G(L \mid \xi) = 0.$$

Let us use again the method of the Fourier sine series (or finite Fourier sine transform). For instance, let us multiply both sides of the DE by $\sin(n\pi x/L)$

---

* This may be very deceiving, however; $f(\xi)$ may be given in a form ill suited for the above integrals, while its Fourier sine series may be very rapidly converging and the first few terms may be known.

† All other frequencies present in an initial Fourier spectrum for $u(x, t)$ will "die out" in due course of time since, in practice, the string is subject to damping, which we have neglected.

and integrate over $(0, L)$ to obtain immediately

$$-\frac{n^2\pi^2}{L^2}\frac{L}{2}\gamma_n(\xi) + k^2\frac{L}{2}\gamma_n(\xi) = \sin\frac{n\pi\xi}{L},$$

where

$$\frac{L}{2}\gamma_n(\xi) = \int_0^L G(x \mid \xi)\sin\frac{n\pi x}{L}\,dx,$$

with $\gamma_n(\xi)$ being the Fourier coefficient of $G(x \mid \xi)$. It follows that

$$\gamma_n(\xi) = \frac{2}{L}\frac{\sin(n\pi\xi/L)}{k^2 - n^2\pi^2/L^2}$$

and

$$G(x \mid \xi) = \frac{2}{L}\sum_{n=1}^{\infty}\frac{\sin(n\pi\xi/L)\sin(n\pi x/L)}{k^2 - n^2\pi^2/L^2}.$$

The appearance of this form is very revealing. First, the symmetry of Green's function is obvious. Secondly, the formula fails if it happens that

$$k^2 = \frac{n^2\pi^2}{L^2}$$

for some positive integer n. This is exactly the situation when $G(x \mid \xi)$ *does not exist*. Indeed, if $k^2 = n^2\pi^2/L^2$, then the homogeneous equation reads

$$\frac{d^2y}{dx^2} + \frac{n^2\pi^2}{L^2}y = 0$$

and it happens to possess a *nontrivial solution*, namely, $\sin(n\pi x/L)$, satisfying the prescribed boundary conditions. If the parameter $k^2 = \lambda$ is viewed as a variable parameter, then $G(x \mid \xi)$ is a function of λ. In the language of functions of a complex variable,* we may say that Green's function possesses simple poles at $\lambda = n^2\pi^2/L^2$ ($n = 1, 2, 3, \ldots$). Note that in our previous example concerning static deflections of a stretched string, this situation did not arise. The homogeneous equation was

$$\frac{d^2y}{dx^2} = 0$$

and did not possess nontrivial solutions satisfying boundary conditions.

    We know from our familiarity with the physics of this problem that those cases where $G(x \mid \xi)$ does not exist are examples of *resonance*. Indeed, in these cases,

$$\omega = \frac{n\pi c}{L},$$

---

* Extension of real physical variables into the complex domain is a powerful analytical tool, whether or not it has any immediate physical significance.

implying that the external frequency matches one of the characteristic frequencies of the string itself. Unless the process is checked by damping (and other moderating factors so far neglected), an external harmonic disturbance in resonance with a natural frequency will excite the corresponding mode of vibration until the rupture occurs. There can be no steady-state solution.

The function $G(x \mid \xi)$ for our problem can also be determined by direct construction, i.e., by joining the solutions of the homogeneous problem at $x = \xi$. A solution of

$$\frac{d^2y}{dx^2} + k^2y = 0$$

which vanishes at $x = 0$ is $\sin kx$; a solution which vanishes at $x = L$ is $\sin k(L - x)$. Their Wronskian is

$$W = -\sin kx k \cos k(L - x) - k \cos kx \sin k(L - x)$$
$$= -k \sin (x + L - x) = -k \sin kL,$$

yielding immediately

$$G(x \mid \xi) = \begin{cases} - \dfrac{\sin kx \sin k(L - \xi)}{k \sin kL} & (x < \xi), \\[2mm] - \dfrac{\sin k\xi \sin k(L - x)}{k \sin kL} & (x > \xi). \end{cases}$$

This form of $G(x \mid \xi)$ also shows that Green's function has poles in the complex k-plane for $k = n\pi/L$, where n is a nonzero integer.* These poles correspond to $\lambda = n^2\pi^2/L^2$ if the λ-plane is used. The equivalence of the two forms of Green's function can be demonstrated by expanding $G(x \mid \xi)$ in the Fourier sine series. Alternatively, the series may be summed, using the techniques of the calculus of residues.

We shall summarize the expansion technique employed in the above two examples by the following statements of a fairly general nature: Suppose that we want to solve the differential equation

$$\mathcal{L}y(x) = f(x),$$

where $\mathcal{L}$ is a Sturm-Liouville differential operator. Also, we want $y(x)$ to satisfy the boundary conditions

$$\mathcal{B}y(x) = 0 \quad \text{(on the boundary)},$$

where $\mathcal{B}$ is the boundary condition operator, namely, an expression of the form

$$\mathcal{B} = \begin{cases} \alpha_1 + \alpha_2 \dfrac{d}{dx} & \text{(at } x = a), \\[2mm] \beta_1 + \beta_2 \dfrac{d}{dx} & \text{(at } x = b). \end{cases}$$

---

* There is no pole at $k = 0$ as easy inspection shows.

We seek Green's function $G(x \mid \xi)$ satisfying

$$\mathcal{L}G = \delta(x - \xi), \qquad \mathcal{B}G = 0.$$

We utilize the set of eigenfunctions $\varphi_\lambda(x)$ of the operator $\mathcal{L}$, namely, the functions satisfying

$$\mathcal{L}\varphi_\lambda(x) = \lambda\varphi_\lambda(x), \qquad \mathcal{B}\varphi_\lambda = 0.$$

If G exists and if the set $\{\varphi_\lambda\}$ is complete, then G can be represented in the form

$$G(x \mid \xi) = \sum_\lambda \gamma_\lambda(\xi)\varphi_\lambda(x),$$

(summation over the entire spectrum of eigenvalues of $\mathcal{L}$). Applying the operator $\mathcal{L}$, we have

$$\mathcal{L}G(x \mid \xi) = \sum_\lambda \gamma_\lambda(\xi)\mathcal{L}\varphi_\lambda(x) = \sum_\lambda \gamma_\lambda(\xi)\lambda\varphi_\lambda(x) = \delta(x - \xi).$$

We multiply both sides by $\varphi_{\lambda'}(x)$ and integrate over x:

$$\sum_\lambda \gamma_\lambda(\xi)\lambda\int_a^b \varphi_{\lambda'}(x)\varphi_\lambda(x)\, dx = \varphi_{\lambda'}(\xi).$$

This set of equations may be used to determine the $\gamma_\lambda(\xi)$. It is easily solved if the eigenfunctions $\varphi_\lambda(x)$ are *orthonormal;** then

$$\int_a^b \varphi_{\lambda'}(x)\varphi_\lambda(x)\, dx = \delta_{\lambda'\lambda} \qquad \text{and} \qquad \gamma_\lambda(\xi) = \frac{\varphi_\lambda(\xi)}{\lambda}.$$

This leads us to the so-called *bilinear formula*

$$G(x \mid \xi) = \sum_\lambda \frac{\varphi_\lambda(\xi)\varphi_\lambda(x)}{\lambda},$$

which permits us to write Green's function at once if the eigenvalues and eigenfunctions of $\mathcal{L}$ are known.

Remarks

1. Very often the DE to be solved has the form

$$\mathcal{L}y - \lambda y = f,$$

where λ is an *arbitrary* parameter. In this case the *actual eigenvalues* of $\mathcal{L}$ are usually denoted by λ_n, the eigenfunctions by $\varphi_n(x)$, and the bilinear formula reads

$$G(x \mid \xi) = \sum_n \frac{\varphi_n(\xi)\varphi_n(x)}{\lambda_n - \lambda}.$$

It is in the framework of this problem that we talk about the poles of Green's function, in the λ-plane, and the resonance phenomena.

---

* The cases of degeneracy may cause some problems.

2. In complex spaces of functions the bilinear formula is modified to read

$$G(x \mid \xi) = \sum_\lambda \frac{\varphi_\lambda^*(\xi)\varphi_\lambda(x)}{\lambda}$$

and Green's function is not symmetric, but rather hermitian under the interchange of x and ξ:

$$G(x \mid \xi) = G^*(x \mid \xi).$$

The eigenfunction expansion approach to Green's function can be extended to two or more variables. It must be remembered, however, that the corresponding partial differential operators and the boundary conditions must be such as to possess complete sets of eigenfunctions necessary for series expansions.

12.4 GREEN'S FUNCTIONS IN TWO DIMENSIONS

Let us consider a nonhomogeneous PDE in two space variables such as, for instance, the Poisson equation

$$\frac{\partial^2 u}{\partial x^2} + \frac{\partial^2 u}{\partial y^2} = f(x, y).$$

To be specific, we shall discuss the static deflection of a rectangular membrane. Then the known function $f(x, y)$ represents the external load per unit area, divided by T (tension in the membrane; see Section 8.8).

The deflection $u(x, y)$ of the membrane must satisfy the boundary conditions

$$u(0, y) = u(a, y) = 0, \qquad u(x, 0) = u(x, b) = 0.$$

A concentrated force F acting at the point (ξ, η) may be simulated by a two-dimensional δ-function†

$$\frac{F}{T} \delta(x - \xi)\, \delta(y - \eta).$$

According to the concepts of superposition, if we solve the equation

$$\frac{\partial^2 G}{\partial x^2} + \frac{\partial^2 G}{\partial y^2} = \delta(x - \xi)\, \delta(y - \eta)$$

and obtain the two-dimensional Green's function $G(x \mid \xi; y \mid \eta)$, then we can represent the solution of the original PDE by the integral

$$u(x, t) = \int_0^a \int_0^b G(x \mid \xi; y \mid \eta) f(\xi, \eta)\, d\xi\, d\eta.$$

Of course, $G(x \mid \xi; y \mid \eta)$ must satisfy the same boundary conditions as $u(x, t)$.

One way to approach the problem of obtaining Green's function is to employ the expansions in terms of the eigenfunctions $\varphi_\lambda(x, y)$ of the Laplace differential

---

† See p. 257.

operator, namely, the functions satisfying

$$\nabla^2 \varphi_\lambda(x, y) = \lambda \varphi_\lambda(x, y)$$

and the same boundary conditions we are dealing with. We know that the eigenvalues are of the form

$$\lambda_{mn} = -\left(\frac{m^2\pi^2}{a^2} + \frac{n^2\pi^2}{b^2}\right) \qquad (m, n = 1, 2, 3, \ldots)$$

and the corresponding eigenfunctions read

$$\varphi_{mn}(x, y) = \frac{2}{\sqrt{ab}} \sin \frac{m\pi x}{a} \sin \frac{n\pi y}{b};$$

we have normalized them to unity, for convenience. Therefore we seek $G(x \mid \xi; y \mid \eta)$ in the form

$$G(x \mid \xi; y \mid \eta) = \frac{2}{\sqrt{ab}} \sum_{m=1}^{\infty} \sum_{n=1}^{\infty} A_{mn}(\xi, \eta) \sin \frac{m\pi x}{a} \sin \frac{n\pi y}{b}.$$

Substituting this into the PDE for G, we obtain, by standard techniques,

$$-\left(\frac{m^2\pi^2}{a^2} + \frac{n^2\pi^2}{b^2}\right) A_{mn} = \frac{2}{\sqrt{ab}} \sin \frac{m\pi \xi}{a} \sin \frac{n\pi \eta}{b},$$

which immediately yields

$$G(x \mid \xi; y \mid \eta) = -\frac{4}{ab} \sum_{m=1}^{\infty} \sum_{n=1}^{\infty} \frac{\sin \dfrac{m\pi x}{a} \sin \dfrac{m\pi \xi}{a} \sin \dfrac{n\pi y}{b} \sin \dfrac{n\pi \eta}{b}}{\dfrac{m^2\pi^2}{a^2} + \dfrac{n^2\pi^2}{b^2}}.$$

This expression is recognized as the bilinear formula for Green's function. The solution of the Poisson equation can now be written as

$$u(x, t) = -\sum_{m=1}^{\infty} \sum_{n=1}^{\infty} \frac{a_{mn}}{m^2\pi^2/a^2 + n^2\pi^2/b^2} \sin \frac{m\pi x}{a} \sin \frac{n\pi y}{b},$$

where a_{mn} are the appropriate expansion coefficients for the function $f(x, y)$,

$$a_{mn} = \int_0^a \int_0^b f(x, y)\varphi_{mn}(x, y) \, dx \, dy.$$

Another way of obtaining Green's function is by means of a *single series*. Let us start by satisfying only two boundary conditions, namely, those along the edges $y = 0$ and $y = b$. This can be done by representing Green's function as a single normalized Fourier sine series with respect to y:

$$G(x \mid \xi; y \mid \eta) = \sqrt{\frac{2}{b}} \sum_{n=1}^{\infty} g_n(x) \sin \frac{n\pi y}{b},$$

where the coefficients g_n are left as undetermined functions of x.* Feeding this series into the PDE for G, multiplying by $\sqrt{2/b}\,\sin(m\pi y/b)$, and integrating over y, we obtain

$$\frac{d^2 g_m(x)}{dx^2} - \frac{m^2\pi^2}{b^2} g_m(x) = \sqrt{\frac{2}{b}}\,\sin\frac{m\pi\eta}{b}\,\delta(x - \xi).$$

This DE shows that the expansion coefficients $g_n(x)$ are one-dimensional Green's functions in their own right.† We may find them by connecting the solutions of the homogeneous DE as in Section 12.2. The solutions of

$$\frac{d^2 g_n}{dx^2} - \frac{n^2\pi^2}{b^2} g_n = 0$$

are exponential or hyperbolic functions. For the region $x < \xi$, we must choose a solution vanishing at $x = 0$; it reads

$$g_n(x) = A_n \sinh\frac{n\pi x}{b} \qquad (x < \xi),$$

where A_n remains arbitrary.

The corresponding solution for $x > \xi$ must vanish at $x = a$ and may be chosen in the form

$$g_n(x) = B_n \sinh\frac{n\pi(a - x)}{b} \qquad (x > \xi).$$

We connect these two forms at $x = \xi$ by requiring the continuity of g_n,

$$A_n \sinh\frac{n\pi\xi}{b} = B_n \sinh\frac{n\pi(a - \xi)}{b},$$

and the appropriate jump discontinuity of dg_n/dx:

$$-\frac{n\pi}{b} B_n \cosh\frac{n\pi(a - \xi)}{b} - \frac{n\pi}{b} A_n \cosh\frac{n\pi\xi}{b} = \sqrt{\frac{2}{b}}\,\sin\frac{n\pi\eta}{b}.$$

Solving for A_n and B_n and simplifying by the use of a formula from "hyperbolic trigonometry,"‡ we obtain

$$A_n = -\frac{\sqrt{2b}}{n\pi}\sin\frac{n\pi\eta}{b}\,\frac{\sinh\dfrac{n\pi(a - \xi)}{b}}{\sinh\dfrac{n\pi a}{b}}, \qquad B_n = -\frac{\sqrt{2b}}{n\pi}\sin\frac{n\pi\eta}{b}\,\frac{\sinh\dfrac{n\pi\xi}{b}}{\sinh\dfrac{n\pi a}{b}}.$$

---

* The g_n-coefficients also depend on ξ and η.
† The factor $\sqrt{2/b}\,\sin(m\pi\eta/b)$ on the right is immaterial since it is constant.
‡ $\sinh\alpha\cosh\beta + \cosh\alpha\sinh\beta = \sinh(\alpha + \beta)$.

This yields the Green function

$$
G(x \mid \xi; y \mid \eta) =
\begin{cases}
-\sum_{n=1}^{\infty} \dfrac{2}{n\pi} \dfrac{\sinh \dfrac{n\pi(a - \xi)}{b} \sinh \dfrac{n\pi x}{b}}{\sinh \dfrac{n\pi a}{b}} \sin \dfrac{n\pi \eta}{b} \sin \dfrac{n\pi y}{b} \quad (x < \xi), \\[4ex]
-\sum_{n=1}^{\infty} \dfrac{2}{n\pi} \dfrac{\sinh \dfrac{n\pi\xi}{b} \sinh \dfrac{n\pi(a - x)}{b}}{\sinh \dfrac{n\pi a}{b}} \sin \dfrac{n\pi \eta}{b} \sin \dfrac{n\pi y}{b} \quad (x > \xi).
\end{cases}
$$

Evidently, this form is the result of summation over m of the double Fourier sine series. A similar formula can be obtained by summation over n:

$$
G(x \mid \xi; y \mid \eta) =
\begin{cases}
-\sum_{m=1}^{\infty} \dfrac{2}{m\pi} \dfrac{\sinh \dfrac{m\pi(b - \eta)}{a} \sinh \dfrac{m\pi y}{a}}{\sinh \dfrac{m\pi b}{a}} \sin \dfrac{m\pi \xi}{a} \sin \dfrac{m\pi x}{a} \\[4ex]
\hspace{10cm} (y < \eta), \\[2ex]
-\sum_{m=1}^{\infty} \dfrac{2}{m\pi} \dfrac{\sinh \dfrac{m\pi \eta}{a} \sinh \dfrac{m\pi(b - y)}{a}}{\sinh \dfrac{m\pi b}{a}} \sin \dfrac{m\pi \xi}{a} \sin \dfrac{m\pi x}{a} \\[4ex]
\hspace{10cm} (y > \eta).
\end{cases}
$$

These two formulas represent the extension of the method of direct construction of a one-dimensional Green function, as opposed to a bilinear formula. For this particular problem this is as close as we can get to the "closed form" of $G(x \mid \xi; y \mid \eta)$.

12.5 GREEN'S FUNCTIONS FOR INITIAL CONDITIONS

The idea of superposition employed in the solution of the nonhomogeneous DE may also be applied to the treatment of the initial conditions for the homogeneous DE. As an example, consider the solution of the one-dimensional heat-conduction equation

$$
\frac{\partial^2 u}{\partial x^2} = \frac{1}{a^2} \frac{\partial u}{\partial t} \quad (-\infty < x < +\infty, \ 0 < t < \infty)
$$

subject to the boundary conditions $u(\pm\infty, t) = 0$ and the initial condition $u(x, 0) = f(x)$.* This problem may represent, for instance, the behavior of an infinite rod insulated on the sides and given an arbitrary initial temperature distribution $f(x)$. It is trivial to verify that the solution $u(x, t)$ depends *linearly* on the initial condition $f(x)$: If $u_1(x, t)$ and $u_2(x, t)$ are the solutions corresponding

---

* Evidently, $f(\pm\infty) = 0$ is required. Alternatively, we may require that $f(x)$ and $u(x, t)$ are bounded.

to initial conditions $f_1(x)$ and $f_2(x)$, respectively, then $C_1u_1 + C_2u_2$ is the solution corresponding to the initial condition $C_1f_1 + C_2f_2$. This property suggests that we try to construct the function $g(x \mid \xi; t)$ satisfying

$$\frac{\partial^2 g}{\partial x^2} = \frac{1}{a^2} \frac{\partial g}{\partial t} \qquad g(\pm\infty \mid \xi; t) = 0 \qquad g(x \mid \xi; 0) = \delta(x - \xi).$$

Then, presumably, the solution for an arbitrary initial condition $u(x, 0) = f(x)$ can be calculated from

$$u(x, t) = \int_{-\infty}^{+\infty} g(x \mid \xi; t)f(\xi)\, d\xi.$$

The function $g(x \mid \xi; t)$ may be called the *initial-condition Green's function*.

The nature of the boundary conditions indicates that we should use the Fourier transform to find $g(x \mid \xi; t)$. Let

$$g_F(k \mid \xi; t) = \mathcal{F}\{g(x \mid \xi; t)\}.$$

Then, transforming the PDE and the initial condition,

$$\frac{dg_F}{dt} = -a^2k^2g_F, \qquad g_F(k \mid \xi; 0) = \frac{1}{\sqrt{2\pi}} e^{ik\xi},$$

solving, and using the formulas

$$\mathcal{F}^{-1}\left\{\frac{1}{\sqrt{2\pi}} e^{ik\xi}\right\} = \delta(x - \xi), \qquad \mathcal{F}^{-1}\{e^{-a^2k^2t}\} = \frac{1}{\sqrt{4\pi a^2 t}} e^{-x^2/4a^2t},$$

and inverting by the convolution theorem, we obtain

$$g(x \mid \xi; t) = \frac{1}{\sqrt{4\pi a^2 t}} \int_{-\infty}^{+\infty} \delta(x' - \xi)e^{-(x'-x)^2/4a^2t}\, dx' = \frac{1}{\sqrt{4\pi a^2 t}} e^{-(x-\xi)^2/4a^2t}.$$

This function is sometimes called the *point-source solution** of the heat-conduction equation. We actually derived it earlier in the salt-diffusion problem in Section 8.5.

We can now build the solution of the heat-conduction equation with arbitrary initial conditions by a "superposition"

$$u(x, t) = \frac{1}{\sqrt{4\pi a^2 t}} \int_{-\infty}^{+\infty} e^{-(x-\xi)^2/4a^2t} f(\xi)\, d\xi,$$

sometimes called the Poisson integral. It is now possible to verify that it actually represents the solution of the problem.

Indeed, using the fact that $f(x)$ is bounded, we can show that the integral converges uniformly for $t > t_0$, where $t_0 \neq 0$ but is otherwise arbitrarily small. Therefore, it can be differentiated under the integral sign with respect to the

---

* The reason for this name will become clear shortly.

parameters x and t and must satisfy the PDE since $g(x \mid \xi; t)$ does. The boundary conditions are verified in a similar fashion. To show that $u(x, t) \to f(x)$ as $t \to 0$, note that $g \to \delta(x - \xi)$ as $t \to 0$ (see Chapter 6). Consequently, if $f(x)$ is infinitely differentiable and vanishes outside a finite region D, the statement follows. The generalization to a piecewise continuous $f(x)$ is obtained by the methods employed in the proof of the smudging theorem of Chapter 6.

While we are dealing with the heat-conduction equation, let us inquire what the analog of the Green's function $G(x \mid \xi; y \mid \eta)$ from the membrane-problem of the preceding section would be. This Green's function will have to deal with the nonhomogeneous PDE of the form

$$\frac{\partial u}{\partial t} - a^2 \frac{\partial^2 u}{\partial x^2} = f(x, t),$$

representing the physical situation in which heat is being generated continuously, with the function $f(x, t)$ representing the *density of heat sources** divided by $c\rho$. The appropriate boundary conditions are still the same,

$$u(\pm\infty) = 0,$$

while the initial condition must now be homogeneous,

$$u(x, 0) = 0.$$

This last condition follows from the fact that the initial conditions are, mathematically speaking, the boundary conditions with respect to the time variable. Since the time t now replaces the second variable y in the membrane problem, the vanishing of u at $t = 0$ is the required analog. There is only one initial condition because the PDE is of the first order with respect to t.

The sought function $G(x \mid \xi; t \mid \tau)$ is then supposed to satisfy

$$\frac{\partial G}{\partial t} - a^2 \frac{\partial^2 G}{\partial x^2} = \delta(x - \xi)\,\delta(t - \tau) \qquad (t > 0, \tau > 0),$$

and

$$G(\pm\infty \mid \xi; t \mid \tau) = 0 \qquad G(x \mid \xi; 0 \mid \tau) = 0.$$

We can find G by transform methods. Taking Fourier transform with respect to x ($G_F = \mathcal{F}\{G\}$), we obtain

$$\frac{dG_F}{dt} + a^2 k^2 G_F = \frac{e^{ik\xi}}{\sqrt{2\pi}}\,\delta(t - \tau).$$

Now, we take the Laplace transform with respect to t ($G_{FL} = \mathcal{L}\{G_F\}$) and use the initial condition to obtain

$$sG_{FL} + a^2 k^2 G_{FL} = \frac{e^{ik\xi}}{\sqrt{2\pi}} e^{-s\tau}.$$

---

* Amount of heat generated per unit volume and unit time (see Section 8.4).

We solve for G_{FL} and invert, using the shifting and attenuation properties (Section 5.3) and deduce

$$G_F = \frac{e^{ik\xi}}{\sqrt{2\pi}}\, e^{-a^2k^2(t-\tau)} S(t-\tau),$$

where $S(t-\tau)$ is the step-function. The inversion with respect to the Fourier transform can be accomplished by the convolution theorem:

$$G = S(t-\tau)\int_{-\infty}^{+\infty} \delta(x'-\xi)\frac{1}{\sqrt{4\pi a^2(t-\tau)}}\, e^{-(x-x')^2/4a^2(t-\tau)}\, dx'$$

$$= \frac{S(t-\tau)}{\sqrt{4\pi a^2(t-\tau)}}\, e^{-(x-\xi)^2/4a^2(t-\tau)}.$$

If we now want to build up the solution of the nonhomogeneous PDE with arbitrary $f(x, t)$, then we must collect the contributions from all sources spread over space and time. Since G vanishes for $\tau > t$,* it is clear that the integration over τ is effectively confined to the interval $(0, t)$ and we will obtain

$$u(x, t) = \int_0^t \int_{-\infty}^{+\infty} \frac{1}{\sqrt{4\pi a^2(t-\tau)}}\, e^{-(x-\xi)^2/4a^2(t-\tau)} f(\xi, \tau)\, d\xi\, d\tau.$$

The proof that this formula solves our problem is straightforward.

Now note that there is a close relationship between the two Green's functions $g(x\mid\xi; t)$ and $G(x\mid\xi; t\mid\tau)$:

$$G(x\mid\xi; t\mid\tau) = g(x\mid\xi; t-\tau).$$

It is instructive to trace this relationship to the physical meaning of both Green's functions. To start with, suppose that in the first problem the initial conditions were not specified at $t = 0$, but rather at time $t = \tau$. Evidently the solution to the problem would become

$$u(x, t) = \frac{1}{\sqrt{4\pi a^2(t-\tau)}}\int_{-\infty}^{+\infty} e^{-(x-\xi)^2/4a^2(t-\tau)} f(\xi)\, d\xi$$

and would be valid for $t > \tau$. What about $t < \tau$? According to the principles of thermodynamics this would be an "unphysical" question, because from a given temperature distribution it is impossible to tell what it should have been a certain time ago.† However, we may attach physical significance to the situation for

---

* This is expected on physical grounds. The temperature at time t and arbitrary x cannot be influenced by heat generated at a later time τ (no matter where).

† The reason is that the theory of thermal phenomena is a *probabilistic* theory: We do not really *predict* them, but rather accept as an answer the *most probable outcome* from given initial conditions.

which we arbitrarily set

$$u(x, t) = 0 \qquad (\text{for } t < \tau).$$

This would mean that the temperature distribution $f(x)$ arose suddenly at time $t = \tau$ and, therefore, there must have been an instantaneous generation of heat at time $t = \tau$. In the "volume element" $d\xi$* there has been generated an amount of heat

$$\delta Q = c\rho f(\xi) \, d\xi \qquad (\text{at time } \tau).$$

This heat contributed an amount δu to the temperature $u(x, t)$ at another point x and at a later time t, given by

$$\delta u = g(x \mid \xi; t - \tau) f(\xi) \, d\xi;$$

note that g depends on $c\rho$. Now, the heat δQ could not really be generated instantaneously, but in some small interval of time $d\tau$. If the *rate* of heat generation per unit volume is $\varphi(\xi, \tau)$, then we can write

$$\delta Q = c\rho\varphi(\xi, \tau) \, d\xi \, d\tau,$$

and

$$\delta u = g(x \mid \xi; t - \tau)\varphi(\xi, \tau) \, d\xi \, d\tau.$$

By the linearity of the heat-conduction equation, the contributions δu arising from the various δQ can be added. Collecting the contributions from all points ξ and all instants of time τ between 0 and t,† we obtain

$$u(x, t) = \int_0^t \int_{-\infty}^{+\infty} g(x \mid \xi; t - \tau)\varphi(\xi, \tau) \, d\xi \, d\tau.$$

We have then solved the second problem (nonhomogeneous PDE) starting from the solution of the first one (homogeneous PDE with initial conditions), because the meaning of $f(x, t)$ in the nonhomogeneous PDE is "heat source density divided by $c\rho$." This identifies $\varphi(\xi, \tau)$ with $f(\xi, \tau)$ and explains the relationship between the two Green's functions.

12.6 GREEN'S FUNCTIONS WITH REFLECTION PROPERTIES

The heat conduction problem treated in the preceding section exhibits very interesting features if the infinite rod is replaced by a semi-infinite rod extending from $x = 0$ to $x = +\infty$. In this case, certain boundary conditions at the end $x = 0$

---

* Recall that we are dealing with a one-dimensional problem. For the case of a rod of cross section A, the volume element is, strictly speaking, $A \, d\xi$.

† If we know that the temperature was zero at $t = 0$ we may assume that no heat was generated prior to this moment, because *no record* of any such heat has been left.

must be prescribed. We shall now consider two cases of such conditions:
a) Homogeneous Dirichlet: $u(0, t) = 0$.
b) Homogeneous Neumann: $\dfrac{\partial u}{\partial x}(0, t) = 0$.

The temperature $u(x, t)$ is then required to satisfy the PDE

$$\frac{\partial^2 u}{\partial x^2} = \frac{1}{a^2}\frac{\partial u}{\partial t},$$

the "boundary condition at infinity" $u(\infty, t) < \infty$ (see the footnote, p. 523), and the initial condition $u(x, 0) = f(x)$, in addition to one of the boundary conditions stated above. As before, we shall attempt to represent the solution in the form of a "continuous" superposition

$$u(x, t) = \int_0^\infty g(x \mid \xi; t) f(\xi)\, d\xi$$

and thereby evaluate the appropriate Green's function $g(x \mid \xi; t)$.

The problem can be solved, for instance, by transform methods (as in Section 12.5) except that now the Fourier sine transform for case (a) and the Fourier cosine transform for case (b) are most appropriate.* It is instructive, however, to utilize the solution for the infinite rod by applying certain symmetry considerations.

It is not hard to verify that if the initial temperature $f(x)$ for the infinite rod is an odd (even) function of x, then the solution $u(x, t)$ must also be an odd (even) function of x.† Indeed, in the explicit form for the solution

$$u(x, t) = \frac{1}{\sqrt{4\pi a^2 t}} \int_{-\infty}^{+\infty} e^{-(x-\xi)^2/4a^2 t} f(\xi)\, d\xi,$$

change x into $-x$, make a change in the dummy variable $\xi = -\xi'$, and deduce the behavior of $u(x, t)$ according to $f(-\xi') = \pm f(\xi')$. An immediate corollary is that if $f(x)$ is an odd function, then $u(0, t) = 0$; also, if $f(x)$ is an even function, then $\partial u(0, t)/\partial x$.

Remark. The mathematical reason for these properties of the solution is the fact that the PDE is *invariant under reflection;* i.e., it does not change its form under the change of variable $x = -x'$. For a given initial temperature, the PDE determines how the temperature develops in time and thus preserves the original symmetry of the temperature distribution.

These observations suggest that the following idea be applied to a semi-infinite rod: For case (a) let us extend the function $f(x)$, defined for $x > 0$, into

---

* The Fourier sine transform is suited for the problems where the value of the function is known at $x = 0$, but the value of its derivative is not. The Fourier cosine transform is suited for the opposite case.

† This idea has been mentioned on p. 310 in connection with the Laplace equation.

the region $x < 0$ in an antisymmetric fashion, i.e., define

$$\bar{f}(x) = \begin{cases} f(x) & (x > 0), \\ -f(-x) & (x < 0). \end{cases}$$

For this initial condition the temperature in an infinite rod would be

$$\bar{u}(x, t) = \int_{-\infty}^{0} \frac{[-f(-\xi)]}{\sqrt{4\pi a^2 t}} e^{-(x-\xi)^2/4a^2 t} \, d\xi + \int_{0}^{\infty} \frac{f(\xi)}{\sqrt{4\pi a^2 t}} e^{-(x-\xi)^2/4a^2 t} \, d\xi.$$

Next we change the dummy variable by $\xi = -\xi'$ in the first integral and then drop the primes to obtain

$$\bar{u}(x, t) = \frac{1}{\sqrt{4\pi a^2 t}} \int_{0}^{\infty} \{e^{-(x-\xi)^2/4a^2 t} - e^{-(x+\xi)^2/4a^2 t}\} f(\xi) \, d\xi.$$

We now claim that for $x > 0$, this formula also represents the solution for the semi-infinite rod; we can write

$$u(x, t) = \int_{0}^{\infty} g(x \mid \xi; t) f(\xi) \, d\xi,$$

where

$$g(x \mid \xi; t) = \frac{1}{\sqrt{4\pi a^2 t}} \{e^{-(x-\xi)^2/4a^2 t} - e^{-(x+\xi)^2/4a^2 t}\}.$$

Indeed, $u(x, t)$ evidently satisfies the PDE and the boundary condition at $x = 0$. As for the initial condition, it is interesting to see that Green's function does not reduce to $\delta(x - \xi)$ for $t = 0$, but rather to

$$g(x \mid \xi; 0) = \delta(x - \xi) - \delta(x + \xi).$$

Note, however, that for $x > 0$ the second δ-function contributes nothing, since

$$\int_{0}^{\infty} \delta(x + \xi) f(\xi) \, d\xi = 0 \quad (x > 0).$$

Therefore

$$u(x, 0) = \int_{0}^{\infty} \delta(x - \xi) f(\xi) \, d\xi = f(x) \quad (x > 0),$$

as required.

It should be obvious that the treatment of case (b), the Neumann boundary condition, parallels the above derivation. We extend the function $f(x)$ into the region $x < 0$ in a symmetric manner,

$$\bar{f}(x) = \begin{cases} f(x) & (x > 0), \\ f(-x) & (x < 0), \end{cases}$$

and proceed in the same fashion as before. This results in the change of sign in the second term for the Green's function:

$$g(x \mid \xi; t) = \frac{1}{\sqrt{4\pi a^2 t}} \{e^{-(x-\xi)^2/4a^2 t} + e^{-(x+\xi)^2/4a^2 t}\}.$$

Remark. The Green's function appropriate for the nonhomogeneous PDE is related to the above Green's functions for the initial condition in the same way as for the infinite rod. The solution of the problem

$$\frac{\partial u}{\partial t} - a^2 \frac{\partial^2 u}{\partial x^2} = f(x, t) \quad \text{with } u(\infty, t) < \infty,$$

$$u(x, 0) = 0,$$

and

$$\begin{cases} \text{either} & u(0, t) = 0, \\ \text{or} & \partial u(0, t)/\partial x = 0, \end{cases}$$

is

$$u(x, t) = \int_0^t \int_0^\infty G(x \mid \xi; t \mid \tau) f(\xi, \tau) \, d\xi \, d\tau,$$

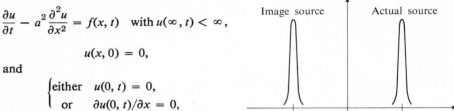

Figure 12.4

where $G(x \mid \xi; t \mid \tau) = g(x \mid \xi; t - \tau)$, with appropriate g for Dirichlet or Neumann boundary conditions. This result means that if we wish to find the temperature due to a point source of heat located at $x = \xi$ subject to, say, the Neumann condition $\partial u(0, t)/\partial x = 0$, then we must actually set up an image source at $x = -\xi$, as shown schematically in Fig. 12.4. As the temperature spreads from each source (Fig. 12.5, dashed lines), the total temperature is obtained by superposition (Fig. 12.5, solid line); the result is that the derivative $(\partial u/\partial x)_{x=0}$ is forced to be zero at all times.*

For Dirichlet conditions the image source is actually a "sink" (Fig. 12.6).† The method of satisfying the boundary conditions by means of construction of

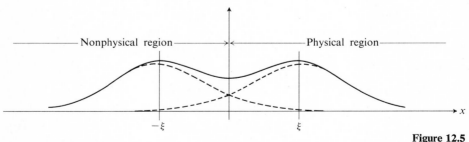

Figure 12.5

---

* Condition $(\partial u/\partial x)_{x=0}$ is equivalent to thermal insulation, i.e., there is no heat exchange, at $x = 0$. In our construction we compensate the loss of heat across the boundary $x = 0$ from the actual source by the influx of heat from the image source.

† This may be a misnomer, since the term "sink" presupposes the presence of heat which is to be absorbed. The mathematical formalism, however, makes no such assumptions at all. The term *source of negative heat* could be introduced, but it is not very illuminating.

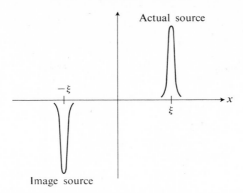

Figure 12.6

image sources can be used for the PDE of other types as well. The best-known examples are from electrostatics (applications to the Laplace equation).

Example. A semi-infinite rod is at a uniform temperature f_0 at a time t_0. Find the temperature at any later time t if the end of the rod ($x = 0$) is maintained at zero temperature.

Solution. The initial conditions at $t = t_0$ are reducible to those at $t = 0$ by replacing t by $t - t_0$ ("turning the clock") in Green's function. Therefore,

$$u(x, t) = \frac{f_0}{\sqrt{4\pi a^2(t - t_0)}} \int_0^\infty \{e^{-(x-\xi)^2/4a^2(t-t_0)} - e^{-(x+\xi)^2/4a^2(t-t_0)}\} \, d\xi \quad (t > t_0).$$

We use the substitutions

$$y = \frac{x - \xi}{2a\sqrt{t - t_0}}$$

and

$$z = \frac{x + \xi}{2a\sqrt{t - t_0}}$$

to obtain

$$u(x, t) = \frac{f_0}{\sqrt{\pi}} \left\{ \int_{-x/2a\sqrt{t-t_0}}^\infty e^{-y^2} \, dy - \int_{x/2a\sqrt{t-t_0}}^\infty e^{-z^2} \, dz \right\}$$

$$= \frac{f_0}{\sqrt{\pi}} \int_{-x/2a\sqrt{t-t_0}}^{+x/2a\sqrt{t-t_0}} e^{-y^2} \, dy = f_0 \operatorname{erf} \frac{x}{2a\sqrt{t - t_0}} \quad (t > t_0).$$

12.7 GREEN'S FUNCTION FOR BOUNDARY CONDITIONS

Since initial conditions are nothing else but boundary conditions in the time variable, it is clear that appropriate Green's functions should exist for solving problems with nonhomogeneous boundary conditions.

Let us consider again a semi-infinite rod, but now with the initial temperature zero and the boundary maintained at a given temperature which may vary in time. The problem is formulated by

$$\frac{\partial u}{\partial t} = a^2 \frac{\partial^2 u}{\partial x^2}, \qquad u(\infty, t) < \infty,$$

$$u(x, 0) = 0, \qquad u(0, t) = v(t).$$

It will be tacitly assumed that $v(t) = 0$ prior to the time $t = 0$.* Any variations in boundary temperature between 0 and t will contribute in a linear fashion to the temperature $u(x, t)$ at some other point x. Therefore we expect $u(x, t)$ to be expressible as

$$u(x, t) = \int_0^t h(x; t \mid \tau) v(\tau) \, d\tau,$$

where $h(x; t \mid \tau)$ is a new type of Green's function representing the influence of boundary conditions on $u(x, t)$. Note that the integration is carried up to time t. Evidently $u(x, t)$ cannot be influenced by $v(\tau)$ at some time τ later than t.† We can solve the problem and evaluate $h(x; t \mid \tau)$ by the transform methods. The Fourier sine transform is very suitable with respect to x.‡

We denote

$$U_s(k, t) = \mathcal{F}_s\{u(x, t)\} = \sqrt{2/\pi} \int_0^\infty u(x, t) \sin kx \, dx.$$

The transformed problem requires

$$\frac{dU_s}{dt} + a^2 k^2 U_s = \sqrt{\frac{2}{\pi}} \, kv(t), \quad \text{(from the PDE and the boundary condition),} \quad (1)$$

$$U_s(k, 0) = 0, \qquad \text{(from the initial condition).} \tag{2}$$

The DE for U_s can be solved by the Laplace transform method, or, perhaps, by the Green's function method as follows: Find Green's function $\gamma(k; t \mid \tau)$ such that $\gamma(k; t \mid \tau) = 0$ for $t < \tau$ and

$$\frac{d\gamma}{dt} + a^2 k^2 \gamma = \delta(t - \tau).$$

For $t > \tau$, γ satisfies the homogeneous equation, so that

$$\gamma = A e^{-a^2 k^2 t} \qquad (t > \tau).$$

---

* Remember that $u(x, 0) = 0$, so that the rod contains no record at $t = 0$ that its boundary has ever been at a nonzero temperature.

† This is known as the *principle of causality*, believed to be a fundamental principle of physics; it applies here, in any case.

‡ The Laplace transform is less useful since $\partial u(0, t)/\partial x$ is not known.

Moreover, from the DE for γ, we have $\gamma(\tau + 0) - \gamma(\tau - 0) = 1$.   Therefore $A = e^{a^2k^2\tau}$ and

$$\gamma(k; t \mid \tau) = e^{-a^2k^2(t-\tau)}S(t - \tau),$$

so that

$$U_s(k, t) = \sqrt{\frac{2}{\pi}}\, k \int_0^t e^{-a^2k^2(t-\tau)}v(\tau)\, d\tau.$$

Now we invert the Fourier sine transform by the direct formula:

$$u(x, t) = \frac{2}{\pi} \int_0^\infty k \sin kx\, dk \int_0^t e^{-a^2k^2(t-\tau)}v(\tau)\, d\tau.$$

Interchanging the order of integration, we obtain*

$$u(x, t) = \frac{2}{\pi} \int_0^t v(\tau)\, d\tau \int_0^\infty e^{-a^2k^2(t-\tau)}k \sin kx\, dk.$$

The integral over k is not difficult.†   The final result reads

$$u(x, t) = \int_0^t \frac{x}{\sqrt{4\pi a^2(t - \tau)^3}}\, e^{-x^2/4a^2(t-\tau)}v(\tau)\, d\tau.$$

Whatever the legitimacy of our procedure, we can now proceed to show that the expression does indeed satisfy the PDE, the initial condition, and the boundary conditions.

Remark: Verification of boundary conditions may call for an elaboration. The formula actually shows $u(0, t) = 0$ rather than $u(0, t) = v(t)$. However, one should never forget that the actual boundary condition, in physics at least, should read

$$\lim_{\substack{x \to 0 \\ x > 0}} u(x, t) = v(t)$$

(see the remark on p. 297). That this condition is indeed satisfied by our solution can be checked, although this may not be so easy. The point is, of course, that the above integral represents a function discontinuous at $x = 0$. It has the limit $v(t)$ if x approaches zero from the right, the limit $-v(t)$ if x approaches zero from the left, and for $x = 0$ it is given by the average of these two values in the standard pattern familiar to us from Fourier Series.

We have derived, therefore, an expression for the boundary condition Green's function that is applicable to the diffusion equation for a semi-infinite one-

---

* Here the theory of distributions can be put to work since the validity of such a procedure may be in doubt.

† For example, evaluate $\int_0^\infty e^{-a^2k^2(t-\tau)} \cos kx\, dk$ and then differentiate with respect to x.

dimensional medium:

$$h(x; t \mid \tau) = \frac{x}{\sqrt{4\pi a^2(t - \tau)^3}} e^{-x^2/4a^2(t-\tau)}.$$

It is interesting that this formula can be inferred from certain considerations which do not actually involve the solution of the stated problem. As a preliminary step, let us recall the solution of the heat-conduction equation for a semi-infinite rod, for the *homogeneous* Dirichlet boundary condition, and the *constant temperature* initial condition at $t = t_0$ (p. 531):

$$u(x, t) = f_0 \operatorname{erf} \frac{x}{2a\sqrt{t - t_0}} \qquad (t > t_0).$$

Now consider the problem with the *homogeneous* initial condition at $t = t_0$ and the *constant temperature* boundary condition, also starting from time $t = t_0$, namely, the problem described by

$$\frac{\partial u}{\partial t} = a^2 \frac{\partial^2 u}{\partial x^2}, \qquad u(\infty, t) < \infty,$$

$$u(x, t_0) = 0, \qquad u(0, t) = f_0 S(t - t_0).$$

Now, a bit of reflection will tell us that we can obtain the solution of the second problem by subtracting from f_0 the solution of the first problem. Indeed, the function

$$\bar{u}(x, t) = f_0 - f_0 \operatorname{erf} \frac{x}{2a\sqrt{t - t_0}} = f_0 \operatorname{erfc} \frac{x}{2a\sqrt{t - t_0}} \qquad (t > t_0)$$

is easily verified to satisfy all the required conditions.

We shall now proceed to investigate, with the help of the function $\bar{u}(x, t)$, a solution to the problem for the arbitrary boundary conditions

$$u(0, t) = v(t).$$

First of all, we build up the solution for the case where $v(t)$ is a rectangular pulse,

$$v(t) = \begin{cases} 0 & (t < \tau), \\ v = \text{const} & (\tau < t < \tau + \Delta\tau), \\ 0 & (t > \tau + \Delta\tau), \end{cases}$$

or, more concisely,

$$v(t) = v[S(t - \tau) - S(t - \tau - \Delta\tau)].$$

It is evident that the corresponding solution can be written as

$$u(x, t) = v \operatorname{erfc} \frac{x}{2a\sqrt{t - \tau}} S(t - \tau) - v \operatorname{erfc} \frac{x}{2a\sqrt{t - \tau - \Delta\tau}} S(t - \tau - \Delta\tau)$$

$$= v[\bar{u}_1(x, t - \tau) - \bar{u}_1(x, t - \tau - \Delta\tau)],$$

where $\bar{u}_1(x, t - \tau)$ is the solution for the homogeneous initial condition and the *unit-step temperature* boundary condition for $t > \tau$.*

If an arbitrary function $v(\tau)$ is given, we represent it, approximately, as a stack of N rectangular pulses (up to $\tau = t$, which is relevant for our purposes), as shown in Fig. 12.7.† Applying the principle of superposition, we can deduce that the solution will now be

$$u(x, t) = \sum_{i=1}^{N} v(\tau_i)[\bar{u}_1(x, t - \tau_i) - \bar{u}_1(x, t - \tau_i - \Delta\tau)],$$

where $\tau_N = t$, and we have defined, for convenience, $\bar{u}_1(x, t - \tau_N - \Delta\tau) = 0$.

By the mean value theorem, we can write

$$\bar{u}_1(x, t - \tau_i) - \bar{u}_1(x, t - \tau_i - \Delta\tau) = -\left.\frac{\partial\bar{u}_1}{\partial\tau}\right|_{\tau=\bar{\tau}_i} \qquad (\tau_i \le \bar{\tau}_i \le \tau_i + \Delta\tau).$$

Now we let $\Delta\tau \to 0$, but $N\,\Delta\tau = t = $ const. Under suitable conditions imposed on $v(\tau)$, the stack of rectangular pulses will approach the true shape of the curve $v(\tau)$, while the sum will go over into the integral

$$u(x, t) = \int_0^t \left[-\frac{\partial\bar{u}_1}{\partial\tau}(x, t - \tau)\right] v(\tau)\, d\tau.$$

It is now seen that the Green's function $h(x; t \mid \tau)$ is related to the function $\bar{u}_1(x, t)$ by means of the formula

$$h(x; t \mid \tau) = -\frac{\partial\bar{u}_1}{\partial\tau}(x, t - \tau),$$

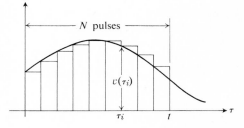

Figure 12.7

which we can easily verify explicitly:

$$-\frac{\partial\bar{u}_1}{\partial\tau}(x, t - \tau) = -\frac{\partial}{\partial\tau}\left(\text{erfc}\,\frac{x}{2a\sqrt{t - \tau}}\right) = -\frac{\partial}{\partial\tau}\left[\frac{2}{\sqrt{\pi}}\int_{x/2a\sqrt{t-\tau}}^{\infty} e^{-y^2}\, dy\right]$$

$$= \frac{2}{\sqrt{\pi}}\left[\frac{x}{4a(t - \tau)^{3/2}}\right] e^{-x^2/4a^2(t-\tau)} = h(x; t \mid \tau).$$

Remarks

1. This idea‡ can be extended to other types of problems with homogeneous initial conditions and given boundary conditions, namely, those involving different geometry and even different partial differential equations. It actually reduces such problems to the case of boundary conditions given by the unit step function $S(t - \tau)$.

---

* Namely, $\bar{u}_1(x, t - \tau) = (1/f_0)\bar{u}(x, t)$.

† Compare with the procedure in Section 5.9.

‡ Known as Duhamel's principle.

2. The function $h(x; t \mid \tau)$ is also related to the *point-source Green's function* for an *infinite* medium, namely, the function $G(x \mid \xi; t \mid \tau)$ on p. 526,

$$G(x \mid \xi; t \mid \tau) = \frac{S(t - \tau)}{\sqrt{4\pi a^2(t - \tau)}} e^{-(x-\xi)^2/4a^2(t-\tau)}.$$

We can check that the following formula holds:

$$h(x; t \mid \tau) = 2a^2 \frac{\partial G}{\partial \xi} (x \mid 0; t \mid \tau) = -2a^2 \frac{\partial G}{\partial x} (x \mid 0; t \mid \tau).$$

This relation can also be shown to follow from general considerations.

12.8 THE GREEN'S FUNCTION METHOD

After considering some applications of various Green's functions and some of their properties, we are now in a position to outline the method in a more general way. However, we shall confine ourselves to a particular type of PDE, namely, to the Helmholtz equation

$$\nabla^2 \psi + \lambda \psi = 0 \qquad (\psi = \psi(\mathbf{r})).$$

There are plenty of good reasons for this choice, because the Helmholtz equation occurs in an extremely wide variety of physical problems. For instance, if we are dealing with the wave equation

$$\nabla^2 u = \frac{1}{c^2} \frac{\partial^2 u}{\partial t^2} \qquad [u = u(\mathbf{r}, t)]$$

and seek solutions which vary harmonically in time,

$$u(\mathbf{r}; t) = \psi(\mathbf{r})e^{-i\omega t},$$

the problem reduces to the Helmholtz equation.* Similarly, the Helmholtz equation arises from the diffusion equation after the separation of variables. Also, the widely encountered Laplace equation $\nabla^2 \psi = 0$ is merely a special case of the Helmholtz equation.

Let us consider the problem of solving the Helmholtz equation in a *bounded region V* of three-dimensional physical space. We shall assume that V is bounded by a piecewise smooth (p. 19) surface S and the sought function $\psi(\mathbf{r})$ will be required to satisfy on S certain boundary conditions which we shall spell out later.

We shall need a couple of formulas from vector calculus, one being the so-called *First Green's formula*

$$\iiint_V (\text{grad } \varphi \cdot \text{grad } \chi) \, dV + \iiint_V \varphi \nabla^2 \chi \, dV = \oiint_S \varphi \, (\text{grad } \chi \cdot \mathbf{dS}),$$

---

* Separation of variables leads to the same conclusion.

which can be obtained from the identity

$$\text{div}\,(\varphi\,\text{grad}\,\chi) = \text{grad}\,\varphi \cdot \text{grad}\,\chi + \varphi\,\text{divgrad}\,\chi$$

by integration and application of the divergence theorem (p. 27).

Exercise. Verify the above identity and derive the first Green's formula.

The other formula is the so-called *second Green's formula,*

$$\iiint\limits_{V} (\varphi\nabla^2\chi - \chi\nabla^2\varphi)\,dV = \oiint\limits_{S} (\varphi\,\text{grad}\,\chi - \chi\,\text{grad}\,\varphi) \cdot d\mathbf{S},$$

obtained from the first Green's formula by interchanging φ and χ and subtracting.

Remark. Analogous formulas may be derived in any number of dimensions. In one dimension, the corresponding transformations have already been employed for the operator d^2/dx^2 (p. 164) and the more general operator $(d/dx)[p(x)(d/dx)]$ (p. 338) showing that Green's formulas may be regarded as examples of integration by parts in three-dimensional space.

Let us now start the investigation of the Green's function appropriate for the solution of the nonhomogeneous Helmholtz PDE (the point-source Green's function) which we denote by $G(\mathbf{r}\mid\mathbf{r}_0)$. We require that it satisfies the equation*

$$\nabla^2 G(\mathbf{r}\mid\mathbf{r}_0) + k^2 G(\mathbf{r}\mid\mathbf{r}_0) = \delta(\mathbf{r} - \mathbf{r}_0).$$

In this notation $\mathbf{r}_0$ indicates the position of the point source and appears in the PDE as a parameter. On the other hand $\mathbf{r}$ is the variable with respect to which the differentiation is carried out. However, since $\mathbf{r}_0$ is arbitrary, it is also a variable under certain conditions. In many cases it is convenient to call $\mathbf{r}_0$ the *source variable* and $\mathbf{r}$ the *field variable.*† We have adopted the convention of writing the field variable *first* in the notation $G(\mathbf{r}\mid\mathbf{r}_0)$.

Let us write the equations for the Green's functions for two different source points $\mathbf{r}_1$ and $\mathbf{r}_2$:

$$\nabla^2 G(\mathbf{r}\mid\mathbf{r}_1) + k^2 G(\mathbf{r}\mid\mathbf{r}_1) = \delta(\mathbf{r} - \mathbf{r}_1),$$
$$\nabla^2 G(\mathbf{r}\mid\mathbf{r}_2) + k^2 G(\mathbf{r}\mid\mathbf{r}_2) = \delta(\mathbf{r} - \mathbf{r}_2).$$

Multiply these equations by $G(\mathbf{r}\mid\mathbf{r}_2)$ and $G(\mathbf{r}\mid\mathbf{r}_1)$, respectively, subtract, and employ the second Green's formula:

$$\oiint\limits_{S} [G(\mathbf{r}\mid\mathbf{r}_2)\,\text{grad}\,G(\mathbf{r}\mid\mathbf{r}_1) - G(\mathbf{r}\mid\mathbf{r}_1)\,\text{grad}\,G(\mathbf{r}\mid\mathbf{r}_2)] \cdot d\mathbf{S} = G(\mathbf{r}_1\mid\mathbf{r}_2) - G(\mathbf{r}_2\mid\mathbf{r}_1).$$

As we already know, the usefulness of Green's functions depends on the fact that they satisfy certain boundary conditions, usually the same as those for the

---

* We shall write $\lambda = k^2$. In most cases k is real.

† Differentiation with respect to the source variable is widely employed in electromagnetic theory.

sought solutions of the nonhomogeneous PDE. The most common boundary conditions required of our Green's functions are:

a) Dirichlet boundary conditions, where G vanishes on the boundary,
b) Neumann boundary conditions, where the normal gradient of G vanishes on the boundary, namely (grad $G \cdot \mathbf{dS}$) = 0, and
c) intermediate boundary conditions, where grad $G + \mathbf{w}(\mathbf{r}')G = 0$ on the boundary and $\mathbf{w}$ is a given vector function of the boundary point $\mathbf{r}'$.*

In any one of these cases, the boundary integral vanishes, and we deduce that $G(\mathbf{r}_1 \mid \mathbf{r}_2) = G(\mathbf{r}_2 \mid \mathbf{r}_1)$. Since $\mathbf{r}_1$ and $\mathbf{r}_2$ are two arbitrary points inside our region, we can write

$$G(\mathbf{r} \mid \mathbf{r}_0) = G(\mathbf{r}_0 \mid \mathbf{r}),$$

establishing the symmetry of Green's function under the interchange of field and source variables.

Remark. Apart from the boundary conditions, the symmetry of Green's function also depends on the partial differential equation. For some partial differential equations, e.g., the diffusion equation, Green's function is not entirely symmetric.† However, a *reciprocity relation* usually exists under the field-source interchange between Green's functions for the so-called *mutually adjoint* problems. We shall not discuss these problems here.‡

Let us derive now the solving properties of our Green's function. We write the nonhomogeneous Helmholtz equation

$$\nabla^2\psi(\mathbf{r}) + k^2\psi(\mathbf{r}) = f(\mathbf{r}),$$

where $f(\mathbf{r})$ is a given function. We also write the equation for $G(\mathbf{r} \mid \mathbf{r}_0)$:

$$\nabla^2 G(\mathbf{r} \mid \mathbf{r}_0) + k^2 G(\mathbf{r} \mid \mathbf{r}_0) = \delta(\mathbf{r} - \mathbf{r}_0).$$

Multiplying these equations by $G(\mathbf{r} \mid \mathbf{r}_0)$ and $\psi(\mathbf{r})$, respectively, subtracting, and integrating, we have

$$\iiint\limits_{V} [G(\mathbf{r} \mid \mathbf{r}_0)\nabla^2\psi(\mathbf{r}) - \psi(\mathbf{r})\nabla^2 G(\mathbf{r} \mid \mathbf{r}_0)]\, dV - \iiint\limits_{V} f(\mathbf{r})G(\mathbf{r} \mid \mathbf{r}_0)\, dV = -\psi(\mathbf{r}_0).$$

We shall now apply the second Green's formula to the first integral. This yields

$$\psi(\mathbf{r}_0) = \iiint\limits_{V} f(\mathbf{r})G(\mathbf{r} \mid \mathbf{r}_0)\, dV + \oiint\limits_{S} [\psi(\mathbf{r})\,\mathrm{grad}\, G(\mathbf{r} \mid \mathbf{r}_0) - G(\mathbf{r} \mid \mathbf{r}_0)\,\mathrm{grad}\,\psi(\mathbf{r})] \cdot \mathbf{dS}.$$

---

* For one-dimensional problems, $\mathbf{w}$ reduces to a scalar. Moreover, since the boundary consists of just two points, left and right ends of an interval, this scalar reduces to a constant (a different one for each point).

† The function $G(x \mid \xi; t \mid \tau)$ from Section 12.5 is symmetric under the interchange $x \leftrightarrow \xi$, but not under the interchange $t \leftrightarrow \tau$.

‡ See, e.g., Morse and Feshbach, Chapter 7, Section 7.5.

This remarkable formula can be specialized in many ways. Before we do this, we shall recast it into a slightly different form. First of all, $\mathbf{r}_0$ is an arbitrary point of V; we prefer to denote it by $\mathbf{r}$.* On the other hand, the variable $\mathbf{r}$ is now merely a dummy variable; we shall denote it by $\mathbf{r}'$ in the boundary integrals and by $\mathbf{r}_0$ in the volume integral. Also, since the gradient operation is to be taken with respect to the variable $\mathbf{r}'$, we shall emphasize this by writing grad' $\psi(\mathbf{r}')$ and grad' $G(\mathbf{r}' \mid \mathbf{r})$. Finally, we shall make use of the symmetry of Green's function, anticipating the corresponding boundary conditions imposed later. This results in what may be called the solving formula:

$$\psi(\mathbf{r}) = \iiint\limits_{V_0} G(\mathbf{r} \mid \mathbf{r}_0) f(\mathbf{r}_0) \, dV_0 + \oiint\limits_{S'} \text{grad}' \, G(\mathbf{r}' \mid \mathbf{r}) \psi(\mathbf{r}') \cdot d\mathbf{S}'$$
$$- \oiint\limits_{S'} G(\mathbf{r} \mid \mathbf{r}') \, \text{grad}' \, \psi(\mathbf{r}') \cdot d\mathbf{S}'.\dagger$$

This formula illustrates how one can represent the influence on $\psi(\mathbf{r})$ of the sources (inside V) and the values of $\psi(\mathbf{r})$ and grad $\psi(\mathbf{r})$ on the boundary. Note, however, that we have not yet completely defined our Green's function, because we have not specified the boundary conditions. They are selected according to the requirements of the problem at hand.

Example 1. *The nonhomogeneous PDE with homogeneous Dirichlet boundary conditions.* In this case it is reasonable to seek $G(\mathbf{r} \mid \mathbf{r}_0)$ which will satisfy the same boundary conditions. If such a Green's function is found, then both boundary integrals in the solving formula vanish, and

$$\psi(\mathbf{r}) = \iiint\limits_{V_0} G(\mathbf{r} \mid \mathbf{r}_0) f(\mathbf{r}_0) \, dV_0.$$

This would solve the problem. We know, however, from the analysis in Section 12.3, Example 2, that the Green's function may fail to exist. This will happen if k^2 is one of the eigenvalues of the corresponding homogeneous problem, namely, if k^2 is such that the Helmholtz equation

$$\nabla^2 \varphi + k^2 \varphi = 0$$

possesses nontrivial solutions vanishing at the boundary. This is the case of resonance.

Remark. Under certain circumstances the solution $\psi(\mathbf{r})$ in the case of resonance still exists. This happens when the function $f(\mathbf{r})$ is orthogonal to the eigenfunction (or eigenfunctions, in the case of degeneracy) corresponding to the eigenvalue k^2. Such a solution is not unique, but if we require, for instance, that $\psi(\mathbf{r})$ must also be orthogonal to the same eigenfunction(s), then it becomes unique. As an illustration, let V be a rectangular

---

* Since we are seeking the value of $\psi = \psi(\mathbf{r})$ at an arbitrary point $\mathbf{r}$.

$\dagger$ The symbols V_0, dV_0, etc., should be self-explanatory in view of our change of notation.

box bounded by the planes

$$x = 0, \qquad x = a,$$
$$y = 0, \qquad y = b,$$
$$z = 0, \qquad z = c.$$

The normalized eigenfunctions are easily seen to be

$$\varphi_{lmn} = \frac{8}{abc} \sin \frac{l\pi x}{a} \sin \frac{m\pi y}{b} \sin \frac{n\pi z}{c} \qquad (l, m, n = \text{positive integers})$$

and the eigenvalues

$$\lambda = \frac{l^2\pi^2}{a^2} + \frac{m^2\pi^2}{b^2} + \frac{n^2\pi^2}{c^2} = k_{lmn}^2.$$

If the ratios $a{:}b$, $b{:}c$, and $a{:}c$ are not rational, the eigenvalues are nondegenerate. Suppose that we want to solve

$$\nabla^2\psi(x, y, z) + k^2\psi(x, y, z) = f(x, y, z),$$

with

$$k^2 = \frac{l'^2\pi^2}{a^2} + \frac{m'^2\pi^2}{b^2} + \frac{n'^2\pi^2}{c^2},$$

where l', m', n' are some fixed positive integers, but

$$\iiint_V f(x, y, z)\varphi_{l'm'n'}(x, y, z)\, dx\, dy\, dz = 0.$$

We expand $f(x, y, z)$ in a triple series of eigenfunctions φ_{lmn}:

$$f(x, y, z) = \sum_{l,m,n}{}' a_{lmn}\varphi_{lmn}(x, y, z),$$

where $\sum'$ indicates that the term with l', m', n' is missing.* We demand that $\psi(x, y, z)$ also be orthogonal to $\varphi_{l'm'n'}$ and expand ψ as well:

$$\psi(x, y, z) = \sum_{l,m,n}{}' c_{lmn}\varphi_{lmn}(x, y, z).$$

Substituting into the PDE and using the orthogonality of eigenfunctions,† we obtain, by the usual techniques,

$$c_{lmn} = \frac{a_{lmn}}{k^2 - k'_{lmn}}.$$

This yields the solution

$$\psi(x, y, z) = \sum_{l,m,n}{}' \frac{\varphi_{lmn}(x, y, z)}{k^2 - k_{lmn}^2} \iiint_{V_0} f(x_0, y_0, z_0)\varphi_{lmn}(x_0, y_0, z_0)\, dV_0,$$

---

* Some other coefficients a_{lmn} may also vanish, but this is not relevant.

† We omit proofs of these details.

where the explicit expression for a_{lmn} has been introduced. If we interchange the order of summation and integration, we see that we may represent $\psi(x, y, z)$ as

$$\psi(x, y, z) = \iiint\limits_{V_0} G'(x, y, z \mid x_0, y_0, z_0) f(x_0, y_0, z_0) \, dV_0$$

with the generalized Green's function

$$G'(\mathbf{r} \mid \mathbf{r}_0) = \sum_{l,m,n}{}' \frac{\varphi_{lmn}(\mathbf{r})\varphi_{lmn}(\mathbf{r}')}{k^2 - k_{lmn}^2},$$

which can be obtained from the bilinear formula for the proper Green's function by discarding the "resonant" term. Note that if $\psi(\mathbf{r})$ and $\varphi_{l'm'n'}(\mathbf{r})$ are not required to be orthogonal, we may add an arbitrary multiple of $\varphi_{l'm'n'}(\mathbf{r})$ to $\psi(\mathbf{r})$. Therefore, $\psi(\mathbf{r})$ is effectively defined up to a scalar multiple of the resonant eigenfunction.*

Example 2. *The homogeneous PDE with nonhomogeneous Dirichlet boundary conditions.* A glance at the solving formula shows that we should select the Green's function satisfying a nonhomogeneous PDE and homogeneous boundary conditions (same Green's function as in Example 1). Then

$$\psi(\mathbf{r}) = \oiint\limits_{S'} \mathrm{grad}'\, G(\mathbf{r}' \mid \mathbf{r})\psi(\mathbf{r}') \cdot d\mathbf{S}' \qquad (d\mathbf{S}' = \text{vector}).$$

This may be rewritten as

$$\psi(\mathbf{r}) = \oiint\limits_{S'} g(\mathbf{r}' \mid \mathbf{r})\psi(\mathbf{r}') \, dS' \qquad (dS' = \text{scalar}),$$

where $g(\mathbf{r}' \mid \mathbf{r})$ is the boundary-value Green's function. Evidently, $g(\mathbf{r}' \mid \mathbf{r})$ is the *normal gradient* of the point source Green's function $G(\mathbf{r} \mid \mathbf{r}_0)$ since

$$\left(\mathrm{grad}'\, G(\mathbf{r}' \mid \mathbf{r}) \cdot d\mathbf{S}'\right) = \frac{\partial G}{\partial n'}(\mathbf{r}' \mid \mathbf{r}) \, dS',$$

where n' is the unit normal to the boundary.† It is needless to stress that questions concerning the existence of a solution now also arise.

Problems involving Neumann boundary conditions are considerably more complicated. The reason is that the values of the normal gradient of $\psi(\mathbf{r})$ are not independent of the PDE itself. Indeed, by the divergence theorem, we have

$$\iiint\limits_{V} \nabla^2\psi \, dV = \iiint\limits_{V} \mathrm{div}\,(\mathrm{grad}\,\psi) \, dV = \oiint\limits_{S} \mathrm{grad}\,\psi \cdot d\mathbf{S}.$$

Suppose that $\psi(\mathbf{r})$ is required to satisfy the nonhomogeneous Helmholtz equa-

---

* In the case of degeneracy the statement would read, "up to a linear combination of resonant eigenfunctions."

† According to the usual convention, it is the "outward normal."

tion with homogeneous Neumann boundary conditions

$$\nabla^2 \psi(\mathbf{r}) + k^2 \psi(\mathbf{r}) = f(\mathbf{r}) \qquad \text{and} \qquad \frac{\partial \psi}{\partial n} = 0 \quad \text{(on } S\text{)}.$$

Integrating and using the above formula, we obtain

$$k^2 \iiint\limits_V \psi(\mathbf{r}) \, dV = \iiint\limits_V f(\mathbf{r}) \, dV.$$

This relation cannot be satisfied, for instance, for $k = 0$ (Poisson PDE) unless it happens that

$$\iiint\limits_V f(\mathbf{r}) \, dV = 0.$$

This condition can be interpreted on physical grounds if we consider, for instance, the steady-state temperature distribution inside a finite region V. The temperature u obeys the Poisson equation $\nabla^2 u = f$,* where f is proportional to the density of the heat sources. The boundary condition $\partial u / \partial n = 0$ implies that there is no exchange of heat across the boundary. Evidently, there can be no steady-state temperature distribution unless the heat sources are balanced by heat *sinks*, where heat is transformed into other forms of energy, as in endothermic chemical reactions. This balance of sources and sinks is given exactly by the above condition on $f(\mathbf{r})$.

Consider now the Green's function. The solving formula indicates that it would be convenient to choose $G(\mathbf{r} \mid \mathbf{r}_0)$ such that it will satisfy the homogeneous Neumann boundary condition:

$$\frac{\partial G}{\partial n} = 0 \qquad \text{(on } S\text{)}.$$

However, the equation $\nabla^2 G + k^2 G = \delta(\mathbf{r} - \mathbf{r}_0)$ then implies

$$k^2 \iiint\limits_V G(\mathbf{r} \mid \mathbf{r}_0) \, dV = 1,$$

which cannot be satisfied for $k = 0$. Nevertheless, physical intuition tells us that if the condition

$$\iiint\limits_V f(\mathbf{r}) \, dV = 0$$

is satisfied, there should be a solution to the problem

$$\nabla^2 \psi(\mathbf{r}) = f(\mathbf{r}) \qquad \frac{\partial \psi}{\partial r} = 0 \quad \text{(on } S\text{)},$$

---

* See Section 8.4. Note that $\partial u / \partial t = 0$ because steady state is considered.

for example, the above mentioned heat-conduction problem. Abandoning the idea $\partial G/\partial n = 0$ on S, we may try the next simplest condition, namely,

$$\frac{\partial G}{\partial n} = \text{const} = C \qquad \text{(on } S\text{)}.$$

Then, integrating $\nabla^2 G = \delta(\mathbf{r} - \mathbf{r}_0)$, we obtain

$$C \oiint_S dS = 1$$

and it follows that $C = 1/A_s$, where A_s is the area of the surface S.

Unfortunately, we have deviated from the choice of boundary conditions which make the Green's function symmetric. However, going over the proof of symmetry of Green's function (p. 538), we see that if we impose an additional condition

$$\oiint_S G(\mathbf{r} \mid \mathbf{r}_0) \, dS = 0,$$

then the symmetry of Green's function will still hold. The solving formula still applies and yields

$$\psi(\mathbf{r}) = \iiint_{V_0} G(\mathbf{r} \mid \mathbf{r}_0) f(\mathbf{r}_0) \, dV_0 + \frac{1}{A_s} \oiint_{S'} \psi(\mathbf{r}') \, dS'.$$

While the last term cannot be evaluated until $\psi(\mathbf{r})$ is known, we note that it is a constant. It is not difficult to verify that this formula yields $\psi(\mathbf{r})$ up to an arbitrary constant. For most physical problems, this is adequate.* We shall omit the proof that $G(\mathbf{r} \mid \mathbf{r}_0)$ satisfying all stated conditions can indeed be found.†

Remark. Solutions of the Helmholtz equation with Neumann boundary conditions cause fewer problems when the region under consideration extends to infinity, for instance, when the region represents the *exterior* of a closed surface S. In these cases, however, additional conditions are imposed on the *asymptotic behavior* (or *behavior at infinity*) of sought functions, as well as of Green's functions.

12.9 A CASE OF CONTINUOUS SPECTRUM

Green's functions for a wide variety of boundary-value problems can be expressed by means of the bilinear formula developed in Section 12.3. In many such problems, however, the eigenvalue spectrum happens to be continuous. It is reasonable to conjecture that the infinite sum in the bilinear formula will "go over" into an integral. We shall illustrate such a situation by an example involving the infinite stretched string.

---

* For example, if $\psi(\mathbf{r})$ is an electrostatic potential.

† See, e.g., Morse and Feshbach, *Methods of Theoretical Physics*, p. 696, D. Jackson, *Classical Electrodynamics*, p. 19.

The concept of the infinite string is, of course, only an idealization of the case where the physical conditions at the ends do not significantly influence the behavior of the string "not far from the middle." In practice, this will happen if the string is very long.

Let us consider such an infinite stretched string subject to an external harmonic force per unit length,

$$F(x, t) = f(x)e^{-i\omega_0 t}.$$

The PDE satisfied by transverse displacements is the same as for the finite string, (p. 289)

$$\frac{\partial^2 u}{\partial x^2} - \frac{1}{c^2}\frac{\partial^2 u}{\partial t^2} = -\frac{1}{T}F(x, t),$$

but the boundary conditions are now different. We shall assume the natural condition that $u(x, t)$ is everywhere bounded: $|u(x, t)| < \infty$. As usual, we seek solutions in the form

$$u(x, t) = y(x)e^{-i\omega_0 t},$$

which reduces the problem to an ordinary DE:

$$\frac{d^2 y}{dx^2} + k_0^2 y = -\frac{f(x)}{T} \qquad \left(k_0 = \frac{\omega_0}{c}\right).$$

The Green's function must satisfy

$$\frac{d^2 G}{dx^2} + k_0^2 G = \delta(x - \xi).$$

If we look into the appropriate eigenvalue problem

$$\frac{d^2 y}{dx^2} = \lambda y$$

for bounded functions y, we see that the only restriction is that $\lambda \leq 0$ and the spectrum is continuous. We denote $\lambda = -k^2$. The eigenfunctions can be taken as

$$\varphi_\lambda(x) = e^{\pm ikx}.$$

It is clear that instead of a series expansion for $G(x \mid \xi)$, we should seek its representation as a Fourier integral,

$$G(x \mid \xi) = \frac{1}{\sqrt{2\pi}} \int_{-\infty}^{+\infty} g(k, \xi)e^{-ikx}\, dk.$$

In this spirit, we subject the DE for G to the Fourier transformation. We multiply by $(1/\sqrt{2\pi})e^{ikx}$ and integrate over x from $-\infty$ to $+\infty$ to obtain

$$-k^2 g(k, \xi) + k_0^2 g(k, \xi) = \frac{1}{\sqrt{2\pi}} e^{ik\xi},$$

so that the Fourier transform of $G(x \mid \xi)$ reads

$$g(k, \xi) = \frac{1}{\sqrt{2\pi}} \frac{e^{ik\xi}}{k_0^2 - k^2} .$$

Inverting, we obtain

$$G(x \mid \xi) = \frac{1}{2\pi} \int_{-\infty}^{+\infty} \frac{e^{ik\xi} e^{-ikx}}{k_0^2 - k^2} \, dk.$$

We have obtained, therefore, an integral representation for the Green's function. It is evident that this integral is the expected generalization of the bilinear formula.

If we desire to evaluate explicitly the integral for $G(x \mid \xi)$, corresponding to the summation of the bilinear formula to the closed form, we are faced with the problem: What should we do about the poles of the integrand at $k = -k_0$ and $k = +k_0$? Without a prescription indicating how the path of integration should be deformed, Green's function cannot be properly defined.*

Let us suppose for a moment that $x < \xi$, meaning physically that the field point (point of observation) is to the left of the source point (point of disturbance). The contour for the evaluation of $G(x \mid \xi)$ by residue calculus must then be closed "up."† If the poles at $k = -k_0$ and $k = +k_0$ *are allowed* to contribute to $G(x \mid \xi)$, their residues will contain the factors

$$e^{-ik_0(\xi-x)} \qquad \text{and} \qquad e^{ik_0(\xi-x)},$$

respectively. Each of these factors will be combined with the time factor $e^{-i\omega t}$ to yield

$$e^{-ik_0\xi} e^{i(k_0x - \omega t)}$$

and

$$e^{ik_0\xi} e^{-i(k_0x + \omega t)}.$$

The first expression corresponds to a wave traveling to the right‡ and the second one to a wave traveling to the left. Now, since the Green's function relates the response to a harmonic disturbance $F(x, t)$ by means of the formula

$$u(x, t) = y(x)e^{-i\omega_0 t} = e^{-i\omega_0 t} \int_{-\infty}^{+\infty} G(x \mid \xi) f(\xi) \, d\xi,$$

our physical intuition tells us that the wave traveling to the right from point ξ should not influence the response at point x lying to the left of ξ.§ Thus for $x < \xi$, the contour should bypass the pole $k = -k_0$ from above and the pole $k = +k_0$ from below, so that only the latter contributes. The contour is shown

---

* See p. 111.

† For the contribution from the large semicircle to vanish.

‡ Traveling waves are discussed in greater detail in Chapter 14 (see, for example, p. 591).

§ Further discussion of this criterion is given on p. 611.

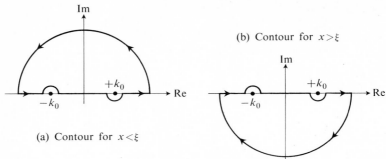

(b) Contour for $x > \xi$

(a) Contour for $x < \xi$

Figure 12.8

in Fig. 12.8(a). The calculation of $G(x \mid \xi)$ is now straightforward:

$$G(x \mid \xi) = 2\pi i \operatorname{Res}\left[-\frac{1}{2\pi} \frac{e^{ik(\xi-x)}}{(k + k_0)(k - k_0)}\right]_{k=k_0} = -\frac{i}{2k_0} e^{ik_0(\xi-x)} \qquad (x < \xi).$$

For $x > \xi$ the contour is closed "down" and only the contribution from the pole $k = -k_0$ is desired. As seen from Fig. 12.8(b), this still means bypassing the left pole from above and the right pole from below. We now have

$$G(x \mid \xi) = -2\pi i \operatorname{Res}\left[-\frac{1}{2\pi} \frac{e^{ik(\xi-x)}}{(k + k_0)(k - k_0)}\right]_{k=-k_0} = -\frac{i}{2k_0} e^{-ik_0(\xi-x)}$$

$$(x > \xi).$$

Instead of bypassing the poles in the manner shown, we could define $G(x \mid \xi)$ by keeping the path of integration straight but displacing the pole $k = -k_0$ slightly below the real axis and the pole $k = +k_0$ slightly above the real axis. Then we can define $G(x \mid \xi)$ by an unambiguous formula*

$$G(x \mid \xi) = \frac{1}{4\pi k_0} \int_{-\infty}^{+\infty} \left[\frac{e^{ik(\xi-x)}}{k - (-k_0 - i\epsilon)} - \frac{e^{ik(\xi-x)}}{k - (k_0 + i\epsilon)}\right] dk,$$

which is applicable to either $x < \xi$ or $x > \xi$.

Remark. The obtained Green's function

$$G(x \mid \xi) = \begin{cases} -\dfrac{i}{2k_0} e^{ik_0(\xi-x)} & (x < \xi), \\[2ex] -\dfrac{i}{2k_0} e^{ik_0(x-\xi)} & (x > \xi) \end{cases}$$

is seen to be symmetric, rather than hermitian, under the interchange of x and ξ. Despite the complex notation, it should be remembered that $G(x \mid \xi)$ serves to calculate a *real*

---

* See p. 111.

function $u(x, t)$ according to

$$u(x, t) = \int_{-\infty}^{+\infty} \text{Re } \{G(x \mid \xi)e^{-i\omega_0 t} f(\xi)\} \, d\xi.$$

If $f(x)$ is real, then the actual physical Green's function is the real part of $G(x \mid \xi)e^{-i\omega_0 t}$. It is easy to check that

$$\text{Re } \{G(x \mid \xi)e^{-i\omega_0 t}\} = \begin{cases} \dfrac{1}{2k_0} \sin [k_0(x - \xi) + \omega_0 t] & (x < \xi), \\[2mm] \dfrac{1}{2k_0} \sin [k_0(\xi - x) + \omega_0 t] & (x > \xi). \end{cases}$$

If the problem were solved by real variable methods, this would be the actual result.

BIBLIOGRAPHY

FRIEDMAN, B., *Principles and Techniques of Applied Mathematics*. New York: John Wiley & Sons, 1956.

JACKSON, J. D., *Classical Electrodynamics*. New York: John Wiley & Sons, 1962.

MORSE, P. M., and H. FESHBACH, *Methods of Theoretical Physics*, New York: McGraw-Hill Book Co., 1953.

PROBLEMS

1. Consider the damped harmonic oscillator governed by the equation

$$\ddot{x} + 2\lambda\dot{x} + \omega_0^2 x = \frac{f(t)}{m},$$

where $\lambda^2 > \omega_0^2$ (overdamped case). Suppose that the external force $f(t)$ is zero for $t < 0$. Develop the Green's function and write the solution $x(t)$ satisfying the initial conditions $x(0) = \dot{x}(0) = 0$. Modify the solution for the case $x(0) = a$, $\dot{x}(0) = b$.

2. We are to solve $y'' - k^2 y = f(x)$ $(0 \leq x \leq L)$ subject to the boundary conditions $y(0) = y(L) = 0$.

a) Find Green's function by direct construction and show that for $x < \xi$,

$$G(x \mid \xi) = -\frac{\sinh kx \sinh k(L - \xi)}{k \sinh kL}.$$

What is the expression for $G(x \mid \xi)$ if $x > \xi$?

b) Solve the equation $G'' - k^2 G = \delta(x - \xi)$ by the Fourier sine series method. Can you show that the series obtained for $G(x \mid \xi)$ is equivalent to the solution found under (a)?

3. Show that the Green's function designed to solve the DE

$$\frac{d}{dx}\left(x\frac{dy}{dx}\right) + \left(k^2x - \frac{m^2}{x}\right)y = f(x) \qquad (m = \text{integer})$$

subject to $y(0) < \infty$ and $y(a) = 0$ reads

$$G(x \mid \xi) = \begin{cases} \dfrac{\pi}{2}\dfrac{[J_m(k\xi)N_m(ka) - J_m(ka)N_m(k\xi)]}{J_m(ka)}J_m(kx) & (x \leq \xi), \\[4mm] \dfrac{\pi}{2}\dfrac{[J_m(kx)N_m(ka) - J_m(ka)N_m(kx)]}{J_m(ka)}J_m(k\xi) & (x \geq \xi). \end{cases}$$

Also consider the case $J_m(ka) = 0$. Show that if $k \neq 0$, then $G(x \mid \xi)$ does not exist, but if $k = 0$ (then, of course, $m \neq 0$) $G(x \mid \xi)$ does exist, although the above form is not applicable. Evaluate $G(x \mid \xi)$ in this case.

4. Consider the boundary-value problem

$$\frac{d^2y}{dx^2} = f(x) \qquad y(0) = 0 \qquad \frac{dy}{dx}(L) = 0 \qquad (0 \leq x \leq L).$$

a) Find the normalized eigenfunctions of the operator d^2/dx^2 for the given boundary conditions.

b) Write the bilinear formula for the Green's function associated with the problem.

c) Obtain $G(x \mid \xi)$ in the closed form.

d) Expand the result of (c) in appropriate series and verify the result obtained in (b).

5. Consider, as in Problem 2, the DE $y'' - k^2y = f(x)$ but for the entire range $(-\infty < x < +\infty)$. The boundary conditions now read $y(\pm\infty) < \infty$.

a) Show, by direct construction, that the Green's function is now

$$G(x \mid \xi) = -\frac{1}{2k}e^{-k|x-\xi|} \qquad \text{(all } x).$$

b) Solve the equation

$$G'' - k^2G = \delta(x - \xi)$$

by the Fourier transform method and show that

$$G(x \mid \xi) = -\frac{1}{2\pi}\int_{-\infty}^{+\infty}\frac{e^{ik'x}e^{-ik'\xi}}{k'^2 + k^2}\,dk'.$$

Comment on the similarity of this expression to the bilinear formula. Evaluate the integral and confirm the result obtained in (a).

6. Suppose that the preceding problem is changed to $y'' - k^2y = f(x)$ for $0 \leq x < \infty$ and with $y(0) = 0$, $y(\infty) < \infty$.

a) Use the ideas of Section 12.6 to set up a source at $x = \xi$ and the appropriate image at $x = -\xi$, and use the Green's function from the preceding problem to show that now

$$G(x \mid \xi) = \begin{cases} -\dfrac{1}{k} e^{-k\xi} \sinh kx & (x < \xi), \\[2mm] -\dfrac{1}{k} e^{-kx} \sinh k\xi & (x > \xi). \end{cases}$$

b) Check this result by solving the equation $G'' - k^2 G = \delta(x - \xi)$ by the Fourier sine transform method. Check also by direct construction.

7. We wish to solve the two-dimensional Laplace equation $\nabla^2 u = 0$ inside the circle of radius a, subject to the nonhomogeneous boundary condition $u(a, \theta) = f(\theta)$, where $f(\theta)$ is a given function of θ.

a) State the reasons why the solution can be expected to be representable as

$$u(r, \theta) = \int_0^{2\pi} g(r; \theta \mid \theta_0) f(\theta_0)\, d\theta_0.$$

b) Set up the relations satisfied by $g(r; \theta \mid \theta_0)$ (PDE and boundary conditions) and develop a complex Fourier series for $g(r; \theta \mid \theta_0)$.

c) Evaluate explicitly the sum of the series to show that

$$g(r; \theta \mid \theta_0) = \frac{1}{2\pi}\, \frac{(a^2 - r^2)}{a^2 + r^2 - 2ar \cos (\theta - \theta_0)}.$$

[*Hint:* Deduce the formula $\sum_{n=0}^{\infty} R^n e^{in\phi} = 1/(1 - Re^{i\phi})$, valid for $|R| < 1$.]

8. Consider the motion of a stretched string satisfying

$$\frac{\partial^2 u}{\partial x^2} = \frac{1}{c^2} \frac{\partial^2 u}{\partial t^2} \qquad u(0) = u(L) = 0.$$

a) Develop, in the form of a single series, the two Green's functions $g_1(x \mid \xi; t)$ and $g_2(x \mid \xi; t)$, yielding the solutions

$$u_1(x, t) = \int_0^L g_1(x \mid \xi; t) u_0(\xi)\, d\xi,$$

and

$$u_2(x, t) = \int_0^L g_2(x \mid \xi; t) v_0(\xi)\, d\xi$$

corresponding to the initial conditions

i) $u_1(x, 0) = u_0(x), \qquad \dfrac{\partial u_1}{\partial t}(x, 0) = 0,$

ii) $u_2(x, 0) = 0, \qquad \dfrac{\partial u_2}{\partial t}(x, 0) = v_0(x)$

respectively.

b) Show that the solution of forced vibrations of the string

$$\frac{\partial^2 u}{\partial t^2} = c^2 \frac{\partial^2 u}{\partial x^2} + f(x, t)$$

can be represented in the form

$$u(x, t) = \int_0^L d\xi \int_{-\infty}^t G(x \mid \xi; t \mid \tau) f(\xi, \tau) \, d\tau,$$

where G satisfies

$$\frac{\partial^2 G}{\partial t^2} = c^2 \frac{\partial^2 G}{\partial x^2} + \delta(x - \xi) \, \delta(t - \tau)$$

and the causal initial condition $G \equiv 0$ for $t < \tau$ (all x, ξ).

c) Having developed $G(x \mid \xi; t \mid \tau)$ in a single-series form, compare it with $g_2(x \mid \xi; t)$ found under (a). Can you produce a physical argument which explains why G is simply related to g_2, rather than g_1? [*Hint:* The *law of impulse* in mechanics may be useful.]

9. Find the Green's function satisfying the two-dimensional Laplace equation $\nabla^2 g = 0$ within the rectangle $0 \le x \le a$, $0 \le y \le b$, and the boundary conditions

$$g(x, 0) = \delta(x - \xi), \qquad g(x, b) = g(0, y) = g(a, y) = 0.$$

a) Do this by direct development of a Fourier sine series for g.
b) Employ the discussion in Section 12.8 to show that

$$g = -\left. \frac{\partial G(x \mid \xi; y \mid \eta)}{\partial \eta} \right|_{\eta=0},$$

where $G(x \mid \xi; y \mid \eta)$ is the Green's function evaluated in Section 12.4. Check the result under (a) by performing the above operation. (*Caution:* The form for $y > \eta$ on p. 523 must be used, since in the limit $\eta \to 0$, the field variable remains fixed.)

10. Certain Green's functions for the Laplace PDE are well known from electrostatics. For instance:

a) Recall the electrostatic potential due to a point charge in space and produce an argument showing that

$$G(\mathbf{r} \mid \mathbf{r}_0) = -\frac{1}{4\pi} \frac{1}{|\mathbf{r} - \mathbf{r}_0|}$$

satisfies $\nabla^2 G = \delta(\mathbf{r} - \mathbf{r}_0)$.

b) Perform an analogous derivation in the two-dimensional case to show that now (compare with p. 258)

$$G(\mathbf{r} \mid \mathbf{r}_0) = \frac{1}{2\pi} \log |\mathbf{r} - \mathbf{r}_0|.$$

Observe that the natural condition that $G \to 0$ or even $G < \infty$ as $|\mathbf{r}| \to \infty$ must now be relaxed.

11. The Green's function stated in the preceding problem can also be obtained in series form. The two-dimensional delta function expressed in polar coordinates reads

$$\delta(\mathbf{r} - \mathbf{r}_0) = \frac{1}{r} \delta(r - r_0) \delta(\theta - \theta_0).$$

a) Obtain the solution of $\nabla^2 G = (1/r) \delta(r - r_0) \delta(\theta - \theta_0)$ in the form of a complex Fourier series

$$G(r \mid r_0; \theta \mid \theta_0) = \sum_{n=-\infty}^{+\infty} g_n(r, r_0; \theta_0) e^{in\theta}$$

by solving the differential equations for functions g_n. (*Caution:* The case $n = 0$ should be treated separately.)

b) Having obtained $G(r \mid r_0; \theta \mid \theta_0)$, set it equal to $(1/2\pi) \log |\mathbf{r} - \mathbf{r}_0|$ and establish the following result:

$$\log \sqrt{r^2 + r_0^2 - 2rr_0 \cos(\theta - \theta_0)} = \begin{cases} \log r_0 - \displaystyle\sum_{n=1}^{\infty} \left(\frac{r}{r_0}\right)^n \cos n(\theta - \theta_0) & (r < r_0), \\ \log r - \displaystyle\sum_{n=1}^{\infty} \left(\frac{r_0}{r}\right)^n \cos n(\theta - \theta_0) & (r > r_0). \end{cases}$$

12. A solution of the two-dimensional Poisson equation $\nabla^2 \psi(\mathbf{r}) = \rho(\mathbf{r})$ is sought in the half-plane $0 \le x < \infty$, $-\infty < y < +\infty$ subject to the boundary condition $\psi(0, y) = 0$. Show that the appropriate Green's function can be cast in the form

$$G(\mathbf{r} \mid \mathbf{r}_0) = \frac{1}{2\pi} \log \frac{|\mathbf{r} - \mathbf{r}_0|}{|\mathbf{r} - \mathbf{r}_0'|}.$$

What is $\mathbf{r}_0'$? Formulate the physical situation in electrostatics and in the conduction of heat which reduce to this mathematical problem.

13. Use the eigenvalues and eigenfunctions for the circular membrane (Section 9.7) to develop a bilinear formula (as in Section 12.4) in polar coordinates for the Green's function satisfying

$$\nabla^2 G = \frac{1}{r} \delta(r - r_0) \delta(\theta - \theta_0) \qquad \text{and} \qquad G = 0 \quad \text{at } r = a.$$

Formulate the idealized physical situation which leads to the deflection of the membrane represented by $G(r \mid r_0; \theta \mid \theta_0)$.

14. Show that, depending on the technique used, the Green's function satisfying

$$\frac{\partial^2 G}{\partial x^2} + \frac{\partial^2 G}{\partial y^2} = \delta(x - \xi) \delta(y - \eta) \qquad (0 \le x < \infty, 0 \le x \le b)$$

and

$$G(0, y) = G(x, 0) = G(x, b) = 0 \qquad (G(\infty, y) < \infty)$$

can be obtained in the following three different forms:

a)
$$G = \begin{cases} -\sum_{n=1}^{\infty} \frac{2}{n\pi} \sin \frac{n\pi y}{b} \sin \frac{n\pi \eta}{b} e^{-(n\pi\xi/b)} \sinh \frac{n\pi x}{b} & (x < \xi), \\ \sum_{n=1}^{\infty} \frac{2}{n\pi} \sin \frac{n\pi y}{b} \sin \frac{n\pi \eta}{b} e^{-(n\pi x/b)} \sinh \frac{n\pi \xi}{b} & (x > \xi); \end{cases}$$

b)
$$G = \begin{cases} -\dfrac{2}{\pi} \displaystyle\int_0^{\infty} \dfrac{\sin k\xi \sin kx \sinh ky \sinh k(b-\eta)}{k \sinh kb} \, dk & (y < \eta), \\ -\dfrac{2}{\pi} \displaystyle\int_0^{\infty} \dfrac{\sin k\xi \sin kx \sinh k\eta \sinh k(b-y)}{k \sinh kb} \, dk & (y > \eta); \end{cases}$$

c)
$$G = -\frac{4}{\pi b} \sum_{n=1}^{\infty} \int_0^{\infty} \frac{\sin (n\pi y/b) \sin (n\pi \eta/b) \sin kx \sin k\xi}{k^2 + (n^2\pi^2/b^2)} \, dk \qquad \text{(all } x, y).$$

Also show that integration over k reduces (c) to (a). (*Suggestion:* Results of Problems 2 and 6 and the idea of a bilinear formula reduce this problem to almost trivial manipulations.)

CHAPTER 13

VARIATIONAL METHODS

13.1 THE BRACHISTOCHRONE PROBLEM

One of the most interesting and important methods used in mathematical physics is the calculus of variations. The following problem is among the oldest that has been solved by variational methods: Consider a particle of mass m sliding down, under the influence of gravity, along some curve Γ from point A to point B (Fig. 13.1a). If points A and B are fixed and the particle starts from rest, what must be the shape of Γ for the time of descent to be minimum? Friction and other dissipative forces are neglected.

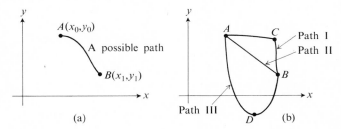

Figure 13.1

The curve possessing this property is known as *the brachistochrone*. We can conjecture the existence of such a curve from the following argument. Among the three conceivable paths shown in Fig. 13.1(b) it is clear that the traveling time along path I can be made arbitrarily long by making the slope between points A and C sufficiently small. It is equally clear that the same effect will be achieved for path III by sufficiently lowering point D. Consequently, it is reasonable to assume that there is an *optimum path*. Whether or not this path is a straight line (path II) remains to be seen.

The mathematical formulation of the problem is as follows: Since path Γ will evidently cross every vertical line between A and B only once, it may be described by a single-valued function $y = y(x)$. Moreover, the origin of coordinates can be chosen to coincide with point A and the y-axis can be directed downward. The sliding particle m when passing through an arbitrary point (x, y) on

Γ (Fig. 13.2) will possess* speed $v = \sqrt{2gy}$ and will cover an element of arc ds in time

$$dt = \frac{ds}{v} = \frac{\sqrt{1 + (dy/dx)^2}\, dx}{\sqrt{2gy}}.$$

The total time of descent is

$$T = \int_0^a dt = \int_0^a \frac{\sqrt{1 + (dy/dx)^2}\, dx}{\sqrt{2gy}}.$$

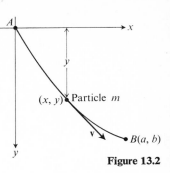

Figure 13.2

Selecting various functions $y(x)$, we shall obtain, in general, different values of T. In other words, T is a number depending on a function or a *functional*. The mathematical problem is then to find such a function $y(x)$ which will produce the minimum of the functional T.

From the physical meaning of the problem, it follows that $y(x)$ must also obey certain restrictions: not only must it be continuous, but it must also be twice differentiable, since the existence of d^2y/dx^2 is directly related to the existence of the acceleration of the particle. It is also obvious that $y(x)$ must satisfy the relations

$$y(0) = 0, \qquad y(a) = b$$

since the curve must pass through A and B.

Formulated in this fashion, the search for the brachistochrone is a particular example of the simplest problem of variational calculus: Among all functions $y(x)$ with fixed values at two distinct points, $y(x_0) = y_0$, $y(x_1) = y_1$, find those which give an extremum (minimum or maximum) to the integral

$$J\{y\} = \int_{x_0}^{x_1} F(y, y', x)\, dx,$$

where $F(y, y', x)$ is an explicitly given function of three variables: y, y', and x.

It is usually assumed that $F(y, y', x)$ possesses the necessary partial derivatives and $y(x)$ is required to be sufficiently well behaved, e.g., twice differentiable.

13.2 THE EULER-LAGRANGE EQUATION

The customary technique of calculus used to locate an extremum of a function of one or many variables consists of the following steps. We select an arbitrary point, defined by a set of independent variables $\{x_0, y_0, z_0, \ldots\}$. Next we introduce arbitrary infinitesimal changes $\{dx, dy, \ldots\}$ and form the total differential of the function $f(x, y, z, \ldots)$,

$$df = \frac{\partial f}{\partial x}\, dx + \frac{\partial f}{\partial y}\, dy + \cdots$$

---

* From the law of conservation of energy, independently of the shape of Γ.

with the understanding that all partial derivatives are evaluated at the point $(x_0, y_0, \ldots)$. Since df must vanish at an extremum,* no matter what dx, dy, ... are, it follows that all partial derivatives must vanish *at the point* $(x_0, y_0, \ldots)$ if it is to qualify as an extremum point:

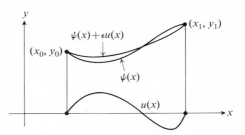

Figure 13.3

$$\left.\frac{\partial f}{\partial x}\right|_{\substack{x=x_0 \\ y=y_0 \\ \text{etc.}}} = \left.\frac{\partial f}{\partial y}\right|_{\substack{x=x_0 \\ y=y_0 \\ \text{etc.}}} = \cdots = 0.$$

Solving these equations, we obtain the coordinates of the point $(x_0, y_0, \ldots)$. At this stage, we omit the label "zero" in $(x_0, y_0, \ldots)$ and we denote the extremum point simply by $(x, y, z, \ldots)$. Variational calculus employs the same general idea. Instead of the point $(x_0, y_0, \ldots)$ we have now a particular selection of the function $y(x)$ which we shall denote by $\psi(x)$. It must satisfy

$$\psi(x_0) = y_0, \qquad \psi(x_1) = y_1.$$

As a second step, a small change in the function is considered. This must obviously be a change in the *functional form* $y(x)$. A simple way of doing this is to add to $\psi(x)$ a small multiple of another function $u(x)$:

$$\psi(x) \rightarrow \psi(x) + \epsilon u(x).$$

Since the new function must again pass through the same points (x_0, y_0) and (x_1, y_1), it is evident that $u(x)$ must vanish at these points:

$$u(x_0) = 0, \qquad u(x_1) = 0.$$

Otherwise, $u(x)$ is almost arbitrary.† In this fashion it is possible to change the form of $\psi(x)$ in an essentially arbitrary manner but keep the new function infinitesimally close to $\psi(x)$ by choosing ϵ sufficiently small. This is illustrated in Fig. 13.3.

Remark. In many texts the term $\epsilon u(x)$ is denoted by $\delta\psi$ and called *variation of the function* ψ. This notation resembles that of a differential dx of a variable x. Observe, however, that a function $\psi(x)$ is, in a sense, equivalent to an infinite number of parameters.‡ Therefore, an *arbitrary* variation of a functional form is equivalent to an infinite number of unrelated changes, one for each parameter. From that point of view, the symbol $\delta\psi$

---

* See, e.g., Kaplan, *Advanced Calculus*, Section 2.15.

† It must be well behaved, just as $\psi(x)$ is.

‡ For instance, a function $\psi(x)$ may be defined by the set of its Fourier coefficients, infinite in number.

is analogous, not to a differential dx of one variable x, but to a *whole set* of such differentials $\{dx, dy, dz, \ldots\}$.

The change in the functional form of $\psi(x)$ results in the change of the *value* of the integral J. Indeed, the value of the integrand changes at each point x by virtue of the fact that the values of y and y', at each point x, are changed. The new values are

$$y(x) = \psi(x) + \epsilon u(x), \qquad y'(x) = \psi'(x) + \epsilon u'(x).$$

Therefore, to the first order in ϵ, the new value of $F(y, y', x)$ is

$$F(\psi + \epsilon u, \psi' + \epsilon u', x) \cong F(\psi, \psi', x) + \left.\frac{\partial F}{\partial y}\right|_{\substack{y=\psi \\ y'=\psi'}} \cdot \epsilon u + \left.\frac{\partial F}{\partial y'}\right|_{\substack{y=\psi \\ y'=\psi'}} \cdot \epsilon u'.$$

Note the meaning of the operations. The function F has to be differentiated with respect to y and y' and the functional forms $\psi(x)$ and $\psi'(x)$ *are to be inserted* after the differentiation.

As a result of these considerations the value of the integral J will undergo a change which is universally denoted by δJ. Explicitly,

$$\delta J = \int_{x_0}^{x_1} F(\psi + \epsilon u, \psi' + \epsilon u', x)\, dx - \int_{x_0}^{x_1} F(\psi, \psi', x)\, dx$$

$$\cong \epsilon \int_{x_0}^{x_1} \left(\left.\frac{\partial F}{\partial y}\right|_{\substack{y=\psi \\ y'=\psi'}} \cdot u + \left.\frac{\partial F}{\partial y'}\right|_{\substack{y=\psi \\ y'=\psi'}} \cdot u' \right) dx.$$

The second term can be conveniently integrated by parts:

$$\int_{x_0}^{x_1} \frac{\partial F}{\partial y'} u'\, dx = \left.\frac{\partial F}{\partial y'} u\right|_{x_0}^{x_1} - \int_{x_0}^{x_1} u \frac{d}{dx}\left(\frac{\partial F}{\partial y'}\right) dx.$$

By virtue of $u(x_0) = u(x_1) = 0$ the "integrated-out" term vanishes, leaving the result

$$\delta J = \epsilon \int_{x_0}^{x_1} \left.\left[\frac{\partial F}{\partial y} - \frac{d}{dx}\left(\frac{\partial F}{\partial y'}\right)\right]\right|_{\substack{y=\psi \\ y'=\psi'}} \cdot u\, dx.$$

As in common calculus, a simple argument is now produced to assert that δJ must vanish at a minimum. If $\delta J > 0$ for some particular choice of $\epsilon u(x)$ (this does not contradict the minimum property), then $\delta J < 0$ when the sign of ϵ is reversed (this does contradict the minimum property). Since for sufficiently small ϵ the sign of δJ is determined by the first-order terms, it follows that $\delta J = 0$ is a *necessary* condition for a minimum. The argument for a maximum is similar. Since this must be valid for arbitrary $u(x)$ and sufficiently small but finite ϵ, it follows that

$$\int_{x_0}^{x_1} \left.\left[\frac{\partial F}{\partial y} - \frac{d}{dx}\left(\frac{\partial F}{\partial y'}\right)\right]\right|_{\substack{y=\psi \\ y'=\psi'}} \cdot u\, dx = 0$$

for *arbitrary* $u(x)$. It appears that this is possible only if

$$\left[\frac{\partial F}{\partial y} - \frac{d}{dx}\left(\frac{\partial F}{\partial y'}\right)\right]\Bigg|_{\substack{y=\psi \\ y'=\psi'}} = 0.$$

A rigorous statement to this effect is found in the

Fundamental theorem of variational calculus. If $f(x)$ is continuous in the interval (x_0, x_1) and the integral

$$\int_{x_0}^{x_1} f(x)g(x)\, dx$$

vanishes for *every* $g(x)$ continuously differentiable (smooth) in (x_0, x_1) and vanishing at $x = x_0$ and $x = x_1$, then $f(x) \equiv 0$ for $x_0 \le x \le x_1$.

Proof. Suppose that $f(\xi) \ne 0$ for some ξ such that $x_0 < \xi < x_1$. Assume that $f(\xi) > 0$. By continuity of $f(x)$ there must exist an interval $(\xi - \epsilon, \xi + \epsilon)$ such that $f(x) > 0$ for $\xi - \epsilon \le x \le x + \epsilon$. Construct the function

$$g(x) = \begin{cases} (x - \xi + \epsilon)^2(x - \xi - \epsilon)^2 & (\xi - \epsilon \le x \le \xi + \epsilon), \\ 0 & \text{(otherwise)}. \end{cases}$$

It is easy to check that $g(x)$ is smooth in (x_0, x_1) and vanishes at $x = x_0$ and $x = x_1$. The integral

$$\int_{x_0}^{x_1} f(x)g(x)\, dx = \int_{\xi-\epsilon}^{\xi+\epsilon} f(x)(x - \xi + \epsilon)^2(x - \xi - \epsilon)^2\, dx$$

is evidently positive since $f(x) > m$, where m is the minimum of $f(x)$ in $(\xi - \epsilon, \xi + \epsilon)$ and m must be positive since $f(x)$ is positive. This eliminates the possibility that $f(\xi) > 0$ for some ξ. The assumption that $f(\xi) < 0$ is rejected by a parallel argument and the theorem is established.

The result of the above analysis is that the expression (at least if it is a continuous function of x)

$$\frac{\partial F}{\partial y} - \frac{d}{dx}\left(\frac{\partial F}{\partial y'}\right)$$

must vanish whenever y is replaced by a function $\psi(x)$ which makes J an extremum. This expression is sometimes called the *Lagrangian derivative* of $F(y, y', x)$ with respect to $y(x)$ and is denoted by $\delta F/\delta y$. To simplify the notation, the function $\psi(x)$ can be renamed $y(x)$ and must satisfy the relation

$$\frac{\partial F}{\partial y} - \frac{d}{dx}\left(\frac{\partial F}{\partial y'}\right) \equiv \frac{\delta F}{\delta y} = 0,$$

known as the *Euler-Lagrange equation*. It is an ordinary DE of second order for $y(x)$. Indeed, the partial derivatives of $F = F(y, y', x)$ are, in general, some functions of y, y', and x:

$$\frac{\partial F}{\partial y} = \varphi(y, y', x), \qquad \frac{\partial F}{\partial y'} = \chi(y, y', x).$$

Then

$$\frac{d}{dx}\left(\frac{\partial F}{\partial y'}\right) = \frac{d\chi}{dx} = \frac{\partial \chi}{\partial x} + \frac{\partial \chi}{\partial y}y' + \frac{\partial \chi}{\partial y'}y''$$

or

$$\frac{d}{dx}\left(\frac{\partial F}{\partial y'}\right) = \frac{\partial^2 F}{\partial x\,\partial y'} + \frac{\partial^2 F}{\partial y\,\partial y'}y' + \frac{\partial^2 F}{\partial y'^2}y''.$$

The Euler-Lagrange equation must have the form

$$\frac{\partial^2 F}{\partial y'^2}y'' + \frac{\partial^2 F}{\partial y\,\partial y'}y' + \frac{\partial^2 F}{\partial x\,\partial y'} - \frac{\partial F}{\partial y} = 0.$$

Since all partial derivatives of F are functions of y, y', and x, this DE involves no higher derivatives of y than the second.

Remark. Functions satisfying the Euler-Lagrange equation, as well as the appropriate boundary conditions, make the variation δJ of the functional J vanish within the first order. This is a *necessary* condition for an extremum but not a *sufficient* one. It is possible to have $\delta J = 0$ to the first order without having an extremum.* In any case, the Euler-Lagrange equation determines the points at which J is *stationary*.† Whether or not it is an extremum needs further investigation.

Let us apply our analysis to the problem of the brachistochrone. Since the factor $1/\sqrt{2g}$ is immaterial, we may set

$$F(y, y', x) = \sqrt{\frac{1 + y'^2}{y}} = (1 + y'^2)^{1/2}y^{-1/2}$$

and calculate

$$\frac{\partial F}{\partial y} = -\tfrac{1}{2}y^{-3/2}(1 + y'^2)^{1/2}, \qquad \frac{\partial F}{\partial y'} = y'(1 + y'^2)^{1/2}y^{-1/2},$$

$$\frac{d}{dx}\left(\frac{\partial F}{\partial y'}\right) = (1 + y'^2)^{-1/2}y^{-1/2}y'' - y'^2(1 + y'^2)^{-3/2}y^{-1/2}y''$$
$$- \tfrac{1}{2}y^{-3/2}y'^2(1 + y'^2)^{-1/2}.$$

We form the Euler-Lagrange equation and simplify it to obtain

$$2y''y + 1 + y'^2 = 0.$$

---

* This situation is analogous to that applying to a function of several variables: The point where all partial derivatives vanish need not be an extremum; it may be, e.g., a saddle point.

† By definition, a stationary point is where $\delta J = 0$ to the first order.

This **DE** does not contain x. The standard substitution

$$y' = p, \qquad y'' = (dp/dy)p$$

permits easy integration resulting in

$$y(1 + y'^2) = k,$$

where k is some undetermined constant. Proceeding further, we obtain

$$dx = \sqrt{\frac{y}{k - y}}\, dy.$$

A convenient substitution is $y = (k/2)(1 - \cos \theta) = k \sin^2 (\theta/2)$; then

$$dx = k \sin^2 \frac{\theta}{2}\, d\theta$$

and

$$x = \frac{k}{2}(\theta - \sin \theta) + k_1 \qquad (k_1 = \text{const}).$$

Choosing $\theta = 0$ at point A (Fig. 13.2), we deduce that $k_1 = 0$. The other constant k, and the corresponding value of θ, can be obtained from the condition that our curve pass through point B:*

$$a = \frac{k}{2}(\theta - \sin \theta), \qquad b = \frac{k}{2}(1 - \cos \theta).$$

The brachistochrone curve is then given in parametric form:

$$x = \frac{k}{2}(\theta - \sin \theta), \qquad y = \frac{k}{2}(1 - \cos \theta).$$

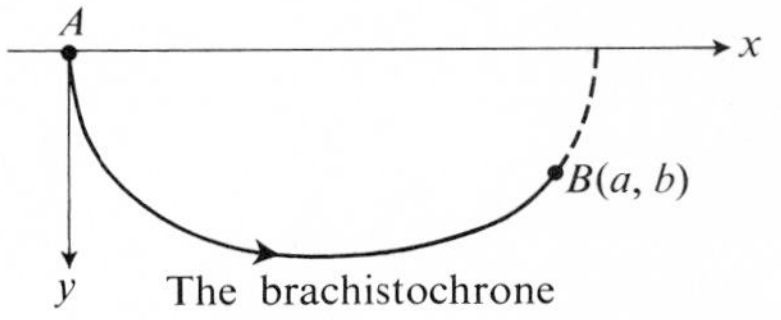

The brachistochrone

Figure 13.4

These equations represent a cycloid which actually yields a minimum for T, as follows from physical considerations.

A curious situation arises if $a > (\pi/2)b$. In this case the brachistochrone descends below point B (Fig. 13.4). The particle must pick up appreciable speed in order to cover the "flat" portion of the cycloid in relatively short time.

Remark. There is a shortcut method which is very helpful in solving the Euler-Lagrange equation when $F(y, y', x)$ happens to be *independent of* x (explicitly). In this case the following identity holds:

$$\left[\frac{\partial F}{\partial y} - \frac{d}{dx}\left(\frac{\partial F}{\partial y'} \right) \right] y' = \frac{d}{dx}\left(F - y' \frac{\partial F}{\partial y'} \right).$$

---

* A simple analysis shows that there is always a unique solution for $a > 0$, $b > 0$.

Exercise. Verify this identity by expanding both sides.

If the Euler-Lagrange equation holds, then the right-hand side vanishes, yielding immediately

$$F = y' \frac{\partial F}{\partial y'} = C = \text{const.}$$

Therefore, if $F(y, y', x)$ contains no x, we can write this relation at once, bypassing the formation of the Euler-Lagrange equation. Further integration yields $y(x)$.

For instance, for the brachistochrone we could have written immediately

$$\sqrt{\frac{1 + y'^2}{y}} - y' \frac{y'}{\sqrt{y}\sqrt{1 + y'^2}} = C,$$

and $y(1 + y'^2) = 1/c^2 = k$ follows, as before. This saves a bit of time and effort.

13.3 HAMILTON'S PRINCIPLE

We have seen that the variational problem of making the integral

$$J = \int_{x_0}^{x_1} F(y, y', x) \, dx$$

an extremum, or at least stationary, is reducible to a differential equation for the unknown function $y(x)$. Conversely, if a DE of second order for an unknown function $y(x)$ is given, then it should be possible, in principle, to relate $y(x)$ to some variational problem. Consider, for instance, the DE for a harmonic oscillator:

$$m \frac{d^2 x}{dt^2} + kx = 0.$$

The independent variable is the time t and the function we are seeking is $x(t)$. It is easy to construct a function $F(x, \dot{x}, t)$ such that the above DE is the Euler-Lagrange equation for F. The function

$$F(x, \dot{x}, t) = \frac{m\dot{x}^2}{2} - \frac{kx^2}{2}$$

will certainly qualify. Note that this function is the difference between the kinetic and potential energies of the oscillator. Since the motion is conservative, F is the *Lagrangian function* $\mathcal{L}(x, \dot{x}, t)$.[*] This is not surprising since the Lagrangian equation of motion

$$\frac{d}{dt}\left(\frac{\partial \mathcal{L}}{\partial \dot{x}}\right) - \frac{\partial \mathcal{L}}{\partial x} = 0$$

is identical in form with the Euler-Lagrange equation.

While the Lagrangian form of equation of motion might have been derived through other considerations, we can relate it to

---

[*] In our case $\mathcal{L}$ does not depend on time.

Hamilton's principle. Among all conceivable motions of a particle under conservative forces* between two given points during a given interval of time (t_0, t_1), the actual motion must be such that the integral

$$J = \int_{t_0}^{t_1} \mathcal{L}(x, \dot{x}, t)\, dt$$

will be stationary.

This statement acquires greater importance for systems with many degrees of freedom, in other words, for variational problems involving more than one function.

Consider the problem of making stationary the integral

$$J = \int_{x_0}^{x_1} F(y, y', z, z', x)\, dx,$$

where the integrand depends on two unknown functions, $y(x)$ and $z(x)$. We can vary J by making small changes in the functional forms of y and z. These changes are independent of each other and we write†

$$y(x) \rightarrow y(x) + \epsilon_1 u_1(x), \qquad z(x) \rightarrow z(x) + \epsilon_2 u_2(x),$$

where‡ $u_1(x_0) = u_1(x_1) = 0$ and $u_2(x_0) = u_2(x_1) = 0$. Within the first order in small quantities ϵ_1 and ϵ_2, we have

$$F(y + \epsilon_1 u_1, \ldots) \cong F(y, y', z, \ldots) + \frac{\partial F}{\partial y} \epsilon_1 u_1 + \frac{\partial F}{\partial y'} \epsilon_1 u_1' + \frac{\partial F}{\partial z} \epsilon_2 u_2 + \frac{\partial F}{\partial z'} \epsilon_2 u_2'.$$

We integrate by parts as before and deduce

$$\delta J = \int_{x_0}^{x_1} \left\{ \left[\frac{\partial F}{\partial y} - \frac{d}{dx}\left(\frac{\partial F}{\partial y'} \right) \right] \epsilon_1 u_1 + \left[\frac{\partial F}{\partial z} - \frac{d}{dx}\left(\frac{\partial F}{\partial z'} \right) \right] \epsilon_2 u_2 \right\} dx.$$

Since u_1 and u_2 are arbitrary, set $u_2 = 0$ and deduce the Euler-Lagrange equation with respect to $y(x)$:

$$\frac{\partial F}{\partial y} - \frac{d}{dx}\left(\frac{\partial F}{\partial y'} \right) = 0.$$

Now set $u_1 = 0$ and deduce the other Euler-Lagrange equation,

$$\frac{\partial F}{\partial z} - \frac{d}{dx}\left(\frac{\partial F}{\partial z'} \right) = 0.$$

Solving these two equations, we can obtain, in principle, the functions $y(x)$ and $z(x)$. Note, however, that the partial derivatives of F will, in general, contain

---

* Forces representable as gradients of some scalar functions (see p. 15).

† To simplify the notation we do not distinguish between the symbol $y(x)$ and some particular form of $y(x)$; similarly for $z(x)$.

‡ Tacitly assuming the condition that the values of y and z are fixed at the ends.

both unknown functions and their derivatives as well as the independent variable x. This means that the Euler-Lagrange equations will yield a *system of coupled differential equations* of second order.

It is evident that the above analysis can be trivially extended to an arbitrary number of variables. In classical mechanics this leads to the formulation of Hamilton's principle for a system of an arbitrary number of degrees of freedom, e.g., a multiparticle system. The Lagrangian is a function of n generalized coordinates $q_1(t), q_2(t), \ldots$ and their derivatives $\dot{q}_1(t), \dot{q}_2(t), \ldots$, and, perhaps, of t itself. The statement of the principle is the same as before, except that *particle* is replaced by *dynamical system* and *point* by *configuration*. The essential result is a set of coupled differential equations of the form*

$$\frac{d}{dt}\left(\frac{\partial \mathcal{L}}{\partial \dot{q}_i}\right) - \frac{\partial \mathcal{L}}{\partial q_i} = 0 \qquad (i = 1, 2, \ldots, n).$$

13.4 PROBLEMS INVOLVING STURM-LIOUVILLE OPERATORS

Many problems in mathematical physics involve, in one way or another, differential operators of the Sturm-Liouville type:

$$\mathcal{L} \equiv \frac{d}{dx}\left[p(x)\frac{d}{dx}\right] - s(x),$$

where the functions p and s are nonnegative,† $p(x) \geq 0$, $s(x) \geq 0$, within the interval under consideration. Let this interval be $(0, L)$ and let us study the DE of the form

$$\frac{d}{dx}\left[p(x)\frac{dy}{dx}\right] - s(x)y = f(x),$$

where $f(x)$ is a given function and $y(x)$ is the unknown function. We have met such problems before (Sections 11.8 and 12.2) and we shall now consider them in their relation to variational calculus. A bit of reflection shows that our DE can be regarded‡ as the Euler-Lagrange equation for the functional

$$J = \int_0^L [py'^2 + sy^2 + 2fy]\,dx.$$

Therefore, the functions which have fixed values $y(0) = a$, $y(L) = b$ and make J stationary must satisfy this DE and vice versa.

---

* See Section 10.1 and 10.2.
† See Section 11.6.
‡ At least this fact is readily verified.

Remark. If $y(x)$ *happens to vanish* at $x = 0$ and $x = L$, which is a rather common case, then we can write

$$\int_0^L py'^2 \, dx = ypy' \Big|_0^L - \int_0^L y \frac{d}{dx} (py') \, dx = -\int_0^L y \frac{d}{dx} (py') \, dx$$

and reduce J to the form ($\mathcal{L}$ as above)

$$J = -\int_0^L (y\mathcal{L}y - 2fy) \, dx.$$

This transformation is important in eigenvalue problems.

To get the full benefit of variational formulation, we shall now prove* that if $p(x) > 0$ and $s(x) \geq 0$, there *exists* a solution of

$$\frac{d}{dx} (py') - sy = f$$

satisfying $y(0) = a$, $y(L) = b$, and that such a solution is *unique*.

It is more convenient to establish the uniqueness first. Suppose that there are two solutions $y_1(x)$ and $y_2(x)$ satisfying the DE and the boundary conditions. Evidently, their difference $u = y_1 - y_2$ must satisfy the *homogeneous* differential equation

$$\frac{d}{dx} \left[p(x) \frac{du}{dx} \right] - s(x)u = 0$$

and *homogeneous* boundary conditions $u(0) = u(L) = 0$. We multiply the DE by $u(x)$ and integrate over $(0, L)$:

$$\int_0^L u \frac{d}{dx} \left[p \frac{du}{dx} \right] dx - \int_0^L su^2 \, dx = 0.$$

However, integrating by parts and using the boundary conditions, we obtain

$$\int_0^L u \frac{d}{dx} \left[p \frac{du}{dx} \right] dx = up \frac{du}{dx} \Big|_0^L - \int_0^L p \left(\frac{du}{dx} \right)^2 dx = -\int_0^L py'^2 \, dx.$$

Therefore

$$\int_0^L (pu'^2 + su^2) \, dx = 0.$$

Since neither term can be negative, each term must be zero. But since $p(x) > 0$, we must have† $u' = 0$ or $u = \text{const}$. However, $u(0) = 0$ so that $u(x)$ must be identically equal to zero. We arrive at the statement: "There can be at most one solution $y(x)$ of our original DE and boundary conditions."

---

* Something that we tacitly assumed earlier.

† By a similar argument as on p. 466.

Proceeding to the proof of existence, we take for granted that *some* solutions of our DE exist. What we want to show is that a solution satisfying $y(0) = a$ and $y(L) = b$ can be selected. We also take for granted that two linearly independent solutions of the corresponding *homogeneous* DE exist.

We let $u_1(x)$ be a nontrivial solution of the homogeneous DE such that $u_1(0) = 0$; then $u_1(L) \neq 0$. Otherwise $u_1(x)$ would be zero (see the proof of uniqueness above). We let $u_2(x)$ be another nontrivial solution of the homogeneous DE such that $u_2(L) = 0$; then $u_2(0) \neq 0$. Finally, we let $y_0(x)$ be any solution of the nonhomogeneous DE, and we form the function

$$y(x) = y_0(x) + C_1 u_1(x) + C_2 u_2(x).$$

Evidently, this function satisfies the nonhomogeneous DE. In order to satisfy our boundary conditions, we must have

$$C_1 u_1(0) + C_2 u_2(0) + y_0(0) = a, \qquad C_1 u_1(L) + C_2 u_2(L) + y_0(0) = b.$$

By virtue of the chosen properties of u_1 and u_2, we can solve for C_1 and C_2; explicitly,

$$C_1 = \frac{b - y_0(L)}{u_1(L)}, \qquad C_2 = \frac{a - y_0(L)}{u_2(L)}.$$

Note that both C_1 and C_2 may vanish. However, they are well defined. Combining this with the uniqueness property, we conclude that a unique solution of our DE and boundary conditions exists.

We are now in a position to prove the following theorem of variational calculus:

Theorem. Within the class of functions that are smooth in $(0, L)$ and satisfy $y(0) = a$, $y(L) = b$, the functional

$$J = \int_0^L (p y'^2 + s y^2 + 2 f y)\, dx \qquad (p(x) > 0,\ s(x) \geq 0)$$

reaches its *minimum* if and only if $y(x)$ is the solution of the Euler-Lagrange equation.

The essence of the theorem is that we are now definitely talking about the minimum, rather than a stationary point.

Proof. We let $\psi(x)$ be the unique solution of the DE and the boundary conditions and let $y(x)$ be any other smooth function satisfying the boundary conditions. Also, we let $y(x) - \psi(x) = \varphi(x)$; then φ is smooth and vanishes at $x = 0$ and $x = L$. We have

$$y^2 = \psi^2 + 2\psi\varphi + \varphi^2, \qquad y'^2 = \psi'^2 + 2\psi'\varphi' + \varphi'^2$$

and
$$\Delta J = J\{y\} - J\{\psi\}$$
$$= 2\int_0^L (p\psi'\varphi' + s\psi\varphi + f\varphi)\, dx + \int_0^L (p\varphi'^2 + s\varphi^2)\, dx.$$

It turns out that the first integral is zero. Indeed, integrating by parts and using boundary conditions satisfied by φ, we have

$$\int_0^L p\psi'\varphi'\, dx = \varphi p\psi' \Big|_0^L - \int_0^L \varphi \frac{d}{dx}(p\psi')\, dx = -\int_0^L \varphi \frac{d}{dx}(p\psi')\, dx$$

so that, using the DE satisfied by ψ, we obtain

$$\int_0^L (p\psi'\varphi' + s\psi\varphi + f\varphi)\, dx = \int_0^L \varphi\left[-\frac{d}{dx}(p\psi') + s\psi + f\right] dx = 0.$$

Therefore
$$\Delta J = \int_0^L (p\varphi'^2 + s\varphi^2)\, dx.$$

Evidently, $\Delta J \geq 0$. Moreover, $\Delta J = 0$ implies $\varphi = 0$. In other words, *any* admissible $y(x)$ not identical with $\psi(x)$ will yield a larger value of J than the value corresponding to $\psi(x)$, as stated.

13.5 THE RAYLEIGH-RITZ METHOD

Consider again the problem of solving the DE

$$\frac{d}{dx}\left[p(x)\frac{du}{dx}\right] - s(x)y = f(x),$$

where $p(x) > 0$, $s(x) \geq 0$, subject to suitable boundary conditions. To be specific, assume $y(0) = y(L) = 0$. We know there exist *complete* sets of functions such that our solution is expressible as

$$y(x) = \sum_{n=1}^{\infty} Y_n\varphi_n(x).$$

According to Section 13.4, our problem is equivalent to the problem of minimizing the functional

$$J = \int_0^L \{p(x)[y'(x)]^2 + s(x)[y(x)]^2 + 2f(x)y(x)\}\, dx.$$

Substituting our expression for $y(x)$ into the integral, we have

$$p(x)[y'(x)]^2 = \sum_{m=1}^{\infty}\sum_{n=1}^{\infty} Y_m Y_n p(x)\varphi_m'(x)\varphi_n'(x).$$

Assuming the validity of term-by-term integration and writing

$$\int_0^L p(x)\varphi_m'(x)\varphi_n'(x)\,dx = C_{mn},$$

we obtain

$$\int_0^L p(x)[y'(x)]^2\,dx = \sum_{m=1}^{\infty}\sum_{n=1}^{\infty} C_{mn}\,Y_m\,Y_n.$$

Treating the other terms in the integral in a similar way, we deduce

$$J = \sum_{m=1}^{\infty}\sum_{n=1}^{\infty} A_{mn}\,Y_m\,Y_n + 2\sum_{n=1}^{\infty} F_n\,Y_n,$$

where

$$F_n = \int_0^L f(x)\varphi_n(x)\,dx,$$

$$A_{mn} = \int_0^L [p(x)\varphi_m'(x)\varphi_n'(x) + s(x)\varphi_m(x)\varphi_n(x)]\,dx.$$

The coefficients A_{mn} and F_n are presumed to be known since the set of the φ_n is known. The unknowns are now the coefficients Y_n. According to the theorem in the preceding section, we can determine these coefficients from the condition that J must be a minimum. This condition requires that

$$\frac{\partial J}{\partial Y_k} = 0 \qquad \text{(all } k\text{)}.$$

Performing the differentiation and using the obvious fact that $A_{mn} = A_{nm}$, we obtain

$$\sum_{n=1}^{\infty} A_{kn}\,Y_n + F_k = 0 \qquad \text{(all } k\text{)}.$$

This is a system of an infinite number of coupled nonhomogeneous equations.

The solution is easy if the system happens to be decoupled, which will be the case if the matrix A of the coefficients A_{kn} is *diagonal*. This will happen if the functions $\varphi_n(x)$ are *eigenfunctions* of the operator

$$\frac{d}{dx}\left[p(x)\frac{d}{dx}\right] - s(x);$$

this can be readily checked. If these eigenfunctions are known, there are no difficulties (except, perhaps, slow convergence), and the coefficients Y_n are easily calculated. Evidently, this technique is nothing but the *method of eigenfunction expansion* described in Section 11.8.

Suppose, however, that the eigenfunctions are not known or the method is deemed too complicated for other reasons, such as, for instance, the evaluation of integrals. In this case the variational formulation allows *approximate* calculation of $y(x)$ by the technique known as the *Rayleigh-Ritz* method. Select a *finite* number N of functions $\varphi_n(x)$. They do not need to be a part of some known complete set, but they should be linearly independent. Suppose that for some choice of coefficients $\bar{Y}_n$ the expression

$$\bar{y}(x) = \sum_{n=1}^{N} \bar{Y}_n \varphi_n(x)$$

is a close approximation to the true solution $y(x)$. Then the corresponding value of J, expressible, as before, by

$$J\{\bar{y}\} = \sum_{m=1}^{N} \sum_{n=1}^{N} A_{mn} \bar{Y}_m \bar{Y}_n + 2 \sum_{n=1}^{N} F_n \bar{Y}_n,$$

will approximate the true minimum $J\{y\}$. Conversely, of all linear combinations of functions $\varphi_n(x)$, we may, in a sense, regard as the best approximation to $y(x)$ that particular one which yields J as close as possible to $J\{y\}$. Evidently, this means that we must choose the *smallest possible* value of $J\{\bar{y}\}$. At this stage the value of the theorem in the preceding section becomes apparent: if we did not know the character of the stationary point of J, we could not tell *how to improve* any given approximation $\bar{y}(x)$.*

The problem of minimizing $J\{\bar{y}\}$ reduces to the set of equations

$$\sum_{n=1}^{N} A_{kn} \bar{Y}_n + F_k = 0 \qquad (k = 1, 2, \ldots, N).$$

This nonhomogeneous system will have a unique solution provided the determinant of matrix A is not zero. However, this must be the case because A is positive definite: For *any* nontrivial choice of the $\bar{Y}_n$, we have

$$\sum_{m=1}^{N} \sum_{n=1}^{N} A_{mn} \bar{Y}_m \bar{Y}_n = \int_0^L (p\bar{y}'^2 + s\bar{y}^2)\, dx > 0.$$

Consequently, all eigenvalues of A are positive and $\det A \neq 0$.

Remark. The quality of the Ritz approximation depends crucially on the choice of the $\varphi_n(x)$-functions. In practice, this means that some informed guess about the shape of the solution $y(x)$ should be made.

13.6 VARIATIONAL PROBLEMS WITH CONSTRAINTS

Maxima and minima problems often involve certain constraints. For instance, an extremum of $F = F(x, y)$ may be sought under the restriction that x and y

---

* This is analogous to the problem of a traveler engulfed in a dense fog and seeking some "stationary point" on an unfamiliar terrain. If the stationary point is a mountain top, he knows that he must climb; similarly, he must descend if it is the bottom of a depression. However, if it is a saddle point, e.g., a mountain pass, there is no way of telling how he should proceed from any given spot.

be related by an equation of the form

$$G(x, y) = C = \text{const.}$$

Suppose that it is inconvenient to solve this equation for y, substitute the result into $F(x, y)$, and reduce the problem to an extremum in a single variable. In this case we can use the *method of Lagrange multipliers* which is based on the following theorem.

Theorem. The problem of stationary values of $F(x, y)$, subject to the constraint $G(x, y) = C$ is equivalent to the problem of stationary values, without constraints, of the function

$$H(x, y) = F(x, y) + \lambda G(x, y)$$

for some constant λ, *provided* at least one of the partial derivatives $\partial G/\partial y$, $\partial G/\partial x$ does not vanish at the critical point.

This theorem can be generalized to an arbitrary number of variables and constraints and has its analog in variational calculus as well. Let us review the ideas behind it.

First, if F is stationary at some point (x_0, y_0), then $dF = 0$ or

$$\frac{\partial F}{\partial x} dx + \frac{\partial F}{\partial y} dy = 0 \qquad (\text{at } x_0, y_0).$$

The new feature introduced by the constraint is that dx and dy *are no longer independent*, and $\partial F/\partial x = 0$, $\partial F/\partial y = 0$ do not follow. From $G(x, y) = C$, it follows that

$$\frac{\partial G}{\partial x} dx + \frac{\partial G}{\partial y} dy = 0.$$

This relation determines dy in terms of dx, or vice versa, provided $\partial G/\partial y \neq 0$ or $\partial G/\partial x \neq 0$, respectively. To be specific, assume the former and write

$$dy = - \frac{\partial G/\partial x}{\partial G/\partial y} dx \qquad (\text{at } x_0, y_0).$$

Substituting into $dF = 0$, we obtain

$$\left(\frac{\partial F}{\partial x} \frac{\partial G}{\partial y} - \frac{\partial G}{\partial x} \frac{\partial F}{\partial y} \right) dx = 0.$$

Since $dx \neq 0$ (otherwise $dy = dx = 0$), we have

$$\frac{\partial F}{\partial x} \frac{\partial G}{\partial y} - \frac{\partial G}{\partial x} \frac{\partial F}{\partial y} = 0.$$

However, then a unique λ must exist such that

$$\frac{\partial F}{\partial x} + \lambda \frac{\partial G}{\partial x} = 0, \qquad \frac{\partial F}{\partial y} + \lambda \frac{\partial G}{\partial y} = 0 \qquad \text{(at } x_0, y_0\text{).}$$

Indeed, such λ is explicitly given by

$$\lambda = -\frac{\partial F/\partial y}{\partial G/\partial y}$$

and satisfies both equations. We have then established the *necessity* of these equations for the "conditional stationary point" of $F(x, y)$. Of course, they also characterize a stationary point of $H = F + \lambda G$. Note that we had to assume that $\partial G/\partial y \neq 0$ or $\partial G/\partial x \neq 0$ in order to carry out the argument.*

The proof of *sufficiency* of the Lagrange equations

$$\frac{\partial F}{\partial x} + \lambda \frac{\partial G}{\partial x} = 0, \qquad \frac{\partial F}{\partial y} + \lambda \frac{\partial G}{\partial y} = 0$$

does not require the condition $\partial G/\partial y \neq 0$ or $\partial G/\partial x \neq 0$. Indeed, suppose that the above equations hold for some λ and some point (x_0, y_0) such that $G(x_0, y_0) = C$. The increments dx and dy consistent with the constraint must satisfy

$$\frac{\partial G}{\partial x} dx + \frac{\partial G}{\partial y} dy = 0 \qquad \text{(at } x_0, y_0\text{).}$$

Multiplying the first of the Lagrange equations by dx, the second by dy, and adding, we obtain

$$\frac{\partial F}{\partial x} dx + \frac{\partial F}{\partial y} dy = 0 \qquad \text{(at } x_0, y_0\text{),}$$

which means that the point (x_0, y_0) is indeed a stationary point of $F(x, y)$ under the constraint.

As for the variational problems with constraints, perhaps the simplest of them is the so-called *isoperimetric problem*. This can be described as follows: Find the stationary points of the functional

$$J = \int_0^L F(y, y', x) \, dx$$

against variations δy that vanish at $x = a$ and $x = b$, but leaving the integral

$$N = \int_0^L G(y, y', x) \, dx$$

invariant at some known constant value C.

---

* There are situations in which the Lagrange method *fails*, but the stationary value of F under $G = $ const exists. In such cases, $\partial G/\partial x = \partial G/\partial y = 0$ at the stationary point.

Remark. The name isoperimetric can be traced to one of the earliest problems of this type. A curve Γ of given length C must be drawn between points $(0, 0)$ and $(0, L)$ (Fig. 13.5) such that the area between the curve and the x-axis is maximum. Assuming Γ to be given by a single-valued function $y = y(x)$, the problem reduces to the statement: Maximize

$$J = \int_0^L y\, dx$$

subject to the constraint

$$\int_0^L \sqrt{1 + y'^2}\, dx = C.$$

The variations in the shape of Γ must be such that the perimeter of the shaded area is kept constant, equal to $C + L$. Hence the term *isoperimetric*.

It is reasonable to conjecture that the isoperimetric problem can be solved by a technique analogous to that of Lagrange multipliers, i.e., by making the integral

$$K = \int_0^L (F + \lambda G)\, dx = J + \lambda N$$

(for some λ) stationary. This implies that the function $y(x)$ that we are seeking must satisfy the equation

$$\left[\frac{\partial F}{\partial y} - \frac{d}{dx}\left(\frac{\partial F}{\partial y'} \right) \right] + \lambda \left[\frac{\partial G}{\partial y} - \frac{d}{dx}\left(\frac{\partial G}{\partial y'} \right) \right] = 0.$$

It is easy to show that this is a *sufficient* condition (for appropriate λ) for the solution of the isoperimetric problem. Indeed, multiply this equation by some variation $\delta y(x)$ and integrate over $(0, L)$:

$$\int_0^L \left[\frac{\partial F}{\partial y} - \frac{d}{dx}\left(\frac{\partial F}{\partial y'} \right) \right] \delta y(x)\, dx + \lambda \int_0^L \left[\frac{\partial G}{\partial y} - \frac{d}{dx}\left(\frac{\partial G}{\partial y'} \right) \right] \delta y(x)\, dx = 0.$$

This holds for *arbitrary* variations $\delta y(x)$. In the isoperimetric problem only those variations are permitted that keep N invariant, namely, for which

$$\delta N = \int_0^L \left[\frac{\partial G}{\partial y} - \frac{d}{dx}\left(\frac{\partial G}{\partial y'} \right) \right] \delta y(x)\, dx = 0.$$

It follows that such variations will also make

$$\int_0^L \left[\frac{\partial F}{\partial x} - \frac{d}{dx}\left(\frac{\partial F}{\partial x} \right) \right] \delta y(x)\, dx = 0$$

or $\delta J = 0$, which means that J is stationary and our function $y(x)$ solves the isoperimetric problem.

To prove the *necessity* of the stationary character of $K = J + \lambda N$, we expect some restriction on $y(x)$, analogous to that in the problem from calculus. This

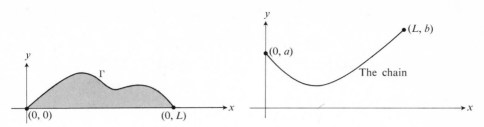

Figure 13.5   Figure 13.6

restriction happens to be

$$\frac{\partial G}{\partial y} - \frac{d}{dx}\left(\frac{\partial G}{\partial y'}\right) \neq 0,$$

that is, $y(x)$ should not be such as to make N stationary in its own right.* This is embodied in a theorem of Euler.

Theorem. The function $y(x)$ which makes J stationary against all variations δy and keeps N constant also makes stationary the functional $K = J + \lambda N$, for some λ, provided $y(x)$ does not cause $\delta N/\delta y$ to vanish; i.e., it does not satisfy the Euler-Lagrange equation for N.

We shall omit the proof of this theorem; the interested reader is referred to standard textbooks on variational calculus.

Example. *The Catenary.* A heavy chain of length C is hung between the points $(0, a)$ and (L, b), as shown in Fig. 13.6. Find its equilibrium shape.

From mechanics, we know that the equilibrium shape must be such that the potential energy will be minimum or, which is the same, its center of gravity will be the lowest possible. This means that we must minimize the functional

$$J = \rho g \int_0^L y \, ds = \rho g \int_0^L y\sqrt{1 + y'^2} \, dx,$$

where $\rho \, ds$ is the mass of the element of arc ds. The function y is subject to the constraint

$$N = \int_0^L ds = \int_0^L \sqrt{1 + y'^2} \, dx = C = \text{const},$$

representing the fact that the length of the chain is C.

---

* Just as δy is the analog of the entire set of differentials $dx, dy, dz, \ldots$ (see p. 556), the expression

$$\frac{\delta N}{\delta y} = \frac{\partial G}{\partial y} - \frac{d}{dx}\left(\frac{\partial G}{\partial y'}\right)$$

is analogous to the entire set of partial derivatives $\partial G/\partial x, \partial G/\partial y, \partial G/\partial z, \ldots$; the condition that it shall not vanish corresponds to the condition that *not all* partial derivatives vanish.

According to the preceding analysis, we may form the function

$$H(y, y', x) = y\sqrt{1 + y'^2} + \lambda\sqrt{1 + y'^2};$$

the factor ρg is irrelevant and may be dropped for our purposes. We must now solve the Euler-Lagrange equation for H. Since H does not explicitly depend on x, we may use the technique from p. 559 and immediately write

$$(y + \lambda)\sqrt{1 + y'^2} - y'\frac{(y + \lambda)y'}{\sqrt{1 + y'^2}} = k = \text{const.}$$

After simple manipulations, we obtain

$$\frac{dy}{\sqrt{(y + \lambda)^2 - k^2}} = \frac{dx}{k}.$$

Integrating by setting $y + \lambda = k \cosh \theta$ or simply using tables of integrals, we obtain

$$y + \lambda = k \cosh\frac{x + h}{k},$$

where h is the second constant of integration. The three constants k, h, and λ are determined from the conditions

$$a + \lambda = k \cosh\frac{h}{k}, \tag{1}$$

$$b + \lambda = k \cosh\frac{L + h}{k}, \tag{2}$$

$$\int_0^L \sqrt{1 + y'^2}\, dx = C. \tag{3}$$

This involves solving some transcendental equations, but the details are relatively simple. First,

$$y' = \sinh\frac{x + h}{k},$$

and the integral in (3) is readily evaluated. Using $\sqrt{1 + \sinh^2 \alpha} = \cosh \alpha$, we obtain

$$k \sinh\frac{x + h}{k}\bigg|_0^L = C.$$

Furthermore, using

$$\sinh \alpha - \sinh \beta = 2 \cosh\frac{\alpha + \beta}{2} \sinh\frac{\alpha - \beta}{2},$$

we reduce (3) to the form

$$C = 2k \cosh\frac{L + 2h}{2k} \sinh\frac{L}{2k}. \tag{4}$$

Next, subtracting (1) and (2) and using

$$\cosh \alpha - \cosh \beta = 2 \sinh \frac{\alpha + \beta}{2} \sinh \frac{\alpha - \beta}{2},$$

we deduce

$$b - a = 2k \sinh \frac{L + 2h}{2k} \sinh \frac{L}{2k}. \tag{5}$$

Dividing the last two equations, we obtain

$$\frac{b - a}{C} = \tanh \frac{L + 2h}{2k},$$

from which the value of $(L + 2h)/2k$ is readily found. Also, squaring and subtracting (4) and (5), we see that

$$C^2 - (b - a)^2 = 4k^2 \sinh^2 \frac{L}{k}$$

or

$$\frac{\sinh (L/k)}{L/k} = \frac{\sqrt{C^2 - (b - a)^2}}{L}$$

which yields the value of L/k. The rest is trivial.

13.7 VARIATIONAL FORMULATION OF EIGENVALUE PROBLEMS

In this section we shall consider the problem of variational formulation of differential equations of eigenvalue type, such as the Sturm-Liouville equation

$$\frac{d}{dx}\left[p(x) \frac{du}{dx} \right] - s(x)y = -\lambda r(x)y,$$

where $y(x)$ must satisfy appropriate boundary conditions. We shall confine ourselves to the case of homogeneous Dirichlet conditions on a finite interval, say $(0, L)$:

$$y(0) = y(L) = 0.$$

Using our experience from Section 13.4, we can deduce without any great difficulties that the functional

$$K = \int_0^L (py'^2 + sy^2 - \lambda ry^2)\, dx$$

will possess the Euler-Lagrange equation of the form we need. It is also worthwhile to observe that, in view of the boundary conditions, the above functional can be rewritten in the form*

$$K = \int_0^L [-y\mathcal{L}y + ysy - y\lambda ry]\, dx,$$

---

* One must, of course, integrate the first term by parts and use the boundary conditions.

where $\mathcal{L} = (d/dx)[p(x)(d/dx)]$. This expression shows that K is made up of inner products in the space of y-functions. In the notation of Chapter 11 we can write

$$K = -(y, \mathcal{L}y) + (y, sy) - (y, \lambda ry),$$

where y is a vector and $\mathcal{L}$, s, and λr are operators in the appropriate linear space.

However, let us return to the original integral for K. Since λ is as yet an unknown parameter, it is logical to associate our functional with the developments of the preceding section and treat the eigenvalue problem as a *variational problem with constraints*. Specifically, $y(x)$ is a function which makes stationary the integral

$$J = \int_0^L (py'^2 + sy^2)\, dx$$

subject to the constraint*

$$N = \int_0^L ry^2\, dx = \text{const.}$$

Remark. The value of the constant for N is irrelevant for the variational formulation, but it is most often taken to be unity. This means that $y(x)$ is normalized with respect to the weight function $r(x)$, a condition which is very convenient in eigenvalue problems.

We have tacitly assumed that all functions involved are real. However, the generalization to complex spaces is straightforward with the necessary changes applied in the spirit of the discussion in Chapters 10 and 11.

The variational formulation of the eigenvalue problem now permits the use of the Rayleigh-Ritz technique. First, if we expand $y(x)$ in terms of some complete set $\{\varphi_n(x)\}$ in our linear space of functions†

$$y(x) = \sum_{n=1}^{\infty} Y_n \varphi_n(x)$$

and substitute into K, then we can obtain

$$K = \sum_{m=1}^{\infty} \sum_{n=1}^{\infty} (A_{mn} - \lambda R_{mn}) Y_m Y_n,$$

where the A_{mn} are defined on p. 566 and

$$R_{mn} = \int_0^L r(x)\varphi_m(x)\varphi_n(x)\, dx.$$

For a chosen set $\{\varphi_n(x)\}$, the coefficients A_{mn} and R_{mn} are fixed and the stationary values of K are determined by the conditions

$$\frac{\partial K}{\partial Y_j} = 0 \qquad (\text{all } j),$$

* We follow the notation of Section 13.6 except that we have $-\lambda$ in place of λ.

† Namely, the space of well-behaved functions vanishing at the ends of the interval $(0, L)$.

which readily results (as on p. 566) in the system of equations

$$\sum_{n=1}^{\infty} (A_{mn} - \lambda R_{mn}) Y_n = 0 \qquad (m = 1, 2, \ldots).$$

This is now an infinite set of homogeneous algebraic equations and is probably more difficult to solve than the original Sturm-Liouville DE. The exception arises if the equations are decoupled (in diagonal form), but this just means that the φ_n are solutions of the DE to start with, leaving us in a vicious circle.

We recall, however, that the major value of the Rayleigh-Ritz method lies in *approximating* a solution $y(x)$ rather than evaluating it exactly. This feature is still in force for eigenvalue problems. Select a finite set of N linearly independent functions $\{\bar{\varphi}_1, \bar{\varphi}_2, \ldots, \bar{\varphi}_N\}$ in our space and form a linear combination

$$\bar{y}(x) = \sum_{n=1}^{N} \bar{Y}_n \bar{\varphi}_n(x).$$

Substituting $\bar{y}(x)$ into the integral for K and performing the same operations as before, we obtain a *finite* set of algebraic equations

$$\sum_{n=1}^{N} (\bar{A}_{mn} - \bar{\lambda} \bar{R}_{mn}) \bar{Y}_n = 0,$$

where $\bar{A}_{mn}$ and $\bar{R}_{mn}$ are defined in the same manner as A_{mn} and R_{mn} except that the φ_n are replaced by the $\bar{\varphi}_n$. For a nontrivial set of $\bar{Y}_n$ to exist, the determinant of this system must vanish, yielding N values* for $\bar{\lambda}$. The corresponding functions $\bar{y}(x)$ then follow.

To see the relation of the $\bar{\lambda}$ to the true eigenvalues λ, we observe that if $y(x)$ is a solution of the Sturm-Liouville equation, then K actually vanishes and we can write

$$\lambda = \frac{\int_0^L (py'^2 + sy^2)\, dx}{\int_0^L ry^2\, dx} = \frac{J\{y\}}{N\{y\}}.$$

A similar relation holds between $\bar{\lambda}$ and $\bar{y}(x)$. From the equations for the $\bar{Y}_n$, it follows (when each is multiplied by $\bar{Y}_m$ and the results are added) that

$$\bar{\lambda} = \frac{\sum_{m=1}^{N} \sum_{n=1}^{N} \bar{A}_{mn} \bar{Y}_m \bar{Y}_n}{\sum_{m=1}^{N} \sum_{n=1}^{N} \bar{R}_{mn} \bar{Y}_m \bar{Y}_n} = \frac{\int_0^L (p\bar{y}'^2 + s\bar{y}^2)\, dx}{\int_0^L r\bar{y}^2\, dx} = \frac{J\{\bar{y}\}}{N\{\bar{y}\}}.$$

Therefore, if $\bar{y}(x)$ is "close" to an exact eigenfunction $y(x)$, then $\bar{\lambda}$ will be close to λ. In practice, the method is most successful in approximating the *lowest* eigenvalue. Note that under the usual assumptions $p > 0$, $s \geq 0$ (see p. 563), we always have $J > 0$. We shall demand, for convenience, that $N = 1$. This means that the spectrum of eigenvalues is bounded from below. It is reasonable to assume, and can be rigorously proved, that for some function $y_1(x)$, the integral J *actually*

---

* They need not be all different.

attains its lower bound, which is then the lowest eigenvalue λ_1. If we have some insight into "what the function $y_1(x)$ looks like," we can select a set of $\bar{\varphi}_n$ such that some linear combination of them will be "close" to $y_1(x)$. This particular linear combination is then obtained by the described procedure as the one which yields the lowest value of $\bar{\lambda}$.

Example 1. Solve the equation* $y'' = -\lambda y$ subject to the boundary conditions $y(\pm 1) = 0$.

Suppose that we do not know the lowest eigenfunction $[y_1(x) = \cos(\pi x/2)]$, but we expect it to resemble the shape of the curve shown in Fig. 13.7. We seek to approximate this function by a parabola $\bar{y}(x) = \bar{Y}(1 - x^2)$, where the parameter $\bar{Y}$ is left undetermined. Using $\bar{y}'(x) = -2\bar{Y}x$, we form the integral ($p = 1$, $s = 0$, $r = 1$)

$$K = \int_{-1}^{+1} \bar{Y}^2[4x^2 - \bar{\lambda}(1 - x^2)^2]\,dx$$

$$= \bar{Y}^2(\tfrac{8}{3} - \tfrac{16}{15}\bar{\lambda}).$$

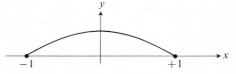

Since $\bar{Y} \neq 0$, we deduce immediately from $\partial K/\partial \bar{Y} = 0$ that

Figure 13.7

$$\tfrac{8}{3} - \tfrac{16}{15}\bar{\lambda} = 0, \quad \text{or} \quad \bar{\lambda} = 2.5.$$

This compares favorably with the correct eigenvalue $\lambda_1 = \pi^2/4 = 2.467\ldots$

In this case we have confined ourselves to a set $\{\bar{\varphi}_n\}$ consisting of only one function. A better approximation is possible with two functions. Let us choose

$$\bar{\varphi}_1 = 1 - x^2, \quad \bar{\varphi}_2 = x^2(1 - x^2)$$

and seek $\bar{y}(x)$ as a linear combination

$$\bar{y} = \bar{Y}_1\bar{\varphi}_1 + \bar{Y}_2\bar{\varphi}_2 = (1 - x^2)(\bar{Y}_1 + \bar{Y}_2x^2).$$

Then

$$\bar{y}' = -2x^2(\bar{Y}_1 + \bar{Y}_2x^2) + 2\bar{Y}_2x(1 - x^2).$$

We find that substitution into the integral K yields

$$K = \tfrac{8}{315}[(105 - 42\bar{\lambda})\bar{Y}_1^2 + (42 - 12\bar{\lambda})\bar{Y}_1\bar{Y}_2 + (33 - 2\bar{\lambda})\bar{Y}_2^2].$$

From the conditions $\partial K/\partial \bar{Y}_1 = 0$ and $\partial K/\partial \bar{Y}_2 = 0$, we obtain

$$(35 - 14\bar{\lambda})\bar{Y}_1 + (7 - 2\bar{\lambda})\bar{Y}_2 = 0, \quad (21 - 6\bar{\lambda})\bar{Y}_1 + (33 - 2\bar{\lambda})\bar{Y}_2 = 0.$$

The characteristic equation $\bar{\lambda}^2 - 28\bar{\lambda} + 63 = 0$ yields the roots

$$\bar{\lambda}_1 = 2.46744\ldots, \quad \bar{\lambda}_2 = 25.6\ldots$$

* This is the original example of Ritz (Crelle, Bd. 135,1909).

The first of these values differs from λ_1 by less than 0.002%. It is of interest to observe that the second value approximates the *third* lowest eigenvalue, rather than the second one, although much less accurately than above, since the correct value is $\lambda_3 = 9\pi^2/4 = 22.2\ldots$ The reason that we have skipped the second lowest eigenvalue is not hard to find. The true eigenfunction $y_2(x) = \sin \pi x$ is an *odd function* while both $\bar{\varphi}_1$ and $\bar{\varphi}_2$ are *even functions* and, consequently, cannot be used to approximate y_2. This example shows clearly the importance of the proper choice of the set $\{\bar{\varphi}_n\}$.

Example 2. *Calculation of the lowest root of Bessel function $J_3(x)$.* It is known that roots of $J_m(x)$ are related to eigenvalue problems. The Bessel DE of mth order

$$\frac{d^2y}{dx^2} + \frac{1}{x}\frac{du}{dx} + \left(k^2 - \frac{m^2}{x^2}\right)y = 0$$

has a solution $y(x) = J_m(kx)$. If the boundary condition $y(1) = 0$ is imposed, then k must be a root of $J_m(x)$. Write the Bessel equation in the Sturm-Liouville form,

$$\frac{d}{dx}\left(x\frac{du}{dx}\right) - \frac{m^2}{x}y = -\lambda xy,$$

so that $p(x) = x$, $s(x) = m^2/x$, $r(x) = x$, and $\lambda = k^2$. It is known that $J_3(x)$ has a third-order zero at the origin (see p. 357). Therefore a trial function of the form

$$\bar{y}(x) = \bar{Y}x^3(1 - x)$$

may be a reasonable approximation. Then

$$K = \int_0^L (p\bar{y}'^2 + s\bar{y}^2 - \bar{\lambda}r\bar{y}^2)\,dx$$

$$= \bar{Y}^2 \int_0^L \left\{ x[9x^4(1-x)^2 - 6x^5(1-x) + x^6] \right.$$

$$\left. + \frac{9}{x}[x^6(1-x)^2] - \bar{\lambda}xx^6(1-x)^2 \right\}dx.$$

This reduces to $K = \bar{Y}^2(\frac{1}{8} - \bar{\lambda}/360)$ and yields $\bar{\lambda} = 45$ so that $k = \sqrt{45} = 6.70$. Since the correct root is 6.379, there is a discrepancy of about 5%.

13.8 VARIATIONAL PROBLEMS IN MANY DIMENSIONS

Up to now we have been dealing with functionals containing only one *independent* variable x. It is not difficult, however, to extend the theory to many independent variables. Consider, for instance, the functional

$$J = \iint_D F\left(u, \frac{\partial u}{\partial x}, \frac{\partial u}{\partial y}, x, y\right)dx\,dy,$$

depending on an unknown function $u(x, y)$ of two variables. The region D is assumed to be a bounded domain in the (xy)-plane with *prescribed values* of $u(x, y)$ at its boundary S. The problem is to find $u(x, y)$ such that J is stationary with respect to small changes in the functional form of u.

The technique that we employ is analogous to that found in Section 13.2. We change function $u(x, y)$ into $u(x, y) + \epsilon v(x, y)$, where $v(x, y)$ is an arbitrary well-behaved function which *vanishes* at the boundary S. If ϵ is small, then the change δJ can be confined to the first-order term in ϵ. For a stationary value of J, this first-order term must vanish, which amounts to the condition*

$$\left.\frac{dJ}{d\epsilon}\right|_{\epsilon=0} = 0.$$

For convenience, we write $\partial u/\partial x = u_x$, $\partial v/\partial x = v_x$, etc. Then

$$\frac{dJ}{d\epsilon} = \iint_D \left[\frac{\partial F}{\partial u}v + \frac{\partial F}{\partial u_x}v_x + \frac{\partial F}{\partial u_y}v_y\right] dx\,dy.$$

The analog of the integration by parts of Section 13.2 is the following relation:†

$$\iint_D \left(\phi\frac{\partial v}{\partial x} + \psi\frac{\partial v}{\partial y}\right) dx\,dy = \oint_S v(\phi\,dy - \psi\,dx) - \iint_D v\left(\frac{\partial\phi}{\partial x} + \frac{\partial\psi}{\partial y}\right) dx\,dy,$$

which we can obtain from Green's theorem

$$\oint_S P\,dx + Q\,dy = \iint_D \left(\frac{\partial Q}{\partial x} - \frac{\partial P}{\partial y}\right) dx\,dy$$

after setting $P = v\phi$ and $Q = -v\psi$.

In our problem we identify $\phi = \partial F/\partial u_x$ and $\psi = \partial F/\partial u_y$ and deduce

$$\frac{dJ}{d\epsilon} = \oint_S v\left(\frac{\partial F}{\partial u_x}dx - \frac{\partial F}{\partial u_y}dy\right) + \iint_D v\left[\frac{\partial F}{\partial u} - \frac{D}{Dx}\left(\frac{\partial F}{\partial u_x}\right) - \frac{D}{Dy}\left(\frac{\partial F}{\partial u_y}\right)\right] dx\,dy.$$

Here a *new notation*, D/Dx and D/Dy, is introduced. To understand its meaning clearly, we note that since $F = F(u, u_x, u_y, x, y)$, we have, in general,

$$\frac{\partial F}{\partial u_x} = \phi(u, u_x, u_y, x, y).$$

The meaning of Green's theorem requires that we differentiate ϕ keeping y constant, but remembering that u, u_x, and u_y are also functions of x. This operation

---

* In Section 13.2 we developed $\delta J = \epsilon J'$ and demanded that $J' = 0$. However, J' is nothing but $(dJ/d\epsilon)|_{\epsilon=0}$.

† See the remark on p. 537.

is explicitly given by

$$\frac{D\phi}{Dx} \equiv \frac{\partial \phi}{\partial x} + \frac{\partial \phi}{\partial u}\frac{\partial u}{\partial x} + \frac{\partial \phi}{\partial u_x}\frac{\partial^2 u}{\partial x^2} + \frac{\partial \phi}{\partial u_y}\frac{\partial^2 \phi}{\partial x\,\partial y},$$

which may be called the *total partial derivative*, as distinct from the *explicit partial derivative* $\partial \phi / \partial x$. Returning to the equation for $dJ/d\epsilon$, we observe that the first term vanishes since $v = 0$ on S. Since v is arbitrary, the vanishing of the second term results in the Euler-Lagrange equation*

$$\frac{\partial F}{\partial u} - \frac{D}{Dx}\left(\frac{\partial F}{\partial u_x}\right) - \frac{D}{Dy}\left(\frac{\partial F}{\partial u_y}\right) = 0.$$

The extension of this technique to three or more dimensions is straightforward.

For the majority of common partial differential equations of mathematical physics, we can construct the necessary functional J without much difficulty by inspection. For instance, the functional

$$J = \iiint \frac{1}{2}\left[\left(\frac{\partial u}{\partial x}\right)^2 + \left(\frac{\partial u}{\partial y}\right)^2 + \left(\frac{\partial u}{\partial z}\right)^2\right] dx\,dy\,dz$$

$$= \frac{1}{2}\iiint (\text{grad } u \cdot \text{grad } u)\,dx\,dy\,dz$$

gives rise to the Laplace PDE in three dimensions,

$$\frac{\partial^2 u}{\partial x^2} + \frac{\partial^2 u}{\partial y^2} + \frac{\partial^2 u}{\partial z^2} = 0,$$

as its Euler-Lagrange equation. Alternatively, variational principles of physics can be used, at least in a heuristic manner.

Example. The stretched string (Section 8.1) can be considered as a system with infinitely many degrees of freedom, each element dx being treated as a particle of mass $\rho\,dx$. Therefore, the formula for kinetic energy of a system of particles,

$$E_{\text{kin}} = \frac{1}{2}\sum_{i=1}^{N} m_i \dot{q}_i^2,$$

becomes an integral,

$$E_{\text{kin}} = \frac{1}{2}\int_0^L (\rho\,dx)\left(\frac{\partial u}{\partial t}\right)^2.$$

The potential energy of the deformed string is most easily calculated as the work done against the force of tension T. The length of the deformed string is slightly

---

* The condition $\epsilon = 0$ in $(\partial J/\partial \epsilon)|_{\epsilon=0}$ is equivalent to replacement of u in the integral by the actual solution u, which makes J stationary; compare with p. 557.

greater than the original length L and is given by

$$L' = \int ds = \int_0^L \sqrt{1 + \left(\frac{\partial u}{\partial x}\right)^2}\, dx.$$

For small deformations, we have

$$\sqrt{1 + \left(\frac{\partial u}{\partial x}\right)^2} \cong 1 + \frac{1}{2}\left(\frac{\partial u}{\partial x}\right)^2.$$

Consequently, the extension ΔL of the string is approximately

$$\Delta L = L' - L \cong \frac{1}{2}\int_0^L \left(\frac{\partial u}{\partial x}\right)^2 dx,$$

and the potential energy (work done against T) is given by

$$E_{\text{pot}} \cong T\,\Delta L \cong \frac{T}{2}\int_0^L \left(\frac{\partial u}{\partial x}\right)^2 dx.$$

This analysis allows us to write the Lagrangian for our system:

$$\mathcal{L} = E_{\text{kin}} - E_{\text{pot}} = \int_0^L \left[\frac{\rho}{2}\left(\frac{\partial u}{\partial t}\right)^2 - \frac{T}{2}\left(\frac{\partial u}{\partial x}\right)^2\right] dx.$$

According to Hamilton's principle (p. 561), the motion of the string must be such that the integral

$$J = \int_{t_0}^{t_1}\int_0^L \left[\frac{\rho}{2}\left(\frac{\partial u}{\partial t}\right)^2 - \frac{T}{2}\left(\frac{\partial u}{\partial x}\right)^2\right] dx\, dt,$$

where t_0 and t_1 are two arbitrary instants of time, will be stationary. The Euler-Lagrange equation for J then takes the form

$$\frac{D}{Dt}\frac{\partial \mathcal{L}}{\partial u_t} + \frac{D}{Dx}\frac{\partial \mathcal{L}}{\partial u_x} = 0,$$

where the quantity

$$\mathcal{L} = \frac{\rho}{2}\left(\frac{\partial u}{\partial t}\right)^2 - \frac{T}{2}\left(\frac{\partial u}{\partial t}\right)^2$$

is customarily called the *Lagrangian density*.* Performing the necessary operations, we reduce our Euler-Lagrange equation to the familiar form

$$-T\frac{\partial^2 u}{\partial t^2} + \rho\frac{\partial^2 u}{\partial x^2} = 0.$$

* The Lagrangian function per unit length, to be precise.

13.9 FORMULATION OF EIGENVALUE PROBLEMS BY THE RATIO METHOD

While discussing the problem of the catenary in Section 13.6, we mentioned that the equilibrium of the chain can be characterized by the lowest possible position of the center of gravity. Referring to Fig. 13.6, we may write the general formula for the height of the center of gravity:

$$Y = \frac{\int_0^L y\rho g \, ds}{\int_0^L \rho g \, ds} = \frac{\int_0^L \rho g y \sqrt{1 + y'^2} \, dx}{\int_0^L \rho g \sqrt{1 + y'^2} \, dx} \, .$$

It is seen that except for the trivial* factor ρ, Y is the ratio of functionals J and N discussed in Section 13.6. Let us vary the function $y = y(x)$. This will induce changes δJ, δN, and δY such that

$$\delta Y = \frac{1}{\rho} \left\{ \frac{J + \delta J}{N + \delta N} - \frac{J}{N} \right\} = \frac{1}{\rho} \frac{N \delta J - J \delta N}{N(N + \delta N)} \, .$$

If, for some particular $y = y_0(x)$, the value of Y is stationary, we must have

$$\delta Y = N \delta J - J \delta N \big|_{y=y_0(x)} = 0,$$

or, dividing by N ($N \neq 0$), we obtain

$$\delta J - \frac{J}{N} \delta N \big|_{y=y_0} = 0.$$

However, the ratio $(J/N)_{y=y_0}$ is nothing but the actual stationary value Y_0 of the ratio Y, multiplied by ρ. Since it is unknown to us, we replace ρY_0 by a parameter $-\lambda$ so that our condition reads

$$\delta J + \lambda \delta N \big|_{y=y_0} = 0.$$

It is now evident that we can obtain the same equation by seeking the stationary values of $K = J + \lambda N$ or, equivalently, stationary values of J subject to $N = $ const. In other words, we obtain the same Euler-Lagrange equation as before. The advantage of this approach is that it gives the physical significance of the Lagrange multiplier λ.

From the discussion in Section 13.7, it should be clear that a similar approach can be employed for eigenvalue problems. In fact, we shall make a sweeping generalization of this idea in terms of the following concepts. We let **x** be a vector in some complex linear space, finite or infinite-dimensional, and let $\mathcal{L}$ and $\mathcal{R}$ be linear operators in this space. Furthermore, we shall assume that $\mathcal{L}$ and $\mathcal{R}$ are *hermitian* and that $\mathcal{R}$ is also *positive definite*.† In the notation used in Chapters

---

* We assume that $\rho = $ const.

† Compare with p. 441.

10 and 11, this means

$$(\mathbf{y}, \mathcal{L}\mathbf{x}) = (\mathcal{L}\mathbf{y}, \mathbf{x}) = (\mathbf{x}, \mathcal{L}\mathbf{y})^*, \qquad (\mathbf{y}, \mathcal{R}\mathbf{x}) = (\mathcal{R}\mathbf{y}, \mathbf{x}) = (\mathbf{x}, \mathcal{R}\mathbf{y})^*$$

for any two vectors $\mathbf{x}$, $\mathbf{y}$ in the space, and

$$(\mathbf{x}, \mathcal{R}\mathbf{x}) \geq 0$$

for any $\mathbf{x}$, with $(\mathbf{x}, \mathcal{R}\mathbf{x}) = 0$ only if $\mathbf{x}$ is the zero vector. The following theorem now holds.

Theorem. The ratio of two functionals

$$\omega = \frac{(\mathbf{x}, \mathcal{L}\mathbf{x})}{(\mathbf{x}, \mathcal{R}\mathbf{x})}$$

will be stationary against small variations $\delta\mathbf{x}$ of the vector $\mathbf{x}$ if and only if $\mathbf{x}$ satisfies the generalized eigenvalue equation

$$\mathcal{L}\mathbf{x} = \lambda\mathcal{R}\mathbf{x},$$

where the eigenvalues λ are the stationary values of the functional ω.

Before proceeding to prove this theorem, let us illustrate it with a few examples.

Example 1. *The Sturm-Liouville problem with homogeneous Dirichlet conditions.* In this case the linear space consists of functions twice differentiable on $(0, L)$ and vanishing at $x = 0$ and $x = L$. The expression for ω reads

$$\omega = -\frac{\displaystyle\int_0^L y(x)\left\{\frac{d}{dx}\left[p(x)\frac{dy}{dx}\right] - s(x)y\right\}dx}{\displaystyle\int_0^L r(x)[y(x)]^2\,dx}.$$

Example 2. *The Helmholtz equation in a bounded region in three dimensions,*

$$\nabla^2\psi(x, y, z) + \lambda\psi(x, y, z) = 0 \qquad \text{(in } V),$$

with the boundary condition

$$\frac{\partial\psi}{\partial n} + h\psi = 0 \qquad \text{(on } S),$$

where S is the closed surface enclosing V, $\partial\psi/\partial n$ is the normal gradient of ψ on S (see p. 323), and h is a constant. The variational formulation is characterized by

$$\omega = -\frac{\displaystyle\iiint_V \psi\nabla^2\psi\,dV}{\displaystyle\iiint_V \psi^2\,dV} \qquad (\psi \text{ is real}).$$

With the help of the first Green's formula (p. 536) and the boundary condition, this expression can also be written as

$$\omega = -\frac{-\iiint_V (\text{grad } \psi \cdot \text{grad } \psi)\, dV + \oiint_S \psi \,(\text{grad } \psi \cdot d\mathbf{S})}{\iiint_V \psi^2 \, dV}$$

$$= \frac{\iiint_V (\text{grad } \psi \cdot \text{grad } \psi)\, dV + h \oiint_S \psi^2 \, dS}{\iiint_V \psi^2 \, dV}.$$

Example 3. *The algebraic eigenproblem in N-dimensional real vector space,*

$$Ax = \lambda x,$$

where x is an N-tuple while A is an $N \times N$ symmetric matrix. In this case, explicitly,

$$\omega = \frac{\sum_{i=1}^N \sum_{j=1}^N a_{ij} x_i x_j}{\sum_{i=1}^N x_i^2}.$$

Example 4. *The Schrödinger equation*

$$-\frac{\hbar^2}{2M} \nabla^2 \psi + U(x, y, z)\psi = E\psi$$

in the space of square-integrable complex functions,† i.e., those for which

$$\iiint_{\text{Space}} \psi^* \psi \, dV < \infty \qquad \text{(boundedness)}.$$

The expression for ω reads

$$\omega = \frac{\iiint_{\text{Space}} \{(\hbar^2/2M)(\text{grad } \psi^* \cdot \text{grad } \psi) + U\psi^*\psi\}\, dV}{\iiint_{\text{Space}} \psi^* \psi \, dV},$$

where the first Green's formula is used again.

Let us now return to the proof of our theorem. We change $\mathbf{x}$ by an arbitrary variation $\delta\mathbf{x}$ and calculate the change $\delta\omega$. Using the linearity and hermiticity of $\mathcal{L}$ and the properties of the inner product, we deduce

$$(\mathbf{x} + \delta\mathbf{x}, \mathcal{L}(\mathbf{x} + \delta\mathbf{x})) = (\mathbf{x}, \mathcal{L}\mathbf{x}) + (\delta\mathbf{x}, \mathcal{L}\mathbf{x}) + (\delta\mathbf{x}, \mathcal{L}\mathbf{x})^* + (\delta\mathbf{x}, \mathcal{L}\,\delta\mathbf{x}),$$

and similarly for $\mathcal{R}$. Consequently, dropping the second-order terms in $\delta\mathbf{x}$ in

---

† In the spirit of the preceding discussion, we allow the normalization integral $\iiint \psi^*\psi \, dV$ to vary. However, it must exist (remain bounded).

the numerator, we have

$$\delta\omega = \frac{(\mathbf{x} + \delta\mathbf{x}, \mathcal{L}(\mathbf{x} + \delta\mathbf{x}))}{(\mathbf{x} + \delta\mathbf{x}, \mathcal{R}(\mathbf{x} + \delta\mathbf{x}))} - \frac{(\mathbf{x}, \mathcal{L}\mathbf{x})}{(\mathbf{x}, \mathcal{R}\mathbf{x})}$$

$$= \frac{[(\delta\mathbf{x}, \mathcal{L}\mathbf{x}) + (\delta\mathbf{x}, \mathcal{L}\mathbf{x})^*](\mathbf{x}, \mathcal{R}\mathbf{x}) - (\mathbf{x}, \mathcal{L}\mathbf{x})[(\delta\mathbf{x}, \mathcal{R}\mathbf{x}) + (\delta\mathbf{x}, \mathcal{R}\mathbf{x})^*]}{(\mathbf{x} + \delta\mathbf{x}, \mathcal{R}(\mathbf{x} + \delta\mathbf{x}))(\mathbf{x}, \mathcal{R}\mathbf{x})}.$$

Now, if $\mathcal{L}\mathbf{x} = \lambda\mathcal{R}\mathbf{x}$ holds, then λ is known to be real.† The numerator reduces to

$$[\lambda(\delta\mathbf{x}, \mathcal{R}\mathbf{x}) + \lambda(\delta\mathbf{x}, \mathcal{R}\mathbf{x})^*](\mathbf{x}, \mathcal{R}\mathbf{x}) - \lambda(\mathbf{x}, \mathcal{R}\mathbf{x})[(\delta\mathbf{x}, \mathcal{R}\mathbf{x}) + (\delta\mathbf{x}, \mathcal{R}\mathbf{x})^*] = 0,$$

and the sufficiency of the eigenvalue equation is established.

Conversely, suppose that $\delta\omega = 0$ and denote the stationary value of ω by λ, so that $(\mathbf{x}, \mathcal{L}\mathbf{x}) = \lambda(\mathbf{x}, \mathcal{R}\mathbf{x})$. From $\delta\omega = 0$, it now follows that

$$[(\delta\mathbf{x}, \mathcal{L}\mathbf{x}) + (\delta\mathbf{x}, \mathcal{L}\mathbf{x})^*] - \lambda[(\delta\mathbf{x}, \mathcal{R}\mathbf{x}) + (\delta\mathbf{x}, \mathcal{R}\mathbf{x})^*] = 0$$

or

$$(\delta\mathbf{x}, \mathcal{L}\mathbf{x} - \lambda\mathcal{R}\mathbf{x}) + (\delta\mathbf{x}, \mathcal{L}\mathbf{x} - \lambda\mathcal{R}\mathbf{x})^* = 0.$$

This must be true for *all* $\delta\mathbf{x}$. Replacing $\delta\mathbf{x}$ by $i\,\delta\mathbf{x}$, we easily deduce

$$(\delta\mathbf{x}, \mathcal{L}\mathbf{x} - \lambda\mathcal{R}\mathbf{x}) - (\delta\mathbf{x}, \mathcal{L}\mathbf{x} - \lambda\mathcal{R}\mathbf{x})^* = 0,$$

and from $(\delta\mathbf{x}, \mathcal{L}\mathbf{x} - \lambda\mathcal{R}\mathbf{x}) = 0$, it follows that $\mathcal{L}\mathbf{x} = \lambda\mathcal{R}\mathbf{x}$, establishing the necessity of the eigenvalue equation.

Remark. A conceivable restriction on $\mathbf{x}$, like the one mentioned on p. 571, does not arise here. Otherwise, the Euler-Lagrange equation for N would read $\mathcal{R}\mathbf{x} = 0$, which is impossible for $\mathbf{x} \neq \mathbf{0}$ since $\mathcal{R}$ is positive definite.

The formulation of eigenvalue problems by means of the relation $\omega = J/N$ is very convenient in the analysis of the eigenvalue spectrum. It can also be used as a starting point for a Ritz-type approximation. We shall illustrate this by treating the problem of the stretched string supporting a discrete mass at the midpoint (Section 11.7). This involves the solution of the Sturm-Liouville equation

$$\frac{d^2 y}{dx^2} = -k^2 \left[1 + \frac{m}{\rho}\,\delta(x) \right] y \qquad \left(k^2 = \frac{\omega^2 \rho}{T} \right)$$

subject to the boundary conditions $y(-L/2) = y(+L/2) = 0$. The eigenvalues $k^2 = \lambda$ are then the stationary values of

$$\omega = - \frac{\int_{-L/2}^{+L/2} y\,(d^2 y/dx^2)\,dx}{\int_{-L/2}^{+L/2} [1 + (m/\rho)\,\delta(x)] y^2\,dx}.$$

---

† A quick general proof: Deduce $(\mathbf{x}, \mathcal{L}\mathbf{x}) = \lambda(\mathbf{x}, \mathcal{R}\mathbf{x})$, take complex conjugates $(\mathcal{L}\mathbf{x}, \mathbf{x}) = \lambda^*(\mathcal{R}\mathbf{x}, \mathbf{x})$, use the hermiticity of $\mathcal{L}$ and $\mathcal{R}$ to obtain $(\mathbf{x}, \mathcal{L}\mathbf{x}) = \lambda^*(\mathbf{x}, \mathcal{R}\mathbf{x})$, and subtract. Since $\mathcal{R}$ is positive definite, the result is $\lambda - \lambda^* = 0$. QED. (Compare with p. 446.)

Integrating the numerator by parts, we find that this expression is easily transformed into

$$\omega = \frac{\int_{-L/2}^{+L/2} (dy/dx)^2 \, dx}{\int_{-L/2}^{+L/2} y^2 \, dx + (m/\rho)[y(0)]^2}.$$

It is now evident that all eigenvalues are *positive* and the lowest eigenvalue is the *absolute minimum* of ω.

If $m = 0$, the lowest eigenfunction is $\cos(\pi x/L)$; if $m \neq 0$, we expect (see Section 11.7) the eigenfunction to have a cusp at $x = 0$ and, perhaps, to have the form shown in Fig. 13.8. We introduce a trial function by joining the arcs of two parabolas to simulate this shape:

$$y(x) = \begin{cases} (x + L/2) + \alpha(x + L/2)^2 & (x < 0), \\ (L/2 - x) + \alpha(L/2 - x)^2 & (x > 0), \end{cases}$$

where α is an adjustable parameter. The problem now is to determine α so that ω has a minimum and then to evaluate this minimum. We have

$$\frac{dy}{dx} = \begin{cases} 1 + 2\alpha(x + L/2) & (x < 0), \\ -1 - 2\alpha(L/2 - x) & (x > 0), \end{cases}$$

and we calculate

$$\int_{-L/2}^{+L/2} \left(\frac{dy}{dx}\right)^2 dx = L\left(1 + \alpha L + \frac{\alpha^2 L^2}{3}\right),$$

$$\int_{-L/2}^{+L/2} y^2 \, dx = \frac{L^3}{4}\left(\frac{1}{3} + \frac{\alpha L}{4} + \frac{\alpha^2 L^2}{20}\right),$$

$$[y(0)]^2 = \frac{L^2}{4}\left(1 + \alpha L + \frac{\alpha^2 L^2}{4}\right).$$

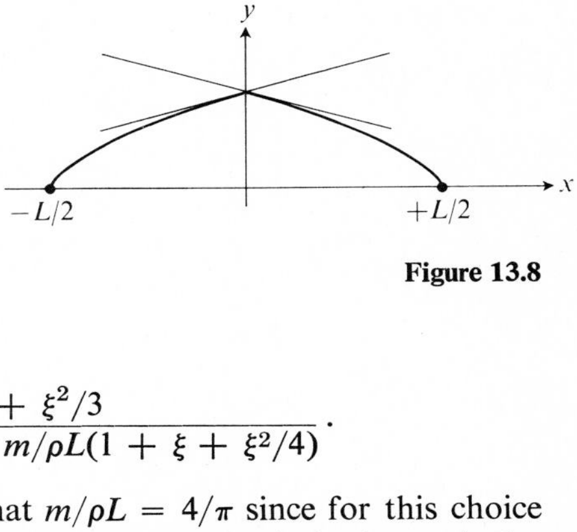

Figure 13.8

Writing $\alpha L = \xi$, we arrive at the expression

$$\omega = \frac{4}{L^2} \frac{1 + \xi + \xi^2/3}{\frac{1}{3} + \xi/4 + \xi^2/20 + m/\rho L(1 + \xi + \xi^2/4)}.$$

For the sake of illustration, let us assume that $m/\rho L = 4/\pi$ since for this choice the exact solution is known:* $\lambda = \pi^2/4L^2$. After some simple algebraic manipulation, this leads to

$$\omega = \frac{80\pi}{L^2} \frac{3 + 3\xi + \xi^2}{a + b\xi + c\xi^2},$$

where $a = 20(12 + \pi)$, $b = 15(16 + \pi)$, $c = 3(20 + \pi)$. Setting $d\omega/d\xi = 0$, we obtain the quadratic equation

$$(3c - b)\xi^2 + 2(3c - a)\xi + 3(b - a) = 0$$

* Set $\gamma = \pi/4$ in the equation for eigenvalues on p. 493.

or, within slide-rule accuracy,

$$3.942\xi^2 + 9.453\xi + 2.355 = 0.$$

The roots are $\xi_1 = -2.11$ and $\xi_2 = -0.283$, and it is a simple matter to verify that the second root yields the minimum of ω equal to

$$\omega_{\min} = \frac{2.37}{L^2}.$$

There is a discrepancy of about 4% between this result and the true eigenvalue $\lambda = \pi^2/4L^2$.

BIBLIOGRAPHY

DETTMAN, J. W., *Mathematical Methods in Physics and Engineering*. New York: McGraw-Hill Book Co., 1962.

ELSGOLC, L. E., *Calculus of Variations*. Reading, Mass.: Addison-Wesley Publishing Co., 1961.

GOULD, S. H., *Variational Methods for Eigenvalue Problems*. Toronto: University of Toronto Press, 1957.

PROBLEMS

1. Show that the shortest curve $y = y(x)$ between two points in a plane, (x_0, y_0) and (x_1, y_1) is obtained by minimizing the functional

$$\int_{x_0}^{x_1} (1 + y'^2)^{1/2} \, dx$$

   and demonstrate that this curve is a straight line.

2. Fermat's principle states that a ray of light in a medium with a variable index of refraction will follow the path which requires the shortest traveling time. For a two-dimensional case, show that such a path is obtained by minimizing the integral

$$\int_{x_0}^{x_1} \frac{\sqrt{1 + y'^2}}{n(x, y)} \, dx,$$

   where $n(x, y)$ is the index of refraction. For the particular case $n = 1/y$, show that the rays of light will follow semicircular paths.

3. We wish to find the point on the curve $y^2 = (x - 1)^3$ which is closest to the origin. Show that the problem is expressible as an extremum under constraint, but that it cannot be solved by the method of Lagrange multipliers. Explain why. Show by a method of your choice that a solution exists and yields the point $(1, 0)$.

4. Solve the isoperimetric problem described in the Remark on p. 570, and show that the curve Γ is an arc of a circle.

5. Let $\mathbf{u}(x, y, z)$ be an eigenvector of the real symmetric matrix

$$A = \begin{bmatrix} 9 & -3 & 0 \\ -3 & 12 & -3 \\ 0 & -3 & 9 \end{bmatrix}.$$

a) Write the algebraic equations for x, y, z, corresponding to the eigenvalue equation $A\mathbf{u} = \lambda\mathbf{u}$.

b) Consider the quadratic form associated with the matrix A, namely,

$$F(x, y, z) = 9x^2 + 12y^2 + 9z^2 - 6xy - 6yz.$$

Show that the problem of finding the extremum of $F(x, y, z)$, subject to the constraint

$$G(x, y, z) = x^2 + y^2 + z^2 = \text{const}$$

leads to the equations found under (a) when treated by the method of Lagrange multipliers. Also show that essentially the same equations are obtained when we wish to obtain the extremum of $G(x, y, z)$ subject to $F(x, y, z) = \text{const}$.

c) Show that the points on the quadratic surface

$$9x^2 + 12y^2 + 9z^2 - 6xy - 6yz = 18,$$

which make the distance from the origin stationary, can be found by solving problem (b). Find these points, show that the given quadric is an ellipsoid, and find its principal axes.

d) What is the relation of the eigenvalues and eigenvectors of the matrix A to the principal axes of the ellipsoid?

6. Generalize the results of the preceding problem to an arbitrary finite-dimensional linear space as follows:

a) Show that the problem of stationary values of a quadratic form $x^T A x$ (A = real symmetric matrix), subject to $x^T x = \text{const}$ reduces to the eigenvalue problem $Ax = \lambda x$.

b) Formulate the generalized eigenvalue problem (see p. 455) $Vx = \lambda K x$ in a similar fashion.

7. It is desired to calculate the first root of the Bessel function $J_0(x)$ by the Rayleigh-Ritz method.

a) Take $y(x) = \overline{Y}(1 - x^2)$ as a trial function and show that the desired root is obtained with an accuracy of about 1.8%.

b) Take $y(x) = \overline{Y}_1\varphi_1(x) + \overline{Y}_2\varphi_2(x)$, where

$$\varphi_1 = 1 - x^2 \quad \text{and} \quad \varphi_2 = (1 - x^2)(x^2 + \alpha);$$

determine α so that φ_1 and φ_2 are orthogonal to each other with respect to the weight function x on the interval $(0, 1)$. Show that the method yields the first and the second roots of $J_0(x)$ with an accuracy of about 0.8% and 10%, respectively

8. Apply the Rayleigh-Ritz method to find the approximate solution of the problem $y'' + y - x = 0$ with $y(0) = y(1) = 0$ in the form

   a) $y_0(x) = \overline{Y}x(1 - x)$,

   b) $y_1(x) = x(1 - x)(\overline{Y}_1 + \overline{Y}_2 x)$.

   Find also the exact solution $y(x)$ and plot y_0, y_1, and y on the same graph, displaying the degree of approximation.

9. If the stretched string of length L is subjected to external forces and is embedded in an elastic medium which produces a restoring force $-ku(x, t)$, then the motion of the string is governed by the equation (see p. 289)

   $$T\frac{\partial^2 u(x, t)}{\partial x^2} + F(x, t) - ku(x, t) = \rho(x)\frac{\partial^2 u(x, t)}{\partial t^2}.$$

   a) Formulate a variational problem which has an Euler-Lagrange equation of this form.

   b) Do the same for a stretched circular membrane of radius a.

10. Show that the boundary-value problem

    $$\frac{\partial^2 u(x, y)}{\partial x^2} + \frac{\partial^2 u(x, y)}{\partial y^2} = -k = \text{const} \qquad (0 \leq x \leq a, \ 0 \leq y \leq b),$$

    $$u(0, y) = u(a, y) = u(x, 0) = u(x, b) = 0$$

    is related to the variational problem of making

    $$J = \int_0^a \int_0^b \left[\left(\frac{\partial u}{\partial x}\right)^2 + \left(\frac{\partial u}{\partial y}\right)^2 - 2ku \right] dx \, dy$$

    stationary. Using the trial function $u_0 = Axy(x - a)(y - b)$, evaluate A by the Rayleigh-Ritz method. Obtain also the exact solution $u(x, t)$ using, e.g., Green's function on p. 521, and estimate the discrepancy between u and u_0 at $x = a/2$, $y = b/2$ for $a : b = 2 : 1$.

11. For a rectangular membrane with sides $a = 1$, $b = \sqrt{2}$, use the Rayleigh-Ritz technique to estimate the two lowest characteristic frequencies. Use a trial function of your choice.

CHAPTER 14

TRAVELING WAVES, RADIATION, SCATTERING

14.1 MOTION OF INFINITE STRETCHED STRING

In this chapter we shall devote some time to a more detailed study of the wave equation in regions which extend to infinity. One of the simple systems with these characteristics is that of the infinite stretched string, already mentioned in Section 12.9. Despite the fact that this idealized concept is not, strictly speaking, physically realizable, the mathematical methods employed in its treatment can serve as an excellent introduction to similar phenomena occurring in empty space, which is indeed considered to extend to infinity.

Transverse displacements of the string, with no external forces present, obey the partial differential equation

$$\frac{\partial^2 u}{\partial x^2} - \frac{1}{c^2}\frac{\partial^2 u}{\partial t^2} = 0 \qquad (c = \sqrt{T/\rho}).$$

The function $u(x, t)$ is usually required to vanish at infinity; that is, the condition

$$\lim_{x \to \pm\infty} u(x, t) = 0$$

must hold for all values of t.* We shall now consider the problem of determining $u(x, t)$ if the initial conditions

$$u(x, 0) = u_0(x), \qquad \frac{\partial u}{\partial t}(x, 0) = v_0(x)$$

are some known functions. Moreover, we shall use a new method, involving the transformation of the PDE by a change of variables.

As in the case of ordinary differential equations, we may attempt to simplify a PDE by introducing the new independent variables

$$\xi = \xi(x, t), \qquad \eta = \eta(x, t)$$

in place of x and t. In particular, we shall select the following new pair:

$$\xi = x - ct, \qquad \eta = x + ct.$$

---

* Sometimes it is only required that $u(x, t)$ be bounded. This creates no difficulties if u is treated as a distribution.

589

The old differential operators can be expressed in terms of the new ones, for example,

$$\frac{\partial}{\partial x} = \frac{\partial \xi}{\partial x} \frac{\partial}{\partial \xi} + \frac{\partial \eta}{\partial x} \frac{\partial}{\partial \eta} = \frac{\partial}{\partial \xi} + \frac{\partial}{\partial \eta},$$

because $\partial \xi / \partial x = 1$ and $\partial \eta / \partial x = 1$. Furthermore, by operator algebra,

$$\frac{\partial^2}{\partial x^2} = \left(\frac{\partial}{\partial \xi} + \frac{\partial}{\partial \eta} \right)^2 = \frac{\partial^2}{\partial \xi^2} + \frac{\partial}{\partial \xi} \frac{\partial}{\partial \eta} + \frac{\partial}{\partial \eta} \frac{\partial}{\partial \xi} + \frac{\partial^2}{\partial \eta^2} = \frac{\partial^2}{\partial \xi^2} + 2 \frac{\partial^2}{\partial \xi \partial \eta} + \frac{\partial^2}{\partial \eta^2},$$

because $\partial / \partial \xi$ and $\partial / \partial \eta$ commute. Similarly, we deduce

$$\frac{\partial}{\partial t} = -c \frac{\partial}{\partial \xi} + c \frac{\partial}{\partial \eta}, \quad \text{and} \quad \frac{1}{c^2} \frac{\partial^2}{\partial t^2} = \frac{\partial^2}{\partial \xi^2} - 2 \frac{\partial^2}{\partial \xi \partial \eta} + \frac{\partial^2}{\partial \eta^2}.$$

Substituting into the wave equation, we obtain

$$\frac{\partial^2 u}{\partial \xi \partial \eta} = 0.$$

The particular choice of the new variables used above seems to be taken "out of a hat." Note, however, that we could have developed general formulas expressing $\partial^2 / \partial x^2$ and $\partial^2 / \partial t^2$ in terms of $\partial^2 / \partial \xi^2$, $\partial^2 / \partial \eta^2$, ... for arbitrary functions $\xi(x, t)$ and $\eta(x, t)$. Substituting into the PDE and requiring some particular simpler form for it, we could have obtained differential equations for the functions ξ and η which would perform the task.*

Now, why is our new form of the PDE simpler than the original one? Because it permits immediate development of the general solution by straightforward integration. Indeed, writing

$$\frac{\partial}{\partial \xi} \left(\frac{\partial u}{\partial \eta} \right) = 0,$$

we conclude that $\partial u / \partial \eta$ must be independent of ξ, so that

$$\frac{\partial u}{\partial \eta} = \phi(\eta),$$

where $\phi(\eta)$ is an arbitrary function of η. Integration with respect to η now yields

$$u(\xi, \eta) = \int^{\eta} \phi(\eta') \, d\eta' + f(\xi),$$

where $f(\xi)$ is an arbitrary function of ξ. Since $\phi(\eta)$ is arbitrary, its indefinite integral is also an arbitrary function of η, say $g(\eta)$, and we obtain

$$u(\xi, \eta) = f(\xi) + g(\eta)$$

---

* For a general theory along these lines, consult, e.g., Tychonov and Samarski, *Partial Differential Equations of Mathematical Physics*, Section 1.1.

or, in terms of the original variables,

$$u(x, t) = f(x - ct) + g(x + ct).$$

This remarkable formula reveals the physical nature of the solutions and explains the name *wave equation*. Indeed, the term $f(x - ct)$ represents a displacement traveling with the speed c in the positive x-direction. Whatever the value of f is at some point x_0 and time t_0, the same value will reappear at a later time $t_0 + \tau$ at the point $x_0 + c\tau$ because

$$f[\underbrace{x_0 + c\tau}_{\text{new } x} - \underbrace{c(t_0 + \tau)}_{\text{new } t}] = f(x_0 - ct_0).$$

Similarly, the term $g(x + ct)$ represents a displacement traveling with the speed c in the opposite direction.

It is now a simple matter to determine the functions f and g in order to satisfy arbitrary initial conditions. Evidently, at $t = 0$ we must have

$$u_0(x) = f(x) + g(x), \qquad v_0(x) = c[g'(x) - f'(x)],$$

where $g'(x) = dg/dx$ and $f'(x) = df/dx$. Integrating the second equation, we obtain

$$c[g(x) - f(x)] = \int_a^x v_0(x') \, dx',$$

where a is an undetermined constant.* Solving now for $f(x)$ and $g(x)$, we obtain

$$f(x) = \tfrac{1}{2}u_0(x) - \frac{1}{2c} \int_a^x v_0(x') \, dx', \qquad g(x) = \tfrac{1}{2}u_0(x) + \frac{1}{2c} \int_a^x v_0(x') \, dx'.$$

Replacing x by $x - ct$ and $x + ct$, respectively, and combining, we arrive at the expression

$$u(x, t) = \tfrac{1}{2}[u_0(x - ct) + u_0(x + ct)] + \frac{1}{2c} \int_{x-ct}^{x+ct} v_0(x') \, dx',$$

known as the *D'Alembert formula*. It represents the *general solution* of our problem since it accommodates arbitrary initial conditions.† Moreover, it shows that for given initial conditions, the solution is unique because *any* solution must have the form $f(x - ct) + g(x + ct)$.

---

* This constant is actually arbitrary because we can always add to f and subtract from g an arbitrary constant without affecting the solution; in that sense, functions f and g are not unique.

† For $u(x, t)$ to satisfy the PDE, it would appear that u_0 must be differentiable twice, and v_0 once. This is actually taken care of by the theory of distributions. Nevertheless, on purely physical grounds, u_0 must be a distribution equivalent to a continuous function and v_0 must be a distribution equivalent to a piecewise continuous one.

14.2 PROPAGATION OF INITIAL CONDITIONS

While the method of change of variables is quite handy in the derivation of the D'Alembert formula, it is by no means indispensable. It may be instructive to derive it in a different way, for instance, through the concept of Green's functions. We observe that a solution $u(x, t)$ of the wave equation plus the boundary conditions depends linearly on the initial conditions

$$u(x, 0) = u_0(x), \qquad \frac{\partial u}{\partial t}(x, 0) = v_0(x).$$

Therefore $u(x, t)$ should be expressible as a continuous superposition over the distribution of initial conditions at various points ξ,

$$u(x, t) = \int_{-\infty}^{+\infty} g_1(x \mid \xi; t) u_0(\xi)\, d\xi + \int_{-\infty}^{+\infty} g_2(x \mid \xi; t) v_0(\xi)\, d\xi.$$

In this formula, g_1 and g_2 are Green's functions for initial displacement and initial velocity. They should satisfy the wave equation plus the boundary conditions and the following initial conditions:

$$\text{for } g_1, \quad g_1(x \mid \xi; 0) = \delta(x - \xi), \qquad \frac{\partial g_1}{\partial t}(x \mid \xi; 0) = 0;$$

$$\text{for } g_2, \quad g_2(x \mid \xi; 0) = 0, \qquad \frac{\partial g_2}{\partial t}(x \mid \xi; 0) = \delta(x - \xi).$$

Let us find g_1 and g_2 by the Fourier transform method with respect to x. We write

$$G_1(k \mid \xi; t) = \mathcal{F}_x\{g_1(x \mid \xi; t)\}.$$

Then $-c^2 k^2 G_1 = d^2 G_1/dt^2$, and $G_1 = A_1 e^{ickt} + B_1 e^{-ickt}$. Transforming the initial conditions, we deduce $G_1(x \mid \xi; 0) = e^{ik\xi}/\sqrt{2\pi}$. Therefore

$$A_1 + B_1 = \frac{e^{ik\xi}}{\sqrt{2\pi}}, \qquad A_1 - B_1 = 0.$$

Solving and inverting, we obtain

$$g_1(x \mid \xi; t) = \frac{1}{4\pi} \int_{-\infty}^{+\infty} [e^{ik(\xi+ct)} + e^{ik(\xi-ct)}] e^{-ikx}\, dk$$

$$= \tfrac{1}{2}[\delta(\xi - x + ct) + \delta(\xi - x - ct)].$$

In a similar fashion the transform of the second Green function reads

$$G_2(k \mid \xi; t) = A_2 e^{ickt} + B_2 e^{-ickt},$$

with

$$A_2 + B_2 = 0, \qquad A_2 - B_2 = \frac{e^{ik\xi}}{ick\sqrt{2\pi}},$$

so that

$$g_2(x \mid \xi; t) = \frac{1}{4\pi ci} \int_{-\infty}^{+\infty} \frac{1}{k} [e^{ik(\xi+ct)} - e^{ik(\xi-ct)}] e^{-ikx} \, dk.$$

We can conveniently evaluate the integral by the calculus of residues. Note that the integrand has no pole at $k = 0$ because we can also write

$$g_2(x \mid \xi; t) = \frac{1}{2\pi c} \int_{-\infty}^{+\infty} \frac{\sin kct}{k} e^{ik(\xi-x)} \, dk.$$

Consequently, we may deform the path of integration as shown in Fig. 14.1 and split the integral into two parts:*

$$g_2 = \frac{1}{4\pi ci} \int_{-\infty}^{+\infty} \frac{1}{k} e^{ik(\xi+ct-x)} \, dk - \frac{1}{4\pi ci} \int_{-\infty}^{+\infty} \frac{1}{k} e^{ik(\xi-ct-x)} \, dk.$$

When evaluating the first integral for $\xi < x - ct$, we must close the contour downward and obtain zero; for $\xi > x - ct$, we must close the contour upward and obtain $1/2c$. In short, the first integral yields the step function

$$\frac{1}{2c} S[\xi - (x + ct)].$$

In a similar manner, the second integral reduces to

$$-\frac{1}{2c} S[\xi - (x + ct)],$$

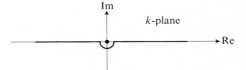

Figure 14.1

yielding

$$g_2(x \mid \xi; t) = \frac{1}{2c} \{S[\xi - (x - ct)] - S[\xi - (x + ct)].$$

We see that g_2 is a *box function*, equal to $1/2c$ in the interval $(x - ct, x + ct)$ and zero elsewhere.

Substituting our Green functions into the formula for $u(x, t)$ and integrating the first term, we rederive the D'Alembert formula:

$$u(x, t) = \tfrac{1}{2}[u_0(x - ct) + u_0(x + ct)] + \frac{1}{2c} \int_{x-ct}^{x+ct} v_0(\xi) \, d\xi.$$

This derivation parallels the approach employed in Section 12.5 for the diffusion equation, and the D'Alembert formula is the analog of the Poisson integral.† It may be of interest to compare Green's functions governing the propagation of

---

* As in Section 2.12, Example 5.

† There is only one initial condition in the diffusion equation because it is of first order with respect to the variable t.

the initial displacement for both equations, namely,

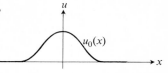

$$g(x \mid \xi; t) = \frac{1}{\sqrt{4\pi a^2 t}} e^{-(x-\xi)^2/4a^2 t}$$

for the diffusion equation, and

Figure 14.2

$$g_1(x \mid \xi; t) = \tfrac{1}{2} \delta(\xi - x + ct) + \tfrac{1}{2} \delta(\xi - x - ct)$$

for the wave equation. Both functions reduce to $\delta(x - \xi)$ at $t = 0$, but their behavior for $t > 0$ is strikingly different. The first one spreads the initial disturbance over the entire space, while the second one splits the disturbance into two equal parts and carries them, without any change in shape, in two opposite directions.

The D'Alembert formula is very helpful in visualizing the propagation of initial disturbances by graphical superposition. Consider, for instance, the case where $v_0(x) = 0$ while the initial displacement $u_0(x)$ has the form shown in Fig. 14.2, where the vertical scale is exaggerated. To construct $u(x, t)$ we represent $u_0(x)$ as the sum of two equal displacements and as the time t increases, we displace their contours in opposite directions with speed c. The superposition of the ordinates shows the shape of the string at various times t, as illustrated in Fig. 14.3.

The other special case, where $u_0(x) = 0$ but $v_0(x) \neq 0$, can be treated as follows: We let $w_0(x)$ be any function such that $w_0'(x) = v_0(x)$. Then

$$u(x, t) = \tfrac{1}{2}[w_0(x + ct) - w_0(x - ct)].$$

Suppose, for instance, that $v_0(x)$ has the shape of the box function, as in Fig. 14.4(a). Then $w_0(x)$ can be chosen as shown in Fig. 14.4(b). Now $u(x, t)$ can be con-

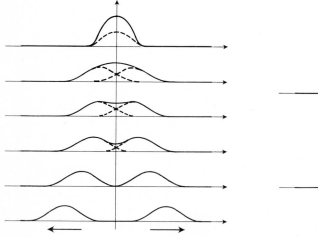

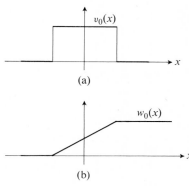

Figure 14.3

Figure 14.4

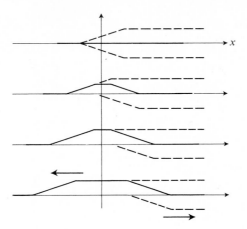

Figure 14.5

structed by allowing the contours $\frac{1}{2}w_0(x)$ and $-\frac{1}{2}w_0(x)$ to travel with speed c in opposite directions, as shown in Fig. 14.5. We see that a distribution of initial velocities leaves the string in a state of permanent deformation and this effect also spreads in both directions.

14.3 SEMI-INFINITE STRING. USE OF SYMMETRY PROPERTIES

Along with the concept of the infinite string, it is often of interest to consider the so-called semi-infinite string. In practical terms, this means the study of phenomena occurring near one of the ends of a very long string. The influence of the other end is deemed to be negligible and the string is, for mathematical convenience, considered to extend to infinity in one direction.

We shall assume that the string extends from $x = 0$ to $x = +\infty$, and consider the basic problem of solving the wave equation subject to the initial conditions

$$u(x, 0) = u_0(x),$$

$$\frac{\partial u}{\partial t}(x, 0) = v_0(x),$$

where u_0 and v_0 are some given functions over the range $0 \leq x < \infty$. As usual, there is a boundary condition at infinity,

$$\lim_{x \to +\infty} u(x, t) = 0 \qquad \text{(all } t),$$

or, at least, $u(x, t)$ should be bounded for all x and t. Beside this, there will be a boundary condition at $x = 0$. The most common situation is that of a string fixed at the end, in which case

$$u(0, t) = 0 \qquad \text{(all } t).$$

Another possibility is when the end of the string is allowed to slide freely* in the vertical direction. Then the force stretching the string must be rigorously horizontal at $x = 0$, and this implies

$$\frac{\partial u}{\partial x}(0, t) = 0 \qquad \text{(all } t\text{).}$$

Armed with the experience acquired with similar problems with the heat-condution equation (see Section 12.6), we may conjecture that it should be possible to apply symmetry considerations to obtain the appropriate solution. In particular, suppose that we are dealing with an *infinite* string where the initial conditions

$$u(x, 0) = u_0(x), \qquad \frac{\partial u}{\partial t}(x, 0) = v_0(x) \qquad (-\infty < x < +\infty)$$

are *odd functions* of x. It should be possible to show that the solution $u(x, t)$ will then be an odd function of x for all times t.† Indeed, consider $u(-x, t)$ as given by the D'Alembert formula

$$u(-x, t) = \tfrac{1}{2}[u_0(-x - ct) + u_0(-x + ct)] + \frac{1}{2c}\int_{-x-ct}^{-x+ct} v_0(\xi)\, d\xi.$$

We may use the antisymmetry of u_0 directly, namely,

$$u_0(-x - ct) = -u_0(x + ct), \text{ etc.,}$$

and change the dummy variable by $\xi = -\xi'$ in the integral; then

$$u(-x, t) = \tfrac{1}{2}[-u_0(x + ct) - u_0(x - ct)] + \frac{1}{2c}\int_{x+ct}^{x-ct} v_0(-\xi')(-d\xi').$$

In view of the antisymmetry of v_0, this reduces to

$$u(-x, t) = -\tfrac{1}{2}[u_0(x + ct) + u_0(x - ct)] - \frac{1}{2c}\int_{x-ct}^{x+ct} v_0(\xi')\, d\xi' = -u(x, t),$$

as conjectured.

Now, if this solution $u(x, t)$ is antisymmetric (odd) in x, we must have

$$u(0, t) = 0 \qquad \text{(all } t\text{).}$$

This fact yields the prescription of how to handle the case of the semi-infinite string with a rigidly fixed end. We extend the initial conditions $u_0(x)$ and $v_0(x)$ (defined, so far, for $0 \leq x < \infty$ only) to the entire x-axis in an antisymmetric manner;

---

* An intermediate case between these two extremes would arise if the string were elastically restrained at $x = 0$. This would mean

$$u(0, t) + \alpha \frac{\partial u}{\partial x}(0, t) = 0.$$

† See the remark on p. 528; note that the wave equation is invariant under reflection.

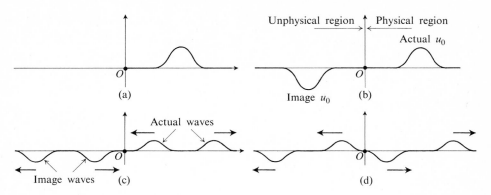

Figure 14.6

i.e., we define $u_0(-x) = -u_0(x)$ and $v_0(-x) = -v_0(x)$. Once this is done, the D'Alembert formula is directly applicable, and the values of $u(x, t)$ for positive x can be regarded as the solution for the semi-infinite string. These values satisfy the PDE, the initial conditions, and both boundary conditions. It is evident that the case where the boundary condition reads

$$\frac{\partial u}{\partial x}(0, t) = 0 \qquad \text{(all } t)$$

should be treated in an analogous fashion, extending the initial conditions in a symmetric manner over the range $-\infty < x < +\infty$.

A graphical illustration of this technique is shown in Fig. 14.6. We assume that the initial velocity distribution is zero while the initial displacement distribution is the same as that shown in Fig. 14.6(a).* If the end $x = 0$ is rigidly fixed, we extend $u_0(x)$ in an antisymmetric fashion, thus creating an "image displacement" (Fig. 14.6b).† As t increases, both patterns split into two equal parts giving rise to two waves moving in opposite directions. In due course of time the left-bound actual wave crosses over into the "unphysical" region ($x < 0$) while the right-bound "image" wave becomes a visible wave in our semi-infinite string. The ultimate state of affairs is characterized by Fig. 14.6(d), with two disturbances traveling to the right in the actual string.

While this method of description may be rather elegant, we should not forget that we are essentially witnessing the physical phenomenon of *reflection* of a wave from the rigid end of a string. Indeed, the left-bound actual wave (Fig. 14.6c) impinges on the fixed end at $x = 0$ and exerts a variable force on it. The fixed end exerts an equal and opposite reaction on the string, or, more precisely, on the element dx of the string adjacent to it. Since the end does not move, the element dx receives an acceleration opposite to the one it had received from the original wave. This additional motion of the element dx, such that the motion of the point

---

* Vertical scale exaggerated.
† Compare with sketches in Section 12.6.

$x = 0$ is canceled out, creates a new wave in the string, propagating to the right. Note that in relation to the original wave, this reflected wave is 180° out of phase, the effect stemming from Newton's third law.

We can apply the technique utilizing symmetry properties to the finite string as well. In this case, as time progresses, the traveling waves will suffer multiple reflections from both ends of the string. In a typical problem of this kind, suppose that the string extends from $x = 0$ to $x = L$ and is fixed at both ends,

$$u(0, t) = u(L, t) = 0 \qquad \text{(all } t\text{)},$$

and the initial conditions are given for the interval $(0, L)$,

$$\left.\begin{array}{l} u(x, 0) = u_0(x) \\ \dfrac{\partial u}{\partial t}(x, 0) = v_0(x) \end{array}\right\} \quad (0 \le x \le L).$$

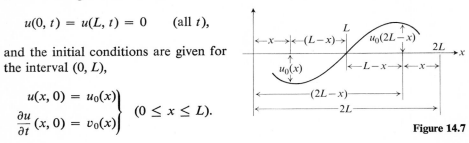

Figure 14.7

The boundary condition at $x = 0$ can evidently be satisfied if $u_0(x)$ and $v_0(x)$ are extended as odd functions for negative values of x. It is reasonable to conjecture that if $u_0(x)$ and $v_0(x)$ are extended beyond the point $x = L$ in such a way that they are antisymmetric with respect to reflection *about the point* $x = L$, then the solution $u(x, t)$ will preserve this property. With the help of Fig. 14.7, we deduce that this implies

$$u_0(2L - x) = -u_0(x), \qquad v_0(2L - x) = -v_0(x).$$

It is not difficult to make use of these relations in the D'Alembert formula and to deduce that $u(x, t)$ will indeed satisfy

$$u(2L - x, t) = -u(x, t).$$

It follows immediately that by extending $u_0(x)$ and $v_0(x)$ in the indicated manner, we obtain a solution which automatically satisfies the boundary conditions.

Remark. The formulas imposed on $u_0(x)$ and $v_0(x)$ imply that these functions are periodic in x with period $2L$. Indeed, it follows that

$$\left.\begin{array}{l} u_0(-x + 2L) = -u_0(x) = u_0(-x) \\ v_0(-x + 2L) = -v_0(x) = v_0(-x) \end{array}\right\} \quad \text{(all } x\text{)},$$

which are the usual periodicity relations.*

The graphical construction of the solution is illustrated in Fig. 14.8 where the actual initial wave packet $u_0(x)$ (v_0 is assumed to be zero) gives rise to an in-

---

* Since x is arbitrary, we can also write $u_0(x + 2L) = u_0(x)$ and $v_0(x + 2L) = v_0(x)$.

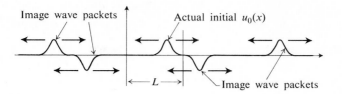

Figure 14.8

finite number of image wave packets, which, according to the D'Alembert formula, split in half, generating waves which travel in both directions. From there on the deformation of the string is given by the superposition of waves which are within the interval $(0, L)$ at a given time t.

14.4 ENERGY AND POWER FLOW IN A STRETCHED STRING

An element dx of the string moving with transverse velocity $\partial u/\partial t$ possesses kinetic energy

$$dE_{\text{kin}} = \frac{1}{2} \left(\frac{\partial u}{\partial t}\right)^2 \rho \, dx.$$

Therefore a portion of the string extending from $x = a$ to $x = b$ has kinetic energy

$$E_{\text{kin}}(a, b) = \frac{1}{2} \int_a^b \rho \left(\frac{\partial u}{\partial t}\right)^2 dx,$$

and the quantity $\frac{1}{2}\rho(\partial u/\partial t)^2$ can be considered to be the linear density of kinetic energy.

The portion (a, b) is under the influence of forces due to adjacent pieces of the string. Consider the left end at $x = a$. The external force in the transverse direction is (Fig. 14.9) $-T \sin \alpha \cong -T \, (\partial u/\partial x)$. The power delivered to the portion (a, b) at the point $x = a$ is the product of the applied force and the velocity of the point of application (more precisely, the inner product of corresponding vectors):

$$P(a, t) = -T\frac{\partial u}{\partial x}\frac{\partial u}{\partial t}\bigg|_{x=a}.$$

This formula actually represents the *power flux* (work per unit time) in the positive x-direction at an arbitrary point $x = a$ of the string.*

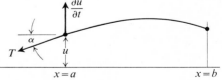

Figure 14.9

Remark. The term *energy flux* is sometimes used for P, tacitly assuming that the concept of flux already presupposes a quantity per unit time. In our discussions no confusion is likely to arise and we may use either of the two expressions.

---

* For instance, the power delivered to the portion (a, b) at the point $x = b$ would be $+T[(\partial u/\partial x)(\partial u/\partial t)]_{x=b}$, since the flow of power is now from the right to the left.

It is important to realize that the power flows in the same direction in which the waves travel. A solution of the form $u(x, t) = f(x - ct)$ yields

$$\frac{\partial u}{\partial x} = f', \qquad \frac{\partial u}{\partial t} = -cf' \qquad \left(\text{where } f' = \frac{df(x - ct)}{d(x - ct)}\right).$$

Therefore
$$P(x, t) = cT(f')^2 \geq 0.$$

Similarly, a solution $u(x, t) = g(x + ct)$ yields

$$P(x, t) = -cT(g')^2 \leq 0.$$

In addition to kinetic energy, the vibrating string also possesses potential energy. However, there is no way to tell how much potential energy is contained in any given element dx because the potential energy is due to the *mutual interaction of all the elements* of the string.* Nevertheless, the following approach is customary and fruitful. We calculate the rate of increase of kinetic energy in the portion (a, b) and compare it with the power delivered to (a, b):

$$\frac{dE_{\text{kin}}}{dt} = \frac{1}{2}\frac{d}{dt}\int_a^b \rho\left(\frac{\partial u}{\partial t}\right)^2 dx = \int_a^b \rho\left(\frac{\partial u}{\partial t}\right)\left(\frac{\partial^2 u}{\partial t^2}\right) dx.$$

We now use $\rho(\partial^2 u/\partial t^2) = T(\partial^2 u/\partial x^2)$ and integrate by parts:

$$\frac{dE_{\text{kin}}}{dt} = \int_a^b T\left(\frac{\partial u}{\partial t}\right)\left(\frac{\partial^2 u}{\partial x^2}\right) dx = T\left(\frac{\partial u}{\partial t}\right)\left(\frac{\partial u}{\partial x}\right)\Bigg|_a^b - \int_a^b T\left(\frac{\partial u}{\partial x}\right)\left(\frac{\partial^2 u}{\partial x \, \partial t}\right) dx.$$

The integrated term reads

$$T\left(\frac{\partial u}{\partial t}\right)\left(\frac{\partial u}{\partial x}\right)\Bigg|_a^b = +T\left(\frac{\partial u}{\partial t}\right)\left(\frac{\partial u}{\partial x}\right)\Bigg|_{x=b} - T\left(\frac{\partial u}{\partial t}\right)\left(\frac{\partial u}{\partial x}\right)\Bigg|_{x=a} = P_{\text{tot}},$$

and represents the total power delivered at both ends to the portion (a, b). Therefore

$$P_{\text{tot}} = \frac{dE_{\text{kin}}}{dt} + \int_a^b T\left(\frac{\partial u}{\partial x}\right)\left(\frac{\partial^2 u}{\partial x \, \partial t}\right) dx.$$

It is now *customary to postulate* that the power input into the portion (a, b) is equal to the rate of change of its total energy. This point of view implies that the potential energy, i.e., the energy of interaction between various portions of the string, is *distributed* over the string in much the same way as the kinetic energy. If $q(x, t)$ is the density of the potential energy, then we must have

$$E_{\text{pot}}(a, b) = \int_a^b q(x, t)\, dx, \qquad \text{and} \qquad \frac{dE_{\text{pot}}(a, b)}{dt} = \int_a^b T\left(\frac{\partial u}{\partial x}\right)\left(\frac{\partial^2 u}{\partial x \, \partial t}\right) dx.$$

---

* A stone of mass m raised to a height y above the ground is said to possess potential energy mgy. Strictly speaking, this energy is due to the mutual separation of the stone and the ground by an amount y. It is completely arbitrary to say that the potential energy resides *within the stone* and not, say, *within the earth*, or *in-between*.

It follows that

$$\frac{\partial q(x, t)}{\partial t} = T \frac{\partial u}{\partial x} \frac{\partial^2 u}{\partial x \partial t}$$

and

$$q(x, t) = \frac{T}{2} \left(\frac{\partial u}{\partial x} \right)^2 + C \qquad (C = \text{const}).$$

The constant term will add a constant contribution $C(b - a)$ to $E_{\text{pot}}(a, b)$. Since the potential energy is usually defined up to an additive constant, it is convenient and customary to set $C = 0$.* In this fashion we have arrived at the concept of the *total energy density*

$$w(x, t) = \frac{\rho}{2} \left(\frac{\partial u}{\partial t} \right)^2 + \frac{T}{2} \left(\frac{\partial u}{\partial x} \right)^2.$$

This quantity, along with the power flux $P(x, t)$, satisfies the equation of continuity

$$\frac{\partial P(x, t)}{\partial x} + \frac{\partial w(x, t)}{\partial t} = 0,$$

which is the analog of $\text{div } \mathbf{j} + \partial \rho / \partial t = 0$ in one dimension. Indeed, we have

$$\frac{\partial P}{\partial x} = \frac{\partial}{\partial x} \left(-T \frac{\partial u}{\partial x} \frac{\partial u}{\partial t} \right) = -T \frac{\partial u}{\partial x} \frac{\partial^2 u}{\partial t \partial x} - T \frac{\partial u}{\partial t} \frac{\partial^2 u}{\partial x^2},$$

while

$$-\frac{\partial w}{\partial t} = -\frac{\partial}{\partial t} \left[\frac{\rho}{2} \left(\frac{\partial u}{\partial t} \right)^2 + \frac{T}{2} \left(\frac{\partial u}{\partial x} \right)^2 \right] = -\rho \frac{\partial u}{\partial t} \frac{\partial^2 u}{\partial t^2} - T \frac{\partial u}{\partial x} \frac{\partial^2 u}{\partial x \partial t}.$$

These two expressions are equal, since $\rho(\partial^2 u / \partial t^2) = T(\partial^2 u / \partial x^2)$. Note that ρ may depend on x; only T must be constant.

The questions of energy and power flow are of particular interest in the case of harmonic wave solutions of the wave equation, namely, solutions of the type

$$u(x, t) = A e^{i(kx - \omega t)} \qquad (\omega = kc = k\sqrt{T/\rho}),$$

where A is a complex constant. Such solutions are particular cases of the D'Alembert formula. Also, they arise in a natural way if the wave equation is solved by the separation of variables or Fourier transform methods. If the real solution is desired, it is often *tacitly understood* that the actual solution is the real part† of the above expression:

$$u_R(x, t) = \text{Re } \{A e^{i(kx - \omega t)}\}.$$

This form takes care of the most general harmonic wave traveling to the right.

---

* This is consistent with the expression for the potential energy for the *finite* string on p. 580. Note that this latter quantity is well defined since a finite string is effectively noninteracting with the surroundings. The potential energy of a *portion* (a, b) of a string is, to some extent, arbitrary. The same is true for the potential energy density.

† The imaginary part would be just as good.

Indeed, if $A = A_R + iA_I$, then

$$u_R(x, t) = A_R \cos (kx - \omega t) - A_I \sin (kx - \omega t).$$

Choosing appropriate A_R and A_I, we obtain arbitrary amplitude and phase of the real harmonic wave, namely,

$$u_R(x, t) = |A| \cos (kx - \omega t + \delta).$$

The transformation formulas read

$$A_R = |A| \cos \delta, \qquad A_I = |A| \sin \delta,$$

$$|A|^2 = A_R^2 + A_I^2, \qquad \tan \delta = \frac{A_I}{A_R}, \qquad A = |A|e^{i\delta}.$$

In connection with these conventions, we should always remember that the imaginary part of the solution does not interfere with the real part in any *linear* relation with *real* coefficients. The energy and power relations are, however, *not linear* with respect to $u(x, t)$ and we must pay attention to this fact. For instance, the power flux must be calculated from

$$P(x, t) = -T \operatorname{Re} \left(\frac{\partial u}{\partial t}\right) \operatorname{Re} \left(\frac{\partial u}{\partial x}\right),$$

and *not* as the real part of complex $P(x, t)$.

Nevertheless, we find that direct use of the complex solution is often possible. For instance, in classical problems,* according to the above formula, the power flux for the harmonic wave reads

$$P(x, t) = Tk\omega(A_R^2 \sin^2 \theta + A_I^2 \cos^2 \theta + A_R A_I \sin 2\theta),$$

where $\theta = kx - \omega t$. We see that the power varies sinusoidally with "doubled" frequency 2ω. In many cases of practical interest only the *average power flux* over a long period of time is important. Evidently, it is sufficient to average $P(x, t)$ over only one period. The factor $\sin 2\theta$ averages to zero while $\sin^2 \theta$ and $\cos^2 \theta$ each yield the factor $\frac{1}{2}$:

$$\int_0^{2\pi/\omega} \sin 2(kx - \omega t)\, dt = 0,$$

$$\int_0^{2\pi/\omega} \sin^2 (kx - \omega t)\, dt = \int_0^{2\pi/\omega} \cos^2 (kx - \omega t)\, dt = \frac{1}{2}.$$

Consequently, the average harmonic power flux is

$$P_{\text{ave}}(x) = \tfrac{1}{2}Tk\omega|A|^2 = \tfrac{1}{2}\rho c\omega^2|A|^2.$$

---

* Most classical problems involving the wave equation have analogous formulas for power flux.

For a wave traveling to the left, the same formula holds except for the sign (due to the reversal of sign in $\partial u/\partial x$). The physical meaning is, of course, that the actual positive power is delivered from the right to the left.

14.5 GENERATION OF WAVES IN A STRETCHED STRING

It is evident on physical grounds that the waves in a stretched string must be generated by some outside influences.* These influences may manifest themselves in the following ways:

a) The string is given initial displacement and velocity at $t = 0$ and then left free.
b) External forces cause motion of the ends of the string, inducing nonhomogeneous boundary conditions.
c) External forces affect the motion of the string along its entire length.

The first situation has already been adequately dealt with in the preceding sections and in Chapter 8.   The second possibility evidently applies only to semi-infinite and finite string.   We shall now consider a typical problem in this category.

   Consider a semi-infinite stretched string with prescribed motion at the boundary $x = 0$.   Without loss of generality, we may assume zero initial conditions† and our problem is to solve

$$\frac{\partial^2 u}{\partial x^2} - \frac{1}{c^2}\frac{\partial^2 u}{\partial t^2} = 0 \qquad \text{(for } x > 0 \quad \text{and} \quad t > 0\text{)},$$

provided $u(x, 0) = \partial u(x, 0)/\partial t = 0$ and $u(0, t) = z(t)$, where $z(t)$ is a given function.   It is tacitly understood that $z(t)$ vanishes prior to $t = 0$; otherwise homogeneous initial conditions would not be possible.   We have already encountered a similar problem involving the heat-conduction equation.   It is instructive to recall the interesting technique described in Section 12.7, which reduces the problem to one already solved.

   Following the discussion on p. 534 et seq., we first construct a solution for the *homogeneous* boundary condition and *unit-displacement* initial conditions, namely, the function $u_1(x, t)$ satisfying

$$\frac{\partial^2 u_1}{\partial x^2} - \frac{1}{c^2}\frac{\partial^2 u_1}{\partial t^2} = 0 \qquad (x > 0, \ t > 0),$$

---

* This follows from the mathematical properties of the wave equation: If the initial and boundary conditions are zero, then the solution is the trivial one, $u(x, t) \equiv 0$.
† A solution $u(x, t)$ satisfying nonhomogeneous boundary conditions and nonhomogeneous initial conditions can be represented as the sum of two solutions: $u_1(x, t)$ satisfying nonhomogeneous boundary conditions and homogeneous initial conditions, and $u_2(x, t)$ satisfying homogeneous boundary conditions and nonhomogeneous initial conditions. This is an important example of how ubiquitous the superposition technique is in linear problems.

with

$$u_1(x, 0) = 1, \qquad \frac{\partial u_1}{\partial t}(x, 0) = 0 \qquad (x > 0),$$

and

$$u_1(0, t) = 0 \qquad (t > 0).$$

According to Section 14.3, we extend the boundary conditions to negative values of x in an antisymmetric fashion:*

$$u_1(x, 0) = \begin{cases} +1 & \text{for} \quad x > 0 \\ -1 & \text{for} \quad x < 0 \end{cases} = 2S(x) - 1 \qquad (\text{all } x),$$

where $S(x)$ is the unit step function. Now applying the D'Alembert formula, we immediately obtain

$$u_1(x, t) = S(x - ct) + S(x + ct) - 1 \qquad (t > 0),$$

which, by the way, reduces to $S(x - ct)$ for $x > 0$ and $t > 0$. From this expression we can obtain a solution to a similar problem with the same initial conditions, but occurring at the time $t = \tau$, rather than $t = 0$; all we need to do is replace t by $t - \tau$:

$$u_1(x, t - \tau) = S[x - c(t - \tau)] + S[x + c(t - \tau)] - 1 \qquad (\text{for } t > \tau).$$

If we now subtract this expression from unity as on p. 534, we should obtain a solution valid for $t > \tau$ to the problem with *homogeneous* initial conditions and nonhomogeneous boundary conditions given by a unit step function starting at $t = \tau$. Explicitly, the function

$$\bar{u}(x, t; \tau) = \begin{cases} 2 - S[x - c(t - \tau)] - S[x + c(t - \tau)] & (\text{for } t > \tau), \\ 0 & (\text{for } t < \tau) \end{cases}$$

is expected to satisfy

$$\frac{\partial^2 \bar{u}}{\partial x^2} - \frac{1}{c^2} \frac{\partial^2 \bar{u}}{\partial t^2} = 0 \qquad (x > 0),$$

with

$$\bar{u}(x, 0; \tau) = \frac{\partial \bar{u}}{\partial t}(x, 0; \tau) = 0 \qquad \text{and} \qquad \bar{u}(0, t; \tau) = S(t - \tau).$$

We find that this is indeed true.

First, observe that for $x > 0$ and $t > \tau$ the second step function is unity so that we can write

$$\bar{u}(x, t; \tau) = \begin{cases} 1 - S[x - c(t - \tau)] & (t > \tau) \\ 0 & (t < \tau) \end{cases} (x > 0).$$

---

* This solution, evidently treated as a distribution, is not physically realizable in view of the discontinuity at $x = 0$. However, we are simply following a formal procedure of heuristic value and need not be worried about this. We shall check the final result.

If $x = 0$, then $S[-c(t - \tau)] = 0$ for $t > \tau$, and $\bar{u}(0, t; \tau)$ does indeed reduce to $S(t - \tau)$. If $t = 0$, then $\bar{u}(x, t; \tau) = 0$ (it is tacitly assumed that $\tau > 0$) and the initial conditions follow. The wave equation is satisfied* by virtue of the fact that x and t appear in the combination $(x - ct)$.

We can now repeat, almost verbatim, the heuristic argument of Section 12.7 and conjecture that the expression

$$u(x, t) = \int_0^t \left[-\frac{\partial \bar{u}}{\partial \tau} (x, t; \tau) \right] z(\tau) \, d\tau$$

is the final solution to our problem for arbitrary boundary conditions. Evaluating this expression, we have†

$$\frac{\partial}{\partial \tau} S[x - c(t - \tau)] = c \, \delta[x - c(t - \tau)]$$
$$= \delta(x/c - t + \tau) = \delta[\tau - (t - x/c)].$$

Integrating, we obtain

$$u(x, t) = \begin{cases} z(t - x/c) & (\text{if } t > x/c), \\ 0 & (\text{if } t < x/c). \end{cases}$$

The success of our technique is now self-evident since $u(x, t)$ clearly satisfies all the desired conditions.

The formula which we have obtained exhibits an important physical feature that is connected with the wave equation. A given point x on the string faithfully follows the motion of the boundary at $x = 0$, but it does so with a delay in time of magnitude $t' = x/c$. This is, of course, the time needed for the wave to reach point x and convey to it the disturbance created at $x = 0$. We say that the motion of point x is *retarded* with respect to the motion of the boundary.

Another worthwhile observation is that the solution contains only the wave moving *to the right*. This is not unexpected either. The disturbance should propagate *away from its source*, which is the point $x = 0$. Within the geometrical setup adopted by us, this implies the right-bound wave.

Let us now turn to the third possibility of generating waves in a stretched string, namely, by means of external forces acting at arbitrary points of the string. In this case we must deal with the *nonhomogeneous wave equation*‡ (see Section 8.1)

$$\frac{\partial^2 u}{\partial x^2} - \frac{1}{c^2} \frac{\partial^2 u}{\partial t^2} = -\frac{F(x, t)}{T},$$

where $F(x, t)$ is the external force per unit length. For convenience, we write

$$-\frac{F(x, t)}{T} = f(x, t).$$

---

* The step function is considered to be a distribution and is, therefore, differentiable.
† See Section 6.3 for the properties of the δ-function.
‡ Sometimes called the D'Alembert equation.

As our first problem of this kind we consider the motion of an infinite string under the influence of external forces which *begin to act* at some instant of time, taken conveniently as $t = 0$. Furthermore, we shall assume that there is no motion of the string prior to that time. We then formulate the problem as follows: We solve

$$\frac{\partial^2 u}{\partial x^2} - \frac{1}{c^2}\frac{\partial^2 u}{\partial t^2} = f(x, t)$$

subject to the initial conditions $u(x, 0) = \partial u(x, 0)/\partial t = 0$ and the usual boundary conditions at infinity (boundedness). In view of the character of initial and boundary conditions, we find that it is reasonable to employ the Fourier transform with respect to x, and the Laplace transform with respect to t. Moreover, it may be instructive to develop a Green's function $G(x, t \mid \xi, \tau)$ by first solving

$$\frac{\partial^2 G}{\partial x^2} - \frac{1}{c^2}\frac{\partial^2 G}{\partial t^2} = \delta(x - \xi)\,\delta(t - \tau)$$

with

$$G(x, 0 \mid \xi, \tau) = \frac{\partial G}{\partial t}(x, 0 \mid \xi, \tau) = 0.$$

We let $G_F(k, t \mid \xi, \tau)$ be the Fourier transform of G and let $G_{FL}(k, s \mid \xi, \tau)$ be the Laplace transform of G_F. Taking the Fourier transform, we obtain

$$-k^2 G_F - \frac{1}{c^2}\frac{\partial^2 G_F}{\partial t^2} = \frac{1}{\sqrt{2\pi}}e^{ik\xi}\,\delta(t - \tau)$$

with

$$G_F(k, 0 \mid \xi, \tau) = \frac{\partial G_F}{\partial t}(k, 0 \mid \xi, \tau) = 0.$$

Further, taking the Laplace transform, we obtain

$$-k^2 G_{FL} - \frac{s^2}{c^2}G_{FL} = \frac{1}{\sqrt{2\pi}}e^{ik\xi}e^{-s\tau},$$

or

$$G_{FL} = -\frac{c^2}{\sqrt{2\pi}}e^{ik\xi}\frac{e^{-s\tau}}{s^2 + k^2 c^2}.$$

Inverting the Laplace transform with the use of the shifting property (see Section 5.3), we obtain

$$G_F = -\frac{c^2}{\sqrt{2\pi}}e^{ik\xi}\frac{\sin kc(t - \tau)}{kc}S(t - \tau).$$

Finally, inverting the Fourier transform, we have

$$G(x, t \mid \xi, \tau) = -\frac{c^2}{2\pi}S(t - \tau)\int_{-\infty}^{+\infty}\frac{\sin kc(t - \tau)}{kc}e^{-ik(x-\xi)}\,dk.$$

The integral is not hard to evaluate. As a matter of fact, we already know from Section 7.2, Example 3, that the inverse Fourier transform of

$$F(k) = \sqrt{\frac{2}{\pi}} \frac{\sin ak}{k} \qquad (a > 0)$$

is the unit box function, namely, a function $f(x)$ which is unity from $x = -a$ to $x = +a$ and zero otherwise.

We shall treat $G(x, t \mid \xi, \tau)$ as a function of ξ with x, t, and τ as temporarily fixed parameters. Setting $k = -k'$ in the integrand and dropping the primes, we may conveniently rewrite it:

$$G(x, t \mid \xi, \tau) = -\frac{c}{2} S(t - \tau) \frac{1}{\sqrt{2\pi}} \int_{-\infty}^{+\infty} \sqrt{\frac{2}{\pi}} \frac{\sin kc(t - \tau)}{k} e^{-ik(\xi - x)} \, dk.$$

It is now evident that apart from the factor $-(c/2)S(t - \tau)$, our Green's function is a unit box function between the limits $\xi = x - c(t - \tau)$ and $\xi = x + c(t - \tau)$. This can be expressed by the analytic formula

$$G(x, t \mid \xi, \tau) = \begin{cases} -(c/2)\{S[\xi - x + c(t - \tau)] - S[\xi - x - c(t - \tau)]\} & (t > \tau), \\ 0 & (t < \tau). \end{cases}$$

The general solution for arbitrary external forces is then given by the integral

$$u(x, t) = -\frac{c}{2} \int_0^t d\tau \int_{-\infty}^{+\infty} G(x, t \mid \xi, \tau) f(\xi, \tau) \, d\xi$$

$$= -\frac{c}{2} \int_0^t d\tau \int_{x-c(t-\tau)}^{x+c(t-\tau)} f(\xi, \tau) \, d\xi.$$

This formula represents the response of the string at point x and time t to the forces which were applied elsewhere in space and time. Again, there is the effect of *retarded response*. To see this more clearly, we consider the Green's function as a function of t with ξ, τ, and x as fixed parameters. Analyzing the formula for $G(x, t \mid \xi, \tau)$, we deduce:

a) If $x > \xi$ and t continues to increase from $t = \tau$, then only the first step function will ever contribute and*

$$G(x, t \mid \xi, \tau) = -\frac{c}{2} S\left[t - \tau + \frac{\xi - x}{c} \right] \qquad (x > \xi, \, t > \tau).$$

b) If $x < \xi$, then, at the beginning (as t begins to increase from $t = \tau$), both step functions contribute and cancel each other; at the time $t = \tau + (\xi - x)/c$ the second term disappears. This behavior can evidently be described by

$$G(x, t \mid \xi, \tau) = -\frac{c}{2} S\left[t - \tau - \frac{\xi - x}{c} \right] \qquad (x < \xi, \, t > \tau).$$

---

* For convenience, we divide the expression in square brackets by c. This does not change a step function since c is a positive number.

Finally, both formulas may be combined into

$$G(x, t \mid \xi, \tau) = -\frac{c}{2} S\left[t - \tau - \frac{|x - \xi|}{c}\right],$$

valid for all x (and for all t since the expression is automatically zero for $t < \tau$). It is now evident that there is no response at the point x to a force at ξ and time τ until the interval of time $|x - \xi|/c$ has elapsed; this is the time needed for a disturbance to reach point x. From there on, the string is left in a state of permanent deformation.*

While the solution of our problem is complete, we may be curious to know whether we could have deduced it from the treatment of the homogeneous wave equation with nonhomogeneous initial conditions. For instance, we know from Section 12.5 that there is a close relationship between the two corresponding Green's functions for the heat-conduction equation. Drawing an analogy from the physical arguments in that section, we may argue as follows: A force

$$F(\xi, \tau) \, \delta(x - \xi) \, \delta(t - \tau)$$

delivers an impulse $F(\xi, \tau) \, dx$ to the element dx within an infinitesimal interval of time near τ. This is equal to a change in momentum and implies an instantaneous increase in velocity equal to

$$v(\xi, \tau) = \frac{dp}{dm} = \frac{F(\xi, \tau) \, dx}{\rho \, dx} = \frac{F(\xi, \tau)}{\rho},$$

where $dm = \rho \, dx$ is the mass of the element dx. This expression can be interpreted as the distribution of newly created velocities† at time τ. If we replace $F(\xi, \tau)$ by $-Tf(\xi, \tau)$, then we can collect the effect of forces occurring at time τ by integrating $v(\xi, \tau)$ with the Green's function for *initial velocities*, namely (see Section 14.2),

$$g_2(x \mid \xi; t) = \frac{1}{2c} \{S[\xi - (x - ct)] - S[\xi - (x + ct)]\},$$

provided we replace t by $t - \tau$, since the initial conditions are now at $t = \tau$. The overall solution should be obtained by integrating this expression further over all the allowed values of τ. We should then be able to prove the following result.

Theorem. The solution $u(x, t)$ of the D'Alembert partial differential equation

$$\frac{\partial^2 u}{\partial x^2} = \frac{1}{c^2} \frac{\partial^2 u}{\partial t^2} + f(x, t)$$

---

* So far as the force proportional to $\delta(x - \xi) \, \delta(t - \tau)$ is concerned; otherwise, there is a cumulative effect from all other sources.

† They come on the top of any velocities already present due to the action of forces prior to τ.

with homogeneous initial conditions $u(x, 0) = (\partial u/\partial t)(x, 0) = 0$ can be obtained from the solution $\bar{u}(x; t \mid \tau)$ of the wave partial differential equation

$$\frac{\partial^2 \bar{u}}{\partial x^2} = \frac{1}{c^2} \frac{\partial^2 \bar{u}}{\partial t^2}$$

with the nonhomogeneous initial conditions

$$\bar{u}(x; t \mid \tau)\big|_{t=\tau} = 0, \qquad \frac{\partial \bar{u}}{\partial t}(x; t \mid \tau)\big|_{t=\tau} = -c^2 f(x, \tau) \qquad \text{(arbitrary } \tau)$$

by means of

$$u(x, t) = \int_0^t \bar{u}(x, t \mid \tau) \, d\tau.$$

Proof. Differentiate $u(x, t)$ with respect to time:

$$\frac{\partial u(x, t)}{\partial t} = \int_0^t \frac{\partial \bar{u}(x, t \mid \tau)}{\partial t} \, d\tau + \bar{u}(x; t \mid \tau)\big|_{\tau=t}.$$

Since the last term is zero, it follows, so far, that $u(x, t)$ satisfies both homogeneous initial conditions. Furthermore,

$$\frac{\partial^2 u(x, t)}{\partial t^2} = \int_0^t \frac{\partial^2 \bar{u}(x; t \mid \tau)}{\partial t^2} \, d\tau + \frac{\partial \bar{u}}{\partial t}(x; t \mid \tau)\big|_{\tau=t}.$$

The last term is equal to $-c^2 f(x, t)$* so that

$$-\frac{1}{c^2} \frac{\partial^2 u}{\partial t^2} = -\frac{1}{c^2} \int_0^t \frac{\partial^2 \bar{u}}{\partial t^2} \, d\tau + f(x, t).$$

Now, since

$$\frac{\partial^2 u}{\partial x^2} = \int_0^t \frac{\partial^2 \bar{u}}{\partial x^2} \, d\tau,$$

it follows that

$$\frac{\partial^2 u}{\partial x^2} - \frac{1}{c^2} \frac{\partial^2 u}{\partial t^2} = \int_0^t \left(\frac{\partial^2 \bar{u}}{\partial x^2} - \frac{1}{c^2} \frac{\partial^2 \bar{u}}{\partial t^2} \right) d\tau + f(x, t).$$

Since the integrand on the right vanishes, it is seen that $u(x, t)$ satisfies the D'Alembert equation.

In view of this theorem, all we need to know is the solution of the wave equation for the initial conditions at $t = \tau$, rather than at $t = 0$. However, this is simply obtained by replacing t by $t - \tau$ in the D'Alembert formula;† since

---

* The notation may be confusing, but the initial condition for $\partial \bar{u}/\partial t$ essentially means: "If we differentiate $\bar{u}(x; t \mid \tau)$ with respect to t and replace both t and τ by the *same* symbol (you may call it θ if you like), then we obtain the functional form $f(x, \theta)$."

† To demonstrate this formally, we make a change of variables $t = t' + \tau$ with fixed τ. Now the D'Alembert formula can be rederived in terms of t', just as before.

we need the effect of initial velocities only, we have

$$\bar{u}(x; t \mid \tau) = -\frac{c}{2} \int_{x-c(t-\tau)}^{x+c(t-\tau)} f(\xi, \tau) \, d\xi,$$

and we have rederived our formula:

$$u(x, t) = -\frac{c}{2} \int_{0}^{t} d\tau \int_{x-c(t-\tau)}^{x+c(t-\tau)} f(\xi, \tau) \, d\xi.$$

As the second problem involving external forces we shall consider an infinite string subject to forces *varying harmonically in time*, with a given frequency ω_0. We seek solutions of

$$\frac{\partial^2 u}{\partial x^2} - \frac{1}{c^2} \frac{\partial^2 u}{\partial t^2} = f(x)e^{-i\omega_0 t} \qquad (\omega_0 > 0).$$

The peculiar feature of this problem is the absence of initial conditions. Instead, we are seeking a solution which also varies harmonically in time with the same frequency, and we write

$$u(x, t) = \psi(x)e^{-i\omega_0 t}.$$

The existence of such solutions is based on our physical experience.* However, it should not come as a surprise that it is *not uniquely determined*. We shall yet have to select a solution which will be physically acceptable. The reasons for this are: A given deflection $u(x, t)$ of the string can arise in a variety of ways; that is, it may be caused by forces acting at x; it may be caused by a wave coming from the left or from the right, and it may be caused by "confluence" of two such waves. We are now lacking the initial conditions which could differentiate between these possibilities.

If we proceed to substitute $u(x, t)$ into the PDE, we obtain

$$\frac{d^2\psi(x)}{dx^2} + k_0^2\psi(x) = f(x) \qquad \left(k_0 = \frac{\omega_0}{c} > 0\right).$$

It is natural to treat this problem by the Fourier transform method, and it is convenient to develop the Green's function $G(x \mid \xi)$ satisfying

$$\frac{d^2 G}{dx^2} + k_0^2 G = \delta(x - \xi).$$

We have actually solved this equation in Section 12.9 and may confine ourselves to some remarks regarding the procedure employed there. Applying the Fourier

---

* Of course, we are idealizing the actual physical conditions: neither the forces nor the motion can exist "forever." What is meant by these formulas is that a *long time* after the beginning of the motion the solution is expected to *approach* a steady-state solution of the above type.

transform method, we deduce

$$G(x \mid \xi) = -\frac{1}{2\pi} \int_{-\infty}^{+\infty} \frac{e^{-ik(x-\xi)}}{k^2 - k_0^2} \, dk.$$

It is clear at this point that the choice of different contours, to avoid the poles $k = -k_0$ and $k = +k_0$, will yield different Green's functions. We must select the contour which yields a physically acceptable $G(x \mid \xi)$.

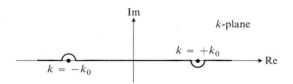

Figure 14.10

The criterion used in Section 12.9 was that $G(x \mid \xi)$, when combined with the factor $e^{-i\omega_0 t}$, must represent a wave traveling *away from the source*. We can strengthen this conclusion on the basis of our experience with other similar problems (e.g., see p. 605). More important, the considerations of energy and power flow (Section 14.4) show that the positive power is transmitted in the same direction as the wave travels. Therefore, the correct choice of Green's function for *radiation processes* is such that it must represent *outgoing waves*. This necessitates, as explained in detail in Section 12.9, the path of integration shown in Fig. 14.10, and yields, by the calculus of residues,

$$G(x \mid \xi) = \begin{cases} -\dfrac{i}{2k_0} e^{-ik_0(x-\xi)} & (x < \xi), \\[2mm] -\dfrac{i}{2k_0} e^{ik_0(x-\xi)} & (x > \xi). \end{cases}$$

14.6 RADIATION OF SOUND FROM A PULSATING SPHERE

Having studied the basic aspects of wave propagation on the simple one-dimensional example of the vibrating string, we can now turn to problems involving the wave equation in more than one dimension. We shall find that they exhibit much the same features as the one-dimensional case, despite the fact that the process of solution may, in general, become quite cumbersome. As one of the simplest examples, let us study the radiation of sound from a pulsating sphere.

Example 1. Consider a sphere of mean radius $R = a$ which pulsates harmonically in time, changing its radius according to the relation

$$R(t) = a + h \cos \omega t,$$

where it will be assumed that $h \ll a$, that is, the oscillations are small. The pulsation of the sphere will cause a motion of the surrounding air which can be described, as follows from the discussion in Section 8.9, by a wave equation, satisfied by the velocity potential $\varphi(\mathbf{r}, t)$:

$$\nabla^2 \varphi - \frac{1}{c^2} \frac{\partial^2 \varphi}{\partial t^2} = 0.$$

To be specific, we shall assume that the frequency of pulsation falls into the acoustic range (say, 20 to 20,000 cps) and describe the waves as sound waves.

It is logical to seek the solution for φ in a spherical coordinate system, so that $\varphi = \varphi(r, \theta, \phi; t)$ and the range of r is restricted to $a \leq r < \infty$. To find the boundary conditions which φ must satisfy at $r = a$, we recall that the macroscopic velocity of the air is given by

$$\mathbf{v} = -\operatorname{grad} \varphi.$$

Now, at $r = a$ the radial component of the velocity of the air must match the velocity of the surface of the sphere* so that we have

$$v_r = -\left.\frac{\partial \varphi}{\partial r}\right|_{r=a} = \frac{dR(t)}{dt} = -h\omega \sin \omega t.$$

It is seen that the potential φ must vary harmonically in time at $r = a$, and it is reasonable to expect that it is a harmonic function of time in general. Moreover, it is convenient to use a complex solution of the form

$$\varphi(r, \theta, \phi; t) = \psi(r, \theta, \phi)e^{-i\omega t}$$

with the understanding that Re φ should represent the actual physical solution. In this spirit, we add an imaginary part to the function $R(t)$ and define a "complex radius"

$$R(t) = a + he^{-i\omega t}.$$

Requiring now that

$$-\left.\frac{\partial \varphi}{\partial r}\right|_{r=a} = \frac{dR(t)}{dt} = -ih\omega e^{-i\omega t},$$

we automatically satisfy

$$-\frac{\partial}{\partial r}(\operatorname{Re} \varphi)\big|_{r=a} = \frac{d}{dt} \operatorname{Re} R(t),$$

which is the actual boundary condition. Solving the wave equation for the complex potential φ subject to the complex boundary condition, we simultaneously solve the actual physical problem. So far as the function $\psi(r, \theta, \phi)$ is concerned, the boundary condition reduces to

$$-\left.\frac{\partial \psi}{\partial r}\right|_{r=a} = -i\omega h.$$

---

* We must assume that the speed of pulsation is considerably smaller than the speed of sound which implies $h \ll c/\omega$; if $h > c/\omega$, supersonic phenomena will occur and our theory will not be applicable.

Now turning to the wave equation, we note that the solution should be spherically symmetric because the boundary condition is spherically symmetric.* Therefore, $\psi = \psi(r)$, and it must satisfy the differential equation

$$\frac{1}{r^2} \frac{d}{dr} \left(r^2 \frac{d\psi}{dr} \right) + k^2\psi = 0 \qquad (k = \omega/c).$$

We may recognize the solutions of this equation as spherical Bessel and Neumann functions of order zero, as described in detail in Section 9.9. Consequently,

$$\psi(r) = Aj_0(kr) + Bn_0(kr).$$

Since our solution does not extend to $r = 0$, there is no reason to discard $n_0(kr)$, and B need not vanish. It is evident that we cannot determine both A and B from the single boundary condition at $r = a$. A clue toward the resolution of this difficulty can be obtained if we recall that (p. 383)

$$j_0(kr) = \frac{\sin kr}{kr}, \qquad n_0(kr) = -\frac{\cos kr}{kr}.$$

Since $\psi(r)$ is to be multiplied by $e^{-i\omega t}$, it is convenient to express it in terms of e^{ikr} and e^{-ikr}, which yields

$$\psi(r) = \frac{A - Bi}{2ikr} e^{ikr} + \frac{A + Bi}{2ikr} e^{-ikr}.$$

The complete solution would then read

$$\varphi(r, t) = \psi(r)e^{-i\omega t} = \frac{A - Bi}{2ikr} e^{i(kr-\omega t)} - \frac{A + Bi}{2ikr} e^{-i(kr+\omega t)}.$$

Since $k = \omega/c$, it is not difficult to see that the first term represents a wave propagating in the direction of increasing r. This is just as in the one-dimensional case, the only difference being that the amplitude of the wave falls off as $1/r$. We call such a wave a *diverging radial wave*. Similarly, the second term represents a *converging radial wave*.

It now stands to reason that our physical solution should entirely consist of the diverging wave which would imply

$$A + Bi = 0,$$

and would provide us with the second relation needed to determine A and B.

This conclusion parallels the argument presented in the preceding section (p. 611), and it is instructive to justify it by the consideration of power flow in acoustics. A volume V of air bounded by a closed surface S is subject to the

---

* This is intuitively clear for a physicist. For a mathematical discussion of this statement, see p. 619. We are already familiar with an analogous phenomenon where the solution preserves the reflectional symmetry of the boundary conditions (Sections 8.3 and 9.6).

total external force*

$$\mathbf{F} = - \oiint_S p \, \mathbf{dS},$$

where p is the pressure; this is, of course, under the usual assumption that body forces (p. 319) are negligible. From this formula, it follows that $\mathbf{dF} = -p \, \mathbf{dS}$ is an infinitesimal force acting at the site of $\mathbf{dS}$, and if $\mathbf{v}$ is the macroscopic velocity of air at that point, then the power produced by this force is $-p(\mathbf{v} \cdot \mathbf{dS})$. To be more precise, this is the power flux *into* the volume V. The power flux *out of* the volume V is obtained by changing the sign so that the total power outflow from V (energy emanating from V per unit time) is given by

$$P_{\text{tot}} = \oiint_S (p\mathbf{v} \cdot \mathbf{dS}).$$

It is customary to define the *power-flux vector*

$$\mathbf{P} = p\mathbf{v},$$

which then represents, in magnitude and direction, the amount of energy passing per second through a unit area normal to it† (compare with p. 599).

Furthermore, in terms of the velocity potential φ we have

$$\mathbf{v} = -\text{grad } \varphi, \qquad p = p_0 + p_0\gamma\delta = p_0 + \rho_0 \frac{\partial \varphi}{\partial t},$$

so that

$$\mathbf{P} = -p_0 \, \text{grad } \varphi - \rho_0 \frac{\partial \varphi}{\partial t} \, \text{grad } \varphi.$$

If we are using complex solutions, then, of course, φ must be replaced by its real part and

$$\mathbf{P} = p_0 \, \text{Re} \, (\text{grad } \varphi) - \rho_0 \, \text{Re} \left(\frac{\partial \varphi}{\partial t}\right) \text{Re} \, (\text{grad } \varphi).$$

As mentioned in Section 14.4, we are most often interested in the *average power* whenever φ varies harmonically in time. In this case, the first term in the above formula will consist of terms proportional to $\sin \omega t$ and $\cos \omega t$ which will average out to zero, and we are left with

$$\mathbf{P}_{\text{ave}} = \left[-\rho_0 \, \text{Re} \left(\frac{\partial \varphi}{\partial t}\right) \text{Re} \, (\text{grad } \varphi)\right]_{\text{ave}}.$$

Applying this formula to spherically symmetric solutions, we can easily calculate

---

* See Section 8.9.

† In electromagnetic theory an analogous vector is called the *Poynting vector*.

(as in Section 14.4) that a diverging wave,

$$\varphi_{\text{div}}(r, t) = D \frac{e^{i(kr-\omega t)}}{r} \qquad (D = \text{const}),$$

yields the power-flow vector (averaged in time) in a positive radial direction:

$$\mathbf{P}_{\text{ave}} = \frac{\rho_0 \omega k |D|^2}{2r^2} \mathbf{r}_0,$$

where $\mathbf{r}_0$ is the unit vector in the r-direction. On the other hand, the power-flow vector due to a converging wave,

$$\varphi_{\text{conv}}(r, t) = C \frac{e^{-i(kr+\omega t)}}{r} \qquad (C = \text{const}),$$

will be in the opposite direction:

$$\mathbf{P}_{\text{ave}} = - \frac{\rho_0 \omega k |C|^2}{2r^2} \mathbf{r}_0.$$

Exercise. Produce the details for the derivation of the above formulas for $\mathbf{P}_{\text{ave}}$.

This derivation confirms the choice of a diverging wave as the solution of our problem and also provides us with the formula for power flow which is of primary practical importance. Thus we have $B = Ai$, and

$$\varphi(r, t) = \psi(r)e^{-i\omega t} = \frac{A}{ikr} e^{ikr} e^{-i\omega t}.$$

To determine A, we use the boundary condition at $r = a$, namely,

$$\left. \frac{\partial \psi}{\partial r} \right|_{r=a} = \frac{A}{a} e^{ika} - \frac{A}{ika^2} e^{ika} = i\omega h,$$

so that

$$\varphi(r, t) = \frac{\omega a^2 h e^{-ika}}{ka + i} \frac{e^{ikr}}{r} e^{-i\omega t}.$$

From this formula all measurable quantities can be determined. In particular, the power-flow vector is

$$\mathbf{P}_{\text{ave}} = \frac{\rho_0 \omega k}{2r^2} \frac{\omega^2 a^4 h^2}{(1 + k^2 a^2)} \mathbf{r}_0 = \frac{\rho_0 a^4 h^2 \omega^4}{2c(1 + a^2/\lambda^2)} \frac{\mathbf{r}_0}{r^2},$$

where k has been replaced by ω/c in the numerator and by $1/\lambda$ in the denominator, λ being the wavelength of the sound waves. This is done to exhibit the transition to the so-called point source when the radius of the pulsating sphere is negligible compared to the wavelength of the radiated sound. If $a \ll \lambda$, then

$$\mathbf{P}_{\text{ave}} \cong \frac{\rho_0 a^4 h^2 \omega^4}{2c} \frac{\mathbf{r}_0}{r^2}.$$

The total power radiated by the source is, of course, the surface integral of this vector over a sphere of arbitrary radius R $(R > a)$:

$$P_{\text{tot}} = \int_0^{2\pi} d\phi \int_0^\pi |\mathbf{P}_{\text{ave}}|_{r=R} R^2 \sin\theta \, d\theta \cong \frac{2\pi\rho_0 a^4 h^2 \omega^4}{c}.$$

In connection with this problem it is useful to introduce some new special functions, widely used in radiation and scattering problems. Recall that the radial factor of our solution was

$$\psi(r) = A[j_0(kr) + in_0(kr)].$$

This particular combination of spherical Bessel and Neumann functions is characteristic for radiation and scattering problems. Let us define, in general, the *spherical Hankel functions* of the first and second kind, respectively, by

$$h_l^{(1)}(kr) = j_l(kr) + in_l(kr), \qquad h_l^{(2)}(kr) = j_l(kr) - in_l(kr).$$

The reason for this idea is the separation of solutions of the wave equation into diverging and converging waves, at least within their asymptotic forms, i.e., for large values of r. Indeed, from Section 9.9 we know* that spherical Bessel and Neumann functions are related to Bessel and Neumann functions of half-integral order by

$$j_l(x) = \sqrt{\frac{\pi}{2x}} J_{l+1/2}(x), \qquad n_l(x) = \sqrt{\frac{\pi}{2x}} N_{l+1/2}(x).$$

Now, from the asymptotic forms of Bessel and Neumann functions (pp. 390 and 391), it follows that $j_l(x)$ and $n_l(x)$ behave asymptotically as

$$j_l(x) \sim \frac{1}{x} \sin\left(x - \frac{l\pi}{2}\right), \qquad n_l(x) \sim -\frac{1}{x} \cos\left(x - \frac{l\pi}{2}\right).$$

Consequently, spherical Hankel functions will possess the asymptotic forms†

$$h_l^{(1)}(x) \sim (-i)^{l+1} \frac{e^{ix}}{x}, \qquad h_l^{(2)}(x) \sim (i)^{l+1} \frac{e^{-ix}}{x},$$

---

* See pp. 382 and 383.

† In general, one defines *Hankel functions* of the first and second kind (and any order) by the formulas

$$H_\mu^{(1)}(x) = J_\mu(x) + iN_\mu(x), \qquad H_\mu^{(2)}(x) = J_\mu(x) - iN_\mu(x).$$

These functions possess asymptotic forms (for real x)

$$H_\mu^{(1)}(x) \sim \sqrt{\frac{2}{\pi x}} e^{ix-(i\pi/2)(\mu+1/2)}, \qquad H_\mu^{(2)}(x) \sim \sqrt{\frac{2}{\pi x}} e^{-ix+(i\pi/2)(\mu+1/2)}.$$

When μ is an integer, these functions are convenient in the treatment of two-dimensional scattering problems.

which do correspond to diverging and converging complex solutions when combined with the factor* $e^{-i\omega t}$. Since $j_l(kr)$ and $n_l(kr)$ are expressible in terms of $h_l^{(1)}(kr)$ and $h_l^{(2)}(kr)$, namely,

$$j_l(kr) = \tfrac{1}{2}[h_l^{(1)}(kr) + h_l^{(2)}(kr)], \qquad n_l(kr) = \frac{1}{2i}[h_l^{(1)}(kr) - h_l^{(2)}(kr)],$$

it is clear that the radial dependence (see p. 384) of the solutions of the Helmholtz equation can be expressed as a linear combination of spherical Hankel functions:

$$R_l(r) = D_l h_l^{(1)}(kr) + C_l h_l^{(2)}(kr).$$

In radiation and scattering problems this representation is of primary interest, since immediate statements can be made about the constants on physical grounds; for example, $C_l = 0$ (all l) in radiation problems, where no waves are coming from infinity.

Remark. Observe that the function

$$f(r) = e^{ikr}/kr$$

has the property $r(\partial f/\partial r) - ikrf = -f$. Neither term on the left-hand side vanishes at infinity, but the one on the right does. Consequently, $f(r)$ satisfies the so-called *Sommerfeld radiation condition*

$$\lim_{r\to\infty}\left(r\frac{\partial f}{\partial r} - ikrf\right) = 0.$$

Since $g(r) = e^{-ikr}/kr$ does not satisfy this condition,† the latter may be used to distinguish between converging and diverging waves. Indeed, since $h_l^{(1)}(kr)$ satisfies the Sommerfeld radiation condition, while $h_l^{(2)}(kr)$ does not, it must hold for the *entire solution* $\varphi(\mathbf{r}, t)$‡ of a radiation problem. Consequently, in such cases, it can be treated as an "asymptotic boundary condition."

Example 2. Consider the acoustic field of a sphere whose surface exhibits *arbitrary* radial harmonic vibrations. Each point on the sphere, characterized by two angles θ and φ, undergoes radial displacements

$$\bar{u}(\theta, \phi; t) = A(\theta, \phi)\cos[\omega t - \delta(\theta, \phi)]$$

from its mean position at $r = a$, where the amplitude A and phase δ both vary from point to point. As before, it is convenient to introduce the complex displacement

$$u(\theta, \phi; t) = A(\theta, \phi)e^{-i[\omega t - \delta(\theta, \phi)]},$$

---

* If the factor $e^{i\omega t}$ were used, then $h_l^{(2)}(kr)$ would correspond to diverging waves and $h_l^{(1)}(kr)$ would correspond to converging waves.

† It satisfies $\lim_{r\to\infty}[r(\partial g/\partial r) + ikrg] = 0$.

‡ It is tacitly assumed that $\varphi(\mathbf{r}, t)$ extends over all angles as $r \to \infty$.

where $\bar{u}(\theta, \phi; t)$ is the real part. This formula can be further rewritten as

$$u(\theta, \phi; t) = u_0(\theta, \phi)e^{-i\omega t},$$

where $u_0(\theta, \phi) = A(\theta, \phi)e^{i\,\delta(\theta,\phi)}$ is the complex amplitude of the displacement.

The acoustic field is now determined by the velocity potential $\varphi(r, \theta, \phi; t)$ which satisfies the wave equation and the boundary condition at $r = a$:

$$-\frac{\partial \varphi}{\partial r}\bigg|_{r=a} = \frac{\partial u}{\partial t} = -i\omega u_0(\theta, \phi)e^{-i\omega t}.$$

As before, $\varphi(r, \theta, \phi; t) = \psi(r, \theta, \phi)e^{-i\omega t}$, and ψ must satisfy the Helmholtz equation for $a \leq r < \infty$. We know (see p. 380) that ψ is then expressible in terms of spherical harmonics as

$$\psi(r, \theta, \phi) = \sum_{l=0}^{\infty} R_l(r) \sum_m C_{lm} Y_{lm}(\theta, \phi).$$

We do not specify the precise form of summation over the label m for the following reason: Since we are dealing with a complex solution, there is no particular advantage of using the classical Y_{lm}, which are real, as defined on p. 380. Instead, we introduce the *quantum-mechanical* definition of spherical harmonics by means of the single formula

$$Y_{lm}(\theta, \phi) = \sqrt{\frac{2l+1}{4\pi} \frac{(l-|m|)!}{(l+|m|)!}} \, P_l^{|m|}(\cos \theta)e^{im\phi},$$

where m is now allowed to take negative values as well (within the limits $-l \leq m \leq l$).

Remark. Unfortunately, there are more than one definition of the Y_{lm} in quantum mechanics. The one we are employing is the so-called Darwin definition, *Proc. Roy. Soc.*, London, A **118,** 645 (1928). The other two commonly used definitions are the Condon-Shortley and Bethe definitions, related to ours as follows:

$$Y_{lm}^{\text{Condon-Shortley}} = \begin{cases} (-1)^m Y_{lm}^{\text{Darwin}} & (m \geq 0), \\ Y_{lm}^{\text{Darwin}} & (m < 0), \end{cases}$$

$$Y_{lm}^{\text{Bethe}} = \begin{cases} Y_{lm}^{\text{Darwin}} & (m \geq 0), \\ (-1)^m Y_{lm}^{\text{Darwin}} & (m < 0). \end{cases}$$

It is not hard to see that the Y_{l0} are the same as in the classical set, while for $m \neq 0$,

$$Y_{lm} = \frac{1}{\sqrt{2}} (Y_{l|m|}^{(+)} \pm i Y_{l|m|}^{(-)}); \qquad (+) \text{ for } m > 0, \ (-) \text{ for } m < 0.$$

The main reason for this choice in quantum mechanics is the fact that the functions Y_{lm} happen to be eigenfunctions of L_z, the z-component of the angular-momentum operator. We are using them now simply because they are somewhat easier to handle than the classical ones. In accordance with their complex nature (see Section 11.1), the orthogonality of the Y_{lm} is given by

$$\int_0^{2\pi} d\phi \int_0^{\pi} Y_{lm}^*(\theta, \phi) Y_{l'm'}(\theta, \phi) \sin \theta \, d\theta = \delta_{ll'}\delta_{mm'}.$$

Turning now to the functions $R_l(r)$ in the expression for ψ, we recognize them as some linear combinations of either $j_l(kr)$ and $n_l(kr)$ or, equivalently, of $h_l^{(1)}(kr)$ and $h_l^{(2)}(kr)$. However, our acoustic field must satisfy the radiation condition; this implies that the terms with $h_l^{(2)}(kr)$ must be absent. It then follows that $\psi(r, \theta, \phi)$ has the form

$$\psi(r, \theta, \phi) = \sum_{l=0}^{\infty} h_l^{(1)}(kr) \sum_{m=-l}^{+l} C_{lm} Y_{lm}(\theta, \phi) \qquad (a \leq r < \infty).$$

Matching $\partial\psi/\partial r$ at $r = a$ with $i\omega u_0(\theta, \phi)$, we obtain

$$i\omega u_0(\theta, \phi) = \sum_{l=0}^{\infty} \frac{dh_l^{(1)}(ka)}{dr} \sum_{m=-l}^{+l} C_{lm} Y_{lm}(\theta, \phi),$$

which determines the coefficients C_{lm} by the standard procedure. Multiplying by $Y_{l'm'}^*(\theta, \phi)$ and integrating over the angles, we have

$$C_{lm} = \frac{i\omega}{[dh_l^{(1)}(ka)/dr]} \int_0^{2\pi} d\phi \int_0^{\pi} u_0(\theta, \phi) Y_{lm}^*(\theta, \phi) \sin \theta \, d\theta.$$

This formula essentially completes the solution of our problem.

Remark. We can now justify, on purely mathematical grounds, the statement made on p. 613 that the solution $\varphi(\mathbf{r}, t)$ must be spherically symmetric if the boundary conditions are independent of angles. Indeed, if $u_0(\theta, \phi) = $ const, then the above formula shows that all the C_{lm} vanish except C_{00}.

14.7 THE RETARDED POTENTIAL

In this section we shall deduce the general solution of the D'Alembert equation

$$\nabla^2\psi - \frac{1}{c^2}\frac{\partial^2\psi}{\partial t^2} = f(\mathbf{r}, t),$$

where the function $f(\mathbf{r}, t)$ is given, and the solution extends over the entire space. This equation represents waves generated by sources distributed over the volume and is not likely to occur in acoustics where the sound waves are usually produced by vibrating surfaces. However, it has wide applications in electromagnetic theory for the following reason: In a nonpolarizable and nonmagnetizable medium, the electric field $\mathbf{E}$ and the magnetic induction field $\mathbf{B}$ must satisfy the Maxwell equations. Expressed in MKSA units, where the charge density $\rho(\mathbf{r}, t)$ and the current density $\mathbf{J}(\mathbf{r}, t)$ are, in general, space and time dependent, these equations are

1. $\operatorname{div} \mathbf{E} = \dfrac{\rho}{\epsilon_0}$,   2. $\operatorname{div} \mathbf{B} = 0$,

3. $\operatorname{curl} \mathbf{E} + \dfrac{\partial \mathbf{B}}{\partial t} = 0$,   4. $\operatorname{curl} \mathbf{B} - \epsilon_0 \mu_0 \dfrac{\partial \mathbf{E}}{\partial t} = \mu_0 \mathbf{J}$

One of the methods of solving this set of equations is to introduce the so-called scalar potential $\varphi(\mathbf{r}, t)$ and the vector potential $\mathbf{A}(\mathbf{r}, t)$ by means of

$$\mathbf{E} = -\operatorname{grad} \varphi - \frac{\partial \mathbf{A}}{\partial t}, \qquad \mathbf{B} = \operatorname{curl} \mathbf{A}.$$

This choice automatically satisfies Maxwell's second and third equations. Moreover, it is convenient* to require that $\mathbf{A}$ and φ satisfy the so-called Lorentz condition†

$$\operatorname{div} \mathbf{A} + \frac{1}{c^2} \frac{\partial \varphi}{\partial t} = 0 \qquad \left(\frac{1}{c^2} = \mu_0 \epsilon_0 \right).$$

Substituting these relations into the remaining two Maxwell's equations, we can verify that φ and $\mathbf{A}$ must satisfy

$$\nabla^2 \varphi - \frac{1}{c^2} \frac{\partial^2 \varphi}{\partial t^2} = -\frac{\rho}{\epsilon_0},$$

and

$$\operatorname{grad} \operatorname{div} \mathbf{A} - \operatorname{curl} \operatorname{curl} \mathbf{A} - \frac{1}{c^2} \frac{\partial^2 \mathbf{A}}{\partial t^2} = -\mu_0 \mathbf{J}.$$

The first of these equations is a D'Alembert equation. The second one is reduced to three D'Alembert equations if $\mathbf{A}$ is written in terms of its cartesian components. Then (see p. 34)

$$\operatorname{grad} \operatorname{div} \mathbf{A} - \operatorname{curl} \operatorname{curl} \mathbf{A} = \nabla^2 \mathbf{A} = \nabla^2 A_x \mathbf{i} + \nabla^2 A_y \mathbf{j} + \nabla^2 A_z \mathbf{k},$$

and we have

$$\nabla^2 A_x - \frac{1}{c^2} \frac{\partial^2 A_x}{\partial t^2} = -\mu_0 J_x,$$

$$\nabla^2 A_y - \frac{1}{c^2} \frac{\partial^2 A_y}{\partial t^2} = -\mu_0 J_y,$$

$$\nabla^2 A_z - \frac{1}{c^2} \frac{\partial^2 A_z}{\partial t^2} = -\mu_0 J_z.$$

---

* This is mandatory in relativistic quantum mechanics.

† The point is that φ and $\mathbf{A}$ have not yet been uniquely specified. If we subtract from $\mathbf{A}$ the gradient of an *arbitrary* scalar function χ and add to φ the term $\partial \chi / \partial t$, then the new potentials $\mathbf{A}' = \mathbf{A} - \operatorname{grad} \chi$ and $\varphi' = \varphi + \partial \chi / \partial t$ will yield the *same fields* $\mathbf{E}$ and $\mathbf{B}$ as the old ones. We can always select (in more than one way) the scalar χ so that the Lorentz condition will be satisfied.

Our electromagnetic problem is, therefore, reducible to solutions of the D'Alembert equation. As in the one-dimensional case, it is convenient to develop Green's function satisfying

$$\nabla^2 G - \frac{1}{c^2} \frac{\partial^2 G}{\partial t^2} = \delta(\mathbf{r} - \mathbf{r}_0)\, \delta(t - t_0),$$

where it is understood that G is a function of the variables $x, y, z; t$ and the parameters x_0, y_0, z_0, t_0; and, by definition,

$$\delta(\mathbf{r} - \mathbf{r}_0) \equiv \delta(x - x_0)\, \delta(y - y_0)\, \delta(z - z_0).$$

Insofar as boundary conditions are concerned, G, being a distribution,* will be required to be bounded only as $x, y, z \to \pm \infty$. With regard to the initial conditions, G must be bounded for a given x, y, z as $t \to +\infty$ and, in addition, it will be required to *vanish identically* for $t < t_0$. This is the principle of causality which we have already met (p. 532, footnote).

We shall tackle the problem by taking Fourier transforms with respect to all three space variables and the time variable.† The amount of labor involved in this derivation can be reduced by the use of vector notation and certain changes of variables. First, we introduce the new variables

$$X = x - x_0, \qquad Y = y - y_0, \qquad Z = z - z_0, \qquad \tau = t - t_0,$$

and observe that in terms of these variables the PDE for G reads

$$\frac{\partial^2 G}{\partial X^2} + \frac{\partial^2 G}{\partial Y^2} + \frac{\partial^2 G}{\partial Z^2} - \frac{1}{c^2} \frac{\partial^2 G}{\partial \tau^2} = \delta(X)\, \delta(Y)\, \delta(Z)\, \delta(\tau).$$

It follows that $G(\mathbf{r}, t \,|\, \mathbf{r}_0, t_0)$ must actually be a function of the scalar τ and the vector $\mathbf{R} = X\mathbf{i} + Y\mathbf{j} + Z\mathbf{k}$; that is, it must depend only on the differences $t - t_0$ and $\mathbf{r} - \mathbf{r}_0$.‡ We can write $G = G(\mathbf{R}, \tau)$.

As we proceed to take the Fourier transform of G, we first multiply G by $(1/\sqrt{2\pi})e^{iK_x X}$ and integrate over X; then we perform analogous operations with Y, Z, and τ. The final result is, evidently,

$$g(\mathbf{K}, \omega) = \frac{1}{(\sqrt{2\pi})^4} \int_{-\infty}^{+\infty} dX \int_{-\infty}^{+\infty} dY \int_{-\infty}^{+\infty} dZ \int_{-\infty}^{+\infty} G(\mathbf{R}, \tau) e^{i(\mathbf{K}\cdot\mathbf{R} + \omega\tau)} \, d\tau,$$

where $\mathbf{K} = K_x\mathbf{i} + K_y\mathbf{j} + K_z\mathbf{k}$. This is the fourfold Fourier transform of G.

---

* A Green's function is more conveniently regarded as a distribution rather than a function (see p. 506).

† Laplace transform with respect to t might have been more logical, but the method used here is so common in physical literature that it is well worth remembering.

‡ In other words, G is invariant with respect to translations in space and time, a direct consequence of the PDE it satisfies.

According to the inversion procedure, $G(\mathbf{R}, \tau)$ will be obtained from

$$G(\mathbf{R}, \tau) = \frac{1}{(\sqrt{2\pi})^4} \int_{-\infty}^{+\infty} dK_x \int_{-\infty}^{+\infty} dK_y \int_{-\infty}^{+\infty} dK_2 \int_{-\infty}^{+\infty} g(\mathbf{K}, \omega) e^{-i(\mathbf{K}\cdot\mathbf{R}+\omega\tau)} \, d\omega.$$

It is now easy to deduce that

$$\frac{\partial^2 G}{\partial X^2} + \frac{\partial^2 G}{\partial Y^2} + \frac{\partial^2 G}{\partial Z^2} - \frac{1}{c^2} \frac{\partial^2 G}{\partial \tau^2}$$

$$= \frac{1}{(2\pi)^2} \iiiint\limits_{-\infty}^{+\infty} \left(\frac{\omega^2}{c^2} - K^2 \right) g(\mathbf{K}, \omega) e^{-i(\mathbf{K}\cdot\mathbf{R}+\omega\tau)} \, d^3\mathbf{K} \, d\omega,$$

where $K = |\mathbf{K}|$, and we employ the commonly used convenient notation

$$d^3\mathbf{K} \equiv dK_x \, dK_y \, dK_z.$$

We also have

$$\delta(X)\,\delta(Y)\,\delta(Z)\,\delta(\tau) = \delta(\mathbf{R})\,\delta(\tau)$$

$$= \frac{1}{(2\pi)^4} \iiiint\limits_{-\infty}^{+\infty} e^{-i(\mathbf{K}\cdot\mathbf{R}+\omega\tau)} \, d^3\mathbf{K} \, d\omega.$$

Substituting this into the PDE, we deduce

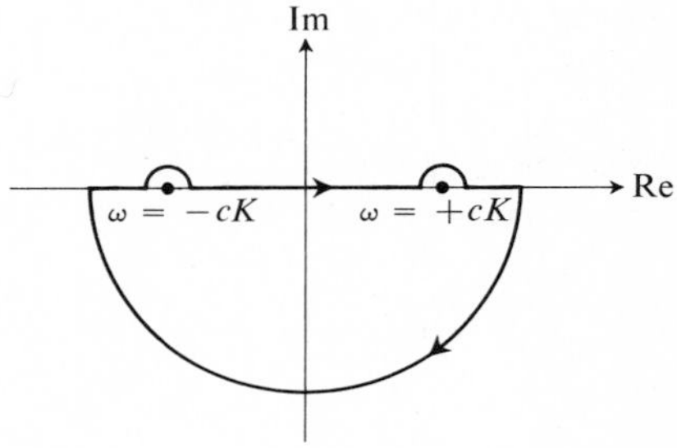

$$g(\mathbf{K}, \omega) = \frac{c^2}{(2\pi)^2} \frac{1}{\omega^2 - c^2 K^2}$$

Figure 14.11

so that our Green's function is given by the integral formula

$$G(\mathbf{R}, \tau) = \frac{c^2}{(2\pi)^4} \iiiint\limits_{-\infty}^{+\infty} \frac{e^{-i\mathbf{K}\cdot\mathbf{R}} e^{-i\omega\tau}}{(\omega + cK)(\omega - cK)} \, d^3\mathbf{K} \, d\omega.$$

It is convenient and customary to perform the ω-integration first. The treatment of poles is dictated by the causality principle, requiring that G must vanish for $\tau < 0$. This implies the contour shown in Fig. 14.11, and integration yields

$$\int_{-\infty}^{+\infty} \frac{e^{-i\omega\tau}}{(\omega + cK)(\omega - cK)} \, d\omega = (-2\pi i) \left\{ \frac{e^{icK\tau}}{(-2cK)} + \frac{e^{-icK\tau}}{2cK} \right\} = -2\pi \frac{\sin cK\tau}{cK},$$

and

$$G = -\frac{c^2}{(2\pi)^3} \iiint\limits_{-\infty}^{+\infty} \frac{\sin cK\tau}{cK} e^{-i(\mathbf{K}\cdot\mathbf{R})} \, d^3\mathbf{K} \qquad (t > 0).$$

Now observe that G is given as an integral over the entire space of **K**-vectors. It may be evaluated in spherical coordinates in such a space* by setting

$$(\mathbf{K} \cdot \mathbf{R}) = KR \cos \theta, \qquad d^3\mathbf{K} = K^2 \sin \theta \, dK \, d\theta \, d\phi,$$

where $R = |\mathbf{R}|$ and the polar axis is chosen in the direction of **R**. Now

$$G = -\frac{c}{(2\pi)^3} \int_0^\infty \frac{\sin cK\tau}{K} K^2 \, dK \int_0^\pi e^{-iKR \cos \theta} \sin \theta \, d\theta \int_0^{2\pi} d\phi \qquad (\tau > 0).$$

Since

$$\int_0^\pi e^{-iKR \cos \theta} \sin \theta \, d\theta = \int_{-1}^{+1} e^{-iKRx} \, dx = \frac{2 \sin KR}{KR},$$

we obtain

$$G = -\frac{c}{4\pi^2 R} \int_0^\infty 2 \sin cK\tau \sin KR \, dK \qquad (\tau > 0).$$

Now write

$$2 \sin cK\tau \sin KR = \cos (cK\tau - KR) - \cos (cK\tau + KR)$$

and use the formula†

$$\int_0^\infty \cos Kx \, dK = \pi \, \delta(x),$$

which is readily established from the integral representation

$$\delta(x) = \frac{1}{2\pi} \int_{-\infty}^{+\infty} e^{iKx} \, dK.$$

Consequently,

$$G(\mathbf{R}, \tau) = -\frac{c}{4\pi} \frac{\delta(c\tau - R)}{R} + \frac{c}{4\pi} \frac{\delta(c\tau + R)}{R}.$$

Since $R \geq 0$, the second term in this expression is always zero (while for $\tau < 0$, G must be identically zero as postulated; this also follows from Fig. 14.11). Using $\delta(ax) = (1/a) \, \delta(x) \, (a > 0)$, we can finally write in terms of the original variables,

$$G(\mathbf{r} - \mathbf{r}_0; t - t_0) = \begin{cases} -\dfrac{1}{4\pi} \dfrac{\delta\left(t - t_0 - \dfrac{|\mathbf{r} - \mathbf{r}_0|}{c}\right)}{|\mathbf{r} - \mathbf{r}_0|} & (t > t_0), \\ 0 & (t < t_0). \end{cases}$$

This formula is the three-dimensional analog of that given on p. 608 and exhibits a similar physical feature. There is no response at **r** to the "δ-like" disturbance

---

* Instead of cartesian coordinates K_x, K_y, K_z as the Fourier transform procedure originally implies.

† The integral is, of course, divergent. However, it is well defined as a distribution; compare with p. 312 (footnote).

created at $\mathbf{r}_0$ at time t_0 until the time interval $(1/c)|\mathbf{r} - \mathbf{r}_0|$ required for the wave to reach point $\mathbf{r}$ has elapsed. However, there is also a difference: As soon as the wave passes, the solution returns to its original value (zero) instead of being permanently changed.

Having found Green's function, we can write immediately the solution of $\nabla^2\psi - (1/c^2)(\partial^2\psi/\partial t^2) = f(\mathbf{r}; t)$ as

$$\psi(\mathbf{r}, t) = \iiiint\limits_{-\infty}^{+\infty} G(\mathbf{r} - \mathbf{r}_0; t - t_0)f(\mathbf{r}_0; t_0) \, d^3\mathbf{r}_0 \, dt_0.$$

Moreover, we can perform the integration over t_0 and deduce

$$\psi(\mathbf{r}, t) = \iiint\limits_{-\infty}^{+\infty} \frac{f\left(\mathbf{r}_0; t - \dfrac{|\mathbf{r} - \mathbf{r}_0|}{c}\right)}{|\mathbf{r} - \mathbf{r}_0|} \, d^3\mathbf{r}_0.$$

This formula defines what is usually called the *retarded potential*.*

14.8 TRAVELING WAVES IN NONHOMOGENEOUS MEDIA

From the preceding sections we know that waves of various physical nature can be described by a wave equation. All waves considered there did propagate through media with *constant* physical characteristics.† Suppose, however, that the characteristics of the medium are no longer constant, but vary from point to point. A simple example is the stretched string of variable density which gives rise to the equation

$$T\frac{\partial^2 u}{\partial x^2} + \rho(x)\frac{\partial^2 u}{\partial t^2} = 0.$$

Strictly speaking, the solutions of such problems cannot be called waves any longer because they are not expressible in the form $f(x - ct)$ or $g(x + ct)$, where c is some constant. What is often the case, however, is that the nonhomogeneity of the medium is *localized*, i.e., confined to a finite region, such as the case of a stretched string with $\rho(x) = $ const except in a region around the origin $(-a \leq x \leq a)$. In these situations the solutions must still obey the usual wave equation outside the region of nonhomogeneity and can be described by *bona fide* waves. Such waves are distorted as they enter the region of nonhomogeneity, and this affects their appearance when they emerge from it. In particular, one observes the appearance of waves *radiating* away from the region of nonhomogeneity.

---

* A term borrowed from electromagnetism. Otherwise, ψ may be called the retarded solution of the D'Alembert equation.

† These media need not be material media: waves in the vacuum are also possible. For instance, electromagnetic waves propagate in the vacuum with the speed $c = 1/\sqrt{\epsilon_0\mu_0}$, where ϵ_0 and μ_0 can be regarded as being characteristic of the vacuum.

These and related phenomena are known under the name of wave *diffraction* or *scattering*.* A variety of special techniques has been developed for such problems. We shall confine ourselves to a brief introductory treatment.

Let the infinite stretched string possess constant density ρ_0 everywhere except for the interval $-a \leq x \leq a$, where the density ρ_1 is somewhat greater but still constant. Then we can say that the density of the string $\rho(x)$ varies according to

$$\rho(x) = \rho_0 + (\rho_1 - \rho_0)B(x),$$

where $B(x)$ is the unit box function for the interval $(-a, a)$. We seek solutions of

$$T\frac{\partial^2 u}{\partial x^2} + \rho(x)\frac{\partial^2 u}{\partial t^2} = 0,$$

which vary harmonically in time and set $u(x, t) = \psi(x)e^{-i\omega t}$, leading to the DE for ψ:

$$\frac{d^2\psi}{dx^2} + \rho(x)\frac{\omega^2}{T}\psi(x) = 0.$$

In our case, this equation reduces to

$$\frac{d^2\psi}{dx^2} + [k^2 + \epsilon^2 B(x)]\psi = 0,$$

where

$$\frac{\rho_0\omega^2}{T} = k^2, \qquad \frac{\rho_1\omega^2}{T} = k_1^2, \qquad k_1^2 - k^2 = \epsilon^2.$$

We know that outside the interval $(-a \leq x \leq a)$ our solution must be a linear combination of e^{ikx} and e^{-ikx}. Let us specify the physical conditions we want to describe. Suppose that we generate a harmonic wave Ae^{ikx} at $x = -\infty$, i.e., at some point far to the left. In the absence of nonhomogeneity near the origin, this wave would continue unchanged into the region $x > 0$. Such a solution will be modified for $x > -a$ if the nonhomogeneity is present, but for $x > a$ it must become a linear combination of e^{ikx} and e^{-ikx}. Now, the presence of the term e^{-ikx} for $x > a$ would imply a generation of waves at $x = +\infty$; this cannot correspond to the physical situation we are describing. Consequently, the solution we seek *must have the form* Fe^{ikx} for $x > a$, and the only question is, What is F?

Turning now to the region $x < -a$, we observe that the solution is given in the form $Ae^{ikx} + Be^{-ikx}$; there is no reason to reject the possibility of a wave reflected from the region of nonhomogeneity, and B is not necessarily zero. As for the constant A, we shall assume that it is known, since we can physically regu-

---

* The term scattering is borrowed from quantum mechanics, where the "waves" represent the motion of particles, and the particles are conceived to be scattered. In modern usage, however, one can find the term scattered wave applied to all kinds of waves. The term diffraction originates from optics, where one usually has some kind of obstacle rather than a nonhomogeneity. The behavior of waves is, however, similar in these two cases.

late the wave generated at $x = -\infty$. In this particular problem we can immediately write the form of the solution for the region $-a \leq x \leq a$ as well, namely, the linear combination of e^{ik_1x} and e^{-ik_1x}, since the DE for this region reads

$$\frac{d^2\psi}{dx^2} + k_1^2\psi = 0.$$

The overall solution must then have the form

$$\psi(x) = \begin{cases} Ae^{ikx} + Be^{-ikx} & (x < -a), \\ Ce^{ik_1x} + De^{-ik_1x} & (-a \leq x \leq a), \\ Fe^{ikx} & (x > a). \end{cases}$$

Physical considerations require that $\psi(x)$ be continuous at $x = \pm a$. Moreover, $d\psi/dx$ must also be continuous because the density $\rho(x)$ is finite everywhere.* This gives us four equations for the unknowns B, C, D, and F:

$$Ae^{-ika} + Be^{ika} = Ce^{-ik_1a} + De^{ik_1a}, \tag{1}$$

$$ikAe^{-ika} - ikBe^{ika} = ik_1Ce^{-ik_1a} - ik_1De^{ik_1a}, \tag{2}$$

$$Ce^{ik_1a} + De^{-ik_1a} = Fe^{ika}, \tag{3}$$

$$ik_1Ce^{ik_1a} - ik_1De^{-ik_1a} = ikFe^{ika}. \tag{4}$$

Omitting the algebraic details, we state the solution:

$$C = A\frac{2k(k + k_1)}{\Delta}e^{-i(k+k_1)a}, \qquad D = A\frac{2k(k_1 - k)}{\Delta}e^{i(k_1-k)a},$$

$$B = A\frac{2i(k_1^2 - k^2)}{\Delta}\sin 2k_1ae^{-2ika}, \qquad F = A\frac{4kk_1}{\Delta}e^{-2ika},$$

where

$$\Delta = 4kk_1 \cos 2k_1a - 2i(k_1^2 + k^2)\sin 2k_1a.$$

Exercise. Solve the above equations and deduce the stated values of C, D, B, and F.

At this stage we shall make some important observations concerning scattering phenomena. First of all, in a vast majority of actual experiments we observe the waves far away from the region of nonhomogeneity (or scattering region). From this point of view, only the amplitudes B and F in the above solution are important for the purpose of comparison with the experiment. Second, what is

---

* From $d^2\psi/dx^2 + \rho(x)(\omega^2/T)\psi = 0$, it follows by integration between $x_0 - \delta$ and $x_0 + \delta$ that

$$\frac{d\psi}{dx}(x_0 + \delta) - \frac{d\psi}{dx}(x_0 - \delta) = \int_{x_0-\delta}^{x_0+\delta}\rho(x)\frac{\omega^2}{T}\psi(x)\,dx.$$

As $\delta \to 0$, the right-hand side approaches zero, so $d\psi/dx$ is continuous for all x_0.

actually being observed is very often not the function $\psi(x)$ itself but rather the energy flux associated with it.* It follows, for instance, that the quantity (see p. 602)

$$P = \frac{\rho_0 c\omega^2}{2}\, |F|^2 \quad (c = \sqrt{T/\rho_0})$$

will represent the average power *transmitted* by the region of nonhomogeneity, i.e., the energy flux in a positive direction past any point with $x > a$. The energy flux to the left of the nonhomogeneity must be calculated from the solution

$$u(x, t) = A e^{i(kx-\omega t)} + B e^{-i(kx+\omega t)}$$

by means of the formula $P = T\,\mathrm{Re}\,(\partial u/\partial x)\,\mathrm{Re}\,(\partial u/\partial t)$. A straightforward calculation† shows that this energy flux (averaged over time) is given by

$$P = \frac{\rho_0 c\omega^2}{2}\, |A|^2 - \frac{\rho_0 c\omega^2}{2}\, |B|^2.$$

Evidently, the first term can be interpreted as *incident power* and the second one as *reflected power*.

Exercise. Produce the details of this calculation.

In view of these observations, it is customary to define the transmission and reflection coefficients:

$$\mathrm{TC} = \frac{|F|^2}{|A|^2}, \qquad \mathrm{RC} = \frac{|B|^2}{|A|^2},$$

representing the fraction of incident power which is transmitted or reflected. Since the region of nonhomogeneity does not generate energy, we must obviously have $|A|^2 - |B|^2 = |F|^2$; in other words, the transmission and reflection coefficients must add up to unity. We can verify this statement in our solution: Writing $k/k_1 = \mu$, we deduce

$$\mathrm{TC} = \frac{4\mu^2}{4\mu^2 \cos^2 2k_1 a + (1 + \mu^2)^2 \sin^2 2k_1 a},$$

$$\mathrm{RC} = \frac{(1 - \mu^2)^2 \sin^2 2k_1 a}{4\mu^2 \cos^2 2k_1 a + (1 + \mu^2)^2 \sin^2 2k_1 a},$$

and observe that

$$4\mu^2 + (1 - \mu^2)^2 \sin^2 \theta = 4\mu^2 \cos^2 \theta + (1 + \mu^2)^2 \sin^2 \theta.$$

A still more compact form for the TC and RC is obtained if we write

$$\frac{1}{\mu} - \mu = \frac{k_1}{k} - \frac{k}{k_1} = \beta,$$

---

* For instance, in the case of optical or acoustical waves this is almost invariably true.
† Bear in mind that A and B are also, in general, complex.

in which case,

$$TC = \frac{4}{4 + \beta^2 \sin^2 2k_1 a}, \qquad RC = \frac{\beta^2 \sin^2 2k_1 a}{4 + \beta^2 \sin^2 2k_1 a}.$$

An interesting feature of the problem is readily revealed. *Perfect transmission* is possible when $\sin 2k_1 a = 0$* or $k_1 a = n\pi/2$ $(n = 1, 2, 3, \ldots)$. Since $k_1 = \omega\sqrt{\rho_1/T}$, it is seen that for a given string, perfect transmission will happen at the frequencies

$$\omega = \frac{n\pi a}{2} \sqrt{\frac{\rho_1}{T}} \qquad (n = 1, 2, 3, \ldots).$$

In a situation of this sort, we have what is called *transmission resonance;* that is, the transmitted amplitude reaches its maximum, which happens to be equal to the incident amplitude so that no scattering actually occurs.

Remark. The mathematical problem treated in this section also arises in quantum mechanics, where it represents one-dimensional scattering of particles by the so-called rectangular potential well.†

14.9 SCATTERING AMPLITUDES AND PHASE SHIFTS

In the preceding section we have acquainted ourselves with, perhaps, the simplest possible scattering problem. Let us now make some generalizations and, at the same time, introduce a somewhat different approach, extremely useful in more complicated scattering phenomena.

We consider again the equation

$$\frac{d^2\psi}{dx^2} + \rho(x)\frac{\omega^2}{T}\psi = 0.$$

Suppose that the density $\rho(x)$ is constant, or nearly so, outside a localized region $|x| < a$ about the origin. Then

$$\rho(x) = \rho_0 + u(x),$$

where $u(x)$ is a function which vanishes, or is negligible, outside the interval $(-a, a)$. The DE can be rewritten as

$$\frac{d^2\psi}{dx^2} + k^2\psi + \epsilon^2 u(x)\psi = 0,$$

where

$$k^2 = \frac{\rho_0\omega^2}{T}, \qquad \epsilon^2 = \frac{\omega^2}{T}.$$

---

* Note that β is zero only if $k = k_1$, i.e., there is no nonhomogeneity in the string.

† For details, see, e.g., Merzbacher, *Quantum Mechanics*, Chapter 6, Section 8.

The essence of scattering problems is that we seek solutions that will *reduce* to a *prescribed solution* of the simpler equation

$$\frac{d^2\psi}{dx^2} + k^2\psi = 0,$$

if we imagine that the function $\epsilon^2 u(x)$ is gradually reduced to zero. The prescribed solution is called the *incident wave*, and we assume that it is given by*

$$\psi_{inc}(x) = Ae^{ikx} \qquad (A > 0).$$

The actual solution of the scattering problem can then be written as

$$\psi(x) = Ae^{ikx} + \psi_{scat}(x) = \psi_{inc}(x) + \psi_{scat}(x),$$

where the so-called *scattered wave* $\psi_{scat}(x)$ must reduce to zero if $\epsilon^2 u(x)$ is reduced to zero.

Furthermore, for large values of $|x|$ the *actual* DE also assumes the form $\psi'' + k^2\psi = 0$. Consequently, $\psi_{scat}(x)$ must, for large $|x|$, reduce to a linear combination of e^{ikx} and e^{-ikx}. The physical conditions† now require that $\psi_{scat}(x)$ satisfy the radiation condition; therefore

$$\psi_{scat}(x) = \begin{cases} A_-e^{-ikx} & (x < -a) \\ A_+e^{ikx} & (x > a) \end{cases} (A_-, A_+ = \text{const}).$$

Remark. This statement is exact only if $\epsilon^2 u(x)$ rigorously vanishes outside the interval $(-a, a)$. In many cases, however, $\epsilon^2 u(x)$ is only "negligible" beyond this range and the above conditions are approximate. It is then customary to say that $\psi_{scat}(x)$ satisfies these conditions *asymptotically* and we write

$$\psi_{scat}(x) \sim \begin{cases} A_-e^{-ikx} & (x \to -\infty), \\ A_+e^{ikx} & (x \to +\infty). \end{cases}$$

Evidently, $\epsilon^2 u(x)$ must decrease sufficiently fast as $|x| \to \infty$ in order to bring about the desired degree of accuracy of the above asymptotic forms.‡

It may be also pointed out that similar ideas can be applied to the equation

$$\frac{d^2\psi}{dx^2} + p(x)\psi(x) + \epsilon^2 u(x)\psi(x) = 0,$$

---

* Physically, we are free to generate $\psi_{inc}(x)$ and it is customary to choose the plane wave that is incident from the left.

† Discussed on p. 625 and evidently applicable no matter what the term $\epsilon^2 u(x)$ may be. These conditions are *in addition* to any other mentioned so far.

‡ We cannot now enter into a rigorous analysis of these questions. The interested reader must consult the literature on asymptotic solutions of differential equations. In most physical problems $\epsilon^2 u(x)$ does, indeed, decrease sufficiently fast (see, however, p. 633, footnote, for an important exception).

where $p(x)$ is not a constant. However, we must essentially possess exact solutions of the equation $\psi'' + p(x)\psi = 0$. The cases where $\epsilon^2 u(x)$ decreases slowly as $|x| \to \infty$ can be treated in this manner.

The complex constants A_- and A_+ are called the *backward* and *forward scattering amplitudes*, respectively. In the problem of the preceding section we had $A_- = B$ and $A_+ = F - A$. It is also customary to define the *backward* and *forward scattering cross sections**

$$\sigma_- = \frac{|A_-|^2}{|A|^2}, \qquad \sigma_+ = \frac{|A_+|^2}{|A|^2}.$$

Evidently, the physical meaning of σ_- is the ratio of the reflected power to the incident power.† In the preceding section it was called the reflection coefficient. Note, however, that the forward scattering cross section *does not* represent the ratio of transmitted power to incident power (or transmission coefficient): The latter is given by

$$TC = \frac{|A + A_+|^2}{|A|^2}.$$

It must be recognized that σ_+ and σ_- characterize the "ability" of a localized nonhomogeneity to scatter waves in forward and backward directions. However, the forward-scattered wave suffers *interference* with the incident wave, while the backward-scattered wave does not. For instance, if it happens that $A_+ = -A$ and $\sigma_+ = 1$, we say that there is strong forward scattering. Nevertheless, no wave actually appears in the forward direction since the incident and scattered waves exhibit complete destructive interference. These peculiar properties of forward-scattering amplitude and cross section are also present in two- and three-dimensional problems. In fact, it is exactly in these problems that the notion of scattering amplitudes‡ is particularly useful. We have considered them in a one-dimensional problem just for introductory purposes.

In this connection we may mention another set of quantities widely used in two- and three-dimensional scattering, namely, the so-called *phase shifts*. To start with, we shall describe the function $\psi(x)$ in terms of the distance from the origin $|x| = r$ and the direction. Since there are only two directions, positive and negative, we may distinguish between them by introducing a so-called *dichotomic variable* μ, namely, a parameter capable of assuming only two values, conveniently chosen as $+1$ and -1. (We actually take $\mu = \text{sgn } x$, the sign of x.)

---

* The term is borrowed from three-dimensional scattering where cross sections are measured in units of area. In one-dimensional problems they are pure numbers.

† In similar problems of classical physics, power is invariably associated with the square of the modulus of the complex amplitude of a harmonic wave. In quantum mechanics the concept of *number of particles* replaces the term *power*.

‡ Instead of two amplitudes A_- and A_+, problems in two and three dimensions involve continuously varying functions, say $f(\theta)$ and $f(\theta, \phi)$, respectively, associated with the scattered wave (see Section 14.10).

This description may not be familiar, but it is just as good as the usual one. For instance, the incident wave $\psi_{\text{inc}}(x) = Ae^{ikx}$ can be written as

$$\psi_{\text{inc}}(x) = \frac{A}{2}\left(e^{ikr} + e^{-ikr}\right) + \mu\frac{A}{2}\left(e^{ikr} - e^{-ikr}\right),$$

which can be verified without any difficulty.* Similarly, the scattered wave is given asymptotically by

$$\psi_{\text{scat}}(x) \sim (A_+ + A_-)e^{ikr} + \mu(A_+ - A_-)e^{ikr} \qquad (r \to \infty).$$

Remark. It is evident that in this notation the term without μ represents the *symmetric part* of a function, and the term containing μ represents the *antisymmetric part*. Now, any function $f(x)$ can be uniquely decomposed into symmetric and antisymmetric parts:

$$f(x) = f_s(x) + f_a(x). \tag{1}$$

It follows that any function $f(x)$ can be written uniquely in our notation as

$$f(x) = f_s(r) + \mu f_a(r). \tag{2}$$

Exercise. Prove statement (1) above, i.e., find the functions $f_s(x)$ and $f_a(x)$ such that $f_s(-x) = f_s(x)$ and $f_a(-x) = -f_a(x)$ in terms of any given $f(x)$.

Returning to the scattering problem, it is now convenient to introduce the symmetric and antisymmetric scattering amplitudes

$$A_s = A_+ + A_-, \qquad A_a = A_+ - A_-.$$

In this notation we can write

$$\psi = \psi_{\text{inc}} + \psi_{\text{scat}} \sim \left\{ \left(\frac{A}{2} + A_s\right)e^{ikr} + \frac{A}{2}e^{-ikr} \right\} + \mu\left\{ \left(\frac{A}{2} + A_a\right)e^{ikr} - \frac{A}{2}e^{-ikr} \right\}$$
$$(r \to \infty).$$

Thus we have actually decomposed the entire solution into four parts according to the following pattern:

$$\psi \sim \underbrace{D_s e^{ikr}}_{\substack{\text{Diverging} \\ \text{symmetric}}} + \underbrace{C_s e^{-ikr}}_{\substack{\text{Converging} \\ \text{symmetric}}} + \underbrace{\mu D_a e^{ikr}}_{\substack{\text{Diverging} \\ \text{antisymmetric}}} + \underbrace{\mu C_a e^{-ikr}}_{\substack{\text{Converging} \\ \text{antisymmetric}}}.$$

This decomposition has the following advantages.

1. The average total power radiated away from the origin is given by

$$P_{\text{out}} = \frac{\rho_0 c \omega^2}{2}\{|D_s|^2 + |D_a|^2 - |C_s|^2 - |C_a|^2\},$$

that is, the four terms do not interfere with each other.

---

* Note that $\cos kr = \cos kx$. Also $\sin kr = \sin kx$ if $x > 0$ and $\sin kr = -\sin kx$ if $x < 0$; therefore $\mu \sin kr = \sin kx$.

Exercise. Verify this statement by straightforward calculation.

2. In all scattering problems we must have

$$|D_s|^2 + |D_a|^2 = |C_s|^2 + |C_a|^2.$$

This follows immediately from the fact that in scattering problems no power is generated at the origin. This is, of course, true for the incident wave as well.

3. If the function $\epsilon^2 u(x)$, which is responsible for the scattered wave, is *symmetric*, then the symmetric and antisymmetric parts of P_{out} must vanish separately, that is,

$$|D_s|^2 = |C_s|^2, \qquad |D_a|^2 = |C_a|^2.$$

To see this, we assume that the incident wave travels from the right to the left. This amounts to changing the sign of the antisymmetric part in the expression for $\psi_{\text{inc}}(x)$. The scattering process is evidently the same as before,* and $\psi(x)$ is the same as before except for the change of sign of the antisymmetric part. In this fashion we have two conceivable solutions of the problem:

$$\psi_1 \sim \left(\frac{A}{2} + A_s\right) e^{ikr} + \frac{A}{2} e^{-ikr} + \mu\left(\frac{A}{2} + A_a\right) e^{ikr} + \mu\left(-\frac{A}{2}\right) e^{-ikr},$$

$$\psi_2 \sim \left(\frac{A}{2} + A_s\right) e^{ikr} + \frac{A}{2} e^{-ikr} - \mu\left(\frac{A}{2} + A_a\right) e^{ikr} - \mu\left(-\frac{A}{2}\right) e^{-ikr}.$$

Adding these solutions, (and this is still a conceivable solution), we obtain

$$\psi_1 + \psi_2 \sim 2\left(\frac{A}{2} + A_s\right) e^{ikr} + 2\frac{A}{2} e^{-ikr}.$$

Applying property 2, we deduce that $|A/2 + A_s| = A/2$, which means that $|D_s| = |C_s|$; then it follows that $|D_a| = |C_a|$.

Our analysis leads us, therefore, to the general statement that

$$\left|\frac{A}{2} + A_s\right| = \frac{A}{2}, \qquad \left|\frac{A}{2} + A_a\right| = \frac{A}{2}, \qquad (A = \text{real}).$$

We see that the complex numbers $A/2 + A_s$ and $A/2$ may differ only in phase; therefore

$$\frac{A}{2} + A_s = \frac{A}{2} e^{2\delta_s i} \qquad (\delta_s = \text{real constant}),$$

and, similarly,

$$\frac{A}{2} + A_a = \frac{A}{2} e^{2\delta_a i} \qquad (\delta_a = \text{real constant}).$$

---

* Figuratively speaking, the term $\epsilon^2 u(x)$ in the DE "cannot distinguish between left and right" (reflection invariance of the DE).

(The factor 2 in $e^{2\,\delta_s i}$ and $e^{2\,\delta_a i}$ is introduced for sheer convenience in our later work.) The constants δ_s and δ_a are called the scattering *phase shifts* for symmetric and antisymmetric scattering. All properties of the scattering process can be expressed in terms of phase shifts, for instance,

$$A_s = \frac{A}{2}\,(e^{2\,\delta_s i} - 1) = Aie^{i\delta_s}\sin\delta_s, \qquad A_a = \frac{A}{2}\,(e^{2\,\delta_a i} - 1) = Aie^{i\delta_a}\sin\delta_a, \quad \text{etc.}$$

14.10 SCATTERING IN THREE DIMENSIONS. PARTIAL WAVE ANALYSIS

Let us consider the three-dimensional analog of the problem treated in Sections 14.8 and 14.9. It concerns solutions of the modified Helmholtz equation

$$\nabla^2\psi(\mathbf{r}) + k^2\psi(\mathbf{r}) + \epsilon^2 u(\mathbf{r})\psi(\mathbf{r}) = 0.$$

In classical physics this equation arises when we study waves in a medium with local nonhomogeneity. As an example, acoustic waves in air are usually described by the velocity potential φ (p. 322) satisfying

$$\nabla^2\varphi = \frac{1}{c^2}\frac{\partial^2\varphi}{\partial t^2} \qquad \text{(where } 1/c^2 = \rho_0/\gamma p_0\text{)}.$$

Now suppose that in some small region, the value of $1/c^2$ is variable. For instance, there may be a pocket of rarefied or condensed air, or a region occupied by a substance other than air where sound propagates with a different speed $c' \neq c$. In such cases we must replace $1/c^2$ by a variable quantity,

$$\frac{1}{c^2}\,(1 + f(\mathbf{r})),$$

where $f(\mathbf{r})$ is some localized function of $\mathbf{r}$; that is, it vanishes outside some bounded region in space. Setting $\varphi(\mathbf{r}, t) = \psi(\mathbf{r})e^{-i\omega t}$, we obtain the modified Helmholtz equation stated above.

In quantum mechanics we have to solve the Schrödinger equation (see p. 469). For the common case where the Hamiltonian function is the sum of kinetic and potential energies, this equation reads

$$-\frac{\hbar^2}{2M}\nabla^2\psi(\mathbf{r}, t) + U(\mathbf{r})\psi(\mathbf{r}, t) = i\hbar\frac{\partial\psi(\mathbf{r}, t)}{\partial t}.$$

If we look for the states of definite total energy E (stationary states), then (p. 471)

$$\psi(\mathbf{r}, t) = \varphi(\mathbf{r})e^{-i(E/\hbar)t},$$

and the function $\varphi(\mathbf{r})$ must now satisfy the stated equation. In the majority of practical problems the potential function $U(\mathbf{r})$ either vanishes or can be neglected outside some bounded region V.*

---

* The function $U(\mathbf{r})$ can be neglected if it approaches zero sufficiently fast as $|\mathbf{r}| \to \infty$. Special treatment is needed for the Coulomb potential which behaves like $1/r$. For mathematical details, see, e.g., Messiah, Chapter 11, Section 7.

Scattering problems arise in practice in the following fashion. An *incident beam* of waves (or particles, in the language of quantum mechanics) emerges from a slit of width d, or a circular opening of diameter d, as shown in Fig. 14.12. Such a beam can be described *approximately* by

$$\varphi(\mathbf{r}, t) = A e^{i(\mathbf{k}\cdot\mathbf{r} - \omega t)},$$

where $\mathbf{k}$ is a constant vector,* called *propagation vector*, with the real components k_x, k_y, k_z, and A a complex constant. The space-dependent part of φ, namely,

$$\psi(\mathbf{r}) = A e^{i(\mathbf{k}\cdot\mathbf{r})} = A e^{i(k_x x + k_y y + k_z z)},$$

evidently satisfies the Helmholtz equation $\nabla^2\psi + k^2\psi = 0$, where $k = |\mathbf{k}|$. It describes a wave propagating in the direction of $\mathbf{k}$ with the speed $c = \omega/k$. This approximation of a physical beam is acceptable for points near the axis of the beam, e.g., point P, but not point Q, in Fig. 14.12, *provided* the slit width is much larger than the wavelength $\lambda = 2\pi/k$.† We shall assume that this last condition will hold.

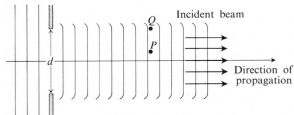

Figure 14.12

Suppose now that there is a localized nonhomogeneity of the medium in the case of classical waves, or a localized potential due to some field of force in the case of particles treated quantum mechanically. The experiment shows that our beam will now be distorted by the appearance of a scattered wave, as shown in Fig. 14.13, diverging from the site of nonhomogeneity (or potential) which we shall call the *scattering center*. We shall assume that the size of the scattering center (region of appreciable nonhomogeneity or potential) is small compared to the width of the beam d.

Remark. The same type of phenomenon occurs when the scattering center is represented by an obstacle that is impermeable to waves, and it can be treated by the same mathematical techniques (see pp. 638–640).

As mentioned before, the steady-state solutions $\varphi(\mathbf{r}, t) = \psi(\mathbf{r})e^{-i\omega t}$ for this situation imply that $\psi(\mathbf{r})$ satisfies

$$\nabla^2\psi + k^2\psi + \epsilon^2 u(\mathbf{r})\psi = 0,$$

---

* It should not be confused with the unit vector in z-direction.

† For a beam of particles treated quantum mechanically, we replace ω by $E/\hbar$ and identify $k\hbar = p$ with the momentum of particles. For details, consult any textbook on quantum mechanics. The above condition then reads $d \gg 2\pi\hbar/\sqrt{2ME}$.

where $u(\mathbf{r})$ is some function which either vanishes or, at least, can be neglected outside a bounded region V_0. Evidently, at points $\mathbf{r}$ outside V_0 the function $\psi(\mathbf{r})$ must essentially satisfy $\nabla^2\psi + k^2\psi = 0$. In a vast number of cases, the value of k^2 is the same as that applicable in absence of a scattering center.* Then we can conveniently represent our solution as the sum of incident and scattered waves,

$$\psi = \psi_{\text{inc}} + \psi_{\text{scat}},$$

such that, by definition, ψ must reduce to ψ_{inc} if the scattering center is removed. Formally, this can be expressed by

$$\psi \to \psi_{\text{inc}} \quad \text{as } \epsilon \to 0.$$

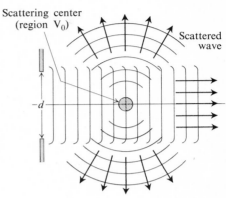

Figure 14.13

The scattering problems are most frequently treated in spherical coordinates with the z-axis along the direction of the beam and the origin at the scattering center. Also, the incident wave may be conveniently chosen to be of unit amplitude so that

$$\psi_{\text{inc}} = e^{ikz} = e^{ikr \cos \theta}.$$

At this stage we shall further restrict ourselves to the condition that the function $u(\mathbf{r})$ is spherically symmetric, i.e., independent of the angles θ and ϕ. Evidently, the entire problem will then possess axial symmetry about the z-axis and $\psi(\mathbf{r})$ will be a function of r and θ only.

Since $\psi(r, \theta)$ must satisfy, at least asymptotically (see p. 629), the Helmholtz equation $\nabla^2\psi + k^2\psi = 0$ for large values of r, we can decompose it in a series of the type (see p. 380)

$$\psi(r, \theta) \sim \sum_{l=0}^{\infty} R_l(r) Y_{l0}(\theta) \qquad (r \to \infty),$$

where only the terms with $m = 0$ have been retained because ψ is independent of ϕ. Furthermore, it is convenient to express $R_l(r)$ as a linear combination of spherical Hankel functions (see p. 616), so that

$$\psi(r, \theta) \sim \sum_{l=0}^{\infty} [D_l h_l^{(1)}(kr) + C_l h_l^{(2)}(kr)] Y_{l0}(\theta) \qquad (r \to \infty).$$

The advantage of using spherical Hankel functions, instead of spherical Bessel and Neumann functions, is that we are separating each $R_l(r)$-function into a diverging part and a converging part (see p. 617). This is analogous to the similar decomposition on p. 631 for the one-dimensional wave, except that instead of just symmetric and antisymmetric terms we now have an infinite series of terms, each

---

* So-called *elastic scattering* in quantum mechanics, where the particles conserve kinetic energy after scattering.

corresponding to a spherical harmonic $Y_{l0}(\theta)$. In line with this analogy, it is again possible to relate the coefficients C_l and D_l to statements about the power flux. In particular, for acoustic waves* we may make the following statements.

1. The average total power radiated away from the origin through a sphere of some large radius R is given by

$$P_{\text{out}} = \frac{\rho_0 c \omega^2}{2} \sum_{l=0}^{\infty} \{|D_l|^2 - |C_l|^2\}.$$

This is readily verified by using the expression for power flux on p. 614 and integrating over a sphere, with the help of the orthogonality property of $Y_{l0}(\theta)$-functions (p. 619).

2. For scattering problems, we have $P_{\text{out}} = 0$ and therefore

$$\sum_{l=0}^{\infty} \{|D_l|^2 - |C_l|^2\} = 0,$$

since no power is generated at the scattering center.

Let us now decompose the incident plane wave e^{ikz} in this manner. For this purpose we shall use the so-called *Bauer formula* (see Chapter 9, Problem 17)

$$e^{ikr \cos \theta} = \sum_{l=0}^{\infty} i^l (2l + 1) j_l(kr) P_l(\cos \theta).$$

Consequently, using the formulas on pages 380 and 617, we can write

$$e^{ikr \cos \theta} = \sum_{l=0}^{\infty} [D_l' h_l^{(1)}(kr) + C_l' h_l^{(2)}(kr)] Y_{l0}(\theta),$$

where $D_l' = C_l' = \frac{1}{2} i^l \sqrt{4\pi(2l + 1)}$. Note that condition 2 above is verified in such a way that each l-term *vanishes separately*.

Let us write the function ψ_{scat} in the same form. From physical considerations we require that it contain *diverging waves only†* so that

$$\psi_{\text{scat}} \sim \sum_{l=0}^{\infty} A_l h_l^{(1)}(kr) Y_{l0}(\theta).$$

Comparing the coefficients in the relation $\psi = \psi_{\text{inc}} + \psi_{\text{scat}}$, we immediately obtain‡

$$C_l = C_l' = \frac{1}{2} i^l \sqrt{4\pi(2l + 1)}, \qquad D_l = D_l' + A_l.$$

Finally, we shall make an assertion analogous to statement 3 on p. 632: "If the

---

* Analogous properties can be derived for other types of classical waves, as well as for the Schrödinger equation in quantum mechanics.

† In other words, we are imposing on ψ_{scat} the Sommerfeld radiation condition (p. 617).

‡ Because of linear independence of spherical harmonics and spherical Hankel functions.

function $u(\mathbf{r})$ is *spherically symmetric*, as we have already assumed, then the contributions to P_{out} from terms with different l must *vanish separately*, just as in the case of the plane wave, namely,*

$$|D_l|^2 = |C_l|^2.$$

We can establish the validity of this formula, using ideas analogous to those given on p. 632. We shall omit the proof.

Since $|D_l| = |C_l|$ and since $C_l = C_l' = D_l'$, it follows that the complex numbers D_l and D_l' have the same magnitude and therefore can differ *only in phase*. We may then write

$$D_l = D_l' e^{2\delta_l i},$$

thereby introducing *the phase shifts* δ_l which are real numbers, and in terms of which we can conveniently express most of the quantities of interest in scattering problems. In particular, each term in the series for ψ_{scat} on p. 636 is called the *l*th *partial wave*. Its amplitude A_l is related to δ_l as follows:

$$A_l = D_l - D_l' = D_l'(e^{2\delta_l i} - 1) = D_l' e^{i\delta_l} 2i \sin \delta_l.$$

For large values of r, the function $h_l^{(1)}(kr)$ can be replaced by $(-i)^{l+1}(e^{ikr}/kr)$ (see p. 616), and ψ_{scat} assumes the form

$$\psi_{scat} \sim \frac{e^{ikr}}{kr} \sum_{l=0}^{\infty} e^{i\delta_l} \sin \delta_l \sqrt{4\pi(2l + 1)}\, Y_{l0}(\theta) = f(\theta)\frac{e^{ikr}}{r},$$

where the angular distribution function $f(\theta)$ is called the *scattering amplitude*. The square of its magnitude,

$$\sigma(\theta) = |f(\theta)|^2,$$

known as the *differential cross section*, is a directly measurable quantity: According to Fig. 14.13, in the regions far from the z-axis, only the scattered wave is present, and therefore the power flux (or particle flux in quantum mechanics) due to ψ_{scat} alone can be measured at all angles θ except those close to $\theta = 0$ or $\theta = \pi$.† We let $p(\theta)\, d\Omega$ be the power flux into an *infinitesimal solid angle* $d\Omega$ (Fig. 14.14). The quantity $p(\theta)$ is, therefore, measurable. Now using the expression for power flux for the diverging wave on p. 615, it is not hard to see that $\sigma(\theta)$ is the ratio of $p(\theta)$ to the power flux per unit area due to the incident wave e^{ikz}.‡ In terms of phase shifts, we have

$$\sigma(\theta) = \frac{1}{k^2} \left| \sum_{l=0}^{\infty} \sqrt{4\pi(2l + 1)}\, e^{i\delta_l} \sin \delta_l\, Y_{l0}(\theta) \right|^2.$$

---

* In quantum mechanics, where the value of l is related to the angular momentum of a particle, this is interpreted by the statement, "A spherically symmetric potential does not scatter particles out of their angular-momentum states."

† For a detailed analysis of the quantum-mechanical case, the reader is referred to the discussion in Messiah, *Quantum Mechanics*, Chapter 10, Section 4.

‡ This is, strictly speaking, the *definition* of $\sigma(\theta)$ as a physical quantity.

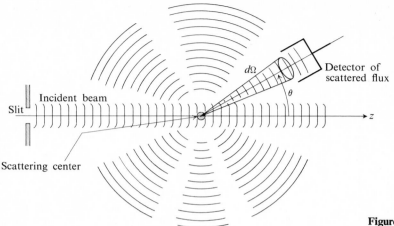

Figure 14.14

If we integrate $\sigma(\theta)$ over all angles to evaluate the so-called *total cross section*

$$\sigma = \iint_{\substack{\text{All} \\ \text{angles}}} \sigma(\theta)\, d\Omega = \int_0^{2\pi} d\phi \int_0^{\pi} \sigma(\theta) \sin\theta\, d\theta,$$

we obtain a particularly simple formula, because of the orthogonality of the Y_{l0}:

$$\sigma = \frac{4\pi}{k^2} \sum_{l=0}^{\infty} (2l+1) \sin^2 \delta_l = \sum_{l=0}^{\infty} \sigma_l.$$

The quantity

$$\sigma_l = \frac{4\pi}{k^2} (2l+1) \sin^2 \delta_l$$

is usually called the *l*th partial cross section.

Remark. The so-called forward-scattering cross section, $\sigma(0)$ is *not measurable* because the scattered beam *cannot be separated* from the incident beam as $\theta \to 0$. Nevertheless, the *total* scattering cross section is measurable, since the value of $\sigma(0)$ does not affect the integral so long as $\sigma(\theta)$ remains bounded for $\theta \neq 0$. The same is true for the backward-scattering cross section $\sigma(\pi)$, although the latter could, in principle, be measurable by the use of a device which would freely transmit waves traveling in one direction, but record the waves traveling in the opposite direction.

This treatment of scattering problems is particularly useful when the phase shifts δ_l can be obtained without great difficulties. As an example, consider the scattering of sound from a solid sphere of radius a. For $r > a$, the velocity potential $\varphi(\mathbf{r}, t)$ satisfies the wave equation

$$\nabla^2 \varphi - \frac{1}{c^2} \frac{\partial^2 \varphi}{\partial t^2} = 0 \qquad (r > a).$$

At the surface of the sphere the motion of air molecules should have no radial component, and we have the boundary condition

$$\left.\frac{\partial \varphi}{\partial r}\right|_{r=a} = 0.$$

Setting $\varphi(\mathbf{r}, t) = \psi(\mathbf{r})e^{-i\omega t}$, we obtain the relations

$$\nabla^2\psi + k^2\psi = 0 \quad (r > a) \qquad \text{and} \qquad \left.\frac{\partial \psi}{\partial r}\right|_{r=a} = 0.$$

Moreover, we are seeking a solution of the type

$$\psi = \psi_{\text{inc}} + \psi_{\text{scat}},$$

where $\psi_{\text{inc}} = e^{ikr \cos \theta}$, while ψ_{scat} must satisfy the radiation condition.

At first glance this problem seems different from the case discussed above: no equation containing the function $u(\mathbf{r})$ ever appears. Nevertheless, it can be solved by the same methods. We can certainly write

$$\psi(\mathbf{r}) = \psi(r, \theta) = \sum_{l=0}^{\infty} [D_l h_l^{(1)}(kr) + C_l h_l^{(2)}(kr)] Y_{l0}(\theta) \qquad (r > a)$$

and make the same kind of statements about D_l and C_l as we did before; in particular,

$$D_l = D_l' e^{2i\delta_l} \qquad \text{and} \qquad C_l = C_l',$$

where $C_l' = D_l' = (i^l/2)\sqrt{4\pi(2l + 1)}$. We now observe that if we use the boundary condition

$$\sum_{l=0}^{\infty} \frac{i^l}{2}\sqrt{4\pi(2l + 1)}\left[e^{2i\delta_l}\frac{dh_l^{(1)}(ka)}{dr} + \frac{dh_l^{(2)}(ka)}{dr}\right] Y_{l0}(\theta) = 0 \qquad \text{(all } \theta),$$

we can immediately claim

$$e^{2i\delta_l}\frac{dh_l^{(1)}(ka)}{dr} + \frac{dh_l^{(2)}(ka)}{dr} = 0 \qquad \text{(all } l).$$

From these relations (one for each value of l) we obtain the phase shifts, and all other quantities follow. For instance, for the purpose of calculating σ_l we need $\sin^2 \delta_l$. We have

$$\sin^2 \delta_l = \tfrac{1}{2} - \tfrac{1}{2}\cos 2\delta_l,$$

and

$$\cos 2\delta_l = \text{Re } e^{2i\delta_l} = -\text{Re}\left.\frac{(d/dr)h_l^{(2)}(kr)}{(d/dr)h_l^{(1)}(kr)}\right|_{r=a}.$$

Now,

$$\left.\frac{d}{dr}h_l^{(1)}(kr)\right|_{r=a} = k\left[\frac{d}{dx}j_l(x) + i\frac{d}{dx}n_l(x)\right]_{x=ka},$$

$$\left.\frac{d}{dr}h_l^{(2)}(kr)\right|_{r=a} = k\left[\frac{d}{dx}j_l(x) - i\frac{d}{dx}n_l(x)\right]_{x=ka}.$$

Therefore

$$\cos 2\delta_l = \left.\frac{n_l'^2 - j_l'^2}{n_l'^2 + j_l'^2}\right|_{x=ka},$$

where $n_l' = dn_l(x)/dx$ and $j_l' = dj_l(x)/dx$. From these relations we have

$$\sigma_l = \frac{4\pi}{k^2}(2l+1)\left.\frac{j_l'^2}{j_l'^2 + n_l'^2}\right|_{x=ka},$$

and

$$\sigma = \frac{4\pi}{k^2}\sum_{l=0}^{\infty}(2l+1)\left.\frac{j_l'^2}{j_l'^2 + n_l'^2}\right|_{x=ka}.$$

Numerical calculation of σ requires tables of the functions $j_l(x)$ and $n_l(x)$. We may, however, note that if $ka \ll 1$, or $a \ll \lambda$, then only the term $l = 0$ contributes significantly. Evaluating $j_0'(ka)$ and $n_0'(ka)$ and retaining the leading term, we are able to show that

$$\sigma \cong \tfrac{4}{9}\pi a^2(ka)^4 \qquad (ka \ll 1).$$

BIBLIOGRAPHY

MERZBACHER, E., *Quantum Mechanics*. New York: John Wiley & Sons, 1961.

MESSIAH, A., *Quantum Mechanics*. Amsterdam: North-Holland, Publ. Co., 1961.

TYCHONOV, A. N., and A. A. SAMARSKI, *Partial Differential Equations of Mathematical Physics*. San Francisco: Holden-Day, Publ. Co., 1964.

PROBLEMS

1. We desire to derive the D'Alembert formula by application of the Laplace transform with respect to time t.
   a) Show that

   $$U(x, s) = \mathcal{L}\{u(x, t)\} = \frac{1}{2c}\int_{-\infty}^{+\infty}\left[u_0(\xi) + \frac{v_0(\xi)}{s}\right]e^{-(s/c)|x-\xi|}\,d\xi;$$

   Problem 5, Chapter 12, may be helpful.
   b) An elegant way of inverting this expression is to split the integrals according to $\xi < x$ or $\xi > x$ and use the changes of variable $(x - \xi)/c = \pm\tau$. Proceed to establish the D'Alembert formula by this technique.

2. The problem involving the semi-infinite string treated in Section 14.5 can be solved by transform methods as well. Which transform would you employ? Solve the problem by a transform method of your choice and show that your result is identical to that given in the text.

3. In Section 14.6, the formulas for power flow for diverging and converging sound waves were given. Show that if $\varphi(r, t)$ is a linear combination of diverging and converging waves,

$$\varphi(r, t) = D\frac{e^{i(kr-\omega t)}}{r} + C\frac{e^{-i(kr+\omega t)}}{r},$$

then

$$\mathbf{P}_{ave} = \frac{\rho_0 \omega k}{2r^2}(|D|^2 - |C|^2)r_0.$$

In other words, the diverging and converging waves do not interfere. Note that the result is far from obvious. Is it true for instantaneous power flow in acoustics?

4. Consider the two-dimensional analog of Example 1 in Section 14.6, i.e., radiation of sound from an infinite cylinder described by

$$\frac{1}{r}\frac{\partial}{\partial r}\left(r\frac{\partial \varphi}{\partial r}\right) + \frac{1}{r^2}\frac{\partial^2 \varphi}{\partial \theta^2} - \frac{1}{c^2}\frac{\partial^2 \varphi}{\partial t^2} = 0.$$

a) Show that if $\varphi(r, \theta, t) = \psi(r, \theta)e^{-i\omega t}$, then

$$\psi(r, \theta) = \psi(r) = AJ_0(kr) + BN_0(kr).$$

b) Study the behavior of $\psi(r)$ for large values of r and produce an argument leading to the requirement that $\psi(r)$ is proportional to the Hankel function $H_0^{(1)}(kr)$ (see p. 616, footnote). Show that $B = Ai$ and complete the problem by evaluating A.

c) Can you suggest a general feature characteristic of divergent waves in two dimensions analogous to the Sommerfeld radiation condition?

5. Consider the acoustic field of a point source located at $\mathbf{r}_0$ and emitting harmonic waves of frequency ω.

a) Show that the velocity potential satisfies

$$\nabla^2 \varphi - \frac{1}{c^2}\frac{\partial^2 \varphi}{\partial t^2} = \delta(\mathbf{r} - \mathbf{r}_0)e^{-i\omega t}.$$

b) Show that the steady state of such a field requires the knowledge of Green's function for the Helmholtz equation

$$\nabla^2 G(\mathbf{r}\,|\,\mathbf{r}_0) + k^2 G(\mathbf{r}\,|\,\mathbf{r}_0) = \delta(\mathbf{r} - \mathbf{r}_0),$$

which satisfies the Sommerfeld radiation condition.

c) The three-dimensional delta function in spherical coordinates reads

$$\delta(\mathbf{r} - \mathbf{r}_0) = \frac{1}{r^2}\delta(r - r_0)\,\delta(\cos\theta - \cos\theta_0)\,\delta(\phi - \phi_0).$$

Using this expression and seeking $G(\mathbf{r}\,|\,\mathbf{r}_0)$ in the form

$$G(\mathbf{r}\,|\,\mathbf{r}_0) = \sum_{l=0}^{\infty}\sum_{m=-l}^{+l} Y_{lm}^*(\theta, \phi)\,Y_{lm}(\theta_0, \phi_0)R_l(r\,|\,r_0),$$

obtain the DE for $R_l(\mathbf{r} \mid \mathbf{r}_0)$ (the Y_{lm} are defined on p. 618). Solve the DE and show that

$$R_l(r \mid r_0) = \begin{cases} -ikj_l(kr)h_l^{(1)}(kr_0) & (r < r_0), \\ -ikj_l(kr_0)h_l^{(1)}(kr) & (r > r_0). \end{cases}$$

6. In the Green's function developed in the preceding problem, let $r_0 \to 0$.

a) Show that $R_l(r \mid 0) = 0$ if $l \neq 0$ while $R_0(r \mid 0) = -(1/r)e^{ikr}$ and deduce

$$G(\mathbf{r} \mid 0) = -\frac{1}{4\pi} \frac{e^{ikr}}{r}.$$

b) Produce an argument (see the technique used in Section 14.7) to claim that, in general, the Green's function of the last problem is simply

$$G(\mathbf{r} \mid \mathbf{r}_0) = -\frac{1}{4\pi} \frac{e^{ik|\mathbf{r}-\mathbf{r}_0|}}{|\mathbf{r} - \mathbf{r}_0|},$$

and the series established above must then be the expansion of this function in terms of spherical harmonics.

c) Specify a general radiation problem in acoustics which can be solved by means of the above Green's function. Can you explain why the problem of Example 2 in Section 14.6 involves the same $G(\mathbf{r} \mid \mathbf{r}_0)$?

7. Let the incident wave $\psi_{\text{inc}}(x) = Ae^{ikx}$ be scattered by a symmetric nonhomogeneity $\epsilon^2 u(x)$, as described in Section 14.9.

a) Show that the total solution ψ can be expressed, at least for large $|x|$, by

$$\psi \cong Ae^{\delta_{si}} \cos(kr + \delta_s) + \mu Ae^{\delta_{ai}} \sin(kr + \delta_a),$$

where δ_s and δ_a are the phase shifts (p. 633).

b) For the particular case of $u(x) = B(x)$ (Section 14.8), show that the above expression is *exact* for $|x| > a$, while for $|x| < a$ the following holds:

$$\psi = P \cos k_1 r + \mu Q \sin k_1 r \qquad (P, Q = \text{const})$$

with $k_1^2 = k^2 + \epsilon^2$.

c) Show that when we match ψ and $d\psi/dx$ at $x = a$, then we can match *separately* the symmetric and antisymmetric parts, and this yields almost immediately

$$k \tan(ka + \delta_s) = k_1 \tan k_1 a,$$
$$k_1 \tan(ka + \delta_a) = k \tan k_1 a.$$

d) Show that, in general, the backward-scattering cross section (reflection coefficient) is given by

$$\sigma_- = \frac{|A_-|^2}{|A|^2} = \sin^2(\delta_s - \delta_a).$$

Calculate σ_- from the relation obtained in (c). *Hint:* Do not solve for δ_s and δ_a, but obtain first tan $(\delta_s - \delta_a)$ through the trigonometric identity

$$\tan(\alpha - \beta) = \frac{\tan\alpha - \tan\beta}{1 + \tan\alpha\tan\beta}.$$

8. From the expression for ψ_{scat} on p. 637, deduce the following formula for the scattering amplitude $f(\theta)$:

$$f(\theta) = \frac{1}{2ik} \sum_{l=0}^{\infty} (2l + 1)(e^{2i\delta_l} - 1)P_l(\cos\theta).$$

Furthermore, setting $\theta = 0$ and comparing with a similar formula for σ, prove the so-called *optical theorem* (or Bohr-Peierls-Placzek relation)

$$\sigma = \frac{4\pi}{k^2} \operatorname{Im} f(0).$$

9. Consider the scattering of the plane wave $\psi_{\text{inc}} = e^{ikr\cos\theta}$, not necessarily acoustical, from the so-called hard sphere where the function $\psi = \psi_{\text{inc}} + \psi_{\text{scat}}$ satisfies $\nabla^2\psi + k^2\psi = 0$ and vanishes at the surface of the sphere $r = a$. Treat the problem by partial wave analysis and show that

$$\sigma_l = \frac{4\pi}{k^2}(2l + 1)\frac{j_l^2(ka)}{j_l^2(ka) + n_l^2(ka)}.$$

Also show that if $ka \ll 1$, then only the term $l = 0$ matters, and the total cross section is approximately

$$\sigma \cong 4\pi a^2 \left(\frac{\sin ka}{ka}\right)^2.$$

CHAPTER 15

PERTURBATION METHODS

15.1 INTRODUCTION

Perturbation methods are among the most widely used approximate methods for problems arising in mathematical physics. The central idea behind such methods, of which there are many varieties, is to use an already existing approximate solution as the starting point to develop a *correction* to it, thereby improving the approximation. This technique can be used in a wide variety of situations and in conjunction with any of the methods described in the preceding chapters. As our first example it would be instructive to treat one of the problems we have already solved. Let us consider the infinite stretched string with a finite portion of somewhat different density (see Section 14.8). The harmonic solutions of the type $\psi(x)e^{-i\omega t}$ are determined by the differential equation

$$\frac{d^2\psi}{dx^2} + [k^2 + \alpha B(x)]\psi = 0,$$

where $k^2 = \rho_0\omega^2/T$, $\alpha = (\rho_1 - \rho_0)\omega^2/T$, and $B(x)$ is the unit box function for the interval $(-a, +a)$, where the density ρ_1 is *slightly different* from the density ρ_0 elsewhere. The last statement implies that the parameter α is small, say, compared to k^2, and this fact is of crucial importance in the entire perturbational approach. Under these circumstances it is customary to say that the term $\alpha B(x)\psi(x)$ represents a small *perturbation* of the unperturbed equation

$$\frac{d^2\psi}{dx^2} + k^2\psi = 0.$$

It is reasonable to suppose that the solution of the original perturbed equation will differ only slightly from the *corresponding* solution $\psi_0(x)$ of the unperturbed equation. In this particular case the solutions of the unperturbed equation are well known, and we are going to seek a solution $\psi(x)$ which reduces to the particular form

$$\psi_0(x) = Ae^{ikx}$$

when the perturbation $\alpha B(x)\psi(x)$ is reduced to zero, which can be formally achieved by letting $\alpha \to 0$. In this spirit we shall assume that the sought solution has the form

$$\psi(x) = Ae^{ikx} + \psi_1(x) = \psi_0(x) + \psi_1(x),$$

where the unknown function $\psi_1(x)$ represents a correction to be added to the approximate solution $\psi_0(x)$.

So far, no actual approximations have been made, and one can, in fact, identify $\psi_1(x)$ with the scattered wave $\psi_{\text{scat}}(x)$ of Section 14.9. However, we shall make no attempt to evaluate $\psi_1(x)$ exactly, but only approximately. We observe that $\psi_1(x)$ must depend on the parameter α, and it is reasonable to assume that it can be expanded in a power series

$$\psi_1(x) = \alpha\varphi_1(x) + \alpha^2\varphi_2(x) + \alpha^3\varphi_3(x) + \cdots,$$

where $\varphi_1, \varphi_2, \ldots$ are some functions independent of α. Note that the leading term is proportional to α, in accordance with the requirement that $\psi_1(x) \to 0$ as $\alpha \to 0$.

Now, if α is very small, we can, presumably, neglect the higher powers of α and represent the overall solution approximately as

$$\psi(x) \cong \psi_0(x) + \alpha\varphi_1(x).$$

When this result is substituted into the perturbed DE, it would be consistent to retain the terms within the first order in α, resulting in the approximate equation

$$\psi_0'' + \alpha\varphi_1'' + k^2\psi_0 + k^2\alpha\varphi_1 + \alpha B(x)\psi_0 = 0.$$

Since ψ_0 satisfies the unperturbed equation, we have $\psi_0'' + k^2\psi_0 = 0$, and the remaining terms, all of first order in α, yield the equation for the correction term $\psi_1(x)$; for convenience, we return to the notation $\psi_1 = \alpha\varphi_1$ and use $\psi_0 = Ae^{ikx}$:

$$\psi_1'' + k^2\psi_1 = -\alpha B(x)Ae^{ikx}.$$

It is now a straightforward task to solve this equation, and this can be done by a variety of methods. When doing this, however, we should remember that the physical conditions of the problem require that ψ_1 satisfy the radiation condition, namely,

$$\psi_1(x) \sim \begin{cases} C_1 e^{-ikx} & (x \to -\infty), \\ C_2 e^{ikx} & (x \to +\infty). \end{cases}$$

Let us employ the Green's function method. The required Green's function is available to us from Sections 12.9 and 14.5 and reads

$$G(x \mid \xi) = \begin{cases} -\dfrac{i}{2k} e^{-ik(x-\xi)} & (x < \xi), \\[2mm] -\dfrac{i}{2k} e^{ik(x-\xi)} & (x > \xi). \end{cases}$$

From the practical point of view we would be interested only in the asymptotic behavior of $\psi_1(x)$ as $x \to \pm\infty$. Therefore, in the integral*

$$\psi_1(x) = \int_{-a}^{+a} G(x \mid \xi)[-\alpha A e^{ik\xi}] \, d\xi,$$

we shall use only one of the two forms of $G(x \mid \xi)$ at a time. For $x \to -\infty$, we have

$$\psi_1(x) \sim \frac{\alpha A i}{2k} \int_{-a}^{+a} e^{-ik(x-\xi)} e^{ik\xi} \, d\xi = A \frac{\alpha i \sin 2ka}{2k^2} e^{-ikx},$$

while for $x \to +\infty$,

$$\psi_1(x) \sim \frac{\alpha A i}{2k} \int_{-a}^{+a} e^{ik(x-\xi)} e^{ik\xi} \, d\xi = A \frac{\alpha a i}{k} e^{ikx}.$$

Summarizing, we have obtained the approximate solution of our scattering problem, at least asymptotically, i.e., when $|x| \to \infty$. Explicitly,

$$\psi(x) \sim \begin{cases} A e^{ikx} + A \dfrac{\alpha i \sin 2ka}{2k^2} e^{-ikx} & (x \to -\infty), \\[2ex] A e^{ikx} + A \dfrac{\alpha a i}{k} e^{ikx} & (x \to +\infty). \end{cases}$$

Remark. These expressions are actually applicable, as approximations, everywhere outside the interval $(-a, +a)$. As mentioned on p. 626, however, only the asymptotic form of the solution is significant, since all physically measurable quantities are calculable from it.

We are now in a position to compare our results with the exact solution of Section 14.8. From our $\psi(x)$ we have the approximate backward- and forward-scattering amplitudes:

$$A_- \cong A \frac{\alpha i \sin 2ka}{2k^2}, \qquad A_+ \cong A \frac{\alpha a i}{k},$$

from which the approximate values of reflection and transmission coefficients follow:

$$\text{RC} = \frac{|A_-|^2}{|A|^2} \cong \alpha^2 \frac{\sin^2 2ka}{4k^4}, \qquad \text{TC} = \frac{|A + A_+|^2}{|A|^2} \cong 1 + \alpha^2 \frac{a^2}{k^2}.$$

The exact values of A_- and A_+ are given by the quantities B and $A - F$, respectively, on p. 626. Expanding them in powers of α, we can demonstrate that our approximate results are accurate within the *first order* in α. The reflection coefficient turns out to be correct to the second order in α, which is the leading term. Observe, however, that the transmission coefficient is *not correct* within the second order. Even the sign of the quadratic term in α is patently wrong: as it

---

* The integration extends only from $-a$ to $+a$ because of the box function, which can now be replaced by unity.

stands, it violates the law of conservation of energy, allowing the transmitted power to exceed the incident power.

It is not difficult to find the reason for this feature. Adding A to A_+ before the calculation of the square of the modulus has a different effect on the approximations from the one observed in the case of A_-.*

Exercise. Perform the expansion (in powers of α) of the results on p. 626 and verify the above remarks.

15.2 THE BORN APPROXIMATION

The results of the preceding section are a particular example of the first-order perturbation technique for scattering problems, commonly known as the *Born approximation*.† Let us state this method formally.

In one dimension, the problem is to find a solution of

$$\frac{d^2\psi}{dx^2} + k^2\psi + u(x)\psi = 0,$$

which reduces to $\psi_0 = e^{ikx}$ (unit amplitude chosen for convenience) whenever the perturbation $u(x)$ reduces to zero. The function $u(x)$ is assumed to be "small," usually proportional to some small parameter α, included for convenience into the expression $u(x)$. Also, $u(x)$ is assumed to vanish outside some interval $(-a, +a)$ or, at least, to be negligible for $|x| > a$.

It is then assumed that $\psi(x)$ can be expressed as

$$\psi(x) = \psi_0(x) + \psi_1(x) + \psi_2(x) + \cdots,$$

where $\psi_k(x)$ $(k = 1, 2, 3, \ldots)$ are functions of the order of magnitude of α^k; they must satisfy the radiation condition. The Born approximation consists in taking $\psi \cong \psi_0 + \psi_1$ and keeping the terms within the first order in α in the DE. As in Section 15.1, we obtain

$$d^2\psi_1/dx^2 + k^2\psi_1 = -u(x)e^{ikx}.$$

Employing Green's function, we obtain the expressions

$$\psi_1(x) \sim \frac{i}{2k} e^{-ikx} \int_{-a}^{+a} u(\xi)e^{2ik\xi}\, d\xi \qquad (x \to -\infty),$$

$$\psi_1(x) \sim \frac{i}{2k} e^{ikx} \int_{-a}^{+a} u(\xi)\, d\xi \qquad (x \to +\infty),$$

which represent the desired first-order corrections to $\psi_0(x)$. Evidently, we are

---

* In principle, one should remember that a first-order approximation is inadequate for calculation of results valid within the second order.

† Or, perhaps, as the *first Born approximation* (see p. 650).

dealing with the backward- and forward-scattered waves and we can write immediately the backward-scattering cross section (see Section 14.9)

$$\sigma_- = \frac{1}{4k^2}\left|\int_{-a}^{+a} u(\xi)e^{2ik\xi}\,d\xi\right|^2 = RC,$$

which is also the reflection coefficient. In view of the discussion in the preceding section, it is *expected** to be a reasonable approximation to the correct value if $u(x)$ is sufficiently small. As for the transmission coefficient, we can use the relation

$$TC = 1 - RC,$$

since direct calculation by means of the Born approximation is inadequate.

Scattering problems in two and three dimensions can be treated by the same type of approach. Suppose, for instance, that we want to solve the three-dimensional problem given by

$$\nabla^2\psi(\mathbf{r}) + k^2\psi(\mathbf{r}) + \epsilon^2 u(\mathbf{r})\psi(\mathbf{r}) = 0 \qquad (\epsilon^2 = \text{const}),$$

where $u(\mathbf{r})$ is a function negligible outside some finite region $r < a$ and can be considered as a small perturbation of the Helmholtz equation. We want a solution which reduces to the plane-wave solution

$$\psi_0(\mathbf{r}) = e^{i(\mathbf{kr})}$$

as the perturbation is reduced to zero ($\epsilon^2 \to 0$). As before, let us set

$$\psi(\mathbf{r}) \cong \psi_0(\mathbf{r}) + \psi_1(\mathbf{r}),$$

where $\psi_1(\mathbf{r})$ is of the order of magnitude of ϵ^2.† Then $\psi_1(\mathbf{r})$ satisfies

$$\nabla^2\psi_1(\mathbf{r}) + k^2\psi_1(\mathbf{r}) = -\epsilon^2 u(\mathbf{r})e^{i(\mathbf{kr})}.$$

We can solve this equation with the help of Green's function $G(\mathbf{r} \mid \mathbf{r}_0)$ satisfying

$$\nabla^2 G(\mathbf{r} \mid \mathbf{r}_0) + k^2 G(\mathbf{r} \mid \mathbf{r}_0) = \delta(\mathbf{r} - \mathbf{r}_0)$$

and the radiation condition, since $\psi_1(\mathbf{r})$ must have this property. We can evaluate $G(\mathbf{r} \mid \mathbf{r}_0)$ by taking Fourier transforms‡ with respect to all three coordinates (the technique is similar to that employed in Section 14.7). Let $\mathbf{R} = \mathbf{r} - \mathbf{r}_0$; then G

---

* It should be remembered that no rigorous conditions have been specified to ensure the validity of the entire approximating procedure. Like most other perturbation methods, the Born approximation is widely used in physics "with the hope that it will work." The proofs that it will indeed work in practical cases of modern scattering theory are usually difficult and rarely available.

† A reasonable condition for this is $k^2 \gg \max |\epsilon^2 u(\mathbf{r})|$.

‡ For other methods of obtaining $G(\mathbf{r} \mid \mathbf{r}_0)$, see Problems 5 and 6 of Chapter 14.

must be a function of $\mathbf{R}$ and must be expressible as

$$G(\mathbf{R}) = \frac{1}{(\sqrt{2\pi})^3} \iiint\limits_{-\infty}^{+\infty} g(\mathbf{K}) e^{-i(\mathbf{K} \cdot \mathbf{R})} \, d^3\mathbf{K},$$

where $g(\mathbf{K})$ is the triple Fourier transform of $G(\mathbf{R})$. Also,

$$\delta(\mathbf{R}) = \frac{1}{(2\pi)^3} \iiint\limits_{-\infty}^{+\infty} e^{-i(\mathbf{K} \cdot \mathbf{R})} \, d^3\mathbf{K}.$$

Substituting into the PDE, we obtain

$$(-K^2 + k^2) g(\mathbf{K}) = \frac{1}{(\sqrt{2\pi})^3},$$

so that

$$G(\mathbf{R}) = \frac{1}{(2\pi)^3} \iiint\limits_{-\infty}^{+\infty} \frac{e^{-i(\mathbf{K} \cdot \mathbf{R})}}{k^2 - K^2} \, d^3\mathbf{K}.$$

It is now convenient to evaluate this integral in spherical coordinates in $\mathbf{K}$-space and perform the integration over the angles first. With the polar axis along the $\mathbf{R}$-direction, we have

$$\int_0^{2\pi} d\phi \int_0^\pi e^{-iKR \cos\theta} \sin\theta \, d\theta = 4\pi \frac{\sin KR}{KR},$$

so that

$$G(\mathbf{R}) = \frac{1}{2\pi^2} \int_0^\infty \frac{\sin KR}{KR} \frac{K^2 \, dK}{(k^2 - K^2)}.$$

Since the integrand is an even function, we may extend the integration to the interval $(-\infty, +\infty)$ and write

$$G(\mathbf{R}) = -\frac{1}{8\pi^2 Ri} \int_{-\infty}^{+\infty} \frac{(e^{iKR} - e^{-iKR}) K \, dK}{(K + k)(K - k)},$$

expressing $\sin KR$ also in terms of exponential functions. The integral can be evaluated by residue calculus, but we must specify the treatment of the poles at $K \pm k$. It is evident that $G(\mathbf{R})$ will, in principle, contain factors e^{ikR} or e^{-ikR}, because the residues will contribute such factors. However, only the terms with e^{ikR} will satisfy the Sommerfeld radiation condition (p. 617).[*] Consequently, the path of integration must be chosen in such a way that only the terms with e^{ikR} occur. This path is shown in Fig. 15.1.

---

[*] An easy way to see this is to observe that e^{ikR} is practically equal to e^{ikr} when $R = |\mathbf{r} - \mathbf{r}_0|$ is large.

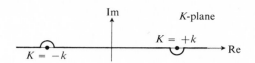

Figure 15.1

Indeed, since $R > 0$, the contour for the first part of the integral with e^{iKR} must be closed upward, yielding

$$\int_{-\infty}^{+\infty} \frac{e^{iKR}K\,dK}{(K + k)(K - k)} = 2\pi i \frac{e^{ikR}k}{2k},$$

while the second part with e^{-iKR} must be closed downward yielding

$$\int_{-\infty}^{+\infty} \frac{e^{-iKR}K\,dK}{(K + k)(K - k)} = -2\pi i \frac{e^{ikR}(-k)}{(-2k)}.$$

Combining these results, we obtain

$$G(\mathbf{R}) = -\frac{1}{8\pi^2 Ri}\{\pi i e^{ikR} + \pi i e^{ikR}\} = -\frac{e^{ikR}}{4\pi R},$$

or, explicitly,

$$G(\mathbf{R}) = G(\mathbf{r} \mid \mathbf{r}_0) = -\frac{1}{4\pi}\frac{e^{ik|\mathbf{r}-\mathbf{r}_0|}}{|\mathbf{r} - \mathbf{r}_0|}.$$

We can now write the expression for $\psi_1(\mathbf{r})$:

$$\psi_1(\mathbf{r}) = \frac{1}{4\pi}\iiint \frac{e^{ik|\mathbf{r}-\mathbf{r}_0|}}{|\mathbf{r} - \mathbf{r}_0|}\,\epsilon^2 u(\mathbf{r}_0)e^{i(\mathbf{k}\cdot\mathbf{r}_0)}\,d^3\mathbf{r}_0,$$

where $d^3\mathbf{r}_0$ is the volume element in the space of the dummy vector $\mathbf{r}_0$ (see p. 622). This expression represents the Born approximation for the scattered wave $\psi_{\text{scat}}(\mathbf{r})$. It is customary to make further approximations in the above integral but we shall not present them here.*

Remark. The procedure employed above to evaluate the Born approximation can also be used to obtain additional corrections to the already developed results. It is in this fashion that the so-called second and higher Born approximations arise.

15.3 PERTURBATION OF EIGENVALUE PROBLEMS

The ideas of perturbation methods can also be applied to eigenvalue problems, namely, problems of the type

$$\mathcal{L}\psi = \lambda\psi,$$

or, even more generally, of the type

$$\mathcal{L}\psi = \lambda\mathcal{R}\psi,$$

---

* The details can be found in many textbooks on quantum mechanics, e.g., Dicke and Wittke, Section 16–2.

where $\mathcal{L}$ and $\mathcal{R}$ are some linear operators and ψ is a vector from the corresponding linear space. For instance, $\mathcal{L}$ and $\mathcal{R}$ may be differential operators (ordinary or partial) and ψ may be a function of one or more variables, or $\mathcal{L}$ and $\mathcal{R}$ may be $N \times N$ matrices and ψ may be a column vector, etc.

As an introduction, consider the already familiar (Sections 11.7 and 13.9) problem of a stretched string of length L with the mass m in the middle. It reduces to the solution of the equation

$$\frac{d^2y}{dx^2} = -k^2\left[1 + \frac{m}{\rho}\,\delta(x)\right]y \qquad \left(k^2 = \frac{\omega^2\rho}{T}\right).$$

This is an equation of the second type mentioned above, with $\mathcal{L} = d^2/dx^2$, $\mathcal{R} = 1 + (m/\rho)\,\delta(x)$, and $\lambda = -k^2$. Let us suppose that the mass m is sufficiently small so that the actual solutions $y_n(x)$ and the actual eigenvalues $\lambda_n = -k^2$ are close to the unperturbed solutions $y_n^{(0)}(x)$ and the eigenvalues $\lambda_n^{(0)}$ which satisfy

$$\frac{d^2y_n^{(0)}}{dx^2} = \lambda_n^{(0)}y_n^{(0)} \qquad \text{(plus boundary conditions)}.$$

These functions $y_n^{(0)}$ represent the normal modes of a homogeneous string of length L (Section 8.2). With the origin at the midpoint of the string, they read explicitly

$$y_n^{(0)}(x) = \left.\begin{cases} \sqrt{\dfrac{2}{L}}\cos\dfrac{n\pi x}{L} & (n = \text{odd}) \\[2mm] \sqrt{\dfrac{2}{L}}\sin\dfrac{n\pi x}{L} & (n = \text{even}) \end{cases}\right\} \quad \lambda_n^{(0)} = -\frac{n^2\pi^2}{L^2}.$$

We shall now suppose that the unknown eigenfunctions $y_n(x)$ and eigenvalues λ_n can be expanded in powers of the parameter $\alpha = m/\rho L$:[*]

$$y_n(x) = y_n^{(0)}(x) + \alpha y_n^{(1)}(x) + \alpha^2 y_n^{(2)}(x) + \cdots,$$
$$\lambda_n = \lambda_n^{(0)} + \alpha\lambda_n^{(1)} + \alpha^2\lambda_n^{(2)} + \cdots$$

Let us confine ourselves to terms of the first order in α and write, for simplicity, $\alpha y_n^{(1)}(x) = \eta_n(x)$ and $\alpha\lambda_n^{(1)} = \Delta\lambda_n$. Introducing this into the DE, we have

$$y_n^{(0)\prime\prime} + \eta_n'' \cong [\lambda_n^{(0)} + \Delta\lambda_n][1 + \alpha L\lambda_n^{(0)}\,\delta(x) + \alpha L\,\Delta\lambda_n\,\delta(x)][y_n^{(0)} + \eta_n].$$

To be consistent, we retain in this equation only the terms within the first order in α and write

$$y_n^{(0)\prime\prime} + \eta_n'' \cong \lambda_n^{(0)}y_n^{(0)} + \lambda_n^{(0)}\eta_n + \lambda_n^{(0)}\alpha L\,\delta(x)y_n^{(0)} + \Delta\lambda_n y_n^{(0)}.$$

In view of $y_n^{(0)\prime\prime} = \lambda_n^{(0)}y_n^{(0)}$, this equation reduces to

$$\eta_n'' - \lambda_n^{(0)}\eta_n \cong \lambda_n^{(0)}\alpha L\,\delta(x)y_n^{(0)} + \Delta\lambda_n y_n^{(0)}.$$

---

[*] A convenient choice since α is a dimensionless quantity.

It now appears that we will have difficulty since we need both $\eta_n(x)$ and $\Delta\lambda_n$.* However, we can take advantage of the fact that $\mathcal{L} = d^2/dx^2$ is a *self-adjoint operator* in the space of functions vanishing at $x = \pm L/2$, namely (see Section 9.4),

$$\int_{-L/2}^{+L/2} y_n^{(0)}(x)\eta_n''(x)\, dx = \int_{-L/2}^{+L/2} \eta_n(x)y_n^{(0)''}(x)\, dx,$$

whatever $\eta_n(x)$ may happen to be, so long as it vanishes at $x = \pm L/2$ as it should. Therefore, if we multiply our equation by $y_n^{(0)}(x)$, integrate over $(-L/2, +L/2)$, and employ $y_n^{(0)''} = \lambda_n^{(0)}y_n^{(0)}$, we obtain

$$0 \cong \lambda_n^{(0)}\alpha L \int_{-L/2}^{+L/2} \delta(x)[y_n^{(0)}(x)]^2\, dx + \Delta\lambda_n \int_{-L/2}^{+L/2} [y_n^{(0)}(x)]^2\, dx.$$

Since the unperturbed eigenfunctions $y_n^{(0)}(x)$ have been normalized, this reduces to

$$\Delta\lambda_n \cong -\lambda_n^{(0)}\alpha L[y_n^{(0)}(0)]^2 = \begin{cases} \dfrac{2m}{\rho L}\dfrac{n^2\pi^2}{L^2} & (n = \text{odd}), \\ 0 & (n = \text{even}). \end{cases}$$

The perturbed eigenvalues are then approximately given by

$$\lambda_n \cong \lambda_n^{(0)} + \Delta\lambda_n = \begin{cases} -\dfrac{n^2\pi^2}{L^2}\left(1 - \dfrac{2m}{\rho L}\right) & (n = \text{odd}), \\ -\dfrac{n^2\pi^2}{L^2} & (n = \text{even}). \end{cases}$$

Since we have analyzed the exact solution of this problem (Section 11.7), it is worthwhile to compare it to the perturbational result.

For even n the exact eigenvalues are $\lambda_n = -n^2\pi^2/L^2$ also obtained above. For odd n the exact eigenvalues are determined from

$$\gamma \tan \gamma = 1/\alpha,$$

where $\lambda = -4\gamma^2/L^2$ and $\alpha = m/\rho L$. To check the perturbational result, it is convenient to rewrite this equation as

$$\cot \gamma = \alpha\gamma,$$

and to seek an approximate solution, within the first order in α, as

$$\gamma_n = n\pi/2 + \alpha\xi.\dagger$$

For odd n we have, in general, $\cot(n\pi/2 + \alpha\xi) = -\tan(\alpha\xi)$; within the first

---

* As distinct from the cases in the preceding sections where only the correction to the function was involved.

$\dagger\ \gamma_n = n\pi/2$ is the exact solution for $\alpha = 0$.

order in α this is equal to $-\alpha\xi$ so that

$$-\alpha\xi \cong \alpha(n\pi/2 + \alpha\xi).$$

Solving, we obtain $\xi = -n\pi/2(1 + \alpha)$. It is prudent to keep this result within the lowest order in α, namely, $\xi \cong -n\pi/2$ since ξ is supposed to be a constant. Then $\gamma_n = (n\pi/2)(1 - \alpha)$ and

$$\lambda_n = -\frac{4\gamma_n^2}{L^2} \cong -\frac{n^2\pi^2}{L^2}(1 - 2\alpha) = -\frac{n^2\pi^2}{L^2}\left(1 - \frac{2m}{\rho L}\right),$$

just as predicted by the first-order perturbation theory.

We shall not pursue this example further, e.g., by evaluating η_n. Instead, let us formulate some general principles of the perturbation theory for eigenvalue problems.

15.4 FIRST-ORDER RAYLEIGH-SCHRÖDINGER THEORY

Let us consider the eigenvalue problem of the type

$$(\mathcal{H} + \mathcal{W})\psi = \lambda\psi,$$

where $\mathcal{H}$ and $\mathcal{W}$ are *linear hermitian operators* and $\mathcal{W}$ can be regarded as a perturbation of $\mathcal{H}$, say $\mathcal{W} = \alpha\mathcal{W}'$, where α is a small parameter. We shall assume to be working in a complex linear space.*

Suppose that we possess complete information about the solution of the unperturbed problem

$$\mathcal{H}\psi_n^{(0)} = \lambda_n^{(0)}\psi_n^{(0)},$$

which is *nondegenerate*, namely, all eigenvalues $\lambda_n^{(0)}$ are different. This condition is of paramount importance in perturbation theory.

Returning to the perturbed problem, it is reasonable to assume that its eigenfunctions and eigenvalues differ only slightly from the unperturbed ones. Moreover, *we can label* by ψ_n and λ_n that eigenpair† of $\mathcal{H} + \mathcal{W}$ which *reduces* to $\psi_n^{(0)}$ and $\lambda_n^{(0)}$ as $\alpha \to 0$. If we confine ourselves to the first-order terms in α, then we can write, approximately,

$$\psi_n \cong \psi_n^{(0)} + \psi_n^{(1)}, \qquad \lambda_n \cong \lambda_n^{(0)} + \lambda_n^{(1)}.$$

Substituting these expressions into the equation $(\mathcal{H} + \mathcal{W})\psi_n = \lambda_n\psi_n$, and retaining the first-order terms in α, we obtain

$$\mathcal{H}\psi_n^{(1)} + \mathcal{W}\psi_n^{(0)} = \lambda_n^{(0)}\psi_n^{(1)} + \lambda_n^{(1)}\psi_n^{(0)}.$$

---

* Many such problems arise in quantum mechanics and we are actually using the customary quantum-mechanical notation, for instance, $\mathcal{H}$ stands for the unperturbed Hamiltonian.

† By *eigenpair* we mean the eigenfunction (or eigenvector) plus the corresponding eigenvalue.

At this stage it is worthwhile to realize that we have not specified the exact nature of our operators and our ψ. Our problem can be a DE with the ψ being functions satisfying some boundary conditions, and thereby forming a linear space. Just as easily, the problem may be a vector-matrix equation, with the ψ being N-tuple column vectors and $\mathfrak{JC}$ and $\mathcal{W}$ being $N \times N$ matrices. Infinite-dimensional vectors and matrices are also possible and we know from Chapter 11 that this may actually be equivalent to the DE-case.

It really makes no difference which of these particular cases is before us. We can always perform an operation common to all these situations, namely, we *take the inner product* of our equation with the vector $\psi_n^{(0)}$. In the notation of Sections 10.6 and 11.1, we write

$$(\psi_n^{(0)}, \mathfrak{JC}\psi_n^{(1)}) + (\psi_n^{(0)}, \mathcal{W}\psi_n^{(0)}) = \lambda_n^{(0)}(\psi_n^{(0)}, \psi_n^{(1)}) + \lambda_n^{(1)}(\psi_n^{(0)}, \psi_n^{(0)}),$$

and it is understood that if ψ happen to be functions of x in (a, b), then

$$(\psi_n^{(0)}, \mathfrak{JC}\psi_n^{(1)}) \equiv \int_a^b \psi_n^{(0)*}(x)[\mathfrak{JC}\psi_n^{(1)}(x)]\, dx, \quad \text{etc.}$$

Alternatively, if ψ are column N-tuples, then

$$(\psi_n^{(0)}, \mathfrak{JC}\psi_n^{(1)}) \equiv \psi_n^{(0)\dagger}\mathfrak{JC}\psi_n^{(1)}, \quad \text{etc.,}$$

where $\mathfrak{JC}$ is now an $N \times N$ hermitian matrix and $\psi_n^{(0)\dagger}$ is a row vector.

Whatever the case is, we must have

$$(\psi_n^{(0)}, \mathfrak{JC}\psi_n^{(1)}) = (\mathfrak{JC}\psi_n^{(0)}, \psi_n^{(1)}) = \lambda_n^{(0)}(\psi_n^{(0)}, \psi_n^{(1)}),$$

because of the hermiticity of $\mathfrak{JC}$. Furthermore, it is customary to simplify the notation by writing

$$(\psi_n^{(0)}, \mathcal{W}\psi_n^{(0)}) = W_{nn},$$

and calling this number the *expectation value* of the operator $\mathcal{W}$ for the vector labeled by n;[*] the unperturbed vectors are tacitly assumed, since, in the perturbation theory, they are the known ones.

All these results, along with the assumption that $\psi_n^{(0)}$ are normalized, so that $(\psi_n^{(0)}, \psi_n^{(0)}) = 1$, yield the fundamental formula

$$\lambda_n^{(1)} = W_{nn},$$

which gives the first-order correction to the unperturbed eigenvalue.

It remains to evaluate the first-order corrections $\psi_n^{(1)}$ to the unperturbed eigenvectors. For this purpose we shall make the assumption that the set of unperturbed eigenvectors is *complete*. In other words, it can serve as a basis for our linear space and $\psi_n^{(1)}$ can be expressed as a linear superposition of unperturbed

---

[*] In quantum mechanics, one commonly uses the term *state* instead of *vector*.

eigenvectors:*

$$\psi_n^{(1)} = \sum_m C_{nm}^{(1)} \psi_m^{(0)},$$

the summation being finite or infinite depending on the nature of the linear space. Substitute this into our equation (p. 653) and take the inner product with a vector $\psi_l^{(0)}$, but such that $l \neq n$ (we have already used the inner product with $\psi_n^{(0)}$). Then

$$\sum_m C_{nm}^{(1)} (\psi_l^{(0)}, \mathcal{K} \psi_m^{(0)}) + (\psi_l^{(0)}, \mathcal{W} \psi_n^{(0)}) = \lambda_n^{(0)} \sum_m C_{nm}^{(1)} (\psi_l^{(0)}, \psi_m^{(0)}) + \lambda_n^{(1)} (\psi_l^{(0)}, \psi_n^{(0)}).$$

Since the eigenvalues are nondegenerate, the eigenvectors $\psi_m^{(0)}$ are orthogonal to each other so that

$$(\psi_l^{(0)}, \psi_m^{(0)}) = \delta_{lm}, \qquad (\psi_l^{(0)}, \psi_n^{(0)}) = 0 \qquad \text{(because } l \neq n\text{),}$$

and

$$(\psi_l^{(0)}, \mathcal{K} \psi_m^{(0)}) = \lambda_m^{(0)} (\psi_l^{(0)}, \psi_m^{(0)}) = \lambda_m^{(0)} \delta_{lm}.$$

This reduces our equation to the form

$$C_{nl}^{(1)} \lambda_l^{(0)} + (\psi_l^{(0)}, \mathcal{W} \psi_n^{(0)}) = \lambda_n^{(0)} C_{nl}^{(1)} \qquad (l \neq n).$$

The quantity $W_{ln} = (\psi_l^{(0)}, \mathcal{W} \psi_n^{(0)})$ is called the matrix element of the operator W between the vectors† labeled by l and n. Solving now for $C_{nl}^{(1)}$, we obtain

$$C_{nl}^{(1)} = \frac{W_{ln}}{\lambda_n^{(0)} - \lambda_l^{(0)}} \qquad (l \neq n).$$

This formula determines all the coefficients in the correction term $\psi_n^{(1)}$ *except one*, namely, the coefficient $C_{nn}^{(1)}$. To obtain some information about $C_{nn}^{(1)}$, we shall use an additional condition. We shall require that our approximate eigenvectors $\psi_n \cong \psi_n^{(0)} + \psi_n^{(1)}$ be *normalized*, at least within the first order.

In general, if we take the inner product of ψ_m and ψ_n, then we have

$$(\psi_m, \psi_n) \cong (\psi_m^{(0)}, \psi_n^{(0)}) + (\psi_m^{(0)}, \psi_n^{(1)}) + (\psi_m^{(1)}, \psi_n^{(0)}),$$

retaining only the first-order terms. If $m \neq n$, then $(\psi_m^{(0)}, \psi_n^{(0)}) = 0$ and the remaining two terms reduce to $C_{nm}^{(1)} + C_{mn}^{(1)*}$ (see p. 437), which vanishes because of the formula for $C_{nm}^{(1)}$ and the fact that for a hermitian $\mathcal{W}$,

$$W_{nm} = (\psi_n^{(0)}, \mathcal{W} \psi_m^{(0)}) = (\mathcal{W} \psi_n^{(0)}, \psi_m^{(0)}) = (\psi_m^{(0)}, \mathcal{W} \psi_n^{(0)})^* = W_{mn}^*.$$

Consequently, the perturbed eigenvectors *remain orthogonal* to each other. If we now set $m = n$ and require that $(\psi_n, \psi_n) = 1$ in our approximation, then the

---

* It is essentially at this point that the Rayleigh-Schrödinger technique starts. It combines the method of eigenfunction expansions for DE problems with the perturbation concepts.
† "between the states . . . ," in the language of quantum mechanics.

following condition on $C_{nn}^{(1)}$ emerges:

$$C_{nn}^{(1)} + C_{nn}^{(1)*} = 0.$$

If we are dealing with real spaces, this condition requires outright that $C_{nn}^{(1)} = 0$. If the space is complex, we can only say that Re $C_{nn}^{(1)} = 0$ while Im $C_{nn}^{(1)}$ remains undetermined.

At this point an important observation is in order. A complex eigenvector, even if normalized to unity, is by no means unique since it can still be multiplied by a phase factor $e^{i\gamma}$ with an arbitrary real phase γ. If we arbitrarily choose for $C_{nn}^{(1)}$ some pure imaginary number $C_{nn}^{(1)} = i\delta$, where δ is real and of the first order, then the perturbed eigenvector will be

$$\psi_n \cong \psi_n^{(0)} + i\delta\,\psi_n^{(0)} + \sum_{m \neq n} C_{nm}^{(1)}\psi_m^{(0)}.$$

However, this can be simply interpreted as though the unperturbed vector $\psi_n^{(0)}$ had been premultiplied by $e^{i\delta}$. Indeed, we can write, within the first order,

$$e^{i\delta}\psi_n^{(0)} \cong \psi_n^{(0)} + i\delta\,\psi_n^{(0)}.$$

It is evident that we can always accept $e^{i\delta}\psi_n^{(0)}$, rather than $\psi_n^{(0)}$, to be the original unperturbed vector, and this would amount to the choice $C_{nn}^{(1)} = 0$ in the first-order perturbation theory.

Remark. Regarding the phase factor $e^{i\gamma}$, it may be pointed out that whenever complex spaces are used, as in quantum mechanics, the physically measurable quantities are of the type $(\psi, \mathcal{Q}\psi)$, where $\mathcal{Q}$ is an operator. They are not affected by the phase factor.

Example 1. Consider the problem of coupled pendula (Fig. 15.2) treated in Sections 10.1 and 10.2 but which is now perturbed by an additional weak spring. By the term "weak" we shall mean

$$k' \ll k$$

and

$$k' \ll mg/L.$$

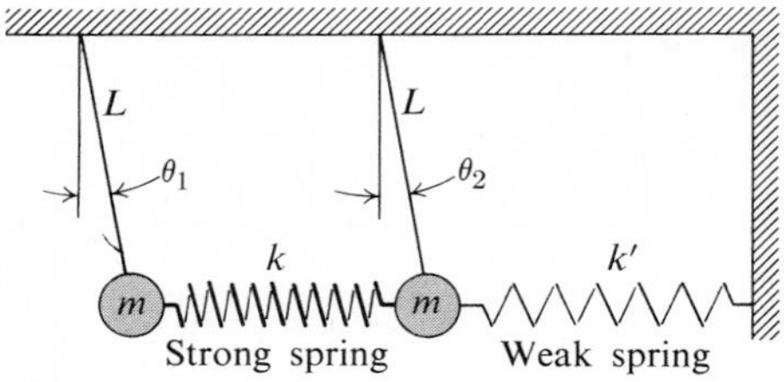

Figure 15.2

In terms of θ_1 and θ_2, the potential energy of the system will be given by

$$V = \underbrace{\tfrac{1}{2}mgL\theta_1^2 + \tfrac{1}{2}mgL\theta_2^2 + \tfrac{1}{2}kL^2(\theta_1 - \theta_2)^2}_{\text{Unperturbed potential energy}} + \underbrace{\tfrac{1}{2}k'L^2\theta_2^2}_{\text{Perturbation}};$$

compare this with p. 409. The unperturbed problem is solved by diagonalizing the quadratic form for the unperturbed potential energy

$$V_0 = \left(\frac{mgL}{2} + \frac{kL^2}{2}\right)\theta_1^2 + \left(\frac{mgL}{2} + \frac{kL^2}{2}\right)\theta_2^2 - kL^2\theta_1\theta_2,$$

or, what amounts to the same thing, by diagonalizing the matrix

$$
\mathcal{V}_0 = \begin{vmatrix} \dfrac{mgL}{2} + \dfrac{kL^2}{2} & -\dfrac{kL^2}{2} \\[2ex] -\dfrac{kL^2}{2} & \dfrac{mgL}{2} + \dfrac{kL^2}{2} \end{vmatrix}.
$$

This has been accomplished by changing the basis from θ_1, θ_2 to the normal coordinates

$$
\psi_1 = \frac{1}{\sqrt{2}}(\theta_1 + \theta_2), \qquad \psi_2 = \frac{1}{\sqrt{2}}(-\theta_1 + \theta_2),
$$

(see p. 412, also p. 450 *et seq.*). We can now express the actual perturbed potential energy in terms of ψ_1 and ψ_2 as

$$
V = \left(\frac{mgL}{2} + \frac{k'L^2}{4}\right)\psi_1^2 + \left(\frac{mgL}{2} + kL^2 + \frac{k'L^2}{4}\right)\psi_2^2 + \frac{k'L^2}{2}\psi_1\psi_2.
$$

The entire problem can now be stated as follows: We must find the eigenvalues and eigenvectors of the operator $\mathcal{V} = \mathcal{V}_0 + \mathcal{W}$, where $\mathcal{V}_0$ and $\mathcal{W}$ are represented by the matrices

$$
\mathcal{V}_0 = \begin{vmatrix} \dfrac{mgL}{2} & 0 \\[2ex] 0 & \dfrac{mgL}{2} + kL^2 \end{vmatrix}, \qquad \mathcal{W} = \begin{vmatrix} \dfrac{k'L^2}{4} & \dfrac{k'L^2}{4} \\[2ex] \dfrac{k'L^2}{4} & \dfrac{k'L^2}{4} \end{vmatrix},
$$

and $\mathcal{W}$ can be considered to be a small perturbation of $\mathcal{V}_0$. In this representation the unperturbed eigenvalues are simply the diagonal elements of $\mathcal{V}_0$:

$$
\lambda_1^{(0)} = \frac{mgL}{2}, \qquad \lambda_2^{(0)} = \frac{mgL}{2} + kL^2,
$$

related to the normal frequencies via $\lambda = (mL^2/2)\omega^2$. The unperturbed eigenvectors are the basis vectors $(1, 0)$ and $(0, 1)$.

Now, according to the first-order perturbation theory, the perturbed eigenvalues are approximately given by

$$
\lambda_1 \cong \lambda_1^{(0)} + W_{11}, \qquad \lambda_2 \cong \lambda_2^{(0)} + W_{22}.
$$

In our representation, W_{11} and W_{22} are nothing but the diagonal elements of the matrix $\mathcal{W}$, and these formulas yield the values

$$
\lambda_1 \cong \tfrac{1}{2}mgL + \tfrac{1}{4}k'L^2, \qquad \lambda_2 \cong \tfrac{1}{2}mgL + kL^2 + \tfrac{1}{4}k'L^2.
$$

The corrections to eigenvectors are also easily evaluated:

$$C_{12}^{(1)} = \frac{W_{21}}{\lambda_1^{(0)} - \lambda_2^{(0)}} = \frac{\frac{1}{4}k'L^2}{(-kL^2)} = -\frac{k'}{4k},$$

$$C_{21}^{(1)} = \frac{W_{12}}{\lambda_2^{(0)} - \lambda_1^{(0)}} = \frac{\frac{1}{4}k'L^2}{kL^2} = +\frac{k'}{4k}.$$

The new eigenvectors are then given by $(1, -k'/4k)$ and $(k'/4k, 1)$. These vectors are orthogonal to each other while the deviation from normalization appears only in the second order.

Of course, the problem is easily solved exactly with the result

$$\lambda_{1,2} = \tfrac{1}{2}(mgL + kL^2 + 2k'L^2) \pm \tfrac{1}{2}kL^2\sqrt{1 + (k'/2k)^2}.$$

If this expression is expanded in powers of k'/k and only the first-order terms are retained, the perturbation results are readily verified.

Exercise. Perform the expansion indicated above and compare with the results of the perturbation theory.

15.5 THE SECOND-ORDER NONDEGENERATE THEORY

It often happens that for one reason or another, the results provided by the first-order theory are not sufficiently accurate. In such cases it becomes necessary to consider second- and higher-order corrections.

Let us consider the general problem of carrying the perturbation calculations to higher orders. We shall still firmly insist on the condition that the unperturbed eigenvalues be nondegenerate. As before, we seek the solutions of the problem

$$(\mathcal{3C} + \mathcal{W})\psi_n = \lambda_n\psi_n,$$

where $\mathcal{W}$ can be considered as a small perturbation of $\mathcal{3C}$. For convenience, we may regard $\mathcal{W}$ as being proportional to a small parameter α (namely, $\mathcal{W} = \alpha\mathcal{W}'$) and assume that λ_n and ψ_n can be expanded in powers of α.* Consequently, we write

$$\lambda_n = \lambda_n^{(0)} + \lambda_n^{(1)} + \lambda_n^{(2)} + \cdots, \qquad \psi_n = \psi_n^{(0)} + \psi_n^{(1)} + \psi_n^{(2)} + \cdots,$$

where $\lambda_n^{(k)}$ and $\psi_n^{(k)}$ are of kth order, i.e., proportional to α^k. Substituting this into our equation,

$$(\mathcal{3C} + \mathcal{W}) \sum_{k=0}^{\infty} \psi_n^{(k)} = \sum_{k=0}^{\infty} \lambda_n^{(k)} \sum_{j=0}^{\infty} \psi_n^{(j)},$$

---

* Effectively, we are assuming that λ_n and the coordinates of vectors ψ_n are analytic functions of the variable α, at least within some circle of convergence about the origin in the complex α-plane. This is a reasonable assumption, although we *do expect* that it will break down for sufficiently large $|\alpha|$.

and separating the various orders of magnitude, we have

zero order: $\mathcal{3C}\psi_n^{(0)} = \lambda_n^{(0)}\psi_n^{(0)}$;

first order: $\mathcal{3C}\psi_n^{(1)} + \mathcal{W}\psi_n^{(0)} = \lambda_n^{(0)}\psi_n^{(1)} + \lambda_n^{(1)}\psi_n^{(0)}$;

second order: $\mathcal{3C}\psi_n^{(2)} + \mathcal{W}\psi_n^{(1)} = \lambda_n^{(0)}\psi_n^{(2)} + \lambda_n^{(1)}\psi_n^{(1)} + \lambda_n^{(2)}\psi_n^{(0)}$;

third order: $\mathcal{3C}\psi_n^{(3)} + \mathcal{W}\psi_n^{(2)} = \lambda_n^{(0)}\psi_n^{(3)} + \lambda_n^{(1)}\psi_n^{(2)} + \lambda_n^{(2)}\psi_n^{(1)} + \lambda_n^{(3)}\psi_n^{(0)}$,   etc.

The idea now is to form the inner products of these equations with the unperturbed vectors $\psi_m^{(0)}$ and use the results from the $(k-1)$-order to evaluate the quantities of the kth order. This program will be carried out within the second order only.

Starting with the zero-order equation, we see that it is trivially satisfied. The first-order equation is exactly the same as in the preceding section. Performing the same operations as before, we still have the formulas

$$\lambda_n^{(1)} = W_{nn}; \qquad C_{nm}^{(1)} = \frac{W_{mn}}{\lambda_n^{(0)} - \lambda_m^{(0)}} \qquad (m \neq n).$$

However, we must review the statements made with regard to $C_{nn}^{(1)}$ since these were confined to the first-order approximations. If we want to invoke the normalization condition within the second order, we must first look into the second-order corrections.

We construct the inner product of the second-order equation with $\psi_n^{(0)}$; we use the fact that $\mathcal{3C}$ is hermitian and $\psi_n^{(0)}$ is normalized, namely,

$$(\psi_n^{(0)}, \mathcal{3C}\psi_n^{(2)}) = \lambda_n^{(0)}(\psi_n^{(0)}, \psi_n^{(2)}) \qquad \text{and} \qquad (\psi_n^{(0)}, \psi_n^{(0)}) = 1$$

to obtain

$$(\psi_n^{(0)}, \mathcal{W}\psi_n^{(1)}) = \lambda_n^{(1)}(\psi_n^{(0)}, \psi_n^{(1)}) + \lambda_n^{(2)}.$$

Further, we use the expansion $\psi_n^{(1)} = \sum_m C_{nm}^{(1)}\psi_m^{(0)}$ and the first-order result $\lambda_n^{(1)} = W_{nn}$ to reduce this relation to

$$\sum_m W_{nm}C_{nm}^{(1)} = W_{nn}C_{nn}^{(1)} + \lambda_n^{(2)}.$$

Note that the terms containing $C_{nn}^{(1)}$ cancel out, and the equation yields

$$\lambda_n^{(2)} = \sum_{m \neq n} W_{nm}C_{nm}^{(1)}$$

or, explicitly,

$$\lambda_n^{(2)} = \sum_{m \neq n}{}' \frac{W_{nm}W_{mn}}{\lambda_n^{(0)} - \lambda_m^{(0)}},$$

where it is understood that the summation is taken over all values of m except $m = n$.

Turning now to the evaluation of $\psi_n^{(2)}$, we also expand it in terms of unperturbed eigenvectors:

$$\psi_n^{(2)} = \sum_m C_{nm}^{(2)} \psi_m^{(0)}.$$

Substituting this into the second-order equation along with the expansion of $\psi_n^{(1)}$ as in the preceding section, and constructing the inner product with the vector $\psi_l^{(0)}$, where $l \neq n$, we obtain

$$\lambda_l^{(0)} C_{nl}^{(2)} + \sum_m W_{lm} C_{nm}^{(1)} = \lambda_n^{(0)} C_{nl}^{(2)} + \lambda_n^{(1)} C_{nl}^{(1)}.$$

Since $C_{nn}^{(1)}$ is still undetermined, we separate this term from the sum over m; we use the first-order formulas to obtain

$$C_{nl}^{(2)} = \frac{W_{ln}}{\lambda_n^{(0)} - \lambda_l^{(0)}} C_{nn}^{(1)} + \sum_{m \neq n} \frac{W_{lm} W_{mn}}{(\lambda_n^{(0)} - \lambda_l^{(0)})(\lambda_n^{(0)} - \lambda_m^{(0)})} - \frac{W_{ln} W_{nn}}{(\lambda_n^{(0)} - \lambda_l^{(0)})^2}.$$

We find that the $C_{nl}^{(2)}$ are not completely determined until $C_{nn}^{(1)}$ is found. Also, $C_{nn}^{(2)}$ remains undetermined. This is all we can get from the original eigenvalue equation considered within the second order.

We now turn to the questions of orthogonality and normalization. If we form, in general, the inner product of ψ_m and ψ_n as represented by the series $\psi_m = \sum_k \psi_m^{(k)}$, we obtain terms of different orders in the expression for (ψ_m, ψ_n) as follows:

zero order: $(\psi_m^{(0)}, \psi_n^{(0)})$;

first order: $(\psi_m^{(0)}, \psi_n^{(1)}) + (\psi_m^{(1)}, \psi_n^{(0)})$;

second order: $(\psi_m^{(0)}, \psi_n^{(2)}) + (\psi_m^{(1)}, \psi_n^{(1)}) + (\psi_m^{(2)}, \psi_n^{(0)})$,   etc.

Let us demand $(\psi_m, \psi_n) = \delta_{mn}$. Since the zero order already yields

$$(\psi_m^{(0)}, \psi_n^{(0)}) = \delta_{mn},$$

it follows that the terms of *any given order* must vanish identically, and it makes no difference whether $m \neq n$ or $m = n$. According to our expansions

$$\psi_n^{(1)} = \sum_m C_{nm}^{(1)} \psi_m^{(0)},$$

the first-order equation immediately yields

$$C_{nm}^{(1)} + C_{mn}^{(1)*} = 0 \qquad \text{(all } m, n).$$

If $m \neq n$, this relation is automatically satisfied; if $m = n$, we obtain $\text{Re } C_{nn}^{(1)} = 0$ as a condition.

In a similar fashion, the second-order equation requires

$$C_{nm}^{(2)} + C_{mn}^{(2)*} + \sum_l C_{ml}^{(1)*} C_{nl}^{(1)} = 0.$$

If we substitute our expressions for $C_{nm}^{(1)}$ and $C_{nm}^{(2)}$, it is possible to show that this relation is satisfied for $m \neq n$ *no matter what* $C_{nn}^{(1)}$ *happens to be.* For the case $m = n$, we obtain, however, the condition

$$\text{Re } C_{nn}^{(2)} = -\tfrac{1}{2} \sum_l |C_{nl}^{(1)}|^2.$$

As in the first-order theory (p. 656), we can argue that we could have used $e^{i\gamma}\psi_n^{(0)}$, instead of $\psi_n^{(0)}$, for the unperturbed eigenvector. We have

$$e^{i\gamma}\psi_n^{(0)} = \psi_n^{(0)} + i\gamma\psi_n^{(0)} - \frac{\gamma^2}{2}\psi_n^{(0)} + \cdots$$

It is evident that if we set $\gamma = \text{Im } C_{nn}^{(1)} + \text{Im } C_{nn}^{(2)}$, then we can incorporate the imaginary parts of $C_{nn}^{(1)}$ and $C_{nn}^{(2)}$ into the arbitrary phase factor $e^{i\gamma}$. This is equivalent to choosing $\text{Im } C_{nn}^{(1)} = \text{Im } C_{nn}^{(2)} = 0$ in the perturbational calculation.

Consequently, we may collect the results of the second-order theory into the following set of formulas:

$$\lambda_n^{(1)} = W_{nn}, \qquad C_{nn}^{(1)} = 0, \qquad C_{nm}^{(1)} = \frac{W_{mn}}{\lambda_n^{(0)} - \lambda_m^{(0)}} \qquad (m \neq n),$$

$$\lambda_n^{(2)} = \sum_{m \neq n} \frac{W_{nm}W_{mn}}{\lambda_n^{(0)} - \lambda_m^{(0)}}, \qquad C_{nn}^{(2)} = -\tfrac{1}{2}\sum_m |C_{nm}^{(1)}|^2,$$

$$C_{nm}^{(2)} = \sum_{l \neq n} \frac{W_{ml}W_{ln}}{(\lambda_n^{(0)} - \lambda_m^{(0)})(\lambda_n^{(0)} - \lambda_l^{(0)})} - \frac{W_{mn}W_{nn}}{(\lambda_n^{(0)} - \lambda_m^{(0)})^2} \qquad (m \neq n).$$

Remark. This type of analysis can be carried out for higher orders. In practice, however, most calculations are confined to first and second orders. Apart from the computational complexities, the point is that if the second-order results are not sufficiently accurate, then the general validity (convergence) of the perturbational series (see the footnote on p. 658) is usually in doubt.

Example. *Perturbational Treatment of Morse potential.* Consider a molecule made up of two atoms with masses M_1 and M_2. Under certain circumstances* such a molecule can be treated as a system of two particles moving under the influence of interatomic forces. Moreover, this so-called two-body problem is reducible† to the motion of a single particle of reduced mass, $M = M_1M_2/(M_1 + M_2)$, moving in the field of some potential $U(\mathbf{r})$. Consequently, the stationary states (see p. 471) of the molecule are described by the Schrödinger equation

$$-\frac{\hbar^2}{2M}\nabla^2\psi(\mathbf{r}) + U(\mathbf{r})\psi(\mathbf{r}) = E\psi(\mathbf{r}).$$

---

* Namely, if the electronic "orbits" in each atom are little affected by the motion of the nuclei and an atom moves "as a whole."

† Consult, e.g., Schiff, *Quantum Mechanics*, Chapter 4, Section 16.

It has been proposed by Morse* that for a variety of diatomic molecules the potential function can be represented by the formula

$$U(\mathbf{r}) = U(r) = U_0[e^{-2(r-r_0)/a} - 2e^{-(r-r_0)/a}],$$

where $r = |\mathbf{r}|$ and U_0, a, and r_0 are constants. This function is represented in Fig. 15.3.

We shall confine ourselves to one-dimensional motion corresponding to pure vibration of the molecule, and, for convenience, transfer the origin in Fig. 15.3 to the "bottom" of the potential well.

$$\xi = r - r_0, \qquad V = U + U_0,$$

so that the Schrödinger equation now reads

$$-\frac{\hbar^2}{2M}\frac{d^2\psi(\xi)}{d\xi^2} + V(\xi)\psi(\xi) = E\psi(\xi),$$

with

$$V(\xi) = U_0[1 + e^{-2\xi/a} - 2e^{-\xi/a}].$$

Expand now $V(\xi)$ in powers of ξ:

$$V(\xi) = U_0\left(\frac{\xi^2}{a^2} - \frac{\xi^3}{a^3} + \frac{7}{12}\frac{\xi^4}{a^4} - \cdots\right).$$

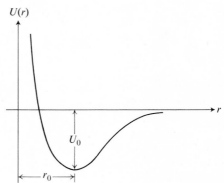

Figure 15.3

As a first approximation,† $V(\xi)$ can be replaced by the leading term $(u_0/a^2)\xi^2$, reducing the problem to that of a harmonic oscillator (see Section 11.3). More accurate results are obtained by including additional terms in the expansion. We shall confine ourselves to terms containing ξ^3 and ξ^4 and treat them as a perturbation of the harmonic oscillator problem. According to Section 11.3, it is convenient to set $\xi = \alpha x$ with $\alpha = (\hbar^2 a^2/2Mu_0)^{1/4}$ and reduce the equation to the form

$$\frac{d^2\psi}{dx^2} - x^2\psi + Ax^3\psi + Bx^4\psi = \lambda\psi,$$

where $A = \alpha/a$, $B = -\frac{7}{12}(\alpha^2/a^2)$, and $\lambda = -2E/\hbar\sqrt{2u_0/Ma^2}$.

The unperturbed eigenvalues are given by‡ $\lambda = -(2n + 1)$ corresponding to energies $E = \hbar\omega(n + \frac{1}{2})$, where $\omega = \sqrt{2u_0/Ma^2}$. The first-order perturbation theory yields the following correction to λ:

$$\lambda^{(1)} = (\psi_n, Ax^3\psi_n) + (\psi_n, Bx^4\psi_n),$$

---

* See, e.g., Schiff, *Quantum Mechanics*, Chapter 11, Section 40.

† In the classical picture, this corresponds to small displacements of the atoms from their equilibrium separation at $r = r_0$.

‡ We conform here to the notation of this chapter so that our λ differs in sign from that used in Chapter 11.

where ψ_n is the nth normalized eigenfunction of the harmonic oscillator. The inner products are now represented by integrals, for example,

$$(\psi_n, Ax^3\psi_n) = A\int_{-\infty}^{+\infty} \psi_n^*(x)x^3\psi_n(x)\,dx, \quad \text{etc.}$$

It now happens that $(\psi_n, Ax^3\psi_n)$ is identically zero, because x^3 is odd and $\psi_n^*\psi_n = \psi_n^2$ is even; the ψ_n are real in our case. Therefore, only the term $(\psi_n, Bx^4\psi_n)$ will yield a first-order correction to λ, and it will be proportional to α^2/a^2. However, the same factor α^2/a^2 would arise from the *second-order correction* due to the term Ax^3 and we cannot ignore it if we want to be consistent. This is an example where the second-order theory is mandatory.*

It should now be evident that our basic task is to evaluate the matrix elements

$$(\psi_m, x^3\psi_n) \equiv (X^3)_{mn}, \quad \text{and} \quad (\psi_m, x^4\psi_n) \equiv (X^4)_{mn}.$$

This can be accomplished in various ways. For instance, we may recall that (Section 11.3)

$$\psi_n(x) = \frac{e^{-x^2/2}H_n(x)}{(\sqrt{\pi}\,2^n n!)^{1/2}},$$

where $H_n(x)$ is the nth Hermite polynomial. The polynomials $H_n(x)$ satisfy the recursion formula

$$xH_n(x) = nH_{n-1}(x) + \tfrac{1}{2}H_{n+1}(x) \qquad (n \geq 1).$$

Multiple application of this formula readily yields†

$$x^3H_n = n(n-1)(n-2)H_{n-3} + \frac{3n^2}{2}H_{n-1} + \frac{3(n+1)}{4}H_{n+1} + \tfrac{1}{8}H_{n+3}.$$

In view of the orthogonality of the ψ_n, the matrix elements of x^3 are now obtained in a straightforward way; as an example, we obtain

$$(\psi_{n-3}, x^3\psi_n) = \int_{-\infty}^{+\infty} \frac{e^{-x^2/2}H_{n-3}(x)}{(\sqrt{\pi}\,2^{n-3}(n-3)!)^{1/2}}\;\frac{e^{-x^2/2}[n(n-1)(n-2)H_{n-3}(x)]}{(\sqrt{\pi}\,2^n n!)^{1/2}}\,dx$$
$$= \sqrt{n(n-1)(n-2)/8}\,,$$

by adjusting the constants and using $\int_{-\infty}^{+\infty} (\psi_{n-3})^2\,dx = 1$. The matrix elements $(X^4)_{mn}$ can be obtained in a similar fashion.

An alternative method is based on the fact that the matrix elements

$$(\psi_m, x\psi_n) \equiv (X)_{mn} = \int_{-\infty}^{+\infty} \psi_m^*(x)x\psi_n(x)\,dx$$

---

* This may be traced to the fact that the perturbation is not of the type $\mathcal{W} = \alpha\mathcal{W}'$, but rather $\mathcal{W} = \alpha\mathcal{W}' + \alpha^2\mathcal{W}''$ with α being a small parameter.

† See Problem 4 in Chapter 11. This formula can be used for $n = 0, 1, 2$ as well, with the usual convention of omitting terms containing $H_{-1}(x)$, $H_{-2}(x)$, $H_{-3}(x)$; compare with p. 345.

are nothing but the elements (or entries) of the matrix X, displayed on p. 481. The matrix elements $(X^3)_{mn}$ are nothing but the elements of the matrix X^3 obtained from matrix X according to the usual rules of matrix multiplication.

Still another procedure may be based on the algebra of operators $\mathcal{G}_+$ and $\mathcal{G}_-$ defined in Section 11.4. They have the properties

$$\mathcal{G}_+\psi_n = \sqrt{2(n+1)}\,\psi_{n+1}, \qquad \mathcal{G}_-\psi_n = \sqrt{2n}\,\psi_{n-1} \quad \text{(or zero vector, if } n = 0)$$

and are related to the operator $\mathfrak{X}$ by means of

$$\mathfrak{X} = \tfrac{1}{2}(\mathcal{G}_+ + \mathcal{G}_-).$$

We can now express $\mathfrak{X}^3$ in terms of $\mathcal{G}_+$ and $\mathcal{G}_-$:

$$\mathfrak{X}^3 = \tfrac{1}{8}(\mathcal{G}_+^3 + \mathcal{G}_+\mathcal{G}_-\mathcal{G}_+ + \mathcal{G}_-\mathcal{G}_+^2 + \mathcal{G}_-^2\mathcal{G}_+ + \mathcal{G}_+^2\mathcal{G}_- + \mathcal{G}_+\mathcal{G}_-^2 + \mathcal{G}_-\mathcal{G}_+\mathcal{G}_- + \mathcal{G}_-^3).$$

All matrix elements of $\mathfrak{X}^3$ follow from this expression by inspection. Suppose, for instance, that we want $(\psi_{n+1}, \mathfrak{X}^3\psi_n)$;* because of the orthogonality of the ψ_n, only the terms containing $\mathcal{G}_+$ twice and $\mathcal{G}_-$ once will contribute, yielding

$$\begin{aligned}(\psi_{n+1}, \mathfrak{X}^3\psi_n) &= \tfrac{1}{8}(\psi_{n+1}, \mathcal{G}_+\mathcal{G}_-\mathcal{G}_+\psi_n) + \tfrac{1}{8}(\psi_{n+1}, \mathcal{G}_-\mathcal{G}_+^2\psi_n) + \tfrac{1}{8}(\psi_{n+1}, \mathcal{G}_+^2\mathcal{G}_-\psi_n) \\ &= \tfrac{1}{8}[\sqrt{2(n+1)}]^3 + \tfrac{1}{8}\sqrt{2(n+1)}\,[\sqrt{2(n+2)}]^2 \\ &\qquad + \tfrac{1}{8}[\sqrt{2n}]^2\sqrt{2(n+1)} = \sqrt{9(n+1)^3/8}\,.\end{aligned}$$

In this fashion we also obtain

$$(\psi_{n+3}, \mathfrak{X}^3\psi_n) = \sqrt{(n+1)(n+2)(n+3)/8}\,, \qquad (\psi_{n-1}, \mathfrak{X}^3\psi_n) = \sqrt{9n^3/8}\,,$$
$$(\psi_{n-3}, \mathfrak{X}^3\psi_n) = \sqrt{n(n-1)(n-2)/8}\,.$$

These are the only nonvanishing elements of $\mathfrak{X}^3$. The elements of $\mathfrak{X}^4$ can be evaluated in an analogous way; we confine ourselves to the only one which we shall use:

$$(\psi_n, \mathfrak{X}^4\psi_n) = (X^4)_{nn} = \tfrac{3}{4}[1 + 2n(n+1)].$$

Let us now proceed to evaluate the corrections to eigenvalues. The term Ax^3 will yield a second-order correction equal to

$$A^2\left\{\frac{\tfrac{1}{8}(n+1)(n+2)(n+3)}{-(2n+1)+[2(n+3)+1]} + \frac{\tfrac{9}{8}(n+1)^3}{-(2n+1)+[2(n+1)+1]}\right.$$
$$\left. + \frac{\tfrac{9}{8}n^3}{-(2n+1)+[2(n-1)+1]} + \frac{\tfrac{1}{8}n(n-1)(n-2)}{-(2n+1)+[2(n-3)+1]}\right\},$$

displaying the origin of each term. After the necessary algebra, this reduces to

$$A^2\frac{30^2n + 30n + 11}{16},$$

---

* For consistency in notation, treat ψ_n as an abstract vector subject to the abstract operator $\mathfrak{X}^3$.

and should be combined with the first-order correction produced by Bx^4 which reads

$$B\tfrac{3}{4}(2n^2 + 2n + 1).$$

Using $B = -\tfrac{7}{12}A^2$ and simplifying, we obtain

$$A^2 \frac{30n^2 + 30n + 11}{16} + B\tfrac{3}{4}(2n^2 + 2n + 1) = A^2(n + \tfrac{1}{2})^2,$$

so that the corrected eigenvalue reads $\lambda = -(2n + 1) + A^2(n + \tfrac{1}{2})^2$, resulting in the energy levels of the molecule given by

$$E = \hbar\omega(n + \tfrac{1}{2}) - (1/4U_0)[\hbar\omega(n + \tfrac{1}{2})]^2.$$

15.6 THE CASE OF DEGENERATE EIGENVALUES

It is by no means uncommon that the treatment of the eigenproblem

$$(\mathfrak{IC} + \mathcal{W})\psi = \lambda\psi,$$

by perturbation methods gives rise to a fundamental difficulty. The unperturbed eigenproblem

$$\mathfrak{IC}\psi_n^{(0)} = \lambda_n^{(0)}\psi_n^{(0)}$$

exhibits degeneracy; that is, certain (or all) eigenvalues $\lambda_n^{(0)}$ are associated with more than one eigenvector. The difficulty stems from the fact that we do not know the unperturbed eigenvectors to which the perturbed ones reduce if the perturbation is reduced to zero. Since such information is vital in any perturbation theory, our first task is to look into this problem.

Let us concentrate our attention on some particular eigenvalue $\lambda_n^{(0)}$ and let us assume that it is g-fold degenerate, i.e., it possesses g linearly independent eigenvectors. Any linear combination of these is also an eigenvector so that we are dealing with a whole *g-dimensional subspace* of eigenvectors. In this subspace we can always select an orthonormal basis* composed of vectors

$$\psi_k \ (k = 1, 2, 3, \ldots, g).$$

Note that *all these vectors* belong to the eigenvalue $\lambda_n^{(0)}$, but we shall omit the label n to simplify the notation and write

$$\mathfrak{IC}\psi_k = \lambda^{(0)}\psi_k \qquad (k = 1, 2, 3, \ldots, g).$$

Now, if a perturbed eigenvalue λ reduces to $\lambda^{(0)}$, then its eigenvector φ must reduce to *some vector* in our subspace. As on p. 658, we write

$$\lambda = \lambda^{(0)} + \lambda^{(1)} + \lambda^{(2)} + \cdots, \qquad \varphi = \varphi^{(0)} + \varphi^{(1)} + \varphi^{(2)} + \cdots$$

_____

* See the Gram-Schmidt process on p. 447.

It is important to realize that $\varphi^{(0)}$ *need not be* one of the vectors ψ_k, but it *must be* some linear combination of them:

$$\varphi^{(0)} = \sum_{k=1}^{g} C_k \psi_k,$$

and it is the set of coefficients C_k that we are after.

As before, we write the exact perturbed equation

$$(\mathcal{H} + \mathcal{W}) \sum_{i=0}^{\infty} \varphi^{(i)} = \sum_{i=0}^{\infty} \lambda^{(i)} \sum_{j=0}^{\infty} \varphi^{(j)}$$

and separate the orders of perturbation:

zero order: $\mathcal{H}\varphi^{(0)} = \lambda^{(0)}\varphi^{(0)};$

first order: $\mathcal{H}\varphi^{(1)} + \mathcal{W}\varphi^{(0)} = \lambda^{(0)}\varphi^{(1)} + \lambda^{(1)}\varphi^{(0)};$

second order: $\mathcal{H}\varphi^{(2)} + \mathcal{W}\varphi^{(1)} = \lambda^{(0)}\varphi^{(2)} + \lambda^{(1)}\varphi^{(1)} + \lambda^{(2)}\varphi^{(0)},$ etc.

While the zero-order equation is automatically satisfied, we may gain some information from the first-order equation by forming inner products with vectors ψ_k. Whatever $\varphi^{(1)}$ may be, we have $(\psi_k, \mathcal{H}\varphi^{(1)}) = \lambda^{(0)}(\psi_k, \varphi^{(1)})$ by hermiticity of $\mathcal{H}$. Expressing now $\varphi^{(0)}$ as

$$\varphi^{(0)} = \sum_{l=1}^{g} C_l \psi_l,$$

we obtain the following equations, g in number, corresponding to each value of k:

$$\sum_{l=1}^{g} C_l(\psi_k, \mathcal{W}\psi_l) = \lambda^{(1)}C_k \qquad (k = 1, 2, 3, \ldots, g).$$

Since the quantities $W_{kl} = (\psi_k, \mathcal{W}\psi_l)$ can be evaluated, we are faced with a system of g algebraic equations with g unknowns $C_1, C_2, \ldots, C_g$. These equations are homogeneous and of "eigenvalue-type"; we display this explicitly:

$$
\begin{aligned}
(W_{11} - \lambda^{(1)})C_1 + \quad W_{12}C_2 \quad + \cdots + \quad W_{1g}C_g \quad &= 0 \\
W_{21}C_1 \quad + (W_{22} - \lambda^{(1)})C_2 + \cdots + \quad W_{2g}C_g \quad &= 0 \\
\vdots \qquad\qquad\qquad\qquad\qquad\qquad\quad \vdots \qquad\qquad & \\
W_{g1}C_1 \quad + \quad W_{g2}C_2 \quad + \cdots + (W_{gg} - \lambda^{(1)})C_g &= 0
\end{aligned}
$$

This set has nontrivial solutions (for the C_k) if the determinant vanishes, and this condition yields the *admissible values of* $\lambda^{(1)}$, which serve as eigenvalues for the above system. If these values of $\lambda^{(1)}$ are *all different*, then there are g of them and *each one* yields a set of C_k which can be made essentially unique* by normalization. If this is the case, we say that the *degeneracy is broken* in the first order.

The entire problem can now be reduced to the theory developed earlier. It is best to switch immediately to a *new basis* in our g-dimensional subspace of

---

* Except for a phase factor $e^{i\gamma}$ (see p. 656).

eigenvectors, with vectors $\varphi^{(0)}$ as basis vectors. We have exactly g such vectors and they are automatically orthogonal to each other, because $\mathcal{W}$ is a hermitian operator and the $g \times g$ matrix of elements W_{kl} is bound to be hermitian.* We shall denote these basis vectors by $\varphi_s^{(0)}$ with $s = 1, 2, 3, \ldots, g$.

The first-order corrections $\lambda_s^{(1)}$ to the original eigenvalue $\lambda^{(0)}$ have already been determined. To find the corrections $\varphi_s^{(1)}$ to the eigenvectors, we expand them as usual in terms of unperturbed eigenvectors. In this expansion it is convenient to separate the terms associated with our degenerate subspace from all others and write

$$\varphi_s^{(1)} = \sum_{p=1}^{g} C_{sp}^{(1)} \varphi_p^{(0)} + \sum_{\alpha} C_{s\alpha}^{(1)} \varphi_\alpha^{(0)}.$$

Here we use Greek letters to label all other unperturbed eigenvectors and eigenvalues except those associated with our particular degenerate eigenvalue. For instance, $\varphi_\alpha^{(0)}$ may be one of the new basis vectors selected, in the same fashion as for $\lambda^{(0)}$, for other degenerate eigenvalues or simply the original eigenvectors, unrelated to $\lambda^{(0)}$ (originally $\lambda_n^{(0)}$).

The reason for this separation is that one can show that the choice of $C_{sp}^{(1)}$-coefficients amounts to the choice of phase factors $e^{i\gamma_s}$ for the vectors $\varphi_s^{(0)}$, in analogy with the nondegenerate case. It is customary to select $C_{sp}^{(1)} = 0$ (all s, p).

The coefficients $C_{s\alpha}^{(1)}$ are uniquely defined from the first-order perturbation equation, by forming the inner product with $\varphi_\beta^{(0)}$ (note the Greek subscript). This yields

$$C_{s\beta}^{(1)}\lambda_\beta^{(0)} + W_{\beta s} = \lambda^{(0)} C_{s\beta}^{(1)}, \qquad \text{or} \qquad C_{s\beta}^{(1)} = W_{\beta s}/(\lambda^{(0)} - \lambda_\beta^{(0)}),$$

exactly as in the nondegenerate theory.

Remark. If some of the g roots determining $\lambda^{(1)}$ are not simple, then it is, in general, necessary to go to a higher-order perturbation theory to break the degeneracy. The interested reader is referred to special literature.

Example. Consider a square membrane which is slightly restrained by a spring attached at the point (ξ, ξ), as shown in Fig. 15.4.

Following the discussion in Section 8.8, it is not hard to see that the characteristic modes of vibration,

$$u(x, y; t) = \psi(x, y)e^{-i\omega t},$$

lead to the following equation for $\psi(x, y)$:

$$\frac{\partial^2 \psi}{\partial x^2} + \frac{\partial^2 \psi}{\partial y^2} + \epsilon \, \delta(x - \xi) \, \delta(y - \xi)\psi = \lambda\psi,$$

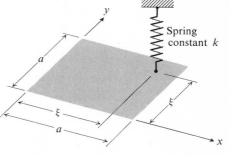

Figure 15.4

---

* Remember that we assume all the roots of the characteristic equation to be different.

where $\lambda = -\omega^2\mu/T$ and $\epsilon = -k/T$. If ϵ is small, the effect of the spring may be treated as a perturbation. The unperturbed normalized eigenfunctions are given by

$$\psi_{mn}^{(0)} = \frac{2}{a}\sin\frac{m\pi x}{a}\sin\frac{n\pi y}{a},$$

and are labeled by a *pair* of subscripts, namely (m, n), where m and n are positive integers. The unperturbed eigenvalues are

$$\lambda_{mn}^{(0)} = -(\pi^2/a^2)(m^2 + n^2).$$

We shall consider a case of twofold degeneracy exhibited by the modes $(2, 1)$ and $(1, 2)$ belonging to the same eigenvalue

$$\lambda_{21}^{(0)} = \lambda_{12}^{(0)} = \lambda^{(0)} = -5\pi^2/a^2.$$

We introduce the simplified notation

$$\psi_1(x, y) = \psi_{12}^{(0)} = \frac{2}{a}\sin\frac{\pi x}{a}\sin\frac{2\pi y}{a}, \qquad \psi_2(x, y) = \psi_{21}^{(0)} = \frac{2}{a}\sin\frac{2\pi x}{a}\sin\frac{\pi y}{a},$$

and seek the reduced eigenfunctions*

$$\varphi = C_1\psi_1 + C_2\psi_2.$$

We need the matrix elements

$$W_{kl} = (\psi_k, \mathcal{W}\psi_l) = \int_0^a\int_0^a \psi_k(x, y)\epsilon\,\delta(x - \xi)\,\delta(y - \xi)\psi_l(x, y)\,dx\,dy,$$

for $k, l = 1, 2$. All four of them happen to be the same:

$$\frac{4\epsilon}{a^2}\sin\frac{2\pi\xi}{a}\sin^2\frac{2\pi\xi}{a} = M.$$

While a special case can arise when $M = 0$ (if $\xi = a/2$), in general we shall have $M \neq 0$. The characteristic equation determining $\lambda^{(1)}$ reads

$$\det\begin{vmatrix} M - \lambda^{(1)} & M \\ M & M - \lambda^{(1)} \end{vmatrix} = 0,$$

and has the roots $\lambda^{(1)} = 0$ and $\lambda^{(1)} = 2M$.

The root $\lambda^{(1)} = 0$ yields the equation†

$$C_1 + C_2 = 0.$$

---

* Those to which the perturbed eigenfunctions reduce as $\epsilon \to 0$.

† Only one equation, since in our case $g = 2$. In general, a $g \times g$ homogeneous system reduces to $g - 1$ *independent* equations if all characteristic roots are different.

A normalized solution $C_1 = 1/\sqrt{2}$, $C_2 = -1/\sqrt{2}$ yields the first reduced eigenfunction:

$$\varphi_1(x, y) = \frac{\sqrt{2}}{a}\left(\sin\frac{\pi x}{a}\sin\frac{2\pi y}{a} - \sin\frac{2\pi x}{a}\sin\frac{\pi y}{a}\right).$$

Similarly, the second root, $\lambda^{(1)} = 2M$, yields

$$\varphi_2(x, y) = \frac{\sqrt{2}}{a}\left(\sin\frac{\pi x}{a}\sin\frac{2\pi y}{a} + \sin\frac{2\pi x}{a}\sin\frac{\pi y}{a}\right).$$

These two modes of vibration have already been mentioned in Section 8.8 as hybrid modes and their nodal lines are displayed in Fig. 8.14. It is worthwhile to observe that the nodal line of $\varphi_1(x, y)$ passes through the point of attachment of the spring and that the perturbed mode, which reduces to φ_1 has *no first-order correction* to the original eigenvalue ($\lambda^{(1)} = 0$ for φ_1). From the physical point of view, this is not surprising; if the unperturbed membrane were set to vibrate in this particular mode, it would continue to do so even if the spring were attached. Since the point of attachment remains at rest, the elastic forces in the spring do not appear and the spring *has no effect on the membrane*.

This observation leads us naturally to conjecture that the mode $\varphi_1(x, y)$ is not perturbed in *any order*. In other words, the mode $\varphi_1(x, y)$, along with the eigenvalue $\lambda^{(0)}$, is also an *exact* solution. This statement can, in fact, be proved quite rigorously.

As for the mode $\varphi_2(x, y)$, it will definitely be perturbed by the spring. The new frequency, in first order, will be given by

$$\omega^2 = -\frac{T}{\mu}(\lambda^{(0)} + \lambda^{(1)}) = \frac{5T\pi^2}{\mu a^2} - \frac{T}{\mu}2M,$$

and will be actually greater than the unperturbed frequency since $M < 0$ (because $\epsilon < 0$).

BIBLIOGRAPHY

SCHIFF, L. I., *Quantum Mechanics*. New York: McGraw-Hill Book Co., 1949.

FONG, PETER, *Elementary Quantum Mechanics*. Reading, Mass: Addison-Wesley Publishing Co., 1962.

PROBLEMS

1. Show that the Born approximation formula for the reflection coefficient on p. 648 yields the same value as that stated on p. 646. Show that this value agrees, within the second order in α, with the exact value (p. 628).

2. The linear density of an infinite stretched string is given by

$$\rho(x) = \rho_0(1 + \epsilon e^{-|x|}),$$

where ϵ is a small parameter ($\epsilon \ll 1$). A traveling wave given asymptotically by $e^{i(kx - \omega t)}$ is incident from "minus infinity" ($k^2 = \omega^2 \rho_0/T$). Calculate the backward-scattering cross section in the Born approximation.

3. Treat the eigenvalue problem

$$\frac{d^2 y}{dx^2} + \epsilon \sin \frac{\pi x}{L} y = \lambda y \qquad (0 \le x \le L),$$

$$y(0) = y(L) = 0,$$

where ϵ is a small parameter, by the first-order perturbation theory. Evaluate the corrections to unperturbed eigenvalues and display the approximate Fourier sine series for the eigenfunctions.

4. Consider the system of three coupled oscillators described in Problem 3, Chapter 10. However, assume that the spring constant k' of the third spring from the left in Fig. 10.13 is slightly different from k. This introduces the additional term

$$W = (\epsilon/2)(x_2 - x_3)^2,$$

with $\epsilon = k' - k$, in the potential energy. This term can be treated as a perturbation.

a) Express the perturbed potential energy $V = V_0 + W$ in terms of normal co-ordinates of the unperturbed problem; use the results of Problem 3, Chapter 10.
b) Display the matrix corresponding to V with respect to the basis supplied by the normal coordinates and read the first-order corrections to the eigenvalues.
c) Calculate the second-order corrections to the eigenvalues as well as the approximate normal coordinates within the second order of the perturbed problem.

5. A rectangular membrane $0 \le x \le a$, $0 \le y \le 2a$ is restrained by a weak spring (as in the Example of Section 15.6) at the point with coordinates $x = a/3$, $y = 2a/3$.

a) Show that the first-order correction to the frequency originally associated with the (1, 1)-normal mode can be calculated using the formula $\lambda^{(1)} = W_{nn}$.
b) Show that this procedure yields incorrect results when applied to the (2, 2)-mode. Explain the reason and perform the correct first-order calculation in this case.

6. Consider the circular membrane (Section 9.7) with a small mass m attached at the center.

a) Regarding m as a perturbation, show that within the first order the formulas of Sections 15.4 and 15.6 are applicable.
b) Show that the eigenvalues with degeneracy will remain unchanged, and that the techniques of Section 15.4 are sufficient.
c) Calculate the first-order corrections to eigenvalues and eigenvectors.

CHAPTER 16

TENSORS

16.1 INTRODUCTION

The intuitive physical definition of vectors from Chapter 1 has been considerably deepened by formal postulates presented in Chapter 10. Observe, however, that these postulates would, strictly speaking, refer to physical vectors of the same kind, say, either to forces or to displacements, but not to both at the same time. This is because only vectors of the same kind can be meaningfully added or subtracted.

Nevertheless, the formation of inner products like $dW = (\mathbf{F} \cdot d\mathbf{s})$ from vectors of different kinds is quite common in physics. It is not difficult to see why this is possible. The force $\mathbf{F}$ and the displacement $d\mathbf{s}$ have components which *transform* in the same fashion under rotation of coordinates, just as though they belonged to the same linear space. It can be said that we are dealing with a whole family of linear spaces, within which certain combinations of vectors are meaningful.

The question now arises: Which combinations of vectors are meaningful? Observe that the quantity $dW = (\mathbf{F} \cdot d\mathbf{s})$ is independent of the orientation of axes of an orthogonal cartesian system. In other words, it is *invariant under rotations*. Suppose that someone claimed that the infinitesimal work dW is given by the formula

$$dW = F_x F_y F_z \, |d\mathbf{s}|.$$

Can such a formula be correct? This can only be answered by experiment, but one thing is certain: The formula can hold only in some particular coordinate systems, and not in general. Relations of this type are, to say the least, inconvenient in physics, because their form must be changed in the transition from one coordinate system to another.*

There is a widespread belief among modern physicists that the fundamental equations of physics should possess the same form in all coordinate systems contemplated within the physical context of a given theory. This view was advanced by Einstein, in particular, and has led to very fruitful developments in the theory of relativity and elsewhere. As an illustration, we consider such equations as Newton's second law, $\mathbf{F} = m\mathbf{a}$, the equation of continuity, div $\mathbf{J} = -\partial\rho/\partial t$, or Maxwell's equations. While not all of them deal with invariants, they still have the same form in all orthogonal cartesian systems. For instance, $\mathbf{F} = m\mathbf{a}$ is

---

* It is tacitly assumed that dW is indeed a scalar.

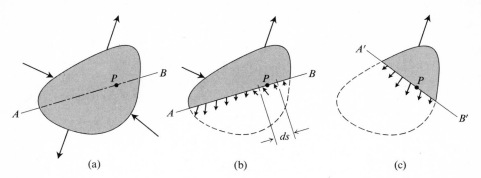

Figure 16.1

equivalent to three equations:

$$F_x = ma_x, \qquad F_y = ma_y, \qquad F_z = ma_z.$$

Despite the fact that both F_x and a_x will change if the coordinate axes are rotated, they will still be related by the same formula as above.

The study of this so-called *covariant* formulation* of physical laws is embodied in tensor analysis to which this chapter is devoted. It paves the way for answers to such questions as: (a) Are all physical laws expressible in terms of scalars and vectors only? (b) With respect to what transformations does a certain equation have covariant form? (c) How do we rewrite a given physical law if a wider class of transformations is introduced?

16.2 TWO-DIMENSIONAL STRESSES

Consider a solid body in equilibrium under the influence of a system of forces as in Fig. 16.1(a). For simplicity we shall first treat the somewhat hypothetical two-dimensional case. All forces are in the plane of the paper, and all effects normal to this plane are ignored.

We separate a portion of the body by a cut AB as in Fig. 16.1(b). This portion is also in equilibrium, but the originally internal forces along the cut AB now appear as external forces. These forces give rise to *stress* at each point P of the cut, defined as the force per unit length.† Note, however, that this quantity will depend not only on the location of point P, but also on the direction of the line AB, since for a different cut the pattern of internal forces will be different Fig. 16.1(c).

To reveal the nature of stress, we consider an infinitesimal element $dx\,dy$ of the body acted upon on all sides by internal forces. We take the resultants of all

---

* The term *form-invariant* or simply *invariant* is probably better, since the concept of covariance has another, more specialized meaning in tensor analysis (see p. 697).

† In three dimensions, the stress is measured as the force per unit area because the cut is then a plane.

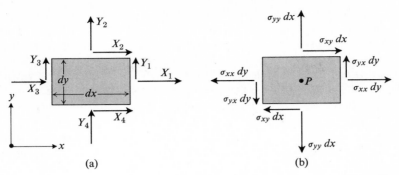

Figure 16.2

such forces on each side of the element and decompose them in the x- and y-directions to arrive at the situation illustrated in Fig. 16.2(a).

It is customary to define *normal stress* at each face by dividing the component of force normal to the face by the length of the face. In this fashion, we write $X_1 = \sigma_1\,dy$, $Y_2 = \sigma_2\,dx$, etc., where $\sigma_1, \sigma_2, \ldots$ are normal stresses on respective faces. Similarly, the tangential components Y_1, X_2, Y_3, and X_4 give rise to *shearing stresses* and can be written $Y_1 = \tau_1\,dy$, $X_2 = \tau_2\,dx$, etc.*

The stresses introduced so far are not independent of each other because the system of forces acting on the element $dx\,dy$ is assumed to be in equilibrium. For instance, the condition $\sum F_x = 0$ reads

$$\sigma_1\,dy + \sigma_3\,dy + \tau_2\,dx + \tau_4\,dx = 0,$$

and immediately leads to the statements $\sigma_3 = -\sigma_1$ and $\tau_4 = -\tau_2$, because dx and dy are arbitrary (as long as they are infinitesimal).

Remark. It may be noted that the above equation did not include the weight $\rho g\,dx\,dy$, where ρ is the mass per unit area of the element, or any other *body force* of the form $f\,dx\,dy$, where f is the force per unit area. Nevertheless, the above result is quite general because these terms will be of higher order in dx and dy, and can always be neglected if the element is sufficiently small.

The task of deducing $\sigma_4 = -\sigma_2$ and $\tau_3 = -\tau_1$ is not difficult either. Moreover, the equilibrium condition for torques then yields

$$(\tau_1\,dy)\,dx - (\tau_2\,dx)\,dy = 0,$$

establishing the result† $\tau_1 = \tau_2$. We see that there are only three independent

---

* The symbols σ and τ for normal and shearing stresses, respectively, are common in engineering texts.

† Rigorously speaking, this relation is true only if there are no body torques other than those due to body forces. It need not hold if there is an additional torque $t\,dx\,dy$, where t (torque per unit area) is not an infinitesimal quantity.

stresses, two normal and one shearing, and the pattern of forces can be revised as in Fig. 16.2(b), where the following notation is adopted: All types of stresses are denoted by σ_{ij}, where the first label i denotes the *direction of the stress*, namely, the direction of the original force, and the second label j denotes the *direction of the normal to the face* at which the stress is acting. Moreover, the directions of forces X_3, Y_3, X_4, and Y_4 have been reversed to avoid symbols like $\sigma_{x,-x}$ (originally σ_3) and to obtain a better physical picture. Note, however, that while both symbols σ_{xy} and σ_{yx} are used, we always have $\sigma_{xy} = \sigma_{yx}$.

It is now important to realize that if the dimensions of the element $dx\,dy$ are sufficiently small, then the stresses σ_{ij} must be the same for *any* such rectangle in the vicinity of point P (Fig. 16.2b), provided its sides are parallel to the x- and y-axes. This means that the σ_{ij} are essentially the stresses *at the point P* along the cuts (as in Fig. 16.1) in the x- and y-directions.

Let us now investigate what the stresses would be at the point P along a cut in an arbitrary direction, i.e., how the stresses transform under rotations.* For this purpose, let us split the element $dx\,dy$ diagonally to form a cut with the unit normal **n** making an angle ϕ with the x-axis, as shown in Fig. 16.3. Proceeding as usual, we can define the normal stress σ_{nn} and the shearing stress σ_{sn}. The equilibrium of forces in the x-direction reads

$$\sigma_{xx}\,dy + \sigma_{xy}\,dx = \sigma_{nn}\,ds\,\cos\phi + \sigma_{sn}\,ds\,\sin\phi,$$

and similarly, for the y-direction:

$$\sigma_{yy}\,dx + \sigma_{yx}\,dy = \sigma_{nn}\,ds\,\sin\phi - \sigma_{sn}\,ds\,\cos\phi.$$

We now use $dx = ds\,\sin\phi$, $dy = ds\,\cos\phi$, and solve for σ_{nn} and σ_{sn}:

$$\sigma_{nn} = \sigma_{xx}\cos^2\phi + \sigma_{xy}\sin\phi\cos\phi + \sigma_{yx}\sin\phi\cos\phi + \sigma_{yy}\sin^2\phi,$$
$$\sigma_{sn} = \sigma_{xx}\sin\phi\cos\phi + \sigma_{xy}\sin^2\phi - \sigma_{yx}\cos^2\phi - \sigma_{yy}\sin\phi\cos\phi.$$

To see the structure of these expressions clearly, we note that $\cos\phi = a_{nx}$ and $\sin\phi = a_{ny}$ are the directional cosines of the **n**-direction, while the directional cosines of the **s**-direction are $a_{sx} = \sin\phi$ and $a_{sy} = -\cos\phi$, so that

$$\sigma_{nn} = a_{nx}a_{nx}\sigma_{xx} + a_{nx}a_{ny}\sigma_{xy} + a_{ny}a_{nx}\sigma_{yx} + a_{ny}a_{ny}\sigma_{yy},$$
$$\sigma_{sn} = a_{sx}a_{nx}\sigma_{xx} + a_{sx}a_{ny}\sigma_{xy} + a_{sy}a_{nx}\sigma_{yx} + a_{sy}a_{ny}\sigma_{yy},$$

or, in compact form,

$$\sigma_{nn} = \sum_i \sum_j a_{ni}a_{nj}\sigma_{ij}, \qquad \sigma_{sn} = \sum_i \sum_j a_{si}a_{nj}\sigma_{ij},$$

where the dummy indices i, j take on specific labels x and y in all possible combinations.

---

* Observe that a rotation of the cut is equivalent to the rotation of the coordinate system.

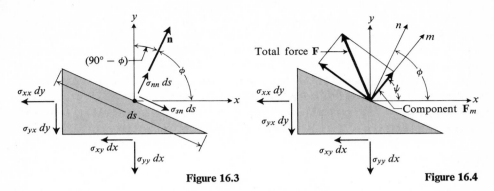

Figure 16.3   **Figure 16.4**

Note that the structure of expressions for the normal stress and the shearing stress are exactly the same and the following generalization is easily established. Let F_m be the component in the m-direction (direction defined by an arbitrary unit vector **m**) of the total force **F** acting on the slanted face with the normal **n**. Then the corresponding stress, which in general, is neither a normal nor a shearing stress, is given by the formula

$$\sigma_{mn} = \sum_i \sum_j a_{mi} a_{nj} \sigma_{ij} = a_{mx} a_{nx} \sigma_{xx} + a_{mx} a_{ny} \sigma_{xy} + a_{my} a_{nx} \sigma_{yx} + a_{my} a_{ny} \sigma_{yy}.$$

The force $\mathbf{F}_m$ associated with this stress by means of $F_m = \sigma_{mn} \, ds$ is represented in Fig. 16.4.

Exercise. Establish the above general formula for the stress in two dimensions.

An expression of the type

$$\sum_{i=1}^{N} \sum_{j=1}^{N} c_{ij} p_i q_j \qquad (i, j = 1, 2, \ldots, N)$$

is known as a *bilinear form* in the variables p_i and q_j; the coefficients c_{ij} are independent of the p_i and q_j.* We conclude that the stress σ_{mn} is a bilinear form in the directional cosines of two directions, namely, those defined by vectors **m** and **n**. In our case, N equals two, and we can, of course, attach index 1 to the x-direction and index 2 to the y-direction. It is now important to realize that for two fixed directions **m** and **n**, *the numerical value* of σ_{mn} must be independent of the original coordinate system, so long as it is a right-handed orthogonal cartesian one. This is evident on physical grounds and can also be verified algebraically.

Remark. The directional cosines a_{mi} and a_{nj} will, of course, be different in a new system of axes. However, so will be the set of original stresses σ_{xx}, σ_{xy}, etc. The new set of stresses $\sigma_{x'x'}$, $\sigma_{x'y'}$, etc., can be obtained from the general formula for σ_{mn} by treating **m** and **n** as the new axes. The bilinear form for σ_{mn} turns out to be numerically the same.†

---

* Compare with the quadratic form defined on p. 409.
† See p. 679 for a general theorem to that effect.

We conclude, therefore, that stress is an *invariant bilinear function of two dimensions* and this is our first example of quantities known as *tensors*. The four coefficients σ_{xx}, σ_{xy}, σ_{yx}, and σ_{yy} in the bilinear form are known as *components* of this tensor and may be viewed as constituting a *representation* of the tensor with respect to a given coordinate system.* They can be arranged in a 2×2 matrix which, in view of $\sigma_{xy} = \sigma_{yx}$, happens to be symmetric.

Note: Many authors define a tensor as the *set of its components*, along with the specification prescribing how this set transforms when the coordinate system is changed. This definition is equivalent to the one given above (see p. 679) and boils down to two different interpretations of the formula

$$\sigma_{mn} = \sum_i \sum_j \sigma_{ij} a_{mi} a_{nj}.$$

Indeed, if m and n are held fixed, then all a_{mi}, a_{nj} and σ_{ij} change, but σ_{mn} remains invariant. If m and n are variable parameters, then the directional cosines a_{mi} and a_{nj} *transform* σ_{ij} into σ_{mn}.

16.3 CARTESIAN TENSORS

The properties of two-dimensional stresses are repeated in three dimensions with only some minor changes. Let us consider a volume element $dx\,dy\,dz$ of a solid body, decompose the forces on its faces into x-, y-, and z-components (Fig. 16.5), and define the stresses σ_{xx}, σ_{xy}, etc., as forces per unit area. The conditions

$$\sum F_x = 0, \qquad \sum F_y = 0, \qquad \sum F_z = 0$$

yield, as before, the statement that the stresses on opposite faces must be equal and oppositely directed, leaving only nine basic components (only these are shown in Fig. 16.5). The three torque equations

$$\sum T_x = 0, \qquad \sum T_y = 0, \qquad \sum T_z = 0$$

yield the symmetry relations for shearing stresses:†

$$\sigma_{xy} = \sigma_{yx}, \qquad \sigma_{yz} = \sigma_{zy}, \qquad \sigma_{zx} = \sigma_{xz}.$$

Exercise. Produce the details leading to all the above statements.

We find that there are six independent components of stress in three dimensions: three normal stresses and three shearing stresses. To find a general expression for stress, we construct a pyramid-shaped body like the one shown in Fig. 16.6,

---

* Compare with the representation of a linear operator with respect to a given basis on p. 425.

† The torques can be calculated with respect to any point. The center of the parallelepiped is, perhaps, most convenient. Recall, however, the qualifying condition in the footnote on p. 673.

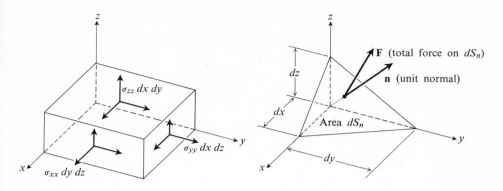

Figure 16.5   **Figure 16.6**

and let $\mathbf{F}$ be the total force acting on the slanted face with area dS_n. We decompose $\mathbf{F}$ into x-, y-, and z-components,

$$\mathbf{F} = F_x\mathbf{i} + F_y\mathbf{j} + F_z\mathbf{k},$$

and define three stresses on the slanted face by means of the formulas

$$F_x = \sigma_{xn}\, dS_n, \qquad F_y = \sigma_{yn}\, dS_n, \qquad F_z = \sigma_{zn}\, dS_n.$$

The condition of equilibrium, $\sum F_x = 0$, now yields*

$$\sigma_{xn}\, dS_n - \sigma_{xx}\tfrac{1}{2}\, dy\, dz - \sigma_{xy}\tfrac{1}{2}\, dz\, dx - \sigma_{xz}\tfrac{1}{2}\, dx\, dy = 0.$$

We use $\tfrac{1}{2}\, dy\, dz = dS_n \cos(\mathbf{i}, \mathbf{n}) = dS_n a_{nx}$, etc., for the projections of dS_n on the coordinate planes, to deduce

$$\sigma_{xn} = \sigma_{xx}a_{nx} + \sigma_{xy}a_{ny} + \sigma_{xz}a_{nz}.$$

Similarly, the conditions $\sum F_y = 0$ and $\sum F_z = 0$ yield†

$$\sigma_{yn} = \sigma_{yx}a_{nx} + \sigma_{yy}a_{ny} + \sigma_{yz}a_{nz}, \qquad \sigma_{zn} = \sigma_{zx}a_{nx} + \sigma_{zy}a_{ny} + \sigma_{zz}a_{nz}.$$

These are the *Cauchy relations*, describing stresses on the slanted face corresponding to the x-, y-, and z-directions. Consider now the projection F_m of the force $\mathbf{F}$ on an arbitrary $\mathbf{m}$-direction giving rise to a stress σ_{mn} such that $F_m = \sigma_{mn}\, dS_n$. Evidently, we can obtain σ_{mn} by projecting the components $F_i = \sigma_{in}\, dS_n$ ($i = x, y, z$) on the direction $\mathbf{m}$, adding them to obtain F_m,

$$F_m = \sigma_{mn}\, dS_n = \sum_i (\sigma_{in}\, dS_n)a_{mi},$$

---

* The stress in the x-direction on the face lying in the yz-plane is $-\sigma_{xx}$ because the normal to the face is in the $-x$-direction, and similarly for the other two minus signs in the equation.

† The torque equations are automatically satisfied.

and canceling the factor dS_n. In view of the Cauchy expressions for σ_{in}, this yields

$$\sigma_{mn} = \sum_i \sum_j \sigma_{ij} a_{nj} a_{mi} \quad (i, j = x, y, z),$$

and shows that σ_{mn} is again an invariant bilinear function of two directions, or a tensor. There are now nine components of the stress tensor, but, in view of the symmetry of shearing stresses, only six are independent. They can be arranged in a 3×3 symmetric matrix.

We have mentioned that a tensor can be alternatively defined as a bilinear invariant or as a set of quantities transforming according to a "bilinear law" (formula for σ_{mn}). We also know (p. 5) that a vector can be treated as a set of components transforming under rotations according to the formula

$$F_i' = \sum_j F_j a_{ij},$$

which is a linear transformation. It is easy to see that a vector can also be defined as an *invariant linear function of direction* if we express its *projection* F_n on an arbitrary fixed direction **n** in terms of its components F_i and the directional cosines a_{ni} of **n**,

$$F_n = \sum_i F_i a_{ni}.$$

If the coordinate system is rotated, both F_i and a_{ni} would change, but the value of F_n must evidently remain invariant.

Bearing in mind the above observation, we shall now formally introduce the concept of *cartesian tensor of rank r* by either of the following two definitions.

a) A cartesian tensor of rank r is an invariant multilinear function of r directions, i.e., an expression

$$T = \underbrace{\sum_i \sum_j \cdots \sum_n}_{r \text{ sums}} T_{ij\ldots n} \cdot \underbrace{\xi_i \eta_j \cdots \lambda_n}_{r \text{ factors}},$$
$$\phantom{T = \sum_i \sum_j \cdots \sum_n T_{ij\ldots n}} \underbrace{\phantom{T_{ij\ldots n}}}_{r \text{ indices}}$$

where $\xi_i, \eta_j, \ldots, \lambda_n$ are various components of *arbitrary* unit vectors, i.e., the directional cosines of directions $\xi, \eta, \ldots, \lambda$, and all summations are from 1 to N, where N is the dimension of the space. The quantities $T_{ij\ldots n}$ are called *components of the tensor** and form a representation with respect to the same basis as the quantities $\xi_i, \eta_j, \ldots, \lambda_n$.

b) A cartesian tensor of rank r is a set of N^r quantities $T_{ij\ldots n}$ which transform under rotations according to the equations

$$\underbrace{T_{ij\ldots n}'}_{r \text{ indices}} = \underbrace{\sum_p \sum_q \cdots \sum_t}_{r \text{ sums}} \underbrace{T_{pq\ldots t}}_{r \text{ indices}} \cdot \underbrace{a_{ip} a_{jq} \cdots a_{nt}}_{r \text{ factors}},$$

---

* In view of the statement on p. 676, and to conform to universal usage, we shall refer to the symbol $T_{ij\ldots n}$ as "the tensor." This is analogous to referring to the triple (F_1, F_2, F_3) as "the vector."

where $a_{ip}, a_{iq}, \ldots$ are the cosines of the angles between the new and the old coordinate axes.

According to these definitions, the stress tensor is a tensor of the second rank and a vector is a tensor of the first rank. It is also customary to consider a scalar as a tensor of zero rank.

Whenever either of these definitions is applied to the three-dimensional physical space, then the x-, y-, and z-directions will be, as a rule, identified by indices 1, 2, and 3, respectively (see p. 5). A similar convention will be used for tensors in the plane. Moreover, at this stage we shall introduce the so-called *summation convention** which is a universally adopted device to dispense with the summation symbol $\sum$ and facilitate the manipulations with tensors.

The Summation Convention. If a letter subscript *appears twice* in a product of quantities with subscripts, whether or not they are tensors, then a summation over the repeated index is automatically implied.

For instance, the expression $a_i b_{ij}$ will stand for the sum $a_1 b_{1j} + a_2 b_{2j} + a_3 b_{3j}$ (any j) in three-dimensional space. Also, in this notation the expressions used above to define tensors are written as

$$T = T_{ij\ldots n}\xi_i\eta_j \cdots \lambda_n \quad \text{and} \quad T'_{ij\ldots n} = T_{pq\ldots t}a_{ip}a_{jq} \cdots a_{nt},$$

respectively. Some authors extend this rule to the multiple appearance of an index, for example,

$$a_i b_i c_i d_i \equiv a_1 b_1 c_1 d_1 + a_2 b_2 c_2 d_2 + a_3 b_3 c_3 d_3.$$

Exercise. Write in a more familiar form the expressions $a_i b_i c_j d_j$ and $a_i b_j c_i d_j$ and convince yourself that they are not equal to each other or to $a_i b_i c_i d_i$.

Remark. Whenever it becomes necessary to talk about some single quantity of the form $a_k b_k$, rather than a sum of such quantities, it is proper to announce this fact explicitly. For instance, the statement "$a_k b_k = 1$ (no summation)" would apply to some particular value of k, like $a_2 b_2 = 1$, or, more commonly, to all values of k, namely, $a_1 b_1 = a_2 b_2 = a_3 b_3 = 1$, but it would not mean $a_1 b_1 + a_2 b_2 + a_3 b_3 = 1$.

Let us now return to the question of definition of tensors and demonstrate that the definitions (a) and (b) are equivalent. For simplicity, we shall do this on the example of a second-rank tensor.

The equivalence theorem. Definitions of a tensor given under (a) and (b) are equivalent.

Proof. Let the components of T_{ij} transform like

$$T'_{ij} = T_{pq}a_{ip}a_{jq}.$$

---

* Also known as the Einstein summation convention.

We know that the components of ξ and η transform according to

$$\xi_i' = \xi_k a_{ik}, \qquad \eta_j' = \eta_l a_{jl}.$$

Therefore

$$T_{ij}'\xi_i'\eta_j' = T_{pq}a_{ip}a_{jq}\xi_k a_{ik}\eta_l a_{jl}$$

$$= T_{pq}\xi_k\eta_l a_{ip}a_{ik}a_{jq}a_{jl}.$$

Now, by orthogonality of the cosines (p. 7), we have $a_{ip}a_{ik} = \delta_{pk}$ and $a_{jq}a_{jl} = \delta_{ql}$ so that

$$T_{ij}'\xi_i'\eta_j' = T_{pq}\xi_k\eta_l\delta_{pk}\delta_{ql} = T_{kl}\xi_k\eta_l,$$

which establishes that $T_{ij}\xi_i\eta_j$ is indeed an invariant.

Conversely, suppose that $T_{ij}'\xi_i'\eta_j' = T_{kl}\xi_k\eta_l$ for an arbitrary choice of unit vectors ξ and η. It is convenient to solve the equations $\xi_i' = \xi_k a_{ik}$ and $\eta_j' = \eta_l a_{jl}$ for ξ_k and η_l. In view of the orthogonality of the transformation matrix, we have

$$\xi_k = \xi_i' a_{ki}^T = \xi_i' a_{ik},$$

and, similarly,

$$\eta_l = \eta_j' a_{jl}.$$

Consequently,

$$T_{ij}'\xi_i'\eta_j' = T_{kl}a_{ik}a_{jl}\xi_i'\eta_j'.$$

Since this must be true for *arbitrary* ξ and η, we are free to choose ξ in, say, the x'-direction and η in the y'-direction. Then only the term with $i = 1$ and $j = 2$ will survive on either side, and the relation becomes

$$T_{12}' = T_{kl}a_{1k}a_{2l},$$

that is, T_{12} transforms as in definition (b). Evidently, identical reasoning can be used for any other pair of values of i and j, and the proof is complete. It is also not difficult to see that the proof of the equivalence theorem for a tensor of arbitrary rank is essentially the same, except for a longer derivation.

Remarks

1. The advantage of the alternative definitions of a tensor is that certain theorems become almost self-evident if a suitable definition is used. This is particularly true of definition (a) because of the simplicity of the concept of an invariant.

2. It has been assumed that the coordinate systems used are always right-handed and the transformations of coordinates represent rotations. Hence, the tensors defined above may be called "tensors with respect to rotations." Observe, however, that the equivalence theorem needs only the fact that the matrix composed of a_{ij} is orthogonal. Consequently, it is equally possible to define "tensors with respect to all orthogonal transformations" (see the Remark on p. 8) and allow the use of left-handed systems as well. Certain distinctions caused by this choice are mentioned in the next section.

3. For the time being (until Section 16.7), the term "tensor" is synonymous with the term "cartesian tensor," defined in *orthogonal* cartesian coordinates. Later, the concept of a tensor will be extended to nonorthogonal cartesian and curvilinear coordinates in general.

16.4 ALGEBRA OF CARTESIAN TENSORS

Tensors possess much the same algebraic properties as vectors. For instance, it is not difficult to verify that a sum of two tensors of the same rank is also a tensor of the same rank. In fact, tensors of a given rank form a linear space, and linear combinations of such tensors can be formed.* In this connection, we may note the existence of a unique zero tensor of any given rank, all components of which are zero in all coordinate systems.

A set of N^2 quantities A_iB_j formed by components A_i and B_j of two vectors is known as the outer product of these vectors. Similarly, one can define an outer product of two tensors, say, P_{ij} and Q_{klm}, to be

$$R_{ijklm} = P_{ij}Q_{klm}.$$

In general, an outer product can be defined for any two sets of multilabeled quantities like X_{ijk} and Y_{lmn}, whether or not they are tensors.†

The outer product theorem. The outer product of a tensor of rank r and a tensor of rank s is a tensor of rank $r + s$.

Proof (using second-rank tensors as an example). Let $A_{ijkl} = B_{ij}C_{kl}$, where B_{ij} and C_{kl} are tensors; then

$$A'_{ijkl} = B'_{ij}C'_{kl} = B_{mn}a_{im}a_{jn}C_{pq}a_{kp}a_{lq} = A_{mnpq}a_{im}a_{jn}a_{kp}a_{lq},$$

which establishes A_{ijkl} as a fourth-rank tensor.‡

Example. The outer product of a unit vector ξ with itself, namely, the set of quantities $\xi_i\xi_j$, constitutes a second-rank tensor. It can be interpreted as the *projection operator* for projecting vectors onto the ξ-direction. Indeed, if a matrix P with elements $p_{ij} = \xi_i\xi_j$ is formed, then the column vector y given by $y = Px$ is readily verified to be the desired projection of the column vector x.

Another common operation with tensors, or any other multilabeled quantities for that matter, consists of setting two of the indices equal and summing over the repeated index. It is known as *contraction*, and the summation convention is extended to this process. For instance, the expression A_{iikl} means, in three dimensions,

$$A_{iikl} = A_{11kl} + A_{22kl} + A_{33kl},$$

and represents the contraction of A_{ijkl} over the first two indices.§

---

* In physics it is, of course, also necessary that the physical meanings and the physical units of such tensors be compatible.

† A set of, say, N^2 quantities X_{ij} may have transformation properties different from those prescribed for tensors. See p. 683 for examples.

‡ By definition (b) on p. 678.

§ Double and multiple contraction is also possible; for instance, from A_{ijkl} one may form A_{iikk}, A_{ijij}, and A_{ijji}.

The contraction theorem. Contraction of a tensor of rank r over a pair of its indices results in a tensor of rank $r - 2$.

Proof (using third rank tensors as an example). From $A'_{ijk} = A_{lmn}a_{il}a_{jm}a_{kn}$, it follows that

$$A'_{iik} = A_{lmn}a_{il}a_{im}a_{kn} = A_{lmn}\,\delta_{lm}a_{kn} = A_{lln}a_{kn}$$

as claimed.

Example. Contraction of a second-rank tensor A_{ij} results in the trace of the matrix A formed by the tensor components, $A_{ii} = \text{tr } A$.

If an outer product of two tensors of ranks r and s is formed and then contracted over a pair of indices *originally belonging to different tensors*, the resulting tensor of rank $r + s - 2$ is called an *inner product* of the original ones.* For instance, $A_{ij}B_{jk}$ is an inner product of tensors A_{il} and B_{mk} with respect to indices l and m. Except for the case $r = s = 1$, the dot product of two vectors, there is more than one inner product because different indices can be paired.

The quotient theorem. If the product, outer or inner, of a set of quantities $X_{ij\ldots n}$ with an *arbitrary* tensor $T_{pq\ldots}$ yields a nonzero tensor of appropriate rank, then $X_{ij\ldots n}$ must be components of a tensor.

Proof. For the outer product, we let $X_{ij}T_{kl} = Q_{ijkl}$, where T and Q are tensors. Then

$$X_{ij}\xi_i\eta_j \cdot \underbrace{T_{kl}\zeta_k\vartheta_l}_{\text{invariant}} = \underbrace{Q_{ijkl}\xi_i\eta_j\zeta_k\vartheta_l}_{\text{invariant}}.$$

Evidently, $X_{ij}\xi_i\eta_j$ is an invariant, as desired.

For the inner product, we let $X_{ij}T_{jk} = Q_{ik}$, where T and Q are tensors. Since T is an arbitrary tensor, we select $T_{jk} = \xi_j\eta_k$, where ξ_j and η_k are components of the unit vectors ξ and η. Multiplication by $\zeta_i\vartheta_k$ yields

$$X_{ij}\zeta_i\xi_j\eta_k\vartheta_k = \underbrace{Q_{ik}\zeta_i\vartheta_k}_{\text{invariant}},$$

again establishing that $X_{ij}\zeta_i\xi_j$ is an invariant. Similar arguments evidently hold for tensors of any rank.

Since second-rank tensors can be represented by matrices, one may ask whether various results of Chapter 10 can be used in tensor algebra. The answer to this question hinges on the following basic observation: A matrix is, in general, just an $N \times N$ array of numbers while the concept of a second-rank tensor implies *definite transformation properties*.

Given arbitrary N^2 numbers arranged in a matrix, we may consider them as components of a tensor in a given coordinate frame.† It means that we must

---

* This operation can be performed with any two multilabeled sets of quantities except that the product will not, in general, possess tensor character.

† This term, popular among physicists, will be used as a synonym for coordinate system.

transform these numbers according to tensor laws. However, if the matrix already presupposes some transformation law, then it may or may not be a tensor. Consider, for instance, the matrix

$$C = \{C_{ij}\} = \begin{vmatrix} y^2 & xy \\ xy & x^2 \end{vmatrix}$$

built from components of a vector $\mathbf{u} = x\mathbf{i} + y\mathbf{j}$ in a plane. If, as it seems logical, it is implied that after a rotation this matrix reads

$$\{C'_{ij}\} = \begin{vmatrix} y'^2 & x'y' \\ x'y' & x'^2 \end{vmatrix},$$

where x' and y' are the new coordinates of the vector $\mathbf{u}$,

$$x' = x \cos \theta + y \sin \theta, \qquad y' = -x \sin \theta + y \cos \theta,$$

then the matrix C *does not* represent a tensor. Using $x = x_1$ and $y = x_2$, we can quickly demonstrate this by forming a bilinear function

$$C_{ij}\xi_i\eta_j = x_2^2\xi_1\eta_1 + x_1x_2\xi_1\eta_2 + x_1x_2\xi_2\eta_1 + x_1^2\xi_2\eta_2.$$

Since ξ and η are arbitrary, we choose

$$\xi = \eta = \mathbf{u}/|\mathbf{u}|,$$

and deduce that

$$C_{ij}\xi_i\eta_j = 4x_1^2x_2^2/|\mathbf{u}|^2 = 4x^2y^2/(x^2 + y^2),$$

which is clearly not an invariant under rotations.

On the other hand, the matrix

$$\{B_{ij}\} = \begin{vmatrix} -xy & x^2 \\ -y^2 & xy \end{vmatrix}$$

does represent a tensor because the bilinear form

$$\begin{aligned} B_{ij}\xi_i\eta_j &= -x_1x_2\xi_1\eta_1 + x_1^2\xi_1\eta_2 - x_2^2\xi_2\eta_1 + x_1x_2\xi_2\eta_2 \\ &= x_1\xi_1(x_1\eta_2 - x_2\eta_1) + x_2\xi_2(x_1\eta_2 - x_2\eta_1) \\ &= (x_1\xi_1 + x_2\xi_2)(x_1\eta_2 - x_2\eta_1) = (\mathbf{u} \cdot \xi)[\mathbf{u} \times \eta] \end{aligned}$$

has been reduced to a rotational invariant.*

---

* Recall (p. 26) that the cross product in a plane is a scalar under rotations.

Suppose now that we are faced with a matrix representing a linear operator acting on vectors. If the vectors are rotated, the matrix undergoes a similarity transformation. Does such a matrix possess tensor character?

The answer is "yes." The transformation of vectors $x' = Ax$ (see Chapter 10)* reads, in tensor notation, $x'_i = a_{ij}x_j$; the transformation of a matrix P, representing an operator $\mathcal{P}$, under *orthogonal* transformations reads

$$P' = APA^T \qquad \text{or} \qquad P'_{ij} = a_{ik}P_{kl}a^T_{lj}.$$

However, $a^T_{lj} = a_{jl}$ so that

$$P'_{ij} = P_{kl}a_{ik}a_{jl},$$

that is, P transforms just as tensors should.†

This result allows us to transplant to tensor algebra a number of statements connected with similarity transformation. For instance, we conclude that if a second-rank tensor is symmetric or antisymmetric in one frame, then this property holds in all frames. This may, in turn, lead us to conjecture a similar property for tensors of arbitrary rank. The conjecture proves to be correct. For instance, suppose that $A_{ijk} = A_{jik}$ in some frame. Since we always have

$$A_{ijk}\xi_i\eta_j\zeta_k = A'_{ijk}\xi'_i\eta'_j\zeta'_k,$$

and (define $B_{ijk} \equiv A_{jik}$ if you wish)

$$A_{jik}\xi_i\eta_j\zeta_k = A'_{jik}\xi'_i\eta'_j\zeta'_k,$$

it follows that if the left-hand sides of these equations are equal, then the right-hand sides are equal as well. However, ξ, η, ζ are arbitrary unit vectors; therefore (as on p. 680) $A'_{jik} = A'_{ijk}$, as desired.

16.5 KRONECKER AND LEVI-CIVITA TENSORS. PSEUDOTENSORS

Consider the 3×3 unit matrix, which has Kronecker deltas as its elements. If it is viewed as the representation of a tensor in some frame, then the corresponding bilinear invariant

$$\delta_{ij}\xi_i\eta_j = \xi_i\eta_i = \cos(\xi, \eta)$$

is the cosine of the angle between the unit vectors ξ and η. Observe now that $\cos(\xi, \eta)$ will be represented by the expression $\xi'_i\eta'_i$ *in any other* orthogonal cartesian system, including the left-handed ones. This implies that the components of our tensor are unchanged when we switch to another orthogonal cartesian frame. This can be verified explicitly,

$$\delta'_{ij} = \delta_{kl}a_{ik}a_{jl} = a_{il}a_{jl} = \delta_{ij},$$

---

* We denote, however, by A the matrix known as T from p. 434 to conform more closely to the notation used in the present chapter.

† The reader may also note that since in the realm of tensors the quantity $y_iP_{ij}x_j$ is an invariant, the tensor P_{ij} must undergo a congruence transformation (p. 442), which, of course, reduces here to similarity transformation.

and also follows from the fact that the unit matrix is invariant under similarity transformation.

Remark. Tensors which have identical components in all frames are called *isotropic tensors*, and they are of great interest in physical applications. We have just demonstrated one such tensor which we may call the *Kronecker tensor* or *unit tensor*. Moreover, it is clear that any scalar multiple of the Kronecker tensor is also an isotropic tensor.

Observing that the Kronecker tensor is involved in the expression for the dot product of two vectors,

$$(\mathbf{x} \cdot \mathbf{y}) = \delta_{ij} x_i y_j,$$

it is logical to seek a similar representation for the cross product,

$$[\mathbf{x} \times \mathbf{y}] = (x_2 y_3 - x_3 y_2)\mathbf{u}_1 + (x_3 y_1 - x_1 y_3)\mathbf{u}_2 + (x_1 y_2 - x_2 y_1)\mathbf{u}_3,$$

where the unit vectors **i**, **j**, **k** are denoted by $\mathbf{u}_1$, $\mathbf{u}_2$, $\mathbf{u}_3$ for convenience.

A bit of reflection shows that if we define the so-called *Levi-Civita symbol* ϵ_{ijk} by means of

$$\epsilon_{ijk} = \begin{cases} +1 & \text{if } (ijk) \text{ is an even permutation* of } (123), \\ -1 & \text{if } (ijk) \text{ is an odd permutation of } (123), \\ 0 & \text{otherwise (some or all subscripts are equal),} \end{cases}$$

then the cross product can be compactly expressed by

$$[\mathbf{x} \times \mathbf{y}] = \epsilon_{ijk} \mathbf{u}_i x_j y_k.$$

Also observe that since the cross product can be expressed as a symbolic determinant,

$$[\mathbf{x} \times \mathbf{y}] = \det \begin{vmatrix} \mathbf{u}_1 & \mathbf{u}_2 & \mathbf{u}_3 \\ x_1 & x_2 & x_3 \\ y_1 & y_2 & y_3 \end{vmatrix},$$

it follows that the Levi-Civita symbol is related to the determinants. Indeed, it is evident that we can write†

$$\det \begin{vmatrix} a_1 & a_2 & a_3 \\ b_1 & b_2 & b_3 \\ c_1 & c_2 & c_3 \end{vmatrix} = \epsilon_{ijk} a_i b_j c_k.$$

---

* Even permutations of (123) are (123), (231), and (312), while odd permutations are (132), (321), and (213). For the general definition of even and odd permutations, consult e.g., Birkhoff and McLane, Chapter 6, Section 10.

† This also follows from the definition of the determinant. See, for instance, Birkhoff and McLane, Chapter 10, Section 1.

In this notation, the 3×3 determinant is interpreted as the triple product of its row vectors **a**, **b**, and **c**, and is equal to the volume of the parallelepiped formed by these vectors, except for the sign (plus for a right-handed triple, minus for a left-handed one).

Exercise. Three vectors are given:

$$\mathbf{a} = (3, -1, 1), \qquad \mathbf{b} = (1, 4, 2), \qquad \mathbf{c} = (-1, 0, 3).$$

Show which of the six possible arrangements into an "ordered triple" yield right-handed triples and left-handed triples, respectively.

Theorem. The 27 quantities ϵ_{ijk} are components of an isotropic tensor of third rank, known as the *Levi-Civita tensor*, provided that the transformation of coordinates is a *rotation*.

Proof. Let ξ, η, ζ be unit vectors forming a right-handed triple. The volume of the parallelepiped formed by these vectors is an invariant under rotations and, therefore, a tensor. However, this volume will be expressed by $\epsilon_{ijk}\xi_i\eta_j\zeta_k$ in *any* right-handed system.* Consequently, the Levi-Civita symbols form an isotropic tensor.

Suppose now that we consider an orthogonal transformation which changes a right-handed system into a left-handed one, or vice versa.† Then the quantity $\epsilon_{ijk}\xi_i\eta_j\zeta_k$ ceases to be an invariant; it changes sign. Consequently, it *ceases to be a tensor* with respect to general orthogonal transformations. A number of other rotational invariants will behave in this way, changing sign whenever the "handedness" of the coordinate system is reversed. Thus it is convenient to introduce the concept of so-called *pseudotensors;* this can again be done in two equivalent ways:

a') A cartesian pseudotensor of rank r is a multilinear function of r directions which transforms according to the law

$$P'_{ij\ldots n}\xi'_i\eta'_j \cdots \lambda'_n = (\det A)P_{ij\ldots n}\xi_i\eta_j \cdots \lambda_n,$$

where $\det A$ is the determinant of the transformation matrix (the matrix of a_{ij}).

b') A cartesian pseudotensor of rank r is a set of quantities (components of a pseudotensor) which transform according to the equations

$$P'_{ij\ldots n} = (\det A)P_{pq\ldots t}a_{ip}a_{jq} \cdots a_{nt}.$$

Since for real orthogonal matrices, $\det A$ can have only two values, $+1$ or -1, it follows that the difference between pseudotensors and tensors is, at most, only in the sign and disappears entirely in the case of rotations. Evidently, the Levi-Civita *symbol* becomes a representation of an isotropic pseudotensor of third

---

* Note that a right-handed triple becomes left-handed if the coordinate system changes its "handedness".

† Such orthogonal transformations are sometimes called *improper rotations*.

rank.*   It is customary to refer to pseudotensors of first and of zero ranks as pseudovectors and pseudoscalars, respectively.

Remark. A number of authors refer to ϵ_{ijk} as the Levi-Civita *tensor density* because pseudotensors are cartesian examples of the concept of tensor density in the general tensor theory (see Section 16.9).

The expression $\epsilon_{ijk}a_ib_jc_k$ represents technically a triple contraction of the pseudotensor ϵ_{ijk} with the tensor $v_{lmn} = a_lb_mc_n$. Many other useful formulas are related to contraction with the Levi-Civita pseudotensor. Perhaps the most widely used expression is $\epsilon_{ijk}\epsilon_{klm}$, which must be† a tensor of rank four.

Theorem. In three-dimensional space,

$$\epsilon_{ijk}\epsilon_{klm} = \delta_{il}\delta_{jm} - \delta_{im}\delta_{jl}.$$

Proof. The quantity $\epsilon_{ijk}\epsilon_{klm}$ (for some fixed k, no summation) is nonzero if and only if i, j, k are all different and k, l, m are all different. Therefore either $i = l$ and $j = m$, or $i = m$ and $j = l$. In the first case, $\epsilon_{ijk} = \epsilon_{klm}$ and whether $\epsilon_{ijk} = +1$ or $\epsilon_{ijk} = -1$, we always have $\epsilon_{ijk}\epsilon_{klm} = +1$ (no summation).   In the second case, $\epsilon_{ijk} = -\epsilon_{klm}$ because the interchange of two indices changes the sign of the value of ϵ_{ijk}. Consequently, $\epsilon_{ijk}\epsilon_{klm} = -1$ (no summation).

Now, if i, j, l, and m are fixed, and k runs through the values 1, 2, 3, then only one term in the sum is nonzero (as explained above), and hence the whole sum is either $+1$ or -1. This can be written as $\delta_{il}\delta_{jm} - \delta_{im}\delta_{jl}$ because this expression yields $+1$ for $i = l$, $j = m$, $i \neq j$, and -1 for $i = m$, $j = l$, $i \neq j$; if neither is the case, it yields zero.   The proof is complete.

Exercise. Verify that

$$\epsilon_{ijk}\epsilon_{lmn} = \delta_{il}\delta_{jm}\delta_{kn} + \delta_{im}\delta_{jn}\delta_{kl} + \delta_{in}\delta_{jl}\delta_{km} - \delta_{in}\delta_{jm}\delta_{kl} - \delta_{im}\delta_{jl}\delta_{kn} - \delta_{il}\delta_{jn}\delta_{km}.$$

16.6 DERIVATIVES OF TENSORS. STRAIN TENSOR AND HOOKE'S LAW

Tensor components may be differentiable functions of (a) coordinates, (b) parameters independent of coordinates, or (c) parameters related to coordinates. Case (b) is the simplest one and yields the following result.

Theorem 1. Differentiation of a tensor with respect to a parameter independent of coordinates results in a tensor of the same rank.

---

* We could still talk about a Levi-Civita tensor, but it would not be isotropic since its components would change sign under improper rotations. Components of a Levi-Civita pseudotensor *do not change sign*, exactly because of the compensating effect of det A.

† A product (outer or inner) of two pseudotensors is evidently a tensor.

Proof. Consider $A'_{ij}(t) = A_{kl}(t)a_{ik}a_{jl}$, where t is the parameter, for instance, time in nonrelativistic physics.* Since the a_{ij} are independent of t, we obtain

$$\frac{dA'_{ij}(t)}{dt} = \frac{dA_{kl}(t)}{dt} a_{ik}a_{jl}$$

as required.

It is instructive to emphasize that in this case the variation of the tensor $A_{ij}(t)$ (characterized by its derivative) may, in principle, be confined to a *single point* in space: the point with which the tensor is associated. In contrast to this, the partial derivatives of a tensor with respect to x, y, z imply the existence of a tensor field and demand the comparison of tensor components at *two different points* in space, say, (x, y, z) and $(x + dx, y + dy, z + dz)$. When the coordinate system is changed, the partial derivatives of new tensor components are taken with respect to new coordinates and case (a) involves the relationship between the new partials $\partial A'_{ij}/\partial x'_k$ and the old partials $\partial A_{ij}/\partial x_k$.

Theorem 2. Differentiation of a tensor field of rank r with respect to cartesian coordinates results in a tensor field of rank $r + 1$.

Proof. If a tensor is treated as a multilinear invariant [Definition (a) on p. 678], namely,

$$T(x_1, x_2, x_3) = T_{ij\ldots n}(x_1, x_2, x_3)\underbrace{\xi_i\eta_j\cdots\lambda_n}_{r\ \text{factors}},$$

then

$$\frac{\partial T}{\partial x_p}\mu_p = \frac{\partial T_{ij\ldots n}}{\partial x_p}\underbrace{\xi_i\eta_j\cdots\lambda_n\mu_p}_{r+1\ \text{factors}},$$

where μ_p are components of a unit vector $\boldsymbol{\mu}$. The left-hand side is the directional derivative of the function $T(x_1, x_2, x_3)$ in the $\boldsymbol{\mu}$-direction and is evidently an invariant.† Inspection of the right-hand side shows that it is a tensor of rank $r + 1$, as stated.

Remark. It may be instructive to produce an alternative proof, based on Definition (b) on p. 678. For instance, we let‡ $A'_{ij}(x'_1, x'_2, x'_3) = A_{kl}(x_1, x_2, x_3)a_{ik}a_{jl}$; then

$$\frac{\partial A'_{ij}}{\partial x'_m} = \frac{\partial A_{kl}}{\partial x'_m} a_{ik}a_{jl}.$$

Using the chain rule

$$\frac{\partial A_{kl}}{\partial x'_m} = \frac{\partial A_{kl}}{\partial x_n}\frac{\partial x_n}{\partial x'_m},$$

---

* In relativistic physics, time is treated as one of the coordinates in the so-called space-time continuum.

† If the coordinates are changed, then μ_p and $\partial T/\partial x_p$ change, but the quantity $\partial T/\partial s \equiv (\partial T/\partial x_p)\mu_p$ remains the same, as is clear from its geometrical meaning.

‡ When the quantities $A_{lm}(x_1, x_2, x_3)a_{il}a_{jm}$ are calculated, they give us nine new functions of x_1, x_2, x_3; we assume that these functions are rewritten in terms of x'_1, x'_2, x'_3 by setting $x_n = a_{mn}x'_m$, of course.

we observe that $\partial x_n / \partial x'_m = a_{mn}$ (because of $x'_m = a_{mn} x_n$ and $x_n = a^T_{nm} x'_m = a_{mn} x'_m$). Consequently,

$$\frac{\partial A'_{ij}}{\partial x'_m} = \frac{\partial A_{kl}}{\partial x_n} a_{ik} a_{jl} a_{mn}.$$

Note that it is crucial that the x_n are related to the x'_m by a *linear* transformation, i.e., that a_{mn} are constants.* Otherwise the theorem would fail (as it indeed does in the case of curvilinear coordinates).

With the help of Theorem 2 it is not difficult to treat case (c), where the differentiation is performed with respect to a parameter related to the coordinates. For instance, suppose that we have a curve in space, given by the parametric equations $x = x_1(s)$, $y = x_2(s)$, $z = x_3(s)$. Then the derivative of a tensor *along the curve* can be defined (the parameter s often represents the length of arc).

Theorem 3. If $x_i = x_i(s)$, then the derivative of a tensor of rank r with respect to s is another tensor of the same rank.

The proof is easily established using the chain rule, and is omitted.

It should come as no surprise that differentiation is one of the basic operations which relates various tensor fields used in physics. We shall illustrate this by discussing the concept of *strain* which arises in the mechanics of continuous media.

A solid body can be translated or rotated, in which case the distances between its points do not change. If, however, the distances between the points are subject to change, then we say that the body is deformed and exhibits strain. An elementary and somewhat vague definition of strain is

$$\text{strain} = \frac{\text{change in distance}}{\text{distance}}.$$

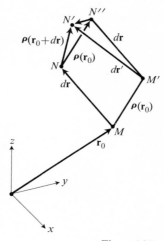

A more rigorous approach considers the mutual position of two points which are very close to each other.† Let point N (see **Fig. 16.7**) be given by a position vector $d\mathbf{r}$ with respect to point M before deformation. Their mutual distance is given by $|d\mathbf{r}|$. Suppose that after the deformation points M and N have moved into positions M' and N', respectively,‡ and the new relative position vector is $d\mathbf{r}'$.

Figure 16.7

---

* Similarly, in the first method of proof, it was necessary that $\xi_i, \eta_j, \ldots$ are constants (independent of x, y, z).

† This is necessary because strain will, in general, vary from point to point, and only over infinitesimal distances may it be considered constant.

‡ The displacements $\overline{MM'}$ and $\overline{NN'}$ need not be small, but this will not affect our arguments which concern only the difference between these displacements, which *must be small*.

Let us study the change in the relative position vector, namely, the vector $d\mathbf{r}' - d\mathbf{r}$. It is evidently equal to $d\boldsymbol{\rho} = \boldsymbol{\rho}(\mathbf{r}_0 + d\mathbf{r}) - \boldsymbol{\rho}(\mathbf{r}_0)$ (see Fig. 16.7), the difference between the displacement vectors (due to deformation) of points M and N. Whatever the nature of the vector function, it must be expressible, on physical grounds, by a Taylor series in the vicinity of point M. If

$$\boldsymbol{\rho}(\mathbf{r}) = \xi(\mathbf{r})\mathbf{i} + \eta(\mathbf{r})\mathbf{j} + \zeta(\mathbf{r})\mathbf{k},$$

then $\xi = \xi(x, y, z)$, $\eta = \eta(x, y, z)$, $\zeta = \zeta(x, y, z)$, and

$$\xi(x, y, z) = \xi(x_0, y_0, z_0) + \frac{\partial \xi}{\partial x}(x_0, y_0, z_0)\, dx$$

$$+ \frac{\partial \xi}{\partial y}(x_0, y_0, z_0)\, dy + \frac{\partial \xi}{\partial z}(x_0, y_0, z_0)\, dz + \cdots,$$

where x_0, y_0, z_0 are coordinates of point M. In cases of greatest practical interest* only the first-order terms are retained. After writing similar formulas for $\eta(x, y, z)$ and $\zeta(x, y, z)$ and setting $x = x_0 + dx$, $y = y_0 + dy$, $z = z_0 + dz$, we have

$$d\boldsymbol{\rho} = \boldsymbol{\rho}(\mathbf{r}_0 + d\mathbf{r}) - \boldsymbol{\rho}(\mathbf{r}_0) = d\xi\mathbf{i} + d\eta\mathbf{j} + d\zeta\mathbf{k},$$

where

$$d\xi = \xi(x, y, z) - \xi(x_0, y_0, z_0) = \frac{\partial \xi}{\partial x}dx + \frac{\partial \xi}{\partial y}dy + \frac{\partial \xi}{\partial z}dz, \quad \text{etc.}$$

Our result can be written in matrix form,

$$
\begin{bmatrix} d\xi \\ d\eta \\ d\zeta \end{bmatrix}
=
\begin{bmatrix}
\dfrac{\partial \xi}{\partial x} & \dfrac{\partial \xi}{\partial y} & \dfrac{\partial \xi}{\partial z} \\[2mm]
\dfrac{\partial \eta}{\partial x} & \dfrac{\partial \eta}{\partial y} & \dfrac{\partial \eta}{\partial z} \\[2mm]
\dfrac{\partial \zeta}{\partial x} & \dfrac{\partial \zeta}{\partial y} & \dfrac{\partial \zeta}{\partial z}
\end{bmatrix}
\cdot
\begin{bmatrix} dx \\ dy \\ dz \end{bmatrix},
$$

or in symbolic notation,†

$$d\boldsymbol{\rho} = T\, d\mathbf{r}.$$

The matrix T evidently represents a tensor (by Theorem 2 on differentiation) which we may call the *displacement tensor*. It connects the relative displacement $d\boldsymbol{\rho}$ with the relative position vector $d\mathbf{r}$. Let us now introduce the definition of

---

* For metals, glass, wood, etc., the deformations represent only a small fraction of undistorted distances and the above theory is quite accurate.

† For convenience, we identify $d\boldsymbol{\rho}$ and $d\mathbf{r}$ with their column-vector representations.

*strain in the direction d***r** by means of the formula

$$S(d\mathbf{r}) = \frac{|d\mathbf{r}'| - |d\mathbf{r}|}{|d\mathbf{r}|}.$$

Since we have assumed that $|d\boldsymbol{\rho}| = |d\mathbf{r}' - d\mathbf{r}|$ is much smaller than either $|d\mathbf{r}'|$ or $|d\mathbf{r}|$, we can replace the change in distance $|d\mathbf{r}'| - |d\mathbf{r}|$ by the projection of $d\boldsymbol{\rho}$ on $d\mathbf{r}$ (see Fig. 16.8), $(d\boldsymbol{\rho} \cdot d\mathbf{r})/|d\mathbf{r}|$. This yields

$$S(d\mathbf{r}) = \frac{(d\boldsymbol{\rho} \cdot d\mathbf{r})}{|d\mathbf{r}|^2} = \frac{(d\mathbf{r} \cdot T\, d\mathbf{r})}{|d\mathbf{r}|^2}.$$

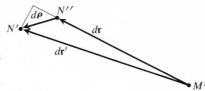

Explicitly, $(d\mathbf{r} \cdot T\, d\mathbf{r})$ is a quadratic form in dx, dy, dz:

$$(d\mathbf{r} \cdot T\, d\mathbf{r}) = \frac{\partial \xi}{\partial x} dx^2 + \frac{\partial \eta}{\partial y} dy^2 + \frac{\partial \zeta}{\partial z} dz^2$$

Figure 16.8

$$+ \left(\frac{\partial \xi}{\partial y} + \frac{\partial \eta}{\partial x}\right) dx\, dy + \left(\frac{\partial \eta}{\partial z} + \frac{\partial \zeta}{\partial y}\right) dy\, dz + \left(\frac{\partial \zeta}{\partial x} + \frac{\partial \xi}{\partial z}\right) dz\, dx.$$

When dividing by $|d\mathbf{r}|^2$, we observe that $dx/|d\mathbf{r}|$, $dy/|d\mathbf{r}|$ and $dz/|d\mathbf{r}|$ are nothing but the directional cosines of $d\mathbf{r}$. We denote them by u_x, u_y, u_z and obtain

$$S(d\mathbf{r}) = \frac{\partial \xi}{\partial x} u_x^2 + \frac{\partial \eta}{\partial y} u_y^2 + \frac{\partial \zeta}{\partial z} u_z^2 + \left(\frac{\partial \xi}{\partial y} + \frac{\partial \eta}{\partial x}\right) u_x u_y$$

$$+ \left(\frac{\partial \eta}{\partial z} + \frac{\partial \zeta}{\partial y}\right) u_y u_z + \left(\frac{\partial \zeta}{\partial x} + \frac{\partial \xi}{\partial z}\right) u_z u_x.$$

We find that strain is a quadratic function of a direction. We may associate it with a symmetric second-rank tensor,* given by the matrix

$$S = \begin{bmatrix} \dfrac{\partial \xi}{\partial x} & \dfrac{1}{2}\left(\dfrac{\partial \xi}{\partial y} + \dfrac{\partial \eta}{\partial x}\right) & \dfrac{1}{2}\left(\dfrac{\partial \xi}{\partial z} + \dfrac{\partial \zeta}{\partial x}\right) \\[2ex] \dfrac{1}{2}\left(\dfrac{\partial \eta}{\partial x} + \dfrac{\partial \xi}{\partial y}\right) & \dfrac{\partial \eta}{\partial y} & \dfrac{1}{2}\left(\dfrac{\partial \eta}{\partial z} + \dfrac{\partial \zeta}{\partial y}\right) \\[2ex] \dfrac{1}{2}\left(\dfrac{\partial \zeta}{\partial x} + \dfrac{\partial \xi}{\partial z}\right) & \dfrac{1}{2}\left(\dfrac{\partial \zeta}{\partial y} + \dfrac{\partial \eta}{\partial z}\right) & \dfrac{\partial \zeta}{\partial z} \end{bmatrix},$$

and is usually called the *strain tensor*. Evidently, S is just the symmetric part† of T.

---

* A quadratic function is a special case of bilinear function. The strain is evidently invariant under rotations because of the tensor character of its components and by virtue of its physical meaning.

† Every matrix can be uniquely decomposed into symmetric and antisymmetric parts (consult Problem 21 in Chapter 10).

Remark. The antisymmetric part of T, namely, the tensor $R = T - S$, does not contribute to strain. We write $d\rho = S \, d\mathbf{r} + R \, d\mathbf{r}$; since R is antisymmetric, we deduce that $(d\mathbf{r} \cdot R \, d\mathbf{r}) = 0$; in other words, $R \, d\mathbf{r}$ is normal to $d\mathbf{r}$. It may be shown that $R \, d\mathbf{r}$ represents an infinitesimal rotation of the $d\mathbf{r}$-vector.

A very instructive application of the tensor theory is the analysis of the relation between the strain tensor S and the stress tensor defined in Section 16.3. The statement that the strain is proportional to stress, known as *Hooke's Law*, is a one-dimensional simplification of the actual state of affairs and must be modified. It seems natural, though, to expect that the components σ_{ij} of the stress tensor are linearly related to the components S_{kl} of the strain tensor. For most solid materials and moderate stress, this conjecture is well supported by experiments.

The most general linear relationship between two second-rank tensors σ_{ij} and S_{kl} reads

$$\sigma_{ij} = \Lambda_{ijkl} S_{kl},$$

where Λ_{ijkl} is a fourth-rank tensor, known as the *elasticity tensor*. This relation may be appropriately called the *generalized Hooke's law*. At first glance it would appear that elastic properties of a solid are described by 81 constants, the number of components of a fourth-rank tensor. Actually, not all of these components are independent. Because of the symmetric nature of stress and strain tensors, we must obviously have $\Lambda_{jikl} = \Lambda_{ijkl}$ as well as $\Lambda_{ijlk} = \Lambda_{ijkl}$. It can also be shown* that an elastic tensor must possess an additional symmetry property, $\Lambda_{ijkl} = \Lambda_{klij}$. All these conditions result in the reduction of the number of independent components of Λ_{ijkl}, from 81 to 21, and this is the actual number of elastic constants in a general crystalline body.

Consider, however, a much more common type of a solid, namely, an *isotropic* body in which the elastic properties are the same in all directions.† In this case, the elastic tensor must have numerically the same components in *all* right-handed cartesian systems:

$$\Lambda'_{ijkl} = \Lambda_{ijkl}.$$

In other words, Λ_{ijkl} must be an isotropic tensor. The isotropy requirement reduces drastically the number of independent components of the elastic tensor, namely, from 81 to only 3, as will be shown in the following analysis.

Let us treat the elastic tensor as an invariant formed with four arbitrary unit vectors:

$$\Lambda = \Lambda_{ijkl} \xi_i \eta_j \zeta_k \vartheta_l.$$

If the components of Λ_{ijkl} are unchanged under all rotations, they are, in particular, unchanged under 180°-rotations about the coordinate axes. In these rotations one component of a vector remains the same while the other two change

---

* See, for instance, Brillouin, *Tensors in Mechanics and Elasticity*, Section 10.8.

† In a crystal, the strains depend not only on the stresses, but also on their orientation with respect to crystalline axes.

sign, for instance, $\xi_1 \rightarrow -\xi_1$, $\xi_2 \rightarrow -\xi_2$, $\xi_3 \rightarrow \xi_3$ for a 180°-rotation about the z-axis. This means that, for instance, a term like $\Lambda_{1232}\xi_1\eta_2\zeta_3\vartheta_2$ will go over into $-\Lambda'_{1232}\xi_1\eta_2\zeta_3\vartheta_2$. Since the unit vectors ξ, η, ζ, and ϑ are arbitrary, it is clear that *each term* in Λ must remain invariant, which implies $\Lambda'_{1232} = -\Lambda_{1232}$. It follows that Λ_{1232} must be zero. Applying 180°-rotations about all three axes, we conclude, in general, that the only nonzero components of Λ_{ijkl} can be those for which either all four indices are equal or for which there are two pairs of equal indices. This leaves four types of nonvanishing components:

$$1. \ \Lambda_{iiii}, \quad 2. \ \Lambda_{iijj}, \quad 3. \ \Lambda_{ijij}, \quad 4. \ \Lambda_{ijji}.$$

Now consider 90°-rotations. A 90°-rotation about the z-axis has the effect $\xi_1 \rightarrow \xi_2$, $\xi_2 \rightarrow -\xi_1$, $\xi_3 \rightarrow \xi_3$, and similarly for η, ζ, and ϑ. This leads to statements such as $\Lambda_{1111} = \Lambda_{2222}$, $\Lambda_{2233} = \Lambda_{1133}$, etc. Generalizing, we conclude that the components of each one of the above types must be equal among themselves. Consequently, the elastic tensor can be tentatively written in the form

$$\Lambda_{ijkl} = \lambda\delta_{ij}\delta_{kl} + \mu\delta_{ik}\delta_{jl} + \nu\delta_{il}\delta_{jk} + \rho\delta_{ijkl},$$

where λ, μ, ν, and ρ are constants and δ_{ijkl} is a generalized Kronecker symbol, equal to unity if all four indices are the same, and zero otherwise.

So far, it has been shown that Λ_{ijkl} is isotropic only under 180°- and 90°-rotations and it must be tested for arbitrary rotations. It is not difficult to verify that each of the first three terms in Λ_{ijkl} is an isotropic tensor in its own right, for instance,

$$(\lambda\delta_{ij}\delta_{kl})' = \lambda\delta_{pq}\delta_{rs}a_{ip}a_{jq}a_{kr}a_{ls}$$
$$= \lambda(a_{ip}a_{jp})(a_{kr}a_{lr}) = \lambda\delta_{ij}\delta_{kl}.$$

The last term, $\rho\delta_{ijkl}$, is, however, not an isotropic tensor, and this can be shown as follows. Since ξ, η, ζ, and ϑ are arbitrary, choose all of them to be equal. Then

$$\rho\delta_{ijkl}\xi_i\eta_j\zeta_k\vartheta_l = \rho(\xi_1^4 + \xi_2^4 + \xi_3^4).$$

Now consider an *infinitesimal* rotation about the z-axis by an angle ϵ. Within the first order in ϵ, we find that the vector ξ becomes

$$\xi'_1 \cong \xi_1 + \epsilon\xi_2, \quad \xi'_2 \cong -\epsilon\xi_1 + \xi_2, \quad \xi'_3 = \xi_3.$$

Solving for ξ_1, ξ_2, ξ_3, we obtain, within the first order in ϵ,

$$\rho(\xi_1^4 + \xi_2^4 + \xi_3^4) = \rho(\xi_1'^4 + \xi_2'^4 + \xi_3'^4 + 4\epsilon\xi_1'^3\xi_2' - 4\epsilon\xi_1'\xi_2'^3)$$
$$\neq \rho(\xi_1'^4 + \xi_2'^4 + \xi_3'^4),$$

which violates the isotropy requirement.

Note: This does not mean that components Λ_{1111}, Λ_{2222}, and Λ_{3333} must be zero; they still occur in the other three terms as special cases. However, they do not form an isotropic tensor on their own.

The above analysis of the elastic tensor was based on the isotropy properties and did not invoke the previously mentioned symmetry requirements. If the condition $\Lambda_{ijkl} = \Lambda_{jikl}$ is applied, then we find that the constants μ and ν must be equal. The other symmetries are readily verified to hold so that the final formula for the elastic tensor of an isotropic solid reads

$$\Lambda_{ijkl} = \lambda \delta_{ij}\delta_{kl} + 2\mu(\delta_{ik}\delta_{jl} + \delta_{il}\delta_{jk}).$$

Substituting this into the generalized Hooke's law, we obtain the relation

$$\sigma_{ij} = \lambda \delta_{ij}\Delta + 2\mu S_{ij},$$

where $\Delta = S_{kk} = S_{11} + S_{22} + S_{33}$ is the volume dilatation of the deformed solid. The constants λ and μ are known as *Lamé coefficients* and μ is also called the *modulus of rigidity*. There is no special name for λ.

Remark. The above relation can also be solved for S_{ij} as follows. Performing the contraction of the stress tensor by setting $i = j$, we obtain the invariant (the trace of σ_{ij})

$$\Sigma = \sigma_{ii} = 3\lambda\Delta + 2\mu S_{ii} = (3\lambda + 2\mu)\Delta.$$

Since Δ can now be expressed in terms of Σ, the original equation is readily solved to read

$$S_{ij} = \frac{1}{2\mu}\sigma_{ij} - \frac{\lambda}{3\lambda + 2\mu}\delta_{ij}\Sigma = \frac{1}{E}[(1 + \kappa)\sigma_{ij} - \kappa\delta_{ij}\Sigma],$$

where the constants

$$E = \frac{\mu(3\lambda + 2\mu)}{\lambda + \mu}, \quad \text{and} \quad \kappa = \frac{\lambda}{2(\lambda + \mu)}$$

are known as *Young's modulus* and the *Poisson ratio*, respectively.

As a second example of the tensor character of physical laws let us consider the question of covariance of Maxwell's equations, which read, in the Gaussian system of units,*

$$\operatorname{div} \mathbf{E} = 4\pi\rho, \quad \operatorname{div} \mathbf{H} = 0$$

$$\operatorname{curl} \mathbf{E} + \frac{1}{c}\cdot\frac{\partial \mathbf{H}}{\partial t} = 0, \quad \operatorname{curl} \mathbf{H} - \frac{1}{c}\cdot\frac{\partial \mathbf{E}}{\partial t} = \frac{4\pi}{c}\mathbf{J}.$$

These equations are usually supplemented by the expression for the Lorentz force density (force per unit volume)

$$\mathbf{f} = \rho\mathbf{E} + \frac{1}{c}[\mathbf{J} \times \mathbf{H}],$$

which represents the connection between the electromagnetic theory and the dynamics of charged matter.

---

* For the purpose of this discussion, the Gaussian system of units is more suitable than the MKSA system employed in Section 8.3.

All five equations given above are covariant with respect to rotations of the cartesian coordinate system, under the usual assumption that **E**, **H**, **J**, and **f** are vectors and ρ is a scalar. Indeed, div **E** can be written as $\partial E_i/\partial x_i$ and must be a scalar since it can be formed by contraction of the second-rank tensor $\partial E_i/\partial x_j$. Consequently, the equation div **E** $= 4\pi\rho$ has definite tensor transformation properties, that is, it is covariant.

Also, if **H** is a vector, then by Theorem 1 of Section 16.6 $\partial \mathbf{H}/\partial t$ also is a vector, since the time t is a scalar.* Related to this is the fact that the ith component of curl **E** can be represented, using the Levi-Civita symbol, by

$$(\text{curl } \mathbf{E})_i = \epsilon_{ijk}\frac{\partial E_k}{\partial x_j},$$

and the vector character of curl **E** is formally exhibited. This makes the equation

$$\text{curl } \mathbf{E} + \frac{1}{c}\cdot\frac{\partial \mathbf{H}}{\partial t} = 0$$

covaraint, since all terms transform like vectors. The covariant character of other equations is established in a similar fashion.

An important point arises if we consider the covariance with respect to all orthogonal transformations. Physically speaking, this implies the possibility of space reflections and, in general, changes from right-handed to left-handed systems and vice versa. If ρ is assumed to remain a scalar, equation div **E** $= 4\pi\rho$ shows that **E** remains a vector under this extended class of transformations. However, the quantity ϵ_{ijk} becomes now a pseudotensor, which implies, as is not hard to verify, that curl **E** is a pseudovector. The equation

$$\text{curl } \mathbf{E} + \frac{1}{c}\cdot\frac{\partial \mathbf{H}}{\partial t} = 0$$

then yields the conclusion that the magnetic field **H** cannot possibly be a true vector but must be a *pseudovector*.

Remark. The most interesting aspect of the covariance of Maxwell's equations is that it can be extended to Lorentz transformations in the special theory of relativity. Here the time variable t is combined with the three space coordinates to form a four-dimensional *space-time continuum* and the Lorentz transformations are such that they leave the quantity $s^2 = x^2 + y^2 + z^2 - c^2t^2$ invariant. This is equivalent to orthogonal transformations in a four-dimensional space with coordinates $x_1 = x$, $x_2 = y$, $x_3 = z$, $x_4 = ict$. The reader is referred to numerous texts on relativity,† where tensor theory finds one of its widest applications.

---

* In the special theory of relativity time is not considered a scalar, but even then it behaves like a scalar under *rotations in space*.

† For example, Lawden, *An Introduction to Tensor Calculus and Relativity*, and Aharoni, *The Special Theory of Relativity*.

16.7 TENSORS IN SKEW CARTESIAN FRAMES.
COVARIANT AND CONTRAVARIANT REPRESENTATIONS

In this section we shall extend the concept of tensors to skew cartesian coordinate systems. Since the use of skew frames is fairly limited, this is not done for the sake of practical considerations but rather, to introduce some new features relevant in the general tensor theory in which noncartesian coordinates are admitted.

Let us start with vectors. Suppose that we switch from an orthogonal cartesian basis given by the unit vectors $\mathbf{e}_i$ to a new basis given by the vectors $\mathbf{g}_i$. This new basis can be represented by a matrix G with the elements g_{ij}, and we may write, using the summation convention,*

$$\mathbf{g}_i = g_{ji}\mathbf{e}_j.$$

The new representation of a vector $\mathbf{x}$, say a column vector x', is related to the old column vector x by $x' = Tx$, which we can write as $x'_i = t_{ij}x_j$, where $T = G^{-1}$. Note that in tensor notation the statement $TG = I$ reads $t_{ij}g_{jk} = \delta_{ik}$.

Now consider the inner product $(\mathbf{y}, \mathbf{x})$ of two vectors $\mathbf{y}$ and $\mathbf{x}$. In the new representation it will no longer be given by the dot product $y'^T x'$, but rather by

$$(\mathbf{y}, \mathbf{x}) = y'^T G^T G x' = y'^T M x',$$

because $(\mathbf{y}, \mathbf{x}) = y^T x$ and $y^T = y'^T G^T$, while $x = Gx'$. In tensor notation this reads

$$(\mathbf{y}, \mathbf{x}) = y'_i g_{ji} g_{jk} x'_k = y'_i m_{ik} x'_k,$$

where m_{ik} are the elements of the metric matrix M (see p. 441). For instance, the length of a vector is now

$$\|\mathbf{x}\| = (x'^T M x)^{1/2}.$$

All these complications arise because the new basis vectors are, in general, neither unit vectors nor mutually orthogonal.†

Exercise. Verify that

$$
\left.
\begin{aligned}
&\text{a)} \qquad \|\mathbf{g}_i\| = \sqrt{m_{ii}} \\
&\text{b) } \cos(\mathbf{g}_i, \mathbf{g}_j) = \frac{m_{ij}}{\sqrt{m_{ii}}\,\sqrt{m_{jj}}}
\end{aligned}
\right\} \text{ (no summation).}
$$

It is not difficult to see that, within the framework of skew systems, which includes, of course, the orthogonal systems as well, we can define *tensors of the first rank* as quantities which transform according to the law

$$A'_i = A_j t_{ij},$$

---

* See p. 433; recall that we have adopted a notation in which the new basis vectors are represented by the *columns* of matrix G.

† The transformation matrix G may be an arbitrary nonsingular matrix.

where t_{ij} form the transformation matrix (as defined on p. 434) from one basis to another. This is the generalization of Definition (b) on p. 678, the difference being that t_{ij} do not represent cosines of angles any longer. Observe, however, that Definition (a) will need a more drastic modification since the construction of invariants is now more complicated. For instance, the contracted product $A'_iB'_i$ of two tensors of the first rank (vectors) is not an invariant; to obtain an invariant we should construct

$$A'_i m'_{ij} B'_j,$$

where $m'_{ij} = g_{ik}m_{kl}g_{lj}$. In other words, we must also transform the metric as we go along (by congruence transformation, as explained in Section 10.7).

Evidently, the metric matrix m_{ij} is a nuisance and a sensible thing to do is to stay with orthogonal cartesian frames. Unfortunately, this is a poor solution because it would deprive us of the use of curvilinear coordinates. It turns out, however, that there exists a simple device allowing us to incorporate the congruence transformation into the transformation of vectors themselves. To achieve this we associate with each n-tuple x, which is a representation of the vector $\mathbf{x}$, another n-tuple Mx which we shall denote by $\tilde{x}$. Then, for a given skew frame, we shall have

$$(\mathbf{y}, \mathbf{x}) = y^T \tilde{x}.$$

If we want to preserve this form for the inner product under all nonsingular linear transformations, then it is clear that when x transforms into x' by means of $x' = Tx$, then $\tilde{x}$ must transform into $\tilde{x}'$ by means of $\tilde{x}' = G^T\tilde{x}$, where $G = T^{-1}$. Indeed, then

$$y'^T\tilde{x}' = (Ty)^T(G^T\tilde{x}) = y^TT^TG^T\tilde{x} = y^T\tilde{x},$$

because $T^TG^T = (GT)^T = I$.

To have this convenience, we now need *two representations* for each vector $\mathbf{x}$, namely, two n-tuples x and $\tilde{x}$. We shall call the first one the *contravariant representation* and the second one the *covariant representation*. If x transforms according to $x'_i = x_i t_{ij}$, then $\tilde{x}$ must transform according to $\tilde{x}'_i = \tilde{x}_j g^T_{ij}$, where the matrix $G^T = \{g^T_{ij}\}$ is the transpose of the inverse of matrix $T = \{t_{ij}\}$. The covariant representation can be obtained at any time from the contravariant representation through the formula

$$\tilde{x}_i = m_{ij}x_j,$$

involving the metric matrix associated with a particular frame.

Remarks

1. The term covariant is related to the fact that the transformation law

$$\tilde{x}'_i = g^T_{ij}\tilde{x}_j = g_{ji}\tilde{x}_j$$

has the same appearance as the relation between the basis vectors*

$$\mathbf{g}_i = g_{ji}\mathbf{e}_j,$$

---

* We regard both $\mathbf{g}_i$ and $\mathbf{e}_j$ as belonging, in general, to skew bases.

so that the $\tilde{x}_i$ transform "in the same fashion" as the basis vectors. On the other hand, the x_i transform "in the opposite fashion" to basis vectors, namely, by an inverse transposed matrix.

2. The covariant representation has the following geometrical interpretation: Apart from the basis composed of $\mathbf{g}_i$ (with metric M), imagine another skew basis composed of vectors $\mathbf{h}_i$, which is related to the $\mathbf{g}_i$-basis by

$$(\mathbf{h}_i, \mathbf{g}_j) = \delta_{ij}.$$

We say that the h-basis and the g-basis are *reciprocal* to each other.* Then the covariant n-tuple with respect to the g-basis is the contravariant n-tuple with respect to the h-basis, and vice versa.

Exercise. Verify this statement; observe also that the h-basis has the metric M^{-1}.

3. Traditionally one speaks about covariant and contravariant *vectors* rather than *representations.* This is due to the fact that in the general tensor theory (see Section 16.8) certain quantities naturally transform covariantly or contravariantly and are classified accordingly. Also, this nomenclature may contribute to brevity of discussion and we shall use it whenever it is convenient.

On the basis of this discussion, it is not difficult to extend the definition of tensors of higher rank to skew cartesian systems. Before we do this, however, let us adopt a special kind of notation which is universally employed in tensor theory. First of all, we note that the coefficients t_{ij} happen to be equal to partial derivatives of new coordinates *of a given point*† with respect to the old ones, because from $x_i' = t_{ij}x_j$, it follows that

$$t_{ij} = \frac{\partial x_i'}{\partial x_j}.$$

Also, the inverse matrix g_{ij} is involved in the relationship $x_i = g_{ij}x_j'$ so that

$$g_{ij} = \frac{\partial x_i}{\partial x_j'}, \quad \text{and} \quad g_{ij}^T = \frac{\partial x_j}{\partial x_i'}.$$

Because of future convenience in the treatment of general tensors, we shall abandon the symbols t_{ij} and g_{ij}^T for matrices T and G^T and use exclusively the partial derivative notation.

As the second step, we shall also abandon the symbol $\sim$ to denote covariant components. Instead, we shall write covariant components in the normal fashion, using *subscripts* as indices. For instance, a covariant vector will, by definition, transform according to

$$A_i' = \frac{\partial x_j}{\partial x_i'} A_j.$$

---

* Note that while the inner product of $\mathbf{h}_i$ and $\mathbf{g}_i$ is unity, neither of these two vectors needs to be a unit vector nor do they need to be collinear.

† The triples (x_1, x_2, x_3) and (x_1', x_2', x_3') may be regarded as coordinates of a point (components of the position vector) in cartesian systems.

On the other hand, contravariant quantities will be labeled by *superscripts*.* Components of a contravariant vector will be written A^i and will transform according to

$$A'^i = \frac{\partial x'_i}{\partial x_j} A^j,$$

where the summation convention is, evidently, extended to cover superscripts as well.

Using this kind of notation, we can define a *covariant tensor* of rank r as the set of quantities transforming according to the scheme

$$T'_{ij\ldots n} = T_{pq\ldots t} \frac{\partial x_p}{\partial x'_i} \frac{\partial x_q}{\partial x'_j} \cdots \frac{\partial x_t}{\partial x'_n}.$$

Similarly, a *contravariant tensor* of rank r is defined by the transformation law

$$T'^{ij\ldots n} = T^{pq\ldots t} \frac{\partial x'_i}{\partial x_p} \frac{\partial x'_j}{\partial x_q} \cdots \frac{\partial x'_n}{\partial x_t}.$$

Beside these two definitions, a third type of tensor can be introduced with equal ease. Tensors of this type are known as *mixed tensors*, with some indices of covariant character and others of contravariant character. For instance, a third-rank mixed tensor with two covariant indices transforms according to

$$T'^k_{ij} = T^n_{lm} \frac{\partial x'_k}{\partial x_n} \frac{\partial x_l}{\partial x'_i} \frac{\partial x_m}{\partial x'_j}.$$

The properties of tensors in nonorthogonal cartesian frames are essentially those of general tensors, which will be discussed later. We shall, however, conclude this section with an observation regarding the metric matrix.

First of all, let us abandon the symbol m_{ij} for the metric matrix and adopt instead the symbol g_{ij} which is almost exclusively used in the entire literature on tensors.† Now, if the contravariant components of a vector, namely, those commonly used until now, undergo a linear transformation by means of a matrix $\partial x'_i/\partial x_j$ (i labels the rows, j labels the columns), then the metric matrix must undergo a congruence transformation by the inverse of this matrix (see Section 10.7). This latter matrix reads $\partial x_k/\partial x'_l$ (it has been previously denoted by g_{kl}). Consequently, in the new coordinate system the metric is given by

$$g'_{ij} = \left(\frac{\partial x_i}{\partial x'_k}\right)^T g_{kl} \left(\frac{\partial x_l}{\partial x'_j}\right) = g_{kl} \frac{\partial x_k}{\partial x'_i} \frac{\partial x_l}{\partial x'_j}.$$

---

* Because of this convention, a symbol such as A^2 will mean the second component of contravariant vector A^i and *not* the quantity "A squared." In order to designate the latter in tensor notation, one should use $(A)^2$.

† Recall that we have discontinued the use of the symbol g_{ij} to denote the elements of the G-matrix involved in transformations. From now on the symbol g_{ij} is strictly reserved for the metric.

This expression shows that the metric matrix is a *covariant tensor of the second rank*, as has been anticipated by placing the indices in subscript position.

16.8 GENERAL TENSORS

The extension of the principles of tensor analysis to arbitrary coordinate systems, curvilinear in general, requires certain modifications. Let us assume that the new coordinates are introduced in physical space by means of the equations

$$u_i = u_i(x_1, x_2, x_3) \qquad (i = 1, 2, 3),$$

and similarly, in a plane, $u_i = u_i(x_1, x_2)$ with $i = 1, 2$. The first difficulty we encounter is that neither u_i nor their differences can serve as components of vectors. They do not satisfy the linear-space postulates (Section 10.3). As an example, we consider the polar coordinates in a plane given by

$$r = \sqrt{x^2 + y^2},$$

$$\theta = \arctan (y/x).$$

As we proceed to add two position vectors (Fig. 16.9), we do not obtain $R = r_1 + r_2$, but rather

$$R = \sqrt{r_1^2 + r_2^2 - 2r_1r_2 \cos (\theta_2 - \theta_1)},$$

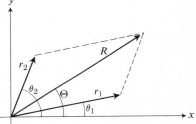

Figure 16.9

which shows that the coordinates are not additive. This is, of course, related to the fact that the transformation from (x, y) to (r, θ) is not linear.

We know, however (Section 1.9), that it is possible to set up, at each point in a plane,* a *local coordinate system*, with axes tangential to the curves of constant u_i, that is, $r = $ const and $\theta = $ const. Physical vectors like forces, velocities, etc., can be decomposed into components referred to these local systems.

In connection with this, we observe that the *differentials* of the functions u_i *can be treated* as components of the infinitesimal displacement vector $d\mathbf{s}$, just as the differentials dx_j of cartesian coordinates. The reason for this lies in the linear relationship between du_i and dx_j. For instance, for polar coordinates (Fig. 16.10),

$$dx = \cos \theta \, dr - r \sin \theta \, d\theta, \qquad dr = \cos \theta \, dx + \sin \theta \, dy,$$

$$dy = \sin \theta \, dr - r \cos \theta \, d\theta, \qquad d\theta = - \frac{\sin \theta}{r} dx + \frac{\cos \theta}{r} dy.$$

Such linear relationships hold in general. Moreover, the differentials should be considered as contravariant components of $d\mathbf{s}$ and labeled by superscripts, according to the convention adopted in Section 16.7. The reason for this is that

---

* We may omit the origin, which has a peculiar character in this respect.

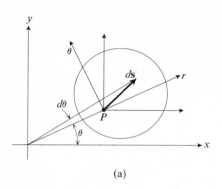

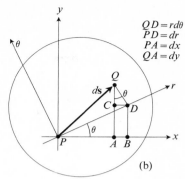

$$QD = rd\theta$$
$$PD = dr$$
$$PA = dx$$
$$QA = dy$$

(a)

(b)

Figure 16.10

they transform according to the formula (compare with p. 699)

$$du^i = \frac{\partial u_i}{\partial x_j} dx^j.$$

The fundamental difference from the case of skew cartesian coordinates is that the quantities $\partial u_i/\partial x_j$ are now *variable*, differing numerically from point to point. Nevertheless, *at a given point* in space it is possible to construct, as we shall do below, the entire edifice of tensor algebra similar to that for cartesian coordinates.

While the differentials du^i are typical quantities transforming as contravariant vectors, we have also a very familiar example of covariant vectors displayed by partial derivatives of a scalar function φ. Indeed, we have

$$\frac{\partial \varphi}{\partial u_i} = \frac{\partial \varphi}{\partial x_j} \frac{\partial x_j}{\partial u_i}$$

in conformity with the formula on p. 698.* Note that the inner product of the covariant vector $\partial \varphi/\partial u_i$ and the contravariant vector du^i is indeed an invariant (in any coordinate system):

$$\frac{\partial \varphi}{\partial u_i} du^i = \frac{\partial \varphi}{\partial x_j} dx^j = d\varphi.$$

It is rather trivial to verify that if further transformations from one coordinate system to another are performed, the differentials and the partial derivatives will follow the general rules†

$$du'^i = \frac{\partial u_i'}{\partial u_j} du^j, \qquad \frac{\partial \varphi}{\partial u_i'} = \frac{\partial u_j}{\partial u_i'} \frac{\partial \varphi}{\partial u_j},$$

---

* In this case, the usual notation $\partial \varphi/\partial u_i$ nicely fits the convention of labeling covariant vectors. Since the index i belongs to the denominator, it is *regarded as a subscript*.

† From now on the symbols x_i or x_i' will be used exclusively to denote orthogonal cartesian coordinates. The symbols u_i or u_i' will apply to arbitrary coordinates, cartesian or otherwise. Note that the subscripts do not refer to covariance since the coordinates are not vectors. Some authors write the transformation coefficients $\partial u^{i'}/\partial u^j$ instead of $\partial u_i'/\partial u_j$. Whatever the notation, these partials must be mixed tensors of rank two (see p. 699) with the i-index contravariant and the j-index covariant.

which represent examples of transformation of contravariant and covariant vectors, respectively, in general coordinate systems.

The next natural step is to extend the definition of tensors of arbitrary rank and character to all coordinate frames.

Definition. A general tensor of rank $r + s$, covariant in r indices and contra-variant in s indices, is a set of quantities which transform according to the formula

$$T'^{mn\cdots}_{ij\cdots} = T^{vw\cdots}_{pq\cdots} \underbrace{\frac{\partial u'_m}{\partial u_v} \frac{\partial u'_n}{\partial u_w} \cdots}_{s\ \text{factors}} \underbrace{\frac{\partial u_p}{\partial u'_i} \frac{\partial u_q}{\partial u'_j} \cdots}_{r\ \text{factors}}$$

under a transformation of coordinates from u_i to u'_j.

Remarks

1. Neither u_i nor u'_j need to be cartesian coordinates, and this definition is, in fact, not tied to any particular coordinate system—a very important point in tensor theory.

2. If $s = 0$, we have a purely covariant tensor; if $r = 0$, we have a purely contravariant tensor; if $s \neq 0$ and $r \neq 0$, we have a mixed tensor. For a zero-rank tensor (an invariant) there is, of course, no distinction between covariance and contravariance.

3. The alternative definition of a tensor, analogous to Definition (a) on p. 678 is still possible, but it is somewhat less lucid: the cartesian unit vectors ξ, η, . . . are not available now, and the invariant would have to be formed as a product of a tensor with an appropriate number of covariant and contravariant vectors which must be defined beforehand.

In Section 16.7, it was mentioned that covariant and contravariant components are supposed to be just two representations of the same vector, and the transition from one set to the other is achieved through the metric matrix. As a general rule, the metric is obtained from the length of an elementary displacement or, more precisely, from the inner product $(d\mathbf{s}, d\mathbf{s})$. In an orthogonal cartesian frame,

$$(d\mathbf{s}, d\mathbf{s}) = (dx)^2 + (dy)^2 + (dz)^2 = dx^i \, dx^i.$$

Let us express dx^i in terms of du^j,[*]

$$dx^i = \frac{\partial x_i}{\partial u_j} du^j.$$

Then

$$(d\mathbf{s}, d\mathbf{s}) = \frac{\partial x_i}{\partial u_j} du^j \frac{\partial x_i}{\partial u_k} du^k = g_{jk} \, du^j \, du^k.$$

We find that $(d\mathbf{s}, d\mathbf{s})$ is a quadratic form in the differentials du^j, and the metric

---

[*] Note that this is still a contravariant transformation. The x_i now serve as "primed coordinates" (see p. 701).

is given by the formula

$$g_{jk} = \frac{\partial x_i}{\partial u_j} \frac{\partial x_i}{\partial u_k},$$

where the x_i are some orthogonal cartesian coordinates.

Using the matrix g_{ij}, it is possible to switch from contravariant components A^j of a vector to its covariant components A_i by means of*

$$A_i = g_{ij} A^j.$$

This allows us, for instance, the introduction of covariant components of the vector $d\mathbf{s}$, namely, the quantities $g_{ij} du^j$, which should be for consistency denoted by du_i. Their use is, however, avoided because they do not transform as the familiar contravariant differentials do, and this may cause confusion.

Example. In polar coordinates in a plane, the contravariant components of $d\mathbf{s}$ are $du^1 = dr$ and $du^2 = d\theta$. The metric is

$$\begin{array}{cc} 1 & 0 \\ 0 & r^2 \end{array}$$

and, therefore, the covariant components of $d\mathbf{s}$ are

$$du_1 = 1\,dr + 0\,d\theta = dr, \qquad du_2 = 0\,dr + r^2\,d\theta = r^2\,d\theta.$$

Remark. In classical vector analysis (outside the tensor theory), the components of $d\mathbf{s}$ in polar coordinates are *neither du^1, du^2, nor du_1, du_2*, but rather dr and $r\,d\theta$ according to the formula

$$d\mathbf{s} = dr\mathbf{r}_0 + r\,d\theta\boldsymbol{\theta}_0,$$

where $\mathbf{r}_0$ and $\boldsymbol{\theta}_0$ are unit vectors in the r- and θ-directions (compare with p. 35). These quantities dr and $r\,d\theta$ are called the *physical components* of vector $d\mathbf{s}$ and *are not used* in tensor theory. What has actually been done is the multiplication of contravariant components (the familiar differentials) dr and $d\theta$ by scale factors h_r and h_θ (see p. 36) which are nothing but $\sqrt{g_{11}}$ and $\sqrt{g_{22}}$, respectively. The disadvantage of this adjustment of the metric to conform to the cartesian pattern† is that it is convenient only for curvilinear coordinates in which the matrix g_{ij} is diagonal. An even more serious objection is that this must be done separately for each particular coordinate system. The whole idea of tensor theory is, actually, to dispense with operations of this kind.

At this stage of the development of the tensor theory, it may be appropriate to make a profound observation about the metric. We can adopt the point of view that for a particular coordinate system, the set of quantities g_{ij}, variable from point

---

* The metric matrix g_{ij} is a second-rank covariant tensor. The proof at the end of Section 16.7 is applicable to general tensors.

† Namely, $(d\mathbf{s}, d\mathbf{s}) = (dr)^2 + (r\,d\theta)^2$, similar to $(d\mathbf{s}, d\mathbf{s}) = (dx)^2 + (dy)^2$.

to point, is *given*, and *need not* be determined with reference to some cartesian frame by means of the formula on p. 703. In this case two possibilities arise within a general space of N dimensions:

1. *It is possible* to find a transformation

$$x_i = x_i(u_1, u_2, \ldots, u_N) \qquad (i = 1, 2, \ldots, N),$$

such that in the x_i-coordinates the metric reduces, *at all points* of the space simultaneously, to the unit matrix and

$$(d\mathbf{s}, d\mathbf{s}) = (dx^1)^2 + (dx^2)^2 + \cdots + (dx^N)^2.$$

By definition, the x_i-coordinates then represent an orthogonal cartesian frame.

2. Conversely, *it may be impossible* to find such a transformation, which means that the N-dimensional space under consideration does not allow for the existence of cartesian coordinates.

So far, we have considered the spaces of the first kind, known as *euclidean spaces*. In particular, we have tacitly assumed that the three-dimensional physical space in which we live admits the existence of cartesian coordinates. However, the spaces of the second kind, called *noneuclidean spaces*, are by no means uncommon. One of the simplest examples is, perhaps, the surface of a sphere of radius R. If the well-known longitude ϕ and colatitude θ are introduced, then the elementary displacement is given by

$$(d\mathbf{s}, d\mathbf{s}) = R^2 \sin^2 \theta (d\phi)^2 + R^2 (d\theta)^2,$$

revealing the metric

$$\begin{array}{|cc|} \hline R^2 \sin^2 \theta & 0 \\[4pt] 0 & R^2 \\ \hline \end{array}.$$

It is intuitively clear, and can be rigorously demonstrated, that it is impossible to introduce a cartesian frame in this space; that is, it is impossible to find two functions $x = x(\phi, \theta)$ and $y = y(\phi, \theta)$ which satisfy the differential equations from p. 703, namely,

$$\left(\frac{\partial x}{\partial \phi}\right)^2 + \left(\frac{\partial y}{\partial \phi}\right)^2 = R^2 \sin^2 \theta, \qquad \frac{\partial x}{\partial \phi}\frac{\partial x}{\partial \theta} + \frac{\partial y}{\partial \phi}\frac{\partial y}{\partial \theta} = 0,$$
$$\left(\frac{\partial x}{\partial \theta}\right)^2 + \left(\frac{\partial y}{\partial \theta}\right)^2 = R^2.$$

The properties of tensors, as defined in this and the next section, apply equally well to euclidean and noneuclidean spaces. It may be fair to say that the development of tensor theory and its applications to physics owe their existence to the study of noneuclidean spaces. In fact, there is no guarantee that our physical space is actually euclidean.*   According to the general theory of relativity, our space is embedded in the four-dimensional space-time continuum, widely believed to be noneuclidean.

16.9 ALGEBRA OF GENERAL TENSORS. RELATIVE TENSORS

The majority of properties of cartesian tensors given in the preceding section have their counterpart in general tensor theory, but certain modifications must be introduced. These modifications are mostly due to the distinction between the covariant and the contravariant methods of transformation. As before, tensors of the same rank and character (matching numbers of covariant and contravariant indices) form a linear space. Their products conform to the following rules.

The outer product theorem. The outer product of two tensors is a tensor, its rank and character being determined in an obvious fashion.

For instance, if R_{ij}^{k} and S^{lm} are tensors, then $T_{ij}^{klm} = R_{ij}^{k}S^{lm}$ is also a tensor. The proof of this theorem follows closely the proof given on p. 681, except that the a_{ij} are replaced by $\partial u_i/\partial u_j'$ or by $\partial u_k'/\partial u_l$ according to the character of a given index (covariant or contravariant).

The contraction theorem. The contraction of a tensor of rank r over a pair of indices, *one covariant and the other contravariant*, results in a tensor of rank $r - 2$.

Exercise. Verify that if T_{ij}^{kl} is a tensor, so is $R_i^k = T_{ij}^{kj}$, by observing that for any two sets of coordinates,†

$$\frac{\partial u_m}{\partial u_j'} \frac{\partial u_j'}{\partial u_n} = \delta_{mn}.$$

Also, show why the quantities T_{il}^{kl} and T_{ij}^{kk} *are not* tensors.

The inner product theorem. An inner product of two tensors of ranks r and s is a tensor of rank $r + s - 2$, provided, of course, that the contraction is over a pair of indices one of which is covariant (a subscript) and the other is contravariant (a superscript).

The quotient theorem. If the product (outer or inner) of $X_{pq\ldots t}^{ij\ldots n}$ with an *arbitrary* tensor yields a nonzero tensor of appropriate rank and character, then the quantities $X_{pq\ldots t}^{ij\ldots n}$ are components of a tensor.

Since the proof on p. 682 was based on Definition (a) of cartesian tensors, an example of an alternative proof using the transformation properties of tensors

---

* Despite the fact that we can use cartesian frames without any apparent contradiction in all practical matters, such frames may not be valid for the universe as a whole.

† It may be more appropriate to write δ_n^m instead of δ_{mn}. See p. 707 for the distinction between these symbols.

is in order. Let, for instance, the equation $P^i_{jk}Q^l_i = R^l_{jk}$ be true in all coordinate systems and let Q^l_i and R^l_{jk} be tensors. As usual, let us denote by primes the result of a tensor-type transformation, so that in a new system we have

$$Q'^l_i = Q^q_p \frac{\partial u'_l}{\partial u_q} \frac{\partial u_p}{\partial u'_i}, \qquad R'^l_{jk} = R^s_{mn} \frac{\partial u'_l}{\partial u_s} \frac{\partial u_m}{\partial u'_j} \frac{\partial u_n}{\partial u'_k}.$$

Suppose now that the quantities P^i_{jk} transform according to some rule, not necessarily in the same manner as tensors, and become P''^i_{jk} in the new frame. Then the following relationship holds in the new system:

$$P''^i_{jk}Q'^l_i = R'^l_{jk}.$$

Let us now *define* the quantities P'^i_{jk} as though P^i_{jk} were indeed a tensor; that is, we *construct* a tensor from the quantities P^i_{jk}:

$$P'^i_{jk} = P^p_{mn} \frac{\partial u'_i}{\partial u_p} \frac{\partial u_m}{\partial u'_j} \frac{\partial u_n}{\partial u'_k}.$$

We shall show that actually $P''^i_{jk} = P'^i_{jk}$. Indeed, by the inner product theorem, the equation

$$P'^i_{jk}Q'^l_i = R'^l_{jk}$$

must also hold in the new system. Subtracting the appropriate equations, we obtain

$$(P''^i_{jk} - P'^i_{jk})Q'^l_i = 0.$$

This is true for all values of j, k, and l. Since Q'^l_i is arbitrary, because Q^l_i is arbitrary, we may choose, say, $Q'^l_2 = 1$ (all l) while $Q'^l_i = 0$ (all l and all $i \neq 2$); then, evidently,

$$P''^2_{jk} = P'^2_{jk} \qquad \text{(all } j, k).$$

However, this argument can be repeated for every value of i, establishing $P''^i_{jk} = P'^i_{jk}$ (all i, j, k), as required.

It was shown in Section 16.4 that the symmetric or antisymmetric nature of a cartesian tensor is a property independent of the coordinate system. This is also true for general tensors *provided*, however, that the indices to be interchanged are either both covariant or both contravariant. Consider, as an example, the tensor A^i_{jk} and let, say, $A^i_{jk} = -A^i_{kj}$. Then

$$A'^i_{jk} = \frac{\partial u'_i}{\partial u_l} \frac{\partial u_m}{\partial u'_j} \frac{\partial u_n}{\partial u'_k} A^l_{mn},$$

while

$$A'^i_{kj} = \frac{\partial u'_i}{\partial u_r} \frac{\partial u_p}{\partial u'_k} \frac{\partial u_q}{\partial u'_j} A^r_{pq}.$$

Now setting $A_{pq}^r = -A_{qp}^r$, we obtain

$$A_{kj}^{\prime i} = -\frac{\partial u_i'}{\partial u_r}\frac{\partial u_q}{\partial u_j'}\frac{\partial u_p}{\partial u_k'}A_{qp}^r.$$

The right-hand side is evidently equal to $-A_{jk}^{\prime i}$, as required. The proof in the case of symmetry is the same, and it should be obvious why it will not hold if a property such as $A_{jk}^i = -A_{ji}^k$ were considered.

The theory of general tensors admits also the definition of the Kronecker tensor. The set of Kronecker deltas may always be used as components of a tensor in *some particular frame*. Whether or not they will yield an isotropic tensor (as in cartesian frames) will depend on how they are allowed to transform. Evidently, we can introduce three such sets of Kronecker deltas and denote them by δ_{ij}, δ^{ij}, and δ_j^i, indicating the character of tensor transformation they will be defined to undergo. It turns out that only the third set will give rise to an isotropic tensor:

$$\delta_j^{\prime i} = \delta_n^m \frac{\partial u_i'}{\partial u_m}\frac{\partial u_n}{\partial u_j'} = \frac{\partial u_i'}{\partial u_m}\frac{\partial u_m}{\partial u_j'} = \frac{\partial u_i'}{\partial u_j'} = \delta_j^i.$$

This tensor represents the generalization of the Kronecker tensor to an arbitrary coordinate system. The symbols δ_{ij} and δ^{ij} also may give rise to tensors (we can force them to be tensors) but they are not isotropic, and for this reason it is preferable to avoid using the letter δ.

Remark. Contraction of a tensor is equivalent to taking an inner product with δ_j^i, for example, $R_{jlm}^{ik}\delta_j^i = R_{ilm}^{ik} = S_{lm}^k$. This will not work with δ_{ij} or δ^{ij} since the operation will not hold in all coordinate frames simultaneously (see p. 705).

The Kronecker tensor δ_j^i is intimately connected with the metric g_{ij} of the space, defined (p. 704) by the formula

$$(d\mathbf{s}, d\mathbf{s}) = g_{ij}\,du^i\,du^j,$$

where the left-hand side represents an invariant (a scalar). As has already been mentioned (p. 703), the metric tensor g_{ij} can be used to obtain the covariant components of a vector from the contravariant ones. This process can be extended to tensors of any rank and is commonly known as the process of *lowering of indices*. Tensors related by this operation are known as *associated tensors*, and it is customary to indicate the spot from which a certain index has been lowered by a dot, for example, $g_{ij}T_{lm}^{jk} = T_{lmi}^{\cdot k}$ or $g_{mn}T_s^{lnp} = T_{sm}^{l\cdot p}$. Since a tensor of rank r has more than one type of associated tensors, this notation is a very useful means of distinguishing between them.

It is natural to inquire how to perform the inverse process, namely, to *raise an index*. This is done by the so-called *associate metric tensor* g^{ij} which is represented by the matrix inverse to the matrix g_{ij} so that

$$g_{ij}g^{jk} = g^{kj}g_{ji} = \delta_i^k.$$

The tensor g^{ij} is contravariant in both indices; this may be shown as follows: Consider the equations $A_i = g_{ij}A^j$. If the A^j are arbitrary, so are the A_i (tacitly assuming g_{ij} to be nonsingular, of course). Solve for A^j to obtain $A^j = g^{jk}A_k$. Now apply the quotient theorem* to claim the tensor character of g^{jk}.

It is customary to define the determinant of the metric matrix by g so that the determinant of g^{ij} is $1/g$. Also, if we denote the cofactor of the matrix element g_{ij} by G_{ij}, then†

$$g^{ij} = G_{ij}/g.$$

As mentioned before, the tensor g^{ij} is used to raise the indices, for example, $A^i = g^{ij}A_j$, $T^{lk}_{.m} = g^{kn}T^l_{nm}$, etc.

By analogy with Kronecker deltas, the Levi-Civita symbols can also be used to generate various tensors. Consider, for instance, a third-rank contravariant tensor, denoted by ϵ^{ijk}, whose components coincide with the corresponding Levi-Civita symbols‡ in *some particular frame*. In a new frame our tensor will have the components

$$\epsilon'^{ijk} = \epsilon^{lmn}\frac{\partial u'_i}{\partial u_l}\frac{\partial u'_j}{\partial u_m}\frac{\partial u'_k}{\partial u_n}.$$

To find the numerical values of ϵ'^{ijk}, we let i, j, k be 1, 2, 3; then the right-hand side is equal to the determinant of the matrix

$$
\begin{vmatrix}
\dfrac{\partial u'_1}{\partial u_1} & \dfrac{\partial u'_1}{\partial u_2} & \dfrac{\partial u'_1}{\partial u_3} \\[2mm]
\dfrac{\partial u'_2}{\partial u_1} & \dfrac{\partial u'_2}{\partial u_2} & \dfrac{\partial u'_2}{\partial u_3} \\[2mm]
\dfrac{\partial u'_3}{\partial u_1} & \dfrac{\partial u'_3}{\partial u_2} & \dfrac{\partial u'_3}{\partial u_3}
\end{vmatrix}
$$

or the Jacobian of new coordinates with respect to the old ones. We shall denote this determinant by J. From a fundamental property of determinants (permutation of rows), it follows that ϵ'^{ijk} will have the value $+J$ for i, j, k forming an even permutation of 1, 2, 3. By antisymmetry properties of tensors, it further follows that ϵ'^{ijk} has the same structure as ϵ^{ijk} except that its components are $\pm J$ and 0, instead of ± 1 and 0. Observe that the Levi-Civita symbols can be retrieved in the new frame if we divide ϵ'^{ijk} by J or, equivalently, if we multiply them by the

---

* The quotient theorem cannot be applied directly to $g_{ij}g^{ik} = \delta^k_i$, because g_{ij} is not an arbitrary tensor.

† It may be noted that the quantities G_{ij} do not transform like a tensor and g is not an invariant (see p. 710).

‡ In other words, $\epsilon^{ijk} = \epsilon_{ijk}$ with the understanding, of course, that this is not a tensor relation and is valid for one frame only.

determinant D of the inverse matrix, namely, the Jacobian of old coordinates with respect to the new ones:

$$D = \det \begin{vmatrix} \dfrac{\partial u_1}{\partial u'_1} & \dfrac{\partial u_1}{\partial u'_2} & \dfrac{\partial u_1}{\partial u'_3} \\[2ex] \dfrac{\partial u_2}{\partial u'_1} & \dfrac{\partial u_2}{\partial u'_2} & \dfrac{\partial u_2}{\partial u'_3} \\[2ex] \dfrac{\partial u_3}{\partial u'_1} & \dfrac{\partial u_3}{\partial u'_2} & \dfrac{\partial u_3}{\partial u'_3} \end{vmatrix}.$$

Because of the necessity of multiplication by D, the set of Levi-Civita symbols as such does not constitute a tensor. To indicate the special character of these symbols, it is customary in tensor calculus to denote them by Gothic letters. We redefine the Levi-Civita symbols by

$$e^{ijk} = \left\{ \begin{array}{ll} +1, & \text{if } i, j, k \text{ is an even permutation of 1, 2, 3} \\ -1, & \text{if } i, j, k \text{ is an odd permutation of 1, 2, 3} \\ 0, & \text{otherwise} \end{array} \right\} \text{ valid in } all \text{ frames.}$$

The transformation law for e^{ijk} therefore reads

$$e'^{ijk} = D \frac{\partial u'_i}{\partial u_l} \frac{\partial u'_j}{\partial u_m} \frac{\partial u'_k}{\partial u_n} e^{lmn},$$

and ensures that $e'^{ijk} = e^{ijk}$. Quantities which transform according to this law are known as *tensor densities* and the set of Levi-Civita symbols can be regarded as an example of an isotropic tensor density (compare with p. 687). This idea can be immediately generalized to introduce a whole class of quantities known as *relative tensors* and denoted, as a rule, by Gothic letters.

Definition. A relative tensor of weight ω (as well as of rank r and appropriate character) is a set of quantities transforming according to the law

$$\mathfrak{T}'^{ij\ldots}_{lm\ldots} = D^{\omega} \frac{\partial u'_i}{\partial u_p} \frac{\partial u'_j}{\partial u_q} \ldots \frac{\partial u_s}{\partial u'_l} \frac{\partial u_t}{\partial u'_m} \ldots \mathfrak{T}^{pq\ldots}_{st\ldots},$$

where D^{ω} is the ωth power of $D = \det \{\partial u_i / \partial u'_j\}$, that is, the Jacobian

$$D = \frac{\partial(u_1, u_2, \ldots)}{\partial(u'_1, u'_2, \ldots)}$$

of the old coordinates with respect to the new ones.

Tensor densities are then relative tensors of weight $+1$. Relative tensors of weight -1 are known as *tensor capacities*. Ordinary (or *absolute*) tensors may be regarded as relative tensors of weight zero.

Relative tensors are by no means uncommon. For instance, the determinant of a covariant tensor of rank two happens to be a relative scalar (relative tensor of rank zero) of weight 2. Indeed, treating A'_{ij} as a product of three matrices (as on p. 699),

$$A'_{ij} = \frac{\partial u_m}{\partial u'_i} \frac{\partial u_n}{\partial u'_j} A_{mn} = \left(\frac{\partial u_i}{\partial u'_m}\right)^T (A_{mn}) \left(\frac{\partial u_n}{\partial u'_j}\right),$$

and using the relation

$$\det \left(\frac{\partial u_p}{\partial u'_q}\right) = \det \left(\frac{\partial u_p}{\partial u'_q}\right)^T = D,$$

we obtain

$$\det (A'_{ij}) = \det \left(\frac{\partial u_i}{\partial u'_m}\right)^T \det (A_{mn}) \det \left(\frac{\partial u_n}{\partial u'_j}\right) = D \det (A_{mn}) D = D^2 \det (A_{mn}),$$

as claimed. Similarly, it is not difficult to prove that the determinant of a second-rank contravariant tensor is a relative scalar of weight -2.

Relative tensors of the same weight, rank, and character form a linear space. The outer product of two relative tensors is another relative tensor of weight equal to the sum of weights of the factors. Contraction of a relative tensor leaves its weight unchanged. These and other properties are easily derived and the proofs will be omitted.

The Levi-Civita tensor density allows the extension of the concept of cross product of two vectors to arbitrary coordinate frames and to noneuclidean spaces. Given two covariant vectors A_j and B_k, we construct the quantities

$$\mathfrak{C}^i = \mathfrak{e}^{ijk} A_j B_k,$$

namely,

$$\mathfrak{C}^1 = A_2 B_3 - A_3 B_2, \qquad \mathfrak{C}^2 = A_3 B_1 - A_1 B_3,$$

and

$$\mathfrak{C}^3 = A_1 B_2 - A_2 B_1.$$

Evidently, the components $\mathfrak{C}^i$ reduce to the usual components of a cross product in cartesian systems, and may be treated as a generalization of this concept. Note, however, that $\mathfrak{C}^i$ is not a vector, but rather a vector density (relative tensor of rank 1 and weight 1). Also, it is contravariant, as opposed to A_j and B_k.

A cross product can also be formed from two contravariant vectors by means of the formula

$$\mathfrak{c}_i = \mathfrak{e}_{ijk} A^j B^k,$$

where $\mathfrak{e}_{ijk}$ is the so-called Levi-Civita tensor capacity, defined by the same formula as $\mathfrak{e}^{ijk}$, but formally transforming in a different way.

Exercise. Verify that $\mathfrak{e}_{ijk}$, transforming as a covariant tensor capacity, is indeed an isotropic relative tensor so that the definition is self-consistent. Deduce that $\mathfrak{c}_i$ is a covariant vector capacity.

Triple products of three covariant or contravariant vectors are also easily formed and given by

$$\mathfrak{p} = \mathfrak{e}^{ijk} A_i B_j C_k = \det \begin{vmatrix} A_1 & A_2 & A_3 \\ B_1 & B_2 & B_3 \\ C_1 & C_2 & C_3 \end{vmatrix}$$

and

$$\mathfrak{v} = \mathfrak{e}_{ijk} A^i B^j C^k = \det \begin{vmatrix} A^1 & A^2 & A^3 \\ B^1 & B^2 & B^3 \\ C^1 & C^2 & C^3 \end{vmatrix}$$

respectively. The first product is a scalar density and the second one is a scalar capacity.

Remark. From the last statement, it follows that the product of differentials

$$d\mathfrak{v} = du^1\, du^2\, du^3$$

used in volume integrals should be treated as a scalar capacity in tensor analysis. This fact is known from advanced calculus where the volume element given by $dx\, dy\, dz$ in a cartesian frame must be *replaced* by $J\, du^1\, du^2\, du^3 = J\, d\mathfrak{v}$ in curvilinear coordinates while the integrand is treated as a scalar. From the point of view of the theory of tensors, the integral

$$\iiint \mathfrak{p}\, d\mathfrak{v} = \iiint \mathfrak{p}(u_1, u_2, u_3)\, du^1\, du^2\, du^3$$

will be an invariant if $\mathfrak{p}$ is a scalar density (and not a scalar). The point is, of course, that the Jacobian J is treated as attached to $\mathfrak{p}$: whenever the coordinates are changed, $\mathfrak{p}$ is replaced by $\mathfrak{p}' = J\mathfrak{p}$ while $d\mathfrak{v}$ is replaced by $d\mathfrak{v}'$ (and *not* by $Jd\mathfrak{v}$). Since $d\mathfrak{v}' = (1/J)d\mathfrak{v}$, the product $\mathfrak{p}'d\mathfrak{v}'$ remains invariant. This observation, incidentally, explains the origin of the term tensor density.

16.10 THE COVARIANT DERIVATIVE

In Section 16.6, it was shown that partial derivatives of a cartesian tensor give rise to a tensor of higher rank. This property *fails to hold* for general tensors, and this failure is one of their fundamental differences from the cartesian ones. Investigation of this problem will lead us to a deeper understanding of the concept of a derivative, and to the definition of a new kind of derivative appropriate in tensor analysis.

To begin with, the partial derivatives of a scalar (tensor of zero rank) $\varphi = \varphi(u_1, u_2, \ldots)$ do form a tensor, namely, a covariant vector, because they transform appropriately:

$$\frac{\partial \varphi}{\partial u'_j} = \frac{\partial \varphi}{\partial u_k} \frac{\partial u_k}{\partial u'_j}.$$

This covariant vector is known as the *gradient* of the scalar φ. Observe, however, that its components are not quite the same as those customarily used in vector calculus (see p. 38). The latter are modified by the scale factors h_i and represent the physical components of the gradient (compare with p. 703). For instance, in polar coordinates in plane, the covariant components of the gradient are $\partial \varphi / \partial r$ and $\partial \varphi / \partial \theta$ while the physical components are $\partial \varphi / \partial r$ and $(1/r)(\partial \varphi / \partial \theta)$. Physical components are not used in general tensor theory because they are convenient only in the case of specially oriented orthogonal coordinates. On the other hand, tensor theory admits contravariant components of the gradient, namely, $g^{ij}(\partial \varphi / \partial u_j)$ which in our example reduce to $\partial \varphi / \partial r$ and $(1/r^2)(\partial \varphi / \partial \theta)$.

Remark. In general, the physical components $\overset{\circ}{A}_i$ of a vector for a frame in euclidean space with a diagonal metric matrix are given by

$$\overset{\circ}{A}_i = \frac{1}{\sqrt{g_{ii}}} A_i = \sqrt{g^{ii}} A_i = \sqrt{A_i A^i} \qquad \text{(no summation)},$$

where g_{ii} (no summation) is the ith diagonal element of the metric matrix.

Now consider the partial derivatives of a covariant vector. From the transformation formula $A'_i = A_j(\partial u_j / \partial u'_i)$, it follows that

$$\frac{\partial A'_i}{\partial u'_k} = \frac{\partial A_j}{\partial u'_k} \frac{\partial u_j}{\partial u'_i} + A_j \frac{\partial}{\partial u'_k}\left(\frac{\partial u_j}{\partial u'_i}\right).$$

Express A_j in terms of A'_m and $\partial A_j / \partial u'_k$ in terms of $\partial A_j / \partial u_l$ to deduce the transformation law for the partials:

$$\frac{\partial A'_i}{\partial u'_k} = \underbrace{\frac{\partial A_j}{\partial u_l} \frac{\partial u_l}{\partial u'_k} \frac{\partial u_j}{\partial u'_i}}_{\text{tensor term}} + \underbrace{A'_m \frac{\partial^2 u_j}{\partial u'_i \, \partial u'_k} \frac{\partial u'_m}{\partial u_j}}_{\text{affine term}}.$$

If it were not for the so-called affine term on the right, the partial derivative of a covariant vector would be a second-rank covariant tensor. Evidently, this extra term is present only because the transformation coefficients $\partial u_j / \partial u'_i$ are not constant. For this reason, it does not appear in cartesian coordinates, no matter whether they are orthogonal or skew (see p. 689).

This peculiar transformation law raises an immediate question: What characterizes a *constant vector*? In a cartesian frame this would mean $A_i = $ const (all i) so that $\partial A_i / \partial x_k = 0$ (all i, k). If this is true in one cartesian frame, it will be true in all others. However, nothing of this sort holds for general coordinates. If a vector is constant, its components *still vary* from point to point.

As an example, let φ be an electrostatic potential in a plane given by $\varphi = -ax$ (a = const). It gives rise to a *constant* electrostatic field $\mathbf{E} = -\text{grad } \varphi$ with cartesian components $E_x = a$, $E_y = 0$. In polar coordinates the potential reads $\varphi = -ar \cos \theta$. Neither the covariant components of its gradient

$$\frac{\partial \varphi}{\partial r} = -a \cos \theta, \qquad \frac{\partial \varphi}{\partial \theta} = ar \sin \theta$$

nor its physical components $-a \cos \theta$ and $a \sin \theta$ are constants. The latter statement is illustrated in Fig. 16.11, where the constant electrostatic field $\mathbf{E} = a\mathbf{i}$ is decomposed at various points into its physical components.

The self-evident conclusion is that if we move from a given point $M(r, \theta)$ to a neighboring point $N(r + dr, \theta + d\theta)$, the covariant components of the vector

$$A_1 = \frac{\partial \varphi}{\partial r} = -a \cos \theta,$$

$$A_2 = \frac{\partial \varphi}{\partial \theta} = ar \sin \theta$$

will acquire infinitesimal changes

$$\delta A_1 = a \sin \theta \, d\theta,$$

$$\delta A_2 = a \sin \theta \, dr + ar \cos \theta \, d\theta$$

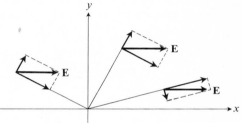

Figure 16.11

which are entirely due to the changes in coordinate axes and not at all due to the changes in the vector itself.

Let us now consider the case of a general covariant vector which is not necessarily constant. As we move from a point M to a neighboring point N, the total change (total differential) dA_i of any given component should consist of two parts: one due to the change of coordinate axes (orientation, angles, etc.), and the other due to the intrinsic variation of the vector field. The former will be denoted by δA_i and the latter by $\mathring{\delta} A_i$, so that $dA_i = \delta A_i + \mathring{\delta} A_i$. These two parts are easily separable in a *euclidean space* because in such a space cartesian frames are available in which the entire change must be attributed to $\mathring{\delta} A_i$.

For the time being, let us confine ourselves to euclidean spaces and use the special symbol $A_i^{\times}$ for covariant components in *cartesian frames*. Transforming the partial derivatives from some selected cartesian frame to an arbitrary frame, according to the formula on p. 712, we obtain*

$$dA_i = \frac{\partial A_i}{\partial u_k} du^k = \frac{\circ A_j^{\times}}{\partial x_l} \frac{\partial x_l}{\partial u_k} \frac{\partial x_j}{\partial u_i} du^k + A_m \frac{\partial^2 x_j}{\partial u_i \, \partial u_k} \frac{\partial u_m}{\partial x_j} du^k.$$

Since a constant vector is characterized by the statement that

$$\partial A_j^{\times}/\partial x_l = 0 \qquad \text{(all } j, l\text{),}$$

---

* Note that the du^k are contravariant vectors, but dA_i *are not vectors at all*, because the partials are not tensors.

it is clear that the second term corresponds to δA_i; it may be written as

$$\delta A_i = \Gamma^m_{ik} A_m \, du^k,$$

where the triple-labeled set of quantities

$$\Gamma^m_{ik} = \frac{\partial^2 x_j}{\partial u_i \, \partial u_k} \frac{\partial u_m}{\partial x_j}$$

will be provisionally called the *euclidean affinity* for the u_i-frame. It is actually independent of the choice of the x_i-frame so long as the latter is cartesian.

Exercise. Verify the last statement by considering another cartesian frame $x'_p = a_{pj}x_j$ with constant a_{pj}.

Observe that if the u_i-frame is also a cartesian frame, then $\Gamma^m_{ik} = 0$ for all m, i, k. From this it follows that the euclidean affinity *cannot possibly be a tensor.* If it were a third-rank tensor, then it would have to vanish in *all* frames once it vanishes in a particular one. This is confirmed by the development of the transformation law for Γ^m_{ik} which is straightforward. From

$$\frac{\partial x_j}{\partial u'_i} = \frac{\partial x_j}{\partial u_p} \frac{\partial u_p}{\partial u'_i},$$

it follows that

$$\frac{\partial^2 x_j}{\partial u'_i \, \partial u'_k} = \left(\frac{\partial^2 x_j}{\partial u_p \, \partial u_q} \frac{\partial u_q}{\partial u'_k} \right) \frac{\partial u_p}{\partial u'_i} + \frac{\partial x_j}{\partial u_p} \frac{\partial^2 u_p}{\partial u'_i \, \partial u'_k}.$$

Also use

$$\frac{\partial u'_m}{\partial x_j} = \frac{\partial u'_m}{\partial u_r} \frac{\partial u_r}{\partial x_j}$$

so that

$$\Gamma'^m_{ik} = \frac{\partial^2 x_j}{\partial u'_i \, \partial u'_k} \frac{\partial u'_m}{\partial x_j} = \frac{\partial^2 x_j}{\partial u_p \, \partial u_q} \frac{\partial u_q}{\partial u'_k} \frac{\partial u_p}{\partial u'_i} \frac{\partial u'_m}{\partial u_r} \frac{\partial u_r}{\partial x_j} + \frac{\partial^2 u_p}{\partial u'_i \, \partial u'_k} \frac{\partial x_j}{\partial u_p} \frac{\partial u'_m}{\partial u_r} \frac{\partial u_r}{\partial x_j}$$

$$= \underbrace{\Gamma^r_{pq} \frac{\partial u'_m}{\partial u_r} \frac{\partial u_p}{\partial u'_i} \frac{\partial u_q}{\partial u'_k}}_{\text{tensor term}} + \underbrace{\frac{\partial^2 u_p}{\partial u'_i \, \partial u'_k} \frac{\partial u'_m}{\partial u_p}}_{\text{nontensor term}}.$$

This formula contains the definition of euclidean affinity as a special case (if the u_i are cartesian) and explains why the index m in Γ^m_{ik} is written as a superscript and the indices i and k as subscripts despite the fact that we are not dealing with a tensor.

Remark. The quantity $A_i + \delta A_i = A_i + \Gamma^m_{ik} A_m \, du^k$ is known as the *parallel displacement of vector A_i* (from point M to point N). It essentially shows how the components of a vector defined at point M would look at point N if the vector were transported there without any intrinsic change.

Turning now to the quantity $\mathring{d}A_i$, we observe that it can be written as

$$\mathring{d}A_i = dA_i - \delta A_i = \left(\frac{\partial A_i}{\partial u_k} - \Gamma_{ik}^m A_m\right) du^k,$$

and that the expression in parentheses may be considered as a new kind of derivative, responsible for the intrinsic change in vector field. It is called the *covariant derivative* of a vector A_i and is often denoted by $A_{i;k}$, where the semicolon symbolizes the operation of covariant differentiation. Incidentally, the partial derivative of A_i is often denoted by a similar symbol, but with a comma instead of a semicolon:* $\partial A_i/\partial u_k = A_{i,k}$ so that $A_{i;k} = A_{i,k} - \Gamma_{ik}^m A_m$.

From our analysis it should be evident that from a physicist's point of view, it is the covariant derivative, namely, the quantity generating the actual changes in the vector field, which should be regarded as the true derivative. It may now be conjectured that $A_{i;k}$ is a second-rank tensor; the reasoning may proceed as follows. The quantity $A_i + \delta A_i$ represents the vector A_i, as defined at point M, but with the components recalculated at a neighboring point N; consequently, $\mathring{d}A_i = (A_i + dA_i) - (A_i + \delta A_i)$ is a difference of two vectors referred to the same point and must be a vector; then, from $\mathring{d}A_i = A_{i;k}\,du^k$, it follows by the quotient theorem that $A_{i;k}$ is a tensor, covariant in both indices.

The tensor character of $A_{i;k}$ can also be verified directly. Using the transformation laws for affinities and partial derivatives, we obtain

$$A'_{i;k} = \frac{\partial A'_i}{\partial u'_k} - \Gamma'^m_{ik} A'_m = \frac{\partial A_j}{\partial u_l}\frac{\partial u_l}{\partial u'_k}\frac{\partial u_j}{\partial u'_i} + A'_m \frac{\partial^2 u_j}{\partial u'_i\,\partial u'_k}\frac{\partial u'_m}{\partial u_j}$$
$$- \Gamma_{pq}^r \frac{\partial u'_m}{\partial u_r}\frac{\partial u_p}{\partial u'_i}\frac{\partial u_q}{\partial u'_k} A'_m - \frac{\partial^2 u_r}{\partial u'_i\,\partial u'_k}\frac{\partial u'_m}{\partial u_r} A'_m.$$

We find that the affine term in $\partial A'_i/\partial u'_k$ is canceled by a similar term arising from Γ'^m_{ik}. We now use $A'_m(\partial u'_m/\partial u_r) = A_r$ and change some dummy indices to get the desired result:

$$A'_{i;k} = \frac{\partial A_j}{\partial u_l}\frac{\partial u_l}{\partial u'_k}\frac{\partial u_j}{\partial u'_i} - \Gamma_{pq}^r A_r \frac{\partial u_p}{\partial u'_i}\frac{\partial u_q}{\partial u'_k}$$
$$= \left(\frac{\partial A_j}{\partial u_l} - \Gamma_{jl}^r A_r\right)\frac{\partial u_l}{\partial u'_k}\frac{\partial u_j}{\partial u'_i} = A_{j;l}\frac{\partial u_j}{\partial u'_i}\frac{\partial u_l}{\partial u'_k}.$$

16.11 CALCULUS OF GENERAL TENSORS

The concept of covariant derivatives can be extended to tensors of all ranks and types. This may be done very conveniently by considering scalars built from tensors of various ranks. The underlying reason is that the changes in coordinate axes have no effect on a scalar φ. The quantity $\delta\varphi$ is always identically zero and

---

* Unfortunately, these conventions are not uniform. Some authors use $A_{i,k}$ rather than $A_{i;k}$ to indicate the covariant derivative. Other symbols, like DA_i/Du_k, are also in use.

the entire change $d\varphi$ during a displacement from a point M to a neighboring point N is entirely due to the intrinsic variation of a scalar field. This is logically expressed by postulating that the covariant derivative of a scalar is identical to its partial derivative:

$$\varphi_{;i} = \frac{\partial\varphi}{\partial u_i} = \varphi_{,i}.$$

Now consider the scalar $A_i B^i$ formed from a covariant and a contravariant vector. On a parallel displacement (see the Remark on p. 714) to a neighboring point, the vectors A_i and B^i would become $A_i + \delta A_i$ and $B^i + \delta B^i$, respectively. Since $\delta(A_i B^i) = 0$, we can write, within the first order,

$$\delta(A_i B^i) = (A_i + \delta A_i)(B^i + \delta B^i) - A_i B^i \cong A_i\,\delta B^i + B^i\,\delta A_i = 0.$$

Since $\delta A_i = \Gamma_{ik}^m A_m\,du^k$, we deduce that $A_m\,\delta B^m = -B^i\,\delta A_i = -B^i\Gamma_{ik}^m A_m\,du^k$. From the fact that A_m is arbitrary, it follows immediately that $\delta B^m = -B^i\Gamma_{ik}^m\,du^k$ and this yields the intrinsic change of a contravariant vector

$$\not\!\delta B^j = dB^j - \delta B^j = \frac{\partial B^j}{\partial u_k}\,du^k + \Gamma_{ik}^j B^i\,du^k.$$

Consequently, the covariant derivative of a contravariant vector is given by

$$B_{;k}^j = \frac{\partial B^j}{\partial u_k} + \Gamma_{ik}^j B^i.$$

It is not difficult to verify that $B_{;k}^j$ is a mixed tensor of the second rank.

The same technique can be used for tensors of higher rank. For instance, in the case of a covariant second-rank tensor, A_{ij}, construct the scalar $\varphi = A_{ij}B^i C^j$ with two arbitrary contravariant vectors and perform the parallel displacement:

$$\delta\varphi = (A_{ij} + \delta A_{ij})(B^i + \delta B^i)(C^j + \delta C^j) - A_{ij}B^i C^j$$
$$\cong B^i C^j\,\delta A_{ij} + A_{ij}C^j\,\delta B^i + A_{ij}B^i\,\delta C^j = 0.$$

Express δB^i and δC^j in terms of the affinity and deduce

$$\delta A_{ij} = \Gamma_{ik}^m A_{mj}\,du^k + \Gamma_{jk}^n A_{in}\,du^k.$$

From this follows the expression for the covariant derivative of A_{ij}, namely,

$$A_{ij;k} = \frac{\partial A_{ij}}{\partial u_k} - \Gamma_{ik}^m A_{mj} - \Gamma_{jk}^n A_{in},$$

which is readily verified to be a covariant tensor of third rank.

It should now be evident that the covariant derivative of any tensor can be deduced in this fashion and the general formula reads

$$A_{ij\ldots;k}^{pq\ldots} = \frac{\partial A_{ij\ldots}^{pq\ldots}}{\partial u_k} - \Gamma_{ik}^m A_{mj\ldots}^{pq\ldots} - \Gamma_{jk}^m A_{im\ldots}^{pq\ldots} - \cdots$$
$$+ \Gamma_{mk}^p A_{ij\ldots}^{mq\ldots} + \Gamma_{mk}^q A_{ij\ldots}^{pm\ldots} + \cdots$$

The structure of this expression is governed by the following three rules:

1. Apart from the partial derivative there is a negative affine term for each covariant index, and a positive affine term for each contravariant index.

2. The *second* subscript in Γ-symbols is always the differentiation index (k in this case).

3. Each index in $A_{ij\cdots}^{pq\cdots}$ is transferred, in turn, to the unoccupied spot of the same character (subscript or superscript) in the Γ-symbol, and its place is taken by a dummy index which also occupies the remaining spot in the Γ-symbol (of opposite character).

The covariant derivative of a tensor is another tensor with rank increased by unity and the extra index is a covariant one. The process of covariant differentiation obeys the two basic rules of ordinary differentiation:

1. The derivative of a sum is the sum of derivatives.

2. The derivative of a product is the sum of similar products where one of the factors, in turn, is replaced by its derivative.

The verification of the first property is trivial. The proof of the second one will be illustrated by a particular example: We let $A_i = T_{ij}B^j$; then

$$A_{i;k} = \frac{\partial}{\partial u_k}(T_{ij}B^j) - \Gamma_{ik}^m(T_{mj}B^j)$$

$$= \frac{\partial T_{ij}}{\partial u_k}B^j + T_{ij}\frac{\partial B^j}{\partial u_k} - \Gamma_{ik}^m T_{mj}B^j.$$

However,

$$\partial T_{ij}/\partial u_k = T_{ij;k} + \Gamma_{ik}^m T_{mj} + \Gamma_{jk}^m T_{im} \quad \text{and} \quad \partial B^j/\partial u_k = B_{;k}^j - \Gamma_{mk}^j B^m.$$

Substituting into the above relation, we observe that all affine terms cancel, yielding the desired result:

$$(T_{ij}B^j)_{;k} = T_{ij;k}B^j + T_{ij}B_{;k}^j.$$

Calculation of covariant derivatives of tensors in euclidean spaces demands, as a prerequisite, the evaluation of euclidean affinity given by

$$\Gamma_{ik}^m = \frac{\partial^2 x_j}{\partial u_i\,\partial u_k}\frac{\partial u_m}{\partial x_j}.$$

This formula shows that the euclidean affinity is symmetric in its subscripts, namely, $\Gamma_{ik}^m = \Gamma_{ki}^m$ but it does not necessarily represent the most convenient way of calculating the coefficients Γ_{ik}^m. Instead, we can develop a formula relating Γ_{ik}^m directly to the metric tensor, and this formula happens to be of great theoretical importance.

Recall that a covariant vector A_i and a contravariant vector A^i are essentially just two representations of an abstract vector field. If this vector field is intrinsically constant, then both $A_{i;k}$ and $A_{;k}^i$ must vanish. Observe, however, that

$$A_{i;k} = (g_{ij}A^j)_{;k} = g_{ij;k}A^j + g_{ij}A_{;k}^j.$$

This leads to the conclusion that for a constant vector we must have $g_{ij;k}A^j = 0$. However A^j is arbitrary at any given point and we obtain an extremely important statement:

$$g_{ij;k} = 0.$$

In other words, the metric tensor *behaves like a constant under covariant differentiation.* Using this, we write explicitly

$$g_{ij;k} = \frac{\partial g_{ij}}{\partial u_k} - \Gamma_{ik}^m g_{mj} - \Gamma_{jk}^m g_{im} = 0.$$

Two other equations of this type can be obtained by the cyclic permutation of indices i, j, and k:

$$\frac{\partial g_{ik}}{\partial u_i} - \Gamma_{ji}^m g_{mk} - \Gamma_{ki}^m g_{jm} = 0, \qquad \frac{\partial g_{ki}}{\partial u_j} - \Gamma_{kj}^m g_{mi} - \Gamma_{ij}^m g_{km} = 0.$$

We add the last two relations and subtract the first one; using the symmetry of both g_{ij} and Γ_{ik}^m with respect to their subscripts, we obtain

$$2g_{mk}\Gamma_{ij}^m = \frac{\partial g_{ki}}{\partial u_j} + \frac{\partial g_{jk}}{\partial u_i} - \frac{\partial g_{ij}}{\partial u_k}.$$

To solve for Γ_{ij}^m, we multiply both sides by $\frac{1}{2}g^{nk}$ (see p. 707) and use $g^{nk}g_{mk} = \delta_n^m$ so that

$$\Gamma_{ij}^n = \frac{1}{2}g^{nk}\left[\frac{\partial g_{ki}}{\partial u_j} + \frac{\partial g_{jk}}{\partial u_i} - \frac{\partial g_{ij}}{\partial u_k}\right].$$

Apart from its practical value, this formula permits the extension of the idea of covariant differentiation to noneuclidean spaces (see p. 704). Spaces in which the metric g_{ij} is defined are called *Riemannian spaces.* In every Riemannian space, whether or not it is euclidean, the affinity may be *defined* by the above formula. In this case Γ_{ij}^n is called *metric affinity* or, more commonly, the *Christoffel symbol of the second kind* and is often denoted by $\{{}^n_{ij}\}$. In this nomenclature the Christoffel symbol of the *first kind* is defined by the expression

$$[ij, k] = \frac{1}{2}\left[\frac{\partial g_{ki}}{\partial u_j} + \frac{\partial g_{jk}}{\partial u_i} - \frac{\partial g_{ij}}{\partial u_k}\right]$$

so that, by definition,

$$\begin{Bmatrix} n \\ i\,j \end{Bmatrix} = g^{nk}[ij, k].$$

Whether or not a Riemannian space is euclidean, the metric tensor is tacitly assumed to be symmetric because it is defined by a quadratic form

$$(ds, ds) = g_{ij}\, du^i\, du^j,$$

in which a conceivable antisymmetric part of g_{ij} would contribute nothing to (ds, ds) and may be omitted. It follows then that the Christoffel symbols $\{{}^n_{ij}\}$ are, by definition, symmetric in their lower indices. Starting with the transformation law for g_{ij}, it is a straightforward task to verify that the quantities $\{^n_{ij}\}$ transform in the same way as euclidean affinities (even in a noneuclidean space), namely,

$$\begin{Bmatrix} n \\ ij \end{Bmatrix}' = \begin{Bmatrix} r \\ pq \end{Bmatrix} \frac{\partial u'_n}{\partial u_r} \frac{\partial u_p}{\partial u'_i} \frac{\partial u_q}{\partial u'_j} + \frac{\partial^2 u_p}{\partial u'_i \partial u'_j} \frac{\partial u'_n}{\partial u_p} .$$

From this, in turn, it follows that if the covariant derivative of a covariant vector is defined by

$$A_{i;k} = \frac{\partial A_i}{\partial u_k} - \begin{Bmatrix} m \\ ik \end{Bmatrix} A_m,$$

then $A_{i;k}$ is a second-rank tensor. Analogous statements can be made regarding covariant derivatives of other tensors. In short, all properties of covariant differentiation remain valid if Γ^m_{ik} is replaced by $\{^m_{ik}\}$ and applied to an arbitrary Riemannian space.

Remark. It is possible to extend further the notion of affinity and covariant differentiation to spaces which *do not possess a metric at all*. In such spaces* tensors are defined, as before, by their transformation properties. However, one cannot say that a certain contravariant vector and a certain covariant vector are just two representations of the *same* abstract vector because the metric connection between A_i and A^i is lacking. In this case an affinity Γ^m_{ik} in the general sense is defined in a particular coordinate system by an *arbitrary* set of values, but is required to transform according to the formula on p. 714. Covariant differentiation is defined as before and produces tensors out of tensors leading to a similar type of calculus as in Riemannian spaces except for the absence of any reference to g_{ij}. The details of interest to a physicist can be found elsewhere.†

The results developed in the last two sections provide us with a mechanism for expressing a great number of physical laws in a form applicable to arbitrary coordinate frames. This will be illustrated by casting the common differential operators, gradient, divergence, curl, and the Laplacian, into forms appropriate for tensor calculus.

The gradient of a scalar φ is usually defined as a covariant vector given by

$$(\text{grad } \varphi)_i = \varphi_{;i} = \frac{\partial \varphi}{\partial u_i},$$

and has already been discussed in Section 16.10. A physical law like grad $\varphi = -\mathbf{E}$ should assume the covariant form

$$\varphi_{;i} = -E_i,$$

where the quantities E_i must be treated as components of a covariant vector.‡

---

* Such spaces, more often called *manifolds*, are simply sets of points $M(u_1, u_2, \ldots, u_N)$ defined by N coordinates which may vary continuously.

† See, for instance, Schrödinger, *Space-Time Structure*, and Brillouin, *Tensors in Mechanics and Elasticity*.

‡ If the vector $\mathbf{E}$ is originally defined in a cartesian frame, then the covariant and contravariant components coincide numerically. The above formula tells, however, how these components must transform when a different coordinate system is introduced.

The divergence of a vector $\mathbf{V}$ is given in cartesian coordinates by $\partial V_i/\partial x_i$ and is obtained by contraction of the cartesian tensor $\partial V_i/\partial x_j$. In general tensor calculus, the partial derivative must be replaced by a covariant derivative, and in order to obtain a scalar by contraction we must have a mixed second-rank tensor (see p. 705). Consequently, we must differentiate *contravariant* components of $\mathbf{V}$ and define

$$\text{div } \mathbf{V} = V^i_{;i} = \frac{\partial V^i}{\partial u_i} + \begin{Bmatrix} i \\ ki \end{Bmatrix} V^k.$$

This expression is a true scalar in all frames and reduces to the familiar form in a cartesian system. It may be rewritten in a different manner. Observe that if g_{ij} is symmetric, then the associated metric g^{ij} is also symmetric so that

$$\begin{Bmatrix} i \\ ki \end{Bmatrix} = \tfrac{1}{2} g^{ij} \left[\frac{\partial g_{ik}}{\partial u_i} + \frac{\partial g_{ij}}{\partial u_k} - \frac{\partial g_{ki}}{\partial u_j} \right] = \tfrac{1}{2} g^{ij} \frac{\partial g_{ij}}{\partial u_k}.$$

Furthermore, consider the partial derivatives $\partial g/\partial u_k$ of the determinant g of a metric tensor. The derivative of an $N \times N$ determinant can be obtained by differentiating each row separately and adding the resulting N determinants. In terms of our summation convention, this reads

$$\frac{\partial g}{\partial u_k} = \frac{\partial g_{ij}}{\partial u_k} G^{ij},$$

where G^{ij} is the cofactor of g_{ij}. However, G^{ij} is equal to $g^{ij}g$ so that the following useful formula holds:

$$\begin{Bmatrix} i \\ ki \end{Bmatrix} = \tfrac{1}{2} g^{ij} \frac{\partial g_{ij}}{\partial u_k} = \tfrac{1}{2} \frac{1}{g} \frac{\partial g}{\partial u_k} = \frac{1}{\sqrt{g}} \frac{\partial}{\partial u_i} (\sqrt{g}).$$

Consequently, the expression for divergence can also be written as

$$\text{div } \mathbf{V} = \frac{1}{\sqrt{g}} \left(\sqrt{g} \frac{\partial V^i}{\partial u_i} + \frac{\partial \sqrt{g}}{\partial u_i} V^i \right) = \frac{1}{\sqrt{g}} \frac{\partial}{\partial u_i} (\sqrt{g} V^i).$$

It is possible to obtain the divergence starting from the covariant components of vector $\mathbf{V}$ by means of the formula $\text{div } \mathbf{V} = g^{ij} \mathbf{V}_{j;i}$. Indeed, it is not hard to show that the associated metric also behaves like a constant under covariant differentiation so that

$$V^i_{;i} = (g^{ij} V_j)_{;i} = g^{ij} V_{j;i}.$$

The Laplacian $\nabla^2 \varphi$ is defined as div grad φ and can be formed by two equivalent methods. The gradient can be made contravariant by

$$(\text{grad } \varphi)^i = g^{ij} (\text{grad } \varphi)_j = g^{ij} \varphi_{;j} = g^{ij} \frac{\partial \varphi}{\partial u_j},$$

and subject to the divergence operation:

$$\nabla^2 \varphi = (g^{ij}\varphi_{;j})_{;i} = \frac{1}{\sqrt{g}} \frac{\partial}{\partial u_i}\left(\sqrt{g}\, g^{ij} \frac{\partial \varphi}{\partial u_j}\right).$$

Alternatively, a second-rank tensor $\varphi_{;j;i}$ can be formed by differentiating φ twice covariantly and contracting with the tensor g^{ij}:

$$\nabla^2 \varphi = g^{ij}\varphi_{;j;i} = g^{ij}\left[\frac{\partial^2 \varphi}{\partial u_i\,\partial u_i} - \begin{Bmatrix} m \\ ji \end{Bmatrix}\frac{\partial \varphi}{\partial u_m}\right].$$

The definition of curl of a vector is somewhat more complicated. It will be recalled that in cartesian coordinates, curl $\mathbf{V}$ is a vector in three dimensions, but a scalar in two dimensions. More precisely, it is a pseudovector or a pseudoscalar, respectively (see Section 16.5). It turns out that in general tensor calculus, in a space of N dimensions, curl $\mathbf{V}$ must be treated as a *second-rank antisymmetric tensor* given by

$$(\text{curl } V_i)_j = V_{j;i} - V_{i;j}.$$

It is interesting to note that the expression $V_{j;i} - V_{i;j}$ happens to be equal to $V_{j,i} - V_{i,j}$ because the affine terms cancel out. In a three-dimensional space this tensor is explicitly displayed by the matrix

$$\begin{vmatrix} 0 & \dfrac{\partial V_2}{\partial u_1} - \dfrac{\partial V_1}{\partial u_2} & \dfrac{\partial V_3}{\partial u_1} - \dfrac{\partial V_1}{\partial u_3} \\[2ex] \dfrac{\partial V_1}{\partial u_2} - \dfrac{\partial V_2}{\partial u_1} & 0 & \dfrac{\partial V_3}{\partial u_2} - \dfrac{\partial V_2}{\partial u_3} \\[2ex] \dfrac{\partial V_1}{\partial u_3} - \dfrac{\partial V_3}{\partial u_1} & \dfrac{\partial V_2}{\partial u_3} - \dfrac{\partial V_3}{\partial u_2} & 0 \end{vmatrix}.$$

From this definition it is clear that in a space of N dimensions, curl $\mathbf{V}$ has $\frac{1}{2}N(N-1)$ independent components, fitting the usual count of three components in three dimensions and one component in two dimensions. Furthermore, the reason that an antisymmetric second-rank tensor can be disguised as a vector in three dimensions is as follows: By means of Levi-Civita tensor density e^{ijk}, we can associate with curl $\mathbf{V}$ a *contravariant vector density*

$$\mathfrak{w}^i = e^{ijk}V_{k;j} = e^{ijk}\frac{\partial V_k}{\partial u_j}$$

so that, explicitly,

$$\mathfrak{w}^1 = \frac{\partial V_3}{\partial u_2} - \frac{\partial V_2}{\partial u_3}, \qquad \mathfrak{w}^2 = \frac{\partial V_1}{\partial u_3} - \frac{\partial V_3}{\partial u_1}, \qquad \mathfrak{w}^3 = \frac{\partial V_2}{\partial u_1} - \frac{\partial V_1}{\partial u_2}.$$

Because of its tensor character, this relation between $\mathfrak{w}^i$ and $V_{k;j}$ is valid in any frame. In other words, while (curl $V_k)_j$ transforms as a second-rank tensor, $\mathfrak{w}^i$ transforms automatically as a first-rank tensor density. Either of these entities carries the same information and is entirely equivalent to the other one.

Remark. It is also possible, in three-dimensional space, to associate with curl **V** a true vector, rather than a vector density. Define the so-called *permutation tensor* e^{ijk} by means of

$$e^{ijk} = \frac{1}{\sqrt{g}} e^{ijk}.$$

Since g is a relative scalar of weight 2 (p. 709), $1/\sqrt{g}$ is a scalar capacity and e^{ijk} must be a tensor, although not an isotropic one.* Consequently, the quantity

$$w^i = \frac{\mathfrak{w}^i}{\sqrt{g}} = e^{ijk} V_{k;j}$$

is a vector and can also be used to represent curl **V**.

In conclusion, it may rightly be asked what the *correct* way of writing curl **V** is. For instance, how do we render the equation curl **A** = **B** in covariant form? The answer is that any of the above methods is equally good. What is important is that both sides of the equation must be written in the *same way*, which is, of course, the whole idea of tensor analysis. This can be done without difficulty. For instance, if **B** is given by contravariant vector components B^1, B^2, B^3, one can always construct a vector density from it by means of $\mathfrak{B}^i = \sqrt{g}\, B^i$ or a covariant antisymmetric second-rank tensor by means of $F_{jk} = \sqrt{g}\, \mathfrak{e}_{ijk} B^i$ which can then be associated with the corresponding form of curl **A**.

BIBLIOGRAPHY

AHARONI, J., *The Special Theory of Relativity.* London: Oxford University Press, 1965.

BRILLOUIN, LEON, *Tensors in Mechanics and Elasticity.* New York: Academic Press, 1964.

LAWDEN, DEREK F., *An Introduction to Tensor Calculus and Relativity.* New York: John Wiley and Sons, 1962.

SCHRÖDINGER, ERWIN, *Space-Time Structure.* Cambridge: Cambridge University Press, 1950.

PROBLEMS

1. An outer product $A_i B_j$ of two vectors is a second-rank tensor. Can every second-rank tensor be represented as an outer product of two vectors? Find the necessary and sufficient conditions which have to be satisfied if a 3×3 matrix is to be represented as an outer product.

---

* In cartesian frames, e^{ijk} reduces to $\pm \epsilon_{ijk}$.

2. Assuming that x and y transform as components of a vector, determine which of the following matrices are tensors.

$$A_{ij} = \begin{vmatrix} x^2 & xy \\ xy & y^2 \end{vmatrix}, \qquad B_{ij} = \begin{vmatrix} xy & y^2 \\ x^2 & -xy \end{vmatrix},$$

$$C_{ij} = \begin{vmatrix} y^2 & xy \\ xy & x^2 \end{vmatrix}, \qquad D_{ij} = \begin{vmatrix} -xy & x^2 \\ -y^2 & xy \end{vmatrix}.$$

3. Show that in a space of N dimensions, second-rank antisymmetric tensor has at most $\frac{1}{2}N(N-1)$ independent components and a symmetric tensor of the second rank at most $\frac{1}{2}N(N+1)$ independent components.

4. Prove the formula $\epsilon_{ikl}\epsilon_{ikm} = 2\delta_{lm}$ and deduce the expression for $\epsilon_{ijk}\epsilon_{ijk}$.

5. Using the properties of Kronecker and Levi-Civita tensors, write, in tensor notation, the proofs of the following identities:

a) $([\mathbf{A} \times \mathbf{B}] \cdot [\mathbf{C} \times \mathbf{D}]) = (\mathbf{A} \cdot \mathbf{C})(\mathbf{B} \cdot \mathbf{D}) - (\mathbf{A} \cdot \mathbf{D})(\mathbf{B} \cdot \mathbf{C})$,
b) $[\mathbf{A} \times [\mathbf{B} \times \mathbf{C}]] + [\mathbf{B} \times [\mathbf{C} \times \mathbf{A}]] + [\mathbf{C} \times [\mathbf{A} \times \mathbf{B}]] = 0$,
c) $[\mathbf{A} \times [\mathbf{B} \times [\mathbf{C} \times \mathbf{D}]]] = (\mathbf{B} \cdot \mathbf{D})[\mathbf{A} \times \mathbf{C}] - (\mathbf{B} \cdot \mathbf{C})[\mathbf{A} \times \mathbf{D}]$.

6. Instead of being represented by a triple (x_1, x_2, x_3), a vector $\mathbf{x}$ in three dimensions can be represented by an antisymmetric matrix

$$X = \begin{vmatrix} 0 & -x_3 & x_2 \\ x_3 & 0 & -x_1 \\ -x_2 & x_1 & 0 \end{vmatrix}.$$

Show that the inner product of the vectors $\mathbf{x}$ and $\mathbf{y}$ is given by $-\frac{1}{2}\operatorname{tr}(XY)$ and the outer product $x_i y_j$ by $YX - \frac{1}{2}\operatorname{tr}(YX)$. Find a similar expression for the cross product.

Relate the elements X_{ij} of matrix X to the components x_k via the Levi-Civita tensor and show that X_{ij} behaves like a second-rank tensor under rotations. Is the matrix X completely equivalent to the triple (x_1, x_2, x_3) under all orthogonal transformations?

7. Let $B_k = \epsilon_{ijk}(\partial A_j / \partial x_k)$. Show that

$$\epsilon_{ijk}B_k = \frac{\partial A_j}{\partial x_i} - \frac{\partial A_i}{\partial x_j}.$$

Furthermore, deduce the first relation from the second one. Comment on the relation of these formulas to curl $\mathbf{A}$.

8. Show that the symmetry conditions

$$\Lambda_{ijkl} = \Lambda_{jikl}, \qquad \Lambda_{ijkl} = \Lambda_{ijlk}, \qquad \Lambda_{ijkl} = \Lambda_{klij}.$$

reduce the number of independent components of an elastic tensor from 81 to 21.

9. Using the definition of general tensors in Section 16.8, demonstrate explicitly that the transformation coefficients $\partial u_i'/\partial u_j$ are themselves mixed second-rank tensors.

10. Given that A^i is an arbitrary contravariant vector and $C_{ij}A^iA^j$ is an invariant, show that $C_{ij} + C_{ji}$ is a covariant second-rank tensor. Give the reasons why this statement cannot be made for C_{ij} and C_{ji} separately.

11. Verify that δ_{ij} and δ^{ij}, as defined in Section 16.9, are not isotropic tensors. Show that if the particular frame within which δ_{ij} and δ^{ij} are defined by Kronecker delta symbols is a cartesian frame, then these tensors are identical with g_{ij} and g^{ij}, respectively.

12. Show that

a) $\det A_j^i$ is a scalar.

b) $\sqrt{g}$ is a tensor density.

c) $e^{ijk} = \dfrac{1}{\sqrt{g}}\, \mathfrak{e}^{ijk}$ is a tensor.

Let A_{ij} be an antisymmetric covariant tensor. Show that the quantities $(1/\sqrt{g})A_{ij}$ may be considered as components of a *contravariant* vector B_k such that the subscripts i, j, k are all different.

13. Consider the vector A_i given (see p. 713) by the components

$$A_1 = -a\cos\theta, \qquad A_2 = ar\sin\theta.$$

Verify explicitly that the covariant derivative of this vector vanishes.

14. Consider a frame with diagonal metric tensor: $g_{ij} = 0$ if $i \neq j$. Show that

$$\left.\begin{aligned}
\begin{Bmatrix} i \\ jk \end{Bmatrix} &= 0, \\[4pt]
\begin{Bmatrix} i \\ jj \end{Bmatrix} &= -\frac{1}{2g_{ii}} \cdot \frac{\partial g_{jj}}{\partial x_i}, \\[4pt]
\begin{Bmatrix} i \\ ji \end{Bmatrix} &= \begin{Bmatrix} i \\ ij \end{Bmatrix} = \frac{\partial}{\partial x_j}(\log\sqrt{g_{ii}}), \\[4pt]
\begin{Bmatrix} i \\ ii \end{Bmatrix} &= \frac{\partial}{\partial x_i}(\log\sqrt{g_{ii}}),
\end{aligned}\right\} \text{ no summation}$$

where it is understood that the summation convention is not applied and different letters *imply different indices*.

15. Calculate all nonvanishing Christoffel symbols $\{^{\,i}_{jk}\}$ for the spherical coordinate system in three dimensions.

INDEX

INDEX

(Boldface numbers refer to pages where the given item is defined or explained.)